CONCISE
ENCYCLOPEDIA
OF
SYNTACTIC THEORIES

CONCISE ENCYCLOPEDIA OF SYNTACTIC THEORIES

Edited by

KEITH BROWN
University of Cambridge

and

JIM MILLER
University of Edinburgh

PERGAMON

UK	Elsevier Science Ltd, The Boulevard, Langford Lane, Kidlington, Oxford OX5 1GB, UK
USA	Elsevier Science Inc, 665 Avenue of the Americas, New York, NY 10010, USA
JAPAN	Elsevier Science Japan, 9-15 Higashi-Azabu 1-chome, Minato-ku, Tokyo 106, Japan

Copyright © 1996 Elsevier Science Ltd

Library of Congress Cataloging in Publication Data
Concise encyclopedia of syntactic theories / edited by E.K. Brown, J.E. Miller.
    p.   cm.
  Includes index.
  1. Grammar, Comparative and general—Syntax.   I. Brown, E. K.   II. Miller, J. E.
P291.C575   1996
415—dc20   96--32931

British Library Cataloguing in Publication Data
A catalogue record for this book is available from the British Library.

ISBN 0–08–042711–1 (HC)

♾™   The paper used in this publication meets the minimum requirements of the American National Standard for Information Sciences—Permanence of Paper for Printed Library Materials, ANSI Z39.48–1984.

Printed and bound in Great Britain by Cambridge University Press, Cambridge, UK.

Contents

Contents

Contents

Editors' Foreword

This book is based on articles which originally appeared in *The Encyclopedia of Language and Linguistics* (*ELL*) published in 10 volumes in 1994 by Pergamon Press, Oxford with R. E. Asher as Editor-in-Chief. Keith Brown was Subject Editor for the syntax articles. Three articles are entirely new: Martin Atkinson's 'Generative Grammar: The Minimalist Program', Adele Goldberg's 'Construction Grammar', and Louisa Sadler's 'New Developments in Lexical Functional Grammar'. Although the title remains the same, 'Role and Reference Grammar' by Robert Van Valin has been substantially updated with new authorship. The articles by Robert Freidin: 'Generative Grammar: Principles and Parameters' and Frits Stuurman: 'Descriptive Grammar and Formal Grammar' are reprinted unchanged from *ELL*. The other articles have been revised and updated where necessary by their authors and some have been significantly modified and enlarged. A few have appeared in their revised form in *Concise History of the Language Sciences*, edited by E. F. K. Koerner and R. E. Asher (Pergamon 1995). The Glossary is a revised and reduced form of relevant entries which have been taken from the glossary that appeared in *ELL*. We are grateful to all the contributors for their support for the present volume.

E. K. B.   J. M.
Cambridge   September 1996   Edinburgh

Introduction

1. Models of Grammar and their Aims

This introduction rests on four basic assumptions: that every model of grammar merits an examination; that models differ with respect to which aspects of language they handle insightfully; that no model is completely independent of other models, totally consistent, and equally developed in all respects; and that there is no single best model in spite of what the proponents of any given model may believe.

These assumptions will be supported throughout the discussion of models currently, or recently, in use. This discussion focuses on models of grammar developed since the 1950s, but it is worthwhile emphasizing that linguistic model-making has long roots and more than one geographical origin. In pre-war Europe, the successors of de Saussure developed a number of different accounts. Martinet developed a version of functional grammar (see *Functional Grammar: Martinet's Model*), Hjelmslev developed a formal approach (see *Glossematics (Hjelmslev)*), and the foundations were laid for the approaches of the Prague School and the London School associated with Firth (see *Firth and the London School*). In Europe the influence of these various schools persisted into the post-war period. In some cases this was a direct influence, as in the influence of Martinet on Axiomatic Functionalism (see *Functionalism, Axiomatic*), of Firth on Systemic Grammar (see *Systemic Functional Grammar*), or in the continuing development of the Prague School (see *Prague School Syntax and Semantics*), or more indirectly as in the continuing functionalist tradition in Europe (see *Functional Grammar*). Meanwhile in pre-war America a different tradition developed from the work of Sapir, Boas, and Bloomfield (see *American Structuralism*). In the post-war period this developed through the work of Harris and other structuralists in a variety of ways. The most influential of these have been the developing versions of Generative Grammar associated with Chomsky and his followers (see *Generative Grammar: Transformational Grammar*; *Generative Grammar: Principles and Parameters*; *Generative Grammar: The Minimalist Program*; *Chomsky's Philosophy of Language*). Bloomfield's ideas were also developed in other models, notably Lamb's Stratificational Grammar (see *Stratificational Grammar*) and Tagmemics (see *Tagmemics*), evolving from the work of Pike and others in the Summer Institute of Linguistics.

Since the mid-1960s there has been a plethora of new models: Halliday's Systemic Grammar (see *Systemic Functional Grammar*) appeared in the mid-1960s; Case Grammar (see *Case Grammar*) and Generative Semantics (see *Generative Semantics*) arrived in the late 1960s; Categorial Grammar (see *Categorial Grammar*) was adopted into linguistics on a large scale in the early 1970s, having been first adopted in the form of Shaumjan's Applicational Grammar (see *Applicational Grammar*); and the late 1970s saw the publication of work in Relational Grammar and Functional Grammar. Then, in the early 1980s, detailed accounts were published of Role and Reference Grammar, Cognitive Grammar, and Word Grammar, and of models in direct competition with Chomskyan Generative Grammar—Lexical Functional Grammar (LFG) and Generalized Phrase Structure Grammar (GPSG). Head-driven Phrase Structure Grammar (HPSG) has taken key ideas from both LFG and GPSG. (See *Role and Reference Grammar*; *Functional Grammar*; *Cognitive Grammar*; *Lexical*

Functional Grammar; *New Developments in Lexical Functional Grammar*; *Generalized Phrase Structure Grammar*; *Head-driven Phrase Structure Grammar*.)

Some of these models have few active adherents. Typically the most popular models borrow and adapt innovative features from the less popular models. Some models are developing rapidly and new models still appear, but it is difficult to predict which new models will find wide acceptance, or at least a modest niche, in the linguistic market, or those which will not be taken up at all.

No model is free of change and free from the influence of other models. The original Chomskyan model developed against the background of American constituent structural analysis with a strong emphasis on distributional criteria. Within Generative Grammar, different models have been developed which concentrate on different aspects of language—arrangements of constituents, dependency relations, compositional semantics, participants' roles, information packaging—which employ different notations and different calculuses. Models change over time; concepts which are developed in one model but rejected by the proponents of another model may subsequently be adopted and adapted by the latter.

To give an example, Fillmore suggested that, in addition to categorial labels (such as noun, verb, etc.) associated with the branching nodes in a tree, the branches themselves should be labeled with terms such as agent, patient, and the like (see Sect. 5 below) to indicate the functional relations between the categorial nodes. This idea has reappeared in certain dependency models such as Allerton's (see *Valency and Valency Grammar*), in Relational Grammar, and most recently in HPSG, where branches are labeled 'H(ead)' or 'C(omplement)'. Case/Participant Roles, introduced into Generative Grammar by Gruber (see Gruber 1976), were integrated into a model by Fillmore (1968), rejected by Transformational Grammar (see the review by Dougherty 1970) but subsequently adopted into Government and Binding in the form of theta-grids (see *Generative Grammar: Principles and Parameters* and Sect. 5 below) and into later models, and are a central part of Starosta's and Anderson's models (the latter contemporaneous with but independent of Fillmore's model of Case Grammar) (see *Lexicase*; *Case Grammar*). Generalized transformations, which in the earliest Chomskyan model did the work of combining clauses but which were abandoned in the 1965 model, have since reappeared in the Minimalist Program (MP), albeit in a sophisticated form (see *Generative Grammar: The Minimalist Program*). The view that in a clause the head is the verb and all the nouns, including the subject, are complements of the verb, is part of traditional Verb-dependency Grammar as described by Tesnière (1959), was a key idea in both Fillmore's and Anderson's versions of Case Grammar, in the dependency grammars of Mel'chuk (1988), in the work of Sgall and his colleagues (1986), and in GPSG and HPSG, but has been resisted in the Government and Binding and Principles and Parameters models. Interestingly, the Principles and Parameters model employs structures in which the verb and the subject and object NPs are initially constituents of a VP; these structures look familiar—in this respect—to verb-dependency linguists.

The term 'Grammar' is ambiguous. It refers to the patterns found in the words, phrases, and clauses—we talk of learning the grammar of a language. 'Grammar' also refers to descriptions of languages. Traditionally grammars of languages describe the structure of words, phrases, clauses, and sentences, employing concepts relating to morphology (e.g., stem, root, affix) and syntax (e.g., phrase, head, modifier, construction, word order). Grammars may be written for beginning, intermediate, or advanced students, or may be written as a reference book for experienced (native or nonnative) users of the language. Grammars of languages with a written variety are typically based on written data (or at least data neutral between written and spoken language); some introductory grammars focusing on communicative competence provide the relevant phrases and vocabulary for dealing with everyday situations. Experienced users of a language probably consult dictionaries more than grammars. They have come to terms with the tense, aspect, mood, case, and transitivity systems of the language and can use word order, highlighting devices, and sentence connectives to construct longer texts out of sentences. Finally, experienced users draw on their general knowledge of the world in order to use a given language appropriately; just as importantly, they draw on their knowledge of the society and culture of the native speakers.

Formal grammars are constructed to handle the various types of information mentioned above, although as yet no grammar handles all the types. Some grammars are designed to generate (give exact specifications of) syntactic constructions, especially the arrangements and dependency relations of constituents. With a given construction some grammars associate a semantic structure, expressed in logical formalism, and a phonological/phonetic structure. With respect to syntax, some grammars specify the structure of words, phrases, and clauses while others focus on words and treat phrases as secondary items. Most grammars recognize syntactic constructions. At the limits, Government and Binding and Principles and Parameters see individual constructions as secondary and give primacy to general constraints each applying to a range of different constructions (see *Generative Grammar: Principles and Parameters*; *Generative Grammar: The Minimalist Program*). Construction Grammar (see *Construction Grammar*) takes constructions as central and fundamental. Some models of grammar neglect basic syntactic structure, attending instead to the functions of different constructions in texts. These models concentrate on the linguistic representation of situations focusing on questions such as: Does a given situation involve an action or a state? What roles are there? Is the agent expressed or not? If it is, is it expressed by a central clause constituent such as a subject noun phrase or by a peripheral constituent such as a prepositional phrase? Is the patient expressed or not? Do the answers to these questions affect the shape of the verb in a given clause? (See *Functional Grammar*; *Role and Reference Grammar*; *Case Grammar*; *Prague School Syntax and Semantics*.)

Along with different central concerns, different grammatical models may have different sources of data. The most explicit models typically make use of idealized examples devised by linguists, who measure the examples against their intuitions as to what is acceptable/grammatical. (Such models are Principles and Parameters, GPSG, HPSG, and LFG.) This type of data is necessary in demonstrations that one model handles complex examples that other models cannot. There is no guarantee that suitably probing examples will occur in even the largest contemporary databases. However, linguists uninterested in such demonstrations or investigating unwritten languages record and transcribe texts. This second set of linguists subdivides into those who supplement their texts with data elicited by various tests (completing sentences, filling in gaps in sentences, forced choice between two alternative structures, and even grammaticality judgments) and those who believe that the only worthwhile data is produced naturally (i.e., not in response to questions or experiments). The latter view has a long history; both in Europe and North America (see *American Structuralism*) the collection, analysis, and publication of texts was considered a major part of linguists' work, a tradition that has now been taken up on a large scale by Australian linguists.

In spite of Chomsky's rejection of corpus data, text-collecting has never stopped; the cassette recorder and computers have made possible the recording, storage, and speedy processing of enormous bodies of text, both written text and transcripts of speech. These are yielding new information about the syntax of written and spoken language and about patterns of collocation among lexical items. This information bears directly on questions of creativity such as the extent to which language-users vary their syntax and vocabulary and the extent to which they employ fixed expressions, both phrases and whole clauses (see *Construction Grammar*). It also bears on whether one can write a grammar of a whole language: how many syntactic and morphological structures occur in any type of text and to what extent different types of text have their own their own grammar. An obvious example is the language of newspaper headlines, but questions have been raised about the grammar of spontaneous spoken language (maximally informal and unplanned) compared with the grammar of formal written language (maximally formal and planned). The answers are not yet clear but syntactic rules may turn out to be unable to generate all and only the sentences of a language. Rather, the latter may have to be handled by a set of grammars. (See *Firth and the London School* for Firth's view that language is heterogeneous.)

Linguists from many schools have been interested in identifying universal properties of language. One early and well-known attempt to establish defining features of human language was by Hockett (during the period of American Structuralism). He proposed a set of Design Features differentiating between human language and other communications systems (e.g., communications systems of bees and apes). Universal features explaining the easy and rapid acquisition of language by children have been postulated and explored within Chomskyan Generative Grammar (see *Generative Grammar: The Minimalist Program*; *Chomsky's Philosophy of Language*). Universals of language, not necessarily connected with design features or language acquisition, were established by Greenberg, who surveyed a sample of languages, drawing up a list of universal properties (see *Greenberg Universals*). This line of investigation has been continued and refined with respect to the sampling of languages and the universal properties proposed (see *Typology and Word Order Change*; *Typology and Areal Issues in Grammar*; *Typology and Grammar*).

Within the Chomskyan paradigm initially there was a notion of formal universals (i.e., rule types) and substantive universals (i.e., parts of speech, etc.) (see *Generative Grammar: Transformational Grammar*). In Principles and Parameters, which is proposed as a theory of Universal Grammar as a mental object, the cross-construction principles are held to constitute universal properties of language, while parameters define permissible variation within the principles, such as differing word order.

The Chomskyan concern with universals is connected with a larger goal, namely the explanation of first language acquisition. Formal models are generally concerned with sentences, but Chomskyan Generative Grammar is centrally concerned, not just with sentences, but with the ability of the speakers of a language to recognize whether a given sentence belongs to their language or not and with the ability of children to acquire this knowledge, that is, to acquire their native language. The Chomskyan position is that the syntax of natural languages is so complex that it would be unlearnable unless children were born with a set of innate principles controlling their acquisition of language (i.e., constituting a strategy for selecting a grammar of the appropriate form compatible with the primary linguistic data). These innate principles are held to be universal. LFG is also concerned with learnability, while Lexicase is said to be relevant to first language acquisition (see *Language Acquisition: Formal Models and Learnability Theory*; *Language Acquisition: Grammar*). HPSG (and earlier GPSG) and Categorial Grammar are more concerned with generative accuracy and coverage; both are used in computer models of language processing and understanding (as was GPSG). In this respect HPSG recalls an earlier view of Generative Grammar as a tool for handling data; that is, as an instrument without any necessary connection with native speakers' knowledge or first language acquisition. In the 1960s and early 1970s Generative Grammar was also regarded as a heuristic device for discovering new syntactic patterns (see *Descriptive Grammar and Formal Grammar*). In contrast, Role and Reference Grammar focuses on communicative function, taking as fundamental the idea that language primarily serves social interaction (see *Role and Reference Grammar*). Cognitive Grammar sets aside the problem of first language acquisition, being constructed around the goal of capturing the human capacity for construing the 'same' situation in alternative way (i.e., focusing on cognition) (see *Cognitive Grammar*).

All the above-mentioned grammars handle clauses and sentences, together with the semantic interpretations attached to them. Interestingly, the earliest Generative Grammar based on the concept of transformations was developed by Zellig Harris in order to analyze relations between different constructions and the relationships holding between the sentences in a text (Harris used the term 'discourse'). Few of the grammars described in this volume deal with text; only the Prague School (see *Prague School Syntax and Semantics*), Tagmemics (see *Tagmemics*), Halliday and his followers (see *Systemic Functional Grammar*), and Functional Grammar (see *Functional Grammar*) have consistently made allowance for discourse; the latter two models were influenced by the Prague

School concept of functional sentence perspective. While sentence grammars have reached an advanced state of formalization, moves to provide an explicit account of the correlation between syntactic structure and discourse factors have come from Artificial Intelligence and Cognitive Science. (For the relationship between sentence structure and discourse, and the concepts required for the analysis of the relationship, see *Information Structure*; *Topic, Focus, and Word Order*; *Word Order and Linearization*).

2. Formalization Past and Present

Formalization, the idea that grammatical patterns should be specified by rules constituting a calculus, must be considered along with the question of abstraction: should linguists keep close to the 'observable' patterns? And how advantageous is it to work with abstract structures, analyzing two or more patterns in terms of a single abstract pattern and thereby revealing relationships that would otherwise remain obscured? The most abstract structures were postulated within the framework of Generative Semantics (see *Generative Semantics*; *Syntax and Semantics*), but the various Chomskyan transformational models are also based on relatively abstract structures. (How abstract the MP will be is not yet clear—see *Generative Grammar: The Minimalist Program*.) GPSG, HPSG, and LFG focus on 'observable' grammatical patterns. Abstract properties are handled by the semantic structures of GPSG, the attribute-value matrices of HPSG, and the functional structures of LFG. Abstract structures are employed in Dependency Grammar to the extent that word order and phrase structure are treated as secondary to dependency relations between words; this applies to traditional Dependency Grammar and to contemporary models such as Hudson's and Anderson's (see *Word Grammar*; *Case Grammar*). Categorial Grammar, both Montague's variety and Shaumjan's, deal with abstract structures, in that word order can be ignored since the models focus on the combinatory properties of constituents in a fashion that also brings head-modifier relationships to the fore (see *Categorial Grammar*; *Applicational Grammar*).

Both formalization and abstractness go back to the first half of the twentieth century; indeed abstractness goes back a lot further, insofar as the nineteenth-century philologists postulated unattested and unobservable forms to account for the variety of forms in the attested stages of Indo-European languages. These forms were employed in some nineteenth-century synchronic grammars of Latin and Greek.

In his work entitled *Language*, Bloomfield treats the word as an abstract unit, stating explicitly that the word is not a phonetic unit (1935: 81) and postulating a unit called the 'word' in order to explain such phenomena as the occurrence of stress, vowel-harmony, and possible consonant clusters. In his *Menomini Morphophonemics*, he establishes a 'theoretical' basic form and states how the basic form changes in combination with other elements. He starts with the basic forms of nouns and verbs and applies his statements in order that they lead from the theoretical basic form to the forms of words as they are actually spoken. This method of description is exactly that of classical generative phonology.

Harris played an interesting and generally unacknowledged role in the development of syntactic formalisms and formal models. He produced his own transformational model but even more interesting is his set of formal statements about the structure of phrases and clauses which anticipates the concern of Chomskyan Generative Grammar with explicit rules and makes use of abstract structures that are different from the apparent structure of observed utterances (Harris 1946). (Harris subsequently extended this type of analysis to discourse.) For example, he treats the verb suffix -*ed* as being a suffix of the whole verb phrase and not just the verb. Harris's paper anticipates other developments: the analysis is categorial and combinatory; also, in that different levels (indicated by superscript numbers) control different combinatory possibilities (adjective and noun on one level, article (adjective) and noun on a higher level), it is X-bar in spirit.

As an example of the use of superscript numbers consider Harris's labels for sequences containing a noun as head. They can be explicated as follows. N^1 is a label for, for example, *paper* plus the position in which the plural ending can be added. *Papers* is N^2, indicating that this form, so to speak, moves up to another position or level, in which the plural ending is not available but adjectives are. In this position any number of adjectives can be added, and the combination of adjectives and noun, say *smooth white paper*, receives the raised number 3, indicating that they move up to another position. In this third position, adjectives are not available but articles and demonstratives are, as in sequences such as *the smooth white paper*. Even a single noun receives the raised number 3, indicating that in a given example, say, *Paper is dear*, a single noun can move up to the level on which it receives no further morphemes suitable as noun modifiers but instead combines with a verb. Harris's notation signals clearly the heads of constructions. All constructions with the label X have X as their head. In Chomskyan Transformational Grammar constructional heads were not clearly signaled until X-bar theory was developed in the late 1960s.

If taken top-down, that is, beginning with N^3 and working down to N^1, Harris's formulas can be converted to phrase structure rules. Another interpretation sees them as categorial rules (see *Categorial Grammar*): a plural suffix is a category that combines with a noun stem to yield a category that no longer combines with suffixes but with adjectives. An adjective combines with an N^2 to yield a category that can combine with another adjective or a category that combines with an article or demonstrative. At the highest level is a nominal category that combines with a verb to yield a clause.

Abstractness and the desire to organize statements about language into a set of rules based on some algebra or calculus were also found in European linguistics in the 1920s and 1930s. For instance, the Glossematics School believed that an algebra should be developed for expressing statements about linguistic structure, although they did not actually develop a calculus, a surprising failure inasmuch as the impetus towards organizing statements into a calculus came largely from the work in Vienna of the Carnap on deriving complex but true propositions from a small set of basic true propositions. In contrast, abstract analyses were abundant, particularly in phonology and morphology. Glossematic linguists, such as Hjelmslev and Uldall (see *Glossematics (Hjelmslev)*), believed that linguists should focus, not on the content of lexical items or the phonetic characteristics of sounds, but on relationships of sameness and difference; they stand in strong contrast with, say, Langacker's Cognitive Grammar with its strong emphasis on content and on representation of content other than by the formulas of predicate logic. In other work, abstractness lay in the principles put forward as underlying systems of morphological and phonological oppositions; for instance, Jakobson's analysis of the Russian case system is as abstract as any current analysis and is still relevant.

Rigorous formalization requires a small number of initial elements and rules deriving other elements from them; in this, formal models merely follow the long-standing practice of mathematics and logic. The initial elements reflect the view of syntactic structure incorporated in a given model. Chomskyan models—but not the Minimalist Program—postulate X-bar constituents, the relationships of Specifier and Complement, and a small number of principles such as the Binding Principle. Dependency models postulate different classes of word and dependency relations. Some dependency models postulate a single head-modifier relation, while others postulate different dependency relations; Glossematics, for instance, postulated relations of interdependence ('a' and 'b' occur together but neither of them without the other), determination ('a' presupposes 'b' but 'b' does not presuppose 'a'), and constellation ('a' and 'b' occur together or independently). Interestingly, 'determination' as defined in Glossematics leads to some of the analyses current in the Chomskyan model; in Noun Phrases, articles presuppose nouns but nouns do not presuppose articles, which makes the article the head of the 'Noun' Phrase.

Grammars with semantic/logical basic structures require primitive elements of a semantic nature. Dik's model has as its primitive categories a set of predicates denoting properties or relations and a set of terms referring to entities, a set of rules for combining terms and predicates into predications, and a set of expression rules for mapping predications into clauses and sentences. These expression rules make crucial reference to states-of-affairs (e.g., actions vs. states), to clause functions such as subject/object and roles such as agent and patient, and to discourse functions such as topic, focus, theme, and tail (see *Functional Grammar*). In Langacker's model (see *Cognitive Grammar*) the primitive elements are a set of semantic units, a set of phonological units, and a set of symbolic units in which semantic and phonological units are linked. Other primitive elements are trajector and landmark, vantage point and orientation, and relations such as being schematic for and being elaborated by.

3. The Structure of Sentences

There is a general consensus that any individual word in a sentence can be assigned to one of a small number of 'lexical classes' or 'parts of speech' and that sentences are not simply strings of words but have a structure.

As far as the categorization of words is concerned, in a sentence like *The hungry mouse is eating the cheese*, *mouse* and *cheese* can be categorized as N(ouns), *hungry* as an A(djective) *eating* as a V(erb), *is* as an (Auxiliary Verb), and *the* as a D(eterminer). Characteristically these word classes are divided into two general subclasses, one contains the 'major' classes, typically Noun, Verb, Adjective, Preposition, and perhaps Adverb, and the other a larger and less well defined set of 'grammatical' or 'functional' classes, typically including Determiners (*the*, *this*, *that*), Quantifiers (*all*, *every*), Auxiliary Verbs (*is, do, did, can, may*), Intensifiers (*very*), Conjunctions (*and, or*), and so on. The major word classes have 'lexical' or 'dictionary' meanings and can typically be used to refer to objects in the world *(mouse, cheese)*, or to describe properties (*hungry*) or actions (*eat*). The minor classes typically have grammatical or functional meanings, which are difficult, if not impossible, to capture in the lexicon; for example, the function of the Auxiliary Verbs is often to carry tense and thus to express temporal relations; *the* is often used when the speaker wants to refer to some identifiable entity in the world, hence its description as a 'definite article' and so on. There is general agreement that this categorization at least is recorded in the 'lexicon', what additional information is recorded differs from theory to theory, and this question will be reconsidered below.

In describing the structure of the sentence, two kinds of structure are generally at issue, 'constituent structure', which focuses on the formal properties of the various parts of the sentence, its constituents and the arrangements in which they occur, and 'functional structure', which is concerned with the relationships between these various constituents. (A third structure, 'information structure' (see Sect. 4 below), encompasses constituent structure and the function of different constituent structures in discourse.) In *The hungry mouse is eating the cheese*, a constituent structure description will identify both *the hungry mouse* and *the cheese* as noun phrases and the string *is eating the cheese* as a verb phrase. In contrast, an account of functional structure would identify *the hungry mouse* as the 'subject of the sentence', *is eating the cheese* as the 'predicate of the sentence', *eat* as the 'main verb of the predicate', *the cheese* as the 'object of the main verb', and so on. Both types of description are necessary, but each focuses on a different aspect of structure. Different models tend to focus major attention on one rather than the other.

The most widely used systems for describing the constituent structure of a sentence derive in one way or another from the work of the American Structuralists of the late 1930s and early 1940s (see *American Structuralism*). As has been observed above, each of the words of a sentence is assigned to a word category (noun, verb, etc.); these are then grouped together to form larger, phrasal categories which in turn are grouped together to form yet further phrasal categories until all the words are accounted for in a single uniform structure. In, for example, *The mouse ran up the clock*, *mouse* and *clock* are N(ouns), and *the* is a D(eterminer), with the Determiner and the Noun together forming a Noun Phrase (NP); *up* is a P(reposition), which together with its following NP form a Prepositional Phrase (PP); *ran* is a V(erb), and it together with the following PP form a Verb Phrase (VP). The NP *the mouse* and the VP *ran up the clock* together form the sentence. This category assignment and constituent structure is commonly represented by a tree diagram like that shown in Fig. 1.

In Fig. 1 the tree is 'rooted' in S (since everything ultimately depends on S) and develops as a 'branching' structure with every branching node labeled for the appropriate category. Descriptions of this kind focus on category assignment (*mouse* is an N; *the mouse* is an NP, etc.) and show a hierarchical constituent structure based on a set of 'constituent structure relations'. Three constituent structure relations are of particular importance: 'dominance', 'order', and 'headedness'. Dominance is the relation between a node and all those other nodes which develop from it: in Fig. 1 S dominates everything; VP dominates the categories that develop from it, which are V, PP, P, NP, D, N, and the lexical items they dominate, but VP does not dominate its 'sister' NP *the mouse*. 'Immediate dominance' is a more specific notion: it is the relation that holds between a 'mother' node and the 'daughters' that immediately develop from it. Thus VP immediately dominates its own daughters V and PP, but whilst it does dominate *their* daughters, it does not *immediately* dominate them. In turn, PP immediately dominates its daughters, P and NP, and so on.

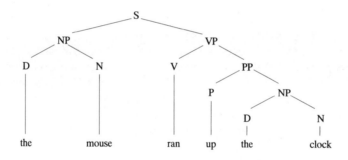

Figure 1. Sentence constituent structure.

Order relates to the fact that constituents can be ordered with respect to each other. So, for example, English prepositions precede their objects, *up the clock* not *the clock up. Order relations are incorporated in the tree of Fig. 1. They are, in principle, independent of dominance relations, since different languages can have the same dominance relations, but different order relations. For example, in both English and French an NP can dominate an adjective as well as a noun, but in English adjectives precede nouns (e.g., *big house*), whereas in French the adjective usually follows (e.g., *maison grande*).

The third constituent structure relation of concern here is that of headedness; within a phrasal category, the head is the principal member and any other constituents within the same phrase are its 'dependents'. For example, a Noun Phrase is headed by a Noun, which is obligatory, and may contain Determiners, Adjectives, and the like, all of which are optional: so *mice run up clocks* is well formed, but *the run up the is not. Note too, that characteristically the phrase takes its name from its head: so a Noun Phrase is headed by a Noun (but see the discussion of Glossematics at the end of Sect. 2, the discussion of Harris in Sect. 2, and the article *X-bar Syntax*), a Verb Phrase by a Verb, and so on. (These issues are discussed, and the relevant arguments summarized, in the article *Constituent Structure*.) The major development and elaboration of this kind of analysis runs from the Structuralists (see *American Structuralism*), through the phrase structure component associated with the early works of Chomsky (see *Generative Grammar: Transformational Grammar*) to the more elaborated models of X-bar syntax (see *X-bar Syntax*) associated with the Principles and Parameters model (see *Generative Grammar: Principles and Parameters*). Chomsky's most recent work (see *Generative Grammar: The Minimalist Program*) returns to a more restrictive notion of constituent structure. (A similar restricted notion is also found in Lexicase (see *Lexicase*).) Models of this kind are also associated with GPSG (see *Generalized Phrase Structure Grammar*).

Sentence structure can also be analyzed as in Categorial Grammar (see *Categorial Grammar* and also the discussion of Harris in Sect. 2 above). In the description illustrated in Fig. 1, the structure of the sentence is derived by grouping categories into larger categories until all are accounted for in a single homogeneous structure. The categories concerned can be words (a D and an N make an NP), phrasal categories (an NP and a VP make an S), or combinations of both (a P and an NP make a PP). The categories within this structure are related to each other by a single set of constituent structure relations.

A radically different way of describing sentence structure is to recognize a number of distinct 'levels' of structure, each with its own particular characteristics. Such systems usually recognize at least the sentence, clause, phrase, and word as distinct levels. In this kind of approach sentences are made up of clauses, a simple sentence consisting of a single clause and a complex sentence of a number of clauses. Each clause is made up of phrases, which are in turn made up of words, and so on. These levels are in principle distinct, though they obviously interrelate, and one could describe a sentence at, say, the 'clause level' or at the 'group level' (roughly equivalent to the 'phrase'). It will be clear that a description of this kind produces a structure different from and flatter than the structure in Fig. 1, in which sentences and phrases are part of the same structure generated by one and the same set of rules; that is, only one level is involved. *The hungry mouse is eating the cheese* is a sentence consisting of a single clause. This clause has the tripartite structure NP VP NP, which yields a structure like that in Fig. 2. Structures of this kind are adopted by Tagmemics and Systemic Grammar (see *Tagmemics*; *Systemic Functional Grammar*).

Figure 2. Tripartite sentence structure.

In contrast with constituent structure, functional structure (see Sect. 5 below) focuses on, not arrangements of constituents, but the relationships between constituents. The most familiar set of relations includes subject, object, indirect object, etc. In a sentence like *John gave a bunch of flowers to his mother*, *John* is the subject of the sentence and *a bunch of flowers* and *his mother* are respectively the direct and oblique objects of the verb. In these terms the sentence would be considered to have a 'Subject Verb Object' (SVO) structure. A second set of relations concerns the 'role' each constituent plays in a sentence; in these terms, *John* might be characterized as 'agent' (the performer of the act of giving), *the flowers* as 'patient' (the object given) and *his mother* as 'recipient' (the person that benefits from the giving). The sentence has an Agent—Patient—Recipient structure (see *Functional Relations; Valency and Valency Grammar*).

Most models identify both constituent and functional structure in one way or another, but different models of grammar take very different positions about them. For most models one is chosen as primary and the other(s) then derive from it. Thus, if constituent structure is chosen as primary, as in Fig. 1, functional relations like subject and object are usually identified in terms of structural positions within trees; the subject NP is the sister of VP and the daughter of S, while the object NP is the sister of V and the daughter of VP. Relations like agent and patient are usually associated with lexical items in the lexicon and are carried into the phrase structure with the lexical item. Chomskyan models take a position of this kind.

Other models take the functional relations as primary. The most syntactic of these is described in the article *Dependency Grammar*, in which relations such as 'head' and 'modifier' are primary. The relations subject, object, etc., are taken as primary by Relational Grammar (see *Relational Grammar*) and Valency Grammar (see *Valency and Valency Grammar*). Such models obviously need to stipulate the way these relations are realized in terms of constituents—subject and object relations are normally realized as a Noun Phrase, an indirect object immediately following the verb is realized as a Noun Phrase (*give his mother the flowers*) or as a Prepositional Phrase when separated from the verb (*give the flowers to this mother*). The relations agent, patient, and the like are primary for various forms of Case Grammar (see *Case Grammar; Lexicase*). These models too must stipulate how the relations are realized in terms of constituents; that the agent and patient are normally realized as Noun Phrases, and that the recipient is realized either as a Noun Phrase or a Prepositional Phrase depending on its order with respect to the patient. Some models adopt a more complex position, describing sentence structure simultaneously in constituent and functional terms: so, for example, at the clause level a sentence might have a description as shown in Fig. 3.

[Subject; Agent, Noun Group, *the cat*]

[Predicator, Active, Verb Group, *chased*]

[Object; Patient, Noun Group, *the mouse*]

Figure 3. Sentence structure at the clause level.

Among theories that proceed in this manner are Tagmemics (see *Tagmemics*) and, to some extent, Systemic Grammar. A more extreme position is taken by Hudson (see *Word Grammar*), who describes the structure of sentence in terms of a variety of dependency relations alone, virtually discarding constituent structure altogether.

4. Information Structure

The mainstream models of grammar are designed to handle the syntactic structure of clauses and sentences but not discourse relations between sentences nor the function of different constructions in discourse. This overly-narrow focus was not considered a weakness in the 1960s, partly because clause and sentence structure were conceived as quite separate from the structure of discourse (at least among Generative Grammarians, but not in the Prague School, Systemic Grammar, Tagmemics, or Dik's Functional Grammar), and partly because concepts for text analysis had just begun to be developed. This is arguably a serious deficiency given the current knowledge of the intimate relationship between sentence syntax and discourse organization. Competence in discourse organization is as important as competence in sentence syntax; language users who can compose sentences correctly but not discourses are unsuccessful communicators, as are language users who fail to associate sentences and semantic interpretations.

Information structure is defined in the article *Information Structure* as the encoding of the relative salience of the constituents of a clause, especially the nominals, the general effect being to foreground certain aspects of the message conveyed by a given clause and to background others. The key concepts in discourse analysis are topic, given-new, and focus. Topic is associated with a number of definitions; the simplest, and the most difficult to apply, defines the topic as what a given clause/ sentence is about, while others define it as expressing given information. Given information is information treated by the speaker as recoverable by the hearer, because it relates to entities physically present in the situational context, or because it has already been mentioned, or because it can be inferred from the situation or from what has been said. New information is presented by the speaker as not recoverable, because it has not been mentioned, does not relate to entities present in the situation, and can not be inferred. Focus has to do with making a constituent salient, because it is contrasted with some other constituent or because the speaker wishes particularly to draw attention to the information.

Central elements of clause and sentence structure correlate closely with the organization of discourse (see *Topic, Focus, and Word Order*; *Information Structure*). In many languages word order in clauses is determined by given-new, with those constituents which convey given information preceding those conveying new information. (The contributors to Payne (1992), mostly analyzing spoken data from Native American languages, argue that in their data new information typically precedes old information. It is not clear whether this is a property of the languages or of the type of text, i.e., spontaneous spoken language. Whatever the correct analysis, there is a correlation between word order and given-new.) Even in languages where the typical order is given-new, the order new-given is found. This order is marked and serves to highlight or focus a constituent—what is new is the focusing: Sornicola in this volume gives the examples *These things we like* and *To Rome I've never been*. In speech, the marked order is associated with emphatic pitch on the focused constituent. In many languages, in both speech and writing, word order signals focus only in conjunction with emphatic pitch and/or particles.

Other factors governing word order are discussed in the article *Word Order and Linearization*: the tendency for heads and modifiers to be adjacent; the tendency for word order to reflect the order of events in the world—*The policeman handcuffed the thief when he had caught him and chased him* is almost impossible, compared with *The policeman chased the thief, caught him and handcuffed him*; the length and complexity of constituents—the strong cross-language tendency (especially in spoken languages) to place short, simple constituents before long, complex ones, indeed to move the latter to the end of the sentence or clause, as in the example of extraposition in the paragraph below or in Siewerska's example *Fred sent to his client several brochures with all the accommodation details*.

Changes in word order may accompany radical changes in construction. Extraposition can move clauses from subject position to clause-final position, as in *That they would lose the election was forecast* vs. *It was forecast that they would lose the election*. Right dislocation moves noun phrases to the right, to a position outside the clause, as in *Running another company he was, the director who had embezzled the pension funds*. Left-dislocation moves constituents to the left, to a position possibly outside the clause: *The policeman we asked, he had no idea where the street was*.

Special constructions may be associated with topic and focus. The English *wh*-construction allows entire clauses to be put into first position in a sentence as the topic: in *What we did next was open the cage very slowly*, the *wh*-clause *what we did next* presents as given a whole clause referring to a whole situation. The English *it*-cleft construction allows noun phrases or preposition phrases to be highlighted: *It was Fiona who kept her head* and *It was in Glasgow that we fell in love with Mackintosh*. *Fiona* is picked out of the relevant set of people and *Glasgow* out of the relevant set of cities. It is pointed out in the article *Information Structure* that voice alternations, such as the alternation between active and passive in English, correlate with alternations in information status. The passive is typically employed when the patient noun in a clause needs to be foregrounded because it is the topic of the clause and given. This discourse pressure is so strong that it can lead speakers and writers to change the syntax of verbs: forms of the verb *embed* occur in the constructions exemplified in *They embedded the nails in the wood* and *The nails were embedded in the wood* but not *The wood was embedded with nails*. Only the last construction could be used by a speaker talking about an ancient tree that survived a bombing raid. Noun Phrases referring to the tree were the subject of a number of clauses, and the final clause was *It* (= *the tree*) *was embedded with bits of shrapnel*.

As emphasized in the article *Word Order and Linearization*, most formal models attempt to handle a limited range of word order patterns and problems have arisen even for their small set of data. The reason suggested is that the models lack adequate provision for information structure, semantic roles, features such as animacy and definiteness, and constituent complexity. This judgment is perhaps too severe, but not undeserved for models identifying a single all-embracing level of sentence structure established to capture the structure of sentences in isolation. That they have difficulty with constructions whose function can only be described in terms of discourse organization is not unexpected. The models that attempt to take communicative functions into account are generally those that recognize layers of structure (see Sect. 3 above). Some versions of Tagmemics identify levels of paragraph and discourse, above that of sentence and with their own structural properties. Some versions of Systemic Grammar identify ranks above the sentence. Dik's Functional Grammar (FG) includes information structure in its core. As explained in Sect. 5 below, in this model basic predications are mapped onto fully specified predications via two sets of rules, one of which assigns grammatical functions such as subject and object and the other of which assigns what are called 'pragmatic functions'. The latter are four in number: theme, tail, topic, and focus. Theme is assigned to constituents preceding the predication, and tail to constituents following it. The constituents are those that would be handled in other models by left-dislocation and right-dislocation. Theme is defined as specifying the universe of discourse for a particular predication while tail presents 'afterthoughts', additional clarifying information. Topic is assigned to the entity of which a predication is made, and focus presents what is the most important or salient information in a given setting. Information may be salient because it is new, or is contrasted with other information, or simply because it is highlighted. (The Functional Grammar treatment is parallel to that found in Systemic Grammar, and in various other models, such as that of Vallduvi's (Vallduvi 1992). The source for the basic ideas is Prague School syntax and semantics; see *Prague School Syntax and Semantics*.)

Functional Grammar in its current state (like Systemic Grammar and even current Prague School work) lacks detailed mappings from predications, through assignments of grammatical and pragmatic functions, to fully specified predications; also, and more importantly, there are no detailed mappings of fully specified predications via expression rules onto linguistic expressions (surface sentences). In contrast, models offering more highly specified rules and/or constraints give no interesting account of information structure. Chomskyan Generative Grammar has been concerned with information structure since Chomsky (1971) proposed a base structure consisting of S' F P, where P is a presupposition structure and F a focus structure. Later Chomskyan models have topic and focus positions (see in particular the treatment of Mayan in Aissen (1992)), which recognizes a topic position immediately dominated by the root node, and to some extent outside the CP and IP structure (and corresponding to theme in FG), and a focus position dominated by IP, capturing the fact that focus applies inside clauses. The Chomskyan model offers nothing corresponding to tail or to the distinction between FG's theme and topic. It does have constituent movement and right-dislocation, but right-dislocated structures are mapped onto logical form, where information structure has no place.

Since features in sorted feature matrices can relate to any aspect of syntactic and semantic structure, it is possible to subcategorize each clause at the highest level by features relating to theme and tail, topic and focus (see Pollard and Sag (1994: Chs. 3, 4, and 8 for HPSG); and see also *New Developments in Lexical Functional Grammar*.) Such treatment would be an interesting application of an analysis employed in Halliday (1967) and Anderson (1968). The feature matrices can in principle specify semantic roles, definiteness and even complexity of given constituents, since a Noun Phrase could be subcategorized for the number and type of modifiers it contained. Such an application of the matrices would answer Siewerska's objections.

5. Functions

Grammatical functions such as subject and object (see Sect. 2 above and Sect. 3 of the article *Functional Relations*) are central to discussions of, for example, subject-verb agreement in person and number, voice or transitivity, and the deletion of Noun Phrases in conjoined clauses. In many languages it is subject Noun Phrases that are deleted, as in *Jane introduced herself to Fiona and chatted to her*, where *Jane* is the subject of *introduced* and the understood subject of *chatted*, and in *Jane was introduced to Fiona and was invited to her party*, where *Jane* is the subject of *was introduced* and the understood subject of *was invited*. Whether the verb is active or passive and whether *Jane* is agent or patient do not matter; what does matter is that *Jane* is the subject of the verb in each clause.

Chomskyan Generative Grammar takes the view that introducing subjects and objects into representations of syntactic structure would involve labeling branches; such labeling is deemed redundant, since information about subject and object functions can be deduced from the position of Noun Phrases in the representations. Relational Grammar, like Dependency Grammar, is based on the view that relations between constituents are more important for many grammatical processes than arrangements of constituents. Dependency Grammar takes the head-modifier relationship as primary whereas Relational Grammar takes grammatical functions as primary. Sentence structure is represented by graphs called 'Relational Networks'; the points on these graphs represent constituents, and grammatical relations/functions are represented by arcs. Instead of the structure of a given sentence being represented by a series of phrase markers, as in Chomskyan Generative Grammar, it is represented by just one relational network graph (see *Relational Grammar*).

Grammatical relations appear in other formal models but less centrally than in Relational Grammar. LFG has one level of syntactic structure, but the structure has two components, constituent structure and functional structure. The latter integrates lexical and structural information; a crucial role is played by grammatical relations, subject, object, and complement. For instance, the link between the active and passive constructions is handled in the lexicon: a rule states that an active verb with a subject and object is mapped into a passive verb such that the subject maps onto an oblique object and the object maps onto a subject. In a sentence such as *Angus considers Finlay boring*, *Finlay* is treated as the object of *considers*, *boring* is the complement (clause) of *considers* and the functional structure contains the information that the object of *considers* is equivalent to the subject of the complement clause.

Another model that explicitly mentions grammatical relations is Dik's Functional Grammar. In this model, terms are inserted into 'predicate-frames' to yield predications containing information about participant roles (see below). The terms in a predication are further specified with respect to grammatical function and pragmatic function (described in Sect. 4 above). For instance, the predication that is mapped into *Kirsty gave Lorna the book* or *Lorna was given the book by Kirsty* or *The book was given to Lorna by Kirsty* has *Kirsty* as agent, *book* as patient (or 'goal' in Dik's terms), and *Lorna* as recipient. The further specification involves labeling one of these terms as 'subject' and the others as 'object'. Depending on which term is labeled as subject, the predication is mapped into a different syntactic construction (with different word order).

Unfortunately, the concept of grammatical subject, while valid for many languages, is not applicable to all languages. Many ergative languages, such as Australian languages, do not offer any evidence of the kind to be found in Indo-European languages, and a number of Native American languages can be analyzed in terms of roles (see below) rather than grammatical functions. Models such as LFG have yet to tackle this difficulty, but Role and Reference Grammar has adopted the solution of recognizing grammatical relations as central but not basic. Instead it takes as basic the function of syntactic pivot; in the examples of conjoined clauses, the subject is pivot in the sense that it is the subject noun phrase which is deleted in the second clause in each example and which acts as the pivot on which the whole compound sentence balances. It is a very old idea that clauses denote situations in which the entities referred to by the Noun Phrases play roles such as agent, patient, instrument, and so on (see the discussion in Sect. 1 above).

Two major questions arise: how are roles established and what is their function in a formal model? (see Sect. 1 in *Functional Relations*). The first question is of no concern to the various Chomskyan transformational models. Thematic roles play a part in marking the links between Noun Phrases and their antecedents, but the semantic content of notions such as 'agent' is irrelevant. How roles are established is likewise unimportant in HPSG, but LFG (see *New Developments in Lexical Functional Grammar*) has adopted the proto-roles developed by Dowty. (In fact proto-roles go back to the early days of Lexicase in the 1970s and were invoked for agent by Cruse (1973), but the supporting arguments differ.) Fillmore (1968) provided a list of unsatisfactory intuitive meaning-based definitions of various roles. Roles in Lexicase are firmly based on grammatical criteria (see Cruse (1973), Anderson (1971), Jackendoff (1976, 1987), and Miller (1989)). Dowty (1991) advocates verbal entailments as criteria for establishing two very general prototypical roles: proto-agent and proto-patient. Dowty's proto-roles are difficult to distinguish from the 'macro-roles' of actor and undergoer employed in RRG and Lexicase, and his general approach is like that of the above-listed advocates of grammatical criteria. (Jackendoff (1987) also proposes entailments as a criterion for differentiating thematic roles.)

Linguists cross-classify further according to their position on two controversial issues. First, some, such as Anderson (see *Case Grammar*), Starosta (see *Lexicase*), and Jackendoff, see roles, or many of them at least, as localist, based on spatial notions such as location, movement to, and movement from. Others do not. Second, some, such as Starosta, see roles as reflecting the speaker's mental representation of an external situation, while others, such as Rappaport and Levin (1988), relate roles directly to 'objective' reality. (Roles are deployed in semantic models, such as Barwise and Perry's Situation Semantics and have long been central in the study of first language acquisition.)

In the 1960s Chomskyan Generative Grammar had no place for roles. Fillmore (1968) put forward the idea of a Case Grammar. He observed that subjects and objects had no single semantic interpretation, and that analysts recognized one and the same role in different languages in which a given role received different case markings. Fillmore proposed that even in languages without case affixes the deep structure of sentences could be seen as consisting of a verb and Noun Phrases, each of which stood in a particular case relationship with the verb. The case relationships received labels such as 'agent', 'instrument', and 'dative'. The Noun Phrases were unordered with respect to the verb and rules of subject selection controlled the linear order of constituents in the surface structure. Fillmore hoped that the arrays of cases would express a universal notion of sentence type independently of surface constituent order.

Fillmore's proposals, criticized by Dougherty (1970) for inadequate subject selection rules and problematic analyses of particular constructions, were subsequently abandoned, but Anderson continued with his localist model and roles play a central part in Jackendoff (1976). Jackendoff (1987) argues that any linguistic model (as opposed to a merely syntactic model) requires rules generating conceptual structures and rules generating syntactic structures. The entities in the conceptual structures are places, events, paths, and states. Roles are not primitives in the model but derive from various combinations of entities in the conceptual structures. Jackendoff, like other linguists, analyzes the control relations in examples such as *Fiona persuaded Angus to help Ruaridh* in terms of thematic roles. (In this example, *Angus* controls the subject of *help*; in traditional terms, it is the understood subject of *help*.)

LFG (see *Lexical Functional Grammar*) recognizes three levels of language—thematic, structural, and functional—which are regarded as parallel information structures. (The parallel here with Halliday (1967) is obvious.) Each level has its own structure and the levels are linked by correspondence/mapping/linking principles. Thematic roles (agent, etc.) are represented in the thematic structures, and subjects and direct/oblique objects in the functional structures. With the different levels, Lexical Functional Grammar offers another way of capturing the fact that there is often a mismatch in every language between role, grammatical function, and syntactic constituent. The obvious English example is the agent expressed by an oblique object prepositional phrase in the passive, as in *The cat was attacked by the dog*, and by the subject noun phrase in the active, *The dog attacked the cat*. LFG shares with Fillmore's Case Grammar the aim of capturing the semantic constancy underlying syntactic variability.

In its treatment of the semantic structure of clause, RRG takes as basic the representation of different types of verb by means of different (combinations of) logical predicates. For instance, in the formula CAUSE (x,e), where x is an individual and e is an event, x has the role of agent. In the formula GO (x,y,z), which relates to sentences like *The marbles rolled from the table to the furthest corners of the room*, x receives the role of theme, y the role of source, and z the role of goal. In Lexicase, roles are specified in the lexical entries for verbs. They figure crucially in statements of subcategorization, where categories such as NP and PP do not appear.

Cases, renamed thematic roles or theta-roles, are deployed in two Chomskyan models, Government and Binding and Principles and Parameters. Verbs and prepositions are generally held to assign roles to argument nouns but not every linguist accepts that nouns and adjectives also assign roles. Each theta-role associated with a verb must be assigned to an argument and each argument must receive one theta-role. Only arguments that have been assigned case can be assigned a theta-role. Theta-roles assigned to arguments function as part of the explanation of the movement of Noun Phrases in the passive construction, and also as part of the constraints that enable links between Noun Phrases and their antecedents to be established and maintained across longer or shorter stretches of syntactic structure. In these models, as opposed to the functional models discussed above, theta-roles have semantic import but the syntax is blind to this content; their crucial function is to help the grammar keep track of the NPs to which they are assigned and to ensure that there are the same number of NPs on each level of structure, that is, ensuring that material is neither deleted or added (see *Generative Grammar: Principles and Parameters*).

6. Lexicon and Syntax

The 'lexicon' in discussions of syntax is a technical construct, rather different from the 'dictionary' of ordinary discourse. The lexicon is a repository of information relevant to a syntactic description, whereas the dictionary, while it may include information of this kind, typically contains information about word etymologies and other aspects of their meaning unrelated to syntax. There is a close relationship between syntax and the lexicon.

Traditionally the syntax handles regularities of sentence structure, and the lexicon is a list of words with information about the syntactic idiosyncrasies of individual words. For example, the syntax may describe the relationship between active and passive sentences by means of a general rule or set of rules and the lexicon will contain the information that, for example, *resemble* only occurs in the active and *rumour* in the passive. Minimally, the lexicon will contain information about the part of speech of individual words (for instance, that *cat* and *mouse* are nouns, *sleep* and *chase* verbs, and so on) and subcategorization information (e.g., *sleep* is intransitive and *chase* is transitive). This information can be encoded in the lexicon with subcategorization frames such as [CHASE, V, — NP] (CHASE is a verb and occurs before an NP, that is, that it is a transitive verb). Early Transformational Grammars held a simple view of this kind, as described in the article *Generative Grammar: Transformational Grammar*. The syntax generated tree structures such as [VP — NP]. This structure then permitted the insertion of a verb like *chase*, since the latter's subcategorization frame met the structure generated by the grammar. An alternative view emerged in connection with developments in phrase structure models, where the kind of account offered above for *chase* came to be seen as replicating information unnecessarily. Since the lexical entry for the verb must contain information on its transitivity, the syntax rules simply seem to recapitulate this information and the lexical items might as well be allowed to 'project' or specify their own syntax (see *Lexicon in Formal Grammar*; *X-bar Syntax*). The changing position of the lexicon in Chomskyan grammar can be seen by comparing the position described in the article *Generative Grammar: Transformational Grammar* with that described in *Generative Grammar: Principles and Parameters*. Chomsky's most recent work in 'bare phrase structure', as reported in the article *Generative Grammar: The Minimalist Program*, carries this approach to one logical conclusion, namely that no syntactic component is required, only a lexicon. (An alternative approach is to recognize a minimal syntax which assembles words into larger structures and moves them from one part of the structure to another.)

A second source of difficulty for early Transformational Grammars was the notion of a transformational rule itself. As mentioned above, one way of conceptualizing the relationship between the syntax and the lexicon is that the syntax describes regularities of sentence structure, and the lexicon contains information about the syntactic idiosyncracies of individual words. This relationship was typically supported with the well-known restrictions on passivization. From the 1970s, however, it became clear that these idiosyncracies are more pervasive than was first thought, so pervasive indeed that to capture them in the lexicon requires a description encapsulating much of the syntax previously handled by transformations. For instance, it turned out that operations within the lexicon performed more efficiently and insightfully syntactic operations assumed in early Chomskyan grammars to be necessarily done by transformation, such as operations relating construction types to each other (like active to passive), rearranging argument structures (like the alternation between *give her the book* and *give the book to her*), and so on (see the discussion in the articles *Lexicon Grammar* and *Lexicon in Formal Grammar*). In models where functional structure is central, the lexicon plays a crucial role, as demonstrated by the names given to some of these models: Lexical Functional Grammar, Lexicase, Autolexical Syntax (see *Autolexical Syntax*). The lexicon is also central where features play a central part, as in HPSG. Role and Reference Grammar, with lexical representations and semantic relations at the heart of its system, is a thoroughly lexicalist model. (See also the contributions on *Case Grammar*; *Relational Grammar*; *Valency and Valency Grammar*.)

7. Formalism

In the early days of Generative Grammar the concept of a rule was close to the traditional notion. There were rules specific to each construction (mostly transformations, as explained below). Lexical items were stored in a lexicon with a certain amount of information relevant to specifying the correct combination of verb and subject/object noun (see *Generative Grammar: Transformational Grammar*).

Two major changes affected this view of rules of grammar. The first was that rules became more general. Transformations were reduced to two simply-stated rules, *wh*-movement and NP movement. Phrase structure rules were simplified so that they specified a single general X-bar schema, a change made possible by the discovery that different phrase types - NP, VP, AP, PP - could be assigned parallel head-specifier-complement structures (see *X-bar Syntax*). The second change came from the realization that lexical items play an important part in clause structure. The first inkling of this idea is found in Lakoff (1970) (which had circulated for a number of years before being published). Lakoff gave an account of how individual lexical items interact with transformations, either requiring a rule to apply or requiring that a rule not apply. That lexical items replace phrase structure rules was advocated and developed by Hudson in a series of papers in the early 1980s and incorporated in his *Word Grammar*. A parallel development was published in more formal detail in Starosta (1988), which demonstrates how a large range of syntactic phenomena can be handled by means of features stored in lexical entries (see *Lexicase*). The latter approach has been adopted into HPSG, and current developments in the Chomskyan model are tending towards a similar central role for lexical items, as discussed in Sect. 6 (for a full discussion, see *Lexicon Grammar*).

In the 1960s Generative Grammar was seen by its practitioners as bringing mathematical rigor to their work. (Mathematical rigor was also prized by Glossematics, Applicational Grammar, and Categorial Grammar.) Their analyses, explicit and predictive, were based on rewriting systems called 'abstract automata'. In the earliest version of Generative Grammar the core of the grammar consisted of an initial symbol and a set of rules. One rule rewrote the initial symbol, S, as NP and VP, and other rules expanded these and other symbols. The operation of the rewrite rules created sequences of strings of symbols; tree diagrams are a condensed representation of such sequences. The rewrite rules generated the core structure of active declarative clauses. It was supposed that rewrite rules could not handle certain central phenomena of natural language such as subject-verb agreement and the relationship between different constructions. Instead, such phenomena were handled by transformations, which operated on whole trees, adding, deleting, and transposing symbols and the structure dominated by them, in order to derive other constructions. Such grammars, neutral between speaker and hearer, were not procedural models but there was (and still is) a general use of procedural, dynamic vocabulary. Constituents move in order to get case (see *Generative Grammar: Principles and Parameters*), features are checked off and items are merged (see *Generative Grammar: The Minimalist Program*), attribute-value matrices are unified (see *Head-driven Phrase Structure Grammar*; *Lexical Functional Grammar*; *New Developments in Lexical Functional Grammar*), and so on. Emphasis moved from detailed rewrite and transformational rules to general constraints that check structures. (The view of transformations as 'node-admissibility-conditions', that is, as filters filtering out incorrect structures, dates at least from McCawley (1968).)

Rewrite rules—phrase-structure rules—were initially conceived as handling unanalyzable symbols, and features were used for the storage of information only in the lexicon, where, for example, nouns carried such features as animate vs. nonanimate, abstract vs. concrete, mass vs. count (see *Generative Grammar: Transformational Grammar*). One development in the late 1960s (e.g., in Postal (1969)) incorporated the idea that rewrite rules generate structures consisting of bundles of features which were spelt out as words. In particular, all morphological information was carried by features and functional items such as articles, and auxiliary verbs resulted from spelling out. The expanded role of features was extended first by GPSG (see *Generalized Phrase Structure Grammar*) and latterly by HPSG (see *Head-driven Phrase Structure Grammar*). HPSG handles features by means of sorted feature structures, also called Attribute-Value Matrices (AVM). For example, where Chomskyan Generative Grammar generated a Noun Phrase containing a determiner and a noun, which acquired features when lexical items were inserted, HPSG has a matrix of features containing submatrices. The top feature in each submatrix specifies the type or sort of the feature-structure, say [noun] or [determiner], and other features convey information about, for example, number, animacy, or case. Each feature consists of a sort (attribute)—say, [case]—and a subsort (value)—say [accusative]. Phenomena such as subject-verb agreement are handled by unification, a constraint ensuring that in a given clause, part of the feature matrix of a subject noun is shared by the feature matrix of the verb. AVMs and unification are also central to LFG and are employed along with other devices in Autolexical Syntax (see *Autolexical Syntax*). Unification, or something analogous, appears to lie behind the MERGE operation invoked in Chomsky's latest work as sketched in the article *Generative Grammar: The Minimalist Program*.

Although favored by computational linguists, unification models have not produced insights into structure or hypotheses about first language acquisition such as were obtained in the 1960s. Indeed, much unification work focuses on problems of syntactic structure flagged in transformational work. On the other hand, it was claimed that GPSG offered a mathematically much tighter structure than Transformational Grammar.

The above comments on unification models, insights and hypotheses also apply to Categorial Grammar. Detailed and rigorous rules were central to Montague Categorial Grammar, which linguists began adopting in the early 1970s, and Shaumjan's Applicational Grammar in the 1960s. Along with Dik's Functional Grammar, these models benefit from the practice of logicians: the basic well-formed formulas are strictly defined, as are the rules for deriving well-formed formulas from the basic ones.

Not all models aim at generative rigor. In its account of the semantics of clauses Role and Reference Grammar employs formulas based on predicate calculus, but primitives and axioms are not defined and rules deriving theorems (generating semantic structures and indeed generating syntactic structures) are not defined. Nonetheless it offers many insights into the semantics of the clause and into the correspondence between semantic and syntactic structures.

The model furthest from the mainstream concern with formal rules is Langacker's Cognitive Grammar. It adopts a view, which would undoubtedly have appealed to Firth (see *Firth and the London School*), that no one formalism can capture all aspects of a given phenomenon. Different notations and descriptive formats are suited to different descriptive and analytical purposes, and no notation translates directly into specific psychological claims. In its current version it is not a generative model but one whose goal is to represent and explore the relationship between cognition and language. Its most important contribution to linguistics has been to introduce and apply to language various concepts from cognitive psychology such as profile, figure and ground, landmark, and trajector, and to develop diagrammatic (almost pictorial) representations of events, entities, and relationships.

The relationship between Cognitive Grammar and formal models parallels two methods in mathematical representation. Stewart (1989: 95) observed that some mathematicians work in terms of visual images and mental pictures and others think in formulas. There are fashions in mathematical presentation. For decades, mathematicians drew pictures. The fashion changes, pictures go out of favor and rigorous formalism is *de rigueur*. But as the formulas become 'ever more impenetrable' (Stewart's words), visual imagery rises once more to the surface of the collective mathematical subconscious. Stewart makes the point that many phenomena cannot be handled by linear algebra but only by topological structures. Similarly, Cognitive Grammar offers representations for concepts and analyses that are not insightfully handled by formulas.

8. Levels of Structure

Grammars fall into two sets: those that handle syntactic constructions by means of different levels or layers of structure and those that have only one layer (see Sect. 3 above). The classic example of a grammar with more than one layer of structure is the Standard Model of Transformational Grammar (see *Generative Grammar: Transformational Grammar*). Phrase-structure rules generate deep structures which are mapped into surface structures by transformations. Transformations move, add, and delete constituents. In the Government and Binding and Principles and Parameters models addition and deletion are not allowed; instead, initial structures with empty nodes are generated and constituents move from one node to another already-existing but empty node. The Minimalist Program envisages initial structures containing no empty nodes; when a constituent moves, the move itself creates a new node (see Sect. 4 in *Generative Grammar: The Minimalist Program*).

The Standard Model had a lexicon, which again was not a separate layer of structure but a store of lexical items. In later models, the extended lexicon plays a large role, without constituting an extra layer of structure. Semantic interpretations are represented in all models by formulas of predicate logic, possibly adapted. These do constitute a separate layer of structure, since different kinds of representations are required for the constituent structure of a given clause and its interpretation. However, since all models require syntactic and semantic structures, the semantic layer does not differentiate one from another. Interestingly, the MP appears to be leading towards a model with one layer of lexico-syntactic structure which is mapped on to Logical Form and Phonetic Form. (Strictly speaking, Logical Form does not constitute a full, rich semantic interpretation but represents certain components of such an interpretation, such as coreference. It is not clear whether the Minimalist Program envisages a level of lexico-syntactic structure or merely a system of rules linking the two levels of Phonetic Form and Logical Form.)

In early work the constraints put on phrase structure rules were such that they were unable to handle various kinds of long-distance dependency such as subject/verb agreement. Instead these phenomena were handled by means of transformations, which led to the creation of two layers of structure ('deep' and 'surface') linked by transformations. Transformations also handled relations between constructions such as active-passive and declarative-interrogative. In the late 1970s the first work within GPSG appeared. This model used only phrase-structure rules and only one layer of structure. As explained in Sect. 7 above, the key idea was that phrase-structure rules could specify complex categories consisting of sets of features carrying information about, for example, word class, X-bar level, agreement, case assignment, and even coreference between a particular item and a constituent elsewhere in a given structure. The latter feature enabled GPSG to handle the long-distance dependencies for which transformations had hitherto been thought essential. An example of such a dependency is the phrase *the book which I knew Fiona wanted to lend to Kirsty*, in which *the book* is the understood direct object of *lend*.

HPSG likewise has a single major layer of structure. The term 'major' is used because Pollard and Sag (1994: 3) talk of 'multiple levels of structure'. In fact, the levels relate mostly to the fact that the values of attributes can themselves function as cover terms for embedded sets of attributes, and the attribute-value matrices (see Sect. 7 above on Formalism) can be converted into tree diagrams showing constituent structure. The relationship between the feature matrices and the tree diagrams recalls the relationship between sequences of strings of symbols and tree diagrams in early Generative Grammar. LFG handles clauses by means of tree diagrams showing constituent structure and by attribute-value matrices showing functional structure and constructed from information stored in lexical entries. The constituent structure and the functional structure are not major different layers of structure but different aspects of one and the same layer.

Dik's Functional Grammar has one layer of syntactic structure. This is achieved, not through phrase-structure rules generating complex categories or through feature matrices, but by making the initial structures semantic, represented by means of predicate logic formulas, by using features on terms to express information about syntactic function (subject, object), role (agent, benefactive), and pragmatic function (topic, theme, focus), and by using operators to encode information about choice of structure, word order, and so on. There is however only one layer of syntactic structure and that is surface syntax, into which semantic representations are mapped by means of expression rules.

9. Features

In linguistics the use of features was first developed in phonology in order to handle processes such as assimilation. Katz and Fodor (1963) introduced features in their modeling of dictionary entries and polysemy. They employed 'semantic markers' such as *Human* and *Male* and more complex 'distinguishers' representing the different interpretations of a given lexical item and functioning like a complex feature. Katz and Postal (1964) introduced features into syntax and Chomsky (1965) used features in the lexicon for subcategorization (see Sect. 6 above; see also *Generative Grammar: Transformational Grammar*) for inherent properties of nouns (count or mass, concrete or abstract, etc.).

Within Chomskyan Transformational Grammar, Postal (1966) proposed that the English articles be derived from features on nouns. For instance, [+Definite] was spelled out as *the*. Jacobs and Rosenbaum (1970) proposed to have only lexical categories and features in deep structure, bundles of features being spelled out as articles and auxiliary verbs. This line of analysis was abandoned and features confined to the lexicon. They were subsequently taken up by, among others, Lieber in her account of morphology. (Features had been used in earlier work on Generative Morphology—see Matthews (1965, 1972).)

Features have been employed intensively in non-Chomskyan models such as Lexicase, GPSG, HPSG, and LFG. In all models the lexicon lists only features not predictable from other features. Whatever model emerges from the Minimalist Program may well join this group.

In Lexicase, lexical features are the basic descriptive mechanism. There are no phrase-structure or transformational rules. (In this respect the MP is following the Lexicase route.) Noncontextual features distinguish lexical items that are not synonymous. Contextual features state which other words may attach to a given word as dependents in sentences. They convey grammatical information and selectional information relating to the semantic properties of the constituents required by a given verb. Information about constituent order is encoded in the contextual features, along with information about agreement and government.

GPSG represents a stage on the route from models handling information mainly by means of arrangements of constituents to models, such as HPSG, handling information mainly by features. Syntactic categories were conceived as sets of features with their values. Features specified a given node as nominal or verbal, its bar level N" corresponds to the features <N +> <V –> and <BAR 2>; that is, a feature N with the value +, a feature V with the value –, and a feature BAR with the value 2. Other features specified whether a noun was singular or plural, what its case was, and even, on the assumption that prepositions are created by the spelling out of features, which preposition a particular verb imposed on a given noun. Features specified whether a verb preceded its subject, as in *Did Shona accept the present?* or whether a sentence contained a null NP: in the structure of *the house which Fergus bought* an S with the feature <SLASH> dominated the sequence *Fergus bought*. <SLASH> indicated that the S dominated an empty Noun Phrase, the one corresponding to *which*. Various constraints controlled the distribution of features; some types of features required a match between the features on a head and the features on its modifiers, while other types of feature were passed from constituents low in a tree to ones higher in the tree, hence the labels 'head features' and 'foot features'.

Like Lexicase, HPSG uses only features as a descriptive device. Unlike Lexicase the features are organized in attribute-value matrices. In Lexicase, agreement is handled negatively; e.g., the relevant feature rule states that a determiner that is [+plural] cannot occur with a noun that has a different feature for number. Whereas GPSG has various principles controlling the distribution of features, HPSG handles distribution by unification alone. For determiner and noun, for example, unification unifies the two feature matrices into one. If unification fails because the values of two attributes are different—here, if the attribute NUMBER has the value SG in one matrix but the value PL in the other, for instance, *this book* vs *this books*—the sentence is rejected. As in GPSG features are used to specify the type of a Verb Phrase: in *wanted to be considered for the post* the entire phrase has the features [finite] and [past-tense]; *to be considered for the post* is a verb phrase with the feature [inf] for infinitive; *be considered* is a verb phrase with the feature [base] specifying that the base form of the verb is required; and *considered for the post* has the feature [pas], specifying that the verb must be passive. Like GPSG, HPSG uses a feature SLASH to specify clauses containing a null Noun Phrase.

LFG specifies arrangements of constituents and functional structures in the form of an attribute-value matrix (see Sect. 7 above; see also *Lexical Functional Grammar*). Unification, first employed in LFG, ensures the correct distribution of features for such phenomena as agreement. With respect to the central role of features and unification, LFG and HPSG are similar, though they differ with respect to the relation between constituent structure and features and with respect to the central role of grammatical functions in LFG.

10. Syntax and Semantics

Related to levels of description within syntax (see Sect. 8) is the linking of syntactic information with semantic and pragmatic information and with phonological information. This section deals with the interface between syntax and semantics/pragmatics, and the following section with the interface between syntax and phonology.

The boundaries between syntax, semantics and pragmatics are not always clearly discernible. This is true of, for instance, the central topic of grammatical meaning, the semantics of grammatical (or functional) categories such as sentence modality (declarative/interrogative/imperative) and negation, of categories associated with the verb, such as tense, mood, and aspect, and categories closely related to the noun, such as definiteness and quantification. All these categories are central to syntax but also have a semantics; declarative and interrogative syntactic structures have a close relationship with semantic types such as assertions and questions. They also have pragmatic implications. For example, declarative and interrogative structures can be used either for statements or inquiries.

These relationships have been accommodated in a variety of ways. The relationship between a syntactic and a semantic representation can be construed as 'directional': from syntax to semantics—a syntactic representation is generated which then receives a semantic representation—or conversely from semantics to syntax—a semantic representation is generated and then interpreted syntactically. Or the relationship can be construed as 'simultaneous', syntactic and semantic representations being generated simultaneously, in which case there is no directionality. Standard Chomskyan models (see *Generative Grammar: Transformational Grammar*) adopted a directional position. A deep structure is generated in the syntax which is sent to the separate 'semantic component' to be assigned a 'semantic interpretation' (and through the transformational machinery to the surface structure and eventually to a phonological interpretation). This position was, in its day, described as involving an 'interpretive semantics'. More recent Chomskyan models postulate among various distinct syntactic levels, a level of logical form, which acts as the interface between syntax and semantics, and perhaps also with pragmatics (see *Generative Grammar: Principles and Parameters*; *Chomsky and Pragmatics*).

Generative Semantics turned the relationship on its head and had the grammar specify semantic structures which were mapped onto syntax (see *Generative Semantics*; *Syntax and Semantics*). Later versions of Generative Semantics sought to include pragmatics too in a single integrated account of sentence derivation. Role and Reference Grammar and Dik's Functional Grammar also map semantic structures onto syntax.

The 'simultaneous' approach handles syntax and semantics in tandem. In GPSG (see *Generalized Phrase Structure Grammar*) each rule pairs a syntactic structure with a semantic representation, so that a derivation simultaneously develops both a syntactic and a semantic structure. There is no 'directionality' and no separate semantic component. HPSG adopts a similar approach, as does Categorial Grammar in a rather different framework (see *Head-driven Phrase Structure Grammar*; *Categorial Grammar*).

The study of grammatical categories such as tense, mood, aspect, and case belongs both to semantics and syntax (with morphology). One part of this study deals with the processes by which grammatical markers develop—tense, mood, and aspect markers, prepositions and case affixes, articles. Typically, a lexical item is reduced in various stages until it becomes a grammatical marker (often in the shape of an affix). The process of development is called 'grammaticalization', although some linguists, mainly in North America, prefer the term 'grammaticization'. Researchers draw attention to the source of grammatical markers in items denoting location, movement, and body parts and regard their work as elucidating the relationship between grammar and cognition, the way in which the speakers of a given language conceive of the world around them (see *Grammaticalization and Lexicalization*).

11. Syntax and Morphology/Phonology

Grammars are traditionally thought of as having two components: syntax and morphology. Syntax deals with the structure of sentences and morphology with the structure of words. Within morphology a distinction is drawn between derivational or lexical morphology and inflexional morphology. The former deals with the structure of words and the creation of new words, for example, *like -likeable;* the latter deals with the realization of grammatical categories such as tense and number: BOY + plural is *boys*, MAN + plural is *men*, and so on. This view supposes that syntax and morphology are different levels, each with its own type of rules and constraints on rules. For example, many rules of derivational morphology change a word from one class to another, as with *like* and *likeable*, but it is arguable that no syntactic rules involve class-changing. Conversely, one expects to find syntactic rules with no morphological counterpart; for instance, there are syntactic rules that move constituents (e.g., *Mary is happy* vs. *Is Mary happy?*) but there are no comparable morphological rules. There is also the question of whether any syntactic processes are affected by morphology, and vice-versa. For example, if the two levels are distinct, the syntax of derived adjectives such as *likeable* should not differ from that of basic adjectives such as *old,* and the syntax of irregular nouns such as *man-men* should not differ from the syntax of regular items such as *boy-boys*. (These general issues are discussed in the article *Syntax and Phonology*.)

There must be an interface between morphology and syntax, and it is possible that inflexional and derivational morphology have different interfaces. Since derivational morphology is concerned with word formation, it must have a close connection with the lexicon. Inflexional morphology is more problematic. It is the traditional interface between syntax and phonology, since the realization of number, tense, case, and so on is relevant both to syntax and the phonological realization of words. Number, for instance, is involved in syntactic operations such as number agreement between subject noun and verb, but it is also relevant to, for example, the realization of the lexical item MAN as *man* or *men*. Some models, as explained in the article *Stratificational Grammar*, keep syntax and morphology relatively separate. In others the distinction is much less clear (see *Generative Grammar: Principles and Parameters*; *Generative Grammar: The Minimalist Program*).

Bibliography

Aissen J L 1992 Topic and focus in Mayan. *Language* **68**: 43–80
Allerton D 1982 *Valency and the English Verb*. Academic Press, London

Anderson J M 1968 Ergative and nominative in English. *Journal of Linguistics* **4**: 1–32

Anderson J M 1971 *The Grammar of Case.* Cambridge University Press, Cambridge

Bresnan J, Kanerva J M 1989 Locative inversion in Chichewa: A case study of factorization in grammar. *Linguistic Inquiry* **20(1)**: 1–50

Chomsky N 1965 *Aspects of the Theory of Syntax.* MIT Press, Boston, MA

Chomsky N 1971 Deep structure, surface structure, and semantic interpretation. In: Steinberg D D, Jakobovits L A (eds.) *Semantics: An Interdisciplinary Reader in Philosophy, Linguistics and Psychology.* Cambridge University Press, Cambridge

Cruse D A 1973 Some thoughts on agentivity. *Journal of Linguistics* **9**: 11–23

Dougherty R 1970 Recent studies in language universals. *Foundations of Language* **6**: 505–61

Fillmore C J 1968 The case for case. In: Bach E, Harms R T (eds.) *Universals in Linguistic Theory.* Holt, Rinehart and Winston, New York

Gruber J 1976 *Functions of the Lexicon in Formal Descriptive Grammars.* Indiana University Linguistics Club, Bloomington, IN

Halliday M A K 1967 Notes on transitivity and theme in English: PART 1. *Journal of linguistics* **3**: 37–81

Harris Z 1946 From morpheme to utterance. *Language* **22**: 161–83

Jackendoff R 1976 Toward an explanatory semantic representation. *Linguistic Inquiry* **7**: 89–150

Jacobs RA, Rosenbaum PS 1970 *English Transformational Grammar.* Ginn, London

Katz J J, Fodor J A 1963 The structure of a semantic theory. *Language* **39**: 170–210

Katz J J, Postal P M 1964 *An Integrated Theory of Linguistic Descriptions.* MIT Press, Cambridge, MA

Lakoff G 1970 *Irregularity in Syntax.* Holt, Rinehart and Winston, New York

McCawley J D 1968 Concerning the base component of a transformational grammar. *Foundations of Language* **4**: 243–69

Matthews P H 1965 The inflectional component of a word-and-paradigm grammar. *Journal of Linguistics* **1**: 139–71

Matthews P H 1972 *Inflectional Morphology: A Theoretical Study Based on Aspects of Latin Verb Conjugation.* Cambridge University Press, Cambridge

Mel'chuk I 1988 *Dependency Syntax: Theory and Practice.* State University of New York Press, Albany, NY

Miller J 1989 Participant roles and truth conditions. In: Arnold D, Atkinson M, Durand J, Grover C, Sadler L (eds.) *Essays on Grammatical Theory and Universal Grammar.* Clarendon Press, Oxford

Payne D (ed.) 1992 *Pragmatics of Word Order Flexibility.* Benjamin, Amsterdam

Pollard C, Sag I A 1994 *Head-Driven Phrase Structure Grammar.* University of Chicago Press, Chicago, IL

Postal P M 1969 On so-called 'pronouns' in English. In: Reibel D A, Schane S A (eds.) *Modern Studies in English.* Prentice Hall, Englewood Cliffs, NJ

Rappaport W, Levin B 1988 What to do with theta-roles. In: Wilkins W (ed.) *Thematic Relations.* Academic Press, New York

Sgall P, Hajicova E, Panevova J 1986 *The Meaning of the Sentence in its Semantic and Pragmatic Aspects.* Academia, Prague

Starosta S 1988 *The Case for Lexicase.* Pinter, London

Stewart I 1989 *Does God Play Dice? The New Mathematics of Chaos.* Blackwell, Oxford

Tesniere L 1959 *Elements de Syntaxe Structurale.* Klincksieck, Paris

Vallduvi E 1992 *The Information Component.* Garland Press, New York

American Structuralism

John G. Fought

The main focus of this article is a theory of language and a corresponding view of linguistics associated primarily with Leonard Bloomfield (1887–1949), to a lesser extent with Edward Sapir (1884–1939), and with their students. Some key elements of their views, however, can be found in the work of Franz Boas (1858–1942), the principal founder of modern American anthropology and the mentor of generations of linguistic anthropologists, including Sapir. It is less well known that Boas was also a friend and mentor of Bloomfield (cf. Bloomfield 1943).

The history of American structural linguistics is often sketched as a mostly linear development from an early, intuitive, anthropological, Boas–Sapir style to a later, more explicitly formal Bloomfieldian style exemplified by Bloomfield himself and his students (cf. Hymes and Fought 1981). This article emphasizes that Sapir and Bloomfield, who had similar backgrounds and were only three years apart in age, also had fundamentally similar approaches to linguistics and, further, that both were strongly influenced by Boas. Finally, it suggests that the main discontinuities in theory and practice within the American structuralist community appeared later, between the group made up of Boas, Bloomfield, and Sapir together with certain of their early students and followers and the younger group of distributionalist structuralists rather misleadingly known as 'Bloomfieldians,' including Bernard Bloch, Martin Joos, Henry Lee Smith, George Trager, and Zellig Harris, whose influence was greatest in the late 1940s and 1950s.

The principal disciplinary contributors to the formation of American structuralist linguistics were the mature fields of dialectology and comparative Indo-European philology and the linguistic side of the young discipline of anthropology. From the first of these came an emergent notion of language structure, exemplified, for instance, in the doctrine of regular, conditioned sound change in comparative philology and of regular phonetic correspondence in dialectology; from linguistic anthropology came an emphasis on the study of spoken language in use within the speech community and a relativistic view of linguistic and cultural categories.

Native American languages have had an important role in giving American structuralist linguistics its distinctive character. The number and diversity of languages that continue to be spoken in North America in Native American speech communities is much greater than those that comprise the linguistic landscape of Western Europe. Native American languages, poorly documented and relatively accessible, have presented a continuing challenge and opportunity to North American scholars.

1. Franz Boas

In the last quarter of the nineteenth century, Boas developed an approach to linguistics that was shaped by his field studies of Native American languages and cultures. Unlike the leaders of European structuralism, he had no academic training in philology, though he apparently studied some standard works on his own (Stocking 1974: 455). His approach to these unwritten languages called for the elicitation, transcription, and analysis of large quantities of spoken discourse of ethnographically significant content. It emphasized proficiency in phonetic transcription that achieved phonetic accuracy but also reflected sound categories relevant to the speakers of the language. In 1889, he published a seminal paper, 'On alternating sounds,' in which he argued that certain apparently variable speech sounds reported for Native American and other 'exotic' languages (such as the range of sound types including both *r* and *l* that make up a phonological unit in Japanese) were actually artifacts of the observers' own categorizations of their perceptions rather than of the subjects' 'primitive' sound systems. Indeed, this was so much the case that the native language of an observer could in some instances be determined from a careful examination of such reports.

Wells (1974) summarized this paper and put its argument in the context of the linguistics and anthropology of the time. Stocking wrote (1968: 159) that it is 'impossible to exaggerate the significance of this article for the history of anthropological thought.' It is

> . . . much more than a critical or methodological exercise. It in fact foreshadows much of Boas' later criticism of late nineteenth-century racial thought and his work in physical anthropology. More importantly, it foreshadows a great deal of modern anthropological thought on 'culture.' At least by implication, it sees cultural phenomena in terms of the imposition of conventional meaning on the flux of experience. It sees them as historically conditioned and transmitted by the learning process. It sees them as determinants of our very perceptions of the external world. And it sees them in relative rather than in absolute terms. Much of Boas' later work, and that of his students after him, can be viewed simply as the working out of implications present in this article.

It must be emphasized that what Boas (and Stocking) say here of culture applies equally to language. It was Boas who made linguistics one of the 'four fields' of anthropological study, along with archaeology, cultural anthropology, and physical anthropology. One especially salient feature of American structuralism traceable to his influence is relativism, the view that cultural and linguistic categorization is imposed on experience in ways that differ, sometimes radically, from culture to culture and from language to language and that these different categorizations have equal claims on the attention of science. In this approach to linguistic description, pioneered and taught by Boas to generations of students, methodological primacy was given to fieldwork as a source of data, that is, to directly observed and carefully recorded speech and behavior, and to methods of analysis and description intended to be free of preconceptions about the nature and interrelationships of specific fundamental categories. Boas emphasized the importance of collecting ethnographically relevant text material by transcribing it phonetically and explicating its form and content with the help of native speakers. By systematically paraphrasing and altering portions of the text after elicitation, and observing the covariation of the meanings and forms in the text, Boas and his students worked out the phonological and grammatical structures of the target languages. 'Perhaps his greatest contribution to science,' wrote Bloomfield (1943: 198) in his deeply felt obituary of Boas, '... was the development of descriptive language study.' And further, 'Boas amassed a tremendous body of observation, including much carefully recorded text, and forged, almost single-handed, the tools of phonetic and structural description.'

For Boas and his first generation of students, much more than for anthropologists since, language lay near the heart of anthropology. Linguistic methods, therefore, were part of the foundation of anthropological training as he organized it. He communicated his emphasis on native classification by generalizing it from his view of linguistics; within linguistics, he extended his conception of the nature of language from its sources in phonology:

> As the automatic and rapid use of articulations has brought it about that a limited number of articulations only, each with limited variability, and a limited number of sound-clusters, have been selected from the infinitely large range of possible articulations and clusters of articulations, so the infinitely large number of ideas have been reduced by classification to a lesser number, which by constant use have established firm associations, and which can be used automatically. (Boas 1911: 21)

Notice first the equal weight given to sounds and ideas in this passage and the notion applied to both of structure emerging from social interaction: systematization through classification, constant use, firm associations, and automaticity. Later American structuralists, however, continued to pay particular attention to phonological structure in developing a model of language, both as a practical matter in analyzing and describing so many hitherto undocumented languages and as a theoretical tenet, whereby a model of structural elements and relations based on phonology was projected into other levels of structure. The structure of semantics, by contrast, remained a mostly anthropological concern.

Since native classifications are imposed on the raw stuff of experience and of language by individuals and are propagated through language use in everyday interactions, there is no reason to expect that different cultures will develop the same scheme of classification. Instead, variation in all aspects of structure from community to community is to be expected. Boas gave expression to this community-oriented relativism in a frequently cited passage from the introduction to the *Handbook* (1911: 39).

> We conclude ... that in a discussion of the characteristics of various languages different fundamental categories will be found, and that in a comparison of different languages it will be necessary to compare as well the phonetic characteristics as the characteristics of the vocabulary and those of the grammatical concepts in order to give each language its proper place.

One offshoot of the linguistic version of cultural relativism was the interpretation of language in culture that came to be known as the Sapir–Whorf hypothesis. This topic has spawned a considerable literature of its own. Hoijer, in an influential symposium volume he edited on this topic (1954), traces this hypothesis to two paragraphs written by Sapir in 1929. The last sentences of each give the idea: 'The worlds in which different societies live are distinct worlds, not merely the same world with different labels attached,' and 'We see and hear and otherwise experience very largely as we do because the language habits of our community predispose certain choices of interpretation' (Sapir 1929, cited in Hoijer 1954: 92). The original formulation claims significantly less than many later, oversimplified paraphrases, whose purport is that language predetermines rather than predisposes. In any event, the close kinship between this view of Sapir's and the corresponding relativism of Boas's linguistic anthropology is manifest.

This relativism implies that individuals may also differ from one another in their personal category systems in the same ways that communities do, but this individual aspect of relativism was kept subordinate in theory to the unity supposed to arise from sharing a common culture or a common language. The largely tacit agreement maintained among most anthropologists and linguists to leave individual variation out of the domain of theory and description, to leave it uncovered, as it were, by the doctrine of cultural and linguistic relativism, has had serious consequences for descriptive practice in both fields. In linguistics, this omission has been a textbook example of anomaly in the sense of Kuhn (1962). Some consequences of the omission of individual variation from structural descriptions are discussed below, in connection with Bloomfield's descriptive work on Algonquian.

A still later sequel to the Boas–Sapir approach to language in culture is the development within American anthropological linguistics in the late 1940s and early 1950s of a structuralist approach to semantics, known as 'componential semantics' and 'ethnoscience' (cf. Goodenough 1956; Lounsbury 1956, 1964). This approach, which simply applied the same analytical tools to meaning that had long been applied to sound, was in sharp contrast to Bloomfield's radically nonstructural view of meaning. This steadfast lack of parallelism between structuralism in language form and atomism in semantics remains the most puzzling aspect of Bloomfield's thinking. At times he came very close to adopting a structural view of semantics, but he apparently never took the final step. Writing in 1927, for instance (1927: 179–80), he evidently relied to some extent on dictionary meaning, even for grammatical formatives and categories. He mentioned numerical systems and botany and kinship terminologies as complex in their relationship to cultural and material realities, 'with troublesome refinements,' such as degrees of affection, respect, and the like. This is an amazingly exact prefiguration of the reasoning that led to structural analyses of these semantic domains, and also of the reaction against those analyses within anthropology when they finally came about 25 years later.

2. Edward Sapir

Both Sapir and Bloomfield produced a large body of published work, including collections of text and analytical studies on a number of Native American languages (see Mandelbaum 1949). Sapir worked especially on the Athabaskan and Uto–Aztecan families. He too published a general book on linguistics, *Language* (1921); like Bloomfield's, it is still in print. Sapir also developed an interest in psychology, which brought him into a close working relationship with Harry Stack Sullivan, whose view of psychology focused on social interactions; from this interest Sapir launched the anthropological subfield of culture and personality studies in the 1930s.

Sapir's and Bloomfield's styles of description are sometimes contrasted as 'item and process' versus 'item and arrangement,' to use terms later introduced by Charles Hockett; in another publication (1970), however, Hockett pointed out that the two models are equivalent in power and descriptive capability. Zellig Harris also noted that Sapir's model of language structure relied on notions of 'pattern' and 'configuration.' Sapir's model of language structure continues the use of processes as one among many of the features of Boas's system. Its reliance on processes rather than on the relational counterparts introduced in later theoretical works by Bloomfield and others is doubtless an important reason for the usual perception of Sapir as an antecedent of Bloomfield.

Sapir (1921: 61–62) listed six types of grammatical processes: word order, composition, affixation, internal modification, reduplication, and accentual differences (in stress and pitch). He explained that composition 'differs from the mere juxtaposition of words in the sentence in that the compounded elements are felt as constituting but parts of a single word-organism' (1921: 64). It is easy to misunderstand his rhetoric of feeling and organism as a kind of naive psychologizing. However, the examples that followed made it clear that compared with mere juxtaposition, semantic changes, stress patterns, and affixation to the compound stem are characteristic of compounds. As usual, Sapir writes of psychology and offers evidence from linguistics. Harris (1951a) commented on this.

> A detailed examination of Sapir's use of *psychology* and kindred words shows they refer not to some new forces within the individual which can affect his language, culture, or personality, but simply to the fact that the individual participates in linguistic, cultural, and personality patterns.

Sapir himself was explicit on this:

> The unconscious nature of this patterning consists not in some mysterious function of a racial or social mind... but merely in a typical unawareness on the part of the individual of outlines and demarcations and significances of conduct which he is all the time implicitly following.

This passage is also an important and eloquent expression of the Sapir–Whorf hypothesis.

One of the aims of his popular book was to classify languages in their patterns of use of the various formal processes as a means of expressing concepts and grammatical relations of different types. His treatment of affixation is an exemplary presentation in terms of process. Distributionalists wedded to item and arrangement descriptive styles often alleged that historical metaphor was inevitable with process descriptions, that process, in other words, always amounted to process through time. Harris did not accept this view:

> The difference between two partially similar forms is frequently described here as a process which yields one form out of the other. Thus when bases or themes have several vocalic forms, the various forms are said to be the result of vowel-change processes operating upon the base or theme (§ 6:2, 22:28). The difference between a base and a base-plus-suffix is described as the result of the process of suffixation (§ 6:1, 20:11). This is a traditional manner of speaking, especially in American Indian grammar (e.g., in the Handbook edited by Boas). It has, of course, nothing to do with historical change or process through time: it is merely process through the configuration, moving from one to another or larger part of the pattern. (Harris 1944: 199)

Although Harris never studied with Sapir, he read his work carefully and wrote penetrating appreciations of Sapir's collected writings and of Stanley Newman's study of Yokuts, as a representative of

Sapir's mature style of description. He emphasized the importance of Sapir's notions of configuration and pattern in understanding the approach:

> The relations between elements in the configuration are always described in terms of the pattern. Therefore Newman says: 'In order to preserve that inflexible rule of Yokuts syllabic structure which does not permit the juxtaposition of two vowels, the glottal stop is interposed as a hiatus-filler between two vowels that should morphologically follow each other' (§ 1:13)[...]. Since the elements are observed only as parts of the system, and occur only in the positions which are mentioned when the system is described, one can picture the configuration as determining the nature of its elements (requiring or employing them): 'The strict vocalic and syllabic requirements of the base do not apply to the theme' (§ 12:1). (Harris 1944: 198)

As in Bloomfield's work, both forms and meanings are related to each other as elements of the pattern: 'The configuration is treated as though it were a pattern of meanings as well as, basically, of forms. Summaries are offered of the meanings of various formal parts of the pattern' (Harris 1944: 199).

3. Leonard Bloomfield

The early career of Leonard Bloomfield was representative of the overall development of linguistics as a discipline in America. His early writings, including his first general book, the *Introduction to the Study of Language* (1914), and his reviews of Braune (1912) and Wundt (1913), show very strong influences from contemporary European work.

However, this same period in American linguistics was also marked by the appearance of descriptive studies of Native American and other non-European languages. Under the editorial and intellectual direction of Boas, the *International Journal of American Linguistics* began to appear in 1917, dedicated to Native American languages; a carefully orchestrated campaign of field studies of selected languages by Boas's closely supervised students resulted in sketches and longer descriptions collected and published in the three volumes of the *Handbook of American Indian Languages* (1911, 1922, 1934). One of these studies was Sapir's landmark dissertation on the Takelma language of Oregon (completed by 1909, published in 1922). Also at about this time, Bloomfield began descriptive linguistic work on Fox by studying texts collected and published by others (Hockett 1970: 94n). Very soon after, he began an analysis of Tagalog, based on elicitation and transcription of material from a native speaker then studying at the University of Illinois. After about two years of part-time work on the language, he published *Tagalog Texts* (1917), his first major venture outside the Indo-European language family and an already mature exercise in the text-based descriptive technique of the time. By some at least, this study is still regarded as the best available description of a Malayo-Polynesian language. During the 1920s, he further shifted the target of his descriptive work, concentrating thereafter on the Algonquian languages.

3.1 Bloomfield's Theoretical System

A characteristic tenet of American structuralism virtually absent from European linguistics is the primacy of the sentence over the word as the basic analytical element. This was asserted by Boas (1911: 23): 'Since all speech is intended to serve for the communication of ideas, the natural unit of expression is the sentence; that is to say, a group of articulate sounds which convey a complete idea.' For both Boas and Bloomfield, this perspective presumably drew support from the analytical techniques worked out for describing languages whose combinations of meaningful elements straddled the range of complexity from word-like structures to sentence-like structures. Sapir (1921: 32–33) takes a broader view of this question, representing the morpheme and the sentence as elements and a range of intermediate formations as more or less relevant to the configuration of a particular language. Bloomfield gave the primacy of the sentence much clearer expression after explicitly rejecting his earlier Wundtian view of the word as fundamental (cf. 1914[1970: 43]), pointing out the inconsistent and arbitrary aspects of conventional word division in European languages, and the lack of clear criteria of any kind for word division in Native American languages (Bloomfield 1927 [in Hockett 1970: 180–81]). Moreover, Bloomfield put this notion into a carefully articulated theoretical and operational context.

3.2 The Introduction to the Study of Language (1914)

The *Introduction* of 1914 feels like a very different book from the *Language* of 1933. The most striking difference between them is in the role played by psychology. The earlier book is a 'traditional' treatment of language, in which language forms are presented as expressing mental acts. The later book is 'formal,' in that language forms are themselves the focus, with types of semantic elements established in correlation with the linguistic forms but left almost completely empty. While this difference affects the exposition in many significant ways, it is the theoretical consequences that were presumably most important for Bloomfield and were certainly the most important in shaping reactions to his later work. In *Language*, Bloomfield advocated basing linguistic analysis on the overt forms of language, using their similarities and differences as the guide to organizing and presenting the grammar and syntax and to establishing the fundamental categories of the structure of each language. It was this, more than anything he said or did about the meaning of linguistic forms or the psychology of language, that ran directly counter to the familiar and dominant pattern of thought in linguistics. For others, as for the younger Bloomfield, it was the presumed underlying mental activities that gave shape and significance both to what was said and to the academic study of language. Moving these putative mental acts away from the focus of linguistics and concentrating instead on overt forms as both the target of analysis and the decisive manifestation of language structure may have been the real motivation for the persistent charges, so puzzling to Bloomfield, that he ignored meaning. His change in orientation toward psychology in linguistics must have taken place not long after the 1914 book was written. It was probably due to several factors; the stimulus of independent descriptive field work in the Boas style and the personal influence of Boas were likely to have been among the more important. Weiss's behaviorist psychology eclipsing the influence of Wundt's system on Bloomfield was also important but must have had its impact somewhat later, after his move to Ohio in 1921.

In any event, as Hymes and Fought (1981) argued, his linguistic practice was scarcely affected by this change in outlook. Bloomfield's approach to linguistics was formed very early in his career, in nearly its full power and generality, but it could only emerge fully through descriptive work. For instance, Moulton remarked (1970: 516) on the courage (and seeming arrogance) of the opening paragraph of 'Etymologisches' (Bloomfield 1912a), a paper based on Bloomfield's dissertation on 'secondary ablaut' and published in German in the premier Germanistic journal when he was only 24. In this paper, Bloomfield stated bluntly that previous treatments of the topic were guilty of either of two errors: treating the vowel alternations of the specific vocabulary sets as instances of sound symbolism or of ad hoc sound laws. Though 'ablaut' patterns of root-vowel alternation are very common in the Germanic vocabulary, comparisons show that many do not date back to proto-Germanic times. Instead, the newer sets of forms were modeled analogically on the older patterns, an example of the 'creative' uses of language to which Bloomfield turned a number of times.

3.3 Language (1933)

The descriptive theory of grammar and syntax expounded in Bloomfield's *Language* (1933) was hierarchical and relational, with elements of form at each level paired with elements of meaning. His methodological precepts made it clear that the formal elements were paramount and the meanings interpretive. Nowadays, the architecture of his theory may seem deceptively familiar in outward appearance. Primary phonemes made up morphemes; morphemes were free or bound, making up words and phrases; these in turn made up constituents and sentences, these last defined (following Meillet) as maximum free forms. To many of his influential contemporaries, however, the book

was shocking, despite its evident borrowings from traditional grammar and from the Pāṇinian tradition of Indian grammar. A closer look at the system outlined in *Language* will help to show why; it is also helpful to compare the less complex theoretical systems of later American structuralists with Bloomfield's to see what features of his system they dispensed with and what they changed.

In his system, there was a hierarchy of grammatical forms as well as the bound and free morphemes; like them, each grammatical form was paired with a semantic unit. Thus, it was not the morphemes themselves that made up grammatical forms; rather, they were the substance of those forms. Bloomfield identified four types of elements of grammatical form, or 'taxemes': these were 'modulation,' 'phonetic modification,' 'order,' and 'selection.' Modulation was the use of secondary phonemes—features of stress, pitch, and intonation—which later, in other structuralist approaches, came to be called suprasegmental phonemes. Phonetic modification was a change in the primary (i.e., segmental) phonemes of a morpheme. Morphemes, for Bloomfield, were composed of primary phonemes and had a single phonemic shape except under 'sandhi,' that is, when occurring with taxemes of modulation or phonetic modification. Taxemes are analogous to phonemes in that they are meaningless elements whose combinations are meaningful. These combinations are 'tagmemes.' Thus, phoneme is to morpheme as taxeme is to tagmeme; just as morphemes are paired with 'sememes,' so tagmemes are paired with 'episememes.'

Bloomfield used the utterance *Duchess!* of the lexical form *duchess* to illustrate his analysis of grammatical form. Each utterance, he emphasized, contains at least one grammatical form; these are arrangements of phonetic (i.e., lexical) forms, not mere naked occurrences of them. His phonemic representations, though interesting, are not the main point here: he transcribed *duchess* ['doces], and its constituent lexical forms *duke* and *-ess* were [djuwk] and [es]. A taxeme of selection establishes the specific form class—subclass of male personal nouns—occurring with *-ess* and the co-occurrence with *-ess*; their sequence is established by a taxeme of order. A taxeme of modulation gives heavy stress to the noun and leaves the affix unstressed. Ironically, in view of later developments, Bloomfield and Noam Chomsky both place stress assignment rules within grammar. Finally, a taxeme of phonetic modification replaces the 'compound primary phoneme' [juw] of [djuwk] with [o], as Bloomfield represented schwa, and the [k] with [c]. These, together with the taxeme of exclamatory final pitch and the taxeme of selection of a substantive expression, make up the utterance *Duchess!*. In this way, every phonological, morphological, and grammatical aspect of the utterance is accounted for.

This system is like the Boas–Sapir model in that

selection, modulation, and phonetic modification are used as if they were processes; Bloomfield describes them as taxemes, however, as elements of form, using relational rather than process terminology. The affixation of -*ess*, for instance, is achieved by a taxeme of selection of a form class and a taxeme of order, not by a process of affixation. Later models of grammar developed by distributionalists (especially Harris) minimized or eliminated these higher order grammatical forms, dealing instead entirely with arrangements of one or more morphemes, some of them grammatical in meaning, some lexical, and some having both kinds of function. As Wells (1963) noted, Harris reduced Bloomfield's four types of grammatical form to one: order.

Bloomfield's episememes, never used in his own practical work, had no counterpart at all in the later model. The *Duchess!* example is also accompanied by a paragraph on semantics that is so typical of his theoretical treatment of meaning that it deserves to be quoted in full (1933: 168):

> If some science furnished us with definitions of the meanings of the units here concerned, defining for us the meanings (sememes) of the two morphemes (*duke* and -*ess*) and the meanings (episememes) of the three tagmemes (arrangement of *duke* and -*ess*; use of exclamatory final pitch; selection of a substantive expression), then the meaning of the utterance *Duchess!* would be fully analyzed and defined.

Bloomfield was a careful writer indeed. The science he mentioned here was not linguistics. He tenaciously held the position that linguistic meaning awaits an exhaustive account of impersonal reality, to be furnished by natural science. Nothing less would be satisfactory. This passage also furnishes an excellent example of the deliberate Pāṇinian concision of Bloomfield's writing. He had noted explicitly earlier (1933: 166) that tagmemes are composed of taxemes, just as morphemes are composed of phonemes. This relationship is implied but not mentioned here by first stating that there are three tagmemes, and then by identifying each of the features of grammatical form in the discussion of the example in such a way that we can see it is a simple taxeme. Consequently, each of these units is a tagmeme made up of a single taxeme.

Bloomfield placed both modulation and phonetic modification within grammar, outside of morphology. Later American structuralists dealt with what he called phonetic modification as a part of morphology, namely, 'morphophonemics.' About the specific grammatical functions of suprasegmentals most had relatively little to say. The explicit identification of these as elements of grammatical form within a system in which individually meaningless components form meaningful combinations is generally absent from the writings of later structuralists. They treated syntax in terms of morpheme order and selection alone. In these later works, grammatical form is a kind of epiphenomenon of combinations of morphemes; all or nearly all meaning is associated with individual morphemes.

Bloomfield's separation of form and meaning into parallel hierarchies was either rejected or misunderstood by Kenneth Pike, whose system of structural linguistics, called Tagmemics, branched off from a fundamentally Bloomfieldian approach on this issue. Pike's system closely associates each form with its meaning but uses a familiar stock of grammatical functions and categories with which each form class (a filler class in tagmemics) is also associated. Except for the lack of relativism about the fundamental categories, the system is like Bloomfield's in the prominence it gives to named constructions and their grammatical meanings (see *Tagmemics*).

There is another parallelism in Bloomfield's system as well, that between word-formation and sentence-formation, or morphology and syntax. The classification of forms in each is more elaborate than the traditional typology of simple, complex, compound, and compound-complex sentences, but it does include such types. Like many American structuralists, Bloomfield paid considerable attention to morphology both in his theorizing and in his descriptive work. There was an obvious reason for this, namely, that the languages he was most concerned with—the older Germanic and the Algonquian language families—had abundant morphologies, compared with that of modern English.

3.4 Bloomfield's Descriptive Linguistic Work

The theoretical system outlined by Bloomfield does not fully prepare the reader for the particular uses he made of it in his descriptive work. It does not presuppose any particular scheme of morphological and grammatical categories. These are expected to arise out of the analysis of forms and meanings in each language. In the analysis of Tagalog, for instance, there are no nouns or verbs. Instead, categories of expressions are built up directly from the formal elements of the language as he segmented and interpreted them. What is most striking about the morphological and syntactic analyses of Tagalog in the *Texts* is their accessibility and apparent simplicity. This is even more striking in the later and much briefer *Outline of Ilocano Syntax* (1942). The descriptive statements are ordered by generality, with the most general given first and the exceptions organized under it, in the method followed by generations of Indo-Europeanists and traditional grammarians as well. There is a straightforward mechanism for supporting cross-references but almost none of the often elaborate notational and classificatory apparatus of later structuralists or of the equally obtrusive and abundant notional terminology of traditional general grammar, as found, for instance, in Bloomfield's own *Introduction* of just three years before. Nevertheless, some major categories are carried forward from that work: the same three major grammatical relations of 'attribution,' 'predication,' and the 'serial relationship' are found in both. Instead of referring to forms by means of a system of hierarchical category labels, however, as many did and still do, Bloomfield cites the forms themselves, often mentioning their category membership just once, the first time they appear. Much use is made in the illustrations of a very few forms that are used many times, each in whatever fresh context or combination is required for illustration. Examples are abundant and are always accompanied by translations. As one moves forward through the syntactic section, they grow progressively longer and more challenging without ever completely abandoning the small, core set of lexical items he chose for this purpose. The text also includes implicit justification for some of the analytical steps taken. For example, Bloomfield refrained from referring to what later scholars call the focus-marking particles of Tagalog as case markers. The examples he cited 'make it possible to speak, in a very wide sense, of three "cases" in which an object expression may stand . . . but it is to be observed that these "cases" are not confined to any class of words, but appear in any word or phrase when it stands in the object construction' (1917: 161). In a note to this passage, he further observed that these Tagalog constructions are 'so different from what is ordinarily understood by cases that the above terminology has been avoided . . .' To Bloomfield at least, these language-specific categories are not simply new labels for old distinctions that could just as well have been called case markers, nouns, and verbs or the like. Instead, they reflect the different structural map of Tagalog, which is unlike European languages in many important respects. It was this aspect of Bloomfield's freedom from preconceptions that seems to have been most irritating to scholars already accustomed to working with a language in terms of traditional (that is, European) grammatical and notional categories. Blake (1919), in his review of the *Tagalog Texts*, complained of such terms as 'static word' and 'transient word' (instead of 'noun' and 'verb'); in his analysis of Ilocano (1942) Bloomfield replaced these by 'object expression' and 'open expression' but not by noun and verb.

Ives Goddard, himself an Algonquianist, has provided a careful analysis of Bloomfield's descriptive and comparative work on these languages (Goddard 1987). He deals at length with Bloomfield's resolution of a fundamental dilemma of structural linguistics: how to reconcile accurate description, necessarily based on the details of language use by individual speakers, with the notion of language as a structural system shared by a speech community. Individuals differ in their usage, not only as individuals, but from situation to situation, and so on. A collection of accurately transcribed texts representing the usage of several speakers shows variation that often seems chaotic, and is at the very least a complex descriptive problem. However, as Goddard points out (1987: 200):

> It is hard to avoid observing that Bloomfield's achievement of the goal of describing the community norm of Menominee sits uncomfortably with his exhortation that in describing the language of a community a 'linguistic observer must record every form he can find and . . . must not select or distort the facts according to his views of what the speakers ought to be saying' not to mention his general condemnatory remarks about normative grammars and about the obliteration of 'linguistically valuable forms' by the over-edition of ancient texts (Bloomfield 1933: 7, 37–38, 295, 497).

Goddard is to be commended for raising this most unpopular issue. It is nearly always resolved by linguists and indeed by other social scientists just as Bloomfield did, but often apparently without reflection, and still more often without a legacy of accurately recorded raw data so that emendations can be undone. Goddard shows how Bloomfield selected and when necessary edited his Algonquian data to compose a community norm of usage, both in phonology and in morphology (Goddard 1987: 200):

> He provided an explicit account only of the pronunciations, forms, and usages that he had determined constituted the norm, an entity that was in the final analysis an abstraction based on evaluation and analysis of the raw materials collected. His editing of the texts shows that he regarded them as providing examples of Menominee that were consistent with the norm and not as attestations of varieties of actual speech.

It is worth repeating that Bloomfield should bear no more than his share of the responsibility for such emendations. Goddard notes that Bloomfield rightly decided to publish his Menominee texts before the analysis, and that unfortunately very few linguists collect or publish texts at all: 'Each age will write its own grammars, but the texts are for all time' (Goddard 1987: 201).

Bloomfield's long-standing interest in mathematics led to a manuscript of some 300 pages on mathematics as *The Language of Science* (ca.1937), in which he 'accepted the discourse of mathematicians as a corpus, and treated that corpus by much the same sort of analysis to which he subjected Tagalog or Menomini texts, or any other body of data' (in Hockett 1970: 333). Only a few pages survive but they are of the highest importance in understanding Bloomfield's thought and its place in the development of linguistics.

The work must be placed at the origin of several traditions within the field: it was apparently the most searching example of an analysis of a technical sublanguage yet produced, and it should also count as a lost forerunner of the generative approach to syntax. It was strikingly free of notational and terminological apparatus except for the mathematical terms themselves, which are after all the object language of the work. Even the few surviving scraps of manuscript make it clear that Bloomfield's work had nothing in common with the caricature presented later as taxonomic linguistics. On page 103 of the manuscript, for instance, Bloomfield is engaged in distinguishing number sequences by means of an 'immediate successor' relation. Having noted that if *two* is the immediate successor of *one*, it may still be the case that *one* is the successor of *two* or of some later number in the sequence:

> Systems of arithmetic where this is the case are *modular* systems. The number system of English and of ordinary arithmetic, by contrast, is an infinite system. For it, we must rule out the recurrence of *one* in the chain of the operator *Immediate successor of*. This demands a recursive definition of the serial operator *Sequent of*, as above given ... (Bloomfield in Hockett 1970: 335).

A later, unnumbered page deals with various ways of naming irrational numbers. In the third of these ways,

> a formula defines an infinite class of rational numbers and orders this class so as to make it approach a limit; this limit then satisfies the definition of a real number, and may be irrational.

On page 213 he describes a formula for naming circulating (i.e., repeating) decimal numbers and mentions some linguistic consequences:

> We now change to a level of discourse where the R's are thing-nouns. They are members of a class O, which is defined as follows. (1) Say *decimal point*; (2) recite any sequence of digits or none; (3) name a second sequence of digits, not all zeros, as a circulating sequence; if you want to avoid duplicates, this sequence must not be the same as the end of the sequence (2). Then any speech-form of the shape (1)–(2)–(3) or of the shape (1)–(3) is a member of the class O.
>   Given the class O, together with a formula for well-ordering it, such as that in the above array, we can define, *as functions of O*, infinite classes of speech forms of the type *N*.

Notice that Bloomfield is here giving explicit grammatical descriptions that generate infinite classes of verbal expressions and that the semantics of these expressions is also explicit, namely, certain parts of arithmetic. It is easy to imagine how much more pretentious this treatment of mathematical English could be made through the use of a quasimathematical notation, but the use of slightly extended English as a medium of expression for the rules should not conceal their explicitness and generative power. For Bloomfield as for other structuralists, there was no necessary limitation of the scope of a description to the content of the corpus it was based on. Moreover, these fragments are certainly evidence of a specific concern with the creative or generative aspect of language use, a concern already present in his doctoral dissertation some 30 years earlier on the analogic productivity of vowel alternations in Germanic vocabulary sets.

4. Distributionalism

After 1945 a new generation of linguists emerged as disciplinary leaders. Bernard Bloch, Zellig Harris, Archibald Hill, Charles Hockett, Martin Joos, Henry Lee Smith, George Trager, and Rulon Wells were prominent figures in this group.

They disagreed on many theoretical issues but shared a commitment to some form of distributionalism, holding that analytic criteria based on the distribution of linguistic forms were preferable in theory to tests of semantic sameness or difference. The distribution of a linguistic element is the sum of the environments in which the element occurs.

The distributionalist program arose indirectly out of the view of meaning as a domain of continuously variable and possibly unknowable details without verifiable internal organization that was held in common by Bloomfield and the distributionalists. Forms, unlike meanings, were observable and easily distinguishable, allowing precise distributional statements *whose outcomes were thought to be equivalent to those that would otherwise be reached through appeal to semantic tests*. Unlike Bloomfield, who made and used judgments of semantic sameness and difference as best he could, the distributionalists took this skepticism about meaning-based criteria as a warrant for relying instead on the distributions of forms alone in making analytical decisions. They were more than willing to leave analytical criteria based on sameness or difference of meaning for the indefinite future when other branches of science had supplied the knowledge necessary to illuminate every aspect of the similarities and differences of, for example, dogs and cats.

Forms were subject to certain candidacy criteria as part of the determination of their contrastive status. These were usually standards of similarity in subtance, for example, phonetic similarity among allophones of a phoneme and phonemic similarity among alternants of a morpheme (in early distributionalist theories). Complementary distribution enjoyed a special status in this approach. This is the relation of two elements such that where one occurs the other does not. Elements in complementary distribution *that also meet the criterion of similarity* are noncontrastive with each other and may be assigned to the same structural element as alternants. In other distributional relationships, elements share some or all of their environments, and may be contrastive or not.

The crucial problem of strictly distributional analysis was to decide whether forms occurring in the same environments were different (contrastive) or equivalent (noncontrastive). For example, were two words contrastive (different forms with different meanings) or synonymous (different forms with the same meaning)? For Bloomfield, the problem did not arise in this way: he used meaning as a criterion of analysis. Distribution for him was contingent on identities and differences established through assessing both formal and semantic sameness and difference. The 'Bloomfieldian' distributionalists' solution to this problem, however, was in effect and sometimes explicitly to deny that 'true' synonymy was possible. The argument was roughly as follows:

(a) Forms identical in meaning would be mutually substitutable in all environments, and thus would not differ in distribution.
(b) Forms differing in meaning are not mutually substitutable in all environments, and therefore differ in distribution.
(c) Observation shows that different forms always differ somewhat in distribution, and therefore must differ somewhat in meaning.
(d) A difference in form implies a difference in distribution and in turn a difference in meaning. There are thus no true synonyms.

The first assumption is not necessarily true: factors other than meaning that influence the co-occurrence of forms are easily brought to mind. Phonological shape, length or metrical factors, situational variables, and historical accidents leading to the fossilization of a particular expression sometimes produce minor differences of distribution that, under the distributionalist theory, must be regarded as implying minor, possibly undefinable differences of meaning.

The positions taken by the distributionalists on the proper role of meaning in linguistics nevertheless covered a wide range. Joos was actively interested in lexicology and semantic structure (1958). Bloch and many others regarded meaning as a practical shortcut to the results best obtained through more laborious but precise distributional analysis. Harris expressed a similar view, but devoted most of his *Methods* (1951a) to establishing a body of distributionally based analytical procedures. Trager was fully committed to excluding meaning from linguistics altogether.

Bloch (1948) remains the clearest statement of a distributional approach to phonology; his note on contrast (1953) was an attempt to redefine the notion distributionally. Much of Harris (1951a) was devoted to establishing methods of distributional analysis for all levels of linguistic description.

4.1 Levels of Structure, Levels of Analysis, and Levels of Description

Distributionalists typically presented language structure in levels, including phonology, morphology, and syntax. It was possible to describe an utterance in terms of the patterning of elements of sound, displaying its structure as a composite of their paradigmatic and syntagmatic relations alone. Alternatively, one could show the same utterance in terms of its morphological elements, and their paradigmatic and syntagmatic relations. The elements belong to different sets and also to different levels; their relations of alternation and substitution are also characteristic of different levels. An utterance is a string of syllables; it is also a string of morphemes. But a syllable is not a morpheme (except by coincidence). Each layer of patterning conveys a part of the overall structure of the utterance and the language.

Wells (1963) regarded a full exploitation of the levels idea as one of the missed opportunities of descriptive linguistics. In early structuralism, there is no clear separation of structural elements into levels such as phonology, morphology, and syntax, such that an element of one type occurring on a higher level was represented by one or more elements of another type on a lower level in the way that a phoneme is represented by its allophones. Morphological and morphophonemic processes were mixed freely with word order and selection in the composition of meaningful grammatical forms. There was some variation in the handling of the levels idea among the distributionalists, but in general they treated it as proper to both analysis and description, whereas others, such as Kenneth Pike, regarded distinguishing levels of description as more important than separation of levels in the course of analysis. In analysis, he argued, structural cues of many kinds must be taken into account all at once, to be sorted out in the presentation of the structure of the language.

4.2 Zellig Harris

Harris's work deserves special attention for several reasons: it is an unusually coherent and formal statement of distributionalist structural linguistics, and it was the variety best known by Noam Chomsky, Harris's student at the University of Pennsylvania and the proofreader of Harris's *Methods* (1951a). The meaningful grammatical categories and construction types of Bloomfield and Sapir are largely replaced in Harris's work by morphemes and morpheme sequences:

> . . . it suffices to define 'meaning' (more exactly 'difference in meaning') in such a way that utterances which differ in morphemic constituency will be considered as differing in meaning . . . Then the meaning of each morpheme in the utterance will be defined in such a way that the sum of the meanings of the constituent morphemes is the meaning of the utterance (Harris 1951a: 190).

Harris also allows for the assignment of meaning to constructions (1951a: 347–48) in instances when all occurrences of a particular construction share some feature of meaning, which is then 'taken out' and not assigned to individual morphemes; he gives a reference to Bloomfield's tagmemes. There is little or no use of this option in Harris's own work, however.

Harris's overall strategy was to reduce grammar (cf. Wells 1963), which he considered either a body of prohibitions or the equivalent body of positive assertions. If by adroitly combining distributionally based classes, the necessary prohibitions could be reduced or made to disappear, then grammar would be reduced by that much, and linguistic elements could be combined more freely. The unattainable end point of this strategy would be a description whose elements were freely combinable without the need for grammatical rules to restrict them. This attitude is close to the surface in his treatment of Sapir's categories, when he suggests that the hierarchical system of named types of word forms could be flattened:

> In general, the technique of classification and naming can be replaced by the technique of stating relations. Thus, Newman calls a base plus non-final suffix a theme, and obtains classes of themes according to the non-final suffix which went into making them. We could just as well speak in terms of base- and base-plus-suffix, and avoid the term 'theme.' We can similarly side-step the stem-classes of bases and themes. (Harris 1944: 203)

5. Summary

Sapir and Bloomfield were much alike in their practice of descriptive linguistics, but less so in their programmatic and theoretical writings. Their styles of presentation of formal patterns differ mostly in rhetoric: form-oriented, distributionalist rhetoric in Bloomfield and psychologistic, pattern-oriented rhetoric in Sapir. But these styles clothe descriptions that are very similar in organization. Between them and the later 'Bloomfieldians,' however, there were quite significant differences. These distributionalists developed a relational mode of descriptive statement, relying on tests of noncontrastive distribution rather than sameness of meaning as a basis for grouping forms together into equivalence classes. They advocated a system of levels of analysis and description to organize distributional relationships among linguistic elements according to the level of each element. The patterning of phonological elements was not to be mixed with the patterning of morphological elements, nor either of these with syntax. An occurrence of the morpheme {pin} was not at all the same thing as an occurrence of the phoneme sequence /pin/, even though /pin/ was the phonemic shape of {pin}. The two are elements of different structural levels.

The 'Sapirians,' students and grandstudents of Sapir, diverged less from the linguistic theory and practice of their mentor, but their influence continued to diminish as linguistics lost some of its standing within anthropology after the passing of Sapir and Boas. By the late 1940s, when linguistics departments were first appearing in major American universities, linguistic anthropologists trained in the Boas–Sapir tradition found themselves scattered among anthropology departments, and deprived of their two most prestigious leaders. Major commitments of time and resources to linguistic research within anthropology eroded, and disciplinary leadership of linguistics passed definitively to the Bloomfieldians. Bloomfield's own work had been stopped by illness in 1946; in any case his personal contribution was not as an academic

political leader but as an intellectual model. This result for the Boas–Sapir–Bloomfield style of linguistic anthropological description is ironic, since all three had signed the call for a Linguistic Society in 1925 in part to ensure closer collegiality among scientists of language, who were then scattered among departments of modern and Classical languages and literatures. A decade or so after the death of Bloomfield, the influence of Chomsky's transformational approach to syntax and its theoretical matrix began to gain ascendancy within the discipline. Though in many particulars Chomsky's linguistics is a continuation of structuralist thinking, it is also in significant ways a reaction against Harris's methods, and in its wider theoretical context it represents a return of pre-Bloomfieldian views, such as mentalism, psychologism, and nativism.

Another link between descriptive structuralism and its successors is formed by the continued teaching of a descriptive approach to linguistics through the use of a number of monographs and textbooks dating from the 1920s to the 1950s until the transformational approach acquired its own in the 1960s. Carroll's collection of Whorf's papers (1956) and Sapir's beautifully written *Language* (1921) attracted many readers to linguistics courses wherever these could be found; there they were exposed to readings drawn from Bloomfield (1933), Francis (1958), Gleason (1955), Harris (1951), Hill (1958), Hockett (1958), Joos (1957), Nida (1946, 1949), Pike (1947), and Trager and Smith (1951). It is noteworthy how strongly the missionary linguistic movement is represented in the list (by Gleason, Nida, and Pike).

It was not only newcomers during the 1950s and 1960s who profited from what these books taught, but also their teachers, whether converts to a transformational approach or not, who had learned linguistics from them. These works exposed their readers to an immense fund of well-organized examples drawn from decades of first-hand experience often gained in fieldwork, an orderly, practical approach to problem solving, and a love of language study shared by all their authors. The debt Transformational Grammar and linguistics itself owes to these now maligned books and their authors is difficult to measure, but is surely far greater than has ever been acknowledged.

Bibliography

Blake F 1919 Review of Bloomfield 1917. *AJPh* **40**: 86–95
Bloch B 1948 A set of postulates for phonemic analysis. *Lg* **24**: 3–46
Bloch B 1953 Contrast. *Lg* **29**: 59–61
Bloomfield L 1943 Obituary of Franz Boas. *Lg* **19**: 198
Bloomfield L 1912a Etymologisches. [Paul und Braunes] *Beiträge zur Geschichte der deutschen Sprache und Literatur* **37**: 245–61
Bloomfield L 1912b Review of Wilhelm Braune, *Althochdeutsche Grammatik*. 3. u. 4. Aufl. (Halle a/S, 1911). *JEGP* **11**: 269–74

Bloomfield L 1913 Review of Wilhelm Wundt. *Elemente der Völkerpsychologie: Grundlinien einer psychologischen Entwicklungsgeschichte der Menschheit*, vol. 2. Aufl. (Leipzig 1913). *American Journal of Psychology* **24**: 449–53

Bloomfield L 1914 *Introduction to the Study of Language*. Holt, New York (Repr., with an introd. by Kess J F 1983 Benjamins, Amsterdam)

Bloomfield L 1917 *Tagalog Texts with Grammatical Analysis*. University of Illinois Studies in Language and Literature, vol. 3, no. 204, University of Illinois, Chicago, IL

Bloomfield L 1927 On recent work in general linguistics. *Modern Philology* **25**: 211–30

Bloomfield L 1933 *Language*. Holt, New York

Bloomfield L 1937 The language of science. Unpublished manuscript. In: Hockett C F (ed.) 1970

Bloomfield L 1942 Outline of Ilocano syntax. *Lg* **18**: 193–200

Bloomfield L 1943 Obituary of Franz Boas. *Lg* **19**: 198

Boas F (ed.) 1911, 1922, 1934 *Handbook of American Indian Languages, Parts 1, 2, 3*. Smithsonian Institution, Bureau of American Ethnology, Washington, D.C.

Boas F 1889 On alternating sounds. *AmA* **2**: 47–53

Francis W N 1958 *The Structure of American English*. Ronald Press, New York

Gleason H A 1955 *An Introduction to Descriptive Linguistics*. Holt, Rinehart and Winston, New York (2nd edn., 1961)

Goddard I 1987 Leonard Bloomfield's descriptive and comparative studies of Algonquian. In: Hall R A (ed.) 1987

Goodenough W 1956 Componential analysis and the study of meaning. *Lg* **32**: 195–216

Goodenough W (ed.) 1964 *Explorations in Cultural Anthropology*. McGraw-Hill, New York

Hall R A (ed.) 1987 *Leonard Bloomfield: Essays on His Life and Work*. Benjamins, Amsterdam

Harris Z 1944 Yokuts structure and Newman's grammar. *IJAL* **10**: 196–211

Harris Z 1951a *Methods in Structural Linguistics*. University of Chicago Press, Chicago, IL

Harris Z 1951b Review of Mandelbaum 1949. *Lg* **27**: 288–333 (Repr. in: Koerner E F K (ed.) 1984 *Edward Sapir: Appraisals of his Life and Work*. Benjamins, Amsterdam)

Hill A A 1958 *An Introduction to Linguistic Structures: From Sound to Sentence in English*. Harcourt, Brace and Co., New York

Hockett C F 1958 *A Course in Modern Linguistics*. Macmillan, New York

Hockett C F (ed.) 1970 *A Leonard Bloomfield Anthology*. Indiana University Press, Bloomington, IN

Hoijer H (ed.) 1954 *Language in Culture: Conference on the Interrelations of Language and Other Aspects of Culture*. University of Chicago Press, Chicago, IL

Hymes D (ed.) 1974 *Studies in the History of Linguistics: Traditions and Paradigms*. University of Indiana Press, Bloomington, IN

Hymes D, Fought J 1981 *American Structuralism*. Mouton, The Hague

Joos M 1957 *Readings in Linguistics*. American Council of Learned Societies, Washington, D.C.

Joos M 1958 Semology: A linguistic theory of meaning. *Studies in Linguistics* **13**: 53–70

Kuhn T 1962 *The Structure of Scientific Revolutions*. University of Chicago Press, Chicago, IL

Lounsbury F 1956 A semantic analysis of Pawnee kinship usage. *Lg* **32**: 158–94

Lounsbury F 1964 A formal account of the Crow- and Omaha-type kinship terminologies. In: Goodenough W (ed.) 1964

Mandelbaum D G 1949 *Selected Writings of Edward Sapir in Language, Culture, and Personality*. University of California Press, Berkeley, CA

Moulton W G 1970 Leonard Bloomfield as Germanist. In: Hockett C F (ed.) 1970

Nida E 1946 *Morphology*. University of Michigan Press, Ann Arbor, MI (2nd edn., 1949)

Pike K L 1947 *Phonemics: A Technique for Reducing Languages to Writing*. University of Michigan Press, Ann Arbor, MI

Sapir E 1921 *Language*. Harcourt, Brace and Co., New York

Sapir E 1922 Takelma. In: Boas F (ed.) 1922

Stocking G W, Jr. 1968 *Race, Culture, and Evolution: Essays in the History of Anthropology*. Free Press, New York

Stocking G W, Jr. 1974 The Boas plan for the study of American Indian languages. In: Hymes D (ed.) 1974

Trager G L, Smith H L 1951 *An Outline of English Structure*. Studies in Linguistics, Occasional Papers 3. Oklahoma Press, Normal, OK

Wells R 1963 Some neglected opportunities in descriptive linguistics. *AnL* **5**: 38–49

Wells R 1974 Phonemics in the nineteenth century, 1876–1900. In: Hymes D (ed.) 1974

Applicational Grammar

Jim Miller

In linguistics, as in all other areas of intellectual activity, ideas catch on not just because they are good but also because they arrive at the right time and in the right place. Developed at the wrong time and in the wrong place, Applicational Grammar (AG) is nonetheless a remarkable, if ultimately unsuccessful, achievement.

1. Background

AG, a type of generative categorial grammar, appeared when categorial grammar had few adherents among linguists. AG's theoretical isolation was increased by being written in Russian: when the English translation came out in 1971, Montague (1970a, b) had been published and Montague (1973) was already known to the specialists in the field. In the excitement of Montague Grammar, Shaumjan's work remained unnoticed, although, for example, his 1965 book proposes a way of handling complement clauses which anticipates Thomason (1976). Shaumjan (1977) is influenced by generative semantics and the lexical decomposition work of Fillmore but was novel in attempting to combine categorial grammar and what is now known as situation semantics.

The focus here is on Shaumjan (1965, 1971), because that model exhibits most clearly the properties distinguishing it from other generative models.

2. The Properties of Applicational Grammar

2.1 The Basic Units

The basic units are *term* and *sentence*, as is usual in categorial grammar. *Term* is represented by α, *sentence* by β. Other units, derived by combining the two basic ones, are interpreted thus: e.g., $\alpha\beta$—a unit or category applying to a term (α) to yield a sentence (β), i.e., a verb; $\alpha\alpha$—a category applying to a term to yield a term, e.g., an adjective; $\alpha\beta.\alpha\beta$—a category applying to a verb to yield a verb, e.g., an adverb; $\alpha\alpha.\alpha\alpha$—a category applying to an adjective to yield an adjective, e.g., an adverb such as *very*.

Shaumjan extends the categorial treatment to the structure of words, adopting Kuryłowicz's view that syntactic and morphological relations are parallel—e.g., that a change in syntactic function from predicate to attribute is paralleled by the change from finite verb to participle: *The child slept* vs. *the sleeping child* (examples are Russian and English).

He also accepts Kuryłowicz's view that different word classes have different primary and secondary functions. For adjectives, the modifying function is primary: they map terms into terms, and include more than the traditional adjectives. For instance, they include derivational affixes deriving nouns from nouns (or terms from terms)—*hood* in *childhood*, and the diminutive suffix *-ik* in Russian *domik* ('little house')—and nouns in the genitive case or with the English possessive affix. *Fiona's* added to *house* yields the term *Fiona's house*. In Russian, a noun in the genitive case—e.g., *studenta* ('of the student')—combines with a noun in the nominative case—e.g., *kniga studenta* ('the book-of the student')—to yield a term. This is a secondary function of the noun *student*, which is signaled by the genitive case. The primary function of nouns is to be a basic term to which verbs apply to yield sentences. This function is signaled by the Russian nominative case.

Other items belonging to the category adjective are prepositional phrases—*about gardening* combines with the term *books* to yield the term *books about gardening*—and participles, such as English *sleeping* from *sleep* and Russian *igrajushchij* ('playing') from the stem *igra-*. The primary function of verbs is to apply to a noun to yield a sentence. One secondary function is to act as an adjective, which is signaled by the participial suffix.

2.2 Derivations

Combinations of items are generated by a single operation called 'application'—whence the title 'applicational grammar.' Application, from Curry's work—cf. Curry (1963), involves an operator applied to an operand. The notation—typical categorial notation—indicates, for a given case, the operator, the operand and the result of the application. Thus, for the item $\alpha\beta$, β labels the category of the operator, α labels the category of the operand and $\alpha\beta$ labels the category into which the operand is mapped. Suffice it to say here that the derivational system is rigorously defined, with a set of primitives and a rule for deriving new items from the primitives or from other derived items.

2.3 Different Levels of Category

To treat *Fiona*'s, etc. merely as instances of a general category $\alpha\alpha$ would be to ignore differences between them: *igrajushchij* derives from a verb, *studenta* is a noun in the genitive and *about gardening* is a prepositional phrase. Moreover, *-ik* in *domik* and *-a* in *studenta* are part of the internal structure of words. Another problem, as mentioned in Sect. 2.1, is that while being an adjective is the primary function for, e.g., *small*, it is a secondary function for the participle *igrajushchij*.

AG solves these difficulties by having a top level of 'episemions,' the general categories presented in Sect. 2.1, and a lower level of 'semions,' which are narrower categories in that a given semion has a structure showing its derivation. Shaumjan captures that structure by means of a 'relator notation' and language (one possible actual 'calculus' of semions).

2.4 Relators: Derivational Morphology and Syntactic Function

There are five relators, R_1 to R_5. R_1 represents the category $\alpha\beta$, $R_2-\alpha$, $R_3-\alpha\alpha$, $R_4-\alpha\beta.\alpha\beta$, and $R_5-\alpha\alpha.\alpha\alpha$. They apply to an empty root 0, or to any combination of relators and 0, or to an entire phrase, i.e., to some sequence of R_n0s. If 0 is the root *uch-*, R_1 applies to yield $R_1$0, corresponding to finite forms of the verb: *uchit* ('teaches'), *uchim* ('we teach'), etc. In turn, R_2 applies to $R_1$0 to yield $R_2R_1$0, corresponding to nouns derived from the verbal stem, such as *uchenie* ('teaching') and *uchitel'* ('teacher').

The sequences of relators correspond to stages in the derivational morphology of a given word. If 0 is *zim-*, R_2 applies to yield $R_2$0—*zima* ('winter'). R_1 applies, yielding $R_1R_2$0, corresponding to a finite verb form—say, *zimuem* ('we pass the winter (somewhere)'). R_2 applies to yield $R_2R_1R_20$, corresponding to *zimovka* ('the act of wintering'), and the formula corresponding to *zimovochnyj* ('winter' as in 'winter quarters') is derived by applying R_3 to yield $R_3R_2R_1R_20$.

Unlike the last Russian example, *winter* can be noun, verb or adjective without derivational affixes. Nonetheless, the adjective *winter* in *winter quarters* would correspond to the formula $R_3R_2R_1R_20$, R_3 signaling its modifying function.

Russian has various cases. Only nouns in the nominative case correspond to R_2, because only they combine with a verb to form a sentence. Nouns in the genitive case correspond to R_3, because they have an adjective function: they map terms onto terms. Nouns in other cases correspond to R_4, because they map verbs onto verbs: the accusative case form *kartu* ('map') combines with *chitaet* ('reads') to yield *chitaet kartu*, which combines with the nominative noun *soldat* ('soldier') to yield the sentence *Soldat chitaet kartu* ('The soldier reads the map'). English has no case, but nouns do have different syntactic functions and correspond to different formulae: in *The soldier is reading the map, the map* is R_4 because it maps the verb *is reading* into the verb *is reading the map*, and the *soldier* corresponds to R_2 because it combines with that verb to yield a sentence.

2.5 Other Primitives in the Relator Calculus

In addition to relators and 0, the relator calculus has 'adnectors,' 'connectors,' and 'propositors.' Adnectors are identity elements interpretable as, e.g., negation and interrogation, which apply to a given linguistic element leaving it identical with itself. Connectors correspond to conjunctions such as *i* ('and'). Propositors convert phrases and clauses into the *determiners* of clauses. Thus, *if* converts the clause *it is raining* into a subordinate clause acting as determiner to another clause: *If it is raining, I am going to stay at home*. The phrase *according to the instructions* can function as an R_4 in, e.g., *We prepared the vegetables according to the instructions*; it can function as a determiner of a clause, as in *According to the instructions, you were to wait there till help arrived*. Subordinating conjunctions such as *if* always function as propositors, whereas phrases such as *according to the instructions* may or may not function as a propositor.

3. Sentences and Transformational Fields

0 with one or more relators corresponds to a word in English or Russian. In turn, an element R_n0 can apply to another R_n0 to create a more complex element. R_30 applied to R_20 generates R_30R_20, which can be interpreted as *splendid parties*. As it stands, R_30R_20 cannot be interpreted as having any particular syntactic function, but the relator R_4 can be applied to generate $\|R_4\| R_30R_20$, i.e., an $\alpha\beta.\alpha\beta$ mapping a verb

onto a verb. $\|R_4\|R_30R_20$ applies to an R_1 item, say R_10 to generate $\|R_4\|R_30R_20R_10$, interpretable as *gives splendid parties*. The above sequence, an instance of $\alpha\beta$, maps a term into a sentence, applying, say, to R_20, to generate $\|R_4\|R_30R_20R_10R_20$—*Gatsby gives splendid parties*.

AG can generate, quite independently of each other, the 'analogs' of *Gatsby ruined that party* and *That party was ruined by Gatsby*. In the relator analog of the active sentence *Gatsby* corresponds to R_20, a term looking for a verb to map it into a sentence. In the analog of the passive sentence, *Gatsby* corresponds to R_4R_20, an item mapping a verb into a verb. These remarks apply, vice versa, to *that party*.

3.1 Transformational Fields

Generative grammar expresses relationships between different constructions, but the independent analogs of active and passive sentences do not. To overcome this defect, AG generates the analogs of sets of sentences by means of graphs.

Down the left-hand side of a given graph are the relators, ordered from top to bottom in the sequence R_5, R_3, R_2, R_1, R_4. This order reflects possible applications: an R_5 item applies to an R_3 item, an R_4 item to an R_1 item, and so on. Across the top of the graph is the expression to be transformed, the 'base,' which can be the analog of a sentence or the analog of a phrase. Each relator is applied to each R_n0 in the expression across the top of the graph and the result is written in the column below the R_n0.

The set of R_n0s generated constitutes a 'transformational field,' represented by a graph with the R_n0s arranged in columns and rows. Two restrictions can be placed on the generative process: (a) the graph is connected; (b) head-modifier links between items in the base expression are preserved in the derived expressions. If (a) and (b) are both imposed, the transformational field is *bound*; if (a) alone is imposed, the field is *semi-bound*; if neither is imposed, the field is *free*. (NB: Head-modifier links relate to phrases only: the subject–predicate link is not one of head and modifier.)

For example, if the base is $R_30\,R_20$—*striking beauty*, one transform is $R_5R_30\,R_3R_20$—*strikingly beautiful*, which maintains the head-modifier links. Suppose that the base is $R_20\,R_10\,R_4R_20$—*The train arrived from Moscow*. One transform is $R_3R_4R_20\,R_2R_20\,R_1R_10$—*The Moscow train arrived*. *From Moscow* is a modifier of the verb in the base expression, but a modifier of the subject noun in the transform: i.e., the head-modifier links are altered.

The base can be a more complex expression, say $\|R_2\|R_30R_20$ (*imaginative students*) R_10 (*write*) $\|R_4\|R_30$ R_20 (*interesting essays*). The initial R_2 applies to the adjective–noun block, and the R_4 applies to the final adjective–noun block. The graph generates, inter alia, $R_4\|R_2\|R_30\,R_20\,R_1R_10\,R_2\|R_4\|R_30\,R_20$, which is the analog of *Interesting essays are written by imaginative students.*

4. Genotype and Phenotype Grammars

The model described above is a 'genotype' grammar; i.e., a grammar handling the generic properties of language. The sequences of semions are mapped onto sequences of, e.g., Russian, English, or Georgian morphs by 'phenotype' grammars which assign word order, morphological categories and phonological shape.

5. The Later Model

Shaumjan (1977) extends the model to semantics. The derivational apparatus is essentially the same, but the relator genotype language represents the analog of semantic structures: the relators correspond to the relations of 'predicate logic,' with the restriction that they are all 'two-place' in the axioms. The axioms belong to the category β, i.e., are sentences, and correspond to components of situation models.

The situation models are 'localist,' that is, based on the assumption that the semantic representation of any situation has as its central components a predicate of location or movement, the case relations of location, movement from or movement to, and the case relation 'objective,' which corresponds to the entity conceived of as being located somewhere or moving somewhere. For instance, *Fiona gave Bill his essay* is derived from a semantic structure which has an event coming from Fiona—represented by a 'two-place predicate'—and the event is the essay coming-to-be-located at Bill, which event is also represented by a two-place predicate.

The axioms state the possible relationships between entities: $R_{oa}T^1T^2$ represents a 'two-place relator,' and the two terms correspond to two entities, one of which moves away from the other. The subscript letters on R represent the case relations and at one stage in the derivation are copied onto the terms. The order is important, since it indicates that the *theme* is ablative and the *rheme* objective: that is, the entity from which the other entity moves away corresponds to the surface subject, and the other entity is in the rheme of the surface sentence. For example, R might correspond to *sent*, T_a^1 to *Bill*, T_o^2 to *telegram*, and the whole axiom to *Bill sent a telegram*. In contrast, $R_{ao}T^1T^2$ corresponds to *A telegram was sent by Bill.*

Rules of derivation generate surface sentences from the sequence of semions representing the semantic structure. One semion, B, triggers the fusion of semions: e.g., the mapping of *cause-be-located* into the single lexical item GIVE. Another semion, labeled C, causes terms to be permuted, as in the derivation of the relator expression corresponding to *They loaded the barges with timber* from the relator expression

corresponding to *They loaded timber on the barges.* The reordering rules with C, like the matrix graphs in the 1965 model, express relations among different constructions.

As in the 1965 AG, once relators and terms have been fused and ordered, a phenotype grammar maps the expressions onto sentences of a given language. The phenotype mappings are organized around particular groups of lexical items. For instance, the general lexeme GIVE$_{ola}$ is a cover term for verbs with a particular valency, such that the theme term corresponds to the giver, the second term (here the direct object)—to the person at whom something comes to be located, and the third term—to the entity that moves, i.e., GIVE$_{ola}$ is a cover term for Z EQUIP X WITH Y, Z PROVIDE X WITH Y, Z PRESENT X WITH Y, Z REWARD X WITH Y, and so on. Each group of lexical items has its own order of nouns, its own prepositions and, for Russian, its own case endings. The valency is crucial: an item with two valencies—Z PRESENT X WITH Y and Z PRESENT Y TO X—is treated in the phenotype grammar as two different items, although the two valencies correspond to one item in the genotype grammar. The corresponding basic relator in the genotype grammar is R_{loa} (Z PRESENT Y TO X), but the order of terms is changed by a derivational rule with C. Even passives and constructions with reflexive verbs (in Russian) are derived by rules with C.

6. A Critique of Applicational Grammar

Like the classical transformational model, the 1965 AG model focuses on syntax while the 1977 model, possibly reflecting generative semantics of the late 1960s, maps semantic expressions onto surface sequences where morphological categories are much in evidence but syntax is absent.

The 1965 model was to contribute to grammatical synonymy and to typology. Given a base expression and the expressions derived from it, two properties could be measured: within a single language, the degree of synonymy between any two of the derived expressions could be measured by the number of sub-expressions they shared; with respect to typology, any two languages could be compared according to which derived formulas are interpretable in both languages and which only in one.

Although AG is remarkable for its rigor and formal consistency, the claim concerning typology highlights a fundamental weakness. The elementary semions are based on certain characteristics of natural languages, but the derivational procedure was devised by Curry to generate completely abstract uninterpreted objects capable of being put in correspondence with any appropriate entities, linguistic or mathematical or whatever. The derivational procedure is defined with great rigor, but, apart from the basic combinatory possibilities, is so remote from natural language that the advantages of the model are outweighed by its limited scope. Offering little for dependency relations and nothing for constituent structure, AG is irrelevant to language acquisition and to typological studies of dependency relations, the order of heads and modifiers, the question of flat vs. hierarchical constituent structure, and the question of clause-embedding vs. clause-chaining.

AG reflects a fundamental tension in formal linguistics: the difficulty of developing a formally rigorous model that expresses interesting and exploitable hypotheses about linguistic structure. Formal rigor comes with systems borrowed from metamathematics, and Shaumjan adopts the notion of a metalanguage formulated so precisely that its reasonings could be seen as derivations according to precise rules, whose correctness of application can be seen by inspecting the symbols of the metalanguage regardless of any meaning they might have. The trouble is that, outside mathematics, the axioms of a given system must have a degree of truth or falsity with respect to a given subject-matter, and a degree of interest. Shaumjan's axioms are true insofar as his categories are not without linguistic support. There is formal rigor in plenty, but in linguistic theory and its major applications the axioms have hitherto failed to arouse excitement.

Bibliography

Curry H B 1963 *Foundations of Mathematical Logic*. McGraw–Hill, New York

Montague R 1970a English as a formal language. In: Visentini B (ed.) *Linguaggi nella Societa e nella Tecnica*. Edizioni di Communita, Milan

Montague R 1970b Universal grammar. *Theoria* **36**: 373–98

Montague R 1973 The proper treatment of quantification in ordinary English. In: Hintikka J, Moravscik J, Suppes P (eds.) *Approaches to Natural Language*. D Reidel, Dordrecht

Partee B H 1976 *Montague Grammar*. Academic Press, New York

Shaumjan S K 1965 *Strukturnaja Lingvistika*. Nauka, Moscow (Transl. by Miller J 1971)

Shaumjan S K 1971 *Principles of Structural Linguistics*. Mouton, The Hague

Shaumjan S K 1977 *Applicational Grammar as a Semantic Theory of Natural Language*. Edinburgh University Press, Edinburgh (Transl. by Miller J)

Thomason R 1976 Some extensions of Montague grammar. In: Partee 1976 *Montague Grammar*. Academic Press, New York

Autolexical Syntax

Jerrold M. Sadock

Autolexical syntax is a variety of nontransformational generative grammar in which fully autonomous systems of rules characterize the various dimensions of linguistic representation. These components, or modules, are coordinated by means of the lexicon and a set of interface principles that limit the degree of structural discrepancy between the autonomous representations given by the various modular grammars. The number, identity, and content of the components remains a matter of debate, but most studies in the framework have assumed at least a syntactic module, a morphological module, and a semantic module, and have assumed that each of these components is a context-free phrase structure grammar. There is neither movement nor deletion in autolexical syntax, the effects of the former being modeled as discrepancies of order or constituency between two autonomous representations, and of the latter as the presence of an element in one dimension to which there corresponds no element in some other dimension.

1. Areas of Application

The theory has been particularly successful in the description of cliticization and incorporation which are analyzed as allowable mismatches between the combinatorics of lexemes in syntax and morphology. There was an attempt, in the early 1990s, to explain the more familiar syntactic phenomena that have been treated in terms of movement or deletion as structural discrepancies between the syntactic position of a lexeme and its position in some other dimension of representation, particularly the semantics (see, for example, Kathman 1996). The goal is clearly to make autolexical syntax a complete theory of grammar, though much work remains to be done.

2. Well-formedness

In this conception of grammar, an expression must satisfy the independent requirements of each of the modules in order to count as fully well-formed. Each

15

module, in other words, acts as a filter on all of the others.

An expression that is well-formed with respect to its projection on each of the levels may still not qualify as grammatical if the interface principles disallow any pair of representations. The investigation of the principles governing the compatibility of autonomous representations from different modules is the subject of much of the research in this framework, as in, for example, Sadock and Schiller (1993).

3. The Components

Each of the major components, the syntax, semantics, and morphology, characterizes an infinite set of phrase-structure trees by means of a set of context-free phrase structure rules. Several of the techniques for capturing grammatical generalizations that are discussed in the article *Generalized Phrase Structure Grammar* are used in autolexical syntax, including:

(a) the definition of categories in terms of features and their values;
(b) the separation of dominance from precedence information (the 'immediate dominance—linear precedence' 'ID–LP' format);
(c) the indication of subcategorization properties of lexemes in terms of rule features (see *Valency and Valency Grammar*); and
(d) the assumption of the important feature-passing mechanism known as the Head Feature Convention.

A fragment of the ID statements needed for the description of the syntax of English might contain the familiar rules in (1–4), where SF is the syntactic rule feature that specifies the subcategorization requirements of lexical heads.

$$S \rightarrow N'', V' \qquad (1)$$

$$N'' \rightarrow DET, N' \qquad (2)$$

$$V' \rightarrow V^0[SF\ 3] \qquad (3)$$

$$V' \rightarrow V^0[SF\ 4], N'' \qquad (4)$$

A phrase structure morphology for English, and a great deal of the morphology of other languages as well, would include the three schemata in (5)–(7).

$$X^{-1} \rightarrow X^{-0}, Y \qquad (5)$$

$$X^0 \rightarrow Y^0, X \qquad (6)$$

$$X^{-2} \rightarrow Y^{-1}, Z \qquad (7)$$

Rule (5) creates inflected words (X^{-1}) from stems (X^{-0}) by adding some morphology (Y). Rule (6) derives stems from other stems by adding a morpheme X that is the head of the complex stem, and rule (7) adds clitics (Z) to fully inflected words, forming a possibly headless unit of greater complexity than the ordinary word.

The semantic component (actually a syntax of logical form), deals with both function–argument relations, and quantifier–binder relations by characterizing trees that correspond closely to the formulas of predicate calculus. (8)–(10) is a fairly representative list of the sorts of rule schemata that have been employed by researchers in autolexical syntax.

$$F^{-(n-1)} = F^{-n}(i) \qquad (8)$$

$$Q = Q^{-1}(F(\ldots x \ldots)) \qquad (9)$$

$$F = Q(F(\ldots x \ldots)) \qquad (10)$$

The schema in (8) is simply the principle of functional application: a function applied to an argument yields a function of one fewer variables, up to F, the category of formulas. Rule (9) yields restricted quantifier phrases by combining a quantifier with an open formula, and rule (10) binds variables in an open formula by combining it with a quantifier phrase.

4. The Interface

The basic vocabulary of each of the modules is to be found in the lexicon, which thus acts as a bridge between and among the autonomous modules (see Sadock 1996). In addition, there exist various cross-modular generalizations including, importantly, what have been called *interface constraints*.

4.1 The Lexicon

It is a commonplace in grammatical theory to divide lexical information into a number of different compartments (or *fields*). In autolexical syntax this practice is of crucial importance, since each field in a lexeme's entry indicates the value of that lexeme with respect to a particular component of the grammar. As an illustration, the lexical entry for the English word *dog* would be as in (11), which shows it to be a lexical noun in syntax, a one-place predicate in semantics, and a noun stem in morphology.

$$\begin{aligned} dog:\ &syntax = N^0 \\ &semantics = F^{-1} \\ &morphology = N^{-0} \end{aligned} \qquad (11)$$

The obvious role that the lexicon plays as part of the interface is thus to insure that the structures that are independently characterized by the several modules contain all and only the same lexemes.

4.2 Interface Constraints

Even if an n-tuple of well-formed representations from n components can be properly lexicalized in terms of a single set of lexemes, there may be no grammatical expression that the set of structures characterizes. The basic insight that autolexical syntax seeks to capture is that structural relationships at one level of representation may differ only to a certain extent from those that obtain at some other level. Various different formulations of the constraints involved exist (e.g., Lapointe 1988). The following version is from Sadock (1991).

Consider the ungrammatical sentences *Winnie's the Pooh here* and *Winnie the's Pooh here*, versus the grammatical *Winnie the Pooh's here*. Assuming that the auxiliary clitic *'s* occurs in syntax as the first element of VP, that is to say after the subject NP, and is a suffix to any sort of word in the morphology, the generalization is simply that the order of elements in the syntax and in the morphology is the same. The idea is illustrated in Fig. 1.

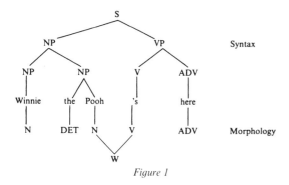

Figure 1

This *strong linearity constraint* is relaxed slightly in the case of the Latin clitic *-que* 'and,' which presumably precedes a conjoined phrase in syntax, as do other conjunctions in that language, and is a morphological suffix, as is the English auxiliary clitic. But the Latin clitic attaches to the end of the word that follows it, rather than the word that precedes it: *puella pulchra puerque bonus* 'a beautiful girl and a good boy.' The clitic must still attach as close to its syntactic position as it can: **puella pulchra puer bonusque*, thus obeying a *weak linearity constraint*.

In the case of incorporation, there seems to be no linearity constraint in effect at all. In West Greenlandic, nominal modifiers follow their nouns, and verbs follow their NP arguments: *Illumik* 'house' *angisuumik* 'big' *aappalaartumik* 'red' *ator-poq* 'rent-he', that is, 'He is renting a big red house.' But no matter how many modifiers are found in an object NP, it is always the head N of that NP that is combined with a suffixal verb in so-called 'noun incorporation': *Angisuumik* 'big' *aappalaartumik* 'red' *illu-si-voq* 'house-buy-he,' that is, 'He bought a big red house.' The generalization, observed also in the Government and Binding framework as the *head movement constraint* is that the two elements that are combined in the morphology are a syntactic head and the head of its syntactic complement. In autolexical syntax, this restriction on incorporative phenomena is known as the *strong constructional integrity constraint*.

Returning to the example of Latin *-que* discussed above, note that the clitic need not attach to the head of the phrase it combines with (e.g., in *puella pulchra bonusque puer*), but does attach to some word of that phrase, namely the first. In other words, it attaches

to that word of its complement that is closest to its syntactic position. A lexeme that combines at one level with an element of the phrase it is a sister to at some other level is said to obey the *weak constructional integrity constraint*.

English auxiliary clitics obey only the strong linearity constraint, West Greenlandic incorporation obeys only the strong constructional integrity constraint, and Latin conjunctive clitics obey both weak constraints. These types seem to represent the maximum degree of allowable discrepancy between morphological and syntactic representations.

5. Intermodular Defaults

Since in this theory lexical information is compartmentalized into fields that refer to independent grammars, a lexeme could in principle display any combination of behaviors in the various components. But there are clearly certain constellations of properties across modules that are more frequent than others, and these correlations are captured in autolexical syntax by means of intermodular default statements.

A transitive verb, for example, ordinarily has the semantics of a function from entity expressions to predicates (an F^{-2} in the notation described above), and conversely, a semantic F^{-2} usually has the syntax of a transitive verb, at least if it is expressed as a verb in syntax. This correlation can be conveniently expressed in an intermodular rule such as (12), where the feature [SF 4] is the subcategorization feature for transitive verbs (see (4) above).

$$\text{syntax} = V^0 \text{ and semantics} = F^{-2}\langle = \rangle \text{syntax} = [\text{SF 4}] \quad (12)$$

If this rule is interpreted as a default setting, rather than a categorical requirement, then individual lexical items may contain information that overrides it. The verb *dispose*, for example, is a two-place predicate in the semantics and a verb in the syntax, but it happens to subcategorize a prepositional phrase in *of*, a fact that can be stipulated in its lexical entry (13):

$$\begin{aligned}
\textit{dispose:} \quad &\text{syntax} = V^0/\_\_[^{PP}\text{of NP}] \quad (13)\\
&\text{semantics} = F^{-2}\\
&\text{morphology} = V^{-0}
\end{aligned}$$

A more typical transitive verb like *remove* could have the simpler lexical entry in (14), the redundant subcategorization feature being filled in by (12).

$$\begin{aligned}
\textit{remove:} \quad &\text{syntax} = V^0 \quad (14)\\
&\text{semantics} = F^{-2}\\
&\text{morphology} = V^{-0}
\end{aligned}$$

6. Other Modules

A great deal of research in the 1980s and early 1990s investigated the utility of employing additional dimensions beyond the traditional triumvirate. It has been suggested that an autonomous level of thematic role structure exists (Faarlund 1996). Other research reveals an independent dimension displaying such discourse-oriented organizational features as topic, focus, and comment (see Sadock 1990). A level at which illocutionary force, as distinct from locutionary content is demonstrated has also been expounded (Eilfort 1986). A few researchers working independently have suggested that the single level called 'morphology' be split into two levels, one of which displays the morphological organization relevant to the syntax, and the other the morphological structure relevant to the phonology (see Chelliah 1996; Woodbury 1996).

7. Comparison with Other Theories

Autolexical syntax differs from all monostratal theories such as generalized phrase structure grammar, head-driven phrase structure grammar, and categorial grammar, in recognizing more than one level of structure, and is thus similar in some respects to transformational grammar.

In the standard theory of transformational grammar, however, the only level that was directly characterized was deep structure (see *Generative Grammar: Transformational Grammar*), whereas each level of representation is directly characterized in autolexical theory. Most work in the Government and Binding framework and its descendents has assumed that all levels are topologically identical through the operation of the 'projection principle.' By contrast, in autolexical syntax every level has its own system of tactics. Inasmuch as the several modular representations may be topologically distinct, autolexical syntax can be seen as based upon a radical rejection of the projection principle.

Since pieces of phonological words can have independent functions in both syntax and semantics, autolexical syntax also rejects the lexicalist hypothesis and to that extent resembles generative semantics (see *Generative Semantics*). But unlike generative semantics with its long and intricate derivations, there are no derivations at all in autolexical syntax, all levels of structure being simultaneously and directly associated without intermediate steps.

In positing autonomous tactics at each level, autolexical syntax bears some kinship to *Stratificational Grammar*, but that theory organizes the various representations into a series of strata (similarly, the theory in Marantz 1984), whereas autolexical syntax does not. Lexical functional grammar (see *Lexical Functional Grammar*) recognizes a small number of independent levels of structure, but they are not of the same formal type, and only the C-structure seems to have a distinct characterization in terms of a set of rules.

Several works within the general tradition of Government and Binding Theory have posited simultaneous structures that strongly resemble those employed in autolexical syntax. These go under the label of 'restructuring' (e.g., in Zubizaretta 1985) or 'co-analysis' (e.g., Di Sciullo and Williams 1987). Unlike autolexical syntax, where each structure represents an independently motivated informational dimension, the simultaneous structures that appear in Government and Binding Theory work are competing syntactic structures.

8. Mathematical Properties

It is well-known that the intersection of context-free phrase structure languages includes noncontext-free languages. Therefore the class of languages describable by autolexical grammars that make use only of strictly context-free components is beyond the set describable in terms of individual single context-free phrase structure grammars. There appear to be languages that can be described by both indexed grammars and context-sensitive grammars, but apparently not by autolexical grammars with a finite number of components. It is not known at present whether the intersection of a finite number of context-free languages is a proper subset of the indexed languages or context-sensitive languages (see Latta 1993).

Autolexical grammars also exceed the strong generative power of their component grammars. Consider a grammar with two components, one a context-free phrase structure grammar describing the mirror-image language on the vocabulary $\{a, b\}$, and the other a right-branching (finite state) grammar describing the regular language $(a*b*)*$. The intersection of these two languages is just the language described by the context-free phrase structure grammar, but taking the structure of the sentences of this language to be that given by the finite state grammar, the result is a language beyond the strong generative capacity of context-free grammar.

Bibliography

Chelliah S L 1996 An autolexical account of voicing assimilation in Manipuri. In: Schiller E, Steinberg E, Need B (eds.) 1996
Di Sciullo A M, Williams E 1987 *On the Definition of Word.* MIT Press, Cambridge, MA
Eilfort W 1986 On the existence and nature of an independent illocutionary level of grammar (Unpublished dissertation, University of Chicago)
Faarlund J T 1996 Autostructural analysis of semantic roles. In: Schiller E, Steinberg E, Need B (eds.) 1996
Kathman D 1996 Control in autolexical syntax. In: Schiller E, Steinberg E, Need B (eds.) 1996
Lapointe S G 1988 Distinguishing types of morphosyntactic cooccurrences: Mismatch resolution, agreement, government. *CLS* **24(2)**
Latta M J 1993 The intersection of context-free languages (Unpublished dissertation, University of Texas)
Marantz A 1984 *On the Nature of Grammatical Relations.* MIT Press, Cambridge, MA
Sadock J M 1985 Autolexical syntax: A theory of noun incorporation and similar phenomena. *NLLT* **8**: 379–440
Sadock J M 1990 A trimodular account of Yiddish syntax. *SLS* **20**: 31–50

Sadock J M 1991 *Autolexical Syntax: A Theory of Parallel Grammatical Representations.* University of Chicago Press, Chicago, IL

Sadock J M 1996 The lexicon as bridge between phrase structure components. In: Rooryck J, Zaring L (eds.) *Phrase Structure and the Lexicon.* Kluwer Academic, Dordrecht

Sadock J M, Schiller E 1993 The generalized interface principle. *CLS* **29**: 391–401

Schiller E, Steinberg E, Need B (eds.) 1996 *Autolexical Theory: Ideas and Methods.* Mouton de Gruyter, Berlin

Woodbury A C 1996 On restricting the role of morphology in autolexical syntax. In: Schiller E, Steinberg E, Need B (eds.) 1996

Zubizaretta M L 1985 The relation between morphophonology and morphosyntax: The case of Romance causatives. *LI* **16**: 247–89

Case Grammar

John M. Anderson

'Case grammar' (CG) is a label used for various developments in grammatical theory originating in the mid-to-late 1960s which are associated more or less closely with a certain hypothesis concerning the organization of the grammar: the hypothesis concerns the status of semantic functions—or relations or roles—such as agentive or locative; functions which label the mode of participation of the denotata of arguments in the situation described by the predication in which they occur. The terms 'various' and 'more or less closely' are used advisedly. Since case grammar is a partial hypothesis, it is compatible with a variety of hypotheses concerning other aspects of the grammar, though it will, of course, interact with them. Since, too, the hypothesis can be formulated in more and less strong forms, not all variants of case grammar are as distinct in their claims from what is embodied in other frameworks which are not usually termed case grammars. The minimum case grammar hypothesis is that semantic functions are relevant to the expression of syntactic (as well as semantic) generalizations; in a stronger, more interesting form it involves the claim that they are basic to the syntax, and that many other aspects of syntactic structure are derivative of them.

The name itself is in part a recognition that what is involved is, again in part, a return to traditional concerns with the semantics and syntax of case, concerns which were neglected by structuralist (including early transformational) frameworks which abolished the morphology/syntax division and were reticent about semantics. The term case grammar specifically devolves from Fillmore's (1965, 1966, 1968a) use of case relation, or simply case, for semantic function, the status of which is fundamental to the case grammar hypothesis. Section 1 outlines some of the basic notions central to the main tradition associated with this hypothesis, while Sects. 2 and 3 give some idea of, respectively, the variety of interpretation to which it has been subjected and the range of attempts to arrive at a definition of case and cases.

1. Some Fundamentals

The use of the term 'case relation' for semantic function is based on the familiar observation that in a number of languages semantic functions are distinguished by differences in nominal inflexion, as in the Old English sentence of (1):

Him ofhreow ðæs mannes   (1)
He/they + DAT pitied the + GEN man + GEN

wherein the dative inflexion signals the locus of the emotion denoted by the verb (discussed below as the experiencer case relation) and the genitive inflexion marks the source of the emotion. However, it must be acknowledged, as is once more familiar from earlier studies (cf. Welte 1987), that in many instances the correlation between case inflexion and semantic function is not simple. Most notoriously, case inflexions can correlate more closely with grammatical functions or relations. Notably, most grammarians would not include subject among the set of semantic functions. At the very least, it is of a rather different character from agentive, etc.; hence its differentiation, along with object, etc., as a 'grammatical relation.' But the inflexions identified by the label nominative in various languages are labeled thus precisely because their occurrence correlates most closely with the nominal identified on other grounds as a subject. Further, apart from the fact that case inflexions typically express other categories simultaneously with case (or grammatical) relations, categories such as gender, number, dimensionality, distinctions in case relation are frequently expressed otherwise than by nominal inflexion. Typically, as well as, or instead of, noun inflexions, adpositions, verbal auxiliaries, word order, verb morphology, and combinations of these may be involved, often in combination in the same language. Consider, for example, the sentences from eastern Pomo in (2):

mîʿp béʿkal duléya 'he them killed'   (2a)

béʿkʰ míʿpal šaʿkakiya 'they him killed'   (2b)

míʿp kaluhuya 'he went-home'   (2c)

béʿkʰ kálpʰiʿlíya 'they went-home'   (2d)

béʿkal ċeʿxéłka 'they slipped.'   (2e)

The shape of the pronoun reflects whether it is agentive or not: *mí·p* and *bé·k*ʰ are agentive, they mark the source of the action, both in the transitive examples (2a–b) and the intransitive (2c–d); but *mí·pal* and *bé·kal* signal the entity undergoing the action or process, what will be described below as an instance of the neutral case relation, both in the transitive examples (2a–b) and in the intransitive (2e). Typically, too, the suppletion illustrated in (2a/b)—the 'kill' verb changes its shape—is in response to the number of the neutral ('them' versus 'him'). However, in (2c/d) the (partial) suppletion is triggered by the number of the argument already (on the basis of the correlation between semantic function and pronoun morphology) labeled agentive. This would seem to confirm that the pronouns in (2c) and (2d) are simultaneously agentive and neutral, as both source of the action and under-goer of the action (of movement), whereas that in (2e) is neutral simply. We return to the association between argument and case relation in Sect. 3; what is most relevant at this point is the interaction of different means of expressing case relations illustrated in (2). There is typically too, with respect to a specific lang-uage, no one-to-one correlation between particular case relation and particular expression, whether by inflexion, adposition, or whatever. Despite occasional claims to the contrary, the English preposition *by*, for instance, is not associated uniquely with agentives, or *to* with goals: both can also mark what is often labeled experiencer (*known by/to*). Nevertheless, given that the expression of distinctions in case relation may be regarded as the prototypical function of case inflexions, this terminology is not unjustified. And its appro-priateness is reinforced to the extent that grammatical relations can be regarded as neutralized case relations.

Such a notion is crucial to the strong case grammar framework developed by Fillmore in the late 1960s. This substituted for the deep structure of a grammar of the type envisaged in Chomsky (1965) basic rep-resentations including nodes associated with a set of case relations. Both surface structures of (3), for exam-ple are derived from the (unordered) deep (case) struc-ture of (4). The proposition consists of a verb and a set of case phrases, each of which includes a case 'flag' (kasus) and a noun phrase. The agentive is the source of the action; the neutral is the least specific case, whose precise relation to the predicate is most obvi-ously dependent on the type of the predicate: it labels the entity which undergoes processes and movements and actions and has locations and states attributed to it. Section 3 discusses more fully the definition of the cases; but notice at this point that n(eutral) appears under a number of different labelings—ergative (an acknowledged misnomer), object(ive), nominative (again, unfortunate), absolutive, patient (usually interpreted more narrowly than neutral). Modality consists of elements of tense, mood, and aspect, including modal cases (such as manner phrases), which are interpreted as modalities of the sentence as a whole. Predicates, such as the verb in (3/4), are subcategorized not in terms of their functionally unlabeled couplements but with respect to the set of case phrases they require, obligatorily, or optionally, as exemplified in (5):

$$+[\text{——} \text{N(eutral) A(gentive)}] \qquad (5a)$$

$$+[\text{——} \text{N (A)}] \qquad (5b)$$

The verb of (5a) (perhaps *kill*, if one ignores instru-mentals, such as *with a handbag*, for the moment: see again Sect. 3) is marked as taking a neutral and an agentive. That in (2b) takes an N and an optional A, perhaps appropriate for *melt*: see (8) below.

Assignment of the status of subject, for example, is based on the set of case phrases present in a sentence, the case frame. Each entry in (5) includes a set of case frame features. Unmarked assignment in a particular predication is specifically in accord with a hierarchy of case relations, as exemplified by (6) (Fillmore 1968a):

$$\text{Agentive} < \text{Instrumental} < \text{Objective} \qquad (6)$$

such that an agentive, if present, will be subject; in the absence of an A, then an instrumental, if present, will be; and so on. With *kill* the agentive takes priority, as in (3a). The surface structure of the passive sentence in (3b) contains signals (the auxiliary construction) that here the hierarchy has been overridden, a marked selection of subject has been made, and the 'rejected' subject is distinguished by an appropriate marker (here *by*). There has been some controversy over the character of the hierarchy, partly as a result of differ-ent views concerning the set of cases, as discussed in Sect. 3 below. It may be too that lexical exceptions to

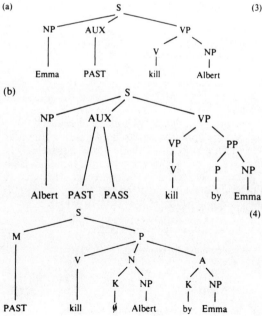

(a), (b), (3), (4) tree diagrams

the hierarchy have to be acknowledged. For instance, if *like* and *please* in English are associated with the same set of case frame features, then one of them will have to be marked as exceptional in subject selection:

Jemima liked the play (7a)

The play pleased Jemima (7b)

whatever the hierarchy, if it is determinate. Anderson (1977: § 2.1.5) and others have denied that this is necessary, in that the two verbs require different sets. But even if such exceptions have to be countenanced, the viability of some such hierarchy is the basis for the strong case grammar hypothesis, which asserts the basicness of cases and the dependence thereon of other syntactic phenomena (including subject selection).

It has been argued too that conventional deep structures, as well as being derivable, also form a poor basis from which to project (deep) grammatical relations, one of their claimed roles: configurational definitions are difficult to maintain across languages; they allow for spurious (or at least never utilized) grammatical relations; and some categories seem themselves to be relational (e.g., 'place'). And the role of deep relations in the grammar (*pace* Katz 1972) remains obscure. (See here, for example, Anderson 1977: § 1.2, 1982; Starosta 1987.) And, the argument proceeds, neither deep structures nor grammatical relations are relevant to lexical relationships.

Fillmore's work throughout has involved a strong interest in lexical semantics (see particularly Fillmore 1987; also, in the present context, 1968b, 1970, 1971b, c, 1972, 1977a, b). And much effort within case grammar has been devoted to showing that subcategorization and lexical relations are sensitive to case relations rather than the configurations and grammatical relations that are derivative in CG. So-called 'ergative' verbs (Lyons 1968) provide a straightforward example with respect to subcategorization. Case grammarians have argued that the basic distributional potential of verbs like that in (8):

Burt melted the ice (8a)

The ice melted (8b)

is most transparently described in terms of the case features of (9):

____ N (A) (9)

rather than, say, the conventional frame of (10):

$(+[\underline{\quad} \text{NP}])$ (10)

which obscures what is constant in the two basic occurrences, the neutral (objective) argument, with selection of subject being determined by the hierarchy. Anderson (1984) attempts to show that a wide range of (lexical) derivational relationships in English make no reference to grammatical relations or the configurations in terms of which they may be defined.

Typical here is -*able*- formation, whose central function is to form adjectives of a certain semantic character on the basis of verbs, such that the argument of the adjective corresponds to the neutral argument of the verb (whatever its grammatical relation); there is again the familiar 'ergative' relation, illustrated in (11):

The cover is removable. (cf. Beppo has removed the
cover) (11a)
The settings are changable. (cf. Beppo has changed the
settings)

The material is perishable. (cf. The material has perished)
(11b)
The weather is changable. (cf. The weather has changed)

and highlighted therein by the derivational pattern associated with a verb like *change*. And reference to grammatical relations again obscures the generalization. The import of this is that if the lexicon (via subcategorization and derivational relationships) has access only to basic syntactic structure, then grammatical relations and the division into subject and objects do not appear to be basic: this is exactly what is claimed by the case grammar hypothesis.

This conclusion can be avoided, with respect to examples like (8) and (11), at least, if there is adopted the unaccusative hypothesis associated with developments in relational grammar and other frameworks. In terms of this hypothesis, the surface subjects of (8a) and (11a) are initial direct objects; their subjecthood is derivative only. (Other intransitive verbs (typically agentive) do have initial subjects; they are unergative.) The relationship in (8) and (11) can then be described without reference to case relations: for example, 'ergative' verbs are transitives with an optionally empty subject; the derivational relationship illustrated by (11) involves uniformly the direct object of the base verb. Case grammarians have argued that such a strategy lacks independent motivation, is unnecessary given the availability of case relations, and leads to incorrect predictions (cf. Anderson 1980).

Such arguments have also been concerned to show not only that grammatical relations are derivative but also that it is inappropriate to attribute subjecthood at all to certain language types, if a definition of subject more restrictive than 'obligatory derived relation' is to be maintained. In most languages, subject is a syntactically motivated grouping (or neutralization) of (whatever else) transitive agentives and intransitive neutrals (cf. (8) again); in the ('ergative') Dyirbal language of Australia such a grouping is at most only marginally relevant syntactically. (Direct) objecthood is also notoriously difficult to identify. Finally with respect to grammatical relations, it has also been argued that indirect object is an incoherent relation, even derivatively (Anderson 1978).

Throughout the late 1960s and the early 1970s, various different versions of CG were proposed, to some extent independently (e.g., apart from the work of Fillmore: Anderson 1968, 1971; Platt 1971; Cook 1971, 1972a, 1972b, 1973, 1978; Nilsen 1972; Longacre 1976; also Chafe 1970); and the framework inspired a number of descriptive and applied studies. However, little agreement on the set and nature of the set of case relations emerged (see further Sect. 3). And it became clear that case grammar was vulnerable to the charge that, apart from the claimed prediction of the distribution of grammatical relations and associated word order properties, little evidence of a syntactic role for case relations was adduced. Thus, for example, the case-based lexicon of Stockwell et al. (1973) plays almost no role in the syntactic descriptions that occupy the rest of the volume. Even more seriously, perhaps, evidence was put forward, on the other hand, for the semantic and syntactic relevance of deep grammatical relations and for the necessity of positing the kind of relation between active and passive sentences prescribed by the passive transformation, which was eliminated from the syntax by Fillmore's (1968a) proposals. Crucial here is the discussion of the role of grammatical relations by S. R. Anderson (1971).

Pairs of sentences such as that in (12):

Ernie loaded the pickup with packs of amaretti   (12a)

Ernie loaded packs of amaretti onto the truck   (12b)

differ in interpretation: the former has been described as 'holistic,' the action exhausts the relevant dimensions of space denoted by the direct object; the latter is 'partitive.' If (12a) and (b) share case features (say 'agentive, neutral, place'), then the basis for the difference must be located elsewhere. It is not a property of surface structure; the difference remains constant under various transformational movements, as illustrated by (13):

The pickup was loaded with packs of amaretti   (13a)

Packs of amaretti were loaded onto the truck   (13b)

and (14):

It was packs of amaretti that Ernie loaded the truck with   (14a)
It was the pickup that Ernie loaded with packs of amaretti

It was packs of amaretti that Ernie loaded onto the pickup   (14b)
It was the pickup that Ernie loaded packs of amaretti onto

What the (12–14a) variants share is deep structure association of the place case relation with direct object function. Their derivations must include a stage at which this association is made, motivating both passive as a transformation and deep object. (This is, of course, not to deny that, given appropriate assumptions, this association could be read off derived structures.)

Fillmore (1977a) concedes the force of this argument, and essentially reinstates deep structure, thereby effectively abandoning the case grammar hypothesis in its strongest form. Others have disagreed. It is possible, for instance, that passive may be accommodated constructionally, as biclausal (see Sect. 2). But even if that possibility is laid aside, it can be argued that the case feature assignments assumed above are inappropriate, that they differ between the (a) and (b) examples. Miller (1985) suggests that the association of argument to case relation is reversed between (12a) and (12b); J. M. Anderson (1977: § 1.8) accepts that the (a) and (b) examples share the same case features and the same associations, but suggests that in addition the place argument in the (a) examples is simultaneously neutral: i.e., it bears two case relations. (On this see Sect. 3.) Under either proposal, holisticness, as elsewhere, can be associated with the neutral case relation: unless this expectation is canceled in some way, neutrals are normally understood as participating as a whole in the process being represented. This is true of the neutrals in (8a) and (8b), for instance. J. M. Anderson also points out that the generalization based on deep object is inadequate. The subject place argument in (12c) is also associated with a holistic interpretation:

The garden is swarming with bees   (12c)
Bees are swarming in the garden   (12d)

He attributes this to the place in (12c) being again simultaneously neutral, which is also associated with its selection as subject. Once more, (12a) and (12c) show the 'ergative' pattern that cuts across grammatical relations.

The syntactic role of case relations has been variously addressed since the mid-1970s. The force of objections based on the paucity of reference by transformations to case relations has been considerably weakened by the apparent demise of individual transformations. For instance, the motivations for a syntactic relationship between pairs such as that in (15):

Anna taught Helen Greek   (15a)

Anna taught Greek to Helen   (15b)

involving a putative dative movement, are disputable, where evident. These pairs can be argued to show a partially shared case frame, with the difference in word order being attributable to the differences in case relations present (cf. again Anderson 1978; also 1987; Böhm 1986). The difference in case frame is reflected in the contrary acceptabilities of (16a) and (b):

*Anna taught an empty room Greek   (16a)

Anna taught Greek to an empty room   (16b)

The *Helen/empty room* argument is involved in the action in a different way in the (a) and (b) examples, suggesting a difference in case relation.

More generally, the development of frameworks in

which transformations are reduced to a small number, including one, or from which they are eliminated altogether, poses the question of the syntactic relevance of case relations in a different way—or rather different possible ways. This is one respect in which different variants of case grammar have evolved in response to decisions about other aspects of the grammar than are encompassed by the basic case grammar hypothesis.

2. Varieties of Case Grammar

Fillmorean case grammar evolved as an alternative to the kind of transformational grammar expounded in Chomsky (1965), with subject-formation as one of a number of transformational rules. Anderson (1968, 1971) talks of rules of realization (including 'sequencing'), implying nontransformational mapping of (unordered) case structures onto surface structures enriched with sequence and configurations; but only a very limited range of constructions is taken into consideration. And Anderson (1977) envisages complex (transformational) derivational relationships between initial structures and surface, including pre-lexical application of syntactic rules (see *Generative Semantics*).

Partly in reaction to such developments, Starosta (1973, 1978, 1987, 1988) and others have formulated a framework, lexicase, which eschews transformations, and, indeed, syntactic derivations altogether. Syntax is monostratal and case relations and case forms (including case inflexions) are marked as features on lexical items, the former on nouns, the latter on nouns, verbs and prepositions. Thus, corresponding to (3) and (4) above one might have (17), with no deep/surface distinction. AGT and PAT, are case relation features, roughly corresponding to A and N; nom, acc, sorc, and goal are case form features. The relationship between the [+AGT] noun in (17a) and the means ([+MNS]) noun in (17b) is expressed by the rule of lexical derivation which forms the adjectival verb in (17b) from the transitive verb in (17a). Corresponding to the case frame features discussed above are contextual features such as [+[+AGT]] and [+[+PAT]] associated lexically with predicates. Contextual features may be either inherent or given by lexical redundancy: e.g., all verbs are redundantly [+[×PAT]] (what Starosta refers to as patient centrality: see Sect. 3). The subject selection hierarchy is also expressed by lexical redundancies such as (18), which requires that an item that occurs with a [+AGT] must also occur with a [+PAT] (generalizable as patient centrality), and also that the [×ACT] is [+nom], subject, and the [+PAT] is [+acc], object. In general the grammar is reduced to what can be expressed via relationships between individual lexical items—though the status of long distance dependencies remains uncertain. It should be noted too that some critics have found it difficult to see how basic word order settings (such as head-

modifier versus modifier-head) can be regarded as part of the lexicon.

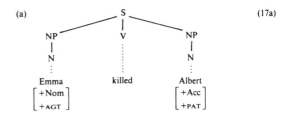

(17a)

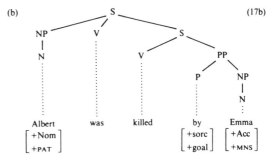

(17b)

It is still possible within such a restrictive framework to reconstruct the fundamental basis for the case grammar hypothesis, the primacy of case relations vis-à-vis case forms; specifically, in terms of redundancies like that in (18). But lexical primacy of case relations is a property shared by a number of other proposals, such as those made within the tradition of functional grammar, as developed by Dik (1978; also 1987) and others. Are these also case grammars? Starosta himself describes various valency grammars as such. This is to some extent a terminological matter. However, the central thrust of work in case grammar (what was called above the strong hypothesis) has involved the *syntactic* primacy of case relations and the exclusion of grammatical relations, etc., from the lexicon (cf. Sect. 1 above). Other developments suggest that this can be maintained within a restrictive theory that does not abandon the syntax/lexicon division.

$$[+[+\text{AGT}]] \rightarrow \begin{bmatrix} +[+\text{PAT}] \\ -\begin{bmatrix} +\text{nom} \\ +\text{AGT} \end{bmatrix} \\ -\begin{bmatrix} +\text{acc} \\ +\text{PAT} \end{bmatrix} \end{bmatrix} \qquad (18)$$

The descriptions proposed by Anderson (1977) involve complex syntactic derivations. But they are conceived of as resulting from the interaction of a small number of universal syntactic rules, and possibly only one involving structure change (raising), regulated by universal constraints, such as strict cyclicity. Roughly, in terms of this last, cyclic structure-changing rules must apply only in derived (non-monoclausal) environments or in an environment resulting from the application of a cyclic rule. Thus, a derivation whereby the subject of the finite verb in (19):

Fran seems to like cheese (19)

is raised out of a subordinate clause, conforms to strict cyclicity, whereas monoclausal rules like dative and the traditional passive, whether interpreted as movements or relation-changes, are illegitimate. Such a requirement outlaws all the advancements of relational grammar, for instance, if conceived in derivational terms. Raising, indeed, it has been argued (e.g., Anderson 1982, 1984, 1986), provides a paradigm instance of the syntactic role of case relations and of the appropriateness of the strong case grammar hypothesis.

In (19) the raised subject of the (nonfinite) subordinate clause assumes the subject function in the main (cyclic) clause. In (20):

Nobody expected Fran to like cheese (20)

the raised subject becomes the object of the finite verb. (Such a formulation clearly rejects attempts to deny such a (derived) status to the *Fran* argument in (20).) The derived relations involved present us with a familiar pattern of distribution, that labeled 'ergative.' The status of subject in (19) and object in (20) is exactly what one would expect of a neutral argument; in (20) it is denied subjecthood by the experiencer argument of the finite verb. Raising confers the neutral case relation in the cyclic clause on the subject argument of the subordinate verb. Formulations of raising invoking grammatical relations or configurations, once again, obscure this generalization. More interestingly still, this interaction of relations is as predicted by the case grammar hypothesis. The identification of grammatical relations is derived, determined by the hierarchy; thus, the identity of the subject of the cyclic clause is not available on the cycle of rules applying to that clause (in the absence of an arbitrary ordering of rules); but, if the subject is identified cyclically, then its identity is available on the next cycle. This is exactly what the formulation of raising requires: the argument involved is identified as the subject of the lower clause (now available, on the raising cycle) and as neutral (a case relation) in the cyclic clause; its grammatical relation in the upper clause is given by the hierarchy. Indeed, if this argument had to be identified in the formulation of raising by its grammatical relation in the cyclic clause, such a formulation would stand as a counterexample to the predictions of the case grammar hypothesis.

Dative and passive, insofar as they involve manipulation of derived properties within a single clause, also violate the case grammar hypothesis, as they do strict cyclicity. The two hypotheses converge in excluding them as monoclausal rules. The dative relationship with examples like (15) can be allowed for in terms of partially shared case features. Such an account is not available, however, for passive. But as an alternative to the lexical proposal described above, a cue can be taken from the overtly two-verb structure involved. Say (passive) *be* is a raising verb, and its subject is raised out of the subordinate clause associated with the accompanying nonfinite (e.g., Anderson 1990, 1991, 1992: § 4.1). It differs from a raising verb like *seem* only in that the raised argument is not the subject of the nonfinite verb; rather, it is the argument next down on the subject selection hierarchy. This stipulation allows for all of (21):

Albert was [killed by Emma] (21a)

That was [known by/to everybody] (21b)

The bed was [slept in by a parrot] (21c)

(with the boundaries of the subordinate clause marked by brackets). In each instance the hierarchically highest argument (agentive, experiencer, agentive/neutral, respectively) is ignored by raising, and is marked with a preposition characteristic of the case relation involved. (On the agentive/neutral assigned to (21c) see Sect. 3.)

More recently, it has been claimed (cf. again Anderson 1990, 1991) that raising (including passive) is structure-building; more generally, that syntactic structure is built up monotonically on the basis of the valencies (specified crucially in terms of case relations) of individual lexical items. Such developments serve to enable us to bring into sharper focus the differences between the lexical case grammar advocated by Starosta and the tradition within which case relations are seen as syntactically basic. Crucially involved is the validity of a syntactic/lexical distinction. Advocates of the distinction (eg., Anderson 1984) argue, for instance, for a differentiation between syntactic and lexical passives (derived adjectives); it is unclear how, if legitimate, this distinction is to be reconstructed in purely lexical terms. Another central question for the lexical approach (apart from those mentioned above) is: how are the alleged asymmetries between the roles of case relations and case forms to be accounted for? This involves both the syntactic asymmetry associated with strict cyclicity (deployed in the description of raising given above) and the lexical asymmetry associated with the claimed failure of lexical rules to make reference to case forms.

Case grammar approaches (including perhaps functional grammar) are united in highlighting the contrastive status of case relations: they have to be stipulated lexically. Many other aspects of syntactic and lexical structure are redundant, derivative of case specifications and, for example, parametric settings for basic word order. The case relations are also semantically identified, though distributionally distinctive. Anderson (1989, 1990, 1991, 1992) thus sees case grammar as a subpart of notional grammar, wherein all the basic elements of the syntax, including word classes, though distributionally established, are identified on the basis of semantic properties displayed by their prototypical members.

As Sect. 2 has in part illustrated, other aspects of case grammar have been much more contentious. To some extent this reflects choice among theoretical alternatives relatively independent of the case grammar hypothesis. Independence of hypotheses within grammatical systems, however, is only ever relative. Thus, whereas Fillmore (1968a, 1971a) remains rather undecided concerning the appropriate representation of syntactic structures including cases, others (e.g., Robinson 1970; Anderson 1971; Tarvainen 1987—and cf. Tesnière 1959) have argued that case relations, specifically, are most appropriately expressed by dependency structures. In terms of the framework of Anderson (1971), for instance, (22) would correspond to (4) (again initially unlinearized), with case nodes dependent on the V(erb) and governing the N(oun); erg = ergative (roughly, agentive—see Sect. 3), nom = nominative (neutral).

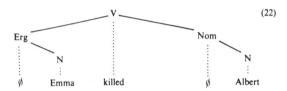

(22)

The correlation between the dependency hypothesis, and other aspects of syntax, and the CG hypothesis itself is controversial. But perhaps the least agreed on aspect of case grammar has been the constitution of the set of case relations themselves, an issue which remains unresolved.

3. Defining Case Relations

The arguments of a predicate identify the entities involved in the situation described by the predicate. The nature of the roles played by these entities can be discriminated in more or less detail. In a sense, each predicate prescribes a unique set of roles. But it is possible to generalize over various 'fields' of the vocabulary; and in certain institutionalized situations, in particular, these roles are made lexically explicit in the language. Thus, in the situations described by English verbs like *sell*, *buy*, *barter*, etc., one recurrent role is occupied by a customer; in those described by *concede*, *justify*, *accuse* etc., there recurs a defendant, perhaps (Fillmore 1971c, 1972: § 42, 1977b). More generally still, one can recognize that in many situations it is possible to attribute to a particular entity the role of source of the action, the agentive role. The customer in (23a) and the defendant in (b):

Algernon bought a Lada from Bert (23a)

Algernon justified his decision unconvincingly (23b)

are both agentive, as sources of the immediate action described by the verb. There is no simple mapping between such generalized roles and the more specific institutionalized functions. The customer in (24), for instance, is not presented as the source of the immediate action:

Bert sold a Lada to Algernon (24)

even though the same 'real-world' event may be being referred to by (23a) and (24). Much of Fillmore's work since the early 1970s has been concerned with the cognitive structures, Frames, within which detailed role specifications are articulated. However, it is generalized roles such as agentive that case grammarians identify as case relations, those semantic functions which are basic to the lexicon and/or syntax.

There has been some agreement, and much disagreement, concerning the set of roles that fulfill this function in the grammar. (For a recent survey see Somers 1987.) The set of case relations offered in Fillmore (1968a: 24–25) was tentative and not intended as necessarily exhaustive. He suggests:

Agentive (A): the case of the typically animate perceived instigator of the action identified by the verb;

Instrumental (I): the case of the inanimate force or object causally involved in the action or state identified by the verb;

Dative (D): the case of the animate being affected by the state or action identified by the verb;

Factitive (F): the case of the object or being resulting from the action or state identified by the verb, or understood as a part of the meaning of the verb;

Locative (L): the case which identifies the location or spatial orientation of the state or action identified by the verb;

Objective (O): the semantically most neutral case, the case of anything representable by a noun whose role in the action or state identified by the verb is identified by the semantic interpretation of the verb itself; conceivably the concept should be limited to things which are affected by the action or state identified by the verb.

Other possibilities are mentioned elsewhere. Fillmore (1971b: § 4) proposes that 'the case notions that are most relevant to the subclassification of verb types include the following:

Agent (A): the instigator of the event;

Counter-agent (C): the force or resistance against which the action is carried out;

Object (O): the entity that moves or changes or whose position or existence is in consideration;

Result (R): the entity that comes into existence as a result of the action;

25

Instrument (I): the stimulus or immediate physical cause of an event;

Source (S): the place from which something comes;

Goal (G): the place to which something moves;

Experiencer (E): the entity which receives or accepts experiences or undergoes the effect of an action (earlier called 'Dative').

Fillmore (1971a) contains a slightly different list, in particular lacking result (regarded there as a goal) and counter-agent and including location, time and path. Starosta (1988) suggests a set much reduced compared to his (and Fillmore's) earlier proposals:

Patient (PAT): the perceived central participant in a state or event (formerly also Object or Theme);

Agent (AGT): the perceived external instigator, initiator, controller, or experiencer of the action, event, or state (formerly also dative, experiencer, force, instrument);

Locus (LOC):
inner: the perceived concrete or abstract source, goal, or location of the patient (formerly also source, goal, or path);
outer: the perceived concrete or abstract source, goal, or location of the action, event, or state (formerly also place);

Correspondent (COR):
inner: the entity perceived as being in correspondence with the patient (formerly dative, experiencer, range, increment);
outer: the perceived external frame or point of reference for the action, event, or state as a whole (formerly benefactive, reference);

Means (MNS):
inner: the perceived immediate affector or effector of the patient (formerly instrument, material, vehicle);
outer: the means by which the action, state, or event as a whole is perceived as being realized (formerly instrument, manner).

And Cook (1978: 299) proposes agent, experiencer, benefactive, object and locative, while Longacre (1976: 27–34) has experiencer, patient, agent, range, measure, instrument, locative, source, goal, path. (The inner/outer distinction invoked by Starosta is discussed below.) These sets at least show some overlap; much less of this is evident in, for example, the rather more exotic set proposed by Tarvainen (1987). Such uncertainty over the set of cases, also well illustrated by the introductory discussion to Stockwell et al.'s (1973: ch. 12, § 11.A) 'sample lexicon,' has often been cited in criticism of the case grammar framework (e.g., Chapin 1972). It might, indeed, be regarded as a sign of lack of responsibility to describe a particular case as a 'wastebasket' (Fillmore 1971a: 42). Unless a

theory of case is properly constrained, new cases are liable to crawl out of (or be rescued from—Radden 1978) the 'wastebasket' or from even less desirable spots.

It should, however, be pointed out that the same challenge, or problem, confronts any framework which includes semantic functions, or thematic roles (Gruber 1965; Jackendoff 1983; and descendants), whose status is now seen by a number of noncase grammarians as central to the grammar (cf., for example, the discussions and references in Wilkins 1988). Moreover, the determination of the set of syntactic categories as a whole remains contentious. How, for instance, does one group and hierarchize the classes indicated by the labels universal quantifier (e.g., *all*), distributive quantifier (e.g., *every*), existential quantifier (e.g., *some*), adjectival quantifier (e.g., *many*), quantificational adjective (e.g., *numerous, various*), cardinal numeral, ordinal numeral, superlative adjective, . . . (see Anderson 1989)? However, the defendant has to concede that the resolution of the question of the constitution of the set of semantic functions is rather more crucial for a framework in which they play such a fundamental role as is advocated by case grammarians. Thus, much effort has been devoted within case grammar not merely to the establishing of definitions and semantic/syntactic properties of the individual cases (cf., for example, Fillmore's (1972: § 32) discussion of experiencer and *personally*), but also to the formulation of general principles governing the distribution of cases and (less commonly) of a general substantive theory of the category of case.

Some case relations seem to be well established: agentives and neutrals, for instance, are generally invoked, with agreement over the central instances of such; and their status as cases is supported by many of the phenomena alluded to in Sects. 1 and 2. And a place or locative case is generally acknowledged, though its relation to source and goal is contentious. It is also generally agreed that predicates of experience like *like* involve a distinct case, which Fillmore (1968a) dubbed dative; but the scope of this case is controversial, with Fillmore (1971a, b), as seen above, for instance, reassigning some former datives to goal or neutral and relabeling the rest experiencer:

> where there is a genuine psychological event or mental state verb, we have the Experiencer; where there is a non-psychological verb which indicates a change of state, such as one of dying or growing, we have the Object; where there is a transfer or movement of something to a person, the receiver as destination is taken as the Goal.
> (Fillmore 1971a: 42)

Many investigators recognize an instrumental case relation, as illustrated in (25):

The vandals dented the BMW *with a hammer* (25a)

A hammer dented the BMW (25b)

and some (cf. Fillmore 1971a: § 9) a path:

Henry traveled *through Celle*. (26)

Anderson (1971, 1977), however, rejects both of these as cases, as well as most of the others that have been proposed, in favor of a very restricted set of case relations. Much of this disagreement can be understood in terms of diverse interpretations of the distributional and substantive constraints which case relations conform to.

The nature of these constraints and the differences in their application can perhaps best be appreciated in terms of an examination of a case on whose validity most researchers seem to be agreed, the agentive. One can provide agentive with a distinctive semantic definition, perhaps along the lines of one of those given above, and we can associate phrases so defined with a distinctive distribution, particularly in relation to their role in the subject selection hierarchy. Occurrence of agentive apparently correlates with other semantico–syntactic properties: zero-manifestation in imperatives (*Kill Albert!*, etc.), adverbial selection:

Emma killed Albert in cold blood/deliberately (27a)

*Albert died in cold blood/deliberately (27b)

where interpretation of (27b) requires some extension of our normal understanding of the argument-type demanded by *die*. Agentives are also, perhaps, 'typically animate' (Fillmore 1968a), even human, as in these examples.

Some phrases that share their basic distribution with agentives like *Emma* in (27a) are not human, or even animate, however:

Lightning killed Albert (28a)

Albert was killed by lightning (28b)

and lack many of the associated properties. This can perhaps be allowed for in terms of Fillmore's '*typically* animate'; perhaps, to elaborate on this somewhat, *lightning* in (28) is a nonprototypical agentive. But what of (29):

The poison killed Albert (29a)

Albert was killed by the poison (29b)

and the like? For Fillmore (1968a) *the poison* is an instrumental, which in the presence of an agentive is necessarily marked by *with*:

Emma killed Albert with the poison (30a)

Albert was killed with the poison (by Emma) (30b)

But the source of *the poison* in (29a) is in fact indeterminate, given Fillmore's definitions (either A or I), or a nonexistent ambiguity is predicted for its role. One solution to this is to suggest that instrumentals only ever occur with predicates that also take an agentive (an instrument presupposes an agent) and to regard *the poison* in (29) as agentive: it is a nonprototypical agentive that one interprets as normally fitting into a frame or scene which includes an (unspecified) ultimate agent. Likewise, there is no distributional reason to recognize a distinct force case (Huddleston 1970) associated with *lightning* in (28): volition and the capacity to wield an instrument are not necessarily to be attributed to nonprototypical agentives. The fact that *the poison* in (29) and (30) is now interpreted as bearing two different cases is analogous to the situation which was associated with the customer role above: an entity bearing the same role, say instrument, in a 'real-world' situation may be represented linguistically in different ways (cf. (23a) and (24)), in this instance as agentive or instrumental. (See Anderson 1977: ch. 1; and for a more general description of instrumentals, Nilsen 1973.)

Similarly, it can be argued that though Fillmore (1971a: § 4) eliminates result (or factitive) uniformly in favor of goal, a particular result situation again may be associated with different case structures. Thus, while it seems appropriate to associate his description of result as 'the end-result role of a thing which comes into existence as a result of the action identified by the predicator,' and thus as a goal, with examples like (31):

I converted my impressions into a poem (31)

this is not the case with the examples, like (32):

I wrote a poem (32)

which Fillmore cites: the goal in (32) is the existing of a poem; the *poem* itself is a neutral (object), it represents the entity which undergoes the action of being brought into existence, just as in (33):

I destroyed a poem (33)

an entity is represented (as a neutral) as being removed from existence (and is, of course, no more a source than *poem* is a goal in (32)).

Such discussions illustrate the need for a set of distributional principles for the cases, as well as for semantic (or notional) definitions which recognize the importance of prototypicality. One can approach a consideration of some of the principles that have been suggested by pursuing discussion of the instrumental. Anderson (1977) argues that the subjects of (28a) and (29a) are not instrumentals. Similarly, the instrument in (34) is not instrumental:

Algy used a clean napkin (34)

but a neutral undergoing the action (of 'using'). If so, prototypical instrumentals such as are realized in (30) do not participate in subject and object selection; indeed, arguably, they are not an independent component of the subcategorization requirements of any predicate. To put it in its strongest form, it has been claimed that instrumentals are available with any agentive predicate. Of course, the class of instrumental will vary with the class of agentive predicate: one *travels by car* rather than *with a car* (unless one is merely accompanying it). If the availability of instrumentals can be allowed for by redundancy, i.e., their occurrence need never be stipulated by the case features of any predicate, then they can be removed from the set of primary cases. They are not participant but circumstantial (Halliday 1967/68; Anderson 1977, 1986); not actants (Tesnière 1959). The drawing of a distinction between participant and circumstantial is the first step in arriving at a delimitation of the set of (participant) case relations. It is only to potential participants that distributional criteria such as Fillmore's (1971a) principles of 'contrast' and 'complementarity' can be fully applied (see below); circumstantials require a rather different approach.

Circumstantials largely correspond to what many case grammarians have dubbed outer cases. (It is less clear to what extent circumstantials as characterized here also correspond in general to Fillmore's modal cases.) And perhaps a less controversial circumstantial is what Fillmore calls the outer locative, illustrated in (35):

Nigel made lots of money in London (35a)

In London Nigel made lots of money (35b)

which (given appropriate choice of lexical terms) can appear with any predicate, and, for example, is readily fronted. Contrast the (inner) locative in (36):

Nigel kept lots of money in a sock (36a)

?In a sock Nigel kept lots of money (36b)

which is part of the case frame (in its absence the lexical item *keep* has a different sense— 'retain') and can be accompanied by an outer locative:

Nigel kept lots of money in a sock in London (37a)

In London Nigel kept lots of money in a sock (37b)

where (b) lacks the additional interpretation available with (a) with respect to which *in London* modifies *sock*.

Anderson (1977: ch. 1) argues that a number of proposed (propositional) cases are circumstantial. Thus, time, for instance, as in (38):

Brenda left on Tuesday (38)

is always circumstantial. For Anderson, the temporal phrases in (39):

The concert lasted from seven to eleven (39)

and (40):

A long period elapsed (40)

are, respectively, source and goal, and neutral, associated here with verbs that require that their source-and-goal or neutral argument involve temporal reference. And *Tuesday* in (41):

Tuesday saw Brenda's departure (41)

is a nonprototypical experiencer. Such a proposal is based on a strategy of eliminating, as distinctions in case, contrasts that are basically signaled elsewhere. As such, it can be said to represent an implementation of Fillmore's (1971a: 40–41) principle of 'complementarity.'

Fillmore (1971a: § 3) also offers two assumptions which he terms principles of 'contrast.' The second principle, unformulated as such, is concerned with the establishment of contrasts in case relation associated with a single (syntactic) position. Fillmore illustrates this with comparative constructions and with the subjects of the same predicate in (42):

I am warm (42a)

This jacket is warm (42b)

Summer is warm (42c)

The room is warm. (42d)

On one interpretation, *I* in (42a) is an experiencer (and *warm* a psychological predicate); *this jacket* in (b) is an instrument; *summer* in (c) is a time; *the room* in (d) is a locative/location. These assignments are supported by the recurrence of such distinctions in subject position with other predicates (Fillmore discusses *sad*), but it is unclear what the syntactic consequences of some of the posited distinctions might be. Fillmore's discussion of comparatives (only noun phrases of identical case can be compared) is inconclusive in this respect, in that it is apparent that many other semantic factors are involved in determining the well-formedness of such constructions. And Anderson's implementation of 'complementarity' would suggest that (c) and (d) (at least) in (42) do not involve a distinction in case (rather, of referential domain). Application of a 'contrast' principle here necessitates that the rest of the environment be kept constant, and thus 'complementarity' eliminated.

The other principle of 'contrast' discussed by Fillmore (1971a) is the one-instance-per-clause principle: i.e., a single clause will contain at most one (possibly compound) noun phrase associated with a particular case. This has been generally accepted (even outside case grammar), and seems to be well supported. The principal area of dissent concerns neutral, which Anderson (1971; also 1977: ch. 1) suggests occurs twice in equatives (*The guy over there is the man she loves*, etc.). He associates this with a further property that has been attributed to neutral; that it is obligatory with every predicate (what Starosta 1987, also 1978, refers to as patient centrality).

This principle has been frequently coupled with a companion principle requiring that each NP bear at most one case relation (Fillmore 1968a: 24). However, it has been argued that this is quite generally inappropriate (not just with respect to specific cases). At issue are, amongst other things, sentences like those in (43):

> Bert has moved the bookcase (43a)
>
> The bookcase has moved (43b)
>
> Bert has moved (43c)

(and see also on this and other areas—such as the *see/look* case frames—Huddleston 1970; Anderson 1968: appendix, 1971: ch. 1). In (43a) *Bert* and *the bookcase* are fairly uncontroversially A and N, respectively; and in (b) *the bookcase* is once more neutral. But what of *Bert* in (c)? It is clearly neutral: *Bert* undergoes the movement; and its status as such is required by patient centrality. But on one interpretation at least *Bert* is also the source of the action, agentive. And there are semantic and syntactic consequences (adverb modification, unergativity, etc.); some of these are also illustrated by the sentences from eastern Pomo given in (2) above. For a contrary view, however, see Starosta (1987), for instance. Somers (1987: ch. 8) surveys some of the arguments involved.

Starosta (1988: § 4.3) introduces a third 'case-like' category (beside case forms and case relations), namely macroroles (cf. Foley and van Valin 1982), of which there are two: actor and undergoer. The actor is the agent of a transitive clause or the patient of an intransitive one. These are 'established to account primarily for morphosyntactic rather than situational generalizations' (Starosta 1988: 145). But one might have expected them to allow for such phenomena as others have associated with attribution of more than one case relation to a single argument, while maintaining the one-instance-per-NP constraint. However, 'it appears that actor, like patient, is present in every clause' (Starosta 1988: 146). Thus, both *the bookcase* in (43b) and *Bert* in (c) would apparently be [+actr, +PAT]. The semantic distinction remains uncaptured. Actor also does not seem to accord well with the syntactic functions Starosta attributes to it. Thus, 'the actant which may be omissible in imperatives . . . is the actor' (Starosta 1988: 151). But not all intransitive patients show unmarked imperativization: this is true of (43b) as well as of the patients associated with verbs like *stumble*, *blister*, etc., under their normal (nonmetaphorical) interpretation.

Anderson (1977: particularly ch. 2) deploys 'complementarity' and nonunary case assignments for NPs to argue, without recourse to macroroles, for a very reduced set of (participant) cases. For instance, he suggests that path is a combination of source and goal; that goal is a variant of locative (with a predicate that also takes a source, a directional predicate). Experiencers are interpreted as a combination of locative with a case relation which, uncombined with locative, characterizes agentives: a case relation he calls ergative. Thus, the case relations in (43) are respec-

tively represented as in (44a–c) and those in (7a) and (42a) as respectively (44d–e):

erg	abs	(44a)
abs		(44b)
erg + abs		(44d)
erg + loc	abs	(44d)
erg + loc + abs		(44e)

(where Anderson's abs(olutive) is N, the nom of 1971). He proposes (Anderson 1977: 115) a set of four cases, given in (45), with each case characterized in terms of combinations of the notional features place and source, such that abs is unmarked and erg is a non-place source, source of the event or situation, physical or mental, potentially in control of it. (See also, more recently, Ostler 1980.)

Case Relations	abs	erg	loc	abl (45)
Case Features			place	place
		source		source

These characterizations incorporate a general substantive principle determining the character of case relations, to complement the distributional and individual properties mentioned above. They instantiate one articulation of the localist hypothesis (cf. localism), whose earlier history is charted by Hjelmslev (1935/37), in terms of which the domain of case is structured by components utilized in our perception of spatial situations: there are no necessarily 'abstract' case relations. The hypothesis is one attempt to provide a general definition of case, avoiding the problems of uncertainty and overlap associated with notional definitions particular to individual cases. The importance of a nonparticularist approach to case is forcibly expressed by Hjelmslev (1935: 4):

> Délimiter exactement une catégorie est impossible sans une idée précise sur les faits de signification. Il ne suffit pas d'avoir des idées sur les significations de chacune des formes entrant dans la catégorie. Il faut pouvoir indiquer la signification de la catégorie prise dans son ensemble.

Apart from within the localist tradition, it is only recently (with developments in cognitive grammar (see *Cognitive Grammar*) and elsewhere) that such a viewpoint has been to the forefront in the mainstream of the structuralist linguistic tradition in the last few decades.

The postulation of a universal theory of case is, of course, not to say that the 'same' situation will be expressed in terms of the same case frame in different languages, or that what can be an erg in language A will necessarily correspond to an erg in language B (cf. Dahl 1987). The English experiencer (erg + loc) in (41) is alien to a large number of languages, for instance. Rather, these relations form the basis for constructing clause structures in any language, and their applicability is limited primarily, within the localist tradition, by the spatial prototypes with which they are associated.

Among the many uncertainties and contentious issues surrounding notions of case, some of which are surveyed here (and see too Cook 1989, for another overview), perhaps the least explored is the character and status of circumstantials. Anderson (1986) suggests that, despite their apparent diversity, the set of circumstantials can be described using the same set of (combinations of) case relations as are appropriate to distinguishing participants, and that the hierarchy of circumstantials in terms of their closeness of relation to the central proposition is associated with the specificity of the verb class with which they are compatible. Thus, instrumentals, insofar as they are compatible only with agentive verbs, are more tightly integrated than outer locatives or circumstantial time phrases. But here in particular much research remains to be done (in any framework). For discussion see Somers (1987: ch. 1).

Bibliography

Abraham W (ed.) 1971 *Kasustheorie*. Athenäum, Frankfurt
Abraham W (ed.) 1978 *Valence, Semantic Case and Grammatical Relations*. Benjamins, Amsterdam
Anderson J M 1968 Ergative and nominative in English. *JL* 4: 1–32
Anderson J M 1971 *The Grammar of Case: Towards a Localistic Theory*. Cambridge University Press, Cambridge
Anderson J M 1977 *On Case Grammar: Prolegomena to a Theory of Grammatical Relations*. Croom Helm, London
Anderson J M 1978 On the derivative status of grammatical relations. In: Abraham W (ed.) 1978
Anderson J M 1980 Anti-unaccusative, or: Relational grammar is case grammar. *RRL* 25: 193–225
Anderson J M 1982 Analysis and levels of linguistic description. In: Siciliani E, Barone A, Aston G (eds.) *La lingua inglese nell'universitá*. Adriatica, Bari
Anderson J M 1984 *Case Grammar and the Lexicon*. University of Ulster Occasional Papers in Linguistics and Language Learning, Coleraine
Anderson J M 1986 Structural analogy and case grammar. *Lingua* 70: 79–129
Anderson J M 1987 Case grammar and the localist hypothesis. In: Dirven R, Radden G (eds.) 1987
Anderson J M 1989 Reflections on notional grammar, with some remarks on its relevance to issues in the analysis of English and its history. In: Arnold D J, et al. (eds.) *Essays on Grammatical Theory and Universal Grammar*. Oxford University Press, Oxford
Anderson J M 1990 On the status of auxiliaries in notional grammar. *JL* 26: 341–62
Anderson J M 1991 Notional grammar and the redundancy of syntax. *SLang* 17: 301–33
Anderson J M 1992 *Linguistic Representation: Structural Analogy and Stratification*. Mouton de Gruyter, Berlin
Anderson J M, Dubois-Charlier F (eds.) 1975 *La grammaire des cas* (= *Langages* 38). Didier–Larousse, Paris
Anderson S R 1971 On the role of deep structure in semantic interpretation. *Foundations of Language* 7: 387–96

Böhm R 1986 Indirect object advancement: From relational to case grammar (via Kalkatungu). *AJL* 6: 73–105
Chafe W 1970 *Meaning and the Structure of Language*. University of Chicago Press, Chicago, IL
Chapin P G 1972 Review of Stockwell R P, Schachter P, Partee B H 1968 *Integration of Transformational Theories on English Syntax*. University of California, Los Angeles, CA. *Lg* 48: 645–67
Chomsky N 1965 *Aspects of the Theory of Syntax*. MIT Press, Cambridge, MA
Cook W A 1971 Case grammar as deep structure in tagmemic analysis. *Languages and Linguistics Working Papers, Georgetown University* 2: 1–9
Cook W A 1972a A set of postulates for case grammar analysis. *Languages and Linguistics Working Papers, Georgetown University* 4: 35–49
Cook W A 1972b A case grammar matrix. *Languages and Linguistics Working Papers, Georgetown University* 6: 15–47
Cook W A 1973 Covert case roles. *Languages and Linguistics Working Papers, Georgetown University* 7: 52–81
Cook W A 1978 A case grammar matrix model (and its application to a Hemingway text). In: Abraham W (ed.) 1978
Cook W A 1979 *Case Grammar: Development of the Matrix Model (1970–78)*. Georgetown University Press, Washington, D.C.
Cook W A 1989 *Case Grammar Theory*. Georgetown University Press, Washington, D.C.
Dahl Ö 1987 Case grammar and prototypes. In: Dirven R, Radden G (eds.) 1987
Dik S C 1978 *Functional Grammar*. North-Holland, Amsterdam
Dik S C 1987 Some principles of functional grammar. In: Dirven R, Radden G (eds.) 1987
Dirven R, Radden G (eds.) 1987 *Concepts of Case*. Gunter Narr, Tübingen
Fillmore C J 1965 Toward a modern theory of case. *Project on Linguistic Analysis, Ohio State University* 13: 1–24
Fillmore C J 1966 A proposal concerning English prepositions. *Monograph Series on Languages and Linguistics, Georgetown University* 19: 19–33
Fillmore C J 1968a The case for case. In: Bach E, Harms R T (eds.) *Universals in Linguistic Theory*. Holt, Rinehart and Winston, New York
Fillmore C J 1968b Lexical entries for verbs. *Foundations of Language* 4: 373–93
Fillmore C J 1970 The grammar of hitting and breaking. In: Jacobs R A, Rosenbaum P S (eds.) *Readings in English Transformational Grammar*. Ginn, Waltham, MA
Fillmore C J 1971a Some problems for case grammar. *Monograph Series on Languages and Linguistics, Georgetown University* 23: 35–56
Fillmore C J 1971b Types of lexical information. In: Steinberg D D, Jakobovits L A (eds.) *Semantics: An Interdisciplinary Reader*. Cambridge University Press, Cambridge
Fillmore C J 1971c Verbs of judging. In: Fillmore C J, Langendoen D T (eds.) *Studies in Linguistic Semantics*. Holt, Rinehart and Winston, New York
Fillmore C J 1972 Subjects, speakers and roles. In: Davidson D A, Harman G H (eds.) *Semantics of Natural Language*. Reidel, Dordrecht
Fillmore C J 1977a The case for case reopened. In: Cole P,

Sadock J (eds.) *Syntax and Semantics 8: Grammatical Relations*. Academic Press, New York

Fillmore C J 1977b Topics in lexical semantics. In: Cole R W (ed.) *Current Issues in Linguistic Theory*. Indiana University Press, Bloomington, IN

Fillmore C J 1987 A private history of the concept 'frame.' In: Dirven R, Radden G (eds.) 1987

Foley W A, Valin R D van 1984 *Functional Syntax and Universal Grammar*. Cambridge University Press, Cambridge

Gruber J S 1965 Studies in lexical relations (Doctoral dissertation, Massachusetts Institute of Technology)

Halliday M A K 1967/68 Notes on transitivity and theme in English. *JL* **3**: 37–81, 199–244; **4**: 179–215

Hjelmslev L 1935/37 La catégorie des cas. *Acta Jutlandica* **7**: i–xii, 1–184; **9**: i–vii, 1–78

Huddleston R D 1970 Some remarks on case grammar. *LIn* **1**: 501–11

Jackendoff R S 1983 *Semantics and Cognition*. MIT Press, Cambridge, MA

Katz J J 1972 *Semantic Theory*. Harper and Row, New York

Longacre R E 1976 *An Anatomy of Speech Notions*. Peter de Ridder, Lisse/Holland

Lyons J 1968 *Introduction to Theoretical Linguistics*. Cambridge University Press, Cambridge

Miller J E 1985 *Semantics and Syntax*. Cambridge University Press, Cambridge

Nilsen D L F 1972 *Toward a Semantic Specification of Deep Case*. Mouton, The Hague

Nilsen D L F 1973 *The Instrumental Case in English: Syntactic and Semantic Considerations*. Mouton, The Hague

Ostler N 1980 *A Theory of Case Linking and Agreement*. Indiana University Linguistics Club, IN

Platt J T 1971 *Grammatical Form and Grammatical Meaning: A Tagmemic View of Fillmore's Deep Structure Case Concepts*. North-Holland, Amsterdam

Radden G 1978 Can 'area' be taken out of the waste-basket? In: Abraham W (ed.) 1978

Robinson J J 1970 Case, category and configuration. *JL* **6**: 57–80

Somers H L 1987 *Valency and Case in Computational Linguistics*. Edinburgh University Press, Edinburgh

Starosta S 1973 The faces of case. *LS* **25**: 1–14

Starosta S 1978 The one per Sent solution. In: Abraham W (ed.) 1978

Starosta S 1987 A place for (lexi-)case. In: Dirven R, Radden G (eds.) 1987

Starosta S 1988 *The Case for Lexicase: An Outline of Lexicase Grammatical Theory*. Pinter, London

Stockwell R P, Schachter P, Partee B 1973 *The Major Syntactic Structures of English*. Holt, Rinehart and Winston, New York

Tarvainen K 1987 Semantic cases in the framework of dependency theory. In: Dirven R, Radden G (eds.) 1987

Tesnière L 1959 *Eléments de syntaxe structurale*. Klincksieck, Paris (2nd edn., 1965)

Welte W 1987 On the concept of case in traditional grammars. In: Dirven R, Radden G (eds.) 1987

Wilkins W (ed.) 1988 *Syntax and Semantics 21: Thematic Relations*. Academic Press, New York

Categorial Grammar

Mark Steedman

Categorial Grammar (CG) is a term which covers a number of related formalisms that have been proposed for the syntax and semantics of natural languages and logical and mathematical languages. All are generalizations of a core context-free grammar formalism first explicitly defined by Ajdukiewicz in 1935, but with earlier antecedents in the work of Husserl, Leśnewski, Frege, Carnap, and Tarski on semantic and syntactic categories, ultimately stemming from work in the theory of types (a tradition to which some work in CG shows signs of returning). The distinguishing characteristics of these theories are: an extreme form of 'lexicalism' where the main and even entire burden of syntax is borne by the lexicon; the characterization of constituents, both syntactically and semantically, as 'functions' and/or 'arguments'; the characterization of the relation between syntax and semantics as 'compositional,' with syntactic and semantic types standing in the closest possible relation, the former in many cases merely encoding the latter; a tendency to 'freer surface constituency'

than traditional grammar, the previously mentioned characteristic guaranteeing that all the nonstandard constituents that CG sanctions are fully interpreted semantically.

Such grammars have been implicated in much work at the foundation of modern theories of natural language semantics. Like their theoretical cousins Tree Adjoining Grammars (TAG), Lexical Functional Grammar (LFG), Generalized Phrase Structure Grammar (GPSG), and Head-driven Phrase Structure Grammar (HPSG), they have also, in the early 1990s, provided an important source of constrained alternatives to transformational rules and their modern derivatives for formal theories of natural language syntax (see also *Lexical Functional Grammar*; *Generalized Phrase Structure Grammar*; *Head-driven Phrase Structure Grammar*). In the syntactic arena, categorial grammars have been claimed to have significant advantages as explanatory and unifying theories of unbounded constructions including coordination and relative clause formation, of constructions that have been held to involve 'reanalysis,' of phonological phrasing associated with intonation, of numerous clause-bounded phenomena including reflexive binding, raising, and control; and also of analogous discontinuous phenomena in morphology.

1. Pure Categorial Grammar

In a categorial grammar, all grammatical constituents, and in particular all lexical items, are associated with a 'type' or 'category' which defines their potential for combination with other constituents to yield compound constituents. The category is either one of a small number of 'basic' categories, such as *NP*, or a 'functor' category. The latter have a type which identifies them as functions mapping arguments of some type onto results of some (possibly different) type. For example, English intransitive verbs like *walks* are most naturally defined as functions from nounphrases *NP* on their left to sentences *S*. English transitive verbs like *sees* are similarly defined as functions from nounphrases *NP* on their right to the aforementioned intransitive verb category. Apart from a language-particular specification of directionality, such categories merely reflect the types of the semantic interpretations of these words.

There are several different notations for directional categories. The most widely used are the 'slash' notations variously pioneered by Bar-Hillel/Lambek (1958), and subsequently modified within the group of theories that are distinguished below as 'combinatory' categorial grammars. These two systems differ slightly in the way they denote directionality, as illustrated in the following categories for the transitive verb *sees* (1):

Lambek: $sees := (np \backslash s)/np$ (1a)

Combinatory CG: $sees := (S \backslash NP)/NP$ (1b)

(Both notations reflect the assumption that multi-argument functions like transitive verbs are 'curried.' Other notations allow 'flat' multi-argument functions. Under an equivalence noted by Schönfinkel in 1924, the assumption is merely one of notational convenience. The categories as shown are simplified by the omission of number and person agreement specifications. In common with most theories, it is assumed that the categories here represented as atomic NPs are in fact feature bundles including agreement features which must unify with corresponding features of their arguments. *np* has been used as the type of NPs in Lambek's notation, rather than *n*, as in the original.)

Lambek's notation encodes directionality in the slash itself, forward slash / indicating a rightward argument and backward slash \ indicating a leftward argument. However, for reasons which will become apparent when the Lambek calculus is examined in detail, Lambek chose to make leftward arguments

appear to the left of their (backward) slash, while rightward arguments appeared to the right of their (forward) slash. This notation has many attractive features, but lacks a consistent left to right order of domain and range. It is therefore rather harder than it might be to comprehend categories in this notation. Readers may judge this difficulty for themselves by noting how long it takes them to decide whether the two functions written $(a/b) \backslash (c/d)$ and $(d \backslash c)/(b \backslash a)$ do or do not have the same semantic type. This property tends to make life difficult, for example, for linguists whose concern is to compare the syntactic behavior of semantically related verbs across languages with different base constituent orders.

It was for this last reason that D. R. Dowty and the author of this article proposed an alternative notation with a consistent left-to-right order of range and domain of the function. In this notation, arguments always appear to the right of the slash, and results to the left. A rightward-leaning slash means that the argument in question is to the right, a leftward-leaning slash, that it is to the left. The first argument of a complex function category is always the rightmost category, the second argument the next rightmost, and so on, and the leftmost basic category is always the result. It is therefore obvious in this notation that the two categories instanced in the last paragraph, which are now written $(C/D) \backslash (A/B)$ and $(C \backslash D)/(A \backslash B)$, have the same semantic type, since the categories are identical apart from the slashes.

All the notations illustrated in (1) capture the same basic syntactic facts concerning English transitive sentences as the familiar production rules in (2):

$$S \to NP\ VP \quad\quad (2)$$

$$VP \to TV\ NP$$

$$TV \to sees$$

That is to say that in order to permit parallel context-free derivations it is only necessary to include the following pair of rules of functional application (3); allowing functor categories to combine with arguments (the rules are given in both notations):

Functional Application:	Functional Application:	(3)
(i) $x/y\ y \Rightarrow x$	(i) $X/Y\ Y \Rightarrow X$	
(ii) $y\ y \backslash x \Rightarrow x$	(ii) $Y\ X \backslash Y \Rightarrow X$	
(a) Lambek	(b) Combinatory	

These rules have the form of very general binary PS rule schemata. Clearly CG is context free grammar which happens to be written in the accepting, rather than the producing, direction, and in which there has been a transfer of the major burden of specifying particular grammars from the PS rules to the lexicon. (CG and CFPSG were shown to be weakly equivalent by Bar-Hillel et al. in 1960.) While it is now convenient to write derivations in both notations as follows (4), they are clearly just familiar phrase-structure 'trees' (except that they have the leaves at the top, as is fitting):

$$
\begin{array}{cccccccc}
\text{Gilbert} & \text{sees} & \text{George} & & \text{Gilbert} & \text{sees} & \text{George} & (4)\\
\hline
np & (np\backslash s)/np & np & & NP & (S\backslash NP)/NP & NP & \\
& \underrightarrow{\hspace{2cm}} & & & & \underrightarrow{\hspace{2cm}} & & \\
\hline
& np\backslash s & & & & S\backslash NP & & \\
\underleftarrow{\hspace{3cm}} & & & & \underleftarrow{\hspace{3cm}} & & & \\
\hline
s & & & & S & & & \\
& \text{(a) Lambek} & & & & \text{(b) Combinatory} & &
\end{array}
$$

(The operation of combination by the application rules is indicated by an underline annotated with a rightward or leftward arrow.) It will be clear at this point that Lambek's notation has the very attractive property of allowing all 'cancelations' under the rules of functional application to be with adjacent symbols. This elegant property is preserved under the generalization to other combinatory operations permitted by the generalization to the Lambek calculus. (However, it will be shown that it cannot be preserved under the full range of combinatory operations that have been claimed by other categorial grammarians to be required for natural languages.)

Grammars of this kind have a number of features that make them attractive as an alternative to the more familiar phrase structure grammars. The first is that they avoid the duplication in syntax of the subcategorization information that must be explicit in the lexicon anyway. The second is that the lexical syntactic categories are clearly very directly related to their semantics. This last property has always made categorial grammars particularly attractive to formal semanticists, who have naturally been reluctant to give up the belief that natural language syntax must be as directly related to its semantics as that of arithmetic, algebra, or the predicate calculus, despite frequent warnings about such optimism from linguistic syntacticians.

At the very time Bar-Hillel and Lambek were developing the earliest categorial grammars, Chomsky was developing an argument that many phenomena in natural languages could not be naturally expressed using context free grammars of any kind, if indeed they could be captured at all. It is therefore important to ask how this pure context-free core can be generalized to cope with the full range of constructions found in natural language.

2. Early Generalizations of Categorial Grammar

Three types of proposal that came from categorial grammarians in response to this challenge should be distinguished. The first was simply to take over the Chomskyan apparatus of transformations, replacing his CFPS base grammar with a pure CF categorial grammar. This proposal was influentially advanced by Lyons (1968: 227ff., 327ff.), and endorsed by D. Lewis in 1972. Lyons's arguments were based on the advantages of a categorial base for capturing the word-order generalizations associated with the then nascent $\bar{X}$-theory (which were explored in categorial terms by M.

Flynn), and were prescient of the subsequent tendency of Chomsky's theory towards lexicalism and a diminished role for PS rules. However, there was increasing awareness at this time that transformational rules themselves needed replacing by some more constrained formal mechanism, and this awareness gave rise to several more radical categorially based alternative proposals.

The paper in which Lewis endorses Lyons's proposal for a categorially based transformational grammar is in fact only peripherally concerned with syntax. Its more central concern is quantifier scope, which motivates Lewis to introduce a transformational rule which would nowadays be recognized as 'quantifier raising,' complete with the suggestion that this rule should operate '*beneath* ... the most ordinary level of deep structure'—that is at what would be called the level of logical form. However, Lewis's account also involves an abstraction operator equivalent to Church's λ, in the form of Ajdukiewicz's operator κ. Implicit in Montague's general approach (though not in his practice), and explicit in the approach of Keenan, Venneman, and the 'λ-categorial' grammars of Cresswell (1973: 7) and von Stechow (1974), is the proposal that with the abstraction operator there is no need for independent movement transformations at all. Compositional interpretations can be assembled on the basis of surface grammar augmented by the completely general variable-binding operation of λ-abstraction, a proposal that was implicit in Ajdukiewicz.

This bold approach was also prescient of coming moves within the transformational mainstream, anticipating (and possibly, via work in Montague Grammar helping to precipitate) the move in Chomsky's theory to small numbers of general purpose movement transformations, perhaps confined to a single most general rule '*move a*,' and the realization that all such 'movements,' even those involving *Wh*-elements and their traces, could be regarded as base-generated. (W. O'Grady, who combines a categorial base with rules for combining nonadjacent elements, can be seen as continuing this tradition within CG.) However, by the same token, the essential equivalence between λ-abstraction ('bind a variable anywhere in the domain') and *move-a* ('co-index any items in the domain') means that the abstraction device is potentially very unconstrained, as Cresswell recognized (1973: 224–27). The approach remains immensely productive in the semantic domain. It remains less clear whether there is any distinct advantage inherent in the syntactic aspects of λ-categorial grammar. Nevertheless, it has made the important contributions of providing a clear and simple interpretation for the notion of movement itself, which might otherwise have appeared semantically unmotivated, and of having directly led, via the work of Emmon Bach, to the third, most recent, and most radical group of proposals for generalizing pure categorial grammar.

As a part of a wider tendency at the time to seek low-power alternatives to transformations, there were during the 1970s a number of proposals for augmenting categorial grammar with additional operations for combining categories, over and above the original rules of functional application. In contrast to the λ-categorial approach, these operations were less general than the abstraction operator of λ-categorial grammar, the chief restriction being that, like the application rules themselves, these operations were confined to the combination of nonempty string-adjacent entities, and were dependent on the directionality of those entities. These proposals had an important historical precedent in the work by Lambek (1958) referred to earlier.

Lambek's short paper can be seen as making two quite separate points. The first was that a number of simple functional operations, importantly including functional composition and type-raising, looked as though they were directly reflected in natural syntax. His second point was that these very operations, together with an infinite set of related ones, could be generated as theorems of a quite small set of axioms and inference rules. In this he drew on even earlier traditions of natural deduction in the work of G. Gentzen, and the analogy drawn between logical implication and functional types by Curry (e.g., Curry and Feys 1958), which he deployed in an important proof of decidability for his syntactic calculus. The effect was to define this version of categorial grammar as a restricted logic.

These two proposals can be seen as reflected in two distinct styles of modern categorial grammar. On the one hand, there is a group of linguists who argue that the addition of a few semantically simple primitive combinatory operations like functional composition yields grammars that capture linguistic generalizations. Sometimes these operations are individual theorems of the Lambek calculus, and sometimes they are not. These theorists are typically not concerned with the question of whether their operations can be further reduced to an axiomatic calculus or not (although they are of course deeply concerned, as any linguist must be, with the degrees of freedom that their rules exhibit, and the automata-theoretic power implicit in their theory).

The other modern school of categorial grammarians is more concerned to identify additional sets of axiom-schemata and inference rules that define other syntactic calculi, primarily as a way of looking at relations among logics, particularly intuitionistic or constructive ones, including modal logics, linear logic, and type-theory. The relation of such logics to natural grammars is often not the central issue.

It will be easiest to discuss Lambek's original proposal in the light of these more recent developments. In adopting this narrative tactic, the history of the subject is recapitulated, for the significance of Lambek's proposals was not appreciated at the time, and his paper was largely forgotten until the rediscovery of many of its principles in the 1970s and early 1980s by Geach, Bach, Buszkowski, and others.

3. Modern Categorial Theories of Grammar

This section begins by examining the 'combinatory' style of categorial grammar, before returning to the 'Lambek' style including Lambek's original proposal. Each of these subsections ends with a brief discussion of the automata-theoretic power inherent in each system. It is convenient to further distinguish certain theories within both frameworks that are mainly concerned with the semantics of quantifier scope, rather than with purely syntactic phenomena. This work is discussed in a separate section.

3.1 'Combinatory' Categorial Grammars

A major impulse behind the development of generalized categorial grammars in this period was an attempt to account for the apparent vagaries of coordinate constructions, and to bring them under the same principles as other unbounded phenomena, such as relativization.

To begin to extend categorial grammar to cope with coordination a rule is needed, or rather a family of rules, of something like the following form (5):

Coordination Rule ($\langle \& \rangle$):   (5)
X' conj $X'' \Rightarrow X'''$

This rule captures the ancient intuition that *coordination is an operation which maps two constituents of like type onto a constituent of the same type*. That is, X', X'', and X''' are categories of the same type X but different interpretations, and the rule is a schema over a finite set of rules whose semantics will be ignored here.

Given such a rule or rule schema, derivations like the following are permitted (6):

Harry	cooked	and	ate	apples	(6)
NP	$(S\backslash NP)/NP$	conj	$(S\backslash NP)/NP$	NP	

$$\frac{}{(S\backslash NP)/NP} \langle \& \rangle$$
$$\frac{}{S\backslash NP}$$
$$\frac{}{S}$$

The driving force behind much of the early development of the theory was the assumption that *all* coordination should be this simple—that is, combinations of 'constituents' without the intervention of deletion, movement, or equivalent unbounded coindexing rules. Sentences like the following are among the very simplest to challenge this assumption, since they involve the coordination of substrings that are *not* normally regarded as constituents (7):

(a) Harry cooked, and *might eat*, some apples   (7)
(b) Harry cooked, and *Mary ate*, some apples
(c) Harry will copy, and *file without reading*, some articles concerning Swahili.

The problem can be solved by adding a small number of operations that combine functions in advance of their arguments. Curry and Feys (1958) offer a mathematics for capturing applicative systems equivalent to the λ-calculi entirely in terms of such operators, for which they coined the term 'combinator'—hence the term 'combinatory' categorial grammars.

3.1.1 A Note on Combinators

A combinator is an operation upon sequences of functions and/or arguments. Thus, any (prefixed) term of the λ-calculus is a combinator. This article will be interested in combinators that correspond to some particularly simple λ-terms. For example, (8):

(a) $\mathbf{I} \equiv \lambda x[x]$ (8)
(b) $\mathbf{K}y \equiv \lambda x[y]$
(c) $\mathbf{T}x \equiv \lambda F[Fx]$
(d) $\mathbf{B}FG \equiv \lambda x[F(Gx)]$
(e) $\mathbf{C}Fy \equiv \lambda x[Fxy]$
(f) $\mathbf{W}F \equiv \lambda x[Fxx]$
(g) $\mathbf{S}FG \equiv \lambda x[Fx(Gx)]$
(h) $HFG \equiv \lambda x[H(Fx)(Gx)]$
where x is not free in F, G, H, y.

(A convention of 'left-associativity' is assumed here, according to which expressions like $\mathbf{B}FG$ are implicitly bracketed as $(\mathbf{B}F)G$. Concatenation as in $\mathbf{T}x$ denotes functional application of $\mathbf{T}$ to x.)

The above are equivalences, not definitions of the combinators. The combinators themselves can be taken as primitives, and used to define a range of 'applicative systems,' that is systems which express the two notions of 'application' of functions to arguments, and 'abstraction' or definitions of functions in terms of other functions. In particular, surprisingly small collections of combinators can be used as primitives to define systems equivalent to various forms of the λ-calculus, entirely without the use of bound variables and the binding operator λ.

3.1.2 **BTS** Combinatory Categorial Grammar (CCG)

One combinatory generalization of categorial grammar adds exactly three classes of combinatory rule to the context-free core. Since two of these types of rule—namely composition and type-raising—have been at least implicit in the majority of combinatory generalizations of categorial grammars, and since a third operation is provably necessary, this system will be taken as the canonical exemplar, comparing it later to a number of variants and alternatives. (This variety, with whose development the present author has been associated is sometimes referred to as CCG (for Combinatory Categorial Grammar), although it is only one of the possible combinatory versions of CG.) The combinatory rules have the effect of making such sub-strings into grammatical constituents in the fullest sense of the term, complete with an appropriate and fully compositional semantics. All of them adhere to the following restrictive assumption (9):

> The Principle of Adjacency: Combinatory rules   (9)
> may only apply to entities which are linguistically realized and adjacent.

The first such rule-type is motivated by examples like (7a), above. Rules of functional composition allow functional categories like *might* to combine with functions into their argument categories, such as *eat* to produce nonstandard constituents corresponding to such strings as *might eat*. The rule required here (and the most commonly used functional composition rule in English) is written as follows:

> Forward Composition ($>$B):   (10)
> $X/Y\ Y/Z \Rightarrow_{\mathbf{B}} X/Z$

The rule permits the following derivation for example (7a):

$$
\begin{array}{ccccccc}
\text{Harry} & \text{cooked} & \text{and} & \text{might} & \text{eat} & \text{some apples} & (11)\\
\hline
NP & (S\backslash NP)/NP & conj & (S\backslash NP)/VP & VP/NP & NP
\end{array}
$$

(derivation)

$$(S\backslash NP)/VP \quad VP/NP \longrightarrow_{B} (S\backslash NP)/NP$$

$$(S\backslash NP)/NP \quad (S\backslash NP)/NP \longrightarrow \langle \& \rangle$$

$$S\backslash NP$$

$$S$$

It is important to observe that, because of the isomorphism that CG embodies between categories and semantic types, this rule is also *semantic* functional composition. That is, if the interpretations of the two categories on the left of the arrow in 10 are respectively F and G, then the interpretation of the category on the right must be the composition of F and G. Composition corresponds to Curry's composition combinator, which he called $\mathbf{B}$, defined earlier as (8d). Hence, the combinatory rule and its application in the derivation are indexed as $>$B because it is a rule in which the main functor is rightward-looking, and has composition as its semantics. Hence also, the formalism guarantees without further stipulation that this operation will compose the interpretations, as well as the syntactic functional types. Formal discussion of this point is deferred, but it should be obvious that if the mapping from VP interpretations to predicate interpretations is known that constitutes the interpretation of *might*, and the mapping from NP interpretations to VP interpretations corresponding to the interpretation of *eat* is known, then everything necessary to define their composition is known, the interpretation of the nonstandard constituent *might eat*.

The result of the composition has the same syntactic and semantic type as a transitive verb, so when it is applied to an object and a subject, it is guaranteed to yield exactly the same interpretation for the sentence

Harry might eat some apples as would have been obtained without the introduction of this rule. This nonstandard verb *might eat* is now a constituent in every sense of the word. It can therefore coordinate with other transitive verbs like *cooked* and take part in derivations like (11). Since this derivation is in every other respect just like the derivation in (6), it too is guaranteed to give a semantically correct result.

Examples like the following (12), in which a similar substring is coordinated with a *di*-transitive verb, require a generalization of composition proposed by Ades and Steedman in 1982:

I *will offer*, and [*may*]$_{(S \backslash NP)/VP}$ [*sell*]$_{(VP/PP)NP}$,   (12)
my 1959 pink cadillac to my favourite brother-in-law.

To compose the modals with the multiple-argument verbs, the following relative of rule 10 is needed (13):

Forward Composition (> B2):   (13)
$X/Y(Y/Z)/W \Rightarrow_{\mathbf{B}^2} (X/Z)/W$

This corresponds in combinatory terms to an instance $\mathbf{B}^2$ of the generalization from $\mathbf{B}$ to $\mathbf{B}^n$ (cf., Curry and Feys 1958: 165, 185). It can be assumed, at least for English, that n is bounded by the highest valency in the lexicon, which is about 4.

The second novel kind of rule that is imported under the combinatory generalization is motivated by examples like (7b) above, repeated here (14):

Harry cooked, and Mary ate, some apples.   (14)

If the assumption is to be maintained that everything that can coordinate is a constituent formed without deletion or movement, then *Harry* and *cooked* must also be able to combine to yield a constituent of type S/NP, which can combine with objects to its right. The way this is brought about is by adding rules of type-raising like the following (15) to the system:

Forward Type-raising (> T):   (15)
$Y \Rightarrow_T X/(X \backslash Y)$

This rule makes the subject NP into a function over predicates. Subjects can therefore compose with functions *into* predicates—that is, with transitive verbs, as in the following derivation (16) for (14):

Type-raising corresponds semantically to the combinator $\mathbf{T}$, defined at (8c). It will be shown later that type-raising is quite general in its application to NPs, and that it should be regarded as an operation of the lexicon, rather than syntax, under which all types corresponding to functions into *NP* (etc.) are replaced by functions into the raised categor(ies). However, for expository simplicity it will continue to be shown in derivations, indexing the rule as $>$ T. When the raised category composes with the transitive verb, the result is guaranteed to be a function which, when it reduces with an object *some apples*, will yield the same interpretation that would have obtained from the traditional derivation. This interpretation might be written as follows (17):

cook' apples' harry'.   (17)

(Here again a convention of 'left associativity' is used, so that the above applicative expression is equivalent to (*cook*' apples') harry'.) It is important to notice that it is at the level of the interpretation that traditional constituents like the VP, and relations such as *c*-command, continue to be embodied. This is an important observation since as far as surface structure goes, both have now been compromised.

Of course, the same facts guarantee that the coordinate example above will deliver an appropriate interpretation.

The third and final variety of combinatory rule is motivated by examples like (7c), repeated here (18):

Harry will copy, and file without reading,   (18)
some articles concerning Swahili.

Under the simple assumption with which this article began, that only like 'constituents' can conjoin, the substring *file without reading* must be a constituent formed without movement or deletion. What is more, it must be a constituent of the same type as a transitive verb, VP/NP, since that is what it coordinates with. It follows that the grammar of English must include the following operation (19), first proposed by A. Szabolsci:

Backward Crossed Substitution (< Sx)   (19)
$Y/Z(X \backslash Y)/Z \Rightarrow_S X/Z$

Harry	cooked	and	Mary	ate	some apples	(16)
NP	$(S \backslash NP)/NP$	*conj*	NP	$(S \backslash NP)/NP$	NP	

$\xrightarrow{\quad} $ T $\xrightarrow{\quad}$ T

$S/(S \backslash NP)$ $S/(S \backslash NP)$

$\xrightarrow{\hspace{3cm}}$ B $\xrightarrow{\hspace{3cm}}$ B

S/NP S/NP

$\xrightarrow{\hspace{4cm}} \langle \& \rangle$

S/NP

$\xrightarrow{\hspace{6cm}}$

S

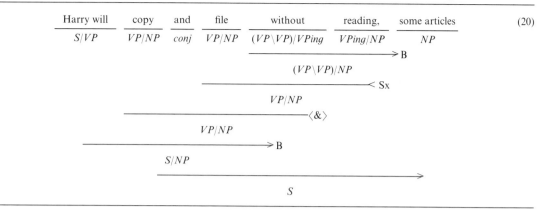

This rule permits the derivation shown in (20) for sentence (18). (Infinitival and gerundival predicate categories are abbreviated as *VP* and *VPing*, and NPs are shown as ground types.)

It is important to notice that the crucial rule resembles a generalized form of functional composition, but that it *mixes* the directionality of the functors, combining a leftward functor over *VP* with a rightward function into *VP*. Therefore it must be predicted that other combinatory rules, such as composition, must also have such 'crossed' instances. Such rules are not valid in the Lambek calculus.

Like the other combinatory rules, the substitution rule combines the interpretations of categories as well as their syntactic categories. Its semantics is given by the combinator **S**, defined at (8g). It follows that if the constituent *file without reading* is combined with an object *some articles* on the right, and then combined with *Harry will*$_{S/VP}$, it will yield a correct interpretation. It also follows that a similarly correct interpretation will be produced for the coordinate sentence (18).

These three classes of rule—composition, type-raising, and substitution—constitute the entire inventory of combinatory rule-types that this version of combinatory CG adds to pure categorial grammar. They are limited by two general principles, in addition to the principle of adjacency (9). They are the following (21 and 22):

The Principle of Directional Consistency: All syntactic combinatory rules must be consistent with the directionality of the principal function. (21)

The Principle of Directional Inheritance: If the category that results from the application of a combinatory rule is a function category, then the slash defining directionality for a given argument in that category will be the same as the one defining directionality for the corresponding argument(s) in the input function(s). (22)

Together they amount to a simple statement that *combinatory rules may not contradict the directionality specified in the lexicon*. They drastically limit the possible composition and substitution rules to exactly four instances each. It seems likely that these principles follow from the fact that directionality is as much a property of 'arguments' as is their syntactic type. This position is closely related to R. S. Kayne's notion of 'directionality of government.'

The inclusion of this particular set of operations makes a large number of correct predictions. For example, once it is seen fit to introduce the forward rule of composition and the forward rule of type-raising into the grammar of English, the degrees of freedom in the theory are not increased any further by introducing the corresponding 'backward' rules. Thus the existence of the coordinate construction in (23) is predicted without further stipulation, as noted

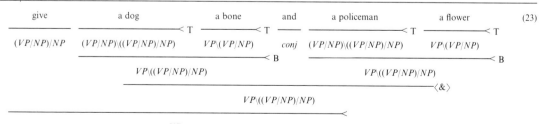

by D. R. Dowty. This and other related examples, which notoriously present considerable problems for other grammatical frameworks, are extensively discussed by D. R. Dowty and others, and constitute strong evidence in support of the decision to take type-raising and composition as primitives of grammar, and moreover for the relegation of raised categories to the lexicon.

The analysis also immediately entails that the dependencies engendered by coordination will · be unbounded, and free in general to apply across clause boundaries. For example, all of the following examples parallel to those in (7) with which the section began are immediately accepted, without any further addition to the grammar whatsoever (24).

(a) Harry cooked, and *expects that Mary will* (24)
eat, some apples
(b) Harry cooked, and *Fred expects that Mary will eat*, some apples
(c) Harry cooked, and *Fred expects that Mary will eat without enjoying*, some apples that they found lying around in the kitchen.

Moreover, if it is assumed that nominative and accusative relative pronouns have the following categories (which simply follow from the fact that they are functions from properties to noun modifiers), then the relative clauses in (26) below are also accepted:

(a) *who/that/which*:=$(N\backslash N)/(S\backslash NP)$ (25)
(b) *who(m)/that/which*:=$(N\backslash N)/(S/NP)$

(a) a man who (*expects that Mary*) *will eat some* (26)
apples
(b) some apples that (*Fred expects that*) *Mary will eat*
(c) some apples that (*Fred expects that*) *Mary will eat without enjoying*

The generalization that 'Wh-movement' and 'right node raising' are essentially the same and in general unbounded is thereby immediately captured without further stipulation.

Rules like the 'direction mixing' substitution rule (19) are permitted by these principles, and so are composition rules like the following (27):

$$Y/Z\,X\backslash Y \Rightarrow X/Z \qquad (27)$$

Such a rule has been argued to be necessary for, among other things, extractions of 'non-peripheral' arguments, as in the derivation (28).

Such rules allow constituent orders that are not otherwise permitted, as the example shows, and are usually termed 'non-order-preserving.' It will be shown later that such rules are not theorems of the Lambek calculus. Friedman et al. showed that it is the inclusion of these rules, together with the generalization to instances of rules corresponding to $\mathbf{B}^2$ (cf. 13) that engenders greater than context free power in this generalization of CG. A language which allowed non-order-preserving rules to apply freely would have very free word order, including the possibility of 'scrambling' arguments across clause boundaries. It is therefore assumed in this version of combinatory categorial grammar that languages are free to restrict such rules to certain categories, or even to exclude some of them entirely.

One of the most interesting observations to arise from the movement analysis of relatives is the observation that there are a number of striking limitations on relativization. The exceptions fall into two broad classes. The first is a class of constraints relating to asymmetries with respect to extraction between subjects and objects. This class of exceptions has been related to the 'empty category principle' (ECP) of GB. In the terms of the combinatory theory, this constraint arises as a special case of a more general corollary of the theory, namely that arguments of different directionality require different combinatory rules to apply if they are to extract, as inspection of the following examples will reveal. The possibility for such asymmetries to exist in SVO languages because of the exclusion of the latter nondirection preserving rule is therefore open, for example, (29):

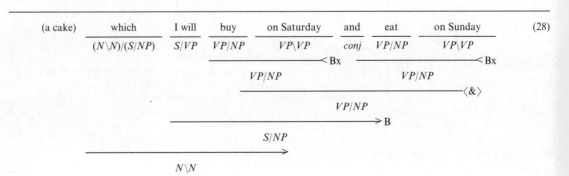

(a) (a man whom) [I think that]$_{S/S}$ [Mary   (29)
    likes]$_{S/NP}$
(b) *(a man whom) [I think that]$_{S/S}$
    [likes Mary]$_{S\backslash NP}$

Indeed, a language like English *must* limit or exclude this rule if it is to remain configurational.

The second class is that of so-called 'island constraints,' which have been related to the principle of 'subjacency.' The fact that adjuncts and NPs are in general islands follows from the assumption that the former are backward modifiers, and that type-raising is lexical and restricted to categories which are arguments of verbs, such as NPs. This can be seen from the categories in the following unacceptable examples (30):

(a) * a book [which]$_{(N\backslash N)/(S/NP)}$ [I will]$_{S/VP}$ [walk]$_{VP}$ (30)
    [without reading]$_{(VP\backslash VP)/NP}$
(b) * a book [which]$_{(N\backslash N)/(S/NP)}$ [I met]$_{S/NP}$ [a man
    who wrote]$_{(S\backslash (S/NP))/NP}$

The possibility of exceptions to the island status of NPs and adjuncts, and their equally notorious dependence on lexical content and such semantically related properties as definiteness and quantification, can be explained on the assumption that verbs can be selectively type-raised over such adjuncts, and lexicalized. Thus the possibility of exceptions like the following (and the generally uncertain judgments that are associated with sentences involving subjacency violations) are also explained (31):

(a) ?a man who I painted a picture of   (31)
(b) ?an article which I wrote my thesis without
    being aware of.

(The subjacency constraints are treated at length by Szabolcsi and Zwarts, and Hepple.)

Other theories on this branch of the categorial family have proposed the inclusion of further combinators, and/or the exclusion of one or more of the above. Perhaps the first of the modern combinatory theories, that of E. Bach, proposed an account of certain bounded constructions, including passive and control, by a 'wrapping' operation which combined functions with their second argument in advance of their first, an analysis which has been extended subsequently. Such operations are related to (but not identical to) the 'associativity' family of theorems of the Lambek calculus. They are also closely related to the **C** or 'commuting' family of combinators. They can also be simulated by, or defined in terms of, the composition and type lifting combinators, as seen in example (31). Curry's combinator **W** has also been implicated in some analyses of reflexives. The theory of related constructions exploits functional composition in accounting for raising, equi, and the like, with important implications for the treatment of VP anaphora.

Since all of the above constructions are bounded, the theories in question can be viewed as combinatory theories of the lexicon and of lexical morphology (however, there are arguments against too simplistic an interpretation of this view). To that extent, the above theories are close relatives of the theories of Keenan and Faltz and of Shaumyan. All of these theories embody related sets of operations in lexical semantics. Shaumyan in particular explicitly identifies these operations with a very full range of Curry's combinators.

3.1.3 Power of Combinatory Grammars

One may ask at this point what the power of such grammars is. Curry and Feys show that collections of combinators as small as the pair **SK** may have the full expressive power of the lambda calculus. **BCWI** and **BCSI** are also implicitly shown by Curry and Feys to be equivalent to the λI-calculus—that is, the lambda calculus without vacuous abstraction. The system of (typed) **BST** is also essentially equivalent to the (simply typed) λI-calculus, although technically it may be necessary to include the ground case of I where its argument is a single variable as a special case. This equivalence means that any restrictiveness that inheres to the theory in automata-theoretic terms stems from the directional sensitivity inherent in the lexicon and in the Principles of Consistency (21) and Inheritance (22) alone. Joshi et al. have shown that a number of 'mildly non-context-free' grammar formalisms including Joshi's Tree-Adjunction Grammars (TAG), Pollard's Head Grammars (HG), and the version of combinatory categorial grammar sketched here can be mapped onto Linear Indexed Grammars.

The consequences of equivalence to linear indexed grammars are significant, as Joshi et al. show. In particular, linear indexed grammars, by passing the stack to only one branch, allow divide-and-conquer parsing algorithms. As a result, these authors have been able to demonstrate polynomial worst-case limits on the complexity of parsing the version of combinatory CG described above.

3.2 Lambek-style Categorial Grammars

Lambek's original proposal began by offering intuitive motivations for including operations of composition, type-raising, and certain kinds of rebracketing in grammars. All of the operations concerned are, in terms of an earlier definition, *order preserving*. The first two operations are familiar but the last needs some explanation. Lambek notes that a possible 'grouping' of the sentence (*John likes*)(*Jane*) is as shown by the brackets. (He might have used a coordinate sentence as proof, although he did not in fact do so.) He then notes that the following operation would transform a standard transitive verb into a category that could combine with the subject first to yield the desired constituency (the rule is given in Lambek's own notation, as defined earlier (32)):

$$(np\backslash s)/np \to np\backslash(s/np) \tag{32}$$

There are two things to note about this operation. One is that it is redundant: that is, its effect of permitting a subject to combine before an object can be achieved by a combination of type-raising and composition, as in example (16). The second is that, while this particular operation is order preserving and stringset-preserving, many superficially similar operations are not. For example, the following rule (33) would not have this property:

$$* (s/np)/np \to s/(np/np) \tag{33}$$

That is, rebracketing of this kind can only apply across opposite slashes, not across same slashes.

However, Lambek was not proposing to introduce these operations as independent rules. He went on to show in his paper that an infinite set of such-order preserving operations emerged as theorems from a logic defined in terms of a small number of axiom schemata and inference rules. These rules included an identity axiom, associativity axiom schemata, and inference rules of application, abstraction, and transitivity. The theorems included functional application, the infinite set of order-preserving instances of operations corresponding to the combinators $\mathbf{B}, \mathbf{B}^2, \ldots, \mathbf{B}^n$, and the order-preserving instances of type-raising, $\mathbf{T}$. They also included the rule shown in (32) and a number of operations of mathematical interest, including the Schönfinkel equivalence between 'flat' and 'curried' function-types, and a family of 'division rules' including the following (34):

$$z/y \to (z/x)/(y/z) \tag{34}$$

The latter is of interest because it was the most important rule in P. T. Geach's proposal, for which reason it is often referred to as the 'Geach Rule.'

This last result is also of interest because an elegant alternative axiomatization of the Lambek calculus in terms of the Geach rule was provided by Zielonka, who dropped Lambek's associativity axioms, substituting two Geach Rules and two Lifting Rules, and dropping the abstraction and transitivity inference rules in favor of two derived inference rules inducing recursion on the domain and range categories of functors. Zielonka's paper also proved the important result that no finite axiomatization of the Lambek calculus is possible without the inclusion of some such recursive reduction law. Zielonka's calculus differs from the original in that the product rule is no longer valid, for which reason it is sometimes identified as the 'product-free' Lambek calculus.

The Lambek calculus has the following properties. If a string is accepted on some given lexical assign-ment, the calculus will allow further derivations cor-responding to all possible bracketings of the string. That is, the calculus is 'structurally complete.' Curi-ously, while W. Buszkowski showed that a version of the calculus restricted to one of the two slash-direc-tions was weakly equivalent to context-free grammar, the nonfinite-axiomatization property of the calculus meant that for many years no proof of the same weak equivalence for the full bidirectional calculus was available. Nevertheless, everyone had been convinced since the early 1960s that the equivalence held, and Buszkowski et al. (1988) had presented a number of partial results. A proof was finally published in 1993 by M. Pentus.

If the Lambek calculus is compared with the com-binatory alternative discussed earlier, then the fol-lowing similarities are seen. Both composition and type-raising are permitted rules in both systems, and both are generalized in ways which can be seen as involving recursive schemata and polymorphism. However, there are important divergences between these two branches of the categorial family. The most important is that many of the particular combinatory rules that have been proposed by linguists, while they are *semantically* identical to theorems of the Lambek calculus, are not actually theorems thereof. For exam-ple, E. Bach's rule of 'right-wrap,' which shares with Lambek's rebracketing rule (32) a semantics cor-responding to the commuting combinator $\mathbf{C}$, is not Lambek-provable. Similarly, examples like (28) have been used to argue for 'nonorder-preserving' com-position rules, which correspond to instances of the combinator $\mathbf{B}$ that are also unlicensed by the Lambek calculus. It is hard to do without such rules, because their absence prevents all nonperipheral extraction and all non-context-free constructions (see below). Finally, none of the rules that combine arguments of more than one functor, including Geach's semantic coordination rule, the coordination schema (5), and A. Szabolsci's substitution rule (19) are Lambek the-orems.

The response of categorial grammarians has been of two kinds. Many linguists have simply continued to take non-Lambek combinatory rules as primitive, the approach discussed in the previous sections. Such authors have placed more importance on the com-positional semantics of the combinatory rules them-selves than on further reducibility to axiom systems. Others have attempted to identify alternative calculi that have more attractive linguistic properties.

Lambek himself was the first to express scepticism concerning the linguistic potential of his calculus, a position that he has maintained to the present day. He noted that, because of the use of a category $(s\backslash s)/s$ for conjunctions, the calculus not only permitted strings like (35a), below, but also ones like (35b):

(a) Who walks and talks? (35)
(b) *Who walks and he talks?

The overgeneralization arises because the conjunction category, having applied to the sentence *He talks* to yield $s\backslash s$, can *compose* with *walks* to yield the predicate category $np\backslash s$. It is exactly this possibility that forces the use of a syncategorematic coordination schema such as (5) in the combinatory approach. However, it has been shown that such rules are not Lambek calculus theorems. Lambek's initial reaction was to restrict his original calculus by omitting the associativity axiom, yielding the 'nonassociative' Lambek calculus. This version, which has not been much used, is unique among extensions of categorial grammar in disallowing composition, which is no longer a theorem.

Other work along these lines, notably by van Benthem (1991), Moortgat (whose 1989 book is the most accessible introduction to the area), and Morrill (1994), has attempted to generalize, rather than to restrict, the original calculus. Much of this work has been directed at the possibility of restoring to the calculus one or more of Gentzen's 'structural rules,' which Lambek's original calculus entirely eschews, and whose omission renders it less powerful than full intuitionistic logic. In CG terms, these three rules correspond to *permutation* of adjacent categories, or 'interchange,' *reduction of two instances of a category to one*, or 'contraction,' and *vacuous abstraction*, or 'thinning' (sometimes termed 'weakening'). In combinatory terms, they correspond to the combinator-families **C**, **W**, and **K**. As Lambek points out, a system which allows only the first of these rules corresponds to the linear logic of D. Girard, while a system which allows only the first two corresponds to the relevance logic **R**_ and the 'weak positive implicational calculus' of Church, otherwise known as the λ_I-calculus.

3.2.1 Power of Lambek-style Grammars

Van Benthem (1991) examined the consequences of adding the interchange rule, and showed that such a calculus is not only structurally complete but 'permutation-complete.' That is, if a string is recognized, so are all possible permutations of the string. He shows (1991: 97) that this calculus is (in contrast to the original calculus) of greater than context-free power. For example, a lexicon can readily be chosen which accepts the language whose strings contain equal numbers of a's, b's, and c's, which is non-context free. However, Moortgat (1989: 118) shows that the theorems of this calculus do not obey the principles of directional consistency (21) and directional inheritance (22)—for example, they include all sixteen possible forms of first-order composition, rather than just four. Moortgat also shows (1989: 92–3) that the mere inclusion in a Lambek-style axiomatization of slash-crossing composition rules like (27) (which of course are permitted by these principles) is enough to ensure collapse into van Benthem's permuting calculus.

There does not seem to be a natural Lambek-style system in between.

However, Moortgat does offer a way to generalize the Lambek calculus without engendering collapse into permutation-completeness. He proposes the introduction of new equivalents of slash, including 'infixing' slashes, together with axioms and inference rules that discriminate between the slash-types (cf. 1989: 111, 120), giving the system the character of a 'partial' logic. While he shows that one such axiomatization can be made to entail the generalizations inherent in the principles of consistency and inheritance, it seems likely that many equally simple formulations within the same degrees of freedom would produce much less desirable consequences. Moreover, unless the recursive aspects of this axiom-schematization can be further constrained to limit such theorems as the composition family **B**^{n} in a similar way to the combinatory alternative, it appears to follow that this calculus is still of greater power than linear indexed grammar.

In the work of Moortgat, the semantic (combinatory) and proof-theoretic (Lambek-style) traditions of CG come close to convergence. Without the restrictions inherent in the principles of consistency and inheritance, both frameworks would collapse. The main difference between the theories is that on the combinatory view the restrictions are built into the axioms and are claimed to follow from first principles, whereas on the Lambek view, the restrictions are imposed as filters.

4. Categorial Grammars and Linguistic Semantics

There are two commonly used notations that make explicit the close relation between syntax and semantics that both combinatory and Lambek-style categorial grammars embody. The first associates with each category a term of the lambda calculus naming its interpretation. The second associates an interpretation with each basic category in a functor, a representation which has the advantage of being directly interpretable via standard term-unification procedures of the kind used in logic programming languages such as PROLOG. The same verb *sees* might appear as follows in these notations, which are here shown for the combinatory categories, but which can equally be applied to Lambek categories. In either version it is standard to use a colon to associate syntactic and semantic entities, to use a convention that semantic constants have mnemonic identifiers like *see'* distinguished from variables by primes. For purposes of exposition it will be assumed that translations exactly mirror the syntactic category in terms of dominance relations. Thus a convention of 'left associativity' in translations is adopted, so that expressions like *see' y x* are equivalent to *(see' y) x* (36):

(a) λ-term-based: $sees := (S \backslash NP)/NP : \lambda y \lambda x [see' \, y \, x]$ (36)
(b) Unification-based: $sees := (S : see' \, y \, x \backslash NP : x)/NP : y$

The advantage of the former notation is that the λ-calculus is a highly readable notation for functional entities. Its disadvantage is that the notation of the combinatory rules is complicated to allow the combination of both parts of the category, as in (37a), below. This has the effect of weakening the direct relation between syntactic and semantic types, since it suggests rules might be allowed in which the syntactic and semantic combinatory operations were *not* identical. In the unification notation (37b), by contrast, the combinatory rules apply unchanged, and necessarily preserve identity between syntactic and semantic operations, a property which was one of the original attractions of CG.

Forward Composition: (37)
$X/Y : f \; Y/Z : g \Rightarrow X/Z : \lambda x [f(g \, x)]$

(a) λ-term-based

Forward Composition:
$X/Y \; Y/Z \Rightarrow X/Z$

(b) Unification-based

Because of their direct expressibility in unification-based programming languages like PROLOG, and related special-purpose linguistic programming languages like PATR-II, the latter formalism or notational variants thereof are widespread in the computational linguistics literature. Derivations appear as follows (for simplicity, type-raising is ignored here):

Gilbert	sees	George	(38)
$NP : gilbert'$	$(S : see' \, y \, x \backslash NP : x)/NP : y$	$NP : george'$	

$S : see' \, george' \, x \backslash NP : x$

$S : see' \, george' \, gilbert'$

All the alternative derivations that the combinatory grammar permits yield equivalent semantic interpretations, representing the canonical function-argument relations that result from a purely applicative derivation. In contrast to combinatory derivations, such semantic representations therefore preserve the relations of dominance and command defined in the lexicon, a point that has obviously desirable consequences for capturing the generalizations concerning dependency that have been described in the GB framework in terms of relations of *c*-command and the notion of 'thematic hierarchy.' This point is important for example, to the analysis of parasitic gaps sketched earlier, since parasitic gaps are known to obey an 'anti-*c*-command' restriction.

By the very token that combinatory derivations *preserve* canonical relations of dominance and command, one must distinguish this level of semantic interpretation from the one implicated in the proposals of P.

T. Geach and others. These authors use a very similar range of combinatory operations, notably including or entailing as theorems (generalized) functional composition (lexical, polymorphic), type-lifting, and (in the case of Geach) a coordination schema of the kind introduced in Sect. 2, in order to free the scope of quantifiers from traditional surface syntax, in order to capture the well-known ambiguity of sentences like the following (39):

Every woman loves some man.   (39)

On the simplest assumption that the verb is of type $e \rightarrow (e \rightarrow t)$, and the subject and object are corresponding (polymorphic) type-raised categories, the reading where the subject has wide scope is obtained by a purely applicative reading. The reading where the object has wide scope is obtained by composing subject and verb before applying the object to the result of the composition. In this their motivation for introducing composition is the combinatory relative of the λ-categorial grammars of Lewis, Montague, and Cresswell (see above). Indeed, one must sharply distinguish the *level* of semantic representation that is assumed in these two kinds of theory, as Lewis in fact suggested (1972: 48), ascribing all these authors' operations to the level of logical form. Otherwise one must predict that those sentences which under the assumptions of the combinatory approach *require* function composition to yield an analysis (as opposed to merely allowing that alternative), such as right node raising, must yield only one of the two readings. (Which reading is obtained will depend upon the original assignment of categories.) However, this prediction would be incorrect: both scopings are allowed for sentences like the following (40), adapted from Geach:

Every girl likes, and every boy detests, some   (40)
saxophonist.

That is not to say that the categorial analysis is without advantages. As Geach points out, one does *not* appear to obtain a third reading in which two instances of the existential each have wide scope over one of the universals, so that all the girls like one particular saxophonist, and all the boys detest one particular saxophonist, but the two saxophonists are not the same. This result is to be expected if the entire substring *Every girl likes and every boy detests* is the syntactic and semantic constituent with respect to which the scope of the existential is defined. However, it remains the case that there is a many-to-one relation between semantic categories at this level and categories and/or rules at the level which has been considered up to now. The semantics itself and the nature of this relationship are a subject in their own right which it is not possible to do justice to here, but the reader is referred to important work by Partee and Rooth, and Hendriks on the question. Much of this work has recently harked back to axiomatic frameworks related to the Lambek calculus.

5. Further Reading

Two indispensible collections of readings in categorial grammar between them contain many important papers in the area, including many of those cited above. (A complete list of references can be found in Steedman 1993.) Buszkowski et al. (1988) includes a number of historically significant older papers, including those by Lambek and Geach. (The most important omissions in the otherwise excellent historical coverage afforded by the Buszkowski volume are the original paper by Ajdukiewicz (1935), which is translated together with other historically relevant material in McCall (1967), and the work of Bar-Hillel (1964). Certain papers crucial to the prehistory of CG, including Schönfinkel (1924), are collected in translation in van Heijenoort (1967).) The review articles by the editors contain valuable survey material in many of the areas touched on here, and the collection is particularly valuable as a source of mathematical results concerning the Lambek calculus and its extensions. The collection edited by Oehrle et al. (1985) also contains important survey articles, largely non-overlapping with those in the previous collection. The overall slant is more linguistic, and the collection includes a large number of important papers which continue to influence current work in natural language syntax and semantics. To some extent, these largely complementary collections epitomize the two approaches distinguished at the start of Sect. 3.

Besides the valuable introductory essays to these two collections, the relevant section of Lyons (1968), which heralded the revival of categorial grammar as a linguistic theory, remains one of the most accessible and inspiring brief introductions to categorial grammar for the general linguist. The 1993 book by M. Wood (which has appeared since the first version of this article was written) is the most complete review of the whole area.

As far as the mathematical foundations of CG go, the most intuitive introduction to the relation between combinators and the λ-calculus remains Curry and Feys (1958: ch. 5 and ch. 6). Hindley and Seldin (1986) provide an excellent modern introduction. Smullyan (1985), in which the combinators take the form of birds, is undoubtedly the most entertaining among recent presentations of the subject, and is a goldmine of useful results. The papers of Richard Montague were collected in Thomason (1974). The related λ-categorial approach of Cresswell is presented in a series of books of which the first appeared in 1973. Important work in Lambek-style categorial grammars is to be found in Moortgat (1989) and van Benthem (1991), the former being aimed at the linguist, the latter at the mathematical logician.

A number of collections bringing together papers on recent linguistic theories include papers on CG, and relate it to other contemporary approaches. The collections by Jacobson and Pullum (1982), Huck and Ojeda (1987), and Sag and Szabolsci (1992) are useful in this respect. These and the two collections mentioned earlier provide references to a large and diverse literature constituting the foundations of the categorial approach. However, for current linguistic work in this rapidly evolving area one must turn to the journals and conference proceedings. Among the former, *Linguistics and Philosophy* has been a pioneer in presenting recent categorial work. Among the latter, the annual proceedings of the West Coast Conference on Formal Linguistics is one important source. Much computational linguistic work in CG also remains uncollected, and here again one must turn to journals and conference proceedings, among which *Computational Linguistics* and the annual proceedings of the meetings of the Association for Computational Linguistics (and of its European Chapter) are important. A more complete bibliography can be found in Steedman (1993).

Bibliography

Baltin M, Kroch A S (eds.) 1989 *Alternative Conceptions of Phrase Structure*. Chicago University Press, Chicago, IL

Bar-Hillel Y 1964 *Language and Information*. Addison-Wesley, Reading, MA

Buszkowski W, Marciszewski W, van Benthem J (eds.) 1988 *Categorial Grammar*. Benjamins. Amsterdam

Cresswell M 1973 *Logics and Languages*. Methuen, London

Curry H, Feys R 1958 *Combinatory Logic*, vol. I. North-Holland, Amsterdam

Hindley R, Seldin J 1986 *Introduction to Combinators and λ-calculus*. Cambridge University Press, Cambridge

Huck G, Ojeda A (eds.) 1987 *Syntax and Semantics 20: Discontinuous Constituency*. Academic Press, New York

Jacobson P, Pullum G K (eds.) 1982 *The Nature of Syntactic Representation*. Reidel, Dordrecht

Lyons J 1968 *Theoretical Linguistics*. Cambridge University Press, Cambridge

McCall S (ed.) 1967 *Polish Logic 1920–1939*. Clarendon Press, Oxford

Moortgat M 1989 *Categorial Investigations*. Foris, Dordrecht

Morrill G 1994 *Type-logical Grammar*. Kluwer, Dordrecht

Oehrle R T, Bach E, Wheeler D (eds.) 1985 *Categorial Grammars and Natural Language Structures*. Reidel, Dordrecht

Sag I, Szabolsci A (eds.) 1992 *Lexical Matters*. CLSI/Chicago University Press, Chicago, IL

Smullyan R 1985 *To Mock a Mockingbird*. Knopf, New York

Steedman M 1993 Categorial Grammar. *Lingua*

Thomason R (ed.) 1974 *Formal Philosophy: The Papers of Richard Montague*. Yale, New Haven, CT

van Benthem J 1991 *Language in Action*. North-Holland, Amsterdam

van Heijenoort J (ed.) 1967 *From Frege to Gödel*. Harvard University Press, Cambridge, MA

Wood M 1993 *Categorial Grammars*. Routledge, London

Chomsky and Pragmatics

A. Kasher

Chomsky's research program of generative linguistics has had syntax in focus, but its conception of objectives, scientific methodology, and philosophical foundations (see *Chomsky's Philosophy of Language*) transcend syntax and lend themselves to interesting applications. Pragmatics is an area to which they have been applied.

1. Pragmatics in Chomsky's Early Writings

The first published appearance of pragmatics in Chomsky's writings is in an early paper (1962). The knowledge of language a speaker has acquired constitutes 'an implicit theory of the language that he has mastered, a theory that predicts the grammatical structure of each of an infinite class of potential physical events, and the conditions for the appropriate use of each of these items' (Chomsky 1962: 528). 'Appropriateness conditions' of sentences to contexts of utterance have often been claimed to form the subject matter of pragmatics, in the sense of a theory of language use (Kasher 1977; van Dijk 1977).

According to the author's own (1973) introduction to Chomsky (1955), 'the overarching semiotic theory in which the theory of linguistic form is imbedded must develop and explain how the notions constructed and applied in the investigation of linguistic form contribute to determining meaning and conditions of appropriate use' (Kasher 1973: 20). This is still a 'thin' notion of pragmatic theory, one that has a certain theoretical objective and bears a certain relation to the theory of linguistic form.

2. Pragmatic Competence

That notion of pragmatic theory is replaced by a 'thicker' one towards the end of the 1970s, when a distinction is introduced between 'grammatical competence,' which is related to form and meaning, and 'pragmatic competence,' which involves 'knowledge of conditions and manner of appropriate use, in conformity with various purposes' (Chomsky 1978: 224). Appropriateness of use is couched in terms of the relations between intentions and purposes and between linguistic means, of certain forms and meanings, within linguistic institutional settings. (See also Chomsky 1980: 59–60 and 93; Kasher 1977.)

The introduction of a theoretical notion of pragmatic competence imports into pragmatics the form of theoretical objectives, the scientific methodology, and the philosophical foundations of Chomsky's research program of generative linguistics.

On a par with the major theoretical objective of the generative study of syntax being an understanding of an innate 'universal grammar,' the major theoretical objective of a similar study of pragmatics would be an understanding of the invariant or innate constraints of language use. Thus, one would replace mere descriptions and classifications of types of speech act, for example, by much deeper attempts to answer questions such as 'What is a cognitively possible speech act type?' (see Kasher 1981).

The very notion of a pragmatic competence involves a variety of abstractions underlying the fruitful distinction between any competence and the related performance (Moravcsik 1990). A prevalent empiricist method of collecting data, classifying it, and making attempts to formulate some generalizations about it is thus replaced by an ordinary scientific method of formulating abstract theories in pursuit of understanding interesting aspects of nature. There is no reason why theoretical studies of natural language, including its pragmatic aspects, should not be carried out the way studies of other aspects of nature are.

At the basic level of the philosophical foundations of the resulting study of the pragmatic competence, the following are the most interesting claims:

(a) Use of language is governed by systems of abstract rules that are universally, most probably innately, constrained.

(b) Use of language is governed by systems that are independent of other linguistic and cognitive systems.

(c) Use of language should not be identified with operation of a communication system. The latter is just a common example of the former (see Chomsky 1975, 1980; Kasher 1991).

3. Use of Pragmatics in Chomsky's Later Publications

In his more recent books (1986, 1988), Chomsky mentioned three 'basic questions' that arise in the study of language, viz. '(i) What constitutes knowledge of language? (ii) How is knowledge of language acquired? (iii) How is knowledge of language put to use?' (Chomsky 1986: 3; see also Chomsky 1988: 3). Question (iii) breaks down into a question about perception and a question about production, which is a question about the character of the creative nature of language use.

The latter question, dubbed 'Descartes's problem,' of the creative aspects of what individuals say and why they say it, has remained unsolved, probably because of the limited nature of human cognitive faculties and intellectual grasp (Chomsky 1988; see also McGinn 1991).

The unsolvability of Descartes's problem has been,

but should not be, interpreted as an argument for the impossibility of pragmatics. Each component of language gives rise to three such basic questions. Question (iii), about putting some linguistic knowledge of that component to use, is not a question about the component itself, but rather about creative aspects of that component, whether it is syntax, semantics, or pragmatics. Pragmatics, being a theory of appropriate language use in context, is a body of knowledge, the subject matter of answers to question (i); it is acquired in a certain way, the subject matter of answers to question (ii); and it is put to use by what embodies the creative aspects of pragmatics, the subject matter of answers to question (iii). Clearly, *use* is used in two different meanings in the delineation of pragmatics and in question (iii), and no argument for the impossibility of the former emerges from Chomsky's arguments about the latter.

Bibliography

Chomsky N 1955 The logical structure of linguistic theory (Manuscript, Harvard University)
Chomsky N 1962 Explanatory models in linguistics. In: Nagel E, Suppes P, Tarski A (eds.) *Logic, Methodology and Philosophy of Science*. Stanford University Press, Stanford, CA
Chomsky N 1975 *Reflections on Language*. Pantheon, New York
Chomsky N 1978 Language and unconscious knowledge. In: Smith J H (ed.) *Psychoanalysis and Language, Psychiatry and the Humanities*, vol. 3. Yale University Press, New Haven, CT
Chomsky N 1980 *Rules and Representations*. Blackwell, Oxford
Chomsky N 1984 *Modular Approaches to the Study of the Mind*. San Diego State University Press, San Diego, CA
Chomsky N 1986 *Knowledge of Language*. Praeger, New York
Chomsky N 1988 *Language and the Problems of Knowledge*. MIT Press, Cambridge, MA
Kasher A 1973 Introduction. In: Chomsky N 1955 *The Logical Structure of Linguistic Theory*. Plenum Press, New York
Kasher A 1977 What is a theory of use? *JPrag* **1**: 105–20
Kasher A 1981 Minimal speakers and necessary speech acts. In: Coulmas F (ed.) *Festschrift for Native Speaker*. Mouton, The Hague
Kasher A 1991 Pragmatics and Chomsky's research program. In: Kasher A (ed.) *The Chomskyan Turn*. Blackwell, Oxford
McGinn C 1991 *The Problem of Consciousness*. Blackwell, Oxford
Moravcsik J M 1990 *Thought and Language*. Routledge and Kegan Paul, London
van Dijk T A 1977 *Text and Context*. Longman, London

Chomsky's Philosophy of Language

F. J. Newmeyer

Given the central role that Noam Chomsky has played in the linguistics of the past few decades, it is important to understand the philosophical system that underlies his ideas. This article traces the development of this system from Chomsky's earliest training to the present, pointing to its relevance to philosophy, psychology, and most importantly, linguistic methodology.

1. Chomsky's Philosophical Training

Noam Chomsky was trained in the most rigidly empiricist linguistic tradition that has ever been practiced, namely that of 'post-Bloomfieldian structuralism.' Leonard Bloomfield, a central figure of American linguistics in the interwar period and the intellectual forefather of this tradition, had pioneered an approach to linguistic methodology that allowed only statements drawn from direct observation of the phenomena under investigation or generalizations that could be derived from observations by a set of mechanical procedures. As he put it, 'The only useful generalizations about language are inductive generalizations. Features which we think ought to be universal may be absent from the very next language that becomes accessible' (Bloomfield 1933: 20). Such a view discouraged not only an inquiry into the universal properties of language, but the study of meaning as well, given the notorious difficulty of making explicit the precise meaning of an utterance.

The 'post-Bloomfieldians' consisted of those students of Bloomfield's, and their colleagues, who dominated American linguistics in the 1940s and 1950s. One of their most prominent members was Chomsky's teacher Zellig Harris. They set to work to devise a set of procedures in accord with Bloomfield's theoretical strictures, while avoiding what they saw as the pitfalls in his actual analytical work, which was prone to make use of 'mentalistic' constructs and nonrigorous procedures. Their goal was explicitly to 'discover' a grammar by performing a set of operations on a corpus of data. Each successive operation was to be one step farther removed from the corpus. Since the physical record of the flow of speech itself was the only data considered objective enough to serve as a starting point, it followed that the levels of a grammatical description had to be arrived at in the following order: phonemics, morphemics, syntax, discourse.

The empiricism that dominated American linguistics from the 1930s to the 1950s was a simple reflection of the fact that this intellectual current dominated *all* the social and behavioral sciences in the USA at the time. Its wide appeal was in large part a function of the fact that there was no other period in American history in which there was greater respect for the methods and results of science. Contemporary philosophy of science (as well as naive common sense) informed linguists and others that what distinguishes science from other types of activity is the ability to generalize laws on the basis of precise measurement of observable data. Post-Bloomfieldian structuralism promised to bring linguistics in accord with what was seen as the practice in physics, chemistry, biology, and the other natural sciences.

Not surprisingly, the post-Bloomfieldians looked to behaviorist psychology for independent support for their approach to language. However, American psychology at this time, under the leadership of B. F. Skinner (1957) was under the grip of a form of empiricism that was so extreme that it would not even tolerate theoretical terms such as 'phoneme,' 'morpheme,' and so on, which could be derived by a set of mechanical operations. Hence, the marriage of structural linguistics and psychology did not take place until a less radical form of behaviorism was developed (Hull 1943) that gave these constructs the status of 'mediating responses,' that is, elements that, while not directly observable, could nevertheless (in principle) be linked deterministically to observable speech.

2. Chomsky's Break with Empiricism

Chomsky's training in the philosophical foundations of linguistics was strictly in this empiricist post-Bloomfieldian tradition—he even published a paper as a student which was designed to sharpen their analytical procedures. But as early as his undergraduate days, he had come to have doubts as to the philosophical worth of the enterprise. These doubts soon led him to rethink the philosophical foundations of the field and to set to work to develop an alternative conception of linguistic theory and practice. This approach was laid out in a 900-page manuscript entitled *The Logical Structure of Linguistic Theory*, written in 1955, but not published until 20 years later (Chomsky 1975a).

The central themes of this manuscript were condensed and published in Chomsky's (1957) book *Syntactic Structures*. This book's conceptual break with post-Bloomfieldianism was not over the question of whether linguistics could be a 'science'—Chomsky never questioned that it could be—but over the more fundamental issue of what a scientific theory is and how one might be constructed with respect to linguistic phenomena. Chomsky argued at length that no scientific theory had ever resulted from the scientist performing mechanical operations on the data. How the scientist happens to hit upon a particular theoretical notion, he pointed out, is simply irrelevant; all that counts is its adequacy in explaining the phenomena in its domain.

Chomsky's rejection of empiricist constraints on theory formation led him to propose a novel conception of what a linguistic theory is a theory *of*. Whereas to earlier structuralists, a theory was no more than a concise taxonomy of the elements extractable from a corpus of data, Chomsky redefined the goal of linguistic theory to that of providing a rigorous and formal characterization of a 'possible human language,' that is, to distinguishing as precisely as possible the class of grammatical processes that can occur in language from that which cannot. This characterization, which Chomsky later came to call 'universal grammar,' specifies the limits within which all languages function. In Chomsky's view, natural scientists set parallel tasks for themselves: the goal of physicists is to characterize the class of possible physical processes, that of biologists to characterize the class of possible biological processes, and so on.

Aside from his extended demolition of empiricist approaches to grammar construction (although the philosophy of 'empiricism' is never mentioned by name), there is little discussion in *Syntactic Structures* of philosophical issues, whether philosophy of language or philosophy of science. Indeed, the only philosophical works referred to in that book are by the arch-empiricists (and Chomsky's teachers) Willard Quine and Nelson Goodman, to whom Chomsky gave credit for his views on simplicity and the evaluation of formal systems.

Nevertheless, philosophers of science had, in the previous decade, been moving away from the empiricist constraints on theory construction and motivation that had generally been espoused earlier. For example, in two important papers (ultimately published in 1965) the philosopher Carl Hempel laid to rest any hope for an empiricist approach to theory formation. As he pointed out, even the more permissive empiricist approaches to this question fail to capture the essence of what it takes for a statement to be considered scientific. He illustrated at length that there is no direct connection between a scientific term or statement and the empirical confirmation of a theory containing that term or statement. Indeed, many fundamental scientific notions, such as 'gravitational potential,' 'absolute temperature,' and 'electric field,' have no operational definitions at all. Hempel concluded that science is more in the business of comparing *theories* than in evaluating *statements*. A theory is simply an axiomatized system which *as a whole* has an empirical interpretation.

Hempel's view, which had begun to gather currency by the late 1950s, signaled the demise of empiricism as a significant force in the philosophy of science. As its philosophical props gave way, post-Bloomfieldian structuralism found itself in a distinctly unstable posture. Not surprisingly, it was relatively simple for a theory that itself rattled these props to topple it completely.

3. Chomsky's Early Approach to Meaning

For all its ground-breaking work about theory construction in linguistics in general, there is nothing particularly innovative in the *Syntactic Structures* approach to meaning. On the one hand, in terms of the *analysis* of meaning, Chomsky adopted the post-Bloomfieldian view that grammar (i.e., syntax and phonology) are autonomous and independent of meaning, though he took pains to stress that this conclusion was based on an analysis of the data, not on some a priori stricture that demanded the exclusion of unobservable semantic phenomena from the domain of linguistic analysis.

As far as his views on the *nature* of meaning are concerned, he endorsed Goodman's (empiricist) attempt to extend the theory of reference to encompass much of meaning. The residue of meaning intractable to this approach was simply ascribed to language use, presumably based on the contemporary influence of the Oxford philosophers and their use of theory of meaning.

Indeed, the terms 'meaning' and 'use' are used interchangeably so often throughout *Syntactic Structures* that Newmeyer (1986: 27) has argued that many of Chomsky's arguments in *Syntactic Structures* for the autonomy of syntax were in reality arguments for (what he would call a few years later) the competence–performance dichotomy. Many aspects of meaning, in his view at the time, were part of performance.

4. The Development of Chomsky's Theory of Mind

The decade following the publication of *Syntactic Structures* saw Chomsky's views mature into a philosophical system in which the boundaries between the fields of linguistics, psychology, and philosophy became ever less distinct.

Chomsky himself did not bring up the question of the psychological implications of transformational generative grammar in either *The Logical Structure of Linguistic Theory* or *Syntactic Structures*; as he wrote later, it would have been 'too audacious' for him to have done so (Chomsky 1975a: 35). But his student, Robert B. Lees, closed his review of *Syntactic Structures* with a frontal attack on inductivist learning theory, arguing that there could be no alternative but to conclude that the grammar the linguist constructed was 'in the head' of the speaker. But if that be the case, then how could these highly abstract principles possibly be learned inductively? 'It would seem,' he wrote, 'that our notions of human learning are due for some considerable sophistication' (Lees 1957: 408).

It was Chomsky's (1959) review of B. F. Skinner's *Verbal Behavior* in which he first stressed that his theory of language is a psychological model of an aspect of human knowledge. Chomsky's review represents, even after the passage of some 20 years, the basic refutation of behaviorist psychology. The review takes in turn each basic construct of behaviorism, and demonstrates that either it leads to false predictions or it is simply devoid of content. Chomsky went on to argue that this ability indicates that rather than being born 'blank slates,' children have a genetic predisposition to structure the acquisition of linguistic knowledge in a highly specific way.

By 1965, with the publication of his *Aspects of the Theory of Syntax*, Chomsky had come to characterize generative grammar explicitly as a 'rationalist' theory, in the sense that it posits innate principles that determine the form of acquired knowledge. As part of the theory's conceptual apparatus, Chomsky reintroduced two terms long out of fashion in academic discussion: 'innate ideas' and 'mind.' For Chomsky, innate ideas are simply those properties of the grammar that are inborn and constrain the acquisition of knowledge. So, for example, generativists believe, based on their abstractness, complexity, and limited amount of relevant information presented to the child, that many grammatical constraints are 'prewired,' so to speak, into the child, rather than acquired by anything one might reasonably call 'learning.' Hence, these constraints are innate ideas.

Mind, for Chomsky, refers to the principles, both innate and acquired, that underlie actual behavior. Such principles, obviously, are not restricted to the realm of language. For example, as recent research has shown, many important aspects of the visual system are also prewired and need only a triggering experience from the environment to be set in motion. In Chomsky's terms, then, the theory of vision is a rationalist theory, and the structures underlying visual perception (innate ideas) form part of mind.

While mind may encompass more cognitive faculties than language, Chomsky believes that linguistic studies are the best suited of all to reveal the essence of mind. For one thing, language is the only cognitive faculty that is *uniquely* human. Not even the study of the communicative behavior of the lower animals sheds any light on it: the mental structures underlying animal communication seem to bear no evolutionary relation to those underlying human language. Also, language is the vehicle of rational thought—another uniquely human ability. And finally, more is known about language and how it functions than about other aspects of cognition. After all, more than two millennia of grammatical research have given us a more detailed picture of the structure of language than a bare century of research has clarified the nature of vision, memory, concept formation, and so on.

Chomsky is happy to refer to the faculty for language as an aspect of 'human nature.' The term 'human nature' for him has real content: it is characterized by the set of innately endowed capacities for language, other aspects of cognition, and whatever else, which, being innate, are immune to environmental influences. Chomsky sees such a conception in an entirely positive political light: our genetic inheritance—our human nature—prevents us from being plastic, infinitely malleable beings subjugable to the whims of outside forces.

Thus at a rather abstract level, there is a connection between Chomsky's philosophy of language and his renowned political anarchism. Just as our innate linguistic endowment shields our language from being shaped in its entirety by external forces, so it is also the case that no oppressive political system has the power to mold our minds entirely to its liking; we are, at root, free agents in this world.

Philosophical critiques of Chomsky's views on language and mind have been legion; while space limitations prevent even a sketchy outline of their content, a sampling may be found in Hook (1969), Harman (1974), and Kripke (1982). They have focused on those aspects of his overall theory that appear most vulnerable: his 'subjectivism,' which entails that a language 'has no existence apart from its mental representation' (Chomsky 1972:95); his 'individualism,' which claims that the explanation of linguistic phenomena rests ultimately on the properties of individual human beings, rather than on their social interactions; his 'mentalism,' which posits that in some real sense speakers 'know' the grammars of their language; and his 'rationalism,' which claims that human language learning is mediated by innate mental schemata. Chomsky defends his views in various works (1972, 1975b, 1980, 1986); for a comprehensive defense of (the bulk of) Chomsky's system of ideas, see D'Agostino (1986).

5. The Further Development of Chomsky's Ideas about Meaning

Returning to more strictly linguistic themes, the decade after the publication of *Syntactic Structures* was also a time of various attempts to integrate a semantic theory into generative grammar. Chomsky, in a 1962 presentation, set the course for this development by raising the question: 'What are the substantive and formal constraints on systems of concepts that are constructed by humans on the basis of presented data?' (1964: 51–52).

Katz and Fodor (1963) attempted to answer Chomsky's question in the following way. First, they distinguished between two faculties involved in the interpretation of a sentence: that provided by a universal theory of meaning, whose primitive terms and principles form part of our strictly grammatical abilities; and that derived from extralinguistic beliefs about the world. The goal of semantic theory would be to explicate only the former faculty, a component of linguistic competence. Second, they developed an analogy between phonetics and semantics. Just as phonetic representations are based on a universal system of phonetic features, semantic representations would be built out of primitive conceptual elements. A reading for a sentence, then, would be determined by the syntactic structure of the sentence and the semantic features ('markers') in the lexical items that comprise it, similar to construction of the phonetic representation of a sentence on the basis of the phonological distinctive features characterizing each lexical item and the language's particular phonological rules.

Chomsky endorsed the Katz–Fodor approach in *Aspects of the Theory of Syntax*. Nevertheless, as time has passed he has become increasingly skeptical that there is a universal semantic system, parallel to a universal phonetic system. As he put it succinctly: 'I doubt that one can separate semantic representation from beliefs and knowledge about the world' (Chomsky 1979: 142).

6. The Generative Semantics Challenge to Chomsky's Philosophy

It seems to be the case that Chomsky believes that the danger of admitting a substantive theory of meaning into generative grammar is a prescription for the ultimate abandonment of a rationalist theory of language in favor of a return of an empiricist one. He would surely point to generative semantics (McCawley 1976) as an object lesson illustrating this point. This approach to grammatical description flourished as a current within generative grammar in the late 1960s and early 1970s. In brief, it took the Katz–Fodor ideas about semantics seriously and attempted to push them to their logical conclusion. Given these ideas, and the related one that deep structure is the locus of semantic interpretation (the 'Katz–Postal Hypothesis'), generative semanticists came more and more to deny that any sensible boundary could be drawn between the syntactic and semantic components of grammar. They had many reasons for coming to this conclusion, but one of the central ones (and the most important for the present discussion) was that, given the existence of a universal semantic system, there exists an overlap between semantic constructs and those participating in what would appear to be strictly grammatical rules (e.g., constructs such as animacy, gender, and the common/proper distinction among nouns). Generative semanticists argued that the redundancy seemingly entailed by this overlap could be eliminated only by erasing the line between syntax and semantics (for detailed discussion of the steps that led them to this conclusion, see Newmeyer 1986).

As this model progressed, it came to challenge any dividing line between semantic and pragmatic facts as well. (Given Chomsky's hypothesis that no such dividing line exists, it would follow naturally that they would be led to this conclusion.) Thus by 1975 or so, the idea that a universal theory of semantic constructs exists had led the competence–performance dichotomy, the linchpin of linguistic rationalism, to be abandoned by generative semanticists.

7. Chomsky and Approaches to Meaning

Chomsky has been equally adamantly opposed to approaches to semantics with roots in the logical tradition, in which, by means of a model, an arbitrary sentence of a language is assigned a truth value with respect to a possible state of affairs. Such approaches began to gain currency among linguists in the mid-1970s and, in one version or another, continue to dominate linguistic semantics today (see Dowty et al. 1981).

Chomsky argues that anyone who believes in possible world semantics is forced to make one of two choices about the status of the constructs that populate such models, and both of them are (in his opinion) unpalatable. On the one hand, they could be regarded in parallel to the way that constructs of syntax and phonology are regarded, namely, as elements of a theory of mind. But, Chomsky argues, it is not at all clear how possible worlds are mentally represented or how people can have access to calculations using possible worlds when they make their judgments. On the other hand, it would be possible to reject any psychological interpretation about possible worlds. But in that case, one would simply be doing some species of mathematics, devoid of linguistic interest. Hence, Chomsky concludes that model–theoretic possible world semantics must be rejected as a component of a linguistic theory.

8. Chomsky's Philosophy and Linguistic Methodology

In debates with his linguistic opponents over even the most seemingly minute aspects of linguistic structure, Chomsky has made it clear that there are philosophical issues at stake that transcend the particular

analysis of the particular phenomenon under discussion. And invariably, Chomsky's position leads to the conclusion that the human mind must be more highly structured than had been heretofore believed. Consider again his debate with generative semantics. This framework took what it described as an 'abstract' view of syntax, in that it attempted to ground syntax in semantics. But Chomsky argued that generative semantics was at the root *anti*abstractionist, since the effect of its reductionist program was to derive unobservable syntactic structure from more accessible semantic structure. To this program, Chomsky counterposed and defended at length a view of syntax populated with null elements, abstract structural relations, and complex constraints, none of which have any direct semantic analogue. Since there is no way that the principles of syntax making use of these syntactic elements could have been learned from exposure to the environment (as, at least in principle, semantic constructs might be), the conclusion follows that the language faculty—i.e., the linguistic aspect of the human mind—must be innately endowed with a complex structure.

The more recent opposition to Chomsky's views of syntax have taken the (seemingly) opposite tack from that of generative semantics. Models such as 'generalized phrase structure grammar' and 'lexical functional grammar' have tended to downplay the need for abstract principles and constraints, arguing that syntactic generalizations can be stated to a much greater degree on surface structure than Chomsky has been wont to believe (see *Generalized Phrase Structure Grammar*; *Lexical Functional Grammar*). Again, in combating the claims of these rival models, Chomsky makes it clear that more is at stake than the particular formulation of some particular principle. Rather, he sees these models as challenging the view of mind that he has developed over the last few decades.

Chomsky's methodology has always been to focus on the broad picture at the expense of working out fine analytic details. In one sense, this is no more than an exemplification of the 'hypothetico–deductive' method of scientific reasoning. As counterposed to the inductive method, which starts from an observed generalization and proceeds to a law, the hypothetico–deductive method begins with a law, derives conclusions from that law, and then matches those conclusions against observed reality. To give a concrete example, a hypothesized universal constraint, proposed on the basis of evidence from one language (or a small number of languages), might lead the investigator to make predictions about the syntactic behavior of some other language, which can then be tested empirically.

By 1980, Chomsky had begun to refer to his variant of the hypothetico–deductive method as the 'Galilean style' of theory construction, a style that carries this method one step farther in the domain of abstractness.

Just as Galileo sought out broad principles governing nature, principles 'falsified' at every turn by a myriad of observable phenomena, Chomsky too has attempted to put forward sweeping generalizations about the structure of the language faculty, ignoring, or postponing the discussion of linguistic phenomena that seem to counterexemplify them. This has led Chomsky to receive many outraged attacks, ranging from mild charges of irresponsibility to the data to the more serious one of being an 'idealist,' rather than a responsible scientist.

Chomsky has dealt with these criticisms in a number of ways. First, he has replied that the 'modular' approach to grammar that he has increasingly espoused allows observed complexity to be derived from the interaction of the general systems that the Galilean style led him to posit. That is, he maintains that complex linguistic phenomena can be explained in terms of the interaction of the autonomous grammatical system with other systems involved in giving language its overall character, such as those based in physiology, cognition, and social interaction.

The modular conception of language, as Chomsky and others have noted, has received independent support from many diverse areas of investigation in recent years, in particular from studies of language acquisition, language–brain relationships, language processing, and language variation. For a summary of some of the most important evidence to that effect, see Newmeyer (1983).

The central principle of Chomsky's more recent approaches to syntax, from the 'government binding theory' (Chomsky 1981) to the 'minimalist program' (Chomsky 1996), is that the internal structure of the grammar is modular as well. That is, syntactic complexity results from the interaction of grammatical subsystems, each characterizable in terms of its own set of general principles. The central goal of syntactic theory thus becomes to identify such systems and characterize the degree to which they may vary from language to language (i.e., the extent to which they may be 'parametrized').

The modular approach to explanation, then, illustrates the internal logic of Chomsky's approach. From an approach to the methodology of science, he derives a linguistic methodology that focuses on broad generalizations at the expense of handling at the outset any number of detailed facts. These broad generalizations bolster his theory of mind, since they tend to be so abstract that they could not have been learned inductively. As a final step in the chain, the broad generalizations, in mutual interaction, do in fact account for a considerable portion of the empirical data.

In sum, Chomsky has moved to a position in which the study of the language faculty, the repository of what he has come to call 'I-language' (i.e., internalized language), has reached a depth of abstractness unprecedented in the development of the theory of generative grammar. But Chomsky considers himself first and foremost an empirical scientist, not (merely) a speculative philosopher. As he would be the first to acknowledge, the philosophical system upon which his approach to linguistic analysis is based will stand or fall depending on the depth of insight attained on the nature of the grammatical processes at work in the 5,000-odd languages of the world.

Bibliography

Bloomfield L 1933 *Language*. Holt, Rinehart, and Winston, New York
Chomsky N 1957 *Syntactic Structures*. Mouton, The Hague
Chomsky N 1959 Review of B F Skinner's *Verbal Behavior*. *Lg* **35(1)**: 26–58
Chomsky N 1964 *Current Issues in Linguistic Theory*. Mouton, The Hague
Chomsky N 1965 *Aspects of the Theory of Syntax*. MIT Press, Cambridge, MA
Chomsky N 1972 *Language and Mind*. Harcourt Brace Jovanovich, New York
Chomsky N 1975a *The Logical Structure of Linguistic Theory*. Plenum, New York
Chomsky N 1975b *Reflections on Language*. Pantheon, New York
Chomsky N 1979 *Language and Responsibility*. Harvester Press, Sussex
Chomsky N 1980 *Rules and Representations*. Blackwell, Oxford
Chomsky N 1981 *Lectures on Government and Binding*. Foris, Dordrecht
Chomsky N 1986 *Knowledge of Language*. Praeger, New York
Chomsky N 1996 *The Minimalist Program*. MIT Press, Cambridge, MA
D'Agostino F 1986 *Chomsky's System of Ideas*. Clarendon Press, Oxford
Dowty D R, Wall R E, Peters S 1981 *Introduction to Montague Semantics*. Reidel, Dordrecht
Harman G 1974 *On Noam Chomsky: Critical Essays*. Anchor Press, New York
Hempel C G 1965 *Aspects of Scientific Explanation*. Free Press, New York
Hook S (ed.) 1969 *Language and Philosophy*. New York University Press, New York
Hull C L 1943 *Principles of Behavior*. Appleton-Century-Crofts, New York
Katz J J, Fodor J A 1963 The structure of a semantic theory. *Lg* **39**: 170–210
Kripke S A 1982 *Wittgenstein on Rules and Private Language*. Blackwell, Oxford
Lees R B 1957 Review of N Chomsky, *Syntactic Structures*. *Lg* **33(14)**: 375–404
McCawley J D 1976 *Grammar and Meaning*. Academic Press, New York
Newmeyer F J 1983 *Grammatical Theory*. University of Chicago Press, Chicago, IL
Newmeyer F J 1986 *Linguistic Theory in America*. Academic Press, New York
Skinner B F 1957 *Verbal Behavior*. Appleton-Century-Crofts, New York

Cognitive Grammar
Ronald W. Langacker

'Cognitive grammar' (originally called 'space grammar') is a highly innovative theory of linguistic structure that has been developed and progressively articulated since 1976. In stark contrast to modular approaches, it regards language as an integral facet of cognition, and grammar as being inherently meaningful. It presupposes a 'conceptualist' account of linguistic semantics that properly recognizes our capacity for construing the same conceived situation in alternate ways. With an appropriate view of meaning, all grammatical elements are reasonably attributed some kind of conceptual import. Grammar is thus considered 'symbolic' in nature: it reduces to the structuring and symbolization of conceptual content.

1. Linguistic Organization

The ultimate goal of linguistic research is to characterize language as a cognitive entity. As envisaged in cognitive grammar, linguistic structure ultimately reduces to recurrent patterns of neurological activity, and owing to its multifaceted complexity, a language is more aptly likened metaphorically to a biological organism than to a computer program or a logical deductive system. Thus it is not presumed that any single formalism can capture all aspects of a given phenomenon, or that any particular notation translates directly into specific psychological claims. The various notations and descriptive formats devised in cognitive grammar are meant to be precise within the limits of our understanding and revelatory for particular descriptive and analytical purposes. They do not however constitute a strict or uniquely privileged formalization, nor is the expectation of such a formalism considered appropriate.

To the extent that a pattern of neurological activity is 'entrenched' and readily elicited as a pre-established whole, it is referred to as a 'unit.' Linguistic knowledge or ability (i.e., a speaker's grasp of linguistic convention) comprises a vast array of such units, which is structured in the sense that units participate in excitatory and inhibitory relationships, and that some units include others as components. This knowledge—the 'internal grammar'—is not conceived as a generative or constructive device. The function of linguistic units is rather to serve as templates for the 'categorization' of expressions. An expression is simultaneously categorized by a multitude of units, each of which corresponds to a particular aspect of its structure and represents a constraint on its possible well-formedness (conventionality). Units compete for activation and the privilege of categorization on the basis of entrenchment and their degree of overlap with the target expression.

Cognitive grammar imposes severe limitations on the kinds of units ascribable to a linguistic system. On the one hand, it posits only (a) semantic units, (b) phonological units, and (c) symbolic units (in which semantic and phonological units are linked by symbolic relationships). This is the bare minimum needed to accommodate the basic semiological function of language, namely the symbolization of conceptualizations by means of phonological sequences. Symbolic units are held sufficient for the description of lexicon, morphology, and syntax, which form a continuum (rather than discrete components). On the other hand, cognitive grammar observes the 'content requirement,' which restricts linguistic units to (a) semantic, phonological, and symbolic structures that occur overtly as (parts of) expressions, (b) 'schematizations' of permitted structures, and (c) 'categorizing relationships' between permitted structures (including 'instantiation' of a schema and 'extension' from a prototype). By virtue of these restrictions, the theory achieves naturalness, conceptual unification, and theoretical austerity.

2. Semantic Structure

Cognitive grammar maintains that grammatical structure is 'symbolic' in nature, being fully describable in terms of symbolic links between semantic and phonological structures. The viability of this conception of grammar depends on a particular view of linguistic semantics.

2.1 Basic Tenets

Cognitive semantics rests on several fundamental notions. First, meaning is not identified with truth conditions, but with 'mental experience' or 'conceptualization' in the broadest sense of that term. Included are novel conceptions (as well as established concepts), all facets of sensorimotor experience, and cognizance of the social, linguistic, and cultural context. Second, a linguistic category is typically 'complex': its adequate description requires not just a single structure, but a set of structures linked by relationships of instantiation and extension to form a network. As a special case of this phenomenon, lexical items are typically 'polysemous.' A lexeme's meaning comprises a network of related senses, some being schematic relative to others, and some constituting extensions vis-à-vis more prototypical values. Third, linguistic semantics is 'encyclopedic' in scope. The meaning of a lexical item (even a single sense) cannot in general be captured by a limited, dictionary-type definition. Everything we know about an entity can in principle be regarded as contributing to the meaning of an expression that designates it, even though certain specifications are far more central and linguistically important than others. One cannot motivate any sharp distinction (only one of degree) between semantics and pragmatics, or between 'linguistic' and 'extralinguistic' knowledge. Finally, an expression's meaning does not consist solely in the conceptual content it evokes (let alone in truth conditions or the objective situation it describes)—equally significant is how that content is 'construed.' Two expressions may invoke the same conceptual content yet differ semantically by virtue of the construals they impose.

2.2 Construal

Numerous aspects of construal have been identified. They are conveniently grouped under several broad rubrics: specificity, scope, background, perspective, and prominence.

We have the capacity to conceive an entity or situation at varying levels of specificity and detail, as witnessed by such hierarchies as *thing > creature > insect > fly > fruit fly*. Each term in the hierarchy is 'schematic' for (and 'elaborated' by) the one that follows, which characterizes the designated entity with greater precision (finer resolution).

An expression's 'scope' comprises the full array of conceptual content that it specifically evokes and relies upon for its characterization. The term 'lid,' for instance, evokes the schematic conception of a container, as well as the notion of one entity covering another. A conception of any type or any degree of complexity is capable of being invoked as part of an expression's meaning. Numerous conceptions—called 'cognitive domains'—typically figure in the meaning of a given expression, which may evoke them in a flexible and open-ended manner (as determined by context). Hence the starting point for semantic description is not a set of semantic features or conceptual primitives, but rather an appropriate array of integrated conceptions, among them higher-order structures representing any level of conceptual organization. At the lowest level, presumably, are cognitively irreducible 'basic domains' such as space, time, and the domains associated with the various senses (e.g., color space).

Another aspect of construal is our ability to conceive of one structure against the 'background' provided by another. Categorization is perhaps the most fundamental and pervasive manifestation of this ability. Another is the relationship between the source and target domains of a metaphor. Words like *even*, *only*, *many*, *few*, *more*, and *less* compare an actual value to some norm or expectation, and the contrast between the truth-functionally equivalent *half-empty* and *half-full* is well known. More generally, such phenomena as presupposition, anaphora, and the given/new distinction all involve construal against a certain kind of background.

Perspective subsumes such factors as *vantage point*, *orientation*, and the *subjectivity* or *objectivity* with which an entity is construed. Vantage point and orientation both figure in the two interpretations of *Jack is to the left of Jill*, where Jack's position may be reckoned from either the speaker's perspective or from Jill's. By subjectivity or objectivity is meant the degree to which an entity functions asymmetrically as the 'subject' or the 'object of conception.' The conceptualizers (i.e., the speaker and addressee) are construed subjectively in *There's a mailbox across the street*, where they remain implicit as 'offstage' reference points. They construe themselves more objectively in *There's a mailbox across the street from us*.

The final aspect of construal is the relative 'prominence' accorded to the different substructures of a conception. Various kinds of prominence need to be distinguished. One is the salience that comes with objective construal and explicit mention, as in the previous example. A second type of prominence is called 'profiling': within the conception it evokes, every expression singles out some substructure as a kind of focus of attention; this substructure—the 'profile'—is the one that the expression 'designates.' For example, *hypotenuse* evokes the conception of a right-angled triangle (its scope) and profiles (designates) the side lying opposite the right angle. *Above* profiles the spatial 'relationship' between two entities. A third type of prominence pertains to the participants in a profiled relationship. One participant, termed the 'trajector,' is analyzed as the 'figure' within the profiled relationship; an additional salient entity is referred to as a 'landmark.' For instance, because *above* and *below* evoke the same conceptual content and profile the same relationship, their semantic contrast can only reside in figure/ground alignment. *X is above Y* is concerned with locating *X*, which is thus the trajector (relational figure), whereas *Y is below X* uses *X* as a landmark to specify the location of *Y*.

3. Grammatical Structure

Grammar is claimed to be 'symbolic' in nature. Only symbolic units (form–meaning pairings) are held necessary for the description of grammatical structure. Thus all valid grammatical constructs are attributed some kind of conceptual import. Rather than being autonomous in regard to semantics, grammar reduces to the structuring and symbolization of conceptual content.

3.1 Grammatical Classes

An expression's grammatical class is determined by the nature of its profile. The most fundamental distinction is between a 'nominal' and a 'relational' expression, which respectively profile a 'thing' and a 'relationship.' Both terms are defined abstractly. A thing is characterized schematically as a 'region in some domain,' where a 'region' can be established from any set of entities (e.g., the stars in a *constellation*) just by conceiving of them in relation to one another. While physical objects occupy bounded regions in space and are prototypical instances of the thing category, the schematic characterization also accommodates such entities as unbounded substances (e.g., *water*), geographical areas (*Wisconsin*), regions in abstract domains (*stanza*), collections of entities (*alphabet*), points on a scale (*F-sharp*; *30°C*), conceptual reifications (*termination*), and even the absence of some entity (*intermission*). The term 'relationship' is also broadly interpreted. It applies to any assessment of entities in relation to one another, regardless of their nature and status; in particular, they need not be distinct, salient, or individually recognized. Expressions classified as relational are therefore not limited to those (like *above*) traditionally considered two-place predicates. For instance, the adjective *blue* profiles the relationship between an object and a certain region in color space. When used as a noun, *square* profiles the region comprising a set of line segments arranged in a particular fashion (or else the area they enclose). When used as an adjective, however, it profiles the complex relationship among subparts of this geometrical figure (involving perpendicularity, equal length of sides, and so on).

Expressions that profile things include such traditional classes as noun, pronoun, and noun phrase (for which the term 'nominal' is adopted in cognitive grammar). Relational expressions subsume those traditionally recognized as adjectives, prepositions, adverbs, infinitives, participles, verbs, clauses, and full sentences. On the basis of the intrinsic complexity of their profiles, relational expressions can be divided into those which designate 'simple atemporal relations,' 'complex atemporal relations,' and 'processes.' A simple atemporal relation is one that comprises a single consistent configuration (or 'state'—hence it is also called a 'stative relation'). For example, adjectives and many prepositions have this character. A complex atemporal relation cannot be reduced to a single configuration but can only be represented as an ordered series of states. In *She walked across the field*, for instance, the preposition *across* designates a series of locative configurations defining the trajector's path with reference to the landmark. A process is a complex 'temporal' relation, i.e., one whose component states are saliently conceived as being distributed through a continuous span of time, and whose temporal evolution is viewed sequentially (rather than holistically). Verbs and finite clauses designate processes, whereas participles and infinitives impose a holistic view on the process specified by a verb stem and are thus atemporal.

3.2 Rules and Constructions

Grammar consists of patterns for combining simpler symbolic structures into symbolic structures of progressively greater complexity. A symbolically complex expression, e.g., *cracked*, represents a 'grammatical construction' wherein two 'component structures' (*crack* and *-ed*) are 'integrated' to form a 'composite structure.' Such integration, both phonological and semantic, is effected by 'correspondences' established between subparts of the component expressions, and by the superimposition of corresponding entities. Typically, one component structure corresponds to, and serves to 'elaborate,' a schematic substructure within the other. Thus *-ed*, being a suffix, makes schematic phonological reference to a stem, which *crack* elaborates to yield *cracked*. Semantically, the adjectival sense of the past participial morpheme profiles the final, resultant state of a schematically characterized process, which corresponds to the specific process profiled by *crack*. By superimposing the corresponding processes, and adopting the profiling of the participial morpheme, one obtains the composite semantic structure of *cracked*, which profiles a stative relation identified as the final state of *crack*.

It is usual for the composite structure to inherit its profiling from one of the component structures, which thereby constitutes the construction's 'head.' The suffix *-ed* is thus the head within the participial construction *cracked*. A component that elaborates the head is a 'complement,' hence *crack* is a complement of *-ed* by virtue of elaborating the schematic process it invokes. Conversely, a component that the head elaborates is a 'modifier.' In *blue square*, for instance, *blue* modifies *square* because the latter—the head—elaborates *blue*'s schematic trajector (the entity located in the blue region of color space).

Grammatical rules take the form of schematized constructions. A 'constructional schema' is a symbolically complex structure whose internal organization is exactly analogous to that of a set of constructions (complex expressions), but which abstracts away from their points of divergence to reveal their schematic commonality. For instance, the rule for adjective + noun combinations in English is a symbolic structure parallel to *blue square*, *cracked sidewalk*, *playful kitten*, etc., except that the adjective and noun are schematic rather than specific: semantically, the constructional schema specifies that the trajector of the adjective corresponds to the profile of the noun, which lends its profile to the composite structure; phonologically, it specifies that the adjective directly precedes the noun as a separate word. A constructional schema may be characterized at any appropriate level of abstraction, and represents the conventionality of a particular pattern of integration. It is available for the categorization of novel complex expressions and can also be thought of as a template used in their assembly.

3.3 Other Grammatical Elements

The foregoing remarks indicate that grammatical classes, rules, and such notions as head, complement, and modifier can all be characterized in terms of configurations of symbolic structures. The same is true of other grammatical elements. For instance, a 'nominal' (noun phrase) profiles a thing and further incorporates a specification of its relationship to the 'ground' (i.e., the speech event and its participants) with respect to fundamental, 'epistemic' cognitive domains; demonstratives, articles, and certain quantifiers serve this function in English. Similarly, a 'finite clause' profiles a process grounded (in the case of English) by tense and the modals. A 'subject' can then be characterized as a nominal which elaborates the trajector of a process profiled at the clausal level of organization, and a 'direct object' as a nominal that elaborates its primary landmark.

Grammatical markers are all attributed semantic values, often quite schematic. For example, the derivational morpheme *-er* (as in *complainer*) profiles a thing characterized only as the trajector of a schematic process; like most derivational morphemes, it is semantically schematic for the class it derives, its primary semantic value residing in the profile it imposes on the specific conceptual content provided by the stem it combines with. Besides schematicity, factors considered compatible with a grammatical marker's meaningfulness include semantic overlap with other elements (e.g., redundant marking, as in agreement), the lack of any option (as in government), and failure to exhibit a single sense in all its uses (polysemy being characteristic of both lexical and grammatical elements—e.g., *-ed* has distinct but related meanings in its adjectival, perfect, and passive uses).

4. Assessment and Outlook

Cognitive grammar has been revealingly applied to a steadily widening array of phenomena in a diverse set of languages. It is rapidly being established as a viable model of language structure, and in view of the restrictiveness and conceptual unification it achieves, it merits serious attention from linguistic theorists. It is fully compatible with 'functional' approaches to linguistic structure, which help explain why certain of the structures it permits have the status of prototypes, or represent language universals or universal tendencies. It also has a natural affinity to 'connectionist' (or 'parallel distributed processing') models of cognition, both because the distinction between rules and data is only one of degree, and also because grammatical structure reduces to form–meaning pairings. The possibility of achieving this reduction has extensive implications for language acquisition, models of language processing, and our conception of the human mind.

Bibliography

Haiman J 1980 Dictionaries and encyclopedias. *Lingua* **50**: 329–57

Lakoff G 1987 *Women, Fire, and Dangerous Things: What Categories Reveal about the Mind*. University of Chicago Press, Chicago, IL

Langacker R W 1986 An introduction to cognitive grammar. *Cognitive Science* **10**: 1–40

Langacker R W 1987a *Foundations of Cognitive Grammar. Vol. 1: Theoretical Prerequisites*. Stanford University Press, Stanford, California

Langacker R W 1987b Nouns and verbs. *Lg* **63**: 53–94

Langacker R W 1988 Autonomy, agreement, and cognitive grammar. In: Brentari D, et al. (eds.) *Agreement in Grammatical Theory*. Chicago Linguistic Society, Chicago, IL

Langacker R W 1990a *Concept, Image, and Symbol: The Cognitive Basis of Grammar*. Mouton de Gruyter, Berlin

Langacker R W 1990b Subjectification. *CognL* **1**: 5–38

Langacker R W 1991 *Foundations of Cognitive Grammar. Vol. 2: Descriptive Application*. Stanford University Press, Stanford, CA

Rudzka-Ostyn B (ed.) 1988 *Topics in Cognitive Linguistics*. Benjamins, Amsterdam

Constituent Structure

P. Jacobson

It has been widely claimed that a sentence of a natural language is not just a sequence of words, but that this sequence also has a structure—generally called the constituent structure of the sentence. After first developing this notion in a somewhat informal and intuitive way, this article turns to a variety of evidence for this claim. But while it is quite clear that a sentence has some kind of structure, there are several open questions and controversies surrounding the precise nature of this structure; some different (although closely related) approaches to sentence structure will be considered. The initial remarks will be developed using the assumptions and terminology of generative grammar, but most of the basic observations concerning constituent structure hold in other views of grammar as well. Indeed, the notion of constituent structure was first made explicit in works like Bloomfield (1933), Harris (1946), and Wells (1947), all of which predate generative grammar. The bulk of this article uses English and English examples to illustrate the points, turning briefly in the final section to the relevance of this notion for languages which are typologically quite distinct from English.

1. The Notion of Constituent Structure

The aim of this section is not to motivate the claim that sentences have a structure, but rather to present the basic idea and terminology as background for the remaining discussion. Thus, consider an English sentence like (1):

Someone who knows everyone in the room said that (1)
Tom hates Bill.

In this sentence, the sequence *someone who knows everyone in the room* forms a unit; the sequence *everyone in the room* forms a unit within the larger unit *someone who knows everyone in the room*; the sequence *Tom hates Bill* forms another unit, and so forth. Each such unit is called a constituent. Since a single constituent such as *everyone in the room* can occur within a larger constituent (here, *someone who knows everyone in the room*), the entire sentence has a hierarchical structure. Moreover, expressions like *Tom, Bill, someone, someone who knows everyone in the room, everyone, everyone in the room*, and *the room* are all units of the same type. What this means is that, roughly speaking, each of these could be substituted for any of the others and still yield a sentence, as in, for example, *Tom said that Bill hates everyone in the room*. Of course, some of these substitutions result in rather strange sentences (as in *The room said that Tom hates Bill*), but this sentence arguably does not violate any principle of English syntax, being strange only by virtue of facts about the world. One could, in fact, imagine a situation where this sentence made sense.

Thus the constituent structure of a sentence like (1) can be represented either as a bracketed structure shown below in (2) or as a tree as in (3). These two representations are merely different graphical conventions to represent the same information; in this article, both kinds of representations are used according to which is more convenient for the purpose at hand. Such representations both show the hierarchical structure and provide names for each constituent. The names themselves are arbitrary; the important point is simply that any two constituents of the same type will have the same name. Here, these constituents are labeled with names which are both mnemonic and relatively standard; the abbreviations in the representations in examples (2)–(4) can be read as follows: S = Sentence; NP = Noun Phrase; VP = Verb Phrase; PP = Prepositional Phrase; R = Relative Clause; CP = Complementizer Phrase (the symbol S′ is also often used here); N = noun; Det = Determiner; C = Complementizer; P = Preposition. Moreover, while words like *die, kill, dash, say*, etc. are often all labeled V (for verb), these actually have somewhat different distributions: *die* is intransitive and occurs without any object; *kill* must be followed by an NP; *dash* must be followed by a PP; and *say* takes a sentential (or CP) object. Accordingly, different names are provided for these: V_1 will refer to intransitive verbs like *die*, V_2 to ordinary transitive verbs like *kill*, V_3 to verbs like *dash*, V_4 to verbs like *say* and *hope*, and so forth.

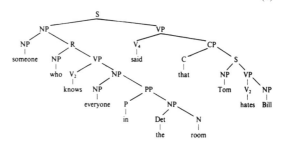

(2)

(3)

It should be noted that many of the details of these representations are unclear or controversial, but the aim here is simply to illustrate the basic notions rather than to justify these particular representations.

Before continuing, some terminology concerning trees will be useful. A tree is a sequence of points or nodes; in the trees used to represent constituent structure, each node has a label (such as NP, VP, etc.). A node A dominates a node B if there is a downward sequence of lines connecting A to B. (Under some definitions of 'dominates,' each node dominates itself; for convenience, 'dominates' is defined here in such a way that no node dominates itself.) For example, in the tree in (4), the node labeled VP dominates the nodes labeled V_3, PP, P, and the 'lowest' NP node:

(4)

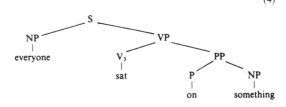

The words themselves (also called the terminal elements) are also considered labels of nodes, and hence the node labeled VP in the tree in (4) also dominates the nodes labeled *sat, on*, and *something*. For expository ease, a node is henceforth referred to by the name of its label. A node A immediately dominates a node B if and only if A dominates B and there is no node C such that A dominates C and C dominates B. Consider any sequence of words in a sentence. If there is some node A which dominates each word in that sequence and no other words, then that sequence forms a constituent. Thus, in (4), the whole sentence is a constituent; the sequence *sat on something* is a constituent; *on something* is a constituent, etc. However, *sat on* is not, for every node dominating these words dominates other words as well.

So far, only constituents of the whole sentence have been considered. However, since the constituent structure is a hierarchical structure, the constituents of smaller units can be considered as well. Thus, *on something* is a constituent of the whole S, but it is also a constituent of the VP *sat on something*. If a sequence of words *x* is a constituent of some larger sequence *y*, and if there is no other sequence *z* such that *x* is a constituent of *z* and *z* is a constituent of *y*, then *x* is an immediate constituent of *y*. Turning again to (4), this means that the immediate constituents of S are *everyone* and *sat on something*; the immediate constituents of *sat on something* are *sat* and *on something*, and the immediate constituents of *on something* are *on* and *something*.

2. Motivation

2.1 Distributional Considerations

The fundamental motivation for the notion of constituent structure was hinted at above: this centers on distributional facts. (Wells (1947) provides a classic and thorough discussion of this, although his discussion is phrased in somewhat different terminology from that adopted here; see also Harris (1946).) The basic idea is perhaps easiest to illustrate with an artificial 'language.' One way to view a language is as a set of sentences, and so one can create a mini-'language' whose 'words' are *a*, *b*, *c*, *d*, and *e*, and whose 'sentences' are only the following sequences of 'words': *abcab, adcab, edcab, ddecab, abcad, adcad, edcad, ddecad, abced, adced, edced, ddeced, abcdde, adcdde, edcdde, ddecdde*. Call this language L_1. L_1 is, of course, not really analogous to a natural language in that it has only 16 sentences, but it will nonetheless serve to illustrate several points.

Consider how one could describe the sentences of this language. One way is simply to list them. But in fact there are simpler ways to characterize these 16 sentences. Note first that each sentence contains a *c*. Note further that immediately before the *c* can go any of the sequences: *ab, ad, ed, dde*, while immediately following the *c* can go any of the sequences *ab, ad, ed, dde*. The interesting point, then, is that what can precede the *c* and what can follow it is the same set of sequences. This can be described by creating an arbitrary name for this set—call it A—and by stating that the strings of this language consist of an expression drawn from the set A followed by *c* followed by an expression drawn from the set A. To put this in slightly different terms, one can posit the existence of a grammatical category A, and specify that the sentences of this language consist of an expression of category A, followed by *c*, followed by an expression of category A. To complete the description, one specifies that the expressions of category A are the sequences *ab, ad, ed,* and *dde*.

Before returning to natural languages, the notion of phrase structure rules will be discussed briefly, for the distributional facts which motivate the notion of constituent structure are intimately tied up with this notion. Much of modern grammatical theory (particularly within the tradition of generative grammar) treats a grammar of a language as a set of rules to predict explicitly which sequences of words are or are not sentences of the language. Among the types of rules which have been most studied are what are known as 'context-free phrase structure rules' (referred to hereafter simply as phrase structure rules), and many grammatical theories posit that the grammars of natural languages contain such rules. The description of L_1 developed above will serve to illustrate the general concept. This description can be seen as a grammar which contains five rules. These rules are stated in prose in the left-hand columns in (5), and each prose description is rewritten in the right-hand column using the standard notation for phrase structure rules (again, the information on the left and on the right is exactly the same; these are merely different notations for the same thing). These rules need not 'apply' in any particular order; they are merely static statements which taken together define the set of sentences of L_1. The numbering on rules is for expository purposes only.

(i) S (a sentence) may consist of A followed by c (5)
followed by A $\qquad$ $S \rightarrow A\,c\,A$
(ii) A may consist of ab $\qquad$ $A \rightarrow ab$
(iii) A may consist of ad $\qquad$ $A \rightarrow ad$
(iv) A may consist of ed $\qquad$ $A \rightarrow ed$
(v) A may consist of dde $\qquad$ $A \rightarrow dde$

(A set of rules such as that in (ii)–(v) can be abbreviated as a single rule schema as follows: A → ab|ad|ed|dde.)

Given a grammar with phrase structure rules, a tree (or the equivalent labeled bracketed representation) is a representation of how the rules of the grammar specify the sentence as well-formed. Continuing to use L_1 for illustration, the sentence *abcad* is well-formed according to (5) because it can be analyzed in the way shown in $[_S[_A ab]\ c[_A ad]]$. Thus *ab* is a constituent of this sentence according to the rules in (5). In other words, the constituent structure of any sentence is a byproduct of the rule system; a sequence *x* forms a constituent in some sentence according to some grammar G if the rules of G provide an analysis of that sentence according to which *x* is an expression of some grammatical category. It should be further noted that a given phrase structure grammar might provide more than one structure for a given sentence. Consider, for example, a grammar with the rules: $S \rightarrow A\,c\,A$ and $A \rightarrow ac|acc|ca|a$. This grammar assigns two different structures to the sentence *accca*: $[_S[_A acc]c[_A a]]$ and $[_S[_A ac]c[_A ca]]$.

The motivation for positing constituent structure for natural language is quite parallel to the reasoning discussed above in conjunction with the grammar in (5). But before applying this to a natural language such as English, there is one further assumption underlying most treatments of constituent structure which should be made explicit. In the artificial language L_1, the simplest set of rules to describe the sentences of this language is the grammar in (5). There are, however, other set of rules (or grammars) which describe the same language. For example, one grammar for L_1 specifies that a sentence of L consists of an A followed by *c* followed by a B, where A can be *ab*, *ad*, *ed*, or *dde*, and B can be *ab*, *ad*, *ed*, or *dde*. Since L_1 is not a natural object, there is no sense in which the grammar in (5) is the 'correct' one—it is merely the simplest. Natural language is, however, a somewhat different matter. While here, too, there might be several different rule systems which yield the same set of sentences, it is generally assumed that only one of these is the correct rule system. Underlying the claim that one grammar is correct is the assumption (made explicit within generative grammar) that a grammar is a set of rules which speakers actually 'know' (in some unconscious way) and which allows them to judge certain sequences of words as well-formed sentences of the language. In this view, the correct grammar is the one which is a (reasonably) close model of a speaker's actual mental representation of the linguistic system. When two different grammars both describe the same language, it is obviously very difficult to determine which is correct. But a working principle subscribed to in most work within linguistic theory is that the simplest grammar is the correct one. In view of this, the claim that some sequence of words within a sentence forms a constituent amounts to the claim that the simplest set of rules to describe the language treats this sequence as a unit.

This principle can be illustrated by considering a portion of English. Consider, for example, sentences of the form *x resembled y*, where *x* and *y* are any sequences of words which can be substituted in here to yield a well-formed sentence. A moment's reflection reveals that there is a large set of sequences which can occur in the position marked *x*, and that a large set can occur in the position marked *y*. What is particularly striking is the fact that these two sets are the same. To give just a few examples, note that all of the following are well-formed sentences: *The man resembles the rock*; *The man resembles the boat*; *The man resembles the woman*; *The rock resembles the man*; *The boat resembles the man*; *The woman resembles the man*; *The rock resembles the woman*. Moreover, this is also exactly the set of expressions which can follow a preposition, as in, for example, *The man sat on the rock*; *The man sat on the boat*; *The man sat on the woman*. Hence the simplest grammar for English will contain rules to define a set of well-formed noun phrases (NPs), and will specify that an NP may precede a verb like *resemble*, may follow a verb like *resemble*, or may follow a preposition. Note too that NPs themselves can be complex and can contain other NPs, as in *the front of the rock*, *the front of the man*, etc. Putting together these various observations, then, it is reasonable to hypothesize that English grammar contains,

among others, the phrase structure rules shown in (6) (the motivation for positing a VP constituent is discussed below):

$$
\begin{array}{llll}
\text{(i)} & \text{S} \to \text{NP VP} & \text{(viii)} & \text{Det} \to \text{the }|\text{a}|\text{every}| \ldots \quad (6) \\
\text{(ii)} & \text{NP} \to \text{Det N} & \text{(ix)} & \text{N} \to \text{woman}|\text{man}|\text{rock}| \ldots \\
\text{(iii)} & \text{NP} \to \text{NP PP} & \text{(x)} & V_1 \to \text{die}|\text{walk}| \ldots \\
\text{(iv)} & \text{PP} \to \text{P NP} & \text{(xi)} & V_2 \to \text{resemble}|\text{kill}| \ldots \\
\text{(v)} & \text{VP} \to V_1 & \text{(xii)} & V_3 \to \text{dash}|\text{sit}|\text{lie}| \ldots \\
\text{(vi)} & \text{VP} \to V_2 \text{ NP} & \text{(xiii)} & \text{P} \to \text{on}|\text{under}| \ldots \\
\text{(vii)} & \text{VP} \to V_3 \text{ PP} & &
\end{array}
$$

The same sort of reasoning can be used to justify some of the other details of the constituent structure shown in (3). Take, for example, the claim that *Tom hates Bill* is a constituent, and a constituent of the same type as the entire sentence. This is motivated by the fact that sequences like this can occur as full sentences in their own right, and conversely, any sequence which constitutes a well-formed declarative sentence can occur in the position following *that* in (1). Consider further the claim that *that Tom hates Bill* is a constituent (which has here been labeled CP). Again, the evidence for this comes from the fact that sequences of the form *that S* occur in a variety of positions. These can, for example, occur in subject position as in (7a), and they can also follow an NP as in (7b):

That Tom hates Bill bothered Mary. (7a)

I told Mary that Tom hates Bill. (7b)

These distributional facts can be accounted for rather simply by adding to the phrase structure rules in (6) the following:

$$
\begin{array}{llll}
\text{(xiv)} & \text{S} \to \text{CP VP} & \text{(xviii)} & \text{C} \to \text{that} \quad (8) \\
\text{(xv)} & \text{VP} \to V_4 \text{ CP} & \text{(xix)} & V_4 \to \text{say}|\text{believe}|\text{think}| \ldots \\
\text{(xvi)} & \text{VP} \to V_5 \text{ NP CP} & \text{(xx)} & V_5 \to \text{tell}|\text{persuade}| \ldots \\
\text{(xvii)} & \text{CP} \to \text{C S} & &
\end{array}
$$

Incidentally, the reader may have noticed that CP has roughly the same distribution as NP—it occurs, for example, in subject position and after certain verbs. However, while there is indeed considerable overlap in the distribution of CP and NP, their distribution is not in fact identical. For example, (9) shows that NPs occur after prepositions while CPs do not (an asterisk in front of a sequence indicates that it is not a well-formed sentence):

*John is happy about that Mary left. (9a)

John is happy about the news. (9b)

While not attempting to justify all of the other details of the structure in (3), the motivation for positing a VP constituent will be briefly mentioned. Note that there are a large number of sequences which can follow subjects; some of these are illustrated by the italicized material in (10):

Mary *walked*. (10a)

Mary *killed the cow*. (10b)

Mary *dashed into the house.* (10c)

Mary *said that Bill left.* (10d)

Mary *told Tom that Bill left.* (10e)

But exactly this same set occurs in a variety of other environments. For example, this is exactly the same set that can follow *Sue helped Mary* in sentences like those in (11):

Sue helped Mary *walk.* (11a)

Sue helped Mary *kill the cow.* (11b)

Sue helped Mary *dash into the house.* (11c)

Sue helped Mary *say that Bill left.* (11d)

Sue helped Mary *tell Tom that Bill left.* (11e)

(The fact that the verbal morphology is slightly different from in the examples in (10) has been ignored here.)

Suppose that the italicized sequences in (10) were not treated as constituents. This would mean that English does not contain the phrase structure rules shown above in (i), (v), (vi), (vii), (xv), and (xvi). Rather, in place of these it would contain the following rules: $S \rightarrow NP\,V_1$; $S \rightarrow NP\,V_2\,NP$; $S \rightarrow NP\,V_3\,PP$; $S \rightarrow NP\,V_4\,CP$; $S \rightarrow NP\,V_5\,NP\,CP$. But although these rules account for the sentences in (10), they do not account for those in (11). Since these are also well-formed sentences, English grammar would need several additional rules: $S \rightarrow NP\,V_6\,NP\,V_1$; $S \rightarrow NP\,V_6\,NP\,V_2\,NP$; $S \rightarrow NP\,V_6\,NP\,V_3\,PP$; $S \rightarrow NP\,V_6\,NP\,V_4\,CP$; $S \rightarrow NP\,V_6\,NP\,V_5\,NP\,CP$; $V_6 \rightarrow$ *help|make|*, *etc.* Moreover, there are even longer sentences like (12), and so yet more rules would be needed:

Sue helped Mary help Tom walk. (12a)

Sue helped Mary help Tom kill the cow. (12b)

But under the hypothesis that English grammar contains a category VP, there is a much simpler set of rules available to account for all of these sentences. Assume, then, that (i), (v), (vi), (vii), (xv), and (xvi) are among the phrase structure rules of English. All of the sentences in (11) and (12) can be accounted for with just two additional rules: (xxi) $VP \rightarrow V_6\,NP\,VP$, and (xxii) $V_6 \rightarrow$ *help|make|* etc.

2.2 Semantic Considerations

While the major motivation for constituent structure centers on distributional facts, the intuition that certain phrases form a unit also receives some confirmation from semantic considerations. Consider a sentence like (13):

Everyone who ate the beef which was raw said (13)
that Bill left.

Distributional evidence indicates that *everyone who ate the beef which was raw* is a single constituent (an NP), as is *the beef which was raw.* Moreover, in terms of the meaning, it is clear that *who ate the beef which was raw* 'goes with' or modifies *everyone* and not *said.* By the same token, *which was raw* goes with *the beef* (or, perhaps, *beef*) and not with *said.* In view of this, there is a close correspondence between the syntactic constituents and the semantic units. Along these lines, *that Bill left* seems to form a meaningful unit in a way in which, for example, *said that Bill* does not (although see Sect. 3.4), and the distributional evidence discussed above similarly shows that *that Bill left* is a constituent.

That syntactic constituents generally also behave as semantic units is not surprising if a tree not only represents the way in which the rules of the grammar work so as to predict that a sentence is well-formed, but also represents the way in which the meanings of words are put together to give the meanings of larger expressions. Put differently, one hypothesis regarding the interaction of syntax and semantics is that each phrase structure rule in the grammar is coupled with a semantic rule specifying how the meanings of the immediate constituents of some expression combine to give the meaning of the whole expression. Just what these semantic rules look like is beyond the scope of this article; suffice it to say that under this conception each syntactic constituent has some kind of meaning, and conversely each semantic unit should therefore be a syntactic unit.

The notion that the semantic composition of a sentence is mirrored by its constituent structure yields interesting accounts of certain ambiguous sentences. As noted in Sect. 1, phrase structure grammars have the property that a single phrase structure grammar might assign more than one constituent structure to a single sentence. In certain cases, these dual analyses correspond to distinct meanings. A classic example is a sentence like (14):

John saw the man with the binoculars. (14)

Note first that PPs can in general occur with any VP, as in (15a, b), and (15c) shows that more than one PP can occur here:

John killed Bill with a knife. (15a)

John sang in the park. (15b)

John killed Bill with a knife in the park on (15c)
Tuesday.

To account for this, assume that in addition to the rules discussed so far, English grammar also contains a rule (xxiii) $VP \rightarrow VP\,PP$. Assume further that the associated semantic rule says that the meaning of the PP modifies that of the VP (there is no attempt here to give a more precise definition of the notion 'modify'). Recall, however, that English grammar also contains the rule (iii): $NP \rightarrow NP\,PP$. Assume that this too has an associated semantic rule to the effect that the PP modifies the NP. Given these rules, there are two different structures for (14) (these trees show only those parts of the structure relevant for the point at hand; a triangle above some sequence indicates that that constituent has further internal structure not being shown here), as example (16) shows:

(16)

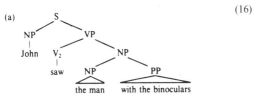

(a)

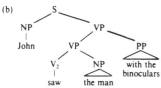

(b)

These two correspond to the two different meanings. Under one meaning, the phrase *with the binoculars* modifies *the man*, and this is represented by the tree in (16a). Under the second meaning, *with the binoculars* describes the way in which the seeing of the man took place, and this is represented by (16b).

Before leaving this, it should be noted that not every sentence with more than one structure is necessarily ambiguous; the semantic rules might be such that two different structures will have the same meaning. Take, for example, the case of sentences connected by *or*, as in *John left or Bill stayed*. Such sentences can be accounted for by a phrase structure rule (xxiv) $S \rightarrow S$ *or* S. The corresponding semantic rule states that the entire sentence denotes a proposition which is true just in case at least one of its immediate constituent sentences denotes a true proposition. Consider now a sentence like (17):

John left or Bill stayed or Mary ran. (17)

Given the rule (xxiv), (17) has two different constituent structures:

$[_S[_S[_S$ John left$]$ or $[_S$ Bill stayed$]]$ or (18a)
$[_S$ Mary ran$]]$

$[_S[_S$ John left$]$ or $[_S[_S$ Bill stayed$]$ or (18b)
$[_S$ Mary ran$]]]$

However, the semantic rule associated with (xxiv) is such that these two structures correspond to the same proposition. In either case, the entire sentence denotes a proposition which is true just in case at least one of the three sentences *John left*, *Bill stayed*, or *Mary ran* denotes a true proposition.

2.3 Additional Considerations

There are a variety of other considerations which have been used both to support the claim that sentences have a constituent structure, and as evidence for the particular structure (or structures) for any given sentence. Many of these considerations are somewhat controversial and/or yield unclear results; nonetheless, a few of these will be mentioned here.

2.3.1 Prosodic Evidence

Although, in this article, written sentences have been used as a medium for discussing English, linguistic theory generally takes the spoken language to be the primary object of description. Sentences, when spoken, have a prosodic structure—this refers to the intonation contour and pause breaks. It has often been noted that the prosodic structure of a sentence meshes—at least to some extent—with its constituent structure. To develop this claim, consider again the tree in (4). Here, there is what is called a more major constituent break between *woman* and *sat* than between *sat* and *on*; thus, a more major break is one which occurs higher in the tree.

The claim, then, is that more major constituent breaks are marked by special prosodic cues; these are often marked by longer pauses and/or rising intonation. Thus, in the spoken version of the sentence shown in (4), there will generally be a longer pause between *everyone* and *sat* than between *sat* and *on*. Or, consider again the ambiguous sentence (14). If this is spoken with a longer pause between *man* and *with* than between *saw* and *the*, then the natural interpretation is the one in which *with the binoculars* modifies *saw the man*; if the longer break is between *saw* and *the*, then the other interpretation is more natural. Hence the pause breaks are taken as cues to the syntactic structure, and the two different structures in turn reflect the two different meanings.

Unfortunately, while the above example demonstrates that there is indeed some connection between the prosodic structure and the constituent structure, this connection is certainly not absolute. For example, even with a longer pause between *man* and *with* than between *saw* and *the*, one can still understand (14) on the meaning represented in (16a), although this interpretation is less natural or less readily accessible than the reading in (16b). There are, moreover, well-known cases where the most natural prosodic structure does not correspond well with the (apparent) constituent structure. A famous case of this sort is the sentence in (19) (Chomsky and Halle 1968):

This is the cat which chased the rat which ate (19)
the cheese.

Distributional evidence of the type discussed in Sect. 2.1 leads to the hypothesis that the structure for this sentence is (20):

(20)

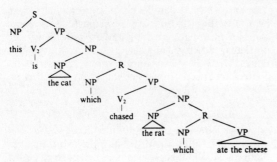

Hence, the constituent break between *is* and *the* is more major than that between *cat* and *which*. By the same token, the break between *which* and *chased* is more major than that between *chased* and the second occurrence of *the*, and the break between *rat* and the second occurrence of *which* is more major than that between *which* and *ate*. Yet the sentence is generally pronounced as shown in (21), where ‖ indicates the major pause breaks:

> This is the cat ‖ which chased the rat ‖ which ate the cheese. (21)

If the constituent structure were directly mapped onto the prosodic structure, one would expect a significant break between *is* and *cat*; but such a break is extremely unnatural.

2.3.2 Interpretation of Pronouns

Another phenomenon which is often adduced in support of the claim that sentences have a structure centers on the distribution and interpretation of pronouns. Pronouns can, in general, be understood as having the same referent as some other NP in a sentence (or in a prior sentence), as in the following:

> John said that he won. (22a)

> John knew the woman who wrote to him. (22b)

> That John lost bothered him. (23a)

> The woman who wrote to John knew him. (23b)

In all of these, *he* or *him* can be understood as referring to John; in this case, *John* and *he* or *him* are said to be coreferential. (The pronouns may, of course, also be understood in all of these as referring to someone else, and so these sentences are ambiguous.) Interestingly, a pronoun can be understood as coreferential to a nonpronominal NP even if the pronoun precedes that NP, as in (24):

> That he lost bothered John. (24a)

> The woman who wrote to him loves John. (24b)

But in some cases, this is impossible:

> He said that John won. (25a)

> He loves the woman who wrote to John. (25b)

> I made him write to the woman who loves John. (25c)

Here, *he* cannot be understood as coreferential to *John*, but must be understood as some other person.

These facts can be described by invoking the notion of the structure of the sentence. The exact conditions under which the coreferential interpretation is impossible are the subject of some controversy, but most formulations of the relevant principle make use of the structure in some way. To develop one standard account (see Reinhart 1983), two further terms concerning trees can be introduced. A branching node is a node which immediately dominates at least two other nodes; thus, in (4), S, VP, and PP are the only branching nodes. A node A c-commands a node B if and only if neither A nor B dominates the other, and the lowest branching node dominating A dominates B. So, for example, in (4) the terminal node *everyone* c-commands all of the other terminal nodes as well as the nodes VP, V_3, PP, P, and the second NP node. With this apparatus, the condition governing the interpretation of pronouns can be described thus: a pronoun may not be understood as coreferential to any nonpronominal NP which it c-commands. The reader can verify that, given the rules developed above, the pronoun in each of the sentences in (25) c-commands *John*, but it does not do so in (22)–(24). Hence, the interpretation of pronouns provides interesting support for the claim that sentences are structured sequences of words.

2.3.3 Conjunction

One additional and very interesting test phenomenon which has been used as a diagnostic for constituent structure is conjunction. Note first that there are a variety of sequences which can be conjoined in English, as in the following:

> The men and the women left. (26a)

> John saw Mary and said that Bill left. (26b)

> John believes that Mary left and that Sam came. (26c)

> John believes that Mary left and Sam came. (26d)

It has often been claimed that the correct generalization regarding conjunction is this: only constituents may conjoin with other constituents (see Chomsky 1957); the two constituents must be of the same category; and the two conjoined constituents themselves form a constituent of the same category as each of the conjuncts (see, for example, Gazdar 1981). In other words, the relevant portions of the structures for (26a) and (26b), for example, are as follows:

[NP [NP the men] and [NP the women]] left   (27a)

John [VP [VP saw Mary] and [VP said that Bill left]]   (27b)

If the above generalization is correct, then it can actually be accounted for in a simple and elegant way. Assume that the grammars of natural languages contain not just phrase structure rules but also phrase structure rule schemata, where a rule schema is an abbreviation for a set of phrase structure rules. Then English grammar can contain the rule schema (xxv) $X \rightarrow X$ and X, where X is a variable over any category. This allows NP constituents which are of the general form *NP and NP*, CP constituents of the general form *CP and CP*, etc. If, moreover, this is the only rule or rule schema introducing conjoined material, then the above generalization follows. In other words, it follows that if two sequences *x* and *y* can conjoin to form a sequence *x and y*, then *x* and *y* are each single constituents, and are constituents of the same type.

There are, however, a number of open questions surrounding the conjunction evidence as a test for constituency. First, there are some cases where apparently unlike categories can conjoin. For example, it was noted above that NP and CP do not have exactly the same distribution; yet in some cases these conjoin:

I believed [CP that Mary came] and   (28)
[NP the other strange things that I heard].

As to the claim that only constituents conjoin with other constituents, there are many well-known instances of so-called nonconstituent conjunction. Consider, for example, the sentences in (29):

John likes and thinks that Bill hates everyone   (29a)
who was here.

John likes and Bill hates Mary.   (29b)

Given the sort of evidence discussed above, there is little reason to posit that *thinks that Bill hates* is a constituent, for this kind of sequence does not occur in a variety of environments. Yet here it conjoins with the constituent *likes*. Similar remarks hold for (29b), in which the apparent nonconstituent *John likes* is conjoined with another apparent nonconstituent (*Bill hates*). This will be returned to in Sect. 3.4.

3. Refinements, Questions, and Alternative Conceptions

Having presented the basic notion of constituent structure and some of the motivation for it, some open questions surrounding this notion will now be considered by presenting some approaches to constituent structure within a variety of a different theories.

3.1 Binary Immediate Constituents

The reader may have noticed that almost all of the phrase structure rules discussed above for English provide trees in which a node immediately dominates at most two other nodes. Put differently, every constituent which contains smaller immediate constituents contains exactly two immediate constituents. In fact, almost all of the rules above are of the general form $A \rightarrow B C$, where B and C are labels for grammatical categories (called nonterminal labels), or of the form $A \rightarrow a$, where a is a single terminal; grammars with only rules of this form are called grammars in Chomsky normal form. There are a few exceptions to this; rules (xvi) and (xxi) allow a node immediately to dominate three nonterminals, and rule (v) allows a nonterminal (VP) to dominate a single nonterminal (V_1). Rule (v), however, could be reformulated as $VP \rightarrow die|walk| \ldots$ (Rules (xvi) and (xxi) are discussed below.) The rule schema in (xxv) is also an exception, but this schema can also be reformulated in such a way that a constituent like *John and Mary* contains the two immediate constituents *John* and *and Mary* (see, for example, Gazdar et al. 1985).

The fact that a constituent in English usually contains two immediate constituents was observed in much of the work in structural linguistics (see Wells (1947) for discussion). Whether or not this is an accidental fact about English grammar or follows from some more general principle regarding natural language grammars has been the subject of a certain amount of controversy, and it is interesting to note in this regard that grammars in Chomsky normal form have played a special role in the work on parsing within computational linguistics. Parsing refers to the process by which a listener (or, perhaps, a computer program) can recover the constituent structure of any sentence given the grammar for the language; if the constituent structure is indeed an indication of the semantic composition, then presumably this would be part of the process of arriving at a meaning for a sentence. Much of the work within computational linguistics, then, seeks to provide an explicit algorithm according to which a sentence can be assigned its constituent structure (or structures), and, if such models are to reflect what it is that humans actually do, then the parsing algorithm must be as efficient as possible, since humans process a sentence almost instantaneously. Interestingly, some of the well-understood algorithms for efficient parsing make use of grammars in Chomsky normal form. In other words, such grammars have been shown to lend themselves to (reasonably) efficient parsing algorithms.

3.2 Discontinuous Constituents

Section 2 developed a view of grammar according to which material which forms a single constituent must be contiguous. This is because a phrase structure rule defines a well-formed expression of some category A by specifying that it may consist of some continuous sequence of smaller expressions. Moreover, if—as suggested in Sect. 2.2—each semantic unit corresponds to a syntactic constituent, then one would expect each semantic unit to be a contiguous sequence within a sentence.

Yet there are numerous instances where what appears to be a single semantic unit is a discontinuous sequence, and such cases are often referred to as discontinuous constituents (see Pike 1943). Consider, for example, the following sentences:

Everyone who was invited arrived. (30a)

Everyone arrived who was invited. (30b)

In (30b), *who was invited* modifies *everyone*, exactly as it does in (30a). Yet, in (30b), *everyone who was invited* is not a continuous sequence.

There are many other examples of discontinuous constituents; just two others will be mentioned here. One is exemplified by what is known as the topicalization construction, shown in (31):

Beans, I like. (31)

The verb *like* is a V_2 and so normally occurs only with a following NP object; thus (32) is not a well-formed sentence:

*I like. (32)

In (31), however, *like* is not followed by an NP object, but there is an NP at the beginning of the sentence which functions as the object of *like*. Thus, here, *like ... beans* is a unit in much the same way that it is in (33), even though in (31) it is discontinuous (and in (31) the object precedes the verb):

I like beans. (33)

Finally, it was mentioned in Sect. 3.1 that rules such as (xvi) and (xxi) are unusual in that they allow for constituents with three rather than two immediate constituents. However, it has often been proposed that these rules are incorrect (see Chomsky (1957) for discussion of a related case). Rather, in a sentence like *John made Mary leave*, *made ... leave* is actually a single discontinuous constituent; hence it is a complex V_2. If this is correct, then here, too, the constituent structure is binary; the VP contains the two immediate constituents *made ... leave* and *Mary*, and *made ... leave* is a discontinuous constituent consisting also of two immediate constituents.

3.2.1 Discontinuous Constituents in Transformational Grammar

The phenomenon of discontinuous constituents is so widespread that a large portion of the research in grammatical theory since about the 1950s has been concerned with discovering the appropriate devices to account for it. The best-known approach to this phenomenon is that which is taken in transformational grammar. Although transformational grammar has undergone considerable evolution since its inception in the mid-1950s, what is presented here is what is sometimes referred to as the 'standard theory,'

developed in Chomsky (1965). Under this theory, the grammars of natural languages contain phrase structure rules of the sort discussed in Sect. 2, but there are additional rules—known as transformations—which map trees onto other trees. The phrase structure rules themselves, then, do not define the set of well-formed sentences of a language, but rather define a set of well-formed deep structures. A deep structure may be mapped onto a different tree by a transformation, and, since several transformations may apply in succession, the resulting tree may in turn be mapped onto yet another tree. A sequence of trees formed in this way is called a derivation, and the last tree in such a sequence is the surface structure. A sentence is well-formed if and only if it is the 'bottom line' (the sequence of terminal symbols) of the last tree in a well-formed derivation; a derivation is well-formed if and only if its first tree is well-formed according to the phrase structure rules and each adjacent pair satisfies the description of some transformation. It should be noted that a derivation can also consist of just a single tree—in this case, no transformation has applied, and so the deep structure and the surface structure are the same.

This can be illustrated by considering the examples in (30). In addition to the phrase structure rules developed in Sect. 2, assume that English grammar also has the rules: (xxvi) $NP \rightarrow NP\,R$ and (xxvii) $R \rightarrow NP\,VP$. These rules, combined with the other rules discussed above, will account for a sentence like (30a) and will assign it the structure in (34):

[$_S$ [$_{NP}$ [$_{NP}$ everyone] [$_R$ who was invited]]] (34)
[$_{VP}$ arrived]]

Suppose that there is a transformation which, informally stated, allows any R constituent to 'move' to the end of the sentence, where it will be attached directly under the S-node. This means that (30b) is well-formed, since (35) is a well-formed derivation.

(35)

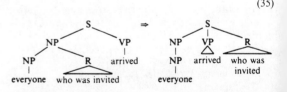

The first tree in (35) is the deep structure for both (30a) and (30b); (30a) is derived by a derivation in which no transformation applies, while (30b) involves the application of a transformation.

Thus, within transformational grammar, a 'discontinuous constituent' is a sequence of material which forms a single constituent in deep structure, but which is broken up by the application of one or more transformations. If deep structures also represent the way in which the meanings of the parts are put together to give the meaning of the whole sentence, then semantic units will be contiguous in deep structure, but need not be contiguous at surface structure. Moreover, within this theory, the application of transformations themselves is also used as a test for constituent structure. Consider the topicalized sentence (31). This can be accounted for under the assumption that the deep structure of (31) is the same as the deep structure for (33), where there is a transformation allowing any NP to 'move' to the front of the sentence. However, it is not only NPs which can front in this way—PPs and CPs may also prepose:

I often sit on the table.	(36a)
On the table, I often sit.	(36b)
I fervently believe that Mary left.	(37a)
That Mary left, I fervently believe.	(37b)

Interestingly, it appears that only single constituents may prepose (and the rule does not apply to its own output). Thus, for example, the following is bad, where an NP–CP sequence which does not form a constituent has preposed:

I told Mary that Bill left.	(38a)
*Mary that Bill left, I told.	(38b)

However, while the preposability of some sequence *x* indicates that *x* is a single constituent, constituency is not a sufficient condition for preposability. There is evidence that the italicized material in (39a) forms a single constituent, but it cannot prepose as shown in (39b). Nor can the italicized S-constituent in (40a) prepose:

I know the woman *who wrote to Mary.*	(39a)
*Who wrote to Mary, I know the woman.	(39b)
I think that *Bill left.*	(40a)
*Bill left, I think that.	(40b)

3.2.2 Other Views of Discontinuous Constituents

While transformational grammar provides perhaps the best-known account of discontinuous constituents, it is by no means the only available account of these phenomena. A number of theories provide rules which directly allow a sentence to be represented as a tree-like object with 'crossed branches'; thus the structure for a sentence like (30b) would be represented as:

(41)

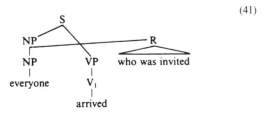

The basic idea behind rule systems which provide representations like (41) is that there are rules roughly like phrase structure rules which specify well-formed expressions in terms of smaller expressions, but these rules do not require the immediate constituents of some expression to be contiguous. Rather, they can allow pieces of smaller expressions to be interrupted by other expressions; hence the NP *everyone who was invited* in (41) can be interrupted by the VP with which it combines to form an S.

The exact formal nature of the rules which yield representations like (41) varies considerably, as such systems have been explored within a variety of theories. Hence there is no attempt to formalize these systems here; proposals along these lines may be found in Harman (1963), Bach (1979), and McCawley (1982), though McCawley derives these structures by transformational rules. There is a variety of other accounts of the phenomenon of discontinuous constituents; for an interesting sample of such approaches, see Huck and Ojeda (1987).

3.3 Alternative Conceptions

The theories considered so far all claim that the structure of a sentence contains information as to dominance relations, linear order, the category labels of each constituent, and nothing else. There are, however, some rather different views of the structure of a sentence in which the objects representing this structure contain somewhat different information from the trees or tree-like representations discussed above. Two such views are considered here (for some additional views, see *Tagmemics* and *Lexical Functional Grammar*).

3.3.1 Relational Grammar

One view rather different from those developed above is taken in relational grammar (hereafter, RG). There are a number of differences between RG and the theories developed above, and space precludes a thorough treatment of this theory here (see Perlmutter (1983) for more exhaustive discussion). The central difference concerns the status of grammatical relations like 'subject,' 'direct object,' and so forth. In the theories discussed above, such notions are not taken as basic; rather, they are usually defined in terms of the tree structure. The subject of some S, for example, is that NP (or CP) which is immediately dominated by S; the direct object is that NP immediately dominated by VP. But proponents of RG have argued that there are certain properties shared by subjects in a wide range of languages; there are other properties shared by direct objects; and such properties need to be captured by grammatical theory. Furthermore, RG argues that no definition of subject or of direct object in terms of tree structure can be given which would characterize these notions in all languages. For this reason, RG simply posits these and other grammatical relations as primitives, and the structure of a sentence thus contains the information as to what grammatical relation is held by each constituent, and various grammatical rules can refer directly to these relations.

Like transformational grammar, RG posits that a sentence has more than one level of representation. Here, though, the majority of rules do not change the tree structure but rather alter the grammatical relations of one or more constituents. Consider, for example, a passive sentence like (42):

> The book was written by John. (42)

In much of the work within transformational grammar, it is assumed that this has a deep structure which is similar to or identical to the deep structure of the corresponding active sentence (43) and that there is a transformation which moves the NP immediately following the verb (here, *the book*) into the position before the verb and postposes the deep-structure subject (here, *John*):

> John wrote the book. (43)

(In some later transformational formulations, (42) and (43) actually have somewhat different deep structures; see, for example, Chomsky (1981).) In RG, these two sentences also have the same representation at the initial level (the level known as deep structure in transformational grammar). However, in RG, the 'transformation' is not formulated so as to alter directly the linear order of the two constituents. Rather, it is what is known as a relation-changing rule, and its formulation is that a direct object becomes a subject, while the original subject takes on a new grammatical relation (called the *chômeur*). Linear order, then, is also not encoded into all levels of representation of a sentence; there would, rather, be language-particular rules mapping the final structure of a sentence into an ordered sequence. In English, these rules specify (among other things) that subjects come first, followed by the predicate, followed by the direct object, followed by the *chômeur*. The full set of structures for (42), then, can be represented as (44), where P is an abbreviation for predicate; Subj for subject; DO for direct object; and Chô for *chômeur*:

(44)

It should be pointed out that this is not quite the standard notational system adopted in RG; various modifications have been made for expository convenience, but these modifications do not affect the points at hand. What is important here is the fact that these representations on the one hand do not directly contain information as to the linear order of the constituents but, on the other hand, do contain information as to the grammatical relation of each constituent. Note, moreover, that category labels like NP or V are missing from these representations. Such information could, however, be added in without any significant change in the theory, although it has often been speculated that this information need not be directly represented but can be deduced from other properties of the representations (a related idea has been put forth within X̄-theory; see Jackendoff 1977). (Note also that the constituent structure is somewhat different from that standardly taken in accounts with phrase structure rules in that here there is nothing analogous to a VP constituent in English.)

One final and very interesting difference between the RG conception of sentence structure and the more standard notion of constituent structure concerns what can be called 'multiattachment structures.' In the standard view of constituent structure developed in Sects. 1–3.2, a node is immediately dominated by at most one other node; this again follows from the way in which phrase structure rules work. A number of different theories, however, have suggested that the correct representations for sentences allow for a case where a single constituent is 'in more than one place'— that is, it is immediately dominated by more than one node. Again, the exact nature of the rules which allow for such representations varies from theory to theory (as one example, see Engdahl 1986). Relational grammar, also makes use of multiattachment structures; in the terms of RG, this means that a single constituent can bear a grammatical relation to more than one predicate, or can bear more than one grammatical relation to a single predicate.

Consider, for example, a sentence like (45):

> John wants to win. (45)

Here, *John* is the 'understood subject' of *to win*, yet is also understood as the subject of *wants*. To account for this, RG posits a multiattachment structure at some level at which *John* is subject of both verbs. Thus, oversimplifying somewhat, (45) would be represented as (46):

(46)

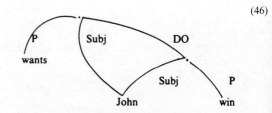

3.3.2 Word Grammar

Another rather different view of sentence structure is taken in word grammar (Hudson 1984) (a related, although somewhat different, view is to be found in Hudson 1976). Like the standard notion of constituent structure, the representation of a sentence in word grammar is a kind of hierarchical structure. However, it represents somewhat different information from the standard constituent structure trees. First, like the version of RG discussed above, constituents are not labeled as to their grammatical category. Second, not only may two or more words form a unit, but any given word may 'depend' on some other word. The intuitive idea here is that, for example, in a simple sentence the verb is central, and the NPs in the sentence depend on that verb (a related idea is embodied in the notion of head within X̄-theory; see Jackendoff 1977). Third, this theory also allows for something like multiattachment structures, in that a single word may depend on more than one other word.

To illustrate these points, consider a sentence like (47), whose representation is shown in (48); each arrow is an indication of a dependency relation:

John seems to like red books. (47)

(48)

Note that this represents some of the same information as does a standard constituent structure tree. Thus, for example, *like red books* in (48) forms a unit in the sense that it constitutes a chain of dependencies, and *red books* constitutes a dependency chain within the larger chain *like red books*. Hence this representation contains something akin to hierarchically arranged constituents. There are, however, also a number of interesting differences between this representation and a standard constituent structure tree. In the latter, *like red books* would be treated as a constituent with two immediate constituents (*like* and *red books*), but these two immediate constituents have the same status within the larger constituent. Here, however, there is an asymmetry between these two, since the structure in (48) represents the facts that *books* depends on *like*. (A similar kind of asymmetry between two immediate constituents is found in categorial grammar; see Sect. 3.4.) Moreover, grammatical categories like NP play no role in the structures of word grammar. Finally, *John* depends simultaneously on *seems*, on *to*, and on *like* (a situation which Hudson labels 'modifier sharing'). Note, then, that this is quite similar to the multiattachment structures of relational grammar.

3.4 Constituent Structure in Categorial Grammar

One of the most unorthodox views of constituent structure is that taken in certain versions of categorial grammar (hereafter, CG)—a theory which derives from the work of Ajdukiewicz (1935), Lambek (1958), Bar-Hillel (1964), and others, and which has enjoyed a resurgence of interest. (There are a number of slightly different versions of CG; just one is discussed here.) In

some sense, the view of constituent structure within CG is quite close to that discussed in Sect. 2; here, the grammar contains phrase structure rule schemata (see Sect. 2.3.3), and hence the structure of a sentence can be represented as a tree which itself is a representation of how the phrase structure rules work to specify a sentence as well-formed. Where the version of CG to be developed here differs from other accounts, though, is that any given sentence has a large number of constituent structures—some of which are quite surprising.

To develop this, first the notion of a syntactic category in CG is considered. Rather than positing a large number of categories such as NP, VP, V_2, etc., CG posits a small set of basic categories, and all other categories are functions from categories to categories. The basic idea is most easily developed by example. Consider a verb like *see*. In Sect. 2.1, this was treated as an item of category V_2 where there is a phrase structure rule $VP \rightarrow V_2\,NP$. One can, however, recast this information by viewing the syntactic category of *see* as a function which maps expressions of the category NP into expressions of the category VP; in particular, *see* combines with an NP to its right to yield a VP. Using the notation $A/_RB$ to designate the syntactic category of any expression which combines with an expression of category B to its right to yield an expression of category A, the category of *see* is $VP/_RNP$. However, this can be broken down further. A VP itself need not be viewed as a primitive category, for it can be seen as something which combines with an NP to its left to yield a S. In other words, a VP like *see Bill* maps an NP like *the women* into the S *the women see Bill*. Hence, the category so far called VP can be recast as $S/_LNP$. Thus, the category of *see* is $(S/_LNP)/_RNP$ and a simple intransitive verb like *die* is of category $S/_LNP$, while a verb like *believe* is of category $(S/_LNP)/_RCP$; *that* is of category $CP/_RS$; a preposition like *on* is of category $PP/_RNP$; etc.

Much of the information contained in phrase structure rules is 'packed into' the categories of the words. In fact, with this view of syntactic categories, the grammar can contain just a few general phrase structure rule schemata. Two of these are: (i) $A \rightarrow A/_RB\ B$ and (ii) $A \rightarrow B\ A/_LB$, for A and B variables over any category. (Note that these rules provide only for structures in which each constituent contains two immediate constituents; see Sect. 3.1.)

So far, this provides constituent structures which are much the same as in standard accounts. A sentence like *Everyone saw Bill* is well-formed because the rules provide the following analysis of this sentence: $[_S\ [_{NP}\ everyone][_{S/_LNP}[_{(S/_LNP)/_RNP}\ saw][_{NP}\ Bill]]]$. The category labels here are of course different from the labels used in Sect. 2, but the only significant difference between this structure and the more standard constituent structure is that it encodes an asymmetry between the two immediate constituents of any expression—one (the one whose category is of the form A/B) is the function, and the other (the one whose category is B) is the argument (see also the discussion of word grammar, Sect. 3.3.2).

But certain versions of CG include rule schemata in addition to those in (i) and (ii). The first pair of additional schemata (known as function composition) are: (iii) $A/_R C \rightarrow A/_R B \; B/_R C$ and (iv) $A/_L C \rightarrow B/_L C \; A/_L B$. The second pair are both nonbinary rules (these allow a single nonterminal immediately to dominate a single nonterminal) and are known as type lifting. These schemata are: (v) $B/_R(B/_L A) \rightarrow A$ and (vi) $B/_L(B/_R A) \rightarrow A$. These schemata may look rather ad hoc, but under the view of syntactic categories as functions which map expressions of one category to expressions of another they actually correspond to very natural operations on functions. (See Oehrle et al. (1988) for discussion of this.)

What is especially interesting about these rule schemata is that they allow a single sentence to have a number of different constituent structures. To take just one example, consider a sentence like *John thinks that Bill hates Tom*. Under 'standard' theories, this has only the following structure (the labels on the constituents will be suppressed here): [*John* [*thinks* [*that* [*Bill* [*hates Tom*]]]]]. This is also a possible structure under CG and is, in fact, the structure which would be obtained by using only the rule schemata in (i) and (ii). But because of these additional schemata, there are other structures; another one, for example, would be as shown in (49) (where the rules which have applied at each point are also shown):

(49)

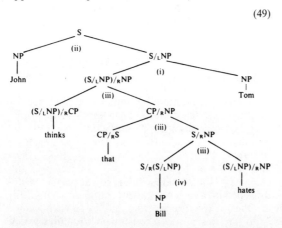

Note that *thinks that Bill hates* is a constituent, and is a constituent of the same category as an ordinary transitive verb like *likes*. Although there will be a great number of constituent structures for every sentence, the semantics is set up in such a way that these extra structures do not yield extra meanings. Note too that in view of the remarks in Sect. 2.2 regarding the fit between the syntactic constituent structure and the semantic composition, it follows that a constituent

like *thinks that Bill hates* is a semantic unit. While such a result appears counterintuitive at first, it can perhaps be made more intuitive by comparing the meaning of such a unit to the meaning of a simple transitive verb. An ordinary transitive verb like *likes* can be thought of as denoting a relation between two individuals; in any situation, it will 'pick out' all pairs of individuals (x, y) such that x stands in the liking-relation to y. A complex transitive verb like *thinks that Bill hates* similarly denotes a (complex) relation between two individuals. It too will, in any situation, pick out all pairs of individuals (x, y) such that x stands in the thinking-Bill-hates relation to y.

In the discussion of conjunction in Sect. 2.3.3, it was pointed out that one hypothesis regarding conjunction is that only constituents may conjoin, and the two constituents must be of the same category. As noted earlier, however, there are apparent counterexamples to this involving cases of so-called nonconstituent conjunction. But in CG these counterexamples disappear, for the flexibility in the constituent structure means that each such case involves constituent conjunction. To clarify, assume that, in addition to the rule schemata discussed immediately above, English also contains the schema (xxv) discussed earlier ($X \rightarrow X$ and X, where X is a variable over any category). Now consider the case of conjunction in (29a) (*John likes and thinks that Bill hates everyone who was here*). As shown above, within CG, *thinks that Bill hates* can be analyzed as a constituent of category $(S/_L NP)/_R NP$; this is the same as the category of an ordinary transitive verb like *likes*. It thus follows that they can conjoin. Similar remarks hold for (29b); using the schemata above, there is an analysis of this in which *John likes* is a constituent (of category $S/_R NP$) and *Bill hates* is also a constituent of this category, and so the two may conjoin.

4. Languages with Free Word Order

This article has focused exclusively on English as a way to demonstrate the notion of constituent structure and some of the controversies surrounding this notion. However, many languages are typologically very different from English. In particular, many languages have much greater freedom of word order than English has. In fact, it has often been noted that English has extremely fixed word order compared to many other languages; at the opposite end of the spectrum are many Australian languages with extremely free word order (and many languages are in between these two poles). The question arises, then, as to whether the sentences of such languages also have a constituent structure where there is simply a great deal of discontinuous constituents or whether, instead, the entire notion of constituent structure needs drastic modification for such languages. Indeed, languages with free word order are occasionally referred to as 'nonconfigurational' languages; a term which itself implies that constituent structure trees (or some similar object) are inappropriate representations for the sentences of such languages. It should be stressed that the question here is more than an issue of representation; as discussed in Sect. 2, a structure itself is simply a representation of how the rules of the grammar work to specify a sentence as well-formed. Thus, if the sentences of languages with free word order do not have a constituent structure in the way that English sentences do, this means that the grammars for such languages work on very different principles.

Although the correct analysis of such languages remains an open question, many researchers have concluded that the sentences of such languages do indeed have a constituent structure of the familiar sort, and that the grammars of these languages simply allow for a great deal of discontinuous constituents. That there is at least a certain amount of structure is evidenced by the following consideration. While the word order in, for example, many Australian languages is quite free (modifiers may be separated from the nouns that they modify; nouns and verbs may appear in any order, etc.), it is not completely free. In many such languages, words may freely 'scramble' within a single S, but words in a subordinate clause may not be freely mixed with words from a higher clause. (A subordinate clause is an S which, in constituent structure terms, is dominated by a higher S-node.) Hence, Blake (1983) reports that Kalkatungu sentences obey this principle. A related phenomenon is discussed in Dixon's classic study of Dyirbal (Dixon 1972). Thus, Dyirbal contains what Dixon refers to as 'iteration of the favorite construction,' as exemplified by (50) (from Dixon 1972: 75); this construction can be analyzed as involving a series of subordinate clauses:

balan   ḍugumbil   baṇgul   (50)
there-nom-II woman-nom there-erg-I

yaṛaŋgu wawun   nayinbagu
man-erg fetch-pres/past girl-pl-dat

walmbilŋaygu bagum   wuḍugu burbilŋaygu
get up-nay-purp there-dat-III fruit-dat pick-nay-purp

'man fetched woman to get the girls up to pick fruit'

Although there is a fair amount of freedom of word order in this construction, Dixon notes that in this construction a word dominated by some S node S_n must generally occur before the verb of some S node S_{n+1} if S_n dominates S_{n+1}. Even to describe this restriction, the notion of one S-node dominating the other has been used; if such sentences did not have any kind of structure, it is unclear how this restriction could be described. A detailed discussion of this general issue is contained in Dixon (1972), who provides an analysis of Dyirbal which relies heavily on the notion of constituent structure.

But even if it is correct that so-called 'non-configurational' languages do have a constituent structure in which there can simply be a great deal of discontinuous constituents, it of course remains an open question as to how best to account for the general phenomenon of discontinuous constituents. This is clearly one of the central issues of syntactic theory, and will undoubtedly occupy research for a long time to come.

Bibliography

Ajdukiewicz K 1935 Die syntaktische Konnexität. *Studia Philosophica* **1**: 1–27 (Repr. as: Syntactic connexion. In: McCall S (ed.) 1967 *Polish Logic: 1920–39*. Oxford University Press, Oxford)

Bach E 1979 Control in Montague grammar. *LIn* **10**: 515–31

Bar-Hillel Y 1964 *Language and Information: Selected Essays on Their Theory and Application*. Addison-Wesley, Reading, MA

Blake B J 1983 Structure and word-order in Kalkatungu. The anatomy of a flat language. *AJL* **3**: 145–75

Bloomfield L 1933 *Language*. Holt, Rinehart and Winston, New York

Chomsky N 1957 *Syntactic Structures*. Mouton, The Hague

Chomsky N 1965 *Aspects of the Theory of Syntax*. MIT Press, Cambridge, MA

Chomsky N 1981 *Lectures on Government and Binding*. Foris, Dordrecht

Chomsky N, Halle M 1968 *The Sound Pattern of English*. Harper and Row, New York

Dixon R M W 1972 *The Dyirbal Language of North Queensland*. Cambridge University Press, Cambridge

Engdahl E 1986 *Constituent Questions: The Syntax and Semantics of Questions, with Special Reference to Swedish*. Reidel, Dordrecht

Gazdar G 1981 Unbounded dependencies and coordinate structure. *LIn* **12**: 155–84

Gazdar G, Klein E, Pullum G, Sag I 1985 *Generalized Phrase Structure Grammar*. Blackwell, Oxford

Harman G H 1963 Generative grammars without transformation rules: A defense of phrase structure. *Lg* **39**: 597–616

Harris Z S 1946 From morpheme to utterance. *Lg* **22**: 161–83

Huck G, Ojeda A (eds.) 1987 *Syntax and Semantics 20: Discontinuous Consistency*. Academic Press, Orlando, FL

Hudson R 1976 *Arguments for a Non-transformational Grammar*. University of Chicago Press, Chicago, IL

Hudson R 1984 *Word Grammar*. Blackwell, Oxford

Jackendoff R 1977 *X̄ Syntax: A Study of Phase Structure*. MIT Press, Cambridge, MA

Lambek J 1958 The mathematics of sentence structure. *American Mathematical Monthly* **65**: 154–69

McCawley J D 1982 Parentheticals and discontinuous constituent structure. *LIn* **13**: 91–106

Oehrle R, Bach E, Wheeler D (eds.) 1988 *Categorial Grammars and Natural Language Structures*. Reidel, Dordrecht

Perlmutter D (ed.) 1983 *Studies in Relational Grammar 1*. University of Chicago Press, Chicago, IL

Pike K 1943 Taxemes and immediate constituents. *Lg* **19**: 65–82

Reinhart T 1983 *Anaphora and Semantic Interpretation*. Croom Helm, London

Wells R S 1947 Immediate constituents. *Lg* **23**: 81–117

Construction Grammar

Adele E. Goldberg

'Construction Grammar' is a linguistic theory concerned with the nature of speakers' knowledge of language. Like traditional grammars, Construction Grammar takes the basic units of language to be form–meaning pairings, or 'constructions.' The theory is nonderivational, nonmodular, and aims to achieve full coverage of the facts of language. Many practitioners of the theory have adopted the unification formalism for representing constructions and an inheritance hierarchy to capture generalizations across constructions.

The research focus of the theory has ranged from general aspects of grammar including agreement, binding, long-distance dependencies, and argument structure constructions, to lexical semantics and more marked constructions.

1. Constructions

A construction is defined to be a pairing of form with meaning/use such that some aspect of the form or some aspect of the meaning/use is not strictly predictable from the component parts or from other constructions already established to exist in the language. On this view, phrasal patterns, including the constructions of traditional grammarians, such as relative clauses, questions, locative inversion, etc. are given theoretical status. Morphemes are also constructions, according to the definition, since their form is not predictable from their meaning or use. Given this, it follows that the lexicon is not neatly delimited from the rest of grammar, although phrasal constructions differ from lexical items in their internal complexity. Both phrasal patterns and lexical items are stored in an extended construct-icon.

Elements within the construct-icon vary in degrees of idiomaticity. At one end of the idiomaticity continuum, we find very general, abstract constructions such as the subject–predicate construction; at the other end, we find simple lexical items and constructions with all of their lexical fillers specified but with noncompositional meanings (e.g., *kick the bucket*). In between, we find the full range of possibilities: for example, idioms which have freely fillable positions (*keep/lose x's cool*); compositional collocations with fixed word order (e.g., *up and down*); phrasal patterns that are only partially productive (e.g., the English ditransitive); and phrasal patterns which are partially morphologically specified (*the Xer, the Yer*).

Construction Grammar shares the basic and fundamental idea that the construction (or *sign*) is central to an account of language with several other current theories including Head-driven Phrase Structure Grammar, Cognitive Grammar, Montague Grammar, and Categorial Grammar (see *Head-driven Phrase Structure Grammar*; *Cognitive Grammar*; *Categorial Grammar*). This view of grammar can be contrasted with the claim made by Principles and Parameters theories that constructions are entirely epiphenomenal, that they are merely taxonomic artifacts, explained through the interaction of the principles of Universal Grammar, once the values of parameters are fixed (Chomsky 1995). Although most aspects of language are highly motivated, in the sense that they are related to other aspects of the grammar and are nonarbitrary, Construction Grammar holds the view that much of language is idiosyncratic to varying degrees and must therefore be learned.

2. No Derivations

Construction Grammar is monostratal: no derivations are posited. A given sentence is licensed by the grammar if and only if there exists in the language a set of constructions which can be combined (or superimposed) to produce an accurate representation of the surface structure and semantics of that sentence. An ambiguous sentence is a sentence for which there exists more than one set of constructions which can be assembled to produce a possible representation. Constructions are represented declaratively, and any constructions which do not conflict may be combined to give rise to grammatical expressions.

Typically, particular sentences (or *constructs*) instantiate several constructions simultaneously. For example, sentence (1) instantiates the subject–predicate construction, the ditransitive construction, the determination construction (*a letter*), the past tense morphological construction (*fax-ed*), and five simple morphological constructions, corresponding to each word in the sentence:

Elena faxed Ken a letter. (1)

3. Nonmodularity

Like the other construction-based theories mentioned above, Construction Grammar is nonmodular, in that conventionalized aspects of both meaning and use are directly related to particular syntactic patterns within individual constructions. This further distinguishes Construction Grammar from current Principle and Parameter approaches.

Construction Grammar also eschews a strict division between the pragmatic and the semantic. Encyclopedic or 'frame-semantic' meaning is considered fundamental to a linguistically adequate understanding of linguistic entities, and as such is integrated with more traditional definitional characterizations.

Generalizations about particular arguments being topical, focused, already relevant to the discourse, etc. are also stated as part of the constructional representation. In addition, facts about the use of entire constructions, including facts about register, restricted dialect variation, etc. are stated as part of the construction. Thus a construction may be posited because of something not strictly predictable about its frame-semantics, its packaging of information structure, or its context of use.

4. Full Coverage

Construction Grammar aims to account for the full range of facts of any language, without assuming that a particular subset of the data is part of a privileged 'core.' In fact there has been some emphasis within the theory on exploring more marked or unusual constructions with the belief that these constructions shed light on more general issues, and make the researcher more sensitive to what is required for a complete account of the grammar of a language (see Sect. 7 below).

4.1 Use of Attested Data

Methodologically, research in Construction Grammar has emphasized the importance of attested data, gathered from discourse or corpora. Serious attention to corpus data has led to the realization that much of attested data falls outside of what is often considered to be 'core' grammar. At the same time, construction grammarians routinely supplement corpus data with data gained from introspection, one obvious reason being that corpora do not contain sentences marked as unacceptable.

4.2 Processing

Although the emphasis in Construction Grammar is on knowledge of language rather than the processing of language, there has been some work exploring the processing implications of the theory (Jurafsky, in press; Bates and Goodman 1996). A central implication of the theory for processing is that words and phrases are the same basic type of entity: pairings of form and meaning/use. Ultimately the theory aims to explicitly articulate the relation between actual linguistic performance and the declaratively represented constructions.

5. Inheritance Hierarchy

Constructions do not form an unstructured set, but rather a highly integrated system. Constructions are typically closely related to other constructions, and are in that sense, not arbitrary. Generalizations across constructions are captured within the theory via an inheritance hierarchy, whereby relationships among constructions are captured by explicit inheritance links.

For example, an abstract Left Isolate (LI) construction is inherited by several different constructions, for example those exemplified by the following:

(a) The woman who she met yesterday (restrictive relative clause)   (2)
(b) Abby, who she met yesterday (nonrestrictive relative clause)
(c) Bagels, I like (topicalization)
(d) What do you think she did? (main clause nonsubject *wh*-question)

Each of the patterns, restrictive and nonrestrictive relative clauses, topicalization, and *wh*-questions, requires a distinct construction of its own, owing to its particular formal and pragmatic properties. But each inherits from the more general LI construction, which specifies the properties that are shared. In particular, the LI construction has two sisters, with the specification that the left sister satisfy the valence requirement of some predicator at an undefined depth in the right sister; the right sister is a maximal verb phrase, with or without a subject.

6. Unification

Many practitioners of this theory have adopted the use of a unification based formalism in order to rigorously detail the specifications of particular constructions. Thus each construction is represented by an Attribute-Value Matrix (AVM). Each attribute can have at most one value. Attributes may be semantic, syntactic, or pragmatic and their values may be binary, ternary, or more complex. The values may also themselves be feature structures.

Any pair of AVMs can be combined to license a particular expression, just in case there is no value conflict on any attribute. When two AVM's unify, they may onto a new AVM, which has the union of attributes and values of the two original AVMs.

7. Research Focus

7.1 Lexical Semantics

There has been a focus on the semantics and distribution of particular lexical items within the framework, owing to the belief that the rich semantic/pragmatic constraints on individual words or idiomatic phrases reveals much about our knowledge of language. For example, work on *even* and *let alone* led to advancements in our understanding of scalar implicatures (Kay 1990; Fillmore et al. 1988); the semantics and distribution of *risk* led to an increased understanding of the importance of specific semantic roles such as in this case, *victim, harm, valued-object* etc. (Fillmore and Atkins 1992). More generally, work on lexical semantics has led to the development of the frame semantic approach to meaning that is used in Construction Grammar. Within the unification based formalism, frame-semantics is captured by allowing semantic attributes to include a frame attribute whose value specifies a particular idealized scene.

7.2 Marked Constructions

In much the same spirit as the work on lexical semantics, there has been a great deal of attention paid to marked constructions within the theory. For example, consider the Covariational Conditional construction, exemplified by *the more you think about it, the less you understand* (see Fillmore et al. 1988; Michaelis 1994). Independent knowledge of *the* and grammatical comparison will not directly predict that the relevant class of expressions will exist or have exactly the form and meaning they have; therefore a distinct construction is posited. Other examples of marked constructions include Kay and Fillmore's 'What's X doing Y?' construction, exemplified by sentences such as *What's that fly doing in my soup?* (Kay and Fillmore 1996), and the Nominal Extraposition construction of Michaelis and Lambrecht (1996) (e.g., *It's amazing the difference!*).

Construction Grammar takes the point of view that the ordinary rules of grammar do not differ qualitatively from these sorts of quantitatively more complex constructions. Thus what some other theories take to be peripheral, Construction Grammar takes to be central to our understanding of language.

7.3 Argument Structure Constructions

In most current linguistic theories, the form and general interpretation of basic sentence patterns of a language are taken to be determined by semantic and/or syntactic information specified by the main verb in the sentence. The sentence patterns given in (3) and (4) indeed appear to be determined by the specifications of *give* and *put* respectively:

> Chris *gave* Pat a ball. (3)

> Pat *put* the ball on the table. (4)

Give is a three argument verb and is expected to appear with three complements corresponding to agent, recipient, and theme. *Put*, another three argument verb, requires an agent, a theme, and a location and appears with the corresponding three complements in (4). However, while (3) and (4) represent perhaps the prototypical case, the interpretation and form of sentence patterns of a language are not reliably determined by independent specifications of the main verb. For example, it is implausible to claim that *sneeze* has a three argument sense in (5):

> Pat *sneezed* the foam off the cappuccino. (Ahrens (5) 1995)

The following attested examples similarly involve sentential patterns that do not seem to be determined by independent specifications of the main verbs:

> 'She *smiled* herself an upgrade.' (D. Adams, *The* (6) *Hitchhiker's Guide to the Galaxy*)

> 'My father *frowned* away the compliment.' (7) (S. McCauley, 1992, *Easy Way Out*)

> 'We *laughed* our conversation to an end.' (J. Hart, (8) 1992, *Sin*)

> 'The Miami quarterback was *boo-ed* to the bench.' (9) (NPR, October 1995)

Moreover, verbs typically appear with a wide array of complement configurations. Consider the verb *sew*:

> (a) Anil sewed all afternoon. (intransitive) (10)
> (b) Nitya sewed a sari. (transitive)
> (c) Anil sewed Nitya a sari. (ditransitive)
> (d) Anil sewed the sleeve shut. (resultative)
> (e) Anil sewed a button onto his jacket. (caused-motion)
> (f) Nitya sewed her way to fame and fortune. (*way*-construction)

In Construction Grammar, instead of predicting the surface form and interpretation solely on the basis of the verb's independent specifications, the lexical verb is understood to combine with an argument structure construction (e.g., the ditransitive, resultative, the caused-motion construction, etc.). Verbs constrain the type of argument structure constructions they can combine with by their frame-specific semantics and particular obligatory roles, but they typically can combine with constructions in several ways.

It is the argument structure constructions which provide the direct link between surface form and general aspects of the interpretation such as something causing something else to move, someone causing someone to receive something, something moving somewhere, someone causing something to change state, etc. The argument structure constructions, which provide the basic sentence patterns of a language, directly reflect these types of basic frames of experience. That is, the skeletal patterns, independently of the main verb, designate such patterns of experience. Thus constructions are invoked both for marked or especially complex pairings of form and meaning, and for many of the basic, unmarked patterns of language.

Bibliography

Ahrens K 1995 The mental representation of verbs (Dissertation, University of California, San Diego)

Bates L, Goodman J 1996 On the inseparability of grammar and the lexicon: Evidence from acquisition, aphasia and real-time processing (Unpublished manuscript, University of California, San Diego)

Chomsky N 1995 *The Minimalist Program*. MIT Press, Cambridge, MA

Fillmore C J 1985 Frames and the semantics of understanding. *QSem* **7(2)**: 222–54

Fillmore C J, Atkins B T 1992 The semantics of RISK and its neighbors. In: Lehrer A, Kittay E F (eds.) *Frames, Fields, and Contrasts*. Lawrence Erlbaum Associates, Hillsdale, NJ

Fillmore C J, Kay P 1987 *Construction Grammar Lecture Notes*. LSA Summer Institute, Stanford, CA

Fillmore C J, Kay P 1993 Construction Grammar (Unpublished manuscript, University of California, Berkeley)

Fillmore C J, Kay P, O'Connor M C 1988 Regularity and

idiomaticity in grammatical constructions: The case of
LET ALONE. *Language* **64**: 501–38
Goldberg A E 1995 *Constructions: A Construction Grammar
Approach to Argument Structure Constructions*. University
of Chicago Press, Chicago, IL
Jurafsky D 1996 A probabilistic model of lexical and syn-
tactic access and disambiguation. *Cognitive Science* **20**:
137–94
Kay P 1990 Even. *L&P* **13(1)**: 59–112
Kay P, Fillmore C J 1996 Grammatical constructions and
linguistic generalizations: The What's X Doing Y? con-
struction (Unpublished manuscript, University of California, Berkeley)
Koenig J-P, Jurafsky D 1994 Type underspecification and

on-line construction in the lexicon. *Proceedings of the
Thirteenth West Coast Conference on Formal Linguistics*
Lakoff G 1987 *There*-constructions. *Women, Fire and
Dangerous Things: What Categories Reveal about the
Mind*. University of Chicago Press, Chicago, IL
Lambrecht K 1994 *Information Structure and Sentence Form*.
Cambridge University Press, Cambridge
Michaelis L 1994 A case of constructional polysemy in Latin.
SLang **18**: 45–70
Michaelis L, Lambrecht K 1996 Toward a construction-
based theory of language function: The case of nominal
extraposition. *Language* **72(2)**: 215–47
Zwicky A 1994 Dealing out meaning: Fundamentals of syn-
tactic constructions. *BLS* **20**: 611–25

Dependency Grammar

N. M. Fraser

A 'dependency grammar' (DG) is one in which syntactic structure is expressed primarily in terms of
'dependency relations.' A dependency relation is a
directed grammatical relation holding between a pair
of elements at the same level in a sentence. One of the
elements *depends* morphologically, syntactically, or
semantically on the other. Dependency relations are
sometimes identified with the traditional 'grammatical
relations.' Dependency relations contrast with constituency relations which hold between elements at
different levels in a sentence (see *Constituent Structure*;
Generalized Phrase Structure Grammar).

1. Dependency and Constituency

Dependency is an asymmetrical relation between two
sentence elements, usually single words. One of the
elements is identified as the 'governor,' 'regent,' or
'head' (each of these terms can be found in the literature, although some writers reserve 'head' for the principal item in a whole phrase rather than the dominant
partner in a pairwise dependency relation); the other
element is identified as the 'dependent' or 'modifier.'

A governor is distinguished from its dependents in
a number of ways. These include: (a) the governor
determines whether a dependent is optional or obligatory, and not vice versa; (b) the governor *subcategorizes* for its dependents, and not vice versa; (c)
the *governor* determines which inflexional form of a
dependent occurs, and not vice versa; and (d) the
governor identifies a semantic object which a dependent further specifies, and not vice versa. Other criteria
for identifying governors have been proposed, but
no single criterion provides a necessary and sufficient
condition for dependency. This is demonstrated by
the fact that dependency grammarians reach different
conclusions about the identity of the governor in a

number of common constructions, such as the determiner–noun construction.

Figure 1 shows a phrase structure tree for the sentence *Tall people sleep in long beds*. Notice that all
words in the sentence appear as terminal nodes in the
tree. These are grouped together under nonterminal
phrasal nodes, with the topmost node S representing
the phrase which includes all others, namely the
sentence.

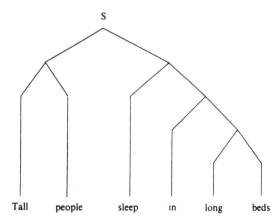

Figure 1. A phrase structure tree.

The most important difference between dependency
structures and constituency (i.e., phrase) structures is
that dependency structures do not include any nonterminal nodes. Structure is expressed solely in terms
of dependency relations between words in the
sentence. There are at least three different conventions
for representing dependency structures. These are
shown in Fig. 2.

The first (due to Tesnière 1959) presents words as

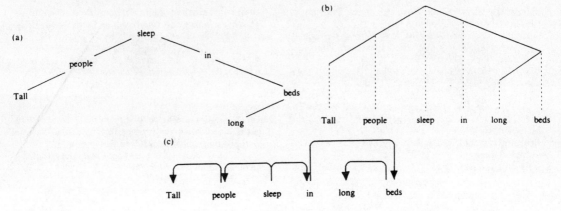

Figure 2. Corresponding dependency structure trees showing the three principal representation schemes. These are (a) stemma, (b) D-marker, (c) arc diagram.

nodes in a graph called a 'stemma' (see Fig. 2a). Dependencies between words are signaled by links between nodes. By convention, governors are located nearer the top of the diagram than their dependents. The first word in a sentence is positioned furthest to the left of the diagram and the Nth word appears to the right of the N−1th word and to the left of the N+1th word. Although stemmas encode sufficient information, they can be difficult to read, especially when the sentence represented is long and involves frequent alternation between 'head first' and 'head second' dependencies.

In the second type of diagram (see Fig. 2b), dependency is represented by the relative vertical position of nodes in a tree; if an *edge* connects a lower node to a higher node then the word corresponding to the lower node depends on the word corresponding to the higher node. Word-node correspondences are indicated by means of broken lines called 'projections.' Diagrams of this kind are known as 'D-markers.'

The third diagrammatic convention moves away from obviously tree-like objects which are confusingly suggestive of phrase structures, and instead represents dependency relations by means of directed arcs. In Fig. 2c, arcs are directed from governors to dependents although there is no generally accepted labeling convention and it is not unusual to find examples of arcs being oppositely directed. Some authors draw arc diagrams with the arcs below the words in the sentence (see Matthews 1981). Hudson (1990) divides the arcs so that those having a particular function appear below the sentence symbols, whilst the rest appear above them.

It is possible to define a phrase solely in terms of word–word dependencies, without making reference to higher nodes. An X phrase consists of an X plus all of its subordinates, where 'subordinates' of X are words which depend directly or indirectly on X. Thus, an arbitrary dependency structure can be mapped

onto a phrase structure of sorts. By bracketing each governor together with its subordinates in the sentence in Fig. 2, the following phrase structure is produced: [[Tall people] sleep [in [long beds]]]. This does not correspond to the desired phrase structure shown in Fig. 1, i.e., [[Tall people] [sleep [in [long beds]]]]. It is not possible to map an arbitrary phrase structure onto a systematically corresponding dependency structure for at least two reasons. First, phrase structures generated by rewrite rules which do not contain a terminal symbol on their right hand side (e.g., S → NP VP) have no dependency structure correlates. This is because a phrase without a lexical head is meaningless in dependency terms. For this reason, the phrase structure shown in Fig. 1 cannot be represented in terms of dependency relations. Second, an arbitrary phrase structure does not identify which sister is the head of a phrase and so the only way to map such a structure onto a dependency structure is to select the head of each phrase arbitrarily. These obstacles can both be overcome if a head-marking phrase structure grammar is employed (see *X-Bar Syntax*). Such grammars encode both constituency and dependency information.

It has been shown (Gaifman 1965) that all DGs subject to a standard set of constraints (described in Sects. 2 and 3) have weakly equivalent context free phrase structure grammars (CFPSGs) and vice versa.

2. Dependency Rules

A number of different dependency rule formalisms have been developed and described in the literature. The oldest and most widely used of these is due to Gaifman (1965). Rules in Gaifman's formalism take three basic forms. In each of the forms, there is an element outside a set of brackets. This element represents the head of the construction. In rule type (1), X is the head and X_1–X_n are its dependents, where $n > 0$. The position of the asterisk marks the position of the head relative to its dependents in the string. Rule type (2) states that X may occur without dependents. Rule type (3) states that X may occur without depending on any other element:

$$X(X_1, \ldots, *, \ldots, X_n) \tag{1}$$

$$X(*) \tag{2}$$

$$*(X) \tag{3}$$

Implicit in discussions of the use of dependency rules is the assumption that each rule may apply a maximum of one time to each head word. This point is important and really needs to be made explicit. A DG is subject to the 'single application constraint' if any rule may apply to a given word at most once. In DGs which are subject to the single application constraint, the number of dependents a head may have is bounded by the grammar and is necessarily finite; in formalisms which are not subject to the single application constraint, there is no upper bound on the number of dependents which any head may have.

A number of early papers on the formal aspects of DGs investigated a class of DGs which were weakly equivalent to the class of CFPSGs (Gross 1964; Hays 1964; Gaifman 1965; Robinson 1970). Some of these papers suggested that *all* DGs shared the same generative capacity. For example, Gross (1964: 49) claimed that 'The dependency *languages* are exactly the context-free languages.' Versions of this claim, though mistaken, have frequently been made in the literature. More accurately, DGs are weakly equivalent to CFPSGs if the DGs (a) have rule sets conforming to Gaifman's rule definitions, and (b) are subject to the standard structural constraints described in Sect. 3.

Chomsky has shown that the generative capacity of a phrase structure grammar (PSG) is dependent on the form of its rules. By progressively relaxing the constraints on the form of rules, it is possible to generate progressively more powerful *languages*. A similar argument can be applied to DGs.

A maximally constrained DG would replace rules of type (1) with rules either of type (4) or type (5):

$$X(X_1, *) \tag{4}$$

$$X(*, X_1) \tag{5}$$

In both kinds of grammar, the maximum number of dependents a head can have is one. Clearly, the set of languages generated by these grammars is properly contained in the set of languages generated by Gaifman-type grammars since rules of type (4) and (5) are well-formed rules of type (1). DGs constrained in this way generate exactly the regular languages. There is a clear similarity between left-linear regular PSGs and DGs expressed in the formalism which includes (4), and between right linear regular PSGs and DGs expressed in the formalism which includes (5). Unlike standard DGs, regular DGs can not generate the string-copying language $a^n b^n$.

More powerful DGs can also be defined. For example, an indexed DG includes a stack-valued feature with push and pop operations. The stack can be represented by means of a pair of square brackets. Thus, [ ] is an empty stack; [i] is a stack containing the single symbol i. It is never necessary to refer to more than the top item on a stack so the notion [i, . .] is used to represent a stack whose top is i. Rules of the form shown in (6) copy the contents of a stack from head to dependent and push i onto the top of the dependent's stack. Rules of the form shown in (7) pop the top of a head's stack and then copy the remainder of the head's stack to the dependent's stack.

$$H[..](\ldots, D[i, ..], \ldots, *, \ldots) \tag{6}$$

or

$$H[..](\ldots, *, \ldots, D[i, ..], \ldots)$$

$$H[i, ..](\ldots, D[..], \ldots, *, \ldots) \tag{7}$$

or

$$H[i, ..](\ldots, *, \ldots, D[..], \ldots)$$

The indexed DG shown in (8) generates the language $a^n b^n c^n$, which cannot be generated either by a CFPSG or by a standard DG:

$$
\begin{aligned}
&*(a[a]) \\
&a[..](*, a[a, ..]) \\
&a[..](*, b[..], c[..]) \\
&b[a, ..](*, b[..]) \\
&b[a](*) \\
&c[a, ..](*, c[..]) \\
&c[a](*)
\end{aligned} \tag{8}
$$

PSG rules are 'rewrite rules'; they allow the symbols which are to be rewritten to be erased and replaced by a new set of symbols. Any further constraints on the number or kind of rewriting operations must be stated separately. By contrast, dependency rules are additive. Each rule application adds at least one new terminal symbol to those which have already been generated in a derivation. Addition is monotonic: once a symbol has been introduced it can be added to but not erased. Thus, the number of steps in a DG derivation is bounded by the number of words in the sentence being generated.

3. Dependency Structures

So far, only the local relations which hold between heads and their dependents have been considered. It is also necessary to make explicit a number of general constraints on the structure of well-formed sentences. The constraints which are usually assumed are described in the next four subsections.

3.1 One Independent Element

In a dependency structure every word must depend on some other word with the exception of one word—

the sentence 'root'—which is free. In DG, a terminal symbol (or class of terminal symbols) rather than a nonterminal (S) symbol is marked as the 'start symbol.'

3.2 Connected Dependency Structures

All of the symbols in a sentence must form part of the same connected dependency structure. A word must be either the root or a subordinate of the root.

3.3 Exactly One Head

Each symbol (except the root) must depend on exactly one other symbol. This is rather like the constraint in PSG which ensures that phrases do not overlap. A number of dependency theorists (Johnson et al. 1985; Hudson 1990) have abandoned this constraint in order to deal with phenomena such as the subject sharing in 'Norman likes flying,' where 'Norman' is the subject of both 'likes' and 'flying.'

3.4 Heads and Dependents are Adjacent

A rule of the form A(B, *) places no constraints on where B may be located, so long as it precedes A in the string. In principle, A and B could be separated by arbitrarily many other symbols which depend on neither A nor B. In practice, most research has concentrated on a class of DG which places an additional constraint on the location of dependents. The 'adjacency' or 'projectivity' constraint, as it is called, requires any two words A and B contracting a dependency relation to be adjacent. A is adjacent to B if either A is next to B or A is separated from B by C and C is a subordinate of either A or B.

Structures which fail to satisfy the adjacency/ projectivity constraint are readily identifiable in two of the dependency diagram styles. In D-markers, at least one projection is intersected by an edge. In arc diagrams, either a pair of arcs intersects or an arc passes over the top of the sentence root.

In order to produce analyses of 'movement' and variable word order, some dependency theorists have abandoned the adjacency/projectivity constraint altogether (Sgall et al. 1986; Covington 1990). Others have developed relaxed versions of the constraint (Hudson 1990).

4. Dependency Grammar in Theoretical Linguistics

The concept of dependency is found in some of the earliest known grammars, for example those of Greek scholars such as Thrax and Apollonius and subsequent Latin scholars, such as Priscian. Traces of dependency can be found in the earlier work of the Sanskrit grammarian Pāṇini. Particularly clear early articulations of the central concepts can be found in the writings of the medieval Arabic grammarians, especially those of the Basra and Baghdad schools. Many details of modern DG were made explicit for the first time in the writings of Ibn Al-Sarrâj (d. 928 AD)

(Owens 1987). Dependency is also found in the writings of medieval European scholars such as the modistic and speculative grammarians, and especially, in the work of Martin of Dacia and Thomas of Erfurt.

Most commentators agree that the most significant contribution to the development of DG in modern times was made in the 1950s by Tesnière, who was the first person to develop a formal apparatus for describing dependency structures. Tesnière's ideas are collected in the posthumously published *Eléments de syntaxe structurale* (Tesnière 1959).

Although early formal work on DG was carried out by North American scholars (Hays 1964; Gaifman 1965; Robinson 1970), DG has been most enthusiastically espoused in Europe, and particularly Germany and Eastern Europe. Prominent German dependency grammarians include Heringer (1970), who combined dependency and constituency in a single representation, Kunze (1975), and Vater (1975) who developed a transformational generative version of DG building on the work of Robinson (1970). Work begun by Mel'čuk and his colleagues in Moscow in the early 1960s has led to the development of meaning-text theory (Mel'čuk 1988). Sgall's group in Prague has developed, in the 1980s, a theory of language structure called 'functional generative description' in which dependency is basic and constituent structure plays no part at all (Sgall et al. 1986). In the UK, John Anderson (a Germanist) developed case grammar, a combination of DG and localist case (Anderson 1971, 1977). Since the mid-1970s, Anderson has also been involved in the development of a dependency-based theory of phonology (Anderson and Durand 1986). Hudson's theory of daughter dependency grammar (Hudson 1976) combines constituency and dependency. His later theory, 'word grammar' (see *Word Grammar*) (Hudson 1990), is based on pure dependency. In addition to these dependency theories, at least two British scholars have used DG in syntax textbooks (Matthews 1981; Miller 1985). In the USA, Starosta has been developing his dependency-based theory of 'lexicase' (see *Lexicase*) since the early 1970s (Starosta 1988).

Amongst the most influential of Tesnière's ideas were those relating to 'valency' (see *Valency and Valency Grammar*). The valency of a verb is its potential for having other words depend on it. The relationship between valency and dependency is rather opaque. Early dependency theorists tended to concentrate on formal issues and to see verbal valency as just one specific example of the general case of dependency—in other words, all words have a valency. Valency theorists, on the other hand, concentrate on the pivotal role played by the main verb in natural language sentences. They tend to focus particularly on the 'case' relations of the verb. Two largely disjointed research communities have thus emerged.

The debate between advocates of dependency and

advocates of constituency (Hudson 1980; Dahl 1980) has lost much of its force as linguistic theories have increasingly come to incorporate aspects of both. Constituency-based theories have expanded the role of the lexicon and diminished the role of grammar rules which refer to phrasal categories. They have also started to refer explicitly to heads and to use them to do significant work (Corbett et al. 1993) (see *Head-driven Phrase Structure Grammar*; *X-bar Syntax*). On the other hand, most dependency grammarians accept that coordinate structures cannot be described adequately in terms of dependency, and that constituency is required at least for this purpose.

5. Dependency Grammar in Natural Language Processing

Much of the formal work in DG carried out in the 1960s was directed towards solving problems in 'machine translation' (MT). After a gap of twenty years during which very few 'natural language processing' systems employed DG, the 1980s saw a resurgence of interest, with several very large MT projects using DG (Johnson et al. 1985; Schubert 1987). DG is now used in a wide variety of natural language processing systems such as parsers, natural language interfaces to databases, and, particularly, speech understanding systems.

Bibliography

Anderson J M 1971 *The Grammar of Case: Towards a Localistic Theory*. Cambridge University Press, Cambridge

Anderson J M 1977 *On Case Grammar: Prolegomena to a Theory of Grammatical Relations*. Croom Helm, London

Anderson J M, Durand J 1986 Dependency phonology. In: Durand J (ed.) *Dependency and Non-linear Phonology*. Croom Helm, London

Corbett G G, Fraser N M, McGlashan S (eds.) 1993 *Heads in Grammatical Theory*. Cambridge University Press, Cambridge

Covington M A 1990 Parsing discontinuous constituents in dependency grammar. *CL* 16: 234–36

Dahl Ö 1980 Some arguments for higher nodes in syntax: A reply to Hudson's 'Constituency and Dependency.' *Linguistics* 18: 485–88

Gaifman H 1965 Dependency systems and phrase-structure systems. *Information and Control* 8: 304–37

Gross M 1964 The equivalence of models of language used in the fields of mechanical translation and information retrieval. *Information Storage and Retrieval* 2: 43–57

Hays D G 1964 Dependency theory: A formalism and some observations. *Lg* 40: 511–25

Heringer H-J 1970 *Theorie der deutschen Syntax*. Hueber, Munich

Hudson R A 1976 *Arguments for a Non-transformational Grammar*. University of Chicago Press, Chicago, IL

Hudson R A 1980 Constituency and dependency. *Linguistics* 18: 179–98

Hudson R A 1990 *English Word Grammar*. Blackwell, Oxford

Johnson R, King M, des Tombe L 1985 EUROTRA: A multilingual system under development. *CL* 11: 155–69

Kunze J 1975 *Abhängigkeitsgrammatik*. Studia Grammatica Akademie-Verlag, Berlin

Matthews P H 1981 *Syntax*. Cambridge University Press, Cambridge

Mel'čuk I A 1988 *Dependency Syntax: Theory and Practice*. SUNY Press, Albany, NY

Miller J E 1985 *Semantics and Syntax: Parallels and Connections*. Cambridge University Press, Cambridge

Owens J 1987 *The Foundations of Grammar: An Introduction to Medieval Arabic Grammatical Theory*. Benjamins, Amsterdam

Robinson J J 1970 Dependency structures and transformational rules. *Lg* 46: 259–85

Schubert K 1987 *Metataxis: Contrastive Dependency Syntax for Machine Translation*. Foris, Dordrecht

Sgall P, Hajičová E, Panevová J, Mey J L (eds.) 1986 *The Meaning of the Sentence in its Semantic and Pragmatic Aspects*. Academia, Prague

Starosta S 1988 *The Case for Lexicase: An Outline of Lexicase Grammatical Theory*. Pinter, London

Tesnière L 1959 *Elements de syntaxe structurale*. Librairie Klincksieck, Paris

Vater H 1975 Toward a generative dependency grammar. *Lingua* 36: 121–45

Descriptive Grammar and Formal Grammar

F. Stuurman

The wide range of 'binding constructions' discussed in this article have constituted a testbed for the adequacy of formal linguistic frameworks for the past 30 years. The Chomskean paradigm current at the time when the article was written was the 'Government and Binding model' and the article looks at the way binding phenomena were handled in that model. Binding phenomena have not yet been seriously addressed in the 'minimalist program'. Although the Chomskean framework has moved on, the issues raised in the article remain relevant and important and for this reason it is reprinted unchanged from the Encyclopedia of Language and Linguistics.

Both descriptive grammar and formal grammar come in many varieties. It is not the purpose of this article to survey diverse manifestations; but to present a fundamental opposition in that descriptive grammar comprehensively includes facts whereas formal grammar is exclusively directed at the underlying system. To demonstrate the fundamentality of this opposition in some of its ramifications in the space available, the focus is on relatively pure types at the extreme ends. Thus, descriptive grammar here includes large grammars such as Jespersen's of English; formal grammar is represented by generative linguistics as it originates from Chomsky. Moreover, the latter is also constructed as an authoritative source for perceived contiguities between descriptive and formal grammar. Chomsky's perceptions have shifted: formal grammar first 'reconstructed,' then 'complements' descriptive grammar; it is argued here that in either sense, contiguity is untenable in view of the fundamental opposition.

1. Descriptive and Formal Grammar: The Fundamental Opposition

Even a focus as above may not make for immediately apparent homogeneity. Thus, Chomsky claims to have led his particular version of formal grammar through a 'conceptual shift': rather intricate rules associated fairly directly with specific grammatical phenomena have made way for relatively simple principles and their parameters, which by modular interaction manifest themselves in a wide range of phenomena. Correspondingly, the perceived relation to descriptive grammar changed from ostensible reconstruction to complementation.

However, over and above Chomsky's shift—and in the very motivation behind it—one can recognize a constant conception: formal grammar is optimally represented in Chomskyan linguistics precisely because its aim of accounting for learnability enforces the view that a system underlies human language which is in principle limited. Grammar is formal if it embodies such a limited conception; and is thus in principle amenable to refutation in terms of whether it can be seen to provide constraints on what are possible accounts of phenomena of human language. More recent principles and parameters may sustain more narrow constraints than earlier rules; but in the conception of constraints as the proper concern of formal grammar, there has not been any fundamental shift.

The true relations between descriptive and formal grammar therefore arise vis-à-vis constraints, and whether they reflect a narrow conception of language

in its systematic aspects. Fundamental opposition obtains in that descriptive grammar proceeds from the assumption that it should reflect the nature of human language as essentially open. Accordingly, descriptive grammar in principle precludes refutation by maintaining an ability to accommodate anything. In actual practice, therefore, descriptive grammar can shift at least as widely as formal grammar between various shapes and forms; even extending to ostensible formal apparatus, a notable instance being Jespersen's 'analytic syntax' (cf. Jespersen 1936, and Sects. 4 and 5 below).

2. Diagnostics

Given shifting practices in both descriptive grammar and formal grammar, the need arises for careful diagnosis, to be able to maintain the distinction. The fundamental opposition between the open nature of descriptive grammar and the narrow restrictions of formal grammar provides for symptomatic contrasts in (at least) two respects. First, opposite methodological predilections accord with the respective conceptions of the object: descriptive grammar proceeds inductively to leave matters open initially; whereas formal grammar starts from narrow limits which it maintains by deduction. Second, descriptive and formal grammar therefore differ as to the ranges of facts they are intended to cover: induction in descriptive grammar fosters aiming for comprehensive coverage; whereas deductive formal grammar determines the relevance of only restricted sets of facts.

It will not be necessary here to argue in detail that Chomskyan generative linguistics has consistently manifested itself as formal grammar on both these scores. For example, Chomsky intimated deduction for early Standard Theory: 'grammar . . . is in no sense an "inductive generalization"' (1965: 133); and equally, for later government-binding theory 'a grammar . . . will in general lack . . . an inductive basis' (1981: 3–4). Accordingly, as early as 1955, Chomsky may be seen to disclaim comprehensive coverage: 'our . . . purpose is not to present a complete picture' (1955: 455–56); rather, the purpose is to cover 'the pertinent facts . . . a notion that is linked to theory' (1979: 107).

Since formal grammar is relatively well-established in its typical manifestation in Chomskyan linguistics, typical descriptive grammar can now be identified by contrast. For English this may be taken to be manifested by, at least, Sweet, Poutsma, Kruisinga, Curme, and Quirk et al.—to leave Jespersen aside for the moment. All of these—if more or less directly—purport induction and/or comprehensiveness. Comprehensive coverage is first aimed at by Sweet: 'by comparison with other grammars . . . my syntax is fairly complete' (1898: v). Poutsma espouses induction: 'above all one ought to abstain from wresting the available evidence into harmony with some preconceived theory' (1928: viii); leaving others to acclaim coverage which is therefore 'exhaustive' (Hill 1958: v). Kruisinga adumbrates induction by stating that 'the study of English is chiefly a matter of observation' (1911: 342); and his coverage too was duly acclaimed 'the most comprehensive' (Grattan 1926: 243). Curme engages in descriptive grammar by aiming 'to describe fully' (1935: v). Finally, the grammars of Quirk et al. are associated with induction from corpora, primarily the Survey of English Usage (1972: v–vi; 1985: 33); and thus (1972) 'aims at ... comprehensiveness' (p. v), and the very title of (1985) flaunts *Comprehensive*.

If there is thus a tradition of descriptive grammar whose open conception is apparent in purporting induction and/or comprehensiveness, Jespersen must be seen to belong to it. In his *Philosophy of Grammar* (*PoG*) (1924), Jespersen avows 'an aversion ... to the idea of a grammar arrived at by deductive reasoning' (p. 48). In *Analytic Syntax* (1937), for all its formalism, Jespersen first subscribes to descriptive grammar by keeping things open to any and all 'extensions' (p. 2); induction is here apparent when Jespersen claims to have 'started everywhere from sentences as occurring in actual living speech' (p. 90). And in *Modern English Grammar* (*MEG*) (1909–49), comprehensive coverage places Jespersen firmly in the descriptive tradition above: 'the great collections of English grammatical data are ... the books of ... Sweet, Jespersen, Poutsma, Kruisinga, Curme' (Sledd 1964: 419).

3. On Chomsky on Jespersen

In fact, on occasion even Chomsky appears to contrast formal grammar to 'the traditional grammars ... of great scope like Jespersen's' (1979: 109). However, the sting in Chomsky's perception of Jespersen is that he takes a dual view: Chomsky distinguishes 'the [descriptive] grammarian' from 'the philosopher' who putatively anticipates formal grammar (1979: 156–57). There appear to be no real grounds for such dualism.

Chomsky's identification of Jespersen as (proto-) formal philosopher rests largely on ascribing to *PoG* the position that native speakers have a 'notion of structure' (1975: 4; 1986: 21); this then putatively anticipates Chomsky's universal grammar, the constrained system which propels deduction. But Jespersen actually wrote about a 'notion of *their* structure' (1924: 19; emphases added). The crucial import of 'their' is to refer to 'innumerable sentences heard and understood' (ibid.) as a basis for Jespersen's notion of structure to develop: i.e., inductively. That Chomsky's appropriation of Jespersen in *PoG* to formal grammar has to involve such blatant perversions only reinforces the consistently descriptive nature of both Jespersen's practice in *MEG* and his philosophy elsewhere.

In fact, Jespersen (1924) explicitly rejects the restrictive philosophy inherent in universal grammar (p. 55);

he only—reluctantly—admits a possibility of universal notional categories. Even if these should exist, however, to avoid the idea that they restrict descriptive grammar, Jespersen leaves relations between notional and grammatical categories fundamentally open: there are 'manifold cross-strands' (p. 46), so that in grammar 'no two languages have the same groupings and make the same distinctions' (p. 49). Once again, Jespersen's is obviously the open philosophy of descriptive grammar, in sharp contrast to Chomsky's narrow philosophy of formal grammar.

Given the fundamentally opposite philosophies, any apparent convergence between descriptive and formal grammar can only be deceptive. In particular, it first deceived Lees in his review of Chomsky (1957), which helped to win the Chomskyan revolution (Newmeyer 1980: 19, 35, 45–46). Lees stated that 'in a sense, transformational analysis is essentially a formalization of a long-accepted, traditional approach ... To cite only a single example, ... Jespersen' (1957: 387). This led to Chomsky's own early perspective: 'transformational ideas are ... an important part of traditional grammar. E.g., Jespersen ... we will reconstruct as transformational' (1958: 124).

Chomsky accordingly defends (1964: 29–30) Jespersen's (1924) descriptions of *the doctor's arrival/the doctor arrived*, and *the barking dog/the dog barks* against Nida's (1960: 27–28) objections, which reflect that these descriptions are fundamentally alien to formal grammar. Chomsky's 'formalization' of Jespersen in transformational terms apparently swayed Nida, who drops his criticisms of Jespersen (see 1966: 60). What was meanwhile lost sight of was that Jespersen's accounts represent descriptive grammar; and are thus—(trans)formalized or otherwise—inherently incompatible with the constrained philosophy of formal grammar. It was inevitable therefore that in due course, Chomsky should in turn retract the transformational reconstruction: as formal grammar restricted itself more effectively, 'transformations ... were gradually reduced'; and this shift 'represents a substantial break from earlier generative grammar, or from the traditional grammar on which it was in part modelled' (1981: 7).

4. 'Reconstruction' of Descriptive Grammar in Formal Grammar

The conception that even Chomsky (1981) maintains is that early generative grammar was—at least partly—modeled on traditional grammar; which still denies that there is always a profound opposition between descriptive and formal grammar. Again, however, such a conception appears to be false, if not a falsification. A notable instance is afforded by the way Chomsky's Standard Theory (1965) was ostensibly modeled: 'The investigation of generative grammar can profitably begin with a careful analysis of the kind of information presented in traditional grammars' (p. 63). Chomsky then presents a 'traditional' account of *sincerity may frighten the boy*: subject *sincerity* + auxiliary *may* + predicate *frighten the boy*.

Chomsky does not cite any traditional grammar which actually has precisely such a tripartition— hardly a 'careful analysis.' Certainly, no descriptive grammar considered in this article provides a model. Kruisinga (1932b: 263ff.) would have just two parts: subject *sincerity* + predicate *may frighten the boy*. And Jespersen (1927: 203ff.) assumes an alternative tripartition: subject *sincerity* + verb *may frighten* + object *the boy*. Most other descriptive grammar goes (implicitly) along with Jespersen.

For Jespersen, there does in fact appear to be something like a philosophy behind his account. Subject *sincerity* and object *the boy* should 'in their relation to the verb stand on nearly the same footing,' because switches from object to subject are so common (1927: 354); e.g., into subject *the boy* + verb *may be frightened* (see also (2), (4), and (5) below). But in descriptive grammar there is nothing which prevents Kruisinga from equally accounting for such switches although by his bipartition of the sentence, subject and object are by no means on the same footing. All this is fundamentally opposed to formal grammar, where subject–object asymmetry deduces directly from constraints on possible grammars. Thus the true source of Chomsky's (1965) tripartition is not any traditional descriptive model, but deduction from a restriction on definitions of grammatical relations such that subject and object can only be distinguished configurationally.

The point about coincidences between descriptive and formal grammar, such as there are, may be that, since in the former essentially anything goes, its apparatus happens to extend to what is necessary in formal grammar. Any apparatus, including what is or might be reconstructed in formal grammar, is inherently fortuitous in descriptive grammar; as long as it does not present an obstacle to comprehensive coverage.

5. 'Complementary' Coverage in Descriptive and Formal Grammar

What is fundamental to descriptive grammar is that it should be open to any facts; such that it is anything but coincidental if descriptive grammar comprehends pertinent facts of formal grammar. This inclusion is, however, in turn denied when Chomsky's purported conceptual shift from rules to principles and parameters in formal grammar is accompanied by abandoning ostensible reconstruction of descriptive grammar; Chomsky intimates that more recently, in (dis)covering deductively pertinent facts such as reflect universal features, formal grammar has become 'complementary' to descriptive grammar with respect to coverage: 'a good ... traditional grammar provides a full list of exceptions' (1986: 6), i.e., language particular features. Still, insofar as descriptive grammar

effectively attains comprehensive coverage, it should cover universal features pertinent to formal grammar as well as anything else.

To take some specific examples, about (1) and (2), Chomsky insinuates that 'It is doubtful that even the most compendious traditional ... grammar notes such simple facts' (1986: 9), 'which were, in fact, noticed only recently, in the course of the study of explicit rule systems in generative grammar' (1986: 8). It is important that Chomsky here raises the issue of whether facts are 'not(ic)ed' or not. There is thus agreement that such facts, once noted, may—or may not—be dealt with quite differently in descriptive and in formal grammar.

John ate an apple	(1a)
John ate	(1b)
(i.e., 'John ate *e*'; *e* = 'something')	
John is too stubborn to talk to Bill	(2a)
John is too stubborn to talk to	(2b)
(i.e., 'John is too stubborn to talk to *e*'; *e* = 'John')	

As indicated, the point about (1) and (2) is the different interpretations of the empty object-positions *e*. Has this point indeed first been noted in formal grammar? Not in the least. In descriptive grammar, (1)/(2) respectively had already been covered before by Sweet (1891: 90, 116), Poutsma (1926: 59, 460), Kruisinga (1932: 205; 1931: 163), Curme (1931: 437, 467); and much the most extensively by—Jespersen.

Jespersen (1927: 319–55) presents a descriptive survey of eight(!) different cases, which comprehend both 'omission of an obvious object' as in (1), and 'shiftings' from object of the infinitive to subject of the sentence as in (2). Jespersen describes cases like (1) as in (3):

he plays	(3)
(i.e., according to the circumstances the piano, football, etc.)	

Shiftings are dealt with in detail by Jespersen (1940: 221ff.), where (4a) is treated as a 'retroactive infinitive': i.e., with 'preceding item as its "implicit object"'; an object–subject shift (see above) formally represented in (4b):

this book is	too long to read	(4a)
S(O*)	V P(3 2 p I*)	(4b)

The paired raised stars in (4) are Jespersen's way in analytic syntax of having subject S *this book* do double duty as implicit object O of infinitive I. But such formalization does not anticipate formal grammar, because there are no associated constraints. That is, there is nothing to prevent (5b) analogous to (4b) instead of (5c) as a description of (5a):

that	made my position	harder to endure			(5a)
S(O*)	V	O	P (2	p I*)	(5b)
S	V	O(O*)	P (2	p I*)	(5c)

Jespersen (1940: 276) duly identifies (5c) as the correct description of (5a): O *my position* doubles as (O*) of

I* *to endure*; but descriptive grammar remains fundamentally open to (5b) as well, as if in (5a) S *that* could (also) double as (O*) of I*, i.e., the implicit object of *to endure*.

With respect to (1) and (2), Chomsky's allegations are not only easy to refute, but they easily backfire. Descriptive grammar duly does not fail to cover (1) and (2); and it is 'doubtful' that (1) and/or (2) are indeed deductively pertinent to Chomsky's current principles and parameters: in which case recent formal grammar had better not have noticed them at all. No such doubts arise with respect to further examples of facts which Chomsky alleges were noticed only recently, by virtue of a focus in current formal grammar on 'binding' (coreference) constrained by 'domains of subjects.' Consider (6), where (6b, d) represent (im)possible interpretations (cf. Chomsky 1986: 8): square brackets enclose domains internal to which coreference is impossible, but external coreference is fine; there are identical subscripts (cf. Jespersen's raised stars in (4) and (5)) for binding, *t* is the trace left by movement of (and cosubscripted with) *who*, PRO is the implicit subject of the infinitive controlled by (cosubscripted with) *the men*:

I wonder who	the men	expected	to see them	(6a)
I wonder who$_i$	the men$_j$	expected [t_i	to see them$_{*i,j}$]	(6b)
	the men	expected	to see them	(6c)
	the men$_j$	expected [PRO$_j$	to see them$_{*j}$]	(6d)

In formal grammar, the pronoun *them* has to be free (not cosubscripted) in the domains [. . .] established by (empty) subjects: the trace *t* of *who* in (6b); PRO controlled by *the men* in (6d). Hence, it will be noticed that only in (6a) but not in (6c) may the pronoun be referentially dependent on the antecedent *the men*; which allegedly 'was not recognized in earlier work' (1986: 8).

But even such facts were duly recognized earlier, in descriptive grammar, although in this case, apparently not by Jespersen. There are more or less explicit discussions of alternations as in (6a, c) in Poutsma (1917: 836), Kruisinga (1931: 206), and Curme (1931: 100; 1935: 10–11). But (6) in formal grammar was most notably preceded in descriptive grammar by more than half a century in Sweet's (1891: 77) observations with respect to (7a); (7b, c) corresponding to (6b, d) are added for exposition:

John	told him	to give himself	plenty of time	(7a)
John$_j$	told him$_h$ [PRO$_h$	to give himself$_h$	plenty of time]	(7b)
John$_j$	told him$_h$ [PRO$_h$	to give himself$_j$	plenty of time]	(7c)

In particular, in (7a) 'the reflexive pronoun *himself*... refers us back to the logical subject of *give*, namely *him*,' as cosubscripts in (7b) indicate; but what in (7a) 'the reflexive pronoun refers back to ... is not the grammatical subject of the sentence,' as by the subscripting in (7c). As Sweet explains, the logical subject

can be recognized in (8a) which is 'equivalent' to (7a); (8b) again for exposition:

John told him that he should give himself . . . time	(8a)
John$_j$ told him$_h$ that he$_h$ should give himself$_h$ . . . time	(8b)

On the other hand (9a) is equivalent to (9b) along the lines of (9c); hence here the personal pronoun *him* takes the place of the 'corresponding' reflexive *himself*:

he	begged me	to defend him	(9a)
he	begged me that I would	defend him	(9b)
he$_h$	begged me$_m$	[PRO$_m$ to defend him$_h$]	(9c)

Descriptive grammar covers alternations between personal and reflexive pronouns dependent on antecedents of 'logical subjects' in (7) and (9), however much Chomsky would like to doubt this; and this refutes privileged access to such alternations through deduction in formal grammar, even if the latter does explicate them, in (6) by cosubscripted PRO or *t*. Note that comprehensive coverage by Sweet is indeed obtained by apparent induction: from (8a) and (9b) respectively. Moreover, Sweet goes on to leave the effect of these alternations on the choice of pronoun explicitly open: in (9) 'in some languages, such as Latin, ... *him* would take the reflexive form ... *oravit ut se defenderem* [he begged that I defended (subjunctive) himself]'; in descriptive grammar, in one language the facts go this way, in another language they may go any other way, without any constraints.

Since binding theory epitomizes formal grammar in its Chomskyan manifestation, the above amounts to a crucial demonstration that coverage in descriptive and formal grammar is not such that the former complements for particular languages the latter's universal features; but rather, if the former's coverage includes the latter's, fundamental incompatibility remains in the approaches taken. The significance of this demonstration is enhanced because it can be extended from English to other languages. That is, since Chomsky takes binding theory to reflect universals, he is logically bound to claim that for instance, facts about binding in Dutch are also the prerogative of formal grammar, to the virtual exclusion of descriptive grammar of Dutch. And indeed, Chomsky is reported as making precisely such a claim in a Dutch newspaper interview (*NRC-Handelsblad*, May 19, 1986; even if the interview transposes original comments of Chomsky's on English, the point stands).

Consider the binding properties of (10a), indicated in (10b, c):

Jan	denkt	dat	Piet	hem aardig vindt	(10a)
Jan	thinks	that	Piet	him nice finds	
'Jan	thinks	that	Piet	likes him'	
Jan$_j$	denkt	dat	Piet$_p$	hem$_j$ aardig vindt	(10b)
*Jan$_j$	denkt	dat	Piet$_p$	hem$_p$ aardig vindt	(10c)

Once again, Chomsky would like to think that such

facts will not be found 'in even the largest ten-volume traditional grammar' of Dutch. But it is easy to find a Dutch counterpart (and contemporary) of Sweet to refute this as well: Den Hertog in his three-volume *Nederlandsche Spraakkunst* (1892–96). Hulshof (1985: 125) identifies Den Hertog's preference for the method of induction; accordingly Den Hertog himself adumbrates descriptive grammar by advertising his extensiveness (1892: iii; cf. Hulshof 1985: 48). And Den Hertog (1896: 71) therefore does discuss (11a) and its 'development' into (11b), such that for (11a), (11c–d) hold; (11a–b) simplified, (11c–d) for exposition:

Jan beval Piet hem de brieven te geven   (11a)
Jan ordered Piet him the letters to give
'Jan ordered Piet to give him [=Jan] the letters'

Jan beval Piet dat hij hem de brieven moest geven   (11b)
J ordered P that he him the letters must give
'Jan commanded Piet that he [=Piet] should
  give him [=Jan] the letters'

Jan$_j$ beval Piet$_p$ [PRO$_p$ hem$_j$ de brieven te geven]   (11c)

*Jan$_j$ beval Piet$_p$ [PRO$_p$ hem$_p$ de brieven te geven]   (11d)

6. Conclusion

Formal grammar as represented by Chomskyan generative linguistics identifies the refutable property of the grammar of human language in its being a closed domain. From this conception derive universal constraints in terms of which the deductively pertinent facts of particular languages are to be accounted for. Descriptive grammar in the tradition to which Jespersen belongs does not restrict its conception of human language a priori; and thus it pre-empts refutation, and purports for each individual language to establish its facts inductively, up to comprehensive coverage. The latter point entails that descriptions may well coincide with accounts in formal grammar. Upon formalization, such coincidence may appear deceptively indicative of significant contiguity: as in two views successively endorsed authoritatively by Chomsky; earlier, that formal grammar reconstructs descriptive grammar, or at least Jespersen; and later, that descriptive grammar for particular languages complements the universals of formal grammar. In the limited space here available, diametrical opposition of descriptive versus formal grammar has been maintained by refuting both of Chomsky's views.

Bibliography

Chomsky N 1955 *The Logical Structure of Linguistic Theory*. Plenum, New York (Repr. in 1975)
Chomsky N 1957 *Syntactic Structures*. Mouton, The Hague
Chomsky N 1958 A transformational approach to syntax [and contributions to discussions]. In: Hill A A (ed.) 1962 *Studies in American English Third Texas Conference on Problems of Linguistic Analysis in English, 1958*. University of Texas, Austin, TX

Chomsky N 1964 *Current Issues in Linguistic Theory*. Mouton, The Hague
Chomsky N 1965 *Aspects of the Theory of Syntax*. MIT Press, Cambridge, MA
Chomsky N 1975 *Questions of Form and Interpretation*. De Ridder, Lisse
Chomsky N 1979 *Language and Responsibility*. Harvester, Brighton (Transl. by Viertel J)
Chomsky N 1981 *Lectures on Government and Binding*. Foris, Dordrecht
Chomsky N 1986 *Knowledge of Language*. Praeger, New York
Curme G O 1931 *Syntax*. Heath, Boston, MA
Curme G O 1935 *Parts of Speech and Accidence*. Heath, Boston, MA
Den Hertog C H 1892–96 *Nederlandsche spraakkunst*. Versluys, Amsterdam (Vol. I, 1892; vol. II, 1892; vol. III, 1896)
Grattan J H G 1926 Review of Kruisinga E, *A Handbook of Present-Day English Part II. English Accidence and Syntax. The Review of English Studies* 2: 243–44
Hill A A 1958 *Introduction to Linguistic Structures*. Harcourt Brace, New York
Hulshof H 1985 *C. H. den Hertog als grammaticus*. Coutinho, Muiderberg
Jespersen O 1909–49 *A Modern English Grammar on Historical Principles*. Allen & Unwin, London (Vol. I, 1909; vol. II, 1914; vol. III, 1927; vol. IV, 1931; vol. V, 1940; vol. VI, 1942; vol. VII, 1949, posthumous, ed. by Haislund N)
Jespersen O 1924 *The Philosophy of Grammar*. Allen & Unwin, London
Jespersen O 1937 *Analytic Syntax*. Holt Rinehart & Winston, New York (Repr. in 1969)
Kruisinga E 1911 *A Grammar of Present-Day English II. A*. Kemink, Utrecht
Kruisinga E 1931–32 *A Handbook of Present-Day English II*. Noordhoff, Groningen (Vol. I, 1931; vol. II, 1932a; vol. III, 1932b)
Lees R B 1957 Review of Chomsky N, *Syntactic Structures. Language* **33**(3): 375–408
Newmeyer F J 1980 *Linguistic Theory in America*. Academic Press, New York
Nida E A 1960 *A Synopsis of English Syntax*. SIL, Norman, OK
Nida E A 1966 *A Synopsis of English Syntax*. Mouton, The Hague
Poutsma H 1904–26 *A Grammar of Late Modern English*. Noordhoff, Groningen (Vol. I–I, 1904, 1928; vol. I–II, 1905, 1929; vol. II-IA, 1914; vol. II–IB, 1917; vol. II–II, 1926)
Quirk R, Greenbaum S, Leech G, Svartvik J 1972 *A Grammar of Contemporary English*. Longman, London
Quirk R, Greenbaum S, Leech G, Svartvik J 1985 *A Comprehensive Grammar of the English Language*. Longman, London
Sledd J 1964 Syntactic strictures. *The English Leaflet* **61**: 14–23 (Repr. in: Allen H B (ed.) 1964 *Readings in Applied English Linguistics*, 2nd edn. Appleton-Century-Croft, New York)
Stuurman F 1990 *Two Grammatical Models of Modern English*. Routledge, London
Sweet H 1900 *A New English Grammar*. Oxford University Press, Oxford (Vol. I, 1891; vol. II, 1898)

Firth and the London School

F. R. Palmer

John Rupert Firth (1890–1960) was Professor and Head of the Department of General Linguistics in the Department of Phonetics and Linguistics in the School of Oriental and African Studies in the University of London from 1941–56, after having served as Senior Lecturer and as Reader in that Department from 1938. The title of Professor of General Linguistics was conferred on him in 1944. He had previously been Professor of English in Lahore, India (1920–28) and from 1928–38 Senior Lecturer in the Department of Phonetics at University College London, of which the renowned phonetician Daniel Jones (1881–1967) was the head. During World War II he was in charge of short intensive training courses in Japanese, which both depended on, and influenced, his linguistic outlook. Firth's was the first and only Chair of Linguistics in Britain until 1960, but his influence is reflected in the rapid growth of the subject in the 1960s and the fact that seven members of his academic staff subsequently held chairs themselves, three of them in other universities.

Firth's earlier works are collected in *Papers in Linguistics 1934–1951* (Firth 1957) and his later works, together with some papers unpublished at his death, in *Selected Papers of J. R. Firth 1952–1959* (Palmer 1968). A collection of original papers by Firth and his colleagues appeared under the title of *Studies in Linguistic Analysis* in 1962, while papers on prosodic analysis (see below) are reprinted in *Prosodic Analysis* (Palmer 1970). A summary of his own views was presented by him in 'A synopsis of linguistic theory 1952–55' (Palmer 1968 [1957]: 168–205). Other accounts of the theory are found in Robins (1963) and in the Introduction to Palmer (1968). For details of Firth's career see the obituary by Robins (1961).

Firth is probably best known for the work produced from 1948 until his death in 1960, but the work of the 'London School' includes the publications of his followers (almost all members of the department) from 1948 until the middle 1960s. His contribution can only be fully appreciated, however, in the light of his earlier works published in the years before the War. Most of his early publications, apart from two popular books *Speech* (1930) and *Tongues of Men* (1937; both reprinted in 1964), were mainly concerned with phonology, although 'The technique of semantics' (Firth 1957 [1935]: 7–33) lays the foundation for his basic theory. It was in the field of phonology that he provided the greatest stimulation, with development of the theory known as 'prosodic analysis' that stemmed from his 'Sounds and prosodies' (Palmer 1970 [1948]: 1–26), for most of the papers published by members of his department during the 1960s were on that topic.

1. Firth's Views on Meaning

A second theory with which Firth is closely associated is that of 'context of situation,' but this (and also, to some degree, prosodic analysis) are best understood in terms of his more general views on meaning. While his contemporary in the early years, Bloomfield, was suggesting that meaning was 'the weak point in language study' (Bloomfield 1933: 140), and later American linguists were to exclude it altogether, Firth was already developing his contextual theory of meaning, which is first clearly stated in 'The technique of semantics,' (Firth 1957 [1935]: 19) where he speaks of meaning as 'situational relations in a context of situation' and says 'I propose to split up meaning or function into a series of component functions. Each function will be defined as the use of some language form or element in relation to some context. Meaning, that is to say, is to be regarded as a complex of contextual relations, and phonetics, grammar, lexicography, and semantics each handles its own components of the complex in its own appropriate context.' (This he applied specifically to phonetics and phonology by distinguishing between the minor function of vowels, which was concerned only with phonetic context, and the major functions, which were situational, lexical, morphological, and phonaesthetic (Firth 1957 [1935]: 37).) This, of course, involves a considerable reinterpretation of the notion of meaning; meaning defined 'in terms of actual situations' (Bloomfield 1935: 144) would relate to only one component. Firth's later exposition of his views in 'Personality and language in society' (Firth 1957 [1950]: 183) held that 'the statement of meaning cannot be achieved by one analysis at one level, in one fell swoop' and talked of linguistics being 'a sort of hierarchy of techniques by means of which the meaning of linguistic events may be, as it were, dispersed in a spectrum of specialized statements' ('rather like the dispersion of light of mixed wavelengths into a spectrum' (Firth 1957 [1951]: 192)). Context of situation is concerned with the 'social level of analysis' and forms the basis of the hierarchy of techniques for the statements of meaning (Firth 1957 [1951]: 183), but Firth could talk also about phonological and even phonetic meaning, with the comment 'surely it is part of the meaning of an American to sound like one' (ibid: 192, 194, 197).

2. Techniques and Abstractions

The title of the 1935 paper, 'Techniques of semantics,' is significant; it is concerned with techniques for language description, which, Firth later stated, consisted of 'a range of abstracted levels, that were not to be confused with Bloomfield's "levels of analysis".' (The term 'semantics' also is intended to refer to his theory; he talks of the integration of the work of the phonetician, grammarian, and lexicographer into experience and situation and wishes to use the term 'semantics' for that; but the term is, perhaps, a little unfortunate because it is also used in the paper in its narrower sense, and he did not use it again in his sense in his later papers.) In particular, there was no direction in the hierarchy of techniques: statements could be made at the different levels either in descending order, beginning with social context, or in the opposite order, beginning with phonetics (Firth 1957 [1951]: 192). Reference to abstraction ('abstracted levels') is also important: both the selection of the text and the operation of the techniques, involved 'abstractions' by the linguist (ibid). There were no '"facts" prior to statement' (Palmer 1968 [1957]: 199). Firth was, in this respect, firmly an empiricist; he had always insisted on a formal approach to grammar: 'No grammar without morphology' (Firth 1957 [1935]: 19) and dismissed any kind of mentalistic approach (Firth 1964 [1930]: 173; 1957 [1935]: 19) and he quoted with approval Wittgenstein's 'the meaning of words lies in their use' (Palmer 1968 [1957]: 179). He also emphasized theory rather than methodology: 'the excessive use of method and procedures is avoided so that theoretical relevance may not be hidden or obscured' (Palmer 1968 [1957]: 168), with particular scorn (in conversation at least) for the methodologies of phonemics with its 'additive' morphemics and 'corrective' morphophonemics (cf. Palmer 1968 [1955]: 40). This might not seem controversial today, when discovery procedures (Chomsky 1957: 51) are no longer in favor, but it gave Firth and his colleagues freedom to break with the dogmas of American structuralism and, in particular, to reject the rigid separation of levels (see *American Structuralism*).

3. Context of Situation

Nevertheless, as quotations above make clear, context of situation was 'a key concept' (Firth 1957 [1950]: 181) of Firth's theory of meaning. He acknowledged that he had taken this expression from the anthropologist Malinowski, with whom he had worked in London, and whose views on meaning are best-known from his 'The problem of meaning in primitive languages,' which is a supplement to Ogden and Richards's (1923) *The Meaning of Meaning* as well as his own (1935) *Coral Gardens and Their Magic*. Malinowski's views on language derived from the difficulties he had experienced in attempting to translate the texts that he had collected, and his conclusion that they could only be understood if placed in the contexts in which they had been uttered. Written language, he suggested, was not the norm, but a far-fetched derivative function of language; language was not a 'mirror of reflected thought,' but a 'mode of action' (1923: 296). Firth felt, however, that Malinowski's

context of situation was 'a bit of the social process which can be considered apart,' that it was 'an ordered series of events considered *in rebus*,' whereas his own context of situation was an abstraction, 'a schematic construct,' 'a group of related categories at a different level from grammatical categories, but rather of the same abstract nature.' The categories, he suggested, were (1):

> (a) The relevant features of participants: persons, personalities.   (1)
>   (i) The verbal action of the participants.
>   (ii) The nonverbal action of the participants.
> (b) The relevant objects.
> (c) The effect of the verbal action.

Firth gives just one example, which represents 'a typical Cockney event' (2):

> 'Ahng gunna gi' wun fer Ber''   (2)
> (I'm going to get one for Bert.)

'What,' Firth asks, 'is the minimum number of participants? Three? Four? Where might it happen? In a pub? Where is Bert? Outside? Or playing darts? What are the relevant objects? "Obvious!" you say. So is the convenience of the schematic construct called "context of situation"' (Firth 1957 [1950]: 182). In addition to these interior relations of the context, he later suggests that there should be reference to more general frameworks such as economic, religious, and other social structures, types of discourse (monolog, narrative, etc.), personal interchanges, and types of speech function such as drills and orders together with the social techniques of flattery, deception, etc. (Palmer 1968 [1957]: 178).

An obvious objection to this is that the technique would deal satisfactorily only with specialized situations, and would fail to account for the meaning of the vast majority of normal utterances. But from the beginning Firth had approached the problem by concentrating on 'common situations' (Firth 1957 [1935]: 30), and always stressed the importance of 'restricted languages' in which the utterances were closely associated with their situation. He would cite as a justification his success in training service personnel in a very short time to interpret Japanese messages during World War II, by recognizing the 'limited situational contexts of war' and their 'operative language' (Firth 1957 [1950]: 182). He did not hope to make a total statement of meaning 'at one fell swoop,' but was content to say what could be said by whatever technique was available. Yet the only paper that attempted, with some success, to put Firth's situational theory into practice is Mitchell's (1957) 'The language of buying and selling in Cyrenaica: a situational statement.' (On this point, and for a more general critique of the theory, see Lyons 1966.)

4. Collocation

One extra 'mode of meaning' that Firth introduced was that of 'collocation'; this is the topic of 'Modes of meaning' (Firth 1957 [1951]: 190–215), and is illustrated by the claim that part of the meaning of *ass* in modern colloquial English could be stated in terms of collocation in (3):

(a) An ass like Bagson might easily do that.   (3)
(b) He is an ass.
(c) You silly ass!
(d) Don't be an ass!

One of the meanings of *ass*, then, is its habitual collocation with *you silly*; there are limited possibilities of collocation, the commonest adjectives being *silly*, *obstinate*, *stupid*, *awful*, and occasionally *egregious*. Firth further illustrated collocation from Lear's limericks, the poems of Swinburne, and letters of the eighteenth and early nineteenth century. He stressed that collocational meaning was not the same as contextual meaning, but also argued that context of situation was necessary for the statement of meaning by collocation to be completed. The notion of collocation may seem similar to that of distribution, a key notion in American structuralism, but, consistently with his general views on meaning, Firth was not concerned with the total distribution of words, but with these restricted co-occurrences, with what he called 'the mutual expectancy' of words, and also within restricted languages (Palmer 1968 [1957]: 180). After prosodic analysis, collocation is the topic that provided the most interest for other scholars who had worked with him or been indirectly influenced by him; three of the papers in his memorial volume (Bazell et al. 1966) are concerned with the subject (those by M. A. K. Halliday, J. McH. Sinclair, and T. F. Mitchell).

5. Structure and System

Within grammar and phonology, Firth laid great emphasis on the notion of syntagmatic and paradigmatic relations, as proposed by Saussure (1959 [1916]: 122–34) and developed by Hjelmslev (1953: 22–25) and the parallel distinction of structure and system, structures always being syntagmatic or 'horizontal,' systems being paradigmatic or 'vertical.' Within each system the units or terms were 'commutable' and received their value from their place within that system. Firth's approach was polysystemic, which meant that different systems could be set up within any one structure, and there was no identification between the terms of different systems. This is well-illustrated in (prosodic) phonology.

Within grammar, Firth illustrates his views by suggesting that a nominative in a four-case system would have a different meaning from a nominative in a two-case or in a fourteen-case system, and that a singular in a two-number system would have a different meaning from a singular in a three-number system or a four-number system such as that of Fijian with its singular, dual, 'little' plural and 'big' plural, and that the meaning of the grammatical category noun would be different in a system of noun, verb, and particle from its meaning in a five-term system in which adjective and pronoun are formally distinct from noun (Firth 1957 [1951]: 227). The grammatical elements of structure were linked by colligation, with, as for collocation, mutual expectation (Palmer 1968 [1957]: 186) between them. These notions of system and structure were adopted by Halliday as a central part of his Systemic Grammar (for early references see Halliday 1962: 254–55, 263–64; Halliday et al. 1964: 29–30; see also *Systemic Functional Grammar*).

6. Grammar

Unfortunately, Firth has very little else of real significance on grammar, although there are interesting observations on the grammars of languages, particularly English, in several of his papers. He emphasized the need for grammar to be formal (Firth 1957 [1951]: 222), rejecting the idea of universal grammatical categories, and insisted on the abstract nature of the grammatical elements. For that reason, he argued that the *order* of the grammatical categories 'is very different from the successivity of bits and pieces in a unidirectional time sequence' (Palmer 1968 [1957]: 173). Grammatical categories are abstracted from the linguistic material, but 'renewal of connection' via their 'exponents' is essential, though these exponents may be discontinuous or cumulative (Palmer 1968 [1957]: 190). This issue is discussed in some detail by Palmer (1964). In one paper specifically on the subject, 'A new approach to grammar' (Palmer 1968: 114–24), he confirms his opposition to dualist theories of meaning and his insistence that grammar is concerned with abstract categories, not words or morphemes, and he suggests that grammatical analysis should first be applied to restricted languages, but the only new idea is in the extension of his 'spectrum' theory of meaning, by suggesting that grammar too should be 'dispersed,' with a series of congruent levels 'such as graphematics, phonology, morphematics, and syntax.'

In his last years Firth devoted much attention to translation (there are two papers in Palmer 1968). This was, in a way, appropriate, since his theoretical views had their origins in the problems that Malinowski had faced.

Anyone who reads Firth's work will inevitably be frustrated. Much of it is programmatic and sometimes unclear and apocryphal, and there is a great deal of repetition in successive papers. Yet it is, and was, stimulating, and offered a whole generation of scholars in the UK a new insight into language study, as well as providing an alternative to the barren structuralism of his time. If some of it appears obvious today, it may be that he was ahead of his time.

Bibliography

Bazell C E, Catford J C, Halliday M A K, Robins R H (eds.) 1966 *In Memory of J. R. Firth*. Longman, London

Bloomfield L 1933 *Language*. Holt, New York
Chomsky N 1957 *Syntactic Structures*. Mouton, The Hague
Firth J R 1957 *Papers in Linguistics 1934–1951*. Oxford University Press, London
Firth J R 1964 *The Tongues of Men and Speech*. Oxford University Press, London
Halliday M A K 1962 Categories of the theory of grammar. *Word* 17: 241–92
Halliday M A K, McIntosh A, Strevens P 1964 *The Linguistic Sciences and Language Teaching*. Longman, London
Hjelmslev L 1953 *Prolegomena to a Theory of Language*. *International Journal of American Linguistics Memoir 7*. IJAL, Bloomington, IN (Transl. by Whitfield F J)
Lyons J 1966 Firth's theory of 'meaning.' In: Bazell et al. (eds.) 1966
Malinowski B 1923 The problem of meaning in primitive languages. Supplement to Ogden C K, Richards I A 1923 *The Meaning of Meaning*. Kegan Paul, London
Malinowski B 1953 *Coral Gardens and Their Magic, II*. Allen and Unwin, London
Mitchell T F 1957 The language of buying and selling in Cyrenaica: A situational statement. *Hespéris* **1957**: 31–71
Palmer F R 1964 'Sequence' and 'order.' In: Stuart C I J M (ed.) Report of the *15th Annual R. T. M. on Linguistic and Language Studies* (*Monograph Series on Languages and Linguistic Series* **17**)
Palmer F R (ed.) 1968 *Selected Papers of J. R. Firth, 1952–1959*. Longman, London
Palmer F R (ed.) 1970 *Prosodic Analysis*. Oxford University Press, London
Philological' Society 1962 *Studies in Linguistic Analysis*. Blackwell, Oxford
Robins R H 1961 John Rupert Firth. *Lg* 37: 191–200
Robins R H 1963 General linguistics in Great Britain 1930–1960. In: Mohrmann C, Norman F, Sommerfelt A (eds.) *Trends in Modern Linguistics*. Spectrum, Antwerp
Saussure F de 1916 *Cours de linguistique générale*. Payot, Paris (Transl. by Baskin W 1959 as *Course in General Linguistics*. McGraw-Hill, New York)

Functional Grammar

Simon C. Dik

updated by J. Lachlan Mackenzie

Functional Grammar (FG) in the sense described in this article is a general theory of the grammatical organization of natural languages, based on a functional view of the nature of language. The theory was initiated by Dik (1978); it has been further developed in a large number of studies on a wide variety of languages and linguistic topics (see the general bibliography in De Groot 1996). The major presentation of the theory is Dik (1989); Part Two of this work is currently in preparation (Dik in press). For a critical assessment of FG, see Siewierska (1991).

This article first discusses some basic metatheoretical principles underlying FG. Sect. 2 then sketches the main modules of the FG clause model: the 'fund,' consisting of the 'lexicon,' the 'term formation component,' and the 'predicate formation component'; the 'underlying clause structure'; and the expression rules. Sect. 3 discusses the potential of the FG clause model as a component in a model of the natural language user. Sect. 4 summarizes some applications of FG, and Sect. 5 describes recent developments in the theory.

1. Metatheoretical Principles

From a functional point of view a natural language is first and foremost conceived of as an instrument of human communication: a means through which speakers and addressees can influence each other's content of mind or 'pragmatic information,' and ultimately each other's action patterns. Seen in this way, a natural language is basically a pragmatic phenomenon. The forms of language are there in order to act as carriers of meanings; and meanings are there in order to transmit messages from one speaker to another within the context and situation of actual speech events. Thus, morphosyntax is subservient to semantics, and semantics is subservient to pragmatics. The 'autonomy of syntax' is explicitly rejected.

A functional theory of the organization of natural languages must be pragmatically and psychologically adequate. Pragmatic adequacy requires that linguistic expressions be described in ways which make one understand how it is that these expressions can be used as carriers of messages. Psychological adequacy is reached to the extent that the language model may be assumed to be compatible with the ways in which natural language users go about producing and interpreting linguistic material. These two requirements may be summarized by saying that a functional grammar should be a viable candidate for serving as the grammatical component of a model of the natural language user. This embedding of FG in a speaker model is further discussed in Sect. 3 below.

Any theory which wishes to be generally applicable to natural languages should be typologically adequate in the sense that it should formulate the rules, structures, and principles of language in a way which generalizes across languages of any type and is unbiased in relation to specific language types. For typological adequacy to be achieved in an interesting way, grammatical analysis should be couched in terms which are sufficiently abstract to be generally valid for natural languages. But in order to actually say something empirically relevant the analysis should be as concrete as possible. This seeming paradox must be solved by seeking, in grammatical analysis, the level of optimal generalization across languages. This is the most concrete level which is yet sufficiently abstract to achieve typological adequacy. One way of avoiding unwarranted abstractness is to avoid structure-changing transformations wherever this is possible. This guarantees that the structures in terms of which linguistic expressions are described will never drift too far away from the actual form the expressions take, and that, given the expression, the underlying structure will be recoverable by effective procedures. Consider two examples of FG decisions based on this reasoning.

1.1 Constituent Ordering

This is notoriously variable both within and across languages. If a specific constituent order is entered into underlying structure as a 'deep' property, then either the underlying structures do not generalize across languages, or an unwarranted amount of transformational 'movement' is required. It is better, then, to assume that constituent ordering is not a 'deep' property of natural languages, but rather one of the means through which underlying structures are mapped onto linguistic expressions. At the same time, this allows one to define the factors which trigger the one or the other constituent order pattern, thus capturing something of the functionality of constituent ordering as an expression device.

1.2 Subject–Predicate

Subject–predicate or NP–VP analysis works well for SVO and SOV languages, those languages, that is, in which the verb and the object are contiguous. For VSO languages, however, this analysis is less adequate: if it is to be maintained, we must adopt one of the following assumptions: (1) VSO languages have a deep SVO or SOV ordering which is transformed into VSO by a rule of V-fronting; (2) they have a discontinuous VP; (3) they have, not a binary, but a ternary (V–NP–NP) underlying structure. With any of these alternatives VSO languages come out as 'exceptional' as compared to SVO and SOV languages. There is, however, not much to warrant this exceptional status apart from the initial assumption that languages in principle have a binary NP–VP structure. From the point of view of typological adequacy, therefore, this assumption is to be rejected. All languages must be assumed to have an underlying nonbinary structure in which a predicate is applied to one or more nominal arguments.

2. The FG Clause Model

The FG clause model consists of three main components: the fund, consisting of the set of predicates and terms available in the language; the component in which underlying clause structures (UCSs) are created; and the expression rules through which UCSs are mapped onto linguistic expressions.

2.1 The Fund

The fund contains the full set of predicates and terms from which UCSs can be formed. Terms are expressions which can be used to identify entities. Predicates are lexical expressions which designate properties of, and relations between entities. Both terms and predicates can be basic or derived. Derived items can be formed by synchronically productive rules; basic items must be learned and memorized as such if they are to be properly used. Basic terms and predicates together constitute the lexicon. Derived predicates are formed through predicate formation rules, derived terms through term formation rules.

2.1.1 The Lexicon

The lexicon plays a central role in the fabric of a functional grammar. Its status is defined by the following properties.

(a) The lexicon contains only lexical material (content items). Grammatical elements such as affixes, particles, auxiliaries, and determiners are specified by the expression rules. Thus, in a sentence such as 'The naughty girl has been kissing the boy,' only girl, naughty, kiss, and boy will be found in the lexicon; all the other elements are specified by the expression rules.

(b) The lexicon contains only basic items. These are items which have formal and/or semantic properties which cannot be derived by productive rules. The lexicon thus contains all the lexical material which a speaker simply has to know in order to be able to speak the language. Basic lexical items need not be words. They may be stems, words, or combinations of words. In the latter case, these word combinations must have unique, nonderivable formal and/or semantic properties. In other words, such word combinations are idioms.

(c) There is no independent syntactic component which generates abstract structures into which lexical items will then be inserted at a next stage. Rather, UCSs are construed around and from lexical items directly. The lexical predicates constitute the nuclei of UCSs.

(d) Lexical items are not isolated forms, but structures with a rich articulation. The lexical entry for a predicate consists of a predicate frame and one or more associated meaning postulates. Consider the sample lexical entry for the English verb, kiss, Fig. 1. The predicate frame specifies the form 'kiss' as a verbal (V) predicate with a valency for two arguments designating human beings, in the roles of Agent and Patient.

KISS

predicate frame:
$$kiss_V (x_1 : \langle human \rangle)_{Ag} (x_2 : \langle human \rangle)_{Pat}$$
meaning postulate:
$$=_{def}$$
$$[touch_V (x_1 : \langle human \rangle)_{Ag} (x_2 : \langle human \rangle)_{Pat}]$$
$$(x_3 : lips)_{Instr}$$
$$(e_1 : [express_V (x_1)_{Ag} (x_4 : affection_N)_{Pat}])_{Purp}$$

Figure 1.

The meaning postulate defines the meaning of the predicate frame as 'x_1 touches x_2 with the lips for the purpose of expressing affection.' Note that the definiens of a meaning postulate has the same formal structure as the definiendum. This implies that when one has a UCS construed around the predicate frame 'kiss,' this structure can be replaced by the defining structure from the lexical entry, thus arriving at a (first-order) paraphrase of the original.

(e) The lexicon also defines the nonderivable (irregular) forms of predicates. For example, the lexicon will contain a 'paradigm' for a verbal predicate such as give, such that the past tense is gave and the past participle is given, rather than *gived. Such forms will be retrieved through a convention of 'lexical priority': for example, whenever the past tense form of a predicate is needed by the expression rules, the convention says, 'first see if there is a paradigm in the lexicon which contains this form; if so, select it and block the regular past tense formation rule; else, apply that regular rule to the stem.'

2.1.2 Term Formation

Terms are expressions which a speaker can use to 'refer' an addressee to an entity. All languages have a restricted number of basic 'ready-made' terms which have to be listed in the lexicon. Personal pronouns and proper names belong to this class, as well as 'ready-made' adverbials such as: today, yesterday, now, here, there, and how. Most terms, however, are construed by means of term formation rules according to a schema which can be most generally represented as:

$$(\omega\ x_i : \phi_1(x_i) : \varphi_2(x_i) : \ldots : \varphi_n(x_i)), n \geq r\ 1. \tag{1}$$

in this schema, x_i represents the term variable (a symbol for the as yet 'unknown' entity that is to be identified through the term), φ indicates one or more term operators, and each $\omega(x_i)$ symbolizes a restrictor, some property through which the potential reference of the term is successively restricted until the intended referent has been sufficiently described. Consider the actual term structure for the term, 'the naughty girl who kissed the boy':

$$(d1x_i : girl_N(x_i): \tag{2}$$
$$naughty_A(x_i):$$
$$Past\ e: [kiss_V (Rx_i)_{Ag} (d1x_j : boy_N(x_j))_{Pat}])$$

'definite (d) singular (1) entity x_i such that x_i has the property 'girl' such that x_i has the property 'naughty' such that x_i has the property of having been involved in the past in a state of affairs e in which x_i kissed definite singular entity x_j such that x_j has the property 'boy''

In (2) the entity x_i is successively restricted by a nominal, an adjectival, and a verbal predicate, where the latter will be expressed by a relative clause in English (the operator R will take care of this). The term structure schema exemplified in (2) is semantically and pragmatically motivated. It can be used for different languages, even though these may have rather different types of expression for terms. Thus, if a language should express term structure (2) in some such form as:

boy the kissed having naughty girl the (3)

this can be regarded as an alternative expression of much the same underlying term structure as (2).

The claim embodied in the term schema is that the underlying semantic relations in the term structure are quite similar, even though the expression rules differ across languages. This also means that a semantic interpretation can more easily be attached to the underlying term structure than to the diverse surface forms of term expressions.

Note that in the structure of terms, operators capture distinctions of a more grammatical nature, while restrictors specify the lexically coded properties and relations in terms of which intended referents are characterized. Note further that term formation procedures are recursive, so that the fund contains a theoretically infinite number of terms.

2.1.3 Predicate Formation

The lexicon contains the basic predicates of a language, together with information on their form, valency, and meaning. Most languages have rules for productively creating derived predicates of various kinds. Such predicates can be formed by predicate formation rules. The term 'predicate formation' rather than 'word formation' is used, since derived predicates, just like basic predicates, need not consist of one word (e.g., 'run away' may be analyzed as a derived predicate), or may consist of less than a word (e.g., a stem such as Greek *hippopotamo-*, formed from *hippo-* 'horse' and *potamo-* 'river'; the derived stem can be inflected for any of the inflexional distinctions that basic stems such as *hippo-* may be inflected for). The question of whether there is an analytic or synthetic expression is thus not essential to the notion of 'predicate.' What is essential is that the predicate should be part of a unified predicate frame, having a single valency pattern.

It was shown above that a predicate necessarily takes the form of a predicate frame, i.e., of a structure including the valency, the semantic functions, and the selection restrictions. It follows that predicate formation rules take one or more predicate frames (which themselves may already have been derived) as input and deliver a new predicate frame as output. At the same time, the meaning of the input and output predicate frames must be specified by general rule.

Since predicate formation rules apply to input predicate frames and deliver output predicate frames, the types of information coded in predicate frames allow for a natural typology of predicate formation rules. Such rules can modify any combination of the following features: (a) the form, (b) the category, (c) the number of arguments, (d) the semantic functions, (e) the selection restrictions, and (f) the meaning of the input predicate(s). A considerable amount of work has been done within FG to further develop and test this predicate formation typology on a variety of languages. For surveys of this work, see De Groot (1987) and Dik (1990).

2.2 Underlying Clause Structure

A UCS is created around a nucleus consisting of a basic or derived predicate frame in a stepwise, layered fashion which can be represented as shown in Fig. 2 (cf. Hengeveld 1989). Here the P-elements stand for operators, and the S-elements stand for satellites of different types and levels within the overall clause structure. The difference between operators and satellites is that the former represent grammatically expressed, and the latter lexically expressed modifiers of the expression type which they take in their scope.

LAYERED CLAUSE STRUCTURE
NUCLEUS = NUCLEAR PREDICATION =
predicate frame, applied to appropriate set of terms.

CORE PREDICATION	= P1 [NUCLEUS] S1
EXTENDED PREDICATION	= P2 [CORE PREDICATION] S2
PROPOSITION	= P3 [EXTENDED PREDICATION] S3
CLAUSE	= P4 [PROPOSITION] S4

Figure 2.

The nuclear predicate frame designates a property of or relation between entities as designated by terms. The predicate operators P1 and predicate satellites S1 provide additional specifications of the State of Affairs (SoA) designated by the nuclear predication. An example of P1 would be the progressive operator, while S1 satellites include satellites of beneficiary, manner, instrument, speed, and direction. An example of a core predication would be:

$$\text{Progr [kiss}_V \text{ (the girl)}_{Ag} \text{ (the boy)}_{Pat}] \text{ (passionate)}_{Man} \quad (4)$$
'the girl kissing the boy passionately'

At the level of the core predication the functions subject and object are differentially assigned to the terms; these functions are interpreted as defining different 'perspectives' from which the SoA as designated by the nucleus can be presented. Thus, the following alternative realizations of the same nuclear SoA are considered as being due to different perspectivizations effected through differential assignment of subject and object function:

Mary (AgSubj) gave the book (PatObj) to John (Rec) (5a)

Mary (AgSubj) gave John (RecObj) the book (Pat) (5b)

The book (PatSubj) was given to John (Rec) by Mary (Ag) (5c)

John (RecSubj) was given the book (Pat) by Mary (Ag) (5d)

Subject and object are not judged to be universally relevant to natural languages. Some languages simply lack this possibility of alternative perspectivization of SoAs. In those languages which do have this possibility, accessibility of terms to subject/object function can be shown to decrease along a hierarchy of semantic functions (roughly, from the most central to the most peripheral semantic functions within the domain of the core predication).

The SoA designated by the core predication can be 'localized' in time and space through P2 operators (e.g., tense) and S2 satellites (e.g., adverbials of time and location). The extended predication thus designates a 'situated event.' The extended predication is the highest structure of the 'representational' part of the clause. An example of an extended predication (with the SoA variable 'e') would be:

$$\text{Past e: [Progr [kiss}_V \text{ (the girl)}_{Ag} \text{ (the boy)}_{PatSubj}] \quad (6)$$
$$\text{(passionate)}_{Man}] \text{ (the library)}_{Loc}$$
'the boy was being passionately kissed by the girl in the library'

At this level pragmatic functions such as Topic and Focus can be assigned to different parts of the predication. These functions are interpreted as signaling the informational status of the constituents in question within the context in which they are used.

The whole extended predication can be placed in a propositional frame by specifying attitudinal operators P3 (e.g., subjective modality, desiderative) and satellites S3 (e.g., probably, in my opinion), which indicate the attitude of the speaker toward the information contained in the extended predication. The resulting proposition thus designates a situated SoA as evaluated by the speaker. The evaluation may consist of elements indicating the speaker's subjective evaluation of the content, and of elements indicating from what source the speaker has received this content (so-called 'validators'). An example of a propositional structure (with the propositional content variable 'X') would be:

(What happened to the boy in the library?)   (7)
Poss X: [Past e: [Progr [kiss$_{VFoc}$ (the girl)$_{AgFoc}$
(the boy)$_{PatSubjTop}$] (passionate)$_{ManFoc}$]
(the library)$_{LocTop}$] (alleged)$_{Val}$]
'Allegedly, the boy may have been being passionately kissed by the girl in the library'

Finally, the proposition can be placed in an illocutionary frame through illocutionary operators P4 (e.g., declarative, interrogative) and satellites S4 (e.g., *frankly*, *briefly*). An example of a fully specified UCS (with a speech act variable E) would be:

DECL E: [Poss X: [Past e: (8)
[Progr [kiss$_{VFoc}$ (the girl)$_{AgFoc}$ (the boy)$_{PatSubjTop}$]
(passionate)$_{ManFoc}$]
(the library)$_{LocTop}$] (alleged)$_{Val}$] (frankly)$_{III}$]
'Frankly, the boy may allegedly have been being passionately kissed in the library by the girl'

Obviously, the overloading with specified operators and satellites makes such productions as (8) rather cumbersome. However, some of the operators and all the satellites are optional, so that the following would also be a potential realization of a UCS:

DECL E: [X: [Past e: (9)
[[kiss$_{VFoc}$ (the girl)$_{AgFoc}$ (the boy)$_{PatSubjTop}$]]]]
'The boy was kissed by the girl'

The layered structure of the clause serves, on the one hand, to define the semantic scope relations of operators and satellites within the overall clause structure and, on the other hand, to specify the formal behavior of such elements in the actual linguistic expression.

2.3 Expression Rules

The expression rules serve to map the UCS onto the linguistic expression through which it can be expressed. The only verbal material in UCSs consists of the various lexical items of which it is composed; all the other elements are more abstract grammatical operators, functions of different levels, and bracketings which indicate scope differences. The task of the expression rules is thus to determine what formal effects these different more abstract elements have on the ways in which the lexical items will be concatenated into linguistic expressions.

There are three aspects of linguistic form which the expression rules will take care of:

(a) the form which constituents of the UCS are going to take;
(b) the order in which they are to be linearized; and
(c) the prosodic contour which is to be assigned to the linguistic expression.

Form-determining expression rules can be generally formulated according to a schema in which one or more morphosyntactic operators, applied to an appropriate input form under stated conditions, yield the correct output form:

[Operator(s)] × [Input Form] → [Output Form]   (10)
   if [Conditions]

For a simple example consider the following expression rules for plural noun formation in English:

[plur] × [Noun] → X   (11a)
   if [X is listed in paradigm of Noun]

[plur] × [Noun] → [Noun + iz]   (11b)
   if [last phoneme of Noun is sibilant]

[Plur] × [Noun] → [Noun + s]   (11c)
   if [last phoneme of Noun is voiceless]

[plur] × [Noun] → [Noun + z]   (11d)

These rules are intended to be applied in the order in which they are given here, stopping when the appropriate plural form has been found. Rule (11a), in fact, exemplifies the general convention of 'lexical priority' mentioned above. Thus, if the input noun is *ox*, the output form, selected from the paradigm, will be *oxen* rather than *ox-iz. Rule (11d) is the 'bottom rule' or default rule to be applied when none of the preceding rules has yielded the form requested.

In terms of schema (10) an interesting typology of morphosyntactic rules can be set up by detailing the various forms which the different components (the operator(s), the input and output forms, the conditions) of such rules can take. For further detail see Dik (1989: ch. 14–15).

The UCS has a hierarchical build-up, but no linear order has as yet been defined for it. The actual order of constituents is therefore determined by placement rules which define which position(s) the constituents may or must take in an ordering template relevant to the language in question. At the moment at which the placement rules operate, the input structures will be identical across languages (apart from the actual phonologically specified material contained in them). Consider the following simplified example of equivalent structures for English and Dutch:

[Int]$_{III}$[has]$_{Vf}$[kissed]$_{Vi}$[who]$_{AgSubjFoc}$[Mary]$_{PatObj}$ (12a)

[Int]$_{III}$[heeft]$_{Vf}$[gekust]$_{Vi}$[wie]$_{AgSubjFoc}$[Marie]$_{PatObj}$ (12b)

ordering template for English interrogatives: (13a)
P1 Vf Subj Vi Obj

ordering template for Dutch: (13b)
P1 Vf Subj Obj Vi

placement rules:

Focus to P1   (14a)

Other constituents to their own position   (14b)

result English: (15a)
Who has kissed Mary?

result Dutch: (15b)
Wie heeft Marie gekust?

The placement rules thus show on account of which properties the different constituents are placed in their appropriate positions, and thus reveal the functionality of constituent ordering as an expression device.

The prosodic contour of the expression is compositionally determined by various relevant properties of the UCS, in particular the illocutionary operator and the pragmatic functions which have been assigned to the constituents. See Dik (1989) for a more detailed treatment.

3. FG as a Component in a Model of the Natural Language User

If FG is to be psychologically adequate it should be a viable component for the linguistic module in a model of the natural language user M*NLU. In order for this to be possible the grammatical model must be recast into a procedural format, showing how linguistic expressions can be actually produced, interpreted, and otherwise used in communicative situations. The following capacities are central to the communicative competence of M*NLU. These capacities are given with their potential FG interpretation.

(a) Producing linguistic expressions: creating, in one way or another, a UCS and mapping it onto a linguistic expression through the expression rules.
(b) Parsing a linguistic expression: reconstructing, for a given input expression, the UCS which it can be taken to express.
(c) Creating and maintaining a knowledge base: an important part of knowledge can be taken to have 'propositional' form; such knowledge can be represented in FG propositions.
(d) Interpreting a linguistic expression: parsing it onto a UCS, interpreting its illocutionary value, reconstructing the speaker's communicative intention, considering the information contained in the propositional part of the UCS, and acting with that information according to the speaker's communicative intention.
(e) Drawing logical inferences from given pieces of knowledge: if (an important part of) knowledge is taken to be represented in FG propositions, then logical inferencing can be simulated in terms of a 'functional logic' which operates on such propositions; at the same time, these propositions can act as components of UCSs.
(f) Translating: parsing an input expression onto its UCS, creating an equivalent UCS$_T$ in the target language L$_T$, and expressing this through the expression rules of L$_T$.

The overall effect of these FG interpretations of capacities of NLU is that UCSs are taken to play a central role not only in the linguistic, but also in the epistemic and the logical capacities of NLUs. This implies a strongly linguistically motivated view of NLU's cognitive and communicative competence.

4. Applications

FG lends itself to application in a number of areas. Of particular importance have been (a) computational implementation, (b) typological research, and (c) the description of individual languages. These will here be dealt with in turn; it goes without saying that the following paragraphs are necessarily highly selective and barely do justice to the plethora of applications of FG.

4.1 Computer Implementation

A number of studies have been devoted to the computer implementation of FG (see Connolly and Dik 1989). Most of these studies use the computer language PROLOG, which has proved eminently suitable for simulating FG rules and principles and thereby testing FG analyses. It has been possible to devise prototype lexica, generators, parsers, translators, and inference machines designed according to the sketches given above. The major PROLOG implementation is the program PROFGLOT (Dik 1992), which contains implementations of most of the rules and principles outlined above for English, French, and Dutch. The following main points have come out of this computational work: (a) using PROLOG, it is possible to translate the mainly 'declarative' FG model into an effective 'procedural' model which can do the various things listed above; (b) the fact that FG is based on an attempt to optimize typological adequacy has the practical advantage of reducing the language-specific modules of the program to a minimum, thus facilitating the transfer to other languages.

4.2 Typological Research

FG offers typologists a language-neutral framework in which to carry out their research. Such notions as noun, verb, Agent, Subject, Topic, etc. are embedded in a coherent theory in which they have stable meanings; this ensures that typological generalizations cast in FG terms are precise and testable. As was mentioned above (Sect. 2.2), Subject and Object are not considered within FG to be universal notions: thus English, which permits both Subject assignment to Recipient or Beneficiary (to yield a so-called indirect object), has both Subject and Object; German, however, permits Subject assignment to Patient (to give the passive) but no Object assignment to Recipient (which is always expressed in the dative case). German thus has Subject but not Object. Hungarian differs from both English and German in permitting neither Subject assignment to Patient nor Object assignment to Recipient; Hungarian is therefore, in FG, a language without syntactic functions (for discussion, see De Groot 1989, Brdar and Brdar Szabó 1993). From this it follows that FG does not typologize languages in terms of the familiar categories SVO, VSO, SOV etc., since S and O are not language-universal phenomena. Rather, FG claims that languages have fundamentally either a Prefield or Postfield organization, according as their expression rules tend to place modifiers before or after heads respectively. English, for example, is regarded as a Postfield language, with the predominantly preverbal position of the Subject and the prenominal position of the Adjective being explained by other factors.

FG also explores the typological consequences of the nonuniversality of wordclasses. Hengeveld (1992) proposes that each of the four classes of lexical predicate, N, Adj, V, and Adv, may be defined as the class that is prototypically available for a particular position within the UCS:

N	first restrictor of term	(16)
Adj	second restrictor of term	
V	head of predicate	
Adv	modifier of predicate	

His typology of languages distinguishes three kinds of wordclass sytem. Languages which line up exactly in the manner shown above are said to have a fully differentiated system. In a flexible system, more than one UCS position may be filled by one and the same wordclass – in Quechua, for example, the nominal, adjectival, and adverbial positions are occupied by one and the same wordclass. In a rigid system, certain UCS positions cannot be realized lexically: in Chinese, for example, the adjectival and adverbial positions are realized by relative clauses rather than a wordclass. The following, precise implicational hierarchy can be formulated for flexible and rigid systems: $V > N > Adj > Adv$. In rigid languages, the wordclasses that are absent are thus just Adv, or Adv and Adj, or Adv and Adj and N. Cayuga is a highly rigid language, having only the wordclass V; Lango is highly differentiated in distinguishing all four; and Tongan is highly flexible in allowing all positions to be filled by the same class ($N = V = Adj = Adv$). Note that this approach allows a sharp distinction between two types of language that lack the full arsenal of wordclasses.

4.3 Description of Individual Languages

FG has been applied not only to typological questions, but also to the description of individual languages. Here, too, the requirement of typological adequacy constrains grammarians to formulate their results with an eye to their cross-linguistic validity. In examining the various nominalizing constructions in English, for example, Mackenzie (1996) observes that there is a remarkable overlap, both formally and semantically, between the various types of nominalization in English and cross-linguistic typologies of such constructions; the formalizations he proposes for English nominalizations thus bid fair to have language-universal pertinence.

FG is at once precise, being an explicit model of grammar, and coherent, in providing a niche in its system for each grammatical phenomenon to be analyzed. This combination of precision and coherence makes it particularly suitable for work that aims to bring order to a field where chaos has reigned. A good example of this is Olbertz (in press), which is an examination of periphrastic verbal constructions in Spanish (e.g. *ir a* 'be going to'), an area that had previously been much studied but remained poorly understood. Olbertz uses FG to provide a precise definition of the periphrastic verbal construction as the productive and indissoluble combination of an auxiliarized lexical verb with a verbal predicate in a specific nonfinite form, progressing to give an FG description and formalization of each construction that satisfies the definition. The result is not only a better understanding of the individual constructions, but also of their mutual relations and of the place of periphrastic constructions in the entire grammar of Spanish.

5. Recent Developments

The FG clause model presented in Sect. 2 is equivalent to that expounded in Dik (1989). Much recent work has been devoted to refining the layered representation of the clause displayed in Fig. 2 above; this has largely taken the form of the addition of layers to the four proposed by Dik (1989). No less attention has been paid to increasing the pragmatic adequacy of the theory with research into the interface between grammar proper and discourse analysis. FG has moreover sought and found contact with other functionalist approaches to language, which has led to a deepening of the theory and greater international recognition of its potential. These three recent developments will be treated in this final section.

5.1 New Layers

On the basis of a suggestion by Dik (1989: 50), Hengeveld (1992) and Keizer (1992) have proposed recognizing a layer for the predicate, with the variable 'f.' One inspiration for this proposal is the desire to give a unified account of anaphora—just as speakers can refer anaphorically to entities, SoAs, propositions, and indeed entire clauses, so they can also refer back to predicates:

Fred is snoring. And so is Gerald (17)

Here the anaphor *so* points back to the verb *snoring*, which is in the scope of a Progr operator. Anaphora of this kind can be captured by giving the predicate its own variable and applying the anaphoric operator A:

DECL E_i: [X_i: [Pres e_i: [Prog f_i: snore$_v$ (f_i) (18)
(Fred)$_\phi$](e_i)](X_i)](E_i)

DECL E_j: [X_j: [Pres e_j: [(Af_i) $(Gerald)_\phi](e_j)](X_j)](E_j)$

At the 'top end' of the clause too, the tendency has been to introduce more layers. Bolkestein (1992: 392 ff.), for example, has pointed out that indirect-speech complements, hitherto analyzed as layer-3 complements, are differentiated according to their illocutionary value, notably as DECL(arative) or IMP(erative). In English, for example, *tell* calls for realization with a *that*-clause where the embedded illocution is declarative but with a *to*-infinitive clause where the embedded illocution is imperative. Hengeveld (1992) accordingly introduces an abstract illocutionary predicate under a capitalized F-variable, which allows a distinction between the entire clause (E_i) and the illocution it contains (F_i). In this approach the highest layer appears as follows:

$(E_i: ([F_i: ILL (F_i)) (Speaker) (Addressee) (X_i:[\ldots] (X_i))] (E_i))$
(19)

Given (19) as the (ultimately six-layered) structure of the clause, it becomes possible to analyze complements with illocutionary value as embedded F-complements (i.e. as clauses stripped of their E-layer), with ILL appearing as DECL, IMP, etc. An added advantage is that illocution-modifying satellites such as *frankly speaking* or *since you want to know* can be situated at the F-layer, with adverbials indicating the positioning of the utterance in the surrounding discourse (such as *finally*) and other interaction-managing devices such as *as far as John is concerned* occurring at E-layer. The E-layer has thus become an important locus for describing the interaction between grammar and discourse in FG

5.2 Grammar and Discourse

This leads us to the second area of major development in the nineties, the growing interest among practitioners of FG in the relation between grammar and discourse (see Connolly et al. in press). One tempting option is to extend the layering model further, allowing new layers to embrace the move, the exchange, and the entire discourse respectively; this is the tack taken by Hengeveld (in press). While this approach appears to have some validity, it cannot contribute to bridging the gap between discourse analysis as a study of communicative processes and grammar as a static account of the outcome of such processes. Relevant proposals have, however, been made by Hannay (1991), who distinguishes a number of communicative strategies available to the speaker for conveying information. In his view, there are five modes of message management, each of which induces distinct assignments of Topic and Focus. These modes may be represented as operators on the abstract illocutionary predicate, i.e. on F_i in (19) above. As their effect percolates down the hierarchy, they have the effect of constraining the assignment of pragmatic functions to elements of the utterance.

The stronger orientation of FG to discourse has gone hand in hand with a growing commitment to corpus analysis. The use of corpora in FG has been prominent from the very outset in the analysis of classical languages (Pinkster 1990; Kroon 1995); this has also been extended to the analysis of unwritten languages, in which large corpora of transcribed text have yielded vital insights (e.g., Reesink 1987); and now corpora of modern written languages are being exploited (e.g., Olbertz in press). Confronting the model with 'real data' has had the salutary effect of bringing out more clearly where the borderline lies between those linguistic phenomena that can be handled within FG and those that must be left to some other component of the model of the natural language user. Another effect has been to provide, alongside the computational testing mentioned in Sect. 4.1 above, another manner of checking the claims of FG.

5.3 FG and Functionalism in General

In the nineties, after the appearance of Dik (1989), FG attracted interest from various branches of functionalist linguistics. Since the model clearly shows the influence of many thinkers in this area, it is not surprising that many opportunities have arisen for fruitful collaboration. Among the major meeting points have been the following: (a) detailed comparison of FG and Systemic Functional Grammar (Butler 1990; see *Systemic Functional Grammar*); (b) work on the quantitative analysis of discourse phenomena, influenced by the approach of 'West Coast functionalists' (Bolkestein in press); (c) collaboration on layering (cf. Sect. 5.1 above) with exponents of Role and Reference Grammar (Van Valin 1996; see *Role and Reference Grammar*); (d) interaction with Cognitive Grammar in developing the semantic side of FG (Harder 1996; see *Cognitive Grammar*); and (e) cooperation with discourse analysts in determining a 'pragmatic' framework for understanding word order alternations (H. Dik 1995). These initiatives are taking place against the backdrop of increasing communication between functionalists across the globe; it seems certain that FG will continue to play a distinctive role in that communication.

Bibliography

Bolkestein A M 1992 Limits to layering: Locatability and other problems. In: Fortescue M, Harder P, Kristoffersen L (eds.) *Layered Structure in a Functional Perspective.* Benjamins, Amsterdam

Bolkestein A M in press Discourse organization and anaphora in Latin. In: Herring S, Van Reenen P, Schøssler L (eds.) *Textual Parameters in Older Languages.* Benjamins, Amsterdam

Brdar M, Brdar Szabó R B 1993 FG and prototype theory: A case study from English, German, Croatian and Hungarian. *Working Papers in Functional Grammar* **51**

Butler C 1990 Functional Grammar and Systemic Functional Grammar: A preliminary comparison. *Working Papers in Functional Grammar* **39**

Connolly J H, Butler C, Vismans R, Gatward R (eds.) in press *Discourse and Pragmatics in Functional Grammar*. Mouton de Gruyter, Berlin

Connolly J H, Dik S C (eds.) 1989 *Functional Grammar and the Computer*. Foris, Dordrecht

De Groot C 1987 Predicate formation in Functional Grammar. *Working Papers in Functional Grammar* **20**

De Groot C 1989 *Predicate Formation in a Functional Grammar of Hungarian*. Foris, Dordrecht

De Groot C 1996 Functional Grammar publications 1978–1996. *Working Papers in Functional Grammar* **61**

Dik H 1995 *Word Order in Ancient Greek*. Gieben, Amsterdam

Dik S C 1978 *Functional Grammar*. North-Holland, Amsterdam

Dik S C 1989 *The Theory of Functional Grammar, Part 1*. Foris, Dordrecht

Dik S C 1990 Some developments in Functional Grammar: Predicate formation. In: Aarts F, Els T van (eds.) *Contemporary Dutch Linguistics*. Georgetown University Press, Washington, DC

Dik S C 1992 *Functional Grammar in* PROLOG*: An Integrated Implementation for English, French and Dutch*. Mouton, Berlin

Dik S C in press *The Theory of Functional Grammar, Part 2*. Mouton de Gruyter, Berlin

Hannay M 1991 Pragmatic function assignment and word order variation in a Functional Grammar of English. *JPrag* **16**: 131–55

Harder P 1996 *Functional Semantics*. Mouton de Gruyter, Berlin

Hengeveld K 1989 Layers and operators in Functional Grammar. *JL* **25**: 127–57

Hengeveld K 1992 *Non-verbal Predication: Theory, Typology, Diachrony*. Mouton de Gruyter, Berlin

Hengeveld K in press Discourse structure in FG. In: Connolly J H, Butler C, Vismans R, Gatward R (eds.) *Discourse and Pragmatics in Functional Grammar*. Mouton de Gruyter, Berlin

Keizer M E 1992 *Reference, Predication and (In)definiteness in Functional Grammar*. Elinkwijk, Utrecht

Kroon C 1995 *Discourse Particles in Latin*. Gieben, Amsterdam

Mackenzie J L 1996 English nominalizations in the layered model of the sentence. In: Devriendt B, Goossens L, Van der Auwera J (eds.) *Complex Structures: A Functionalist Perspective*. Mouton de Gruyter, Berlin

Olbertz H in press *Verbal Periphrases in a Functional Grammar of Spanish*. Mouton de Gruyter, Berlin

Pinkster H 1990 *Latin Syntax and Semantics*. Routledge, London

Reesink G 1987 *Structures and Their Functions in Usan, a Papuan Language of Papua New Guinea*. Benjamins, Amsterdam

Siewierska A 1991 *Functional Grammar*. Routledge, London

Van Valin 1996 Toward a functionalist account of so-called extraction constraints. In: Devriendt B, Goossens L, Van der Auwera J (eds.) *Complex Structures: A Functionalist Perspective*. Mouton de Gruyter, Berlin

Functional Grammar: Martinet's Model

André Martinet

1. Functional Linguistics: A Short Historical Survey

In the course of the twentieth century, the term 'functional' has been applied, on several occasions, to different types of linguistic practice: first of all, by members of the Prague Linguistic Circle, from the late 1920s onward, with a value close to the one that will be retained here, and later on, by Louis Hjelmslev with a sense reminiscent of its mathematical use and akin to that found in 'grammatical functions,' i.e., pointing to relations between items. More recently, it has been used by some followers of the transformational and generative trends, or by people initially influenced by, but departing from, them. As will appear from what follows, the functional linguistics recommended employ 'functional' in its most usual meaning of 'adapted to achieve some end.' This use has been adopted, to some extent at least, by the members of the International Society for Functional Linguistics (= SILF standing for the French *Société internationale de linguistique fonctionnelle*).

The first linguists who pointed to the necessity of a conscious functional approach were the Prague phonologists. In the wake of Karl Bühler (1931), they operated with the principle of abstractive relevance according to which any scientific approach chooses a viewpoint that determines what observable facts shall be retained and what shall be disregarded as irrelevant for a given research. Experience has shown that the functioning and evolution of languages depends first and foremost on their use as communicative mediums. Therefore communicative relevance is the first, if not the sole, relevance to be reckoned with.

In the same way as glossematics took shape as a reaction to Prague teachings, functional linguistics, stemming from the same Saussurian stock, has, in many respects, developed in contrast to glossematic positions (Martinet 1977). The main features that characterize glossematics are: (a) the constant parallelism between the two faces of the sign presented as expression and content, (b) the rejection of phonic and semantic substances in favor of pure relations, this leading to (c) the disregard of changes affecting substance, resulting in a tendency to equate the successive stages of a language and thereby leading to a purely static approach.

On these three points, functionalism is in total disagreement: (a) the asymmetrical pattern of double articulation into phonemes and monemes contrasts with Hjelmslev's isomorphic approach; (b) relevant substance is retained in order to qualify relations; and (c) changes in substance are found to pave the way toward a reshuffling of the relational network.

Operating with relevant substance leads to positing a functional linguistic reality. Linguistic structures are thus deemed to be facts with a real existence in human behavior, and by no means, as widely assumed, mere contrivances of the descriptivists.

Contrasting with the enrichment derived from the permanent, even if antithetic, contacts between glossematicians and functionalists, the reaction of the latter to generativism has always been totally negative (Martinet 1975: 82–88). The assumption of an innate language organization distinct from the various mental equipments of man was rejected from the start as gratuitous. The arbitrary and conflicting statements regarding a so-called 'deep structure' were denounced as entirely subjective (Martinet 1975: 231–32). The transformative operation was described as an unnecessary departure from an observation and comparison of real utterances leading to the establishment of syncretisms.

Functionalism was introduced into the UK by Jan Mulder, and later developed at St Andrews University by Mulder and Sándor Hervey (1980). Its basically axiomatic basis has been emphasized and a logical apparatus devised that anticipates a confrontation with a large variety of linguistic facts, a procedure that contrasts with the more pragmatic, step-by-step 'continental' approach.

2. An Empirico-deductive Approach

The obvious fact that languages differ through space and time is indicative of the nature of human language. It points to its constant adaptation to the varying needs of human communities. Contacts will breed linguistic convergence, with concomitant divergence among those who do not participate in the same contacts. This amounts to saying that communicating with language may be conducive to linguistic changes and, in short, that languages change because they function. Those who describe languages should take this into consideration, and, by comparing the usages of co-existing generations, try to determine the direction and rhythm of their evolution.

The observation of natural languages has shown that they have a number of features in common. First of all their communicative function. No one would deny their fundamental contribution to the ordering of human experience. But this results from the analysis

of that experience made necessary by the need to communicate it from person to person.

The next common feature is their use of vocal utterances. This is often forgotten, nay, intentionally omitted by those who want to operate with relations rather than substance or do not feel at ease in phonic matters. The argument that some languages practically exist only in a written form is invalidated by the fact that they originated as spoken mediums and are organized accordingly. The linearity of speech could, in Saussurian terms, be considered irrelevant for 'language' proper, the occasional use of respective position in the spoken chain for indicating relations being by-passed as belonging to substance and not to the relational pattern. But it should be clear that if mankind had resorted to visual signs for inter-human communication, the analysis of experience, prior to its transmission, would have been of a totally different nature. Functionalists (Martinet 1975: 26–29) do away with linearity in their two-dimensional visualizations. But they do not mean thereby that the auditory nature of linguistic exchanges which imposes that linearity has no bearing upon the way man perceives the world.

A third common feature is the double articulation of utterances into significant units whose perceptible form is, in its turn, articulated into distinctive units. Many linguists, even among functionalists, are tempted to argue that one could distinguish between more than two articulations, such as that of significant units into semantic features and that of distinctive units into distinctive features, which no one denies. But what is essential is the distinction between what is significant and what is just distinctive. Here again, those who refuse to consider the written form of a language as an additional code could argue that ideographic writing systems do not go beyond a first articulation. But they would thereby forget that all ideographic systems must, at some point, have recourse to phonic, i.e., distinctive non-significant features.

By stipulation, we shall call 'a language' any form of human behavior that shares the above-mentioned three features. Arguing that the validity of our assertion has not been checked for all the past, present, and future 'languages' of the world does not make sense because, by means of our stipulation, we actually redefine the term 'language' and decide that it shall not be used in reference to any object that would not conform to our definition. All scientific terms should of course be carefully redefined.

Some linguists take exception to our stipulation by arguing that it leaves out some features that are obviously present in what all would agree to call a language, as, for instance, 'intonation,' or more generally prosodic or suprasegmental traits. The answer is that 'vocal,' in reference to linguistic utterances implies 'voice' which, in its turn, implies 'melodic curve,' which takes care of 'intonation.' Intensity and duration are similarly implied. For what purposes individual languages make use of the ingredients is not of concern here.

Our stipulatory, or should we say 'axiomatic,' approach takes care of what it has been fashionable to refer to as 'universals.' It would defeat our purposes to posit universals which are not implied in our formulation. Whatever does not conflict with it cannot be excluded from a language, be it positive or negative. For instance, the assumption that the distinction between noun and verb is universal cannot be made because it is not implied by our definition. It should go without saying that being rendered in English by means of a verb or a noun does not make a foreign significant unit a verb or a noun. In other words, what is relevant in language A does not make it relevant in language B.

3. Functional Grammar

Functional grammar is concerned with the identification, classification, and functioning of significant units. It presupposes a phonology whose main task is the identification of distinctive units. It precedes a study of the lexicon, i.e., an examination of each significant unit, not taken care of in the grammar, in its relations to the analysis of man's experience.

The minimal linguistic unit combining an acoustically perceptible form and a reference to some aspect of experience is called a 'moneme.' Utterances are analyzed into monemes by means of the commutation test which consists in looking for and comparing utterances that differ only on account of one minimal meaningful segment. A meaningful element is said to be minimal if it cannot be further analyzed into such segments. Many linguists refer to minimal significant units as 'morphemes.' But it is preferable to avoid this term which suggests form rather than meaning. Once form has played its identifying role, only meaning should count as implied by the term 'significant.' The linguistic ideal would seem to require that each meaning should always correspond to one and the same form and that one and the same form should always correspond to the same meaning. Actually, it frequently happens that the same meaning assumes different forms in different contexts as, e.g., -s in *cows* and -en in *oxen* with the same meaning 'plural,' and the same form assumes different meanings, as in *last* ≠ *first* and *last* = *to endure*. Here, -s and -en stand for the same moneme, *last*[1] and *last*[2] for different ones.

Among monemes identified by means of the commutation test, a first distinction is to be made between joint and free monemes: *farm* is free in *the farm was sold*, but joint in *farmer*, *farm-yard* and *farm hand*. A free moneme refers to a definite element of experience; a joint moneme, as such, does not. A combination of joint monemes is called a 'syntheme.' Free monemes and synthemes may receive determinations: *a big farm*, *a large farm-yard*, *a strong farm hand*; joint monemes

cannot. Synthemes commute with free monemes and maintain the same relations within the utterance. Therefore what is said henceforth about monemes applies to free monemes and to synthemes as well. Complex monemes, such as participles, that share the compatibilities of different classes or present their own set of compatibilities are said to be 'parasynthemes.' Since individual speakers are free to make new synthemes according to certain patterns, 'synthematics,' which partially coincides with traditional 'word-building,' belongs to grammar as an aspect of the functioning of significant units.

Speakers are not free to combine monemes at will if they want to be understood. The appearance of some type is often dependent on the presence of some other type. In such a case, the monemes of the former type are said to be 'subordinated' to those of the latter. Where no such restrictions exist, the monemes that are found to maintain the same relations to the context are said to be 'coordinated.'

Utterances consisting of several monemes are normally found to center around one of them, or two or more coordinated ones, which can be designated as the nucleus, the rest being its satellites. In *I worked on my father's farm*, the nucleus is *work-*; *I* enjoys a special status because its elimination would destroy the utterance. It is traditionally interpreted as what is talked about and accordingly called the 'subject.' Both *-ed*, as the form of the preterite moneme, and what follows are dispensable satellites. In *my father's farm*, *farm* acts as the nucleus of its satellite *my father's*. A specific designation was needed for the nucleus of the complete utterance. The term 'predicate' was chosen for that purpose although it originally covered, not only the nucleus, but all its satellites except the subject.

What is called a 'verb' is a moneme which is only used as a predicate (or a predicatoid, i.e., the nucleus of a subordinate clause or, in other words, a full statement functioning as the satellite of another). Predicates are not necessarily verbs: in Russian *dom nov* 'the house is new,' the predicate is *nov* 'new,' but *nov* can function as a satellite in *nov-yj dom* 'new house.'

Some monemes never act as nuclei, but always as satellites. They are called 'modalities' or 'modifiers.' They often appear as grammatical endings, such as the *-ed* of *worked*. But *my*, in *my father's*, is also a modality. A modality requires, of course, the presence of a nucleus.

A 'relator' (or 'functional') is a moneme that connects two monemes or moneme clusters, either coordinated or subordinated. Traditionally, coordinators such as *and, or, but* are called conjunctions; subordinators are conjunctions when they connect two clauses. They are prepositions, postpositions, or case endings elsewhere. A relator obviously requires the presence of two or more than two monemes or moneme clusters.

Another way of expressing the relation between nuclei and satellites is the use of 'determine' or its derivatives: the nucleus is said to be determined by its satellites and the satellites are the determinants of the nucleus.

Monemes are said to be compatible with one another if they can meaningfully combine in an utterance. This does not necessarily imply contiguity: *farm* is found to be compatible with the article *the* in *the rich and big farm*.

Moneme classes are established on the basis of their mutual compatibilities. They are found to differ from one language to another. This was not generally assumed for the traditional parts of speech. Describers should not be led astray by the translations into their own language of the utterances they are analyzing. What appears as an adjective in a translation may well be a verb or a noun in the original. If, as has just been done here, the terms 'adjective,' 'verb,' and 'noun' are retained in reference to the moneme classes of a new language, they should be carefully redefined after a complete survey of the compatibilities of each class. It should not be assumed that all languages distinguish between adjective, verb, and noun classes.

Monemes belonging to a class are apt to be transferred to other classes: by dropping the moneme which a relator connects with the rest of the utterance, the relator ceases to be one and becomes the determinant of what precedes, as in *go through*, *stand for*; *blind* remains an adjective when it designates those who cannot see, but it is transferred to the noun class in *the blinds of the windows*. Cardinals, in French, that are constantly transferred from one class to another, may as well be considered as forming a class of their own.

Beginners should be warned against assuming the existence of a moneme when a formal distinction does not contribute any new information. This is the case of gender in a language like French. Except in some derivatives, the feminine gender, in that language, is not manifested in the noun itself, but in its determinants, articles, or adjectives. The word *classe* 'class' happens to 'be' feminine. All French speakers know that, accordingly, it requires feminine concord, which means that the use of the article *la* instead of *le* contributes no information whatsoever. Therefore the feminine gender is not a moneme. In the same language, there is a female sex moneme which appears as -*esse* in *poétesse* 'female poet' or as -*ière* in *épicière* 'female grocer' as opposed to *épicier*, her male equivalent. But since the gender mark, in the adjective *entière* 'entire' versus *entier* is homonymous, traditional grammarians are apt to confuse feminine gender, a morphological accident, and female sex, a full moneme.

In the same vein, no moneme should be posited for a gap in a grammatical paradigm. In a language with a past tense moneme and a future tense moneme, one is tempted to assume the existence of a present tense moneme. But, in such languages, it is frequent that what is called the 'present' is formally identical with the bare stem of the verb, i.e., the verbal moneme itself. Should that form be restricted to the expression of events taking place precisely when the speech is being delivered, one would have to posit a present moneme with the positive meaning 'present' even if its form is zero. But, as a rule, the bare stem is also found in reference to past and future events (cf. *call me before you come*) and generally when no definite time period is implied. In French, for instance, where personal endings are added to the bare stem in the so-called 'present tense,' no present tense moneme should be identified. In English, where the present tense is positively characterized by 3rd pers sg -*s*, the existence of a present tense moneme could be argued.

The same remark applies to the singular number in languages where the bare stem is used for the species as well as for a unit, e.g., *man, the lion*. The same could be said about the indicative mood which, again, normally coincides with the bare stem and just points to the existence of an event. But a zero form does not necessarily coincide with the absence of information: in Russian, the endingless *ryb*, among full forms such as *ryba*, *ryby*, harbors three distinct monemes with the meanings of 'fish,' 'plural,' and 'genitive.' Here again, what counts, when dealing with significant units, is meaning.

Generally speaking, concord amounts to repeating the same information in different places in the utterance, as, e.g., in Latin *bonorum vinorum* 'of good wines' where 'plural' and 'genitive' appear twice, but are meant once. In the case of French gender, the -*a* of the article *la* is properly a part of the 'feminine' moneme *classe*. It is precisely what distinguishes *la voile* 'the sail' from *le voile* 'the veil.' In such cases, one operates with the discontinuous form of a moneme or, for short, a discontinuous moneme.

It is quite frequent that the commutation test confirms the presence of a moneme, but in such conditions one is not in a position to ascribe to it a definite segment of the utterance. This applies to Latin *vinorum* where it cannot be discerned which parts of the total should be ascribed to 'wine,' 'genitive' or 'plural' respectively. In such cases, the forms of the monemes are said to be 'amalgamated.'

These various accidents should not prevent us from operating with monemes and incite us to resort to the traditional notion of 'word.' Even if it may prove useful in the description of a language like Latin, it cannot be accurately defined in general linguistics except in reference to the written forms of languages that make use of an alphabet. The closest one can get to pinning down the 'word' in the basic spoken form of language is by starting from the grammatical phrase, or syntagm. This consists in a nucleus with its various determinants and, as the case may be, a relator connecting it to the rest of the utterance. The largest grammatical phrase is the sentence where whatever sounds as a relator (e.g., *but*) is actually transferred to some adverbial class, i.e., used as a determinant of the predicate. As an illustration of a full grammatical phrase, with all its ingredients, one can choose *of the large gardens* where *garden-* is the nucleus, *large* is a determinable determinant (as in *very large*), *the* and *-s* are modifiers, and *of* is the relator. The term 'syllemma' has been proposed for a grammatical phrase limited to its nucleus, its modifiers, and its relator. If the determinable determinant *large* is removed, the grammatical phrase is reduced to the syllemma *of the gardens*. Now, if, in a syllemma, the modifiers and the relator come before the nucleus, they are likely to be words in their own rights, as is the case, here, with *the* and *of*. If they come after, they will probably constitute a single word with the nucleus, as in *garden-s*. In *havernes*, the Danish equivalent of our syllemma, both the modifiers, *-er-* 'plural' and *-ne-* definite article, and the relator *-s* follow the nucleus, and the syllemma corresponds to what is called a 'word.' The reason for this difference of treatment is clear: significant segments are normally identified in speech before their final phonemes are uttered. It is therefore essential to preserve the identity of the initial part of each of them by avoiding amalgamation with what precedes, whereas that of the final part is less important and offers less resistance to blurring. One could be tempted to define the word as a syllemma where determinants and relator follow the nucleus. But there are exceptions like Greek *elabon* 'I took' written as a single word in spite of the initial position of the modifier *e-*, a past tense moneme. Besides, such 'words' as *of* or *the* being modifiers cannot be identified as the nuclei of syllemmas. It should be clear that a functional grammarian is under no obligation ever to operate with the notion of syllemma.

Syntax is often conceived as dealing with the combinations of significant units (usually conceived as 'words') in utterances. Functionally, it is best understood as the study of how the hearer can manage to derive a meaning from a succession of significant units, or, in other terms, to reconstruct, beyond the articuli of speech, the experience the speaker wants to communicate. It is, from the start, clear that relators like *-s* in *man's speech* or *of* in *the speech of man* should play a great role in such matters. But plain contiguity is often resorted to: the identification of a moneme as belonging to a certain class may suffice to indicate the nature of its relations to its neighbors: *good*, as an adjective, is known to qualify a following noun; *-ed* is known as a modifier of the verb to which it is tagged, and so forth. In other words, the first chapter of syntax will consist in the inventory of moneme classes including, of course, all the compatibilities of each class.

This will suffice in a number of cases. But stating that, in English, verbs and nouns are compatible, the former as a nucleus, the latter as a satellite, does not give all the required information, because the mutual relations between verb and noun vary from one utterance to another and within the same utterance: the noun may act as a subject, an object, a beneficiary, an indication of time, space or manner, and so on. These different functions may be indicated by means of the respective positions of verb and noun, e.g., the noun in subject function appearing before and that in object function after the verb. But this will have to be eked out by means of some relators, also referred to as 'functional indicators.' Another possibility is to coordinate several verbs, each one requiring its own determinants, as when *I write a letter to my son* becomes *I letter write give my son*. But, of course, *give*, in such a case, may be interpreted as resulting from a transfer from the verb class to that of subordinating relators.

Within a class, the nature of possible relations varies from one moneme to another. This is illustrated by the traditional distinction established between transitive and intransitive verbs. But in order to be exhaustive, one shall have to tell which verbs can combine with a beneficiary (e.g., *to give*), which verbs do not need a real subject (e.g., *to snow*) because the action referred to is conceived as self-sufficient, which verbs cannot appear without an object (e.g., *to put*), and so forth. In short, each moneme likely to act as a nucleus can be expected to maintain different relations with its satellites. The listing of all of these is best left to the lexicon, the grammarian, as such, being satisfied with the identification of the different types of relations for each moneme class.

As pointed out above, the form of a moneme may vary from one context to another: *keep* appears as *kep-* before the preterite moneme /-t/, *have* is reduced to *ha-* before the /-d/ variant of the same modifier; *go* + the preterite appears amalgamated as *went*; the genitive moneme of Latin presents ten different avatars. Concord is widely responsible for the formal variations of monemes. As was suggested before, the material changes determined by concord should be ascribed to the moneme whose choice had caused them. This rule, if strictly applied, would not only ascribe the *-a* of the definite article to the feminine noun that it accompanies, but also every additional element that the choice of such a noun entails in the determining adjectives: if the French moneme for 'chair' is supposed to assume the form /-aʃɛ/ in *la chaise*, it will become /-a...-dʃɛ/ in *la grande chaise* since no /d/ is sounded in the masculine *grand*. Of course, once such variations have been identified as zero for the communication of information, one may be allowed to list the ones implied by the feminine gender of nouns in the chapter devoted to adjectives. In a similar way, using declensional patterns is probably the most sensible approach to the presentation of the forms of Latin cases. But one should not forget that the *-ibus* of *civibus* and the *-is* of *dominis* are linguistically identical, viz. datives and ablatives.

All of this belongs to the chapter of morphology. The unfortunately widespread opinion that morphology involves, and even consists in, the study of the relations between the components of the 'word,' just like syntax takes care of the relations between 'words,' should by all means be denounced as a misinterpretation of the contents of classical grammars.

Morphology, or accidence, is nothing but the presentation of the formal accidents that may complicate the task of youthful or adult learners, but do not have the least bearing upon the information utterances are meant to convey. Formal accidents may of course be prosodic as well as phonematic and also include deviations in the respective positions of monemes.

The insistence on a strict distinction between morphology and syntax as respectively negative and positive from the point of view of the success of communication and ease in the handling of the linguistic tool does not entail that each should be dealt with in two different chapters. The presentation of each class should include a thorough survey of the various accidents every one of the monemes involved may incur. But this should by no means exclude the possibility of dealing with some morphological facts prior to the listing of the classes. Such features as German Umlaut that affects the morphology of several moneme classes are best presented in an introductory part of the grammar, and referred to later when dealing with specific problems such as plural of nouns, personal inflexion of verbs, and so on. This means that the way morphology will be introduced in the grammar will depend on the nature of the formal accidents in the language at issue.

Grammar dealing with significant units, it is to be expected that semantics will not be absent from it. The problem is how much of it will be handled here and how much will be left for the lexicon. Spelling plays a role in this connection because written 'words' will all be included in the lexicon, but endings will be left out. This conflicts with the functional approach which implies that modifiers and relators be handled together irrespective of whether they appear as 'words' or as parts of 'words.' Linguistic reality, as distinct from its formal vagaries, demands that, e.g., relators should be handled together and confronted, whatever form they may assume: endings, prepositions, or respective position. With this reservation, there is no reason to depart from the habit of dealing, in the grammar, with the semantic values of the units belonging to classes where they can be exhaustively listed and leaving those of others to the dictionary. In the same way as linguists distinguish in phonic matters between phonetics dealing with objective reality irrespective of its function, and phonology where matters are handled in reference to communicative relevance, it is recommended to distinguish between semantics proper where differences of meaning are considered irrespective of whether they correspond to some formal difference, and axiology where only relevant significant features are retained, namely those that are orally perceptible.

The describer of a language cannot hope to give an exhaustive presentation of all its varieties. Whether he should concentrate on an idiolect or a sociolect or try to cover a number of different usages depends on what his aims are. He might choose to concentrate on the spoken practice or cover the written form as well, and the problem arises of whether the two aspects should be dealt with separately, particularly in the case of an ideographic writing system. But even with an alphabetically written language it may be advisable to present two different analyses, at least for some of the moneme classes. In standard written French, personal endings may differ from one verb to another. For present indicative 1., 2., 3. sg, there is for *dorer* 'to gild,' *-e*, *-es*, *-e*, in *je dore, tu dores, il dore*, but, for *dormir* 'to sleep,' *-s*, *-s*, *-t* in *je dors, tu dors, il dort*. In daily oral practice, all these endings are silent and all the forms sound /dɔr/ (note, with linking, the same pronunciation /dɔrtil/ for *dore-t-il*? 'does he gild?' and *dort-il*? 'does he sleep?'). This means that one has to operate, in one case, with two different conjugations, in another, with verbs with the same radical throughout versus verbs with varying radicals: cf. e.g., *nous dorons* 'we gild' /dɔr-/ versus *nous dormons* 'we sleep' /dɔrm-/. Here is a situation where the distinction between spoken and written coincides with two different levels, one more solemn and one more spontaneous. But these are not necessarily confused: to familiar and slangy forms normally correspond written renderings, and rhetoric and ritual usages often present some specific oral features. All of this goes beyond grammar, involving, as it does, phonetics, phonology, and vocabulary, but it includes it.

Bibliography

Bühler K 1931 Phonetik und Phonologie. *Travaux du Cercle Linguistique de Prague* **IV**

Martinet A 1962 *A Functional View of Language*. Clarendon Press, Oxford

Martinet A 1964 *Elements of General Linguistics*. Faber, London (Transl. by Palmer E)

Martinet A 1975 *Studies in Functional Syntax*. W. Fink, Munich

Martinet A 1977 Some basic principles of functional linguistics. *Linguistique* **13(1)**: 7–14

Martinet A 1979 Grammatical function. In: Allerton D J et al. *Function and Context in Linguistic Analysis*. Cambridge University Press, Cambridge

Martinet A 1981 Synthematics. *Word* **31(1)**: 11–14

Martinet A 1982 Grammatical phrases and lexical phrases. In: *Linguistics and Philosophy: Essays in Honor of Rulon S. Wells*. Benjamins, Amsterdam

Martinet A 1983 What is syntax? In: *Ninth* LACUS *Forum*. Hornbeam, Columbia, SC

Martinet A 1985 *Syntaxe générale*. Colin, Paris

Mulder J W F, Hervey S 1980 *The Strategy of Linguistics*. Scottish Academic Press, Edinburgh

Functional Relations

R. D. Van Valin, Jr

Syntactic structure may be divided into two fundamental types: relational and nonrelational structure. 'Relational structure' refers to the relations that exist among major constituents in a sentence, e.g., between a predicate and its arguments or between a head and its modifiers, and these relations may be syntactic, semantic, or pragmatic in nature. 'Nonrelational structure' denotes the hierarchical organization of phrases, clauses, and sentences, however it may be conceived in a particular theory; the commonest conception of nonrelational structure is the X-bar theory of phrase structure (see *X-bar Syntax*). The focus here is on relational structure only, and in particular with the different 'functional relations' that play a role in grammatical description and linguistic theory. Functional relations fall into three basic categories: semantic, pragmatic, and syntactic.

1. Semantic Functional Relations

Semantic functional relations are one of the two major types of relation between a predicate and its argument(s); the other type is syntactic relations (see Sect. 3). They are important for a variety of reasons. They are empirically important because they capture the basic structure of the events denoted by the verb. In other words, they are a way of talking about who did what to whom. When a verb, for example, is associated with an 'agent' argument and a 'patient' argument, something is ultimately being said about the events in the world which this verb could be used to express. Such an event has a participant in it who willfully and intentionally instigates the event, and then there is a less willful participant who is somehow affected by that event. There should be some relationship between the structure of the event and the linguistic encoding of it, since otherwise it would be very difficult to describe events and, more generally, states of affairs linguistically. Semantic functional relations are also called 'participant roles,' because they can be viewed as the linguistic encoding of the parts (in the sense of parts in a play) participants play in an event. They are, therefore, a central component of the semantic structure of the clause. They must be universal, because if a language is going to function, to convey information, it needs to have ways of coding these kinds of relationships.

Semantic functional relations are also very important in linguistic theory. Almost every syntactic theory makes use of these notions in some way, either overtly or covertly (see Sect. 1.3). They have a variety of names in the different theories: semantic roles, case roles, semantic case roles, thematic relations, θ-roles,

participant roles, and so on. They were first seriously proposed by Gruber (1965), who termed them 'thematic relations,' and by Fillmore (1968), who called them 'case roles.' Thematic relations and 'θ-roles' are the terms standardly used for them in generative grammar.

The terms 'agent' and 'patient' are often employed in two distinct senses. First, they are used to refer to narrowly defined participants, i.e., to the willful instigator of an event or action (agent) and to the involuntary affected participant (patient). In this sense they are distinguished from other narrowly defined relations, e.g., experiencer, instrument, or locative. Second, they are often used in a very general sense to refer to the two primary arguments in a transitive predication; in this use, agent and patient are each a cover term for a range of relations. In this broad sense agent subsumes roles like experiencer or force, while patient subsumes theme and goal. Thus semantic functional relations may be divided into two general types, which will be called 'specific thematic relations' and 'generalized thematic relations.' Each will be discussed in the following sections.

1.1 Specific Thematic Relations

Thematic relations describe the semantic function of an argument with respect to the predicate in a sentence. Two very fundamental issues must be raised: first, the level of generality of semantic function that thematic relations should capture, and second, the right inventory of relations, for both descriptive and theoretical purposes. Definitive resolutions of these issues have not been propounded, but they must be addressed.

The issue of generality is as follows. A verb like *kill* has a 'killer' and a 'killed' as arguments, *hear* a 'hearer' and a 'heard,' and *send* a 'sender,' a 'sent,' and a 'sendee.' There are, therefore, three relations with *send*, two with *hear*, and two with *kill*. The issue is whether it is possible to generalize from these statements, e.g., compare the sender of *send* with the killer of *kill* and with the hearer of *hear*. *Believe*, a cognition verb, has a 'believer' and a 'belief.' The debate is whether one can conclude that the believer and the hearer have something in common. Or, similarly, that a killer, a sender, and a dancer have something in common. While it is true that a killer and a sender are not the same thing, they both instigate an event or action, usually volitionally. Therefore, they are purposefully instigating some event. Similarly, with the hearer and the believer, both are having some sort of internal experience, one perceptual and one cognitive.

No event or action is being instigated in either case, nor is the experience normally volitional. Thus they do have something in common. The generality problem can be formulated as follows. Given relations that are similar (for example, hearer, see-er, smeller, and taster can be classed together as perceivers; and believer, thinker, and knower can be classed together as cognizers), is it appropriate to postulate 'perceiver' and 'cognizer' as distinct thematic relations? Or is it appropriate to establish a more general role of 'experiencer,' and then set up 'cognizer' and 'perceiver' as allorelations of that one more general relation?

These questions cannot be answered purely semantically, because both possibilities can be justified in semantic terms. The answer must, therefore, come from grammatical facts. This should not be surprising, since thematic relations are part of a general theory of grammar. It is necessary, then, to look and see if languages systematically treat perceivers and cognizers as different grammatically, or if they tend to treat them alike. It is generally the case that they do tend to be lumped together, receiving the same morphosyntactic treatment. But, on the other hand, many languages systematically treat experiencers differently from killers, senders, and dancers. In other words, an experiencer, which undergoes an internal state, is treated very differently in the grammar from purposeful instigators. In many languages, for example, subjects which are experiencers appear in the dative case, whereas those which are willful instigators appear in the nominative or ergative case. An example of this can be found in many Indo-European languages, e.g., Russian, German, and Italian, in which some verbs of internal state use the so-called 'inverse construction': the experiencer is in the dative and the thing being experienced is in the nominative, e.g., German *das gefällt mir* (that[NOM] pleases me[DAT]) 'I like that.' This is opposed to *kill*, *send*, and *dance*, where the entities killing, sending, and dancing are in the nominative. Underlying the common treatment of experiencers is a neutralization of otherwise valid semantic contrasts within the grammar. It would be hard to argue, on any kind of reasonable 'grammatical' grounds, that believers ought to be separated from knowers, thinkers, expecters, and assumers. Since it would be hard to justify this, they are all grouped together as cognizers. Similarly, it would be hard to justify see-ers, feelers, hearers, touchers, smellers, and tasters as all being different; hence they are all grouped together as perceivers. Clause-internal phenomena like case marking tend to treat them alike, and on these grounds they are often classed together under the general label of experiencer.

The fundamental issue here is to justify these distinctions on grammatical grounds, because ultimately, thematic relations act as an interface between lexical semantics and syntax. In other words, they do double duty. On the one hand, they are semantic in nature and related to the lexical semantic representation of the verb, because they are a function of the meaning of the verb. And the richer and more detailed the representation of the meaning of the verb, the more distinctions can be made. For example, a richer representation would permit the representation of the nuances which separate a believer from a knower. This is ultimately a part of a speaker's linguistic competence. But this distinction does not appear to be necessary for the grammar. On the one hand, these roles are a part of the lexical semantic representations of verbs, while on the other hand, they have grammatical implications. The thematic relations posited have to be faithful to their semantic basis, but they also have to be sensitive to the demands of grammar.

The solution to the problem of the correct inventory of thematic relations is ultimately a theory-internal issue; different theories and approaches have proposed inventories ranging from three to several dozen thematic relations. Since, as argued above, thematic relations must be justified grammatically as well as semantically, the grammatical justifications would be couched in terms of particular grammatical theories. Moreover, the size of the inventory depends crucially on the task(s) which thematic relations are assigned. There are two basic functions they can serve: (a) they can be part of the system of lexical representation, wherein they represent aspects of the verb's meaning (as in, e.g., Fillmore 1968); and (b) they can play a role in the statement of grammatical rules, principles, or constraints. It is the first function that has led to large inventories of thematic relations: if they are used to capture meaning contrasts among verbs, then a large number will be needed to express the great variety of verbal semantic contrasts. If, on the other hand, their function is limited to the second one, then only as many will be needed as the syntax requires, and this is a much smaller number than that required for a lexical representation function.

While it would be quite impossible to review all of the inventories proposed by different theories, it is possible to construct a list of thematic relations that are standardly referred to in most accounts. This is given in Table 1.

One solution to the inventory problem suggested in Foley and Van Valin (1984) and elaborated in Van Valin (1993) is not to propose an absolute universal list of roles but rather to posit a universal semantic continuum in terms of which languages may make a varying number of distinctions. In this continuum of thematic relations, agent defines one end and patient the other; all of the other thematic relations represent points along the continuum, and there is no absolute number of distinctions which every language must make, although there is strong evidence that certain of these distinctions are universal. The continuum may be represented as in Fig. 1. The anchor points of the thematic relations continuum are agent (the will-

Table 1.

agent: a willful, purposeful instigator of an action or event, such as in *John broke the glass*.

experiencer: things that experience internal states, such as perceivers and emoters (subjects of verbs like *think*, *believe*, *love*, and *hate*) as in *John thought about the question*.

instrument: usually inanimate things that are manipulated by an agent in the carrying out of an action, as in *John broke the window with the rock* or *The rock broke the window*. In both cases *rock* is the instrument of an agent, whether the agent is specified or not.

force: involuntary causal participant which, unlike an instrument, cannot be manipulated. They can include things like *tornados*, *storms*, and *acts of God*, as in *The flood washed away the village*.

patient: things that are in a state or condition, or undergo a change of state or condition as in *John is tall*, *John is sick*, *The window broke*, and *John died*.

theme: things which are located or are undergoing a change of location (motion), as in *The book is on the table* or *John put the book on the table*.

recipient: someone who gets something (recipients are almost always animate), as in *He sent the book to John* or *He sent John the book*.

goal: destination, which is similar to recipient, except that it is inanimate, as in *He sent the book to Philadelphia*.

source: the origin of an event or action. It is used in a variety of situations, which can conflate the ambiguity between recipient and goal:

$$\text{source } x - y \xrightarrow[\text{motion}]{\text{transfer}} z \quad \begin{array}{l}\text{recipient}\\\text{goal}\end{array}$$

(x = initial position, y = object, and z = final position)
If there is a transfer of *y* then *z* is a recipient. If *y* is in motion, then *z* is a goal. In either case, *x* is the source, and *y* is the theme. No distinction is usually made between source of motion and source of transference, even though there is a distinction between recipient and goal.

locative: a location. Path, source, and goal can be viewed as elaborations of different aspects of locatives. Locatives contrast with the others by referring to a situated location, such as in *The book is on the table*.

path: a route, as in *He ran from the house*, *along the creek to the park*.

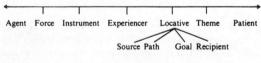

Figure 1.

ful, volitional, instigating participant) at one end and patient (the non-willful, non-instigating, maximally affected participant) at the other. In between the polar entities, there is a continuum of semantic relations of more agent-like and patient-like roles. This continuum is flexible, for languages divide it up in different ways. There are, however, certain restrictions upon the ways that it can be divided up.

Furthermore, the divisions are not random, for there are common divisions across languages. Languages distinguish entities which are affected in terms of their state or condition from those which are affected in terms of location. Therefore, they differentiate patients from things that are clearly at the right end of the scale but are less patient-like, namely themes. Themes are not affected in the same way and to the same degree, because they do not get crushed and chopped, but they do get moved around. Therefore, themes are clearly at the right end of the continuum, and are not agent-like. On the other hand, there are things on the left side of this continuum which can be causal, but not instigating or controlling. Examples of this include instruments and forces. Further to the right, toward the center of the continuum, is the experiencer, which is the locus of an internal event, but is certainly not willful, volitional, and instigating. Many perceptual events are not volitionally instigated. The difference between verbs like *look at* and *see* is that the subject of *look at* is an experiencer which is also an agent, while the subject of *see* is simply an experiencer. In the middle of the continuum, there are all of the various types of locatives. In fact, many more can be found in the world's languages than are represented in Fig. 1. Typically things like recipient, source, goal, and path do not interact with each other, but rather with the theme. Figure 1 represents a continuum of distinctions, and languages may make more or fewer of them than what is listed above. This seems to be the semantic range that needs to be expressed in all languages. There appear to be as many roles as can be motivated, as long as they fall on the continuum in Fig. 1. And, in fact, the same distinctions recur across languages; the same contrasts between experiencer and agent, instrument and agent, theme and locative, and so on, are found in language after language.

Holisky (1987) and Van Valin and Wilkins (1996) argue that with many verbs the interpretation of the subject as an agent is an implicature involving animate arguments. They maintain that there is a more general role, 'effector' (first proposed in Foley and Van Valin 1984), which is neutral with respect to agency, which most verbs in English take; when the effector is human, the default interpretation of it is as an agent. This implicature can be blocked by adverts like *inadvertently* or *accidentally* or strengthened by adverbials like *intentionally* or *on purpose*. The fact that many English verbs like *break* and *kill* (but not *murder*) can take inanimate subjects is evidence that their subject is really an effector which can be construed as an agent when it is human.

Jackendoff (1987) takes a somewhat different approach to specific thematic relations. He posits several tiers of thematic relations: an action tier and a temporal tier in addition to the basic level of the thematic tier. The thematic tier deals with motion and location, the action tier with attributions of responsibility and affectedness, and the temporal tier with aspectual properties of events. The thematic tier is primarily concerned with the roles of theme, goal, and source, while agent and patient appear only on the action tier. This is exemplified in (1), with examples from Jackendoff (1987).

(a) The car [Theme$_{TH}$] hit the tree [Goal$_{TH}$; Patient$_{AC}$].   (1)
(b) Pete [Source$_{TH}$; Agent$_{AC}$] threw the ball [Theme$_{TH}$; Patient$_{AC}$].
(c) Bill [Theme$_{TH}$; Agent$_{AC}$] entered the room [Goal$_{TH}$].

('TH' denotes a role from the thematic tier, 'AC' one from the action tier.)

In this scheme, an argument may bear multiple specific thematic relations, each reflecting one facet of its interpretation.

1.2 Generalized Thematic Relations

It has been proposed that a second, more general type of semantic relation must be posited: 'semantic macroroles' or 'semantic proto-roles.' Originally proposed in Van Valin (1977) and further developed in Foley and Van Valin (1984) and subsequent work, semantic macroroles are generalized semantic relations which subsume groups of specific thematic relations. There are two macroroles, 'actor' and 'undergoer.' They are the two primary arguments of a transitive predication, corresponding to the general senses of 'agent' and 'patient' discussed in Sect. 1, either one of which may be the single argument of an intransitive verb. They correspond to what is pretheoretically commonly called 'logical subject' and 'logical object.' Macroroles are motivated by the fact that in grammatical constructions groups of thematic relations are treated alike. This is illustrated in (2)–(4).

(a) *Fred* broke the window.   Agent   (2)
(b) *The bomb* destroyed the car.   Instrument
(c) *Mary* received a parking ticket.   Recipient
(d) *The farm animals* sensed the earthquake.   Experiencer
(e) *Stars* emit light.   Source

(a) Max tossed *the book* to the teacher.   Theme   (3)
(b) The tidal wave destroyed *the harbor*.   Patient
(c) The rock hit *the wall*.   Locative
(d) The mugger robbed *Tom* of $45.00.   Source
(e) Will presented *Sheila* with a bouquet.   Recipient

(a) The window was broken by *Fred*.   Agent   (4)
(b) The car was destroyed by *the bomb*.   Instrument
(c) The earthquake was sensed by *the farm animals*.   Experiencer
(d) *The book* was tossed to the teacher by Max.   Theme
(e) *The harbor* was destroyed by the tidal wave.   Patient
(f) *The wall* was hit by the rock.   Locative

In (2) agent, instrument, recipient, experiencer, and source are all treated as the actor and subject of a transitive verb, while in (3) theme, patient, locative, source, and recipient are treated alike as the undergoer and object of a transitive verb. These groupings are not equivalent to (surface) grammatical relations like subject and direct object, for they hold in passive constructions as well, as illustrated in (4); here the

undergoer is subject and the actor the object of *by*. If this alternation were to be stated in terms of specific thematic relations, then long disjunctive lists of thematic relations would be required: in an active clause, the agent, instrument, recipient, experiencer, or source is subject and the theme, patient, locative, source, or recipient is object, while in a passive clause the theme, patient, locative, source, or recipient is subject and the agent, instrument, recipient, experiencer or source is the object of *by*. This is an undesirable analysis, as it clearly does not capture what is going on. Alternatively, a formulation in terms of macroroles is much simpler: in an active clause, the actor is subject and the undergoer direct object, while in a passive clause the undergoer is subject and the actor is the object of *by*.

With intransitive verbs similar generalizations hold. Some intransitive verbs take an actor as their single argument, while others take an undergoer. This is illustrated in (5)–(6).

(a) *David* sang loudly.   Agent   (5)
(b) *The ball* flew over the fence.   Theme
(c) *The motor* is running well.   Instrument

(a) *The dog* was sitting on the table.   Theme   (6)
(b) *Larry* got fat.   Patient
(c) *Marge* felt sick.   Experiencer

The subjects in (5) are all actors, despite the range of thematic variation, and those in (6) are undergoers. As with transitive verbs, each macrorole subsumes a number of specific thematic relations.

Dowty (1991) proposes two generalized thematic relations which he calls 'proto-roles'; they are 'proto-agent' and 'proto-patient.' They are similar in certain respects to actor and undergoer, but they are embedded within a very different theoretical outlook: Dowty claims that proto-roles are the only valid thematic relations, and he denies the validity of specific thematic relations like agent, theme, and patient. Proto-roles are constellations of features which define a prototype; they are not generalizations of specific thematic relations, unlike macroroles.

The relationship between specific and generalized thematic relations is captured in Fig. 2, which represents the increasing generalization and neutralization of semantic distinctions involved in them. (Not all specific thematic relations and not all groupings of specific thematic relations into generalized relations are illustrated.)

1.3 Role of Semantic Relations in Syntactic Theories

Most syntactic theories employ semantic relations in some way; Generalized Phrase Structure Grammar (GPSG) (Gazdar et al. 1985) and Montague Grammar (MG) (e.g., Dowty 1979) are the major exceptions (see also *Generalized Phrase Structure Grammar*). Specific thematic relations are a central feature of lexical entries for verbs in both Government-Binding Theory

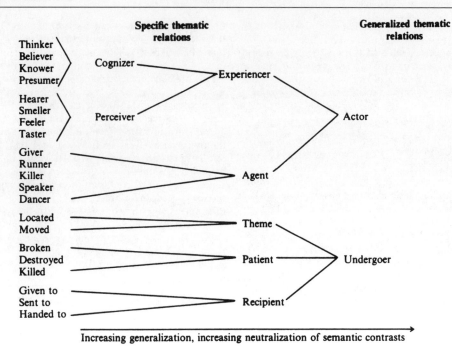

Figure 2.

(GB) (Chomsky 1981) and Lexical Functional Grammar (LFG) (Bresnan 1982); they are assumed to be part of the lexical entries for verbs in work in Relational Grammar (RELG) (Perlmutter 1982), but there is no explicit discussion of either thematic relations or lexical entries within RELG (see also *Lexical Functional Grammar*; *Relational Grammar*).

Thematic relations function differently in GB and LFG. The list of (specific) thematic relations associated with a verb, its *θ-grid*, plays a central role in the GB system; syntactic subcategorization information is deduced from it, and this in turn underlies the constraints imposed by the Projection Principle. D-structure is assumed to be a *pure* syntactic representation of the argument structure of a verb, which is represented by the θ-grid. Moreover, θ-role assignment is an important part of the derivation of a sentence, and the principle which governs it, the θ-criterion, is one of the major constraints in the GB system. In LFG, on the other hand, θ-roles are associated with grammatical relations (called, 'grammatical functions' in LFG) in the lexical entries of verbs, and lexical rules operate to change the linkings between thematic relations and grammatical functions, e.g., passive relinks the agent from subject to oblique and the theme from object to subject. In both theories θ-roles serve as the primary means for representing the *meaning* of a verb, but neither theory assumes an explicit theory of lexical semantics or proposes any independently motivated principles which govern the assignment of specific θ-roles to particular verbs. This is more of a problem for LFG than GB; in GB nothing depends on which θ-role an argument receives, as long as it receives one (and only one), whereas in LFG the validity of the syntactic analysis depends crucially in many instances on the identity of the θ-role assigned, e.g., the analysis of locative inversion in Chicheŵa in Bresnan and Kanerva (1989). Hence, without independent criteria for determining which θ-role an argument is linked to, the validity of such analyses is open to serious question. Thus, while thematic relations are an important feature of the GB and LFG systems of lexical representation for verbs, their respective functions within the overall theory are very different in the two frameworks.

The only theory which makes use of both specific and generalized thematic relations is Role and Reference Grammar (RRG) (Foley and Van Valin 1984; Van Valin 1993; see *Role and Reference Grammar*). RRG posits only one level of syntactic representation, unlike GB and RELG, and θ-roles, especially macroroles (generalized thematic relations), serve a crucial function in the linking of semantic and syntactic representations. Some of the generalizations captured by macroroles (see (2)–(6) above) are handled in other theories by D-structure (GB)/initial stratum (RELG) grammatical relations, but macroroles are not equivalent to underlying grammatical relations (see Van Valin 1990). Unlike GB and LFG, θ-roles are not part of the scheme for lexical representation of verbs; that is accomplished by a modified version of the system of lexical decomposition proposed in Dowty (1979). Moreover, there are independent principles governing the association of specific θ-roles with particular verbs, and therefore RRG is the only theory in which the assignment of thematic relations to verbs is independently motivated. In RRG, thematic relations are derived from argument positions in the decompositional semantic representation of a verb, following Jackendoff (1987), and therefore the role labels are mnemonics for the argument positions in the semantic representations which define them.

2. Pragmatic Functional Relations

Pragmatic functional relations are concerned with the distribution of information in utterances, in particular with respect to what is assumed by the speaker to be known to interlocutors and what is presented as new and informative. Research on this type of functional relation goes back at least to the Prague School linguists (see *Prague School Syntax and Semantics*) of the 1920s, e.g., Mathesius, and has continued in modern work, e.g., Firbas (1966) and Sgall, Hajičová, and Panevová (1986). Pragmatic relations have played a role in contemporary linguistic theory and description in the work of Halliday (1967, 1985), Jackendoff (1972), and Kuno (1972a, 1972b, 1975), among others.

There is a fundamental distinction in information structure which all of these different approaches seek to capture, namely that between the material in an utterance which is presented by the speaker as assumed to be known, accessible, or recoverable from context by interlocutors and that which is presented by the speaker as unknown, inaccessible, and not recoverable, hence as new and informative. Different approaches vary both with respect to how this contrast is labeled and exactly how the opposition is defined, but this basic distinction underlies all of them. In Prague School work, for example, 'theme' (known, given) is distinguished from 'rheme' (unknown, new), while in most contemporary work the terms 'topic,' 'focus,' and 'presupposition' are employed. They may be characterized as follows, following Lambrecht (1986, 1987, 1988).

> *Pragmatic presupposition*: 'the proposition or set of propositions which the speaker assumes the hearer considers true (believes, knows) and is aware of at the time of the utterance and which is relevant in the context of utterance.'
>
> (Lambrecht 1988: 1)

> *Topic*: 'What must be presupposed in the case of a topic is not the topic itself, nor its referent, but the status of the topic reference as a possible center of interest or matter of concern in the conversation. . .[T]he topic reference is *active* or *accessible* in the discourse. . .[T]he topic is contained in the pragmatic presupposition or is an element of the pragmatic presupposition.'
>
> (Lambrecht 1986: 102)

> *Focus*: The focus of an utterance is the nonpresupposed part of the utterance; it is the part that is asserted in a declarative utterance and questioned in an interrogative utterance. In English and many other languages, it is indicated by prosodic prominence.

These notions are derivable from Kempson's (1975) reformulation of Grice's (1975) maxim of quantity (see Van Valin 1991). They are universal, as they follow from the essential communicative function of language.

Lambrecht proposes a typology of information structure patterns with different topic–focus arrangements. The least marked one distributionally involves a topical subject and a focal predicate and corresponds to the traditional 'topic–comment' bifurcation of clauses; he labels it a 'predicate focus construction.' Presentational sentences like *There arose a great storm* lack a topical lexical subject NP and contain virtually all focal material; these are termed 'sentence focus constructions' by Lambrecht and 'neutral description utterances' by Kuno (1972a, 1972b). Finally, utterances in which the focus is restricted to a single constituent, e.g., the answer to a wh-question, are called 'narrow focus constructions.' These constructions are found in all languages, and a variety of means are employed to signal them. English distinguishes them primarily by means of prosody and clefting. Japanese uses particles: unstressed *wa* marks the topic(s) in a predicate focus construction, stressed *wa* and stressed *ga* ('exhaustive listing *ga*' in Kuno) mark narrow focus constructions, and unstressed *ga* indicates sentence focus constructions. Italian employs word order, prosody, and clefting: predicate focus involves (S)VO order, sentence focus VS order, and narrow focus a cleft in which the focus NP appears postverbally in the matrix clause (see Lambrecht 1986, 1987, 1993 for detailed discussion).

It has long been noticed that there appear to be correlations between information structure and grammatical structure. Given that in the vast majority of languages topical, presupposed material tends strongly to precede focal, nonpresupposed material in utterances, constructions which involve displacement of elements from their default position to the left toward the onset of the utterance could be analyzed as having a topicalizing function, while those which entail the displacement of elements to the right toward the end of the utterance could be analyzed as having a focalizing function. Subject inversion in Romance languages like Italian and Spanish, for example, can be viewed as motivated by the need to place the subject in the immediately postverbal focus position in these languages in a sentence focus or narrow focus construction. Similarly, passivization can be interpreted as a construction in which the undergoer, which would normally appear in the pre(OV)-/post(VO)-verbal focus position, occurs instead in the normally topical subject position, as a reflection of its topical status in the discourse context, while the actor, the topical subject in the default case, appears in the normally focal portion of the utterance (if it appears at all). The occurrence of normally clause-internal material in utterance-initial position, as in topicalization and left-dislocation constructions, is another example of pragmatically motivated syntax (see, e.g., Prince 1981a, 1981b; Horn 1986).

Most syntactic theories simply ignore pragmatic functions. To the extent that the correlations noted above between syntactic structures and pragmatic functions is acknowledged, it is nevertheless considered to fall outside of the realm of grammar. Only two of the theories mentioned in Sect. 1.3 make any systematic use of these functions, namely LFG and RRG. Both theories recognize all three types of functional relation, but they are treated differently in them. LFG views them as autonomous, and an argument can be described in terms of all three independently; that is, a subject can be an agent or a theme and a topic or a focus, for example. In RRG, on the other hand, focus structure is treated as a separate aspect of clause structure which interacts with constituent structure. The focus structure patterns identified by Lambrecht play an important role in explaining grammatical phenomena in RRG.'

3. Syntactic Functional Relations

Syntactic functional relations, or grammatical relations, are the focus of considerable controversy within syntactic theory. Some theories, e.g., RELG and LFG, consider them to be a fundamental and indispensable component of linguistic theory and analysis. Others, e.g., GB and RRG, treat them as derivative of other, putatively more basic concepts, while GPSG ignores them altogether. GB derives grammatical relations from phrase-structure configurations: subject is the NP immediately dominated by S (Chomsky 1965), or, more recently, SPEC(ifier) of IP ($=$INFL$''=$S) (Chomsky 1986), while object is the NP immediately dominated by VP (Chomsky 1965) or V$'$ (Chomsky 1986). The RRG theory of grammatical relations differs markedly from all generative accounts, and it will be discussed below.

3.1 Grammatical Relations

Since both LFG and RELG claim to be theories of universal grammar, their postulation of grammatical relations as fundamental components of linguistic theory raises the vital issue of their universality. If valid cross-linguistic universals are to be stated in terms of them, then they must themselves be universally valid constructs. The first step in ascertaining their validity as primitive (nonderived) theoretical constructs is characterizing them in such a way that their existence in a grammatical system can be demonstrated.

A grammatical relation exists when there is a restricted neutralization of semantic roles for syntactic purposes. Grammatical relations result from the extension of the pattern of neutralization represented in Fig. 2 to the neutralization of all semantic role contrasts. Consider the following examples from English (7):

(a) Henry seems to be singing in the shower. (7)
(b) Henry seems to be elated.
(c) Henry seems to be listening to a new CD.
(d) *Henry$_i$ seems Louise to have embarrassed____ $_i$.
(e) Henry seems to have been embarrassed by Louise.

In (7) an argument of the dependent clause appears in the matrix clause. In (7a) the 'raised' argument is the actor of the intransitive verb *sing*, while in (b) it is the undergoer of the intransitive predicate *be elated*. The verbs in the remaining examples are transitive; the raised argument in (c) is the actor of *listen to*, while in (d) and (e) it is the undergoer of *embarrass*. It is clear that the restriction on which argument can be raised cannot be stated in semantic role terms: it can be either an actor or an undergoer, and the crucial contrast between (d) and (e) cannot be explained in purely semantic terms. Rather, it must be accounted for syntactically: the argument which can be raised is the one which bears a particularly syntactic relation in the dependent clause, and it bears this relation in the passivized dependent clause in (e) but not in the active clause in (d) in which it has a different syntactic function. Hence there is a restricted neutralization of semantic roles with regard to which argument of the dependent clause can appear in the matrix clause, and the relation that this neutralization defines is the traditional notion of 'subject' for English. The same argument can be made with respect to the relation which triggers finite verb agreement in (7); it cannot be characterized semantically, because all semantic role possibilities are represented in (7a, b, c, e). (Note that it makes no difference for this argument whether specific or generalized thematic relations are assumed.) Here again a restricted neutralization defines the same syntactic relation as in the raising construction.

Grammatical relations are defined only by restricted neutralizations of semantic roles; neither unrestricted neutralizations nor restrictions without neutralization define a syntactic relation. An example of an unrestricted neutralization is relativization with a wh-relative pronoun in English. This clearly involves a neutralization of semantic roles, as the relativized NP can bear virtually any thematic relation, specific or general, to the predicate in the relative clause. This is illustrated in (8).

Mary talked to the man (8)
  (a) who [actor, agent] bought the house down the street.
  (b) who [undergoer, patient] the dog bit.
  (c) to whom [recipient] Bill showed the house.
Mary looked at the box
  (d) in which [locative] the jewelry was kept.
  (e) out of which [source] the jewelry had been taken.

There appear to be no semantic restrictions of the relevant type on the relativization strategy in English, and therefore this is an example of a neutralization of semantic roles for syntactic purposes. However, this construction does not define a grammatical relation in English, unlike raising and finite verb agreement, because it is not restricted. The converse, a restriction without neutralization, can be found in possessor ascension in Acehnese, an Austronesian language spoken in Sumatra. The basic facts are presented in (9), from Durie (1987).

(a) Seunang até lôn. (9)
    happy liver 1SG
    'I am happy.' (lit: 'My liver is happy.')

(b) Lôn seunang-até.
    1SG happy-liver
    'I am happy.'

(c) Ka lôn-tët   rumoh gopnyan.
    IN 1SGA-burn house 3SG
    'I burned her house.'

(d) Gopnyan ka lôn-tët-rumoh.
    3SG   IN 1SGA-burn-house
    'I burned her house,' or 'She had her house burned by me.'

(e) *Gopnyan ka aneuk-woe.
    3SG   IN child-return
    'His/her child returned.'

Possessor ascension is possible only if the possessed argument functions as an undergoer in the clause; the transitivity of the verb is irrelevant. In (9a) the single argument of *seunang* 'be happy' is *até lôn* 'my liver,' which is the undergoer of the stative predicate. In (9b) *lôn* 'I' functions as subject and *até* is compounded with *seunang*. In (9c) the undergoer of the transitive verb *tët* 'burn' is *rumoh gopnyan* 'his/her house,' while in (9d) the possessor *gopnyan* 'he/she' appears as an independent argument and *rumoh* 'house' is incorporated into the predicate. This is impossible with the possessor of an actor argument, as (9e) shows. Thus possessor ascension in Acehnese involves a definite restriction, i.e., the possessed NP must be an undergoer argument, but there is no neutralization of semantic roles; consequently, the relation specified is not a syntactic (grammatical) relation but rather a semantic one. It is only when there is both a restriction and a neutralization that a grammatical relation is involved.

If one were to investigate every major syntactic construction in English, it would be seen that the results were either like that in (7), in which a particular restricted neutralization is found, or like that in (8) in which there is a neutralization without a restriction. The pattern of restricted neutralizations across constructions is very consistent in English, and it is this pattern which constitutes and defines the grammatical relation 'subject' in English. Grammatical relations are consistent patterns of restricted neutralizations in a language.

3.2 Universal Grammatical Relations

There are two senses in which grammatical relations could be considered universal, a strong one and a weaker one. The strong sense is that there are grammatical relations in every human language. That is, in the grammar of every human language there is at least one construction in which there is a restricted neutralization of semantic roles for syntactic purposes. If it can be demonstrated that there is at least one language in which this is not the case, then grammatical relations are not universal in the strong sense. The weaker sense of universality is that in all of the languages that have grammatical relations, they play the same role in every language. This is based on the Saussurean notion of linguistic 'value': two linguistic entities are the same if they have the same value, i.e., they enter into the same relations of co-occurrence and contrast within the linguistic system. This weaker sense of universality is, then, the claim that grammatical relations in different languages have the same value in each linguistic system. In this domain, value is determined by the restricted neutralizations defining the relations: two systems of grammatical relations are the same if they are defined by the same (or comparable) restricted neutralizations.

As noted above, grammatical relations are not universal in the strong sense if there is a single language which exhibits no restricted neutralizations in its grammar. Acehnese is such a language, as argued in Durie (1987): there are restrictions without neutralizations, as in (9), and neutralizations without restrictions, as in (8), but there are no restricted neutralizations of semantic roles for syntactic purposes in the language. The full range of Acehnese data cannot be presented here, but three representative sets can be given. Grammatical constructions fall into three groups in this language: those in which only actor arguments may be involved, those in which only undergoer arguments may be involved, and those in which any argument of the verb may be involved. The second type has already been exemplified in (9). Before presenting the other two, it is necessary to give a brief introduction to verb classes and agreement in Acehnese. All examples are from Durie (1987).

Acehnese transitive may carry agreement clitics cross-referencing both primary arguments, the actor and the undergoer. This is illustrated in (10).

(a) Gopnyan geu-mat lôn./geu-mat-lôn. (10)
    3SG   3A-hold 1SG/3A-hold-1SGU
    '(S)He holds me.'

(b) (Lôn) lôn-mat   gopnyan.
    1SG   1SGA-hold 3SG
    'I told him/her.'

The clitics for actor and undergoer have the same basic form; they are distinguished by position, with actor signaled by a proclitic and undergoer by an optional enclitic. Thus *geu-* cross-references the actor and *-lôn* the undergoer in (10a), while *lôn-* cross-references the actor in (10b). Intransitive verbs fall into two general classes in terms of which agreement they take: some take only actor proclitics, e.g., *jak* 'go,' while the others take only the undergoer enclitics, e.g., *rhët* 'fall.' This is exemplified in (11).

(a) (Gopnyan) geu-jak./*gopnyan jak(-geuh). (11)
    3SG   3A-go   go(3-U)
    '(S)He goes.'

(b) (Lôn) lôn-jak./*lôn jak(-lôn)
    1SG 1SGA-go   go(-1SGU)
    'I go.'

(c) Gopnyan rhët(-geuh)./*gopnyan geu-rhët
    3SG   fall(-3U)   3A-fall
    '(S)He falls.'

(d) Lôn rhët(-lôn)/*lôn   lôn-rhët
    1SG fall(-1SGU)   1SGA-fall
    'I fall.'

Constructions involving the verb *tém* 'what' can only have complements in which the verb takes an actor argument, and the cross-reference clitic for the actor is obligatorily omitted; intransitive verbs which take only an undergoer argument are impossible in this construction, and with a transitive verb the omitted argument must always be the actor, never the undergoer. This is illustrated in (12).

(a) Gopnyan geu-tém [(*geu-)jak]. (12)
    3SG   3A-want   go
    '(S)he wants to go.'

(b) Geu-tém [(*geu-)taguen bu].
    3-want   cook rice
    'She wants to cook rice.'

(c) *Gopnyan geu-tém [rhët].
    3SG   3A-want fall
    '(S)he wants to fall.'

(d) *Aneuk agam nyan ji-tém [geu-peuréksa lé dokto].
    child male that 3A-want 3A-examine by doctor
    'That child wants to be examined by the doctor.'

(The Acehnese construction in (12d) is not a passive; see Durie 1988 for detailed arguments. *Geu-* and *ji-* are both third person but differ in the social status they code; *geu-* cross-references the higher status doctor, while *ji-* agrees with the lower status child.) Both *jak* 'go' and *taguen* 'cook' take actor arguments, and the actor clitic is obligatorily omitted in the dependent clause in (12a, b). *Rhët* 'fall,' on the other hand, takes only an undergoer argument, and it is impossible in this construction, as (12c) shows. In (12d) the omitted argument in the complement clause must be interpreted as the undergoer, and the result is ungrammatical. Thus this construction is restricted to verbs which take an actor argument, and the actor argument must be omitted; this is an example of a restriction without a neutralization. The difference between this construction and the one in (9) is that possessor ascension is restricted to undergoer arguments only, while this one is restricted to actor arguments

only. These two constructions are representative of the majority of syntactic constructions in Acehnese.

There are, however, constructions which involve an unrestricted neutralization, e.g., raising. This is exemplified in (13).

(a) Gopnyan teuntèe [geu-woe]. (13)
    3SG   certain 3A-return
    '(S)he is certain to return.'

(b) Gopnyan teuntèe [meungang-geuh].
    3SG   certain win-3U
    '(S)he is certain to win.'

(c) Gopnyan teuntèe [geu-beuet hikayat prang sabi].
    3SG   certain 3A-recite epic
    'He is certain to recite the Prang Sabi epic.'

(d) Hikayat prang sabi teuntèe [geu-beuet].
    epic   certain 3A-recite
    'The Prang Sabi epic is certain to be recited by him.'

(e) Gopnyan lôn-anggap [na neu-bi pèng baroe].
    3SG   1SG-consider be 2A-give money yesterday
    'I believe him to have been given money by you yesterday.'
    (lit.: 'I consider him$_i$ [you gave money [to]___$_i$ yesterday].')

The raised argument is an actor in (13a, c), an undergoer in (b, d), and a recipient argument in (e); Durie states that any core argument of the verb can be raised in this construction. Hence in this construction, unlike the others, there is a neutralization of semantic roles for syntactic purposes, but it is not restricted. Therefore it does not define a grammatical relation. Neither actor nor undergoer nor 'any argument of the verb' constitutes a grammatical relation.

Acehnese thus presents an example of a language which exhibits no restricted neutralizations of semantic roles in its syntax and therefore lacks grammatical relations as defined in Sect. 3.1. Another example of such a language is Mandarin Chinese; Li and Thompson (1976) argue that pragmatic functional relations are the relevant relations in Mandarin grammar, and LaPolla (1990) shows that there is no evidence to support the positing of purely syntactic relations in Mandarin syntax. Consequently, the strong sense of universality cannot be maintained. The validity of the weaker sense can be tested by contrasting English with Warlpiri (Andrews 1985), a language of Central Australia. The construction to be examined involves omission of an argument in a dependent clause; it is illustrated in (14).

Ngaju-rlu Ø-rna yankirri pantu-rnu, ngapa (14)
I-ERG   AUX-I emu (ABS) spear-PAST water (ABS)
nga-rninyja-kurra
drink-INF-while
'I speared the emu while it (not I) was drinking water.'

Andrews states that the missing argument in the *-kurra* construction is always the subject of the nonfinite clause. In semantic role terms, the omitted argument is the actor of *nga-* 'drink.' The actor argument of an intransitive verb can also be omitted, and in the sentences in (15) the omitted argument in each is the undergoer of an intransitive verb.

(a) Ngaju ka-rna-ngku mari-jarri-mi   (15)
I(ABS) PRES-I-you grief-being-NONPAST
nyuntu-ku, murumuru nguna-nyja-kurra-(ku)
you-DAT sick   lie-INF-while-(DAT)
'I feel sorry for you while you are lying sick.'

(b) Karli   ∅-rna nya-ngu pirli-ngirli wanti-nyja-kurra
boomerang(ABS) AUX-I see-PAST stone-ELATIVE fall-INF-while
'I saw the boomerang fall from the stone.'

In (15a) the verb is *nguna* 'lie' as part of the expression 'lie sick,' which can plausibly be assumed to be non-volitional since people do not volitionally lie sick, and in (15b) it is *wanti* 'fall.' These two verbs do not take actors as their single argument, and yet it is possible for it to be omitted in this construction. This shows that the restriction on which argument is omitted in the dependent clause cannot be stated in purely semantic role terms. Therefore, with intransitives, there is an example of a restricted neutralization of semantic roles for syntactic purposes in Warlpiri, and this shows that the language has grammatical relations.

Is there an analogous neutralization in sentences with transitive verbs? The restricted neutralization in (14) and (15) parallels that in English in (7a, b) with intransitive verbs and (7c) with an active voice transitive verb. In English there is a restricted neutralization with transitive verbs, as shown in (7c, d, e); the relevant Warlpiri example is given in (16).

*Yankirri ∅-rna nya-ngu ngarka-ngku pantu-nyja-kurra. (16)
emu(ABS) AUX-1SG see-PAST man-ERG   spear-INF-while
'I saw the emu$_i$ while the man speared____$_i$.'

It is impossible for the omitted argument in the dependent clause to be interpreted as the undergoer, in sharp contrast to (7e) in English, and therefore the restricted neutralization in Warlpiri is limited to intransitive verbs. The facts in (14–16) are representative for the language as a whole. The situation in Acehnese, English, and Warlpiri is summarized in Table 2. Even though grammatical relations can be motivated in both English and Warlpiri, the restricted neutralizations defining them are not the same: in English the neutralization applies to the arguments of both transitive and intransitive verbs, whereas in Warlpiri it is only with intransitive verbs. Thus subject in Warlpiri cannot be considered to be exactly the same as subject in English, and therefore the weaker sense of universality is also in- supportable. It must be emphasized that the reason for this contrast is not due to the fact that Warlpiri has ergative morphology and English accusative; Dyirbal, another Australian language (Dixon 1972), has both ergative morphology and syntax, and yet with respect to these criteria it patterns like English, not Warlpiri, in that it exhibits restricted neutralizations with both intransitive and transitive verbs. While this discussion has focused on just these three languages, many examples of English-type and Warlpiri-type languages could be adduced (see Foley and Van Valin 1985; Van Valin 1993). It appears, then, that grammatical relations are not universal in either sense.

3.3 Types of Systems of Grammatical Relations

Systems of syntactic relations vary along three primary dimensions: the pattern of the relations, the factors affecting the relations, and the consistency of the relations. Each of these will be discussed below.

The pattern of grammatical relations refers to the contrast between languages with accusative syntax and those with ergative syntax. In characterizing ergativity, it is useful to distinguish what Andrews (1985) calls 'grammatical functions' from grammatical relations. Dixon (1972) proposes that there are three grammatical functions: 'S,' the single argument of an intransitive verb; 'A,' the actor of a transitive verb; and 'O,' the object of a transitive verb. Grammatical relations are constituted of combinations of the functions. In English, the grammatical relation 'subject' includes both S and A, while the 'direct object' encompasses only O. This is clear from the facts in (7): S and A are treated alike, as in (7a, b, c), while O is excluded from the construction, as (7d) shows. In order for an undergoer of a transitive verb (which is normally realized as the O) to be raised in this construction, it must function as the derived intransitive subject of a passive verb; this grammatical function will be labeled 'd-S.' This pattern (subject = [S, A, d-S], object = [O]) defines an 'accusative' pattern. The name comes from the case marking pattern in languages like German in which S and A receive nominative (unmarked) case and O receives accusative (marked) case. In an ergative language, the grouping of functions is different, at least for some grammatical phenomena. With respect to case marking, S and O are assigned absolute (unmarked) case, while A receives ergative (marked) case. There are also syntactic phenomena in some ergative languages, e.g., Dyirbal (Dixon 1972), Sama (Walton 1986), and Jacaltec (Craig 1977), which treat S, O, and d-S the same and exclude A, e.g., relativization. Thus in a morphologically ergative language, case marking groups S and O together and treats A differently, and in a syntactically ergative language, the restricted neutralizations treat S, O, and d-S the same and A differently. These two patterns can be represented as in Fig. 3.

Table 2. Restricted neutralization of semantic roles

	Intransitive Vs	Transitive Vs	Grammatical Relations
Acehnese	NO	NO	NO
English	YES	YES	YES
Warlpiri	YES	NO	YES

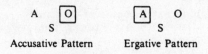

Accusative Pattern   Ergative Pattern

Figure 3.

This difference in patterns of grammatical relations is relevant to the issue of universality. If [S, A, d-S] defines the traditional notion of subject found in English and many other languages, what is the grammatical relation defined by [S, O, d-S]? If [O] is the traditional notion of direct object, what grammatical relation is [A]? The decomposition of grammatical relations into grammatical functions also permits a restatement of the contrast presented in Table 2, as in (17).

(a) English subject   [S, A, d-S]   (17)
(b) Warlpiri subject [S, A]
(c) Dyirbal 'subject' [S, O, d-S]

Both English and Dyirbal have restricted neutralizations with both intransitive and transitive verbs, hence the d-S component of subject, which Warlpiri lacks. Thus even though the syntactic pattern in English and Warlpiri is accusative, the notion of subject is not the same in the two languages. And even though Dyirbal and Warlpiri are both morphologically ergative, they differ syntactically both in terms of pattern and types of restricted neutralizations. There are, therefore, three distinct notions of syntactic subject operative in the grammatical systems of these three languages.

The second parameter of variation among grammatical systems is the factors affecting the relations. By this is meant the factors, syntactic, semantic, or pragmatic, which affect the determination of which argument of a verb will bear which grammatical relation. That is, given the set of thematic relations associated with a multiple-argument verb, there is, in some languages, more than one possible morphosyntactic realization of these arguments. With a transitive verb in Warlpiri and the North American Siouan language Lakhota (Van Valin 1977), for example, there is no variation as to which argument will be subject and which will be object: the actor is always subject, and the undergoer is always object. In these languages the lexical semantic properties of the verb determine how the arguments will be realized; there is no variation. With a transitive verb in English and Dyirbal, on the other hand, either the actor or the undergoer may function as subject; what conditions this choice? The fact that both roles are possible shows that the choice is not strictly semantically conditioned, as in Warlpiri and Lakhota. A major factor affecting the selection of the argument to function as subject is the pragmatic status of the argument in the discourse. It has long been noted that there is a correlation

between subjecthood and topichood, and in some languages the relative topicality of arguments affects subject choice: the most topical argument will be realized as subject, *ceteris paribus*. An analysis of subject selection in texts provides strong evidence of discourse influences on subject selection (see Van Valin 1993). Thus, pragmatic relations of the kind discussed in Sect. 2 play a significant role in the grammar of some languages, and in these languages subject can be viewed as a grammaticalization of the discourse relation of topic within the clause. It is important to emphasize that while subjects appear to be highly topical in all languages that have grammatical relations, pragmatic factors influence subject selection in only some languages, e.g., English and Dyirbal. Hence in some languages grammatical relations represent an interaction between all three types of functional relations, and in these languages grammatical relations cannot be considered purely syntactic.

The final dimension of variation is the consistency of the relations defined by restricted neutralizations. In all of the languages discussed to this point the major constructions in the language all involve basically the same restricted neutralization. When one talks about the notion of subject in English, what is meant is that the restricted neutralization found in (7) is found in all of the major constructions in the language. Grammatical relations are thus generalizations across the consistent restricted neutralizations found in a language, and therefore consistency is a crucial feature of these relations. Not all languages have consistent systems of grammatical relations. A very extreme example of an inconsistent or split system can be found in Jacaltec, a Mayan language (Craig 1977). Table 3, taken from Van Valin (1981), summarizes the pattern of neutralizations in seven major grammatical constructions. The inconsistency here is indeed striking: there are *five* distinct patterns in only seven constructions. It is not at all clear what 'subject in Jacaltec' in the traditional sense could mean, other than S, the only common denominator in all seven constructions. Thus while most languages are like

Table 3.

Construction	Pattern
1. 'Subject'[S, A]-triggered equi-NP-deletion	[S] only
2. 'Object'[O]-triggered equi-NP-deletion	[S, d-S(passive)] only
3. Promotion ('subject' copying with verbs like *begin*)	Dialect 1: [S] only
	Dialect 2: [S, d-S(both)] only
4. Relativization	[S, O, d-S(antipassive)]
5. *wh*-question formation	[S, O, d-S(antipassive)]
6. Clefting	[S, O, d-S(antipassive)]
7. Cross-clause coreference (preferred)	[S, A, d-S(passive)]

English, Dyirbal, and Warlpiri in having a relatively consistent system of grammatical relations, there are languages such as Jacaltec in which there does not appear to be a set of syntactic relations which applies consistently through their grammar.

3.4 Implications for Syntactic Theories

As noted at the beginning of Sect. 3, grammatical relations are treated differently in different syntactic theories. They play only an indirect role in GB; while reference is often made to subject, it is always interpreted in a strictly structural way, i.e., as the NP which is SPEC of IP or the 'external argument' of the verb. This approach crucially assumes that subject can be given the same structural definition in every language, and this is problematic. It would be possible to claim that in a syntactically ergative language like Dyirbal or Sama S and O are the external argument and A is the VP-internal argument, but this runs into serious theory-internal difficulties (see Van Valin 1992). Phenomena like those in Jacaltec potentially pose a serious problem, since in some constructions S and O would be the external argument, in others the S alone would be external; and in yet others S and A would appear to be the external argument.

Theories like LFG and RELG which take traditional English-like grammatical relations as basic run into greater difficulties. The nonuniversality of grammatical relations in both senses is a significant problem. The existence of languages like Acehnese which lack grammatical relations is an obvious difficulty; this would appear to pose a severe challenge to the descriptive adequacy of the theories. RELG nevertheless proposes grammatical-relations-based analyses of the language (e.g., Perlmutter 1982), while no analysis of these phenomena has yet been proposed in LFG. The variation in grammatical relations across languages is also problematic. In RELG this has been dealt with in terms of grammatical relations at different strata in a derivation, e.g., initial versus final grammatical relations, and combinations thereof, e.g., 'working 1' = an argument which is a subject (1) in the initial stratum and a term in the final stratum (Perlmutter 1982). Researchers in LFG have not addressed this issue, either; there are no accounts of syntactic ergativity in LFG, for example. Finally, both theories assume consistent systems of relations, and split systems like Jacaltec present another challenge. RELG approaches split systems the same way as it deals with cross-linguistic variation, namely, with formulations based on grammatical relations at different levels in a derivation and combinations thereof. An LFG account of these phenomena remains to be developed.

RRG takes a radically different approach to these problems: it rejects traditional grammatical relations as theoretical constructs, and instead proposes only a single syntactic relation, which it terms 'the syntactic pivot of a construction.' Syntactic pivot is a con-

struction-specific notion, and a pivot is defined by a restricted neutralization of the type discussed above. Thus RRG views grammatical relations systems as being composed of syntactic pivots; languages which have the same pivot for all or most major grammatical constructions have what appears to be the traditional system of grammatical relations, but this is a derived rather than basic concept. Languages with ergative or split syntactic systems pose no particular challenge, because there is no assumption that the [S, A, d-S] accusative pivot of English is in any way the unmarked pivot universally or that a language must have the same pivot for every construction. Languages like Acehnese simply lack syntactic pivots, and grammatical constructions are characterized directly in terms of semantic functional relations. RRG integrates pragmatic relations in such a way that in languages like English and Dyirbal their influence on the determination of the pivot in a construction can be captured.

Bibliography

Andrews A 1985 The major functions of the noun phrase. In: Shopen T (ed.) *Language Typology and Syntactic Description. Vol. I: Clause Structure.* Cambridge University Press, Cambridge

Bresnan J (ed.) 1982 *The Mental Representation of Grammatical Relations.* MIT Press, Cambridge, MA

Bresnan J, Kanerva J M 1989 Locative inversion in Chicheŵa: A case study of factorization in grammar. *LIn* **20**: 1–50

Chomsky N 1965 *Aspects of the Theory of Syntax.* MIT Press, Cambridge, MA

Chomsky N 1981 *Lectures on Government and Binding.* Foris, Dordrecht

Chomsky N 1986 *Barriers.* MIT Press, Cambridge, MA

Craig C 1977 *The Structure of Jacaltec.* University of Texas Press, Austin, TX

Dixon R M W 1972 *The Dyirbal Language of North Queensland.* Cambridge University Press, Cambridge

Dowty D 1979 *Word Meaning and Montague Grammar.* Reidel, Dordrecht

Dowty D 1991 Thematic proto-roles and argument selection. *Lg* **67**: 547–619

Durie M 1985 *A Grammar of Acehnese.* Foris, Dordrecht

Durie M 1987 Grammatical relations in Acehnese. *SLang* **11**: 365–99

Durie M 1988 The so-called passive of Acehnese. *Lg* **64**: 104–13

Fillmore C J 1968 The case for case. In: Bach E, Harms R (eds.) *Universals in Linguistic Theory.* Holt, Rinehart and Winston, New York

Firbas J 1966 Non-thematic subjects in contemporary English. *Travaux linguistiques de Prague* **2**: 239–56

Foley W A, Van Valin R D Jr 1984 *Functional Syntax and Universal Grammar.* Cambridge University Press, Cambridge

Foley W A, Van Valin R D Jr 1985 Information packaging in the clause. In: Shopen T (ed.) *Language Typology and Syntactic Description. Vol. I: Clause Structure.* Cambridge University Press, Cambridge

Gazdar G, Klein E, Pullum G, Sag I 1985 *Generalized Phrase Structure Grammar*. Blackwell, Oxford

Grice H P 1975 Logic and conversation. In: Cole P, Morgan J (eds.) *Speech Acts (Syntax and Semantics 3)*. Academic Press, New York

Gruber J 1965 Studies in lexical relations (Unpublished PhD dissertation, Massachusetts Institute of Technology)

Halliday M K 1967 Notes on transitivity and theme in English. *JL* **3**: 37–81, 199–244

Halliday M K 1985 *An Introduction to Functional Grammar*. Arnold, London

Holisky D A 1987 The case of the intransitive subject in Tsova-Tush (Batsbi). *Lingua* **71**: 103–32

Horn L 1986 Presupposition, theme and variations. *CLS* **22(2)**

Jackendoff R S 1972 *Semantic Interpretation in Generative Grammar*. MIT Press, Cambridge, MA

Jackendoff R S 1987 The status of thematic relations in linguistic theory. *LIn* **18**: 369–411

Kempson R 1975 *Presupposition and the Delimitation of Semantics*. Cambridge University Press, Cambridge

Kuno S 1972a Functional sentence perspective: A case study from Japanese and English. *LIn* **3**: 269–320

Kuno S 1972b Pronominalization, reflexivization, and direct discourse. *LIn* **3**: 161–95

Kuno S 1975 Three perspectives in the functional approach to syntax. In: Grossman R E, San L J, Vance T J (eds.) *Papers from the Parasession on Functionalism*. Chicago Linguistic Society, Chicago, IL

Lambrecht K 1986 Topic, focus and the grammar of spoken French (Unpublished PhD dissertation, University of California, Berkeley)

Lambrecht K 1987 Sentence focus, information structure, and the thetic-categorial distinction. *BLS* **13**: 366–82

Lambrecht K 1988 When subjects behave like objects: A markedness analysis of sentence focus constructions across languages (Unpublished manuscript, University of Texas)

Lambrecht K 1993 *Information Structure and Sentence Form*. Cambridge University Press, Cambridge

LaPolla R 1990 Grammatical relations in Chinese (Unpublished PhD dissertation, University of California, Berkeley)

Li C N, Thompson S A 1976 Subject and topic: A new typology of language. In: Li C (ed.) *Subject and Topic*. Academic Press, New York

Perlmutter D M 1982 Syntactic representation, syntactic levels, and the notion of subject. In: Jacobson P, Pullum G K (eds.) *The Nature of Syntactic Representation*. Reidel, Dordrecht

Prince E 1981a Topicalization, focus-movement and Yiddish-movement: A pragmatic differentiation. *BLS* **7**: 249–64

Prince E 1981b Toward a taxonomy of given-new information. In: Cole P (ed.) *Radical Pragmatics*. Academic Press, New York

Sgall P, Hajiĉová E, Panevová J 1986 *The Meaning of the Sentence in its Semantic and Pragmatic Aspects*. Reidel, Dordrecht/Academia, Prague

Van Valin R D Jr 1977 Aspects of Lakhota syntax (Unpublished PhD dissertation, University of California, Berkeley)

Van Valin R D Jr 1981 Grammatical relations in ergative languages. *SLang* **5**: 361–94

Van Valin R D Jr 1990 Semantic parameters of split intransitivity. *Lg* **66**: 221–60

Van Valin R D Jr 1992 Incorporation in universal grammar: A case study in theoretical reductionism. *JL* **28**: 199–220

Van Valin R D Jr 1993 A synopsis of Role and Reference Grammar. In: Van Valin R D Jr (ed.) *Advances in Role and Reference Grammar*. Benjamins, Amsterdam

Van Valin R D Jr, Wilkins D P 1996 The case for 'effector': Case roles, agents and agency revisited. In: Shibatani M, Thompson S (eds.) *Grammatical Constructions*. Oxford University Press, Oxford

Walton C 1986 *Sama Verbal Semantics: Classification, Derivation and Inflection*. Linguistic Society of the Philippines, Manila

Functionalism, Axiomatic

S. G. J. Hervey

Axiomatic Functionalism (AF) is the name given to the paradigm in core-linguistic theory and description initiated by J. W. F. Mulder in the 1960s and further developed, especially at the University of St. Andrews between 1968 and 1985, by Mulder in association with Hervey. Research along axiomatic functionalist lines has been conducted in the 1980s and 1990s at the University of Freiburg in Germany. An excellent recent publication applying axiomatic functionalist principles to a simple presentation of English syntax in particular is Paul Rastall's *A Functional View of English Grammar* (1995). An axiomatic functionalist

view of language also underpins the translation theory developed by Hervey at St. Andrews since the late 1980s (see for instance, Hervey and Higgins 1992).

AF is best described as a 'paradigm'—rather than a 'linguistic theory'—for a number of reasons. First, the approach claims a unique position with respect to the philosophy of science, in particular to theory-building and the evaluation of theories and descriptions. Second, its theoretical scope far exceeds that of linguistics by virtue of creating a semiotic theory that acts as the matrix for an embedded theory of language. Third, the axiomatic-deductive formulation of the theory—as a network of postulates, supporting definitions, and theorematically derived tenets—makes the approach fundamentally unlike any other within the social sciences. Finally, the descriptive models and methods employed, and the degree of rigor with which they are applied, constitute a further aspect of the singularity of the approach, in even a structuralist, let alone a 'post-structuralist' context.

In broad terms, AF is a typically 'European,' post-Saussurean enterprise: the location of linguistic theory strictly within a newly-constituted semiotics, the 'oppositionally' conceived identity of semiotic (including linguistic) items, the dualistic conception of *signum* as an indissoluble correlation between an 'expression' and a 'content,' the rigorous abstraction of self-contained synchronic systems as objectives of description: all these testify to Saussurean origins.

Still speaking impressionistically, AF has marked affinities with French functionalism (see *Functional Grammar: Martinet's Model*)—even though, in effect, it rejects most of the tenets held by Martinet as either insufficient or lacking in rigor. It also has notable affinities with glossematics (see *Glossematics (Hjelmslev)*)—even though the extent of common ground was only recognized post hoc. As an instance of the link with Martinet's functionalism one may usefully cite the concept of the 'double articulation' of language: both approaches use this concept in their definition of 'language,' but 'articulation' is given an explicit technical definition in AF which renders the resulting conception of 'double articulation' (*tactic* relations in both phonology and grammar) substantially different from its French namesake; furthermore, 'double articulation' is used (in AF) to define a minimal type of 'language,' while natural languages are expected to conform to a more elaborate prototype referred to as 'proper language' (cf. Mulder and Hervey 1975). As for the similarity to glossematics, a typical case in point is the epistemological notion of 'theories without an *existential postulate*' (i.e., theories that do not make an inbuilt claim for the existence of the phenomena to which they are subsequently applied; cf. Hjelmslev 1953). This notion was explicitly formulated in AF in terms of a rigorous ontological separation between theories and descriptions (the former having, ideally, potential empirical applicability, the latter having, necessarily, direct empirical content; cf. Mulder 1975), some time before the authors of the approach became aware of Hjelmslev's different, but equivalent, formulation.

On the level of the philosophy of science, the unique position of AF may be summarized by reference to two main points. First, AF explicitly rejects all forms of speculativism (e.g., the claim that a 'grammar' is a 'model of (mental) competence'; the search for substantive phonic or cognitive universals), operationalism (e.g., the notion of generative rules operating on ad hoc formatives acting as contentless

'dummy' elements in a calculus), and inductivism (e.g., the claim that phenomena should/can be described without predescriptive a priori, or that a 'general' linguistic theory can be inductively justified as a high-level generalization over a sufficient number of linguistic descriptions). Second, AF adopts its own neo-Popperian version of hypothetico-deductivism based on the idea that theories should be deductive, but not hypothetical, while descriptions should be hypothetical, but not deductive. Thus, it is only descriptions, not theories, that actually contain refutable (testable) hypotheses; theories (primarily evaluated in terms of their deductive-logical consistency) can only be 'indirectly tested' in the light of the 'quality' (consistency, adequacy, relative simplicity) of the descriptions they engender. As such, theory and description must be rigidly differentiated sets of statements, particularly in the social sciences where a single theory may be used for an indefinite number of descriptions pertaining to different, parallel, fields of phenomena (e.g., speech data drawn from different speech communities).

Assessing AF in a semiotic context (cf. Hervey 1982), it is significant that the major postulates, as well as many of the attendant definitions, theorems, and analytic models of the theory are applicable to conventional systems for communication in general, not merely to languages in particular. The theory is, in other words, as much a framework and instrument for the structural–functional analysis of semiotic systems at large as it is for the description of natural languages. Thus, for instance, the concept of 'cenological articulation' (tactic relations between figurae in combinations) is no less applicable to a description of Morse Code than it is to the phonotactic level of a language, or the graphotactic level of a system of alphabetic writing. Similarly, the concept of *signum* is no less applicable in the analysis of, say, systems of musical notation than it is in the analysis of the grammatical level of languages.

A characteristic, and at first glance daunting, aspect of axiomatic functionalist theory is its explicitly axiomatic–deductive formulation as a network of postulates, supporting chains of definitions, and theorematic statements establishing theoretical notions and models. Yet the forbidding appearance of the presentation—with postulates (labeled *Axiom A* to *Axiom F*) interspersed by series of technical definitions carefully numbered in accordance with the position each occupies in a network of definitional chains (chains through which the terms used in axioms and definitions can be reduced to a small set of primitive terms)—is not a mere stylistic device in the service of a formulistic pose, nor the window-dressing of a sterile and pretentious formalism. The layout genuinely reflects the intrinsic synthetic structure of the theory, and, looked upon as a whole, systematically expresses not only everything that the authors of AF take for granted in advance of describing fields of semiotic (including linguistic) phenomena, but also the rationale of the logical relationships linking the concepts deployed. Above all, the explicit organization of the tenets of AF (cf. Mulder and Hervey 1980; Mulder 1989) is a device for making transparent the 'deductive' structure of the theory, in order to facilitate evaluation of the coherence and consistency required of the theory. In fact, the theory indulges in a minimum of 'formulization' (i.e., the formulaic labeling of concepts and models); these being restricted to such items as formulas for the representation of, say, various kinds of tactic relation modeled in syntactic descriptions. For the most part, technical terms are not expressed by 'algorithmic' symbols, but by words and phrases borrowed from 'ordinary' language. The ultimate primitive terms of the theory are, of course, relatively unambiguous 'ordinary' language items drawn from English.

As for formalization, miscomprehension of the epistemological character of AF may be attributed to the way in which the terms 'axiomatic system' and 'deductive calculus' have been used in transformational–generative linguistics. Where axiomatic functionalist theory has been described as an axiomatic system and a deductive calculus (cf. Hjelmslev 1953), this was meant to indicate that the theory is systematically constructed by the juxtaposition of a closed set of 'first principles' (axioms interpreted by definitions) and the elaboration of deduced theorems. This theory is not in any sense an 'algorithmic' program for generating some external output through the operation of ad hoc rules on initial input symbols. Thinking of AF theory as a 'generative' system is, therefore, misleading, since (unlike in the case of generative grammars) its main concern at this juncture is with ontogenesis: the actual accumulation of that body of tenets to which adherents of the approach subscribe. Furthermore, the 'calculus' behind this ontogenesis is simply that of 'ordinary' deductive logic (e.g., syllogistic inference, *reductio ad absurdum*) used in order to determine tenets already theorematically implicit, but perhaps not yet explicitly recognized, in the theory. This 'deductive calculus' is a means of progressive self-exploration within the framework circumscribed by the axioms. Thus, the most practical suggestion for grasping in what sense AF theory is an axiomatic system and a deductive calculus is to forget what the transformational–generative paradigm might make of these terms, and to relate them to Euclidian geometry instead.

The axioms on which AF theory rests (cf. Mulder 1989) are:

Axiom A (the axiom of scope): *All features in semiotic sets are functional.* When interpreted through supporting definitions, this axiom postulates that every constitutive item in any semiotic system must derive its identity from opposition to other items making a different contribution to communicative import within the system.

Axiom B (the axiom of 'systemology'): *Semiotic systems contain simple, and may contain complex ordered, and/or complex unordered signa and figurae.*

When interpreted, this axiom postulates that, both in phonology and in grammar (or in comparable sub-systems of nonlinguistic semiotic systems), there *are* unanalyzable, minimal units, and there *may* also be asymmetrically constituted constructions, as well as symmetrically constituted ones.

Axiom C (the axiom of para-tactics): *Cenological entities may have para-cenotactic features and plerological entities may have para-syntactic features.*

As far as languages are concerned, this axiom postulates that phonological systems have, over and above the tactic combination of phonemes, a level of prosodic organization; and that grammatical systems have, over and above the level of syntax, a further level of para-syntactic organization.

Axiom D (the axiom of sentence-formation): *All semiotic systems contain sentences constituted by a base and para-syntactic features.*

This axiom postulates that sentences—the self-contained units of communication in any semiotic system—are not *syntactically* formed entities, but are the 'output' of a further structural level whose role is to endow grammatical 'base' units—words, phrases, parts of phrases, juxtapositions of phrases—with markers of sentential function.

Axiom E (the axiom of realization): *There may be a many-to-one relation between cenetic form and figura (allophony), and between cenological form and signum (allomorphy), and vice versa (homophony and homomorphy respectively).*

This axiom postulates that there may be 'formal' variants of figurae (e.g., [r] and [R] as allophones of the French /r/ phoneme), and of signa (e.g., /iz/ and /ar/ as allomorphs of English 'to be')—and that there may be formal coincidence between variants of different figurae (e.g., flapped [ɾ] as a variant of either /t/ or /d/ in American English), or between variants of different signa (e.g., /iz/ as a variant of either 'to be' or 'plural' in English).

Axiom F (the axiom of denotation): *Signa may be realized an unlimited number of times (in actual communication), each resulting utterance denoting a denotatum which may belong to a potentially infinite denotation class.*

In a nutshell, this axiom postulates a particular 'denotational' account of the meaning of signa according to which the putative denotation of a signum can be tested against the extension of the class of individual denotata denoted by token utterances of that signum. That is, the axiom postulates an interpretation of the relationship between the 'constant' denotation of a signum and contextual meanings of its utterances.

AF has proved itself capable of producing highly original (some may say 'idiosyncratic'), structural analyses in all the traditional areas of core-linguistics (distinctive feature analysis of phoneme systems, phonotactics, prosody, word-formation, syntax, semantics). Its additional level of sentential para-syntax reaches far into areas that are generally relegated to pragmatics or to text-linguistics. AF is susceptible to further extension in the direction of illocutionary theory and discourse analysis. It is also a suitable framework for semiotic analysis of nonlinguistic systems. Given these considerations, the 'narrowness' and 'sterility' that critics perceive in the approach should perhaps be seen as a reaction against the extreme methodological rigor of AF, and, in particular, against its outright refusal to pursue fashionable lines of speculation.

Bibliography

Hervey S G J 1982 *Semiotic Perspectives*. Allen and Unwin, London
Hervey S G J, Higgins I 1992 *Thinking Translation*. Routledge, London
Hjelmslev L 1961 *Prolegomena to a Theory of Language*. University of Wisconsin Press, Madison, WI
Mulder J W F 1975 Linguistic theory, linguistic descriptions, and the speech-phenomena. *Linguistique* 11(1): 87–104
Mulder J W F 1989 *Foundations of Axiomatic Linguistics*. Mouton de Gruyter, Berlin
Mulder J W F, Hervey S G J 1975 Language as a system of systems. *Linguistique* 11(2): 3–22
Mulder J W F, Hervey S G J 1980 *The Strategy of Linguistics: Papers on the Theory and Methodology of Axiomatic Functionalism*. Scottish Academic Press, Edinburgh
Rastall P R 1995 *A Functional View of English Grammar*. Mellen Press, Lampeter

Generalized Phrase Structure Grammar

A. R. Warner

Generalized Phrase Structure Grammar (GPSG) is a theory of syntax (with associated semantic interpretation) which marks a radical return to earlier ideas. It is a development of Phrase Structure Grammar (PSG), a framework which was explicitly rejected by Chomsky in the 1950s as an adequate model for natural-language syntax, in a judgment generally accepted over the following two decades. But the development of fresh ways of expressing generalizations which retain the essential characteristics of this approach had led to insightful accounts of a wide range of phenomena. The resulting theory belongs to generative grammar, but it has some distinctive characteristics. Among the more salient are its concern with an explicit formalism, its possession of a semantic interpretation, its highlighting of the issue of the potential capacity of types of grammars, the fact that it characterizes syntax (and semantics) using only one level of structure, and the fact that its practitioners generally avoid claims about the psychological relevance of linguistic theory.

1. Phrase Structure Grammar (PSG)

Phrase Structure Grammar formalizes essential aspects of the constituent structure approach found in much post-Bloomfieldian American syntactic analysis. In such analyses a sentence is divided up into contiguous parts or 'constituents,' which are themselves subdivided, until the smallest units are reached. Each constituent carries a label indicating category membership, such as S (sentence), NP (noun phrase), N (noun), DET (determiner), VP (verb phrase), V (verb), etc. The resulting analyses can be presented as 'labeled trees' like Fig. 1.

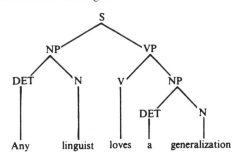

Figure 1. A Phrase Structure Grammar labeled tree.

Phrase structure rules provide an unambiguous way of specifying or 'generating' such labeled trees. In the usual notation for such rules a single label precedes an arrow which is followed by one or more labels, as in S → NP VP, or VP → V NP. This corresponds to a subpart of the tree in which a single node (the 'mother') stands directly above ('immediately dominates') one or more 'daughter' nodes, as S immediately dominates NP and VP, or VP immediately dominates V and NP in Fig. 1. The subtrees defined here are necessarily 'local' in the sense that they involve the immediate domination of daughters by their mother: this follows from the formalism. Rules which like these expand a node without reference to its context of occurrence are said to be 'context free.' Corresponding, grammars which contain only such rules are called 'Context-free Phrase Structure Grammars' and they are capable of generating 'context-free languages.' It is this type of grammar of which GPSG is a development.

There have been two major lines of argument against Context-free Phrase Structure Grammar (CFPSG) as a theory of natural-language syntax. The first, developed by Chomsky in *Syntactic Structures* (1957), is that PSGs (including CFPSGs) are incapable of making the simple and revealing general statements needed in an adequate account. It was claimed that they could not deal revealingly with interrelationships like that between active and passive sentences (*linguists love generalizations, generalizations are loved by linguists*), or with discontinuities within such structures as English *wh*-questions, where an apparently displaced phrase corresponds to a later gap (*What did you say linguists loved?*). Arguments based on facts like these led Chomsky to the conclusion that a more powerful formalism was required, in which more than one tree structure was associated with each sentence, and a distinct rule type, the 'transformation,' related such structures to one another. This conclusion was apparently supported by a second line of argument against CFPSG, which depends on the mathematical interpretation of the capacities of such grammars. Here it has been claimed that they are in principle incapable of generating some human languages when the latter are construed as sets of strings.

2. From Phrase Structure Grammar to Generalized Phrase Structure Grammar

GPSG was developed from the late 1970s by Gerald Gazdar and others. Its plausibility depends on the subversion of the two lines of argument against CFPSG just outlined. The first has been tackled by writing grammars which capture generalizations appropriately. Some of the analyses are strikingly elegant and have the important property that they derive from the theory with a minimum of stipulation. The second, mathematical, argument was countered by demonstrating that the proofs of the inadequacy of CFPSG which were generally accepted at that date were flawed (see Pullum and Gazdar 1982). GPSG importantly established a candidate theory of natural-language syntax which was of limited and relatively well-understood capacity and which did not use transformations. Doubts about the descriptive appropriacy of particular transformations had been growing among some linguists, and other transformationless theories were developed, notably Lexical Functional Grammar (see *Lexical Functional Grammar*). Moreover, transformations, if unconstrained, give grammars much more power than is required for human language, and (as Gazdar noted) the strongest way to constrain a component of grammar is to eliminate it. It now seems likely, however, that GPSG is in fact too restrictive, for more recent claims that CFPSG is

insufficient in principle as a model of natural-language syntax seem better founded than those rebutted by Pullum and Gazdar. But what is striking about such claims is the uncommonness with which the relevant data is to be found in language. Thus GPSG seems to be very close to an appropriate characterization of natural-language syntax in terms of 'weak generative capacity' (under which languages are construed as sets of strings), and to those who accept the relevance of such considerations (which are disputed) it forms a basis for research into the minor increase in capacity needed.

Like CFPSG, GPSG generates labeled trees which are specified in terms of the local trees of which they consist. But there is a crucial difference, and on this the possibility of generalizations hangs. The labels of a PSG are unanalyzable wholes, so that there is no formal relationship between the label for a verb (V) and the label for a verb phrase (VP) despite the convenient and informal notation (V, VP) which seems to imply such a relationship. But in GPSG, as elsewhere in generative grammar, constituent labels are 'complex symbols,' decomposable along such dimensions as finite/nonfinite, verbal/nominal, lexical/phrasal. This enables GPSG to make general statements which relate local trees to one another, and to abstract general conditions on local trees. Where particular nodes are required to share certain properties this may establish identities between quite remote parts of a structure. In the example of Fig. 1, subject–verb agreement can be mediated via three local trees: in one, the grammatical number of N (*linguist*) is identical to that of its mother NP, in another that NP and its sister VP agree, in a third the number of VP is identical to that of its daughter V (*loves*). Thus agreement between N and V, though not itself local, is dealt with as a chain of local identities, and generalizations across and between trees are captured by local rules and principles. The degree of generalization in GPSG is, indeed, so considerable that it has the surprising consequence that a grammar contains no actual Phrase Structure rules. Despite this, such a grammar is claimed to be mathematically equivalent to a CFPSG in essential respects. This follows because it generates a set of local trees, and each can be placed in unique correspondence with a rule 'mother → daughter(s)' in which distinct complex symbols are interpreted as single, monadic labels without internal structure. For this purpose, the label for VP (namely [N−, V+, BAR 2]) can be seen as a calligraphically ornate writing of what is mathematically a single symbol.

3. Mechanisms of GPSG

Like other theories of generative grammar, GPSG has undergone considerable development. Its most important statement is given in *Generalized Phrase Structure Grammar* (Gazdar et al. 1985) and it is this account that will be followed here.

GPSG essentially works by admitting labeled trees which meet the conditions of the grammar. A tree is admitted provided (a) it is labeled with well-formed categories, (b) each local tree in it corresponds to a rule of the grammar, and (c) no principle of the grammar is violated in any local tree. Basic to this is an account of features and categories, and a statement of the universal principles which control rule-to-tree mapping (Feature Instantiation Principles, Sect. 3.3). Beyond this GPSG captures two further types of generalization: about the order of elements (Linear Precedence Statements) and about interrelationships between rules (Metarules). These are dealt with in Sects. 3.7 and 3.8.

3.1 Categories and Features

GPSG has a precise and explicit theory of features and categories which is formalized in function theory. This reflects the importance of the decomposition of categories for the capture of generalizations. The dimensions along which categories differ are assigned feature names, each having a range of possible values. A category is then simply a set of feature names each with a value, so that (to exemplify) a 'finite verb phrase' is partly characterized for English as [V+, N−, VFORM FIN, BAR 2]. The features involved in this example with their range of possible values and a rough gloss are given in Table 1.

A category must, however, be internally consistent: it cannot assign more than one value to a feature name, so that [V+, V−] or [BAR 0, BAR 2, V+, N−] are not categories. Moreover, not all combinations of features are allowed in legitimate categories (the restriction being variously a universal or language particular matter). Since the finite/nonfinite dimension is a property of verbs and verb phrases, which are [V+, N−] ('verbal and nonnominal') in the above system, the grammar of English will contain a 'Feature Cooccurrence Restriction' VFORM ⊃ [V+, N−]. Thus the combination [V−, N+, VFORM PSP] will not be a category of English. But a category need not be fully specified, so that [BAR 2] (=phrase) is a category, as is [V+, N−, BAR 2] (=morphosyntactically unspecified VP). Note that the symbols V, N, VP, etc., as in Fig. 1, abbreviate feature complexes, so that V may either be a feature name or stand for [V+, N−, BAR 0]. The context will make clear which of these is intended.

3.2 The Introduction of Lexical Items

The occurrence of lexical items is sensitive to their context. The expansion of V as a transitive verb like *love* (which is said to be 'subcategorized' for the NP which is its direct object) is allowed where V has a sister NP as in Fig. 1, and this seems to need a context-sensitive rule, 'V → *love* before NP.' But the use of complex symbols allows the grammar to subclassify lexical items directly, using a feature name SUBCAT (for 'subcategorization') whose values are (arbitrarily chosen) integers {1, 2, 3, ...}. This feature is introduced on lexical nodes by rule and appears in lexical entries: for example, VP → V[SUBCAT 2] NP, where *love* is V[SUBCAT 2]. Thus context is dealt with here by a context-free mechanism.

3.3 Feature Instantiation

'Feature instantiation' is the central mechanism of GPSG. Essentially it allows features to be freely assigned to categories in a local tree corresponding to a rule, provided that they do not violate the conditions of the grammar. This permits very general statements. Consider the local tree which dominates *loves a generalization* in Fig. 1 (given with fuller but still partial specification in Fig. 2).

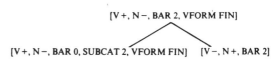

Figure 2. Local tree illustrating a (partial) GPSG feature specification.

There is a substantial similarity here between the mother VP and the head daughter V (where 'head' is a technical term for the daughter which characterizes the identity of its constituent). Both share [V+, N−, VFORM FIN]. Moreover parallel partial identities between mother and head will hold very generally across phrase types. This is captured by the 'Head Feature Convention' which requires identity in a particular subset of features (the 'Head features') between mother and head. The grammar can then allow the free instantiation of features in the local tree corresponding to a rule provided this convention (and other principles of the grammar) are not violated.

This means that rules can be given in a simpler and

Table 1. Features used for the category 'finite verb phrase' in English, and their range of values.

Feature name	Range of values	Gloss
V	{+, −}	verbal, nonverbal
N	{+, −}	nominal, nonnominal
VFORM	{FIN, INF, PSP, PRP, PAS, ...}	finite, infinitive, past participle, present participle, passive participle, ...
BAR	{0, 1, 2}	lexical level, intermediate level, phrasal level

more general form. The rule admitting the tree of Fig. 2 becomes (1):

$$[V+, N-, BAR\ 2] \rightarrow H[SUBCAT\ 2]\ [V-, N+, BAR\ 2] \quad (1)$$

where *H* is not a feature name but identifies the category which is the head. The categories in Fig. 2 correspond to those of the rule. Each is required to contain at least the information given in the corresponding category in the rule, so that it is an 'extension' of that category. Features 'inherited' from the rule are in roman type in Fig. 2. Instantiated features are in italics. To exemplify, the first daughter has inherited [SUBCAT 2] from the rule, and shows the instantiation of [V+, N−, BAR 0, VFORM FIN]. Here [V+, N−] are required by the Head Feature Convention since the rule requires their presence on the mother. VFORM has been freely added, as it has on the mother: it could have carried any value, provided only that the values on the mother and head were identical. Finally, [BAR 0] shows disagreement between mother and daughter although BAR is a Head feature. This is imposed by the rule together with the grammar since there is a Feature Cooccurrence Restriction which requires all major categories which carry SUBCAT also to be [BAR 0]. This has priority over the Head Feature Convention which imposes identity as a default, that is only in cases where the grammar does not make an exceptionless statement requiring lack of identity.

3.4 Control Agreement Principle

This principle is semantically driven. Its main case involves categories which are semantically 'functor' and 'argument,' like VP and its subject NP, or V and its object NP. In various languages such structures may show overt agreement of the functor with the argument. In GPSG such agreement is represented by a 'Control feature' AGR whose values are categories, and the 'Control Agreement Principle' requires AGR on a functor to carry the value of its argument for the subset of universal cases relevant to the language in question. With more fully specified labels the topmost local tree in the example of Fig. 1 would contain the argument NP[PLU−, PER 3] (nonplural and third person) and the functor VP[AGR NP[PLU−, PER 3]]. Since the value of AGR here is identical to the category of the argument NP the Control Agreement Principle is satisfied. Since AGR is a Head feature as well as a Control feature [AGR NP[PLU−, PER 3]] will also appear on V because of the requirements of the Head Feature Convention on the local tree dominated by VP, and this convention will also ensure that [PLU−, PER 3] appears on the subject N as well as the subject NP. Thus English subject–verb agreement can be dealt with by context-free mechanisms, despite occasional claims to the contrary.

3.5 Unbounded Dependencies

Unbounded dependencies are found in such constructions as English WH-questions or topicalizations like *Who did John take the money from e?*, *This book, John took e from Harry*, where a constituent corresponds to a later gap (here indicated by *e* for 'empty') and has apparently been displaced.

This phenomenon is also described in GPSG by the percolation of information through a chain of local subtrees. Intuitively this involves the establishment of a distinct series of categories which contain a gap: *took the book from Harry* is VP, but *took e from Harry* is a distinct category, a VP with an NP gap in it. After all, as Gazdar has argued, such pairs of phrases have quite distinct distributions, and they fail the common test that identical categories may be conjoined, contrast (2a) and (2b):

> *This book, John [took e from Harry] and [gave an offprint to Mary]. =VP-with-NP-gap *and* VP   (2a)

> This book, John [took e from Harry] and [gave e to Mary]. =VP-with-NP-gap *and* VP-with-NP-gap   (2b)

These categories are identified by a feature called SLASH whose value is the category of the gap itself. Thus *took e from Harry* is VP[SLASH NP] (commonly written VP/NP). The information [SLASH NP] 'with an NP gap' is not simply subject to the Head Feature Convention since, for example, the VP[SLASH NP] *took the book [from e]* has head V and contains the PP[SLASH NP] *from e*. The relevant principle of feature instantiation must ensure that the information passes from mother to nonlexical daughter, and it is dubbed the 'Foot Feature Principle.' This holds for a designated set of features (the 'Foot features,' including SLASH), and it requires any Foot feature instantiated on the mother of a local tree to be matched by the instantiation of that Foot feature on at least one daughter. Then in the example of Fig. 3, the Foot feature in the topmost local tree (i) is introduced by the rule for topicalization: it is inherited, not instantiated, and the Foot Feature Principle is not relevant. But in

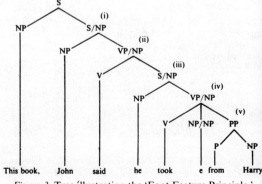

Figure 3. Tree illustrating the 'Foot Feature Principle.'

trees (ii), (iii), (iv), and (v) [SLASH NP] is not specified by rule: it is instantiated subject to the Foot Feature Principle. Finally NP[SLASH NP] is realized as a null element. Thus the filler–gap relation can be conceptualized in terms of the introduction, percolation, and elimination of the SLASH category: separate rules are responsible for its introduction and elimination, but its percolation between these subtrees depends on a chain of local relationships established by the Foot Feature Principle.

SLASH, however, is not only a Foot feature. It is also a Head feature and, when inherited, it is a Control feature. This gives a graphic illustration of GPSG's ability to capture generalizations. Because it is a Control feature the Control Agreement Principle requires the categorial identity of filler and SLASH in (i) of Fig. 3, so that the general possibility of an initial filler in English clauses (whether topicalized phrase or *wh*-phrase) is stated in the single rule $S \rightarrow X^2 H/X^2$ (where X is an underspecified category). Moreover, coordination is analyzed as multiply headed, so that each conjunct is a head. Then by a simple extension of the Head Feature Convention, if the mother carries SLASH each of the conjunct daughters must also carry SLASH. Thus if one conjunct contains a gap related to a filler, all must (cf. (2)), and at one stroke the grammar accounts for the Coordinate Structure Constraint and its systematic across the board exceptions. Moreover, where a phrasal head and phrasal adjunct are sisters, as in *filed the paper* (VP head)— *without reading it* (Adverb Phrase adjunct), the Head Feature Convention will require a SLASH feature instantiated on the construction's mother to appear on the head, while the Foot Feature Principle will permit it also to appear on the adjunct. But percolation onto the adjunct alone is not permitted. Thus GPSG has a persuasive account of the distribution of multiple (parasitic) gaps, and of the fact that adjuncts do not permit nonparasitic gaps.

> This paper, Dana filed e without reading e.
>   = VP/NP AdvP/NP.   (3a)

> This paper, Dana filed e without reading the abstract.
>   = VP/NP AdvP.   (3b)

> *This paper, Dana filed the abstract without reading e.
>   = VP AdvP/NP.   (3c)

3.6 Default Conditions

The labels in a tree must also comply with 'default' conditions. In English a passive participle carries the feature [VFORM PAS]. Clearly this cannot be freely instantiated on V or the grammar would admit transitive structures carrying [VFORM PAS] and falsely predict the existence of grammatical passive VPs such as *bitten a dog*, hence of the sentence *John was bitten a dog*. Equally the grammar must be able to specify the occurrence of *bitten* in appropriate circumstances. This type of markedness condition is dealt with by

Feature Cooccurrence Defaults, such as [BAR 0] $\supset \neg$[VFORM PAS]. These must hold unless the grammar specifies otherwise (as V[VFORM PAS] will be specified in rules for passive VPs) or unless the local subtree essentially involves the percolation of information between 'nonlexical' nodes (hence [VFORM PAS] will be specified across a coordination of passive participles [*attacked and bitten*] *by a Rottweiler* since these are not 'lexical' in the technical sense relevant here).

3.7 Ordering

A local structure like that of the VP in Fig. 1 contains two sorts of information. First, the mother immediately dominates the daughters. Second, the daughters have a particular left–right order. GPSG separates these two types of information. Immediate Dominance rules (ID rules) specify mother/daughter relationships and Linear Precedence statements (LP statements) establish permitted orders. This IDLP format gives a simple but general account of ordering facts. Thus, for English, a single statement can be made about the ordering of lexical heads: that they are initial in their local tree. The information need not be repeated in each of a series of lexical phrase structure rules as in example (1). Some ordering can also be left free. English syntax requires no statement about the ordering of PPs introduced as sisters to V (*talk to Gerald about GPSG*, *talk about GPSG to Gerald*), and languages which like the Bantu language Makua have free (or virtually free) word order have a simpler rather than a more complex grammar: instead of a battery of Phrase Structure rules, one for each ordering of daughters, there are just fewer LP statements. Moreover, the framework is a restrictive one. If lexical heads were introduced by a series of Phrase Structure rules, then the placement of the head could in principle vary idiosyncratically from rule to rule. But such idiosyncratic variation is precluded in IDLP format. Indeed, this format is only possible where ordering conditions (including both the restrictions and the freedoms) hold without exception across their domain, and this Exhaustive Constant Partial Ordering in fact provides a surprisingly restrictive account.

3.8 Metarules

GPSG has no device like the transformation for relating structures directly. It can, however, capture a range of generalizations about relationships between local structures by interrelating the rules which underlie such structures. The 'metarule' maps one set of ID rules into another. To exemplify: to each basic rule of English which introduces a transitive verb, like those in (4) (here the comma indicates lack of ordering on the right-hand side), there will correspond a derived rule (given in (5)) lacking the object NP and carrying a feature [VFORM PAS] to characterize the distinct morphology and distribution of passive verb phrases.

The metarule in (6) is essentially a statement of this mapping. Note that the passive is here treated as a VP category, capable like other nonfinite VP categories of occurring after *be*.

VP → H[SUBCAT 2], NP	V[SUBCAT 2] = *maul*, etc.	(4a)
VP → H[SUBCAT 5], NP, NP	V[SUBCAT 5] = *spare*, etc.	(4b)
VP → H[SUBCAT 8], NP VP[VFORM INF]	V[SUBCAT 8] = *persuade*, etc.	(4c)
VP[VFORM PAS] → H[SUBCAT 2]		(5a)
VP[VFORM PAS] → H[SUBCAT 5], NP		(5b)
VP[VFORM PAS] → H[SUBCAT 8], VP[VFORM INF]		(5c)
PATTERN TARGET		(6)

VP → W, NP ⊃ VP[VFORM PAS] → W

(Here *W* stands for any string of categories. A fuller version of the metarule would provide for the optional *by*-phrase of passives.)

There will be a similar mapping between the basic rules of English and the derived rules which legitimize gaps and correspond to subtrees like (v) in Fig. 3 above which terminate the downward percolation of SLASH. Metarules are, however, subject to the restriction that they apply only to rules which have a lexical head. This predicts that gaps can only occur as sister to a lexical item (either straightforwardly, as above, or less obviously in *The girl who John knew was happy* where *knew was happy* is analyzed as V VP without a subordinate S). Thus GPSG has an account for data covered in GB by the stipulation that empty categories should be 'governed' by a lexical head.

3.9 Semantic Interpretation

GPSG is associated with a version of Montague Grammar. Within this approach semantic interpretation is essentially a matter of establishing the real world conditions for the denotation of expressions, and the manner of their combination. Thus GPSG has a 'truth-conditional' semantics. Gazdar et al. (1985) give an account in which the principles of semantic composition follow directly from the syntax and the lexical semantics of individual items. Thus there is no independent level of semantic representation. The translations into formulas of 'intensional logic' are simply an aid to the analyst, not a formal level of the theory, and the grammar has only a single level of representation.

The semantics does, however, give the theory a very limited capacity to capture nonlocal generalizations which are treated as syntactic in some other theories, hence its treatment of 'raising' and 'equi' verbs such as *seem* and *try*. When these occur with the infinitive, they have a semantic structure which does not correspond to their overt syntactic structure: an argument is in the 'wrong' place, or must be supplied. *He seems to run* is semantically *seems* (*he run*); *he tries to run* is semantically *he tries* (*he run*). The lexical semantics associated with *seem* and *try* in these structures in GPSG contains a functor which has the effect of stating this equivalence, thus capturing 'control' properties of 'equi' verbs and the 'transparency' of 'raising' verbs.

3.10 Summary

A GPSG admits trees consisting of local trees each of which meets the following conditions.
(a) It is labeled with legal categories which violate no Feature Cooccurrence Restrictions.
(b) Its categories are extensions of corresponding categories in a basic Immediate Dominance rule, or in an Immediate Dominance rule which is the output of a metarule.
(c) It does not violate any Linear Precedence statements.
(d) It does not violate any feature instantiation principle, or any Feature Specification Default. The feature instantiation principles are:
Head Feature Convention;
Control Agreement Principle;
Foot Feature Principle.

4. Prospect

As noted above it seems likely that natural-language syntax requires more than the power of a CFPSG, hence that that classical GPSG is too restrictive. But it provides a clear basis for research into the increase in power which is needed. Major components of the theory will be of continuing importance: the detailed account of features and categories which is soundly based in function theory; some of the principles of feature instantiation, especially the Head Feature Convention and the Foot Feature Principle; and the distinction between principles of dominance and of order. These are prominent (in modified form) in Head-driven Phrase Structure Grammar (HPSG), GPSG's most direct descendant (see *Head-driven Phrase Structure Grammar*). GPSG is also of major interest to computational linguistics, and to theories of parsing (though here there is much dispute). The most obviously problematic area in the theory presented in Gazdar et al. (1985) is the account of metarules. First their availability must be restricted to avoid increasing the generative capacity of the theory, but it is not clear that the restriction imposed by Gazdar et al. (1985) (that is, that a metarule should not be allowed to apply to its own output) is either natural or descriptively appropriate. Second, the fact that metarules are restricted to ID rules with lexical heads means they essentially interrelate subcategorization possibilities. This suggests that GPSG's syntactic account of subcategorization should be replaced by a lexical account, so that this area of syntax is a projection from the lexicon with metarules reinterpreted as lexical rules, and this line of development has been pursued in the theory of Head-driven Phrase Structure Grammar.

Bibliography

Note: For a straightforward introductory book, see Bennett (1995). Briefer introductions can be found in Horrocks (1987) and Sells (1985). Borsley (1991) introduces GPSG in a comparative context alongside HPSG and GB. The central work is Gazdar et al. (1985). It is demanding, and Hukari and Levine (1986) is a useful companion. Gazdar (1982) is valuable for its discussion and for a clear exposition of an early version of the theory.

Bennett P 1995 *A Course in Generalized Phrase Structure Grammar*. UCL Press, London
Borsley R 1991 *Syntactic Theory. A Unified Approach*. Arnold, London
Gazdar G 1982 Phrase Structure Grammar. In: Jacobson P, Pullum G K (eds.) *The Nature of Syntactic Representation*. Reidel, Dordrecht
Gazdar G, Klein E, Pullum G K, Sag I A 1985 *Generalized Phrase Structure Grammar*. Blackwell, Oxford
Horrocks G 1987 *Generative Grammar*. Longman, London
Hukari T E, Levine R D 1986 Generalized Phrase Structure Grammar: A review article. *LA* **16**: 135–260
Pullum G K, Gazdar G 1982 Natural languages and context-free languages. *L&P* **4**: 471–504
Sag I A, Gazdar G, Wasow T, Weisler S 1985 Coordination and how to distinguish categories. *NLLT* **3(2)**: 117–72
Sells P 1985 *Lectures on Contemporary Syntactic Theories*. Center for the Study of Language and Information, Stanford, CA

Generative Grammar: Principles and Parameters

R. Freidin

Syntactic models within the general framework of generative grammar have been in constant change and development. This article, reprinted unchanged from the Encyclopedia of Language and Linguistics, *admirably summarizes the 'Principles and Parameters' model of the late 1980s and early 1990s. Recent developments of the past few years are outlined in the article* Generative Grammar: The Minimalist Program.

The main task of linguistic theory 'must be to develop an account of linguistic universals that, on the one hand, will not be falsified by the actual diversity of languages and, on the other, will be sufficiently rich and explicit to account for the rapidity and uniformity of language learning, and the remarkable complexity and range of the generative grammars that are the product of language learning' (Chomsky 1965: 27–28). The framework of generative grammar at the end of the twentieth century attempts to fulfill this goal by postulating a specific set of general principles of grammar, each of which is formulated in terms of a fundamental notion of grammatical analysis (e.g., case and binding). Such principles are assumed to be part of the innate knowledge that a language learner brings to the task of language acquisition—more precisely, the acquisition of a grammar of a human language. To the extent that much of a speaker's knowledge of his/her language can be derived from this system of general principles, the need for language-particular rules of grammar diminishes—thus contributing to an explanation for the rapidity and uniformity of language acquisition. From the perspective of these principles of grammar, much of the diversity across languages can be viewed as the result of systematic differences in the way in which certain principles apply to the grammars of various languages. These differences seem to fall within a restricted range of options, referred to as parameters. Research is based on the working hypothesis that much of the apparent diversity among languages can be reduced to instances of parametric variation. Though in the early 1990s it is too soon to say whether this hypothesis is correct, it has generated a substantial amount of promising research in the area of comparative grammar (see Jaeggli and Safir 1989; Freidin 1991).

It is worth noting that comparative grammar as practiced in the late twentieth century has a much more ambitious and wide-ranging goal than its nineteenth-century predecessor. Both are concerned with establishing an explanatory basis for the relationships between human languages. The neogrammarians of the nineteenth century were focused primarily on relationships between languages and groups of languages in terms of common ancestry. Over a century later, generative grammar is concerned with a theory of grammar that is postulated to be an innate component of the human mind/brain, a faculty which all humans share as part of their genetic identity and which guides the acquisition of language. Thus the theory of grammar establishes the relationship among all human languages—not only those that happen to be related by historical accident (e.g., common ancestry).

The system of grammatical principles under investigation in the 1990s evolved out of the study of conditions on the application of transformations, beginning with Chomsky's work on the A-over-A Principle in the early 1960s (see Chomsky 1964) and continuing with Ross's work from the 1960s on island constraints (Ross 1985) and Chomsky's extension of the conditions framework (Chomsky 1973). One of the first important breakthroughs in modern comparative grammar came from the work of Kayne (1975) and Quicoli (1976a, 1976b), which demonstrated that certain abstract conditions on the application of transformations, postulated for the analysis of English in

Chomsky (1973), also applied to some very different constructions in Romance languages involving clitics and quantifiers. Another crucial step in the development of the subsequent approach was achieved with the demonstration (Chomsky 1976) that under trace theory the behavior of transformational rules followed from general principles and therefore that transformations could be stated in an optimally general form—essentially as bare elementary transformational operations (e.g., 'substitute α' or adjoin 'α to β'). Transformational rules in such general form could be viewed as rules of universal grammar (the theory of grammar) rather than as language-specific rules of a particular grammar, or as construction-specific rules (e.g., a relative clause transformation).

The study of filters (conditions on representations) provides another major element of the framework under discussion (see Chomsky and Lasnik 1977)—one which raises important empirical questions regarding the status of various levels of syntactic representation. This line of research led to the realization of the central role of the notions of case and government for the theory of grammar (due to Jean-Roger Vergnaud; see Rouveret and Vergnaud 1980)—and ultimately to Chomsky's 1981 reformulation and extension of the entire theory, commonly referred to as government and binding (or GB) theory. It should be noted that the designation 'GB theory' is somewhat misleading because, (a) the theory covers more than government and binding (see below); (b) government is not the only important concept in the theory; (c) to the extent that a concept of government is intrinsic to the structure of language, any theory of language must include a theory of government; and (d) binding is not unique to this theory.

Labels aside, Chomsky (1981) relates phrase structure theory and the theory of transformations in a new way. Up until this version of the theory of generative grammar, the theory of phrase structure and the theory of transformations had developed more or less independently. By defining a notion of government in terms of the theory of phrase structure and then establishing the major role that it plays in the various conditions that determine the behavior of transformations, Chomsky identifies a conceptual thread that links the two theories.

1. Organization of the Grammar

Within the principles and parameters framework, a grammar provides structural descriptions of expressions in the language which serve as the basis for correlating the sound and meaning of each expression. The grammar also provides structural descriptions (or partial structural descriptions) for deviant expressions (e.g., strings of words in the language which violate some principle of grammar or fail to conform to some specific lexical property). The structural description

of an expression involves four levels of representation, as illustrated in Fig. 1.

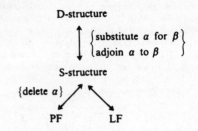

Figure 1. Levels of syntactic representation.

D-structure provides a structural description of lexical strings in accordance with the principles of phrase structure and the principles of predicate/argument structure. Thus D-structures are free of syntactic dislocations of the sort indicated in the examples in (1) below, where the italicized phrase has been moved from the underlined empty position:

the boy was stopped ＿＿ by the police. (1a)

who did you say Mary wants to invite ＿＿? (1b)

an article on string theory ＿＿ just appeared *which I want to read.* (1c)

S-structure is related to D-structure via the application of movement transformations (substitution and adjunction). S-structure is also the interface between the levels of phonetic form (PF) and logical form (LF). PF is derived from S-structure via deletion and the application of phonological rules. Note that the purely phonetic form of an expression involves no structural information and hence not even word boundaries. Since many discussions of PF assume the presence of syntactic structure (e.g., Aoun et al. 1987), PF should not be equated with the level of pure phonetic form. LF is derived from S-structure via further movement operations (e.g., quantifier raising, which creates quantifier variable structures—see Sect. 4.5.5).

The existence of these four levels is determined by the theory of principles, which act as well-formedness conditions (filters) on the various levels. The level of representation to which a given principle applies is an empirical issue. At the time of writing, the empirical evidence that has been brought to bear on the issue still allows a certain range of interpretation and thus is not always conclusive. The relation between these levels of representation and a theory of principles and parameters is documented in Sect. 4.

2. Phrase Structure Theory

The syntactic representation of an expression in a language is largely determined by principles of phrase structure. In the principles and parameters framework, this is achieved via X-bar theory, which is based on the central concept of phrasal projection. In essence, most words in a language constitute lexical heads that project phrasal categories which contain the lexical head and other phrases or lexical items as constituents. A lexical head may project one or more phrasal categories, as illustrated by the examples in (2), where X* indicates a phrasal projection of X, a lexical category (X = N, P):

$$[_{N^*} \text{ complaints}] \qquad (2a)$$

$$[_{N^*} \text{ those } [_{N^*} \text{ complaints } [_{P^*} \text{ against the company}]]] \qquad (2b)$$

(Alternative notations use bars over the category label or primes superscripted to it.) The noun *complaints* projects only one phrasal category N* in (2a), but two such categories in (2b). The highest projection of a lexical head in a given structure is called the *maximal phrasal projection*, sometimes indicated as XP (e.g., NP for the examples in (2)). In some versions of X-bar theory, it is assumed that the maximal phrasal projection is categorially distinct from an intermediate phrasal projection and that both occur in a structural description even if XP contains only X* as a constituent (for discussion, see Stuurman 1985; Speas 1990).

Initially, it was thought that only major lexical categories (i.e., nouns, verbs, adjectives, and prepositions) constitute heads that project phrases. These categories are assumed to be nonatomic—that is, analyzable into feature complexes $[\pm n, \pm v]$, giving $[+n, -v]$ for nouns, $[-n, +v]$ for verbs, $[+n, +v]$ for adjectives, and $[-n, -v]$ for prepositions. It is generally believed in the 1990s, however, that certain functional categories (e.g., I (for inflexion) and C (for complementizer)) are also structural heads that project phrases. Thus the sentential complement in (3) would have the phrase structure given in (4):

$$\text{I believe that you will win the prize.} \qquad (3)$$

$$[_{CP} \text{ that } [_{IP} \text{ you } [_{I^*} \text{ will } [_{VP} \text{ win the prize}]]]] \qquad (4)$$

This analysis brings the major sentential structures (formerly S (= IP) and S′ (= CP)) into line with the basic idea of X-bar theory, that phrasal categories are projections of a structural head. A basic assumption of X-bar theory is that every head projects to a maximal phrasal projection.

X-bar theory also assumes that constituents within a projection are organized according to the schema in Fig. 2. A complement (generally an argument of the head when the head is some form of predicate, for example, verb, adjective, or derived nominal) is always a sister of the head and thus an immediate constituent of the first phrasal projection of the head. A specifier is an immediate constituent of a maximal phrasal projection distinct from the immediate phrasal projection of the head. In some cases, it bears an agreement relation to the head of its projection (as in (5)), but apparently not in all cases (e.g., (6)):

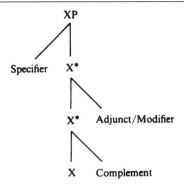

Figure 2. The X-bar projection.

$$[_{NP} \text{ this/*these } [_{N^*} \text{ book}]] \qquad (5a)$$

$$[_{NP} \text{ *this/these } [_{N^*} \text{ books}]] \qquad (5b)$$

$$[_{AP} \text{ very } [_{A^*} \text{ happy } [_{PP} \text{ about her good fortune}]]] \qquad (6)$$

This characterization generalizes to the subject NP of a finite sentence since the subject must agree in number and person with the inflected form of the verb or auxiliary. Thus a subject is considered to be a specifier position in IP.

Evidence for a specifier position in CP is based on the specifier–head agreement relation, as illustrated in (7) in the paradigm for sentential complements of the verb *wonder*:

I wonder whether/if the economy will recover in 1993.

$$(7a)$$

*I wonder that the economy will recover in 1993. (7b)

I wonder in which year the economy will recover. (7c)

Example (7) shows that a sentential complement of *wonder* must be an indirect question. Presumably this follows from a selectional restriction (a head-to-head relation—in this case V-to-C) that the verb imposes on the head of its CP complement—namely that C must be realized as some form of question word. Example (7b) violates the selectional restriction, whereas (7a), assuming that *whether* and *if* are instances of C, satisfies it. Example (7c) does not directly satisfy this restriction because the PP *in which year* cannot be taken as an instance of C. Example (7c) satisfies the selectional restriction indirectly, assuming specifier–head agreement between an empty C and the PP in the specifier position of CP. The selectional feature imposed on C by the matrix verb is lexically realized by the PP via the agreement mechanism. This suggests that the position of the *wh*-phrase at the front of a sentence is one determined by X-bar theory, rather than one which is created by an adjunction transformation.

The treatment of adjuncts or modifiers other than the specifier is open to interpretation at this point in the development of X-bar theory. Under one proposal, an adjunct or modifier will be a constituent within the maximal phrasal projection of the head which it modifies. Alternatively, an adjunct is a constituent which is adjoined (via a transformation) to a maximal phrasal projection, creating an adjunction structure as in (8) which X-bar theory alone could not account for:

$$[_{XP} \text{ XP Adjunct}] \text{ or } [_{XP} \text{ Adjunct XP}] \qquad (8)$$

This follows under the assumption that the XP which is a sister of the adjunct remains the maximal phrasal projection of X.

The relationship between the head of a projection and the immediate constituents of its phrasal projections is that of *government*. This relation is defined in terms of the relation of m-command:

m-command (9)
A category α *m-commands* a category β if and only if the first maximal projection dominating α dominates β, and neither α nor β dominates the other.

A head m-commands all the constituents of its maximal phrasal projection, but does not m-command any constituent outside its phrasal projections. In (2b), for example, the head noun *complaints* m-commands the determiner *those*, the PP *about the company*, and each of its constituents. The relation of government, which is more restrictive, is defined in terms of symmetric m-command as in (10):

government (10)
A head α *governs* a category β if and only if α m-commands β *and* β m-commands α.

Since the constituents of the PP in (2b) do not m-command the N *complaints*, that N governs the PP but not its constituents. Under this definition, a maximal phrasal projection constitutes a *barrier* to government. The domains created by the government relation play a central role in several subtheories of grammar, as will be discussed below.

C-command is another important phrase structure relation. In contrast to m-command, which is based on the character of phrasal projection, c-command is based on the branching property of phrase structure:

c-command (11)
A category α *c-commands* a category β if and only if the category which immediately dominates α also dominates β, and neither α nor β dominates the other.

Given the stipulation about nondominance, this relation holds only between categories that are in a linear relation. In Fig. 2, the specifier position c-commands the complement position, but not conversely. Support for this schema with respect to noun phrases comes from the analysis of anaphoric relations, where c-command plays a central role (see Sect. 4.5). The examples in (12) illustrate the well-established fact that a pronoun cannot be anaphoric on an expression that it c-commands (in these examples and elsewhere,

anaphoric relations will be expressed in terms of coindexing and interpreted essentially as coreference):

$$*[_{NP} \text{ his}_i \, [_{N^*} \text{ admiration } [_{PP} \text{ for } [_{NP} \text{ John's}_i \text{ mother}]]]] \quad (12a)$$

$$[_{NP} \, [_{NP} \text{ his}_i \text{ mother's}] \, [_{N^*} \text{ admiration } [_{PP} \text{ for John}_i]]] \quad (12b)$$

In (12a), the anaphoric interpretation of the pronoun is impossible because the pronoun c-commands the name, in contrast to (12b), where the pronoun does not c-command *John*, and so an anaphoric interpretation is possible.

The perspective on phrase structure under X-bar theory is essentially bottom-up, in contrast with the top-down character of phrase structure rules. Because phrase structure rules tend to be language-specific stipulations, whereas the concept of phrasal projection and the constituent schema for projections are part of universal grammar (UG), several researchers have attempted to eliminate phrase structure rules entirely and rely instead on the principles of X-bar theory and other principles of UG to predict the details of phrase structure. The general idea is that whatever is stipulated in phrase structure rules is redundant because this follows from various parts of the UG in conjunction with the lexical properties of words in a language (see Sects. 4.2 and 4.4 for further discussion, and also Stowell 1981 and Speas 1990).

3. Transformations

Transformational mappings among the four levels of representation are performed by three elementary transformational operations: substitution, adjunction, and deletion. Substitution is a structure-preserving operation which replaces one category (phrasal projection or head) with a corresponding category under a condition of nondistinctness that essentially prohibits the operation from eliminating information from the phrase marker to which it applies, for example, the substitution of one *wh*-phrase for another. Adjunction is a structure-building operation. As illustrated in (8) above, it creates new hierarchical structure in a phrase marker. Deletion is a structure-destroying operation subject to a recoverability condition, which prohibits the elimination of information from a phrase marker that cannot be reconstructed from what remains after the operation. It should be noted that there is a strong family resemblance between the nondistinctness and recoverability conditions, though the exact nature of this resemblance depends on the precise formulation of the conditions.

In terms of X-bar structure, substitution appears to be limited to maximal phrasal projections and heads. Direct questions in English involve both kinds of substitution, as illustrated in the S-structure (13), where the coindexed categories containing no lexical material indicate the D-structure positions of the correspondingly coindexed lexical elements:

[$_{CP}$ what$_i$ [$_{C^*}$ is$_j$ [$_{IP}$ Bernie [$_{I^*}$ I$_j$ [$_{VP}$ working on NP$_i$]]]]] (13)

In (13), the interrogative pronoun object of the preposition *on* is moved into the specifier position of CP, and the progressive auxiliary which instantiates I at D-structure substitutes for C—an instance of head-movement. At D-structure, the specifier position of CP and the head of CP are bare categories, NP and C respectively. Presumably nondistinctness between the functional categories C and I is met, even though they are not categorially identical. The landing site of substitutions involving maximal phrasal projections seems to involve only specifier positions. There seems to be no evidence that a substitution ever moves a maximal phrasal projection to a complement or adjunction position.

The phenomenon of subject raising constitutes another instance of substitution between two NP positions. As illustrated in (14), the subject of the sentential complement of *seem* must be moved to matrix subject position when the complement is infinitival and cannot move to this position when the complement is a finite clause.

infinitival complement (14a)
  (i) *it seems [the situation to be getting worse]
  (ii) the situation$_i$ seems [NP$_i$ to be getting worse]

finite clause complement (14b)
  (i) it seems that the situation is getting worse.
  (ii) *the situation$_i$ seems [(that) NP$_i$ is getting worse]

Assume that at D-structure the matrix subject position is a bare NP. As (14) demonstrates, there are two options for lexicalizing this position: insert a pleonastic element (expletive *it*), or fill it with a lexical NP from some other position in the phrase marker. Both operations are instances of substitution, though the former is an insertion operation whereas the latter is a movement operation. Since the theory of transformations under the principles and parameters framework does not allow the formulation of a transformation with a structural description that distinguishes between finite and infinitival complements, both the well-formed (14a.ii) and the ill-formed (14b.ii) could result from the application of substitution to NP. The explanation for the proper behavior of the substitution operation cannot therefore be given in terms of the formulation of the transformational rule. Rather, the proper behavior of this and other transformations must follow from other general principles of grammar, as will be illustrated below.

In previous theories of generative grammar, substitution was utilized for lexical insertion under the assumption that phrase structure rules generated structural descriptions minus lexical items and that lexical items were then introduced into phrase markers by a substitution operation which mediated between the output of phrase structure rules and the lexicon.

In the absence of phrase structure rules, this approach is no longer necessary. It could be that the principles of phrase structure generate structural descriptions minus lexical items, as before. Alternatively, it could be that the input to the system of principles, including phrase structure theory, is simply strings of words which are then assigned structural descriptions via the principles of UG in conjunction with the lexical properties of the particular words in the string. Those strings that satisfy the principles and yield a viable interpretation are considered nondeviant—the rest being deviant in one or more ways. This theory departs radically from previous theories in which the phrase structure component provided an algorithm for generating syntactic structures. Whether a fully interpretive theory of grammar of this sort is viable remains to be demonstrated, though it seems to be the direction in which syntacticians' work is moving.

In terms of X-bar structure, adjunction sites appear to be limited to maximal phrasal projections, and in particular those which are not complements to the major lexical heads (N, V, A, and P). Example (15) illustrates an adjunction which results in the movement of a relative clause (CP), and (16) shows the effects of an adjunction which inserts a grammatical formative ('s) into a phrase marker.

[$_{NP}$ an article on string theory CP$_i$] [$_{VP}$ [$_{VP}$ just appeared] (15)
  [$_{CP_i}$ which I want to read]]

[$_{NP}$ [$_{NP}$ the [$_{N^*}$ philosopher [$_{NP}$ from Princeton]]]'s] beard. (16)

Thus adjunction, like substitution, can be used to perform insertion as well as movement. Various analyses differ as to whether adjunction to a head is possible. For example, the analysis of incorporation phenomena in Baker (1987) is based on adjunction to heads, whereas in Freidin (1992) the analysis of heads precludes such adjunction. Under the assumption that heads are instantiated by lexical items, it is unclear how adjunction to heads would be possible, since the category dominating the head and the element adjoined to it in the adjunction structure could not be a head—that is, an X^0 category—nor could it be a phrasal projection of a head. If adjunction to heads is excluded, then the internal structure of phrasal projections should be immune to structure-building operations throughout the derivation.

Substitutions and adjunctions that result in the movement of an element from one position in a phrase marker to another are referred to under the designation 'Move α,' where α stands for some category. It has been assumed that 'Move α' does not involve the deletion operation, which is structure-destroying. As a result, 'Move α' leaves behind a *trace* of the moved element, an empty category which bears the categorial designation of the moved element and is coindexed with it. Thus, in (15), CP$_i$ is a trace of the extraposed relative clause adjoined to VP. This follows from the stronger constraint prohibiting grammatical transformations formed from compounds of elementary operations (Chomsky 1980; see also Freidin 1992).

The precise nature of deletion operations is less well determined than substitutions and adjunctions for several reasons. The effect of deleting certain lexical material also follows from the optionality of lexical insertion, which is independently motivated. Thus, for example, the optionality of complementizers in certain contexts (e.g., *they think that he lied* versus *they think he lied*) could result from the optionality of lexical insertion. Given the optionality of lexical insertion and the availability of interpretive rules, it is possible to account for apparent deletion-effects via interpretation of empty categories. VP anaphora provides one illustration:

> the boy has [vp read that book] and his friend (17)
> as [vp e] too.

The logical form of this sentence could just as well be derived via a rule which interprets the empty VP as anaphoric on the lexical VP, as via a rule which deletes an identical copy of the lexical VP in the second conjunct (see Williams (1977) for a telling argument in favor of the interpretive analysis as opposed to the deletion analysis). Given these alternatives to deletion, and in the absence of strong motivation for deletion analyses with respect to lexical material, one might conjecture that once lexical material is introduced into a derivation it cannot be removed. This conjecture leaves open the possibility that deletion may eliminate empty categories during a derivation via deletion.

The deletion of empty categories is realized in those analyses which assume that traces need not be left by movement unless their presence is required to satisfy a principle of grammar (see Lasnik and Saito 1984, 1992)—which means that trace deletion at least may compound with either substitution or adjunction operations. Under this analysis, deletion operations are not limited to the interface between S-structure and PF as in earlier analyses (see Chomsky and Lasnik 1977) and so need not be considered independently of substitution and adjunction. Therefore the three elementary operations can be identified under the single rubric 'Affect α.'

4. The System of Principles

The set of principles assumed under this theory of grammar predicts the proper behavior of transformational operation, so that it is unnecessary to stipulate this behavior in terms of highly articulated structural descriptions and structural changes for language-specific transformational rules. Rather, the set of principles provides an account of this behavior at the level of the theory of grammar. Thus the properties of constructions that involve the various transformational operations follow from a theory of UG—

a significant advance over an analysis in which these properties were merely stipulated in the formulations of rules that are specific to one particular language.

The theory of UG in the early 1990s consists of a group of general principles that incorporate basic syntactic notions such as c-command, government, case, and binding, among others. The full set of principles operate in a modular fashion to account for the syntactic properties manifested in natural languages. Thus the theory of UG is viewed as a set of independent subtheories, each with its autonomous principle(s). The standard set includes, in addition to the X-bar theory of phrase structure, the subtheories and principles shown in Table 1.

Table 1. The theory of UG.

Theory	Principle(s)	Mediates
Bounding	Subjacency Condition	The syntactic distance between a phrase and the position in which it receives an interpretation
Case	Case filter	The distribution of phonetically realized NPs
Government	Empty Category Principle	The distribution of traces
Argument structure	θ-criterion	The distribution of arguments with respect to predicates
Binding	Binding principles	The distribution of bound elements (anaphors, pronouns, and referential expressions)

The precise formulation of these principles and their interaction continue to be major topics of research, as is the investigation of other principles that may supplement or replace these standard examples.

4.1 Bounding Theory

Although movement transformations have the capability of moving a constituent indefinitely far away from its D-structure position, actual movement phenomena in languages demonstrate that certain syntactic boundaries may not be crossed—in effect, transformations may not move a constituent 'too far' away. Thus, movement operations are bounded within a particular syntactic domain. The paradigm in (18) involving extraposition of relative clauses (see also (15)) provides one illustration of bounding phenomena:

> [NP an author of [NP an article on string theory] CP$_i$] (18a)
> [vp [vp just arrived] [CP:i who I want to meet]]

> *[NP an author of [NP an article on string theory CP$_i$]] (18b)
> [vp [vp just arrived] [CP:i which I want to read]]

A relative clause that modifies the head of the subject NP (i.e., *author*) may be extraposed as in (18a), whereas extraposing one that modifies a more deeply imbedded noun in the subject NP (e.g., *article*) results in a deviant sentence, as (18b) illustrates. In terms of syntactic distance, the extraposed relative clause in (18b) crosses only one more NP boundary than the one in (18a).

The boundedness of movement operations is accounted for in terms of a general principle of grammar that designates certain categories as bounding categories and sets a limit for bounding categories that may be crossed in a single movement operation. This limit is fixed in UG at one bounding category. Two syntactic positions are said to be *subjacent* to one another if they are separated by no more than one bounding category. The principle for bounding, the Subjacency Condition, has the effect of prohibiting movement across more than one bounding category. This principle can be formulated as a condition on trace binding between a trace and its nearest antecedent, in which case it constitutes a condition on representations rather than a condition on the application of rules (Freidin 1978; Browning 1991). Alternatively, it has been argued that the Subjacency Condition must be formulated as a condition on the application of 'Move α' (Lasnik and Saito 1984, 1992).

A trace and its antecedent form a *chain*—thus, in (18), the relative clause and its trace CP_i form a chain of two members, the chain consisting of a single *link*. The number of links in a chain depends on the number of traces in the chain. Example (19) contains a three-member chain with two traces (given as italicized *e* and *e′*) and hence two links ($\{John_i, e′\}$ and $\{e′, e\}$):

$$John_i \text{ is believed } [_{IP} e′ \text{ to be likely } [_{IP} e \text{ to win}]] \quad (19)$$

The Subjacency Condition, viewed as a constraint on trace binding, may therefore be formulated as a locality condition on chains (or, more precisely, on links of a chain), as in (20):

Subjacency Condition (20)
    The members of each link in a chain must be subjacent.

Example (18b) violates (20) under the assumption that NP is a bounding category for English. IP constitutes another bounding category for English, as (21) illustrates:

$$[_{IP} [_{CP} \text{ that } [_{IP} [_{NP} \text{ a man } e_i] [_{VP} [_{VP} \text{ is coming to dinner}] \quad (21a)$$
$$[_{CP \cdot i} \text{ who I want to meet}]]] [_{VP} \text{ is unusual}]]$$

$$*[_{IP} [_{CP} \text{ that } [_{IP} [_{NP} \text{ a man } e_i][_{VP} \text{ is coming to dinner}]]] \quad (21b)$$
$$[_{VP} [_{VP} \text{ is unusual}] [_{CP \cdot i} \text{ who I want to meet}]]]$$

Example (21a) shows that the relative clause may extrapose out of NP within IP, whereas (21b) demonstrates that this extraposition may not cross both NP and IP at once. Thus the chain in (21b) violates (20). A further principle of grammar rules out the derivation where (21a) serves as an intermediate step

in the derivation of the ill-formed *that a man is coming to dinner is unusual who I want to meet* (Freidin 1992), since this derivation would not violate the Subjacency Condition.

The Subjacency Condition also accounts for the boundedness of *wh*-movement phenomena, as illustrated in the contrast between (22a) and the deviant (22b):

who does John believe Mary claimed that Fred admires? (22a)

*who does John believe the claim that Fred admires? (22b)

Example (22) would have the analysis given in (23):

$$[_{CP} \text{ who}_i \text{ does } [_{IP} \text{ John believe } [_{CP} e\rangle [_{IP} \text{ Mary claimed} \quad (23a)$$
$$[_{CP} e′ \text{ that } [_{IP} \text{ Fred admires } e]]]]]]$$

$$*[_{CP} \text{ who}_i \text{ does } [_{IP} \text{ John believe } [_{NP} \text{ the claim} \quad (23b)$$
$$[_{CP} e′ \text{ that } [_{IP} \text{ Fred admires } e]]]]]$$

In (23a), each link of the chain satisfies Subjacency, whereas in (23b) the link $\{who_i, e′\}$ violates the condition since the link is formed across two bounding categories, NP and IP. The condition applies more generally to many other constructions involving chain links formed across two NPs or across two IPs (see Freidin 1992 for discussion and references).

Bounding effects appear to vary across grammars. In some idiolects of Italian, it is possible to extract a relative pronoun out of an indirect question (Rizzi 1982).

$$il \text{ mio primo libro, } [_{CP} \text{ che } [_{IP} \text{ credo } [_{CP} e_i \text{ che } [_{IP} \text{ tu} \quad (24)$$
$$\text{sappia } [_{CP} \text{ a chi}_j [_{IP} \text{ ho dedicato } e_i e_j]]]]]] \text{ me è}$$
$$\text{sempre stato molto caro.}$$
    'my first book, which I believe that you know to whom I dedicated, has always been very dear to me.'

This sentence is well-formed even though the chain link $\{e_i, e_i\}$ crosses two IPs, suggesting that IP is not a bounding category in this idiolect of Italian. Nonetheless, Subjacency holds in Italian, since movement across two CPs is prohibited, as in (25):

$$*il \text{ mio primo libro, } [_{CP} \text{ che}_i [_{IP} \text{ so } [_{CP} \text{ a chi}_j [_{IP} \text{ credi} \quad (25)$$
$$[_{CP} e_i \text{ che } [_{IP} \text{ abbia dedicato } e_i e_j]]]]]] \text{ me è sempre}$$
$$\text{stato molto caro.}$$
    'my first book, which I know to whom you believe that I dedicated, has always been very dear to me.'

The link $\{che_i, e_i\}$ is formed across two CPs in violation of Subjacency if CP is taken as a bounding category for this idiolect of Italian. Similar phenomena pointing to the same conclusion can be found in French and Spanish (Sportiche 1981; Torrego 1984). Thus the choice of IP versus CP as a bounding category for Subjacency constitutes one parameter of UG. If both IP and CP are chosen as bounding categories, then Subjacency would prohibit so-called long-distance *wh*-movement, the movement of a *wh*-phrase from one clause to another. Some languages (e.g., Russian) prohibit this kind of *wh*-movement, a fact that would follow from bounding theory if both IP and CP were bounding categories for Subjacency in these languages.

4.2 Case Theory

The basic ideas of case theory are, first, that lexical NPs can only occur in positions to which case assignment is possible or in chains where one element occupies such a position; and, second, that case assignment occurs only to a NP in a proper configuration with a case-assigning element. The most straightforward instances of case assignment occur with the NP objects of verbs and prepositions, where the NP object is governed by the V or P. It is not the actual morphological case assigned to NP which is at issue, but rather the fact that the NP is assigned some case in a configuration. Thus it is not relevant for case theory that V assigns accusative case while P assigns oblique case, or that in some languages certain Vs assign specific oblique cases as a lexical property (see Freidin and Babby 1984; Freidin and Sprouse 1991). Under this view, the assignment of case in the abstract (sometimes referred to as 'abstract case') is the central factor in case theory (Babby 1992).

This notion of case plays a central role in the analysis of infinitival constructions in English and other languages. In certain syntactic configurations, an infinitival construction may occur with an overt lexical subject; in other configurations, it may only occur with a null (hence nonlexical) subject.

$[_{CP}$ for $[_{IP}$ John to win]] would take a miracle   (26a)

*$[_{CP}$ $[_{IP}$ John to win]] would take a miracle   (26b)

$[_{CP}$ $[_{IP}$ PRO to win]] would take a miracle   (26c)

John was happy $[_{CP}$ for $[_{IP}$ Bill to win]]   (27a)

*John was happy $[_{CP}$ $[_{IP}$ Bill to win]]   (27b)

John was happy $[_{CP}$ $[_{IP}$ PRO to win]]   (27c)

Examples (26a) and (27a) show that an overt lexical infinitival subject can occur in the presence of the complementizer *for*. When the complementizer is absent, only the null subject PRO is allowed in this position, as illustrated in (26b–c) and (27b–c). It is generally assumed that the complementizer *for* has some of the properties of a preposition, a [-n] category like verb—in particular, the ability to assign case.

Under this analysis, the complementizer assigns case to the lexical infinitival subject because it is in a proper government configuration with the NP, on a par with the object of a verb or preposition. This requires that the infinitival IP not be a barrier to government by the case-assigning complementizer and hence that not all maximal phrasal projections be barriers to government. (The transparency of IP for government from outside and the question of what constitutes a barrier for government are discussed further in Sect. 4.3.)

In (26b) and (27b), where the complementizer is absent, the lexical subject of the infinitival will not be marked for case because it is not governed by a case-assigning element. This is ruled out by the Case Filter, a principle of UG formulated as a condition on representations which prohibits any lexical NP that is not marked for case.

Case Filter   (28)
Each phonetically realized NP must be marked for case.

Thus the Case Filter accounts for the deviant status of constructions like (26b) and (27b).

Note, however, that lexical infinitival subjects can occur without the presence of the complementizer *for* when the infinitival construction occurs as the complement of certain verbs.

John believes $[_{IP}$ Smith to be the culprit]   (29a)

John wants $[_{IP}$ the police to arrest Smith]   (29b)

In (29), the infinitival subject is governed by the matrix V, assuming the transparency of IP and the absence of CP (presumably by a rule which deletes the CP boundary—called CP-deletion) at the point in the derivation where case assignment occurs. Given the Subjacency Condition, example (30) constitutes some evidence that the infinitival complement of *believe* must be a CP at some point:

$[_{CP}$ who$_i$ does $[_{IP}$ John believe $[_{CP}$ e$_i$ $[_{IP}$ e$_i$ to be the culprit]]]]   (30)

If the infinitival complement of *believe* were just an IP, then the movement of the *wh*-phrase would cross two IP boundaries in violation of Subjacency. Yet in order for the lexical *wh*-phrase to be assigned case by the matrix verb in the same way that the lexical infinitival subject is assigned case in (29a), the imbedded CP and the trace that it contains must be deleted so that the trace in subject position is governed by and adjacent to the matrix verb. The *wh*-phrase is assigned case via inheritance of the case assigned to its trace in a grammatical function position. The paradigm in (31) provides further evidence for this analysis:

I wonder $[_{CP}$ who$_i$ $[_{IP}$ PRO to visit e$_i$]]   (31a)

*I wonder $[_{CP}$ who$_i$ $[_{IP}$ he/him to visit e$_i$]]   (31b)

*I wonder $[_{CP}$ who$_i$ $[_{IP}$ e$_i$ to visit Bill]]   (31c)

In (31a), the *wh*-phrase inherits accusative case via its trace in the complement object position. Example (31b) is excluded by the Case Filter because the infinitival subject is not governed by an adjacent case-assigning element. Example (31c) is also ruled out by the Case Filter because the trace of the *wh*-phrase is not marked for case, and the *wh*-phrase itself cannot be directly marked for case by the matrix verb since CP is a barrier to government.

The Case Filter also accounts for the obligatory character of some NP movements, as illustrated in (14a) above, and recast here as (32):

*it seems [IP the situation to be getting worse] (32a)

the situationᵢ seems [IP eᵢ to be getting worse] (32b)

An infinitival complement of *seem* cannot occur with a *for*-complementizer, nor does this verb assign structural case to an object. Example (32a) therefore violates the Case Filter even under the assumption that the matrix verb governs the infinitival subject. As (32b) illustrates, the D-structure infinitival subject can be properly assigned case by moving to the matrix subject position, where it receives nominative case as the subject of a finite clause. Subject raising of this sort is obligatory. This follows from the Case Filter, and therefore no stipulation about the obligatory character of this operation is necessary.

As illustrated in (33), passive predicates that take infinitival complements manifest the same properties.

*it was reported [IP the situation to be getting worse] (33a)

the situationᵢ was reported [IP eᵢ to be getting worse] (33b)

Example (33a) is also a Case Filter violation. Note that this is a special property of passive predicates. In the case of *report*, the active verb does assign case across an IP boundary, as in (34):

they reported [IP the situation to be getting worse] (34)

This suggests that passive morphology somehow blocks the assignment of structural case. In (33b), as in (32b), the lexical infinitival subject moves from a caseless position in D-structure to a case-marked position in S-structure. The obligatory character of this movement also follows from the Case Filter.

The interaction of the Case Filter and movement operations can be expressed by taking the Case Filter as a well-formedness condition on chains. Thus, some member of a chain containing a lexical phrase must be marked for case. Under this formulation, Case inheritance is just a property of chains, since the lexical member of a chain (e.g., a *wh*-phrase) need not be the case-marked member, provided that some other member of the chain occurs in a case-marked position.

The Case Filter is also responsible for the obligatory character of certain language-specific rules. In English, for example, the rule which inserts the possessive marker *'s* is an obligatory rule—that is, it must apply when the conditions for its application are met.

[NP [NP the boy]'s jacket] (35a)

*[NP [NP the boy] jacket] (35b)

Taking *'s* to be a case marking for a NP in a certain configuration, if the rule fails to apply, the result (e.g., (35b)) violates the Case Filter (Freidin 1992).

In some languages, case-marked NPs must meet an additional configurational requirement aside from being governed by and adjacent to a case-assigning element. In Icelandic, where a verb may select the case of its subject as a lexical property (called 'lexical' or 'quirky' case), a lexical subject may not occur in an infinitival even though the verb selects and therefore assigns a lexical case to it. As the paradigm in (36) from Icelandic illustrates, the infinitival clause may have a null subject, but not a lexical one:

Jóni batnaði veikin (36a)
John-DAT recovered-from the-disease-NOM

Ég tel [IP Jóni hafa batnað veikin] (36b)
I believe John-DAT to have recovered-from the-disease-NOM

[CP að [IP PRO batna veikin]] er venjulegt (36c)
PRO-DAT to-recover-from the-disease-NOM is usual

*[CP að [IP Jóni batna veikin]] er mikilvægt (36d)
John-DAT to-recover-from the-disease-NOM is important

Although the verb *batna* ('recover from') selects a dative subject, (36c) illustrates that the null subject PRO can satisfy this requirement even though it is not lexical. Yet, as (36d) shows, lexical satisfaction of the case requirement is not sufficient, since the lexically case-marked NP cannot be lexical. The subject of the infinitive in (36d) is not appropriately governed by a case-assigning element, in contrast to (36b) where the dative NP is governed by the matrix verb *tel* (assuming that the infinitival complement has undergone CP-deletion). In (36b), the element which assigns case is different from the element that licenses case. A similar situation occurs in Portuguese involving configurational case assignment, as illustrated in (37–38) (from Freidin and Quicoli 1992):

José viu nós chegarmos (37)
Jose saw us-NOM to-arrive-1st-plural
'Jose saw us arrive'

José cre [CP termosᵢ [IP nós eᵢ chegado a um (38a)
acordo]]
Jose believes to-have-1st-plural us-NOM reached
an agreement

*José cre [CP [IP nós termos chegado a um acordo]] (38b)
Jose believes us-NOM to-have-1st-plural reached an
agreement

In (37), nominative case is assigned via the agreement element of the sentential complement. If case assignment were the only requirement on a lexical NP, then (38b) should be well formed. The fact that it is deviant indicates that a further requirement must be involved. Example (38a), where the lexical auxiliary has been raised into the head of CP, suggests that some form of lexical government plays a role in licensing lexical NPs. The same element both licenses and assigns nominative case to the lexical NP in (38a), in contrast to (37), where the agreement element assigns nominative case while the matrix verb lexically governs and hence licenses the lexical subject of the infinitival complement. Such examples demonstrate the need for distinguishing case assignment and case licensing as distinct grammatical processes.

4.3 Government Theory

The core of the theory of government is the Empty Category Principle (ECP), which determines the distribution of traces (as opposed to the base-generated empty categories (e.g., the null subject PRO—see Sects. 4.4 and 4.5 for further discussion). The exact formulation of the ECP is a topic of intensive investigation and debate. It can be formulated schematically as in (39):

Empty Category Principle
A trace must be properly governed. (39)

Given X-bar structure, every trace will be a constituent of a projection of some head and therefore will be governed by some head of a phrase. However, since traces may not occur in all governed positions, it is assumed that a further requirement holds which distinguishes the instances that are allowed from those that are not. The paradigm case concerns a subject/object asymmetry involving *wh*-movement.

$[_{CP}$ who$_i$ does $[_{IP}$ Mary believe $[_{CP}$ e$_i$ that $[_{IP}$ Bill $\quad$ (40a)
$[_{VP}$ admires e$_i]]]]]$

*$[_{CP}$ who$_i$ does $[_{IP}$ Mary believe $[_{CP}$ e$_i$ that $[_{IP}$ e$_i$ $\quad$ (40b)
$[_{VP}$ admires Bill$]]]]]$

Wh-movement from complement object position yields a well-formed construction, in contrast to the corresponding movement from subject position. The two cases can be distinguished in terms of government, since the complement object trace is lexically governed (by the complement verb), whereas the complement subject trace is not lexically governed by V. Thus, lexical government provides one way to satisfy the proper government requirement of the ECP.

If the ECP is a general condition on all traces, there must be another way to satisfy the proper government requirement, since the intermediate trace in (40a) does not appear to be lexically governed. This has been handled by postulating another relation called *antecedent government* that satisfies proper government. Antecedent government concerns the antecedent–trace relation, where the basic idea is that the trace, which is coindexed with and c-commanded by an antecedent, is not structurally 'too far' from its nearest antecedent. Thus, in (40a), *who* must antecedent-govern its trace in CP. Note that even if intermediate traces were excluded from having to satisfy the ECP, some notion of antecedent government would be necessary to account for constructions like (41), where the subject trace is not lexically governed:

$[_{CP}$ who$_i$ did $[_{IP}$ Mary say $[_{CP}$ e$_i$ $[_{IP}$ e$_i$ $[_{VP}$ admires $\quad$ (41a)
Bill$]]]]]$

*it is disturbing $[_{CP}$ the situation$_i$ to be reported $\quad$ (41b)
$[a$ e$_i$ is getting worse$]]$
(cf. it is disturbing (that) it has been reported that
the situation is getting worse)

In contrast to (41a), where the complement subject trace satisfies the ECP, the complement subject trace in (41b) does not. It is assumed that trace in (41b) is not lexically governed by the matrix predicate *reported* and that therefore *a*, whether it be a CP or IP boundary, constitutes a barrier to government. Thus it appears that the ECP must be a disjunctive condition where the proper government condition is satisfied either by lexical or antecedent government.

The ECP analysis extends beyond subject–object asymmetries to complement–noncomplement asymmetries more generally. Objects are always complements of a lexical head, whereas subjects and adjuncts are not. Some evidence that movement of adjuncts is restricted by the ECP comes from the relative grammaticality judgments concerning complement movement versus adjunct movement. Both examples in (42) are deviant sentences in English under the interpretation that the leftmost *wh*-phrase in each comes from the infinitival complement:

*how are you wondering which car to fix? $\quad$ (42a)

?*which car are you wondering how to fix? $\quad$ (42b)

However, the degree of deviance seems greater in (42a) compared to (42b).

This distinction follows from an ECP analysis of (42a–b), which would have the representations (43a–b):

$[_{CP}$ how$_j$ $[_C$ are$]$ $[_{IP}$ you $[_{VP}$ wondering$]$ $[_{CP}$ $[_{NP,i}$ which car$]$ $\quad$ (43a)
$[_{IP}$ PRO to $[_{VP}$ fix e$_i]$ e$_j]]$

$[_{CP}$ $[_{NP,i}$ which car$]$ $[_C$ are$]$ $[_{IP}$ you $[_{VP}$ wondering$]$ $\quad$ (43b)
$[_{CP}$ how$_j$ $[_{IP}$ PRO to $[_{VP}$ fix e$_i]$ e$_j]]$

Both structures violate the Subjacency Condition because the binding relation between the *wh*-phrase in the matrix CP and its trace in the infinitival complement crosses two bounding categories (i.e., the two IPs). Example (43a) also violates the ECP because the trace of *how* is neither lexically governed nor antecedent-governed. In (43b), the trace of *what* is lexically governed and the trace of *how* is antecedent-governed, and thus both chains in (43b) satisfy the ECP.

The notion of antecedent government has been more closely aligned with the concept of government in Chomsky (1986a) and subsequent work. This formulation is based on the idea that relation between a trace and its antecedent may cross no barrier. Presumably, although each maximal phrasal projection is a potential barrier with respect to government, not every one is an actual barrier for antecedent government (i.e., movement). (The analysis of barriers given in Chomsky (1986a) and elsewhere is quite intricate and can only be briefly sketched here.)

As an illustration, consider a barriers analysis of the ECP for the failures in antecedent government in examples (41b) and (43a) above. However, before looking at violations of antecedent government, it is necessary to understand how well-formed sentences involving long-distance movement satisfy antecedent government. In (41a), for example, the complement subject trace can be antecedent-governed by the trace in the complement CP because IP is not an inherent barrier. The connection between the lexical *wh*-phrase and the trace in the complement CP must also satisfy antecedent government. This relation holds across the complement CP boundary, and the matrix VP and IP boundaries. The complement CP is not a barrier in this instance because it is a complement of the matrix verb and hence 'L-marked' by that verb. The matrix IP is not a barrier via the stipulation that IP is not an inherent barrier. The barrierhood of the matrix VP can be handled in one of two ways. Either the auxiliary verb L-marks VP (see Kayne 1989), or the *wh*-phrase adjoins to VP on the way to the matrix CP (resulting in (44)) under the assumption that adjunction structures do not constitute barriers with respect to the adjoined phrase (see Chomsky 1986a).

$$[_{CP} \text{ who}_i \text{ did } [_{IP} \text{ Mary } [_{VP} \text{ e}_i [_{VP} \text{ say } [_{CP} \text{ e}_i [_{IP} \text{ e}_i \quad (44)$$
$$[_{VP} \text{ admires Bill}]]]]]]]]$$

In contrast to (41a), the CP in (41b) constitutes a barrier, and hence the chain formed by the matrix subject and its trace in complement subject position violates antecedent government. Even though the complement CP is L-marked by the matrix predicate, it is counted as a barrier because it dominates IP, designated as a 'blocking category' (defined as a category that is not L-marked), and therefore inherits barrierhood as a result. (Inheritance of barrierhood by CP is blocked when the chain satisfies the antecedent-government relation across the IP that CP dominates, as in (41a).) In (42a), the complement CP also constitutes a barrier with respect to the chain created by adjunct movement. Under the barriers analysis, (42a) would have a representation (45), where both *wh*-phrases move via adjunction to VP:

$$[_{CP} \text{ how}_j [_{C} \text{ are}] [_{IP} \text{ you } [_{VP} \text{ e}_j [_{VP} \text{ wondering}] [_{CP} \quad (45)$$
$$[_{NP_i} \text{ which car}] [_{IP} \text{ PRO to } [_{VP} \text{ e}_j [_{VP} \text{ e}_i [_{VP} \text{ fix e}_i] \text{ e}_j]]]$$

In (45), the complement CP also inherits barrierhood from the IP which it dominates.

To account for the *that*-trace effect in (40b) under a barriers analysis of antecedent government, it is necessary to introduce another condition on government, the Minimality Condition.

Minimality Condition (46)

In ... α ... $[\gamma ... \delta ... \beta ...]$ ..., α does not govern β if γ is a projection of δ excluding α. (Chomsky 1986a: 42)

Example (40b) fits the structural description of the Minimality Condition, as illustrated in (47), where

β = the trace in IP, δ = the complementizer *that*, γ = C*, and α = the trace in CP:

$$[_{CP} \text{ e}_i [_{C*} \text{ that } [_{IP} \text{ e}_i ... \quad (47)$$

Thus the Minimality Condition blocks antecedent government between the two traces in (47) and therefore accounts for the *that*-trace effect in (40b).

Although the barriers analysis of the ECP is quite intricate and to some extent stipulative, it is conceptually more elegant than the previous analysis. As a further example of this, consider how this analysis allows for the partial unification of the ECP and the Subjacency Condition. Under a barriers analysis, the Subjacency Condition may be reformulated as a constraint against crossing more than one barrier, where the optimal movement crosses no barriers. Example (48) violates this reformulation in the following way:

*a politician $[_{CP} \text{ who}_i [_{IP} [_{NP} \text{ an article by e}_i] \text{ appeared in}$ (48) today's *Times*

Neither IP nor NP is L-marked; therefore both are blocking categories. NP is also a barrier, and therefore IP inherits barrierhood from the blocking category (NP) which it dominates. The movement of the relative pronoun *who* crosses two barriers in violation of Subjacency. Note that the trace satisfies the ECP because it is lexically governed by the preposition *by*.

Given the barriers formulations of the ECP and the Subjacency Condition, there is a potential contradiction if both apply to the same level of representation. That is, the ECP says that the antecedent–trace relation may not cross any barrier; whereas the Subjacency Condition allows the antecedent–trace relation to cross one barrier at most. If the two conditions hold at different levels of representation, then no contradiction need arise. There is some evidence that the ECP applies at LF. In contrast, there is no compelling evidence that the Subjacency Condition holds at LF. The empirical motivation for this condition is compatible with the analysis that it holds at S-structure.

This LF analysis of the ECP is motivated in part by superiority effects, as illustrated in (49):

$$[_{CP} \text{ who}_i [_{IP} \text{ e}_i [_{VP} \text{ wrote what}]]] \quad (49a)$$

$$*[_{CP} \text{ what}_j [_{C} \text{ did}] [_{IP} \text{ who } [_{VP} \text{ write e}_j]]] \quad (49b)$$

In the underlying structure of both (49a–b), the subject *who* asymmetrically c-commands the object *what* and is therefore said to be superior to the object. In earlier versions of generative grammar, a Superiority Condition (Chomsky 1973), which prevented a transformation from moving a phrase over a superior phrase of the same type (e.g, *wh*-phrase), accounted for the deviance of (49b). Under the ECP, it is possible to subsume the effects of the Superiority Condition if the ECP holds at LF. Assuming that a *wh*-phrase functions as a quasiquantifier, each *wh*-phrase must bind a variable at LF. At S-structure, the examples in (49) contain only a single *wh*-trace that can be interpreted as a variable. Thus, in each example, the *wh*-phrase which has not moved at S-structure must move at LF to create an appropriate quantifier–variable structure. The LF movement results in the adjunction of the hitherto unmoved *wh*-phrase to the *wh*-phrase in the specifier of CP position (a process referred to as 'absorption'—see Higginbotham and May 1981). Of the resulting LF representations of (49), (50a) satisfies the ECP and (50b) violates it:

$[_{CP} [_i [_j \text{ what}]] [_i \text{ who}]] [_{IP} e_i [_{VP} \text{ wrote } e_j]]]$ (50a)

$[_{CP} [_j [_i \text{ who}] [_j \text{ what}]] [_C \text{ did}] [_{IP} e_i [_{VP} \text{ write } e_j]]]$ (50b)

In (50a), the trace of *what* is lexically governed and the trace of *who* is antecedent-governed. In (50b), however, the trace of *what* is both lexically governed and antecedent-governed, while the trace of *who* is neither. In particular, antecedent government between *who* and its trace fails because the *wh*-phrase does not c-command its trace (for discussion of a similar analysis concerning complement–adjunct asymmetries and the LF analysis of the ECP, see Huang 1982; Lasnik and Saito 1984).

In addition to the Superiority Condition, it has been argued that the barriers analysis of the ECP subsumes other conditions on rules, including the Head Movement Constraint (Travis 1984) and the Constraint on Extraction Domains (Huang 1982) (see also Chomsky (1986a) for discussion, and Browning (1989) on the claim that the ECP is distinct from the latter constraint).

The disjunctive nature of the ECP has been a focus of investigation since its initial formulation in Chomsky (1981). Following Stowell (1981), some discussions (Lasnik and Saito 1984; Chomsky 1986a) assume that lexical government for the ECP occurs only between a lexical head and its complement. Thus the trace in (32b) is antecedent-governed but not lexically governed. Whether it is possible to eliminate lexical government from the ECP and rely entirely on antecedent government remains to be determined.

4.4 Argument Structure

The three subtheories of bounding, case, and government provide strong constraints on movement transformations to the extent that they restrict how far a constituent may be moved, when it can be moved, and when it must be moved (case theory with respect to NP movement). However, these subtheories together do not cover all the possibilities that must be prohibited. An ill-formed construction like (51a) derived from a D-structure (51b) via simple NP movement is not excluded by any of these subtheories.

*it is easy $[_{CP} C [_{IP} \text{ him}_i \text{ to like } e_i]]$ (51a)

it is easy $[_{CP} C [_{IP} \text{ NP to like him}]]$ (51b)

This option for a base-generated empty NP, indicated

as NP in (51b), is required for the derivations of both the simple passive construction (e.g., (52)) and the raising construction (e.g., (32b)).

Seymour$_i$ was $[_{VP} \text{ arrested } e_i \text{ in Shanghai}]$ (52)

Since NP movement from object to subject position violates no locality restrictions (e.g., Subjacency and the ECP) in passive constructions, it should not violate any in active constructions. The Case Filter plays no role in (51a) because the chain formed via NP movement contains a case-marked position, and only one— just like the chain in (52).

An account of why (51a) is prohibited by a general principle of grammar concerns the analysis of predicate-argument structures in syntax. In a sentence, a predicate (e.g., verb or adjective) assigns a specific semantic function to its complements and sometimes to its subject. These semantic functions have been characterized as 'thematic relations' (or θ-roles) (see Jackendoff 1972, 1990). In an active sentence, a subject and object are both assigned independent θ-roles by the active verb. In a passive sentence, however, the θ-role corresponding to the subject of an active sentence is not assigned to the syntactic subject position, but rather to the object of the preposition *by* should it occur in the passive sentence. Thus the subject position in a passive construction is nonthematic. In raising constructions (e.g., (53a)), the nonthematic nature of the matrix subject position is demonstrated by the fact that pleonastic, nonreferential *it* may occur there, as in (53b):

the situation$_i$ seems $[_{IP} e_i \text{ to } [_{VP} \text{ be getting worse}]]$ (53a)

it seems $[_{CP} [_C \text{ that}] [_{IP} \text{ the situation is } [_{VP} \text{ getting worse}]]$ (53b)

Given this characterization of predicate-argument structure, the NP movement chain in (51a) is easily distinguished from the one in (52) (and also (53a)). Example (51a) involves movement from a thematic position (object) to a thematic position (subject), whereas the movement in (52) and (53a) is from a thematic position to a nonthematic position. Assuming that trace binding between two thematic positions results in the assignment of two θ-roles to a single argument, the former possibility can be prohibited by a constraint against arguments that bear more than one θ-role (cf. the 'functional uniqueness' constraint of Freidin 1978). Functional uniqueness is limited to trace binding. It does not apply to the relationship between a null subject PRO and its antecedent, as in (54) where PRO is anaphoric on the matrix subject:

John$_i$ tried hard $[_{CP} [_{IP} \text{ PRO}_i \text{ to win}]]$ (54)

Example (54) is fully grammatical, and thus *John* does not violate the functional uniqueness condition. Only trace binding involves θ-role inheritance. It follows therefore that there are at least two distinct types of empty category in syntax, namely trace and PRO.

Another predicate-argument condition, which complements functional uniqueness, requires every argument in a sentence to bear a θ-role (cf. the 'functional relatedness' constraint of Freidin 1978). This excludes the possibility of having arguments occur in nonthematic positions where they are not linked to some other thematic position via trace binding. Example (55) illustrates this possibility, which must also be prohibited.

*the student was praised the boy by the teacher.   (55a)

*the situation seems that the economy is getting worse.   (55b)

Although (55a) involves a Case Filter violation, (55b) does not; thus this second constraint on predicate-argument structure is independently motivated.

These two conditions have been incorporated into a more general condition, the θ-criterion:

θ-criterion
Each argument bears one and only one θ-role   (56)
and each θ-role is assigned to one and only one argument. (Chomsky 1981: 36)

The second part of the θ-criterion prohibits two structural arguments of a predicate from bearing the same thematic function (see Freidin 1975: n. 20). In English double object constructions, for example, the thematic function assigned to an indirect object may alternatively be assigned to the object of an appropriate preposition as illustrated in (57), where *Mary* bears the same semantic function with respect to the predicate *give*:

John gave Mary a present.   (57a)

John gave a present to Mary.   (57b)

This part of the θ-criterion prohibits the possibility that both an indirect object and a *to*-phrase will occur simultaneously with *give*, as in (58).

*John gave Mary a present to Bill.   (58)

Since both *Mary* and *Bill* cannot be assigned the same θ-role, one will lack a θ-role in violation of the first part of the θ-criterion. The other half of the θ-criterion's second part excludes constructions containing a predicate which cannot discharge all its thematic functions onto arguments.

*Bill mentioned.   (59)

Given that *mention* assigns at least two thematic functions, and assuming that there is only one argument available for thematic assignment, (59) violates this part of the θ-criterion. The formulation of this last subpart requires some adjustment, since it could be argued that *mention* assigns three θ-roles, as in *Bill mentioned that book to Mary*, whereas the sentence *Bill mentioned that book* is fully grammatical even though the thematic function associated with *Mary* in the previous example is presumably not discharged.

The θ-criterion concerns some lexical properties of predicates—namely, how many θ-roles each assigns and which θ-roles they are. The theory of grammar at the time of writing contains another principle concerning lexical properties, the Projection Principle, which states that lexical structure must be represented categorially at every syntactic level (i.e., D-structure, S-structure, and LF). With these two principles, certain properties of phrase structure follow—in particular, the number of complements that may and in many cases must occur with a given head follows from lexical properties of heads. If particular θ-roles correlate with particular syntactic categories (i.e., some θ-roles can only be realized by propositions (i.e., CP), others by NPs, and so on), then the category of complements and subjects could be fully determined by lexical properties as well. In earlier versions of generative grammar, this information was stipulated in language-particular phrase structure rules. In the principles and parameters theory, it is assumed that this information follows from general principles (the θ-criterion in conjunction with the Projection Principle) and therefore that a grammar of a language need not include phrase structure rules. Case theory also contributes to this conclusion to the extent that it determines facts about the ordering of complements: for example, when a verb takes both a NP and CP complement, the order of the complements must be with the NP adjacent to V so that adjacency for case assignment is satisfied.

4.5 Binding Theory

In addition to an antecedent–trace binding relation, the theory of grammar also accounts for the binding relation that holds between an anaphoric expression and its antecedent. Languages contain two types of anaphoric expressions: those that require the presence of an antecedent in the same sentence, called bound anaphors (i.e., reflexive pronouns and reciprocal expressions—henceforth 'anaphors'); and pronouns, which can occur in a sentence without an antecedent. Binding theory is concerned in part with the conditions under which anaphors and pronouns can be bound to an antecedent.

4.5.1 Bound Anaphors

Formally, an antecedent binds an anaphoric expression when it c-commands and is coindexed with the expression. The paradigm for anaphors in (60) illustrates that not all possible binding relations are permissible:

Simple sentence: (60a)
    we$_i$ help each other$_i$

Finite clause complement: (60b)
(i) *we$_i$ expect [$_{CP}$ (that) [$_{IP}$ each other$_i$ will win]]
(ii) *we$_i$ expect [$_{CP}$ (that) [$_{IP}$ Mary will help each other$_i$]]

Infinitival complement: (60c)
  (i) we$_i$ expect [$_{IP}$ each other$_i$ to help Mary]
  (ii) *we$_i$ expect [$_{IP}$ Mary to help each other$_i$]

While all the anaphors in (60) are bound, only those in (60a) and (60c.i) are properly bound. Proper binding of anaphors falls under a principle of grammar, referred to as Principle A of the binding theory, which is given schematically in (61).

Principle A
  An anaphor must be antecedent-bound in (61)
  local domain δ.

Example (61) constitutes a principle of UG which, by specifying the local domain δ, is instantiated in the grammar of a particular language as binding condition A.

The local domain for anaphors in English is the domain of an accessible SUBJECT, where SUBJECT stands for a syntactic subject or the agreement element associated with the head of finite IP (given that specifier–head agreement between a syntactic subject and the head I is mandatory in finite clauses). Any syntactic subject is accessible to an anaphor if it c-commands the anaphor. Thus (60a) and (60c.i) satisfy binding condition A because the only accessible subject in each example is the main clause subject to which the anaphor is bound. In (60b.ii) and (60c.ii), the complement subject is accessible to the anaphor, but the anaphor is antecedent-free (i.e., not coindexed to a c-commanding antecedent) in the domain of this subject. Therefore these examples violate binding condition A. In (60b.i), the agreement element of the sentential complement constitutes an accessible SUBJECT, and in that domain the anaphor is antecedent-free in violation of binding condition A. (The precise formulation of the local domain δ for English is somewhat more intricate; see Chomsky (1986b) and Freidin (1992) for details.)

Crosslinguistically, some variation is found in the local domain δ for binding condition A. In Korean, for example, the binding domain for reciprocals is that of any c-commanding NP. Thus, within a single clause, a direct object may create a binding domain for the object of a PP in VP, as illustrated in (62) (from Hong 1985):

kitil-i   [$_{NP}$ John-kwa Mary]-lil sero-eke   sogehetta   (62)
they-NOM John and Mary-ACC   each other-to introduced
they$_i$ introduced [$_{NP}$ John and Mary]$_j$ to each other$_{\{*i, j\}}$

In the corresponding English example, either the subject or the direct object may be the antecedent of the reciprocal. Hence the binding domain for reciprocals in Korean is more restricted than that of English. This indicates that the binding domain for Principle A is subject to parameterization.

A comparison of the distribution of reflexive pronouns in English and Icelandic provides another example of the parameterization of Principle A. English reflexives have essentially the same distribution as reciprocals, so that (60) could be converted into a paradigm for reflexives simply by replacing *each other* with *themselves*. The corresponding Icelandic paradigm is identical to English with one exception: (60c.ii) is not deviant in Icelandic. The difference between English and Icelandic reflexive binding is that the binding domain for the Icelandic is the domain of an antecedent-bound SUBJECT, whereas for English whether the SUBJECT is antecedent-bound is not relevant (as (60c.ii) demonstrates). Assuming that a null subject PRO with an antecedent constitutes an antecedent-bound subject, (63) (from Thraínsson 1979) supports this formulation of the binding domain for Icelandic reflexives:

*ég$_i$ lofaði   Haraldi$_j$[$_{CP}$ að [$_{IP}$ PRO$_i$ raka   sig$_j$]]   (63)
I   promised Harold   to-shave self
I$_i$ promised Harold$_j$[$_{CP}$ [$_{IP}$ PRO$_i$ to shave himself$_j$]]

The crosslinguistic evidence concerning the binding domain of Principle A suggests that the parametric differences fall within a narrow range of options (for further discussion of anaphor binding, including some alternative analyses, see Koster and Reuland (1991)).

4.5.2 Pronouns

In contrast to anaphors, which must be bound within a certain domain, pronouns cannot be bound within certain domains. The paradigm for pronoun binding corresponding to (60), given in (64), illustrates a complementarity between bound anaphors and bound pronouns—where a bound anaphor can occur, a bound pronoun may not.

Simple sentence: (64a)
  *the politician$_i$ voted for him$_i$

Finite clause complement: (64b)
  (i) Clara$_i$ expects [$_{CP}$ (that) [$_{IP}$ she$_i$ will win]]
  (ii) Clara$_i$ expects [$_{CP}$ (that) [$_{IP}$ Sam will help her$_i$]]

Infinitival complement: (64c)
  (i) *Clara$_i$ expects [$_{IP}$ her$_i$ to help Sam]
  (ii) Clara$_i$ expects [$_{IP}$ Sam to help her$_i$]

Thus, pronoun binding is accounted for by a principle of grammar complementary to Principle A, referred to as Principle B of the binding theory:

Principle B
  A pronoun must be antecedent-free in local (65)
  domain δ.

As with Principle A, Principle B is instantiated in the grammar of a particular language as binding condition B by specifying the local domain δ. As with anaphor binding, this domain varies across languages. For example, pronoun binding in the Icelandic sentence corresponding to (64c.ii) is not possible.

Given the complementarity of anaphors and bound pronouns illustrated in (60) and (64), it would appear that the specification of the local domain for pronoun binding is identical to that of anaphor binding. Although this complementarity holds for binding within IP and across IP boundaries, it collapses with respect to binding across NP boundaries, as (66–67) illustrate:

> they$_i$ never discuss [$_{NP}$ each other's$_i$ work]　(66a)

> they$_i$ never discuss [$_{NP}$ their$_i$ work]　(66b)

> every man$_i$ heard [$_{NP}$ a story about himself$_i$]　(67a)

> every man$_i$ heard [$_{NP}$ a story about him$_i$]　(67b)

These examples show that the domain statement for binding condition B in English cannot be identical to that of binding condition A, since if it were, then (66b) and (67b) should be unacceptable on a par with (64a) and (64c.i), contrary to fact. These examples show that NP constitutes a binding domain for pronouns, and the paradigm in (64) shows that IP constitutes another binding domain with one exception, (64c.i), where the matrix verb governs the complement subject across IP. One property that NP and IP share in common is that they both constitute domains in which predicates (e.g., verbs and derived nominals) may discharge their θ-roles (θ-domains, or complete functional constructs, in the terminology of Chomsky (1986b)). Example (64c.i) shows that the binding domain for pronouns is not the minimal θ-domain containing the pronoun, but rather the minimal θ-domain of the governor of the pronoun (for further discussion of the representation and interpretation of pronoun binding, see Lasnik 1989).

4.5.3 R-expressions

In addition to trace binding and the binding of an anaphoric expression to an antecedent, coindexing in grammatical representation may also occur between two nonanaphoric, nonpronominal, and nonpleonastic expressions, that is, R-expressions (where R designates 'referential' in a loose sense). For a sentence like (68), the representation of the reading in which there is only one person named 'George' requires the two instances of *George* to be coindexed:

> [$_{IP}$ [$_{NP}$ no-one who knows George$_i$ well]　(68)
> [$_{VP}$ respects George$_i$]]

Thus, coindexing between R-expressions is possible, and necessary if the grammar is to distinguish between the two readings—where in the second reading there are two different individuals with the same name.

While coindexing between R-expressions is allowed in the case just cited, it appears to be unacceptable when an R-expression is c-commanded by the phrase it is coindexed with.

> Simple sentence:　(69a)
> 　*Clara$_i$ voted for Clara$_i$

> Finite clause complement:　(69b)
> 　(i) *Clara$_i$ expects [$_{CP}$ (that) [$_{IP}$ Clara$_i$ will win]]

> 　(ii) *Clara$_i$ expects [$_{CP}$ (that) [$_{IP}$ Sam will help Clara$_i$]]

> Infinitival complement:　(69c)
> 　(i) *Clara$_i$ expects [$_{IP}$ Clara$_i$ to help Sam]
> 　(ii) *Clara$_i$ expects [$_{IP}$ Sam to help Clara$_i$]

Read with normal sentence stress, these sentences do not allow the coindexing interpretation. In contrast, the two instances of *George* in (68) are not in a c-command relation. This demonstrates that R-expressions are subject to another principle of the binding theory:

> **Principle C**
> An R-expression must be free in domain δ.　(70)

As (69) indicates, an R-expression in English must be free in all domains—that is, it can never be bound.

Like Principles A and B, Principle C is subject to some degree of parameterization. In Vietnamese, for example, an R-expression may bind another R-expression across a clause boundary, but not within a single clause; whereas in Thai, such binding may occur even within a single clause (see Lasnik 1991 for details). However, like English, neither Thai nor Vietnamese allows a pronoun to bind R-expressions, as in (71):

> *she$_i$ expects [$_{CP}$ (that) [$_{IP}$ Sam will help Clara$_i$]]　(71)

As Lasnik points out, the prohibition against a pronoun binding an R-expression appears to be an absolute constraint for all languages.

4.5.4 Binding Theory and Empty Categories

The principles of binding theory apply to the distribution of empty categories, both PRO and various types of trace. This approach works well for the distribution of *wh*-trace and PRO, but runs into problems with NP-trace. Assuming NP-trace to be the empty category analog of a lexical bound anaphor, much of the distribution of NP-trace follows from Principle A. Thus, NP-trace binding has exactly the same properties illustrated in the paradigm in (60) for lexical anaphors. Nonetheless, the binding-theoretic approach to NP-trace is redundant with respect to case theory, the ECP, and the Subjacency Condition. Once the effects of these principles have been factored out of the distribution NP-trace, there is nothing left for Principle A to account for.

The binding-theoretic analysis for the distribution of PRO is based on the assumption that PRO has the properties of both anaphors and pronominals and hence is subject to Principles A and B—an analysis referred to in the literature as 'the PRO Theorem.' For the PRO Theorem to go through, the binding domains for Principles A and B must be formulated, details aside, in terms of government so that neither condition applies to PRO when PRO is in a position which is not lexically governed—that is, when PRO is the subject of an infinitival complement which does not undergo CP-deletion.

Wh-trace is the analogue of an R-expression under the binding-theoretic analysis of empty categories and therefore subject to Principle C. This analysis accounts for two different properties of *wh*-movement, one involving the impossibility of a certain type of *wh*-movement not excluded by other grammatical principles, and the other involving the effect of *wh*-movement on interpretation.

Once a *wh*-phrase has moved into the specifier position of CP, it may not move into a grammatical function position, but only into a c-commanding specifier position of a higher CP. Thus, the *wh*-movement pattern illustrated in (72) is prohibited:

$$*[_{CP} \text{ who}_i [_C \text{ was}] [_{IP} e_i [_{VP} \text{ tried } [_{CP} e_i [_{IP} e_i \text{ to } [_{VP} \text{ to leave}]]]]]] \quad (72)$$

(Note that (72) is analogous to the well-formed *who was believed to have left*.) The application of Principle C to *wh*-trace requires a further refinement of Principle C along the following lines. Basically, a *wh*-trace may be bound by an antecedent in the specifier position of CP but not by one in a grammatical function position. Thus, there must be a distinction between argument positions (grammatical function positions where arguments can occur in D-structures) and nonargument positions like the specifier position in CP. Given this distinction, Principle C can be sharpened as a prohibition against an R-expression which is argument-bound. Example (72) violates Principle C because the trace in the complement subject position is argument-bound by the trace in the matrix subject position.

The fact of interpretation addressed by the binding-theoretic analysis of *wh*-trace is this: a sentence like (73) allows two distinct interpretations, whereas the analogous sentence (74) in which the *wh*-phrase and the pronoun have switched positions only allows one of these interpretations.

who wants me to take him to the concert? (73)

who does he want me to take to the concert? (74)

Example (73) can be interpreted as a question about three different people, or alternatively as a question about just two people. These interpretations are given in (75), where (75a) represents the former and (75b) the latter:

$$[_{CP} \text{ who}_j] [_{IP} e_j [_{VP} \text{ wants } [_{IP} \text{ me}_j \text{ to } [_{VP} \text{ take him}_k \quad (75a)$$
$$\text{to the concert}]]]]]$$

$$[_{CP} \text{ who}_j] [_{IP} e_j [_{VP} \text{ wants } [_{IP} \text{ me}_j \text{ to } [_{VP} \text{ take him}_i \quad (75b)$$
$$\text{to the concert}]]]]]$$

In contrast, (74) cannot have the representation where the *wh*-phrase and the pronoun are coindexed. Thus, only the representation (76a) is allowed for (74)—a phenomenon referred to in the literature as 'crossover' on the grounds that *wh*-movement over a pronoun

affects the possibilities for the anaphoric interpretation of the pronoun.

$$[_{CP} \text{ who}_i [_C \text{ does}_m] [_{IP} \text{ he}_k e_m [_{VP} \text{ want } [_{CP} e_i [_{IP} \text{ me}_j \quad (76a)$$
$$\text{to}[_{VP} \text{ take } e_i \text{ to the concert}]]]]]]$$

$$*[_{CP} \text{ who}_i [_C \text{ does}_m] [_{IP} \text{ he}_i e_m [_{VP} \text{ want } [_{CP} e_i [_{IP} \text{ me}_j \quad (76b)$$
$$\text{to}[_{VP} \text{ take } e_i \text{ to the concert}]]]]]]$$

Example (76b) violates Principle C, since the *wh*-trace in complement object position is argument-bound by the pronoun in matrix subject position. Thus, this reading is excluded for the same reason that a pronoun cannot be anaphoric on an R-expression that it c-commands, as in *he said that John was brilliant*.

The binding theoretic analysis of *wh*-trace establishes a principled distinction between *wh*-trace on the one hand, and NP-trace and PRO on the other. NP-trace is necessarily argument-bound, and PRO is when it has an overt antecedent. Thus it follows from this analysis in conjunction with the θ-criterion and the ECP that there are at least three distinct empty categories, each with its own special properties. In this way, the analysis of empty categories demonstrates the abstract nature of the human language faculty, as well as its computational complexity (for further discussion of the binding theoretic analysis of empty categories, see Brody (1984) and Lasnik (1991)).

4.5.5 Binding Theory and LF

The three principles of binding theory apply to representations at some syntactic level. Aside from which level or levels of syntactic representation are subject to binding theory, there is also the question of whether the three principles operate as a unit on the same levels of representation, or whether one principle or another applies at a different level from the others. If it can be shown that all three principles apply at the same level of representation, there is a strong indication that the three principles operate as a unit within the grammar. Whether the principles of binding theory hold at the same levels of representation crosslinguistically remains to be determined.

In English, Principle A does not apply at D-structure, as illustrated by the example in (77) of NP-movement:

$$[_{IP} \text{ they}_i \text{ seemed to each other}_i [_{IP} e_i \text{ to be hiding} \quad (77)$$
$$\text{something}]]$$

The anaphor in (77) is properly bound at S-structure, but not at D-structure; therefore applying Principle A at D-structure would give the wrong result. Example (77) shows that Principle A applies after D-structure—that is, to S-structure or LF (or both). The case of *wh*-movement in (78) provides evidence that Principle A does not apply at S-structure, since at S-structure the anaphor is not properly bound.

$$[_{CP} [_{AP:k} \text{ how angry at himself}_i] [_C \text{ did}_j] [_{IP} \text{ Mary } e_j \quad (78)$$
$$[_{VP} \text{ say } [_{CP} e_k [_{IP} \text{ John}_i [_{VP} \text{ was } e_k]]]]]]]$$

At LF, however, the anaphor is properly bound, assuming that (78) has the representation (79) at LF:

$[_{CP}$ to what degree x_l $[_C$ did$_j]$ $[_{IP}$ Mary e_j $[_{VP}$ say $[_{CP}$ e_k (79) $[_{IP}$ John$_i$ $[_{VP}$ was $[_{AP·k}$ x_l angry at himself$_i]]]]]]]]$

In (79), the *wh*-phrase has been reconstructed in its original D-structure position. Given reconstruction of this sort, the ill-formed (80a) yields a Principle A violation at LF, since the anaphor in the LF representation (80b) is antecedent-free in the domain of the sentential complement subject *Mary*.

*how angry at himself did John say Mary was? (80a)

$[_{CP}$ to what degree x_l $[_C$ did$_j]$ $[_{IP}$ John$_i$ e_j $[_{VP}$ say (80b) $[_{CP}$ e_k $[_{IP}$ Mary $[_{VP}$ was $[_{AP·k}$ x_l angry at himself$_i]]]]]]]]$

Thus, (77–80) provide some empirical support for concluding that Principle A applies at LF.

Reconstruction effects also support the LF analysis of Principle B. In the S-structure (81a), the pronoun is not bound, in contrast to its LF representation (81b):

*$[_{CP}$ $[_{AP·k}$ how angry at him$_i]$ $[_C$ was$_j]$ $[_{IP}$ John$_i$ (81a) $[_{VP}$ $e_j e_k]]]$

$[_{CP}$ to what degree x_l $[_C$ was$_j]$ $[_{IP}$ John$_i$ $[_{VP}$ e_j $[_{AP·k}$ x_l (81b) angry at him$_i]]$

In this way, (81b), but not (81a), yields a Principle B violation. A similar argument can be constructed for Principle C simply by switching the positions of the R-expression and the pronoun in (81a–b).

The contrast between (82a) and (82b) on the bound readings provides further striking evidence that Principle C holds at LF:

which recommendation that John$_i$ revised did he$_i$ (82a) submit?

*which recommendation that John$_i$ should be promoted? did he$_i$ submit? (82b)

At D-structure as well as S-structure, the relative positions of the coindexed pronoun and R-expression in both examples are identical. Therefore, the difference between (82a) and (82b) cannot be captured at either of these levels. At LF, the two *wh*-phrases receive different analyses based on the difference between the relative clause in (82a) versus the nominal complement in (82b). In the LF representation of (82a), the relative clause modifies the variable and therefore remains as part of the quantifier structure, as in (83):

(for which x such that $[_{CP}$ John$_i$ revised $x]$, (83) $x =$ a recommendation) did$_j$ $[_{IP}$ he$_i$ e_j submit $x]$

Coindexing between the R-expression and the pronoun violates no principle of the binding theory and therefore is possible. In contrast, the LF representation of (82b) leads to a Principle C violation.

(for which x, $x =$ a recommendation $[_{CP}$ that John$_i$ (84) should be promoted]) did$_j$ $[_{IP}$ he$_i$ e_j submit $x]$

In (84), the variable x stands for the nominal plus its sentential complement which contains the R-expression. Since the variable is c-commanded by the pronoun, the expression which it stands for is likewise c-commanded via interpretation of the variable. This results in a Principle C violation at LF.

5. New Directions

For the most part, the principles of UG discussed above are formulated as conditions on representations—more specifically, as licensing conditions on particular elements in syntactic representations. Thus the Case Filter licenses the occurrence of lexical NPs, and the functional relatedness requirement of the θ-criterion licenses the occurrence of nonpleonastic NPs. Traces must be properly governed according to the ECP and must be local with respect to their closest antecedent via the Subjacency Condition. As noted above, these licensing conditions determine when movement rules must apply and also when they cannot apply (because the application results in an ill-formed structure). In this way, they determine the design of language.

Chomsky (1991) has suggested that the principles and parameters approach can be interpreted in terms of more general guidelines for language design. In essence, these guidelines legislate against 'superfluous steps' in deviations and 'superfluous elements' in representations. For example, the principle of Full Interpretation (Chomsky 1986b) requires that every PF and LF element interfacing with systems of language use must receive an appropriate interpretation. From Full Interpretation, it follows that LF representations for natural languages may not contain vacuous quantifiers or arguments that are not functionally related to some predicate in the representation (as in (55)). Therefore the functional relatedness requirement of the θ-criterion follows from the principle of Full Interpretation, a more general requirement that representations be minimal in some sense.

With respect to derivations, the guidelines appear to move in the direction of 'least effort' in a sense still to be made explicit. With respect to NP-movement, for example, a 'least effort' guideline would proscribe movement unless necessitated by some principle of UG. In certain constructions (e.g., (32b)), the Case Filter requires that the lexical subject of an infinitival complement move to the matrix subject position in order to receive case. In similar constructions where the complement subject is case-marked in its D-structure position, there is no motivation for the NP to move at all. Thus, if it moves, the derivation is in violation of the 'least effort' guideline. Under this analysis, it is no longer necessary to treat constructions like (41b) as ECP violations, since they are ruled out by a more general condition.

Note that, although least effort is clearly a condition on derivations, it addresses the issue of language design in a very general way, in contrast to previous conditions on derivations—e.g., the Strict Cycle Condition (Chomsky 1973)—which were more closely tied to the application of transformational rules. Until there is a more precise formulation of this guideline, exactly how the 'least effort' analysis interacts with the principles and parameters theory remains an intriguing open question.

The material covered in this article is merely a sketch of some of the most central topics being investigated within the principles and parameters framework. Ongoing research extends the empirical coverage of various subtheories, including parametric variation across languages. It also explores a number of promising alternative analyses for various parts of the theory. As in any area of rational inquiry, no assumption is immune to critical inquiry.

For further discussion of these and other topics within this approach to generative grammar, see van Riemsdijk and Williams (1986), Lasnik and Uriagereka (1988), Haegeman (1991), and Freidin (1992). Many of the topics under investigation have had a long and rich history in generative grammar since the mid-1950s—see Newmeyer (1986) for a historical account.

The principles and parameters framework of generative grammar attempts to establish the common biological basis for all the world's languages. The ongoing work in comparative grammar illuminates the human language faculty as an intricate computational structure of the human mind that is unique to the genetic endowment of the species. In this way, work in comparative grammar makes a major contribution to the emerging cognitive science enterprise.

Bibliography

Anderson S, Kiparsky P (eds.) 1973 *A Festschrift for Morris Halle*. Holt, Rinehart and Winston, New York

Aoun J, Hornstein N, Lightfoot D, Weinberg A 1987 Two types of locality. *LIn* **18**: 537–77

Babby L 1992 Case theory. In: Otero C P (ed.) *Noam Chomsky: Critical Assessments*. Routledge, London

Baker M C 1987 *Incorporation: A Theory of Grammatical Function Changing*. Chicago University Press, Chicago, IL

Brody M 1984 On contextual definitions and the role of chains. *LIn* **15**: 355–80

Browning M A 1989 ECP ≠ CED. *LIn* **20**: 481–91

Browning M A 1991 Bounding conditions on representation. *LIn* **22**: 541–62

Chomsky N 1964 *Current Issues in Linguistic Theory*. Mouton, The Hague

Chomsky N 1965 *Aspects of the Theory of Syntax*. MIT Press, Cambridge, MA

Chomsky N 1973 Conditions on transformations. In: Anderson S, Kiparsky P (eds.) *A Festschrift for Morris Halle*. Holt, Rinehart and Winston, New York

Chomsky N 1976 Conditions on rules of grammar. *LAn* **2**: 303–51

Chomsky N 1980 On binding. *LIn* **11**: 1–46

Chomsky N 1981 *Lectures on Government and Binding*. Foris, Dordrecht

Chomsky N 1986a *Barriers*. MIT Press, Cambridge, MA

Chomsky N 1986b *Knowledge of Language: Its Nature, Origin, and Use*. Praeger, New York

Chomsky N 1991 Some notes on the economy of derivation and representation. In: Freidin R (ed.) *Principles and Parameters in Comparative Grammar*. MIT Press, Cambridge, MA

Chomsky N, Lasnik H 1977 Filters and control. *LIn* **8**: 425–504

Freidin R 1975 The analysis of passives. *Lg* **51**: 384–405

Freidin R 1978 Cyclicity and the theory of grammar. *LIn* **9**: 519–49

Freidin R (ed.) 1991 *Principles and Parameters in Comparative Grammar*. MIT Press, Cambridge, MA

Freidin R 1992 *Foundations of Generative Syntax*. MIT Press, Cambridge, MA

Freidin R, Babby L 1984 On the interaction of lexical and structural properties: Case structure in Russian. In: *Cornell Working Papers in Linguistics* **6**. Department of Modern Languages and Linguistics, Cornell University, Ithaca, NY

Freidin R, Quicoli A C 1992 On the licensing of lexical subjects (Unpublished manuscript, Princeton University)

Freidin R, Sprouse R A 1991 Lexical case phenomena. In: Freidin R (ed.) *Principles and Parameters in Comparative Grammar*. MIT Press, Cambridge, MA

Haegman L 1991 *Introduction to Government and Binding Theory*. Blackwell, Oxford

Higginbotham J, May R 1981 Questions, quantifiers, and crossing. *LRev* **1**: 41–80

Hong S 1985 A and A′-binding in Korean and English (Doctoral dissertation, University of Connecticut)

Huang C-T J 1982 Logical relations in Chinese and the theory of grammar (Doctoral dissertation, Massachusetts Institute of Technology)

Jackendoff R 1972 *Semantic Interpretation in Generative Grammar*. MIT Press, Cambridge, MA

Jackendoff R 1990 *Semantic Structures*. MIT Press, Cambridge, MA

Jaeggli O, Safir K (eds.) 1989 *The Null Subject Parameter*. Kluwer, Dordrecht

Kayne R 1975 *French Syntax: The Transformational Cycle*. MIT Press, Cambridge, MA

Kayne R 1989 Null subjects and clitic climbing. In: Jaeggli O, Safir K (eds.) *The Null Subject Parameter*. Kluwer, Dordrecht

Koster J, Reuland E (eds.) 1991 *Long-distance Anaphora*. Cambridge University Press, Cambridge

Lasnik H 1989 *Essays on Anaphora*. Kluwer, Dordrecht

Lasnik H 1991 On the necessity of binding conditions. In: Freidin R (ed.) *Principles and Parameters in Comparative Grammar*. MIT Press, Cambridge, MA

Lasnik H, Saito M 1984 On the nature of proper government. *LIn* **15**: 235–89

Lasnik H, Saito M 1992 *Move α*. MIT Press, Cambridge, MA

Lasnik H, Uriagereka J 1988 *A Course in GB Syntax*. MIT Press, Cambridge, MA

Newmeyer F J 1986 *Linguistic Theory in America*, 2nd edn. Academic Press, Orlando, FL

Quicoli A C 1976a Conditions on clitic-movement in Portuguese. *LAn* **2**: 199–223

Quicoli A C 1976b Conditions on quantifier movement in French. *LIn* **7**: 583–607

Riemsdijk H C van, Williams E S 1986 *Introduction to the Theory of Grammar*. MIT Press, Cambridge, MA
Rizzi L 1982 *Issues in Italian Syntax*. Foris, Dordrecht
Ross J R 1985 *Infinite Syntax!* Ablex, Norwood, NJ
Rouveret A, Vergnaud J-R 1980 Specifying reference to the subject: French causatives and conditions on representations. *LIn* **11**: 97–202
Speas M J 1990 *Phrase Structure in Natural Language*. Kluwer, Dordrecht
Sportiche D 1981 On bounding nodes in French. *LRev* **1**: 219–46
Stowell T 1981 Origins of phrase structure (Doctoral dissertation, Massachusetts Institute of Technology)

Stuurman F 1985 *Phrase Structure Theory in Generative Grammar*. Foris, Dordrecht
Thráinsson H 1979 *On Complementation in Icelandic*. Garland Publishers, New York
Torrego E 1984 On inversion in Spanish and some of its effects. *LIn* **15**: 103–29
Travis L deM 1984 Parameters and effects of word order variation (Doctoral dissertation, Massachusetts Institute of Technology)
Williams E S 1977 Discourse and logical form. *LIn* **8**: 101–39

Generative Grammar: The Minimalist Program

Martin Atkinson

The Minimalist Program (MP) is, in some respects, a natural development from Principles and Parameters Theory and the varieties of Generative Grammar which preceded the latter (see *Generative Grammar: Principles and Parameters*). However, as Chomsky himself has noted, it represents a radical departure from these earlier models in a variety of fundamental respects, some of which will be introduced below. Additionally, it is important to be clear that in the mid-1990s it remains a *program*; as we shall see, it is quite unlike the preceding innovations initiated by Chomsky (1981, 1986). These earlier works, which represented milestones in the development of Principles and Parameters Theory, contained detailed attempts to come to terms with a range of complex linguistic structures. While the plea for explanation was readily apparent, the requirement to adequately describe syntactic phenomena, which had hitherto resisted insightful treatment, was also overt. The best-known primary literature introducing the MP (Chomsky 1989, 1992, 1994, 1995) is quite different in this respect, with the proportion of text devoted to conceptual and technical matters far outweighing analysis of example structures. Further, the structures which do receive detailed attention are often those of simple clauses; in short, the MP urges that we should carefully review the status of much of the generative grammar of the previous 40 years, bringing to bear on it a small set of fundamental and, it is argued, attractive principles.

Given the tentative nature of many of the foundations of the MP, it would be quite inappropriate in a volume of this kind to attempt to engage the fast-changing and somewhat elusive technical developments of the last five years. What follows, therefore, is a sketch of what seem to be some of the major differences between the MP and its generative predecessors.

Driving the MP are provisional views on a small number of basic issues. Chomsky (1994: 385) articulates these issues in two questions: 'What conditions on the human language faculty are imposed by considerations of virtual conceptual necessity?' And: 'To what extent is the language faculty determined by these conditions, that is, how much special structure does it have beyond them?' The first of these questions has two distinct perspectives, and it is important to have a sense of these before going further.

Throughout the development of Chomsky's approaches to generative grammar, a constant theme has been that there is an identifiable language module in the mind/brain, which constitutes a legitimate object of enquiry under appropriate idealizations and which is embedded in a set of other cognitive systems. Alternatives to this conception are possible, hence Chomsky's use of 'virtual' as a modifier for 'conceptual necessity' above, but insofar as such alternatives have been pursued, perhaps assimilating the study of language to the study of general cognition, they have failed to yield any significant insights. To accept the conception is to acknowledge that, in a complete account of mental organization, the language module will interface with other cognitive systems, and that in order for such an interface to function, the language module will need to satisfy conditions imposed by these systems. Thus the idea is reached that some aspects of the language faculty will be determined by these external requirements.

The second perspective arises from adopting what some might regard as determinants of good practice in science; these involve being attracted by simplicity and elegance and being suspicious of redundancy and 'ugliness.' Of course, notions such as these are not sharp, but it is undeniable that they do regularly inform argumentation. To the extent that they can be given content, it can be considered whether the language faculty conforms with them. That such conformity exhibits conceptual necessity even of the virtual kind is far from apparent, but Chomsky's intention here is clear enough. In short, there is a second set of external conditions, against which the properties of the language faculty can be assessed.

Turning to the second question Chomsky poses, note that the success of the MP is predicated on the answer 'not much.' If it turns out that the language faculty has a large number of properties which are not reducible to the requirements of interfacing cognitive systems, nor to general simplicity or economy conditions, then the MP will have been shown to be misguided.

It is customary for discussions of the MP to begin with notions of economy. This article however will follow a different course by first discussing levels of representation, turning then to phrase structure and to Chomsky's recent attempts to eliminate X-bar Theory from Universal Grammar by deriving its consequences in a theory of 'bare phrase structure.' This is followed by an account of Case Theory in the MP and how this is linked to an insistence on the locality of grammatical relations. Finally, Principles of Economy and their role in derivations will be briefly described.

1. Levels of Representation

The overall organization of a grammar in Principles and Parameters Theory is discussed in detail by Freidin elsewhere in this volume (see *Generative Grammar: Principles and Parameters*). This organization appears in (1):

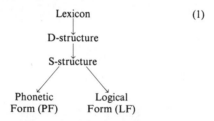

(1)

In (1), the relationship between the lexicon and D-structure is mediated by a notion of lexical items 'projecting' their selectional and subcategorizing properties into a syntactic configuration. Between D-structure and S-structure and between S-structure and LF are applications of 'Move α' (or 'Affect α'); and between S-structure and PF is the phonological component, along with some poorly understood non-phonological operations.

Now, it is readily apparent that the various levels of representation in (1) are motivated in quite different ways. Supposing that the language module interfaces with systems of articulation and auditory perception, PF is the linguistic side of that interface; similarly, since the language faculty is crucially involved in enabling understanding, inferencing, and the derivation of 'meaning' in some suitably broad sense, there must be an interface (LF) with the nonlinguistic cognitive systems responsible for these processes. The conclusion that PF and LF are levels of linguistic

representation by reason of 'virtual conceptual necessity' follows. Furthermore, the properties of these levels of representation will need to take account of whatever precisely is on the other side of the interface; to the extent that such taking account exhausts the properties of PF and LF, this gives an affirmative answer to the second of Chomsky's questions introduced above.

It is easy to see that the same immediate motivation is not available for the 'internal' levels of syntactic representation, D-structure, and S-structure. Their motivation, while considerable within Principles and Parameters Theory, is empirical and theory internal. In short, while there are arguments for the necessity of postulating these levels of representation, there are no such arguments in the case of PF and LF (although there may be disputes about their nature); to question the status of PF and LF, as levels of representation, is to question a whole way of construing linguistic theorizing. From the MP perspective, it follows that a conception of linguistic theory should be developed which eschews reference to these intermediate levels. The consequences of this will be addressed presently, but first the overall organization of linguistic theory will be sketched out from the requirements obtained so far.

As in (1), suppose that a language contains a lexicon and the linguistic levels PF and LF. One immediate condition which must be imposed on the interface levels, and which is quite consistent with the spirit of the MP, is that of 'Full Interpretation.' Taking the notion of interface level seriously, it would be inappropriate for a well-formed PF to contain elements which are not interpretable by the articulatory-acoustic systems; equally, it would be inappropriate for a well-formed LF to contain anything other than elements which are interpretable by systems of general understanding, although it must be acknowledged that very little is known about the latter. Supposing, then, that items in the lexicon consist of sets of features which fall into various categories. Among others, there will be phonological features, relevant to articulation and perception, and semantic features, relevant to understanding. In a well-formed derivation, phonological features must not survive to LF and semantic features must not survive to PF. It must be the case then that a derivation, starting from a set of lexical choices, will branch. The point at which this occurs coincides with an operation known as SPELL-OUT, which effectively involves stripping the phonological features off the representation. This leads to the schematic organization in (2):

$$\text{Lexicon} \longrightarrow \text{SPELL-OUT} \longrightarrow \text{LF} \qquad (2)$$
$$\downarrow$$
$$\text{PF}$$

At this point, it is legitimate to ask how SPELL-OUT differs from the S-structure which appears in (1). The answer to this is straightforward. First, SPELL-OUT is not a linguistic level but an operation. Secondly, and related to the first reason, SPELL-OUT can occur at any point in a derivation. As will become clear, if it occurs at the 'wrong' point, the derivation will not be well-formed; however, the suggestion that S-structure could occur at any point in a derivation makes no sense.

The rejection of intermediate levels of syntactic representation poses a challenge. As noted already, D-structure and S-structure have been regarded as legitimate constructs because of their role in theory. For example, S-structure has been seen as the level at which the principles of the Binding Theory operate and the level at which the Case Filter checks the properties of NPs. The integrity of the level is a consequence of the generalizations expressed by the Binding Theory and the Case Filter. Whether S-structure is the appropriate level for the Principles of the Binding Theory to operate has given rise to considerable discussion within the Principles and Parameters framework (e.g., Belletti and Rizzi 1988). Chomsky (1992) discusses one case which has been cited as supporting the traditional view. Consider the examples in (3):

I said he bought the car that Bill drove   (3a)
Which car that Bill drove did I say he bought?   (3b)
Who said he bought which car that Bill drove?   (3c)

Principle C of the Binding Theory says that an r-expression (*Bill*) must be free everywhere (see *Generative Grammar: Principles and Parameters*). Thus, in (3a), *Bill* cannot be coindexed with *he* (i.e., cannot have *he* as an antecedent). In (3b), the phrase *which car that Bill drove* has been moved into a position in which *he* no longer c-commands *Bill*, and coindexing of *he* and *Bill* is possible. Finally, in (3c), at S-structure the configuration correctly predicts that coindexing is not possible—such coindexing would lead to *Bill* being bound by *he*. Crucially, however, at LF the phrase *which car that Bill drove* is assumed to move into an operator position, as in (4a), ultimately yielding the paired question interpretation along the lines of (4b):

[Which car that Bill drove$_i$ [Who$_j$]][e$_j$ said he bought e$_i$]   (4a)
(Who is the x, x a person, and which is the y, y a car that Bill drove)(x said he bought y)   (4b)

In (4a), *Bill* is no longer c-commanded by *he*, so coindexing ought to be possible if Principle C operates at LF; coindexing is not possible, so Condition C does not operate at LF.

In response, as Chomsky notes, the assumption in (4a) that LF-movement of *which car that Bill drove* moves the whole *wh*-phrase may not be correct. As an alternative, consider the possibility of extracting just

the *wh*-word by LF-movement, giving the outline representation in (5) at LF:

[which$_i$ [who$_j$]](e$_j$ said that he bought [e$_i$ car that Bill drove])   (5)

In (5), *Bill* is again c-commanded by *he*, so coindexing of these items would lead to a Principle C violation at LF. From the point of view of this analysis, then, Principle C could be construed as an LF-condition. On the assumption that the analysis can be defended, this becomes a small part of the process of migrating the Binding Theory to LF.

In fact, there is what is plausibly a more direct pointer to the same conclusion in May (1991). He considers examples such as (6):

John introduced himself to everyone that Bill did   (6)

This sentence is ambiguous, but the interpretation we are concerned with here is that in which John and Bill both introduce themselves to exactly the same set of people (the other interpretation is that both John and Bill introduce John to exactly the same set of people). This interpretation appears to require that *himself* takes both *John* and *Bill* as antecedents, as is indicated in (7):

John$_i$ introduced himself$_{i,j}$ to everyone that Bill$_j$ did   (7)

The difficulty here is that, whereas *John* c-commands *himself* at S-structure, *Bill* does not, and it is unclear how to make Principle A of the Binding Theory work for this example. Note now that in the derivation of an appropriate LF for (7), it will be necessary to raise the quantifier phrase *everyone that Bill did* into an operator position and to reconstruct the VP into the position of *did*. The first of these operations yields (8a) and the second (8b):

[everyone that Bill did]$_k$ [John introduced himself to e$_k$]   (8a)
[everyone that Bill introduced himself to e$_k$]$_k$[John introduced himself to e$_k$]   (8b)

It is easy now to see that this process has introduced two tokens of *himself* into the representation, in positions which permit one to be bound by *Bill* and the other by *John*. Crucially, this account requires the Binding Theory to operate at LF.

It is important to be clear that the above arguments only serve to establish that the level of operation of the Binding Theory is not finalized absolutely. It would be quite mistaken to suppose that they convincingly establish that it applies at LF. Further, note that there is an additional layer of the MP which is not touched by the above. Ideally, the principles of the Binding Theory will themselves be reducible to properties of the interface; nothing we have said here engages this question.

The theory of structural Case will be revisited in the next section, but something should first be said about the remaining intermediate level, D-structure, so as to begin to develop a view on derivations. D-structure is construed as a configurational representation of the selectional properties of the lexical items appearing in a structure constructed in accordance with the principles of X-bar Theory (see *Generative Grammar: Principles and Parameters*; *X-bar Syntax*). Speaking somewhat metaphorically, a D-structure is 'created' by simultaneously ensuring that the appropriate lexical properties are satisfied and that the resulting structure also satisfies X-bar Theory. From the MP perspective, there are at least two ways in which this conception might be challenged. First, the notion of an autonomous X-bar Theory is clearly at odds with the spirit of the MP and this will be considered later in this article. Secondly, the idea that lexical items come together simultaneously into a single structure is not the only conceivable way to build representations; an alternative whereby substructures are built up and progressively combined is at least intelligible.

The assault on simultaneity is somewhat oblique. Alongside the observation that structures could be built up piecemeal, Chomsky (1992) notes that there are well-known problems for the traditional view of D-structure. These are provided by complex adjectival constructions such as (9):

A linguist is difficult to employ （9）

In (9), *employ* is a transitive verb and *a linguist* is construed as its logical object. It would be natural, then, to suggest that *employ* projects into a transitive VP with *a linguist* occupying an appropriate position to be θ-marked by the verb and subsequently moving to clause-initial position. Similar consideration of the lexical properties of *difficult* will, it is supposed, ensure that it projects into an appropriate configuration and the 'Extended Projection Principle' (see *Generative Grammar: Principles and Parameters*) will guarantee that there is a subject position which can be filled by pleonastic *it* (*it is difficult to employ a linguist*) or by moving the phrase *a linguist* to this position. Unfortunately, there are at least two problems with this intuitively attractive account. First, the supposed movement of *a linguist* to produce (9) is not motivated; the direct object position of *employ* is a Case-marked position, unlike the direct object position of a passive verb form or the subject of an infinitival complement of a raising verb. Thus, the movement would be entirely stipulative. Secondly, there is evidence from *wh*-movement that complex adjectivals contain an empty operator binding a variable in the position we are considering. That is, an appropriate structure for (9) is (10):

A linguist is difficult [OP$_i$[PRO to employ e$_i$]]   （10）

In (10) though, *a linguist* does not occupy a θ-position (pleonastic *it* can also occur in this position), and the characterization of D-structure as the level at which θ-marked arguments appear in appropriate positions

is seriously questioned. Accordingly, an alternative where *a linguist* is integrated into the structure as the derivation proceeds should at least be seriously considered. Again, it is important to be clear that this observation, while casting doubt on the integrity of D-structure, can hardly constitute the last word on the topic.

The arguments that have been briefly considered here are intended to establish the possibility that the weighty empirical arguments for the necessity of D- and S-structure are spurious. A major task for the MP is to demonstrate that the descriptive and explanatory advantages associated with these levels can be maintained in a system which does not contain them.

2. Bare Phrase Structure

As noted above, in Principles and Parameters Theory the principles of X-bar Theory are stipulated and D-structures are built on the schematic structures which the theory provides. Chomsky (1994, 1995) offers an alternative.

Returning to (2), it should be noted that a derivation commences by consulting the lexicon. Suppose that this process of consultation amounts to no more than a random selection of items. Such a selection (suppressing certain complexities) is referred to as a numeration. A derivation is construed as a computation which maps a numeration N into a pair consisting of a PF(π) and an LF(λ). In general, the computational system for human language C_{HL} is a function mapping numerations into such pairs:

$$C_{HL}(N) = (\pi, \lambda) \qquad (11)$$

At some point in this process the operation SPELL-OUT occurs, but it needs to be further considered how complex syntactic objects are constructed from the numeration if these are not produced by simultaneously projecting lexical items into an X-bar schema. The simplest conception is that the derivation proceeds by selecting an item from the numeration. Thus, alongside SPELL-OUT can be postulated SELECT. It is immediately apparent that something akin to this will be necessary in any intelligible, compositional theory. Suppose that nothing happens beyond this selection process: LF will be presented with a non-integrated set of lexical items, which it will not be able to interpret. So, on the basis of fundamental considerations, there must be a second operation of merger. MERGE takes two syntactic objects (one or both of which may be the result of previous operations of MERGE) and creates a single object from them. Note that MERGE, just like SELECT, readily passes the test of being ultimately justified in terms of interface conditions. If there is no selection, there will be nothing to interpret; if there is no merger, the objects presented to the interfaces will be non-interpretable.,

Recall that items in the numeration are here supposed simply to be sets of features. Chomsky (1995) formulates the 'Inclusiveness Condition,' which says that the output of syntactic operations must not extend the vocabulary of the input(s). This, he refers to as a 'natural condition' and one consequence is that the complex objects presented to the interfaces can be nothing more than rearrangements of (subsets of) lexical features. A more revealing consequence is that the vocabulary of bar-levels, long familiar in the literature on X-bar Theory, becomes illegitimate. Suppose, then, that SELECT has selected two objects from the enumeration, α and β. It constructs an object from α and β. What is this object? The most basic notion of composition is the bringing together of two objects into a set, so it is proposed that the set $\{\alpha, \beta\}$ is part of this object, with α and β regarded as its constituents. However, conditions operative at the LF interface require that something more is necessary; specifically, complex nominal expressions are interpreted differently to complex verbal expressions, so LF must have access to the 'character' of a complex object. Suppose that this is indicated in the complex object by giving it a label γ; the result of merging α and β is thus the object $\{\gamma, \{\alpha, \beta\}\}$. At this point the inclusiveness condition comes into play, since γ cannot extend α and β. Candidates for the identity of γ satisfying this requirement are: (a) the intersection of α and β; (b) the union of α and β; and, (c) either α or β. Straightforward considerations rule out (a); the intersection could well be empty. Similarly (b) is implausible as the union of α and β will typically contain contradictorily specified features. This leaves (c) and the conclusion that the result of a simple merger of α and β is either $\{\alpha, \{\alpha, \beta\}\}$ or $\{\beta, \{\alpha, \beta\}\}$. Now, it should be immediately apparent from these possibilities that when two constituents come together to form a complex object, one of them functions as the head of the complex object and projects, one of the fundamental principles of X-bar Theory. In the case of $\{\alpha, \{\alpha, \beta\}\}$, α projects and is the head of the complex object; for $\{\beta, \{\alpha, \beta\}\}$, β has this role. With this much elementary set theory, supplemented by the 'natural' inclusiveness condition, it is possible to extend this simple system to allow familiar definitions of complement and specifier; an extension to include ordered sets is sufficient to deal with adjunction structures. Levels of projection are, of course, not available in the notation, but can be easily defined relationally; thus X is a maximal projection of α if α is the label of X and not the label of any object resulting from merging X, and X is a minimal projection of α if X = α and α is not a projection at all. Any other projection of α is an X'. At this point, it might be useful to compare a rather traditional way of representing clause structure with the results of applying this notational system. Consider (12) with the familiar representation in (13):

The dog will run   (12)

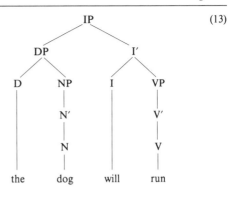

(13)

The system introduced above has no place for the various node labels and bar levels appearing in (13). Continuing to use tree notation first and adopting the convention that **X** is an abbreviation for the set of features corresponding to X, (13) will be replaced by (14):

(14)

Using the set-theoretic representation, which Chomsky views as untainted by nonminimalist terminology, the corresponding representation will be (15):

$\{$**will**, $\{\{$**the**, $\{$**the**, **dog**$\}\}$, $\{$**will**, $\{$**will**, **run**$\}\}\}\}$ (15)

Particularly noteworthy in (14) and (15) is the fact that there are no nonbranching configurations corresponding to the relation between, say *the* and D in (13); all the features of a lexical item are taken forward in the derivation. Additionally, all branching is binary, this being a consequence of the status of MERGE as a binary operation. Summarizing a rather fuller version of the above, Chomsky (1995: 249) says: 'We thus have the outlines of a "bare phrase structure" theory that derives fairly strictly from natural minimalist principles.'

More will be said about bare phrase structure in the final section, but before this the other major component of C_{HL}, MOVE, will be introduced.

3. Local Relations

In Sect. 1, Case Theory was mentioned as a module of Principles and Parameters Theory which can be used to motivate the level of S-structure. Freidin, elsewhere in this volume, outlines the central components of Case Theory (see *Generative Grammar: Principles and Parameters*); for the purposes of this article, consider the following sub-part of the theory (for English):

(a) Objective Case is assigned by a transitive verb to its complement.
(b) Nominative Case is assigned by a finite I to its specifier.
(c) Exceptionally, objective Case is assigned across a maximal projection boundary in exceptional case marking (ECM) constructions.

It could be viewed as suspicious that the core structural Cases are assigned under different relations, albeit local ones, but this suspicion becomes urgent when noting the phenomenon of ECM, illustrated in the following examples:

John believes [him to work hard]   (16a)
John considers [him a fool]   (16b)

In (16a), the standard account holds that *him* is assigned objective Case exceptionally by *believes*, the exceptionality being due to the need to perhaps delete a CP-boundary and to regard IP as transparent to external government. A similar maneuver is necessary for (16b), where the Small Clause, *him a fool*, whatever its categorial status, must also be transparent to external government. Cases such as these, as well as extending the relation of government to a nonlocal relation, raise a range of complex questions about the barrier status of various maximal projections. These questions were the focus of Chomsky (1986) and much of the theoretical literature during the next few years. The problem arrived at can be simply stated: the unified concept of Case is being treated in a nonunified way in Principles and Parameters Theory. The challenge is to produce a unified account, and it is the mechanism of nominative Case assignment which provides the basis for such an account within the MP.

The concepts enabling the development of a unified theory of Case emerged from Pollock's (1989) influential comparative study of English and French. Of course, this study was conducted before the emergence of the MP, and assumes a level of D-structure. For this discussion, then, the concerns of Sect. 1 are set aside, and Pollock's own usage is followed. For finite verbs, Pollock reiterates well-known observations concerning the placement of such verbs with respect to negation and VP-initial adverbs, which lead to the conclusion that lexical verbs raise to I in French but not in English (such raising in English is restricted to the auxiliaries *have* and *be*). Examples justifying this claim involving adverbs appear in (17):

Jean embrasse souvent Marie   (17a)
*John kisses often Mary   (17b)
John often kisses Mary   (17c)
*Jean souvent embrasse Marie   (17d)

To account for the distribution in (17), along with a range of related observations, Pollock assumes that clauses in both English and French have the schematic D-structure in (18):

$$[_{IP} \text{ NP} - \text{I} - (\text{NEG}) - (\text{ADV}) - [_{VP} \text{ V} - ....]]$$ (18)

If V raises to I in such structures, this will produce the orders V-NEG and V-ADV found in French. For English, where the V remains *in situ* the attested orders NEG-V and ADV-V will be obtained.

Turning to infinitive clauses, Pollock notes that French lexical verbs do not raise to a pre-NEG position:

Ne pas sembler heureux est une condition ...   (19a)
*Ne sembler pas heureux est une condition ...   (19b)

At this point, the appropriate generalization would appear to be that French infinitival lexical verbs, like finite lexical verbs in English, remain *in situ*. However, consideration of collocations of French infinitives with adverbs shows that this is incorrect:

Souvent paraître triste ...   (20a)
Paraître souvent triste ...   (20b)

It seems, then, that French lexical infinitives can (optionally) be raised, but the position to which they are raised cannot be I—if it were, they would also appear before negation, but (19) shows that this is not possible.

Pollock's response to these observations is to suggest that I, traditionally viewed as the locus of Tense and Agreement features, should be split so that each of these elements can head its own projection. The additional head position which is thereby available can then be the target of verb raising in (20). Thus, the proposal in (18) is replaced by (21):

$$[_{TP} \text{ NP} - \text{T} - (\text{NEG}) - [_{AgrP} \text{ Agr} - (\text{ADV}) - [_{VP} \text{ V} - ...]]]$$ (21)

Given this level of articulation, it can now be maintained that French lexical nonfinite verbs can raise to Agr but not to T and this accounts for the pattern in (19) and (20).

Commenting on Pollock's account, Chomsky (1989) acknowledges the case for splitting I in some way. However, he takes issue with Pollock's claim that T is higher than Agr in the structure. This is principally on the grounds of Agr being construed as the locus of subject agreement features and therefore needing to be in a local relationship with the subject. However, a head position for French infinitive verbs to target in examples like (20b) is still necessary. Acknowledging that many languages display overt object agreement leads Chomsky to suggest that clause structure should contain two agreement heads (AgrS and AgrO). Additionally, following Koopman and Sportiche (1991), he maintains that the position of the subject at D-structure should be within the projection of its θ-marking head, the V. The available position is the specifier position of VP, and the canonical D-structure for clauses (omitting intervening elements such as negation and the system of C-projections) is as in (22):

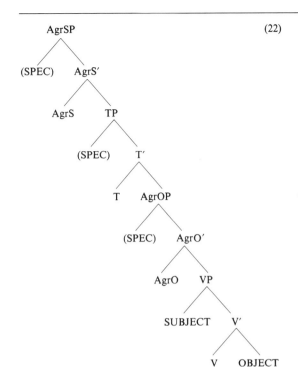

(22)

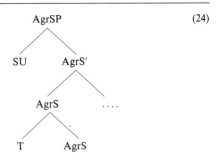

(24)

To this point, apart from the subject originating in VP, the analysis is fairly traditional. However, suppose further that the object also raises to the specifier position of AgrO. This gives (25), which structurally parallels (24):

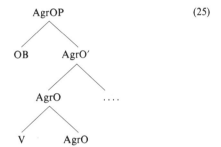

(25)

In this schema, T, if finite, is associated with nominative Case and V, if transitive, with objective Case. Suppose, then, that T raises to AgrS and V raises to AgrO, both of these movements producing 'Case-Agreement complexes' as indicated in (23):

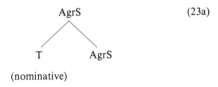

(23a)

(nominative)

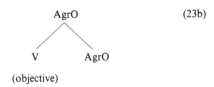

(23b)

(objective)

Then assume that the subject raises to the specifier position of AgrS, yielding the partial configuration in (24):

It was required that a unified theory of Case be found, and that this should be consistent with the view that all grammatically relevant relations should be local. Looking at (24) and (25), it can be seen immediately that the agreement relationships between the subject and AgrS on the one hand, and the object and AgrO on the other, are specifier-head relationships. What is not so clear is the nature of the relationships between the subject and T, and between the object and V, the relationships which are fundamental to the theory of Case. Transparently, these are not specifier-head relations, as T is not the head of the projection of which the subject is the specifier and V is not the head of the projection of which the object is the specifier.

Chomsky (1992) develops a fairly complex set of definitions for various domains of a head. Unfortunately there is not the space to go into this in detail here, but suffice it to say that among these domains is the 'complement domain' (which corresponds to the traditional notion of complement) and the 'checking domain.' This latter contains a residue of head-related elements, including the specifier. Crucially, however, it is defined for T and V in (24) and (25) so as to include the subject and the object respectively. Thus, the subject in (24) is in the checking domain of both AgrS and T, and the object in (25) is in the checking domain of both AgrO and V. Maintaining that one way for α to be in a local relation with β is to be in the latter's checking domain, the mechanisms outlined here guarantee that both agreement and Case (nominative and objective) are construed as local relations.

ECM constructions such as those in (16a) will now be considered within this framework. If it is supposed that the embedded subject enters the derivation in the specifier position of the lower VP, then raising it to the specifier of the embedded AgrSP will not be sufficient to satisfy its Case requirements. This is because the embedded T is nonfinite and is not associated with either nominative or objective Case. Therefore, the embedded subject has to be raised further to the specifier position in the matrix AgrOP. Here it is associated with objective Case, as it is now in the checking domain of the matrix verb, which has itself been raised to AgrO. It can thus be concluded that the assumptions developed here achieve the goal of articulating a unified theory of Case, where the relevant relations are always local in the defined sense.

There remain two points to make before closing this section. The first is the obvious one that the movements postulated above as applying to (22) might be viewed as somewhat fanciful, particularly from the perspective of English. Recall Pollock's initial observation that lexical verbs in English, unlike in French, do not raise out of the VP. Yet the mechanisms described previously clearly depend upon V raising to AgrO so as to create the appropriate complex of Case and Agreement. Furthermore, if V does not raise in English, it follows that the object does not raise either; if the object were to raise without V-raising, this would give the word-order SOV.

The second point can be linked to the first. The process of raising V to I in the Principles and Parameters framework was construed as moving the verb to a position where its Tense and Agreement morphology was independently generated. Thus, in a French sentence like (26), the idea was that the I position not only hosted features encoding 1st Person Plural and Non-Past, but also a representation of the suffix *-ons*:

> Nous aimons des chiens   (26)

Before verb raising, the structure of (26) would be (27):

> [$_{IP}$ Nous [$_I$-ons] [$_{VP}$ aime- des chiens]]   (27)

Supposing that part of the motivation for raising is that the verb must join its affix, else the affix remains unattached, then the situation in English, which appears to lack this sort of verb raising, becomes difficult to account for. It might be supposed that the affix lowers to the verb position in English, but lowering operations are viewed with considerable suspicion, since they create a chain in which the moved item does not c-command its trace. Chomsky (1989), mindful of this consequence, suggested that in English the affix does indeed lower in the overt syntax, but the

verb plus its affix subsequently raise non-overtly in the mapping to LF, precisely to avoid postulating illformed chains. However, a lowering followed by a raising, the function of the latter being to annul partly the effects of the former, is hardly a comfortable option.

An alternative construal is possible, and is adopted in the MP. For simplicity, (26) will again be used as the example, with the supposition that there is a unified I-constituent to illustrate this. If verbs do not enter derivations lacking their affixes, but instead are taken from a numeration fully inflected then, in (27), in the V position, there will be a collection of features representing the pronunciation of *aimons* along with abstract morphological features ([1 Plural], [−Past], [objective Case]), syntactic categorial features ([−n], [+v]) and semantic features. Suppose also that inflexions do not appear in I, although abstract features do. Thus, in the I position in (27), there will be no representation of *-ons*, but there will be features such as [+Plural] and [−Past].

As was mentioned in Sect. 1, Full Interpretation requires that features which are not interpretable at one of the interfaces should not be presented to that interface in a well-formed derivation. Among the features of *aimons*, those concerning its pronunciation will be dealt with by SPELL-OUT. However, among its abstract morphological features, there are some ([1 Plural], [objective Case]) which are arguably not interpretable at LF. Therefore, they too must be removed in a well-formed derivation. Raising of the verb to I places the verb in the checking domain of I, and the checking of features in an appropriate checking domain can now be identified with the removal of those features from the derivation. To put the contrast between Principles and Parameters Theory and the MP simply: in the former V raises to I to be united with its inflexions; in the latter V raises to I to check its features.

Of course, it is intended that these considerations will extend to the more articulated structure in (22). In that structure, the verb raises successively to AgrO, T, and AgrS, where it checks in turn its object agreement features, its tense features and its subject agreement features. In a simple transitive clause, the direct object will include the feature [objective Case], and the subject the feature [nominative Case]. These too are checked by the object moving to the specifier of AgrO, within the checking domain of the raised verb, and the subject moving to the specifier of AgrS, within the checking domain of the raised T.

Returning now to English, it can be seen that there is no longer any necessity to suppose that English verbs raise to I (equivalently, to AgrO, T, and AgrS) overtly, since they enter the derivation appropriately inflected. However, they still need to check their agreement features, and the obvious proposal to make is that this checking can take place either before SPELL-

OUT, as in French, in which case the results of verb raising are reflected at PF or after SPELL-OUT, as in English, in which case, its results are not apparent at PF. The urgent question now is: why do French and English behave differently in this respect. Chomsky (1992) proposes that those features which must be checked by LF in order to avoid a violation of Full Interpretation should be regarded as either 'strong' or 'weak.' He then extends the metaphor so that 'strong' means 'visible at PF' whereas 'weak' means 'invisible at PF.' The idea is that any abstract morphological feature which is visible at PF and is presented to PF will lead to an illformed derivation. Accordingly, 'strong' features must be eliminated before SPELL-OUT, i.e., as part of the overt syntax (Chapter 4 of Chomsky (1995) contains a different attempt to come to terms with this contrast between 'strong' and 'weak'—there Chomsky assumes that the mapping from a numeration to LF is 'uniform' and this entails that it cannot be stipulated that certain results need to be achieved before SPELL-OUT). In the original problem being discussed here, it it merely necessary to note that agreement features are 'strong' in French, but 'weak' in English. This accounts for why overt verb raising is found in French, but does not yet account for the nonovert verb raising found in English. This latter point will be considered further in the next section.

Taking the idea of the above paragraph to (22), it can readily be seen how to generalize it; Case features can be 'strong' or 'weak' in the same way as agreement features. Strong nominative Case features will require a subject to raise overtly, before SPELL-OUT; strong objective Case features will impose a similar condition on an object. The contrast between 'strong' and 'weak' morphological features is the source of linguistic variation in the MP, and it is easy to see how major word-order differences can be approached from this perspective (for relevant discussion, see Marantz 1995). Finally, it can now be seen what has become of PPT's Case Filter; its consequences are dealt with by requiring Case features to be checked before an expression arrives at the interfaces, since they are not interpretable there. There is no 'level' at which they are checked, such as S-structure, and the fact that they must be checked is due to Full Interpretation being operative at the interfaces.

4. Movement and Principles of Economy

In this section the notion of a derivation is now considered in more general terms. In connection with (22), and supposing that there is no autonomous X-bar module in the theory, an important question arises. To grasp the nature of this, note that (22) contains two empty positions into which phrases will move in the course of a derivation. These are the specifier of AgrS, which will receive the subject, and the specifier of AgrO, which will receive the object (the specifier of

T is ignored in this discussion). According to X-bar Theory, there is nothing mysterious about these positions: they are simply there as empty slots as a consequence of every head projecting a specifier position. But if X-bar Theory is no longer available, the question arises of where these positions come from. Starting in his 1994 paper, Chomsky has sought to develop an answer to this question.

The brief answer is that the process of movement itself creates the position. To see how this works, suppose that a derivation has proceeded to the point shown in the partial structure in (28) (again tree structures are used for clarity of exposition along with the convention that bold expressions abbreviate sets of features):

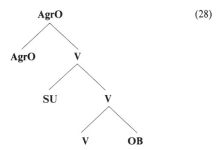

(28)

Given a language in which the Case features of **OB** are 'strong,' these features must be checked before SPELL-OUT. One way to do this is to move **OB** at this point in the derivation. This is done by introducing another binary operation, MOVE, into $\mathcal{C}_{HL}$. MOVE (α, β) moves α and targets β so as to produce a new merged structure $\{\gamma, \{\alpha, \beta\}\}$. In the case in point, MOVE moves **OB** and targets the higher **AgrO** to produce $\{\gamma, \{\textbf{OB}, \textbf{AgrO}\}\}$, which could be represented as in (29) (where t_{OB} represents the trace of the moved phrase):

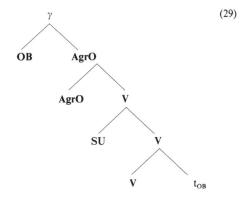

(29)

Thus, movement becomes a species of merger on this account. However, (29) is still incomplete as nothing has yet been said about the nature of the label of the new syntactic object γ. This should be **AgrO**, but there is nothing in the spare system adopted here which will guarantee this. In general, it is desirable to assert that in a movement configuration it is always the **target** which projects, a conclusion which was built directly into the X-bar principles responsible for (22).

Chomsky (1994, 1995) adopts the 'Chain Uniformity Condition' in (30) for dealing with the above dilemma:

> A chain is uniform with respect to phrase structure status (30)

It is easy to see how this deals with the present case. Suppose that **OB** projects in (29); then the chain (**OB**, t_{OB}) would violate (30), as t_{OB} is maximal in (29), but if $\gamma = $ **OB**, then the moved token of **OB** is non-maximal. Extension to other cases of movement introduces additional complexities, but ways of overcoming these have been developed.

Finally, in this connection, it can be seen that with one additional speculation, (30) itself may be motivated by properties of the LF interface. LF must be able to access lexical items and maximal projections—for example, nominal maximal projections are interpreted quite differently to verbal maximal projections. However, it is not clear that LF must be able to access intermediate projections. Suppose, then, that C_{HL} (and LF itself) is 'blind' to intermediate projections. If this were so and if **OB** projected in (29), the chain (**OB**, t_{OB}) would be uninterpretable at LF and a violation of Full Interpretation would result. Thus a further property of the X-bar system is derived within minimalist assumptions.

MOVE, unlike SELECT and MERGE, is not a necessary component of C_{HL} on conceptual grounds (Chomsky speculates that the appearance of movement operations in grammars is a consequence of the products of C_{HL} having to be 'externalized' at PF). Tokens of MOVE are 'costly,' and the final feature of the MP that will be considered here is the proposition that this cost is minimized, i.e., languages seek to minimize their divergence from perfectly designed systems, once due account is taken of conditions imposed by the interfaces.

The most approachable of the conditions governing the operation of MOVE is SHORTEST MOVE. Locality conditions on movement are well-known from earlier versions of generative grammar (cf. Travis (1984) on the Head Movement Constraint, and Rizzi (1990) on Relativized Minimality). To take just one example, consider the contrast in (31):

> It seems he is believed t to have won the race   (31a)
> *He seems it is believed t to have won the race   (31b)

In (31b), *he*, which must move to a suitable position to check its nominative Case features, cannot skip the embedded subject position in this movement, i.e., superraising is not possible (for more extensive discussion, see Marantz 1995).

In the previous section, the question of why English lexical verbs do not raise overtly was left unanswered. Unlike French verbs, they do not have to; but, surely, they could. A second economy principle, PROCRASTINATE, provides the answer here. According to this principle, nonovert movement is 'cheap,' this being linked to the fact that nonovert processes are going to be 'wired in' to C_{HL}, as there is no evidence for the child to determine their properties. From this perspective, the conclusion can rapidly be derived: if an item does not have to move overtly, it will not do so.

Lastly, GREED, subsumed under LAST RESORT in Chomsky (1995), where it is the focus of extended and complex discussion, seeks to link movement explicitly to the need for certain features to be checked. Since it is features, such as Case features and Agreement features which must be checked, minimalist prescription states that only the features needing to be checked will move. In fact, this cannot be maintained for overt syntax pre-SPELL-OUT, as should be clear from the overt movement of lexical items (sets of features) and phrases. Chomsky suggests that this 'generalized pied-piping' of whole lexical items may itself be reducible to properties of the PF-interface. To put it crudely, if only languages were not spoken, signed or externalized in some other way, all movement would consist of the movement of features into appropriate checking environments. Not surprisingly, Chomsky maintains that this ideal obtains in the post-SPELL-OUT part of the mapping to LF.

Overall, the shifting picture presented here can be summarized in the following terms. A derivation in C_{HL} is a mapping from a numeration N to a pair (π, λ). If π and λ satisfy Full Interpretation, the derivation converges (derivatively, it will converge at PF or LF). A nonconvergent derivation crashes (again, derivatively, at PF or LF). Thus, the notion of convergence is linked explicitly to conditions derived from the interfaces. Within the class of convergent derivations, economy conditions such as those briefly reviewed here determine which are optimal. For instance, (31b) above converges, but because SHORTEST MOVE would be violated in its derivation, it does not constitute a linguistic expression. The economy conditions emerge from the second type of external constraint on the design of C_{HL}, that it should be simple, economical, nonredundant, etc.

As pointed out at the beginning of this discussion, many problems remain to be adequately addressed within the MP. The reconstruction of the achievements of generative grammar within this new set of assumptions is a massive task, which has only just begun. Additionally, it would be misleading to suggest that 'minimalism' denotes much more than a *Geist* in its current formulations. Metaphors abound, and references to maneuvers as 'natural' or assumptions as the 'most simple' are not always backed up by detailed argument. Nonetheless, it is proving to be an exciting and thought-provoking approach to syntactic theory, the coherence of which will only be properly evaluated by pushing it to the limit.

Bibliography

Belletti A, Rizzi L 1988 Psych-verbs and θ-theory. *NLLT* **6**: 291-352
Chomsky N 1981 *Lectures on Government and Binding*. Foris, Dordrecht
Chomsky N 1986 *Barriers*. MIT Press, Cambridge, MA
Chomsky N 1989 Some notes on economy of derivation and representation. In: Laka I, Mahajan A (eds.) *Functional Heads and Clause Structure*. Department of Linguistics and Philosophy, MIT, Cambridge, MA (Repr. in: Chomsky N 1995 *The Minimalist Program*)
Chomsky N 1992 A minimalist program for linguistic theory. *MIT Occasional Papers in Linguistics, Vol. 1*. Department of Linguistics and Philosophy, MIT, Cambridge, MA (Repr. in: Chomsky N 1995 *The Minimalist Program*)
Chomsky N 1994 Bare phrase structure. *MIT Occasional Papers in Linguistics, Vol. 5*. Department of Linguistics and Philosophy, MIT, Cambridge, MA (Repr. in: Webelhuth G (ed.) 1995 *Government and Binding Theory and the Minimalist Program*. Blackwell, Oxford)
Chomsky N 1995 *The Minimalist Program*. MIT Press, Cambridge, MA
Koopman H, Sportiche D 1991 The position of subjects. *Lingua* **85**: 211-58
Marantz A 1995 The Minimalist Program. In: Webelhuth G (ed.) *Government and Binding Theory and the Minimalist Program*. Blackwell, Oxford
May R 1991 Syntax, semantics and logical form. In: Kasher A (ed.) *The Chomskyan Turn*. Blackwell, Oxford
Pollock J-Y 1989 Verb movement, Universal Grammar and the structure of IP. *LIn* **20**: 365–424
Rizzi L 1990 *Relativized Minimality*. MIT Press, Cambridge, MA
Travis L 1984 Parameters and the effects of word order variation (Doctoral dissertation, Massachusetts Institute of Technology)

Generative Grammar: Transformational Grammar

Stephen J. Harlow

Transformational grammar was developed in the mid-1950s by Noam Chomsky. Over the next two decades it became the dominant paradigm in syntactic theory and description and its descendant, government binding theory, is still one of the most influential current theories. Transformational grammar forms a wide-ranging theory, whose central tenets are the use of hypothetico-deductive methodology to construct formal models of certain aspects of human linguistic capabilities. Such models are called 'grammars' in the theory and are taken to be an encoding, in some form, of the native speaker's linguistic knowledge (or 'competence'). Much of the work of transformational grammar has consisted of constructing models of (fragments of) individual languages, but equally important has been the task of exploring and defining the properties which are required by such grammars to provide accurate and revealing accounts of the linguistic data under consideration. Such general properties are taken to form the content of 'linguistic theory' (also termed 'universal grammar') and therefore do not need to be stated in individual linguistic descriptions. While a grammar for an individual language is a representation of the linguistic knowledge of the native speaker of that language, linguistic theory represents the properties (possibly very abstract in nature) which constrain all languages and thus defines the notion 'possible human language.' The content of universal grammar is taken to be a characterization of the human language acquisition device—those antecedent conditions that make language acquisition possible and which constrain the learning space available to the child acquiring a native language. Transformational grammar has undergone significant evolution since its initial development and one of the slightly ironic consequences of the pursuit of the goals listed above is that transformations themselves have come increasingly to play a less and less significant role in the theory. This article traces that development.

1. Early Transformational Grammar

Transformations, from which the theory derives its name, were developed during the 1950s by Zellig Harris and Noam Chomsky. The central idea underlying the concept of transformation was that of capturing systematic relationships between different syntactic representations. However, because of fundamental differences in the metalinguistic goals of Harris and Chomsky, the role played by transformations in the work of the two and the consequences of their introduction also were radically different.

1.1 Harris on Transformations

For Harris, transformations offered a way of allowing structural linguistics to transcend the limits of the sentence and offer a method of approaching discourse-level structures. For Harris, transformations are a device that extends the descriptive linguistic techniques of segmentation and classification to texts larger than a single sentence. They allow the linguist to establish equivalences between sequences of words in a text which would otherwise resist analysis. For example, suppose that a text contains the sentences:

He played the cello. (1)

The cello was played by Casals. (2)

but no sentences of the form:

Casals played the cello. (3)

The cello was played by him. (4)

In other words, there are no environments which show that *Casals* and *he/him* are grammatically equivalent (i.e., belong to the same grammatical category).

If, however, the text contains active/passive sentence pairs:

He plays the guitar. (5)

The guitar was played by him. (6)

an equivalence can be established between the two sentence types, as follows:

$$N_x V N_y \leftrightarrow N_y \text{ was } V ed \text{ by } N_x \qquad (7)$$

Assuming that *He*, *him*, *Casals*, and *the`guitar* belong to the category *N*, and that *played* is a member of the category *V*, (7) captures the relationship between the two; and between all other pairs of sentences possessing the same structure. With the equivalence given in (7) above, 'we can show that all the environments of *Casals* are equivalent to all those of *he*; and this in turn can make other equivalences discoverable textually' (Harris 1952: 129).

1.2 Chomsky on Transformations

For Chomsky, on the other hand, transformations formed part of a program directed at characterizing the nature and properties of the human language faculty. Chomsky states:

> The development of these ideas that I would like to report on briefly, however, follows a somewhat different course. It begins by questioning the adequacy of a certain view of the nature of linguistic theory that has dominated much recent work, and it attempts to reformulate the goals of linguistic theory in such a way that questions of a rather different nature are raised. And finally, it attempts to show that the concept of grammatical transformation, in something like Harris' sense, but with certain differences, is essential to answering these questions.
>
> (Chomsky 1964b: 212)

One major difference between Chomsky's and Harris's applications of transformations was the nature of the representations between which a transformational mapping held. For Harris, the kinds of relationships captured by transformations were essentially those

which in terminology developed later were called 'surface structure' relationships (Chomsky 1965a). That is to say, the mappings defined by transformations were limited to those which could be expressed in terms of the categories and linear order of the actually occurring words/morphemes in a sentence. For Chomsky, no such restriction was applicable. This is apparent in one of Chomsky's earliest and most well-known transformational analyses: that of the English auxiliary system. The abstractness permitted by Chomsky's conception of transformations allowed him to propose an elegant and simple analysis of the auxiliary system which, in the words of Newmeyer (1980: 24), '[...] probably did more to win supporters for Chomsky than all of his metatheoretical statements about discovery and evaluation procedures.' In *Syntactic Structures*, the book in which transformational grammar first became accessible to the linguistic community, Chomsky states:

> The study of these 'auxiliary verbs' turns out to be quite crucial in the development of English grammar. We shall see that their behaviour is very regular and quite simply describable when observed from a point of view that is quite different to that developed above. Though it appears to be quite complex if we attempt to incorporate these phrases directly into a [S, F] grammar [i.e. a phrase structure grammar].
>
> (Chomsky 1957: 38)

and proposes the following phrase structure rules:

(i) *Verb → Aux → V* [28]

(ii) *V → hit, take, walk, read, etc.*

(iii) *Aux → C (M) (have + en) (be + ing) (be + en)*

(iv) *M → will, can, may, shall, must*

(i) $C \to \begin{cases} S \text{ in the context } NP_{sing}^- \\ \emptyset \text{ in the context } NP_{pl}^- \\ past \end{cases}$ [29]

Rule [28iii] states that an *Aux* phrase must contain as its initial element the tense/agreement morpheme *C*, and that this initial element can be followed by zero or more of *M, have + en, be + ing, be + en* in that order. *M* can then take any of the forms in [28iv]. Chomsky (1975: 232–33) observes, however, that:

> the seqence of morphemes which results from an application of [28] is not in the correct order. Thus to complete the statement we give the following rule [which later became known as 'affix hopping']:
>
> (ii) Let *Af* stand for any of the affixes *past, S, Ø, en, ing*. [29]
>
> Let *v* stand for any *M* or *V*, or *have* or *be* (i.e., for any nonaffix in the phrase *Verb*). Then:
>
> $$Af + v \to v + Af \#$$
>
> where # is interpreted as word boundary.
>
> (iii) Replace + by # except in the context *v → Af*. Insert # initially and finally.

When the items S, $have + en$ and $be + ing$ in rule [28iii] are selected to give the string:

$$the + man + S + have + en + be + ing + read + the + book \quad (8)$$

and rule [29ii] is applied three times (first to $C + have$, then to $en + be$, and finally to $ing + read$), followed by the application of rule [29iii], the following is derived:

$$the \ \# \ man \ \# \ have + S \ \# \ be + en \ \# \ read + ing \ \# \ the \ \#$$
$$book \quad (9)$$

Chomsky's analysis thus depends upon an abstract structure in which the affixes of the auxiliary system do not appear in their 'surface' order. The question of what kind of syntactic representations could legitimately constitute the input and output of a transformation came to be one of the most significant issues in the development of transformational theory.

In Chomsky's interpretation of the notion, a transformation is a mapping which converts a sentence (= a string of words) with an associated constituent structure analysis (= a 'phrase marker'), defined by a set of phrase-structure rules, into a new sentence with a 'derived constituent structure.' A transformation consists of a 'structural analysis' (often also called a 'structural description,' and abbreviated to SD), which specifies the sequence of categories into which a phrase marker must be analyzable for the transformation to apply to it, and a 'structural change,' which specifies the changes effected on the input phrase marker by the transformation. For example, the passive transformation is given by Chomsky (1957: 112) in the following form:

Structural analysis: (10)
$$NP - Aux - V - NP$$
Structural change:
$$X_1 - X_2 - X_3 - X_4 \rightarrow X_4 - X_2 + be + en - X_3 - by + X_1$$

(An alternative notation, which merges the structural analysis and structural change into a single statement of the form:

$$NP_1 - Aux - V - NP_2$$
$$\rightarrow NP_2 - Aux + be + en - V - by + NP_1$$

was also commonly used in later transformational work.)

The structural analysis specifies that for the transformation to apply to a string, the phrase marker associated with that string must be analyzable into a sequence of $NP - Aux - V - NP$. In the structural change, the variables $X_1 - X_4$ identify the four categories listed in the structural analysis and the string to the right of the arrow defines the mapping effected by the transformation: the relative positions of the two NPs are interchanged, the morpheme by is adjoined to the left of X_1 in its new position and the morphemes be and en are adjoined to the left of X_2 ($= Aux$). Each transformation is thus the composition of a number of more elementary operations, which include deletion, substitution of one element for another, adjunction,

and permutation. For example, Chomsky (1965b: 120) specifies the operation of the passive transformation in terms of the following 'elementary transformation,' which details the operations performed by the rule:

$$tp(Y_1; Y_1, \ldots, Y_4) = Y_4 \quad (11)$$
[substitute Y_4 for Y_1]
$$tp(Y_1, Y_2; Y_2, Y_3, Y_4) = Y_2 \hat{\ } be \hat{\ } en$$
[adjoin be and en to the right of Y_2]
$$tp(Y_1, Y_2, Y_3; Y_3, Y_4) = Y_3$$
[leave Y_3 unchanged (identity)]
$$tp(Y_1, Y_2, Y_3, Y_4; Y_1) = b\hat{e} \ Y_1$$
[adjoin be to left of Y_1]
$$tp(Y_1, \ldots, Y_n; Y_n, \ldots, Y_r) = Y_n \text{ for all } n \leqslant r \neq 4$$
[identity]

This notation identifies each term in the structural description of the transformation by successively splitting the structural description into two substrings (indicated in (11) by the semicolon), one of which terminates with that item and the other of which begins with it. For each such item, the elementary transformation specifies what operation is performed on it.

As stated above, Chomsky's motivation for the introduction of transformations was radically different from that of Harris. Chomsky had established a hierarchy of language types, which could be used to model the properties of human languages. Each of the languages on the Chomsky hierarchy is defined in terms of the possible sequences of symbols it admits. Chomsky presented a proof that English possesses properties which mean that it cannot be analyzed in terms of the most restricted type of language on the hierarchy: 'finite state languages.' He also argued that any attempt to describe the syntactic properties of English in terms of the kind of devices available for characterizing the next weakest language type on the hierarchy ('phrase structure languages') leads to the loss of generalizations and greater complexity. The simple and elegant analysis of the English auxiliary system or of the passive outlined above, for instance, which require the capacity to rearrange the order of elements in a string cannot be accomplished within the limits of these more restricted grammatical systems. Chomsky concludes (1957: 44) 'By further study of the limitations of phrase structure grammars with respect to English we can show quite conclusively that these grammars will be so hopelessly complex that they will be without interest unless we incorporate such rules [i.e., transformations].' (It is, however, important to note that Chomsky did not *prove* that English could not be analyzed by phrase structure grammars at all. Rather, he argued that any such analysis would be unacceptably complex and unrevealing. Indeed, later developments in phrase structure grammars in the 1980s demonstrated that even this assertion is too strong.)

A grammar for Chomsky is a device which defines the language under investigation via a system of rules.

In the earliest stages of transformational grammar (e.g., *Syntactic Structures*), the grammar consisted of three sets of rules:

> Phrase structure rules (12)
> Transformations
> Morphophonemic rules

As seen above, the phrase structure rules defined the constituent structures which form the input to the transformational component. The morphophonemic rules are responsible for ensuring, for example, that *take + en* is realized as *took*.

1.3 Subtypes of Transformations

Transformations in the early period fell into two categories, 'singulary' transformations, whose domain consisted of a single sentence, and 'generalized' (or 'double-based') transformations, with a structural description containing reference to more than one sentence. All the examples mentioned so far have been of singulary transformations. An example of a generalized transformation is the rule for coordination (Chomsky 1957: 113):

> Structural analysis: of S_1: $Z - X - W$ (13)
>   of S_2: $Z - X - W$

where X is a minimal element (e.g., *NP*, *VP*, etc.) and Z, W are segments of terminal strings.

> Structural change:
> $(X_1 - X_2 - X_3; X_4 - X_5 - X_6) \rightarrow (X_1 - X_2 + and + X_5 - X_6)$

For example:

> (Yesterday – John – left home; Yesterday – Sam – left home) → (Yesterday – John – and + Sam – left home), where *John* and *Sam* are both instances of NP.

A further major class of generalized transformations were those that embedded one sentence in another. Chomsky (1964b) lists 19 such transformations, of which the following are representative examples:

> Nominalization (14)

> Structural analysis: S_1: $T, it + \varphi, VP$
> S_2: NP, C, VP_1

> Structural change:
> $X_4 + S$ or φ replaces X_1; $ing + X_6$ replaces X_2

For example:

$$\left\{ \begin{array}{llll} T & - it + C - be + a + great + surprise \\ X1 & X2 \qquad X3 \\ John - C & - prove + the + theorem \\ X4 & X5 \qquad X6 \end{array} \right\}$$

$\rightarrow John + S - ing + prove + the + theorem - C - be + a + great + surprise$

giving 'John's proving the theorem was/is a great surprise.'

> Complement (15)

Structural analysis: S_1: $X, V_T, Comp, NP$
                     S_2: $NP, Aux, be, Pred$

Condition: X_2 is a member of the class of verbs containing *consider*, *believe*, ...

Structural change: X_5 replaces X_4; X_8 replaces X_3

For example:

$$\left\{ \begin{array}{llll} They + C & - consider - Comp - the + assistant \\ X_1 & X_2 \qquad\quad X_3 \qquad\quad X_4 \\ the + assistant - C & - be \quad - qualified \\ X_5 & X_6 \qquad\quad X_7 \qquad X_8 \end{array} \right\}$$

$\rightarrow They + C - consider - qualified - the + assistant$

Following the application of an obligatory transformation which permutes the last two factors in the derived phrase marker, this gives *They consider the assistant qualified*.

This class of generalized transformation exemplified by (15) formed the locus of recursion in early transformational grammar, and was thus the mechanism by which grammars make available an infinite set of sentences from finite resources.

1.4 Rule Ordering

Transformations, in principle, could be ordered arbitrarily relative to one another (i.e., they were extrinsically, rather than intrinsically ordered). For example, the derivation of an interrogative sentence such as *Did John eat an apple* involved the application of the (optional) question-formation transformation:

> Structural analysis: $\left\{ \begin{array}{l} NP - C - V \ldots \\ NP - C + M - \ldots \\ NP - C + have - \ldots \\ NP - C + be - \ldots \end{array} \right\}$ (16)

> Structural change: $X_1 - X_2 - X_3 \rightarrow X_2 - X_1 - X_3$

In other words, the tense formative C moves to the front of the sentence. The resulting derived P-marker requires the obligatory application of the word-boundary transformation [29iii] and the *do*-insertion transformation:

> *do*-insertion (17)

> Structural analysis: $\# - Af$

> Structural change: $X_1 - X_2 \rightarrow X_1 - do + X_2$

(Adjoin the word *do* to the left of any affix immediately preceded by a word boundary.)

The successive stages of the derivation would look like this:

Phrase structure:	John – C – eat – the apple
Question-formation:	C – John – eat – the apple
Word-boundary:	# C # John # eat # the apple
Do-insertion:	# do + C # John # eat # the apple

($do + C$ is then converted to *did* by a morphophonological rule).

In order to correctly derive the sentence *Who ate*

the apple, it was necessary to stipulate that T_w, the rule which moves an interrogative element such as *who* to sentence initial position, must apply *after* the question-formation transformation:

Phrase structure rules:	John – C – eat – the apple
Question-formation:	C – John – eat – the apple
T_w:	Who – C – eat – the apple
Word-boundary:	# Who # C eat # the apple

Do-insertion cannot apply to this structure, so 'affix hopping' [29ii] applies obligatorily instead:

Affix Hopping:	# Who # eat + C # the apple

Applying the two transformations in the reverse order would have the following effect:

Phrase structure rules:	John – C – eat – the apple
T_w:	Who – C – eat – the apple
Question-formation:	C – who – eat – the apple
Word-boundary:	# C # who # eat # the apple
Do-insertion:	# do + C # who # eat # the apple

This would give the ungrammatical *Did/does who eat the apple*. The only way in this analysis to avoid the generation of this ungrammatical string is to stipulate the ordering which gives the correct results.

In addition, a stipulation was required as to whether the application of a given transformation was either obligatory or optional. In the examples given above, the passive transformation is an instance of an optional rule, 'affix hopping,' [29ii] an instance of an obligatory rule—it must apply to any structure which meets the terms of its structural analysis. A sentence that is generated solely by the application of obligatory rules was termed a 'kernel' sentence. These corresponded to the class of simple, active, declarative sentences. Associated with the transformational derivation of each sentence was a representation called a 'T-marker,' which recorded which transformations had applied and in which order.

1.5 Transformations and Mental Processes

Although transformational grammar is intended as a model of the linguistic knowledge of the native speaker, it was not Chomsky's claim that the components of the theory were a model of the way the construction or comprehension of linguistic utterances is computed in the brain. Nonetheless, a number of experiments carried out in the 1950s and 1960s seemed to show that the transformational grammars developed for English during the early period did indeed make accurate predictions if taken as models of mental processing. In brief, these experiments seemed to show that there was a correlation between the number of transformations involved in the derivation of a sentence and the processing complexity associated with the sentence, measured in terms of some behavioral index such as response time—the greater the number of transformations involved, the greater the processing difficulty. For example, passive sentences take longer to process than their active counterparts and negative sentences take longer to process than their affirmative counterparts.

However, subsequent studies and a more mature assessment of the results of these experiments have shown that those experiments which seemed to show a positive correlation between transformational complexity and processing load did so because of a failure to control for other variables. It is well attested that processing load increases with sentence length. In the case of passive sentences, for example, *Albert was eaten by a lion* is two words longer than *A lion ate Albert*. Once such factors as this were controlled for, it became apparent that the derivational complexity hypothesis could not be maintained. It is universally agreed that the relationship between the form of a transformational grammar and the manner in which it is implemented in the brain is much more abstract and indirect than these early experiments suggested. It is therefore important to note that when linguists talk of a grammar 'generating' a set of sentences, there is no implication in the use of the term that the grammar is a model of human sentence production (see Carroll and Bever 1976).

2. The 'Standard Theory'

As Chomsky comments (1975: 23), 'The theory of transformations developed in *The Logical Structure of Linguistic Theory* was far too unrestricted. It seems that there are much narrower conditions that determine the applicability of transformations and the kinds of mapping that they can perform.' The subsequent development of transformational grammar can be seen as a progressive transfer of many of the functions originally assigned to transformations to other components of the grammar.

There are five major areas in which this pattern of development can be seen:

1. rule interaction;
2. recursion;
3. derived constituent structure;
4. the relationship of syntax to semantic interpretation;
5. the degree of abstractness permitted for underlying representations.

Rule interaction had presented a problem in the early theory of transformations because it was not clear what kind of ordering relationships could exist between singular and generalized transformations. It was not clear whether, for example, singular transformations could apply to an incomplete sentence structure *before* a generalized transformation embedded material in it. Various suggestions were made concerning the 'traffic rule' problem, but the most significant contribution was that of Fillmore (1963) who observed that it did not appear that there were any cases in which a singular transformation had to apply to a structure before a generalized transformation embedded material in it. Second, it did not appear that it was necessary in practice to stipulate any ordering between generalized transformations, and third, there were attested cases where a singulary transformation could apply to a sentence before it was embedded in a larger structure (passive, for example, in sentences such as *The director believed the keeper to have been eaten by one of the lions*). Fillmore's conclusion from these facts was that singulary transformations should apply first to (what would be) the most deeply embedded sentence. This sentence would then be embedded in the matrix sentence by a generalized transformation. This sentence would then become the domain of the singulary transformations again, and the process would be repeated as often as necessary.

Since transformations are mappings from phrase markers to phrase markers, it is essential that there be some well-defined way of specifying the constituent structure that results from the application of a transformation. The passive, for example, requires that the word *by* be adjoined to the left of the NP which has been moved into final position. It is clear that the resulting constituent should be a prepositional phrase, and that *by* itself should be a preposition. This information is not derivable, however, from the version of the transformation given above. Some linguists resolved this issue by specifying the details of the derived constituent structure in the structural change of the transformation itself:

$$NP_1 - Aux - V - NP_2 \qquad (18)$$
$$\rightarrow NP_2 - Aux + be + en - V - [_{PP}[_P by] + NP_1]$$

This increasingly came to be considered an undesirable enrichment of the theory and alternatives were sought.

The problem of derived constituent structure also arose in the context of the application of generalized transformations. As can be seen from the complement example above (15), the transformation not only embeds material from one clause into another, but also deletes the subject of the embedded clause. The question then arises as to what the category of the embedded constituent is. The idea rapidly developed (Katz and Postal 1964) that clauses into which a sentence was to be embedded should contain a 'dummy' node, defined by the phrase structure component of the grammar, which would provide a host (and a category) for the embedded material.

These issues were addressed in the 'standard theory,' the name given to the revised version of transformational grammar developed by Chomsky in his book *Aspects of the Theory of Syntax* (1965a).

2.1 Rule Interaction: The Transformational Cycle

In *Aspects* the issues listed above received a radical answer, which reduced the role which transformations

played in the theory. Most dramatically, the class of generalized transformations was eliminated entirely and their role as the locus of recursion was allocated to the phrase structure component. The issue of rule interaction was resolved by combining Fillmore's proposals with this innovation. Their joint effect is to require that transformations apply first to the most deeply embedded sentential structure, and, only when all possibilities have been exhausted, is the next 'higher' sentential level considered as a transformational domain. Graphically, the situation is illustrated in the schematic tree in Fig. 1.

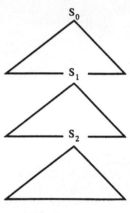

Figure 1.

All transformations apply first to S_2, then to S_1, and only then to S_0. This principle of transformational rule application is known as the ('transformational') cycle.

By way of specific illustration, take the analyses of complementation by Rosenbaum (1967) whose thesis has proved a reference point for most subsequent work. Rosenbaum's work is concerned with the analysis of sentences such as the following:

Sam prefers to stay here.	(19)
I believe Bill to have been convinced by John.	(20)
John is believed by me to have convinced Bill.	(21)

Each of these sentences would earlier have involved a generalized transformation. In the *Aspects* framework, the structures underlying them are provided by the following phrase structure rule:

$$VP \rightarrow V \ (NP) \ S \qquad (22)$$

This rule pre-empts the role of generalized transformations by introducing the symbol S on its right-hand side. The structure associated with (19) by Rosenbaum's phrase structure rules (suppressing some details) is given in Fig. 2.

On the lowest cyclic domain (the structure dominated by S_1) no rules apply. When the next highest cyclic domain (S_0) is reached, a 'complementizer place-

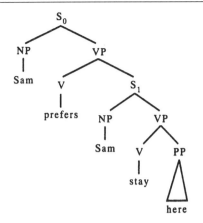

Figure 2.

ment' transformation is responsible for transforming this basic structure into:

Second Cycle: Sam prefers [for Sam [$_{VP}$ to stay here]]

This structure meets the structural description of what Rosenbaum termed the 'identity erasure transformation' (now generally known as 'equi NP deletion,' or simply 'Equi'):

Equi NP Deletion   (23)

Structural Description:

W   (NP)   X   +D   NP   Y   (NP)   Z
1   2   3   4   5   6   7   8

(Where + D identifies the complementizer *for – to*.)

Structural Change: 5 is erased (deleted) by 2

The effect of the application of this rule on *Sam prefers [for Sam [$_{VP}$ to stay here]]* is to delete the second occurrence of the NP *Sam*:

Second Cycle: Sam prefers [for [$_{VP}$ to stay here]]

which finally gives *Sam prefers [$_{VP}$ to stay here]]*, through the application of a rule of 'complementizer deletion.'

For (20) and (21), Rosenbaum's analysis would provide the derivations in (20a) and (21a). (Note the use of the substructure [$_{MAN}$ by + P] in these derivations to provide a trigger for the passive transformation and a landing-site for the NP moved from subject position by the passive.)

(20a)

First Cycle: I believe [$_{NP}$ it [$_S$ [$_{NP}$ John] [$_{VP}$ have + en convince Bill] [$_{MAN}$ by + P]]]]

Passive: I believe [$_{NP}$ it [$_S$ [$_{NP}$ Bill] [$_{VP}$ have + en *be* + *en* convince [$_{MAN}$ by + *John*]]]]]

Affix Hopping: I believe [$_{NP}$ it [$_S$ [$_{NP}$ Bill] [$_{VP}$ have *be* + *en* convince + *en*] [$_{MAN}$ by + *John*]]]]]

Second Cycle:
Complementizer   I believe [$_{NP}$ it [$_S$ *for* [$_{NP}$ Bill] [$_{VP}$ *to* have

Placement: be + en   convince + en]   [$_{MAN}$ by + John]]]]

Extraposition: I believe [$_{NP}$ it] [$_S$ for [$_{NP}$ Bill] [$_{VP}$ to have be + en convince + en] [$_{MAN}$ by + John]]]

Raising to object: I believe [$_{NP}$ *Bill*] [$_S$ for [$_{VP}$ to have be + en convince + en] [$_{MAN}$ by + John]]]]

Complementizer   I believe [$_{NP}$ Bill] [$_S$ [$_{VP}$ to have be + en
Deletion: convince + en] [$_{MAN}$ by + John]]]]
Post Cycle:
Morphophonemic   I believe [$_{NP}$ Bill] [$_S$ [$_{VP}$ to have *been*
Rules: *convinced*] [$_{MAN}$ by + John]]]]

('Extraposition' is a transformation that takes a structure of the form [$_{NP}$ it S] and moves the S rightwards out of the NP.)

(21a)

First Cycle: I believe [$_{NP}$ it [$_S$ [$_{NP}$ John] [$_{NP}$ have + en convince Bill]]] [$_{MAN}$ by + P]

Affix Hopping: I believe [$_{NP}$ it [$_S$ [$_{NP}$ John] [$_{VP}$ have *convince* + *en* Bill]]] [$_{MAN}$ by + P]

Second Cycle:
Complementizer   I believe [$_{NP}$ it [$_S$ *for* [$_{NP}$ John] [$_{VP}$ *to* have
Placement: convince + en Bill]]] [$_{MAN}$ by + P]

Passive: [$_{NP}$ it [$_S$ for [$_{NP}$ John] [$_{VP}$ to have convince + en Bill]]] *be* + *en* believe [$_{MAN}$ by + I]

Extraposition: it be + en believe [$_{MAN}$ by + I] [$_S$ for [$_{NP}$ John] [$_{VP}$ to have convince + en Bill]]]

Raising: *John* be + en believe [$_{MAN}$ by + I] [$_S$ for [$_{VP}$ to have convince + en Bill]]]

Affix Hopping: John be *believe* + *en* [$_{MAN}$ by + I] [$_S$ for [$_{VP}$ to have convince + en Bill]]]

Complementizer   John be believe + en [$_{MAN}$ by + I] [$_S$ [$_{VP}$
Deletion: to have convince + en Bill]]]
Post Cycle:
Morphophonemic   John is *believed* [$_{MAN}$ by + *me*] [$_S$ [$_{VP}$ to
Rules: have *convinced* Bill]]]

In (20a) the passive transformation applies on the first cycle (inside the subordinate clause), whereas in (21a) it applies on the second cycle (in the main clause). In both derivations affix hopping applies twice, once on the first cycle and once on the second. Both these sentences also exemplify the rule of raising (called 'pronoun replacement' by Rosenbaum), which moves the subject of a non-finite subordinate clause (here *John*) into the next higher clause on the second cycle. The existence of this rule was to become a major issue in the subsequent development of transformational grammar.

2.2 The Organization of the Grammar

With the adoption of the transformational cycle, many of the problems of rule interaction were satisfactorily resolved and, by the time of the publication of *Aspects of the Theory of Syntax*, the organization of the grammar took the following form (shown in Fig. 3).

The 'lexicon' (formerly part of the phrase structure component) and Phrase Structure Rules were split into separate subcomponents of the 'base component' of the grammar and jointly determined a level of syn-

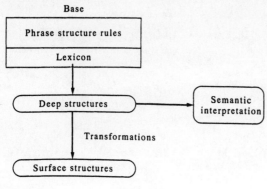

Figure 3.

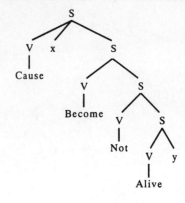

Figure 4.

tactic representation called 'deep structure.' This, on the one hand, provided the input to rules of semantic interpretation and, on the other, the input to the transformational component of the grammar, which mapped deep structure representations on to surface structure representations in the manner illustrated in (20a) and (21a) above.

3. Generative Semantics

The proposal that deep structure formed the level at which both lexical insertion and semantic interpretation took place came under strong challenge during the late 1960s. The branch of transformational grammar which became known as generative semantics argued that this conception of the organization of the grammar led to a loss of generalizations, a situation which could be remedied if underlying representations were allowed to be more abstract than Chomsky's deep structures (see *Generative Semantics*). This aspect of generative semantics was driven by the Katz–Postal hypothesis (Katz and Postal 1964) concerning the relationship between syntax and semantics. This proposed that all the information necessary for semantic interpretation is represented in the underlying structure of a sentence. Corollaries of this proposal are that synonymous sentences have a single underlying structure and that ambiguous sentences have more than one underlying structure. It also implies that transformations do not change semantic interpretation.

For many sentence pairs, such as actives and passives, this proposal seems eminently reasonable. The assumption that *John saw Bill* and *Bill was seen by John* have the same deep structure and acquire their different surface forms through the application of transformations provides a basis for accounting for the fact that the two sentences have the same truth conditions. However, this logic, when applied to *Bill is dead* and *Bill is not alive* leads to the conclusion that they too must share a single underlying structure. In this case, however, such an identity in underlying

structure must exist *before* lexical insertion, contradicting Chomsky's hypothesis about deep structure. This led McCawley (1968) to propose that the underlying structure of a sentence of the form *x killed y* should receive the analysis in Fig. 4 (note that McCawley is assuming here that in its underlying structure English is verb-initial; see McCawley 1970 for details).

By the repeated cyclic application of an optional transformation of 'predicate raising,' the verbs in this structure could be adjoined to one another to give the structure in Fig. 5.

McCawley proposed that 'if lexical insertion did not apply until after that transformation, then the "dictionary entry" for *kill* could be expressed as a transformation which replaces the subtree at the left [of the above tree] by *kill*' (McCawley 1968: 73). If lexical insertion is constrained to apply before all transformations, as in the *Aspects* approach, the semantic relationship between *x killed y* and *x caused y to become not alive* could not be expressed using transformations.

As an example of ambiguity prompting the postulation of different underlying structures, where purely syntactic evidence might not warrant them,

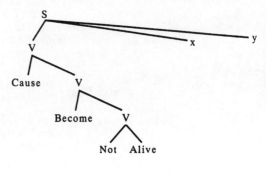

Figure 5.

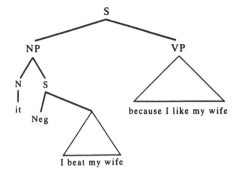

Figure 6.

take Lakoff's (1970) argument that the ambiguity of the sentence (24), with its two paraphrases (25) and (26):

I don't beat my wife because I like her. (24)

It is because I like her that I don't beat my wife. (25)

It is not because I like her that I beat my wife. (26)

could be accounted for by the assumption that the two readings correspond to different underlying structures. For (25), Lakoff proposed the structure in Fig. 6. For (26), he proposed the structure in Fig. 7. Transformations called 'it-deletion' and 'neg lowering' apply to these structures to give (24).

A further modification of standard transformational grammar made within generative semantics concerned the nature of the relationship which held between the various levels of a derivation. In standard transformational grammar, transformations are in effect relations between adjacent stages in a derivation. There was no possibility of a transformational 'looking forward' to a future stage in the derivation, for example. Generative semanticists, on the other hand, argued that such extensions were necessary. Lakoff (1971) observed that sentences like *Many men read few books* and *Few books are read by many men* seem to differ in their interpretations. The first is paraphrasable as *There are many men who read few books*

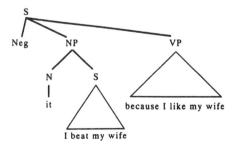

Figure 7.

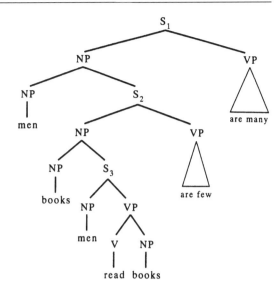

Figure 8.

and the second as *There are few books that are read by many men*. Lakoff proposed that these two interpretations are derived from different underlying structures. The first has the underlying structure in Fig. 8, the second that in Fig. 9.

The surface structures are derived by a transformation of 'quantifier lowering.' A problem remains, however, in ensuring that structure in Fig. 8 must undergo passive and the structure in Fig. 9 must not. Lakoff's solution was to propose that passive and quantifier lowering could freely apply to both structures, but that a 'global derivational constraint' checked the relationship between the underlying and surface forms, requiring that the quantifier which was highest in underlying structure must be the leftmost one in surface structure. Global constraints allow the application of a transformation to have access to any level of representation in the derivation, not merely the information coded in its structural description and structural change.

In essence, what generative semantics did was to pursue the use of transformations to express linguistic regularities and subregularities to its logical conclusion. It assumed that transformations were the *only* way that such regularities should be captured, incorporating into syntactic description phenomena from semantics, pragmatics, and even social interaction. Ultimately, however, this central tenet of generative semantics was rejected by the majority of linguists working in the transformational framework. (A more comprehensive discussion of generative semantics and the factors both linguistic and nonlinguistic involved in its rise and fall can be found in Newmeyer 1980: ch. 4 and 5.)

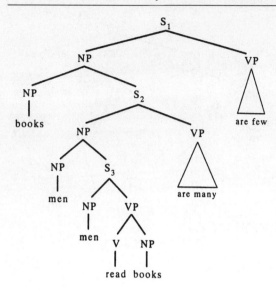

Figure 9.

4. The Extended Standard Theory

Subsequent developments in transformational grammar were motivated by a desire to constrain the expressive power of the transformational component. These took two forms. One was to seek to impose restrictions on transformations themselves, with the goal of limiting their expressive power; the other was to reallocate the responsibility for certain classes of phenomena to other components of the grammar, in particular the lexicon, the phrase structure component, and the semantic component. The name given to the version of the theory incorporating these revisions, which developed during the 1970s, was the 'extended standard theory.'

The work of Peters and Ritchie (1973) too undoubtedly encouraged a climate in which constraining the power of transformations was seen as desirable. They provided a proof that transformational grammars of the *Aspects* type had the weak generative capacity of the most powerful device on the Chomsky hierarchy, unrestricted rewriting systems (Turing machines). This meant that human languages, as characterizable by transformational grammars, had no particular properties other than that they could be generated by some set of well-defined rules. *Aspects*-style transformational grammar did not place any interesting constraints on the class of possible human languages. In terms of language acquisition, this implies that the formal properties of transformational grammars provided no interesting restrictions on the search space accessible to the learner. There was undoubted merit, in the light of these results, in any program which sought to constrain the power of existing transformational grammars.

156

4.1 The Lexicalist Hypothesis

'Nominalization,' referred to above, had been one of the earliest transformational rules proposed (see Lees 1966). Yet in 'Remarks on nominalization,' Chomsky (1970) developed the argument that at least some nominals which had previously been assumed to be transformationally derived were in fact simply basic lexical entries. His argument had two prongs. First, he demonstrated that the basis for the purported generalization was unsound and, second, that there were alternative ways of capturing the generalizations which remained.

In arguing against a transformational analysis of nominalization, Chomsky noted that what he termed 'derived nominals' (such as *refusal, easiness, revolution, belief*) do not occur in structures which are themselves derived by transformations. (The term 'derived nominal' does not imply any transformational derivation. Rather, the term is an allusion to the fact that such nominals form part of the derivational morphology of English.) So the sentences on the right of the arrows in (27) and (29) below are well-formed, but their corresponding derived nominals in (28) and (30) are not:

To please John is easy ⇒ John is easy to please   (27)

*John's easiness to please   (28)

For John to win the prize is certain ⇒ John is certain to win the prize   (29)

*John's certainty to win the prize   (30)

Furthermore, the semantic relationship which holds between a derived nominal and the item it is supposed to be derived from is frequently idiosyncratic. *John's deeds*, for example, are not the same as *things which John did*, nor is *John's ignorance* the same as *what John ignores*. In the common situation where there is no verb or adjective corresponding to a derived nominal (such as *'book,' 'poem'*), the proponent of a transformational analysis is forced to postulate abstract underlying verbs such as *poetize* and to formulate mechanisms to ensure that these nonexistent items do not show up in surface structures (see, for example, Lakoff 1970).

To capture the regularities that do occur, such as *John refused to leave/John's refusal to leave, The enemy destroyed the city/The enemy's destruction of the city* and *The city was destroyed by the enemy/The city's destruction by the enemy*, Chomsky proposed first that in cases where there exists a verb/derived nominal pair, the lexical entry should be neutral with respect to grammatical category, but should specify what complements the pair require. In addition, he proposed an extension of the theory of phrase structure, known as 'X-bar theory,' to allow generalizations to be made across different linguistic categories.

For example, sentences and NPs have a similar internal structure (cf. Chomsky 1970: 211). In (31) *the theorem* is the direct object of the noun *proof* and *John* is its subject. (This structure also requires the later insertion of the preposition *of.*)

(31)

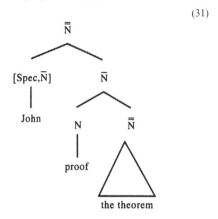

In the corresponding sentence, *the theorem* and *John* hold exactly the same grammatical relations to the verb *prove.*

(32)

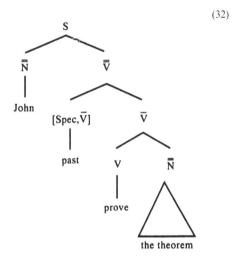

Chomsky also proposed that cyclic transformations such as passive could apply not only within sentences, but also within NPs, and proposed factoring the passive transformation into two subrules: 'NP-preposing' and 'agent-postposing.' The derivation of *The city's destruction by the enemy* would look like this (with various details omitted):

(33)

	The enemy('s) destruction the city by Δ
Agent-postposing	The destruction (of) the city by the enemy
NP-preposing	The city('s) destruction by the enemy

Note that the intermediate stage, resulting from agent-postposing, is also grammatical, provided that the NP's subject position is filled by a determiner. Exactly the same transformations apply in the case of the sentential passive *The city was destroyed by the enemy*, with the additional proviso that, for independent reasons, NP-preposing is obligatory.

Chomsky's argument, then, was that the generalizations captured by the nominalization transformation were spurious and, to the extent that genuine generalizations exist (such as the existence of active/passive pairs of nominalizations) there are alternative analyses available. The upshot of this was the proposal that transformations cannot change the syntactic category of an item. Thus, the rule of nominalization, as posited in early transformational grammar is not a possible transformation. This proposal was termed the 'lexicalist hypothesis,' because it assumes that any relationship of a cross-categorical kind is represented in the lexicon, and not by a transformational relationship.

4.2 Interpretive Semantics

The lexicalist hypothesis removes from the transformational component the power to alter syntactic categories and hence results in the reallocation of one class of linguistic phenomena to another component of the grammar. This is a tendency that is seen to be repeated with respect to other linguistic phenomena as the theory develops.

From the early days of transformational grammar, it had been assumed that the relationship that exists between an anaphoric pronoun and its antecedent, in sentences such as (34), where *Alice* and *she* can be interpreted as referring to the same individual, was to be captured by a transformation:

Alice said that she should go. (34)

The standard analysis of anaphoric pronouns (Lees and Klima 1969) assumed that they were derived from an underlying structure containing two identical occurrences of an NP. One of the NPs would be obligatorily converted into a pronoun by the pronominalization transformation:

Pronominalization (35)

$$X - NP_1 - Y - NP_2 Z \rightarrow X - NP - Y - NP_2[+ Pro]Z$$

where $NP_1 = NP_2$ [and various conditions on the topological relations between the two NPs were satisfied].

Jackendoff (1972) argued instead for a treatment of pronominal anaphora which relied on rules of semantic interpretation (an 'interpretive' approach to pronominalization). Jackendoff pointed out that the condition requiring identity between the two NPs (which must include not only syntactic identity but also identity of reference) is unexpected given that coreference is not generally a condition on the application of transformations; no movement rule, for example, is constrained to apply only to coreferential NPs.

Jackendoff's proposal assumed that anaphoric pronouns were base-generated in underlying structure and that rules of semantic interpretation established the necessary connection between them and their antecedents; no transformation of any kind was involved. This approach had a number of empirical consequences. It provided the basis for a solution to the problem that, in sentences containing quantified NPs such as *every runner*, the transformational treatment of prominalization predicts incorrectly that *Every runner expects that she will win* should have the interpretation associated with *Every runner expects that every runner will win*.

Furthermore, there are cases of anaphora which do not involve pronouns. Such sentences as *I wanted to help Harry, but the fool wouldn't let me* allow a coreferential interpretation of *Harry* and *the fool*. In addition, the conditions on the configurations in which anaphora is possible are shared by pronominal anaphors and by 'epithets' like *the fool*. For example, neither permit an anaphoric interpretation in sentences like the following *He/the fool said Harry would leave*. It is implausible to envisage a transformation giving rise to epithets, but no problems arise in principle in assuming that epithets are assigned interpretations by the same semantic rules that interpret pronouns. Note also that Jackendoff's proposal is consonant with the lexicalist hypothesis in not allowing a transformation to radically alter the morphological shape of lexical material.

The net conclusion of these and other arguments is that pronominalization is not a transformation and that the phenomenon of pronominal anaphora falls within the domain of the semantic component of the grammar.

Similar arguments apply to two other long-established transformational analyses; those of reflexivization and equi-NP deletion. Reflexivization was assumed to work in complementary distribution with pronominalization; roughly, where the latter applied to identical NPs which were separated by a clause boundary, the former applied to identical NPs in the same clause. Thus *Mary was proud of Mary* would give *Mary was proud of herself*. Note, however, that when a quantified NP is involved, the result is the same as in the case of pronominalization; *Every runner is proud of herself* does not have the same interpretation as *Every runner is proud of every runner*. Equi-NP deletion, which derives *Mary wanted to win* from *Mary wanted Mary to win* exhibits the same phenomenon; *Every runner wanted to win* does not have the same interpretation as *Every runner wanted every runner to win*. As a consequence, proponents of the interpretive semantics position argued that neither reflexives nor the control phenomena handled by equi-NP deletion were the responsibility of the trans-

formational component. Instead, reflexive pronouns should be base-generated and interpreted by the semantic component. For 'equi' sentences it was proposed that the subject position of the nonfinite subordinate clause was filled by a base-generated phonologically empty pronominal (PRO), also interpreted by the semantic component.

The result of these proposals was the removal from the transformational component of responsibility for a whole class of linguistic phenomena—those involving coreference—resulting in a more constrained theory of transformations and a superior account of the empirical data.

4.3 Constraints on Movement Rules

4.3.1 Structure Preservation

The lexicalist hypothesis and interpretive semantics reduced the range of phenomena to be accounted for by the transformational component. For those transformations that remained, a major goal of the extended standard theory was to remove from the theory the capacity for individual transformational rules to contain detailed specifications of the conditions of their application, and to replace them with general conditions applying to all transformations, or to whole classes of transformations. This goal may be summarized as that of restricting the expressive power of transformations.

It was noted above that the precise manner in which the derived constituent structure resulting from the application of a transformation was determined was unclear and that various ad hoc measures were adopted, such as stipulating derived constituent structure in the structural change of the rule or introducing 'dummy' elements to act as the landing site of a moved constituent. This issue received a more highly-motivated solution in proposals by Emonds (1976). Emonds established three different classes of movement transformations:

Root transformations   (36)
Those that crucially involved the root (roughly speaking the topmost) S node, and hence do not apply in subordinate clauses. Examples include Subject-Auxiliary Inversion (*Isn't it cold today*), Directional Adverb Preposing (*Down the street rolled the baby carriage*) and Topicalization (*Our daughters we are proud of*).

Local transformations   (37)
Those that involve the reordering of two adjacent constituents, one of which is phrasal and the other nonphrasal. An example is Particle Movement (cf. *She picked up the book* and *She picked the book up*).

Structure Preserving Transformations   (38)
Those that involve the replacement of a node by one of the same syntactic category. Examples include Passive, Raising, There-insertion (*A book is on the table* ⇒ *There is a book on the table*) and

Dative Movement (*gave a ticket to John ⇒ gave John a ticket*).

The phenomena handled by root and local transformations have been subject to reanalysis more recently, but the essence of the structure preserving hypothesis has been accepted by all subsequent work.

Emonds argued, like Chomsky, that the passive transformation is in fact a composition of two separate rules: one that postposes the agent NP into the position of *by*-phrase object; and one that preposes the object NP into the vacant subject NP position. This requires that the derivation of *Germany was defeated by Russia* looks like this:

Agent Postposing: (39)

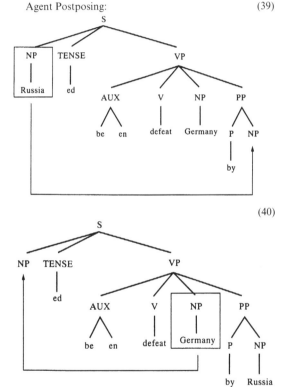

(40)

The structure-preserving hypothesis requires that the *by*-phrase be present in deep structure and that the NP within it be lexically empty (note that this implies that lexical insertion need not take place at deep structure). This analysis accounts for the fact that the passive *by*-phrase is like any other PP with respect to its internal structure and transformational behaviour.

Emonds points out that the fact that PPs under VP are generally optional in English, when combined with the structure-preserving analysis of passive, accounts automatically for the existence of agentless passives (*Germany was defeated*), in contrast to early analyses which had postulated a rule of by-phrase deletion.

Emonds's proposals constituted a step in the direction of removing from the structural description and structural change of a transformation the necessity, or even the possibility, of specifying where a constituent could be moved to; e.g., if the structure involved is not a root S and the transformation does not involve two adjacent constituents, the only possibility is for the moved constituent to move to a location in which the phrase structure rules permit a constituent of that type to be generated.

4.3.2 Blind Application of Transformations

The 1970s saw major steps toward the goal of replacing conditions on specific transformations with general conditions which, instead of forming part of individual grammars, were a component of universal grammar. Chomsky (1973) noted that, if the structural description of the passive transformation in English were taken to be essentially:

$$X, NP, V, NP, Y \qquad (41)$$

with no reference to conditions requiring the two NPs to be members of the same clause (as had been standardly assumed), the transformation would apply to the deep structure analysis of a sentence like *I believe the dog to be hungry*, namely [$_S$ *I believe* [$_S$ [$_{NP}$ *the dog*] [$_{VP}$ *to be hungry*]] without the necessity for raising to move the NP *the dog* into the higher clause. Without any restriction on its operation, passive (and other transformations) would apply 'blindly' to any structural configuration meeting the structural description. Viewed in this way there is no problem in accounting for sentences such as *The dog is believed to be hungry by me*. Instead, there is a question as to why passive does not apply to *I believe the dog is hungry* to give **The dog is believed is hungry by me*. Chomsky's conclusion was that the failure of the passive to apply to the latter sentence is to be attributed to a general condition on transformational rules to the effect that no item may be extracted from a tensed (finite) clause. This constraint is phrased as follows:

The Tensed-S Condition (TSC) (42)

No rule can involve X, Y in the structure

$...X...[_a...Y...]...$ [where a is a tensed sentence]

Chomsky's discussion of reciprocals (*each other*) illustrates the application of the TSC. Following Dougherty (1970), he assumes that *each* in sentences such as (43):

The men hated each other. (43)

originates in deep structure as part of the subject NP as in (44):

The men each hated the others. (44)

and is moved out of it by a transformation ('each' movement) to give the structure in (43). The TSC explains why this movement is not possible in sentences like *The men each expected [$_S$ the others would win]* to give **The men expected [$_S$ each other would win]*, and why movement of *each* is possible in the nonfinite counterpart *The men each expected [$_S$ the others to win]*, giving *The men expected [$_S$ each other to win]*.

However, given the grammaticality of *The men expected [$_S$ to shoot each other]*, in which *each* appears in the object NP of the lower clause, the TSC does not account for the ungrammaticality of **The men expected [$_S$ the soldier to shoot each other]*. To account for this paradigm, Chomsky proposed the specified subject condition:

Specified Subject Condition (SSC)   (45)

No rule can involve *X*, *Y* in the structure

$$\ldots X \ldots [_\alpha \ldots Z \ldots - WYV \ldots] \ldots$$

where Z is the subject of *WYV* in α, α is a cyclic node (NP or S) and α contains a subject distinct from *Z* and not controlled by *X*.

'Control' is the relationship which holds between PRO and its antecedent in 'Equi' constructions, or between a 'trace' (see below) and its antecedent. Any subject meeting the additional criterion in (45) is a 'specified subject.'

This provides an account of the difference between:

We promised Bill [$_S$ PRO to kill each other].   (46)

and:

*We persuaded Bill [$_S$ PRO to kill each other].   (47)

In (46) *each* originates in the deep structure as part of the NP containing *we*, which is the controller of PRO and moves into the subordinate sentence by 'each movement' (cf. (44) above); whereas in (47) the controller of PRO is the NP *Bill* which does not contain *each* at any level of representation. PRO in (47) is therefore a specified subject. Note that any phonologically realized NP (such as *the soldier* in (45)) is a specified subject, and also blocks the application of 'each' movement.

Under standard assumptions, there was an immediate counter-example to these conditions: the rule of *wh*-movement (so called because it moves phrases which contain the class of interrogatives and relatives that begin with the letters 'wh,' such as *who*, *which*, and *what*—as well as various others not fitting this description, such as *how*). *Wh*-movement is the rule responsible for deriving sentences such as:

Who did John kill?   (48)

Since *kill* is a transitive verb, it is expected to have a direct object, yet no NP follows the verb in (48). The reason for this is that the requirement for an object

NP is satisfied at deep structure, and the NP concerned, *who*, is moved to its surface structure position by a transformation.

In contrast to the transformations discussed so far, *wh*-movement has the property of being 'unbounded.' That is to say, that there seems to be no principled limit on the amount of material that can intervene between the deep structure position of the *wh*-item and its surface structure position, as the following examples illustrate (the underscore marks the position from which *who* has moved):

Who does Max think John killed__?   (49)

Who did Sam say Max thinks John killed__?   (50)

Note that in these examples the clause which contains the extraction site of *who* is a finite one and, in addition, contains a specified subject (*John*). According to the TSC and SSC these sentences should not be possible.

Chomsky's solution to this problem was the radical proposal that, contrary to appearances, *wh*-movement is a cyclic rule. He adopted a proposal made by Bresnan (1970) that *wh*-movement involves moving the *wh*-phrase into the complementizer position of a clause—roughly speaking, the clause-initial position occupied by *that* or *whether*. This position, known as COMP, has the status of an 'escape hatch' for movement; movement to or from the COMP position does not violate the TSC or SSC.

The derivation of (50) would thus proceed as in (51):

(51)

[$_S$who[$_S$ did Sam say [$_{S'}$ COMP [$_S$ Max thinks [$_{S'}$ COMP [$_S$ John killed__]]]]]]

To enforce the cyclic application of *wh*-movement (and prevent the movement of *who* in (51) from its deep to surface structure positions in one fell swoop), Chomsky proposed a further condition on movement rules: 'subjacency.' A node *X* is 'subjacent' to another node *Y* only if *Y* is higher in the tree than *X* and there is at most one cyclic node that dominates *X* and does not dominate *Y*. This is illustrated diagrammatically below, where α is a cyclic node (that is, NP or S):

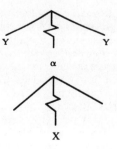

The subjacency condition requires that no movement can take place from X to Y unless X is subjacent to Y. Checking (51) will confirm that the combination of COMP as the landing-site for *wh*-movement and subjacency precludes any other derivation than the one indicated.

Subjacency also provides an account for a class of phenomena known, since Ross (1967), as 'islands.' Despite the apparent unboundedness of *wh*-movement, it had been known for some time that there are constructions out of which *wh*-movement is prevented for some reason from moving *wh*-items. Chomsky (1964a) had observed that while the sentence *John kept the car in the garage* is ambiguous (meaning either that the car in the garage was kept by John, or that the car was kept in the garage by John), the sentence *Which car did John keep in the garage* is not, having only the latter reading. The nonexistent reading is the one in which the NP *the garage* is contained within the larger NP *the car in the garage*. Chomsky had proposed that in a situation like this, where a transformation might in principle apply to either of two NPs, in fact it must apply only to the larger one. This proposed constraint he termed the 'A-over-A principle.'

Ross (1967) gave a detailed investigation of a wide range of situations in which the application of unbounded movement rules was blocked. Ross pointed out that the A-over-A principle proved too strong in certain cases and identified the defining characteristics of the phenomenon as a set of structural configurations which he termed 'islands,' and proposed a corresponding set of 'island constraints' to restrict the application of unbounded movement rules:

Complex NP Constraint (CNPC)　　　　　(52)

No item may be moved out of a complex NP by transformation, where a 'complex NP' is a structure of the following form.

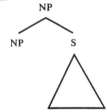

Example:　　Max met a man that sells books/what
　　　　　*What did Max meet [NP [NP a man] [S that sells ___]]

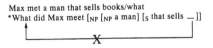

Sentential Subject Constraint　　　　　(53)

No item may be moved out of a sentential subject by a transformation.

Coordinate Structure Constraint (CSC)　　(54)

No conjunct in a coordinate structure may be moved,

nor may any item in a conjunct be moved out of that conjunct.

Example:　　That John gave the book to Max/who surprised Sam
　　　　　*Who did [NP [S that John gave the book to ___]] surprise Sam

Left Branch Condition　　　　　　　　(55)

No NP on the left branch of another NP may be moved out of that NP.

Example:　　Max spoke to Sam/who and Fred
　　　　　*Who did Max speak to[NP ___ and Fred]

The subjacency principle serves to provide a unified account of all these island phenomena except the coordinate structure constraint. Note that in all other cases but coordinate structures, the movement involves a violation of subjacency. To illustrate with the last example, in *Whose [S did you read [NP___book]] two cyclic nodes, S and NP, intervene between *whose* and the extraction site.

Chomsky also proposed that subjacency would account for the prohibition on moving two (or more) *wh*-phrases out of the same clause (the *wh*-island constraint), as in *What [S do you wonder [who [S___saw___]]. On the assumption that, once the COMP node of the lower clause is occupied by *who*, it is no longer a possible landing-site for *what*, the only route to the topmost COMP will involve crossing two S nodes – a subjacency violation.

4.4 Trace Theory

The developments outlined in the preceding sections resulted in a situation where the substantive content of transformations had been severely reduced. Lexicalism had removed many linguistic phenomena from the domain of the transformational component, as had the reanalysis of phenomena involving coreference; structure preservation reduced the need to specify details in the structural descriptions of transformations, and subjacency limited the domain of application of transformations.

Chomsky (1973) had introduced the idea that movement of an NP left behind a 'trace' of itself. He developed this idea further (Chomsky 1976). He proposed that all movement transformations leave behind a phonetically empty copy (a 'trace') bound by the moved constituent and inheriting all its relevant properties. He points out the pattern of reciprocal interpretation (now effected by an interpretive rule, rather than the transformation of 'each' movement) supports the postulation of such an empty category in sentences involving raising to subject. There is a parallel between (56) and (57), where reciprocal interpretation in (57) allows *each other* and *the men* to be construed together, just as if they were in the same clause, as in (56):

The men like each other. (56)

The men seem to John [*t* to like each other]. (57)

There is a similar parallel between (58) and (59), where reciprocal interpretation is blocked by the SSC. This insight is captured explicitly by the occurrence of a trace of NP preposing in (57) which participates in the interpretation of *each other* and one in (59) which forms a specified subject since it is bound by the singular moved NP *John*, blocking reciprocal interpretation with *men* just as the overt occurrence of *John* does in (58):

*The men want [John to like each other]. (58)

*John seems to the men [*t* to like each other]. (59)

Lasnik (1977) drew a parallel between the relationship which exists between traces and their binders and that which exists between PRO and its controller and between a reciprocal and its antecedent: always the binder must precede or asymmetrically 'command' the trace. (A commands B if the first S node that dominates A also dominates B.) This means that movement must always be leftward or to a higher position in a tree. Hence raising is a possible movement rule, but its inverse, 'lowering,' would not be. Similarly, *wh*-movement must always be to a higher COMP node and never to a lower one.

With these developments, Chomsky proposed a constraint on transformations to the effect that the only categories that may be explicitly mentioned in a structural description are those that are changed (i.e., moved, deleted etc.) by the rule. He also suggests that a further step can be taken in the light of the structure preserving hypothesis, which entails that, for example, an NP can only be moved into another NP position. 'Thus the rules in question [e.g., passive] reduce to the following formulation: move NP' (Chomsky 1976: 313).

All other details of the operations carried out by the rule are determined by general principles, the landing site being determined by a combination of the structure preserving hypothesis, subjacency, and Lasnik's condition.

This move was accompanied by a reinterpretation of the status of conditions like the TSC and the SSC, which ultamtely spells the end of transformational grammar as such and its evolution into government-binding theory. At their inception, these conditions were construed as constraints on rules, blocking their application. Chomsky now proposed construing them as conditions on surface structure well-formedness. That is to say, 'move NP' can apply freely, but the resulting representations must satisfy the TSC and the SSC. To take a specific example, *John seems [t to like Bill]* is the result of move NP and the trace is bound by an NP (*John*) as required by Lasnik's proposal. In *John seems [Bill to like t]*, although NP movement has applied, the resulting configuration violates the

SSC, on the assumption that the relationship between an NP and its trace is just like the one that holds between a reciprocal and its antecedent. The trace does not stand in the appropriate relationship to *John*, any more than *each other* does to *they* in *They expect [Bill to like each other]*.

In 'On binding' Chomsky (1980) took this development a stage further and proposed that the SSC (renamed the 'opacity condition') and the TSC (renamed first the 'propositional island condition,' or PIC, and then the 'nominative island condition,' or NIC) should be reinterpreted as constraints on the occurrence of anaphors alone, rather than as relations between anaphors and their antecedents. The opacity condition took the form 'if α is an anaphor in the domain of the subject of β, β minimal, then α cannot be free in β, $\beta = $ NP or S'. The nominative island condition took the form: A nominative anaphor cannot be free in S'. 'In the domain of' means 'c-commanded by,' where A c-commands B if the first branching node which dominates A also dominates B (a revision of Lasnik's 'precede or command'). 'Free' means not coindexed with a c-commanding antecedent. Nominative case is assigned only to the subjects of finite clauses.

To take up the analysis of *each other* to exemplify the revised framework, Chomsky suggests that all that need now be said about the distribution of *each other* is that it is a reciprocal. From this, within an appropriately articulated theory of grammar, will follow the requirement that it be bound by a plural antecedent within the same S' or NP, if it is not itself a subject, so that (60) is grammatical with *each other* bound by *the students* within the minimal S':

John expected [$_{S'}$ the students to like each other]. (60)

(61), however, is ill-formed, because *each other* has no acceptable antecedent within S':

*The students expected [$_{S'}$ John to like each other]. (61)

(62) is ill-formed because the lower clause is finite. Its subject *each other* is therefore nominative and, according to the NIC, must be bound in S'. But, in this structure there is no possible c-commanding binder within S', so the sentence is defined as ungrammatical:

*The students expected [$_{S'}$ to each other would to like John]. (62)

Earlier, Chomsky (1977) had argued that what had been considered a range of different transformations should all be interpreted as expressions of *wh*-movement. These included not only *wh*-questions and relative clauses, but also topicalization (63a) (and its associated analysis in 63b), *Tough*-movement (64a) and (64b), comparatives and cleft sentences, although most of these do not occur with overt *wh*-phrases in them:

This book, I asked Bill to get his students to read. (63a)

$[_S'[_{TOP}$ This book] $[_{S'}[_{COMP}$ what] (63b)
I asked Bill to get his students to read t]].

John is easy for us to please. (64a)

John is easy for us $[_S[$ who for] PRO to please t]]. (64b)

John is taller than Mary is. (65a)

John is taller than $[_S[$ what] Mary is t]]. (65b)

Chomsky's argument was founded on the claim that all these constructions exhibit the defining characteristics of *wh*-movement:

  a. it leaves a gap; (66)
  b. there is an apparent violation of subjacency, PIC and SSC;
  c. it observes the complex NP constraint;
  d. it observes *wh*-island constraints.

For example, the comparative in (67) and the *wh*-question (68) both demonstrate a violation of the complex NP constraint, while the comparative in (69) and the *wh*-question (70) both demonstrate parallel violations of the *wh*-island constraint:

*Mary is taller than (what) Bill believes $[_{NP}$ the claim that she is__]. (67)

*Who does Bill believe $[_{NP}$ the claim that she met__]. (68)

*Mary is taller than (what) [I wonder [whether she used to be__]]. (69)

*Who [does Bill wonder [whether she met__]]. (70)

The set of transformational movement rules was now reduced to two: 'move NP' and 'move *wh*' and in *On binding* Chomsky proposed that it could be reduced still further to 'move α,' where α is some category of the grammar. Move α will apply freely, but the resulting structures must satisfy the relevant constraints.

Transformational grammar, as it had been envisaged originally, was about to evolve into a theory in which transformations themselves played a relatively minor role. The task of specifying the operations which transformations were entitled to perform was to be replaced by the task of specifying well-formedness conditions on the representations which resulted from the operation of transformations and other kinds of rules. The only constraint specific to transformations was, and remains, subjacency.

Transformational grammar constituted a major breakthrough in the investigation of the syntax of human languages and spawned an unprecedented amount of research, providing many new insights into language and its structure. It has been a topic of controversy since its inception, and a variety of alternatives now exist which challenge the very bases of transformational theory; but it is fair to say that many of them have developed in response to positions articulated within transformational grammar and it is doubtful that they would have come about without the stimulus and insights provided by transformational grammar. It is certainly true that our understanding of human language would be much impoverished had it not existed.

Bibliography

Bresnan J 1970 On complementizers: Toward a syntactic theory of complementation. *Foundations of Language* **6**: 292–321

Carroll J M, Bever T G 1976 Sentence comprehension: A case study in the relation of knowledge and perception. In: Carterette E C, Friedman M P (eds.) *The Handbook of Perception.* Academic Press, New York

Chomsky N 1957 *Syntactic Structures.* Mouton, The Hague

Chomsky N 1964a *Current Issues in Linguistic Theory.* Mouton, The Hague

Chomsky N 1964b A transformational approach to syntax. In: Fodor J A, Katz J J (eds.) *The Structure of Language.* Prentice-Hall, Englewood Cliffs, New Jersey

Chomsky N 1965a *Aspects of the Theory of Syntax.* MIT Press, Cambridge, MA

Chomsky N 1965b Three models for the description of language. In: Luce R D, Bush R R, Galanter E (eds.) *Readings in Mathematical Psychology.* Wiley, New York

Chomsky N 1970 Remarks on nominalization. In: Jacobs R, Rosenbaum P S (eds.) *Readings in English Transformational Grammar.* Blaisdell, Waltham, MA

Chomsky N 1973 Conditions on transformations. In: Kiparsky P, Anderson S (eds.) *A Festschrift for Morris Halle.* Holt, Rinehart and Winston, New York

Chomsky N 1975 *The Logical Structure of Linguistic Theory.* Plenum, New York

Chomsky N 1976 Conditions on rules of grammar. *LAn* **2**: 303–51

Chomsky N 1977 On *wh*-movement. In: Culicover P, Wasow T, Akmajian A (eds.) *Formal Syntax.* Academic Press, New York

Chomsky N 1980 On binding. *LIn:* **11**: 1–46

Dougherty R S 1970 A grammar of coordinate conjoined constructions. *Lg* **46**: 850–98

Emonds J 1976 *Transformational Approach to English Syntax: Root, Structure-preserving and Local Transformations.* Academic Press, New York

Fillmore C 1963 The position of embedding transformations in a grammar. *Word* **19**: 208–31

Harris Z S 1952 Discourse analysis. *Lg* **28**: 18–23

Jackendoff R 1972 *Semantic Interpretation in Generative Grammar.* MIT Press, Cambridge, MA

Katz J J, Postal P M 1964 *An Integrated Theory of Linguistic Descriptions.* MIT Press, Cambridge, MA

Lakoff G 1970 *Irregularity in Syntax.* Holt, Rinehart and Winston, New York

Lakoff G 1971 On Generative Semantics. In: Steinberg D, Jakobovits L (eds.) *Semantics.* Cambridge University Press, Cambridge

Lasnik H 1977 On trace theory. *LIn* **8**: 35–61

Lees R B 1966 *The Grammar of English Nominalizations.* Mouton, The Hague

Lees R B, Klima E S 1969 Rules for English pronominalization. In: Reibel D A, Schane S (eds.) *Modern Studies in English.* Prentice-Hall, Englewood Cliffs, NJ

McCawley J D 1968 Lexical insertion in a transformational grammar without deep structure. In: *Papers from the Fourth Regional Meeting of the Chicago Linguistic Society.* Chicago, IL

McCawley J D 1970 English as a VSO language. *Lg* **46**: 286–99
Newmeyer F J 1980 *Linguistic Theory in America*. Academic Press, New York (2nd edn., 1986)
Peters S, Ritchie R W 1973 On the generative power of transformational grammars. *Information Sciences* **6**: 49–83
Rosenbaum P 1967 *The Grammar of English Predicate Complement Constructions*. MIT Press, Cambridge, MA
Ross J R 1967 *Constraints on variables in syntax* (Doctoral dissertation, Massachusetts Institute of Technology)

Generative Semantics

James D. McCawley

The term 'generative semantics' (GS) is an informal designation for the school of syntactic and semantic research that was prominent from the late 1960s through the mid-1970s and whose best-known practitioners were George Lakoff, James D. McCawley, Paul M. Postal, and John Robert Ross.

1. GS Positions on Controversial Issues

The name GS gives undue prominence to one of many issues on which GS-ists took positions that conflicted with those of more orthodox generative grammarians, an issue that in hindsight seems arcane because it is intelligible only against the background of the once widely accepted assumption (shared then by GS-ists and their adversaries) that there must be a single level of linguistic structure for which it is appropriate to give a system of 'generative rules' (i.e., rules giving a complete specification of what structures are well-formed on that level) and to which all other levels of structure are related by 'interpretive rules.' The issue commemorated in the name GS was that of whether the privileged level was semantic structure (the GS position) or was a level of syntactic structure as distinct from semantic structure (the position of Chomsky and other 'interpretive semanticists'). The prominence that has been given to that arcane issue should not obscure the fact that GS-ists disagreed with other generative grammarians on many far more substantial issues, such as the following:

(a) Whether sentences were 'grammatical' or 'ungrammatical' in themselves rather than relative to (linguistic and extralinguistic) contexts and to possible interpretations. GS-ists rejected the then popular idea that a language can be identified with a set of sentences and took syntactic derivations as implying that the surface form in question was grammatical not absolutely but only relative to the meaning represented in its deep structure and to any contextual factors to which steps in the derivation are sensitive.

(b) The nature of semantic structure. GS-ists held that semantic structures have the same formal nature as syntactic structures, except for having semantic rather than morphological entities as their ultimate constituents, while interpretive semanticists either were reluctant to make any concrete claims about the nature of semantic structure (e.g., Chomsky 1972: 137) or adopted a conception of semantic structure that differed considerably in formal nature from syntactic structure (e.g., Jackendoff 1972).

(c) The nature of syntactic categories. Much work in GS attempted to reduce syntactic category distinctions to distinctions of logical category, supplemented by lexical 'exception features' (e.g., verbs and adjectives would both belong to the category 'predicate,' usually confusingly called 'V' by GS-ists, with adjectives differing from verbs in bearing a feature licensing the application of a transformation that inserts a copula), while other generative grammarians took syntactic categories to have at most a tangential relation to semantic categories.

(d) The linguistic level or levels relevant to the choice of the lexical material of a sentence. One who holds that there is no level of syntactic deep structure as distinct from semantic structure is forced to recognize syntactic structures whose ultimate units are semantic rather than morphological in nature, such as a syntactic structure [Brutus DO SOMETHING$_X$ (X CAUSE (BECOME (NOT (Caesar ALIVE))))] underlying *Brutus killed Caesar*. (Here and below, capitalization is used as an informal way of representing semantic units corresponding roughly to the words in question.) GS-ists accordingly proposed transformations that combined semantic units into complexes that could potentially underlie lexical items, e.g., 'predicate-raising' (proposed in McCawley 1968) adjoined a predicate to the immediately superordinate predicate, thus allowing the derivation of such complexes as NOT-ALIVE, BECOME-NOT-ALIVE ($= die$), BECOME-NOT ($= cease$), and CAUSE-BECOME-NOT-ALIVE or CAUSE-*die* ($= kill$). Intermediate derivational stages involving both lexical and semantic units (such as CAUSE-*die*) needed to be recognized in order to account for, e.g., the parallelism between idiomatic combinations with *come* (*come about, around, to, ...*) and their counterparts with *bring*: as Binnick (1971) noted, *bring* corresponded not to CAUSE plus some determinate complex of semantic material but to CAUSE plus *come*, irrespective of whether *come* was used as an independent lexical unit or as part of such combinations as *come about*. Consequently, lexical insertion could not be restricted to a single linguistic level: applications of certain transformations had to be interspersed between lexical insertions. The combinations that could be derived through the application of predicate-raising and other 'prelexical' transformation were supposed to underlie 'possible lexical items.' Since there are infinitely many such combinations but only finitely many actual lexical items in any given language, most correspond to no actual lexical item of the language and were supposed to reflect accidental gaps in the lexicon of the language.

Lexical decomposition analyses were criticized in such works as Fodor 1970, where it was argued that the simple and complex surface forms that supposedly corresponded to the same deep structure (e.g., *Brutus killed Caesar* and *Brutus caused Caesar to die*) did not in fact have the same meanings. It was noted subsequently (McCawley 1978) that such discrepancies in interpretation can be explained by a version of Grice's (1967/1989) maxim of manner according to which a simple surface form is preferred to a more complex alternative except when the referent is a peripheral instance of the category defined by the given semantic structure, e.g., using indirect means to cause someone to die would be a peripheral instance of the category defined by 'cause to cease to be alive' and thus would not be in the part of that category where *kill* would preempt the use of *cause to die*. (Syntactic analyses involving lexical decomposition also figured prominently in Gruber 1965, a work that early GS-ists found congenial despite some important differences between its framework and theirs.)

2. GS Policies on the Conduct of Research

Of equal importance to these points of theory in their influence on the directions that GS research took and the reception that GS work received were several policies about the conduct of linguistic research, of which the following deserve mention here:

(a) A lack of concern about the compartmentalization of the parts of a linguistic analysis or of a linguistic theory, as contrasted with the concern among Chomskyan generative grammarians with the drawing of boundaries among, e.g., syntax, semantics, and pragmatics. One important facet of this lack of concern was an egalitarian position regarding the different kinds of data that had a bearing on a linguistic analysis: whereas most generative grammarians held that syntactic analyses needed to be supported by arguments in which only syntactic facts figured, GS-ists held that facts about truth conditions, possible denotations, etc., were as relevant as any other kind of facts to evaluating analyses that purported to specify how meanings corresponded to surface forms in the given language, and that supposed syntactic facts were usually at least partly semantic in nature, in that what a speaker of a language judges acceptable is not a sentence in itself but that sentence relative to an assumed understanding of it. Another facet of this policy was GS-ists' insistence that all parts of a linguistic analysis were subject to the same standards of explicitness, simplicity, and factual accuracy, irrespective of how one might wish to demarcate syntax and semantics; by contrast, interpretive semantics has come only gradually and often grudgingly to subject the semantic parts of analyses to the same standards of appraisal as the syntactic parts.

(b) Rejection of the dogma of generative grammar that a fixed notational system is essential to a linguistic theory and that precision can be achieved only by formulating one's analyses in the privileged notational system.

(c) Adoption of a 'static' conception of linguistic rules: rules were thought of not in terms of the popular metaphor of assembling linguistic structures and converting structures on one level into corresponding structures on another, but as 'derivational constraints,' that is, as specifications of what a structure may or may not contain and of how a structure on one level may or must differ from the corresponding structure on another level. This difference in the conception of rules resulted in differences with regard to what theoretical notions posed 'conceptual problems' (Laudan 1976) for each approach; thus GS-ists readily accepted rules that specified relations among nonadjacent levels of structure (what Lakoff 1970b dubbed 'global rules'), a notion that was unproblematic from their conceptual vantage point but outlandish from the vantage point of the 'operation' metaphor for rules, while rejecting the idea of ordering among rules, a notion that was unproblematic for those who accepted the 'operation' metaphor but was difficult to make coherent with the GS conception of rules as derivational constraints.

(d) Disdain for those concerns of Chomskyan generative grammarians that had little connection with linguistic facts or with detailed linguistic description, such as mathematical models and speculation about the extent to which linguistic structure is biologically determined. While GS-ists were receptive to the idea that linguistic structure is profoundly influenced by neuroanatomy, they demanded (e.g., Lakoff 1974: 171) that claims to that effect be backed up with solid linguistics and solid biology rather than with what they dismissed as arguments from ignorance (i.e., hasty leaps from one's failure to see how some characteristic of languages could be learned to the conclusion that it must be innate).

(e) Eagerness to put in practice in their professional lives many of the ideas of the 1960s counterculture, such as policies of antiauthoritarianism, antielitism, and demystification of science and scholarship, and a belief that one's work should be pleasurable. One of many facets of the GS ethos that these policies helped to shape is what Newmeyer (1986: 133) has disparaged as 'data-fetishism': joy in the unearthing of novel and intriguing facts for which one is not yet in a position to provide a satisfactory analysis; GS-ists, by contrast, regarded Chomskyan generative grammarians as 'scientific Calvinists' (McCawley 1980: 918).

3. Prominent and Influential Analyses Proposed within the GS Approach

Kuhn (1970) notes that one major component of the paradigm of a scientific community is a set of 'exemplars': prestigious solutions to problems, presented to neophytes in the field as paragons of good science, and serving as models for solutions to new problems. (For discussion of the history of generative grammarians' analyses of English auxiliary verbs in terms of Kuhnian notions such as 'paradigm' and 'exemplar,' see McCawley 1985.) The exemplars for the GS community included a number of analyses that bore an intimate relation to central tenets of GS, for example, lexical decomposition analyses such as were discussed in Sect. 1, and analyses of quantified expressions as being external to their host sentences in deep structure (e.g., *John has read many books = many books + John has read x*) and as being moved into their surface positions by a transformation of Quantifier-Lowering (QL). (The term QL was in fact applied indiscriminately to a variety of transformations that differed according to the specific deep structure that was assumed; proposals differed with regard to whether just a quantifier or a whole quantified expression was external to the host S, what filled the deep structure position into which the quantified expression was to be moved, and where the quantifier or quantified expression was in relation to the host S.) The best-known arguments given for a QL analysis consisted in demonstrations that the many syntactic rules that were problematic when applied to structures that contained quantified elements became unprob-

lematic if the deep structure position of a quantified expression was external to its host sentence and consequently (in virtue of the principle of the cycle) the rule had as its domain of application a structure that does not contain the quantified expression; for example, this view of the interaction between QL and the transformation of 'Reflexivization' explained why such pairs of sentences as *Every philosopher admires himself* and *Every philosopher admires every philosopher* differed in meaning in the way in which they did, and why reflexivization was applicable only in the derivation of the former. A thorough survey of arguments for a QL analysis is given in McCawley (1988: ch. 18).

Several other GS exemplars were in fact as consistent with the substantive claims of interpretivist transformational grammar as with those of GS, but were embraced by GS-ists and rejected by interpretive semanticists as much because of policies on the conduct of research (see Sect. 2) as because of any points of linguistic theory, or simply because of the historical quirk that a particular idea occurred to a member of the one camp before it occurred to any of his counterparts in the other camp. One such exemplar is the analysis of English auxiliary verbs as being verbs that take nonfinite sentential complements in the manner of such verbs as *seem* (Ross 1969; McCawley 1971), which Pullum and Wilson 1977 subsequently argued for from within an interpretive semantic framework. (A similar treatment of auxiliary verbs is found in Jespersen 1937: 92). A second was the proposal (McCawley 1970, subsequently disavowed by the author) that English had underlying verb–subject–object (VSO) word order, a hypothesis that is, if anything, harder to reconcile with the assumptions of GS than with those of interpretive semantics in view of the dubious nature of the assumption that the order of elements is significant in semantic structure; by contrast, there is no general policy in interpretive semantic versions of generative grammar against discrepancies between deep and surface constituent order, and indeed languages with surface VSO word order are commonly analyzed by interpretive semanticists as having deep SVO word order. Another such exemplar is the 'performative analysis' (Ross 1970), in which sentences are assigned underlying structures in which a 'hypersentence' (Sadock 1969, 1974) specifies the illocutionary force of the sentence, e.g., *Birds fly* would have an underlying structure of the form [*I tell you* [*birds fly*]].

4. The History of GS

The term 'generative semantics' first appears in Lakoff (1963/1976), a work that antedates the development of the Katz–Postal–*Aspects* approach to syntax and prefigures some of Lakoff's subsequent GS work. GS originated in attempts by Postal and Lakoff to exploit novel possibilities that were opened up by the revisions of the transformational syntactic framework proposed in Katz and Postal (1964) and Chomsky (1965) and to fill gaps in the evolving framework. For example, Lakoff's PhD thesis (Lakoff 1965/1970) originated as an attempt to develop a precise and coherent account of the way in which a lexical item could affect the applicability of transformations to structures containing the given item, and thereby to put on a solider footing those analyses in Chomsky (1965) in which the choice of lexical items affected the possibilities for derivations. In the course of providing such a theory of 'rule government,' Lakoff realized that it could be exploited in ways that narrowed the distance between semantic structure and syntactic deep structure, for example, by treating inchoative and causative clauses in terms of underlying structures that contained a corresponding stative clause (e.g., the structures underlying *The door opened* and *He opened the door* would contain an embedded sentence corresponding to *The door is open*) and by treating certain part-of-speech distinctions as differences in the applicability of transformations that inserted a copula or adjoined a preposition to an NP. Similarly, an attempt to refine and add substance to Chomsky's hesitant suggestion (1965: 145) that referential indices were a part of underlying syntactic structures gave rise to the line of research in which McCawley (1968) argued that all rules whose application is contingent on the identity of two units are sensitive to the purported reference of those units and of their parts, provided one identifies correctly what units purport to refer and what units figure in identity requirements.

An identifiable GS research community came into being during the 1966–67 US academic year, when Lakoff and Ross taught year-long courses at (respectively) Harvard and MIT, in which they proposed and refined a large body of 'abstract syntax' analyses that provided much of the core of subsequent GS research and stimulated a considerable amount of research within their evolving framework by students at the two institutions. GS first attained prominence outside of the Harvard–MIT linguistic community at a conference at the University of Texas at Austin in March 1967 whose proceedings were published as Bach and Harms (1968). The GS community increased considerably in size during the Linguistic Institute held at the University of Illinois in summer 1968, at which numerous students were exposed to large doses of GS syntax and semantics in courses taught by Lakoff, McCawley, and Ross, including for the first time a detailed presentation of the conception of semantic structure that figured with increasing prominence in GS research. The fifth annual conference of the Chicago Linguistic Society (CLS), in April 1969, attracted a large proportion of those who were engaged in GS research and dwarfed all previous CLS conferences in attendance, number of submissions, and number of papers presented. For the next several years, the CLS conference served as a gathering of the GS clan, and the volumes of its proceedings contain a sizeable proportion of the published GS research that was done during those years.

The GS community rapidly decreased in numbers during the mid-1970s, until by the end of the decade no real GS community existed any longer. The reasons for this decline are a matter of controversy. It was not simply a matter of interpretive semanticists and others refuting theoretical claims of GS, since GS-ists and interpretive semanticists had comparable success in refuting the others' theoretical claims (see, e.g., the detailed dissection in McCawley 1975 of the positive claims put forward in Chomsky 1972 and of Chomsky's arguments against various tenets of GS). In several of the factual domains that figured prominently in disputes between GS and interpretive semantics, the facts were not what either camp predicted them to be. For example, adverbials that modified semantic constituents of the meaning of a semantically complex word (as in *He lent me his bicycle until Tuesday*, where *until Tuesday* modifies 'I have his bicycle') were neither always possible (as GS analyses in their pristine form implied) nor never possible (as tenets of interpretive semantics implied); neither camp ever succeeded in explaining which cases did and which did not allow such modifiers, though each continued to cite the cases that worked in the desired way as confirmations of its own position and refutations of the opposing position. (Situations in which two factions have solid grounds for claiming to have refuted the other's position are by no means rare in the history of science; Musgrave 1976 documents such a state of affairs in the dispute between phlogiston chemistry and oxygen chemistry between 1771 and 1785.) While the grammar of nominalizations played a major role in interpretive semanticists' attacks on GS and in the rationale for their 'lexicalist' framework, no detailed study of nominalizations was produced by any interpretive semanticist, and the only at all comprehensive study of normalizations produced in the 1970s (Levi 1978) was done in a GS framework.

Some factors that clearly played a role in the precipitous decline of GS are (a) the development of a variety of alternative approaches to syntax and semantics that for various reasons attracted substantial numbers of neophyte linguists and a certain number of erstwhile GS-ists; (b) the fact that leading figures of early GS devoted much of their attention during the 1970s to topics that were widely regarded as peripheral or irrelevant to syntax; and (c) the fact that the leading figures of GS stimulated few students to engage in GS research during that period (Postal held an industrial research position and thus did no teaching; Lakoff taught at Harvard and Michigan for only brief periods, and none of his Berkeley students finished their PhDs until after the decline of the GS community was far advanced; and after the departure of some congenial colleagues, Ross was the sole GS-ist on the faculty of a department that was otherwise openly hostile to GS). Newmeyer (1986: 132–38) speculates that the factors contributing to GS's rapid decline included the casual and at times flippant, vulgar, and dadaist style that GS-ists often affected, the willingness of leading GS-ists to allow the factual domain for which they held themselves and their theories accountable to expand beyond reasonable limits (Harris (1993: 230) refers to a popular view that GS 'tried to swallow the world and choked on it'), and that 'Generative semanticists simply gave up on attempting to *explain* grammatical phenomena.' The latter claim does not fit the historical facts, but a widespread impression of its truth may have been fostered by some of the policies on the conduct of research listed above in Sect. 2, as well as by the infrequency with which GS-ists used the word *explain* and its derivatives, as contrasted with the high frequency of that set of words in interpretive semantic works.

The one part of GS theory that can plausibly be implicated in the demise of the GS community is the GS treatment of syntactic categories, which is one of the few parts of GS theory that any prominent GS-ists have subsequently recanted (McCawley 1977, 1982). (One other recantation should be mentioned, namely Lakoff's (1987: 583–85) recantation of the GS policy of adopting a conception of semantic structure that was closely tied to formal logic and model theory.) Coincidentally, the radical revisions that interpretive semanticists were making in their versions of generative syntactic theory included the adoption of the 'X-bar' conception of syntactic categories, which identified two of the factors that affect the syntactic behavior of a linguistic unit, namely, the difference between a word unit and a phrasal unit, and the part of speech of the unit or of its head. Once a descriptive framework was available that allowed linguistic generalizations to be stated in terms of those factors, considerable progress was made in the analysis of the many syntactic phenomena in which those factors play a role.

No important tenets of GS rule out the adoption of a conception of syntactic categories as defined by these factors *in addition to* logical categories, and indeed a conception of syntactic categories as reducible to those and other factors (with logical category being merely one of several factors that influence a unit's syntactic behavior) is adopted in McCawley (1977, 1982) and subsequent works. However, in the 1960s and early 1970s, an assumption shared by GS-ists and interpretive semanticists impeded GS-ists from adopting such a conception of categories, namely the assumption that syntactic categories must remain constant throughout derivations: a word (with a determinate part of speech) that replaced a complex of semantic material (thus, a unit not having a part of speech) could not differ in category from the replaced unit and thus parts of speech could not be part of the category system. (The widespread misconception that GS analyses allowed linguistic units to change category in the course of derivations in their analysis of, for example, nominalizations overlooks the fact that, according to GS-ists' assumptions, verbs and their nominalizations belonged to the same category. Anyway, analyses of any kind in which the verb *invent* is a constituent of the noun *invention* are not committed to any assumption that the former changes its category in the derivation of the latter: it is whatever it is, regardless of what it is contained in.) Since interpretive semanticists did not require that deep structures match semantic structures (and indeed took delight in arguing that they did not match), there was no obstacle to their having the same categories in deep as in surface structures while drawing the full range of category distinctions provided for by X-bar syntax. The interpretive semantic research program was thus able to become 'progressive' in the sense of Lakatos (1978) because of something extraneous to the issues that were the loci of the substantive disputes between GS and interpretive semantics.

Bibliography

Bach E, Harms R T (eds.) 1968 *Universals in Linguistic Theory*. Holt, Rinehart and Winston, New York

Binnick R I 1971 'Come' and 'bring.' *LIn* **2**: 260–67

Chomsky N A 1965 *Aspects of the Theory of Syntax*. MIT Press, Cambridge, MA

Chomsky N A 1972 *Studies on Semantics in Generative Grammar*. Mouton, The Hague

Fodor J A 1970 Three reasons for not deriving 'kill' from 'cause to die.' *LIn* **1**: 429–38

Grice H P 1967 Logic and conversation. In: Grice H P 1989 *Studies in the Way of Words*. Harvard University Press, Cambridge, MA

Gruber J S 1965 Studies in lexical relations. In: Gruber J S 1976 *Lexical Structures in Syntax and Semantics*. North-Holland, Amsterdam

Harris R A 1993 *The Linguistics Wars*. Oxford University Press, Oxford

Jackendoff R S 1972 *Semantic Interpretation in Generative Grammar*. MIT Press, Cambridge, MA

Jespersen O 1937 *Analytic Syntax*. Allen and Unwin, London

Katz J J, Postal P M 1964 *An Integrated Theory of Linguistic Description*. MIT Press, Cambridge, MA

Kuhn T 1970 Postscript. *The Structure of a Scientific Revolution*, 2nd edn. University of Chicago Press, Chicago, IL

Lakatos I 1978 Falsification and the methodology of research programmes. In: Lakatos I, Musgrave A (eds.) *Criticism and the Growth of Knowledge*. Cambridge University Press, Cambridge

Lakoff G 1963 Toward generative semantics. In: McCawley J (ed.) 1976 *Notes from the Linguistic Underground* (*Syntax and Semantics*). Academic Press, New York

Lakoff G 1970a *Irregularity in Syntax*. Holt, Rinehart and Winston, New York

Lakoff G 1970b Global rules. *Lg* **46**: 627–39

Lakoff G 1974 (interview conducted by H Parret). In: Parret H *Discussion Language*. Mouton, The Hague

Lakoff G 1987 *Women, Fire, and Dangerous Things.* University of Chicago Press, Chicago, IL

Laudan L 1976 *Progress and Its Problems.* University of California Press, Berkeley, CA

Levi J N 1978 *The Syntax and Semantics of Complex Nominals.* Academic Press, New York

McCawley J D 1968a The role of semantics in a grammar. In: Bach E, Harms R T (eds.) 1968

McCawley J D 1968b Lexical insertion in a transformational grammar without deep structure. *Chicago Linguistic Society Papers* **4**: 71–80

McCawley J D 1971 Tense and time reference in English. In: Fillmore C, Langendoen D T (eds.) *Studies in Linguistic Semantics.* Holt, Rinehart and Winston, New York

McCawley J D 1975 Review of Chomsky 1972. *Studies in English Linguistics* **5**: 209–311

McCawley J D 1977 The nonexistence of syntactic categories. *Second Annual Metatheory Conference Proceedings.* Michigan State University, East Lansing, MI

McCawley J D 1978 Conversational implicature and the lexicon. In: Cole P (ed.) *Pragmatics* (Syntax and Semantics 9). Academic Press, New York

McCawley J D 1980 Review of 1st edn. of Newmeyer 1986. *Linguistics* **18**: 911–30

McCawley J D 1982 *Thirty Million Theories of Grammar.* Croom Helm, London

McCawley J D 1985 Kuhnian paradigms as systems of markedness conventions. In: Makkai A, Melby A (eds.) *Linguistics and Philosophy. Studies in Honor of Rulon S. Wells.* Benjamins, Amsterdam

McCawley J D 1988 *The Syntactic Phenomena of English,* 2 vols. University of Chicago Press, Chicago, IL

Musgrave A 1976 Why did oxygen supplant phlogiston? Research programmes in the Chemical Revolution. In: Howson C (ed.) *Method and Appraisal in the Physical Sciences.* Cambridge University Press, Cambridge

Newmeyer F J 1986 *Linguistic Theory in America,* 2nd edn. Academic Press, Orlando, FL

Postal P M 1974 *On Raising.* MIT Press, Cambridge, MA

Pullum G K, Wilson D 1977 Autonomous syntax and the analysis of auxiliaries. *Lg* **53**: 741–88

Ross J R 1969 Auxiliaries as main verbs. *Studies in Philosophical Linguistics* **1**: 77–102

Ross J R 1970 On declarative sentences. In: Jacobs R, Rosenbaum P S (eds.) *Readings in English Transformational Grammar.* Ginn, Waltham, MA

Sadock J 1969 Hypersentences. *Paper in Linguistics* **1**: 283–371

Sadock J 1974 *Toward a Linguistic Theory of Speech Acts.* Academic Press, New York

Glossematics (Hjelmslev)

Erik C. Fudge

'Glossematics' was an approach to the study of language carried on mainly in Denmark between the mid-1920s and the mid-1950s under the leadership of Louis Hjelmslev (1899–1965). It represents in general a development of certain principles first put forward by Ferdinand de Saussure, in particular the principle that the importance of the units of a language is that they are distinct from one another, rather than that they exhibit particular concrete properties.

The glossematicians aimed to devise a universal framework within which the description of particular languages could be carried out. Their approach was intended as a thoroughgoing attempt to reshape linguistics as an exact science: this reflects important features (see Sect. 2) of 'logical positivism,' the most influential philosophical movement of the time.

1. Outline of the History of the Glossematic Movement

Denmark has a strong tradition of linguistic study going back at least as far as Rasmus Kristian Rask (1787–1832). It was therefore not surprising that an active movement in structural linguistics should originate in Copenhagen. After studying Romance philology and comparative philology, and working on Lithuanian, Hjelmslev published his first major book *Principes de grammaire générale* in 1928.

As early as 1924 Hjelmslev had spent time in Prague (before the foundation of the Linguistic Circle there), but it was not until 1931 that he became particularly concerned with phonology. In that year the phonologists of the Prague School had made striking contributions to the International Congress of Linguistics held in Geneva; this resulted in the formation of bodies analogous to the Linguistic Circle of Prague in a number of places, Copenhagen among them.

From the beginning, Hjelmslev's approach to sound structure differed considerably from Prague phonology, which he criticized as being excessively phonetic in its definition of basic units such as the phoneme. He and his principal collaborator Hans Jørgen Uldall (1907–57) coined the term 'phonematics' to refer to the theory on which they were working: the titles of the papers they gave in 1935 to the International Congress of Phonetic Sciences in London include this new term.

The Copenhagen Circle aimed to publicize its work from quite early on—a regular *Bulletin* appeared from 1934; however, their series of *Travaux* (analogous to the series of highly influential linguistic studies emanating from the Prague Circle in the years 1929–39) was not inaugurated until 1944. Before then, most of the important Copenhagen contributions appeared in periodicals, or in the proceedings of a number of international congresses. The one full-length book produced in this period was Hjelmslev's *La catégorie des cas* (1935; see Anderson 1971, 1977).

Coincidentally, the term 'glossematics' itself dates from 1935; Hjelmslev and Uldall felt that they were now ready to proceed to the construction of a general theory of language which was rather different from most of the theories hitherto proposed under the title of 'linguistics.' The two scholars planned a joint book on the theory, to be entitled *An Outline of Glossematics*. Although a very brief *Synopsis* was produced in 1936, little progress was made on the complete work. Separation during World War II meant they had to work independently on the theory; by the time they were able to get together again (in 1951), they found their ideas had diverged to the point of making the production of a joint publication difficult.

In the meantime, in 1943 Hjelmslev had produced what became his major work, *Omkring sprogteoriens grundlæggelse*: being written in Danish, it was for some while inaccessible to the majority of linguists. Hjelmslev's visit to the USA in 1952 to teach at the Summer Institute of the LSA led to the production of the authorized English translation *Prolegomena to a Theory of Language* in 1953 (2nd edn. 1961).

Hjelmslev's fiftieth birthday in 1949 was marked by the publication of a volume of essays *Recherches structurales 1949*, subtitled *Interventions dans le débat glossématique*. Although 16 of the 24 contributions are by other Danish scholars (including Uldall), the remaining eight clearly show that Hjelmslev enjoyed an international reputation by this time: the authors include Roman Jakobson (Harvard, USA, formerly of the Linguistic Circle of Prague), Jerzy Kuryłowicz (Kraków, Poland), Emile Benveniste (Paris), and André Martinet (Paris, but at the time attached to Columbia University, USA).

A further important indication of Hjelmslev's growing reputation outside Denmark was the appearance in 1955 of Berthe Siertsema's *A Study of Glossematics: Critical survey of its fundamental concepts* (2nd edn., 1965), a book which remains one of the most detailed and constructively critical treatments of Hjelmslev's theory.

Most of the large-scale works emanating from the movement at this time were general and theoretical in nature. One exception is the book published in 1951 by Knud Togeby (1918–74) entitled *Structure immanente de la langue française*: although set within the framework of a version of glossematic theory, it is a sustained treatment of the form and substance of French (see Sect. 6 for more detail). Another extended treatment of a particular language (Spanish) in a glossematic framework, also published in 1951, was Emilio Alarcos Llorach's *Gramática estructural* (*según la escuela de Copenhague y con especial atención a la lengua española*).

Uldall completed his Part I of the projected *Outline*

of *Glossematics* (in page proof as early as 1952), but the divergence of their views meant that Hjelmslev found himself unable to write his Part II to fit with it. Part I was eventually published on its own in 1957, the year of Uldall's death. Between then and his own death in 1965, Hjelmslev produced no other large-scale works.

For a fuller historical account of the movement, see Fischer-Jørgensen (1975: ch. 7).

2. Logical Positivism and Glossematics

The following four characteristics of logical positivism exerted a strong influence on glossematics:

    (a) metaphysical sentences are not false but meaningless, and must therefore be avoided (Sect. 2.1);

    (b) science must account for as many empirical facts as possible by means of logical deduction from as few axioms (initial assumptions) as possible (Sect. 2.2);

    (c) structural statements are to be preferred to statements of content (Sect. 2.3);

    (d) scientific language should be a kind of algebra, with all terms being unambiguously defined (Sect. 2.4).

2.1 Avoidance of Metaphysical Claims

Traditionally, the glossematicians claimed, the view had been taken that methods appropriate for the humanities were quite different from those appropriate for the sciences. According to this traditional view, the basis for the difference was that the unpredictable 'human factor' was central in the study of the humanities, but missing from the sciences, in which all variables were controllable.

A refutation of this position was attempted in terms of an analogy: 'If two candles on the dining-table do not burn exactly alike[...]it might, analogously, be inferred that the candle factor is too strong to permit physics and chemistry to be merely mechanical in operation' (Uldall 1957: 2). Clearly the 'candle factor' could be made explicit in terms of structural differences in the candles, the influence of air currents, and other controllable physical and chemical aspects of the situation. So the issue was whether or not linguistics could attempt to make relevant aspects of the 'human factor' more explicit.

To account for linguistic phenomena in terms of this human factor (or 'mind,' 'world-view,' etc.) without further explanation would clearly be to use language in a metaphysical way which the logical positivists would have found objectionable. This avoidance of metaphysical language makes an interesting comparison with the antimentalism of the linguistics of the same period in the USA.

2.2 Deductive Reasoning

'Inductive' reasoning argues from observed data to inferred theory. However, any theory which is arrived at by this method cannot be tested by the same method. Testing needs a different method, 'deductive' reasoning, which proceeds in the opposite direction from inductive reasoning.

Deductive reasoning in fact assumes a theory and on that basis predicts the kinds of data that will be observed; the validity of the assumed theory may be tested by comparing these predictions with the data that actually occur—if the predictions are at variance with the data, the theory is thereby shown to be false, while if the fit between predictions and data is good, the theory is thereby supported, though not shown incontrovertibly to be true.

It is clear that, in any type of scientific enquiry, both types of reasoning are needed. There is, however, an important difference between the two: inductive methods are a matter of trial-and-error, and so are difficult, if not impossible, to describe coherently—deductive methods are a matter of drawing conclusions from premises using well-defined logical processes.

Glossematicians certainly use the two terms 'inductive' and 'deductive,' but it is important to bear in mind that their usage does not conform exactly to the more usual explanation of the terms given here.

2.3 Importance of Structural Statements

There are some areas, for example color perception, where it is difficult to make a precise statement of content, e.g., 'A sees this color as a shade of green tending towards turquoise'; it is often easier to achieve precision by making relational statements such as 'A sees colors X and Y as distinct from each other, whereas B sees X and Y as the same color.' This relational statement leaves out of account the 'greenness' or 'turquoiseness' or other specific property of colors X and Y.

Extension of this approach to aspects of language description was one of the key elements in the thought of Saussure. When dealing with the inner system of a language, it was for him much less important to ask 'What are the physical properties of this sound?' than to ask 'Are these two sounds the same, or distinct?' The glossematicians took this approach to a conclusion judged by some scholars to be beyond the limits of feasibility.

2.4 Reduction of Scientific Language to an Algebra

Sentences using constructions of the kind which are typical of metaphysical discourse (such as 'the form of this utterance is governed by certain ideas present in the speaker's mind') should be excluded from scientific discourse; furthermore, all terms used should be defined unambiguously. Although suitable algebras were available to glossematics for its purpose, its proponents, notably Uldall, seem to have expended a good deal of energy in attempting to evolve an algebra of their own.

3. Form and Substance in Glossematics

Saussure viewed the structural system of a language as a form linking two kinds of substance: phonic (sounds) and conceptual (ideas). Both kinds of substance were described by him as formless masses ('*masses amorphes*'), one phonetic and the other semantic. The worlds of sound and idea can be conceptualized only by having form superimposed on them by the structural system of a language.

Although glossematicians also use the term 'substance,' they take it in a different sense—they view it, not as the formless masses themselves (to refer to which Hjelmslev uses a term translated into English as 'purport'), but as the *result* of operating on purport in terms of the abstract distinctions of which the 'form' consists. Thus form is logically prior to substance.

3.1 Form and Substance in the Area of Sounds

In the area of phonology and phonetics, for example, the purport is the whole range of possible sounds which the human vocal apparatus is capable of producing, i.e., the subject matter of general (language-independent) phonetics. On the other hand, the substance is the (comparatively restricted) range of sounds actually used by speakers of a language or language variety, i.e., the subject matter of language-specific phonetics.

Thus, for instance, the continuum formed by the pharynx, palate, teeth, and lips is a matter of general human anatomy; it is therefore language-independent, and belongs to purport. However, this continuum will be divided up differently in different languages: the form of the particular language acts on the purport to produce the substance of that language.

Many languages will have a substance exhibiting a division of this particular continuum into three, giving a three-way distinction of place of articulation: a back [k]-area, a middle [t]-area, and a front [p]-area. In other languages, the continuum is divided into four parts: the [k]-area may be further divided (as in Eskimo—uvular consonants distinguished from velar), or the [t]-area may be further divided (as in Hindi—retroflex consonants distinguished from dental).

From the point of view of the form of a language, the fact that the 'place of articulation' continuum is divided into three, or four (or in some languages more) is more important than what the three, or four (or more) places of articulation within the substance actually are.

3.2 Form and Substance in the Area of Ideas

Here one might take as an example of purport the infinite range of different color hues which exist. Each language specifies this infinite range in terms of a number of basic categories, most notably in the area of hue; some languages have a larger number of basic color terms than others.

Not only words are involved in form in this area: examples are very common in which prefixes or suffixes relate to each other formally in this way. Take, for instance, the aspect of purport represented by the (language-independent) continuum of time. On the level of form, many languages have a two-way distinction which, when applied to this continuum, often gives rise to a basic 'past' versus 'non-past' division on the level of substance, a division made manifest in two different sets of inflexions.

3.3 Logical Priority of Form

Glossematicians recognize that form as well as purport is twofold, and that therefore substance is twofold; this yields four areas of study within every language:

(a) 'content-substance' (roughly meanings of words and of morphosyntactic properties of the language);

(b) 'content-form' (roughly morphological, syntactic, and lexical structure of the language);

(c) 'expression-form' (roughly phonology of the language);

(d) 'expression-substance' (roughly phonetics of the language).

Content and expression are on a footing of equality—each of them is presupposed by the other. On the other hand, form is logically prior to substance—there can be no substance unless form has done its work.

The conclusion drawn by glossematicians from this logical priority is that the scientific description of form must be entirely independent of substance, and, a fortiori, of purport. The science of the expression is thus not a phonetics, nor is the science of the content a semantics. Expression-form was claimed to be independent of phonetics, on the grounds that expression-form may be manifested not only in sounds (as in a spoken language) but also in, for example, writing, morse code, or manual signs. For both expression and content, a language must be described in terms of its own 'immanent' structure.

3.4 Form: Discovery and Verification

Critics of glossematics often raised the objection: 'How can anything be discovered about form without reference to substance?' After all, the basic tool for investigating how languages work has to be to ask the question 'Does changing a sound in an utterance change its meaning, and vice versa?' Glossematicians certainly used this tool in the form of the so-called 'commutation test': in their terminology, 'Does a change on the level of the expression entail a change on the level of the content, and vice versa?'

The apparent paradox is resolved by noting that it is not on the level of discovery that substance must be excluded from consideration. The discovery phase of any scientific enterprise is inductive (see Sect. 2.2) in

nature: the investigator must begin by examining observable data, which of course must involve physical properties of substance. He or she then proceeds to set up hypotheses about what must be the abstract formal system capable of accounting for the data.

The workings of this formal system, on the other hand, are deductive (see Sect. 2.2); here the starting point is the hypothesized basic entities, the relations between them being stated formally, i.e., in terms which are not related to substance. As the deductive process continues, the elements concerned are put into correspondence with more and more properties of substance.

This is what Hjelmslev meant when he claimed (1961:79) that glossematics 'would be an algebra of language, operating with unnamed entities, i.e., arbitrarily named entities without natural designation, which would receive a motivated designation only on being confronted with the substance.' This approach is exemplified in Sect. 6 below, from Togeby's work.

4. The Analytical Procedure of Glossematics

The complete procedure, including both inductive and deductive aspects, is said by Siertsema (1965: 24–25) to be best understood in terms of seven steps. The important features of each step can be summarized as follows:

(a) For a particular language, the expression units (phonemes, syllables, etc.) and the content units (word-roots, prefixes, etc.) must be discovered by means of:

  (i) relationships holding between content units and (combinations of) expression units, established by applying the commutation test (see Sect. 3.4); and

  (ii) properties of substance of these units.

(b) Relationships holding between an expression unit and other expression units of that language, and relationships holding between a content unit and other content units of that language, must be described without reference to their substance.

(c) The units and their relationships are tentatively drawn up into a hypothesized system for the language.

(d) Steps (a)–(c) must be repeated for as many languages as possible.

(e) Extrapolation must be made from the total of relations actually found in these languages to the total of theoretically possible relations.

(f) These theoretically possible relations must be combined into a calculus which constitutes the system of language, rather than the system of a particular language or of many particular languages.

(g) Each particular language will then be characterized by the subset of actually occurring relations which it has 'selected' from the total of theoretically possible relations. This characterization will enable the tentative systems set up under (c) to be revised and brought nearer to their definitive form.

Steps (a)–(d) are clearly inductive, leading to a set of tentative language systems. Steps (e) and (f) introduce a deductive system which is universal, i.e., language-independent; this is then used in step (g) to make predictions which will be the means of making revisions to the tentative language systems.

This approach diverges markedly from that of the post-Bloomfieldians in American Structuralism (see *American Structuralism*), who believed that a sound theory should be based on the correct method of proceeding from observable data to hypothesized system. For them the inductive method alone was scientifically respectable, and they sought to work in terms of a completely specified discovery procedure. Only steps (a) and (c) of the glossematic procedure would have won their full approval.

5. Basic Relations in Glossematics

If, as glossematicians held, relations between entities in a theory are more basic than the physical properties of those entities, then it is of fundamental importance to have a typology of such relations. The relations in fact constitute an important part of the axioms of the theory.

The basic dependence is '*a* presupposes *b*' (i.e., 'if *a* occurs, then *b* occurs' or '*a* cannot occur without *b*'). A more complex set of dependences can be built up on this foundation: for example, three complex dependences which crop up frequently in linguistic study are:

(a) Interdependence—*a* presupposes *b* and *b* presupposes *a*. Here *a* and *b* may occur together, but neither of them without the other.

(b) Determination—*a* presupposes *b* but *b* does not presuppose *a*. Here *a* and *b* may occur together, and *b* may occur alone, but *a* may not occur alone (in which case *a* is referred to as the *variable* and *b* as the *constant*).

(c) Constellation—*a* and *b* are compatible but neither presupposes the other. Here *a* and *b* may occur together, *b* may occur alone, and *a* may occur alone.

There are other logical possibilities, such as '*a* precludes *b*,' which are not given labels, on the grounds that they play no real part in the analysis of language systems or texts.

A further distinction is brought in, between syntagmatic ('both–and') relations and paradigmatic ('either–or') relations. Each resulting type of relation is referred to by a label as shown in Fig. 1. Thus in

looking at a language system, the relation between vowel and consonant is always a 'complementarity,' since there are no languages which do not have both vowels and consonants. However, in looking at texts in languages, the situation will depend on the language. In those languages where all syllables have a vowel and at least one consonant, the relation is a 'solidarity'; in languages where some syllables consist of a vowel alone, the relation is a 'selection.'

Dependence	'Both–and'	'Either–or'
determination	selection	specification
interdependence	solidarity	complementarity
constellation	combination	autonomy

Figure 1. Types of dependence in glossematics.

The importance of this system of relations is not the terminology, but the fact that such relations, rather than any properties of substance, are felt to be of prime importance in glossematics.

6. The Procedure Exemplified

Togeby's *Structure immanente de la langue française* of 1951 puts forward a deductive system whose aim is to account for the whole range of possible texts in French. Some of the more detailed statements are specific to French (e.g., statement (c), Phonology, §6.2), but many statements are to be taken as general (universal) (e.g., statement (f) in §6.3, Syntax). Some statements are included with the aim of completeness on the general level, but with the specific caveat that they do not hold for French (e.g., statement (d), Phonotactics, §6.2).

The summary of this work given below is intended to show what glossematicians believed the description of a language had to cover. This included an inventory of the items which were important within a language, and a statement of how these items could be combined. The scope of the description should be noted: unlike some other grammatical theories, this one went beyond the level of the sentence, and attempted to give an account of the structure of larger bodies of material. Thus 'text' in the previous paragraph is intended to mean any discourse—not only written, but also spoken.

The description begins by introducing the entity 'text.' No definition of the term 'text' is given directly, but in fact the sequence of statements which follows, if applied correctly, produces something which does constitute a correctly constructed text in French. All other terms in the description will gain a definition in analogous fashion. This illustrates Hjelmslev's claim about how the theory works (see Sect. 3.4).

One type of statement within the theory deals with constructions: a 'syntagmatic' statement of the form X: Y + Z. This may be read as 'X has components Y and Z': the order of Y and Z is not necessarily sequential, at least as far as the 'content' part of the grammar is concerned. The similarity between these statements of the glossematic theory and phrase-structure rules in generative grammar (X → Y+Z) is noteworthy.

The other type of statement deals with systems: a 'paradigmatic' statement of the form X: Y, Z, W, meaning 'Xs are either Ys or Zs or Ws.' Alternatively this may be cast in the form:

X: Y
 Z
 W

Again the parallel with one type of rule in generative grammar is noteworthy.

The set of operations is divided into three main sections:

(a) a set of operations which applies in parallel fashion to expression and content alike (see Sect. 6.1);
(b) a set of operations which applies to expression alone (see Sect. 6.2);
(c) a set of operations which applies to content alone (see Sect. 6.3).

Each set is then further subdivided into a syntagmatic subset (dealing with constructions on a particular level) and a paradigmatic subset (dealing with the elements from which a choice may be made at the appropriate point).

6.1 French: Description Involving both Expression and Content

The syntagmatic subset is named 'syntagmatics,' and consists of the following operations:

(a) *Text*: expression line+content line. (The text is divided into two simultaneous parts, one on the level of expression, the other on the level of content.)
(b) *Line*: modulation sentences. (Each of the two lines is divided into successive units consisting of intonation plus sentence; see operation (c).)
(c) *Modulation sentence*: modulation unit+sentence. (The modulation unit is a sentence-length sequence of intonation groups.)
(d) *Modulation unit*: modulation elements. (The modulation element is the intonation pattern associated with a single tone-group.)

The paradigmatic subset is named 'systematics,' and consists of the following operations:

(a) *Elements*: phonemes; morphemes; morpho-phonemes; onomatopoeias. This division is carried out on the basis of whether the element is associated with the expression ('phonemes'), with the content ('morphemes'), with both ('morpho-phonemes'—elements further defined in operation (b)), or with neither ('onomatopoeias'—expressions like *pstt* which

do not enter into constructions, and which need not obey the normal phonological rules of the language).
(b) *Morpho-phonemes*: modulations; emphases. (Modulations are intonation elements; emphases are emphatic or contrastive stresses.)

6.2 French: Description of the Expression

The syntagmatic subsection is named '*Prosodie*,' which might best be translated 'phonotactics'. This consists of the following operations:

(a) *Sentence*: syllable-groups. (Syllable-groups are very much like words, but that term is reserved for the content; see Sect. 6.3).
(b) *Syllable-group*: word-accent+syllable-group. (An operation which does not apply for French; 'word-accent' refers to the tonal elements in languages like Swedish.)
(c) *Syllable-group*: syllables.
(d) *Syllable*: accent+syllabic base. (Another operation which does not apply for French; 'accent' refers to tone in languages like Chinese, or word-stress in languages like English.)
(e) *Syllabic base*: nucleus+margin. (The syllabic base consists of the segments (vowels and consonants) which go to make up the syllable; the nucleus is formed of vowels, or, in the absence of vowels, of consonants of high sonority (nasals or liquids)—the margin is formed of consonants.)
(f) *Margin*: consonants. (The fact that some consonants may precede the nucleus and others may follow it is not specifically noted in the operation: linear order of elements is not part of this section of the theory.)
(g) *Nucleus*: marginal vowel+central vowel +marginal vowel. ('Central vowel' not in the sense of 'midway between front and back,' but indicating centrality within the nucleus—more prominence than the others, and often a greater degree of openness.)

The paradigmatic subsection is named 'phonology,' and consists of four operations:

(a) *Phonemes*: accents; vowels; consonants. (French has no accents, i.e., distinctive stresses.)
(b) *Accents*: strong; weak.
(c) *Consonants* (inventory of 17 for French).
(d) *Vowels* (inventory of 10 for French).

6.3 French: Description of the Content

The syntagmatic subsection is named 'syntax,' and consists of seventeen operations, beginning with 'sentence,' and proceeding in a fashion resembling the phrase-structure rules of generative grammar via 'words' down to the smallest grammatical elements, 'morphemes.' Examples of the operations involved:

4. *Clause*: circumstantial complement + clause-nucleus
5. *Circumstantial* ⎰preposition + object
    complement: ⎱subordinating conjunction + clause
6. *Clause-nucleus*: subject + predicate
7. *Subject*: apposition + nominal phrase
8. *Predicate*: object ⎱
              attribute⎰ + verbal phrase

15. *Word*: stem + inflexions
16. *Stem*: root + derivational marker

NB: the numbering of the above subset of operations follows that of the text, and differs from the summary table appearing later in the book.

The paradigmatic part is entitled 'morphology' and consists of the following statements:

2. *Morphemes*:
    inflexions
    roots
    derivational markers
    particles
3. *Inflexions*:
    verbal: mood, aspect, tense
    verbo-nominal: person, number
    nominal: case, comparison, gender
4. *Roots*:
    verbs: auxiliary verbs, ordinary verbs
    nouns: proper nouns, pronouns, numbers, substantives, adjectives
5. *Derivational markers*:
    prefixes, suffixes, non-finite verb
6. *Particles*:
    adverbs, linking words, interjections
    linking words: subordinating conjunctions, prepositions, co-ordinating conjunctions

7. Conclusion

Although the theory of glossematics has not been further elaborated since Hjelmslev's death, there can be no doubt that many linguistic scholars in Denmark, and also some outside Denmark, have been greatly stimulated by the views he put forward and the questions he raised. Fischer-Jørgensen's work (1975: ch. 7) is a good starting point for understanding the theory and how it developed; Siertsema (1965) gives a profound exposition and critique of Hjelmslev's work.

Perhaps the best exemplification of the theory with special reference to a particular language is Togeby (1965). There is also in this work a considerable amount of valuable comparison with other approaches.

Of Hjelmslev's own works, Hjelmslev (1961) is in many ways central for the understanding of his theory; on the other hand, some of his collected essays (Hjelmslev 1959, 1973) are considerably less difficult for the nonspecialist.

Bibliography

Anderson J M 1971 *The Grammar of Case: Towards a Localistic Theory*. Cambridge University Press, Cambridge

Anderson J M 1977 *On Case Grammar: Prolegomena to a Theory of Grammatical Relations*. Croom Helm, London

Fischer-Jørgensen E 1975 *Trends in Phonological Theory*. Akademisk Forlag, Copenhagen

Hjelmslev L 1959 *Essais linguistiques*. Nordisk Sprog- og Kulturforlag, Copenhagen

Hjelmslev L 1961 *Prolegomena to a Theory of Language*, 2nd edn. University of Wisconsin Press, Madison, WI (Transl. by Whitfield F J)

Hjelmslev L 1973 *Essais linguistiques II*. Nordisk Sprog- og Kulturforlag, Copenhagen

Recherches structurales 1949. Nordisk Sprog- og Kulturforlag, Copenhagen

Siertsema B 1965 *A Study of Glossematics*, 2nd edn. Brill, Leiden

Togeby K 1951 *Structure immanente de la langue française*. Larousse, Paris

Uldall H J 1957 *An Outline of Glossematics*, Part I. Nordisk Sprog- og Kulturforlag, Copenhagen

Grammatical Units
R. E. Longacre

The structure of a language is essentially threefold: (a) its sound structure, commonly called phonology; (b) its lexical structure, as seen in its dictionary items, its synonyms, antonyms, and items from the same or different semantic domains; and (c) its grammatical structure. A systematic account of the grammar of a language treats of the units and relations that hold within its grammar. This can best be illustrated by resort to an example (1):

College freshmen don't always enjoy Orientation Week. (1)
In fact some find it a great bore.

This passage is a one-paragraph discourse which consists of two sentences. Speaking this way, there has already been occasion to mention three grammatical units: 'discourse,' 'paragraph,' and 'sentence.' Discourse (or text) is the most inclusive unit and reflects the realities of oral and written communication. This particular discourse could, for example, have been spoken in a faculty meeting called to consider the value of 'Orientation Week' in the calendar of a private college. But, while discourse is the most inclusive unit and ultimately of almost universal relevance in grammar it is taken for granted in this article and little is said about it. Paragraph is also seen by some as a grammatical unit, and is mentioned briefly in Sect. 3.

In example (1) each sentence is a one-clause, or simple sentence. The clause is a unit of predication; most clauses consist of a verb (or predicate) and its arguments, as encoded in the verb phrase and noun phrases. The study of the internal structure of clauses, and similar and contrasting structures from clause to clause has been a very important part of grammar whether traditional, structural, or generative.

The first sentence of (1) consists of a clause composed of three phrases: the noun phrase *college freshmen*, the verb phrase *don't always enjoy*, and a second noun phrase *Orientation Week*. The first and third parts of the clause are related to the central part as subject and object respectively. In this clause each noun phrase is internally complex and consists of two or more words: (a) *college freshmen* consists of two nouns, the first of which modifies (or qualifies) the second; (b) this is likewise true of *Orientation Week*; (c) the central verb phrase *don't always enjoy* is composed of four words: *do*, *not* (with phonological contraction between them), *always*, and *enjoy*. The internal structure of the phrases again reflects grammatical relations; beginning with the predicate note that *enjoy* is the main verb, *do not* is a negated auxiliary, and *always* is an adverb which is closely related to the verb. In regard to the two noun phrases, where clearly the former element modifies the latter, it needs to be pointed out that, while such noun–noun phrases are very prolific in English, other noun phrase types such as the following also occur: *those two incoming freshmen*, and *this particularly obnoxious week*, and *John's haircut*.

The word and its internal composition is a further concern. Here the concept of word is tied to that of morpheme as a name for a component-meaningful part of a word. Thus, *freshmen* is a plural of *freshman*; this internal complexity must be recognized as parallel to *boys*, *girls*, *fiefs*, *houses*, and *cruises* which also are plural formations. Here an isolable morpheme /-z/, /-s/, /-əz/, and /-əs/ marks plural with forms varying according to simple phonological rule. *Freshmen*, however, has a plural which is indicated by internal change; this is discussed below under Sect. 1.4.1. The form *freshmen* is complex even if not pluralized, i.e., the form *freshman*. Here the compound form acts exactly like a simple noun, so that *man : men :: freshman : freshmen*. *Freshman* is, then, a derived form consisting of *fresh + man*.

To return again to example (1). While the first clause-sentence can be summarized in three phrases, the second such unit is slightly more complex.

(a) It has an initial conjunctive phrase *in fact*, which serves to contrast the second one-clause sentence with the first in the grammar of the paragraph.

(b) Besides the subject–verb–object structure,

which is similar to that of the first sentence, and besides the initial conjunctive phrase, it also has a final complement *a great bore*. The latter is an attributive noun phrase with a determiner *a*, an adjectival modifier *great*, and a head noun *bore*.

(c) The second sentence has pro-forms *some* and *it* as its subject and object respectively. *Some* is a pro-word which indicates a logical partitioning of its antecedent *college freshmen* into those who like and those who do not like *Orientation Week*. *It* is another pro-word; it refers back to *Orientation Week* of the first sentence. *Some* and *it* are pronouns which are used anaphorically to tie the second sentence into the first.

In this discussion of example (1), the terms 'discourse,' 'paragraph,' 'sentence,' 'clause,' 'word,' and 'morpheme' as names for grammatical units have been illustrated. Certain grammatical relations have also been briefly referred to in the course of the discussion. The latter will not figure very prominently in the ensuing sections since the focus here is on the units rather than the relations. Here the clause, sentence, and paragraph are highlighted.

1. The Clause

The clause is the natural language counterpart of the predicate calculus, i.e., it consists of a predicate and its terms or arguments. As such the clause is the domain of the verb and of the nouns that are associated with it. A language may or may not have case endings marked in its noun morphology. But even in a language with such marking (Latin, Greek, Sanskrit, Lithuanian, northeastern Caucasian languages), a noun with a given case ending often encodes several distinct functions or roles. So, a Latin grammar must list uses of the nominative, genitive, dative, accusative, and ablative. Apparently, semantic roles such as agent, patient, experiencer, and goal are more basic than the case marking as such.

A case-frame classification is a semantic classification of clauses according to verb types and nouns in accompanying roles. A sampling of such a semantic classification of clauses is given here (from Longacre 1983).

(a) Ambient clauses refer to the environment or the weather. English uses a third person impersonal 'dummy' word *it* in such clauses: *It's hot*, *it's windy*, *it's snowing*, *it's raining*. Trique is an example of a language which employs an inflected verb without any surface structure subject: $a^3m\tilde{a}^{35}$ʔ 'raining,' $ga^3m\tilde{a}^{35}$ʔ 'rained,' $ga^5m\tilde{a}^5$ʔ 'will rain.' Korean must use a noun such as 'weather' or 'climate' in meteorological clauses. For 'rain' or 'snow' some languages employ a verb 'fall,' i.e., 'rain's falling.'

(b) Desire/cognition clauses include not only

want/desire, love, but also verbs of acquaint-
ance knowledge such as *know, come to know,
introduce*, and 'evaluation' clauses such as
those containing such verbs as *disdain, praise,
judge, accuse*, and *pardon*. In these verbs there
is an experiencer and a goal as in *John loves
Mary* where *John* is experiencer, and *Mary*
(who may not even be conscious of John's
feelings towards her) is the goal.

(c) Sensation and speech clauses often take special
treatment as well, for example, verbs such as
*hear, smell, see, tell, speak, show, sing, listen,
watch*. To some degree these two sorts of
clauses go their separate ways. Korean
requires one to say 'we heard the sound of the
train,' not just 'we heard the train,' i.e., the
source must be specified.

(d) Physical clauses include clauses referring to
physical state, process, action-process, and
action. State verbs are such verbs as *(be)
broken, (be) wet*. Process includes such clauses
as: *the dish broke; the bolt came loose; the pig
died*. Action–process clauses include the prototypical transitive verbs which occur with an
agent and a patient. They often express an
instrument as well: *John broke the dish; Sue cut
the rope with a knife*. In motion verbs the agent
and patient coalesce: *Stephen ran the race;
They fought a good fight; John ate a full meal*.
In these clauses there is an agent/patient and
often a surface structure complement (*the race,
a good fight, a full meal*).

The surface structure of these semantically differing
clauses varies considerably from language to language. At one extreme stands such a verb–subject–
object language as Trique which has no cases and
marks only a few distinctions in the surface structure,
but which marks subject versus object by word order.
At the other extreme are languages with a proliferation of cases marked with endings or postpositions, e.g., Japanese, Korean, Finnish, and
Daghestan (Caucasian) languages.

1.1 Surface Structure Variations

Here brief mention is appropriate of active versus
passive, and ergative versus accusative structures.
While all these concerns relate to the surface structure
organization of clauses, characteristically these variations and contrasts are responsive to the discourse
structure (i.e., context on some level).

Active versus passive is well-established in English
where it is easy to produce paradigmatic examples
such as *John purchased the book* versus *The book was
purchased by John*. In both clauses *John* is agent and
book is patient. But in the former *John* is surface
structure subject and *the book* is object while in the
latter *the book* is surface structure subject and the
agent *John* occurs in a *by* adjunct phrase.

While passive variants of most English transitive
clauses are paradigmatically possible, in actual dialog
and monolog discourse passives have restricted and
specialized functions: (a) to avoid mention of the
agent, when to specify a further participant, i.e., the
agent, would distract from the thematic unity of a
stretch of discourse; (b) to underscore the affectedness
of the patient; and (c) to mark generic statements in
expository sentences, instead of specific statements in
narrative sentences (Longacre 1983).

Passives in some languages include a type where the
agent cannot be mentioned. In still other languages
(traditional Japanese and some other Asian languages) passives have an adversative connotation.
That is, one might say 'Tarou was scolded by the
teacher' but not 'Tarou was praised by the teacher.'

Unlike passive, ergative is a nontraditional term
recently introduced into contemporary linguistics.
Ergative structures treat as the same morphological
(or even morphosyntactic) category the subject of an
intransitive verb and the object of a transitive verb as
over against the agent of a transitive verb.

Thus, in Zoque there is a special suffix *-ʔs*, which
occurs only on the subject (agent) of a transitive verb
while the subject of an intransitive verb and the object
of a transitive verb are unmarked. In the agreement
of the verb with subjects and objects in Mayan languages the same (or, at least, very similar) pronominal
affixes indicate subject of an intransitive verb and
object of a transitive, while a special set of pronominal
affixes express agreement with the subject (agent) of a
transitive verb. In ergative languages with systems of
case endings or nouns there is an absolutive case ending for nouns which are either subjects of intransitive
verbs or objects of transitives, and there is an ergative
case ending for nouns that are subjects (agents) of
transitive verbs. Australian and Caucasian languages
provide many examples of such usage (Dixon 1979).

1.2 Types of Nonindependent Clauses

Besides independent clauses there are three types of
non-independent clauses: complement clauses, relative clauses, and adverbial clauses.

The complement clause is an argument of another
clause (2):

    (a) *His going there surprised me.*   (2)
    (b) *I remember that he went there.*

In (a), *his going there* is subject of the verb *surprised*.
In (b) *that he went there* is object of the verb *remember*;
it could have taken the same form as in (a). Both *his
going there* and *that he went there* fill noun slots within
their sentences.

The relative clause qualifies a head noun in a variety
of syntactic positions (3):

    (a) *The house that Jack built fell down.*   (3)
    (b) *I tore down the house that Jack built.*
    (c) *I put a new front door on the house that Jack built.*

The adverbial clause corresponds to a variety of adverbial functions. Furthermore, the function of such a clause, while primarily related to the main clause with which it occurs, may involve structures on paragraph and discourse levels. Example (4) illustrates very briefly something of the range of adverbial clauses in English (temporal, causal, conditional, concessive, circumstantial, and purpose respectively):

(a) *When Mary came in, Jack stalked out.* (4)
(b) *Because Mary came in, Jack stalked out.*
(c) *If Mary comes in, Jack will stalk out.*
(d) *Although Mary came in, Jack stalked out.*
(e) *In that Mary had come in, Jack saw no reason for staying.*
(f) *Mary came home so that Jack could go out for a while.*

1.3 Word Order in the Surface Structure

Most languages have a word order (or, properly speaking, a constituent order) which is either its statistically most common ordering, or which at least offers the best base for a description of alternative orderings. The basic word order is characteristically found in sentences which move the story forward in narrative discourse.

English is strongly subject–verb–object, i.e., noun phrase, verb phrase, noun phrase, in surface structure. So prevalent is this order that grammatical dummies for the subject are resorted to in meteorological clauses, and in some existential structures. Thus in the following *it* and *there* perform such dummy subject functions (5).

(a) *It's raining.* (5)
(b) *It's a fact that soup requires crackers.*
(c) *There is still another angle to the situation.*

In spite of the fact that English is strongly SVO in structure, there are conditions under which English employs alternative ordering. An older form of postposed quotation formula regularly had VS order: '*I'm not going to go,' said George.* Here, a detail of sentence structure, the structure of quotation sentences calls for a departure from the SVO ordering, with subject and verb changing places. A further departure from the normative ordering in English is occasioned by discourse structure, i.e., marking the high point of a story (6).

Into the pot fell the wolf with a great splash. (6)

Most native languages of Mesoamerica, Biblical Hebrew, Classical Arabic, and some Nilotic languages are verb-first languages, commonly expressed as VSO. Occasionally one finds a language such as Teposa (Nilotic) where deviation from the standard order is extremely rare. Many VSO languages have, however, a preverbal slot X into which one noun phrase (and characteristically only one phrase) can be shifted, giving, on occasion, such orders as SVO, OVS, and T/LVS(O), where T and L represent time and location expres-

sions. The X slot can be termed 'emphatic,' but this cover term must in every case be replaced by a more adequate description in the grammar of each VSO language.

Many languages around the world are of SOV structure, viz. New Guinea and some surrounding islands; much of South America; Indic; Omotic, Cushitic and Ethio–Semitic languages of Ethiopia; Caucasian languages; Turkish; Japanese; and Korean. Some such languages are strongly SOV, to the point where any noun phrase which occurs out beyond the verb is considered to be an afterthought which may occur in oral text or speech but which is corrected by rotating it to its usual preverb position in edited, written transcription. A few SOV languages, however, systematically exploit an X slot, i.e., SOV(X) for special discourse purposes. A signal instance of this is in Cayapa text (Ecuador) where a noun phrase in regular position versus one in position X has to do with the aggressor–victim (or antagonist–protagonist) structure of a story (Weibe 1979).

2. The Sentence

The sentence is the grammatical unit which embraces clause combination. As such, it is the natural-language counterpart to the statement or propositional calculus of logic. Sentences may be put together internally according to co-ranking or chaining.

2.1 Co-ranking Sentence Structures

Here a further division between languages that have sentences built around internal conjunction and those that do not is posited.

The nucleus of conjunctive sentences turns on the use of conjunctions such as *and, but,* and *or.* Again, languages vary greatly in this regard; there may be several sorts of 'and's,' 'but's,' or 'or's' in a given language. Subtle differences in the semantics of conjunctions present a challenge to the analyst—not to speak of problems for translators. Typically *and*-like conjunctions are default connectors; *but*-like conjunctions express contrast and counterexpectation; and *or*-like conjunctions express alternation or at least alternative wordings.

The English conjunction *and* typically joins predications from the same semantic domain (7):

(a) *My wife collects coins and I do ceramics.* (7)
(b) *Rudolf plays chess and participates in a string quartet.*

Here leisure time activities is the semantic domain. Example (7a) couples the leisure time activities of two people, while (7b) couples two such activities of the same person. But *and* is a default connector; as such it is sometimes employed where more specific connectors are avoided (8):

OK, Mary is rich and I'm poor—so what! (8)

In this example had the speaker meant to foreground

contrast he would have employed *but* instead of *and*. Contrast, however, is deliberately played down by employing *and*.

The conjunction *but* foregrounds contrast. This semantic notion can be defined as turning on two sets of lexical oppositions: one set embraces a pair of antonyms or antonym-like terms; the second such set may or may not be antonymically opposed but must be a pair of differing entities/participants. The first set can turn on positive versus negative values of the same/similar predicates (9):

> (a) *He's naive about women but sophisticated about*
>   *computers.* (9)
> (b) *Jim works outdoors during the summer, but indoors*
>   *during the winter.*
> (c) *I don't like western movies but my brother loves them.*

In the above, (9a) turns on *naive* versus *sophisticated* and *women* versus *computers*; (9b) turns on *outdoors* versus *indoors* and *summer* versus *winter*; while (9c) turns on *I* versus *my brother* and *don't like* versus *loves*.

The same conjunctive *but* in English (but not necessarily in other languages) expresses counterexpectation or frustration (10):

> (a) *John has long legs but is a very poor runner.* (10)
> (b) *Maple says that Horace is intelligent but he really*
>   *isn't.*

In (10a) above, long legs might imply that John was a good runner, but the second part of the sentence denies this implication. In (10b) Maple's attributing intelligence to Horace might lead one to believe him to be intelligent, but, again, the latter part of the sentence denies this.

The English conjunction *or* is used in sentences which express alternation—typically of the exclusive variety (not 'and/or'). In English *or* is sometimes reinforced with *either* in the first clause (11):

> (a) *Either Harry should be forced to get up and go to work* (11)
>   *or his wife should at least phone in that he is sick.*
> (b) *I'll either go to work or I won't.*
> (c) *Did he go to work or stay home?*

Notice that alternation requires only one set of lexical opposites; this is evident in (11b) 'go to work' versus 'not go to work' and (11c) 'go to work' or 'stay at home.' In (11a) the opposed set is internally complex: 'be forced to get up and go to work' versus 'have someone phone in that he is sick.' But a second set of opposites is not present as in contrast.

The conjunction *or* is sometimes used in English to express alternative verbalizations (12):

> *We should get some legal protection, call the police,* (12)
> *or something on that order.*

For a detailed presentation of conjunctive sentences in a family of non-Indo-European languages (Phi-

lippine), see Longacre (1968: 2); for English, see Longacre (1979).

2.1.2 Juxtaposed (Nonconjunctive) Sentence Patterns

Still another type of co-ranking structure does not use sentence–internal conjunction but rather patterns of juxtaposition with restrictions on the internal structure of component clauses. This has been the prevailing pattern of sentence formation in the Otomanguean languages of Mesoamerica, as described for Otomi by Lanier (1968), for Chatino by Pride (1965), and for Trique by Longacre (1966). Take the following pair of Trique sentences (13):

(a) $gi^3da^3\hat{r}a^{34}$ $neh^3 zi^3$ zi^{21} $d\bar{a}h^3$ $ga^3\check{c}ih^2$ (13)
    seized   they   man   that   put

    $neh^3 zi^3 du^3gwa^3ga\hat{r}a^3$.
    they (in) jail.
    'They seized that man (and) put him in jail.'

(b) $gi^3da^3\hat{r}a^{34}$ neh^3 zi^3 zi^{21} $d\bar{a}h^3 ga^5\check{c}ih^5$ $du^3gwa^3ga\hat{r}a^3$
    seized   they   man $neh^3 zi^3$ they (in) jail
    'They   seized   that   man   that will-put   him in jail.'
                                     to put

In both the above sentences there is no internal conjunction such as 'and' or 'in order to.' There are, however, aspectual-modal restrictions on the verbs in the juxtaposed clause. The verbs in (13a) are indicative and punctiliar (the *gi-* prefix on the first verb and the *g-* prefix on the second). Consequently (13a) is a narrative sentence which records two successive events. In (13b), however, the second verb is modal (lowered tones). Marked this way sentence (13b) expresses an event and its purpose; there is no other way to express purpose in Trique.

With a continuative nonpunctiliar verb in both juxtaposed clauses, overlap or simultaneity is expressed (14):

$a^3g\bar{a}r^{34} ni^3 yah^2 n\ddot{i}h^3 a^3di^3y\bar{a}^{34} ni^3 ri^3\tilde{a}^{34} ni^2ma^3$ (14)
beat   they   drum   precede they   corpse
'They beat a drum as they walked before the corpse (funeral procession).'

Here both verbs are continuative (the punctiliar verbs have a *g-* prefix); the activities indicated are represented as simultaneous.

In the Philippines, juxtaposed sentence types are found side-by-side with sentence types which employ internal conjunction. However, only the former will be examined here. Inibaloi sentences constitute a crucial witness in regard to the fact that two clauses are involved, not one clause with two predicates. The crucial nature of the Inibaloi witness is seen in the fact that that language does not employ equideletion where it might be expected but instead repeats the pronoun (15):

> (a) *Onbowas ira   ira   man-obda* (15)
>   go-early they they work
>   'they go early in the morning to work'
> (b) *daw ka mo bayshi*

go   you you pay
'you go and pay it'

In these examples not only is the pronoun repeated but the whole construction is arranged in chiastic or mirror image order: VS, SV. In (5a) the pronoun *ira* 'they' is repeated; in (15b) the repeated pronoun changes form according to the requirements of the focus system, i.e., *ka* is subject-as-topic in the first clause and *mo* 'you' is subject-as-nontopic in the second clause— since money to be paid is the unstated topic of the second clause.

In all other Philippine languages encountered by the author equideletion is applied to reduce the sequence of two pronouns to one in such sentences as those illustrated by Inibaloi. The following Ata Negrito example is given (16):

makkido ka parúban   ta bale ta   (16)
as   you try   for house our
'Try asking for a house for us.'

2.2 Chaining Structures

The sentences which are considered above indicate two patterns of clause combination: (a) adverbial clause with *when, while, if*, etc. plus main clause (Sect. 1.1); and (b) main clause plus main clause either with or without sentence-internal conjunction (Sect. 2.1). This summary sketch of sentence structures around the world would, however, be quite incomplete without a presentation of chaining structures.

In a chaining structure (which is often equivalent to a sentence) only one fully inflected verb occurs in the chain; other verbs are less than fully inflected. In English one can say *John got up, put on his clothes, and went outside.* Here the verbs *got up, put on,* and *went* are all of the same rank, i.e., they are all independent indicative verbs. But in chaining structures in SOV languages only the equivalent of the last verb would be fully inflected; the first two verbs would be a structure variously called 'converbs,' 'co-verbs,' 'gerunds,' 'participles,' or 'medial' verbs. While semantically the chaining structure is still coordinant, structurally the final verb outranks the first two. Conversely, in VSO and SVO chaining structures the first verb is a special initial verb and subsequent verbs in the sentence are variously called 'sequential' or 'consecutive.' The two kinds of chaining are mirror images of each other. Medial-final chaining is the more widespread of the two and is found in the following areas: New Guinea and surrounding islands, many languages of South America, Ethiopian languages, Indic, Korean, Japanese, Turkish, Caucasian, and some native languages of the southwest USA. The reverse structure with initial-consecutive chaining is at present documented only in certain VSO and SVO languages of Africa (Longacre 1990). The latter sort of chaining is not illustrated here.

The following example (17) illustrates medial-final chaining in Wojokeso, a language of Papua New Guinea; note the rudimentary structure of the medial verbs in this sentence versus the structure of the final verb—which is the last word in the sentence (West 1973: 12–13):

(17)

Uhwon -ontae nowe -ntae sosyo		*ife'n-*		*ontae*
see -we go -we (name)		pick- we		
	sikunofo l-	*ontae toho*	*yohoj-*	*ontae*
	dark speak -we wood	gather -we		
	toho	*hiyamno sof-ontae*	*nop-*	*ontae*
	wood	carry carry-we	come -we	
nowe- ntae toho	*nomo'n- ontae*			
go- we wood	carry-we (with rope from head)			
yafe	*lo'mo p-*	*ontae mijo*	*lomo -wekapmmalohwoyofoho.*	
incline in	come -we	water in	crossed = we (indicative)	

'We looked and we went and picked some sosyo and we said "It's getting dark," and we gathered firewood and carried the firewood and came and went and carried the firewood by a rope hanging from our head and came down the incline and crossed the stream.'

The medial verbs *uhwonontae*, 'see-we'; *nowentae*, 'go-we'; *ife'nontae*, 'pick-we'; etc. have a suffix, (*o*)*ntae* which indicates nonfuture, 1st person plural (and also redundantly marks the same subject referent, since this tense–person–number category is not used with different subject referents). For the most part the sentence indicates successive events.

3. Paragraph

It has been argued (Longacre 1979) that there is a grammatical unit spaced midway between the sentence and the discourse, and that this unit can be given the traditional name paragraph. This structural unit in a given text in a given language, e.g., English, is not necessarily congruent with the orthographic unit which is marked by indentation in English and other languages.

As a grammatical unit, the paragraph (a) has closure (starts and stops); (b) has thematic unity; (c) is sometimes needed to make the grammar of the sentence or clause intelligible; and (d) can be shown to constitute a system. In reference to (a) the use of conjunctions and backreferential adverbial clauses should be noted as well as the occurrence of a sentence or two of introductory/setting nature at paragraph beginning and sentences that conclude the paragraph (a narrative can have static verbs in these places as opposed to the dynamic verbs in the body of the paragraph). In regard to (b) observe not only repetitions of key lexical items (often at beginning and end of the paragraph) but also topicalizations, left shifts, and cleft structures that are theme-establishing. Therefore, in regard to both (a) and (b) there is concern with surface features in grammar and lexicon. There is not space to argue (d) in this article.

In regard to (c) an example from the Ica language of Colombia is very instructive. Within isolated one-clause sentences of a narrative text there simply is no marking of the subject versus objects and complements. Apparently the clause-level grammar of the language is inconclusive at this point and one can go only on lexical probability, e.g., the probability that the dog bit the man instead of the man bit the dog. This is, however, not the whole story. On analyzing structural paragraphs in narratives within the language it turns out that: (a) in the first sentence or by the second sentence of the paragraph a noun (phrase) is marked with the suffix -*ri*; (b) once so marked the indicated noun and the participant which it encodes is the unstated subject of following sentences in the paragraph; (c) if a sentence introduces a subject other than the thematic participant of the paragraph, then the noun phrase in question is suffixed with -*seʔ*; (d) if part way through the paragraph the narration decides to switch the thematic participant of the paragraph, then the noun in question is suffixed with -*seʔri*. Clearly, in respect to rules (a)–(d) above the grammar of individual clauses and sentences waits upon the grammar of the paragraph. To insist under these conditions that the paragraph is 'simply a lexical unit' seems untenable. But the Ica situation is simply an extreme illustration of the interweaving of the grammar of the paragraph with the grammar of lower level units.

Bibliography

Dixon R 1979 Ergativity. *Lg* **55**: 59–138
Greenberg J H 1966 *Universals of Language*, 2nd edn. Mouton, The Hague
Lanier N 1968 Three structural layers in Mezquital Otomi clauses. *Linguistics* **53**: 32–85
Longacre R E 1966 Trique clause and sentence: A study in contrast, variation, and distribution. *IJAL* **32**: 242–52
Longacre R E 1968 *Philippine Languages Discourse, Paragraph, and Sentence Structures*, vol. 2: *Sentence Structures*. Summer Institute of Linguistics, Publications in Linguistics **21**
Longacre R E 1970 Sentence structure as a statement calculus. *Lg* **46**: 783–815
Longacre R E 1979 The paragraph as a grammatical unit. In: Givon T (ed.) *Discourse and Syntax (Syntax and Semantics 12)*. Academic Press, New York
Longacre R E 1983 *The Grammar of Discourse*. Plenum, New York
Longacre R E 1990 *Storyline Concerns and Word-order Typology in East and West Africa. Studies in African Linguistics, Supplement 10*. Department of Linguistics and James S. Coleman African Studies Center, University of California, Los Angeles, CA
Nida E A 1949 *Morphology: The Descriptive Analysis of Words*. University of Michigan, Ann Arbor, MI
Pride K 1965 *Chatino Syntax. Summer Institute of Linguistics, Publications in Linguistics* **12**
Shopen T 1985 *Language Typology and Syntactic Description*, vol. 1: *Clause Structure*; vol. 2: *Complex Constructions*; vol. 3: *Grammatical Categories and the Lexicon*. Cambridge University Press, Cambridge
West D 1973 *Wojokeso Sentence, Paragraph, and Discourse Analysis*. Pacific Linguistics, Series B. No. 28. Australian National University, Canberra
Wiebe N 1979 The structure of events and participants in Cayapa narrative discourse. *Summer Institute of Linguistics, Publications in Linguistics* **52**: Part 2

Grammaticalization and Lexicalization
Elizabeth C. Traugott

Much work in historical syntax, especially morphosyntax, and morphophonology can be considered related to or even exemplary of 'grammaticalization' (sometimes called 'grammaticization'). Grammaticalization is the linguistic process whereby grammatical categories such as case or tense/aspect are organized and coded. Typical examples involve a lexical item, construction, or morpheme, that, when used in certain highly specific frames, may come to code an abstract grammatical category. Some synchronic work can also be considered exemplary of grammaticalization; this work rejects static definitions of synchrony and focuses instead on dynamic, typically discourse, perspectives on language.

What distinguishes work on grammaticalization from much other work on morphosyntax is the perspective taken: focus on the interdependence of *langue* and *parole*, of the categorial and less categorial, of the fixed and the less fixed in language, of the motivated and the arbitrary. The study of grammaticalization therefore highlights the tension between relatively unconstrained lexical expression and more constrained morphosyntactic coding, and points to relative indeterminacy in language. In this sense, much work on grammaticalization challenges some of the fundamental theoretical constructs of linguistics since Saussure, including categoriality, homogeneity, arbitrariness, and (more recently) the discreteness and autonomy of syntax.

1. Grammaticalization as a Diachronic Phenomenon

From the diachronic perspective, grammaticalization is usually thought of as that subset of linguistic changes whereby lexical material in highly constrained pragmatic and morphosyntactic contexts becomes grammatical, and grammatical material becomes more grammatical. A simple example is the development of *be going to/gonna* as a marker of prospective temporality in English. Originally the progressive form of the main verb *go* plus a subordinator introducing a purposive clause, in certain contexts *be going to* came to function as an auxiliary.

This example illustrates many factors typically involved in grammaticalization (see Hopper and Traugott 1993: chs. 3, 4).

(a) The change occurs only in a very local context, that of purposive directional constructions with nonfinite complements, such as *He is going to help Bill* (i.e. *He is leaving/traveling to help Bill*). It does not occur in the context of purposive directionals in which the locative adverb is present, such as *He is going to London* or even *He is going to London to help Bill.*

(b) The change is made possible by the fact that there is an inference of prospective action from purposives: if a person is traveling in order to help someone, the help is to be expected in the future. In the absence of a directional phrase, prospective eventhood can be interpreted as salient. (This suggests that syntactic change is triggered by pragmatic factors, and therefore is not autonomous; furthermore that the change is by no means arbitrary.)

(c) The shift from purposive *be going to* to auxiliary *be going to* involves reanalysis not only of the *going to* phrase but also of the clause following it; thus [*He is going* [*to help Bill*]] is rebracketed as [*He is going to help Bill*].

(d) The reanalysis is discoverable (that is, manifest) only when the verb following *be going to* is incompatible with a purposive meaning, or at least unlikely in that context, for example, *He is going to like Bill.* In other words, the reanalysis is apparent only because the linguistic contexts in which *be going to* can occur have been generalized (or analogized) to contexts which were unavailable before.

(e) Once the reanalysis has occurred, *be going to* can undergo changes typical of auxiliaries such as phonological reduction. Note that the reduction of the three morphemes *go + ing + to* into one in the development of *gonna* is enabled only because there is no longer an internal bracket.

(f) Although the process started in the fifteenth century, the various stages of the grammaticalization of *be going* [*to.* .] are still present in Modern English. (This points to variation rather than homogeneity.)

(g) The original purposive meaning continues to constrain the use of the auxiliary: *be gonna* is a future of intention, plan, or schedule, in fact a prospective aspect rather than a deictic tense, and can therefore occur in constructions where a deictic future cannot. Compare *If she's going to go to London, we'll have to change our plans* with **If she'll go to London, we'll have to change our plans* (the only reading under which the

latter is acceptable is the *will* of agreement or intention, not of futurity).

(h) The verb *go* is a semantically rather empty verb, an inclusive hypernym for verbs of movement.

(i) In the process of grammaticalization, some of the original semantics of *go* has been lost, specifically motion and directionality; however, this loss has been balanced out by the development of temporal meanings, albeit more abstract ones.

Cross-linguistic studies show that only certain lexical items or classes of lexical items are likely to be used to code grammatical categories. For example, it is unlikely that *wallpaper* or *digress* would become grammaticalized directly, without intervening semantic changes. This is because they are semantically highly specific, and are unlikely to be used frequently in restricted syntactic contexts. What is found cross-linguistically is that for any given grammatical domain, there is only a limited set of lexical fields, and within them only a limited set of lexical items (those with general hypernymic meaning), that are likely to undergo grammaticalization. For example, case markers, whether prepositions or postpositions, typically derive from terms for body parts or verbs of motion, giving, and taking; temporal from spatial terms; middles from reflexives; articles and certain grammatical gender markers from demonstratives (for several examples, see Greenberg et al. 1978; Givón 1979: ch. 9; Traugott and Heine 1991; Lehmann 1995[1982]). Furthermore, the paths of change are highly restricted, and evidence minimal step-by-step developments, not large leaps across semantic or pragmatic domains. Accounts of why these restrictions apply appeal to cognitive constraints (Langacker 1977), communicative strategies (Slobin 1985), or the competing motivations of iconicity, economy of expression, and arbitrary grammatical structure (Haiman 1983; Du Bois 1985).

Among mechanisms of change leading to grammaticalization, the most usual is reanalysis (Langacker 1977), although not all reanalysis involves grammaticalization. Reanalysis involving boundary loss, such as is illustrated by *be going to*, is a prototypical case of grammaticalization, since it involves reduction and subsequent phonological attrition. Other cases, however, may involve scope expansion. For example, in the process of the development of complementizers or sentence connectives, a preposition introducing an NP can come to introduce an S, for example, *since evening > since he left*, or in the development of epistemic from deontic modals or of tense from aspect, the scope of the operator increases (Bybee 1985; Bybee et al. 1994).

Another type of reanalysis is word order change. Although Meillet (1912) included it among instances of grammaticalization, many linguists have specifically excluded it because it is not phonologically expressed and because word order changes occur in both directions, OV to VO and vice versa. Nevertheless, word order changes have extensive effects on the morphological structure of a language. For example, postfixal inflexions are typically replaced by prepositions in the shift from OV to VO (cf. the gradual replacement in English of the genitive inflexion by the preposition *of*, as in Old English *þara* [*dem + gen*] *tweo*, Modern English *two of them*; cf. also discussion of the Romance perfect below). Word order changes therefore figure centrally in work on grammaticalization, and recently efforts have been made to include it once again (e.g. Claudi 1994).

Another major mechanism in the morphosyntactic changes involved in grammaticalization is analogical spread. As indicated in (d) above, reanalysis cannot be discerned in the absence of evidence from analogical spread. Analogy also operates in the specialization of one grammatical form over another; for example, English had both a *be*-perfect and a *have*-perfect, cf. *She is gone, She has taken the book*; the loss of the *be*-perfect is effected by the analogical extension of the *have*-perfect from transitive to intransitive (specifically unergative) verbs.

Whereas the reanalysis is necessarily abrupt, the spread to new environments is actuated gradually and in small steps (Lichtenberk 1991). The result of the accumulation of changes may be a significant category change (e.g., the development of AUX in English), but individual changes may occur at different rates and may never reach categorial status. For example, *will* and *must* participated in the change to the category AUX that developed in Early Modern English, but started on the path from main verb to AUX in Old and Middle English respectively; and some verbs, such as *ought* and *dare*, have acquired only a subset of the characteristics of AUX. The result is considerable variability in structure at any one synchronic moment.

1.1 Unidirectionality

Although many examples of morphological changes that resemble cases of grammaticalization were discussed by nineteenth-century scholars, the term was apparently first used by Meillet (1912). He defined it as the evolution of grammatical forms (function words, affixes, etc.) out of earlier lexical forms, and much work has been done in this tradition.

Alongside the lexical item > morpheme tradition which derives from Meillet, there has been a more recent tradition that focuses on the 'packaging' of information in discourse and evolution of syntactic and morphological structure through fixing of discourse strategies. For example, Givón (1979: 209), characterizes the process as one of cyclic waves (1) involving:

discourse → syntax → morphology → morphophonemics → zero.   (1)

The definition proposed at the beginning of this article that grammaticalization is that subset of linguistic changes whereby lexical material in highly constrained pragmatic and morphosyntactic contexts becomes grammatical, and grammatical material becomes more grammatical, combines the two models, by specifying that grammaticalization arises from the use of lexical items, constructions, or morphemes in particular, highly localized, discourse contexts.

Firmly entrenched in diachronic perspective on grammaticalization and in the various definitions outlined above is the hypothesis of a 'cline of unidirectionality,' that is, a pathway that channels change through a limited number of structures that are minimally different from one another. This does not mean that all unidirectionality involves grammaticalization; for example, the well-known tendency for [sy] to become [š], but not vice versa, is in itself not an instance of grammaticalization. However, if it results from morpheme boundary loss, then it is an instance of a stage in grammaticalization. The question is precisely what kinds of unidirectionality are necessary or at least typical of grammaticalization.

One kind of semantic-pragmatic undirectionality often associated with grammaticalization is increase in abstractness. For example, *gonna* is less concrete than *go*; so is the use of French *pas* as a negative marker in *ne...pas* (derived from *not...a step*). But increased abstractness is not definitional of grammaticalization. For example, when French negative *ne...pas* is simplified to *pas*, or Old English negative *ne* becomes fused to *habb-* 'have,' forming *nabb-* 'not to have,' greater abstractness is not involved. Furthermore, not all increased abstractness involves grammaticalization. For example, the shift in meaning from *tongue* (as body part) to 'language' is merely a case of semantic change because the nominal status of *tongue* has not changed.

Much of the literature on unidirectionality characterizes the development of grammatical meaning from lexical meaning in terms of desemanticization, bleaching, and emptying or loss of semantic or pragmatic content. However, grammaticalization has been shown in its early stages typically to involve pragmatic specification and strengthening through 'inferencing.' This inferencing may be metaphorical: in the case of *be going to* the spatial motion of *go* is projected onto temporality (or, to put it another way, temporality is represented by a term from the spatial domain) (Sweetser 1988; Heine et al. 1991). The inferencing may also be metonymically derived from contiguity in the discourse world (Traugott and König 1991); for example, contiguity with purposive *to* enables projection of the inference of futurity onto *go* in the development of *gonna*. In either case, what is involved is a decline in concrete semantics balanced with an increase in pragmatic content. Typically, the direction of semantic-pragmatic change in early stages of grammaticalization is to greater subjectivity. A particularly clear case is the development of imperative *let us go* (cf. *let us go, will you!* > hortative *let's go* (cf. *let's go, shall we!*) (see papers in Stein and Wright 1995).

Another kind of unidirectionality often considered characteristic of grammaticalization is increase in structural bondedness. Typically, at the clause level independent clauses are combined, and a cline may develop from independent clauses through some kind of loose juxtaposition to subordination. A well-known example is the development in Indo–European of adjunct and nucleus into relative clauses, cf. Hittite (Held 1957: 43) (2–4):

| nu | U-NU-TUM | ku-it | ku-e-da-ni | (2) |
| and | utensil | INDEF | to-someone | |

| pe-es-ki-it | na-at | U-Ul | si-i-e-es-ki-it | (3) |
| he-gave | and-it | not | he-stole | |

'Which utensil he gave to someone, he did not steal it'   (4)
(= 'he did not steal a utensil which he gave to someone').

Eventually the *ku-* came to function as a relativizer in an embedded clause. Another example is the development in West African and Asian languages of a verb of saying into a complementizer. In the earliest stages, the verb introduces a direct quotation, for example, Ewe (Lord 1976: 179) (5–6):

me-bé mewɔe   (5)

I-said 'I-did-it.'   (6)

The general verb *bé* 'say' comes to introduce indirect quotation; it is semantically weakened by use after a range of other locutionary verbs, such as 'agree,' and sensory-intellectural verbs such as 'think,' loses its ability to take temporal inflexions, and eventually becomes an invariant particle.

At the phrasal level, forms may become less free and more bound via grammaticalization, for example, postpositions become affixes. Although the phenomenon is not confined to grammaticalization, one of its effects is that morphemes undergoing this process move away from cardinal categoriality, and in their later stages lose the ability to refer and to associate with the inflexional and derivational trappings of their morphosyntactic category (cf. Hopper and Thompson 1984). Nouns which develop into adpositions (e.g., *in the stead of* 'in the place of' > *instead of*) lose nominal characteristics such as the ability to be marked for definiteness or number, and verbs which are grammaticalized to case markers tend to lose the ability to be inflected for person, tense, aspect, and mood.

Later stages of grammaticalization typically also involve morphonological changes such as those illustrated by the development of *gonna*. The changes demonstrate not only the phonological effects of boundary loss, but the differentiation associated with it (only

the prospective *be going to* undergoes this change, hence *I'm gonna go*, but not *I'm gonna London*).

Unidirectionality may suggest a single path of evolution. However, in most cases of grammaticalization, multiple processes are at work. Heine and Reh (1984) suggest a tripartite classification of correlations of change: semantic–pragmatic status, grammatical behavior, and phonological substance. Lehmann (1985, 1995[1982]) uses a bipartite classification according to paradigmatic and syntagmatic processes, that is, according to the alternatives available on the one hand and the effect of linguistic context on the other. Whichever view is taken, an additional factor needs to be considered: 'frequency.' Given that a form A is a candidate for grammaticalization both because of its semantic generality and its discourse context, the further condition of frequent use has to apply for grammaticalization to take place. The seeds of grammaticalization are therefore to be found in a correlated set of phenomena: semantic suitability, constructional contiguity, and frequency. It is the last that leads to fixing, freezing, idiomatization, etc.

Although structural unidirectionality is a robust concept in grammaticalization, it is by no means definitional for grammaticalization. Nichols and Timberlake (1992) have suggested that sometimes morphological forms may be reassigned to different functions, without there necessarily being any clear directionality. Their example is the redistribution of nominative and instrumental case markers in Russian. Others have pointed to the existence of real counterexamples, for example, the use of prepositions like *up* as main verbs, as in *up the ante* (for more counterexamples, see Joseph and Janda 1988; Harris and Campbell 1995). Of particular interest is the fact that discourse particles appear frequently to involve disjunction rather than bonding. For example, in Modern Japanese the following pair exists, along with others of similar structure (based on Matsumoto 1988: 340) (7–8):

| Taro-wa | wakai(*-yo)-ga, | yoku | yar-u(-yo) | (7) |
| Taro-TOPIC | young(PART)-but, | well | do-PRES(-PART) | |
'Although Taro is young, he does a good job.'

| Taro-wa | wakai(-yo). | Ga, | yoku yar-u(yo) | (8) |
| Taro-TOPIC | young(PART). | But, | well do-PRES(-PART) | |
'Taro is young, but he does a good job.'

In (7) the particle *-ga* is bound intonationally to the preceding lexical item, and the structure is constrained (*-yo* is not permitted). In (8) *ga* is part of the intonational pattern of the following clause. Unidirectionality would suggest that (7) is a later form than (8). However, the reverse is true: (7) type constructions are quite old, whereas (8) type constructions date only from the seventeenth century (see also Onodera 1995).

It appears that direction of structural change may be correlated with the type of functional change in question (main verb > auxiliary, adposition > case, clause connective > discourse marker). What is common to all changes that count as grammaticalization is the shift from relatively open class to relatively closed class status.

Such change of status results naturally from frequent use of forms in highly specific frames. Another phenomenon that arises from frequent use of forms in highly specific frames is renewal of forms that have become grammaticalized. It used to be argued that renewal typically occurs after a form is lost, for example, prepositions were thought to replace case inflexions in English after the inflexions were lost through phonological attrition, that is, a cyclical model is assumed of the type (9):

lexicon > syntax > morphosyntax > morphophonology > zero. (9)

However, such a model would entail communicative dysfunction. What is seen repeatedly is the competition of two coexisting forms, one older and one newer, where the motivating force seems to be speakers' attempts to express abstract notions in novel ways instead of more idiomatized, frozen ones; these novel ways, after frequent use, may themselves become idiomatized. Sometimes a construction is renewed more or less in the same constituent position. An example is the development in late Latin of the periphrastic future *cantare habeo* 'I have to sing' (lit. 'sing-INF have-I'). This construction was eroded via morphological boundary loss, bonding, and phonological reduction to forms like French *chanterai*. However, in the process, no significant change in overall coding structure occurred, since the earlier form that it replaced was also inflexional (*cantabo*). By contrast, when a word order shift is in process, the newer form often conforms to the newer word order. Thus late Latin inflexional perfect *amavi* 'I have loved' was replaced by the periphrastic *habeo amatum*, eventually French *j'ai aimé*, presumably as the word order change from Latin OV to Romance VO was occurring (Fleischman 1982).

1.2 Some Questions for the Further Study of Grammaticalization from the Diachronic Perspective

Among a number of questions still to be answered is what the language–external motivation for grammaticalization may be. If semantic suitability, salience, and frequency are among the prerequisites for grammaticalization to start, then the question still remains as to what motivates the beginning of the process. Is it discourse-pragmatic pressure, that is, the need to be informative and processable and expressive all at the same time (cf. Langacker 1977), the phenomenon of gaps in grammatical paradigms or in the universe of abstract concepts, a 'natural propensity' for signaling metalinguistic relations in nonlexical ways (cf. Bybee and Pagliuca 1985), or some other factor(s)? These possibilities all point to linguistic problem-solv-

ing as a clue to motivations for grammaticalization (Lehmann 1985; Heine et al. 1991). Any claim about problem-solving and functional purpose raises issues of teleology. Because grammaticalization does not necessarily happen in any given instance of potential grammaticalization, considerable caution needs to be taken in proposing teleological explanations (cf. Keller 1994). Not enough is known yet about communication to argue that 'communicative necessity' motivates the development of grammatical categories. It is primarily through the study of what prevents grammaticalization, or simply fails to trigger it, that the answer to the question of motivation will be discovered. Here the fundamental question is how so much potential ambiguity as evidenced by extensive polysemy is tolerated in language.

Yet another unsolved puzzle is what motivates the differential speed with which grammaticalization takes place in different functional domains. Observations on African languages suggest that some kinds of development proceed faster than others. For example, new categories of tense and aspect have emerged within a relatively short period, and in some cases a new morphology evolving along the same grammaticalization pattern is already emerging, competing with the old one. The development of noun class systems or of verbal derivation, on the other hand, has been much more conservative: morphological paradigms found today can be reconstructed as having already existed in a similar form and function several millennia ago.

2. Grammaticalization from the Synchronic Perspective

Although most work on grammaticalization has been done from a historical perspective, there is a growing body of synchronic work considered to be conducted from the perspective of grammaticalization (although the term grammaticization is typically used). One line of this work tends to be a detailed study of alternative uses of the same form (e.g., Ford and Thompson 1986 on uses of *if-then*); the fundamental task is to identify a cline from more to less categorial or prototypical uses. Another line is typological, and explores ways of coding the same kind of discourse-pragmatic structure cross-linguistically (always through space and sometimes through time), for example, topic continuity (Givón 1983), evidentiality (Chafe and Nichols 1986), ergativity (DeLancey 1981), and middle voice (Kemmer 1993). Usually the unidirectionality of change is assumed; therefore, that which is less categorial, more bonded, etc., is assumed to be more grammaticalized. Common to this work is the view that language cannot be understood without attention to its use, and to the fluidity of its patterns. Questions are raised about whether 'grammar' preexists use, for example, whether it is innate. Hopper (1988), for example, argues that grammar, in so far as it exists at all, arises out of language use, especially the fixing of forms through frequent use.

3. Lexicalization

Like grammaticalization, the term 'lexicalization' is used in a number of different ways.

It has been used to refer to the expression as a linguistic form of a semantic property. Thus in English *have* and *be* can be said to 'lexicalize' ownership, location, possession, existence (Bickerton 1981). Another, related use of the term lexicalization is to name the process whereby an originally inferential (pragmatic) meaning comes to be part of the semantics of a form, that is, has to be learned. For example, in speaking of the fact that the inference of prospective eventhood in the purposive *be going to* construction became part of the meaning of *be going to* as an auxiliary, it can be said that the inference of prospectivity is lexicalized. Lexicalization in the sense described is as much part of semantic change in general as of grammaticalization.

In another, more restricted, sense of the word which pertains more particularly to grammaticalization, lexicalization is the process whereby independent, usually monomorphemic, words are formed from more complex constructions (Bybee 1985); this process is often called 'univerbation.' One example is the development of words like *tomorrow*, which originated in a prepositional phrase; the boundary between preposition and root was lost, and a monomorphemic word developed. This is an example of the kind of morphological detritus that can result from processes of reanalysis typical of grammaticalization. (Note that *to* is recognizable as a unit that also occurs in *today*, *tonight*, and so there may be different opinions about whether *tomorrow* is or is not monomorphemic.)

Another example is provided by phonological changes that result in morphological loss and the development of idiosyncratic lexical items, such as the English pairs *lie—lay*, *sit—set*, *stink—stench*, all of which have their origins in *i*-umlaut. This *i*-umlaut results from the loss of an original causative marker, so what occurs is morphological loss resulting in a more elaborate lexicon. Although the individual instances cited are further counterexamples to the unidirectionality from lexical item to bound morpheme, nevertheless their development is part of an overall shift in causative word formation in English away from post root affixation (still found, but recessively, in e.g., *redden*), to periphrasis (e.g., *make red*), or separate lexical expression; this itself is part of a larger shift to stem–invariance in the English lexicon (cf. Kastovsky 1989). From this perspective, the lexicalizations are part of a shift in coding to a simpler, more streamlined system of word formation than was typical in earlier Germanic and especially older Indo–European. They can therefore be considered part of a larger framework of grammatical recoding (i.e., of grammaticalization broadly defined), in which several local changes took place at different rates and at different times. As a result, Modern English (like any other language) exhibits characteristics from many layers of coding practices, and is far from homogeneous.

Bibliography

Bickerton D 1981 *Roots of Language*. Karoma, Ann Arbor, MI

Bybee J L 1985 *Morphology: A Study of the Relation between Meaning and Form*. Benjamins, Amsterdam

Bybee J L, Pagliuca W 1985 Cross linguistic comparison and the development of grammatical meaning. In: Fisiak J (ed.) *Historical Semantics and Historical Word Formation*. De Gruyter, Berlin

Bybee J L, Perkins R, Pagliuca W 1994 *The Evolution of Grammar: Tense, Aspect, Modality in the Languages of the World*. University of Chicago Press, Chicago, IL

Chafe W, Nichols J (eds.) 1986 *Evidentiality: The Linguistic Coding of Epistemology*. Ablex, Norwood, NJ

Claudi U 1994 Word order change as category change: The Mande case. In: Pagliuca W (ed.) *Perspectives on Grammaticalization*. Benjamins, Amsterdam

DeLancey S 1981 An interpretation of split-ergativity. *Lg* **57**: 626–57

Du Bois J W 1985 Competing motivations. In: Haiman J (ed.) *Iconicity in Syntax*. Benjamins, Amsterdam

Fleischman S 1982 *The Future in Thought and Language: Diachronic Evidence from Romance*. Cambridge University Press, Cambridge

Ford C E, Thompson S A 1986 Conditionals in discourse: A text-based study from English. In: Traugott E C, Meulen A ter, Reilly J S, Ferguson C A (eds.) *On Conditionals*. Cambridge University Press, Cambridge

Givón T 1979 *On Understanding Grammar*. Academic Press, New York

Givón T (ed.) 1983 *Topic Continuity in Discourse: A Quantitative Cross-Language Study*. Benjamins, Amsterdam

Greenberg J H, Ferguson C A, Moravcsik E A (eds.) 1978 *Universals of Human Language*, 4 vols. Stanford University Press, Stanford, CA

Haiman J 1983 Iconic and economic motivation. *Lg* **59(4)**: 781–819

Harris A C, Campbell L 1995 *Historical Syntax in Cross-Linguistic Perspective*. Cambridge University Press, Cambridge

Heine B, Reh M 1984 *Grammaticalization and Reanalysis in African Languages*. Helmut Buske, Hamburg

Heine B, Claudi U, Hünnemeyer F 1991 *Grammaticalization: A Conceptual Framework*. University of Chicago Press, Chicago, IL

Held W M 1957 The Hittite relative sentence. *Language Dissertation* **55**

Hopper P J 1988 Emergent grammar and the A Priori Grammar postulate. In: Tannen D (ed.) *Linguistics in Context: Connecting Observation and Understanding*. Ablex, Norwood, NJ

Hopper P J, Thompson S A 1984 The discourse basis for lexical categories in universal grammar. *Lg* **60(4)**: 703–52

Hopper P J, Traugott E C 1993 *Grammaticalization*. Cambridge University Press, Cambridge

Joseph B D, Janda R D 1988 The how and why of diachronic

morphologization and demorphologization. In: Hammond M, Noonan M (eds.) *Theoretical Morphology: Approaches in Modern Linguistics*. Academic Press, San Diego, CA

Kastovsky D 1989 Typological changes in the history of English morphology. In: *Meaning and Beyond: Ernst Leisi zum 70. Geburtstag*. Gunter Narr, Tübingen

Keller R 1994 *On Language Change: The Invisible Hand*. Routledge, London

Kemmer S 1993 *The Middle Voice: A Typological and Diachronic Study*. Benjamins, Amsterdam

Langacker R W 1977 Syntactic reanalysis. In: Li C N (ed.) *Mechanisms of Syntactic Change*. University of Texas Press, Austin, TX

Lehmann C 1985 Grammaticalization: Synchronic variation and diachronic change. *LeSt* **20**(3): 303–18

Lehmann C 1995[1982] *Thoughts on Grammaticalization*. Lincom Europa, Munich

Lichtenberk F 1991 On the gradualness of grammaticalization. In: Traugott E C, Heine B (eds.) 1991

Lord C 1976 Evidence for syntactic reanalysis: From verb to complementizer in Kwa. In: *Papers from the Parasession on Diachronic Syntax*. Chicago Linguistic Society, Chicago, IL

Matsumoto Y 1988 From bound grammatical markers to free discourse markers: History of some Japanese connectives. *Berkeley Linguistics Society* **14**: 340–51

Meillet A 1912 L'évolution des formes grammaticales. In: *Linguistique générale et linguistique historique*. Champion, Paris

Nichols P, Timberlake A 1991 Grammaticalization as retextualization. In: Traugott E C, Heine B (eds.) 1991

Onodera N O 1995 Diachronic analysis of Japanese discourse markers. In: Jucker A (ed.) *Historical Pragmatics*, Benjamins, Amsterdam

Slobin D I 1985 Cross-linguistic evidence for the language-making capacity. In: Slobin D I (ed.) *The Cross-Linguistic Study of Language Acquisition, vol. II: Theoretical Issues*. Erlbaum, Hillsdale, NJ

Stein D, Wright S (eds.) 1995 *Subjectivity and Subjectivisation*. Cambridge University Press, Cambridge

Sweetser E E 1988 Grammaticalization and semantic bleaching. *Berkeley Linguistics Society* **14**: 389–405

Traugott E C, Heine B (eds.) 1991 *Approaches to Grammaticalization*, 2 vols. Benjamins, Amsterdam

Traugott E C, König E 1991 The semantics–pragmatics of grammaticalization revisited. In: Traugott E C, Heine B (eds.) 1991

Greenberg Universals
B. G. Hewitt

A view was growing in the early 1960s among Transformational Grammarians that linguistic investigation should concentrate on producing highly abstract grammars of individual languages, from which a set of common features might prove amenable to extraction. These could then be proposed as the defining characteristics of human language in general. As such they would be both universal and possibly innate to the human mind. Contrary to this view, Joseph H. Greenberg amassed data from a wide variety of languages dealing with aspects of the surface ordering of certain grammatical elements (chiefly complete words fulfilling select grammatical roles, such as verb, object, adjective, etc.). Presenting his results in the seminal article 'Some universals of grammar with particular reference to the order of meaningful elements' (Greenberg 1966), he tried to demonstrate not only how certain ordering combinations predominate across languages but also that, given these patterns, certain predictions can be made of the form: if order-p exists, order-q will (tend to) accompany it. Such are the universals discussed below, which have formed the basis of much of the subsequent work on language typology.

1. The Original Concept

Since input from all the languages of the world could not be included both because of the size of the data base and because of the frequent absence of (adequate) grammars, a representative sample had to be selected. Greenberg chose 30 languages, which he lists, from a variety of families, in order to avoid duplicating features shared through common inheritance, and covering a wide geographical spread, in order to avoid duplicating features shared through areal contact. In his Appendix II Greenberg lists all possible permutations (=24) found with the three most common basic clause types (i.e., SOV, SVO, VSO) for the orderings he investigated together with, where they exist (=15), a list of languages illustrating each permutation—in this Appendix many more than the core 30 languages are named (for comments see Sect. 3).

1.1 Basic Order Typology

The first task was to establish the dominant clausal word order for the elements nominal subject (S), verb (V), and nominal object (O) in simple declarative sentences. This presupposes that each such item is identifiable, which in the case of subjects especially is problematical for some languages (cf. Keenan 1976). Of the logically feasible six combinations (SOV, SVO, VSO, VOS, OSV, OVS) the first two are the most widely attested, whilst the third is not rare. Clearly, though, there seems to be a distinct preference for subject to precede object. For convenience Greenberg referred to the three most widespread clausal orders by capital Roman numerals, with the numeral indicating the position of the verb (viz. I = VSO, II = SVO, III = SOV). Then the relative placements of noun (N) and adjective (A), noun and adnominal genitive (G), and noun and adposition, this being the superordinate for preposition (Pr) and postposition (Po), were noted. In his Table 1, reproduced below, Greenberg presented the distribution amongst his 30 languages for three of these parameters, thus (1):

(V relative to S and O)	I	II	III	(1)
Po-A	0	1	6	
Po-N	0	2	5	
Pr-A	0	4	0	
Pr-N	6	6	0	

Universal 3 easily follows from this, namely:

> Languages with dominant VSO order are always prepositional.

This is a universal implication of the form: if p, then q. Such formulations allow three possible combinations, namely: (a) VSO + prepositions, (b) non-VSO + prepositions, (c) non-VSO + postpositions; only the combination VSO + postpositions is excluded. And Greenberg explicitly cautioned against assuming the inverse of his universals to be also valid (viz. the presence of prepositions does not necessarily imply VSO-ordering). The same table leads to *Universal 4*:

> With overwhelmingly greater than chance frequency, languages with normal SOV order are postpositional.

This represents a universal tendency, and, by taking into consideration the relative positions of noun and genitive Greenberg was able to capture a double tendency in *Universal 2*:

> In languages with prepositions, the genitive almost always follows the governing noun, while in languages with postpositions it almost always precedes.

This confirmed the close relationship between placement of adposition and genitive that had long been recognized.

Most of Greenberg's universals repeat the pattern already illustrated whereby the consequence depends upon the fulfillment of a single condition. However, *Universal 5* incorporates a double condition:

> If a language has dominant SOV order and the genitive follows the governing noun, then the adjective likewise follows the noun.

Though genitive and adjective can be viewed as sharing the function of qualifying their noun, genitive-placement is seen to correlate better with other phenomena than adjective-placement.

Whilst it is statements of the kind already alluded to that generally come to mind at the mention of Greenberg's name, he by no means limited his purview to the question of basic order. In fact, only seven of his 45 universals belong in this subsection.

1.2 Syntax

Eighteen universals concern the link between a range of syntactic phenomena and basic word order. Question formation, ordering of elements internal to the NP and VP, and the relative placement of main vs. subordinate clauses are among the features examined. *Universal 12* is an illustration of the first feature:

> If a language has dominant order VSO in declarative sentences, it always puts interrogative words or phrases first in interrogative word questions; if it has dominant order SOV in declarative sentences, there is never such an invariant rule.

The placement of the relative clause figures in *Universal 24*:

> If the relative expression precedes the noun either as the only construction or as an alternate construction, either the language is postpositional or the adjective precedes the noun or both.

Research into relatives was later taken further by Keenan and Comrie (1977).

1.3 Morphology

Of the final 20 universals some again are linked to basic word order, e.g., *Universal 27*:

> If a language is exclusively suffixing, it is postpositional; if it is exclusively prefixing, it is prepositional.

Universal 42, however, illustrates an absolute universal:

> All languages have pronominal categories involving at least three persons and two numbers.

1.4 Explanation

Greenberg made no attempt to account for all of his proposed universals. He did, however, try to draw some conclusions, hypothesizing in part relations of harmony and disharmony between some of the individual features he examined. He states:

> A dominant order may always occur, but its opposite, the recessive, occurs only when a harmonic construction is likewise present.

He assumes two sets of internally harmonic relations: (a) prepositions, NG, VS, VO, NA, and (b) postpositions, GN, SV, OV, AN. In a language like Basque (SOV/Po/NA/GN) the problematic feature NA is accounted for by treating it as a dominant order, though, as Greenberg observes, 'It is more difficult to account for the dominances than for the harmonic relations.'

It is likely that no single explanation for universals exists; Comrie (1981: 23) talks of 'cognitive, functional, and pragmatic explanations, as these seem particularly fruitful sources of explanation of formal properties of language.'

2. Applications of the Basic Concept

In the late twentieth century, it is a commonplace that no language spoken in the world can be regarded as more primitive, or less developed, than any other. Examination of the oldest stages of languages for which documentary evidence is extant similarly reveals that the essentials of linguistic structure seem not to have altered during this time-span. This has led to the (perhaps dubious) proposal that universals established on the basis of, and applicable to, documented languages must apply (have applied) to any human language at any stage in its development. It is, therefore, hardly surprising that the results of typological investigation have been employed by historical linguists. Even in pre-Greenbergian days the traditional reconstruction of the Proto-Indo–European consonant system with its series of voiceless, voiced, and voiced aspirated stops was challenged as a result of Roman Jakobson's observation that 'as a rule, languages possessing the pairs voiced/voiceless, aspirate/non-aspirate have also a phoneme /h,' for no such proto-phoneme had been reconstructed for Proto-Indo–European.

2.1 Winfred Lehmann and Theo Vennemann

Of the 15 attested permutations in Greenberg's Appendix II four are by far the best represented:

(a) VSO/Pr/NG/NA
(b) SVO/Pr/NG/NA
(c) SOV/Po/GN/AN
(d) SOV/Po/GN/NA

Types (a) and (b) differ only in the placement of the subject, and so Lehmann (1973), in developing his Structural Principle, suggested ignoring it with the result that the set of features VO/Pr/NG/NA becomes prototypical for a language with object following verb. Types (c) and (d) are collapsible (apart from AN vs. NA) if the position of the subject is again ignored. And since VO languages seem to anticipate NA, AN is argued to be most consistent for OV languages in view of the fact that OV/Po/GN/AN provides the mirror-image of what is proposed as being consistent for a VO language.

Vennemann (1974) subsequently developed his Natural Serialization Principle. He drew the distinction between 'operands' (or heads) and 'operators' (or adjuncts) and proposed the following classification (2):

Operators	*Operands*	(2)
Object	Verb	
Adjective	Noun	
Genitive	Noun	
Relative Clause	Noun	
Noun Phrase	Adposition	
Main Verb	Auxiliary/Modal	
Determiner	Noun	
Adverbial	Adjective	

The Principle then states that languages tend to serialize all operator–operand pairs unidirectionally. But, since it is evident from Greenberg's Appendix II that many languages exist in a state of disharmony with this hypothesis, Vennemann further suggested that his principle be invested with predictive power within the realm of language-change, so that in effect it becomes a proposed explanation for those instances of so-called 'drift' that affect alterations to word order—natural serialization will eventually be achieved as a result of evolutionary re-ordering(s). Also a crucial difference now arises between Greenberg's original relations (whereby if p implies q, q does not necessarily imply p) and those following from Vennemann's suggestion. Referring back to *Universal 4*, SOV generally predicts postpositions. But, if OV and N + Po illustrate natural serialization of the type operator–operand, then from the presence of postpositions one should equally be able to predict the order OV, and yet a glance at Appendix II proves the unreliability of such an expectation.

Lehmann himself employed the notion of consistency in the matter of word orders in his endeavor to reconstruct aspects of Proto-Indo–European syntax (1974). The oldest attested Indo–European language, Hittite, seems to have basic order (S)OV, which is paralleled by some of the older related languages like Latin. This order was assumed to be inherited. The parent language was then further assumed to be *consistent* in its OV-characteristics, for which evidence was provided by adducing the anticipated features (GN, AN, etc.) from the various reflex languages.

3. John Hawkins

Hawkins (1980) returned to Greenberg's raw data to see whether it might not be possible to state the implicational relations in such a way as to reduce even further the number of exceptions. Though the article takes as its base the language classifications from Appendix II, Hawkins's own investigations revealed some examples of misassignment in this list, and these were noted in a late addition to the article as Footnote 2. However, not all the inaccuracies were even then corrected, for still included under Type 23 (SOV/Po/GN/AN) was the entry 'Abkhaz and other Caucasian languages.' Firstly, this should presumably read 'and other *Northwest* Caucasian languages.' But more importantly, the whole of this family (Abkhaz–Abaza, Circassian, Ubykh) behave like a number of other languages in placing the bulk of their adjectives after the noun, whilst inverting this order for certain easily defined subtypes of epithet. This entry, thus, belongs in Type 24 (SOV/Po/GN/NA). This demonstrates how careful the typologist has to be in gathering data from others' descriptions.

Hawkins adopted the pattern of *Universal 5* with its double condition and proposed as his first implicational network (a):

(a) SOV → (AN → GN)

which is to be interpreted as: if in an SOV language adjectives precede nouns, then genitives will also precede them. His second network was (b):

(b) VSO → (NA → NG)

His two remaining networks were (c):

(c) Pr → (NA → NG)

and (d):

(d) Po → (AN → GN)

In fact, (c) admits of exceptions, like Arapesh (Greenberg Type 12), which are SVO languages. Such anomalies from SVO languages then led to the refinement of (c) into (c′):

(c′) Pr & (VSO v SOV) → (NA → NG)

which states that a prepositional VSO or SOV language when coupled with NA necessitates NG.

These formulations were supplemented by a distributional universal called the principle of cross-category harmony, which states:

> The more similar the position of operands relative to their operators across different operand categories considered pairwise (verb in relation to adposition order, noun in relation to adposition order, verb in relation to noun order), the greater are the percentage numbers of exemplifying languages.

There are similarities here with Vennemann's natural serialization and Lehmann's structural principle, but for the first time a sort of scale of deviation is hypothesized whereby the greater the degree of disharmony in ordering-phenomena, the fewer should be the languages attested, it is claimed.

4. Criticism

Lehmann's attempt to apply his ideas about consistency in word order to the reconstruction of Proto-Indo–European word order was quickly challenged by Calvert Watkins (1976), who pointed to the circularity of argumentation—once the assumption had been made that Proto-Indo–European was a consistent (S)OV language, any phenomena from the daughter languages that the structural principle predicted should accompany OV were seen as supporting the OV-hypothesis, whilst simultaneously their ancient status was defended on the grounds that they must have been inherited from the parent language. Equally any indication from the daughter languages of an inherited feature at odds with the supposed consistent OV-nature of Proto-Indo–European was ignored. For example, OV presupposes preposed relative structures without relative pronoun. And yet there is evidence that at least two variants of a relative pronominal stem should be traced back to Proto-Indo–European, which argues for the presence of postposed, full relative clauses.

In a comprehensive critique, Neil Smith (1981: 53) is led to the following conclusion: 'Typology provides data which need explanations and which hence form a testing ground for any linguistic theory with pretensions to universal relevance. It provides no explanations itself.' His argument is described below.

First the concept of 'consistent language' is queried, for, as noted earlier, 15 of the logically possible 24 types of permutations were confirmed by Greenberg himself, even if some networks are better represented than others. However, if the existence of (relatively) consistent languages is nevertheless allowed, either (a) such languages will be normal (i.e., unmarked) or (b) consistency vs. inconsistency has nothing to do with markedness but is 'a statistical property which is itself in need of explanation'—this latter is Smith's preference. He reaches it by testing the four predictions that would follow from option (a) above, namely that consistent languages should be: (i) statistically predominant, (ii) easier to learn for children, (iii) more stable in maintaining their characteristics, while change should always be towards consistency rather than vice versa, (iv) easier to process.

Regarding (i), Smith stresses the almost equal number of languages (including families) confirmed by Greenberg as belonging to his Types 23 and 24, both being SOV and differing only with respect to adjective-noun ordering. The greater precision in stating implications achieved by Hawkins is recognized, though he wonders whether it might not ultimately prove impossible to produce a counterexample as new ad hoc statements might always be devisable. If the implications are not ad hoc, they must be part of the defining characteristics of human language. But it is difficult to encapsulate the results of typological research into more than one language within the competence of a speaker of possibly just a single language, unless perhaps the sort of scale of deviation from an ideal pattern as captured by Hawkins's principle of cross-category harmony can be accommodated within the familiar notion of markedness. This leads to a consideration of whether there is evidence from the learning process for the notion that inconsistent/marked languages (or at least such individual features) are more difficult for the child to master. The evidence is not favorable, and so the conclusion is that: 'It is possible that markedness has a role to play in language acquisition, but that role still has to be demonstrated. Until this is done the linking of markedness and consistency is unrevealing' (Smith 1981: 48). Parallel consideration of (iii) and (iv) leads to the view that 'there is no good evidence that "consistency" constitutes an independent principle controlling language change or language use' (1981: 51).

Despite such a negative conclusion, the importance of Greenberg's original insights cannot be denied.

They led to a wholly justifiable renewal of interest in the comparative study of language, now called 'language typology', as exemplified in the works of Bernard Comrie and the Leningrad group (under the original direction of A. A. Xolodovič). If the mechanisms behind the results thrown up by such surveys are not yet fully understood, that is no excuse for abandoning the investigations.

Bibliography

Comrie B 1981 *Language Universals and Linguistic Typology*. Blackwell, Oxford
Greenberg J H 1966 Some universals of grammar with particular reference to the order of meaningful elements. In: Greenberg J H (ed.) *Universals of Language*, 2nd edn. MIT Press, Cambridge, MA
Hawkins J A 1980 On implicational and distributional universals of word order. *JL* **16**: 193–235
Keenan E L 1976 Towards a universal definition of subject. In: Li C N (ed.) *Subject and Topic*. Academic Press, New York
Keenan E L, Comrie B 1977 Noun phrase accessibility and universal grammar. *LIn* **8**: 63–99
Lehmann W P 1973 A structural principle of language and its implications. *Lg* **49**: 47–66
Lehmann W P 1974 *Proto-Indo–European Syntax*. University of Texas Press, Austin, TX
Smith N V 1981 Consistency, markedness and language change: On the notion 'consistent language.' *JL* **17**: 39–54
Vennemann T 1974 Topics, subject and word-order: From SXV to SVX via TVX. In: Anderson J, Jones C (eds.) *Historical Linguistics*. North-Holland, Amsterdam
Watkins C 1976 Towards Proto-Indo–European syntax: Problems and pseudo-problems. In: Steever S B, Walker C A, Mufwene S S (eds.) *Papers from the Parasession on Diachronic Syntax, April 22, 1976*. Chicago Linguistics Society, Chicago, IL

Head-driven Phrase Structure Grammar

Richard P. Cooper

Head-driven Phrase Structure Grammar (HPSG) is a formal linguistic theory which borrows insights from a number of contemporary linguistic theories and combines them, together with further insights, in a declarative, unification-based framework. The theory is, therefore, somewhat eclectic, but the unification-based framework allows a high degree of precision in the statement of a grammar, and the declarative approach frees the linguistic theory from psychological claims concerning language processing.

1. Elements of the Theory of HPSG

HPSG adopts the view that linguistic theory should follow the approach of other scientific theories, and as such, a fundamental concept is the mathematical modeling of linguistic entities. The theory then consists of statements in a formal language about the models. The language employed by HPSG is based on sorted feature structures which model the linguistic entities. Though the use of feature structures in modern linguistic theories is not peculiar to HPSG, the underlying methodology of HPSG requires that all linguistic entities be described within a single domain, and so, unlike other linguistic theories which employ feature structures, HPSG restricts itself to only employing sorted feature structures: no other descriptive devices are employed.

A sorted feature structure consists of a set of features, where each feature consists of an attribute and a value. The attributes appropriate to a particular feature structure are determined by its sort. Attributes are atomic entities, but values may be either atomic or other feature structures. No two features within a single feature structure may be based on the same attribute, but different attributes may share a value. As such, a feature structure may be viewed as a partial function from a set of attributes to a set of values, where the set of values consists of both atoms and other sorted feature structures. Within HPSG, sorted feature structures are represented orthographically as attribute value matrices preceded by a subscript indicating the sort. Examples of these matrices are given throughout this article.

Feature structures are partially ordered by the subsumption relation. A feature structure ϕ subsumes a feature structure ψ, written $\phi \sqsubseteq \psi$, if and only if the set of objects described by ϕ includes the set of objects described by ψ, or alternately if and only if ψ is at least as informative as ϕ. Given this partial ordering, the operation of unification, for which the symbol $\sqcup$ is used, may be defined as the least upper bound (with respect to the subsumption ordering) of a set of feature structures. Intuitively, the unification of two (or more feature structures) is the least feature structure which is at least as informative as each of the operands. If no such feature structure exists unification is said to fail. Unification is thus a way of putting together information and checking that the result is consistent. It is the fundamental information combining operation employed by HPSG.

A number of augmentations to the basic feature structure language are employed by HPSG. On the logical side, these include disjunction, negation, and implication. If ϕ and ψ are feature structures, then so is $\phi \vee \psi$, $\neg\phi$ and $\phi \Rightarrow \psi$. A form of conjunction is given by unification, and logical conjunction is not required. These logical operations add a great deal of expressive power to the description language, allowing disjunctive, negative, and implicational constraints to be stated: an object is described by $\phi \vee \psi$ if and only if it is described either by ϕ or by ψ; an object is described by $\neg\phi$ if and only if it is not described by ϕ; an object is described by $\phi \Rightarrow \psi$ if and only if either it is not described by ϕ or it is described by ψ. Further augmentations include the use of list and set valued features, and the use of values which are functionally dependent on other values. List values are represented within angle brackets, and set values are represented within braces. Functionally dependent values are represented by function symbols with their arguments represented by boxed indices. The notion of subsumption is augmented in accordance with each of these augmentations to the language, leading to an augmented notion of unification suitable for the extended language.

HPSG consists of grammar principles, grammar rules, and lexical entries, all of which are represented in terms of feature structures. Each licensed constituent is described by a feature structure, and this feature structure must be subsumed by each grammar principle (corresponding to the fact that the constituent must satisfy each grammar principle), and either by one grammar rule (if the constituent is phrasal) or by one lexical entry (if the constituent is lexical). Any such feature structure is necessarily of sort *sign*. Given the augmented language, an HPSG grammar may thus be stated as a single feature structure which takes the form:

$$P_1 \sqcup \ldots \sqcup P_l \sqcup (R_1 \vee \ldots \vee R_m \vee L_1 \vee \ldots \vee L_n)$$

where the P_i are the grammar principles, the R_i are the grammar rules, and the L_i are the lexical entries.

2. The HPSG Sign

Each constituent admitted by an HPSG grammar is described by a feature structure of sort *sign*. Such a feature structure is referred to as a 'sign.' An HPSG sign contains at least two attributes: *phonology* (abbreviated to PHON) and *syntax/semantics* (abbreviated to SYNSEM). Signs which describe phrases also contain a *daughters* attribute (abbreviated to DTRS).

The PHON attribute takes as its value a list representing the phonological structure of the constituent. As HPSG is primarily a theory of linguistic structure at the level of the word and above, this value is often glossed as the corresponding list of words.

The fact that HPSG uses feature structures to model phrasal constituents, as well as lexical constituents, requires that phrase structure be encoded within those feature structures. This is accomplished by the DTRS attribute, which is only defined for descriptions of phrasal constituents. The value of the DTRS attribute is a complex feature structure normally having attributes including HEAD-DTR and COMP-DTRS. The value of HEAD-DTR is the feature structure description of the head daughter of the phrase. The value of COMP-DTRS is a list of feature structure descriptions where each element of the list describes a complement daughter. The description of a phrasal constituent thus includes the descriptions of all its subconstituents, imbedded somewhere in the value of the phrasal constituent's DTRS attribute.

3. Syntactic Categories

Broadly speaking the value of the SYNSEM attribute encodes the syntactic category of a constituent. Syntactic categories in HPSG are similar to those in GPSG (see *Generalized Phrase Structure Grammar*) in that rather than being atomic they are complex feature structures. In HPSG these feature structures have two attributes, LOCAL and NONLOCAL, whose values are themselves complex feature structures.

The value of the LOCAL attribute is a feature structure having three attributes: CATEGORY, CONTENT, and CONTEXT. Three further attributes are appropriate for the value of the CATEGORY attribute: HEAD, SUBCAT, and LEX. The HEAD attribute encodes all syntactic features that a head and its phrasal projection have in common. This invariably includes whether the constituent is nominal, verbal, prepositional, etc. For nominal constituents, case and form (whether normal or expletive) are also head features. For verbal constituents, the head features include binary features indicating whether the constituent is inverted, whether the constituent is headed by an auxiliary, and whether the constituent is predicative, as well as a feature indicating verb form (base, present participle, passive participle, etc.). For prepositional constituents, the head features include a feature indicating the prepositional form (determined by the preposition which heads the phrase) of the constituent.

That a head and its phrasal projection share their head features is ensured by the Head Feature Principle, the HPSG analogue of GPSG's Head Feature Convention, which is claimed to be a principle of Universal Grammar. In feature structure terms the Head Feature Principle may be stated as:

$$\begin{bmatrix} \text{DTRS} & \textit{headed-structure}[\ ] \end{bmatrix} \longrightarrow$$

$$\begin{bmatrix} \text{SYNSEM|LOCAL|CATEGORY|HEAD} & \boxed{1} \\ \text{DTRS|HEAD-DTR|SYNSEM|LOCAL|CATEGORY|HEAD} & \boxed{1} \end{bmatrix}$$

The boxed indices represent shared values.

As a principle of Universal Grammar, every HPSG sign must unify with the above feature structure. Consequently, every sign bearing a DTRS attribute whose value is of sort *headed-structure* (i.e., every description of a headed phrase) must extend the consequent of this feature structure.

The degree of saturation of a sign is indicated by the sign's SUBCAT attribute which takes as its value a list of feature structures of sort SYNSEM. Each element of the list corresponds to one unfilled complement of the sign. A sign whose SUBCAT list is the empty list is fully saturated.

The final CATEGORY attribute, the LEX attribute, is a binary attribute indicating lexicality. The attribute has value '+' for all lexical signs and '−' for all non-lexical signs. Lexicality in HPSG is important in determining word order and phrase structure.

The remaining local attributes, CONTENT and CONTEXT, are employed in the HPSG account of semantics (including certain agreement phenomena). The underlying theory behind these values is situation semantics, the relevant aspect of which is that it employs a semantic domain of structured objects, rather than a semantic domain of functions. These objects, by virtue of their structured nature, are easily modeled within the domain of sorted feature structures.

Unbounded dependencies, *wh*-marking, and the marking of relative clauses are treated via the NONLOCAL attribute. This has two attributes, INHERITED and TO-BIND, which between them encode any unfilled dependencies within the phrase which the sign models. The value of each NONLOCAL attribute has in turn three attributes—SLASH, QUE, and REL—each of which is set-valued. In the case of SLASH this set corresponds to the set of extracted elements from the constituent in question. In the case of QUE this corresponds to the set of *wh*-words in the constituent. In the case of REL this corresponds to the set of relative pronouns in the constituent. For canonical word orderings in nonquestions and nonrelative clauses these sets are all empty. The propagation of the values of these attributes between a constituent and its subconstituents is governed by the Binding Inheritance Principle, which is the HPSG correlate of GPSG's Foot Feature Principle.

An HPSG sign thus takes the form:

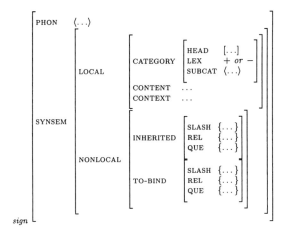

4. Subcategorization

As explained above, the SUBCAT attribute indicates the degree of saturation of a sign. The SUBCAT list includes all unfilled complements and, in particular, there is no distinction between *internal* and *external* arguments, as in Government-Binding Theory. Thus the SUBCAT list of a transitive verb consists of two elements, one which is a partial description of the object of the verb and one which is a partial description of the subject of the verb.

The elements of the SUBCAT list are ordered according to obliqueness, with least oblique elements first. Obliqueness is a function of grammatical relation: subjects are less oblique than direct objects, which are in turn less oblique than indirect objects. Obliqueness plays a crucial role in several areas of HPSG theory, including word order, control, and binding.

HPSG's Subcategorization Principle, which is taken to be a second principle of Universal Grammar, requires that, for any headed phrase, the subcategorization requirements of the phrase are those of the head daughter less those filled by any complement daughters. Within the formalism of HPSG this principle is stated via a functional dependency as shown in Fig. 1. Like the Head Feature Principle, the Subcategorization

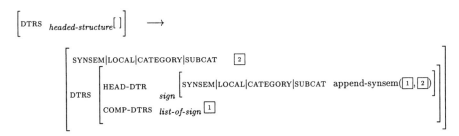

Figure 1

Principle is also claimed to be a principle of Universal Grammar. Consequently, every sign describing a headed phrase must extend the consequent of the principle. The Subcategorization Principle thus ensures that complement daughters are unified with their corresponding elements on the SUBCAT list of their sister head, and hence that only those signs which actually do unify with the elements on a head's SUBCAT list can act as complements to that head.

The requirement of the Subcategorization Principle that the head daughter be of sort *sign* and that all complement daughters be of sort *sign* captures the requirement that all subconstituents of any constituent must also be constituents licensed by the grammar.

Semantics interfaces with syntax via the SUBCAT attribute. As the elements on any SUBCAT list are of sort SYNSEM, they contain a CONTENT attribute. The unification of complement daughters with these elements thus includes the unification of the values of the CONTENT attributes of the complement daughters with the corresponding CONTENT attributes of the subcategorized-for signs. In general, these subcategorized-for signs share the value of (some attribute imbedded in) their CONTENT attribute with the appropriate argument role of the head which subcategorizes for them. Consequently, when a complement unifies with an element on a head's SUBCAT list, the appropriate semantic information supplied by that complement will be unified with the appropriate argument role of the head. The Semantics Principle then requires that the semantic content of the entire head/complement phrase is just the semantic content of the head of the phrase.

Agreement in HPSG is treated semantically via the parameters which fill the argument roles of verbs. All parameters are assumed to have language specific attributes for agreement. For English these are PERSON, NUMBER, and GENDER. Appropriate agreement features are marked lexically on the SUBCAT lists of all verb forms, indicating the agreement features which the complements of the verb forms require. Thus different forms of the same verb have different lexical entries, each one indicating its own specific requirements. These verb forms are related by lexical rules (see Sect. 6).

HPSG's treatment of subcategorization is illustrated by the lexical sign for the intransitive verb *meows*, which can be partially specified as shown in Fig. 2. The SUBCAT attribute of this sign encodes the fact that the verb is not saturated, and requires a single complement, a third person singular nominative noun phrase, such as *Tigger*. This lexical treatment of subcategorization owes much to that of categorial grammar (see *Categorial Grammar*).

5. Grammar Rules

Although HPSG is a phrase structure grammar, phrases within the grammar are not licensed by formal rewrite

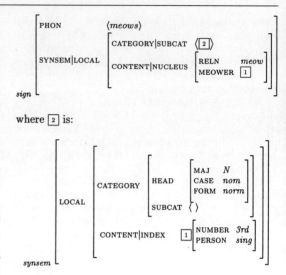

Figure 2

rules as in other phrase structure grammars. Given the encoding of phrase structure trees within sorted feature structures and the corresponding use of sorted feature structures to describe phrasal constituents, the grammar rules are instead expressed as well-formedness constraints on the feature structure descriptions of phrases. Each grammar rule takes the form of a feature structure and each feature structure which describes a phrase must extend the feature structure corresponding to one grammar rule. The highly lexicalist nature of HPSG means that very few grammar rules are required, and much of the coverage is achieved by just two grammar rules. Furthermore, following GPSG, word order is factored out of the grammar rules, which only state immediate dominance relations. Grammar rules are thus referred to as 'Immediate Dominance (ID) Schemata.'

ID Schema 1 states that a saturated phrase may consist of a nonlexical head together with a single complement. This is stated in terms of a sorted feature structure as:

$$\begin{bmatrix} \text{SYNSEM|LOCAL|CATEGORY|SUBCAT} & \langle \rangle \\ \text{DTRS} \begin{bmatrix} \text{HEAD-DTR|SYNSEM|LOCAL|CATEGORY|LEX} & - \\ \text{COMP-DTRS} & \langle [\ ] \rangle \end{bmatrix} \end{bmatrix}$$

By the Subcategorization Principle the head of such a phrase must require exactly one complement, and that complement must be identical to the single element on the COMP-DTRS list. This rule corresponds to the rules standardly expressed as 'S→NP VP' (where VP is the head of S), 'NP→Det Nom,' and 'NP→NP[Gen] Nom' (where Nom is the head of NP).

In X′-syntax the rule corresponds to X″→Spec X′ (see *X-bar Syntax*).

ID Schema 2 states that a phrase may consist of a noninverted lexical head together with all but its least oblique complement. In terms of feature structures this means that a phrasal constituent may be described by an extension of:

$$
\begin{bmatrix}
\text{SYNSEM|LOCAL|CATEGORY|SUBCAT} & \langle [\ ] \rangle \\
\text{DTRS|HEAD-DTR|SYNSEM|LOCAL|CATEGORY} & \begin{bmatrix} \text{HEAD|INV} & - \\ \text{LEX} & + \end{bmatrix}
\end{bmatrix}
$$

This rule subsumes all standard rules for VPs, as well as rules for combining nouns with nondeterminer complements. The corresponding rule in X′-syntax is X′→X Comp*.

Although the above two grammar rules have close correlates in X′-theory, HPSG is very different from most incarnations of X′-theory. The main difference stems from the fact that HPSG takes the verb phrase (which is headed by a verb) to be the head of a sentence. There is no category such as Inflexion posited as a carrier of tense. Rather, the auxiliary chain is analyzed as a series of verb phrases, each headed by an auxiliary verb followed by a single complement which happens to also be a verb phrase.

Inverted clauses are licensed by ID Schema 3, which states that a phrase may consist of a lexical head followed by all of its complement daughters, provided that the phrase bears the head feature +INV to indicate that it is inverted. Linear precedence rules ensure that the lexical head precedes all other subconstituents.

The order of subconstituents within a constituent is functionally dependent on the subconstituents. For English, this functional dependency ensures that lexical heads precede their complements and nonlexical heads follow their complements. The ordering of complements is, for the most part, determined by their relative obliqueness, with least oblique complements preceding more oblique complements. However, other factors, most notably lexicality, do come into consideration and word order is not a direct reflexion of obliqueness, nor vice versa.

6. Lexical Organization

The lexical approach of HPSG leads to a very small number of highly schematic phrasal rules accompanied by a very rich and complex lexicon. Rather than treating the lexicon as an unstructured set of word-feature structure pairs, the lexicon in HPSG is organized in terms of several inheritance hierarchies, with each lexical item being cross-classified according to all relevant hierarchies. The nodes of each hierarchy correspond to sorted feature structures, with dominance relations in the hierarchy corresponding to sub-

sumption relations in the domain of sorted feature structures. This approach reduces redundancy in the lexicon and allows generalizations across classes of words (such as all intransitive verbs, for example) to be captured. Further generalizations are stated in terms of lexical rules, which relate feature structure descriptions corresponding to different inflexional classes.

As an example, one inheritance hierarchy is based on subcategorization requirements. The root node, corresponding to the sort *major-lexical-sign* (for which subcategorization is appropriate), is partitioned into nodes corresponding to the sorts *saturated* and *unsaturated*. Any sign of sort *saturated* must have the empty list as the value of its SUBCAT attribute. The sort *unsaturated* is further partitioned into *unsaturated-non-nominal* and *common*. Any sign of sort *unsaturated-non-nominal* has a noun phrase as the last element on its SUBCAT list. Any sign of sort *common* has a determiner as the last element on its SUBCAT list. Each of these sorts is further partitioned. This partitioning continues for several more layers, giving a hierarchical structuring to the lexicon which terminates with leaf sorts including *strict-intransitive*, *strict-transitive*, *ditransitive*, etc. Other hierarchies, apart from the hierarchy based on subcategorization, include hierarchies based on head features, verb form, and the auxiliary/main verb distinction.

Given these hierarchies, the lexicon may be stated as a set of triples consisting of a word, the leaf sorts that the word is an instance of, and any idiosyncratic features of that word. The lexical entry for *meows*, for example, states that the word is of the sorts *main*, 3 SG, and *strict-intransitive*, and that it has several idiosyncratic features, including its phonology and its semantic content.

The HPSG lexicon also includes lexical rules, capturing various generalizations between forms of words. A lexical rule of passive, for example, relates feature structure descriptions of base form verbs to the descriptions of their passive participles. Other lexical rules relate all forms of verbs, various adjectival forms, and singular and plural nominal forms.

HPSG takes lexical rules as being functional, in general mapping base forms to inflected forms. Given such rules, the lexicon may be stated compactly solely in terms of base forms. The complete lexicon may then be determined by taking the closure of the base forms under the application of the lexical rules.

7. Ongoing Research

The basic formalism of HPSG sketched above leaves many issues unresolved and, as a relatively new theory, it continues to develop. Work in the late twentieth century is aimed at extending the scope of phenomena under consideration. This includes the treatment of adjunction, control constructions, extraction and topicalization, binding, and coordination. HPSG is also a theory that is very amenable to computational work. Several implementations of large parts of the theory exist and research into the issues raised by such implementations is continuing.

Bibliography

Pollard C J, Sag I A 1987 *Information-based Syntax and* Semantics. *Vol. 1: Fundamentals*. CSLI Lecture Notes Number 13. Center for the Study of Language and Information, Stanford, CA

Pollard C J, Sag I A 1994 *Head-driven Phrase Structure Grammar*. University of Chicago Press, Chicago, IL

Iconicity
J. Haiman

The idea that there is no resemblance between the signs of language and the thoughts they stand for, is one of the oldest in linguistic thought. The first significant challenge to this dogma in the respectable philological tradition is Roman Jakobson's famous article 'Quest for the essence of language' (1965), which exploited Peirce's idea of the diagram as an attenuated icon.

1. Diagrammatic Iconicity

In his typology of signs, Charles S. Peirce drew attention to the existence of different kinds of icons. The most common icon is the image which, like a photograph, attempts to resemble its referent completely. Much more important than the *image*, however, in all sign systems, is the *diagram*.

Although the component parts of a diagram may not resemble what they stand for, the relationships among those components may approximate the relationships among the ideas they represent. Onomatapoeic words like 'moo'—iconic auditory images—are of peripheral importance in languages. Word order patterns like Caesar's 'Veni, vidi, vici,' on the other hand, are diagrammatic icons, wherein the order of words corresponds to the order of events.

Aside from the independence of simultaneously uttered segmental and suprasegmental signs, spoken language is essentially a one-dimensional medium, in which the possible formal relationships among the parts, both syntagmatic and paradigmatic, are basically linear. Nevertheless, these relationships are exploited in almost all languages for the iconic representation of both banal and highly complex concepts. Some of these are alienation and its converse, empathy; symmetry; and predictability.

2. Alienation

Alienation, or conceptual distance, may be of many different kinds, and formally reflected in different ways. The most obvious, and frequently noted, formal manifestation of conceptual distance is on the segmental level, and consists of the distance between arbitrary morphemes X and Y in the speech chain.

2.1 Causation

In almost all languages which distinguish between direct and indirect causation, the semantic difference between the two constructions mirrors the formal difference between them. For example, in the English pair of sentences:

I killed the chicken. (1a)
I caused the chicken to die. (1b)

the formal distance between 'causing' and 'dying' is obviously less in (1a) than in (1b). The conceptual distance between them is also less: typically, in (1a) causing and dying occur at the same time and place, and there is a strong imputation of physical contact. In (1b), there is an even stronger imputation that there is no physical contact between causer and causee, and that the action is in some sense magical.

2.2 Coordination

The formal difference between structures which have been related by the now discredited transformation of '*coordination reduction*' is, in part, one of different distances between conjuncts:

X a Y and X b Y (2a)
X a and b Y (2b)

The conceptual distance between the conjuncts 'a' and 'b' is again greater in (2a) than in (2b). The inference in (2a) is that 'a' and 'b' are separate and contrasting. The inference in (2b) is that they constitute a group and are alike in various ways. For the simplest example of this contrast, consider the difference between:

red ribbons and white ribbons. (3a)
red and white ribbons. (3b)

There is a reading of (3b) which is synonymous with the only possible meaning of (3a): the colors 'red' and 'white,' on this reading, are on separate ribbons. But there is also a possible, perhaps preferred, reading of (3b), on which the different colors are on the same ribbons. Other examples, which have been frequently discussed, are more complex. In each case, however, formal distance between conjuncts reflects the conceptual distance between them.

2.3 Quotation and Titles

Another kind of formal distance between linguistic elements is reflected in the degree to which they affect each other grammatically. Intuitively, if an element 'a' is affected in any way by the presence of another element 'b,' then the formal distance between 'a' and 'b' is less than in cases where 'a' is grammatically independent of 'b.' Now, it has been widely noted that quoted material is grammatically independent in this formal sense. Compare for example:

I don't like *myself*.   (4a)
I don't like '*I*' in essays.   (4b)

The quoted 'I' in (4b) is neither in the oblique case nor in the reflexive form: that is, there is no grammatical recognition of its status as a direct object of any sort, let alone one which is coreferential with the subject of the sentence. This failure of quoted material to undergo syntactic incorporation in a way reflects its temporary divorce from its actual meaning. The reason for the peculiar status of direct quotes (they are mentioned rather than used), is that in uttering them, the speaker is adopting an alien framework—literally, play-acting. The quote is valid only 'on the stage,' not 'in real life.' Spoken language, like conventional orthography, marks and enforces the distinction between the stage and the real world in suspending the usual processes whereby words are incorporated into a text, or associated with real events. As the sentiments uttered by the actors on the stage have no validity beyond the proscenium, so too, words directly quoted have no grammatical status in the surrounding text.

Titles are similar to quotes. Although the words of a title may designate real referents, those referents do not play their customary role in the sentence where they are uttered. Their conceptual separation is reflected in their ability to resist being affected by other elements in the sentence:

He believed in *us*.   (5a)
Zamyatin depicts a brave new world in '*We*.' (5b)

2.4 Argument Status of Protasis Clauses

Another index of incorporation besides agreement and case marking is the ability to condition word order. Not surprisingly, quoted material does not have this ability:

Not a word did she say.   (6a)
'Not a word' she said.   (6b)
                   *did she say.

Again, other kinds of alienation are possible, although not all languages mark them equally. English, for example, makes no grammatical distinction between conditionals like those of (7):

If you're hungry, you can have a banana.   (7a)
If you're hungry, there's a banana on the table. (7b)

In (7b), there is no causal relationship between *protasis* and *apodosis*. This distinction is graphically marked in German (8), where subordinate clauses like the protasis either do or do not count as arguments with respect to the verb–second rule. In the German translation of (7a), the protasis counts as an argument, and the verb of S2 must follow it immediately, causing subject-verb inversion in S2. However, the translation of (7b) has no subject-verb inversion, indicating that S1 does not act as a constituent of the sentence containing S2:

Wenn du hungrig bist, kannst du eine   (8a)
   Banane haben.
Wenn du hungrig bist, es gibt auf dem Tisch (8b)
   eine Banane.

2.5 Social Distance

Another kind of formal distance is that which exists between the meaning of an utterance and its actual form. In 'plain speech,' there is no difference between the two, while in various kinds of baroque styles, including gobbledygook, metaphor, and sarcasm, the meaning of an utterance may diverge significantly from its outward form.

A pragmatic universal is that politeness mirrors social distance between equals. The greater the politeness, the longer the message. What is reflected in the length of the message is not simply social distance between interlocutors, which is the same in both symmetrical and asymmetrical relationships. Rather, it is respect for the interlocutor, and the speaker's need to preserve this interlocutor from the contents of the message itself. Given an arbitrary message X, plain speech consists of the sign 'X,' while baroque polite speech (bafflegab or gobbledygook being extreme manifestations of this) consists of a string of signs 'pdq X aby' within which 'X' is hidden. Alternatively, euphemisms are longer than 'four-letter words,' in all languages. Prolixity is an icon of concealment; concealment is motivated by the need, for whatever reason, to estrange a hearer from the facts.

In European languages, where politeness is not grammaticized as extensively as in Javanese or many Australian languages, alienation of the listener is achieved by highly motivated baroque terms of address. Almost all European languages, with the recent exception of modern English, distinguish T and V forms in personal pronoun systems (e.g., French *tu* and vous). In many of these languages, the polite V form is third person: the addressee is not so much addressed (where address is a kind of verbal aggression), as referred to.

2.6 Sarcasm

Another kind of formal distance is possible where the unit 'a' is segmental and the unit 'b' is intonational, and they occur simultaneously. Intuitively, the formal distance between 'a' and 'b' is greater when there is a 'dissonance' between them, than when they 'harmonize.'

Sarcasm is expressed by the incongruity between a speaker's actual words and the intended meaning, which is often conveyed by an 'emotively inappropriate' intonation. For example, two varieties (9) out of several are:

inappropriate flatness (e.g., Wow)	(9a)
inappropriate exaggeration (e.g., Poor baby!).	(9b)

Given that sarcasm by definition communicates two opposed meanings simultaneously, the fact that it is conveyed by an incongruous or inappropriate intonation overlaid over the ostensible text is again perfectly iconic. Sarcasm is a complex notion not in that it requires both segmental text and intonational melody (all spoken language does), but in that it must presuppose and deviate from an implicit model of appropriate melody or melodic coincidence.

3. Empathy

Where sarcasm marks the speaker's alienation from other people or the sentiments that they may utter, empathy marking indicates the speaker's identification with others, including most importantly the actors in the events s/he describes. There is considerable evidence, mainly assembled by S. Kuno, that the subject role is that with which the speaker indicates empathy. The most iconic possible indication of speaker's empathy occurs in ASL, where it is not the subject, but the 'role-prominent NP' with which the signer indicates empathy—

> by a subtle shift of the body into a specific position in the signing space. The NP which also agrees with this position is thereby marked with role prominence.
> (Kegl 1986: 289, and 289 footnote)

Empathy is a sublimated form of identity. The identity of coreferential NP is marked in ASL by the same device (Kegl 1986: 287):

> [The index] is a pointing gesture which establishes a relationship between some NP and a unique point in space. Subsequent reference to this point in space . . . constitutes reference to the original NP.

4. Symmetry

It might seem that spoken language, as opposed to ASL, is poorly qualified to express symmetry iconically: auditory symmetry is expressed in palindromic devices which human beings either do not appreciate or have genuine difficulty in processing. Musical palindromes, too, like Bach's Crab Canon, are—as palindromes—a delight to the eye and the brain rather than to the ear. But symmetry in language, as in music, is expressed by parallelism: repetition of what is the same or similar units from left to right. Thus allit-

eration, antithesis, and rhyme; and thus the opening bars of Beethoven's Fifth or Mozart's 40th symphony. Thus also coordination in general: coordinated elements must be formally and conceptually parallel.

Formal parallelism characterizes a number of structures in which conceptual symmetry is expressed. One of the most striking is the reciprocal construction. There seems to be no language which fails to distinguish between, say:

Max hit Harry, and (then) Harry hit Max.	(10a)
Max and Harry hit each other.	(10b)

The first suggests a sequence of cause and effect: the second, by avoiding repetition of the event verb, suggests simultaneity. Languages with rich inflexion (like Hua, Tauya, and Amele), may suggest the same simultaneity by the use of various devices which heighten the formal parallelism between conjoined sentences. Their parallelism then overrides the fact that the clauses occur serially.

As with coordination, so also with comparison: it is necessary that contrasted elements are on a par both semantically and formally. This constraint may be responsible for the widely noted, and apparently idiosyncratic, English pattern:

I am more sad than I am angry.	(11a)
I am sadder than I am angry.	(11b)
I am more sad than angry.	(11c)
*I am sadder than angry.	(11d)

In (11a) and (11b) the contrasted elements occur in the same syntactic frame, that is, they follow the words *I am*. In (11a) and (11c) the contrasted elements occur in the same morphological frame, that is, they both occur in the analytic root form. In (11d), however, the contrasted elements are neither morphologically nor syntactically parallel. The demand for symmetry is even stronger than the requirement for logic. There are languages in which structures like:

I am sadder than angrier.	(11e)

are permitted, for example, Latin, Greek, and Sanskrit. Thus, the Latin (12):

Long-	ior	quam	lat-	ior	acies	erat	(12a)
long	er	than	wide	er	line	was	(12b)
The battle-line was longer than it was wide.						(12c)

Formal symmetry may be more subtle than in these examples (12). For example, in the sentence:

I want *me* to win.	(13)

the contrastively stressed word *me* is *treated in exactly the same way as any other noun phrase that could potentially appear in this position.* None of them is reflexive: and so, neither is *me*. There is thus a paradigmatic symmetry between *me* and these other NP. Sentences like this are only acceptable if the stressed noun phrase is contrasted with others. The conceptual parity between contrasted elements which is iconically represented here is the loss of 'speaker privilege' on the subject's part.

5. The Unexpected

The fundamentally iconic nature of markedness is a virtual cliché: marked form corresponds to marked meaning.

In a number of publications, Givón (1983, 1985) has argued that the physical segmental bulk or suprasegmental amplitude of a nominal expression varies inversely with its predictability: the more predictable the referent, the less effort is expended on signaling its presence.

5.1 Expectations of Noncoreference

The functional motivation of the passive construction is well brought out in the following passage:

> If I were to change, the changing would have to be (14) mine alone. I could not *be* changed, since there was no-one to do it for me.

The usual raison d'être of the passive is the non-specification of the agent. When the passive is one which involves a promotion of the underlying patient, the normal expectation is that the superficial subject is not the agent. This is the expectation which the author of (14) exploits in: 'being changed' contrasts with 'changing by oneself.' It is of course possible for this expectation (the listener's) to be frustrated, as in (15):

> He was changed—but by *himself*. (15)

but the unexpected coreference of subject and agent is then obligatorily signaled by contrastive stress on the agent noun.

Similar expectations of noncoreference apply to patient and recipient noun phrases:

> The senator sold the slave—to the slave *himself*. (16a)
> The slave was sold— to *himself*. (16b)

In other languages, the contrast between stressed and unstressed forms of the reflexive is also marked by a change in their relative position, but the same distinction applies: unexpected coreference must be signaled by the stressed form of the reflexive. Consider the Italian sentences in example (17):

> E stato presentato a se stesso (17a)
> is been presented to self emphatic
> He was introduced to *himself*.
> *S' è stato presentato (17b)
> self is been presented
> He was introduced to himself.

The contrast between predictable and unpredictable objects of ordinary transitive verbs is similar. Some transitive verbs, typically those of grooming or posture, are typically *introverted*: their objects are usually coreferential with their subjects. Others are typically *extroverted*: their objects are typically distinct from their subjects. In the formal contrast

> He shaved (himself). (18a)
> He kicked himself. (18b)

English patterns like a large number of other languages. The construction 'he shaved' is typically used, since shaving is an action one normally performs on oneself. The analogue of (18a) in languages like Russian, Hungarian, and Turkish, is the *middle voice*, marked by some bound morpheme. The expression 'he kicked,' is not used because kicking is an action typically performed on others. The analogue of (18b), and of other sentences like 'know thyself' in those languages which allow it, must use the pronoun which marks unexpected coreference.

5.2 Unexpected Noncoreference

Most European languages mark middle voice with some bound morpheme, thus Hungarian *mos-akod* 'wash (middle)' versus *mos-* 'wash (transitive).' Some languages, however, leave introverted verbs unmarked: English is such a language, as is the Papuan Hua of New Guinea. In order to make such a typically introverted verb transitive, Hua, unlike English, must mark the marked function of the verb with a special auxiliary *to-* 'put' (3rd sg te-e):

> ehi – e (19a)
> stand = up 3rd sg
> S/he stood up.
> ehi – na te – e (19b)
> stand = up – 3rd sg medial put – 3rd sg final
> S/he stood him/her up.

All of the examples discussed in this section deal with familiar examples of markedness. The phenomenon of markedness reversal indicates that markedness is context sensitive. What is marked by more complex form is therefore never a more complex concept but a more surprising one, given the context.

6. Competing Motivations

The iconicity of word order is one of the most widely recognized types in the literature, from Jakobson's 'Veni, vidi, vici' onwards. The basic idea is that the order of clauses or phrases corresponds to the order of thoughts. This simplistic view runs counter to the incontestable fact that languages differ considerably in their preferred word order, at least within the clause.

Countervailing Behaghel's universal that the given comes first is Jespersen's 'principle of actuality.' The first puts topics at the beginning of their sentences, while the second puts focused elements there. Not atypically, English conforms with both conflicting universals. Protasis clauses typically precede apodoses (given precedes new), while question words typically are *fronted* (focus precedes everything else).

That competing motivations may exist is perhaps an inevitable consequence of the limitations of the medium of spoken language. But unless they are resolved, with a clear understanding of the domains within which they have priority, it is difficult to avoid charges of Panglossianism.

Some recent approaches to this problem which show promise are demonstrations that where no competition exists, no variation of forms exists either. For example, although languages differ in their placement of interrogative pronouns, they agree in their placement of the frequently homophonous relative pronouns. A possible explanation for this is that there are competing motivations for the placement of focused elements, but no competition for the placement of relative pronouns.

Similar in spirit is Du Bois' demonstration that competing motivations may account for nominative/accusative and nominative/ergative split patterns in languages, but that where there is no competition, as in first and second person pronouns, nominative/accusative patterns overwhelmingly predominate.

Bibliography

Bolinger D, Gerstman L 1957 Disjuncture as a clue to constructs. *Word* **13**: 246–55
Bybee J 1985 *Morphology*. Benjamins, Amsterdam
Du Bois J 1985 Competing motivations. In: Haiman (ed.) *Iconicity in Syntax*. Benjamins, Amsterdam
Givón T 1980 The binding hierarchy and the typology of complements. *SLang* **4(3)**: 333–77
Givón T (ed.) 1983 *Topic Continuity in Discourse*. Benjamins, Amsterdam
Givón T 1985 Iconicity, isomorphism, and non-arbitrary coding in syntax. In: Haiman J (ed.) *Iconicity in Syntax*. Benjamins, Amsterdam
Greenberg J 1966a *Language Universals, with Particular Reference to Feature Hierarchies*. Mouton, The Hague
Greenberg J 1966b Some universals of language, with particular reference to the order of meaningful elements. In: Greenberg J (ed.) *Universals of Language*, 2nd edn. MIT Press, Cambridge, MA
Haiman J 1983 Iconic and economic motivation. *Lg*. **59**: 781–819
Haiman J 1985a *Natural Syntax*. Cambridge University Press, Cambridge
Haiman J (ed.) 1985b *Iconicity in Syntax*. Benjamins, Amsterdam
Haiman J 1988 Incorporation, parallelism, and focus. In: Hammond M et al. (eds.) *Studies in Syntactic Typology*. Benjamins, Amsterdam
Jakobson R 1965 Quest for the essence of language. *Diogenes* **51**: 21–37
Kegl J 1986 Clitics in American sign language. In: Borer H (ed.) *The Syntax of Pronominal Clitics*. Academic Press, New York
Kuno S 1987 *Functional Syntax*. University of Chicago Press, Chicago, IL
Peirce C S 1932 *Philosophical Writings*. Harvard University Press, Boston, MA
Rappoport G 1979 Detachment and adverbial participle clauses in Russian (Unpublished PhD dissertation, UCLA)
Schachter P 1977 Constraints on coordination. *Lg* **53**: 86–103
Tai J 1985 Temporal sequence and Chinese word order. In: Haiman (ed.) *Iconicity in Syntax*. Benjamins, Amsterdam

Information Structure
W. A. Foley

Information structure is the encoding of the relative salience of the constituents of a clause, especially nominals, and is realized as choices among alternative syntactic arrangements. The information structure of a particular clause is determined by the larger sentence or discourse of which it is a part (i.e., its context). The communicative effect of the information structure is to foreground certain aspects of the message of the clause, but to background others. The need to encode information structure is a language universal, but the formal means to do so vary widely across the languages of the world.

1. Definition of the Basic Terms: Focus and Topic

English is often referred to as a fixed-order language. This is because changing the word order typically alters the basic meaning of the sentence: for example, *John killed Bill* has quite a different meaning from *Bill killed John*; Russian, on the other hand, is commonly called a free word order language. For example, the sentence *Maksím zaščiščájet Viktora* has the following alternative orders, all of the same meaning (Comrie 1979a):

Maksím Víktora zaščiščájet	(1)
Víktora Maksím zaščiščájet	(2)
Víktora zaščiščájet Maksím	(3)
zaščiščájet Maksím Víktora	(4)
zaščiščájet Víktora Maksím	(5)
'Maksím defends Viktor.'	(6)

In all these sentences *Maksim* is nominative case, indicating it is the subject, while *Viktora* is accusative case, for the direct object. Thus, the word order of Russian can vary freely without changing the basic meaning of which nominal is subject or object. To make that change the case endings must be transposed: *Maksíma zaščiščájet Viktor* 'Viktor defends Maksim.'

But it is not truly accurate to claim that the word order of Russian is absolutely free. Word order is used by Russian, as well as many other languages, to encode the information structure of the clauses. Each of the above alternatives (1–6) expresses the same meaning, but encodes it within different information structures; this is made clear by a study of the following mini-dialogs (Comrie 1979a):

Q:	Któ zaščiščájet Víktora?	(7)
	'Who defends Viktor?'	(8)
A:	Víktora zaščiščájet Maksím.	(9)
	'Maksim defends Viktor.'	(10)
Q:	Kogó zaščiščájet Maksím?	(11)
	'Whom does Maksim defend?'	(12)
A:	Maksím zaščiščájet Víktora.	(13)
	'Maksim defends Viktor.'	(14)

Note that while the answer to both questions can have the same word order in English, this is not possible in Russian. Rather the nominal which provides the answer to the question word always occurs finally in the answer, while the material already established by the question must precede it. The question sets up certain expectations which must be realized in the information structure of the answer. The nominal corresponding to the question word is the *focus* of the clause, expressing the new information which the utterance of the clause is expected to provide, while the remainder expresses what is taken for granted (presupposed). Thus the information structure of both question and answer in the first mini-dialog could be represented as:

Q:	Presupposed: someone is defending Viktor	(15)
	Focus: who is that someone?	(16)
A:	Presupposed: someone is defending Viktor	(17)
	Focus: that someone is Maksim.	(18)

With the exception of question words which always occur initially, Russian has a fairly rigid rule of information structure that presupposed information precedes focused information. Focused information typically occurs at the end of the sentence:

Presupposed:	someone is defending Viktor	(19)
Focus:	that someone is Maksim.	(20)

Víktora zaščiščájet	‖	Maksím.	(21)
PRESUPPOSED	‖	FOCUS	

The above sentence (21) presents an obvious question as to the information status of the first noun, *Víktora*. This corresponds to the *topic* of the sentence, another notion of information structure best illustrated by mini-dialogs (Comrie 1979a):

S:	Maksím ubivájet Alekśeja.	(22)
	'Maksim kills Alekséj.'	(23)

Q:	a Víktora?	(24)
	'and Viktor?'	(25)
A:	Víktora Maksím zaščiščájet	(26)
	'Maksim defends Viktor.'	(27)

Typically a sentence expresses a comment about some entity. This entity is really what the sentence is about, its presupposed starting point. It is referred to by a nominal which corresponds to the topic of the sentence. The topic is presupposed information that the remainder of the sentence comments upon. In Russian, as in many languages, the topic of the sentence always occurs initially. Thus, the initial nominal in the answer in the above mini-dialog has the following topic-comment information structure (28–9):

Topic:	concerning Boris	(28)
Comment:	(he) defends Viktor	(29)

Thus, there are two systems expressed in the information structure of the Russian clause, that of *presupposed-focus* and *topic-comment*. The information structures of the final answer in the mini-dialog (28–9) is (30).

TOPIC	‖	COMMENT		(30)
Boris	‖	zaščiščájet	‖ Víktora	
	‖	PRESUPPOSED	‖ FOCUS	

Thus, the basic word order rules that encode information structure of Russian clauses is that topic precedes comment and presupposed information precedes focused information. This typically results in an order with the topic nominal sentence initially and the focus nominal sentence finally. This ordering constraint is often referred to as *functional sentence perspective* in the Slavic grammatical tradition.

2. Information Structure in English

Word order in English is strongly determined by syntactic conditions, such as the encoding of grammatical relations like subject and object (Sect. 1). So an important issue is how English indicates information structure. It does it through word order as Russian does. Topic occurs sentence initially and focus, finally. For example, not all of English word order is rigidly fixed. Some alternatives are commonly found, for example, *today Brian is reading* and *Brian is reading today*, and *the children are playing in the yard* and *in the yard the children are playing*. That these differences encode information structure is apparent from constructing mini-dialogs (31–3):

Q:	When is Brian reading?	(31)
A:	Brian is reading ‖ today.	
	PRESUPPOSED ‖ FOCUS	

A:	?Today ‖ Brian is reading.	(32)
	FOCUS ‖ PRESUPPOSED	

Q:	Is Brian writing today?	
A:	No, today Brian ‖ is reading.	(33)
	PRESUPPOSED ‖ FOCUS	

The normal position for focused information in English is sentence finally, as in Russian. English is more flexible than Russian and does allow some deviations from this rule, however, the language does require that this deviation be signaled. Thus, one common way in English to encode focused information which is not sentence final is by a high falling pitch on the constituent (sometimes called 'emphatic stress'). Consider (34–9):

Q:	Who saw Bill?	(34)
A:	Bill was seen ‖ by John.	(35)
	PRESUPPOSED ‖ FOCUS	
A:	John ‖ saw Bill.	(36)
	FOCUS ‖ PRESUPPOSED	
Q:	Which one is John?	(37)
A:	John is ‖ the chairperson.	(38)
	PRESUPPOSED ‖ FOCUS	
A:	The chairperson ‖ is John.	(39)
	FOCUS ‖ PRESUPPOSED	

Another way of altering the normal English ordering of presupposed information before focused is through *it*-cleft constructions. Thus the meaning of the sentence *Ron ate a sandwich* could be expressed in *it*-cleft constructions, indicating unusual encodings of information structure (40–1):

It was Ron ‖ who ate a sandwich.	(40)
FOCUS ‖ PRESUPPOSED	
It was a sandwich ‖ that Ron ate.	(41)
FOCUS ‖ PRESUPPOSED	

The relative clauses in *it*-cleft constructions are typically used to reintroduce information already known, but not foregrounded in the present discourse context (Prince 1978). They are presupposed information, but are now being reintroduced and partially highlighted in this context; hence, their appearance sentence finally, the position of focused information. *It*-clefts, contrast with *wh*-clefts, which have the expected ordering of presupposed information before focused (42–3):

The one who ate the sandwich was ‖ Ron.	(42)
PRESUPPOSED ‖ FOCUS	
What Ron ate was ‖ a sandwich.	(43)
PRESUPPOSED ‖ FOCUS	

Given their different information structure, it should come as no surprise that *wh*-clefts are found in different discourse contexts than *it*-clefts. The relative clauses of *wh*-clefts (presupposed) express information already foregrounded, assumed to be in the hearer's mind at the moment. Hence, they have no need to

appear in focus position, in fact, rather properly belonging in the topic position they do indeed occupy.

The encoding of the topic-comment information structure in English is complicated by the common sentence initial position for the subject nominal. There is, in fact, a very strong correlation between the concepts of topic and subject in English, a salient typological fact about this language as opposed to Russian. Thus, the typical way to express alternatives of topic choice is to select different subjects. This is very common in English. For example (44–5):

Tears ‖ streamed down her face.	(44)
TOPIC ‖ COMMENT	
Her face ‖ streamed with tears.	
Blood ‖ flowed in the streets.	(45)
TOPIC ‖ COMMENT	
The streets ‖ flowed with blood.	

In these two examples the same predicate is used with different subject/topic choices. In other cases different predicates must be used (46–51):

Q:	Where is the dot?	(46)
	TOPIC ‖ COMMENT	
A:	The dot ‖ is ‖ inside the circle.	(47)
	PRESUPPOSED ‖ FOCUS	
A:	? The circle surrounds the dot.	(48)
Q:	Where is the circle?	(49)
	TOPIC ‖ COMMENT	
A:	The circle ‖ is ‖ around the dot.	(50)
	PRESUPPOSED ‖ FOCUS	
A:	? The dot is inside the circle.	(51)

Any construction in English which affects subject selection also typically encodes the topic-comment information structure. For example, extraposition is a topic-altering device (52–3):

TOPIC ‖ COMMENT	(52)
that John will attend ‖ is certain	
TOPIC ‖ COMMENT	(53)
John ‖ is certain to attend	

And, perhaps, the most common information-structure encoding device in English (and many other languages) is the alteration between active and passive voice (discussed further in Sect. 5.1), for example (54–5):

TOPIC ‖ COMMENT	(54)
the manager ‖ sacked the pilots	
TOPIC ‖ COMMENT	(55)
the pilots ‖ were sacked by the manager	

Thus, the immediate discourse context determines the proper choice between active and passive, as with all information-structure alternatives. Consider these mini-dialogs (56–9):

Q: Who saw Bill? (56)

TOPIC	COMMENT	(57)
A: Bill	was seen by John	

Q: Whom did Bill see? (58)

TOPIC	COMMENT	(59)
A: ? John	was seen by Bill	

The second answer is bizarre because *Bill* is the natural topic, as established by the question. Hence, Bill should be subject and the answer is properly in the active voice: *Bill saw John*.

While there is a very close correlation in English between the notions of topic and subject, it is not the case that they are isomorphic; these are clear cases of topics which are not subjects. These are topics occurring sentence initially and preceding the subjects as in (60–2):

TOPIC	COMMENT	
Last night	I saw three movies in town.	(60)
As for John	he is such a clown.	(61)
Soukous	I think it's the great African twentieth-century contribution to civilization.	(62)

Such constructions are especially common in informal spoken speech styles. The first example is an ordinary topicalization, while the second and third examples illustrate left-dislocations, in which a pronoun marks the position where otherwise the topic nominal would be found. Left-dislocations are used in English to express a change in topic in discourse, such as when a new topic is introduced which supersedes a previous one (this is especially noticeable with *as for*). Ordinary topicalizations, on the other hand, can be used to present as topic any constituent which is presupposed. It may not be explicitly mentioned previously, but must be presupposed, for example (63–4):

Q: What's your favorite dance music? (63)

TOPIC	COMMENT	(64)
A: Soukous	my feet find irresistible.	

Soukous, a type of African dance music, is presupposed by the general cover term 'dance music' in the question.

3. Other Means of Encoding Information Structure

Both Russian and English largely employ word order to express information structure, and it is sometimes assumed that this is the natural way to do so. Although a widespread device, used probably by all languages to some extent, word order is superseded in some languages as the primary means to encode information structure by other strategies. One of the most common alternative means is specific morphemes which encode the information-structure function of a nominal. Japanese, for example, has a special

postposition *wa*, which makes a topic nominal (Inoue 1979) (65–6):

Hanoko ni wa	Taroo ga	hon o	watashi-ta	(65)
Hanoko to TOPIC	Taroo SUBJ	book OBJ	give-PAST	

'As for Hanako, Taroo gave her a book.'

Nihon wa	Tookyoo ga	sumiyoi	(66)
Japan TOPIC	Tokyo SUBJ	easy to live in	

'As for Japan, Tokyo is easy to live in.'

As in English and Russian, topics in Japanese are set up by the discourse context. Consider this mini-dialog (67–8):

X:	yuube	Sakai san ga	asobi ni	(67)
	last night	Sakai Mr SUBJ	play to	
	ki-mashi-ta yo			
	come-POLITE-PT AFFIRM			

'Last night Mr Sakai come for a visit.'

Y:	soo	des-u	ka? Sakai san wa/?ga	(68)
	thus	be-NON PT	QUES Sakai Mr TOPIC/SUBJ	
	genki	des-u	ka?	
	healthy	be-NOW PT	QUES	

'Is that so? Is Mr Sakai healthy?'

Note that *Sakai san* 'Mr Sakai' is simply marked with the subject marker *ga* in *X*, not the topic marker *wa*; hence it is being presented as nontopical information, likely the focus of the sentence. But by the *Y* utterance *Sakai san* has been established as topical and so is encoded as the topic with *wa*; it is ungrammatical to simply use the subject particle *ga* in *Y*.

Japanese has a strict separation of topic and focus. A subject which is the focus must be encoded with *ga*; it may never co-occur with a *wa* topic. Consider this mini-dialog (69–70):

Q:	dare ga	mado o ake-ta ka?	(69)
	who SUBJ	window OBJ open-PT QUES	
	FOCUS	PRESUPPOSED	

'Who opened the window?'

A:	watashi ga/?wa	ake-ta	(70)
	I SUBJ/TOPIC	open-PT	
	FOCUS	PRESUPPOSED	

'I opened (it).'

The focused nominal *watashi* 'I' can only be encoded with the subject marker *ga*; *wa* topic is ungrammatical. Note that the presupposed information *mado o* 'the window' is omitted completely in the answer; this is very common in Japanese, the so-called *zero anaphora*.

Perhaps, the most unusual device for encoding information structure is through verbal agreement affixes, a common feature of Bantu languages and some Papuan languages, like Yimas. Chicheŵa, a Bantu language of Malaŵi and neighboring areas is a good representative of this type (Bresnan and Mchombo 1987). In Chicheŵa an object nominal can function as focus or topic of its clause. As a focused nominal, it may not be crossreferenced by a verbal prefix and must immediately follow the verb, resulting in a rigid presupposed-focus ordering (71–2):

njûchi   zi-ná-lum-a ‖ alenje (71)
10 bees 10 SUBJ-PAST-bite-INDIC ‖ 2 hunters
PRESUPPOSED ‖ FOCUS
'The bees stung the hunters.'

*alenje ‖ njûchi   zi-ná-lúm-a (72)
2 hunters ‖ 10 bees 10 SUBJ-PAST-bite-INDIC
FOCUS ‖ PRESUPPOSED

(The numbers indicate gender classes.) However, an object nominal which is also topic must be cross-referenced with a verbal prefix and then can occur in any position in the clause, the syntactic position of the topic in Chicheŵa being free, not fixed sentence initially as in Russian or English (73–4):

njûchi zi-ná-wá-lum-a ‖ alenje (73)
10 bees 10 SUBJ-PAST-2 OBJ-bite-INDIC ‖ 2 hunters
     COMMENT ‖ TOPIC

zináwáluma alenje njûchi (74)
alenje zináwáluma njûchi
zináwáluma njûchi alenje
njûchi alenje zináwáluma
alenje njûchi zináwáluma

Note that *wá-* 2 OBJ indicates that *alenje* 'hunter' is the topic of its clause and hence the nominal can occur in any position, as the grammaticality of the six sentences above (73–4) demonstrates. Thus, unlike Russian and English, word order does not encode the topic comment information structure in Chicheŵa; the verbal morphology does.

This analysis is clearly supported by the behavior of questions. Question words, being the focus of the sentence, can never be crossreferenced by a verbal prefix, nor can the focused nominal in the answer (75–8):

Q: mu-ku-fún-á ‖ chíyáni (75)
   you SUBJ-PRES-want-INDIC ‖ 7 what
   PRESUPPOSED ‖ FOCUS
   'What do you want?'

(*mu-ku-chí-fún-á ‖ chíyáni) (76)
 you SUBJ-PRES-7 OBJ-want-INDIC ‖ 7 what
   COMMENT ‖ TOPIC

A: ndi-ku-fún-a ‖ chipêwa (77)
   I SUBJ-PRES-want-INDIC ‖ 7 hat
   PRESUPPOSED ‖ FOCUS
   'I want a hat.'

(?? ndi-ku-chí-fún-a ‖ chipêwa) (78)
 I SUBJ-PRES-want-INDIC ‖ 7 hat
   COMMENT ‖ TOPIC

The answer with *chipêwa* 'hat' as topic could be acceptable if the speaker was choosing from some articles he/she could see and had decided on one of these objects, the hat. In this case, it is topical by being among the immediate objects of discussion. Otherwise, *chipêwa* 'hat' is a focused nominal and may not occur with a crossreferencing verbal prefix.

In questions in which the focused question word is other than the object, it is possible, of course, for the object to function as topic in both question and answer, as in these Swahili examples:

Q: nani ‖ a-na-i-tak-a ‖ nazi (79)
   1 who ‖ 1 SUBJ-PRES-9 OBJ-want-INDIC ‖ 7 coconut
   FOCUS ‖ ‖ TOPIC
   'Who wants the coconut?'

A: nazi ‖ ni-na-i-tak-a (80)
   7 coconut ‖ I SUBJ-PRES-9 OBJ-want-INDIC
   TOPIC ‖ FOCUS
   'I want the coconut'

Nazi 'coconut' is topic in both question and answer. The question might occur when a man is holding a coconut in his hand and offering it to a group of children. It is already the topic of the discourse. One of the children might then answer as above, continuing with the coconut as topic.

4. Categories of Information Status

4.1 Given versus New Information

Topics are typically presupposed information. They are the starting point of the sentence, what it is about. Focused nominals, on the other hand, are the end goal of the sentence, the information which the speaker intends to introduce into the discourse. Hence the topic tends to occur toward the beginning of a sentence and the focus toward the end. Topics are closely correlated with the given or old information, which is currently in the speaker's awareness, while focused constituents are new information, just being introduced into the discourse. The concept of given information is more or less equivalent to presupposed, but new information need not (although it usually does) correspond only to the focused constituent.

Q: What happened? (81)

A: An enormous storm devastated Manila. (82)

Arguably, all the information in the answer (82) is new, but only the nominal *Manila* is really the focus, as demonstrated by its high falling pitch.

There are other types of mismatches between topic and presupposed/given and focus and new. Some of these are exemplified by contrastive nominals. These are marked like focused constituents by a high falling pitch. Contrastive nominals are typically focused, but presupposed (83).

Considering the suspects, only Egbert has a motive. (83)

Egbert is one of several suspects in a crime investigation; he is thus presupposed, yet new information is provided about him, as focus, as being the only person among them with a motive. Thus, he is set up in contrast to the other suspects, presupposed but focused. Another example of a focus-presupposed nominal would be in the following sentence (84) in a discourse about dances.

I like the lambada, but Sa͞m likes the cha-cha.   (84)

People who like dancing are presupposed, Sam among them. But he is focused as being unusual in liking the cha-cha; the goal of the sentence is to communicate this piece of gossip.

There are also examples of topics which are new information. Perhaps the best-known examples of these are found in the opening lines of stories, such as fairy tales (85):

Once upon a time, a little old woman lived in a dark cave. (85)

Little old woman is the topic of this sentence, but as it initiates a discourse, it is *obviously* not given information, but new.

4.2 Referential versus Nonreferential

Besides given/presupposed versus new, nominals may bear other kinds of information statuses, depending on the speaker's view of the listener's knowledge of their referents. A nominal is referential if the speaker intends that it refer to a particular entity in the world. For example, if someone rings a friend and asks *What are you doing?* and the response is *I'm looking for a snake*, the nominal *snake* could be either referential or nonreferential. If the respondent has a particular snake in mind, for example, a pet boa constrictor, then *snake* would be referential as in (86):

I'm looking for a snake. Moses escaped from his cage. (86)

Here, Moses is the boa constrictor's name. If, on the other hand, she/he is lonely and just wants a pet snake, then *snake* would be nonreferential, as in (87):

I'm looking for a snake. I want a new pet.   (87)

Pronouns like *I, we, you, they* are typically referential, but at least two, *you* and *it*, have nonreferential uses (88–9):

You pay your money and you take your chances.   (88)

It's raining in Melbourne, as usual.   (89)

4.3 Definite versus Indefinite

A nominal is mark definite when the speaker presupposes the listener can uniquely identify its referent; otherwise a nominal is indicated as indefinite. So if X goes up to Y and announces *Egbert bought the snake*, the definite article indicates that X presupposes Y knows which snake she/he is talking about. If X does not, X would probably come back with a request for additional information to help identify the referent of *the snake*, such as *which snake?* On the other hand, if X believed that Y had no knowledge of the particular snake, X would have initiated the conversation with

the nominal indicated as indefinite: *Hey, Egbert just bought a snake!*

Topic nominals are closely correlated with definiteness, and because subject selection is largely equivalent to topic choice in English, indefinite subjects are sometimes impossible. Consider (90–1):

TOPIC	COMMENT		(90)
John	has	a new camera	
PRESUPPOSED		FOCUS	

TOPIC	COMMENT		(91)
the/*a new camera		is John's	
PRESUPPOSED		FOCUS	

Note that the variant with the indefinite nominal as subject and, hence, topic, is ungrammatical.

English, like many languages, has articles to mark the difference between definite and indefinite nominals. Other languages may use other devices. Mandarin, for example, uses word order: definite nominals precede the verb (92), indefinite follow (93) (Li and Thompson 1975):

ši rén le   (92)
die person PRF
'a person has died/someone has died'

rén ši le   (93)
person die PRF
'the person has died'

Other languages may use distinctive case endings to indicate definite nominals. In Iranian, for example, there is a special accusative case, but only if the nominal is definite (Comrie 1979b):

Hasan yek ketāb did   (94)
Hasan a   book saw
'Hasan saw a book.'

Hasan ketāb-rā did   (95)
Hasan book-ACC DEF saw
'Hasan saw the book.'

Personal pronouns like *I, you,* and *they* and proper nouns like *Hasan, Egbert,* and *Australia* are usually definite; they refer to entities which the speaker presupposes the listener can uniquely identify. There can be exceptions, however; for example, when two people are looking over a map and one says to the other (96):

Hey Sue, I found an Athens in Georgia!   (96)

Here, *Athens*, although a proper noun, is indefinite, because the speaker assumes the listener does not have this particular Athens in mind.

The distinction between definiteness and indefiniteness interacts with the two previous definitions discussed. Definite nouns are presupposed and hence typically given information. They can be new, however, as in (97):

Hey, get up! The sun has already come up!   (97)

Here *the sun* is new information being introduced for

the first time. Yet the speaker treats it as definite, for she/he assumes the listener can uniquely identify the referent: there is only one sun in the real world. Definiteness interacts with referentiality to form all four possible combinations:

   (a) definite and referential: *I'm looking for the snake* (our pet boa constrictor);

   (b) indefinite and referential: *I'm looking for a snake* (my pet boa constrictor just escaped from its cage);

   (c) definite and nonreferential: *I'm looking for the friendliest snake I can find* (I haven't got it yet, but you and I know what kind it would have to be) and

   (d) indefinite and nonreferential: *I'm looking for a snake to buy* (said to a pet store keeper).

4.4 Generic versus Specific

This distinction indicates whether a nominal refers to the entire class of its possible referents or a specific one (98–9):

> Snakes are easy pets to care for. (98)

> The snake is my favorite among my pets, but it keeps escaping. (99)

Snakes in the first example is generic; the statement is meant to cover all animals classed as snakes. The nominal *the snake* in the second example is specific, as the sentence only applies to a particular snake, my pet snake. Generic nominals can be definite (100) or indefinite (101–2):

> The snake is an easy pet to care for. (100)

> A snake is an easy pet to care for. (101)

> Snakes are easy pets to care for. (102)

In other languages, the distinction between generic and specific can be realized quite differently. For example, in Fijian specific nominals functioning as direct object co-occur with an article while the verb is overtly marked transitive, while generic nominals are article-less and, further, are incorporated into the verb phrase, so that the verb is formally intransitive (103–4):

> e ra gunu-va na wai (103)
> 3PL drink-TR ART water
> 'They drank the water.'

> e ra gunu wai (104)
> 3PL drink water
> 'They drank water.'

This incorporation of generic direct objects is widely attested crosslinguistically; even English exhibits it: *they went snake-hunting*.

4.5 The Animacy Hierarchy

The distinctions of information status for nominals considered above were all established by the discourse context. Now it is time to assess the information status of nominals as determined by inherent properties of their referents, the most significant of which properties is being one of the immediate speech act participants: the speaker or the addressee. Speaker and addressee generally correspond to the personal pronouns *I* and *you*. The traditional definition of a pronoun as a word which stands for a noun is inaccurate in the case of *I* and *you* in that there is no possible nominal for which they stand. The referents *I* and *you* are not constant, but rather they change in the course of an interaction, depending on who is doing the speaking and who is being spoken to. This interplay of the shifting referents of *I* and *you* in the continuing speech act is a fundamental fact of language.

The elements which do fit the traditional definition of pronouns as the forms which take the place of nouns are the third-person pronouns: in English *he*, *she*, *it*, *they*. These are fundamentally different from *I* and *you*. Whereas *I* and *you* have the present speech participants as referents, a third-person pronoun may refer to any referent, other than the speech act participants. The third person is, in fact, a non-person, its possible referents being restricted to nonparticipants in the speech act.

There is a fundamental principle of salience in the system of persons. The speech act participants, speaker and addressee, are more salient than the absent participants of the third person (Silverstein 1976). In some languages the addressee is more salient than the speaker. In other languages the speaker is more salient than the addressee. And, in still other languages, speaker and addressee have equal salience. Many languages make further distinctions between different types of third person nominals. Nominals with animate referents are more salient than those with inanimate referents, and among animates, human referents are the most salient. Some languages make a further distinction among nominals with human referents, with proper nouns more salient than common nouns. Finally, third-person pronouns are generally more salient than full nominals. A hierarchy of inherent salience can be established (105–6):

> speaker/listener > third-person pronouns (105)
>   > human proper

> nouns > human common nouns
>   > other animate nouns > inanimate nouns. (106)

The inherent salience of a nominal often determines the packaging of a particular expression. Nominals higher on the animacy hierarchy tend to occupy more prominent syntactic positions than nominals lower on it. Many languages have grammatical systems which are sensitive to the distinctions along this hierarchy. Yimas of New Guinea is one such language: its version of the animacy hierarchy is:

speaker > listener > third-person human   (107)
   > animate > inanimate.

In Yimas, grammatical relations like subject and object are signaled by verbal crossreferencing prefixes. These are not in a fixed order: whichever has a referent higher on the animacy hierarchy occurs closer to the verb stem. Consider the pair (108):

na-ka-tay   na-ŋa-tay   (108)
3SG OBJ-1SG SUBJ-see 3SG SUBJ-1SG OBJ-see
'I saw him.'   'He saw me.'

Note that the prefixes for the speaker *ka-* 1SG SUBJ and *ŋa-*1SG OBJ always occur closer to the verb stem than the prefix for third person *na-*. This is because the speaker outranks third person human in the animacy hierarchy. The same applies if the listener is substituted for the speaker (109):

na-n-tay   na-nan-tay   (109)
3SG OBJ-2SG SUBJ-see 3SG SUBJ-2SG OBJ-see
'You saw him.'   'He saw you.'

And in combinations with the speaker and listener, the prefix for the speaker is closer to the verb stem, as speaker outranks listener on the animacy hierarchy (110):

ma-ŋa-tay   (110)
2SG SUBJ-1SG OBJ-see
'You saw me.'

5. Voice Alternations for Information Structure

Perhaps the most studied of syntactic devices for encoding information structure are voice alternations like passives and antipassives. They typically cause some major rearrangements of clause structure.

5.1 Passive

The usual choice for subject in English (and hence topic), is the actor, the entity performing the action. This results in active sentences, for example (111–12):

The boy ate the sandwich.   (111)

The keeper fed the python.   (112)

When the speaker chooses the entity affected by the action (the patient) as subject, he uses a passive construction. The actor then appears in a prepositional phrase with *by*:

The sandwich was eaten by the boy.   (113)

The python was fed by the keeper.   (114)

Note that the passive construction diverges from the active in two important respects: (a) the patient is foregrounded in being presented as subject and, hence, topic and (b) the actor is backgrounded, appearing in a prepositional phrase. This corresponds to the two basic functions of passive in English and crosslinguistically: *foregrounding*, in which a nonactor is sub-ject and topic, and *backgrounding*, in which the actor is removed from the forefront of the clause.

Perhaps the most common type of backgrounding passives are agentless passives with no mention of the actor (115–16):

The house was sold from under us.   (115)

Egbert got robbed yesterday.   (116)

These are used when the referent or the actor is unknown or the speaker wishes to avoid mentioning them. The impersonal passives of European and other languages also have a backgrounding function, as in these Dutch examples (Krisner 1976):

er   woorden   daar huizen gebouwd   (117)
there became(3PL) there houses built
'There were houses built there.'

er   wordt   door de jongens gefloten   (118)
there became(3SG) by the boys   whistled
'There is whistling by the boys.'

These impersonal passives may have overt actors, but they are strongly backgrounded.

Passives are strongly favored when there is a large imbalance between a definite or highly animate patient and an indefinite or lowly animate actor. Because the patient has high information status in comparison to the actor, it is preferred as topic. Hence a passive commonly results (119–20):

I got run over by a bus.   (119)

Egbert was stung by a bee!   (120)

Whereas if the actor is of high information status, and the patient low, passives are marginal at best (121–23):

? A bee was killed by Egbert.   (121)

? A bus was run off the cliff by me.   (122)

The/? A CD player was lent to me by Dad. (123)

The foregrounding function of passives is most apparent when a patient needs to be subject and topic for the purposes of discourse cohesion. Note, if the sentences *Oscar went to the store* and *Oscar saw Bill* are conjoined, they produce (124):

Oscar went to the store and saw Bill.   (124)

where Oscar as subject and topic of the second clause can simply be omitted. However, if the same exercise is attempted with *Oscar went to the store* and *Bill saw Oscar*, the ungrammatical sentence (125) is produced:

*Oscar went to the store and Bill saw   (125)

in which the patient *Oscar* has been omitted. This is impossible: rather the passive must be used to make Oscar subject and topic, and then the conjunction is fine (126):

Oscar went to the store and was seen by Bill. (126)

This is an example of the foregrounding function of passive: the patient is made subject and topic in order to meet discourse conditions, in this case, constraints on conjunction.

5.2 Antipassives

Antipassives are the mirror-image constructions to passives. They most transparently occur in languages in which the usual choice for topic is not actor, as in English, but is the patient (so-called 'ergative' languages). In these languages antipassives are functionally parallel to passives: they indicate that instead of the usual choice for topic, the patient, there is a marked choice, the actor. Dyirbal of Australia is such a language (Dixon 1979a):

TOPIC					(127)
balan	dyugumbil	baŋgul	yaṛaŋgu	buṛa-n	
FEM ABS	woman ABS	MASC ERG	man ERG	see-PT	
'man saw women'					

ABSOLUTIVE is the case of the topic and the ERGATIVE the case of the actor. Example (127) is the basic sentence type with the patient as the topic choice. If the actor was chosen as topic, then the antipassive construction must be employed:

TOPIC					(128)
bayi	yaṛa	bagun	dyugumbilgu	buṛal-ŋa-ɲu	
MASC ABS	man ABS	FEM DAT	women DAT	see-ANTIPASSIVE-PAST	
'man saw women'					

Now the actor has the ABSOLUTIVE case marking and is topic, while the patient is in the dative case (parallel to the prepositional phrase with *by* in the English passive). Note the verb has an overt antipassive suffix -ŋa(*y*).

Antipassives further parallel passives in having both foregrounding and backgrounding functions. Suppose the following two Dyirbal sentences (129–30) are conjoined:

TOPIC			(129)
bayi	yaṛa	bani-ɲu	
MASC ABS	man ABS	come-PAST	
'man came'			

TOPIC				(130)
balan	dyugumbil	baŋgul	yaṛaŋgu	buṛa-n
FEM ABS	woman ABS	MASC ERG	man ERG	see-PAST
'man saw women'				

The topics of the two clauses 'man' and 'woman' are not identical so they may not be conjoined in this form. Rather the foregrounding function of the antipassive must apply to the second clause, making the actor 'man' the topic:

TOPIC					(131)
bayi	yaṛa	bagun	dyugumbilgu	buṛal-ŋa-ɲu	
MASC ABS	man ABS	FEM DAT	women DAT	see-ANTIPASSIVE-PT	
'man saw women'					

Now *bayi yaṛa* 'men' is topic of both clauses and the two clauses can be conjoined, with omission of the topic in the second clause:

TOPIC			
bayi	yaṛa	bani-ɲu	
MASC ABS	man ABS	came-PAST	
	bagun	dyugumbilgu	buṛal-ŋa-ɲu
	FEM DAT	women DAT	see-ANTIPASSIVE-PAST (132)
'man came and saw women'			

Backgrounding antipassives also occur. These typically result in the omission of the patient of the clause with a number of semantic effects. For example, in Yidiɲ (Dixon 1979b) the backgrounding function can imply a generalized action with no specific affected patient or a reflexive action:

TOPIC			(133)
yinu	bunya	buga·-dyi-ŋ	
this ABS	woman ABS	eat-ANTIPASSIVE-PRES	
'this woman is eating'			

TOPIC		(134)
wagu·dya	bambi·-dyi-ɲu	
man ABS	cover-ANTIPASSIVE-PAST	
'the man has covered himself'		

Bibliography

Bolinger D 1986 *Intonation and Its Parts: Melody in Spoken English*. Arnold, London

Bresnan J, Mchombo S 1987 Topic, pronoun and agreement in Chicheŵa. *Lg* **63**: 741–82

Brown G, Yule G 1983 *Discourse Analysis*. Cambridge University Press, Cambridge

Chafe W 1976 Giveness, contrastiveness, definiteness, subjects, topics, and point of view. In: Li C (ed.) *Subject and Topic*. Academic Press, New York

Comrie B 1979a Russian. In: Shopen T (ed.) *Languages and Their Status*. Winthrop, Cambridge, MA

Comrie B 1979b Definite and animate direct objects: A natural class. *Linguistica Silensiana* **3**: 13–21

Dixon R M W 1979a Ergativity. *Lg* **55**: 59–138

Dixon R M W 1979b *A Grammar of Yidiɲ*. Cambridge University Press, Cambridge

Foley W A, Van Valin R D Jr 1985 Information packaging in the clause. In: Shopen T (ed.) *Language Typology and Syntactic Description. Vol. 1: Clause Structure*. Cambridge University Press, Cambridge

Givón T 1979a *On Understanding Grammar*. Academic Press, New York

Givón T (ed.) 1979b *Syntax and Semantics. Vol. 12: Discourse and Syntax*. Academic Press, New York

Halliday M A K 1967 Notes on transitivity and theme in English. *JL* **3**: 37–81, 199–244

Hawkins J 1979 *Definiteness and Indefiniteness: A Study in Reference and Grammaticality Prediction*. Croom Helm, London

Inoue K 1979 Japanese: A story of language and people. In: Shopen T (ed.) *Languages and their Speakers*. Winthrop, Cambridge, MA

Krisner R 1976 On the subjectless "pseudo-passive" in standard Dutch and the semantics of background agents. In: Li C (ed.) *Subject and Topic*. Academic Press, New York

Kuno S 1973 *The Structure of the Japanese Language*. MIT Press, Cambridge, MA

Lambrecht K 1981 *Topic, Antitopic and Verb Agreement in Non-standard French*. Benjamins, Amsterdam

Li C N (ed.) 1976 *Subject and Topic*. Academic Press, New York

Li C N, Thompson S A 1975 The semantic function of word order: A case study of Mandarin. In: Li C N (ed.) *Word Order and Word Order Change*. University of Texas Press, Austin, TX

Prince E F 1978 A comparison of WH-clefts and *it*-clefts in discourse. *Lg* **54**: 883–906

Prince E F 1981 Topicalization, focus-movement and Yiddish-movement: A pragmatic differentiation. *BLS* **7**: 249–64

Silverstein M 1976 Hierarchy of features and ergativity. In: Dixon R M W (ed.) *Grammatical Categories in Australian Languages*. Australian Institute of Aboriginal Studies, Canberra

Thompson S A 1978 Modern English from a typological point of view: Some implications of the function of word order. *LBer* **54**: 19–35

Thompson S A 1987 The passive in English: A discourse perspective. In: Channon R, Shockey L (eds.) *In Honour of Ilse Lehiste*. Foris, Dordrecht

Weiner E J, Labov W 1983 Constraints on the agentless passive. *JL* **19**: 29–58

Language Acquisition: Formal Models and Learnability Theory
Martin Atkinson

One way to approach an understanding of first language acquisition is to adopt a view on a small set of fundamental questions.

First, it is necessary to characterize the child's initial state, and this amounts to taking a stance on what the child brings to the acquisition task in the form of a priori knowledge (see *Chomsky's Philosophy of Language*). Such knowledge can be seen as delimiting a set of hypotheses which is available to the child regarding the nature of the ambient language.

Second, the nature of the data to which the child is exposed is in need of clarification. The importance of a child's linguistic environment is demonstrated by the fact that children come to speak a language L (and not L′) when they are surrounded by L, but what exactly this environment consists of is not determined—for example, whether it contains only well-formed sentences from L or whether there are also occurrences of ill-formed strings. Is there any explicit or implicit information for the child about what is ill-formed? Is there any information about ambiguity?

Third, it is important to have a view on the interaction between the data and the procedures the child implements in sorting through the options available to him. What determines the rejection of an option and how does the child select an alternative?

Finally, this way of looking at things requires taking a position on just what it means to have acquired a language. Is some absolute notion appropriate, whereby all mature speakers of a language L can be said to have identified exactly the same option, or is some approximate or probabilistic notion of identification to be preferred?

To formulate a reasonably explicit stance on these four issues is to offer a formal model of language acquisition. To pursue the consequences of this stance in precise mathematical terms is the concern of learnability theory. Both of these activities are to be contrasted with traditional approaches to the study of first language acquisition in which the emphasis has been on data collection and the search for inductive generalizations emerging from these data. This article is concerned with what is sometimes termed the logical problem of language acquisition, i.e., how to account for the fact of language acquisition, rather than the real-time, descriptive issues.

1. Learnability Theory

In accordance with the above outline, a theory of first language acquisition which falls within the bounds of learnability theory will have four components. These consist of: (a) a set of hypotheses which is definitive of the learner's initial state; (b) an assumption about the data available to the learner; (c) a proposal for how the learner maintains, selects, and rejects hypotheses in the light of data; and (d) a criterion for acquisition.

Within this framework, a large number of options have been pursued and a number of important formal results obtained. These can be seen as minimally establishing the feasibility of studying learnability within a formally precise framework and, more importantly, as determining certain boundary conditions for acquisition.

1.1 Identification in the Limit

The notion of 'identification in the limit,' introduced by Gold (1967), is a criterion of acquisition and forms the basis of one of the most important learning-theoretic paradigms. Its intuitive content is that acquisition is equated with a situation where a learner selects (identifies) the correct ambient language from a set of possibilities after some finite time (in the limit) and subsequently retains this selection. If a learner can achieve this for a language L on the basis of exposure to any legitimate set of data (see below), L is said to be identifiable in the limit. If L is a class of languages, each of which is identifiable in the limit, then L is itself identifiable in the limit, and it is easy to see the attraction of taking L as the class of possible human languages and manipulating other aspects of the framework to try to ensure that L has this property.

This course has not been pursued for reasons which are easy to comprehend. The formal properties of human languages are not sufficiently well understood to enable them to be studied as mathematical objects. However, there are well-known classes of languages which are appropriately formalized, viz. recursively enumerable languages (L_0), context-sensitive languages (L_1), context-free languages (L_2), and finite state (or regular) languages (L_3), these collectively constituting the Chomsky Hierarchy. Each of these classes properly contains those lower on the Hierarchy (i.e., $L_0 \subset L_1 \subset L_2 \subset L_3$) and, at the time of Gold's work, there was debate as to the position the class of possible human languages might occupy in the Hierarchy. It was therefore significant to consider the problem of identifying (in the limit) these classes of languages.

Regarding data, two obvious assumptions can be investigated. The first (text presentation) has the learner presented with sentences from the target language in no particular order, the only constraint being that for any sentence in the language, there should be some finite time at which it appears. The second (informant presentation) presents the learner with sentences and nonsentences along with information as to which is which; again, the only constraint on a data-sequence is that for any sentence or nonsentence, there should be a finite time at which it has been presented. The notion of a legitimate set of data is thus fixed in two ways.

Finally, it can be assumed that the candidate languages are enumerated for the learner and that the procedure for selecting a new language is based on this enumeration. Thus, the learner adopts the first language in the enumeration as his initial hypothesis. For text presentation, if the first datum is a sentence in this language, the language is maintained as the learner's guess; if not, the learner moves through the enumeration, adopting the first language which does contain this sentence. At any subsequent point, a shift from the current guess is occasioned by error and the learner continues to move through the enumeration until a language is found containing the new sentence and all previously presented sentences. This procedure is generalizable to informant presentation in an obvious way.

It is easy to demonstrate a class of languages which cannot be identified from text on these assumptions.

Consider the class $L = \{L_0, L_1, L_2, \ldots\}$ where $L_0 = \{a, aa, aaa, \ldots\}$ (i.e., the language consisting of all strings on the single 'word' a), $L_1 = \{a\}$, $L_2 = \{a, aa\}$, etc. Assume an enumeration of these languages. L_0 occupies a position in this enumeration and there are two possibilities to consider: (a) there is a finite language L_n after L_0 in the enumeration; (b) there is no finite language which is ordered after L_0. Consider (a) when L_n is the target language. Because L_0 occurs before L_n and is consistent with any legitimate data set from L_n, it will be selected at some point and not subsequently rejected, i.e., L_n will be incorrectly identified as L_0 and L will not be identifiable. So consider (b) when L_0 is the target. Now, the learner will continue to modify his guess as longer strings are presented, but there will be no finite time at which guesses stabilize on L_0, i.e., in this case, no language will be identified and again L will not be identifiable. But (a) and (b) exhaust the possibilities, so L is not identifiable.

This example might be thought of marginal interest, but its significance becomes apparent if one notes that each of the languages in L is a finite state language. Thus, L is properly contained in L_3, the smallest class in the Chomsky Hierarchy. It is provable, but intuitively obvious, that any superset of a set of unidentifiable languages is itself unidentifiable, from which it follows that each of the classes of languages in the Chomsky Hierarchy is unidentifiable on these assumptions.

Responses to the above conclusions can take a number of forms. Most obviously, their significance for natural language acquisition can be denied by not accepting the desirability of locating human languages on the Chomsky Hierarchy. Justification for such a response is provided by the observation that the classes in the hierarchy all contain the class of finite languages, and there is every reason to believe that no possible human language is finite. In short, the class of human languages is delimited by linguistic (ultimately biological) and not mathematical criteria.

Alternatively, it is easy to see that the conclusions do not follow if one moves to informant presentation—L_0 appears first in the enumeration and remains the learner's guess until a nonsentence is presented with the ordering of the finite languages being inconsequential. In fact, Gold proved that with informant presentation, a class properly containing the class of context-sensitive languages is identifiable, but the significance of this within the context of actual language acquisition is dubious, as there is considerable evidence that children do not receive systematic information about nonsentences.

1.2 Modifications to Identifiability in the Limit

Gold's work initiated an abstract, formal approach to the problem of first language acquisition and demonstrated the feasibility of obtaining results. However, it only begins to explore the consequences of modifying assumptions in the four components of a learnability model, and systematic investigation of a wide range of such modifications has been undertaken by Osherson and his colleagues (see, particularly, Osherson et al. 1986).

These enquiries construe a learner as a function, in the mathematical sense, from data sets to hypotheses, and one aspect of the work has been to explore the consequences of constraining this function in certain ways. The crucial question is whether membership of the classes of identifiable languages is affected by such manipulations as other aspects of the learnability model are held constant. Exactly the same question can be raised if the nature of the learner (as a particular type of function) is constant and modifications are introduced into other components of the model. Here attention is restricted to a small sample of the results of this research.

Consider first the function which the learner is assumed to embody. It seems plausible that such a function will be computable, since there is considerable support in cognitive science for the view that human mental operations are simulable by computational devices. The set of computable functions is a subset of the set of all functions, and it can be proved (other aspects of the learnability model being fixed in some way) that there are classes of languages which are identifiable by unrestricted functions but not by any computable function. Thus, restricting the learning function in this way constitutes a genuine constraint on the classes of identifiable languages.

Somewhat more surprising is the fact that computable learning functions which are constrained so as not to include finite languages in their values (equivalent to restricting the learner's set of hypotheses to exclude finite languages) cannot identify certain classes of infinite languages that can be identified by computable functions which lack this constraint. Thus, for a learner to be equipped with the information that no possible language is finite is restrictive in a way which goes beyond the obvious non-identification of finite languages.

Turning to considerations of data, the empirical implausibility of informant presentation was noted above; what seems to be a much more likely situation is one in which the child is confronted by (perhaps small) numbers of ungrammatical intrusions which are not labeled as such. If this is so, one might expect it to make learning more difficult in some sense, so it is noteworthy that it is provable that there are classes of languages which are not identifiable by any computable learning function when data can include such intrusions despite being identifiable in this way when data consist entirely of grammatical sentences.

Perhaps the most surprising conclusion demonstrated within this approach is that a specific set of empirically plausible assumptions requires the class of identifiable languages to be finite. The spirit of these assumptions is: (a) ungrammatical intrusions do characterize the learner's data; (b) the learning function is 'local' in the sense that it does not have access to the full range of previously presented data; and (c) the learning function is 'conservative' in that it is reluctant to produce a new value if new data can be accommodated by the current guess (note that the framework of Sect. 1.1 is strictly conservative in this sense). If these assumptions are realistic in the context of actual first language acquisition, it follows that the class of possible human languages is itself finite, an interesting conclusion in the light of the claims of the Principles and Parameters model discussed in Sect. 2.2.

1.3 The Learnability of Transformational Grammars

The research summarized in Sects. 1.1 and 1.2 has taken place outside the development of mainstream theoretical syntax. Within the Chomskian approach to syntactic theory, a continued focus has been on grammars which have a number of components, and an immediate question to raise is whether such grammars and the languages generated by them are amenable to learnability considerations. In a series of important studies, Wexler and his colleagues have investigated this issue. These studies culminate in Wexler and Culicover (1980), where it is proved that a class of transformational components is learnable on a set of specific assumptions.

Note first that it is easy to establish negative results in this domain. If one considers the class of languages generated by transformational grammars on a context-free base with text presentation, it is immediately apparent that this class is a superset of the class of context-free languages; any context-free language will fall within this class, as it will be generated by a context-free grammar with an empty transformational component or with a transformational component comprised solely of the identity mapping. So the class of transformational languages generated by such grammars will properly contain the class of context-free languages, and the unlearnability of the former follows from the unlearnability of the latter.

Because of this, it is perhaps appropriate to put aside questions concerning the learnability of the base and to concentrate on the transformational component itself. Thus, the learner's hypotheses are to be possible transformational components. Here, if it is assumed that transformational components are functions, it is easy to achieve a positive learnability result on the basis of the notion of function learnability. Assume that the learner is confronted with determining the identity of a function drawn from a given set which can be enumerated and that he has access to the enumeration. Data consist of argument-value pairs for the target function. The learner takes the first function in the enumeration, applies it to the argument in the first datum and checks whether the function yields the presented value. If it does, the function is retained and the learner moves on to the second datum; if it does not, the learner tries the second function in the enumeration and so on. At any point, a function will be rejected if it leads to error and the learner will move through the enumeration until he finds a function which will give the right result for the current datum and for all previous data. On the assumption that the correct function is in the enumeration, the learner will eventually select it and retain it from thereon. Given certain assumptions about the nature of transformations, the class of possible transformational components can be enumerated and the positive result follows.

There are a number of reasons for being cautious about the significance of this result. The requirement that the learner retains information about all previous data is empirically implausible, but is necessary in order for the procedure outlined above to work. A related point is that on this account the learner accepts and rejects whole transformational components as he moves through the enumeration, and this is inconsistent with the intuition that the acquisition of a grammar involves gradual modifications as the child approximates to the target.

In obtaining a more significant result, Wexler and Culicover retain the assumption that the child's data are argument-value pairs; more specifically, a datum is a (b, s) pair, where b is a base structure and s is a surface string, the mapping between b and s being achieved by the target transformational component. But enumeration is rejected as a procedure for selecting hypotheses and is replaced by a gradual, hence empirically more plausible, notion. The essence of this is that if a learner applies his current transformational component to a base structure from the current datum and derives a surface string distinct from that in the datum, this is a detectable error which constitutes a signal that modification of the transformational component is necessary. This modification can take one of two forms: dropping a transformation from the current component or selecting a transformation not currently included in the component. Both of these maneuvers involve selection from finite sets so there is a nonzero probability that the move will be correct from the adult perspective. This introduction of probabilistic considerations necessitates a change in the criterion of learnability away from identification in the limit, and Wexler and Culicover adopt a definition of learnability which identifies it with there being a finite time at which the probability of the learner being correct is arbitrarily close to 1.

There is one further important consideration which underlies the proof. Since learning (hypothesis modification) only takes place in the light of detectable errors, if the child is to converge on the correct hypothesis, it is necessary to ensure that such errors will occur with some appropriate probability. If errors only

become detectable on data which are so complex that they are extremely unlikely to form part of the input, there will be no guarantee that convergence will occur. To this end, it is useful to contemplate some upper bound on the complexity of the data on which an error will be revealed. An important feature of Wexler and Culicover's proof is that this upper bound is set at two degrees of embedding.

It is important to be clear that the strategies outlined above weaken the components of the system in two ways: first, the rejection of enumeration as a learning mechanism requires the adoption of a 'weaker,' if empirically more plausible, method for selecting hypotheses; second, in insisting on an upper bound for the detection of errors, the system must function on only a subset of the possible range of data. As might be anticipated, the positive result obtained for function learnability can no longer be established on these assumptions. What Wexler and Culicover have to do to ensure learnability is restrict the set of possible transformational components. The form of these restrictions enabled their work to make contact with work in theoretical syntax. Thus, they found it necessary to impose what they refer to as the Binary Principle on the functioning of transformations. To all intents and purposes, this is a locality condition restricting the operation of transformations to the current and immediately preceding cycles and, as such, it bears a striking resemblance to Subjacency, a principle formulated independently in theoretical syntax. With this principle and a number of others (these having various degrees of independent linguistic motivation), Wexler and Culicover were able to prove that transformational components were learnable on the basis of data which displayed no more than two degrees of embedding. This is referred to as Degree-2 Learnability.

That the Degree-2 result required the learner to have access to (b, s) pairs is a controversial aspect of the proof, and Wexler and Culicover's justification for the accessibility of base-structures in terms of the child being able to work out the meanings of a significant number of utterances and somehow project these into base-structures is not compeling. On the other hand, the suggestion that the child has access to surface strings may be too weak, and Morgan (1986) documents observations which argue for the availability of unlabeled surface bracketings. According to this view, a datum will consist of a (b, sb) pair, where the sb is the surface bracketing arising from b by application of the target transformational component. Intuitively, this is a strengthening of one component of the framework: there is now more information available to the learner in the data, and one might expect that this will have implications for learnability. Indeed, this is so and Morgan shows that Degree-1 Learnability can be established within this model. Of course, Degree-1 Learnability requires the learner to converge on data involving no more than one degree of embedding, so the richer information in the data via the surface bracketing assumption allows for a corresponding reduction in the recursive complexity of the data required to ensure learnability. Substantial modifications to Wexler and Culicover's set of constraints on transformations are also involved in producing this result.

The general research strategy which emerges from the above considerations is clear. On the one hand, there are purely logical considerations whereby modifications in one of the components of a learnability model are likely to have implications for the other components. On the other hand, the modifications made are subject to empirical considerations if they are to be of more than purely formal interest. The positive result for function learnability is empirically uninteresting, since it is implausible to assume that a child has access to all previous data; the Morgan result is of empirical interest, since it is plausible that children are not exposed to many tokens of sentences involving even two degrees of embedding.

2. Formal Modeling of Language Acquisition

It is possible to pursue theoretical questions in first language acquisition outside the rigorous framework of learnability theory by investigating in a more notional way the consequences of taking a view on the way in which the learner's hypotheses are constrained, the data available to the learner, etc. and such an activity has been a constant backdrop to the development of one variety of generative grammar (see *Generative Grammar: Transformational Grammar*). Certainly since the 1960s Chomsky and his associates have consistently claimed that the fact of language acquisition can only be accounted for by assuming that the child brings to the task a set of constraints on possible grammars, these constraints comprising the contents of Universal Grammar (UG). Typically, such assertions are supported by alluding to the limited nature of the data available to the child, and are often referred to as arguments from the poverty of the stimulus.

2.1 Learning Grammatical Rules

In the 'Standard Theory of Transformational Grammar,' UG is viewed as largely comprising a set of constraints on rules (see *Generative Grammar: Transformational Grammar*). A grammar for a possible human language comprises a number of components, each made up of rules that satisfy certain constraints. For example, such a grammar contains a base comprising a set of context-free phrase structure rules which generate a set of deep structures. Operating on these deep structures is a transformational component, made up of transformational rules, which converts deep structures to surface structures. The notion of what is a legitimate rule of a particular

type is supplied by UG, and the child's task is that of hypothesizing specific tokens of these types which make up the grammar of his language on the basis of exposure to data. While the details of this process were not discussed in detail, it is clear that some version of a hypothesis selection and testing mechanism was centrally involved (see the discussion of Wexler and Culicover's model, Sect. 1.3).

A number of difficulties for this perspective have become apparent. First, from a descriptive viewpoint, the constraints imposed by UG were sufficiently coarse-grained to admit a range of possibilities which were not attested in the world's languages. Furthermore, there was reason to believe that they never would be attested. Second, children acquiring their first language, while making a range of errors, fail to produce many errors which a hypothesis selection and testing procedure operating with relatively unconstrained hypotheses would predict as likely. Finally, those who attempted to chart grammatical development in terms of these assumptions found themselves having to indulge in theoretically ad hoc manipulations to deal with their data; the ensuing descriptive accounts were unattractive and lacking in insight.

Starting in the early 1970s, there was a shift in the linguistic orthodoxy towards the Principles and Parameters account which informs a great deal of current work, both in theoretical syntax and in acquisition.

2.2 Principles and Parameters Theory

The theory of principles and parameters differs from the Standard Theory in a number of ways. Most notably, the emphasis on rule types and instantiations of these disappears, and it is often claimed that this approach to linguistic theory does not recognize rules except derivatively (see *Generative Grammar: Transformational Grammar*; *Generative Grammar: Principles and Parameters*). Instead, the theory recognizes a number of linguistic levels (D-structure, S-structure, Logical Form, and Phonetic Form), each subject to wellformedness constraints. These are stated in terms of principles which belong to modules of grammar. Some modules with their associated principles are specific to particular levels; others operate at all levels. The intention is that the principles should be universal, simple, and relatively small in number. Complexities which were handled by language- and construction-specific rules in the Standard Theory are accounted for by the interactions between principles from different modules.

Consider, for example, the passive in English. In the Standard Theory, a passive transformation had the effect of promoting the direct object to subject position, relegating the subject to object of *by*, introducing an auxiliary and adjusting the verbal morphology. This rule was construction-specific and not generalizable in detail to other languages which have passives similar in certain respects to English. In Principles and Parameters Theory, the idiosyncracies of the English passive are seen as largely following from the θ criterion (operative at all levels), the Extended Projection Principle (again operative at all levels), and the Case Filter (operative at S-structure) (see *Generative Grammar: Principles and Parameters*). Given these principles, the properties of the English passive are not only appropriately described, but become necessary. The passive emerges as the consequence of a set of general, abstract principles, and it is these, playing a part in the understanding of a wide range of different structures in English and other languages, which form the proper subject matter of grammatical investigation rather than the constructions themselves.

This approach accommodates linguistic variation by the recognition of a set of parameters, each with a small number of values. For example, consider the X-bar module which is concerned with the projection of information in lexical entries into syntactic configurations (see *X-bar Syntax*). Like other modules, this contains a set of universal principles, e.g., all phrases are endocentric with NPs being headed by Ns, VPs by Vs, etc. However, the relative order of heads and their complements within a phrase is not universal, so here there is a locus of parameterization. Oversimplifying for purposes of illustration, in a language like English, this parameter will be specified so that heads precede their complements, whereas in Japanese the opposite situation obtains.

During the last decade, a number of parameters in different modules of the theory have been proposed and investigated. These have included direction of θ-role assignment (for the θ-module), direction of Case assignment (for the Case module), the identity of bounding nodes (for the Bounding module), the values for α in the single principle of movement, Move α, the definition of governing category (for the Binding module) and properties of agreement systems (for the distribution of certain phonetically null elements) (see *Generative Grammar: Principles and Parameters*). In general, the postulation of a parameter of this type has been seen as legitimate if it has proved possible to identify a small range of values for the parameter and the consequences of setting the parameter one way or another have been reasonably extensive.

Returning now to first-language acquisition, in the Principles and Parameters account, the learner is assumed to come to the process equipped with the set of universal principles and knowledge of where parametric variation is possible. This a priori knowledge constrains the hypotheses available to the child in the familiar way. Notably, a finite set of principles and a finite set of parameters each with a finite number of possible values allows for only a finite number of possible grammars, and from this perspective, the acquisition of a grammar for L amounts to setting the

parameters appropriately. It is further assumed that the data available in this parameter-setting process are restricted so as to include neither negative instances labeled as such nor complex constructions which are unlikely to be heard and processed by the child.

A large number of questions which are stimulating research arise within this framework. First, the process of parameter setting is often presented as being distinct from hypothesis selection and testing (i.e., learning). Recall that one of the motivations for the move away from the Standard Theory was the non-occurrence of a range of errors in child speech that inductive mechanisms might lead one to expect. Now parameter setting is sometimes likened to the setting of a switch. The idea is that a simple choice at one point in the grammar can have proliferating and deterministic consequences over a wide range of phenomena, these consequences being forced by the complex interactions between the modules sanctioned by UG. Of course, deterministic consequences rule out other possibilities (those which are not so determined), and the result is that the child will never be tempted by these possibilities. However, it does not seem appropriate to rule out an attenuated role for learning in this sort of account, since the notion of parameter re-setting appears to be taken for granted by most authors, i.e., it is generally acknowledged that children may make mistakes in their initial parameter settings. It is difficult to see the setting and subsequent resetting of a parameter as qualitatively distinct from the selection and rejection of hypotheses in the light of available data.

Second, one might wonder whether the situation illustrated by the simple example in Sect. 1.1 arises within this paradigm, i.e., one in which hypothesization of a language (or grammar) which is too general leads to circumstances in which the learner would not receive data enabling him to retreat from this hypothesis. More concretely, are there parameter values which yield set-theoretically nested languages? And if there are, how are they to be handled in this framework?

A positive answer to the first question has been suggested in connection with parametric variation in Binding Theory, that module which deals with the distribution of anaphors (such as *himself* in English), pronouns (such as *him*), and names (such as *John*) (see *Generative Grammar: Principles and Parameters*). Restricting attention to anaphors, they must have their antecedent within some local domain. Thus, in *John believes that Bill hates himself*, *himself* cannot have *John* as antecedent because it is 'too far away.' This local domain is referred to as the Governing Category of the anaphor, and one principle of the Binding Theory states that an anaphor must be bound within its governing category.

Consideration of other languages shows that while anaphors universally have to be bound in some domain or other, the identity of this domain can vary; there are languages in which the equivalent of *himself* in the above example could be coreferential with the equivalent of *John* (or, of course, *Bill*). This sort of observation leads to the conclusion that the notion of Governing Category is parameterized, and it is easy to see that a language with a 'liberal' setting of this parameter will be a superset (for the relevant structures) of a language with a more restricted setting. Now, assume that a learner is in fact confronted with a language for which the restricted setting is correct, but chooses the liberal one. For such a learner, in the absence of negative information, no subsequent data will disconfirm this guess, and he will be stuck with the wrong hypothesis.

How can this predicament be avoided? If the learner's hypothesis selection mechanism is constrained to choose the most restrictive value for a parameter consistent with presented data, the liberal setting will only be adopted when positive data justify it. This constraint on the operation of the learning mechanism is an informal statement of the Subset Principle of Manzini and Wexler (1987), and an interesting question concerns the extent of parametric variation which necessitates a mechanism of this kind.

A third question of interest is whether it is appropriate to assume that all principles and parameters of UG are available at the onset of acquisition or that some of them only enter the system at some later stage. To adopt the former position is to subscribe to the Continuity Hypothesis and leads to a dilemma. This is that language acquisition is not instantaneous and appears to follow a fixed course. If all principles and parameters are available at the onset and furthermore the child's linguistic environment contains the information necessary to set parameters, why is acquisition not instantaneous or at any rate compressed into a very short time span with individual differences in development being referred directly to chance encounters with linguistic stimuli?

Attempts to answer this question take a number of forms. For example, it might be maintained that the child's representation of his linguistic environment changes significantly due to general cognitive factors such as increased memory span. Thus, while principles and parameters are all available immediately, they are not immediately effective because the data to engage them, while present in the distal environment, are not available as proximal stimuli for the child.

Alternatively, if the Continuity Hypothesis is abandoned one is faced with giving an account of the mechanism whereby the newly available principles emerge at some stage in development. It is fashionable in the 1990s to speculate that maturation may have a role to play here. After all, once a subscription is taken out on extensive genetic endowment, and all contemporary approaches concede that this much is necessary, it becomes plausible to suggest that aspects of this become available according to a maturational schedule. This perspective, which is adopted by Borer and Wexler (1987) in connection with the development of passives and causatives and by Radford (1990) for inflexional elements, complementizers, and determiners, also provides a genuine alternative to learning as a developmental mechanism.

Finally, it is increasingly recognized that it is important to constrain the locus of parametric variation if descriptive profligacy is to be avoided. A provocative idea which is being investigated in some detail is that parametric variation may be restricted to the properties of functional categories. Functional categories bear some resemblance to the closed classes of traditional grammar and include various inflexional classes, complementizers, determiners, and some prepositions.

As an example, the *pro*-drop parameter (see Hyams 1986, for an influential discussion in the context of language acquisition) was investigated in some detail during the 1980s. Roughly, languages can be partitioned into those that do or do not allow phonetically empty subjects in tensed clauses. English does not (**saw that film*), but Spanish does (*vio ese film*). The standard view on this variation has been that its source can be located in the properties of agreement inflexions in languages, with English having relatively impoverished subject–verb agreement and the Spanish system being much richer. This difference allows the identification of an empty subject in Spanish where this is not possible in English, and a number of other grammatical phenomena follow from the same difference.

Naturally, such an example does not establish the general proposition and there remain formidable obstacles to overcome in this enterprise, but there are several other examples that could be cited, and collectively these do lend an element of plausibility to the claim that linguistic variation is restricted to properties of functional categories. This claim takes on additional perspectives when account is taken of two further contexts. First, congenitally deaf children creating their own signing systems appear not to create the equivalent of functional categories. Second, there is some evidence to suggest that it is the development of functional category systems and not what might be referred to as 'basic predicate-argument structure' which is sensitive to variations in maternal speech style. If linguistic variation is restricted to the properties of functional categories, it follows that these properties must be fixed by a linguistic environment. In the absence of such an environment (the deaf children) no such categories will appear; variations in linguistic environments in the relevant respects will lead to variations in developmental rate.

Bibliography

Atkinson M 1992 *Children's Syntax: An Introduction to Principles and Parameters Theory*. Blackwell, Oxford

Borer H, Wexler K 1987 The maturation of syntax. In: Roeper T, Williams E (eds.) *Parameter Setting*. Reidel, Dordrecht

Clark R 1992 The selection of syntactic knowledge. *LAcq* **2**: 93–149

Gibson E, Wexler K 1994 Triggers. *LIn* **25**: 407–54

Gold E M 1967 Language identification in the limit. *Information and Control* **10**: 447–74

Hyams N M 1986 *Language Acquisition and the Theory of Parameters*. Reidel, Dordrecht

Lightfoot D 1989 The child's trigger experience: Degree-0 learnability. *Behavioral and Brain Sciences* **12**: 321–75

Manzini M R, Wexler K 1987 Parameters, binding theory, and learnability. *LIn* **18**: 413–44

Morgan J L 1986 *From Simple Input to Complex Grammar*. MIT Press, Cambridge, MA

Osherson D N, Stob M, Weinstein S 1984 Learning theory and natural language. *Cognition* **17**: 1–28

Osherson D N, Stob M, Weinstein S 1986 *Systems that Learn*. MIT Press, Cambridge, MA

Radford A 1990 *Syntactic Theory and the Acquisition of English Syntax: The Nature of Early Child Grammars of English*. Blackwell, Oxford

Roca I M (ed.) 1991 *Logical Issues in Language Acquisition*. Foris, Dordrecht

Wexler K, Culicover P W 1980 *Formal Principles of Language Acquisition*. MIT Press, Cambridge, MA

Language Acquisition: Grammar

H. Tager-Flusberg

Within a few months of acquiring an initial vocabulary of about 50–100 words, young children, usually in the latter half of the second year, begin combining words together to form their first sentences. This new stage in language acquisition marks an important milestone because even the simplest two-word utterances show evidence of early grammatical development. Research on children's grammatical development began with descriptive studies in the 1930s; however, it was not until the publication of Chomsky's seminal work that theoretically focused research began in earnest, with an emphasis on studies of the acquisition of English, but also including since the 1980s some important cross-linguistic studies.

The child's task in acquiring the grammar of her native language is complex: she must be able to segment the stream of language she hears into basic units such as words, morphemes, and phrases; she must discover the major parts of speech of noun, verb, article, etc. and map the appropriate lexical items into them; she must acquire the major phrase structure rules for organizing basic phrasal units like noun phrase and verb phrase, as well as for organizing basic sentence structures for declaratives, questions, and negation; and finally she must figure out the syntactic rules for complex sentences involving the coordination and imbedding of multiple clauses. Research has indicated that children use a variety of clues to facilitate the process of grammatical development. Prosodic cues may help the child break into the linguistic stream to help identify word and phrase boundaries, and later on children make use of semantic and pragmatic as well as syntactic and morphological information in developing the underlying grammatical knowledge that allows them to produce and understand the full range of unlimited and novel sentences in their native language.

1. Measuring Grammatical Development

1.1 Mean Length of Utterance (MLU)

The most significant transition children make in acquiring grammar is the move from single words to the use of word combinations and simple sentences. Data from a recent large-scale normative study using a parent report measure called the Communicative Development Inventories suggest that there is a wide variability in the age at which children make this transition, with the average age at about eighteen months.

One of the most obvious ways in which children's sentences subsequently change over time is that they gradually grow longer. This fact is the basis of one of the most widely used measures of grammatical development: the MLU or mean length of utterance, which is the average length of a child's utterances as measured in morphemes, based on a sample of 100 utterances (Brown 1973). Thus it is a measure of production rather than comprehension. The basic assumption of this measure is that each newly acquired element of grammatical knowledge adds length to the child's utterances. Longitudinal studies of language acquisition have confirmed that children's MLU increases gradually over time, though at different rates for different children, and norms for MLU between the ages of 2 and 5 have been developed. Despite its widespread use in research and clinical studies, MLU has received some criticism; it is quite limited in use and only valid up to an average sentence length of 4.0 morphemes.

To overcome some of these problems, other measures of grammatical development have been introduced which analyze more directly the grammatical content of a child's productive language.

1.2 Language Assessment, Remediation, and Screening Procedure (LARSP)

The LARSP profile analysis, introduced by David Crystal and his colleagues, provides a comprehensive measure of a child's phrases and clauses (Crystal et al. 1976). On the basis of this analysis, the child is assigned to one of seven developmental stages: (a) one-word utterances; (b) two-word utterances; (c) three-word utterances; (d) four-word utterances; (e) complex sentence formation defined in terms of coordination or subordination; (f) consolidation of grammatical systems, including complex complementation and fewer error patterns; and (g) remaining structures such as connectivity between sentences, emphatic expression, etc. This sequence of stages reflects the order of emergence of these structural patterns identified in the general literature on language acquisition. This measure is widely used in clinical settings with diverse populations of children; it is useful both because of its hierarchical organization and because it allows one to identify specific problems at either the phrasal or clausal level.

1.3 Assigning Structural Stage (ASS)

Another measure that assigns a child's productive language to a structural stage is the ASS (Miller 1981). The child's utterances are analyzed in five main categories: (a) noun phrase elaboration; (b) verb phrase elaboration; (c) negatives; (d) questions; and (e) complex sentences. On the basis of this categorization a child's language is assigned to a stage that is parallel to MLU ranges. The limitation of this approach is that the product of this measure is simply a stage assignment, and details about the structures used or those that are omitted are not taken into consideration.

1.4 Index of Productive Syntax (IPSyn)

More recently, the ASS has been modified and adapted into a new measure, the IPSyn, which consists of 56 items divided into four subscales: (a) noun phrase; (b) verb phrase; (c) question/negation; and (d) sentence structure (Scarborough 1990). Within each subscale the items are sequenced developmentally based on current knowledge about patterns of language acquisition. A child is credited with a point system for the use of one or two different examples of each item; scores are summed within and across the subscales to yield a total IPSyn score (maximum 120), but there is no stage assignment. This is a reliable measure that correlates with MLU but is useful

beyond an MLU of 4.0. Thus far, it has been used mainly in research studies with a variety of populations.

1.5 Tests of Comprehension

Comprehension of grammatical structures is much more difficult to measure than production. Although in naturalistic contexts young children give the impression they understand more than they produce, this may reflect the child's use of nonlinguistic context rather than grammatical structure to figure out the underlying meaning relations of sentences. Methods to assess comprehension typically include: (a) the use of diary studies, which document the conditions and contexts in which a child does or does not understand a particular structure; (b) act-out procedures, in which the experimenter asks the child to act out a sentence or phrase using toys; (c) direction tasks, in which the child is asked to carry out a direction; (d) picture-choice tasks, in which the child is asked to select from a set, the picture that best represents the linguistic form presented; and (e) preferential-looking paradigm, in which the child is placed equidistant between two video-monitors on which different scenes are simultaneously presented. A linguistic message, which corresponds to one of the scenes, is played in synchrony with them and the amount of time the child spends watching each scene is recorded. If the child spends significantly longer watching the correct scene, then she is credited with understanding the linguistic form of the message. This paradigm is complex and lengthy but it avoids some of the limitations of other methods and can be used with infants as young as 9 months old (Golinkoff et al. 1987).

2. Two-word Utterance Stage

2.1 Semantic Relations

When children begin to combine words to form the simplest sentences most are limited in length to two words, although a few may be as long as three or four words. These early sentences are often unique and creative composed primarily of nouns, verbs, and adjectives. In English, function words and grammatical morphemes are usually omitted, making the child's productive speech sound 'telegraphic'; however, this is less true for children learning other languages that are rich in inflexional morphology.

Crosslinguistic studies of children at this stage have shown that there is a universal small set of meanings or semantic relations that are expressed (Brown 1973). Table 1 lists the eight most prevalent semantic relations together with examples of each. These examples illustrate that children talk a lot about objects by naming them, and by discussing their locations or attributes, who owns them, and who is doing things to them. They also talk about people, their actions, their locations, their actions on objects, and so forth. Objects, people, actions, and their interrelationships

Table 1. Set of prevalent semantic relations expressed in two-word stage.

Semantic relation	Examples
Agent + Action	*Mommy come. Daddy sit.*
Action + Object	*Push car. Eat cookie.*
Agent + Object	*Mommy sock. Dog book.*
Action + Location	*Go out. Sit floor.*
Entity + Location	*Cup table. Truck box.*
Possessor + Possession	*My bottle. Mommy shirt.*
Entity + Attribute	*Big book. Box shiny.*
Demonstrative + Entity	*Dat milk. Dis paper.*

preoccupy the young child universally. These are precisely the concepts that the child has differentiated during the infancy period according to the developmental psychologist, Jean Piaget.

2.2 Limited Scope Formulae

Initial studies of utterances produced in the two-word stage found that children used highly consistent word order. Indeed, the semantic relations approach assumed that the child uses a productive word order rule which operates on broad semantic rather than syntactic categories. This research was limited by focusing primarily on languages that make extensive use of order to mark basic relations in sentences, and on a small number of subjects. It is now acknowledged that there is considerable individual variation among children learning different languages, and even for children learning English. Nevertheless, word order rules are used at this early stage of grammatical development, but they are more limited and more narrowly defined in semantic scope than is suggested by the semantic relations approach and therefore have been called 'limited scope formulae' (Braine 1976). For some children ordered combinations of words may even be based on specific lexical items rather than on semantic categories. Over time, these more limited rules expand to encompass broader semantic and later syntactic categories, and begin to resemble the adult grammar.

2.3 Null Subjects

One characteristic of children's two-word sentences is that they often omit the subject. Recently this has been interpreted from the perspective of current linguistic theory, which proposes a parameter-setting approach. Hyams (1986) argues that all children begin with the subject parameter set in the null position (which holds for languages like Italian or Spanish) so that children learning English must eventually switch the parameter setting to the position marked for required subjects.

Although this proposal is attractive because it connects early grammar to linguistic theory, there are several criticisms of this approach. While English-speaking children do omit subjects, in fact they include them significantly more often than Italian-speaking

children, which suggests that they know that subjects need to be expressed. Subjects are probably omitted because young children have limited processing capacity, and for pragmatic reasons, subjects are more readily omitted than objects as they are often provided by the context.

2.4 Lexical Categories

The most detailed view of this early stage of grammatical development that is based on Chomsky's Government Binding Theory has been proposed by Radford (1994). Radford argues that during the early stages of word combinations much of the linguistic system is absent, but the child does have a lexicon and limited set of phrase structure rules in d-structure. Specifically, Radford claims that English-speaking children at this stage only have lexical categories; what is missing from their grammars are the functional categories such as INFL and COMP. There is also no transformation rule and the d-structure is assigned thematic roles to yield the s-structure. Broadly, this hypothesis does fit with the general descriptions of English-speaking children's very early two-word utterances.

2.5 Comprehension of Word Order

Studies of children's comprehension of grammar at this stage of development has focused on their ability to use word order to interpret the basic relations in a simple sentence. Studies using a variety of methods, including act-out and picture-choice tasks, have led to conflicting findings: some suggest that children can use word order in their productive speech before they can in comprehension, while others suggest the opposite. In a study using the preferential-looking paradigm, which makes less extraneous processing demands on the child, it was found that children aged 18 months, who were not yet producing two-word utterances, looked reliably longer at the correct scene corresponding to sentences like *Cookie Monster is tickling Big Bird*. Thus it appears that comprehension of word order does precede its production.

3. Development of Grammatical Morphology

3.1 Brown's 14-morpheme Study

As children progress beyond the two-word stage, they gradually begin to fill in the inflexional morphology and function words that are omitted in their early language. The process of acquiring the major grammatical morphemes in English is gradual and lengthy and some are still not fully controlled until the child enters school, i.e., at around 5 years. The most comprehensive study of morphological development was conducted by Roger Brown (1973), using the longitudinal data collected from three children.

Brown selected for his study a set of 14 English morphemes that are among the most frequently used. These included two prepositions (*in, on*), articles (*a, the*), noun inflexions marking possessive (*'s*), and plural (*-s*), verb inflexion marking third person singular present tense for regular (*-s*), and irregular verbs (e.g., *does*), past tense for regular (*-ed*) and irregular verbs (e.g., *went*), and the verb *to be* used as auxiliary and main verb (copula) in both contractible and uncontractible forms. Brown coded for each transcript the percentage of each morpheme supplied in its obligatory contexts, counting 90 percent as the point marking full acquisition. The most significant finding was that the order in which these morphemes was acquired was strikingly similar across the three children, and this has been confirmed in later studies including larger samples of children. The order of acquisition is not accounted for by frequency of use by the child or mother; instead it is related to measures of linguistic complexity—both semantic and syntactic. From a syntactic point of view it is interesting to note that the morphemes that are acquired early involve only lexical categories, whereas the later acquired morphemes all involve functional categories, particularly INFL (present and past tense; auxiliary verbs).

3.2 Overgeneralization and Rule Productivity

One striking error that children make in the process of acquiring grammatical morphemes is the overgeneralization of regular forms to irregular examples. For example, the plural *-s* is frequently added to nouns that take an irregular plural, such as *mans* instead of *men*, or *mouses* instead of *mice*; and the regular past tense ending *-ed* is sometimes used on verbs that are marked with an irregular form, such as *falled*, *goed*, or *teached*. These errors may not be frequent, but they can persist well into the school years and are quite resistant to feedback or correction. They are taken as evidence that the child is indeed acquiring a rule-governed system, rather than learning these inflexions on a word-by-word basis.

Steven Pinker (1991) argues that two different mechanisms are involved in acquiring regular and irregular forms. Regular forms involve a rule-governed mechanism that applies the *-ed* ending in contexts requiring the expression of a past tense, while irregular forms are retrieved directly from the lexicon, and thus involve a memory storage system. This dual-mechanism hypothesis has come under attack from models developed within a *connectionist* framework, in which only a single mechanism is needed to compute the correct past tense ending for both regular and irregular forms.

Other evidence for the productive use of morphological rules comes from an elicited production task introduced by Jean Berko (1958), called the 'Wug test.' The child is shown drawings depicting novel creatures, objects, and actions and asked to supply the appropriate description which would require the inclusion of noun or verb inflexions. For example, a creature was labeled a wug, and then the child had to

fill in the blank for *there are two* ____. Preschoolaged children performed well on this task demonstrating their internalized knowledge of English morphological rules that can be applied productively.

3.3 Crosslinguistic Data

There is a growing literature on the acquisition of morphology in other languages. Overgeneralization errors have been recorded in children learning many different languages suggesting this is a universal pattern for this aspect of grammatical development. However, the slow and gradual development of English morphology does not hold for languages that have richer morphological systems. For example, children acquiring Turkish include case-marking suffixes on nouns at even the earliest stages of language development, and children learning Italian acquire verb inflexions marking person, tense, and number very rapidly and in a less piecemeal fashion than has been found for English morphology. These crosslinguistic variations seem to reflect differences among languages in the amount of inflexional morphology within a language and the degree to which inflexions are optional. For example, English marks verbs only for the past tense or third person singular present tense or progressive aspect, while Italian verbs are always marked in various ways. Children appear to be highly sensitive to these differences from the beginning stages of acquiring grammar (Slobin 1985).

4. Sentence Modalities

4.1 Simple Declaratives

As children progress beyond the two-word stage, they begin combining words into three-, and then four-word sentences. In doing so, they link together two or more basic semantic relations that were prevalent early on. For example, *agent + action* and *action + object* may be linked to form *agent + action + object*. These simple declarative sentences include all the basic elements of adult sentences. Gradually these may get enriched with the addition of prepositional phrases, more complex noun phrases that include a variety of modifiers, and more complex verb phrases including auxiliary and modal verbs. All these additions add length to the declarative sentences of young children.

4.2 Negation

Although children do express negation even at the one-word stage, e.g., using the word *no!*, the acquisition of sentential negation is not fully acquired until much later. Ursula Bellugi (Klima and Bellugi 1966) identified three stages in the acquisition of negation in English:

- (a) the negative marker is placed outside the sentence, usually preceding it (e.g., *not go movies*; *no Mommy do it*);
- (b) the negative marker is sentence internal, placed adjacent to the main verb but without pro-

ductive use of the auxiliary system (e.g., *I no like it*; *don't go*);

(c) different auxiliaries are used productively and the child's negations approximate the adult forms, (e.g., *you can't have it*; *I'm not happy*).

Although the existence of the first stage has been questioned by some researchers, there does appear to be crosslinguistic support for an initial period when negative markers are placed outside the main sentence.

Negation is used by children to express a variety of meanings. These emerge in the following order, according to studies of children learning a wide range of languages: 'nonexistence'—to note the absence of something or someone (e.g., *no cookie*); 'rejection'— used to oppose something (e.g., *no bath*); and finally, 'denial'—to refute the truth of a statement (e.g., *that not mine*). Some children show consistent patterns of form–meaning relations in their negative sentences. For example, one child used external negation to express rejection, while at the same stage reserved sentence internal negation forms to express denial. These patterns may have had their source in the adult input.

Studies of children's comprehension of negative sentences find that they are influenced by the pragmatic context in which the sentence is presented. Thus sentences expressing denial are more easily understood in plausible rather than implausible nonlinguistic contexts. Together, these studies suggest that the development of negation is influenced by grammatical and semantic, as well as pragmatic factors.

4.3 Questions

There are several different forms used to ask questions. These include rising intonation on a declarative sentence; *yes–no* questions, which involve subject–auxiliary verb inversion; *wh*-questions, which involve *wh*-movement and inversion; and tags, which are appended to declaratives and may be marked lexically (e.g., *we'll go shopping, okay?*) or syntactically (*we'll go shopping, won't we?*). Children begin at the one- or two-word stage by using rising intonation and one or two fixed *wh*-forms, such as *what that?* Gradually, over the next couple of years syntactic forms of questions develop with inversion rules acquired simultaneously for both *yes–no* and *wh*-questions. Some data suggested that for *wh*-questions, inversion rules are learned sequentially for individual *wh*-words such as *what*, *where*, *who*, *why*, and may be closely linked in time to the appearance of those words used as *wh*-complements. Thus syntactic rules for question formation may be *wh*-word specific in early child language.

Several studies of English and other languages have investigated the order in which children acquire various *wh*-questions and the findings have been consistent. Children generally begin asking and understanding *what* and *where* questions, followed by *who*, then *how*, and finally *when* and *why*. One expla-

nation for this developmental sequence is that it reflects the semantic and cognitive complexity of the concepts encoded in these different types of questions. Thus, questions about objects, locations, and people (i.e., *what*, *where*, *who*) involve less abstract concepts than those of manner, time, and causality (i.e., *how*, *when*, *why*). The early emerging *wh*- questions are also syntactically less complex in that they involve simple noun phrase replacement, whereas the later developing questions involve prepositional phrases or full sentence complements.

Children use questions to express a range of functions. Most questions asked by 2- and 3-year-olds seek information or facilitate the conversation by asking for clarification or expressing agreement. Older children begin asking questions more to direct the behavior of others, especially to gain attention. Typically there are strong form-function relationships, that may reflect the input directed to children: *wh*-questions are used to seek information, while yes–no forms are used for conversational and directive functions. Thus, as for negation, the development of questions is determined not only by linguistic complexity, but also by semantic and pragmatic factors that interact with the acquisition of the requisite syntactic rules.

4.4 Passives

Despite the rarity of the passive construction in everyday conversations in English, a good deal of attention has been paid to how children use and understand passive sentences. Because the order of the agent and patient is reversed, this particular construction can reveal a great deal about how children acquire word order rules that play a major role in English syntax.

Elicited production tasks have been used to study how children construct passive sentences, typically using sets of pictures that shift the focus to the patient. Younger children tend to produce primarily truncated passives (e.g., *the window was broken*) in which no agent is specified. These truncated passives generally have inanimate subjects, while full passives are produced by children when animate subjects are involved, suggesting that full and truncated passives may develop separately and be unrelated for the younger child. It has been suggested that truncated passives are really adjectival whereas the later appearing full forms are complete verbal passives.

Numerous studies have used an act-out procedure to investigate children's comprehension of passive voice sentences. Typically these studies compare children's comprehension of passive sentences to active sentences that are either reversible—in which either noun could plausibly be the agent (e.g., *the boy kisses the girl*; *the boy is kissed by the girl*), or semantically biased—in which one noun is more plausibly the agent than the other (e.g., *the girl feeds the baby*; *the girl is fed by the baby*). Studies find that children correctly interpret the plausible passive sentences before they do the reversible sentences. Preschoolers acquiring English tend to make errors systematically on the reversible passive sentences, suggesting the use of a processing strategy, called the word-order strategy, whereby noun–verb–noun sequences are interpreted as agent–action–object. Children learning languages other than English may develop different processing strategies that closely reflect the canonical ways of organizing the basic relations in a sentence in their native language. For example, Japanese is a verb-final language that marks the agent with a suffix -*ga*, rather than with a fixed word order, although there is a preference for an agent–object–verb order. Preschool-aged Japanese children tend to use a strategy that takes the first noun marked with -*ga* as the agent of the sentence. Thus children's processing strategies are tailored to the kind of language they are acquiring and show that preschoolers have already worked out the primary ways their language marks the basic grammatical relations.

Studies of the acquisition of other languages such as Sesotho, in which the passive construction is very frequent because subjects always mark sentence topic, find that children acquire the passive much earlier and use it much more productively than do English-speaking children. Again, this suggests that children are sensitive to the typology of their language and that these factors influence the timing of development for the passive.

The semantic characteristics of the verb also influence the child's comprehension of passive sentences. While 5-year olds do correctly understand passive sentences which have action verbs, they find it more difficult to interpret passive sentences with nonaction verbs (e.g., *Donald was liked by Goofy*) are difficult to interpret. Thus the acquisition of passive voice continues into the school years as the child's knowledge becomes less constrained by semantic aspects of the verb.

5. Complex Sentence Structures

5.1 Coordinations

As early as 30 months of age, children begin combining sentences to express compound propositions. The simplest and most frequent method children use to combine sentences is to conjoin two propositions with *and*. One question that has been investigated in numerous studies is the order in which different forms of coordination develop. Both sentential (e.g., *Mary went to school and Peter went to school*) and phrasal coordinations (e.g., *Mary and Peter went to school*) tend to emerge at the same time in development suggesting that these forms develop independently and are not, for young children, derived from one another. Children form phrasal coordinations by directly conjoining phrases, not via deletion rules.

From the beginning children are sensitive to the different contexts in which phrasal and sentential forms of coordination are used appropriately in both production and comprehension. Children use sentential forms to describe events that are separated in time or space or involve different referents, while phrasal forms are used when events occur at the same time, in the same place, or involve the same referents. Semantic factors also influence the course of development of coordination. Children use coordinations first to express additive meaning, where there is no dependency relation between conjoined clauses (e.g., *maybe you can carry this and I can carry that*). Later temporal relations (e.g., *Joey is going home and take her sweater off*) and then causal relations (e.g., *she put a bandaid on her shoe and it maked it feel better*) are expressed, suggesting that children begin demonstrating greater semantic flexibility even while limiting themselves to the use of a single connective *and*.

5.2 Relative Clauses

Sometime after children begin using coordination, relative clauses emerge in their spontaneous speech. Initially they are used to specify information exclusively about the object of a sentence (e.g., *let's eat the cake what I baked*), and often the relative pronoun is omitted or incorrect. The use of relative clauses in the spontaneous speech of young children is quite rare, perhaps because children avoid these syntactically complex constructions, or because they lack the occasion to use them when the context is shared by the speaker and listener.

Elicited production techniques have been used successfully with preschoolers. These studies have also found that children find it easiest to add relative clauses to the ends of sentences rather than to embed them within the matrix clause. This suggests that some processing constraints operate on young children's productive capacities. Studies of children's comprehension of relative clause constructions, which typically involve act out procedures, confirm that object relatives are easier to process than subject relatives (which are usually embedded), though different theoretical interpretations have been offered for these findings. Some suggest this is related to processing limitations and the use of comprehension strategies, while others offer interpretations from linguistic theory. There is also evidence to suggest that children are sensitive to semantic and prosodic factors in tasks that require children to interpret sentences with various types of relative clauses.

5.3 Anaphoric Reference

Children's knowledge of grammar continues to develop beyond the preschool years. One area that has received a good deal of attention from researchers is their knowledge of coreference relations within sentences; especially how anaphoric pronouns and reflexives link up with referents. This research has been conducted primarily within a Government-Binding theoretical framework, investigating children's knowledge of the main binding principles. Spontaneous productions of pronominal forms suggest that quite young children use them correctly in their productive speech; however, the limits of their knowledge cannot be accurately assessed in naturalistic contexts.

More controlled studies have utilized a variety of methods including comprehension, picture-matching, and judgment tasks. Generally, children appear to develop knowledge of the main principles in the following order. By the age of 6 children know 'principle A,' which states that reflexives are bound to referents within the same clause (e.g., *John watched Bill wash himself; himself* must refer to Bill, not John). Sometime later, knowledge of 'principle B' emerges, which states that anaphoric pronouns cannot be bound to referents within the same clause (e.g., *John asked Bill to hit him; him* must refer to John in the *ask*-clause, not Bill in the *hit*-clause). The last principle to emerge sometime during middle childhood, is 'principle C,' which states that backward coreference is only allowed if the pronoun is in a subordinate clause to the main referent (e.g., *when he came home, John made dinner*). Some researchers have argued that the grammatical knowledge of these principles is acquired much earlier that the research would suggest but that children's performance on tasks that tap this knowledge is limited by processing factors, pragmatic knowledge, or lexical knowledge. This debate continues in the developmental psycholinguistic literature.

6. Basic Theoretical Approaches

6.1 Semantic Bootstrapping

Current theories in language acquisition attempt to address the central question of how the young child achieves the learnability task in acquiring the abstract and formal syntactic system of their language. In the 1970s and 1980s one idea that gained prominence in the literature was that children may use semantics or meaning to help them break into the grammar of their language. This approach was taken up by analyses of two-word utterances in the semantic relations approach, outlined in Sect. 2.1. Pinker (1984) has been the main proponent to argue that children may use semantics as a bootstrap into syntax, particularly to acquire the major syntactic categories on which grammatical rules operate. Thus children can use the correspondence that exists between names and things to map on to the syntactic category of noun, and physical attributes or changes of state to map on to the category of verb. At the initial stages of development all sentence subjects tend to be semantic agents, and so children use this syntactic-semantic correspondence to begin figuring out the abstract relations for more complex sentences that require the category of subject.

6.2 Functionalism

A very different theoretical approach has been taken up by those who view the central task of the child

as gaining communicative competence. Much of the research conducted within this framework has focused on the acquisition of pragmatic aspects of language, including the functions of utterances and their use in discourse and other communicative contexts. Within research on grammatical development the functional approach does not take formal syntactic theory as its primary model. Instead the structure of language is viewed from a functional, or processing perspective. One example is the competition model of language acquisition proposed by Elizabeth Bates and Brian MacWhinney (MacWhinney 1987). On this model, the child begins by establishing the basic functional categories: topic-comment and agent. Different surface representations of these functional categories then compete for expression and initially the child may use a simple one form–one function mapping. Eventually children move toward the adult system of form-function mappings (see *Functional Grammar*).

6.3 Distributional Learning

At some point all theories of acquisition need to consider how the child learns the major syntactic categories, even if they begin with a simple lexically specific, functional, or semantic approach. One important approach to this learning problem is the distributional learning view, proposed by Maratsos and Chalkley (1980). According to this view children not only use semantic mappings to acquire a category like verb, they also use distributional factors, such as it takes an *-ed* ending to express pastness, or an *-ing* or *-s* in present tense contexts, it occurs with auxiliary verbs and so forth. Gleitman (1990) has also suggested that children must use syntactic information to learn something about the meanings of terms, such as using the argument structure of a verb to learn something about its meaning. Other kinds of distributional learning, using morpho-phonological patterns may be central in acquiring aspects of morphology such as noun gender in languages other than English. This kind of approach argues that children are sensitive to all kinds of distributional patterns in the linguistic input to which they are exposed and some of the research summarized in previous sections supports this view (see also *Cognitive Grammar*; *Syntax and Semantics*).

6.4 Parameter-setting Models

Linguists working within a Government-Binding framework who have taken an interest in the question of how children acquire the grammar of their language claim that the central task of acquisition is to set the parameters of universal grammar in the direction appropriate for the language that is being acquired. Some argue that the parameters start off set in one position, which may then have to be switched. One example of this is Hyams's proposal about the null subject parameter, presented in Sect. 2.3. An alternative view would hold that parameters start off neutrally, that is they are not set in any position. As the child is exposed to her native language she uses linguistic evidence present in the environment to set the parameters accordingly. This kind of approach to child language is still relatively new and awaits further refinements from linguistic theory (see *Generative Grammar: Principles and Parameters*).

6.5 Reorganizational Processes

Numerous approaches have been proposed to explain how the child acquires the complex and abstract grammatical system of language. Children may indeed begin with functional or semantic categories, which may serve their needs during the early stages of acquisition, but these approaches are limited for the child. Eventually the child must come to employ abstract syntactic categories though these may still have correlates in meaning and function. Some theorists, taking a developmental approach, argue that the child must undergo some radical reorganization of their grammar at certain stages in development, rather than simply generalizing the categories they start off with. For example, the child may begin with categories that are defined semantically (e.g., agent, experiencer) that later become reorganized and restructured into syntactic categories (e.g., subject).

These kinds of reorganizational processes are seen as central not only to grammatical development but also to the acquisition of lexical and phonological knowledge. In this way children piece together and reformulate through a series of stages using the same fundamental developmental processes and integrated foundation of knowledge of the language they are acquiring (see *Cognitive Grammar*; *Syntax and Semantics*).

Bibliography

Berko J 1958 The child's learning of English morphology. *Word* **14**: 150–177

Braine M D S 1976 Children's first word combinations. University of Chicago Press, Chicago, IL (*Monographs of the Society for Research in Child Development*, 41)

Brown R 1973 *A First Language*. Allen and Unwin, London

Crystal D, Fletcher P, Garman M 1976 *The Grammatical Analysis of Language Disability: A Procedure for Assessment and Remediation*. Elsevier-North Holland, New York

Fenson L, Dale P, Reznick S, Thal D, Bates E, Hartung J P, Pethick S, Reilly J S 1993 *The MacArthur Communicative Development Inventories: User's Guide and Technical Manual*. Singular Publishing, San Diego

Fenson L, Dale P, Reznick S, Bates E, Thal D, Pethick S 1994 Variability in early communicative development. University of Chicago Press, Chicago, IL (*Monographs of the Society for Research in Child Development*, 59)

Fletcher P, MacWhinney B (eds.) 1995 *The Handbook of Child Language*. Blackwell, Oxford

Gleitman L 1990 The structural sources of verb meanings. *LAcq* **1**: 3–56

Golinkoff R, Hirsh-Pasek K, Cauley K M, Gordon L 1987 The eyes have it: Lexical and syntactic comprehension in a new paradigm. *JChL* **14**: 23–45

Hyams N 1986 *Language Acquisition and the Theory of Parameters*. Reidel, Dordrecht

Klima E, Bellugi U 1966 Syntactic regularities in the speech of children. In: Lyons J, Wales R (eds.) *Psycholinguistic Papers*. Edinburgh University Press, Edinburgh

MacWhinney B (ed.) 1987 *Mechanisms of Language Acquisition*. Erlbaum, Hillsdale, NJ

Maratsos M P, Chalkley M A 1980 The internal language of children's syntax: The ontogenesis and representation of syntactic categories In: Nelson K E (ed.) *Children's Language*, vol. 2. Gardner Press, New York

Miller J F 1981 *Assessing Language Production in Children*. University Park Press, Baltimore, MD

Pinker S 1984 *Language Learnability and Language Development*. Harvard University Press, Cambridge, MA

Pinker S 1991 Rule of language. *Science* **253**: 530–35

Plunkett K, Marchman V 1993 From rote learning to system building: Acquiring verb morphology in children and connectionist nets. *Cognition* **48**: 21–69

Radford A 1994 The syntax of questions in child English. *JChL* **21**: 211–36

Scarborough H 1990 The index of productive syntax. *AP* **11**: 1–22

Slobin D I (ed.) 1985 *A Cross-Linguistic Study of Language Acquisition*. Erlbaum, Hillsdale, NJ

Lexical Functional Grammar

C. Neidle

The term 'Lexical Functional Grammar' (LFG) first appeared in print in the 1982 volume edited by Joan Bresnan: *The Mental Representation of Grammatical Relations*, the culmination of many years of research. LFG differs from both transformational grammar and relational grammar in assuming a single level of syntactic structure. LFG rejects syntactic movement of constituents as the mechanism by which the surface syntactic realization of arguments is determined, and it disallows alteration of grammatical relations within the syntax. A unique constituent structure, corresponding to the superficial phrase structure tree, is postulated. This is made possible by an enriched lexical component that accounts for regularities in the possible mappings of arguments into syntactic structures. For example, the alternation in the syntactic position in which the logical object (theme argument) appears in corresponding active and passive sentences has been viewed by many linguists as fundamentally syntactic in nature, resulting, within transformational grammar, from syntactic movement of constituents. However, LFG eliminates the need for a multi-level syntactic representation by allowing for such alternations to be accomplished through regular, universally constrained, productive *lexical* processes that determine multiple sets of associations of arguments (such as 'agent,' 'theme') with grammatical functions (such as 'subject,' 'object')—considered within this framework to be primitives—which then map directly into the syntax.

This dissociation of syntactic structure from predicate argument structure (a rejection of Chomsky's Projection Principle, in essence) is crucial to the LFG framework. The single level of syntactic representation, 'constituent structure' ('c-structure'), exists simultaneously with a 'functional structure' ('f-structure') representation that integrates the information from c-structure and from the 'lexicon.' While c-structure varies somewhat across languages, the f-structure representation, which contains all necessary information for the semantic interpretation of an utterance, is claimed to be universal.

Phenomena that had been explained by the interaction of transformations are accounted for in LFG by the regular interaction of lexical processes. Bresnan shows that some of the classic arguments for syntactic transformations do not, in fact, distinguish between a transformational and a lexical account of the regularities. Bresnan (1982b) argues that the lexical account of passivization is superior to the transformational approach, e.g., in explaining why passivized forms can undergo further lexical rules, such as Adjective Conversion and compounding (giving rise to such forms as 'snow-covered').

Bresnan and other contributors to Bresnan (1982a) offer evidence and arguments in support of the formulation of such alternations in terms of alternative assignments of grammatical functions to arguments rather than syntactic movement. They suggest that the model has psychological validity, and is consistent with evidence about grammatical processing and acquisition. It also captures cross-linguistic generalizations about languages that have comparable alternations in the realization of arguments as grammatical functions despite the use of very different syntactic means for expressing functions like subject and object. Bresnan suggests that the 'illusion' of NP-movement in the English active/passive alternations

is just an artifact of the structural encoding of object and subject through word order in English. This is in contrast with languages like Malayalam (see Mohanan 1982), in which word order is much freer; accordingly, passivization in Malayalam involves an apparent change in morphological case. In LFG, the different realizations of active and passive sentences in Malayalam and English follow directly from independent principles that determine how subject, object, and oblique phrases are expressed syntactically in those languages.

Work in Lexical Mapping Theory, an outgrowth and extension of Lexical Functional Grammar, has been refining the principles for association of arguments with grammatical functions, so some of the earlier work could now be recast accordingly to simplify the lexical component. Thanks to a more general set of mapping principles, the associations of grammatical functions with arguments no longer need to be stipulated, and many lexical redundancy rules can be eliminated or greatly simplified since many characteristics of the associations are now predictable. Sects. 1–5 below summarize the 1982 framework; Lexical Mapping Theory will be discussed in Sect. 6. (For a discussion of more recent work in LFG, see *New Developments in Lexical Functional Grammar*.)

1. Levels of Representation

Lexical Functional Grammar postulates three distinct but interrelated levels of representation: lexical structure, functional structure, and constituent structure, which are present simultaneously. See Kaplan and Bresnan (1982) for details of the LFG formalism, which is briefly summarized below.

1.1 Lexical Structure

The lexical entry (or 'semantic form') includes information about the meaning of the lexical item, its argument structure, and the grammatical functions (e.g., subject, object, etc.) that are associated with those arguments. The verb 'hit,' for example, has a predicate argument structure that consists of an agentive argument associated with 'subject' and a patient or theme argument associated with the 'object' function.

(SUB)   (OBJ)   ← lexical assignment of grammatical functions
  | |
'hit (agent, theme)'   ← predicate argument structure

Grammatical functions are universal primitives within this framework, and since they are associated both with lexical items and with syntactic positions—by means of annotated phrase structure rules—they mediate between lexical and constituent structure representations. Grammatical functions play an essential role in Lexical Functional Grammar; however, they have no intrinsic significance and are situated at the interface between the lexicon and the syntax. LFG imposes the restriction of 'Direct Syntactic Encoding,' which prevents any syntactic process from altering the initial assignment of grammatical function.

Each lexical entry consists of a pairing of arguments and grammatical functions. The principle of 'function–argument biuniqueness' requires that each argument be associated with a unique grammatical function (even if that assignment is $\emptyset$, which entails that the argument will be interpreted as a bound variable, as in 'John ate' where it is implied that there is something John ate), and conversely that no grammatical function may occur more than once within a predicate argument structure. An actual lexical entry for the verb 'hit,' then, might look something like this:

> *hit*, Verb
> ($\uparrow$ PRED) = '{meaning of hit}$\langle$SUB, OBJ$\rangle$'

where the PRED feature has as its value some representation of the *meaning* of 'hit,' which in this case is a two-place predicate. The variable '$\uparrow$' in this representation refers to the lexical item under which this entry is found, here 'hit.'

A grammatical function may, however, be directly associated with no logical argument of the predicate with which it occurs. This is the situation for the object of 'consider' in the sentence

> John considered *her* to be a fine candidate.

where 'her' is the logical subject of the infinitival complement. This is indicated in the lexical entry for 'consider' by placement of the function OBJ outside of the angled brackets containing the arguments of the verb. So, the verb 'consider' would be represented as:

> *consider*, Verb
> ($\uparrow$ PRED) = '{meaning of consider}$\langle$SUB, XCOMP$\rangle$(OBJ)'
> ($\uparrow$ OBJ) = ($\uparrow$ XCOMP SUB)

where the XCOMP is an open complement, i.e., a complement whose subject is controlled grammatically; the control equation is added (by default).

Any other grammatical information associated with a lexical item will also be encoded in the semantic form. The name 'Mary,' for example, comes with the grammatical information about gender and number features (expressed here using '—' to indicate the unmarked value of the feature in the Jakobsonian sense; cf. Neidle 1988), which may also be expressed by equations:

> *Mary*, Noun
> ($\uparrow$ PRED) = '{meaning of 'Mary'}'
> ($\uparrow$ NUM) = −PL
> ($\uparrow$ GEND) = +FEM

These equations are referred to as 'constituting equations' because the information contained in them will be incorporated into any f-structure that contains this semantic form. It is also possible to have 'constraint equations' in a lexical entry; in such a case the f-structure would only be well-formed if the equation holds, but the information expressed by the equation

would not be added to the functional structure. Verb agreement in English may be accomplished in this way, by associating a constraint equation with a form like 'speaks' (contributed by a redundancy rule added to all forms that have the same inflexional ending):

> *speaks*, Verb
> ($\uparrow$ PRED) = '{meaning of 'speak'}$\langle$SUB$\rangle$'
> ($\uparrow$ SUB NUM) = $_c$ −PL

A sentence like 'They speaks' would be ill-formed since the constraint equation is not satisfied.

'Lexical redundancy rules' relate alternate pairings of arguments to grammatical functions. So, for example, passivization may involve suppression of the first argument (associated with SUB in the active form) and realization of the second argument (the OBJ in the active) as SUB; the morphological form associated with this operation is the participial form of the verb.

> (i) (SUB) $\rightarrow$ $\emptyset$
> (ii) (OBJ) $\rightarrow$ (SUB)

Notice that function–argument biuniqueness ensures that part (ii) of the passivization rule is contingent upon part (i); there can be only one subject. The output of that lexical redundancy rule on the previous lexical form given for 'hit' would be:

$$
\begin{array}{cc}
\emptyset & (\text{SUB}) \\
| & | \\
\end{array}
$$
'hit (agent, theme)'

However, the rule applies quite generally to lexical items having the appropriate grammatical functions. Notice that the rule would apply as well to grammatical functions contained within control equations, so the passivized version of 'consider' would be:

> *consider*, Verb
> ($\uparrow$ PRED) = '{meaning of consider}$\langle\emptyset$, XCOMP$\rangle$(<u>SUB</u>)'
> ($\uparrow$ <u>SUB</u>) = ($\uparrow$ XCOMP SUB)

Some support for formulation of such rules in terms of grammatical functions rather than structural configuration comes from the contrast illustrated by the following two sentences, distinguished by the fact that 'a doctor' is an 'object' in the first but is a 'nominal complement' in the second. Only the first may be subject to passivization.

> John hit a doctor.   A doctor was hit.
> John became a doctor.   *A doctor was become.

While the configuration of the post-verbal NP in both cases may be the same, it is the difference in grammatical function that accounts for the contrast with respect to passivization.

1.2 Constituent Structure

Constituent structure encodes linear order, hierarchical groupings, and syntactic categories of constituents, and is the input to the phonological component of the grammar. Language-specific annotations of phrase structure rules identify the grammatical functions that may occur in specific syntactic positions. Examples of phrase structure rules for English:

$$S \rightarrow \underset{(\uparrow SUB)=\downarrow}{NP} \quad \underset{\uparrow=\downarrow}{VP} \qquad VP \rightarrow \underset{\uparrow=\downarrow}{V} \quad \underset{(\uparrow OBJ)=\downarrow}{NP}$$

The arrows are variables; '↑' is to be instantiated by the node immediately dominating the constituent under which the arrow is placed, and '↓' by that node itself. So, the first equation for the rule on the left states that the NP under which the equation is written is the SUB of the S that dominates it. The '↑ = ↓' equation beneath VP indicates that the features of that node are shared with the higher node. This is the default assignment to phrasal heads, which share information with the dominating phrasal node. These equations are used to construct the f-structure representations described in Sect. 1.3.

It should be noted that the equations illustrated here are in the form in which LFG phrase structure rules were written in 1982. Similar associations of grammatical functions could be made with phrase structure rules conforming to current versions of X'-theory.

The terminal nodes of the tree are lexical items. The 'Lexical Integrity Hypothesis' requires that fully formed lexical items are inserted into the syntax. A rule like Affix-hopping would be disallowed. Syntactic rules are prohibited from moving any element into or out of lexical categories.

1.3 Functional Structure

Structural and lexical information is integrated and unified within functional structure (f-structure), which consists of hierarchically organized attribute-value matrices. A straightforward algorithm for transferring information from c-structure to f-structure is presented in Kaplan and Bresnan (1982). When the lexical items that occupy the terminal nodes of the tree are inserted into f-structure, the information contained in the lexical entry (including relevant equations) is retrieved and included in the f-structure. It is in this way that lexical information is combined with the structural information available from the c-structure tree.

So, the f-structure corresponding to the sentence 'John hit Bill'—constructed from the c-structure representation generated by the phrase structure rules illustrated in Sect. 1.2 and the lexical information from the entry for 'hit' discussed in Sect. 1.1—would include the following information:

$$\begin{bmatrix} \text{SUB} & [\text{PRED 'John'}] \\ \text{PRED} & \text{'hit}\langle\text{SUB, OBJ}\rangle\text{'} \\ \text{OBJ} & [\text{PRED 'Bill'}] \end{bmatrix}$$

The validity of the f-structure representation is ensured by a number of well-formedness conditions.

2. Well-formedness Conditions on Functional Structure

The following basic well-formedness conditions, which have counterparts in other frameworks, apply to f-structures.

2.1 Coherence

Coherence requires that every meaningful semantic form be a grammatical function mentioned in the predicate argument structure (or in a constituting equation) of a predicate in its clause. This prevents extraneous material from appearing.

2.2 Completeness

An f-structure is ill-formed if it does not contain values for the grammatical functions that are subcategorized by the predicate. The following sentence, for example, lacks a value for the SUB, and is therefore incomplete:

* Speaks.

2.3 Consistency

'Consistency,' also known as 'functional uniqueness,' requires that each attribute in the matrix have a unique value. So, for example, if an f-structure contained a matrix with the following:

$$\begin{bmatrix} \text{GEND} & +\text{FEM} \\ \text{GEND} & -\text{FEM} \end{bmatrix}$$

the f-structure would be inconsistent.

Notice that this common sense principle can also be used to guarantee the complementary distribution of elements that may fulfill a single grammatical function. This kind of complementary distribution has motivated many syntactic movement analyses, such as clitic-movement. In French, for example, both a full NP object appearing post-verbally and a pre-verbal direct object clitic may be associated with the *object* function. Thus, both of the following are grammatical:

Jean le voit
John him sees
'John sees him'

Jean voit l'homme
John sees the man
'John sees the man'

However, the following is ungrammatical without a pause before the final NP:

*Jean le voit l'homme
John him sees the man

While this distribution could be accounted for by a movement analysis (such as Kayne's 1975 proposal that both clitics and full NP's are generated in post-verbal position, and that a rule of clitic-placement applies), there is a straightforward account of these facts without movement. As discussed in Grimshaw (1982), the object function is associated with the pre-verbal clitic and with the post-verbal NP, both of which are optionally included in the phrase structure expansion of VP. If either a direct object clitic or full NP occurs with a verb that does not subcategorize for an object, then the f-structure is incoherent. If a lexical item like 'voit' requires an object, then either the clitic or the full NP must be present; otherwise the sentence will be incomplete. However, if both are present with 'voit,' then the f-structure is inconsistent because the value of the object's PRED would not be unique. Many phenomena for which arguments of functional equivalence and distributional complementarity have been used to argue for syntactic movement (not only NP-movement but also V-movement, for example) could be analyzed in similar fashion.

2.4 Semantic Coherence

All semantic forms that are not semantically empty (i.e., that are not dummy elements) must be linked to the logical argument of another lexical form—in order to be coherently interpreted.

3. Control and Complementation

Among the universal set of grammatical functions are complements and adjuncts. Complements are an essential part of the argument structure (part of the subcategorization frame), while adjuncts provide additional information and are interpreted by association with some other subcategorized argument. Adjuncts are not required for grammaticality, while omission of a complement results in an ill-formed sentence. Adjuncts have greater mobility than complements and are often set off by pauses. The following contrasts illustrate this:

Complement	John didn't sound *ashamed of himself.*
	*John didn't sound.
	*John, ashamed of himself, didn't sound.
Adjunct	John looked down, ashamed of himself.
	John looked down.
	John, ashamed of himself, looked down.

Complements and adjuncts may either be 'closed,' i.e., semantically complete, containing within them all the elements required for logical interpretation of the predicate, or 'open,' lacking a subject argument, which is then 'controlled' by another argument in the sentence. Open complements may be phrases of any lexical category (AP, NP, VP, PP) and so the abbreviation XCOMP is used to designate that set of complements. The same is true for open adjuncts, and the abbreviation XADJ is used.

Open complements predicate something of either the subject or the object of the main predicate with which they occur; this relation is expressed by a control equation (which can be filled in by a lexical redun-

dancy rule on the basis of the argument structure provided), as illustrated here:

consider, Verb
 ($\uparrow$ PRED) = '{meaning of consider}$\langle$SUB, XCOMP$\rangle$(OBJ)'
 ($\uparrow$ OBJ) = ($\uparrow$ XCOMP SUB)

This control equation sets the object of the main predicate equal to the subject of the XCOMP. This is indicated formally by either coindexing the two f-structures that are set equal, or by drawing an arrow from one to the other. Consider the sentence:

Mary considers John boring.

$$
\begin{bmatrix}
\text{SUB} & \begin{bmatrix} \text{PRED} & \text{'Mary'} \\ \text{NUM} & -\text{PL} \\ \text{GEND} & +\text{FEM} \\ \text{PERS} & \text{3rd} \end{bmatrix} \\
\text{PRED} & \text{'consider} \langle \text{SUB, XCOMP} \rangle \text{(OBJ)'} \\
\text{TENSE} & -\text{PAST} \\
\text{OBJ} & \begin{bmatrix} \text{PRED} & \text{'John'} \\ \text{NUM} & -\text{PL} \\ \text{GEND} & -\text{FEM} \\ \text{PERS} & \text{3rd} \end{bmatrix}_i \\
\text{XCOMP} & \begin{bmatrix} \text{SUB} & [\quad]_i \\ \text{PRED} & \text{'boring} \langle \text{SUB} \rangle \text{'} \end{bmatrix}
\end{bmatrix}
$$

This notation indicates that the two coindexed f-structures are identical in all respects. This relation of f-structure identity is referred to as 'grammatical' or 'functional' control. It is important to note that the subject of XCOMP is not present in c-structure. It is introduced into f-structure only through the lexical information contained in the entry for 'consider.' A similar analysis applies to the lexical entry for the verbs 'seem' and 'want,' which involve subject control over the complement:

seem, Verb
 ($\uparrow$ PRED) = '{meaning of 'seem'}$\langle$XCOMP$\rangle$(SUB)'
 ($\uparrow$ SUB) = ($\uparrow$ XCOMP SUB)

want, Verb
 ($\uparrow$ PRED) = '{meaning of 'want'}$\langle$SUB, VCOMP$\rangle$'
 ($\uparrow$ SUB) = ($\uparrow$ XCOMP SUB)

Thus, LFG grammatical control structures include some constructions that would be analyzed in recent Chomskyan frameworks as involving exceptional case marking, NP-movement, and controlled PRO. In each instance, the constituents that are postulated to be structurally present in LFG are those which are observable and which pass the syntactic constituency tests for the grammatical function assigned to them. So, for example, in the sentence 'John considered her to be a fine candidate,' 'her' is an object; it bears object case; it passivizes; it behaves syntactically like an object. Its semantic role as a subject argument of the following complement is not encoded in constituent structure in LFG. The kind of structural adjustments that are required in Chomskyan frameworks to compensate for the mismatches between surface syntactic constituency and the underlying argument structure (projected into d-structure) are not required in LFG, since the link between argument structure and c-structure is mediated by grammatical functions and since control properties are functionally rather than structurally encoded.

The analysis of open complements extends naturally to open adjuncts, although there is greater freedom in the argument that may serve as the controller, since this is not lexically determined; the subject of the adjunct may be set equal to a grammatical function from among those that are acceptable adjunct controllers in a given language.

Closed complements contain all arguments required for interpretation, as in the following sentence, where the closed sentential complement is italicized:

Mary thought *that it might rain.*

Such closed sentential complements may contain a phonetically null subject in f-structure (equivalent to PRO) that is then subject to principles of 'anaphoric control' for interpretation. The interpretation of PRO is subject to many of the same constraints that hold for interpretation of lexical pronouns, and is freer than in the case of grammatical control.

4. Long-distance Dependencies and Scrambling

To account for the kind of long-distance dependencies that are traditionally analyzed by *wh*-movement, the 1982 version of LFG utilizes 'constituent control.' The basic idea is that syntactic identity is established between the element that appears outside the clause and the position left empty within the clause. Long-distance associations are composed of local binding relations that are established. For details of the formalism see Kaplan and Bresnan (1982), or Sells (1985) for a more recent version. Unlike cases of grammatical control—where control information for the lexicon is used to construct functional structure representations of the controlled arguments—constituent control is not lexically determined and involves empty nodes that are syntactically present. The presence of this type of syntactic gap is associated with well-known processing effects and phonological effects (relating to contraction), unlike alternative assignments of arguments to grammatical functions as found in the passive construction, e.g., for which no null c-structure is postulated in LFG.

Rules that change the order of syntactic constituents without modifying their grammatical functions are handled as operations on c-structure rules. Thus, 'scrambling' rules are treated as rules that affect c-structure but not f-structure.

5. Case

5.1 What Case is and is not in LFG

Within the LFG framework, 'case' is not invoked to account for the distribution of lexically filled NP's, as it is in recent Chomskyan frameworks. The distribution of arguments that may be subject to grammatical or anaphoric control is handled in LFG by the theory of control, in terms of grammatical functions rather than syntactic positions. Similarly, while case is used in the Chomskyan framework to trigger movement (as in the passive construction, where the d-structure object cannot remain in that position without causing a violation because lexical forms can only occur in casemarked positions and past participles do not assign case), in LFG such alternations are determined by the mapping from argument structure to grammatical functions.

The term 'case' is used in LFG in the more traditional sense, to describe the use of inflexion to encode syntactic relations. Case is most easily observed and studied in languages that have rich case morphology, and in such languages, the claim that the existence of lexically empty subjects of tenseless clauses correlates with their caselessness has not been validated. As has been shown for many such languages, these empty elements can bear case. For example, in Russian, Neidle (1988) (following a 1974 proposal of Comrie's) argues that the subject of the embedded clause in the following sentence is, in fact, marked with Dative case, as can be seen from the case marking of case-agreeing modifiers.

On   poprosil Ivana   [**PRO**]$_{NP}$ pojti.
he$_{Nom}$ asked   Ivan$_{Acc}$ to go

On   poprosil Ivana   [**PRO**$_i$]$_{NP}$ pojti odnomu$_i$/*odnogo.
he$_{Nom}$ asked   Ivan$_{Acc}$ to go alone$_{Dat}$/*$_{Acc}$

Also, subjects of adverbial participle clauses bear Nominative case:

[**PRO**$_i$]$_{NP}$ Podbežav   k stancii **odin**$_i$, ...
              having-run to station alone

To accommodate evidence of this kind, a modified notion of case, 'Abstract case' is now required to license NP's in the Chomskyan model; LFG has no such device.

5.2 Syntactic Case Assignment

In LFG syntactic case is associated with either a specific grammatical function or syntactic configuration, and a morphological form that comes from the lexicon with the compatible case inflexion is required in that slot. Case-marked forms are generated in the lexicon (according to the regularities appropriate for the morphological class to which a given word belongs) and lexical entries include information about case features. It is in f-structure that appropriate use of case forms is ensured; if the morphological form inserted into c-structure is inconsistent with the case features assigned to the NP, then the corresponding f-structure will be ill-formed.

5.3 Case as a Reflex of Structural and Grammatical Relations

In languages that have rich case systems, overt case marking can provide evidence of grammatical relationships. In Neidle (1988), for example, it is argued that case marking in Russian provides evidence for the distinction between grammatical control and anaphoric control. In instances of grammatical control, the controlled NP shows identity in case with the controller. This can be shown by looking at the case marking of adjuncts that necessarily agree in case with the controlled element, since adjuncts exhibit case agreement with the noun they modify, as shown below:

Ivan prišel **odin**.
Ivan$_{Nom}$ came alone$_{Nom}$

Ivan xotel prijti **odin**/*odnomu.
Ivan$_{Nom}$ wanted to come alone$_{Nom}$/*$_{Dat}$

In the second sentence, '**odin**' is agreeing with the functional subject of 'prijti,' which is controlled by the higher subject in f-structure and is thus identical in all respects, including its case features. In cases involving anaphoric control, however, a separate f-structure corresponding to the subject of the embedded infinitive is present, and is casemarked independently of the higher subject. It is with this independently casemarked f-structure that the adjunct agrees in case.

On poprosil Ivana [**PRO**]$_{NP}$ pojti **odnomu**/*odnogo.
He$_{Nom}$ asked Ivan$_{Acc}$ to go alone$_{Dat}$/*$_{Acc}$

5.4 Case Alternations and Case Feature Decomposition

Neidle (1988) presents an analysis of Russian case alternations that uses an analytical decomposition of case into case features (in the Jakobsonian tradition). She argues that the same features that are relevant to morphological case syncretism are relevant to syntactic case assignment. Case alternations such as the Nominative/Dative alternation in subject position and the Accusative/Genitive alternation found on postverbal NP's in Russian (giving rise to the so-called Genitive of Negation) are accounted for by assignment of partially specified feature matrices, where the alternation in case can be attributed to the difference in the value of a single case feature. These basic case features may, in fact, be related to the features into which grammatical functions are decomposed within Lexical Mapping Theory.

6. Developments: Lexical Mapping Theory

Much work of the late 1980s (cf. Bresnan and Zaenen 1990; Bresnan and Kanerva 1989; Bresnan and Moshi 1990) is focused on Lexical Mapping Theory, which is an outgrowth of the work of L. Levin (1985) on unaccusativity. The basic idea is that syntactic functions may be analytically decomposed into two binary features: [$\pm$r] ($\pm$thematically unrestricted) and [$\pm$o] ($\pm$objective), which are associated with arguments according to universal mapping principles (although there may be some parametric variation in those principles across languages). Syntactic alternations are a result of feature underspecification in the initial assignment.

With these two features, grammatical functions are grouped into natural classes:

	non-objective [−o]	objective [+o]
thematically unrestricted [−r]	SUB	OBJ
thematically restricted [+r]	OBL$_\theta$	OBJ$_\theta$

where 'OBL$_\theta$' and 'OBJ$_\theta$' are abbreviations for sets of grammatical functions differentiated by their thematic restriction; thus 'oblique goal' and 'oblique instrumental' would both fall within the class represented by 'OBL$_\theta$' but are distinct grammatical functions. The '+' and '−' values represent the marked and unmarked values of the features. A markedness hierarchy can be established on this basis: subjects are the least marked grammatical function and restricted objects are the most marked. Not all languages even contain thematically restricted objects. The relative markedness of these functions is significant for the mapping of arguments onto grammatical functions.

The arguments appear in 'A-structures' ordered according to their relative role prominence, according to the following thematic hierarchy:

agent < beneficiary < experiencer/goal < instrument < patient/theme < locative

The most prominent role in a predicate may be represented by θ. Each thematic role in the argument structure is also associated with an intrinsic feature classification, a single syntactic feature compatible with that role:

patientlike roles	θ [−r]
secondary patientlike roles (as found with ditransitives)	θ [+o]
other roles	θ [−o]

Illustrations of A-structures:

hit ⟨ agent, theme ⟩
      [−o]   [−r]

fall ⟨ theme ⟩
       [−r]

The second feature specification, which completes the determination of the grammatical function to be fulfilled by each argument, can be filled in freely, in accordance with a few mapping principles. Basically, if the highest argument on the hierarchy is [−o], then that becomes the subject, otherwise a $[-r]$ argument is mapped onto subject. Function–argument biuniqueness, discussed earlier, still holds: no grammatical function can be associated with more than one thematic role, and no thematic role can be associated with more than one grammatical function. (There can, however, be more than one thematically restricted object, as long as the two are distinct grammatical functions.)

So, unless $\hat{\theta}$ is suppressed by the following association (a simplified statement compared with that from 1982):

$$\text{Passive} \quad \begin{array}{c} \hat{\theta} \\ | \\ \varnothing \end{array}$$

the agent of the verb 'hit' (whose A-structure is illustrated above) will be assigned $[-r]$ and will be realized as the grammatical subject. The $[-r]$ argument will receive the least marked assignment of the second feature compatible with mapping principles. It cannot be assigned $[-o]$, however, because the subject function is already filled and the assignment of $[-o]$ would constitute a violation of function–argument biuniqueness; therefore it will be $[+o]$, a thematically unrestricted object. If that $\hat{\theta}$ argument *is* suppressed, however, then the $[-r]$ argument, the theme, of the verb 'hit' will be assigned $[-o]$ and will appear as subject.

In other words, the alternations that occur in the grammatical functions that may be associated with a given argument are a result of the intrinsic feature assignment, which is only a partial feature specification. So an argument that is intrinsically specified to be $[-r]$ could potentially appear in the syntax as either a subject or an object, depending upon the subsequent assignment of $[\pm o]$. A second example of this kind of alternation is given here:

A book fell.
There fell a book.

This alternation results, within Lexical Mapping Theory, not from syntactic movement but from alternative assignments of grammatical functions to the argument.

Another alternation that is predicted is that between a subject and a thematically-restricted oblique, such as is found in the following English sentences:

John hit Bill.
Bill was hit by John.

Similar alternations occur with experiencers, which may occur either as thematically-restricted obliques or as subjects, and with locatives (see Bresnan and Kanerva 1989).

While many of the mapping principles are claimed to be universal, there appears to be slight parametric variation in the constraints that apply. In Bresnan and Moshi (1990), an explanation is proposed for a

clustering of differences between Kichaga (and languages like it) on the one hand and Chicheŵa (and languages like it) on the other, in terms of a restriction on assignment of intrinsic syntactic features (requiring that not more than one argument have an intrinsic classification of $[-r]$, based on a proposal by Alsina and Mchombo) that holds only for the latter group.

7. Summary

Thus, the three simultaneous levels of representation in LFG have different formal characterizations. No syntactic derivational process is involved. Syntactic generalizations of the type that inspired transformations such as passivization are instead viewed as resulting from productive relations in the lexicon. In instances where the arguments of a lexical entry may be associated with more than one set of grammatical functions, each different association corresponds to a different mapping from argument structure to syntactic functions, as expressed in a unique lexical entry, and lexical entries themselves may be productively related by 'lexical redundancy rules.' This is in contrast to the Government-Binding approach, which assumes an initial mapping of arguments into the syntax determined on the basis of the argument structure and from which alternative structures may be derived by syntactic movement. Thus, in LFG the cross-linguistic generalization about passive constructions is stated in terms of the alternate realization of arguments as grammatical functions, and the generalization about the syntactic position in which particular grammatical functions occur in a given language is stated independently. Lexical Mapping Theory further analytically decomposes grammatical functions into distinctive features, and establishes principles by which intrinsic syntactic features are associated with logical arguments and by which those arguments map into grammatical functions in conformity with universal principles, with slight parametric variation.

Bibliography

Alsina A, Mchombo S A 1989 Lexical mapping in the Chichewâ applicative construction (manuscript). Departments of Linguistics, Stanford University, Stanford, CA; University of California, Berkeley, CA

Bresnan J (ed.) 1982a *The Mental Representation of Grammatical Relations*. MIT Press, Cambridge, MA

Bresnan J 1982b The passive in lexical theory. In: Bresnan J (ed.) 1982a

Bresnan J, Kanerva J M 1989 Locative inversion in Chichewâ: A case study of factorization in grammar. *LIn* **20(1)**: 1–50

Bresnan J, Mchombo S A 1987 Topic, pronoun, and agreement in Chichewâ. *Lg* **63**: 741–82

Bresnan J, Moshi L 1990 Object asymmetries in comparative Bantu syntax. *LIn* **21(2)**: 147–85

Bresnan J, Zaenen A 1990 Deep unaccusativity in LFG. In: Dziwirek K, Farrell P, Mejías-Bikandi E (eds.) *Gram-*

matical Relations: A Cross-Theoretical Perspective. CSLI, Stanford, CA

Chomsky N 1982 *Lectures on Government and Binding*. Foris, Dordrecht

Comrie B 1974 The second dative: A transformational approach. In: Brecht R D, Chvany C V (eds.) *Slavic Transformational Syntax*. Michigan Slavic Publications, University of Michigan, Ann Arbor, MI

Grimshaw J 1982 Romance reflexive clitics. In: Bresnan J (ed.) 1982a

Kaplan R M, Bresnan J 1982 Lexical–functional grammar: A formal system for grammatical representation. In: Bresnan J (ed.) 1982a

Kayne R 1975 *French Syntax: The Transformational Cycle*. MIT Press, Cambridge, MA

Levin L 1985 *Operations on Lexical Forms: Unaccusative Rules in Germanic Languages* (MIT Dissertation. Pub. 1989 by Garland Press, New York)

Mohanan K P 1982 Grammatical relations and clause structure in Malayalam. In: Bresnan J (ed.) 1982a

Neidle C 1988 *The Role of Case in Russian Syntax*. Kluwer, Dordrecht

Sells P 1985 *Lectures on Contemporary Syntactic Theories*. CSLI, Standford, CA

Lexicase

Stanley Starosta

Lexicase is a type of European-style dependency/valency grammar which evolved out of American-style generative-transformational grammar. From its American origins lexicase retains the requirements that a linguistic theory, as a scientific hypothesis, be generative (formal and explicit) and maximally simple and general. Compared to analyses proposed by most other grammatical frameworks, lexicase representations are extremely simple: there is only one level of representation, so there can be no D-structure distinct from S-structure, no f-structure distinct from c-structure, or initial versus final stratum. There are no traces, PROs, or other empty categories, and no node labels are needed. In spite of this simplicity, lexicase is able to capture the same kinds of grammatical facts as other theories, frequently in a much more general and explicit way (see Starosta 1988).

The *lexi-* part of the name 'lexicase' reflects a strategy of regarding all linguistic generalizations as statements about the internal structure and external distribution of words, while the *-case* part reflects the prominent part played in a grammar by the syntactic–semantic relations that obtain between nouns and the words on which they depend, and the morphological and syntactic mechanisms that overtly mark the presence of these relations.

A lexicase grammar is very simple in concept. Each word can be thought of as an atom with its own valence, a specification of the kinds of other words/atoms it may or must combine with. A phrase then is like a molecule, any combination of words which are linked to each other in accordance with their individual valences, and a sentence is a free molecule, a phrase whose central word is a predicator. For example, a simple lexicon might consist of the entries in (1):

$$
\begin{array}{ll}
\text{a} & [+\text{Det}] \qquad\qquad\qquad\qquad (1)\\
\text{big} & [+\text{Adj}]\\
\text{dog} & [+\text{N},?[+\text{Det}],?([+\text{Adj}])]\\
\text{man} & [+\text{N},?[+\text{Det}],?([+\text{Adj}])]\\
\text{saw} & [+\text{V},?[+\text{N}],?[+\text{N}]]\\
\text{the} & [+\text{Det}]
\end{array}
$$

Here simple features like $+\text{Det}$ specify class membership and contextual features like $[?([+\text{N}])]$ specify valences. Thus *dog* $[+\text{N},?[+\text{Det}],?([+\text{Adj}])]$ is a member of the class N (noun). It may be linked to a member of the class Det $[?([+\text{Det}])]$ and may also be linked to a member of the class Adj $[?([+\text{Adj}])]$. Configuration (2), for example, satisfies these requirements; in the terminology of generative grammar, it can be said to be 'generated' by the grammar implicit in the lexicon:

231

If sequential ordering is built in, indices are added to show which word satisfies which valency specification of which other word, and the valence-bearing elements ('regents') are elevated to make the direction of the dependency more easily discernible. This gives a dependency diagram, or 'stemma,' as in (3):

(3)

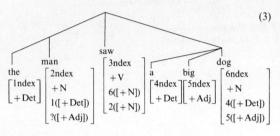

If node labels are added based on the class features of the controlling elements ('heads') of each sequence or subsequence, the result is an X-bar representation (in the strict sense of the term), as in (4):

(4)

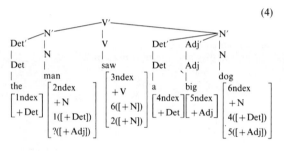

In principle, then, the grammar is the lexicon, and no additional rules are necessary to generate the sentences of the language. If grammatical rules are generalizations about the composition of words and sentences, then it follows that grammatical rules in a lexicase grammar must be statements of the regularities that can be extracted from the lexicon (see below).

The system just illustrated evolved out of an earlier Chomsky-style X-bar notational system in the course of testing what kinds of formal constraint could be imposed to limit its excessive expressive power. In this process, it was found that limiting X^n to X^1 (the one-bar constraint) resulted in a kind of dependency representation which was in effect a straightforward version of European dependency grammar. Similarly, in the process of devising a system of 'case relations' (comparable to thematic relations in several other frameworks) which accounted directly for generalizations about grammatical structures rather than just mapping subjectively perceived extralinguistic situations onto linguistic structures by brute force, lexicase found itself to have become a kind of Eur-

opean valency grammar rather than 'case grammar' in the conventional Fillmorean sense.

Lexicase is intended to be generative grammar in Noam Chomsky's original sense: a formal and explicit description of the internalized system which accounts for a speaker's ability to recognize well-formed sentences of his language. This requirement for generativity reflects the view that a linguistic theory is a scientific hypothesis about a native speaker's linguistic competence, and that a scientific theory can only be tested and corrected if it is absolutely clear what claims the theory makes. A proper lexicase description of a linguistic system is one which meets the requirement that it be explicit enough to be processed by a computer with no modification by the user, and in fact lexicase descriptions have been being routinely computer-tested since 1977.

In addition to the generativity requirement, lexicase maintains the old slogan that a stronger grammar makes a weaker claim. A theory that says that in principle all things are possible says nothing at all, and can never be disproved by evidence. Conversely, a theory which states that certain things are not at all possible makes a testable empirical claim, one which can in principle be disproved by observations. The content of a theory is its constraints. For this reason, the research strategy within lexicase at the meta-theoretical level is to propose new formal constraints on the theory and then determine whether descriptions of real language data can be written within these constraints, and if so, whether the constraints inhibit or facilitate the capture of language-internal and cross-linguistic generalizations.

This requirement for testability and a related requirement for psychological reality have resulted in a restriction on the domain of the theory: a lexicase grammar is an account of the linguistic competence of a single native speaker, rather than a description of the union or intersection of the linguistic competences of some arbitrarily selected group of individuals. As a practical research strategy, lexicase research has been conducted almost exclusively at the sentence level, based on the hypothesis that the sentence boundary is a natural boundary and that a prerequisite for doing serious discourse analysis is a good knowledge of the linguistic components of a discourse. Similar considerations apply to linguistic pragmatics, individual and social variation, first and second language acquisition, neurolinguistics, and psycholinguistics.

As in the case of traditional transformational-generative grammar, lexicase descriptions of specific languages are regarded as a means of getting at universal grammar, here regarded as a characterization of the ultimately neurological species-specific mechanisms which underlie the striking cross-linguistic commonalities which emerge when languages are described within a constrained theory, and which explain the ability of human beings to learn such complex systems so effortlessly. How much of this machinery is innate remains an open empirical question, but the current consensus in lexicase is that most if not all of the universal properties of languages can only be regarded as genetically preprogrammed.

Lexicase is *word grammar* in Richard Hudson's sense, although there are some significant differences in the two approaches. Grammar comes from the lexicon: phonology is the description of the internal structure of words, and morphology accounts for lexical relations among words with similar shapes and meanings. Syntax is a description of the 'pairwise' dependencies obtaining between words in phrases; coreference relationships are described in terms of coindexing words; and linguistic semantics in this framework is a function of the differential semantic features of lexical items plus interpretations imposed by regent words on their dependent words. Syntactic and semantic properties of words are characterized in terms of contextual and noncontextual features of their lexical entries, and rules of grammar are implicational statements about relations between features within a matrix (redundancy rules and subcategorization rules), relations between features, shapes, and sytactic distribution (inflexional rules), analogical rules relating sets of lexical entries (lexical derivation rules), or coindexing rules assigning the index of one word as the value of a contextual feature in the matrix of a grammatically related word (linking and chaining rules). The relationships among these rules can be represented in terms of a flow chart (see Fig. 1), the components of which will be considered in turn below.

1. Lexical Entries

Figure 2 shows partially specified example lexical entries. In these sample entries, features without

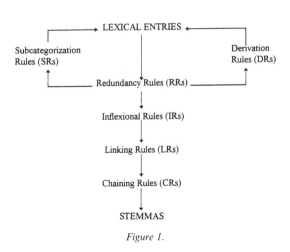

Figure 1.

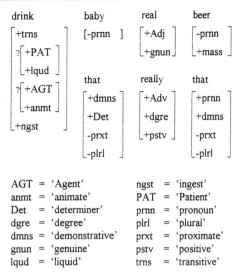

AGT = 'Agent'   ngst = 'ingest'
anmt = 'animate'   PAT = 'Patient'
Det = 'determiner'   prnn = 'pronoun'
dgre = 'degree'   plrl = 'plural'
dmns = 'demonstrative'   prxt = 'proximate'
gnun = 'genuine'   pstv = 'positive'
lqud = 'liquid'   trns = 'transitive'

Figure 2.

internal brackets ($+$trns, $-$prxt) are noncontextual features, while:

$$\left[\begin{bmatrix} ^? + AGT \\ + anmt \end{bmatrix} \right]$$

is a contextual implicational feature (a kind of Chomskyan Selectional Feature) which imposes the interpretation of 'animate' on any Agent dependent. Two other kinds of contextual features will be illustrated below.

Lexicase grammatical categories are limited and atomic. The set includes eight members: Adj, Adv, Cnjc (conjunction), Det, N, V, P, and Sprt (sentence particle). These primary categories cannot be broken down into components of $[\pm N, \pm V]$ etc., though they can certainly be divided into subcategories such as $[\pm xlry]$ ('auxiliary') for verbs and $[\pm prnn]$ for nouns. Semantic features such as $[+$ngst] 'ingest' in these examples are intended to suggest a full semantic componential analysis in which every pair of items which differ in denotation are distinctly marked for at least one such feature. Thus lexical semantics in a lexicase grammar is emic rather than etic.

It is assumed in writing a lexicase lexicon that a lexicon is maximally compact and nonredundant, and that everything that can be predicted by a general rule will be extracted from the lexical entries concerned. This is probably not a psychologically tenable position, however: in language use, there is a trade-off between storage and processing, and it is probable that frequently used words are stored with all their predictable features specified so that they can be used 'right off the shelf,' thus saving accessing time, while less frequent items may be stored in their maximally nonredundant forms, à la Bloomfield, and reconstructed 'from scratch' as needed, to minimize storage requirements.

2. Redundancy Rules (RRs)

In lexicase, Redundancy Rules state implicational relationships between features within a single matrix. They should not be confused with 'redundancy rules' in Jackendoff's sense, which refer to lexical derivational processes which typically do not specify redundant features. A redundancy rule states simply that if a matrix contains one or more particular features, it will also contain certain other features, as shown in (5):

RR-1
$[\pm \text{prnn}] \rightarrow [+\text{N}]$

Examples (5)

baby → baby
$[-\text{prnn}]$ → $\begin{bmatrix} -\text{prnn} \\ +\text{N} \end{bmatrix}$

beer → beer
$\begin{bmatrix} -\text{prnn} \\ +\text{mass} \end{bmatrix}$ → $\begin{bmatrix} -\text{prnn} \\ +\text{mass} \\ +\text{N} \end{bmatrix}$

that → that
$\begin{bmatrix} +\text{prnn} \\ +\text{dmns} \\ -\text{prxt} \\ -\text{plrl} \end{bmatrix}$ → $\begin{bmatrix} +\text{prnn} \\ +\text{dmns} \\ -\text{prxt} \\ -\text{plrl} \\ +\text{N} \end{bmatrix}$

Lexicase rules are monotonic, that is, they are not allowed to alter preexisting features. This property makes it possible to use RRs as marking conventions. For example, if it is determined that nouns are normally count ($[-\text{mass}]$), this can be stated as a general RR. Mass nouns will already be lexically marked for $[+\text{mass}]$, and will not be affected by the rule:

RR-2
$[+\text{N}] \rightarrow [-\text{mass}]$

Examples (6)

baby → baby
$\begin{bmatrix} -\text{prnn} \\ +\text{N} \end{bmatrix}$ → $\begin{bmatrix} -\text{prnn} \\ +\text{N} \\ -\text{mass} \end{bmatrix}$

beer → beer.
$\begin{bmatrix} -\text{prnn} \\ +\text{mass} \\ +\text{N} \end{bmatrix}$ → $\begin{bmatrix} -\text{prnn} \\ +\text{mass} \\ +\text{N} \end{bmatrix}$

Redundancy Rules also specify regular distributional characteristics of classes of words. For example, RR-3 states that nouns may have Det dependents, but that such dependents may not follow the nouns, while $[+\text{V}]$ dependents (relative clauses) may not precede the HEAD noun (the common regent of the other words in the NP), etc., as in (7):

RR-3 Example: (7)
$[+\text{N}] \rightarrow$
$\begin{bmatrix} @\text{ndex} \\ ?([+\text{Det}]) \\ @ > ?([+\text{Det}]) \\ ?([+\text{Adj}]) \\ @ > ?([+\text{Adj}]) \\ ?([+\text{P}]) \\ @ < ?([+\text{P}]) \\ ?([+\text{N}]) \\ @ < ?([+\text{N}]) \\ ?([+\text{V}]) \\ @ < ?([+\text{V}]) \end{bmatrix}$

baby → baby
$\begin{bmatrix} -\text{prnn} \\ +\text{N} \\ -\text{mass} \end{bmatrix}$ → $\begin{bmatrix} -\text{prnn} \\ +\text{N} \\ -\text{mass} \\ @\text{ndex} \\ ?([+\text{Det}]) \\ @ > ?([+\text{Det}]) \\ ?([+\text{Adj}]) \\ @ > ?([+\text{Adj}]) \\ ?([+\text{P}]) \\ @ < ?([+\text{P}]) \\ ?([+\text{N}]) \\ @ < ?([+\text{N}]) \\ ?([+\text{V}]) \\ @ < ?([+\text{V}]) \end{bmatrix}$

Optional positive contextual features such as $[?([+\text{Det}])]$ can be read as 'may take a $[+\text{Det}]$ dependent.' Such features are meaningless in themselves, since they can never be violated by any context. In a lexicase grammar, however, they have an important function: they are used to indicate dependency links between regents and endocentric dependents (see the discussion of linking rules below), and thereby establish a sentence skeleton which allows government and agreement requirements, grammatical relations, and selectional restrictions to be imposed by regents on their immediate dependents.

3. Subcategorization Rules (SRs)

Subcategorization Rules state that a given class of words is composed of two or more subtypes. There are two kinds of such rules, although it has not been found necessary to distinguish them notationally. The first kind may be referred to as 'Lexical Subcategorization Rules.' For example, see (8):

SR-1 Examples: (8)
$[+\text{N}] \rightarrow [\pm \text{prnn}]$

beer → beer
$\begin{bmatrix} -\text{prnn} \\ +\text{mass} \\ +\text{N} \end{bmatrix}$ → $\begin{bmatrix} -\text{prnn} \\ +\text{mass} \\ +\text{N} \end{bmatrix}$

that → that
$\begin{bmatrix} +\text{prnn} \\ +\text{dmns} \\ -\text{prxt} \\ -\text{plrl} \\ +\text{N} \end{bmatrix}$ → $\begin{bmatrix} +\text{prnn} \\ +\text{dmns} \\ -\text{prxt} \\ -\text{plrl} \\ +\text{N} \end{bmatrix}$

As can be seen from the examples, lexical Sub-categorization Rules have no actual effect on the matrices to which they apply. They specify subclass membership, a property which is part of the inherent lexical specification for every word and which cannot be altered by the application of monotonic lexical rules. Nevertheless such rules are necessary as part of the characterization of 'well-formed lexical items in language X,' and are very useful in presenting a grammar in a compact and easily graspable form.

The second group of Subcategorization Rules can be referred to as 'Inflexional Subcategorization Rules.' They break up stems into paradigms of inflected forms, e.g., (9), which describes the set of non-pronominal nouns as consisting of pairs of words distinct only in the feature of plurality:

$$\text{SR-2} \qquad [-\text{prnn}] \rightarrow [\pm\text{plrl}]$$

Example: (9)

$$
\text{noun}_{1a} \begin{bmatrix} -\text{prnn} \\ -\text{plrl} \\ \alpha F_i \end{bmatrix} : \text{noun}_{1b} \begin{bmatrix} -\text{prnn} \\ +\text{plrl} \\ \alpha F_i \end{bmatrix}
$$

$$
\text{noun}_{2a} \begin{bmatrix} -\text{prnn} \\ -\text{plrl} \\ \alpha F_i \end{bmatrix} : \text{noun}_{2b} \begin{bmatrix} -\text{prnn} \\ +\text{plrl} \\ \alpha F_i \end{bmatrix}
$$

$$
\text{noun}_{ia} \begin{bmatrix} -\text{prnn} \\ -\text{plrl} \\ \alpha F_i \end{bmatrix} : \text{noun}_{ib} \begin{bmatrix} -\text{prnn} \\ +\text{plrl} \\ \alpha F_i \end{bmatrix}
$$

4. Inflexional Rules (IRs)

Lexical items may occur in inflexional paradigms, n-ary sets of words belonging to the same syntactic distribution class and related to each other in shape and meaning in fairly consistent ways. Thus in the example in (9), nonpronominal nouns occur in binary sets, identical to each other in semantic and grammatical features except that one member of the set is singular ($[-\text{plrl}]$) and the other is plural ($[+\text{plrl}]$). The elements in such a set will normally also differ in shape in some fairly consistent way. Thus the $[+\text{plrl}]$ forms will differ from their singular counterparts in that the plural forms will end in /s/, /z/, or /iz/, the choice among the three forms being predictable from the final segment of the nonplural counterpart.

The relationships among the members of a paradigm are described by 'Inflexion Rules' (IRs), analogical rules that relate pairs or n-ads of words to each other in terms of consistent differences in features and phonetic shape. For example, IR-1 in (10) relates the members of one subset of English noun pairs to each other.

$$
\text{IR-1} \qquad [XV] \begin{bmatrix} +N \\ -\text{plrl} \end{bmatrix} : [XVz] \begin{bmatrix} +N \\ +\text{plrl} \end{bmatrix}
$$

Examples: (10)

$$
\begin{array}{ll}
\text{/tri/} & \text{/triz/} \\
\text{tree} & \text{trees}
\end{array}
$$

$$
\begin{bmatrix} +N \\ \alpha F_i \\ -\text{plrl} \end{bmatrix} : \begin{bmatrix} +N \\ \alpha F_i \\ +\text{plrl} \end{bmatrix}
$$

$$
\begin{array}{ll}
\text{/tre/} & \text{/trez/} \\
\text{tray} & \text{trays}
\end{array}
$$

$$
\begin{bmatrix} +N \\ \beta F_j \\ -\text{plrl} \end{bmatrix} : \begin{bmatrix} +N \\ \beta F_j \\ +\text{plrl} \end{bmatrix}
$$

$[\alpha F_i]$ and $[\beta F_j]$ in these examples represent the features that the two lexical entries have in common.

For those pairs that are related in a way that is completely consistent with such a formula, each of the forms is predictable from the other, so one can be omitted from the lexicon and reconstituted as necessary from the other, which is referred to as the 'base word.' For paradigms whose shapes are not describable in terms of a general rule such as IR-1, all members of the paradigm are separately listed in the lexicon.

Note that this 'word and paradigm' approach to morphology does not assume the listing of 'stems' or 'affixes' in the lexicon. Instead, the lexicon contains only full words, complete with inflexional morphology if any. There are no abstract truncated or underspecified forms from which the actual forms have to be projected. The result is the disappearance of a number of problems that have long vexed conventional item-based morphological analysis which attempt to analyze words by slicing them up into nonoverlapping sequences of morphs, and using implausible ad hoc evasions ('portmanteau morphs,' 'tiers,' etc.) when this turns out not to work.

The features which constitute inflexional paradigms are typically grammatically significant. They may for example differentiate the subclasses of words selected by regent words in agreement or government dependencies. Thus the verb *appear* selects a $[+\text{plrl}]$ (or non-third person) Nominative dependent, while *appears* selects a $[-\text{plrl}]$ Nominative dependent.

In addition to agreement relationships, IRs may assign contextual features which mark grammatically significant word order patterns. For example in (12) the rule accounts for English 'Subject–AUX Inversion' in yes–no questions:

$$
\text{IR-2} \qquad [X] \begin{bmatrix} +\text{xlry} \\ +\text{root} \\ -\text{ntrg} \\ @>?\begin{bmatrix} +N \\ +\text{Nom} \end{bmatrix} \end{bmatrix} : [X] \begin{bmatrix} +\text{xlry} \\ +\text{root} \\ +\text{ntrg} \\ @<?\begin{bmatrix} +N \\ +\text{Nom} \end{bmatrix} \end{bmatrix}
$$

(11)

Examples:

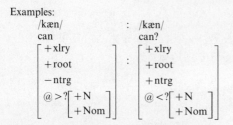

IRR-2 states that a root auxiliary verb marked [+ntrg] ('interrogative') must co-occur with a following subject and never with a preceding subject, while a declarative root verb requires a preceding subject. This rule allows structures (12a) and (12c) but excludes (12b) and (12d):

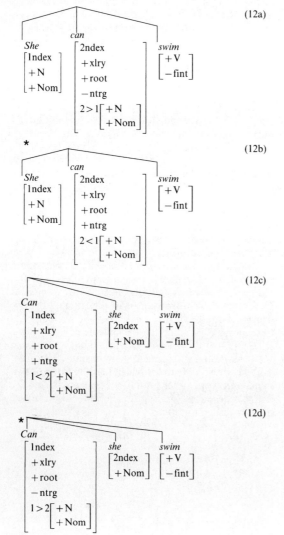

5. Linking Rules (LRs)

Lexicase is a kind of dependency grammar, and grammatical representations are stated not in terms of layers of constituents, but in terms of pairwise dependency relations between a dominant word (the regent) and a dependent word. This relationship is formalized in lexicase by contextual features related by external and internal linking rules. External linking rules copy the index of another word into the regent matrix as the value of one of its contextual features. External links are either exocentric (structurally obligatory) or endocentric (structurally optional). Linking rules for endocentric dependents have the form shown in (14):

LR-1 (14)

$$[?([+WC_i])] \rightarrow [n([+WC_i])] / \begin{bmatrix} +WC_i \\ nndex \end{bmatrix}$$

A word which allows a dependent bearing the word class ('part of speech') feature $[+WC_i]$ takes on the index n of a neighboring word bearing the feature $[+WC_i]$, thereby establishing a dependency link between the two. Exocentric linking rules are identical except in lacking the parentheses, as illustrated by LR-2 in (15). Specific examples are shown in (16) and (17).

LR-2 (15)

$$[?[+WC_i]] \rightarrow [n[+WC_i]] / \begin{bmatrix} +WC_i \\ nndex \end{bmatrix}$$

LR-3 (16)

$$[?([+Det])] \rightarrow [n([+Det])] / \begin{bmatrix} +Det \\ nndex \end{bmatrix}$$

Examples:

that $\begin{bmatrix} @ndex \\ +Det \end{bmatrix}$ baby $\begin{bmatrix} @ndex \\ +N \\ ?([+Det]) \end{bmatrix}$ → that $\begin{bmatrix} 1index \\ +Det \end{bmatrix}$ baby $\begin{bmatrix} 2ndex \\ +N \\ 1([+Det]) \end{bmatrix}$

LR-4 (17)

$$[?[+V]] \rightarrow [n[+V]] / \begin{bmatrix} +V \\ nndex \end{bmatrix}$$

Examples:

drink $\begin{bmatrix} @ndex \\ +V \end{bmatrix}$ to $\begin{bmatrix} @ndex \\ +P \\ ?[+V] \end{bmatrix}$ → to $\begin{bmatrix} 1index \\ +P \\ 2[+V] \end{bmatrix}$ drink $\begin{bmatrix} 2ndex \\ +V \end{bmatrix}$

Tom $\begin{bmatrix} @ndex \\ +N \end{bmatrix}$ Jerry $\begin{bmatrix} @ndex \\ +N \end{bmatrix}$ and $\begin{bmatrix} @ndex \\ +Cnjc \\ ?[+N] \\ ?[+N] \end{bmatrix}$

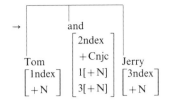

The external linking rule can be called valence linking, since the contextual feature is like a potential chemical bond which may be satisfied by an external atom bearing the appropriate complementary valence. In one sense the analogy is not appropriate, however, since the lexicase valence links are unidirectional: the regent indexes its dependent, but the dependent is not aware of its regent. A well-formed lexicase dependency representation is one in which every word (except one, the head of the construction as a whole) is dependent on one and only one other word. The output of the external linking rules is the dependency skeleton of the phrase or sentence. Such a representation is referred to as a 'stemma.' In lexicase stemmas, a vertical line indicates the head of a construction, slanted lines indicate the head's endocentric dependents, and horizontal lines indicate its exocentric dependents.

The external LRs bring the indices of dependents into the lexical matrices of a regent, where they may be used as the values of other contextual features. If an endocentric dependent is linked internally to an obligatory contextual feature, it is a 'complement,' otherwise it is an 'adjunct.' A construction is ill-formed if any of its complement features are left unsatisfied. *The* in (18) is a complement of *angel* while *some* and *sly* in (19) are adjuncts of *demons*.

(18a) / (18b)

(19a) / (19b)

Internal LRs may link external dependents to other contextual features which assign interpretations to them. Thus a dependent may be interpreted as having particular grammatical roles or features (government, agreement) or semantic features (selection).

6. Case Marking and LRs

Among the most important of contextual features are those referring to case forms. For example, in accusative languages such as English, a transitive verb requires a nominative and an accusative complement, and these complements must be linked to external nouns, as illustrated in (20).

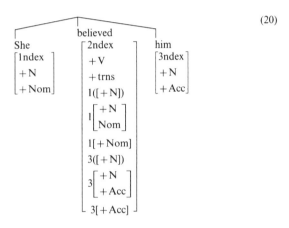

(20)

The bridging features which establish links between two other contextual features, for example, [?[+N, +Nom]] in LR-5 and LR-6, (21) and (22), are referred to as TOBIISI features.

LR-5

$$\begin{bmatrix} n([+N]) \\ ?\begin{bmatrix} +N \\ +Nom \end{bmatrix} \end{bmatrix} \rightarrow \begin{bmatrix} n\begin{bmatrix} +N \\ +Nom \end{bmatrix} \end{bmatrix}$$ (21)

LR-6

$$\begin{bmatrix} n\begin{bmatrix} +N \\ +Nom \end{bmatrix} \\ ?[+Nom] \end{bmatrix} \rightarrow [n[+Nom]]$$ (22)

Lexicase case relations differ from conventional Fillmorean case grammar and other 'thematic relation' systems in that lexicase case relations are established by grammatical rather than language-independent situational criteria. As a consequence, lexicase has so far been able to make do with only five case relations and one macrorole:

Case relations:
PAT   Patient
AGT   Agent
LOC   Locative
MNS   Means
COR   Correspondent

Macrorole:
actr (actor)

Case relations are assigned to constituents bearing case forms such as Nom and Acc by linking rules which apply inside the matrix. A fundamental postulate of lexicase case grammar is that every verb has a PAT complement, and that every transitive verb has an AGT complement. PAT links to Nom in all intransitive clauses, and actr links to PAT in an intransitive clause and AGT in a transitive clause.

These assumptions are primarily responsible for the large number of universal and language-specific generalizations that can be captured in this framework. Only one will be mentioned here, the characterization of accusative as opposed to ergative case-marking systems. In accusative languages, Nom links to actr, and in ergative languages, Nom links to PAT. Accusative languages in addition link PAT to Acc in transitive clauses, while ergative languages have a rule linking AGT to an ergative case in transitive clauses. The result can be illustrated as in (23) and (24):

Ergative case marking (schematic)   (24)

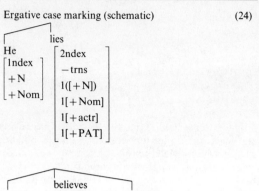

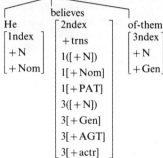

7. Chaining Rules (CRs)

Linking rules apply to links between words and their immediate dependents. However, there are some dependencies which obtain between words in different dependency domains. For such cases, Chaining Rules (CR) are used to copy indices from items in higher or lower domains to satisfy contextual features. Two examples will be illustrated here: infinitival complementation ('control') and unbounded dependency ('*wh*-movement').

An infinitive is defined in lexicase as a verb form which does not allow its grammatical subject to appear overtly as a dependent, as in (25):

John wanted to [graduate]   (25a)
$\begin{bmatrix} 4\text{ndex} \\ -\text{fint} \end{bmatrix}$

*John wanted to [John   graduate]   (25b)
$\begin{bmatrix} 4\text{ndex} \\ +\text{Nom} \end{bmatrix}$ $\begin{bmatrix} 5\text{ndex} \\ -\text{fint} \end{bmatrix}$

Mary told John to [bring   the book]   (25c)
$\begin{bmatrix} 5\text{ndex} \\ -\text{fint} \\ 7[+\text{acc}] \end{bmatrix}$ $\begin{bmatrix} 7\text{ndex} \\ +\text{Acc} \end{bmatrix}$

*Mary told John to [John   bring   the book]   (25d)
$\begin{bmatrix} +\text{Nom} \\ 5\text{ndex} \end{bmatrix}$ $\begin{bmatrix} 6\text{ndex} \\ -\text{fint} \\ 8[+\text{acc}] \end{bmatrix}$ $\begin{bmatrix} 8\text{ndex} \\ +\text{Acc} \end{bmatrix}$

Accusative case marking   (23)

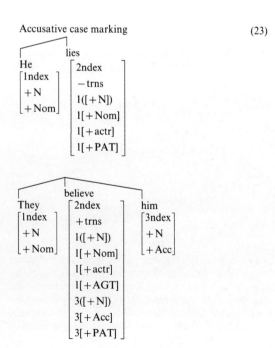

238

Nevertheless, speakers of a language are consistently able to identify the missing subject without reference to any external context, so a grammar must account for this ability. Formally, the problem is how to satisfy case frame requirements for such verbs without being able to copy an index from an overt subject. This is done by means of the most prevalent infinitival complement Chaining Rule (26):

CR-1   (26)

$$\begin{bmatrix} ?[+\text{actr}] \\ -\text{fint} \\ \text{nndex} \end{bmatrix} \rightarrow \quad [m[+\text{actr}\ ]\ ] \setminus \begin{bmatrix} m[+\text{PAT}\ ] \\ n[-\text{fint}\ ] \end{bmatrix}$$

Here the '\' environment refers to the lexical matrix of the word's regent. This rule copies the index of the PAT of the matrix clause (transitive or intransitive) onto the actr feature of the infinitive, as shown in (27) and (28), for instance:

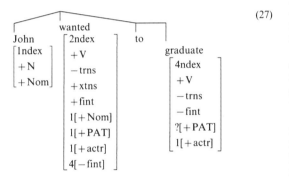

(27)

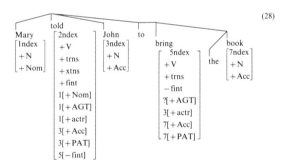

(28)

Regular internal Linking Rules then copy 1 onto [?[+PAT]] in (27) and 3 onto [?[+AGT]] in (28), identifying *John* as the PAT of *graduate* and *John* as the AGT of *bring*. The infinitival complement rule can apply recursively to successively embedded complements to any arbitrary depth of embedding.

Chaining Rules for unbounded dependencies use an adjunct feature [?([+prtr])] ('operator') to carry an index along through a tree and establish a coindexing chain between a contextual feature and some 'displaced' argument, such as an interrogative pronoun or a topic, as seen in (29):

CR-2   (29)

$$[?([+\text{prtr}])] \rightarrow [n([+\text{prtr}])] \setminus [n([+\text{prtr}])]$$

Only elements in appropriate dependency relationships to each other can be chained together in this way, but there is no formal limit on the length of such chains. The rule assigns an index to a [?([+prtr])], where the index is taken from a previously indexed [?([+prtr])] feature marked on the head verb of the next clause up. The index on the higher verb in turn may have come from the next clause up or from an external adjunct, such as a *wh*-pronoun. Figs. 3 and 4 are examples of *wh*-questions analyzed in this way.

In both examples, the [1([+prtr])] feature in the highest verb, *do*, gets its index from the external interrogative pronoun by external valency linking. The [1([+prtr])] on *tell* gets its index from the [1([+prtr])] on *did*, and the [1([+prtr])] on *send* gets its index from the [1([+prtr])] on *tell*. The 'complementizer' preposition *to* takes the 1 index from its regent verb and passes it down to the dependent infinitive. This index is then copied onto the thus far unindexed case frame feature, [?[+LOC]] in Fig. 3 and [?[+COR]] in Fig. 4, and this is in turn copied onto the unindexed case form feature, [?[+lctn]] in Fig. 3 and [?[+Acc]] in Fig. 4. This last step imposes a case form requirement on the interrogative pronoun: [1[+lctn]] states that the item with the index 1 must be [+lctn] in Fig. 3, and [1[+Acc]] in Fig. 4 states that the item with the index 1 must be [+Acc]. This system will take care of more complex case-marking in displaced interrogative pronouns in languages such as German without modification.

8. Derivation Rules (DRs)

Derivation rules state analogical relationships among subsets of lexical entries. For example in (30), DR-1 states that there is a correspondence between the set of demonstrative pronouns and the set of demonstrative determiners in English, while DR-2 states a similar analogical relationship between the sets of quality adjectives and manner adverbs:

DR-1   (30)

$$\begin{bmatrix} +\text{Det} \\ +\text{dmns} \end{bmatrix} : \begin{bmatrix} +\text{prnn} \\ +\text{dmns} \end{bmatrix}$$

DR-2

$$\quad\quad\quad\quad]\ :\ \text{li}]$$

$$\begin{bmatrix} +\text{Adj} \\ +\text{qlty} \end{bmatrix} : \begin{bmatrix} +\text{Adv} \\ +\text{qlty} \\ +\text{mnnr} \end{bmatrix}$$

Words created by DRs do not contain any internal boundaries, and phonological alterations connected with various kinds of lexical derivation are part of the DR itself, not synchronic phonological rules conditioned by Rule Features or ad hoc boundary

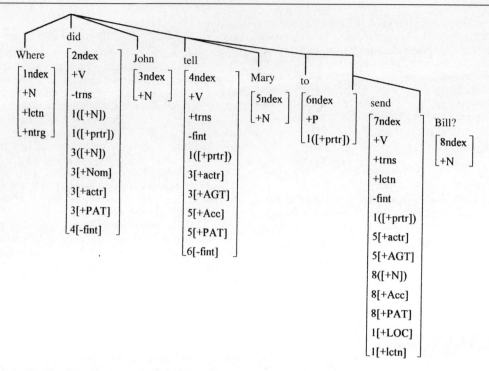

Figure 3. 'Where did John tell Mary to send Bill?'

symbols. Similarly, affixes that may be added by DRs are not separate lexical entries. Rather, they exist in the grammar only as elements of the phonological change part of a DR. The analogies depicted by such rules may involve correspondences between syntactic features, semantic features, or both. Typically, they also involve a correspondence between phonological forms, such as the presence of /li/ at the end of manner adverbs and its absence at the end of corresponding quality adjectives in DR-2. However, this is not always true, as shown by DR-1, and languages such as English and Chinese are especially prone to the use of such 'zero derivation' processes.

As derivation, the analogies depicted by DRs are subject to irregularities. Thus in the pattern a : b :: c : d, either c or d may not exist at all, or may exist with some unpredicted semantic or phonological deviations from the expected pattern. Thus while DR-1 is quite regular, DR-2 is not; not all quality adjectives have corresponding manner adverbs or vice versa (real: *real-ly, friendly: *friendlily, fuchsia: *fuchsialy), and the meanings of some manner adverbs are not completely predictable from the meanings of their source adjectives.

The analogical patterns depicted in DRs are psychologically real to the extent that a speaker notices the patterns and can use them in creating or decoding new words. Using such a rule to coin a new word is an individual historical event, and because the occurrence of such an event and the precise form of the result of this event are not completely predictable, the output form must be separately listed in the lexicon. As independent forms, the output items are then subject to semantic or phonological changes for the most part independent of their historical derivational sources. DRs are then not normally invoked in the production or interpretation of a new sentence. Rather, the derived forms are accessed from the lexicon like any other lexical item.

The DR component of a lexicase grammar carries most of the burden of accounting for relationships between classes of sentences. To take a simple example, a lexicase grammar of English will have a rule such as DR-3, as in (31):

DR-3 (31)

$$\begin{bmatrix} +\text{trns} \\ {}^?\begin{bmatrix} +\text{AGT} \\ \alpha F_i \end{bmatrix} \end{bmatrix} : \begin{bmatrix} -\text{trns} \\ {}^?\begin{bmatrix} +\text{PAT} \\ \alpha F_i \end{bmatrix} \end{bmatrix}$$

This rule is needed to account for the relationship between sentence pairs such as (a) and (b) in (32):

John drinks   buttermilk (32a)

$$\begin{bmatrix} +\text{trns} \\ {}^?\begin{bmatrix} +\text{AGT} \\ +\text{anmt} \end{bmatrix} \end{bmatrix}$$

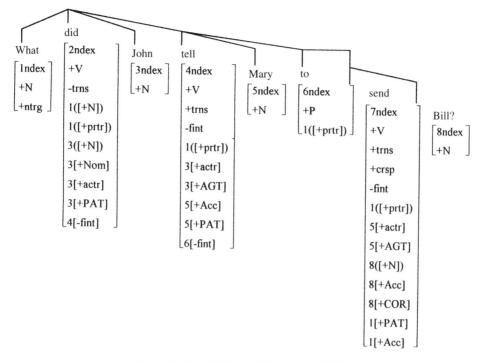

Figure 4. 'What did John tell Mary to send Bill?'

John drinks   (32b)

$$\left[\begin{array}{l} -\,\text{trns} \\ ?\left[\begin{array}{l} +\,\text{PAT} \\ +\,\text{anmt} \end{array} \right] \end{array} \right]$$

anmt = 'animate'

The rule states that corresponding to a transitive verb which interprets its AGT to be $[\alpha F_i]$ (here $[+\,\text{anmt}]$), there may be a homophonous intransitive verb which imposes the same selectional requirements on its PAT. Similar rules will be needed to account for the active–passive relationship, 'raising' to subject and object, 'dative movement,' 'spray paint' sentences, causatives, etc.

Most work in lexicase has been done at the University of Hawaii, much of it by or under the supervision of Stanley Starosta. Since its beginnings in 1970, the framework has been employed in the study of more than seventy languages, mostly Pacific and Asian languages and English, with some limited work on Greek, Swahili, and Native American languages. Several papers have also appeared proposing ways of applying lexicase in natural language processing. Linguistic journals in Britain and the US have generally been inhospitable to dependency grammar contributions, and most of the published work has appeared in Asia and on the European continent. Currently the most accessible sources of information on the theory and its applications are one book (Starosta 1988) and a number of University of Hawaii doctoral dissertations available through University Microfilms International.

Bibliography

Starosta S 1988 *The Case for Lexicase: An Outline of Lexicase Grammatical Theory.* Pinter, London

Lexicon in Formal Grammar
R. L. Humphreys

The lexicon in Formal Grammar refers to that component of the theory which deals with linguistic singularities rather than generalities. That is, the lexicon is the repository of basic items on which grammar rules operate (words) together with word-related constraints on the free operation of those rules (see *X-bar Syntax* for an introductory discussion).

For the purposes of syntax, the lexicon has traditionally been supposed to consist of a list of basic words, their syntactic categories, and their subcategorization properties, e.g., for verbs, whether they take a noun phrase, a prepositional phrase, a clause, or nothing at all in object position. Subcategorization properties are deemed to be lexical givens; that is, the syntactic transitivity of a verb may not be predictable even when semantic class is taken into account. For example, syntacticians note that there is no obvious reason in virtue of meaning why *eat* can have both transitive and intransitive forms whilst the near-synonymous *devour* can only be realized as a transitive; similarly, there is no obvious semantic explanation for the exclusion of sentential subjects by verbs like *result* or *make*.

A lexical entry for the syntactic component of one form of *bake* in Government and Binding Theory (GB) might look thus:

bake: V, +[NP]

that is, *bake* takes an NP object. The subject NP is not specified in the lexical entry because its existence will be determined by the interaction of other grammar principles such as X-bar theory.

In early structuralist theory, the listing of complements was ordered, e.g., an entry for *put* as in *put the box on the table* would explicitly indicate that the NP came before the PP. In all contemporary theories of grammar complements are unordered; ordering information is supplied by rules/principles such as an Adjacency Principle putting case-markable elements such as NPs before those which are not case-markable GB, or a small ordered constituency Phrase Structure Grammar in Lexical Function Grammar (LFG), or linear precedence rules which are statable as write-out constraints on syntactic types in Generalized Phrase Structure Grammar (GPSG) and Head Phrase Structure Grammar (HPSG).

In LFG the lexical entry explicitly specifies subject information.

bake, V, bake⟨(SUBJ)(OBJ)⟩

The realized verb form *bake* is associated with the predicate 'bake,' which has two thematic role slots realized as subject and object functions. An explicit subject representation is claimed to allow for the possibility of non-NP subjects (*In the cave dwells a dragon*), the assignment of case to the subject by the verb in languages like Icelandic, and a clear path for the assignment of thematic role to the subject by the verb.

A subject is also specified in the corresponding HPSG entry (see Fig. 1). This entry is a sign which includes both semantic information about the predicate 'bake' and its syntactic environment; NPs are explicitly

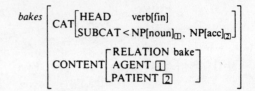

Figure 1. HPSG lexical entry for *bakes*.

linked to predicate-argument positions by structure-sharing tags (⏌, ⏋). The two NPs are in positions in the subcategorization list which correspond to subject and object function.

Redundancy in the lexicon is minimized by specifying a range of types or classes (of which the traditional 'transitive/intransitive' is a simple example) and assigning each individual predicate to a class. HPSG presupposes an elaborate cross-cutting type hierarchy which allows individual lexical entries to inherit features from several specified general types. This can be extended right down to inflected form, allowing *bakes* to be described as (or 'typed to') 'main & 3rdsing & transitive,' where each of these conjuncts is the name of a type with an appropriate internal structure. In principle, the use of type hierarchies as a representational device is available to any formal theory of grammar.

1. Variant Forms

1.1 Alternations

The treatment of valency alternations and changes such as active/passive, dative/double-object, causative/anticausative and completive/anticompletive (as with verbs like *spray/load*) varies substantially from theory to theory (see *Valency and Valency Grammar*). As was seen from the entry for *bake*, at least some of these, including active/passive, are treated by general syntax rules and principles in GB. By contrast, LFG and HPSG treat alternations in terms of operations on lexical entries; as Pollard and Sag (1987) note in the context of HPSG, such lexical rules are type-construction operations. One could thus view passives, and so on, as part of a potential lexicon available by a regular process from an actual lexicon of unmarked active forms.

1.2 Derived Forms

Because HPSG and LFG both eschew many of the specifically syntactical operations, rules and principles of GB such as movement and its concomitant traces, the proponents of the former pair are rather less concerned than GB theoreticians to establish the precise division of labor between a class of specifically lexical rules and those of 'general' syntax. GB theoreticians tend to talk of something being 'in the lexicon' if it is thought to require localist lexical rules which cannot be assimilated to more general structural syntactic principles. This concern is particularly apparent in discussions of the relationship between source and derived forms, e.g., the relationship between a verb and nouns derived from it.

Chomsky's influential 1970 paper *Remarks on Nominalization* highlighted the differences between gerunds and derived nominals in their relationship to their source verb/adjective.

(a) Mary manages the company.	*Source*	(1)
(b) Mary's management of the company.	*Derived nominal*	
(c) Mary's managing the company.	*Gerund*	

Whilst the gerund has a constant interpretation with respect to the source verb and is regularly produced from all of them by *-ing* suffixation, derived nominal forms may not be available, are constructed with a wide variety of suffixes, and may have varied (and not readily predictable) interpretations. The claim was that whilst gerundives might be derived by meaning-preserving syntax rules (transformations, in the theory of the time), derived nominals would require special lexical rules which permit shifts in meaning and may have limited productivity.

Consider, for example, affixation in *-er* to verbs, as in *bake → baker*. The noun form seems to inherit the argument structure of the verb in that it forms a compound where the nonhead corresponds to the object, or it forms a phrasal construction where the head noun takes the noun correlate of an object—an *of* PP:

(a) Alfred bakes cakes	(2)
(b) Alfred is [a baker of cakes]	
(c) Alfred is [a cake baker]	

Is the relationship between *cake* and *baker* to be handled with elements of the syntactic rule system which characterize the relationship between a verb and its object, or does one appeal to a special category of lexical rules to do the job? In the first case, the internal structure assigned to the compound might have to reflect structural requirements that hold between a verb and its arguments so that, for example, *bake* in the compound is able to govern *cake* in the sense of the term within GB. In the second case, it is still necessary to explain how it is that the compound or phrasal construction apparently inherits the thematic role corresponding to the verb argument, and how this thematic role structure is affected by the affixation process. Indeed, one might ask whether it is the affix or the abstract process it is involved in (Agentive Nominalization) that is responsible for the final properties of the derived form (see Spencer (1991) for an extensive review of this area).

Another morphological phenomenon with implications for the theory of the lexicon is blocking (Aronoff 1976). For example, whilst many adjectives in *-ous* form nouns in *-ity*, as with *audacious → audacity*, others such as *glorious* and *furious* do not—pre-sumably because their realization is blocked in some way by the prior availability of the lexicalized noun forms *glory* and *fury*. However, there is no such 'prior alternative' blocking of nouns derived by the highly productive *-ness* affixation—*gloriousness* and *furiousness* are both acceptable.

2. Semantics in the Lexicon

Thematic roles can be explicitly linked with grammatical functions, e.g., in LFG by stating in the entry that the SUBJ and OBJ functions of *bake* realize Agent and Patient respectively. Work in LFG attempts to capture subregularities in the relationship between functions and roles by linking lexically specified roles to appropriate functions by rules.

$$bake\langle\text{agent patient}\rangle$$
$$\quad\quad -\text{o} \quad\; -\text{r}$$

By default, the syntactic features $+/-$(o)bjective and $+/-$(r)estrictive are assigned to the roles in the lexical entry by general and/or parameterized rules, e.g., patient-like roles (including Theme) are assigned *-r*. Finally, a small set of additional rules ensures that the correct functions are assigned.

There are considerable difficulties in characterizing an adequate set of thematic roles. They may be reanalyzable in terms of Lexical Conceptual Structure (LCS), a new—or perhaps merely revived—level of lexical semantic description currently receiving considerable attention (see Jackendoff 1985). An LCS entry for *bake* in *bake a cake* might look thus:

CREATE[A, cake] FROM B BY BAKE(A, B)

Presumably a lexicon constructed with a developed LCS theory would assign each predicate to an LCS schema or schema class. Thematic roles (if still used) and subcategorization frames would be obtained by linking rules. Furthermore, the rich internal structure of LCS opens the possibility of an elaborate lexical semantics (see Pustejovsky 1991).

3. Meaning-Text Theory and the Explanatory/Combinatory Dictionary

Mel'cuk's Meaning-Text Model (cf. Mel'cuk 1988: ch. 2) attempts a comprehensive formal account of the relationship between a lexical semantic form and the set of its surface-syntax paraphrases. The Explanatory/Combinatory dictionary or ECD (Mel'cuk et al. 1984) is in part a realization of the lexicon for the Meaning-Text model. Amongst its many innovations, attention should be drawn in particular to its highly developed treatment of collocation and idiom phenomena. The ECD has been significantly (and deservedly) influential in the fields of Lexicography and Computational Linguistics.

Bibliography

Aronoff M 1976 *Word Formation in Generative Grammar.* MIT Press, Cambridge, MA

Bresnan J, Zaenen A 1990 Deep unaccusativity in LFG. *Proceedings of the Fifth Biannual Conference on Grammatical Relations*

Chomsky N 1970 Remarks on nominalization. In: Jacobs R A, Rosenbaum P S (eds.) *Readings in English Transformational Grammar.* Ginn, Waltham, MA

Gazdar G, Klein E, Pullum G, Sag I A 1985 *Generalized Phrase Structure Grammar.* Blackwell, Oxford

Jackendoff R 1985 *Semantics and Cognition.* MIT Press, Cambridge, MA

Jackendoff R 1987 The status of thematic relations in linguistic theory. *LIn* **18**(3): 369–411

Mel'cuk I 1988 *Dependency Syntax: Theory and Practice.* SUNY Press, New York

Mel'cuk I, Abatchewsky-Jumarie N, Elnitsky L, Iordanskaja L N, Lessard A 1984 *Dictionnaire explicatif et combinatoire du français contemporain. Recherches lexico–sémantiques*, 1. Les Presses de l'Université de Montréal, Montreal

Pollard C J, Sag I A 1987 *Information-based Syntax and Semantics*, vol. 1. CSLI Lecture Notes 13, CSLI, Stanford, CA

Pustejovsky J 1991 The generative lexicon. *CL* **17**(4): 409–41

Spencer A 1991 *Morphological Theory: An Introduction to Word Structure in Generative Grammar.* Blackwell, Oxford

Lexicon Grammar
Maurice Gross

Lexicon grammar is a model of syntax limited to the elementary sentences of a natural language. Its main theoretical features are presented here, mostly inferred from large-scale empirical studies aimed at obtaining a large coverage of French. French is the earliest application, but other studies, in varied lànguages, have also been performed (cf. Sect. 5).

1. Principles

The major principle is that the unit of meaning is not located at the level of the word, but at the level of elementary sentences; it will be seen how coherent descriptions of natural languages have been built on this basis. The point of departure was the construction of a transformational grammar of French (Gross 1968, 1975) based on Z. S. Harris's theoretical framework. Adding the requirement of providing a significant coverage of the language led to the development of an extensive list of transformations, and a lexicon of verbs (or elementary sentences) to which these transformations applied.

The intended program consisted in marking each verb (or sentence) with the transformations it underwent. This approach is necessary for obvious reasons, even though there has been little theoretical or practical discussion of the basic phenomena. Consider, for example, the traditional notion of transitive verb, or equivalently, the notion of a sentence with a direct object. Attempts to formalize it lead first to the basic structure: $N_0 V N_1$ of which examples are (1 and 2):

Bob enjoyed all his vacation. (1)

Bob rested all his vacation. (2)

The main notations are the following: in a sentence,

the noun phrases (*NP*s) are numbered from left to right starting with the subscript zero: N_0 is the subject, N_1 is the first complement, N_2 is the second complement, etc.

Both sentences (1) and (2) have a direct complement, but only (1) has a direct object. Transformational properties show (define) the difference (3–8):

Interrogative pronoun formation:

What did Bob enjoy? All his vacation (3)

*What did Bob rest? All his vacation (4)

Relative pronoun formation:

The vacation which Bob enjoyed (was lost time). (5)

*The vacation which Bob rested (was lost time). (6)

Passive formation:

All his vacation was enjoyed by Bob. (7)

*All his vacation was rested by Bob. (8)

Just one of these three properties is enough to discriminate (1) from (2) and hence could provide a basis for a syntactic definition of direct object. But the original intention of the notion of object seems to be also semantic, hence it usually associates meaning and form. Then a question arises: do these three syntactic properties coincide as in the case of *to enjoy*? Moreover, do they coincide with some semantic notion? In fact, if sentence (9) is considered:

Bob spent all his vacation sleeping. (9)

only two possibilities out of three observed are a priori relevant (10):

Relativization: All the vacation which Bob spent sleeping
(was lost time).
Passive: All Bob's vacation was spent sleeping.
(10)

and one impossibility (11):

wh-question: *What did Bob spend sleeping? (11)

Since there is no theoretical reason why the three 'properties' should coincide, they ought to be described independently of each other. Notice that relativization and *wh*-question could be correlated; for example, if a common basic pronoun (e.g., *something*) could be shown to be the source of both pronouns *what* and *which*. Such a hypothesis needs to be strengthened, which can only be done through a thorough examination of the verbs. There is no hint whatsoever that passive forms have a grammatical link to the other two properties.

Consider another example. In the notations used here, the nonoriented passive relation can be written (12):

$$N_0 V N_1 = N_1 \text{ be V-ed by } N_0. \qquad (12)$$

Now, it is largely assumed that the agent complement *by N_0* can be omitted, that is, the resulting structure N_1 *be V-ed* always corresponds to an acceptable sentence (13):

Bob briefed Max. (13)
Max was briefed by Bob.
Max was briefed.

However, there are paradigms, such as (14):

This assumption underlies Bob's whole discourse. (14)
Bob's whole discourse is underlied by this assumption.
*Bob's whole discourse is underlied.

Where omission of the *by*-agent is not possible. There is no way to detect and describe these patterns of relation, except by looking individually at each verb and marking them.

This situation is fairly general, given a structure $N_0 V W$, where W is a sequence of complements: the transformations that apply to this structure are found to be dependent on the choice of the verb V (hence on the complements W).

It is now possible to be more explicit about the form of a lexicon grammar. First, it describes the syntax of ordinary verbs, which means that it describes verbs in their minimal environment: subjects and essential complements. Separating essential from circumstantial complements is a classical question, for which the traditional answer is largely based on the shape of interrogative pronouns. Considering again examples (1) and (2), the following difference can be observed (15):

*When did Bob enjoy? All his vacation (15)
When did Bob rest? All his vacation

Upon examination of more than 10,000 verbs, deli-

neating a border between essential and circumstantial complements has proved to be a varied enterprise, more dependent on individual verbs than initially thought: tests for characterizing essential complements are highly lexical and tend to apply more to individual verbs or small groups than to broad semantic classes.

The choice of verbs (over 10,000) and of transformational properties (over 500) is an interdependent process performed by a team of linguists who have to carry out acceptability judgments on sentences, which included: (a) deciding whether several sentences had the same meaning or transformationally related meanings (e.g., for (1), (3), and (7) or for (2) and (9)); (b) deciding whether two sentences had unrelated meanings (e.g., (1) and (2)); (c) deciding whether a sentence form was acceptable or not (e.g., for (4), (6), (8)).

The linguistic activity aims: (a) at separating the meaning or uses of the morphological verbs; (b) at marking syntactic verbs (i.e., elementary sentences) for the properties they do or do not have.

A crucial requirement in such descriptive work is reproducibility of judgments. Only when a consensus was reached by the team of linguists, was a verb retained for study in the lexicon, and only when the evaluation of a syntactic shape could be reproduced by the team, was this syntactic shape retained as a property (a rule) of the grammar. Judgments are binary: a verb has or does not have a given property. This ideal representation cannot be reached directly. For example, it has been observed in written corpus that intuitions of acceptability underestimate the actual production of forms. The effect has been corrected by a rule of thumb: when acceptability is dubious, the form is considered acceptable.

More precisely, verbs, that is, elementary sentences of the form subject–verb–essential complements, are considered as elementary units for syntactic as well as for semantic composition. The set of elementary sentences is structured by Z. S. Harris's (1968) transformation rules, construed as equivalence relations between sentences.

2. Classification of Verbs

The principle of all classifications is formal, i.e., it is based on reproducible categories such as the traditional parts of speech. A rather simple example will be considered first: the classification of English frozen adverbial phrases. The categories PREP (preposition), DET (determiner), N (noun), ADJ (adjective) are used. The following types are distinguished (16):

PREP N, (16)
PREP DET N,
PREP DET N PREP N, etc.

which lead respectively to the construction of the corresponding tables (Tables 1–3).

Table 1.

Prep	N
above	all
by	chance
in	effect
for	example
in	fact

Table 2.

Prep	Det	N
at	this	point
in	this	respect
by	the	way
in	a	way
on	the	whole

Table 3.

Prep	Det	N	Prep	Nh	N-h	PDC
at	the	beginning	of	−	+	+
on	—	behalf	of	+	−	−
by	—	comparison	with	+	+	+
—	—	thanks	to	+	+	−
by	—	virtue	of	−	+	−

Table 4.

Structures	Examples	Numbers of entries
N_0 V	Guy flâne	450
N_0 V N_1	Max boit du vin	3,700
N_0 V à N_1	Luc pense à Jo	350
N_0 V de N_1	Guy rêve de trains	400
N_0 V Prép N_1	La mer compte pour Max	1,000
N_0 V N_1 N_2	On nomme Luc chef	60
N_0 V N_1 à N_2	Guy donne un lit à Max	900
N_0 V N_1 de N_2	Max reçoit un lit de Guy	1,300
N_0 V N_1 Prép N_2	Max pose le lit sur le sol	1,700
N_0 V à N_1 à N_2	Le lit sert à Luc à cela	5
N_0 V à N_1 de N_2	Le lit sert à Luc de bureau	10
N_0 V à N_1 Prép N_2	Ce texte équivaut à une insulte pour Jo	30
N_0 V Prép N_1 Prép N_2	Max s'allie avec Luc contre Guy	200

There are practically no examples with three objects; one candidate is the verb *parier* (to bet) in the sentence:

Jo a parié cent francs avec Luc que Max partirait.
(Jo bet one hundred francs with Luc that Max would leave.)

These last adverbial phrases are semifrozen: their first part PREP DET N PREP is fixed and listed in the table, whereas the remaining part is a variable noun phrase which is described by means of binary properties; its nouns can be '+' or '−' human (i.e., column Nh), or non-human (i.e., column N-h). The second part PREP N, can be omitted or not, depending on each expression, this possibility being indicated in the last column named PDC.

Other such tables have to be defined, in order to reach a complete coverage of this family of adverbial complements. For example, the table PAC would contain the structure (17):

PREP DET ADJ N = by the same token + in the long run + etc. (17)

It is now necessary to describe the classification of verbs, or rather of elementary sentences. The general approach to the construction of classes will be the same as in the preceding example.

All verbs have a subject N_0, but their sequence W of essential complements is quite variable. Thus, the examples of verbs discussed above have the following basic declarative structures (18):

N_0V = Bob rested. (18)

N_0VN_1 = Bob enjoyed his vacation.

N_0VN_1 (V^1-ing W)$_2$ = Bob spent his vacation sleeping.

The notation of the last structure is with a second complement subscripted $_2$ and made of a verbal struc-

ture whose subject is indicated by the superscript [1], that is N_1.

The classification is based on several parameters, the main ones being the number of complements and their shape. For French, it was necessary to consider first three basic shapes: direct (i.e., 'zero' preposition), indirect with prepositions *à* and *de*. It turns out that other prepositions (PREP) introduce few essential complements. Table 4 gives the typology on which the classification of French verbs has been made (Boons et al. 1976a, 1976b; Gross 1975; Guillet and Leclère 1991; Leclère 1990).

A second parameter of the classification is the content of the noun phrases N_i. Two types have been distinguished: (a) sentential, that is accepting one of the forms *que S* or *V-inf W* (infinitive clause), then, predicative nouns are also possible in general; (b) nonsentential, that is only nouns. This classification results in the distribution shown in Table 5, where the main structures are displayed with the corresponding number of verbs. The structures are more specific than in Table 4. They each define a syntactic class whose description is given in the form of a binary matrix (cf. Fig. 1).

Such a classification has to be completed by the properties that depend on individual verbs. This is done in a uniform way. Each row of the matrix is an entry of the lexicon grammar, that is, an elementary sentence in the declarative form defining a class (e.g., Table 5). Each column is a particular sentence shape, into which the verb may or may not enter. A plus or a minus sign is placed accordingly at the intersection

Table 5. The subclasses of elementary sentences with at least one sentential argument.

Table codes	Structures	Sizes
1	N_0 U Prép V_0 W	100
2	N_0 V V_0 W	150
3	N_0 V N_1 V_1 W	50
4	Qu P V N_1	650
5	Qu P V Prép N_1	180
	Il V Prép N_1 Qu P	
6	N_0 V Qu P	420
7	N_0 V à ce Qu P	170
8	N_0 V de ce Qu P	250
9	N_0V Qu P à N_2	360
10	N_0 V Qu P Prép N_2	150
11	N_0 V N_1 à ce Qu P	180
12	N_0 V Qu P	60
	N_0 V N_1 de V_1 W	
13	N_0 V N_1 de ce Qu P	150
14	N_0 V à ce Qu P Prép N_2	20
15	N_0 V de ce Qu P Prép N_2	80
16	No V Prép$_1$ N_1 Prép$_2$ ce Qu P	60
17	Il V Prép ce Qu P Prép N_2	20
18	N_0 V Prép N_1 Prép N_2 Prép Qu P	20
19	Qu P V N_1 Prép N_2	50
	Total	3,120

of the corresponding row and column. The main properties are:

(a) Distributional properties of *N*s, such as human or non-human. They are defined by means of interrogative pronouns. Consider the entry N_0 *influence* N_1. Both subject and complement are marked $+Nhum$, $+N\text{-}hum$, as the result of accepting the following sentences (19):

(What + Who) influences Bob?   (19)
(What + Who) does Max influence?

Columns containing the specifications $N_i = Nhum$, $N_i = N\text{-}hum$ correspond to sentence forms such as (20):

Who VN_1?, What do N_0V?   (20)

Hence, distributional properties are defined as sentence shapes.

(b) Transformational properties can be seen as sentence shapes associated with the declarative form that defines the class. Hence, the passive transformation is noted as accepted by a verb of the class N_0VN_1, when the matrix has a '+' sign in the column that contains the simple form (21):

N_1 be influenced by N_0.   (21)

The general description of verbs can then be visualized as a single matrix of 10,000 rows by 500 columns. There is considerable redundancy in this matrix: for example, when a verb is intransitive, marking '—' the properties of its objects carries no information. Hence, the classes allow a more tractable representation, by means of submatrices of a smaller size: they have an

average of 250 rows (verbs) and 25 columns. A sample of a class is given in Fig. 1.

3. Frozen Sentences

Frozen sentences (one could use alternatively the terminology 'compound verbs') include elementary sentences described from a variety of stylistic points of view, but all sharing one feature. They include verb–noun combinations which are not distributional, that is, not semantically predictable (22):

idioms:	Max took the bull by the horns.	(22)
metaphors:	Max burned his bridges.	
cliché:	The house burst into flames.	
technical:	Max integrated the function by parts.	

This nonreproducible classification is replaced by using distributional criteria. Consider, for example, the common sentence type (23):

N_0VN_1 Prep N_2.   (23)

In the same way as verbs were subclassified by separating them according to their acceptance of a sentential N_i, the sentences are described according to the position of the nouns frozen with respect to the verbs; note in passing C_i, the frozen nominal positions. It is then possible to write (24):

N_0VC_1 Prep C_2:	Max took the bull by the horns.	(24)
N_0VN_1 Prep C_2:	The news took Bob by surprise.	
N_0VC_1 Prep N_2:	Bob took part in the inquiry.	
C_0VC_1 Prep C_2:	Money burns a hole in Bob's pocket.	

The last example should be noted more precisely as follows (25):

C_0VC_1 Prep (N's C)$_2$ (25)

since a variable *human* noun N must be attached to the frozen head noun *pocket*. Table 6 gives the present state of the description of frozen sentences. (In general, the tables named **Cx** contain verbs different from the 'auxiliary' verbs *être* (to be), *avoir* (to have), *faire* (to make). These verbs are described in other tables named respectively **Ex** and **Ax** (Danlos 1980; Labelle 1974; Meunier 1977, 1981; Négroni-Peyre 1978; Vivès 1983), **Fx** (Giry-Schneider 1978, 1987). Also see Sect. 4.) The description of frozen sentences does not differ from the description of the free sentences discussed in Sect. 2. Figure 2 contains an example of a syntactic table which is to be read in the same way as Fig. 1. Frozen sequences appear explicitly.

4. Support Verbs

4.1 Nominalizations

The fundamental principle, according to which it is elementary sentences and not words that carry units of meaning, may be further justified. The frozen sentences are clearly a case of meaning not being located in individual words, but in whole sentences. That meaning is not compositional is obviously true for

247

Sujet			Auxiliaire avoir	Auxiliaire être	No être Upp W	No U		Compléments indirects																	
										Infinitives															
Nhum	Nnc							que P	que Psubj	Tp = Tc	Tc = "passé"	Tc = "présent"	Tc = "futur"	Vc = devoir	Vc = pouvoir	Vc = savoir	ppv	No U Prép N₁	Nhum	N-hum	ppv	dans N₁	No U N₁	Nhum	N-hum
+	-	négliger	+	-	-	-	de	-	-	+	-	-	-	-	-	-	-	-	-	-	-	-	-	-	-
+	-	oeuvrer	+	-	-	-	pour	-	+	-	-	-	+	-	-	+	-	+	-	+	-	-	-	-	-
+	-	s'offrir	-	+	-	-	de	-	-	-	+	+	+	-	-	-	-	-	-	-	-	-	+	-	+
+	-	omettre	+	-	-	-	de	-	-	+	-	-	-	-	-	-	-	-	-	-	-	-	-	-	-
+	-	opter	+	-	-	+	pour	-	+	-	-	-	+	-	-	+	-	+	-	+	-	-	-	-	-
+	-	oser	+	-	-	+	-	-	-	+	-	-	-	-	-	+	+	-	-	-	-	-	+	-	+
+	-	oublier	+	-	-	-	de	-	-	+	-	-	-	-	-	-	-	-	-	-	-	-	-	-	-
+	-	s'oublier	-	+	-	-	à	-	-	+	-	-	-	-	-	-	-	-	-	-	-	-	-	-	-
+	-	partir	-	+	-	-	à	-	-	+	-	-	-	-	-	-	-	-	-	-	-	-	-	-	-
+	+	partir	-	+	-	+	pour	-	+	-	-	-	+	+	-	+	-	+	-	+	-	-	-	-	-
+	-	passer	+	-	-	-	pour	-	-	-	+	+	-	+	+	+	-	+	+	+	-	-	-	-	-
+	-	en passer	-	+	-	-	par	-	-	+	-	-	-	-	-	-	-	+	+	+	-	-	-	-	-
+	-	pencher	+	-	-	-	pour	-	+	-	-	+	+	-	-	-	-	+	-	+	-	-	-	-	-
+	-	se permettre	-	+	-	-	de	-	-	-	+	+	+	-	-	+	-	-	-	-	-	-	+	-	+
+	-	persévérer	+	-	-	+	à	-	-	+	-	-	-	-	-	-	-	-	-	-	-	+	-	-	-
+	+	persister	+	-	-	+	à	-	-	+	-	-	-	-	-	-	-	-	-	-	-	+	-	-	-
+	+	pouvoir	+	-	-	-	-	-	-	+	+	+	+	+	+	+	+	-	-	-	-	-	-	-	-
+	-	pouvoir	+	-	-	-	-	-	-	+	-	-	-	-	-	-	-	+	-	-	-	-	-	-	-
+	-	pouvoir	+	-	-	-	-	-	-	-	+	-	-	-	-	-	-	+	-	-	-	-	-	-	-

Figure 1.

other categories of frozen or compound terms: (a) adverbs, such as *time and again*, *by and large*; (b) compound nouns, from the idiomatic *red herring* to technical terms such as *cathode ray tube* or *transgenic mouse*.

The category of frozen adjectives can also be defined for examples such as (26):

> Bob is well-to-do. (26)
> The decision is clear-cut.

It does not differ essentially from verbs.

Both of the major categories noun and adverb raise a question about the localization of meaning: these expressions do appear to contain their meaning, hence the basic assumption would not hold for them. There are however reasons to describe them as elementary sentences.

Consider the relation of nominalization as defined by Z. S. Harris (1964), as a relation between sentences, not between a sentence and a noun phrase; as in, for example, (27 and 28):

> (27)=(28)   This proposal contradicts your ideas. (27)
>
> This proposal is in contradiction with (28) your ideas.

This pair may be considered similar to the pair active–passive: the verb has become a noun (in the passive it becomes adjective-like), the preposition *with* has been introduced (*by* in the passive form), and an auxiliary verb *to be in* has been inserted *to be* in the passive). Hence Passive and this rule of Nominalization differ formally only by the fact that word order is not affected in this nominalization. In other nominalizations, the word order can change (29):

> That Jo left satisfied Bob. (29)
>
> (29)=(30)   Bob had the satisfaction that Jo left. (30)

Another example is adjective nominalization (31 and 32):

> (31)=(32)   This office is convenient. (31)
>
> This office has a certain convenience. (32)

Since it is not oriented, the relation (31)=(32) could also be called Adjectivization of a noun, and one can look at Passive forms as adjectivized verbs. The auxiliary verbs *to be* (*in, into*), *to have* may be called support verbs. Support verbs may have variants such as in (33–36):

> (27)=(33)   This proposal (comes in+remains (33) in+stays in+enters into) contradiction with your ideas.

Table 6.

Table codes	Structures	Examples	Sizes
C1	N_0 V C_1	Il a loupé le coche	4,450
CAN	N_0 V (C à = de N)$_1$	Cela a délié la langue de Max (lui)	810
CDN	N_0 V (C de N)$_1$	Il bat le rappel de ses amis	610
CP1	N_0 V Prép C_1	Il charrie dans les bégonias	1,850
CPN	N_0 V Prép (C de N)$_1$	Il abonde dans le sens de Max	320
C1PN	N_0 V C_1 Prép N_2	Il a déchargé sa bile sur Max	2,010
CNP2	N_0 V N_1 Prép C_2	Ils ont passé Max par les armes	1,610
C1P2	N_0 V C_1 Prép C_2	Il met de l'eau dans son vin	1,040
CPP	N_0 V Prép C_1 Prép C_2	Il tape du poing sur la table	210
CPPN	N_0 V C_1 Prép C_2 Prép C_3	Il se met le doigt dans l'œbil jusqu'au coude	370
C5	Que P V Prép C_1	Que Max reste milite en sa faveur	170
C6	N_0 V Qu P Prép C_2	Il a pris du bon côté que Max reste	300
C7	N_0 V C_1 à ce Qu P	Il a dit non à ce que Max reste	140
C8	N_0 V C_1 de ce Qu P	Il se mord les doigts de ce qu'il est resté	290
CPQ	N_0 V C_1 Prép ce Qu P	Il partira à temps pour voir Luc	330
CPPQ	N_0 V C_1 Prép C_2 Prép ce Qu P	Il rend grâce au ciel de ce qu'il a réussi	210
CADV	N_0 V Adv	Cela ne pisse pas loin	350
CV	N_0 V (Prép) VW	Il est parti sans laisser d'adresse	450
C0	C_0 V W	La moutarde monte au nez de Max	1,320
C0Q	C_0 V Prép N Qu P	Peu lui importe s'il part	300
C0E	(V + X) W	Minute papillon!	1,100
A1	N_0 avoir C_1	Il a eu le mot de la fin	280
A1PN	N_0 avoir C_1 Prép N_2	Il a barre sur Max	110
ANP2	N_0 avoir N_1 Prép C_2	Il a Max en horreur	90
A12	N_0 avoir C_1 Adj$_2$	Il a la vue basse	110
A1P2	N_0 avoir C_1 Prép C^2	Il a mal aux cheveux	340
E01	C_0 de N extre Adj	La barbe de Max est fleurie	830
E0P1	C_0 être Prép C_1	Le temps est à la pluie	340
		Total	20,340

= (34) There is a contradiction between this proposal and your ideas. (34)

(31) = (35) This office (retains + keeps) a certain convenience. (35)

= (36) This office lost its convenience. (36)

where the support verbs *to enter, to keep, to lose* are not semantically minimal: they carry aspect or other modalities. More complex examples are (37 and 38):

Her remark puts this proposal in contradiction with your ideas. (37)

Jo's appointment gave some convenience to this office. (38)

and *to put, to give* (together with their causative or agentive subject) are called operator verbs on sentences with support verbs. Since operator verbs apply to elementary sentences, they leave invariant the relations holding in the original sentence: (37) and (38) contain respectively (32) and (34), in some sense. In the same way, by applying the 'causative' operator $N_0 put$ to the sentence (39):

The child is at Bob's mercy. (39)

where various relations hold between *mercy, child,* and *Bob,* one obtains (40):

The accident put the child at Bob's mercy. (40)

an outcome that contains all the relations of (39). Other operators introduce new relations. For example, the binding operators $N_0(have + keep)$, also applied to (38), lead to (41):

Bob (has + keeps) the child at his mercy. (41)

where the subject of *have, keep,* must be bound to *his* (42):

*Bob (has + keeps) the child at your mercy. (42)

The syntactic study of relations between the various parts of elementary sentences has not been much developed so far. Lexical decompositions such as those of generative semantics are such attempts. But one is dealing here with a quite general problem that may go beyond the study of operator verbs as exemplified above. The following examples show that the overall syntactic structure does not reflect the basic relations observed between parts of elementary sentences (43):

Bob attributed the crime to Max. (43)
Bob confessed the crime to Max.
Bob described the crime to Max.

Max is the subject of *crime* with *to attribute; Bob* is

Sujet			Compl. dir.				Complément figé			
Nhum	*N-hum*		*Passif*	*Nhum*	*N-hum*	*N₀VN₁*			*N spc*	
+	+	noyer	+	+	+	+	sous	un	-	flot de détails
+	-	noyer	+	+	-	-	sous	certaines	-	paroles
+	-	noyer	+	-	+	-	dans	le	+	sang
+	-	occuper	+	+	+	+	-	-	-	militairement
+	+	offrir	+	+	-	-	à	les	-	coups de "Nhum"
+	-	offrir	+	+	+	-	en	-	-	holocauste
+	+	offrir	+	+	+	-	à	le	-	regard de "Nhum"
+	+	offrir	+	+	+	-	à	la	-	vue de "Nhum"
+	+	offrir	+	+	+	-	à	les	+	yeux de "Nhum"
+	-	ordonner	+	+	-	+	-	-	-	prêtre
+	+	orienter	+	-	+	-	à	la	-	baisse
+	+	orienter	+	-	+	-	à	la	-	hausse
+	+	ôter	+	+	-	-	de	un	-	doute
+	-	ôter	+	-	+	-	de	les	+	mains de "Nhum"
+	-	ôter	+	+	+	-	de	la	-	vue de "Nhum"
+	+	n' oublier pas	+	-	+	+	dans	Poss-0	-	pensées
+	+	ouvrir	+	-	+	+	à	la	-	circulation
-	+	ouvrir	+	+	+	-	à	le	-	monde de "N-hum"
+	+	ouvrir	+	-	+	+	à	la	-	navigation

Figure 2.

the subject with *to confess*; *Max* and *Bob* have no relation to the *crime* with *to describe*. Notice that other lexical items and syntactic structures may be used to express the same relations, such as (44):

> Bob accused Max of the crime. (44)
> Bob informed Max of the crime.

Support and operator verbs are quite different from ordinary verbs. They do not select their subjects and objects in the way ordinary verbs do; thus, it is clear that in (28) and (33), *proposal* is not selected by *to come* or *to enter*, but by the noun *contradiction*; and the same is true for *to have*, *to keep*, *to lose* in (32), (35), and (36), where it is *convenience* that selects the subject *office*. Second, the complement structure of support and operator verbs is different. Consider, for example, the sentences (45–47):

> Bob opposed John's scheme. (45)
>
> (45)=(46) Bob took opposition to John's scheme. (46)
>
> =(47) Bob discussed opposition to John's scheme. (47)

(46) is a nominalized form of (28) with support verb *to take*; (45) contains an ordinary verb; (47) has a very different nature, although its structure is identical to the structure of (46). Semantically (45) and (46) are synonymous, while in (47) *Bob* is not the subject of

opposition. In fact, although the sequences *opposition to John's scheme* appear to be identical in (46) and (47), differences are observed with respect to extractions (48 and 49):

> It is to John's scheme that Bob took opposition. (48)
> *It is to John's scheme that Bob discussed opposition.

> Opposition was taken to John's scheme. (49)
> *Opposition was discussed to John's scheme.

4.2 Stand-alone Nouns

Support and operator verbs also apply to stand-alone nouns, that is, they are not only auxiliaries in nominalization relations. The following pair involves a nominalization relation (50 and 51):

> Bob (murdered + assassinated) someone. (50)
>
> (50)=(51) Bob committed (a murder + an assassination). (51)

where the support verb is *to commit*. The following sentence (52):

> Bob committed a crime. (52)

has exactly the same properties as the nominalized forms, but *crime* has no corresponding verb. *Crime* is called a stand-alone noun, with respect to nominalization of verbs. Notice that (52) is to be related to another nominal sentence with support verb 'to be' (53):

> Bob is a criminal. (53)

In sentences such as (54 and 55):

> Bob's proposal is at variance with (54)
> John's scheme.
> Bob (is + goes) at war against John's scheme.
>
> Bob is under pressure. (55)
> (54) = (55) Jo's arrival put Bob under pressure.

the same properties of the verbs can be observed, that is, they are support verbs, and the nouns *variance*, *war*, and *pressure* are not (any longer) related to verbs similar in form (*to vary*, *to press*, *to pressurize*). This observation is crucial from a theoretical point of view, since it provides a sentential framework for the description of nouns. It has been argued that it is a necessary form of description for various reasons:

(a) Noun complementation which includes shape of prepositions and distribution of their noun arguments is defined at the level of support verbs. When a complex noun phrase is combined with an ordinary verb, as in (47), its properties are derived by systematic rules from the elementary structure with support verb, not from the verbal structure.

(b) Nominalizations, as they have been extended, increase the syntactic coverage of equivalence classes of elementary sentences, hence extending the syntactic variety that hides the meaning of sentences. Such equivalence classes provide a new approach to derivational morphology: words will enter a morphological family only if they occur in sentences related by relations of nominalizations and adjectivizations.

(c) Various frozen (idiomatic) forms can only be related by support or operator verbs (56–60):

> This story has neither head or (56)
> tail.
>
> (56) = (57) The story is without head or tail. (57)
>
> (57) = (58) Bob cannot make head or tail of (58)
> this story.
>
> This story broke Bob's heart. (59)
>
> (59) = (60) This story was heart-breaking to (60)
> Bob.

It is interesting to observe that ambiguous nouns have different support verbs for each of their meanings: consider the noun *order* in the following sentences (61–68):

> The room is in order. (61)
>
> For Bob to leave at 2 pm is in order. (62)
>
> Bob (is in + took) orders. (63)

> The machine (is in running + out of) order. (64)
>
> The books have a certain order on these shelves. (65)
>
> The police kept order. (66)
>
> Bob gave Max a clear order. (67)
>
> Bob placed an order for books with Max. (68)

Furthermore, the noun *order* appears in other forms with other functions and meanings:

(a) determiner in: (*of* + *on*) *the order of one thousand*;
(b) adverbial in: *till further orders*;
(c) subordinating conjunction in: *in order* (*that he* + *to*) *succeed*; and
(d) in many compound terms such as frozen sentences: *Bob called Max to order, Bob makes shirts to order, Pay to the order of BMC*...; compound nouns: *alphabetical order, lexicographic order, order of magnitude, law and order*, etc., some of which combine with support verbs.

All the meanings of *order* are different, but placing *order* in an elementary sentence with a support verb or in other characteristic contexts eliminates ambiguities.

It may be remarked that a seemingly simple rule such as plural formation can be shown to have been overlooked in numerous cases. Consider the plural of *order*: in sentences (61), (62), (64), and (66), 'order' has no plural, in (63) it has obligatory plural, in (65), (67), and (68) it may have the plural *orders*. Such cases of syntactic plurals of nouns are quite numerous, and they are described in a natural way at the syntactic level where they co-occur with support verbs.

From an empirical point of view, selecting or discovering the (main) support verb of a given noun has proved possible and reproducible for most abstract nouns (i.e., predicative, relational, etc.). The question does not seem to be relevant to concrete nouns, at least in the same sense.

4.3 Other Nouns

The problem of the integration of concrete nouns in a lexicon grammar has already been mentioned. The difficulty is in the choice of a support verb. Whereas with abstract nouns, a basic support verb imposes itself most of the time, with concrete nouns there are too many candidates. Given the noun *chair*, the question is whether it should be introduced through classificatory sentences such as (69):

> A chair is a seat. (69)
> A seat is a piece of furniture.
> A chair is a piece of furniture.

or whether a physical description of a chair made in terms of elementary sentences should be considered (70):

> A chair has a back. (70)
> A chair has four legs, etc.

or a functional description (71):

Table 7.

NA	N Adj	cordon bleu	48,000
NDN	N de N	pomme de pin	28,000
NAN	N à N	ver à soie	2,500
AN	Adj N	fin gourmet	1,500
PN	Prép N	à-côté	500
VN	VN	lave-glace	1,000
NN	N N	télé-couleur	2,300
NAV	N à V	bon à tirer	200
etc.			

A person sits on a chair, etc. (71)

or whether one should enter all this encyclopedic knowledge in the lexicon grammar at all. These difficulties do not differ essentially from traditional semantic questions about synonymy, hyperonymy, etc., except that they take on a different form when they are stated in terms of elementary sentences rather than in terms of words. For example, the synonymy of words has to be relativized as soon as the words are presented in sentences: semantic relations (e.g., synonymy between two nouns) are not discussed outside of elementary sentences where they occur, hence only relations between words embedded into a given set of elementary sentences are considered, hence sentences such as the following are compared, in order to make explicit the situations in which both nouns *chair* and *seat* are synonymous (72):

Take a chair! (72)
Take a seat!

One sits on a chair.
One sits on a seat.
One sits on a piece of furniture.

There are five hundred seats in this concert hall.
There are five hundred chairs in this concert hall.

Bob put the chairs around the table.
Bob put the seats around the table.

A lexicon of compound nouns has been built (G. Gross 1988; Silberztein 1993). This lexicon has been classified according to the internal constitution of the nouns, as shown in Table 7.

The intended coverage of this lexicon is of the order of magnitude of 300,000 entries, which would give it the same level of coverage as the one reached for the electronic lexicon DELA of simple words that has already been built (Courtois 1989, 1990). Among compound nouns, there are abstract nouns such as *first degree murder*, *economic future* which will have to be described with their support verbs in the lexicon grammar (73):

N_0 commits a first degree murder. (73)
N_0 has a certain economic future.

There are also numerous concrete nouns including technical terms: *boat basin, electron microscope, resolving power, light-collecting mirror, short range nuclear*

missile. More complex compound nouns have also been classified according to their internal structure.

The DELA dictionary of simple words contains 80,000 word forms as entries. Information about inflexions is associated to each of them, which allows for automatic generation of over 700,000 inflected forms together with the corresponding grammatical properties (Courtois 1990) and a phonemic representation (Laporte 1988). This dictionary is intended to serve as an access key to the lexicon grammar and to the dictionary of compound nouns: given a word found in a text, a look-up program extracts the different entries corresponding to this word and the lexical and syntactic properties attached to each of the entries. Then, an analyzer can determine the (single) solution present in the text by exploring the context of the word. This system has various applications to automatic processing of texts (from spelling-error correction to the more ambitious mechanical translation). The coverage of the DELA dictionary system is comparable to that of current dictionaries, which are incomplete in various respects:

(a) Proper names are missing, and also their derived forms (verbs, nouns, adjectives: *to russify, russification*, etc.).

(b) Many forms derived from common dictionary entries are absent from all dictionaries, because they are easy to interpret when the canonical entry is known: this is the case for the word *unrecommercializability*, well formed and easy to interpret by means of the entry *to commercialize*, the prefixes re-, un-, and the suffixes -able, -ability. These gaps are to be filled at the level of the lexicon grammar, by adding new properties according to derivations such as (74):

Passive sentence with modal:	This product can be commercialized by our firm.	(74)
Adjectivization:	This product is commercializable by our firm.	
Prefixation from negation:	This product is uncommercializable by our firm.	
Nominalization:	This product has a certain commercializability by our firm.	

where each of these sentence forms constitutes a column of the lexicon grammar. This is another example (cf. Sect. 4.2) of the syntactic treatment of derivational morphology.

4.4 Adverbs

Z. S. Harris (1968) has proposed the following scheme of derivation for various adverbs, circumstantial complements, and most subordinate clauses (75):

That Bob left occurred yesterday. = Bob left yesterday. (75)

Table 8.

Table codes	Structures	Examples	Sizes
PADV	Adv	soudain	520
PC	Prép C	en bref	590
PDETC	Prép Det C	contre toute attente	750
PAC	Prép Adj C	de sa belle mort	670
PCA	Prép C Adj	à gorge déployée	710
PCDC	Prép C de C	en désespoir de cause	620
PCPC	Prép C Prép C	des pieds à la teκte	240
PCONJ	Prép C Conj C	en tout et pour tout	290
PCDN	Prép C de N	aʼu moyen de N	450
PCPN	Prép C Prép N	par rapport à N	140
PV	Prép V W	à dire vrai	240
PF	P (phrase figée)	Dieu seul le sait	360
PECO	(Adj) comme C	comme ses pieds	300
PVCO	(V) comme C	comme un cheveu sur la soupe	330
PPCO	(V) comme Prép C	comme dans du beurre	40
PJC	Conj C	et tout le tremblement	150
		Total	6,400

The sentential subject contains an elementary sentence, that is, with no adverb of time or of place, and the verb is a support verb for adverbs, belonging to a small class (*to take place, to happen*, etc.). Hence, certain families of adverbs (of time and place) are going to be described as elementary sentences of the form (76):

> That S Vsup Adverb. (76)

that can be naturally entered into the lexicon grammar of the language. For other adverbs, the derivation can take a different form, but the principle is the same (78 and 79):

> That Bob entered the smoky room (78)
> was courageous (of him + on his part).

> (78) = (79) Bob entered the smoky room (79)
> courageously.

where the pronoun or the possessive adjective *his* must refer to *Bob* and is the subject of *courageous*. This constraint does not hold in the following otherwise similar relation (80 and 81):

> That Bob entered the smoky room was (80)
> unfortunate.

> (80) = (81) Unfortunately Bob entered the smoky (81)
> room.

Adverbs or more generally nonobject complements have been little studied, and their relations to elementary sentences are far from being understood (for French, cf. Gross 1990). As is often the case, frozen forms can be quite revealing about the nature of relations which can be hidden under apparently regular structures. The following description of frozen and compound adverbs was undertaken, and resulted in the classification given in Table 8.

Although this study is primarily about the internal constitution of adverbial phrases, some relations with the sentences where they occur have been studied; for example, coreference relation such as in the examples (82):

> Bob is an active person, in his way. (82)
> In his madness, Bob hurt Jo badly.

where adverbs have a status different from those in the following pair, where changes of level occur:

> Bob told Max in all honesty that he should (83)
> apologize to Jo.
> In all honesty, Max should apologize to Jo.

Other detailed studies have been made in the framework of lexicon grammar: of time adverbials (Maurel 1988), of manner adverbials (Molinier 1982), of subordinating conjunctions (Piot 1978), but many more are needed in order to get a comprehensive picture of the phrases that have been called circumstantial complements; they are much more varied than the classification based on the half dozen *wh*-interrogative pronouns might lead one to believe.

5. Results and Discussion

The lexicon grammar is stored in a computer database and maintained on a regular basis: new properties are added, and new entries are still introduced, mainly so-called 'metaphors' or figurative meanings of already existing sentences. One tends to consider a proper and a figurative meaning of a given word as unrelated, except at some etymological level.

Given an entry, the '+' signs that appear in the corresponding row (cf. Fig. 1) provide a syntactic paradigm of the entry. The following question can be asked. How many of these paradigms can be found in the lexicon grammar? For the 10,000 verbs, the answer is 8,000. Hence, there are few verbs which have the same set of constructions. Even more, when deri-

vational properties are added, then no two verbs have the same syntactic paradigm. This observation can be seen as an a posteriori justification of the lexicon grammar: every verb has to be described on an individual basis.

The compilers have proposed a number of criteria to separate objects from other complements (mainly adverbial). As a consequence, they observed that ordinary verbs practically never had three objects. Verbs with two objects often have a relation between both objects or between the subject and one of the objects (cf. Sect. 4.1). With frozen sentences, where one complement (possibly an adverb) is often frozen with the verb, they record more entries with three complements, but they are still exceptional, or at any rate much less numerous. For example, in the sentences (84):

> Bob used (the cold)₁ as (a pretext)₂ (for leaving (84) early)₃.
> The cold provides (Bob)₁ with (a pretext + an excuse)₂ (for leaving early)₃.

the three complements are obligatory. They have no explanation for this numerical limitation, nor for another fact they observed, that verbs with two prepositional complements are rare (cf. Table 1). They consider such data important, since they have direct structural implications for sentences.

The compilers would like to insist on the fact that in the lexicon, there are many more sentences containing a verbal expression, that is, which are frozen (i.e., noncompositional), than sentences containing an ordinary verb (i.e., compositional). This should come as a surprise, unless the sentences thought to be compositional turned out to be less so, as further studies tend to show; then truly compositional constructions would be quite rare.

The lexicon grammar framework together with the requirement of substantial coverage leads to a uniform and consistent description of elementary sentences. Many features have been shown to be lexical, for example, the choice of the determiners and modifiers of the subject or object of a verb can be lexical, whether with ordinary or support verbs; compare (85 and 86):

> Bob is building a palace. = Bob is building a future palace.
> Bob is selling a palace. = Bob is selling a future palace. (85)

> *Bob has (a + the) courage. (86)
> Bob has (a + the) courage we are all missing.

Also, the distribution of adverbials appears to obey rules of co-occurrence with sentences. As a consequence, the grammar of complex sentences may be quite different from what has been proposed so far. For example, S.-Y. Kuroda (1968) has shown the existence of complex dependencies between determiners and relative clauses; such phenomena could be more general and more complex, that is, more lexical. Thus, lexicon grammar may have to be extended to nonelementary sentences, as is already the case for frozen complex sentences (M. Gross 1988).

Some of the phenomena mentioned may be language dependent. For example, in English, verb–particle combinations seem to correspond to verb–adverb combinations in French, but too little is yet known about such phenomena to draw any conclusion. One of the main advantages of lexicon grammar is that it allows comparisons between languages both at the lexical and the syntactic levels. In fact, large segments of lexicon grammars have already been built, for Italian (Elia 1984; Elia et al. 1981), for Portuguese (Ranchhod 1990; Maceido-Oliveira 1984), and for Spanish (Lamiroy 1983; Pellat-Masso 1990; Subirats-Ruddeberg 1987) which allows for comparisons of Romance languages.

Many classes of constructions have also been described for English (Freckleton 1985; Machonis 1988; Salkoff 1983), for German (Caroli 1984; Treig 1977), for Arabic (Chad 1988; El Hannach 1988), and for Korean (Hong 1984).

All this work confirms the possibility of constructing lexicon grammars of varied languages in a comparable way.

As mentioned above, the evolution of lexicon grammar is toward increased structure, because derivational properties are being added. As a consequence, there is a tendency to use roots of words as entries. In fact, this is a tendency to render descriptions more abstract: parts of speech become equivalent and thus lose significance inside a dictionary article. It is one of the features that make feasible comparisons between languages.

6. Local Grammars

Local grammars constitute a generalization of the lexical entries discussed above. Their introduction is motivated by a variety of phenomena that can all be termed 'description of the variant forms of a given utterance.' The same formal device is used to represent families of utterances: finite automata (Gross and Per-

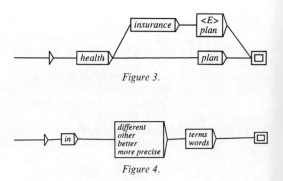

Figure 3.

Figure 4.

rin 1989), and, quite often, the restricted version of finite automata without cycles (i.e., either directed acyclic graphs or DAGs).

Consider the compound noun *health insurance plan.* In most contexts where it is used, it can be replaced by one of the abbreviations *health insurance* or *health plan.* A way of representing the three equivalent forms is by means of the graph of Fig. 3, where each path starting from the leftmost arrow (initial state) and ending in the rightmost square (final state) corresponds to an utterance. Such a graph can be automatically translated into a parser that locates in a text all the member strings, and that states their equivalence. The equivalence classes one can represent in

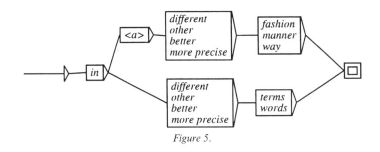

Figure 5.

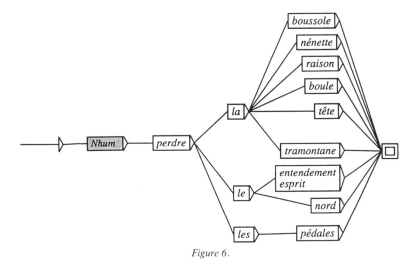

Figure 6.

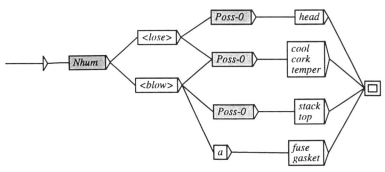

Figure 7.

255

this way are quite varied. For example, one might decide to represent a semantic family of adverbial phrases such as those of Fig. 4. This small class can then be generalized to a few more adverbials of the same kind, such as those of Fig. 5.

Such graphs are the natural extension of the entries of compound words discussed in Sects. 4.3 and 4.4. The name of the graph becomes itself an entry of a dictionary of graphs, it holds for a set of 'lexical entries.' In many cases, graphs reduce the redundancy of the description and avoid the introduction of a large number of entries closely resembling each other, but entered as independent of each other, unless some system of cross reference is set up to link entries. The same approach has been applied to elementary sentences, and in particular, to frozen sentences that often have lexical variants. Consider the graph of Fig. 6, which represents variants of the idiomatic sentence *Bob a perdu la tête* (Bob lost his head).

From a formal point of view, all these sentences are cognate: they all have a free human subject (*Nhum*), they share the same verb *perdre*, they all have one complement formed of a noun preceded by the definite article (*le*, *la*, *les*), they differ only by the noun, which ranges over an unpredictible set of nouns. These nouns arose through anecdotal proposals, at various periods of time, at different levels of expression (literary or popular). Hence, the decision to include all these sen-

tences into one single equivalence class is a generalization of the procedure used when deciding whether two sentences are related by a formal transformation. A combination of semantic and formal criteria come into play. Figure 7 presents the equivalent graph for English, and it can be seen that the simple factorization that was available in the French case is not possible here. Instead of limiting the class by means of syntactic criteria (both in the French and the English examples), meaning could have been relied upon totally. Other more or less synonymous sentences, with other syntactic structures, could then have been added to the graph as in Fig. 8.

This approach can be generalized to the description of elementary sentences whose vocabulary is restricted, for example to a given technical field. Figure 9 shows a class of sentences that express the variations of an index of the Stock Exchange.

So far, a few thousand graphs have been built. The estimate is that a large number of them will be necessary for the representation of nouns corresponding to technical terms. Many others will be necessary to describe frozen sentences, and it is difficult to foresee the limits of applications, since the phenomenon of sentences with restricted vocabulary appears to be so general that it could well extend to most, if not all, of the lexicon grammar of free sentences (Roche 1993).

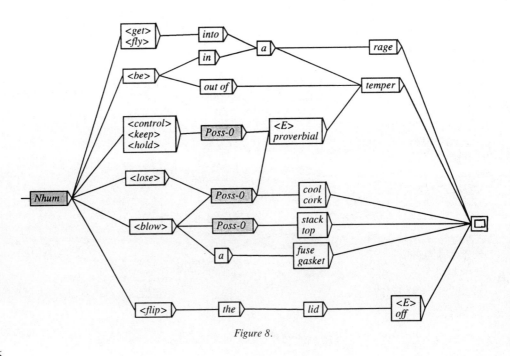

Figure 8.

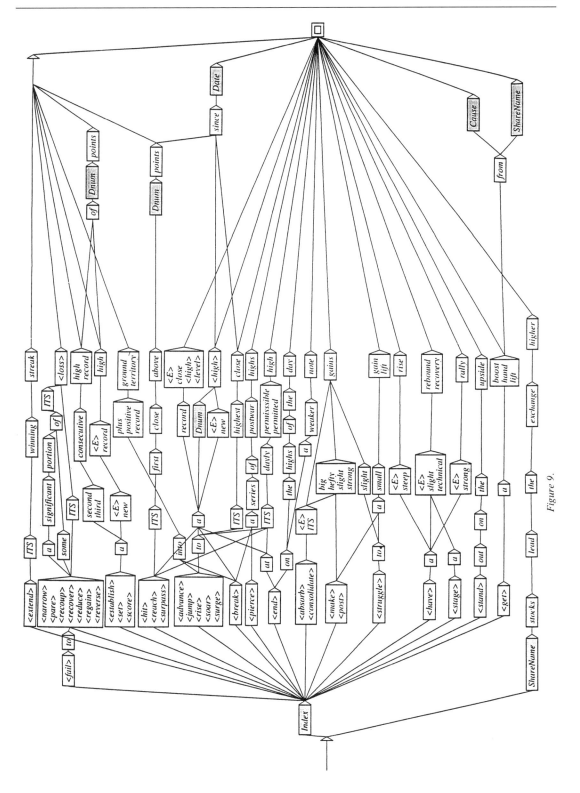

Figure 9.

257

Bibliography

Boons J-P, Guillet A, Leclère C 1976a *La structure des phrases simples en français, I Constructions intransitives.* Droz Geneva

Boons J-P, Guillet A, Leclère C 1976b *La structure des phrases simples en français, II Constructions transitives.* LADL, Paris (Rapport de recherches du LADL, No 6)

Caroli F 1984 Les verbes transitifs à complément de lieu en allemand. *Lingvisticae Investigationes* **8(2)**: 225–67

Chad M 1988 Système verbal arabe. Régime des constructions transitives (Unpublished PhD thesis, University of Paris)

Courtois B 1989–90 *Dictionnaire électronique du LADL pour les mots simples du français.* DELAS V06/2. LADL, Paris (Rapport technique du LADL, No 20)

Courtois B 1990 Un système de dictionnaires électroniques pour les mots simples du français. *LFr* **87**: 11–22

Courtois B, Silberztein M (eds.) 1990 Dictionnaires électroniques du français. *LFr* **87**

Danlos L 1980 Représentation d'informations linguistiques: les constructions être Prép X (Unpublished PhD thesis, University of Paris)

El Hannach M 1988 Syntaxe des verbes psychologiques de l'arabe (Unpublished PhD thesis, University of Paris)

Elia A 1984 *Le verbe italien, les complétives dans les phrases à un complément.* Schena-Nizet, Bari-Paris

Elia A, D'Agostino E, Martinelli M 1981 *Lessico e strutture sintattiche. Introduzione alla sintassi del verbo italiano.* Liguori, Naples

Freckleton P 1985 Une comparaison des expressions de l'anglais et du français (Unpublished PhD thesis, University of Paris)

Giry-Schneider J 1978 *Les nominalisations en français. L'opérateur* FAIRE *dans le lexique.* Droz, Geneva

Giry-Schneider J 1987 *Etude de prédicats nominaux en français. Les constructions faire N.* Droz, Geneva

Gross G 1988 Degré de figement des noms composés. *Langages* **90**: 57–72

Gross G 1989 *Les constructions converses du français.* Droz, Geneva

Gross M 1968 *Grammaire transformationnelle du français. 1– Syntaxe du verbe.* Cantilène, Paris

Gross M 1975 *Méthodes en syntaxe.* Hermann, Paris

Gross M 1981 Les bases empiriques de la notion de prédicat sémantique. *Langages* **63**: 7–52

Gross M 1982 Une classification des phrases figées du français. *RQLTA* **11(2)**: 151–85

Gross M 1988 In: Gross G, Piot M (eds.) *Syntaxe des connecteurs.* *LFr* **77**: 151–85

Gross M 1990 *Grammaire transformationnelle du français. 3– Syntaxe de l'adverbe.* ASSTRIL, Paris

Gross M, Perrin D (eds.) 1989 *Electronic Dictionaries and Automata in Computational Linguistics.* Springer, Berlin

Guillet A, Leclère C 1991 *La structure des phrases simples en français. Verbes à complément direct et complément locatif.* Droz, Geneva

Harris Z S 1952 Discourse analysis. *Lg* **28**: 1–30

Harris Z S 1964 Elementary transformations. In: 1970 *Papers in Structural and Transformational Linguistics.* Reidel, Dordrecht

Harris Z S 1968 *Mathematical Structures of Language.* Wiley, New York

Hong C 1984 La classe des verbes de mouvement en coréen contemporain. *Lingvisticae Investigationes Supplementa.*

Kuroda S-Y 1968 English relativization and certain related problems. *Lg* **44**: 2

Labelle J 1974 Etude de constructions avec opérateur AVOIR (nominalisations et extensions) (Unpublished PhD thesis, University of Paris)

Lamiroy B 1983 Les verbes de mouvement en français et en espagnol. Etude de syntaxe comparée de leurs infinitives. *Lingvisticae Investigationes Supplementa*

Laporte E 1988 Méthodes algorithmiques et lexicales de phonétisation du français (Unpublished PhD thesis, University of Paris)

Leclère C 1990 Organisation du lexique-grammaire des verbes français. *LFr* **87**

Maceido-Oliveira E 1984 *Syntaxe des verbes psychologiques du portugais.* Instituto Nacional de Investigação Científica, Centro de Lingüística da Universidade de Lisboa, Lisbon

Machonis A P 1988 Support verbs: An analysis of *be Prep X* idioms. *The* SECOL *Review* **12(2)**: 95–125

Maurel D 1988 Grammaire des dates. Etude préliminaire à leur traitement automatique. *Lingvisticae Investigationes* **12(1)**: 101–28

Meunier A 1977 Sur les bases syntaxiques de la morphologie dérivationnelle. *Lingvisticae Investigationes* **1(2)**: 287–332

Meunier A 1981 Nominalisation d'adjectifs par verbes supports (Unpublished PhD thesis, University of Paris)

Molinier C 1982 Etude syntaxique et sémantique des adverbes en *-ment* (Unpublished PhD thesis, University of Toulouse–Le Mirail)

Négroni-Peyre D de 1978 Nominalisation par *être en* et réflexivation (*admiration, opposition, révolte et rage*). *Lingvisticae Investigationes* **2(1)**: 127–64

Pellat-Masso L 1990 Une description formelle des expressions figées de l'espagnol. *Mémoires du* CERIL **5**: 22–290

Piot M 1978 *Etudes transformationnelles de quelques classes de conjonctions de subordination* (Unpublished PhD thesis, University of Paris)

Ranchhod E 1983 On the support verbs *ser* and *estar* in Portuguese. *Lingvisticae Investigationes* **7(2)**: 17–53

Ranchhod E 1990 *Sintaxe dos Predicados Nominais com Estar.* Instituto Nacional de Investigação Científica, Centro de Lingüística da Universidade de Lisboa, Lisbon

Roche E 1993 Une représentation par automate fini des textes et des propriétés transformationnelles des verbes. *Lingvisticae Investigationes* **17(1)**: 189–222

Roche E, Schabes Y (eds.) 1996 *Finite-State Devices for Natural Language Processing.* MIT Press, Cambridge, MA

Salkoff M 1983 Bees are swarming in the garden. *Lg* **59(2)**: 288–346

Silberztein M 1993 *Dictionnaires électroniques et analyse automatique de textes.* Masson, Paris

Silberztein M 1990 Le dictionnaire électronique des mots composés. *LFr* **87**: 71–83

Subirats-Ruddeberg C 1987 Sentential complementation in Spanish. A lexico-grammatical study of three classes of verbs. *Lingvisticae Investigationes Supplementa* **14**

Treig T 1977 Complétives en allemand. Classification. *Rapport de recherches du LADL* **7**: 39–203

Vivès R 1983 *Avoir, prendre, perdre:* constructions à verbe support et extensions aspectuelles (Unpublished PhD thesis, University of Paris)

New Developments in Lexical Functional Grammar

Louisa Sadler

This article provides a brief introduction to a number of key advances in Lexical Functional Grammar (LFG) since the late 1980s. A description of the framework itself is given in Neidle (see *Lexical Functional Grammar* in this volume), which provides an overview of the 1982 version of the theory, together with a sketch of a major subsequent development, Lexical Mapping Theory (LMT).

LFG as a framework for linguistic description has its roots in the desire to elaborate a fully explicit, mathematically precise and computationally oriented model of linguistic structures which would support a psychologically plausible model of human linguistic processing. Since that time, LFG has been applied to the description of a wide variety of different languages, and has enjoyed a significant degree of influence in computational linguistics.

A very striking aspect of LFG is its stability as a framework. The fundamental architecture of the theory has remained constant since the late 1970s. A very important facet of LFG syntax which singles it out from many other syntactic theories is the representation of different dimensions of the syntax (c-structure and f-structure, or external and internal syntax) by means of different formal entities: the architecture combines a context-free grammar formalism (for c-structure) with attribute value structures (for f-structures). These (and other) different dimensions are related by structural correspondence functions, or projections, the most familiar of which is the function mapping c-structure nodes into f-structure, ϕ.

As the theory has progressed, light has been cast on the nature of other structures and work has proceeded on the mapping functions. This brief review, which focuses on LFG syntax, touches on the nature of one dimension (in addition to f-structure and c-structure), namely argument structure, and the argument structure to f-structure projection. Section 1 discusses recent work in Lexical Mapping Theory, which concerns both the nature of argument structure and the mapping from argument structure of f-structure.

Much other work in LFG has been concerned with extending the description languages of LFG (for c-structure and f-structure), and on the c- to f-structure projection. The rest of this review of recent development focuses on this, and on the range of syntactic analyses made available in the LFG architecture. We pick out for particular attention three aspects of this work: that on principles of c-structure organization and the mapping to f-structure; that on the extension of the f-structure description language to include functional uncertainty equations and some linguistic analyses which exploit this; and the role of empty categories in the syntax.

The work on anaphoric binding, which is considered in Sect. 2.3, presupposes the existence of a projection relating f-structure to semantic structure. Space precludes any significant discussion of semantic interpretation in LFG, or of computational aspects of the theory, although both areas have been the focus of significant work in recent years.

1. Lexical Mapping Theory

1.1 Capturing Lexical Regularities

Since the late 1980s a good deal of work has focused on the mapping from (semantic) roles to (grammatical) functions, responsible for projecting predicate argument structures into the syntax. An important tenet of LFG, expressed in the Principle of Direct Syntactic Encoding, is that the syntax is monotonic. From this requirement it follows that all grammatical relation changing operations, or relational alterations, are lexical. The principle of monotonicity is related to two facets of LFG: (a) the surface-oriented nature of syntax, and (b) the fact that partial information about the f-structure is contributed by (potentially many) different parts of the constituent structure, and must combine in a well-behaved manner.

In the 1982 model of LFG, the lexicalization of relational alternations had a serious effect on the size of the lexicon, because all surface configurations of roles had to be expressed by alternative lexical forms, related by lexical redundancy rules which remapped grammatical functions. The grammatical function assignment was simply lexically specified on a case by case basis, along the lines of (1), which shows the number and type of participants and expresses an ordering over them, although the assignment to (semantic) roles was suppressed in the notation for semantic forms (2):

$$\text{'lean } \langle \text{AGENT THEME LOCATION} \rangle \text{'} \qquad (1)$$
$$\uparrow\text{SUBJ} \quad \uparrow\text{OBJ} \quad \uparrow\text{OBL}$$

$$(\uparrow\text{PRED}) = \text{'lean } \langle (\uparrow\text{SUBJ}) (\uparrow\text{OBJ}) (\uparrow\text{OBL}) \rangle \text{'} \qquad (2)$$

The Dative Shift alternation might be formulated as follows in such a model:

$$(\uparrow\text{OBJ}) \rightarrow (\uparrow\text{OBJ2}) \qquad (3)$$

$$(\uparrow\text{OBL}_{to}\text{OBJ}) \rightarrow (\uparrow\text{OBJ})$$

Lexical Mapping Theory attempts to replace the stipulated mapping between the (predicate) argument structure and functional structure in (1) by a more explanatory approach. In LMT, canonical and non-canonical linkings are accounted for by a small number of classification and mapping principles. Early work used a small set of thematic roles, ordered by a universally valid thematic role hierarchy (see *Lexical Functional Grammar*; see also Levin 1986; Bresnan and Kanerva 1989; Bresnan and Moshi 1990; Bresnan and Zaenen 1990).

More recent work has extended the approach to a number of lexical alternation phenomena, but has also questioned the assumption that thematic roles are the relevant descriptive device to capture those elements of the semantics which are relevant to the mapping of participants to the syntax. Recent work by Zaenen (1993), Alsina (1992a, 1992b), and others has replaced theta roles with Dowty's Proto-Agent and Proto-Patient properties.

1.2 Using Dowty Roles

1.2.1 Unaccusativity

In many languages intransitive verbs may be partitioned into two groups—the unergatives and the unaccusatives—according to a number of aspects of their syntactic behavior. These aspects include choice of auxiliary, partitive cliticization, participle formation, the interpretation of null pronominal subjects, impersonal passivization, secondary result predication and many others. A key aspect of this distinction is that the single argument of unaccusative verbs often seems to exhibit object properties at some level of syntactic representation. Deep unaccusativity refers to the case where this single argument is like both an underlying object and a surface subject, and may be accounted for in a two level syntax by assuming movement of the NP from object to subject position. At first sight, deep unaccusativity appears to be something of a challenge for LFG, but Bresnan and Zaenen (1990) show that it is simply accounted for in LMT—the unaccusative predicates are those in which an argument classified as [-r] by the LMT syntactic underspecification features (on the basis of the thematic role) is mapped to subject, by the mapping principles (for details of classification using the features +/-r and +/-o and mapping, see *Lexical Functional Grammar*).

> John arrived (4)
>
> arrive ⟨theme⟩
>   −r

Bresnan and Zaenen suggest that only [-r] arguments can be the focus of result predication, thus accounting for the fact that result predications may be formed on the objects of transitive verbs, the subjects of unaccusative verbs and the so-called fake reflexives and nonthematic objects of unergative intransitive verbs (by definition, nonthematic arguments are not semantically restricted, and therefore [-r]). Note that nonthematic arguments appear outside the ⟨ ⟩ in semantic forms—see *Lexical Functional Grammar*.

> John hammered the metal flat. (5)
> The river froze solid.
> They shouted themselves hoarse.

She drank the teapot dry.

In subsequent work on Dutch, Zaenen (1993) shows that, by replacing thematic roles by Dowty proto-roles, and thus taking a slightly more abstract view of the argument structure, various semantic correlates can be found for the shared syntactic behavior of different classes of verbs, namely the unaccusative verbs and a class of psychological predicates with stimulus subjects. She first shows that auxiliary selection and prenominal *ge-* participle formation in Dutch are diagnostic of the unaccusative/unergative distinction in that language, and that they are semantically grounded in the property of lexical Aktionsart (specifically, telicity). Lexically telic predicates occur with *zijn*, while lexically atelic predicates occur with *hebben*.

> Hij heeft gezwommen. (6)
> He has swum.
>
> Hij is weggezwommen. (7)
> He has swum away.

Similarly, prenominal *ge-* participles are only derivable from intransitive telic predicates (i.e., those that take *zijn*).

The lexically telic verbs can be semantically characterized as those in which one participant role undergoes a change of state or position, and this observation permits the syntactic distinctions at issue (auxiliary selection and *ge-* participle formation) to be grounded in the Dowty proto-patient properties:

Proto-Agent Properties:	Proto-Patient Properties: (8)
volition	change of state
sentience	incremental theme
causes event	causally affected
movement	stationary
independently referential	possibly referential

Zaenen goes on to show that these same syntactic tests partition the class of psychological predicate with experiencer objects, but that different semantic properties seem to characterize the subclasses (the experiencer subject verbs in fact constitute a third class). Specifically, those psychological predicates which occur with *zijn* and form *ge-* participles modifying a noun corresponding to the subject (the stimulus) are generally stative, not controllable (essentially, not volitional) and not potentially causative. The former property is illustrated by embedding under *dwingen*:

> Hij dwong me hem te bevallen. (9)
> He forced me to please him.
>
> Hij dwong me je te ergeren. (10)
> He forced me to irritate you.

Zaenen brings these classes of *zijn* taking verbs together, observing that they have themelike or non-agentive subjects (viewed in terms of proto-role properties, the experiencer object psychological predicates which take *zijn* have subjects which lack proto-agent properties). This may be captured by assigning intrinsic classification features [+/-r, +/-o] on the basis of proto-role properties rather than thematic roles:

> If a participant has more patient properties than (11)
> agent properties, it is marked -r.
> If a participant has more agent properties than
> patient properties, it is marked -o.

1.2.2 Morpholexical Operations

The use of LMT to replace the relation changing rules of early LFG alters grammatical function assignment to roles, but leaves unaltered the lexical semantics or the predicate argument structure of the verb. That is, only morphosyntactic operations (to do with variable encoding) were accounted for.

In work on the Hungarian locative alternation, Ackerman (1990) shows how the theory can be extended to deal with morpholexical relations which extend, redistribute or alter the semantic properties of predicates.

> A paraszt (rá=)rakta a szénát a szekérre. (12)
> the peasant (PV=)loaded-3SG/DEF the hay-ACC the wagon-SUBL
> The peasant loaded the hay onto the wagon.

> A paraszt tele=rakta a szekeret szénával. (13)
> the peasant (PV=)loaded-3SG/DEF the wagon-ACC hay-INSTR
> The peasant loaded the wagon full with hay.

He uses the classification and mapping principles (using the underspecification features +/-o, +/-r) of LMT but, like Zaenen, combines this with a level of role structure based on Dowty's proto-role properties rather than thematic roles. The key point is that the argument with the greatest number of Proto-Patient properties is assigned -r. He argues that the verbal prefixes in the Hungarian locative alternation associate the Proto-Patient properties of incremental theme and change of state with the location (*tele*) and the locatum (*rá*) respectively and hence effectively determine which of these two arguments is intrinsically classified [-r] and consequently maps to the OBJ.

Ackerman's own formulation of this idea is somewhat curious in that he assumes (without argumentation) that the arguments of a basic predicate are assigned underspecification features in some way *before* prefixation takes place, and that these assignments are then overwritten ([-r] gets reassigned as [-o]). This gives a nonmonotonic aspect to the approach, requiring one to specify that the classification feature coming along with the prefix is to take precedence, and relies on a form of default unification. This is odd, especially given that the machinery is there to support an alternative approach in which the assignment of underspecification features takes place on the fully

formed word by counting up (possibly weighted) proto-role properties.

1.3 Complex Predication

Work on complex predication in LFG has begun to liberate the mapping theory (relating role structure to functional structure) from the confines of the lexical domain (Butt 1995; Alsina 1992a, 1993). In this discussion, complex predicate is used to refer to cases in which one f-structure PRED corresponds to two semantic predicators; that is, there is one head at functional structure but two heads at (semantic) role structure. When this is the case, there is a structural mismatch between the two levels for which the mapping theory must be extended to take into account. In many languages, causatives are complex predicates in this sense. In the Chicheŵa example in (14), the causative morpheme and verb stem are each semantic predicators which fuse to form one f-structure domain (with a SUBJ *farmer*, OBJ *poem*, and an OBL *lion*):

> Mlĩmi a-ku-lémb-éts-a ndakatulo (kwá mkângo). (14)
> 1-farmer 1s-PR-write-CST-FV 9-poem to 3-lion
> The farmer is having the poem written (by the lion).

Alsina argues that causatives involve argument structure composition, with an argument of the causative predicate being identified or fused with an argument of the embedded predicate. This 'complex' role structure may then be mapped to the functional structure without any alteration of the classification and mapping principles. Interestingly, both Alsina (1993) (for Romance causatives) and Butt (1995) (for Urdu light verbs) argue that precisely the same sort of complex predication occurs where the semantic predicators are lexical items, rather than morphological structures, as for example in the Catalan (15):

> Els pagesos fan escriure un poema al follet. (15)
> the farmers make write a poem to-the elf
> The farmers are making the elf write a poem.

If this is right then we must permit argument structure and PRED value composition in the syntax as well as in the morphology—this in turn releases the mapping theory from the domain of the strictly lexical.

2. Internal and External Syntax

Recall that LFG postulates a single level of syntax, with different aspects of the (surface-oriented) syntax represented in distinct, simultaneous or parallel dimensions, c-structure and f-structure, related by a projection or mapping ϕ from c-structure nodes to f-structures. The function ϕ is many to one (many pieces of c-structure can contribute information about the same f-structure) and into (there may be pieces of f-structure which do not correspond to any c-structure node). This section looks at a number of recent developments concerning the relation between and role of these two syntactic dimensions.

2.1 Principles

In early LFG the c-structure to f-structure projection for a language was effectively stipulated by the grammar writer on a case by case basis by means of functional annotations to phrase structure rules (see *Lexical Functional Grammar*). While this captured the variability of the mapping across languages, with some languages encoding grammatical functions configurationally, and some morphologically, with a relatively or even totally free word order, it was inadequate in various respects. Firstly, general principles across languages, where they exist, were not captured (the annotations were language specific), and secondly, cross-categorial generalizations within a single language were not expressed (although this could be simulated to a certain extent by the introduction of metavariables over category labels).

In some very recent work, Bresnan (1996) replaces this approach with a set of encoding principles, which she argues are of universal validity. She proposes that there are two orthogonal sets of principles at work universally determining c-structures and ultimately the mapping to f-structure. These are 'predicate argument locality' and 'endocentricity.'

Endocentricity refers to the set of c-structure principles known as X′ syntax (see *X-bar Syntax*). Bresnan assumes three bar levels (with adjunction) and the existence of both lexical (N, V, A, and P) and functional categories (C, I, and D). Note however that in LFG the functional categories are viewed as specialized subclasses of the lexical categories, and the surface c-structure is directly admitted by the principles of endocentricity viewed as node admissibility conditions. The mapping to f-structure (the f-annotations in earlier LFG) follow from the Principles of Endocentric Structure-Function association, which are:

> c-structure heads are f-structure heads;   (16)
> specifiers of functional categories are the syntacticized discourse functions (TOPIC, FOCUS and SUBJ) or absent;
> complements of functional categories are f-structure co-heads;
> specifiers of lexical categories are a subclass of adjuncts or absent;
> complements of lexical categories are the nondiscourse argument functions (OBJ, OBJ$_\theta$, OBL$_\theta$, XCOMP, COMP); and
> constituents adjoined to maximal projections are non-argument functions.

Some languages organize their external syntax in terms of an orthogonal principle, predicate-argument locality, using a flat, exocentric phrase structure (S → C*). In such languages the mapping to functional structure is effectively determined morphologically (rather than configurationally) either by case or agreement marking.

The principles of endocentricity and predicate argument locality then serve to constrain the range of possible c-structures, and permit a more adequate approach to structure-function association in LFG. In recent work on weak crossover, Bresnan further suggests that the mapping function ϕ may also be subject to an additional constraint, namely the Principle of Lexical Expression, which states that:

> The mapping ϕ from c-structure to f-structure must satisfy this condition: for every c-structure node N there is a lexical element w such that $\phi(N) = \phi(w)$.

This principle reflects the strong surface orientation of LFG syntax and constrains the postulation of null constituents in the external syntax, as shall be seen below.

2.2 Empty Categories and Unbounded Dependency Constructions

In early LFG, which was very much under the influence of the approach taken in contemporary transformational grammar, a constituent structure oriented account was given of unbounded dependencies. The crucial features of this account (see *Lexical Functional Grammar* for details) were:

> (a) that c-structure nodes corresponding to the canonical 'gapped' position were posited;
> (b) that constraints on the filler gap relationship were expressed in terms of c-structure configurations; and
> (c) that the displaced element (e.g., topicalized, or fronted in an interrogative structure) was the value of two attributes in the f-structure, a within clause grammatical function and a so-called discourse oriented function.

In later work, Kaplan and Zaenen (1989) observed that the original LFG proposal was much influenced by the (necessarily) constituent structure oriented accounts available in transformational grammar, and showed that it was not necessary to express the filler gap constraints in c-structural terms. They extended the LFG description language to permit a further type of equation, known as a functional uncertainty equation. The function argument expression is extended to permit the use of regular expressions (denoting sets of strings) in the argument position. This means that the grammar writer is able to abbreviate what may be an infinite disjunction of identities between the value of the discourse oriented function (TOPIC or FOCUS) introduced at the 'fronted' node and a within clause function. This is illustrated below (the f-structure is abbreviated to show only essential details).

the man *who Mary likes*   (17)

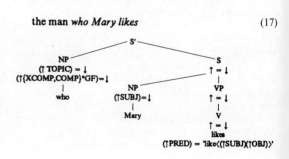

$$\begin{bmatrix} \text{TOPIC} & [1] \\ \text{SUBJ} & [\text{PRED 'mary'}] \\ \text{PRED} & \text{'like} \langle(\uparrow \text{SUBJ})(\uparrow \text{OBJ})\rangle' \\ \text{OBJ} & [1][\text{PRED 'who'}] \end{bmatrix} \quad (18)$$

The functional uncertainty equation ($\uparrow$ TOPIC) = ($\uparrow$ {COMP, XCOMP}* GF) annotating the fronted NP node specifies that the f-structure associated with this node is the value of both the path TOPIC and of some path in the (infinite) set {XCOMP, COMP, XCOMP SUBJ, COMP SUBJ, XCOMP OBJ, COMP OBJ, XCOMP XCOMP SUBJ, . . .}. Given this way of relating the fronted NP to a within clause grammatical function, the c-structure representation of an empty node is clearly superfluous. Island constraints on unbounded dependencies can be stated over PATHS in the f-structure (by constraining the functional uncertainty expression appropriately) as easily as they can be stated over configurations of c-structure nodes. Moreover, as Kaplan and Zaenen observe, a category based account gets into trouble with data such as (19):

(a) That he might be wrong he didn't think of.   (19)
(b) *That he might be wrong he didn't think.
(c) *He didn't think of that he might be wrong.
(d) He didn't think that he might be wrong.

On a constituent matching approach, in which fronted NPs must correspond to empty NP slots in the c-structure, and fronted S′ to empty S′, (19a) would be predicted ungrammatical and (19b) grammatical. The functional approach, on the other hand, is able to make the correct predictions in these cases.

This approach to unbounded dependency constructions appears to remove the motivation for null constituents in gap positions, since the constraints on filler gap constructions are no longer stated in terms of c-structure configurations, and the within clause f-structure of the 'displaced' constituent can be indicated without introducing an empty node. The use of functional uncertainty for unbounded dependency constructions permitted the complete elimination of null constituents from LFG. No null categories are postulated in the theory for the various sorts of empty pronominal in (20); since the c-structure to f-structure mapping is not an onto function, the theory admits f-structures which have no c-structure image (see Kaplan and Bresnan 1982 for further discussion of null pronominals).

(a) Giving an oral presentation always troubles   (20)
John. (Coreferential PRO)
(b) Sharing rides to work is a responsible thing to do. (PRO ARB)
(c) Vió a Juan.
saw-3S-PAST to Juan
He/she saw John.

The Principle of Lexical Expression given above prevents the postulation of null c-structures corresponding to the pronominals in (20), for it requires that every c-structure node be 'sanctioned' by a lexical element. This does not, however, prevent the postulation of empty nodes in unbounded dependency constructions, since the filler maps into the same piece of f-structure as the putative empty node. In very recent work on weak crossover, Bresnan (1995) shows that, contrary to the prevailing assumption in lexicalist approaches to syntax, there is evidence for empty constituents in unbounded dependency constructions. She argues that there are *two* conditions on the binding of pronominals by operators, a syntactic rank condition, which makes reference to the rank of phrases on a functional hierarchy (SUBJ > OBJ > OBL > COMP/XCOMP . . .) and a linear order condition. The former prevents an operator binding a pronoun which outranks it, while the latter prevents an operator binding a pronoun which f-precedes it. (The precise definition of f-precedence is irrelevant to the point at issue, but is as follows, where μ is the projection we are calling ϕ (Bresnan 1995): f_1 f-precedes f_2 if and only if there are c_1 and c_2 such that c_1 is a rightmost element in $\mu^{-1}(f_1)$, c_2 is a rightmost element in $\mu^{-1}(f_2)$, and c_1 precedes c_2.)

Because English is a configurational, SVO language, these two properties often coincide, but they do not always do so. Consider the following data from Bresnan (1995):

?*Everyone$_i$ in the room, I talked about his$_i$ (21)
coursework with.

Everyone$_i$ in the room, I talked about the   (22)
coursework with.

If there is no empty category within the PP in the topicalization in (21), then the operator–pronoun binding indicated violates neither the syntactic rank condition nor the linear precedence condition. If, on the other hand, there is an empty category, the operator chain (the fronted material and the empty category) will in fact be f-preceded by the pronominal, in violation of the linear order condition. A similar argument can be made on the basis of the following data (in terms of syntactic rank, the OBL PP outranks the XCOMP AP):

?*To whom$_i$ did Mary seem proud of him.   (23)

*Clinton seems proud of her$_i$ to every woman   (24)
appointee$_i$.

Clinton seems to every woman appointee$_i$ to be   (25)
proud of her$_i$.

That is, the contrast in grammaticality between (23) and (25) follows from the conditions on pronominal operator binding if there is an empty node corresponding to the fronted material in (24), in which case the pronominal would f-precede the operator.

2.3 Using Functional Uncertainty

The extension of the LFG description language to permit regular expressions over paths has also opened the way to the development of a lexicalist theory of anaphoric binding (Dalrymple 1993; Dalrymple et al. 1990; Dalrymple and Zaenen 1991). This approach rejects the mainstream view which divides referential NPs into three groups: full referential expressions (names), which may not be syntactically bound; pronouns, which may be syntactically bound but must be disjoint in reference within a certain local syntactic domain; and anaphors, which are required to be syntactically bound within a certain (local) domain. In Dalrymple's (1993) fully lexicalist approach, the familiar Binding Theory is no longer stipulated as an external well-formedness condition on grammars, but instead Binding equations are directly associated with lexical items. This in theory permits many more than three types of NPs to be recognized. For example, the reflexive *himself* in English, which must be bound within its clause (that is, within the minimum domain containing a PRED and SUBJ) is associated with a constraint which says just that in the lexicon. In LFG, an f-structure which contains a PRED and all its subcategorized arguments is called a 'nucleus' and a nucleus containing a SUBJ function is a 'complete nucleus.' Intuitively, the anaphor (in this case *himself*) is associated with a constraint which says it can bind to any piece of f-structure within the minimal f-structure which contains it, a PRED and a SUBJ (i.e., within its minimal complete nucleus). A pronoun, such as *him*, on the other hand, may bind to (take as antecedent) any piece of f-structure within the f-structure(s) which contains it, excluding those f-structures within the minimal nucleus (the locality disjointness condition). Binding constraints such as these are expressed using functional uncertainty equations which essentially express an infinite disjunction over the possible f-structures which may contain the anaphor or pronoun. The uncertainty equations differ from those presented above in that they give paths out rather than paths in (and hence this is known as Inside Out Functional Uncertainty). Thus the expression (XCOMP$^+$ ↑) abbreviates all the f-structures from which ↑ (call it f1) is reachable by traversing a path of one or more XCOMPS. Clearly such descriptions can be used to specify the f-structures within which a pronoun or anaphor may appear: an anaphor which must be subject bound and is limited to OBJ position might be associated in the lexicon with the functional uncertainty expression in (26) to pick out its antecedent:

$$((GF^* \ OBJ \ \uparrow) \ SUBJ) \tag{26}$$

In this approach, the theory of binding is viewed as essentially a set of (lexical) constraints (using functional uncertainty) constraining the mapping into the semantics: expressions such as these pick out pieces of f-structure, and then the equation itself states that the anaphoric element and the antecedent (so described) will map into the same element in the semantics. The

full equation, then, uses the mapping function σ which maps f-structure into semantic structure. The following should be read as saying that the OBJ and the SUBJ have the same semantics:

$$\sigma \ ((OBJ \ \uparrow) \ SUBJ) = \sigma \ (\uparrow) \tag{27}$$

3. Summary

LFG is a surface-oriented lexicalist linguistic theory. Different aspects of the syntax are expressed by means of different structures, which are related by mapping functions or projections. The basic architecture of LFG has remained remarkably stable over the years. Work in Lexical Mapping Theory has developed a theory of the mapping between argument structure and f-structure. The f-structure description language has been extended to permit sets of strings in paths, and this has made possible a number of new linguistic analyses. In other work, it is proposed that the structure–function association may follow from a small set of universal principles. A number of other recent advances (most notably to do with the computational interpretation of LFG and with semantic interpretation) are not mentioned here.

Bibliography

Ackerman F 1990 Locative Alternation vs. Locative Inversion. In: Halpern A (ed.) *Proceedings of Ninth West Coast on Formal Linguistics*. CSLI, Stanford, CA

Alsina A 1992a On the Argument Structure of Causatives. *LIn* **23(4)**: 517–55

Alsina A 1992b *Predicate Composition: A Theory of Syntactic Function* (PhD thesis, Stanford University)

Alsina A 1993 A Theory of Complex Predicates: Evidence from Causatives in Bantu and Romance (Unpublished work, Stanford University)

Bresnan J 1995 Linear Order, Syntactic Rank, and Empty Categories. In: Dalrymple M, Kaplan R, Maxwell J T III, Zaenen A (eds.) *Formal Issues in Lexical Functional Grammar*. CSLI, Stanford, CA

Bresnan J 1996 Lexical functional syntax. (Unpublished work, Stanford)

Bresnan J, Kanerva J M 1989 Locative Inversion in Chicheŵa: A Case Study of Factorization in Grammar. *LIn* **20**: 1–50

Bresnan J, Moshi L 1990 Object Asymmetries in Comparative Bantu Syntax. *LIn* **21(2)**: 147–85

Bresnan J, Zaenen A 1990 Deep Unaccusativity in LFG. In: Katarzyna Dziwirek P F, Mejías-Bikandi E (eds.) *Grammatical Relations: A Cross-Theoretical Perspective*. CSLI, Stanford, CA

Butt M 1995 *The Structure of Complex Predicates in Urdu*. CSLI, Stanford, CA

Dalrymple M 1993 *The Syntax of Anaphoric Binding*. CSLI, Stanford, CA

Dalrymple M, Maxwell J T III, Zaenen A 1990 Modeling Syntactic Constraints on Anaphoric Binding. In: *Proceedings of COLING-90*. University of Helsinki, Helsinki

Dalrymple M, Zaenen A 1991 Modeling Anaphoric Superiority. In: *Proceedings of the International Conference on Current Issues in Computational Linguistics*, Penang

Kaplan R, Bresnan J 1982 Lexical Functional Grammar:

A Formal System for Grammatical Representation. In:
Bresnan J (ed.) *The Mental Representation of Grammatical
Relations*. MIT Press, Cambridge, MA
Kaplan R M, Zaenen A 1989 Long-distance Dependencies,
Constituent Structure, and Functional Uncertainty. In:
Baltin M, Kroch A (eds.) *Alternative Conceptions of
Phrase Structure*. Chicago University Press, Chicago, IL

Levin L 1986 *Operations on Lexical Forms: Unaccusative
Rules in Germanic Languages*. MIT Press, Cambridge,
MA
Zaenen A 1993 Unaccusativity in Dutch: Integrating syntax
and lexical semantics. In: Pustejovsky J (ed.) *Semantics
and the Lexicon*. Kluwer Academic Publishers, Dordrecht

Prague School Syntax and Semantics
Eva Hajičová

The Prague School of Linguistics, though better
known for its research into the domain of phonology,
has brought many valuable insights into syntax and
semantics as well, especially with its due regard to the
character of language as a system of signs (with its
specific relation between grammar and semantics) and
to the communicative function of language. In formulating these issues as early as the 1930s, the Prague
School was well ahead of most of the linguistic trends
in the USA (where meaning was excluded from
linguistic research for a long time) and in Europe
(where, in fact, it had such important adherents as
Lucien Tesnière). Even in the early 1990s, the elegance
and economical character of dependency syntax, for
which formal frameworks were formulated (both for
generation and for parsing) in Prague, represents a
challenge for the main approaches to theoretical
linguistics.

1. The Main Roots of Prague School Syntax and Semantics

1.1 Sentence and Utterance
The distinction made between 'sentence,' as a unit of
the language system and 'utterance event,' as a unit
of discourse, or a verbal 'communicate,' can be traced
back to Karcevskij (1931, 1937), with whom 'proposition' denotes a predicative syntagm, while 'phrase'
refers to a function of dialog having two sides: from
the point of view of the conceptual layer, 'phrase' is a
communicative unit, while from that of the phonic
layer, it is an intonational unit.

Closely connected with this issue is the notion of
'sentence pattern' as introduced by Vladimír Skalička
(1935, *Satzcliché*) and characterized by him as a sentence structure that is 'normalized' for some language
or some part of the sentences of a certain language.
Vilém Mathesius (1936) regards 'sentence' as an
abstract pattern that belongs to the field of language
and sees the task of functional syntax as consisting
in a systematic analysis of the repertoire of sentence
patterns.

A systematic investigation into the dichotomy of
sentence and utterance was carried out by Dokulil

and Daneš (1958), who characterize 'utterance' as the
smallest situationally anchored linguistic communication unit and 'sentence' as a typicized, common
grammatical form of utterance.

1.2 Linguistic Meaning and Extralinguistic Content
The functional orientation of the Prague School (often
characterized as a 'means–ends' model, especially by
R. Jakobson) involves a view of language as a system
of means expressing the (ontological, cognitive)
content. Following F. de Saussure, the Praguians
distinguished between content itself (or its different
nonlinguistic patternings) and its (linguistically patterned) form, which was called (linguistic, literal)
'meaning'; a similar dichotomy is known from Louis
Hjelmslev, and also from Eugenio Coseriu. The
relationship between meaning and the outer (phonic
or written) shape of linguistic units was regarded as the
proper object of 'functional grammar' by Mathesius.
This relationship between the two aspects of the
linguistic sign was viewed as articulated into several
levels of language system, every two adjacent levels
being connected by the relation of form (signifying)
and function (signified). As for sentence structure,
Dokulil and Daneš (1958) showed persuasively that
along with the grammatical patterning of the sentence
(which later was called its 'surface structure') there
exists a fully organized layer of meaning (understood
as 'the content in its mirroring by the form'), which
should be studied on the basis of grammatical form
and consequently distinguished both from content
and from form; this level corresponds to what later
was distinguished in different linguistic models as the
level of underlying or deep, tectogrammatical structure.

1.3 The Verb as the Center of Sentence Structure
Mathesius (1936) distinguished two processes involved in every communicative act of speech: (a) a
selection of elements from reality that are expressed by
means of the vocabulary existing in the given language
(the study of which is the matter of functional onomatology), and (b) bringing the naming units into

mutual relations so as to constitute an organic whole (studied by functional syntax). The central role in the organization of this organic whole is the predicate (cf. Thèses 1929: 13, on the study of predicational forms). The starting point for the study of the verb from a syntactico–semantic point of view was presented by Pauliny (1943), whose approach in certain aspects continued Jakobson's (1936) analysis of the meaning of cases. He distinguished several basic types of verbal 'intention' in accordance with the 'roles' semantically patterned with a verb and grammatically shaped, while others are only implicitly present (coalescing with the meaning of the verb, or with another role).

The main contributions to the general questions of verbal valency were formulated by members of the Prague School outside the country of its origin (first of all by Tesnière 1959 with his elaborate system of '*actants*' and '*circonstants*' and consistent distinction between two levels of sentence patterns; cf. also Kuryłowicz's (1949) syntactically based analysis of the functions of cases; these were two of the sources of Fillmore's case grammar), or outside the Prague Circle for Czech (Šmilauer 1947).

1.4 Functional Sentence Analysis

One of the basic aspects of Prague functionalism is the treatment of language as a functioning system, adapted to its communicative role. If a linguistic description is to be well integrated into a complex account of communication, due regard is to be paid to those features of sentence structure which reflect the impact of the communicative function of language. One of these features is functional sentence perspective (or topic and comment, theme and rheme, topic and focus). The importance of the phenomena now subsumed under the above-mentioned headings was well known since H. Weil, G. von der Gabelentz, P. Wegener, H. Ammann, and A. Marty. It was Mathesius who introduced these notions into the Prague School and anchored them in a systematic linguistic study. He pointed out various interrelations of the topic/focus articulation (TFA) with the grammatical sentence structure (e.g., the topic is characterized—in the Prague terminology of function and form, see Sect. 1.2 above—as one of the functions of subject; see especially Mathesius 1929) as well as its bearing on word order. One of the main results of this analysis (Mathesius 1928) was the confrontation of Czech and English in this respect: in Czech, TFA is the prevailing factor determining word order; in English, word order is determined mainly by the grammatical factor. If the actor belongs to the focus of a sentence and the goal belongs to its topic, the unmarked order is goal–verb–actor which, in English, is only made possible by the passive form of the verb (e.g., 'Shane was killed by Kim.') The order topic–focus is the natural order, called 'objective' by Mathesius, as opposed

to the order focus–topic, which in Czech is 'subjective,' emphatic.

As will be seen in Sect. 4 below, the issues of topic and focus, in their interrelations with syntax and semantics, were widely discussed and the theory of TFA was further developed by the next generations of Czech linguists.

1.5 Other Work

This brief outline has to leave aside many important contributions concerning syntax and semantics in connection with stylistics, with the functional and social stratification of the national language, or with the development of individual languages, and so on. The writings of such prominent scholars as Trubetzkoy, Trnka, Vachek, and others here deserve the reader's attention (see especially Vachek 1964).

2. The Sentence Patterns Model

The sentence patterns model in syntax as developed by Daneš and his followers (Daneš 1968, 1987; Daneš et al. 1981) is based on the following two main assumptions:

(a) a distinction is made between three levels of sentence analysis: the level of (formal) grammatical structure, the level of semantic sentence structure, and the level of the communicative organization of the utterance (Daneš 1964); and

(b) the construction of a sentence is based on predication.

Two types of sentence patterns are distinguished: a formal grammatical sentence pattern and a semantic ('propositional') sentence pattern. The structure of the sentence can be described by a complex sentence pattern, which is a correlation of patterns of the two types. Thus, for example, the structure of the English sentence 'Mary cleaned the cloth' can be described by a complex sentence pattern N/Agent ← VF/Action → N/Patient. Each grammatical sentence pattern can be viewed as a generalization over a class of verbs with identical valency; it contains a number of functional positions, which are filled in a particular sentence with particular lexical items. The number of these positions, as well as their syntactically bound morphological characteristics, is determined by the valency potential of the finite verb, which acts as the organizational center of the sentence structure both on the grammatical and on the semantic level. On the semantic level, the (meaning of the) finite verb determines the number and type of roles of the participants involved; the choice of particular participants is influenced by the semantic selectional restrictions associated with the meaning of the given verb.

The correlation of grammatical and semantic sentence patterns is not biunique; grammatical sentence patterns may exhibit both polysemy (a single grammatical sentence pattern may correspond to two or more semantic sentence patterns) and synonymy (two or more grammatical sentence patterns correspond to a single semantic sentence pattern).

Semantic sentence patterns are supposed to be language specific and to belong to the domain of linguistic meaning in the sense of the meaning/content distinction mentioned in Sect. 1.2 above. A description of the content structure of the sentence is aimed at by semantic formulas. Daneš's (1987) example of the following three sentences (1–3) illustrates the distinction between the two layers:

English: *Peter stole a book from his brother.* (1)

German: *Peter stahl ein Buch seinem Bruder.* (2)

Russian: *Petr ukral knigu u svojego brata.* (3)

The common semantic formula describing the given situation is A ((z LC y) T (z LC x)), containing the relators A for action, LC for local co-occurrence, and T for transitional change, and three components x for agent, y for the initial holder, and z for the held thing. The semantic formula has a hierarchical structure relating the agentive and the action–contents components on the highest level, the two situation components are related on the next lower level and these situation components themselves represent the lowest level in the hierarchy. This underlying semantic formula is reflected in different language specific semantic sentence patterns, where the initial holder is structured as the source of acquisition (in English), as the deprivation (in German), or as the location of acquisition (in Russian).

The relation between semantic formulas and the corresponding grammatical sentence patterns can be used to illustrate different perspectives in which a given action can be presented or a different hierarchization of participants of one and the same event: both 'She cleaned the cloth' and 'She cleaned the stain' correspond to the same semantic formula, namely x A ((y LC z) T (y LC z)), where LC denotes the relator of 'local co-occurrence,' the two occurring items y and z being 'a container' and its 'contents,' respectively, and the final situation is a negation of the one before the transition T. In the first of the two sentences, the given action is presented from the point of view of the participant 'container' (with the right-hand valency position of Direct Object being filled with the name of this participant), while the second sentence presents the action from the point of view of the participant 'contents'; in both cases, the given participant acquires the meaning of patient. Predicate structures are classified into two major classes, namely static predicates and dynamic predicates; the latter class is in turn subdivided into simple processes ('She is dancing.' 'It rained.') and mutations ('They are building a new house.' 'He marched the soldiers.')

Daneš's conception has found several followers especially among the Czech linguists studying Russian syntax and it represents one of the important stages in the development of valency theory. It also supplies many valuable stimuli for a many-sided classification of the lexical meanings of verbs.

3. Valency in the Prague Generative Approach

Prague School principles deeply influenced also the main tenets of the functional generative description (FGD) as proposed by P. Sgall in the early 1960s (Sgall 1964; for a more recent formulation, see Sgall et al. 1986). FGD is conceived as a multilevel type of description (see Sect. 1.2), with a generative component enumerating the representations of meanings of sentences (tectogrammatical representations, TRs), which basically have the shape of dependency trees defined in such a way that the number of sister nodes is not limited; the root of the tree is the verb. A more complex form of the framework accounts also for coordination and apposition, which are relations of another kind than dependency. The TRs contain nodes with complex labels which include terminal symbols only; in these nodes all the information needed for the derivation of the surface shapes of sentences as well as that relevant for semantic interpretation is present. The dependency relation between the verb as the root of the tree and its immediate dependents is divided into different valency relations (see Sect. 1.3); the same holds true for the relations between nouns (adjectives, adverbs, embedded verbs) and their immediate dependents. The necessity of operational criteria for the specification of the linguistically patterned oppositions on the level of meaning has always been recognized in Prague, and is especially stressed in FGD.

The valency slots are classified into two types (see Panevová 1974, 1977; Hajičová and Panevová 1984): inner participants (cases) and free (adverbial) modifications. They can be operationally distinguished on the basis of two criteria: (a) Do the rules of the language described allow the occurrence of the given modification with every verb? (b) Can the modification occur more than once as a dependent of a single verb token? These two criteria classify the two surface objects as inner participants; with Actor, the answer to (a) might seem to be positive, but there are also impersonal (subjectless) verbs in inflexional languages (Latin *pluit*, *piget*) and the English surface subject in 'it rains,' 'it is snowing,' etc. appears to have no counterpart in the meaning of the sentence. This, as well as the negative answer to (b), corroborates the view that Actor should be classed as one of the inner participants. The adverbials of origin and of effect are similar to direct and indirect objects in that they are connected with a negative answer to (a) as well as to (b); their tectogrammatical counterparts thus are considered as inner participants. The outcome is five inner participants to be distinguished:

(a) Actor or Actor/Bearer (corresponding also to

the cognitive role of Experiencer, and primarily expressed as a surface subject);

(b) Patient (Objective), as the primary underlying counterpart of the direct complement; cognitively it is the goal, the object affected by the action; 'cook potatoes,' 'touch the wires,' 'speak about the holiday';

(c) Addressee (known from traditional syntax under the heading of indirect object); 'tell someone,' 'bring something to someone,' 'pay somebody';

(d) Origin; 'build something from something,' 'change something from something';

(e) Effected object (which includes, in particular, the predicative complement with verbs like 'elect somebody a president,' 'nominate somebody a chairman,' and the traditional adverbial of result as in, e.g., 'he tore it into pieces').

Other complementations are classified as free modifications; though some types of adverbials are seldom found with a verb of a certain class, such combinations are not excluded by the language system; they are just made improbable or practically excluded by the conditions of the world we live in, i.e., by cognitive content.

The morphemic forms (means) corresponding to the valency relations have either the shape of affixes (endings, stem alternations) or of words (prepositions, subordinating conjunctions) which appear as such only due to shallow rules. This is similar to the morphemic counterparts of values of such grammatical categories as number, tense, modality. In the TRs all these units, which do not play an essential syntactic role, have the shape of indices (parts of complex labels), rather than of nodes.

When a unit of a TR is deleted by a surface rule, the speaker assumes that the hearer can easily recover the deleted item. It can happen that the speaker's assumption is mistaken and in this event the hearer can then ask for the suppressed item to be stated explicitly. In such a case the dialog is disturbed to a certain extent, as can be illustrated by (4a) and (4b). On the other hand, with (4c) following (4a) the situation is different: the hearer asks for an additional piece of information and the acceptability of the dialog is by no means disturbed.

Charles came by train. (4a)

Where did he come to? (4b)

When did he come? (4c)

The utterer of (4a) must be able to answer (4b); he cannot merely say 'I don't know' without disqualifying himself as a speaker. However, he need not know the answer to (4c), which he can explicitly admit without disturbing the connectedness of the dialog. As seen in example (4), this dialog test can serve as an operational criterion distinguishi between obligatory

complementations of verbs deletable on the surface and optional ones.

It is assumed that each lexical entry has a valency frame (cf. the more recent notion of theta grid) assigned to it, where all the inner participants are listed for the given lexical unit, with an indication whether they are obligatory or optional. Free modifications may be listed once for all the verbs (nouns, adjectives, adverbs) in the grammar (see criterion (a) above for distinguishing between participants and modifications); only if a certain modification is obligatory with a given lexical head (as the direction 'where to' with 'come,' 'arrive,' etc., or manner with 'behave,' or location with 'stay,' etc.), then it should be also listed in its frame (for a classification of valency slots of nouns, see Piťha 1980).

Within this approach the participants are defined, essentially, on a semantic basis; however, if the verb does not have all the inner participants in its frame, then the tectogrammatical participants partly differ from the cognitive roles in a regular way. If the cognitive role which would primarily correspond to Patient is absent from the frame, while the role primarily corresponding to Addressee, Origin, or Effect is present, then this latter role is linguistically structured on the level of TRs as a Patient; in a similar vein, the cognitive role primarily corresponding to the Patient may be shifted to the position of Actor. This correspondence can be illustrated by the following shifts (5):

Patient → Actor (*the book appeared*) (5a)

Effect → Patient (*John became a teacher*) (5b)

Origin → Patient (*Bill abandoned his family*) (5c)

Addressee → Patient (*The chairman has addressed the audience*) (5d)

Under such a treatment it is possible to state that every verb having a single (inner) participant in its frame has an Actor there; if the verb has two participants, they are Actor and Objective; in this, FGD comes close to Tesnière's treatment of his first and second participants. Only if a verb has more than two participants, then one of them is Origin, Addressee or Effect, but Actor and Objective are always present in the valency frame of such a verb (as obligatory or optional participants).

4. Topic/Focus Articulation

4.1 A Specification of the Basic Notions

The main notions connected with topic/focus articulation (TFA; see Sect. 1.4 above for other terms referring, with some slight differences, to this issue) were characterized by Firbas (1956) first of all on the basis of the hierarchy of communicative dynamism (CD). By 'degree of CD carried by a linguistic element,' Firbas (1987: 23) understands 'the relative extent to which the element contributes towards the development of the communication within the sentence.' According to Firbas (1971: 141) the theme is then 'constituted by an element (elements) carrying the lowest, the rheme by an element (elements) carrying the highest degree(s) of CD within the distributional field. Elements ranking between theme and rheme constitute a kind of transition.' Though no overt criteria were then given for distinguishing the degrees of CD as determining the theme, the rheme and the transitional elements, the framework using the degrees of CD has brought many convincing results.

Sect. 4.3 below shows that a certain operational criterion can be found in the so-called 'question test'; the use of this test and the tests based on negation leads to the necessity of another underlying notion, namely that of contextual boundness. Contextual boundness corresponds directly to the distinction between pieces of information processed by the speaker as (a) points assumed to be readily available in the hearer's memory, and (b) ways of modification of these points attempted by the speaker through her/his message. The distinction between elements which are contextually bound and those which are nonbound also has an independent justification, e.g., on such grounds as the conditions for the use of weak (unstressed) pronouns or the semantic specification of the scope of negation.

Following up his previous considerations on the so-called 'communicative importance,' but working in more abstract terms, Firbas (1979, 1992) postulates 'a natural order (ordo naturalis)' of contextually non-bound elements of the sentence and suggests two context independent semantic scales reflecting a gradual rise of CD:

(a) scene (settings)—appearance/existence—phenomenon appearing/existing (possible prospective quality bearer); and

(b) scene (settings)—quality bearer—quality—specification—further specification(s).

In his more recent works, Firbas (1985) takes up the problem of the interrelations between TFA (functional sentence perspective), intonation, and emotiveness, throwing new light on the place of intonation as one of the means of expressing the distribution of the degrees of communicative dynamism over the sentence. The analysis is illustrated by a most detailed analysis of a continuous stretch of conversation.

More recently, Svoboda (1981) proposes to work with the concept of 'diatheme,' which he characterizes in several ways (not fully identical, as shown by Sgall 1987):

(a) as the thematic element carrying the highest degree of CD (p.5);

(b) as a temporary center of the scene, the newly introduced or just chosen quality bearer (p.42);

(c) as what was called by Mathesius 'the center of the theme' (p.42).

It is necessary to make a distinction between TFA and the cases of the so-called 'second instance,' i.e., of a correction of some misunderstanding concerning a part of a sentence (be it a slip of the tongue, a fault of perception, or an actual error); these sentences can be—at least in many cases—preceded by a string of the form '*Not*' ('that') ..., 'but,' where ... equals the given sentence, only the element bearing contrastive heavy stress being replaced by one of its antonyms: 'The book WAS published by Mouton'; 'To London he sent only FIFTY dollars.'

4.2 An Explicit Account of Topic/Focus Articulation (TFA)

The Prague research group of formal linguistics, following up the intuitive observations of the Prague School linguists presented since the 1930s, formulated an explicit, formal framework which makes it possible to describe TFA within a dependency-based account of the meaning of the sentence (see Sect. 3 above and Sgall et al. 1986). The empirical background and the theoretical framework of this approach can be briefly sketched as follows.

In a theoretical description of language one has to account jointly for three layers of phenomena belonging to the same domain, namely

(a) the individual lexical items occurring in the sentence as contextually bound or as nonbound, the former use being possible only with items the speaker assumes to be salient, activated in the hearer's memory, Sect. 4.4. below;

(b) the division of the underlying (tectogrammatical) representation (TR) of the sentence into its topic and its focus; and

(c) the hierarchy of communicative dynamism (CD, 'deep word order'), rendered by the left-to-right ordering of the nodes of this representation (see above in Sect. 4.1 for Firbas's pioneering formulations on CD).

Informally, the focus of a TR of a sentence treated (with a simplification concerning coordination) as a dependency tree, can be specified as follows (see Sgall 1979):

(a) if the main verb or some of the nodes which directly depend on it (i.e., some of the 'deep cases' and other modifications) are contextually nonbound, then these nodes belong to the focus of the TR;

(b) if a node other than the root of the tree belongs to the focus, then also all nodes subordinated to it belong to the focus;

(c) if the root and also all its daughter nodes are contextually bound (cf. (a) in the previous paragraph), then it is necessary to specify the rightmost of the daughter nodes of the root and ask whether (some of) its own daughter node(s) is (are) nonbound; if so, then these nodes belong to the focus; if not, one again specifies the rightmost of the last set of sister nodes and asks whether some of its daughter nodes are nonbound, etc.

The nodes that do not belong to the focus of a sentence constitute its topic.

Attempting to describe the three layers of phenomena mentioned above in a unified way, functional generative description works with two rather strong hypotheses:

(a) the boundary between topic and focus is always placed so that there is a node A such that any node that is less dynamic than A belongs to the topic, and any which is more dynamic, to the focus; and

(b) the hierarchy of CD within focus is determined by an ordering of the kinds of complementations (of valency relations) which is given by the grammar (called 'systemic ordering'); on the other hand, within the topic permutations of the complementations are possible (see Hajičová and Sgall 1987; Hajičová 1994).

It is assumed that every sentence has a focus, since otherwise it would convey no information relevant for the communication, it would lack any illocutionary force; however, there are sentences without any topic (corresponding to thetic judgments).

An examination of Czech in comparison with English and several other languages has led to the conclusion that the systemic ordering of some of the main participants is identical for many languages, having the form: Actor–Addressee–Objective. As for Instrument, Origin, and Locative, it seems that English differs from Czech (and from German) in that these three complementations follow Objective in English, though they precede it in Czech.

Various questions of TFA are still open for a more detailed and systematic investigation, but the framework has been already built allowing for an explicit description of many of these phenomena. In addition, this framework helps to bring a better insight into such important linguistic issues as presuppositions and the semantic scope of linguistic negation (Hajičová 1973, 1974, 1984). Especially, it can be stated that the prototypical scope of negation is identical with the focus of the sentence. In connection with this, definite noun groups trigger presuppositions if they are included in the topic, not in the focus of a sentence: 'Our victory was (not) caused by Harry' presupposes that the victory took place, although 'Harry did not cause our victory' entails neither the presence nor the absence of victory (a case of allegation); 'The king of France is (not) bald' cannot be appropriately used as referring to the actual world, but 'Yesterday London was not visited by the king of France' may be used as a true utterance.

4.3 An Operational Test for Topic and Focus

As noted above one should look for operational criteria to identify the different phenomena from TFA. One of these tests, indicated by Hatcher (1956) and further developed especially by Daneš (1970) and Sgall and Hajičová (1977), is based on the assumption that for every sentence the intuitions of the speakers of the given language determine a set of *wh*-questions that can be appropriately (although redundantly) answered by the given sentence in different contexts. Thus, with the intonation center on a 'problem,' (6) can answer (7a) to (7d) while it cannot answer (7e) or (7f).

John talked to his neighbor about a problem. (6)

(a) What did John do? (7)
(b) What did John talk about to whom?
(c) What did John talk about to his neighbor?
(d) What was John's attitude towards his neighbor?
(e) Who talked to his neighbor about a problem?
(f) To whom did John talk about a problem?

The following rules (formulated here in terms of TRs, Sects. 3 and 4.2 above) may be understood as the basis of the question test.

(a) If the set of all those questions for which the given sentence can serve as an appropriate answer (called 'the set of relevant questions' in the following) fulfills the condition, for some phrases A and B included in the given sentence, that (the referent of) A is (referred to by a phrase) included in every question from the set in which B is included, and also in such a question (from the set) that does not include B, then in (all TRs of) the given sentence the (source of the) phrase A is less dynamic than the (source of the) phrase B;

(b) if A (from the given sentence) occurs in no element of the set of relevant questions, it is the focus proper (i.e., the most dynamic element) of the given sentence;

(c) if A (from the given sentence) occurs in every element of the set of relevant questions, then it belongs to the topic of the given sentence;

(d) if (a) is met by A and B, but either A or B breaks (b) and also (c), then the sentence is ambiguous in that the phrase breaking these two conditions belongs to its topic in some of its TRs and to its focus in some others;

(e) if there is a pair of phrases, A, B, in the given sentence such that A and B break (a) and neither A nor B meets (c), then the sentence is ambiguous not only with respect to the position of the boundary between topic and focus but also in that A is less dynamic than B in some of its TRs, being more dynamic than it is in some other; at most in one of these two cases both A and B belong to the focus.

If these conditions are applied to example (6) above,

(7a) is fulfilled by the pairs 'John' and 'talked,' 'John' and '(to his) neighbor,' and also by every pair containing 'problem' as B and any other constituent (the verb or one of its participants) as A; thus in the scale (or linear ordering) of CD of all TRs of (6) 'John' precedes 'talk' as well as 'neighbor,' while each of the three precede 'problem.' The condition (b) is met by 'problem,' which is the focus proper of all TRs of (6), while 'John' belongs to the topic in all TRs since it fulfills (c). Since the condition (d) is met by the pair in which A and B are assigned the values of 'John' and 'neighbor,' respectively, or 'John' and 'talk' (and, trivially, also 'neighbor' and 'problem'), it may be stated that 'talk' (and 'neighbor') belongs to the topic in some TRs of (6) and to the focus in others.

If 'talk' is substituted for A and 'neighbor' for B (or vice versa), point (e) is fulfilled, so that there are such TRs in which 'neighbor' is more dynamic than 'talk' as well as others in which 'neighbor' is less dynamic, whereas only in the former case both the phrases may belong to the focus.

This shows that to a certain degree the question test is useful not only for drawing the boundary between topic and focus, but also for identifying the degrees of CD; the elements that belong to the topic only in some of the TRs of the sentence are more dynamic than those belonging to the topic in all the TRs, but less dynamic than the element that in all the TRs belongs to the focus (and thus constitutes the focus proper).

4.4 TFA *and the Structure of the Discourse*

As for the relationship between TFA of a sentence and the corresponding aspects of the patterning of the text, Daneš (1970, 1974) distinguishes three types of 'thematic progressions,' the first of which consists in the comment of a given utterance U_1 reappearing as the theme of the following utterance U_2 (as 'Last week I visited Lund. It is a nice university town . . .'); in the second type the theme of U_1 is identical (or in an associative link, etc.) to that of U_2 (as, e.g., in 'Charles came to his AUNT. He wanted first of all to show his POLITENESS'); with the third type, the two utterances derive their topics from a hypertheme (as, e.g., in 'Three of the four rooms are rather LARGE. The windows lead into a GARDEN' with the hypertheme 'the apartment').

The interrelations between TFA of the sentences and the dynamic aspects of discourse can be also viewed from the point of view of a pragmatically understood psychological layer, taking into account the speaker's assumptions about the relative salience of the pieces of knowledge she/he assumes to share with the hearer (see Hajičová and Vrbová 1981; Sgall et al. 1986: ch. 3; more recently, Hajičová 1993).

At the initial point of a discourse, the interlocutors share a certain stock of information (the stock of shared knowledge, SSK), a part of which is activated by the situational context. During the discourse, the SSK changes in accordance with what is in the center of attention at the given point of the discourse. The changes of the degree of salience depend to a great extent on the TFA of the sentence uttered.

(a) The items referred to by the focus of the immediately preceding utterance are the most activated ones at every time-point of the discourse.

(b) If an item is mentioned in the topic, then at least two issues are to be taken into consideration:
  (i) a pronominal reference strengthens the activation of the item referred to to a lesser degree than a reference with a full (definite) noun group;
  (ii) the activation of the items referred to in the topic fades away less quickly than that of the items referred to (only) in the focus of the preceding utterance(s).

(c) Also an item lacking a high degree of activation can be mentioned in the topic (or, more exactly, as contextually bound), if natural language inferencing makes it possible without much effort on the hearer's side to identify the item mentioned (on the basis of various associative links).

(d) If an item of SSK is not referred to in the given utterance, then its activation decreases (cf. point (b) (ii) above).

(e) Also other scales or hierarchies should be considered. Thus, there is a hierarchy of prominence with regard to the individual utterances and their positions in the discourse; e.g., utterances metatextually opening a narration or one of its portions, or headings are more prominent than other parts of the discourse, in that the items which the former introduce retain their activation to a higher degree than items introduced in the latter parts.

These observations were formulated, to a certain degree, in a framework that allows one to understand how the issues of reference assignment can be captured by finite means and to describe such notions as that of the topic of (a part of) a discourse.

5. Semantics

5.1 *Meaning of Morphemes*

Within the Prague School, semantics has always been understood as belonging to the core of the system of language. A first major contribution to the theoretical approach to semantics was Jakobson's (1936) analysis of the meanings of cases, which he understood as based on invariant units arranged in binary oppositions (analogically to phonological systems). This approach was shown by Pauliny (1943) to exhibit only a limited applicability within an account of the meaning of the sentence; however, it was elaborated into a much more general account of the meaning of morphemes of different kinds by van Schooneveld (1978) and others, whose approach offers many insights important for the classification of the units of the level of meaning.

5.2 Meaning and Intensional Semantics

Only in the second generation of the School did the semantic (or pragmatico–semantic) structure of the sentence start to be studied (see above Sects. 2–4), and in the 1980s a direct connection with research in formal semantics was achieved thanks to the joint efforts of the authors of FGD and of a group of logicians, who based their research on intensional semantics (using Tichý's 1971, 1988 transparent intensional logic). A certain division of labor is postulated: the proper task of linguistics is seen in an adequate description of the relationship between the outer shape of linguistic items and the level of meaning, while the transduction from the latter level to a formal system of intensional logic constitutes the task of an interdisciplinary cooperation; for the first attempts at a treatment of this transduction see especially Materna et al. (1980, 1987) searching for formal correlates of the topic–focus articulation of the sentence and communicative dynamism, and Materna and Sgall (1984) relating the predicates of formal logic (with their fixed arity) and the verbs of natural language (having obligatory and optional complementations).

It is proposed to deal with problems of semantic interpretation on the basis of the concept of sense, understood as linguistic (literal) meaning combined with a specification of reference (see Sgall et al. 1986: 51ff.). If each of the meanings of a sentence is conjoined with a specification of the reference of the referring expressions contained in the sentence, then the sense obtained in this way determines a proposition, viewed as a partial function from possible worlds into truth values. This allows an assertion not to assign a truth value to a possible world, if the presuppositions of that assertion are not satisfied in that world.

The meaning of a (declarative) sentence can thus be understood as a procedure enabling the hearer to find the sense h of a sentence token, provided the proper reference assignment is known to her/him; as far as she/he knows the relevant features of possible worlds, the hearer is then enabled by Prop(h) to find the truth value of the particular utterance, if the presuppositions of h are met (see Sgall 1994).

5.3 A Criterion for the Identity of Meaning

The distinction between linguistic meaning and cognitive content (see Sect. 1.2 above) can be operationally specified on the basis of the following delimitation of synonymy (cf. Sgall et al. 1986: ch. 1).

Two expressions (morphemes or elementary surface syntactic constructions) a and b are strictly synonomous (have a meaning in common) if, for every pair of sentences A and B, where A differs from B only in that A contains a in the same position in which B contains b, it holds that for every utterance of A and of B there is a set of corresponding propositions they have in common. (A and B should not contain quotational contexts so that such contexts as 'The noun' stay/sojourn 'has two syllables' are excluded.)

The following pair of sentences illustrates how the criterion operates: 'Charles sold a car to Paul' and 'Paul bought a car from Charles.' The set of possible worlds with regard to which the two sentences are true is identical; however, the so-called 'converse predicates' 'buy/sell' are not synonymous because if they are inserted in a different context (lexical setting), the synonymy condition is not met; 'Charles was selling a car to Paul' and 'Paul was buying a car from Charles' certainly do not share their truth conditions since in the former situation, before the action was completed, the addressee may not be willing to buy a car, which cannot be the case for the latter situation. Another point is that the two word order patterns are not synonomous, expressing different instances of TFA.

This operational criterion makes it possible to establish a set of units of the level of meaning (specifying expressions which share a meaning they convey). In this way one of the fundamental issues of structural semantics can be settled, since the delimitation of the level of meaning can be used to draw the borderline between the linguistically structured part of semantics and the cognitive content, as has been postulated since Saussure.

Bibliography

Daneš F 1964 A three-level approach to syntax. In: *Travaux linguistique de Prague 1*. Academia, Prague

Daneš F 1968 Some thoughts on the semantic structure of the sentence. *Lingua* **21**: 55–69

Daneš F 1970 Zur linguistischen Analyse der Textstruktur. *FoL* **IV**: 72–78

Daneš F 1974 Functional sentence perspective and the organization of the text. In: Daneš F (ed.) *Papers on Functional Sentence Perspective*. Academia, Prague

Daneš F 1987 Sentence patterns and predicate classes. In: Steele R, Threadgold T (eds.) *Language Topics*. Benjamins, Amsterdam

Daneš F, Hlavsa Z, Kořenský J 1981 *Větné vzorce v češtině*. Academia, Prague

Dokulil M, Daneš F 1958 K tzv. významové a mluvnické stavbě věty. In: *O vědeckém poznání soudobých jazyků*. Nakladatelství ČSAV, Prague

Firbas J 1956 Poznámky k problematice anglického slovního pořádku z hlediska aktuálního členění větného. *Sborník prací filosofické fakulty brněnské university* (Brno) **A4**: 93–107

Firbas J 1971 On the concept of communicative dynamism in the theory of functional sentence perspective. *Brno Studies in English* **7**: 12–47

Firbas J 1979 A functional view of 'ordo naturalis.' *Brno Studies in English* **13**: 29–59

Firbas J 1985 Thoughts on functional sentence perspective,

intonation and emotiveness. *Brno Studies in English* **16**: 11–48

Firbas J 1987 On two starting points of communication. In: Steele R, Threadgold T (eds.) *Language Topics I*. Benjamins, Amsterdam

Firbas J 1992 *Functional Sentence Perspective in Written and Spoken Communication*. Cambridge University Press, Cambridge

Hajičová E 1973 Negation and topic versus comment. *Philologica Pragensia* **16**: 81–93

Hajičová E 1974 Meaning, presupposition and allegation. *Philologica Pragensia* **17**: 18–25

Hajičová E 1984 Presupposition and allegation revisited. *JPrag* **8**: 155–67

Hajičová E 1993 *Issues of Sentence Structure and Discourse Patterns*. Charles University, Prague

Hajičová E 1994 Topic/focus and related research. In: Luelsdorff P A (ed.) 1994: 245–75

Hajičová E, Panevová J 1984 Valency (case) frames of verbs. In: Sgall P (ed.) *Contributions to Functional Syntax. Semantics, and Language Comprehension*. Academia, Prague

Hajičová E, Sgall P 1987 The ordering principle. *JPrag* **11**: 435–54

Hajičová E, Vrbová J 1981 On the salience of the elements of the stock of shared knowledge. *FoL* **XV(3–4)**: 291–303

Hatcher A G 1956 Syntax and the sentence. *Word* **12**: 234–50

Jakobson R 1936 Beitrag zur allgemeinen Kasuslehre. In: *Travaux du Cercle linguistique de Prague* **VI**. Jednota československých matematiků a fyziků, Prague

Karcevskij S J 1931 Sur la phonologie de la phrase. In: *Travaux du Cercle linguistique de Prague* **IV**. Jednota československých matematiků a fyziků, Prague

Karcevskij S J 1937 Phrase et proposition. In: *Mélanges de linguistique et de philologie offerts à J. van Ginneken*. Librairie C. Klincksieck, Paris

Kuryłowicz J 1949 Le problème de classement des cas. *Builetyn polskiego towarzystwa językoznawczego* **IX**: 20–43

Luelsdorff P A (ed.) 1994 *Prague School of Structural and Functional Linguistics*. Benjamins, Amsterdam

Luelsdorff P A, Panevová J, Sgall P (eds.) 1994 *Praguiana 1945–1990*. Benjamins, Amsterdam

Materna P, Hajičová E, Sgall P 1987 Redundant answers and topic–focus articulation. *L&P* **10**: 101–13

Materna P, Sgall P 1980 Functional sentence perspective, the question test and intensional semantics. *SMIL—Journal for Linguistic Calculus* **1(2)**: 141–60

Materna P, Sgall P 1984 Optional participants in a semantic interpretation. In: Sgall P (ed.) *Contributions to Functional Syntax, Semantics, and Language Comprehension*. Academia, Prague

Mathesius V 1928 On linguistic characterology with illus-
trations from Modern English. *Actes du 1er Congrès International des Linguistes*: 56–63

Mathesius V 1929 Zur Satzperspektive im modernen Englisch. *Archiv für das Studium der neueren Sprachen und Literaturen* **155**: 202–10

Mathesius V 1936 On some problems of the systematic analysis of grammar. In: *Travaux du Cercle linguistique de Prague* **VI**. Jednota československých matematiků a fyziků, Prague. Repr. in: Vachek J 1964

Mathesius V 1975 *A Functional Analysis of Present Day English on a General Linguistic Basis*. Mouton, The Hague (Ed. by Vachek J)

Panevová J 1974–75 On verbal frames in functional generative description 1, II. *PBML* **22**: 3–40; **23**: 17–52

Panevová J 1977 Verbal frames revisited. *PBML* **28**: 55–71

Pauliny E 1943 *Štruktúra slovenského slovesa*. Bratislava

Pitha P 1980 Case frames of nouns. In: *Linguistic Studies Offered to Berthe Siertsema*. North Holland, Amsterdam

Schooneveld C H van 1978 *Semantic Transmutations*, vol. 1. Physsardt, Bloomington, IN

Sgall P 1964 Zur Frage der Ebenen im Sprachsystem. In: *Travaux linguistiques de Prague* **I**. Academia, Prague

Sgall P 1979–80 Towards a definition of focus and topic. *PBML* **31**: 3–25; **32**: 24–32. Repr. 1981 in: *PSML* **7**. Academia, Prague

Sgall P 1980 Case and meaning. *JPrag* **4**: 525–36

Sgall P 1987 The position of Czech linguistics in theme–focus research. In: Steele R, Threadgold T (eds.) *Language Topics*. Benjamins, Amsterdam

Sgall P 1994 Meaning, reference and discourse patterns. In: Luelsdorff P A (ed.) 1994: 277–309

Sgall P, Hajičová E 1977–78 Focus on focus. *PBML* **28**: 5–54; **29**: 23–41

Sgall P, Hajičová E, Panevová J 1986 *The Meaning of the Sentence in its Semantic and Pragmatic Aspects*. Reidel, Dordrecht/Academia, Prague

Skalička V 1935 *Zur ungarischen Grammatik*. Universita Karlova, Prague

Svoboda A 1981 *Diatheme*. Universita J E Purkyně, Brno

Šmilauer V 1947 *Novočeská skladba*. Prague

Tesnière L 1959 *Eléments de syntaxe structurale*. Librairie C. Klincksieck, Paris

Thèses présentées au Premier congrès de philoloques slaves 1929. In: *Travaux du Cercle linguistique de Prague* **I** 5–29. Jednota československých matematiků a fyziků, Prague

Tichý P 1971 An approach to intensional analysis. *Noùs* **5**: 273–97

Tichý P 1988 *The Foundations of Frege's Logic*. De Gruyter, Berlin

Vachek J 1964 *A Prague School Reader in Linguistics*. Indiana University Press, Bloomington, IN

Relational Grammar

B. Blake

Relational grammar (RG) is a theory of grammar developed primarily by David Perlmutter and Paul Postal. In this theory grammatical relations are taken to be primitive. The theory is multistratal. In a passive clause like *Tom was seen by Fred*, *Tom* is a direct object in the initial stratum which advances to subject in the final stratum displacing the initial stratum subject *Fred*.

1. Basic Notions

RG recognizes the following grammatical relations: subject, direct object, indirect object, and a number of oblique relations such as locative, instrumental, and benefactive. Subject, direct object, and indirect object are called terms and with the obliques they form the following hierarchy:

$$\text{subject direct object indirect object obliques} \tag{1}$$
$$1 \qquad 2 \qquad 3$$

The terms are often referred to by their position on the hierarchy, a subject being 1, a direct object 2, and an indirect object 3. 1 and 2 are called nuclear relations, and 2 and 3 are collectively object relations.

Clause structure is represented by networks of arcs. An arc is a curved arrow joining a tail node and a head node. Each arc bears a label for a relation and one or more coordinates indicating the stratum or strata at which the relation is held. The structure of the active clause (2a) is shown in (2b). (The lowercase c stands for coordinate and the subscript numeral indicates the level or stratum. P stands for predicate.)

Fred saw Tom (2a)

(2b)

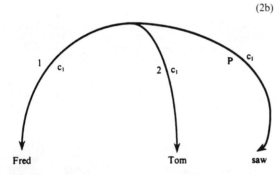

The structure of the corresponding passive (3a) is displayed in (3b):

Tom was seen by Fred (3a)

(3b)

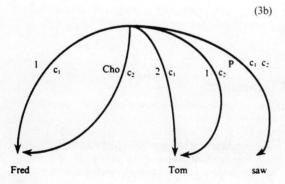

Example (2b) indicates that the active clause is interpreted as having a single stratum in which *Fred* holds the subject relation, *Tom* the direct object relation and *saw* the predicate relation. The passive equivalent (3a) has two strata. As can be seen from (3b), the initial stratum is the same as the sole stratum of the active clause, but the second and final stratum involves revaluations. The initial 2 *Tom* advances to 1 and forces the initial 1 *Fred* to demote to *chômeur* (Cho). The word *chômeur*, which is French for unemployed person, denotes the relation held by nominals that are displaced from term status (1, 2, or 3). *Fred* in (3a) lacks properties of the corresponding term. It is an optional, peripheral prepositional phrase unable to control verb agreement.

Relational networks are difficult to read when more than two strata are involved and it is common practice to use instead a stratal diagram with one arc for each relation and 'horizontal arcs' to mark off the strata. Here is the stratal diagram equivalent of the relational network in (3b):

(4)

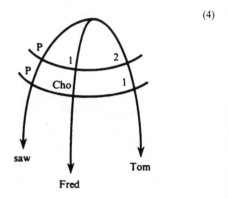

In early RG the assignment of initial grammatical relations was made in accordance with a principle known as the universal alignment hypothesis whereby agents, experiencers, and cognizers were taken to be initial 1s, patients and themes to be initial 2s, and recipients initial 3s. This hypothesis in its strong form has been abandoned, but it remains generally true that agents are taken to be initial 1s and patients or themes initial 2s. The alignment principle can be seen at work in the treatment of the two constructions used with *give* in English.

The construction with *to* is held to reflect initial grammatical relations directly while the double object construction is interpreted as involving the advancement of an initial indirect object to direct object. The relational networks for (5a) and (5b) are given in (6a) and (6b) respectively:

Fred gave a book to Tom (5a)

Fred gave Tom a book (5b)

(6a)

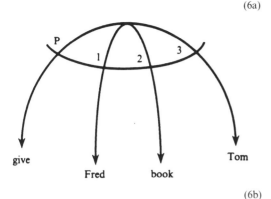

(6b)

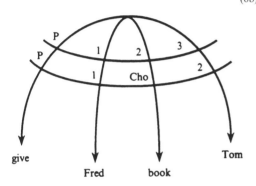

Some syntactic evidence for the interpretation given in (6b) lies in the fact that the putative 2 can be advanced to 1 via passive. Correspondence with (5b) produces *Tom was given a book by Fred*. The relations borne by the nominals in the three strata of this passive are displayed in (7) which is a stratal chart. Each column shows the career of a nominal through the strata. The stratal chart is a convenient substitute for relational networks and stratal diagrams:

Tom was given a book by Fred			(7)
3	2	1	
2	Cho	1	
1	Cho	Cho	

In some varieties of English one can have a passive of the form *A book was given Tom by Fred*. This can be interpreted as the result of 2–1 advancement (passive) with 3–2 advancement in a subsequent stratum:

A book was given Tom by Fred			(8)
2	3	1	
1	3	Cho	
1	2	Cho	

However, the analysis presented in (8) is controversial within RG. Bickford (1987) seeks to constrain RG theory by not allowing 3–2 advancement to follow 2–1 advancement since he finds no language where such a configuration is needed. He points out that there is little evidence to show that nominals like *Tom* in (8)

are direct objects and suggests that they may be indirect objects that are not flagged (marked) as such.

The relational network is unordered. Surface structure order is handled by linearization rules which are normally based on final grammatical relations. The basic word order of English, for instance, can be specified as: 1–P–2–3–nonterm.

RG recognizes a class of overlay relations which can be held in addition to the central relations (1, 2, 3, obliques, and *chômeur*). These include topic, overweight, focus (illustrated in (23a, b)), relative, and question (see *Topic, Focus, and Word Order*). In the relative clause of *I saw the book which you wrote*, the pronoun *which* would bear the 2 relation and the overlay relation of relative. The linearization rules would place relative first in the clause.

2. Relational Laws

RG does not allow unconstrained revaluation. In order to characterize language as narrowly as possible, RG proposes well-formedness conditions on revaluations including the following:

(a) Stratal Uniqueness Law. There can be only one dependent bearing a particular term relation in a particular stratum.

(b) Final 1 Law. Every final stratum must have a subject. This does not mean there must be a surface subject. In *Go away!* there is a second person final 1 that is deleted in surface structure.

(c) Oblique Law. A dependent bearing an oblique relation bears that relation in the initial stratum. In other words, no revaluations to oblique.

(d) Motivated *Chômage* Law. *Chômeurs* are not created spontaneously, but as the result of advancement, ascension (see Sect. 6.2), or dummy birth (Sect. 5.5).

(e) *Chômeur* Advancement Ban. A *chômeur* cannot advance.

Here is a summary of licit revaluations:

Advancements	Demotions	(9)
2–1	1–2	
3–1	1–3	
Oblique-1	1-*Chômeur*	
3–2	2–3	
Oblique-2	2-*Chômeur*	
Oblique-3	3-*Chômeur*	

3. Motivation

RG began as a reaction to transformational grammar in which subject and direct object were defined in terms of structural configuration, the subject being the relation held by the noun phrase immediately dominated by the sentence node and the direct object being the relation held by the noun phrase immediately dominated by the verb phrase node (10). In such a system subject and object are derived entities, whereas in RG they are undefined primitives. An

275

important argument put forward by Perlmutter and Postal (1983) in support of RG as opposed to transformational grammar concerned the universal characterization of the passive. They claimed that RG could characterize the passive universally in terms of the advancement of 2 to 1 from a transitive stratum, whereas an attempt to capture the universal character of the passive in structural terms would have to cope with language particular differences. In Tzotzil, for instance, active and passive have the same word order whereas in English the agent/experiencer and patient/theme change positions. In Russian the *chômeur* appears in the instrumental case whereas in English it appears in a prepositional phrase.

(10)

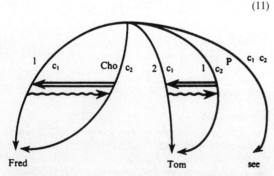

4. Arc Pair Grammar

Arc pair grammar (APG) is an offshoot of relational grammar developed by Paul Postal and David Johnson in the late 1970s (Johnson and Postal 1980). Example (11) is the APG relational network for the passive sentence *Tom was seen by Fred* previously given as (3a):

(11)

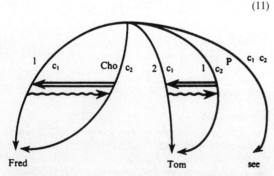

Two notions peculiar to APG that are shown in (11) are the sponsor relation and the erase relation. The initial 1 is said to sponsor the Cho arc. This is indicated by the wiggly arrow. The Cho arc on the other hand erases the initial 1 arc, i.e., replaces it at a later stra-

tum. The erase relation is indicated by a double arrow. Example (11) illustrates that the initial 2 sponsors the final 1 and the final 1 erases the initial 2. The initial 1 is referred to as the predecessor of the Cho arc; conversely the Cho arc is the successor of the initial 1 arc.

5. Some Clause-internal Revaluations

5.1 Unaccusatives

RG distinguishes intransitive subjects that are initial 1s from intransitive subjects that are initial 2s. In English one can form a pseudo-passive with verbs like *sleep*, *dream*, *ski*, and *jump* but not with verbs like *exist*, *melt*, and *vanish*:

The bed was jumped on by the children	(12)
*The bed was existed in by the children	(13)

RG attributes the difference to a difference in initial stratum relations. Predicates like *jump* are analyzed as having an initial 1 and predicates like *exist* as having an initial 2. The former group are called unergative predicates (a stratum with a 1 but no 2 is unergative); the latter group unaccusative (a stratum with a 2 but no 1 is unaccusative). With unaccusative predicates the initial 2 advances to 1 in accordance with the Final 1 Law (Perlmutter and Postal 1984: 85):

Martians dream (14a)

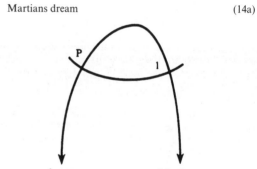

Martians exist (14b)

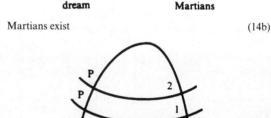

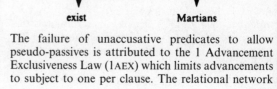

The failure of unaccusative predicates to allow pseudo-passives is attributed to the 1 Advancement Exclusiveness Law (1AEX) which limits advancements to subject to one per clause. The relational network for the pseudo-passive, it is argued, would have 2–1 advancement plus the advancement of an oblique to 1. Here is a stratal chart showing the analysis of *The bed was existed in by the children.*

2	Loc	P	(15)
1	Loc	P	
Cho	1	P	

children	bed	exist

Rosen (1984), developing earlier work of Perlmutter, demonstrates that in Italian intransitive predicates fall into two classes with respect to at least three separate criteria. Verbs like *arrivare* 'to arrive,' *venire* 'to come,' and *partire* 'to leave' conjugate with *essere* 'to be' in the compound tenses; allow the proclitic *ne* 'of it,' 'of them' as in *Ne sono venuti tre* (of-them are come three) 'Three of them came,' and appear in absolute constructions like *Partiti gli amici, Giovanni si è addormentato* 'The friends having departed, Giovanni fell asleep.' On the other hand verbs like *dormire* 'to sleep,' *telefonare* 'to telephone,' and *tacere* 'to be silent' conjugate with *avere* 'to have,' do not allow the proclitic *ne*, and do not appear in absolute constructions. The first group are interpreted as unaccusative, the second group as unergative. The behavior of the putative unaccusative initial 2s parallels the behavior of initial 2s in transitive strata. The proclitic *ne*, for instance, can be used to refer to an initial and final 2 as in *Ne ho visti tre* (of-them I-have seen three) 'I saw three of them.'

5.2 Antipassive and 2–3 Retreat

In a great number of languages there are two-place intransitive constructions which are a regular alternative to the transitive construction or peculiar to certain predicates. There are two analyses available in RG which involve interpreting such constructions as having an initial transitive stratum. If there is evidence that the nonsubject complement is an indirect object, then the intransitive construction can be interpreted as reflecting 2–3 retreat. If the nonsubject complement is neither a 2 nor a 3, then it can be considered a *chômeur*. The following pair of sentences (16) is from Yup'ik Eskimo. Example (16a) is a transitive sentence, and (16b) the intransitive counterpart. In this dialect the detransitivized construction is used to express a nonspecific patient, as here, or it is used in the negative (Blake 1990: 41):

Qimugte-m	neraa	neqa	(16a)
dog-ERG	eat:3s:3s	fish	

'The dog ate the fish.'

Qimugta	ner'uq	neq-mek	(16b)
dog	eat:3s	fish-ABL	

'The dog ate fish.'

In the transitive sentence (16a) the subject is marked by the ergative case and the direct object is in the unmarked absolutive case. In the intransitive counter-part the subject is in the absolutive and the erstwhile direct object in the instrumental and hence a candidate for interpretation as a *chômeur*. However, the Motivated Chômage Law (Sect. 2) specifies that a dependent cannot go into *chômage* spontaneously. Postal's solution to this problem is to analyze sentences like (16b) as follows (Postal 1977):

1	P	2	(17)
2	P	Cho	
1	P	Cho	

qimug-	ner-	neq-

In the second stratum the initial 1 demotes to 2 and pushes the initial 2 into *chômage*. In the final stratum the 2 advances to 1 in accordance with the Final 1 Law.

The construction in (16b) as analyzed in RG is called antipassive, but a note on terminology is in order here. The term antipassive in the general literature is usually used to cover detransitivized constructions in ergative languages, but in RG a distinction is made between 2–3 retreat (see (23b)) and antipassive and the term is not restricted to ergative languages.

5.3 Inversion

In some languages one finds nominals marked like indirect objects which exhibit subject properties. This happens with a verb like Italian *piacere a* 'to please to' as in (18):

A Giorgio	piace	Roma	(18)
to George	pleases	Rome	

'George likes Rome.'

For such a predicate RG supplies an 'inversion analysis.' The experiencer is taken to be an initial 1 that demotes to 3 and the theme is taken to be an initial 2 that advances to 1 in accordance with the Final 1 Law:

1	2	P	(19)
3	2	P	
3	1	P	

Giorgio	Roma	piacere

Some evidence for the analysis is provided by the fact that the inversion nominal (*Giorgio* in (18)) behaves like a subject in that it can control the missing subject of various nonfinite constructions. In (20) *Giorgio*, the subject, controls the missing subject of the infinitive *far(e)*. In (21) it is the putative inversion nominal that controls the missing subject of *lasciar(e)* (adapted from Perlmutter 1982):

Giorgio	mi	ha	rimproverato	tante	volte	da farmi	paura.
George	me	has	reproved	so:many	times	to make:me	fear

'George rebuked me so many times that he scared me.' (20)

A	Giorgio	è	talmente	piaciuta	una	compagna d'ufficio	da lasciarci.
To George	is so	pleased	a	companion-of-office	to leave:us

[lit.] 'To George was so pleasing an office co-worker that he left us.'
'George was so taken with a girl at the office that he left us.' (21)

This is significant when one considers that an 'ordinary indirect object' (initial and final 3) does not have these control properties. RG is able to distinguish between indirect objects that are initial 3s and those that are initial 1s.

5.4 Dummies

Nonreferring nominals like *it* in *It rained* and *there* in *There's a fly in the soup* are treated as dummies and do not appear in the initial stratum but have a *birth* in a later stratum. Here is an analysis of *There's a fly in the soup* (22). Note that *be* is taken to be an unaccusative predicate so *fly* is an initial 2. The dummy is introduced in the second stratum as a 2. It pushes the initial 2 into *chômage* in accordance with the Stratal Uniqueness Law and then advances to 1 in accordance with the Final 1 Law:

(22)

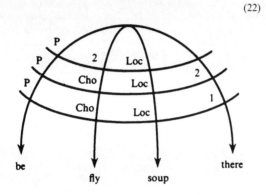

6. Some Multinode Analyses

6.1 Cross-clausal Multiattachment

In a sentence like *Rosa will go to buy the meat*, *Rosa* appears in the main clause, but is also understood to be the subject of the dependent verb. In early transformational grammar *Rosa* would have appeared as the subject of the nonfinite clause in deep structure and been deleted under identity with the controlling nominal in the governing clause by a transformation known as 'equi noun phrase deletion.' In RG *Rosa* would be multiattached. Here is an example from K'ekchi (23). The example illustrates two points: cross-clausal multiattachment (*Rosa* is a 1 in both clauses) and a clause-internal multiattachment arising from the fact that *Rosa* heads an overlay arc (focus) as well as a central relation arc (1). The fact that *Rosa* is focused is apparent from its position before the verb in what is a verb–object–subject language (Berinstein 1985: 137–38):

Lix Rosa ta:-Øxic   chi   lok'oc   re   li   tib (23a)
Rosa FUT-3ABS-go PREP buy:INF DAT the meat
'It's Rosa who will go to buy the meat.'

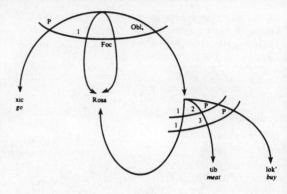

6.2 Ascension

The verb *seem* can take a subject that is sensitive to the selectional restrictions of a dependent verb rather than to *seem* itself. For such predicates an 'ascension' or raising analysis is used. In *Fred seems to work* (24), for instance, *Fred* is taken to be an initial stratum subject of *work* that ascends to become a dependent of *seem*. *Seem* itself is taken to be an unaccusative predicate with a clause as initial 2:

Fred seems to work   (24a)

(24b)

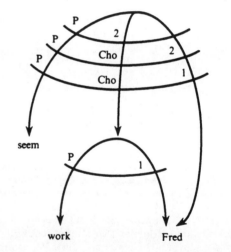

When *Fred* ascends it takes on the relation of the dependent out of which it ascends in accordance with the Relational Succession Law (ascendees assume the grammatical relation of their host).

Ascension analyses are also posited for sentences like *I expect the glass to fall* where *glass* ascends to become the final 2 of the governing clause, and also for sentences with predicates such as *be tough*, *be easy*, etc., as in *John is easy to please*. This would be analyzed as involving the ascension of *John* from initial 2 of *please* to second stratum 2 and final stratum 1 of *be easy*.

Besides cross-clausal ascension RG also posits

ascension out of possessor phrases. Consider the following pair of sentences (25) from Stoney (Frantz 1981:30):

> Ma-thiha n-uzazach (25a)
> my-foot 2s-wash
> 'You washed my foot.'

> Thiha ma-n-uzazach (25b)
> foot 1s-2s-wash
> 'You washed my foot.'

In (25a) the possessor is expressed as a proclitic or prefix to the possessed, whereas in the synonymous or nearly synonymous (25b) the erstwhile possessor is expressed as a direct object realized via a prefix on the verb. RG seeks to relate pairs like this in the following way. Sentence (25a) would be taken to reflect initial stratum relations directly with the first person POSS(essor) a dependent of the H(ead) *thiha* 'foot.' Example (25b) on the other hand would be interpreted as reflecting the ascension of the possessor out of the possessor phrase into the clause proper. This analysis is displayed in (26). Note that the ascendee takes on the relation borne by its host (namely direct object) in accordance with the Relational Succession Law and pushes the initial direct object into *chômage* in accordance with the Stratal Uniqueness Law.

(26)

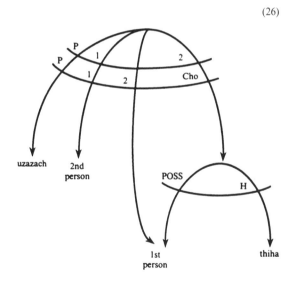

7. Clause Union

If the synonymous sentences (27a and b) are compared one can see that while (27a) contains two clauses, (27b) has amalgamated the two, as evidenced by the position of the clitic pronouns which are proclitic to the finite modal *deve* though they represent arguments of the infinitive *spiegare*:

> Ugo deve spiegar-te-lo. (27a)
> Ugo must explain-thee-it

> Ugo te lo deve spiegare (27b)
> Ugo thee it must explain
> 'Ugo must explain it to you.'

RG provides an analysis in terms of 'clause union' which is applicable here. (27a) is given a biclausal analysis and (27b) is given a biclausal analysis in the initial stratum, but one in which there is a union in a later stratum. The analysis of (27b) is given in (28):

(28)

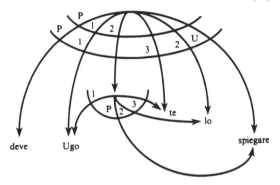

Ugo is an initial 1 in both the upstairs (matrix) and downstairs (embedded) clauses (multiattachment). In the second stratum, the union stratum, *te* and *lo* ascend into the higher clause. *Spiegare* ascends to become a union predicate which can be considered a predicate *chômeur* and indeed, in the analysis of Davies and Rosen presented below, this notion is used. Essentially such an analysis provides for the dependents of a downstairs verb to ascend and become dependents of an upstairs verb leaving the downstairs verb stripped. It has the advantage that it is applicable in cases where the upstairs and downstairs verbs are not even adjacent.

Most of the examples of clause union in the literature concern 'causative clause union.' In Italian, for instance, the verb *fare* 'to make' is used to form the causative of verbs as illustrated in the following (Davies and Rosen 1988:71) where the position of *mi*, a final 3 expressing the recipient of *regalare*, is indicative of union:

> Il babbo mi ha fatto regalare una torta da Nino (29)
> the daddy me has made give a cake by Nino
> 'Father made Nino give a cake to me.'

RG also extends biclausal analyses to morphological causatives. The following example (30) is from Georgian (Davies and Rosen 1988:71):

> Mamam Ninos miacemina torti čemtvis
> father:ERG Nino:DAT he:caused:give:her:it cake me:for
> 'Father made Nino give the cake to me.' (30)

The biclausal analysis is shown in (31). Note that *mama* is an initial 1 in the upstairs clause. This means that the initial 1 of the downstairs clause must be revalued. As can be seen it revalues to 3 which in turn means that the downstairs 3 must revalue. It becomes a *chômeur* as in (31).

(31)

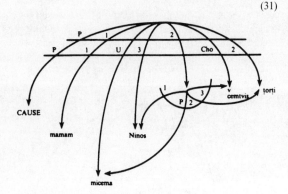

Davies and Rosen (1988) have also proposed a new analysis in which unions are interpreted as multipredicate uniclausal constructions. Example (32) displays the new analysis of (27b) above; the older analysis is in (28):

(32)

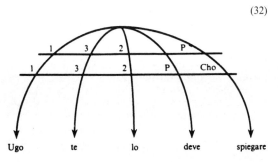

In this analysis there is only one clause node and the inner clause consisting of the lexical verb and its dependents occupies the first stratum. The modal predicate is introduced in the second stratum and puts the inner predicate in *chômage*.

Here is the uniclausal analysis (33) of the Georgian sentence given above as (30) with a biclausal analysis as (31):

		P	1	2	3	(33)
P	1	Cho	3	2	Cho	
CAUSE	mama	micema	Nino	ṭorṭi	čem	

The inner clause consists of *micema* and its dependents. The causative predicate is introduced in the second stratum which puts the lexical predicate in *chômage*.

There are a number of arguments in favor of the new analysis. Under the old analysis violations of the Motivated *Chômage* Law occur. Consider *čem* 'me' in (31). It heads a *cho−meur* arc in the second stratum, but it does not head a term arc in an earlier stratum with the same tail, i.e., in the same clause. According

to the Motivated *Chômage* Law it should. This deficiency is made good under the new analysis as can be seen from (33) since *čem* does head a term arc in an earlier stratum of the same clause.

A second argument concerns the asymmetry between union and ascension. In ascension the ascendee takes over the relation of the host pushing the host or the remnant thereof into *chômage* under the Relational Succession Law (see Sect. 6.2). However, in unions it is the raised nominals that are put in *chômage* when they encounter occupied relations. Under the new analysis there are no raised nominals or ascendees in clause union.

8. Overview

RG is one of a number of theories that began as a reaction to transformational grammar, but whereas some saw transformational grammar with its deep, intermediate, and surface structures and a proliferation of transformations as too unconstrained and moved in the direction of surface structure only models, Perlmutter and Postal retained multilevel analyses and indeed allowed rules to make reference to any level (global rules). The distinctive feature of RG is that it deals in grammatical relations as primitives. Its limitation up to the present has been that it generates relational networks consisting of predicates, central relations, and overlay relations but not surface structures. With a few exceptions, some within the framework of arc pair grammar, it has not spelt out the realization in terms of linear sequences of morphemes. It has not dealt with the internal structure of noun phrases, for instance.

Given the large number of competing theories the future of RG must be in some doubt, but it is certain that RG has made a contribution of permanent value that is translatable into other frameworks. This would include the explication of the hierarchical nature of grammatical relations, the unaccusative hypothesis, and the notion of *chômage*.

Bibliography

The principal sources are two volumes of papers:
    Perlmutter D (ed.) 1983 *Studies in Relational Grammar 1*; Perlmutter D, Rosen C (eds.) 1984 *Studies in Relational Grammar 2*.
A general overview is provided in Blake B J 1990 *Relational Grammar*.
Berinstein A 1985 *Evidence for Multiattachment in K'ekchi (Mayan)*. Garland, New York
Bickford J A 1987 Universal constraints on relationally complex clauses (Doctoral dissertation, University of California)
Blake B J 1990 *Relational Grammar*. Routledge, London
Davies W, Rosen C 1988 Unions as multi-predicate clauses. *Lg* **64**: 52–88
Frantz D 1981 Grammatical relations in universal grammar. Indiana University Linguistics Club, Bloomington, IN
Johnson D, Postal P 1980 *Arc Pair Grammar*. Princeton University Press, Princeton, NJ

Perlmutter D 1982 Syntactic representation, syntactic levels, and the notion of subject. In: Jacobson P, Pullum G (eds.) *The Nature of Syntactic Representation*. Reidel, Dordrecht

Perlmutter D (ed.) 1983 *Studies in Relational Grammar*, vol. 1. University of Chicago Press, Chicago, IL

Perlmutter D, Postal P 1983 Toward a universal definition of the passive. In: Perlmutter D (ed.) 1983

Perlmutter D, Postal P 1984 The 1-Advancement exclusiveness law. In: Perlmutter D, Rosen C (eds.) 1984

Perlmutter D, Rosen C (eds.) 1984 *Studies in Relational Grammar*, vol. 2. University of Chicago Press, Chicago, IL

Postal P 1977 Antipassive in French. *Linguisticae Investigationes* 1: 333–74

Rosen C 1984 The interface between semantic roles and initial grammatical relations. In: Perlmutter D, Rosen C (eds.) 1984

Role and Reference Grammar

Robert D. Van Valin, Jr.

Role and Reference Grammar (RRG) (Van Valin 1993; Van Valin and LaPolla, in press) grew out of an attempt to answer two basic questions: (a) what would linguistic theory look like if it were based on the analysis of Lakhota, Tagalog, and Dyribal, rather than on the analysis of English? and (b) how can the interaction of syntax, semantics, and pragmatics in different grammatical systems best be captured and explained? RRG takes language to be a system of communicative social action, and accordingly, analyzing the communicative functions of grammatical structures plays a vital role in grammatical description and theory from this perspective. It is a monostratal theory, positing only one level of syntactic representation, the actual form of the sentence. The overall organization of the theory is given in Fig. 1.

1. Central Concepts of the Theory

1.1 Clause Structure

RRG rejects the standard formats for representing clause structure (grammatical relations, X-bar syntax), because they are not universal and hence necessarily impose aspects of structure on at least some languages where it is not appropriate. The RRG conception of clause structure (originally proposed in Foley and Van Valin (1984) and further refined in Van

Valin (1993); Van Valin and LaPolla (in press)), the 'layered structure of the clause' (LSC), is made up of the 'nucleus,' which contains the predicate(s), the 'core,' which contains the nucleus plus the arguments of the predicate(s), and the 'periphery,' which contains adjunct temporal and locative modifiers of the core. These aspects of the LSC are universal. This is summarized in Fig. 2.

Some languages have a 'pre-core slot' (PrCS), which is the position of *wh*-words in languages like English and Icelandic, and a 'left-detached position,' (LDP), which is the position of the preclausal element in a left-dislocation construction. In addition, some verb-final languages have a 'post-core slot' (PoCS) (e.g. Japanese; see Shimojo 1995), and some languages also have a 'right-detached position' (RDP), which is the position of the post-clausal element in a right-dislocation construction. Each of the major layers (nucleus, core, clause) is modified by one or more operators, which include grammatical categories such as tense, aspect, modality, and evidentiality. The LSC applies equally to fixed word-order and free word-order languages, to head-marking and dependent-marking languages, and to languages with and without grammatical relations. It is assumed that noun phrases and adpositional phrases have a comparable layered structure; operators in the NP include determiners, quantifiers, and adjectival and nominal modifiers. In the formal representation of the LSC (proposed in Johnson 1987), operators are represented in a distinct projection of the clause from the predicates and arguments (the constituent projection). This is presented in Figs. 3–6. In Fig. 3, the periphery has been omitted from the diagram for the sake of simplicity. In Fig. 4, *did* is labeled both 'tense' and 'IF' in the operator projection, because the position of the tense operator signals illocutionary force in English: core-medial tense signals declarative IF, core-initial (pre-core) tense signals interrogative IF, and the absence of tense in a matrix core signals imperative IF.

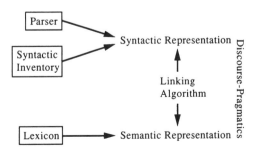

Figure 1. General structure of Role and Reference Grammar.

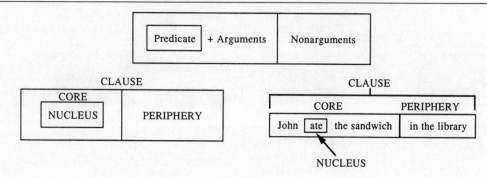

Figure 2. Components of the layered structure of the clause.

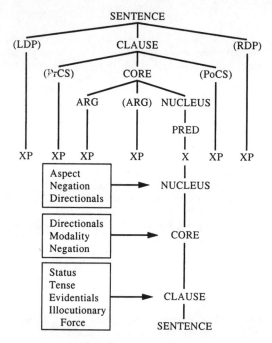

Figure 3. The layered structure of the clause.

they are intended to be concrete, in the sense that they should represent the actual form of the sentence, including the linear sequence of its constituent elements and their morphological properties. The representation may be abstract with respect to phonology or morphophonology; for example, the output could be in terms of abstract morphophonological units rather than concrete phonetic ones.

Representations of constituent projections such as these should be viewed as 'syntactic templates,' the inventory of which in a language constitutes an important component of its grammar. It may be termed the 'syntactic inventory' and complements the lexicon.

The three central components of the LSC also turn out to be the three fundamental building blocks of complex sentences in human language. The unmarked pattern for the construction of complex sentences involves combining nuclei with nuclei, cores with cores, or clauses with clauses. These are called levels of 'juncture' in RRG, specifically nuclear juncture, core juncture, and clausal juncture. Clausal junctures, as the name implies, involve sentences containing multiple clauses. Examples of nuclear junctures from French, English, and Mandarin are given in (1), and their representations are shown in Fig. 7. Justifications for these structures can be found in Van Valin and LaPolla (in press).

Je ferai   manger les gâteaux à Jean. (1a)
1sg make.FUT eat   the cakes to John
'I will make John eat the cakes.'
[Two nuclei, *faire* and *manger*, in a single core.]

John forced open the door. (1b)
[Two nuclei, *force* and *open*, in a single core.]

Tā qiāo pò   le   yī ge fànwǎn. (1c)
3sg hit break PRFV one CL bowl
'He broke (by hitting) a ricebowl.'
[Two nuclei, *qiāo* 'hit' and *pò* 'break,' in a single core.]
    (Hansell 1993)

Core junctures involve two or more cores (which may themselves be internally complex) in a clause. Examples from French, English, and Mandarin are

The operator projections of the clause have been omitted in the Dyirbal (Dixon 1972) and Lakhota examples. The lines connecting the determiners to the head nouns are the operator projection within the NP, analogous to the operator projection within the clause, as in Figs. 3 and 4. In head-marking languages like Lakhota, the bound pronominals on the verb are considered to be the core arguments; overt NPs are within the clause in apposition to them (Van Valin 1985, 1987). Note that despite the differences between the three languages in Figs. 5 and 6, comparable structural relations, such as core argument and peripheral adjunct, are represented in the same way. It should be noted that these representations are not abstract, unlike relational networks or functional structures;

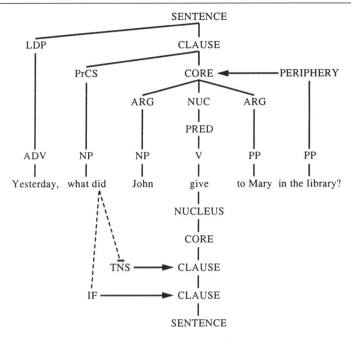

Figure 4. The LSC in English.

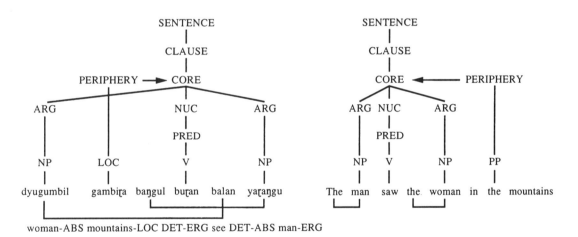

Figure 5. The LSC in Dyirbal and English.

given in (2), and their structures in Fig. 8. In this type of core juncture, the two cores share a core argument; 'sharing a core argument' is defined formally in terms of the linking algorithm mapping syntactic and semantic representations into each other.

> Je laisserai Jean manger les gâteaux.   (2a)
> 1sg let.FUT John eat   the cakes
> 'I will let John eat the cakes.'

> I ordered Fred to force the door open.   (2b)

> Tā jiāo wǒ xiě zì.   (2c)
> 3sg teach 1sg write characters
> 'She teaches me to write characters.'

Of equal importance in the RRG theory of complex sentences is the set of possible syntactic and semantic relations between the units in a juncture; the semantic relations will be discussed in Sect. 1.2. The syntactic relations between units are called 'nexus' relations in RRG. Traditionally, only two basic nexus relations are

283

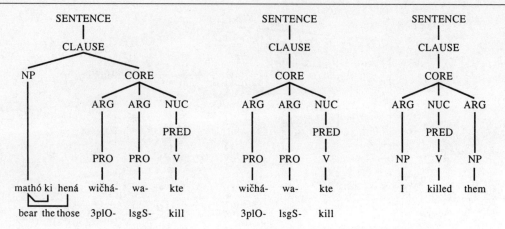

Figure 6. The LSC in Lakhota (head-marking) and English (dependent-marking).

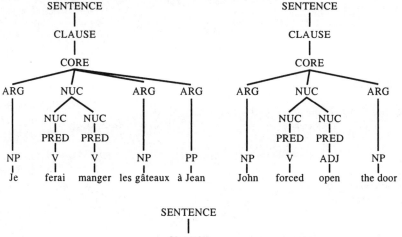

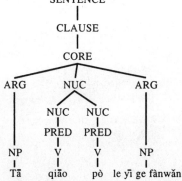

Figure 7. Nuclear junctures in French, English, and Mandarin.

recognized, coordination and subordination, but RRG, following Olson's (1981) analysis of clause linkage in Barai (a Papuan language), posits three nexus types: coordination, subordination, and cosubordination, which is essentially dependent coordination. The dependence is operator dependence; that is, in cosub-

ordination, the units obligatorily share one or more operators at the level of juncture. In the Mandarin example in (2c), aspect obligatorily has scope over both nuclei, and therefore the nexus is cosubordination. This is represented as in Fig. 9.

The following examples from Turkish (in (3) below

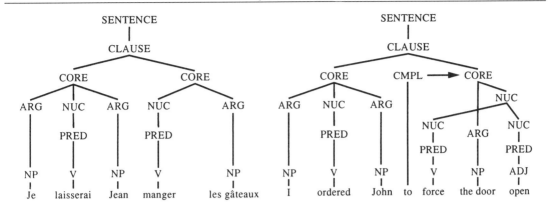

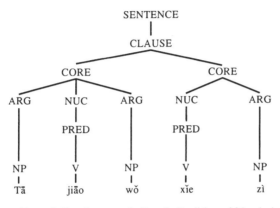

Figure 8. Core junctures in French, English, and Mandarin.

and in Fig. 10, from Watters (1993)) illustrate obligatory operator sharing and the lack of it in Turkish core cosubordination and coordination, respectively. The term 'coordination' here is being used for an abstract linkage relation referring to a relationship of equivalence and independence at the level of juncture. It is distinct from conjunction, which is a construction type of the general form 'X conj Y,' which may be one of the formal instantiations of coordinate nexus.

Core   cosubordination: (3a)
Gid-ip   gör-meli-yiz.
go-CMPL see-MODAL-1pl
'We ought to go and see.'

Core coordination: (3b)
Müzik dinle-yerek,   uyu-yabil-ir-im.
music listen-CMPL sleep-MODAL-AOR-1sg
'While listening to music, I can sleep.'

In (3a), the modal operator -*meli*- ('ought') has scope over both cores, and therefore the nexus is cosubordinate; in (3b), on the other hand, the modal operator -*yabil*- ('able') has scope only over the final core, hence coordinate nexus. The following sentences from Kewa (Franklin 1971) are a minimal triple for the three nexus types at the clause level.

Coordination: (4a)
Nipú ípu-la   pare ní paalá na-pía.
3sg come-3sgPRES but 1sg afraid NEG-be.1sgPRES
'He is coming, but I am not afraid.'

Cosubordination: (4b)
(Ní) Épo lá-ri   épa-wa.
1sg whistle say-SIM.SS come-1sgPAST
'I whistled while I came,' or 'I came whistling.'

Subordination: (4c)
(Ní) Épo lá-lo-pulu   irikai épa-lia.
1sg whistle say-1sgPRES-CAUSAL dog come-3sgFUT
'Because I am whistling, the dog will come.'

The three levels of juncture combine with the three nexus types to generate nine possible complex sentence types. Not all of them are instantiated in every language; for example, Korean appears to have all nine (Yang 1994), while English appears to have six and Jacaltec seven. The juncture-nexus types found in a language may be realized by more than one formal construction type; for example, both *Mary sat playing the guitar* and *Robin tried to open the door* instantiate core cosubordination, while both *For Sam to leave now would be a mistake* and *Lisa's losing her job shocked everyone* instantiate core subordination in English.

285

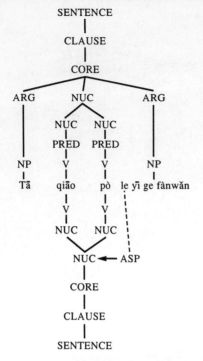

Figure 9. Nuclear cosubordination in Mandarin.

The nine juncture-nexus types may be ordered into a hierarchy in terms of the tightness of the syntactic link between the units (see the hierarchy in Fig. 12 in Sect. 1.2).

1.2 Semantic Structure

The heart of the RRG approach is the system of lexical representation and semantic roles. The system of lexical representation is based on Vendler's (1967) *Aktionsart* classification of verbs into states, activities, achievements, and accomplishments. Each of these classes has a causative counterpart, and the telic alternative uses of activity verbs are termed active accomplishments. Examples of each class and their formal representation are given in (5) and (6). This system differs in important ways from the one proposed in Foley and Van Valin (1984) and assumed in Van Valin (1990, 1991a, 1993).

State:	The boy is afraid of the dog.	(5a)
Causative state:	The dog frightens/scares the boy.	(5a′)
Achievement:	The balloon popped.	(5b)
Causative achievement:	The cat popped the balloon.	(5b′)
Accomplishment:	The ice melted.	(5c)

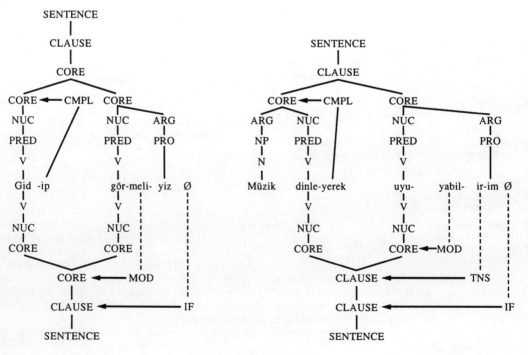

Figure 10. Turkish core junctures.

Causative accomplishment:	The hot water melted the ice.	(5c′)
Activity:	The ball bounced around the room.	(5d)
Causative activity:	The girl bounced the ball around the room.	(5d′)
Activity:	The boy drank milk.	(5e)
Active accomplishment:	The boy drank a glass of milk.	(5e′)
State:	**predicate′** (x) or (x,y)	(6a)
Activity:	**do′** (x, [**predicate′** (x) or (x,y)])	(6b)
Achievement:	INGR(ESSIVE) **predicate′** (x) or (x,y)	(6c)
Accomplishment:	BECOME **predicate′** (x) or (x,y)	(6d)
Active accomplishment:	**do′** (x, [**predicate₁′** (x, (y))]) ∧ BECOME **predicate₂′** (z, x) or (y)	(6e)
Causative:	α CAUSE β, where α, β are representations of any type	(6f)

Achievements are punctual, and accomplishments are durative, as are their causative counterparts.

A crucial component of this system is a set of syntactic and semantic tests for determining the class membership of a verb in a particular sentence, since the class of the verb determines the lexical representation or 'logical structure' (LS). Examples of English verbs with their LSs are given in (7):

States: (7)

Leon is a fool.	**be′** (Leon, [**fool′**])
The window is shattered.	**shattered′** (window)
Fred is at the house.	**be-at′** (house, Fred)
John saw the picture.	**see′** (John, picture)

Activities:

The children cried.	**do′** (children, [**cry′** (children)])
The wheel squeaks.	**do′** (wheel, [**squeak′** (wheel)])
Carl ate snails.	**do′** (Carl, [**eat′** (Carl, snails)])

Achievements:

The window shattered.	INGR **shattered′** (window)
The balloon popped.	INGR **popped′** (balloon)
John glimpsed the picture.	INGR **see′** (John, picture)

Accomplishments:

The snow melted.	BECOME **melted′** (snow)
The sky reddened.	BECOME **red′** (sky)
Mary learned French.	BECOME **know′** (Mary, French)

Active accomplishments:

Carl ate the snail.	**do′** (Carl [**eat′** (Carl, snail)]) ∧ BECOME **eaten′** (snail)
Paul ran to the store.	**do′** (Paul, [**run′** (Paul)]) ∧ BECOME **be-at′** (store, Paul)

Causatives:

The dog scared the boy.	[**do′** (dog, ∅)] CAUSE [**feel′** (boy, [**afraid′**])]
Max broke the window.	[**do′** (Max, ∅)] CAUSE [BECOME **broken′** (window)]
The cat popped the balloon.	[**do′** (cat, ∅)] CAUSE [INGR **popped′** (balloon)]
Felix bounced the ball.	[**do′** (Felix, ∅)] CAUSE [**do′** (ball, [**bounce′** (ball)])]

Examination of the verbal systems of a number of languages had led to the conclusion that this set of distinctions is one of the fundamental organizing principles of verbal systems in human language.

The RRG theory of semantic roles is rather different from that of other theories, in that it posits two types of semantic roles (see *Functional Relations*). The first are specific thematic relations, the traditional (since Fillmore 1968 and Gruber 1965) notions of agent, theme, patient, experiencer, etc. The second are generalized semantic roles called 'semantic macroroles'; they were introduced in Van Valin (1977) and have no exact analogue in other theories, although Jackendoff's 'action tier' and Dowty's proto-roles bear some resemblance. Following the ideas of Gruber (1965) and Jackendoff (1976), RRG defines thematic relations in terms of argument positions in LSs such as those in (8) and (9). All thematic relations are defined in terms of argument positions in state and activity LSs; all other LS types are composed of them plus elements like BECOME, INGR and CAUSE. Since thematic relations have no independent status, they are really just mnemonics for the argument positions in LSs. That is, 'experiencer' stands for 'the first argument of a two-place state predicate of internal experience,' for example. In verbs that lexicalize agency, e.g., *murder*, agent is represented by 'DO (x, ...' (following Dowty 1979). However, in most cases agent is an implicature related to human effectors with certain types of activity predicates and would not be represented in the LS of the verb (see Holisky 1987; Van Valin and Wilkins 1996).

The second type of semantic role plays a crucial role in the theory; macroroles act as the primary interface between the LS and syntactic representations. There are only two macroroles, 'actor' and 'undergoer,' corresponding to the two primary arguments in a prototypical transitive relation. They are called 'macroroles' because each subsumes a number of specific thematic relations; the relationship between the macroroles and

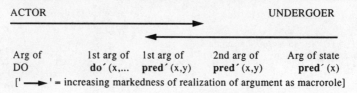

Figure 11. The Actor-Undergoer Hierarchy.

the argument positions in LS is captured in the Actor-Undergoer Hierarchy in Fig. 11. Given the LS of a verb, the most agent-like argument will be actor, the most patient-like undergoer, in the default case. Macroroles are not equivalent to grammatical relations, as shown in (8):

Der Junge [SUBJ, ACTOR] hat den Kuchen   (8a)
[OBJ, UNDERGOER] aufgegessen.
'The boy ate the cake.'

Der Kuchen [SUBJ, UNDERGOER] wurde   (8b)
vom Jungen [ACTOR] aufgegessen.
'The cake [SUBJ, UNDERGOER] was eaten by the boy [ACTOR].'

Der Hund [SUBJ, ACTOR] ist um das Haus   (8c)
herumgelaufen.
'The dog [SUBJ, ACTOR] ran around the house.'

Der Hund [SUBJ, UNDERGOER] ist gestorben.   (8d)
'The dog [SUBJ, UNDERGOER] died.'

The exact role of macroroles in the mapping (or linking) between semantic and syntactic representations will be sketched in Sect. 1.4 and summarized in Fig. 15.

As mentioned in the previous section, an important component of the theory of complex sentences is the semantic relations that obtain between units in a juncture. These include causality, psych-action, direct perception, cognition, propositional attitude, conditional, and varieties of temporal sequence. These may be ordered into a hierarchy in terms of whether the units in the juncture express facets of a single event, state, or action, or of distinct events, states, or actions. This semantic hierarchy interacts with the syntactic hierarchy of juncture-nexus types as follows: there is an iconic relation between the semantics and syntax of clause linkage, such that the tightness of the syntactic linkage directly reflects the semantic integration of the units in the linkage (cf. Silverstein 1976; Givón 1980). This is expressed in the Interclausal Relations Hierarchy in Fig. 12. Van Valin and Wilkins (1993) employ this hierarchy, together with an enriched version of the system of lexical representation introduced above, to show how it is possible to predict the syntactic form of certain types of complex sentences from their semantic representations.

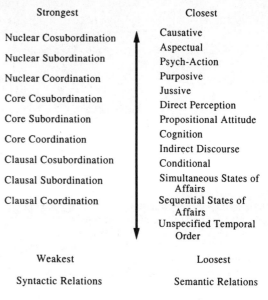

Figure 12. Interclausal Relations Hierarchy.

1.3 The Lexicon

The lexicon plays a very important role in RRG, and it should be considered a lexicalist theory. Lexical entries for verbs are built around LSs; the lexical representation of nouns is based on the theory of nominal qualia proposed in Pustejovsky (1995). RRG takes the position that lexical entries for verbs should contain only idiosyncratic information, with as much as possible derived from general lexical principles or rules. Information about transitivity is very important, and RRG defines transitivity in terms of the number of macroroles that a verb takes: transitive = two, intransitive = one, atransitive = zero. In RRG, no syntactic subcategorization information is included in lexical entries; all of the relevant information is derivable from the LS of the verb plus information about its transitivity. Thus these principles have the effect of predicting the syntactic subcategorization of a verb from its semantic representation. (See Van Valin (1990, 1991a) for application of this to the analysis of syntactic issues in Italian, Georgian, and Icelandic.) All theories must stipulate the transitivity of exceptional verbs, and this is done in RRG by specifying their transitivity in terms of [MRα], where 'α' is zero, one, or two. Sample lexical entries for some English verbs are given in (9):

kill	[**do′** (x, ∅)] CAUSE [BECOME **dead′** (y)]	(9a)
own	**have′** (x,y)	(9b)
belong (*to*)	**have′** (x,y) [MR1]	(9c)
arrive	BECOME **be-at′** (x,y) [MR1]	(9d)
seem	**seem′** (x,y) [MR0]	(9e)
see	**see′** (x,y)	(9f)
watch	**do′** (x, [**see′** (x,y)])	(9g)
show	[**do′** (w, ∅)] CAUSE [INGR **see′** (x,y)]	(9h)
run	**do′** (x, [**run′** (x)])	(9i)
melt	BECOME **melted′** (x)	(9j)

The prepositions that mark oblique core arguments can in many instances be predicated from the LS of the verb and therefore need not be listed in the lexical entry (cf. Jolly 1993).

RRG distinguishes lexical from syntactic phenomena in terms of the linking scheme, as will be discussed below. Basically, any process which affects LSs or the arguments therein or the mapping between LSs and macroroles is considered to be lexical. Examples include causativization, regardless of whether it is morphologically unmarked (as in English) or marked (as in Japanese and Lakhota), noun incorporation, the 'dative alternation' (which is analyzed as variable linking to undergoer; cf. Van Valin 1993), and some types of passivization and antipassivization. Syntactic phenomena involve the mapping between macroroles and the syntactic representation, e.g., some types of passivization and antipassivization, *wh*-question formation in languages like English and Icelandic, and 'raising' constructions (cf. Van Valin 1993).

1.4 Focus Structure

The issue of the distribution of information in clauses and sentences was not addressed in Foley and Van Valin's original work (1984). In Van Valin (1993), Lambrecht's (1986, 1987, 1994) theory of 'focus structure' is integrated into RRG. Focus structure is the grammatical system which serves to indicate the scope of the assertion in an utterance in contrast to the pragmatic presupposition, and it is vital to the RRG analysis of many grammatical phenomena. An innovation in RRG is the distinction between the 'potential focus domain' (PFD), i.e., the syntactic domain in the sentence where focus may fall, and the 'actual focus domain,' i.e., the part that is focused in a particular sentence. Languages vary in terms of how the PFD is restricted, both in simple sentences and in complex sentences, and this variation underlies important

grammatical differences across languages (cf. Van Valin 1993, 1995). The focus structure of an utterance is represented in a distinct projection of the clause from the operator and constituent projections; this is exemplified in Fig. 13 for a predicate focus construction in English ('predicate focus' is Lambrecht's term for the traditional 'topic-comment' structure with a topical subject and a focal predicate). It is possible to represent all three projections in a single representation, as in Fig. 14.

1.5 Grammatical Relations and Linking

In the earliest work on RRG it was argued that grammatical relations like subject and direct object are not universal and cannot be taken as the basis for adequate grammatical theories. In place of these notions, RRG employs the notion of 'syntactic pivot,' which is a construction-specific relation and is defined as à restricted neutralization of semantic roles and pragmatic functions for syntactic purposes (see *Functional Relations*). The other arguments in a clause are characterized as direct or oblique core arguments; there is nothing in RRG corresponding to direct or indirect object.

Syntactic functions like pivot and direct core argument represent the syntactic pole of the system, while LSs represent the semantic pole. In every language with grammatical relations, there is an accessibility to pivot hierarchy for multiple-argument verbs; it is the actor-undergoer hierarchy interpreted from the actor end, i.e. arg of DO > 1sg arg of **do′** > 1st arg of **pred′** (x,y) > 2nd arg of **pred′** (x,y) > arg of **pred′** (x). In syntactically accusative languages like English and German, the highest ranking macrorole is the default choice for pivot, whereas in syntactically ergative languages like Dyirbal and Sama (Austronesian, Philippines; Walton 1986), it is lowest ranking macrorole which is the default choice. That is, in a syntactically accusative language the unmarked choice for syntactic pivot of a transitive verb is the actor, with the undergoer being a marked choice possible only in a passive construction. On the other hand, in a syntactically ergative language, the unmarked choice for syntactic pivot of a transitive verb is the undergoer, with the actor being a marked choice possible only in an antipassive construction. With an intransitive verb, the hierarchy is irrelevant, as the single macrorole functions as pivot regardless of whether it is actor or undergoer.

The overall linking system is summarized in Fig. 15. We have discussed logical structures, macroroles, and the hierarchy linking them. This part of the system is universal, in that there is very little cross-linguistic variation; this is the domain of lexical processes, as mentioned in Sect. 1.3. Where languages differ substantially is how macroroles and other arguments link into the syntax. The reason the arrows in Fig. 15 are double-headed is that the linking system works both

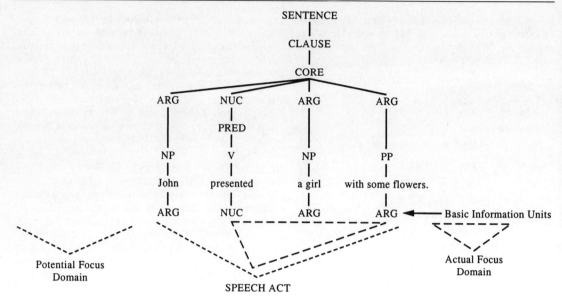

Figure 13. Predicate focus construction in English.

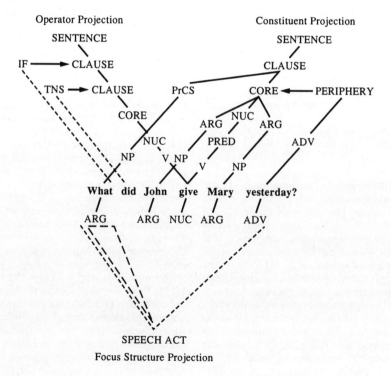

Focus Structure Projection

Figure 14. Clause structure with constituent, operator and focus structure projections.

290

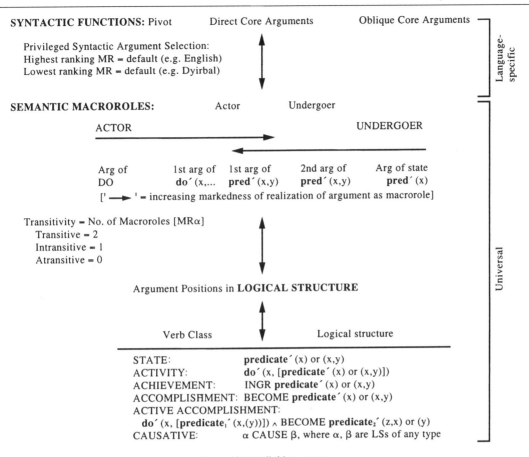

SYNTACTIC FUNCTIONS: Pivot   Direct Core Arguments   Oblique Core Arguments

Privileged Syntactic Argument Selection:
Highest ranking MR = default (e.g. English)
Lowest ranking MR = default (e.g. Dyirbal)

Language-specific

SEMANTIC MACROROLES: Actor   Undergoer

ACTOR   UNDERGOER

Arg of	1st arg of	1st arg of	2nd arg of	Arg of state
DO	**do′** (x,...	**pred′** (x,y)	**pred′** (x,y)	**pred′** (x)

[' → ' = increasing markedness of realization of argument as macrorole]

Transitivity = No. of Macroroles [MRα]
   Transitive = 2
   Intransitive = 1
   Atransitive = 0

Argument Positions in **LOGICAL STRUCTURE**

Verb Class   Logical structure

STATE: **predicate′** (x) or (x,y)
ACTIVITY: **do′** (x, [**predicate′** (x) or (x,y)])
ACHIEVEMENT: INGR **predicate′** (x) or (x,y)
ACCOMPLISHMENT: BECOME **predicate′** (x) or (x,y)
ACTIVE ACCOMPLISHMENT:
   do′ (x, [**predicate₁′** (x,(y))]) ∧ BECOME **predicate₂′** (z,x) or (y)
CAUSATIVE: α CAUSE β, where α, β are LSs of any type

Universal

Figure 15. RRG linking system.

from semantics to syntax and from syntax to semantics. A theory which could describe the linking from semantics to syntax only could be part of a language production system, but it would not be adequate for a comprehension system. In such a system, the parser, as an idealization, would take the input and produce a structured syntactic representation of it, identifying the elements of the layered structure of the clause and the cases, adpositions, and other grammatically relevant elements in the sentence. It is then the grammar's job to map this structure into a semantic representation, as the first step in interpreting it, and this is where the syntax → semantics linking algorithm is required. The details of the linking algorithm are given in Van Valin and LaPolla (in press).

Most of what counts as 'syntax' in many theories, for example, case assignment, agreement, *wh*-movement, and reflexivization, is handled in RRG in terms of the syntactic phase of the linking. The analysis of reflexivization in RRG follows the approach in Jackendoff (1992) and states the constraints for core-internal ('clause-bound' in other theories) reflex-ivization at the LS level, not with respect to the syntactic representation. The linking in a *wh*-question in English is illustrated in Fig. 16; the subscripts ('ACV' and 'ACS') stand for 'activated' and 'accessible,' and they refer to different cognitive statuses that a referent of the element may have (cf. Lambrecht 1994).

Constraints on *wh*-question formation and other 'extraction' constructions is explained in terms of the interaction of focus structure and syntax, in particular in terms of restrictions on the potential focus domain (Van Valin 1993, 1995). The interaction of the three projections of the clause with linking is represented in Fig. 17.

2. Some implications of RRG

RRG illustrates one possible answer to the questions stated at the beginning of this article, and it shows that it is possible to have a rigorous, typologically-sensitive grammatical theory which takes semantics and pragmatics as central features.

With respect to cognitive issues, RRG adopts the criterion of psychological adequacy formulated in Dik

291

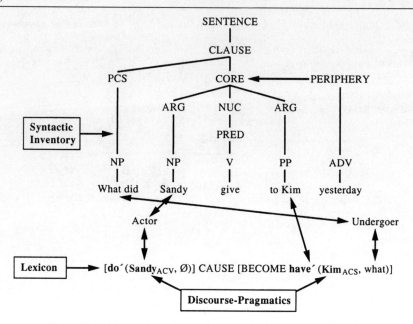

Figure 16. Linking syntax and semantics in a simple sentence in English.

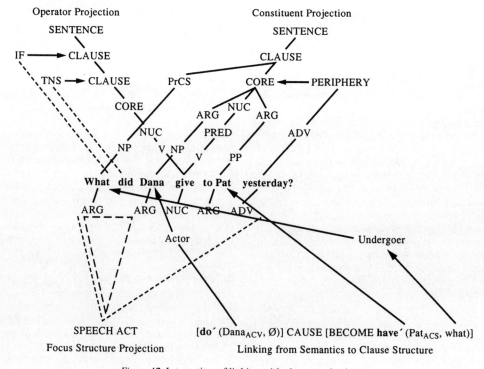

Figure 17. Interaction of linking with clause projections.

(1991), which states that a theory should be compatible with the results of psycholinguistic research on the acquisition, processing, production, interpretation and memorization of linguistic expressions (1991: 248). It also accepts the related criterion put forth in Kaplan and Bresnan (1982) that theories of linguistic structure should be directly relatable to testable theories of language production and comprehension. The RRG approach to language acquisition, sketched in Van Valin (1991b, 1994), rejects the position that grammar is radically arbitrary and hence unlearnable, and maintains that it is relatively motivated (in Saussure's sense) semantically and pragmatically. Accordingly, there is sufficient information available to the child in the speech to which it is exposed to enable it to construct a grammar. For example, Braine (1992) shows how a conception of clause structure very much like the layered structure of the clause could be constructed developmentally by the child. Rispoli (1991a, 1991b, 1994, 1995) shows how the lexical representations in Sect. 1.2 and the conception of grammatical relations in Sect. 1.4 could be learned. Bowerman (1990) provides evidence in favor of the view that rules linking syntactic and semantic representations of the type symmarized in Fig. 15 are learned, and Van Valin (1994) puts forward an account of how some of the constraints on linking between syntactic and semantic representations in complex sentences (i.e., subjacency) could be learned.

Bibliography

Bowerman M 1990 Mapping semantic roles onto syntactic functions: Are children helped by innate linking rules? *Linguistics* **28**: 1253–89

Braine M D S 1992 What sort of innate structure is needed to 'bootstrap' into syntax? *Cognition* **45**: 77–100

Dik S 1991 Functional Grammar. In: Droste F, Joseph J (eds.) *Linguistic Theory and Grammatical Description.* Benjamins, Amsterdam

Dixon R M W 1972 *The Dyirbal Language of North Queensland.* Cambridge University Press, Cambridge

Dowty D 1979 *Word Meaning and Montague Grammar.* Reidel, Dordrecht

Fillmore C J 1968 The case for case. In: Bach E, Harms R (eds.) *Universals in Linguistic Theory.* Holt, Rinehart and Winston, New York

Foley W A, Van Valin R D Jr 1984 *Functional Syntax and Universal Grammar.* Cambridge University Press, Cambridge

Franklin K 1971 *A Grammar of Kewa, New Guinea.* Pacific Linguistics C16. Australian National University, Canberra

Givón T 1980 The binding hierarchy and the typology of complements. *SLang* **4**: 333–77

Gruber J 1965 *Studies in Lexical Relations* (Unpublished PhD dissertation, Massachusetts Institute of Technology)

Hansell M 1993 Serial verbs and complement constructions in Mandarin: A clause linkage analysis. In: Van Valin R D Jr (ed.) *Advances in Role and Reference Grammar.* Benjamins, Amsterdam

Holisky D A 1987 The case of the intransitive subject in Tsova-Tush (Batsbi). *Lingua* **71**: 103–32

Jackendoff R 1976 Toward an explanatory semantic representation. *LIn* **7**: 89–150

Jackendoff R 1992 Mme. Tussaud meets the Binding Theory. *NLLT* **10**: 1–31

Johnson M 1987 A new approach to clause structure in Role and Reference Grammar. *Davis Working Papers in Linguistics* **2**: 55–59

Jolly J 1993 Preposition assignment in English. In: Van Valin R D Jr (ed.) *Advances in Role and Reference Grammar.* Benjamins, Amsterdam

Kaplan R, Bresnan J 1982 Lexical-Functional Grammar: A formal system for grammatical representation. In: Bresnan J (ed.) *The Mental Representation of Grammatical Relations.* MIT Press, Cambridge, MA

Lambrecht K 1986 *Topic, Focus and the Grammar of Spoken French* (Unpublished PhD dissertation, University of California, Berkeley)

Lambrecht K 1987 Sentence focus, information structure, and the thetic-categorial distinction. *BLS* **13**: 366–82

Lambrecht K 1994 *Information Structure and Sentence Form.* Cambridge University Press, Cambridge

Olson M 1981 *Barai clause junctures: Toward a functional theory of interclausal relations* (Unpublished PhD dissertation, Australian National University)

Pustejovsky J 1995 *The Generative Lexicon.* MIT Press, Cambridge, MA

Rispoli M 1991a The acquisition of verb subcategorization in a functionalist framework. *First Language* **11**: 41–63

Rispoli M 1991b The mosaic acquisition of grammatical relations. *JChL* **18**: 517–52

Rispoli M 1994 Structural dependency and the acquisition of grammatical relations. In: Levy Y (ed.) *Other Children, Other Languages: Issues in the Theory of Language Acquisition.* LEA, Hillsdale, NJ

Rispoli M 1995 Missing arguments and the acquisition of predicate meanings. In: Tomasello M, Merriman W (eds.) *Beyond Names for Things: Young Children's Acquisition of Verbs.* LEA, Hillsdale, NJ

Shimojo M 1995 *Focus Structure and Morphosyntax in Japanese: Wa and Ga, and Word Order Flexibility* (Unpublished PhD dissertation, SUNY at Buffalo)

Silverstein M 1976 Hierarchy of Features and Ergativity. In: Dixon R (ed.) *Grammatical Categories in Australian Languages.* Australian Institute of Aboriginal Studies, Canberra

Van Valin R D Jr 1977 *Aspects of Lakhota Syntax* (Unpublished PhD dissertation, University of California, Berkeley)

Van Valin R D Jr 1985 Case marking and the structure of the Lakhota clause. In: Nichols J, Woodbury A (eds.) *Grammar Inside and Outside the Clause.* Cambridge University Press, Cambridge

Van Valin R D Jr 1987 The role of government in the grammar of head-marking languages. *IJAL* **53**: 371–97

Van Valin R D Jr 1990 Semantic parameters of split intransitivity. *Language* **66**: 221–60

Van Valin R D Jr 1991a Another look at Icelandic case marking and grammatical relations. *NLLT* **9**: 145–94

Van Valin R D Jr 1991b Functionalist linguistic theory and language acquisition. *First Language* **11**: 7–40

Van Valin R D Jr 1993 A synopsis of Role and Reference Grammar. In: Van Valin R D Jr (ed.) *Advances in Role and Reference Grammar.* Benjamin, Amsterdam

Van Valin R D Jr 1994 Extraction restrictions, competing theories and the argument from the poverty of the stimulus. In: Lima S et al. (eds.) *The Reality of Linguistic Rules.* Benjamin, Amsterdam

Van Valin R D Jr 1995 Toward a functionalist account of so-called 'extraction constraints.' In: Divriendt B et al. (eds.) *Complex Structures: A Functionalist Perspective.* Mouton de Gruyter, Berlin

Van Valin R D Jr, LaPolla R J in press *Syntax: Structure, Meaning and Function.* Cambridge University Press, Cambridge

Van Valin R D Jr, Wilkins D P 1993 Predicting syntactic structure from semantic representations: *Remember* in English and its equivalents in Mparntwe Arrernte. In: Van Valin R D Jr (ed.) *Advances in Role and Reference Grammar.* Benjamins, Amsterdam

Van Valin R D Jr, Wilkins D P 1996 The case for 'effector':

case roles, agents and agency revisited. In: Shibatani M, Thompson S (eds.) *Grammatical Constructions.* Oxford University Press, Oxford

Vendler Z 1967 *Linguistics in Philosophy.* Cornell University Press, Ithaca

Walton C 1986 *Sama Verbal Semantics: Classification, Derivation and Inflection.* Linguistic Society of the Philippines, Manila

Watters J 1993 An investigation of Turkish clause linkage. In: Van Valin R D Jr (ed.) *Advances in Role and Reference Grammar.* Benjamins, Amsterdam

Yang B-S 1994 *Morphosyntactic phenomena of Korean in Role and Reference Grammar: Psych-verb constructions, inflectional verb morphemes, complex sentences, and relative clauses.* Hankuk, Seoul

Stratificational Grammar

David C. Bennett

An account of syntax within the framework of stratificational grammar (SG) needs to be understood in the context of the theory as a whole. Developed by Sydney M. Lamb from the late 1950s onwards, SG has inevitably undergone various kinds of revisions over the years, but most versions reflect the following three basic assumptions: (a) the information constituting a language is appropriately represented as a network of relationships; (b) within the network as a whole can be identified certain distinct levels, or 'strata'; and (c) to model various linguistic processes, networks need to be considered also from a dynamic point of view. Section 1 expands briefly on each of these basic assumptions; Sect. 2 reviews relevant accounts of syntax; and Sect. 3 summarizes work on modeling linguistic processes. Section 4 re-examines the notion of stratification.

1. The Basic Assumptions

1.1 A Network of Relations

The view of a language as a network of relations is present in Saussure (1949) but is even more prominent in Hjelmslev (1961), from where it was taken into SG. Figure 1 shows a highly simplified fragment of a network grammar of English. Of particular interest is the fact that part of the network corresponds to a simple phrase structure grammar (PSG) whereas the remainder of the network represents part of the lexicon. Thus, the section of the diagram on the right is a network version of the following PSG:

S → NP V (NP) (PP)
NP → Det N (S)
V → {*enter, arrive,*...}
PP → prep NP
prep → {*to, into, at, in,*...}.

The lexicon, on the other hand, contains the items *enter, arrive, to, into, at,* and *in,* and shows the concepts to which these items are connected (at the top of the diagram) and something of their phonological structure (at the bottom). Wherever two items are similar in some respect—either semantically or phonologically, or in terms of their syntactic distribution— what they share is explicitly represented in the connections within the network.

In the terminology of SG, the vertical dimension of the diagram, which connects semantic components such as 'goal' ultimately to phonological components such as /Nasal/, is known as the 'realizational structure.' On the other hand, the section corresponding to a PSG would be referred to as the 'lexotactics.' (This term is modeled on the more familiar term 'phonotactics,' with 'lex-' substituted for 'phon-' since the ultimate constituents of the lexotactics are 'lexemes,' or lexical items.) The lexotactics can be thought of as being horizontal and located at a particular level of the realizational structure. Diamond-shaped nodes are used where lines of the lexotactics connect to lines in the realizational structure. They represent a special kind of AND node: lexemes have a particular meaning *and* a particular phonological structure *and* a particular syntactic category membership. Otherwise, AND nodes are triangular in shape. The three AND nodes in the lexotactics represent constructions: the sentence, noun phrase, and prepositional phrase constructions. These three nodes are also 'ordered': the left-to-right order of the lines at the bottom shows the order in which the various constituents occur. They are also 'downward' ANDs: they branch in a downward direction. The ordered downward ANDs in the bottom half of the realizational structure represent the phono-

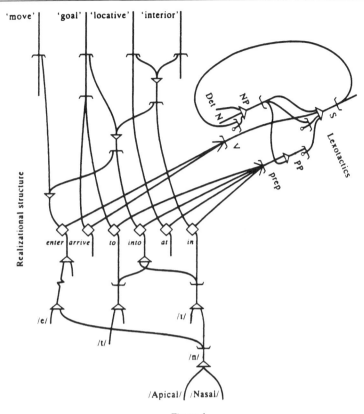

Figure 1.

logical structure of particular lexemes (either in terms of syllables or in terms of phonological segments). On the other hand, the AND node showing /n/ as having the phonological components /Apical/ and /Nasal/ is an 'unordered' downward AND (since the components are simultaneous rather than sequential). In the top half of the realizational structure, unordered AND nodes occur also with 'upward' branching, representing particular combinations of semantic components. The remainder of the nodes in Fig. 1 are OR nodes. They represent, inter alia, alternative members of syntactic categories (e.g., the category of prepositions), alternative slots in which noun phrases may occur, and alternative realizations of particular concepts or combinations of concepts (for more detailed discussion of the notation, see Lamb 1966; Lockwood 1972).

1.2 Strata

One way in which the grammar of Fig. 1 can be improved upon is by including a phonotactics, so that it would specify possible combinations of phonological elements of various sizes (including phonological components, segments, and syllables). Similarly, a further PSG can be added to specify possible

combinations of concepts such as 'goal' and 'interior.' This would indicate, for instance, that 'goal' is related syntagmatically to the concepts 'source' and 'path,' the three concepts representing the three phases of a change of position; and that 'interior' is related paradigmatically to concepts such as 'surface,' 'anterior,' and 'posterior' (see Sect. 2.2 and Bennett 1975: 132–76). If concepts such as 'goal' and 'interior' are referred to as 'sememes,' this latter PSG can be referred to as the 'semotactics.' Finally, if a separate 'morphotactics' is included, to characterize the composition of words in terms of morphemes, the result is an overall grammar that can be represented schematically as in Fig. 2, which corresponds to a SG with four strata.

A stratum is a level of language, or module of the overall grammar, but with the proviso that each stratum is regarded as having essentially the same kind of structure as all the other strata. In particular, each stratum of Fig. 2 has its own 'tactic pattern,' or PSG, and the implication is that there is independent patterning of language at these four levels. The similarities between strata extend also to the realizational structure. Thus, the alternation between *a* and *an* (as in *a banana* versus *an orange*) involves the same

295

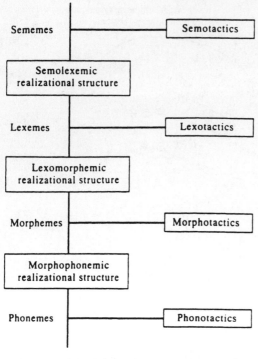

Figure 2.

relationship as that between *although* and *despite* (as in *although it was raining* versus *despite the rain*), but at a different level—the former morphophonemic, the latter semolexemic.

1.3 Linguistic Processes

Stratificational grammar has never been content to concentrate on 'competence' to the exclusion of 'performance.' Rather, it has set out to provide an account of a language that can be used as the basis for a performance model. The processes of producing and understanding specific utterances are thought of in terms of signals passing through the network of the grammar, either from semantics to phonetics or from phonetics to semantics. Besides production and comprehension, attention has been given also to the network modification involved in the processes of language acquisition and linguistic change.

For two reasons, SG claims to represent a brand of 'cognitive linguistics,' constituting an improvement on 'generative linguistics.' First, its main objective is to model linguistic processes. Second, it assumes not only that a speaker's linguistic system takes the form of a network but also that all of his/her knowledge, both general and specific, is stored in a similar form in a 'cognitive' network; and it is therefore concerned with the interrelationship between the linguistic network and this wider cognitive network.

2. Syntax

2.1 Selected Topics in Syntax

Stratificational accounts of the relationship between active sentences such as (1) below and corresponding passives such as (2) and (3) are to be found, for instance, in Lockwood (1972: 144–49) and Sullivan (1980: 320–23):

> The teacher gave a prize to the two most helpful pupils. (1)

> A prize was given to the two most helpful pupils (by the teacher). (2)

> The two most helpful pupils were given a prize (by the teacher). (3)

Although the analyses differ in certain respects, on crucial details they are in agreement. They involve the semotactics and lexotactics and the intervening realizational structure. The semotactics incorporates a set of participant roles, and in these examples *the teacher*, *a prize*, and *the two most helpful pupils* are associated with the roles of 'agent,' 'patient,' and 'recipient' respectively. The choice of subject in the lexotactics, or surface structure syntax, is determined by the selection of the sememe 'focus' in the semotactics. This sememe can be attached either to the 'patient' or to the 'recipient.' In either case, the particular combination of sememes triggers a lexotactic order in which the noun phrase in question is realized as the subject. It also causes the verb to be marked as passive. The 'agent' noun phrase (if present) then occurs postverbally, its function signaled by the preposition *by*. In the unmarked case where 'focus' is not attached to 'patient' or 'recipient,' the 'agent' noun phrase occupies the subject position. One characteristic feature of the analysis is that there is no linear order in the structure produced by the semotactics. Thus, in realizing it as a surface syntactic structure, there is no transformation of one linear order into another. Instead, the order of constituents is determined by the lexotactics on the basis of the sememes present in the sememic representation.

Sullivan's (1978: 58) analysis of 'raising' data such as the examples in (4) and (5) below depends on the possibility of a noun phrase having two distinct participant roles simultaneously:

> I expect that Ed will leave. (4a)

> I expect Ed to leave. (4b)

> I ordered that Ed remove Bob from the room. (5a)

> I ordered Ed to remove Bob from the room. (5b)

In the sememic representation of the (b) examples, 'Ed' has one role in relation to the first verb and one in relation to the second, whereas in the (a) examples it has no role in relation to the first verb. Thus, in (5b), 'Ed' is 'recipient' with respect to 'order' and 'agent' of 'remove,' whereas in (5a) it is only 'agent' of 'remove.' The presence of two roles associated with the same participant then triggers the production, by the lexotactics, of the infinitival construction rather than a clause introduced by *that*. Support for this analysis comes from (6):

I ordered that Bob be removed from the room by Ed.
(6a)

?I ordered Bob to be removed from the room by Ed.
(6b)

The oddity of (6b) depends on the fact that 'Bob' is the 'recipient' in relation to 'order' but only 'patient' of 'remove.' In other words, Bob is apparently being ordered to carry out an action over which he has no control. (There is no problem with (6a), since Bob is not the 'recipient' of 'order' in this example.)

While agreeing in general with Sullivan's dual-role analysis, Anderson (1978: 155–63) draws attention to the problem of (7):

I expect that it will be raining by 3 pm at the latest. (7a)

I expect it to be raining by 3 pm at the latest. (7b)

As the dummy subject of a weather verb, 'it' can hardly be an argument of 'expect' in (7b). But if the sememic structure of (7b) does not parallel that of the other (b) examples, this must be an analogical extension of a surface-structure pattern. Moreover, such an interpretation of the data supports the claim of independent semantic and syntactic patterning reflected in the distinction between semotactics and lexotactics.

This discussion of selected topics in syntax concludes by referring to Sampson's (1980: 182) comments on relative clauses. In general Sampson is sympathetic to SG and lists a number of respects in which it compares very favorably with Chomskyan linguistic theory, including its greater overall conceptual simplicity, the notion of independent patterning at different levels and its plausibility as a model of the production and comprehension of utterances (1980: 172–80). He also mentions the simplicity measure for grammars that was developed within the framework of SG (Reich 1973). However, Sampson ends on a negative note. While agreeing with Bloomfield (1933: 213) that a 'process' account of the relationship between *knife* and *knives*—according to which *first* the [f] at the end of *knife* is voiced and *then* the [z] form of the plural is added—is merely a convenient descriptive fiction, Sampson continues (1980: 181)

... when one investigates syntax more deeply than Bloomfield did, one finds the data to be such that, arguably, only process rules can handle them.

He regards English relative clauses as a case in point (1980: 182):

The obvious way of stating the facts is to say that relative clauses are formed from normal sentences by deleting one of their nominal phrases, or replacing it with a relative pronoun.

Within the SG framework as he sees it (1980: 182):

... while a tactic pattern might be designed so as to allow zero as an option at each nominal-phrase position in a relative clause, it seems impossible ... to prevent the zero option being chosen more (or less) than once in a single clause.

It is certainly to the discredit of proponents of SG that they have never given a detailed account of relative clauses but it seems to the present author that the outline of such an account is clear. Moreover, it presupposes that SG is crucially concerned with modeling the processes of producing and comprehending utterances rather than merely generating sentences. Elsewhere Sampson gives appropriate emphasis to this distinction: compared with 'the "unnatural" task of enumerating all-and-only the well formed sentences' (1980: 178), the 'chief attraction' of SG is its concern with 'how speakers and hearers actually operate' (1980: 177). But at the point at which he doubts SG's ability to provide an adequate characterization of relative clauses he loses sight of his own earlier discussion and is thinking exclusively in terms of generating sentences. As was pointed out in Sect. 1.3, SG assumes not only that a speaker's linguistic system takes the form of a network but also that all of his/her knowledge, both general and specific, is stored in a similar form in a cognitive network. The cognitive network of a particular person contains a vast amount of information about an enormous number of entities, including details of events that they have participated in. Such information represents properties of the entities in question and is utilisable in identifying them. A relative clause incorporating such information is a 'downgraded predication' (Leech 1974: 149–54) from which one participant is omitted, namely the participant that is identified by reference to the remainder of the predication in question. Thus when the structure of the relative clause is produced, the fact that there is one, and only one, gap in it by comparison with an independent sentence is determined by what is being read off from the relevant portion of the speaker's cognitive network.

2.2 Syntax and Lexical Semantics

The studies referred to in Sect. 2.1 were not concerned specifically with lexical semantics and were content therefore to treat lexemes such as *give* and *kill* as realizations of the 'event sememes' 'give' and 'kill.' Yet *give* and *kill* are certainly amenable to lexical decomposition. Moreover, in view of SG's assumption that there is independent patterning at the semantic and surface-syntactic levels, it is natural to formulate the semotactics not in terms of 'give' and 'kill' as such but in terms of the separate components of their meaning. An analogous point can be made particularly clearly in relation to sentences describing a change of position.

Such sentences may contain a 'source expression,' 'path expression,' and 'goal expression':

We drove from York over the Pennines to Manchester. (8)

However, what is involved here is not so much a syntactic classification of prepositional phrases as a semantic distinction which cuts across syntactic categories such as 'preposition' and 'verb.' Admittedly, the goal expression underlying *to Manchester* is realized as a prepositional phrase, but there are goal expressions also in *The first runner is just about to enter the stadium* and *A rabbit has just appeared from behind that tree*, and these are realized not as prepositional phrases but as *enter the stadium* and *appear*, respectively. Similarly, 'means of locomotion' is a semantic category. Particular instances of the category may be realized as verbs, e.g., *drive* in (8), but another possible realization is as the prepositional phrase *by car*.

There should be no duplication of information between the semotactics and lexotactics. Thus, any facts that are deemed to be semantic are thereby excluded from the lexotactics, with the result that the latter is correspondingly simpler. The difference in acceptability of *from behind the door* and **from to the door* depends on the meaning of the prepositions in question. Moreover, it is a straightforward matter to allow the semotactics to produce a sememic representation corresponding to the first of these phrases but not the second. The lexotactics can therefore state merely that one kind of prepositional phrase consists of a preposition followed by a prepositional phrase. It does not need to exclude **from to the door*, since it will never be called upon by the semotactics to produce such a phrase.

Within some approaches to syntax, it has been customary to invoke 'subcategorization features' to reflect the difference in grammaticality between, say, *The journey from Ostende to Vienna was very tiring* and **The fact from Ostende to Vienna was rather unexpected*. Thus, *journey* and *fact* are sometimes subcategorized as follows:

> *journey*: N, +[____ (*from* NP) (*to* NP)]
> *fact*:   N, +[____ *that* S]

If, however, the concept 'path' is attributed to *journey* as one of its semantic components, it would follow automatically from the information in the semotactics about source, path, and goal expressions that this noun could be accompanied by prepositional phrases introduced by *from* and *to*, and would not need to be stated as though it were an idiosyncratic syntactic property of the lexeme *journey*.

298

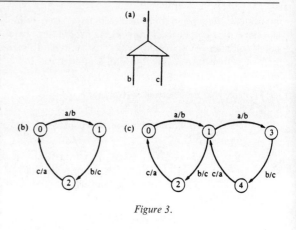

Figure 3.

3. Performance Models

3.1 Finite-state Node Definitions

To simulate the production and comprehension processes by sending signals through a network grammar, it is necessary to define the operation of each type of node in such a way that any input signal arriving at a particular type of node along a particular line results in the appropriate output signal. Reich (1969) treated each type of node as a finite-state device. Figure 3(b) is a very preliminary definition of the ordered downward AND node shown in Fig. 3(a). In its initial state—state 0—the node can accept a signal along line *a*, whereupon it sends a signal out along line *b* (hence 'a/b') and switches to state 1. This is equivalent to starting to produce some construction by sending out a signal corresponding to the first constituent. In state 1, the node can accept a signal along line *b*, whereupon it sends a signal out along line *c* and switches into state 2. This is equivalent to receiving a feedback signal to the effect that the first constituent has been produced, which informs the node that it is now time to produce the second constituent. A similar feedback signal up line *c* informs the node that the whole construction is now complete. This information is passed on to whatever node is above the downward AND by sending a signal up line *a*, and at the same time the node switches back to its initial state.

Given that the sentence construction is one instance of an ordered downward AND, examples such as [*The cat* [*that the dog worried*] *killed the rat*] require an elaboration of the preliminary definition given in Fig. 3(b). To produce an embedded sentence as part of the subject noun phrase of *The cat killed the rat*, the node needs to be able to interrupt the transition from state 1 to state 2 and allow signals to pass through in the sequence a/b, followed by b/c, followed by c/a. This is achieved by adding states 3 and 4 (see Fig. 3(c)). As is seen from the labels on the arrows (a/b, etc.), the state-transitions $0 \rightarrow 1 \rightarrow 2 \rightarrow 0$ parallel the transitions 1 → 3 → 4 → 1; but, whereas the former represent an unembedded sentence, the latter correspond to an embedded sentence. The node thus keeps track of where it is in the processing of the matrix and embedded sentences. If speakers were able to produce (and comprehend) an indefinite amount of self-embedding, it would be necessary to add an indefinite number of states to the definition of the ordered downward AND, which would then no longer be a finite-state device. However, three self-embeddings, as in [*The rat* [*that the cat* [*that the dog* [*that the cow tossed*] *worried*] *killed*] *ate the malt*], are already beyond what speakers can process. Thus, the desired amount of self-embedding can be achieved with no more than seven states.

Right-branching and left-branching structures differ in an important respect from self-embedded structures: they may be extended to an arbitrary depth, as is seen from the right-branching structure [*The cow tossed the dog* [*that worried the cat* [*that killed the rat* [*that ate the malt* [*that . . . .* The crucial fact about such examples is that, as each new sentence is begun, the previous sentence is otherwise complete. There are thus no interrupted sentences to which the speaker has to return, for which reason it is unnecessary to keep track of how many sentences one has produced. The structure is therefore 'iterative' rather than 'recursive' (Reich 1969: 839–40). The node definition requires no further states, merely an additional transition (labeled 'a/b') from state 2 to state 1, which allows the node to loop an arbitrary number of times between states 1 and 2. (For more complete discussion of this and other details, see Reich 1969; Schütze and Reich 1990).

The approach outlined above rejects the suggestion that there is a central short-term memory involved in the production and comprehension of syntax. Instead, it claims that short-term memory is spread out over all the nodes of the grammar, since each type of node needs to be able to remember a limited amount of information. It also rejects Chomsky's (1957: 18–25) claim that finite-state grammars are inadequate to describe natural languages. Since there is a sharp cut-off point with regard to recursion proper, and since there is no need to keep track of the amount of iteration, a network grammar containing a finite number of nodes, each of which is a finite-state device, is adequate to the task.

3.2 Spreading Activation

The only aspect of performance considered in Sect. 3.1 was the difference in processing between self-embedding, on the one hand, and right-branching and left-branching, on the other. The signals with which the model operated were either present or absent on a given line at a given time. Later work involving computer simulation of slips of the tongue (Dell and Reich 1980) replaced the earlier on/off signaling by numerical values and allowed a proportion of the signal on a given node to spread to all neighboring nodes. Selection of one or another of a set of competing items then depended on which had the highest level of activation. Among the results obtained in the simulations were that the likelihood of slips was proportional to the similarity between the target word and the influencing word; and the spreading activation mechanism had the effect of editing potential slips that would result in non-words of the language, especially at slower speech rates. Although most of the discussion was concerned with phonology, the same general approach is applicable also in syntax.

3.3 Micronotation

Lamb adopts a different approach to modeling linguistic processes from that of Reich, and one which has much in common with models of neural networks. In place of the nodes and lines of the standard network notation (as of Fig. 1), which allow signaling in either direction, Lamb employs a 'micro-notation' in which nodes and lines carry signals in only one direction. Varying degrees of activation are implemented in terms of frequency of pulsation, and in addition to positive activations there are also inhibitory activations. Nodes have activation thresholds, and lines have varying strengths. (A stronger line carries more activation than a weaker one for the same frequency of pulsation.) Learning in the model consists in building new network structure by bringing latent connections into use.

4. Stratification

Throughout much of the history of SG, the number of strata posited was under continuous review. While the four-stratum model of Fig. 2 enjoyed the most popularity, other versions posited as many as six strata or as few as three. As of the early 1990s, Lamb attaches less importance than before to the distinction among morphemes, lexemes, and sememes, each being a case of lexical units that connect to the conceptual system. The overall architecture of language thus involves a phonological (and graphological) system, a lexical system, and a conceptual system. Alternatively, the conceptual system may be thought of as separate from a more narrowly defined linguistic system, and serving as a bridge between the linguistic system and other mental modalities such as the visual system.

In any case, with the increasing emphasis that is now placed on dynamic aspects of relational networks, the idea of stratification has become less important—with the result that the label 'stratificational grammar' may well have outlived its usefulness. 'Dynamic grammar' has been proposed as a possible alternative label; but, at the time of writing, no clear successor has emerged.

Bibliography

Anderson L B 1978 Stratificational and transformational grammars on 'raising': Comments on Sullivan's paper and a comparison. In: Wang J P (ed.) *Proceedings of the Second Annual Linguistic Metatheory Conference, 1977*. Michigan State University, East Lansing, MI

Bennett D C 1975 *Spatial and Temporal Uses of English Prepositions*. Longman, London

Chomsky N 1957 *Syntactic Structures*. Mouton, The Hague

Dell G S, Reich P A 1980 Slips of the tongue: The facts and a stratificational model. In: Copeland J E, Davis P W (eds.) *Papers in Cognitive–Stratificational Linguistics*. Rice University Studies **66**

Hjelmslev L 1961 *Prolegomena to a Theory of Language*. University of Wisconsin Press, Madison, WI (Transl. by Whitfield F J)

Lamb S M 1966 *Outline of Stratificational Grammar*. Georgetown University Press, Washington, D.C.

Lamb S M 1987 Linguistics, semiotics, and the human information system. In: *Georgetown University Round Table on Languages and Linguistics, 1986*. Georgetown University Press, Washington, D.C.

Lamb S M 1995 *Toward Outlines of a Cognitive Theory of Language*

Leech G 1974 *Semantics*. Penguin, Harmondsworth

Lockwood D G 1972 *Introduction to Stratificational Linguistics*. Harcourt Brace Jovanovich, New York

Reich P A 1969 The finiteness of natural language. *Lg* **45**: 831–43

Sampson G R 1980 *Schools of Linguistics*. Hutchinson, London/Stanford University Press, Stanford, CA

Saussure F de 1949 *Cours de linguistique générale*, 4th edn. Payot, Paris

Schütze C T, Reich P A 1990 Language without a central pushdown stack. In: Karlgren H (ed.) *COLING-90: Papers presented to the 13th International Conference on Computational Linguistics on the occasion of the 25th Anniversary of COLING and the 350th Anniversary of Helsinki University*. Yliopistopaino, Helsinki, **3**: 64–69

Sullivan W J 1978 Raising: A stratificational description and some metatheoretical considerations. In: Wang J P (ed.) *Proceedings of the Second Annual Linguistic Metatheory Conference, 1977*. Michigan State University, East Lansing, MI

Sullivan W J 1980 Syntax and linguistic semantics in stratificational theory. In: Moravcsik E A, Wirth J R (eds.) *Current Approaches to Syntax*. Academic Press, New York

Syntax and Phonology

Arnold M. Zwicky

Syntax, phonology, and the lexicon are the central and indispensable parts of the mediation between meaning and sound in language. The lexicon provides (at least) the irreducible basis of sound–meaning associations, in lexemes and idioms. Syntax and phonology together concern the rule-governed portion of this association, syntax serving (together with morphology) as the gateway to semantics, phonology as the gateway to phonetics. Both are complex systems involving units of various sizes (in syntax, these include words, phrases, clauses, and sentences; in phonology, these include features, segments, syllables, phonological words, and phonological phrases) and also involving (language-particular) generalizations about how units combine to make larger units. How syntax articulates with phonology is then a central question in the description of any particular language, as well as a major issue in the framing of a general theory of grammar.

1. Phenomena and Components

The labels 'syntax' and 'phonology' are used both for classes of phenomena and for components of a grammar.

In the first sense, syntax concerns the meaningful free units (of word size or larger) in a language and comprises everything that has to do with the combination of these into meaningful composites, and consequently with the distribution of such units with respect to one another. ('Morphology' in this sense concerns the expression of meaning by form within words.) Also in the first sense, phonology concerns those properties of sound that are relevant in a language and comprises everything that has to do with the combination of these into pronounceable units of various sizes.

The divisions thus made between syntax and phonology are not necessarily those appropriate for a theory of grammar, which divides components according to differences in the types of generalizations (also known as 'rules') applicable within them. The distribution of meaningful units in a language can be contingent on their stylistic values (as in the anomalous conditional clause *were I to buzz off* 'if I left,' with its conflict between the formal style of the inversion in it and the casual style of the idiom *buzz off*), or on their semantics (as in the anomalous clause *I am containing DNA*, with its conflict between the ongoing-event semantics of the progressive and the state semantics of the VP *contain DNA*), or on their morphological properties (as when clauses with modals, like *I can sing*, fail to occur in a wide variety of constructions—*I want to can sing*, versus *I want to be able to sing*—because the modals lack nonfinite inflexional forms), or their phonological properties (as in the anomalous clause *to would make me happy*—cf. *to do so would make me happy* and *not to would make me happy*—with its accentually stranded *to*).

But that does not necessarily mean that rules in the syntactic portion of a grammar attend to the stylistic values, semantic properties, morphological properties, and phonological properties of syntactic units. In these particular cases a sufficient account is available in other parts of grammar, based on the assignment of pragmatic, semantic, morphological, or phonological properties to the elements of syntax and lexicon.

It is also true that the distribution of phonological properties in a language can be contingent (a) on the morphological function of the material involved (as in the contrast between the phonological effects of the /i/ suffixes in *piracy*, based on *pirate*, and *carroty*, based on *carrot*), (b) on its syntactic function (as when the auxiliary *is* can be unaccented and contracted to /z/ in *I know the party's tonight* but not in **I know where the party's tonight*), (c) on its semantics (as when the auxiliary must be contracted in the idiomatic *What's with him?*, the uncontracted *What is with him?* having some quite different literal meaning), or (d) on its pragmatic values (as when a falling intonation on *what* makes *My name is what?* a quiz question, while a high rising intonation makes it an incredulity or reclamatory question).

In examples like (d), it is plausible to suggest that pragmatic values are assigned to phonological elements, but in (a–c), something rather different seems to be going on. It appears that another component of grammar (morphology or syntax) or the lexicon is imposing conditions on the makeup of phonological units.

2. The Modularity of Grammar

The picture just sketched presumes a modular view of linguistic organization, in which (at least) phonology, phonetics, morphology, syntax, semantics, pragmatics, and lexicon are treated as to some degree autonomous domains. Most theorists adopt such a 'separation of levels,' but there are some (including many of the 'generative semanticists' of the 1970s) who have seen linguistic organization as a seamless web, in which stipulations and generalizations about the association of sound with meaning can make reference to any properties of expressions, even properties of very different sorts, and will treat these properties as all on a par with one another.

Autonomous levels of analysis are posited partly out of a desire to restrict the expressive power of grammars, so as to constrain the range of languages consistent with the analytic framework, and partly as a way of embodying the observation that interactions between two domains of linguistic organization often turn out to be quite limited, both in that the interacting properties are only a subset of those relevant within the domains and in that there is a logical directionality to the relationship, rather than a mutual conditioning.

3. Morphology-free and Phonology-free Syntax

In particular, it is generally assumed that syntax has only limited access to morphological organization. Many would say syntax is morphology-free (the 'lexicalist hypothesis'), in the sense that syntactic rules do not distribute specifically morphological properties of expressions. On this hypothesis, syntax can be sensitive to abstract properties realized in morphology, but not to specific inflectional marks for these properties (to dative case, say, but not to a particular dative case marking, or to a declension class for nouns); and it can be sensitive to syntactic subcategories of lexemes, but not to specific derivational marks for these subcategories (to abstract Ns, say, but not to just those abstract Ns with the derivational suffix *-ness*).

It is also generally assumed that syntax has only limited access to phonological properties. Indeed, it has been claimed (Pullum and Zwicky 1988) that syntax is phonology-free, in the sense that syntactic rules do not distribute specifically phonological properties of expressions. On this hypothesis, syntax can be sensitive to abstract properties realized in the distribution of phonological features, but not to the specific phonological features. Though the conditions in a syntactic rule can have certain sorts of indirect or ultimate phonological consequences (like the temporal ordering of the parts of an expression), these conditions never seem to distribute phonological properties directly; no language has a syntactic rule stipulating that some constituent begin with an obstruent, or have no more than two syllables, or contain only unrounded vowels, or have stress on its penultimate syllable.

The literature on the connection between syntax and phonology contains many apparent counterexamples to the hypothesis that syntax is phonology-free. But Pullum and Zwicky (1988) maintain that all of these dissolve on closer examination. Some are merely incorrect statements of the generalization; it is sometimes said that the inverted material in English subject-auxiliary inversion must constitute a *phonological* word (*Wouldn't I sing?* versus **Would not I sing?*), but it can be argued that the correct condition requires a *syntactic* word, that is, a constituent of word (rather than phrase) rank in the syntax. Others involve preferences or tendencies in language use that should not be seen as rules of grammar, in particular as rules of syntax; an instance in point is the preference for having long, complex, and prosodically heavy constituents ordered at the end of their constructs (favoring the alternative ordering *We saw with pleasure sixteen beautiful birds that none of us could find in our guide books* over *We saw sixteen beautiful birds that none of us could find in our guide books with pleasure*).

Still others involve genuine regularities, but ones that belong to some extragrammatical domain; here belongs the requirement in certain forms of verse that each part of an utterance must have a fixed number of syllables in it, a requirement that is not part of the grammar of the language in question, but rather is a matter of a set of conventions for language use that build upon, or are overlaid on, the rules of grammar. A fourth collection of cases comprises genuine regularities in the grammar, regularities that belong, however, not to syntax but rather to morphology/lexicon; the presence (in *geschlagen* 'hit') or absence (in *trompetet* 'trumpeted') of a prefix *ge-* in German past participles turns on phonological properties of the verb (it is present only for a verb stem with stress on its first syllable), but the rule in question is one of (inflexional) morphology, not of syntax.

A final group of cases is exemplified by the acceptability of coordinations like *They have never and will never come to our parties*, where the existence of syntactically distinct verb forms (bare infinitive and past participle) that happen to be phonemically identical (*come*) permits one word to serve simultaneously in two different, and normally incompatible, syntactic functions. There is evidently an interaction here between phonological properties of syntactic words and their ability to occur in syntactic constructions, an interaction that Pullum and Zwicky (1988) suggest is not stipulated in the syntactic rules of individual languages, but rather is made available by a general condition on the applicability of such rules.

4. Submodularity

The large domains of linguistic organization might themselves turn out to comprise several autonomous subdomains. Pragmatics certainly embraces principles of quite different sorts, and the same has been argued for syntax, phonology, and morphology/lexicon.

4.1 Modularity in Syntax

In the case of syntax, Bloomfield (1933) distinguished rules describing sentence types (the declarative type of *Penguins cannot fly*, the yes–no question type of *Can penguins fly?*, the fragment type of *more penguins*), those describing the distribution of anaphoric elements (the reflexive pronoun in *We congratulated ourselves*, the anaphoric gap in *I ordered sushi, and Robin sashimi*), and those describing the combination of immediate constituents into constructs (for instance, the combination of the head V *donated* with its direct and indirect object arguments *huge sums* and *to good causes* to yield the VP *donated huge sums to good causes*). Modern theoretical frameworks would further separate rules describing syntactic valency (for instance, the fact that there is a class of verb lexemes, *donate* among them, eligible to occur with three syntactic arguments—a (nominative) subject, an (accus-

ative) direct object, and an indirect object marked by the preposition *to*) from those describing how heads, their arguments, and their modifiers are assembled into constructs (for instance, the fact that a head V and its non-subject arguments can be assembled into a VP).

4.2 Modularity in Phonology

Most phonological theories have distinguished at least two subcomponents, either one concerned with morphophonemic alternants (like the word-final /z/–/s/ alternation in *dogs–cats*) versus one concerned with allophonic variants (like the partial devoicing word-finally in *tag* as against the full voicing medially in *tagging*), or one concerned with nonautomatic—morphologically, lexically, or syntactically targeted and/or triggered—phenomena (like the morphologically triggered /t/–/s/ alternation in *pirate–piracy* and the lexically targeted /Ø/–/n/ alternation in *a/an*) versus automatic, entirely phonologically targeted and triggered, phenomena (as in *dogs–cats* and *tag–tagging*).

4.3 Modularity in Morphology/lexicon

The internal organization of a phonological component is clearly not independent of the organization of a morphological component and of the lexicon. Morphological theories building on the Greco-Roman tradition distinguish at least two subcomponents that incorporate phonological generalizations about the stock of lexemes: derivational morphology, relating the phonological properties of different lexemes' stems (*sane–sanity, anaphoric–anaphoricity*); and inflexional morphology, relating the phonological properties of inflexional forms of a lexeme to the properties of one of its stems (*dream–dreamt, sleep–slept*). To these subcomponents can be added one dealing with phonological relationships between the different stems of a lexeme (Latin present versus perfect stems *amā* versus *amāv* 'love,' *curr-* versus *cucurr-* 'run') and one dealing with lexeme-specific facts about the phonological make-up of forms—their 'shapes'—in external sandhi (*an* versus *a*). Each of these subcomponents concerns itself, at least in part, with phonological relationships, all of them nonautomatic and morphophonemic.

A rather different division of morphology (that of 'lexical morphology and phonology'; see Kaisse and Shaw 1985) posits several layers of morphology, along with its (again, nonautomatic and morphophonemic) phonological concomitants, arranged out from the stem, without any assumption that these 'levels,' or 'strata,' necessarily correspond to derivational versus inflexional morphology.

In addition to these subcomponents of morphology, there are in every language several types of generalizations about the properties of lexemes: rules that predict some such properties from others. Since they describe redundancies in the lexicon, they are sometimes called 'lexical redundancy rules.' There are, for instance, rules relating some phonological properties of forms to others (though these are usually classed as a species of phonological rule rather than as lexical redundancy rules). For instance, in German the default rule for stress placement is that if a syllable is the first one in a form (of some lexeme), then it is stressed. And there are rules relating phonological properties of lexemes to their morphological properties. For instance, in English the default rule for adjectives and adverbs with stems of more than two syllables to lack an inflexional comparative and superlative (*shyer*, *worldlier*, **fatherlier*).

Lexical redundancy rules do not necessarily involve phonological properties. There are, for instance, such rules relating semantic properties of lexemes to their paradigm classes (in English, nouns referring to creatures hunted for sport—*quail*, *moose*—belong, at least as a default, to the 'zero plural' declension class) or their grammatical categories (as when the default is for nouns referring to male creatures to belong to the gender labeled 'masculine').

The lexical redundancy rules of special interest here are those expressing some association between phonological properties of lexemes, in particular, phonological properties of their stems, and their syntactic properties, in particular, membership in a major syntactic category or in a syntactic subcategory. There are two types of such associations: those in which syntactic (sub)category predicts aspects of stem phonology, and those in which aspects of stem phonology predict syntactic (sub)category. Associations of the first type—e.g., the default in English is that if a lexeme is an interrogative proform, then its stem begins with /hw/—have been reported with modest frequency in the literature, though it is not always clear whether they represent generalizations that should be captured by rules of grammar, preferences or tendencies in language use, or accidental co-occurrences of the properties in question (having no place in a description of regularities in linguistic organization).

It appears that associations of the second type are even less secure than those of the first type. It is unclear whether there are any firm examples of real linguistic generalizations that predict syntactic (sub)category of a lexeme from phonological properties of its stem. For instance, it has been claimed that the default in English is that if a verb lexeme with semantics involving agent, patient, and recipient roles has a monosyllabic stem, then it can occur as head in the double-NP-object construction of *I'll give Chris flowers* and *We told Robin stories*; indeed, it has been claimed as well that membership in this syntactic subcategory also predicts (at least as a default) the monosyllabicity of stems. The first claim says that *give* and *tell* should belong to the subcategory, the second that *donate* and *divulge* should not. But when semantic regularities are factored out of the data—for example, means-of-communication verbs like *cable* and *telegraph* generally belong to the subcategory (however many syllables they happen to have), and manner-of-speaking verbs like *lisp* and *scream* generally do not (again, regardless of their number of syllables)—there seem to be no significant generalizations left, beyond the overall tendency in English for lexemes, or at least frequent lexemes, to have monosyllabic stems.

5. Phonological and Syntactic Rules

The discussion to follow does not further explore the relationship between syntax and the phonological side of morphology. Instead it focuses on automatic phonology—simply 'phonology' in this discussion—and its relationship to syntax.

Rules of the syntactic and phonological components of a grammar distribute *target* properties of very different sorts and operate within *domains* of different types.

5.1 Phonological Rules

Phonological rules describe the content of phonological (or 'prosodic') domains of various sizes, from segments and syllables through phonological words, phonological phrases, intonational phrases, and phonological utterances. (The inventory of domains is a matter of controversy; in particular, several domain types lying between the phonological word and the phonological phrase, and between the phonological phrase and the intonational phrase, have been proposed.) The ultimate units are purely phonological properties like syllabicity, voicing, nasality, obstruency, and high tone. For each type of domain, rules describe how phonological constituents of some smaller domain are distributed with respect to one another—how they are organized in time, by simultaneous or successive occurrence—so as to form instances of the larger domain.

Phonological rules can stipulate that some property is distributed within a domain (e.g., nasality in the coda of an English syllable spreads to the nucleus of that syllable, but not to an adjacent syllable, as in the second syllable of *iron*, *Haldane*, and *balloon*), at the edge of a domain (e.g., syllable-final obstruents in German are devoiced, as in *Bund* 'band, covenant' and *Bundbruch* 'treaty violation'), or across domain boundaries (e.g., in fast speech, syllable-final /n/ in English assimilates in point of articulation to a following syllable-initial obstruent, so that *infamous* can have a labio–dental nasal in its first syllable and *incongruous* a velar one).

It can often be unclear as to whether the domains within which, at the edge of which, or between which phonological properties are distributed are phonological or morphosyntactic. Given that there are generalizations about the phonology of stems of lexemes (the default Latin perfect stem is the present stem plus -*v*/-*u*), forms of lexemes (the default English past tense verb form is the stem plus /d/), and shapes these forms take in syntactic combinations (the 'reduced' shape of a form of an English auxiliary verb is its final consonant: /z/ for *is* and *has*, /d/ for *would* and *had*, etc.), it might not be clear whether a particular phenomenon involves a generalization about forms of lexemes versus phonological words, or about shapes of forms versus phonological words/phrases.

5.2 Syntactic Rules

To a large extent syntactic rules distribute purely *syntactic* properties of various sorts: major syntactic category (e.g., V), syntactic subcategory (e.g., auxiliary V eligible to invert with a subject), rank (word, phrase, or clause), grammatical relations (e.g., subject-of), and constituency (e.g., divisibility into a subject constituent and a VP constituent).

But there are also properties that are 'cashed out' in inflexional morphology (e.g., case in government; person, gender, and number in agreement), in the selection of particular 'grammatical marker' lexemes (like infinitival *to* in English), and in phonology—in prosodic properties like intonation contours and boundary tones (e.g., the rising terminal intonation of English yes–no questions), in phonological alternations (in effect, 'phrasal inflexions') affecting the edge segments of syntactic constituents (like the Welsh consonant mutations affecting the first word of a phrase and triggered by, among other things, certain specific prepositions, as in *wedi pob cath* 'before every cat,' *ar bob cath* 'on top of every cat,' *â phob* /fob/ *cath* 'with every cat'; or the English possessive suffix /z/, attached to the last word of a phrase, as in *one person I know's opinions*), in the presence or absence of some constituent with phonological content (e.g., the gap in information questions like *What did you make?* or the missing subject in imperatives like *Behave yourself!*), and indeed in the temporal ordering of words.

6. Stacking of Domains

A striking difference between syntactic and phonological organization is that in syntax it is common for units of some type to properly contain units of the same type (as in the stacked VPs in *might have been being attacked*), even to the point of recursivity (as when finite clauses contain finite clauses: *That your evidence demonstrates the point demonstrates that my argument demonstrates nothing*). Stacking is rare for the units of phonology—many would maintain that it does not occur at all (the strict layer hypothesis of Nespor and Vogel 1986)—and recursivity is unknown; there is no such thing as a syllable containing other syllables, or a phonological phrase containing phonological phrases of similar type. This difference pre-

sumably follows from the different functions of syntax and phonology, syntax providing units (syntactic constituents) that are semantically interpreted, phonology providing units (phonological domains) that are phonetically interpreted.

7. The Morphosyntax–phonology Interface

Given the very different functions served by syntactic constituents and phonological domains, it is no surprise that a single expression can be subject to very different hierarchical organizations in the two components.

This point is familiar from morphology. Though phonology for the most part pays little attention to morphological structure, there are circumstances in which morphological structure conditions phonological organization. For instance, in English the strong (secondarily stressed and semantically transparent) prefixes *mis-*and *dis-*, as in *mistabulate* and *distaste*, can be maintained in separate syllables, whereas /s/ is otherwise obligatorily syllabified with a following voiceless stop, as in *pastiche*.

Phonology *always* pays some attention to syntactic structure. The organization of an expression into syntactic words, phrases, and clauses serves as the basis for its organization into phonological words and phrases. For instance, there is normally a phonological phrase break in English between the subject of a clause and its VP: [*All of us*] [*love spinach*], [*People from Italy*] [*all love spinach*].

But phonological domains can cut across syntactic constituents, as frequently happens with syntactic words that are phonologically dependent on adjacent material: English complementizer *that*, phonologically dependent on immediately following material, as in the phonological phrasing [*I know*] [*that soon*] [*I'll win*]; and infinitival *to*, phonologically dependent on immediately preceding material if it cannot 'lean' on following material, as in the phonological phrasing [*I'll soon*] [*persuade them to*]. Consequently it is not enough for a grammar to specify for each expression what constituents of morphology/syntax it has within it and what domains of phonology it has within it. The grammar must also include generalizations about how (morpho)syntactic spans are associated with phonological domains: rules of 'prosodic domain formation.'

7.1 Prosodic Domain Formation

The investigation of prosodic domain formation rules is in its infancy. Some such rules are specific to individual lexemes or small classes of them; this is the case for the facts just cited about *that* and *to*, and it also applies to the distribution of unaccented object pronouns in English, which must form phonological phrases with their immediately preceding heads: *I gave the fight up*, *I gave it up* (where *gave* is *it*'s head), *gave up the fight*, **I gave up it* (where *up* is not *it's* head). Other prosodic domain formation rules are more general, gathering a variety of different syntactically related items into phonological domains.

A number of proposals have been put forward for such general mappings between syntactic constituency and phonological domain organization; see Kaisse and Zwicky (1987) for a variety of these. It has been suggested that phonological domain formation is sensitive, among other things, to the difference between maximal and nonmaximal phrases in syntax (in *They might have been being attacked*, *might have been being attacked* is a maximal VP, and all the other VPs are nonmaximal), to the location of the edges of syntactic phrases, to the location of the edges of clauses, to the difference between syntactic constituents that are (nonbranching) syntactic words and those that are multi-word phrases (unmodified nouns versus modified nouns, or intransitive verbs versus transitive verbs), and to syntactic relations between adjacent constituents, in particular to the difference between modifying (or adjunct) dependents of a head and argument (or complement) dependents.

A typical proposal is that of Chen (in Kaisse and Zwicky 1987) for tone groups in Xiamen Chinese. These domains, within which tone sandhi rules apply, are picked out (in part) by requiring that every end of a maximal phrase in syntax is also the end of a tone group in phonology.

7.2 Direct versus Indirect Syntactic Conditioning

Prosodic domain formation rules provide a means for indirect syntactic conditioning of phonological rules. Syntax specifies one set of properties of expressions; prosodic domain formation rules relate these to a different set of properties, phonological in character, which include organization into phonological domains; and phonological rules apply within the domains of the latter sort.

The discussion in Sect. 4.2 and 4.3 above also allowed for direct syntactic conditioning of rules distributing phonological properties, though such rules would be classified as lexical/morphological rather than properly phonological. These are nonautomatic phonological rules that must be viewed as applying within, at the edges of, or between syntactic constituents—rules governing 'shapes' in the terminology used above, 'P1 rules' in the terminology of Kaisse (1985), 'precompiled lexical phonology' in the terminology used by Hayes (in Inkelas and Zec 1990). There is some controversy as to whether there are any such rules; the alternative is to maintain that any syntactic conditioning is indirect, to claim that prosodic domain formation rules, themselves sensitive to (morpho)syntactic organization, establish the appropriate spans, within which entirely automatic phonological rules apply.

The alternative has a theoretical point in its favor, since it entirely eliminates one class of rules (syntactically constrained nonautomatic rules) in favor of types of rules (prosodic domain formation rules sensitive to syntactic organization; automatic phonological rules) whose existence is not in question. In practice, deciding between direct and indirect syntactic conditioning is not an easy matter, turning largely on the question of whether generalizations are better captured in nonautomatic phonological rules or in prosodic domain formation rules. The literature covers a wide range of phenomena, both clitics, such as the English reduced auxiliaries, and external sandhi, in a variety of languages including Italian (syntactic doubling), French (liaison), Mandarin Chinese (tone sandhi), and Matumbi (vowel shortening).

7.3 Surface versus Remote Syntactic Conditioning

Some syntactic theories posit more than one level at which the syntactic properties of an expression are described—one or more levels of 'remote' representation, in addition to the 'surface' level. In such theories the question arises of whether factors available only at a remote level can condition phonological rules (either directly or indirectly). Though there is some tradition for permitting such a relaxation in theoretical assumptions, the weight of opinion is in favor of the simpler theory, in which all syntactic conditioning is superficial.

Several English phenomena have been the focus of discussion on this point: the reduction of auxiliaries (*I know where it's been* versus **I know where it's*), contraction of *to* with a preceding verb (*What do you wanna make?* versus **What do you wanna vanish?*), and the assignment of stress and intonation contours to sentences (the infinitival relative interpretation favored for *I have* <u>plans</u> *to* <u>leave</u> versus the noun-complement interpretation favored for *I have plans to* <u>leave</u>).

Bibliography

Bloomfield L 1933 *Language*. Holt, New York

Inkelas S, Zec D (eds.) 1990 *The Phonology–syntax Connection*. University of Chicago Press, Chicago, IL

Kaisse E M 1985 *Connected Speech: The Interaction of Syntax and Phonology*. Academic Press, New York

Kaisse E M, Shaw P A (eds.) 1985 *Phonology Yearbook. Vol. 2: Phonology and the Lexicon*. Cambridge University Press, Cambridge

Kaisse E M, Zwicky A M (eds.) 1987 *Phonology Yearbook. Vol. 4: Syntactic Conditions on Phonological Rules*. Cambridge University Press, Cambridge

Nespor M, Vogel I 1986 *Prosodic Phonology*. Foris, Dordrecht

Pullum G K, Zwicky A M 1988 The syntax–phonology interface. In: Newmeyer F J (ed.) *Linguistics: The Cambridge Survey*, vol. 1. Cambridge University Press, Cambridge

Syntax and Pragmatics

R. Carston

A Rottweiler bit me last week.	(1a)
I was bitten by a Rottweiler last week.	(1b)
It was a Rottweiler that bit me last week.	(1c)
Last week I was bitten by a Rottweiler.	(1d)
What bit me last week was a Rottweiler.	(1e)

There are few lexical differences among these five sentences but each of them has a distinct syntactic structure. These differences in the type and order of phrases seem to make no difference to the objective information content of the sentences. They are all true at a given time if and only if a member of the class of Rottweilers is in the relation of having bitten the speaker a week prior to the time of utterance; otherwise they are all false. So a speaker who wants to convey that information has at least these five means at her disposal. The differences between the examples appear to concern the way the information is 'packaged' or tailored, the different packagings perhaps suited to particular cognitive or communicative aspects of the transfer of the propositional content (see Vallduvi 1993). The questions of interest here are what governs the speaker's choice of one rather than any other of these options—is it random?—and what, if any, difference does the option chosen make to the hearer's understanding of the utterance? Before responses to these questions are considered some preliminaries are necessary.

1. Syntax, Semantics, and Pragmatics

The subject here is the relation between syntax and pragmatics but coming to grips with this is difficult without bringing in a third participant, semantics. In order to appreciate the peculiarly pragmatic effects that particular syntactic structures may have some understanding of the difference between semantics and pragmatics is needed. Traditionally, syntax is taken to be the study of the combinatorial properties of words, semantics to be the study of meaning and pragmatics to be the study of language usage. 'Meaning' is a very vague term and a distinction between semantics and pragmatics along these lines leaves open a wide range of quite different ways of construing the subject matter of the two fields. A sharper distinction can be made between two aspects of utterance meaning: (a) those elements of meaning that can be directly decoded from the linguistic expressions used, that is, meaning which they have across all contexts of use, and (b) those which depend on extralinguistic contextual information and the interpreter's inferential abilities. So, for example, B's response to A in (2) communicates information about B's impression of the person referred to by A in the previous utterance

as Mary. A would most likely understand B as making a remark about Mary's personality rather than her temperature and might well infer that B did not very much like Mary, on the assumption that coldness of personality is not a likable feature:

A: Did you like Mary?	(2)
B: I found her very cold.	

Now the words actually uttered fall far short of encapsulating this information in and of themselves: *her* is a word that can be used to refer to any female creature, *cold* is ambiguous between the temperature and the personality understandings, and the sentence contains no words encoding concepts to do with liking. These processes of assigning a referent to the pronoun, of disambiguation and of deriving certain implications from an utterance are pragmatic processes. What is meant by this is that they depend on the assumption that speakers observe certain standards of rational cooperative behavior when they communicate and that hearers interpret utterances with these standards in mind. Without this assumption A (and the reader) would have no grounds for thinking that B is talking about Mary and is making a remark about her personality. Just what these standards guiding communication are will be considered in the next section.

So utterance understanding is a two-phase process. The first phase is the automatic decoding of linguistic content and it employs linguistic knowledge alone, that is, the grammar and the lexicon. The second phase is inferential, taking as its input the decoded content together with information derived from other sources, such as visual perception or memory; for example, the interpretation of B's utterance above might well involve accessing the assumption that a cold personality is not a likable one. Building on the conceptual outline or blueprint which is the result of decoding, the pragmatic processes deliver up an enriched version, for example, B experienced Mary Thomas at such and such a time as having a cold personality, plus (perhaps) additional assumptions derived inferentially such as that B did not much like Mary, etc. One way of understanding the semantics/pragmatics distinction is in terms of these two phases: the subject matter of semantics is linguistic meaning, that is decoded content, while the domain of pragmatics is all those additional processes which must be carried out in order to arrive at the speaker's intended message.

This semantics/pragmatics distinction is a psychological one; linguistic meaning is taken to be something conceptual or cognitive, a mental representation of a certain sort. There is another, perhaps even more established, approach to semantics which takes as central the relation between linguistic expressions and the world, so meanings on this view are things in the world rather than mental entities. The meaning of a word is the individual or set of individuals in the world it refers to and the meaning of a sentence is its truth-conditions, that is, the conditions that must hold for the sentence to be true. Truth-conditional content was implicitly adverted to in discussing the five syntactic structures given in (1) above, when it was said that they were true if and only if a member of the class of entities picked out by 'Rottweiler' was in a relation with the speaker of having bitten him/her a week prior to the time of utterance. The point being made there was that those sentences are truth-conditionally equivalent; the conditions in the world that make any one of them true make the other four true too. However, one might object that, as in the case of (2B), they don't actually have a full set of truth-conditions until some pragmatic work is done on them; the identity of the speaker needs to be known and the time of utterance. In other words, it looks as if this way of understanding semantics requires a prior operation of pragmatics, in order to fix reference, choose among the senses of ambiguous words, and enrich vague linguistic content, so as to provide a representation that can be evaluated with regard to whether it is true or false of the world. The propositions that utterances express have truth-conditions; the sentences used for their expression generally do not. Three levels are being studied here: cognitive semantics (of the linguistic code), pragmatic processes which build on decoded content, and truth-conditional semantics (of full-fledged propositional representations).

When it is said that the five *sentences* in (1) are truth-conditionally equivalent what is meant is that they make identical contributions to the truth-conditional content of utterances employing them, though they do not fully encode that content. The argument will be that they are not, however, cognitively equivalent: differences in the order of syntactic constituents naturally give rise to differences in the order in which hearers access the concepts they encode, so that hearers cannot help but process the truth-conditional content differently in each case and may thereby derive distinct cognitive effects. That is, these structures differ pragmatically.

2. A Relevance Approach to Pragmatics

Various different systems of principles or rules have been proposed in an attempt to develop Grice's original important observation that communication depends on the assumption that speakers and hearers observe certain standards of rational cooperative interaction. Atlas and Levinson (1981) develop a system of principles which is a direct descendant of Grice's (1975) set of conversational maxims and Horn (1988) summarizes various approaches. Sperber and Wilson's (1986) Relevance-based pragmatics is perhaps the most radical of these approaches in that it proposes a single criterion governing all those aspects of understanding an utterance which are not decoded from linguistic form but have to be inferred. This approach to pragmatics rests on a few basic ideas: (a) every utterance has a range of possible interpretations, all compatible with the information encoded by the linguistic expressions used ((2B) above gives a clear illustration of this point), (b) not all of these interpretations are equivalently easy for the hearer to access on any given occasion of utterance, (c) hearers have a particular means of evaluating interpretations as they occur to them.

The criterion or means for evaluation that hearers employ rests on the assumption that human cognition in general is relevance-oriented: that is, our attention is automatically drawn to what seems relevant in the environment. What's meant by 'relevant' here is 'capable of yielding large cognitive effects relative to small cognitive effort,' i.e., relevant information is information which interacts productively with a context of accessible assumptions. On this general cognitive assumption rests the particular claim about utterance interpretation. By producing an utterance a speaker makes a request for attention from a hearer, but since focusing attention on some phenomenon in the environment involves effort, the hearer can reasonably expect the speaker to be offering him relevant information in exchange for his effort. So utterances come with a tacit guarantee of optimal relevance, that is, a guarantee that the hearer's attention will be rewarded by a satisfactory range of cognitive effects and that he won't be required to expend any gratuitous effort in deriving these effects.

Cognitive effects arise when newly presented information interacts with a context of assumptions in any of three ways: (a) by strengthening contextual assumptions, (b) by contradicting and eliminating contextual assumptions, and (c) by acting as a premise together with contextual assumptions in the deduction of further assumptions (called contextual implications) that could not be derived from the context alone nor from the new information alone. For instance, returning to B's response in example (2), the newly presented information that B found Mary a cold person might strengthen A's own view of Mary as an unfriendly person or it might contradict an assumption of his that Mary and B would get on well. Given the immediate context of A's question it is quite likely to have the contextual implication, mentioned above, that B didn't particularly like Mary, arrived at deductively through the interaction of the new information with the highly accessible assumption that coldness of personality is not a very likable trait.

What the guarantee of relevance entitles the hearer to expect is that he will derive an adequate array of such contextual effects. Of course he will have to expend some mental effort in arriving at these: he has to decode the linguistic content, to access contextual assumptions and to compute the effects of the utterance in the context. This is where the second part of the guarantee comes in, which says that the hearer won't have to go to unnecessary effort to recover the effects. The point here is that the speaker has a particular message she wants to communicate to the hearer and it's in her interest to make the interpretation she has in mind as easy as possible for the hearer to recover. In particular it's in her interest to avoid formulating her utterance in such a way that it has a satisfactory and immediately accessible interpretation which is not the intended one, since a hearer is liable to stop there and not consider any other interpretation. Of course speakers are fallible and sometimes fail to produce utterances that fulfill the guarantee of optimal relevance. So the pragmatic criterion of 'consistency with the principle of relevance' that Sperber and Wilson propose does not entail that utterances are in fact always optimally relevant. The criterion is as follows: an utterance, on a given interpretation, is consistent with the principle of relevance if and only if *the speaker might rationally have expected* it to be optimally relevant to the hearer on that interpretation. Note that the first interpretation accessed and found consistent with the principle of relevance is the only interpretation consistent with the principle of relevance since any other possible interpretation will fail to fulfill the minimal processing part of the definition.

The quite general cognitive goal of keeping effort to a minimum in processing incoming information coupled with the speaker's aim to shape the utterance in such a way as to help the hearer's recovery of the intended interpretation raises a certain expectation about natural languages. That is, linguistic codes might be expected to contain formal devices (lexical items, syntactic structures) that give the hearer some guidance with regard to the allocation of his effort. So perhaps lexical and syntactic differences between truth-conditionally equivalent sentences guide the hearer in the choice of the context against which the truth-conditional content is to be processed, or shape the sort of inferential relation it has with that context, or indicate which of the many logical implications of the utterance can be expected to have the greatest yield in contextual effects. The five sentences given at the beginning seem to have the same truth-conditional content. The idea will be explored that their structural differences constrain the way the hearer processes their conceptual (or truth-conditional) content and that the speaker's choice of structure is determined by her bid to keep the processing demands on the hearer to a minimum.

3. Truth-conditional Equivalence and Pragmatic Effects

Consider the following pairs of sentences:

It's done.	(3a)
It's done, and if it's done it's done.	(3b)
He is my father.	(4a)
I am his daughter.	(4b)
The room was half empty.	(5a)
The room was half full.	(5b)
She passed the physics exam but failed Latin.	(6a)
She passed the physics exam and failed Latin.	(6b)
The meeting's at half past six, then.	(7a)
The meeting's at half past six, though.	(7b)
If you eat some bread, I'll cook hamburgers all week.	(8a)
If you eat any bread, I'll cook hamburgers all week.	(8b)

Despite their truth-conditional equivalence the members of each pair differ in the contextual effects a hearer would derive from them and therefore in the sort of contexts they would most likely occur in. That is, it can be said that although they are truth-conditionally synonymous they are not cognitively synonymous. For example, as Atlas and Levinson (1981: 1) point out, (3a) is a more likely answer to the question (9a) than (3b) is, whereas (3b) is a more likely response to (9b) than (3a):

Have you done it yet ?	(9a)
Oh dear, I wish I hadn't done that.	(9b)

Green (1989) considers cases where distinct but truth-conditionally equivalent constructions convey different information about attitudes, beliefs, or feelings, as in her examples in (8). Although *some* and *any* make the same contribution to truth-conditional content, the use of *some* in conditional and hypothetical constructions indicates a positive attitude toward the situation described by the proposition it refers to, whereas *any* seems to indicate a neutral or negative attitude. So (8a) might well be understood as an attempt to get the hearer to eat bread with the bribe of hamburgers as inducement, while (8b) has the effect of a threat, intending to keep the hearer from eating bread. Examples (4) and (5) convey different attitudes or feelings towards the same fact, and in (6) and (7) the hearer is required to process the same proposition differently in each case, to relate it differently to the context. The functions of these lexical items which do not seem to make a contribution to truth-conditional content are explored in detail in Blakemore (1987), and Wilson and Sperber (1993).

These are cases where the effects depend on lexical differences. Move now to the central issue of *structural* differences between sentences which do not affect truth-conditional content but which have effects on interpretation. The groups of examples in (10)–(14) are a small sample of this phenomenon:

A Rottweiler bit Mary.	(10a)
Mary was bitten by a Rottweiler. (passive)	(10b)
It was a Rottweiler that bit Mary. (*it*-cleft)	(10c)
What bit Mary was a Rottweiler. (*wh*-cleft)	(10d)

Sam has given his old car to Julie.	(11a)
Sam has given Julie his old car. (dative movement)	(11b)
His old car, Sam has given to Julie. (topicalization)	(11c)

Bill's twin sister lives in Berlin.	(12a)
Bill has a twin sister who lives in Berlin.	(12b)

The little bunny scampered into its hole.	(13a)
Into its hole, the little bunny scampered. (adverbial preposing)	(13b)
Into its hole scampered the little bunny. (adverbial preposing and subject–verb inversion)	(13c)

It rained on MONDAY.	(14a)
On Monday it RAINED.	(14b)
On MONDAY it rained.	(14c)

These examples are taken from Sperber and Wilson (1986: 202) and Green (1989: 129); the first of these sources is called on extensively in the following discussion. In each of these sets the canonical declarative word order is given in (a) and the bracketed labels beside the others are the standard names in generative grammar for the noncanonical (or marked) structures. Capitalization in (14), and hereafter, indicates main stress placement so (14c) is marked both with regard to its syntactic structure and its stress. An important and complicated issue is ignored here concerning the nature of the logical forms encoded by these sentences. There can be no doubt that different logical forms may make the same contribution to truth-conditional content; this is especially obvious in the lexical cases, such as (4) and (5) where *father*, *daughter* and *full*, *empty* encode discrete concepts. It may also be true of the truth-conditionally equivalent structures in (10) that each has a distinct logical form. The general point to make about all of these sets is that although they are arguably semantically equivalent they clearly make a difference to interpretation and they are appropriate in different contexts.

So, for example, the cleft constructions in (10c) and (10d) are appropriate answers to the question *What bit Mary?* but, unlike (10a) or (10b), would not be appropriate answers to the question *What's the matter?* and are less likely than them as discourse initial utterances. Similarly, the topicalized structure in (11c) would be appropriate in the context of a discussion about Sam giving away various of his possessions, but would be odd in certain contexts where (11a) or (11b)

would be fine, for example, in a discussion of what's been going on in Julie's life recently, or discourse-initially. The differences in stress placement and phrasal order in (14) constrain the use of the examples as answers to questions, so (14a) or (14c), unlike (14b), would be an appropriate answer to the question *When did it rain?*, whereas (14b), unlike (14a) or (14c), would be an appropriate answer to the question *What was the weather like on Monday?* The differences between (14a) and (14c) are harder to pinpoint but (14a) is a more likely discourse-initial utterance than (14c).

The different effects of the distinct linguistic forms have been described in terms of various (non-equivalent) distinctions. For example, Prince (1981) outlines several dichotomies between old and new information which have been used to explain these effects. Prince (1978) employs two of these old/new distinctions in her discussion of the different structurings of information effected by *it*-clefts and *wh*-clefts, such as those in (10c) and (10d) above. In both cases the new information concerns the identity of the biter, that is, that it is a Rottweiler, so the idea is that these structures provide a slot marked out for new information, directly after the copula (*is*) in both cases. The complement clauses of the two structures (*that S*, *what S*) house the 'old' information and what distinguishes the two structures, in Prince's view, is that there is a difference in the nature of this old information in the two cases. In the *wh*-cleft case the information in the clause (*what bit Mary*) is indicated as being 'given,' that is, the speaker assumes it is currently in the hearer's consciousness; in the *it*-cleft complement (*that bit Mary*) the speaker takes the information to be 'known,' that is, to be factual and believed by certain persons, though not necessarily the hearer. This accounts for the slight but perceptible difference in appropriateness of the two structures in certain contexts such as the following:

So I learned to sew books. They're really good books. It's just the covers that are rotten.	(15a)

So I learned to sew books. They're really good books. What's rotten is just the covers.	(15b)

(Prince 1978: 896)

It is known or knowable, from the fact that the speaker sews books, that something is 'rotten' or wrong with them. But what is being talked about, and therefore what the speaker can take the hearer to be currently thinking about is 'books,' not 'what is rotten'; so the *it*-cleft is more appropriate than the *wh*-cleft.

In addition to these sorts of informational distinctions there are several linguistic distinctions including topic/comment (Reinhart 1981) and theme/rheme (Halliday 1967, 1968). Reinhart's 'sentence topic' is an unstressed syntactic constituent occurring early in the utterance, whose referent is what the sentence is about. She compares it with the headings in the subject-catalogue in a library, which give access to existing information on the subject and provide a place to store the new information on it. For example, the sentence topic in (10b) is *Mary*: it makes stored information about the person it refers to available for use as context in interpreting the rest of the utterance. The topicalized structure in (11c) marks out as topic the constituent *his old car*, which would otherwise be in noninitial position as in (11a) and (11b) and so not able to play this role. There are various further distinctions, both linguistic and pragmatic, between presupposition and focus or presupposition and assertion. In (10c) and (10d) 'A Rottweiler' is the focus and what is presupposed or given is the assumption that something bit Mary; the information that Bill has a twin sister is treated as given or presupposed in (12a) whereas it is treated as new or asserted in (12b). It is unclear to what extent these various dichotomies overlap with each other and whether or not any of them covers the full range of data.

One or two generally agreed observations emerge from all these discussions. One is the view that it is natural for old information (i.e., information the speaker is treating as known or available or uncontroversial) to come before new information, as this somehow facilitates comprehension. In accordance with this intuition is another, concerning stress, which is that its natural or unmarked position is towards the end of the utterance. These two observations go together, given the apparent function of stress to highlight or draw attention to a particular constituent in an utterance, that is, to make it the *focus*. Of course it's not the case that old information always precedes new, nor that focal stress always comes at the end of the utterance. For instance, the *it*-cleft construction, as in (10c), lends itself to the presentation of new information before old, another factor which distinguishes it from the *wh*-cleft, which presents old before new information. The structure with a preposed phrase carrying focal stress in (14c) is another case where the intuition is that new information precedes old, and Green (1980) gives many other examples of this. Nevertheless it is generally felt that the natural or *unmarked* case is that of old before new. So what is required is a theory that accommodates both the unmarked and the marked cases and which explains these intuitions regarding markedness.

4. Relevance and Linguistic Form

The Relevance account of utterance interpretation provides the tools for a developed account of the pragmatic effects that these variations in syntactic

structure give rise to. Sperber and Wilson claim that there is a direct link between linguistic form (both phonological and syntactic) and pragmatic interpretation, explainable in terms of the two components of their definition of optimal relevance. That is, differences in the linguistic structure of utterances which are truth-conditionally equivalent may result in differences in contextual effects or in differences in the processing effort they require or the way in which processing effort is allocated. First, it will be considered what an account in these terms has to say about a case which is unmarked as regards syntactic structure and stress placement, given in (16a). Then, maintaining the canonical word order, the difference that a change of stress placement makes will be studied, as in (16b) and (16c), and finally move to the effects of such syntactic structures as clefts, passive, and preposed adverbials:

John invited LUCY.	(16a)
John INVITED Lucy.	(16b)
JOHN invited Lucy.	(16c)

Because any utterance is produced and processed over time a hearer naturally accesses some of the concepts encoded by the utterance before others and forms anticipatory hypotheses about the overall structure of the utterance on the basis of what he has already heard. The purpose of these hypotheses is to resolve ambiguities and referential indeterminacies as quickly as possible in order to reduce processing costs, which are heavier the wider the range of possible interpretations that has to be entertained. So, for example, at an early stage of the on-line processing of (16a) the hearer assigns *John* to the syntactic category NP and makes the anticipatory syntactic hypothesis that it will be followed by a VP. Then, as part of the decoding process, syntactic variables (NP, VP, PP, etc.) are mapped onto semantic variables (something/someone, do something/have some property, somewhere/sometime, etc.) in this case yielding the semantic hypothesis: John do something. On the assumption that the hearer knows several people called *John* (say, John Reed, John Holmes, John Sim), his assignment of reference to the name depends on the guarantee of optimal relevance. If, for instance, the first candidate that he accesses is his concept of John Sim and if the information that John Sim did something is relevant (has cognitive effects) in some context he currently has accessible, then he will assume that this is the referent the speaker intended. Alternatively, if there is no obvious assignment of reference which would make (16a) relevant, as is likely at this early stage of comprehension, it may be that some assignment of reference raises a relevant question in the hearer's mind. For example, an answer to the question *What did John Reed do?* may be relevant in some context currently accessible to the hearer, in which case he will assume that this is the question the speaker intended to raise and that the rest of the utterance will answer.

As the hearer proceeds through the utterance, constituent by constituent, he makes a series of anticipatory hypotheses:

John did something/What did John do?	(17a)
John invited someone/Who did John invite?	(17b)

Finally, he arrives at his hypothesis about the proposition the speaker has expressed, for instance, that John Sim invited Lucy Scott. Notice that these three hypotheses are logically related to each other. They are a subset of the logical implications of the utterance and they form a scale in which each member logically implies the immediately preceding member. If the speaker has done her job properly, each hypothesis will either be directly relevant by having some cognitive effect, or contribute indirectly to relevance by speeding up disambiguation, reference assignment, or context construction, that is, by reducing processing costs. The implications that contribute directly to relevance are *foreground implications* and those that contribute indirectly to relevance are *background implications*. This distinction provides the concepts for a description of the intuitive notion of the focus of an utterance. Note that stress seldom picks out a unique focus since the word it falls on is usually a part of larger phrasal constituents. For instance, in (16a) the focally stressed NP *Lucy* is a constituent of the VP *invited Lucy* which is a constituent of the sentence as a whole; any one of these three might be the focus of the utterance. Sperber and Wilson define the focus as the smallest syntactic constituent whose replacement by a variable yields a background rather than a foreground implication. In other words, the focus is the syntactic constituent which dominates all the information that contributes directly to relevance. For example, if the hypothesis (17a), John (Sim) did something, is relevant in its own right, that is, is a foreground implication, the focus must be the sentence as a whole. If (17a) merely contributes indirectly to relevance but (17b), John (Sim) invited someone, is directly relevant then the focus is the VP *invited Lucy*, since this is the smallest syntactic constituent whose replacement by a variable *did something* yields a background implication, that is (17a).

This background/foreground distinction partially parallels the distinctions mentioned above, given–new, presupposition–focus, etc. However background and foreground are distinguished by the way they contribute to the relevance of the utterance, whether by reducing processing effort or by having cognitive effects. Background information need not be given or presupposed though it often is; foreground information need not be new though it often is. Backgrounding and foregrounding of information are automatic effects of the hearer's bid to maximize

relevance, and of the speaker's exploitation of that tendency.

This approach sheds light on the robust intuition that it is natural for given information to come before new, or for the focus to come at the end of the utterance. Our cognitive life is such that we generally seek answers to questions previously raised and we consider freshly impinging information in a context of existing (background) information; it is difficult to conceive of a system that worked otherwise. So it is natural to organize utterances such that the focus comes at the end, where 'natural' here means in accordance with the principle of relevance: this arrangement places the least demands on the hearer's processing resources. In the unmarked case, (16a), the scale of anticipatory hypotheses determined by left-to-right word order coincides with the scale which is formed by considering the potential foci of the utterance: the NP *Lucy*, the VP *invited Lucy*, or the whole sentence. These potential foci in effect form the same logically ordered scale; this is more easily seen if each potential focus is replaced by a variable:

Something happened.	(18a)
John did something.	(18b)
John invited someone.	(18c)

Of course placing the focal stress on one of the other words of the sentence defines a different focal scale, made up of a different subset of logical implications of the utterance. For example, if *John* is stressed, as in (16c), the focal scale is as in (19):

Something happened.	(19a)
Someone invited Lucy.	(19b)

and if stress is placed on *invited* as in (16b) another scale is defined. What accounts for the intuitive unmarked/marked distinction between (16a), on the one hand, and (16b) and (16c), on the other, is that the focal scale induced by (16a) coincides with the natural order of hypothesis formation, shown in (17), which is determined by word order.

Despite the naturalness of the final position for focus it seems that in some circumstances it appropriately falls elsewhere. The question then is when is it appropriate (that is, in accordance with the principle of relevance) to use a marked focal stress as in (16c), thereby inducing the scale in (19)? How could a hearer working step by step through the utterance as it is presented across time recover the implication (19b)? The obvious answer is that (16c) is appropriate when (19b) is antecedently available to the hearer, for instance, via the immediately preceding utterance:

Who invited Lucy?	(20a)
JOHN.	(20b)
JOHN did.	(20c)
JOHN invited Lucy/her.	(20d)

Each of these responses has the NP *John* as focus and the assumption *Someone invited Lucy* as background.

When a question has been raised by the immediately preceding utterance and an initial context thereby established, it is often a waste of processing effort to repeat it. Responses to explicit questions can thus be fragmentary as in (20b) and (20c), and when the background assumption is made fully explicit as in (20d) it may follow the focus, acting merely as a reminder. The question is explicitly asked here, but (20d) could be appropriately used when the background question is merely implicated by the preceding utterance, say *Lucy's here*, or when the speaker has reason to think it's a question that the hearer is currently entertaining.

5. Relevance and Syntactic Variation

In the light of this discussion of foregrounded and backgrounded information and their contributions to the relevance of an utterance, consider some of the syntactically marked constructions mentioned above, starting with the cleft structures, repeated here as (21b) and (21c):

A ROTTWEILER bit me.	(21a)
It was a Rottweiler that bit me. (*it*-cleft)	(21b)
What bit me was a Rottweiler. (*wh*-cleft)	(21c)
A Rottweiler was what bit me. (reverse *wh*-cleft)	(21d)

Considering first just the *it*-cleft, the idea is that this construction distinguishes the focus from the remainder of the sentence by syntactic means and thereby constrains the sort of context in which it can be appropriately used. While the focus of (21a), which has focal stress on the initial NP, could be either the NP *A Rottweiler* or the sentence as a whole, the *it*-cleft in (21b) narrows the options to the NP *A Rottweiler* alone. So while (21a) would be an appropriate answer to the questions *What's the matter?* or *What happened to your hand?* and (21b) would not, either might do as responses to queries about what had bitten the speaker, and the cleft would be the more natural means for correcting a mistaken assumption about the identity of the biter: *It was a Rottweiler, not an Alsatian, that bit me.* Conversely, a hearer of (21b) would be led by the form of this construction to treat as a background assumption the information that something bit the speaker and to derive cognitive effects from the information that the entity responsible is a Rottweiler. For example, in interaction with ready assumptions of the hearer it might yield contextual implications regarding the speaker's likely attitude to and future reactions to Rottweilers; it might strengthen the hearer's own existing opinion of these dogs; it might eliminate an earlier tentative hypothesis that the speaker had been bitten by her next-door-neighbor's Alsatian.

The *wh*-cleft construction might appear to function pretty similarly, the post-copular position being syntactically marked out as focus. Then the only significant difference from the *it*-cleft would be that the ordering of information is the unmarked one of background preceding focus. However, the existence of reverse *wh*-clefts as in (21d) indicates that more needs to be said here. It may well be that Prince's (1978) distinction, mentioned above and exemplified in (15), between two kinds of background information, 'given' and 'known,' will be central to an explanation of the differences in appropriateness and effects of these two structures:

A: Hi! I'm Martha.	(22)
B: a. Hi! It was your office I used when I was at MIT.	
b. Hi! Your office is what I used when I was at MIT.	
(adapted from an example of J. Delin)	

In Relevance terms, the idea would be that 'known' background assumptions and 'given' ones differ in their accessibility and so the two types of construction give hearers different indications regarding the accessing of context. For instance, 'given' information (as in the *wh*-clefts) should either be part of the existing context or be directly retrievable from the immediately preceding utterance while information which is merely 'known' might require more inferential work for its recovery. Then the slightly more natural feel of (22a) as a response to Martha's greeting might be due to the reasonable supposition that she cannot be expected to be currently entertaining the assumption that B was in MIT or that she used someone's office when she was there, though she (Martha) might be able to recall this under prompting or to infer it. Much work is needed to tease out the subtle differences between these three cleft types but it may be that this distinction between degrees of accessibility of background assumptions, together with the effects on processing which the different orderings of focus and background have, play a central role in the explanation:

It is—focus—*that*—'known' background.	(23a)
Wh—'given' background—*is*—focus.	(23b)
Focus -*is*—*wh*—'given' background.	(23c)

For a more fine-grained account of the discourse effects of *it*-clefts with different stress possibilities, see Delin (1995) and Delin and Oberlander (1995).

The active/passive alternation, exemplified in (10a) and (10b), obviously makes a difference to the scale of anticipatory hypotheses, dictated by word order. Assuming unmarked focal stress, each indicates different backgrounding and foregrounding of assumptions: the initial NP in (10a), *A Rottweiler*, makes accessible stored assumptions about Rottweilers which can serve as context for the processing of the rest of the utterance, while in the passive case of (10b) it is information about Mary that first becomes available as context. The different structurings of information determine which of the implications of the utterance contribute directly to relevance (by yielding cognitive effects) and which contribute indirectly by, for instance, guiding the hearer's choice of context. Sperber and Wilson (1986: 215) show how this Relevance approach gives an explanation for the different effects of referential expressions in different syntactic positions. It has been observed in the literature on existential presupposition that in the case where there is no identifiable referent for the referring expression *The King of France* it is generally felt that (24a) is less acceptable than (24b), that while (24b) makes a false assertion, (24a) does not succeed in making any assertion at all.

> The King of France visited the EXHIBITION. (24a)
> The exhibition was visited by the
>   King of FRANCE. (24b)

Now, if the focus of (24a) is *the exhibition* or *visited the exhibition*, and so the background is *The King of France visited something* or *The King of France did something*, the information that there is a King of France is logically implied by this background, and a hearer who rejects it will be unable to access a context in which the utterance might be relevant. In (24b), on the other hand, the focus might be *the King of France* or *was visited by the King of France*, and the background *The exhibition was visited by someone* or *The exhibition had some property*. Then at least the hearer will be able to access the appropriate context and see what sort of cognitive effects the speaker must have had in mind, even though he will regard the speaker as mistaken.

Finally, consider the examples in (14). (14a) could be understood as an answer to any of the questions: *On what day did it rain?*, *When did it rain?* and *What happened?*, that is, the focus could be *Monday*, *On Monday* or the whole sentence. The variations in word order and focal stress in (14b) and (14c) alter the background/foreground relations and so channel processing effort in particular directions and influence the sort of effects derived. The effect of preposing the unstressed constituent *On Monday* is to push it into the background, thereby indicating to the hearer that there is some question about what happened on Monday which the speaker thinks is relevant to him. On the other hand, stressing the preposed phrase, as in (14c), selects it as focus, so by the time the hearer has processed the phrase he knows that it gives the answer to some question he is taken to have accessible, such as *When did it rain?* As with all the examples considered, the different effects they have on interpretation are the outcome of the interaction of syntax, stress placement, and the principle of relevance. For a detailed account of the discourse functions and the cognitive effects of preposing different constituents, see Ward (1985, 1990).

6. Conclusion

Natural languages encode conceptual and hence truth-conditional content, thereby enabling hearers to construct propositional representations from utterances. However, as has been seen, there are aspects of phonological and syntactic form which do not contribute to truth-conditional content but function to direct the hearer's processing effort along particular lines. A variety of syntactic structures have been considered whose differences in phrasal type and order seem to perform just this function. Given the Relevance-based approach to pragmatics this comes as no surprise; it is clearly in the interest of both speakers and hearers to have such effort-directing structures available to guide the interpretation process.

Bibliography

Atlas J D, Levinson S C 1981 *It*-clefts, informativeness, and logical form: Radical pragmatics (revised standard version). In: Cole P (ed.) *Radical Pragmatics*. Academic Press, New York
Blakemore D 1987 *Semantic Constraints on Relevance*. Blackwell, Oxford
Delin J 1995 Presupposition and shared knowledge in *it*-clefts. *LCProc* **10**: 97–120
Delin J, Oberlander J 1995 Syntactic constraints on discourse structure: The case of *it*-clefts. *Linguistics* **33**: 465–500
Green G M 1980 Some wherefores of English inversions. *Lg* **56**: 582–660
Green G 1989 *Pragmatics and Natural Language Understanding*. Erlbaum, Hillsdale, NJ
Grice H P 1975 Logic and conversation. In: Cole P, Morgan J (eds.) *Syntax and Semantics. Vol. 3: Speech Acts*. Academic Press, New York
Halliday M A K 1967, 1968 Notes on transitivity and theme in English. *JL* **3**: 37–81, 199–244; **4**: 179–215
Horn L 1988 Pragmatic theory. In: Newmeyer F (ed.) *Linguistics: The Cambridge Survey*, vol. 1. Cambridge University Press, Cambridge
Prince E 1978 A comparison of *wh*-clefts and *it*-clefts in discourse. *Lg* **54**: 883–906
Prince E F 1981 Towards a taxonomy of given–new information. In: Cole P (ed.) *Radical Pragmatics*. Academic Press, New York
Reinhart T 1981 Pragmatics and linguistics: An analysis of sentence topics. *Philosophica* **27**: 53–94
Sperber D, Wilson D 1986 *Relevance: Communication and Cognition*. Blackwell, Oxford
Vallduví E 1993 *Information Packaging: A Survey*. Centre for Cognitive Science and Human Communication Research Centre, University of Edinburgh, Edinburgh
Ward G 1985 *The Semantics and Pragmatics of Preposing* (Dissertation, University of Pennsylvania. Repr. 1988. Garland, New York)
Ward G 1990 The discourse functions of VP preposing. *Lg* **66**: 742–63
Wilson D, Sperber D 1993 Linguistic form and relevance. *Lingua* **90**: 1–25

Syntax and Semantics

P. A. M. Seuren

The question of the relation between syntax and semantics originates with the modern syntactic conception of grammar, as developed in the tradition of American structuralism (see *American Structuralism*). In this tradition, which began in the early 1920s, a grammar of **L** is an exhaustive description or specification of all the combinations of atomic elements (called 'morphemes' in linguistics) that are permissible in **L**. A combination (construction) is permissible just in case it is, or is part of, a well-formed (grammatical) sentence of **L**. This syntactic concept of grammar is found not only in linguistics but also in logic, where it relates to the formal or symbolic languages in which logical calculi are conducted.

Before the 1920s, as far as linguistics is concerned (and before the 1940s, as regards logic), there was hardly any explicit notion that the syntax and the semantics of any language, natural or formal, could or should be distinguished at all. A language was seen as a system manifesting itself in the use of meaningful signs or symbols, whose form and meaning were, so to speak, hand in glove with each other. It was only with the discovery, in the context of modern structuralism, of the relative autonomy of form versus meaning that the distinction could be properly made. The distinction was made more quickly and more clearly in logic than in linguistics.

As regards the notion of semantics there is hardly any common ground between the linguistic and the logical traditions in the twentieth century. In linguistics, due to the enormous influence of behaviorism, the notion of meaning, and thus also of semantics, remained for a long time ill-understood and badly defined, if at all. This situation has improved a little but the effects are still clearly felt. In logic, on the other hand, much greater clarity was achieved about what was (is) meant by 'meaning' and 'semantics,' and thus also about the relation between syntax and semantics in formal logical languages.

When these logical notions were, after 1960, transferred and applied to the study of natural language (where they proved useful in many ways but defective in others) linguists were faced with an entirely novel way of looking at the facts of grammar and meaning. And although there is now a lively and fruitful dialog between representatives of both traditions, the division is still clearly marked. It is, therefore, necessary to consider the question of the relation between syntax and semantics from two different angles. This question will be considered first in the light of the more strictly linguistic tradition of the twentieth century. It will then become clear that there are two main schools of thought in linguistics concerning the status of syntactic and semantic descriptions. After that the question will be considered in the light of the logical tradition.

1. The Linguistic Tradition

In the structuralist conception, a 'grammar' of **L** is a full specification of all permissible (grammatical) constructions in **L**. Most authors in the linguistic tradition (e.g., Bloomfield 1933: 184) distinguish two parts of grammar, 'syntax' and 'morphology,' defining morphology as the complete specification of all constructions that form words, and syntax as the full specification of all constructions that consist of words and form sentences or parts of sentences (phrases). But often the term syntax is also used, in a wider sense and perhaps a little sloppily, to cover the totality of all constructions of **L**, both the morphological and the strictly speaking syntactic ones. Unless otherwise specified the term syntax will be used, in this article, in this wider sense.

Semantics, on the other hand, is taken to consist of the description or specification of the meanings of the morphemes and the constructions that the morphemes enter into to form larger structures (words, phrases, sentences). It is normally taken for granted in an implicit way that meanings, whatever they may be, are themselves structured in certain ways and that there exist regular, systematic relations between grammatical (syntactic) and semantic structures. A full description of **L** will thus consist of both a grammar (syntax) and a semantics of **L**, the latter being a (full) specification of the meanings of the structural elements distinguished and specified in the former.

Whereas the notions of grammar (syntax), grammatical construction and grammatical structure appeared reasonably manageable and lent themselves without too many serious problems to operational treatment in the form of formally precise specifications, this was not so for the notions of meaning and semantic structure. In fact, as a result of the then extremely influential movement in psychology known as behaviorism, Bloomfield and many of his students and followers proclaimed that a semantic description of a language was scientifically unattainable because, in their view, meaning was either of a mental nature and hence not a proper object for scientific investigation, or, if it were to be scientifically investigated, required a pairing of all morphemes and grammatical structures occurring in actually uttered sentences with a scientifically exact description of all objects, properties, and states of affairs referred to or specified by them. And such a pairing is intrinsically impossible, if only because it would require a description of objects, properties, or states of affairs referred to or specified in *future* utterances.

This idea that a semantic description of a language is either scientifically improper or at least scientifically unattainable is now universally considered erroneous. Yet it led to a situation where all attention was focused on the specification of syntactic structures, their semantic description being entirely neglected and even considered illegitimate. This extreme position reached its brief apogee in the work of Harris (Harris 1951), one of Bloomfield's more prominent students. This work was written between 1945–48, and at the time of its eventual publication, in 1951, antisemanticism in linguistics was already beginning to wane. In structuralist linguistic publications throughout the 1950s a certain category of semantic phenomena was rapidly gaining recognition: structural ambiguities, such as are found in constructions like *old men and women*, or *the fat major's wife* were provided as examples of the disambiguating power of structuralist syntactic analyses, which allowed one to associate different tree diagrams with each of the different readings.

After 1960 behaviorism rapidly declined and was replaced by a new and richer theoretical basis known as cognitivism in psychology. The difference from behaviorism consisted mainly in the admission that behaviorist theory, which explains all behavior in terms of associative mechanisms linking stimuli and responses, is inadequate and needs to be replaced by an essentially richer set of assumptions including the postulate of rich and powerful 'computational mechanisms' in the mind. Insofar as the concept of 'mind' can be made explicit in terms of such machinery it is now no longer considered unscientific to operate with that concept.

In this context, understandably, the linguistic world largely freed itself from its previous semantic fears. Around 1960 it was again fully acceptable to mention meaning in linguistic writings. In Chomsky (1957), semantic criteria, in particular ambiguity phenomena, are exploited more systematically than in other structuralist writings of that period. They are now used as a formal means of testing the adequacy of a syntactic description and of the general theory in terms of which it is cast. Since Chomsky came up with cases of ambiguity that could not be made to correspond to different tree diagrams, such as the famous 'the shooting of the hunters,' it was felt that a grammar whose power was restricted to the direct generation of tree diagrams for sentences was bound to be inadequate. This semantic criterion greatly contributed to the birth of transformational generative grammar (TGG) in the late 1950s.

Soon after, in the early 1960s, an algorithmically precise description of the constructions of a language L, i.e., a generative grammar of L, came to be regarded as a scientific hypothesis aiming at an explicit specification of a (native) speaker's competence in L (see *Generative Grammar: Principles and Parameters*). This way of looking upon grammar or syntax immediately led to the insight that a generative grammar specifying just well-formed structures can only be a partial description of a native speaker's competence in L, since 'competence' or 'knowledge' of a language L involves not only the ability to distinguish between structures (sentences) that are well-formed and those that are not, but, obviously, also a knowledge of what the well-formed structures mean. Hence it was concluded (Katz and Fodor 1963; Katz and Postal 1964), that an adequate hypothesis (theory) describing a native speaker's competence in L must comprise at least two distinct components, a 'syntactic component' specifying the well-formedness constraints on the structures of L, and a 'semantic component' specifying the meanings of the structures defined by the syntax. The syntactic component, it was felt, was more or less available in the shape of the existing model of transformational generative grammar, but the semantic component had yet to be designed.

In the then current theory of TGG a sentence S is specified ('generated') first in terms of its 'deep structure' (DS), and then in terms of its 'surface structure' (SS). The DS of a sentence is produced by a set of 'formation rules,' standardly called 'phrase structure rules' (PS-rules), which specify the set of all possible DS trees in L. A different set of rules, the 'transformations' (T-rules) convert the DS into the SS of S. The PS-rules and the T-rules together form the syntax of L, which is thus seen to be a device for generating all and only the well-formed sentences of L, at the same time assigning a structure to each sentence generated.

In Katz and Fodor (1963) it is proposed that the semantic component of the full description of L should be conceived as consisting of 'projection rules' which take as their input syntactically defined structures and produce meaning descriptions or 'semantic representations' (SRs) as output. Each sentence S of L will thus have a double specification, in terms of its SS and in terms of its SR. The specific proposal contained in Katz and Fodor (1963) is that DSs 'project' certain semantic elements of sentences while SSs 'project' other elements. They thus envisage two kinds of projection rules, P1-rules which take DSs as input, and P2-rules which take SSs as input. Both sets of rules contribute to the one intended output, the SRs of the sentences of L. A full, 'integrated' description of L will thus have the overall structure presented in Fig. 1, where the triangles stand for sets of structures and the boxes for sets of rules. The symbol 'S' (sentence) at the top specifies the class of the products delivered as output by the apparatus.

In contrast to this, it is proposed in Katz and Postal (1964) that all projection rules of the semantic component should take DSs as their sole input, so that the P2-rules disappear from the model and only P1-rules remain. The argument supporting this proposal is that the syntactic description of any language L is simpli-

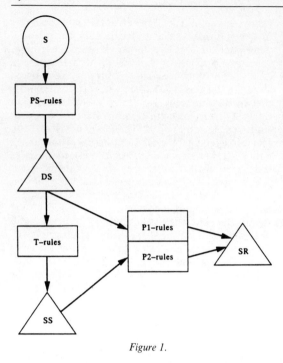

Figure 1.

fied, and hence improved, if it is assumed that all semantic information carried by a sentence S is contained in the DS of S. This amounts to postulating that the T-rules of the grammar are 'meaning invariant': no semantic change may be induced by the application of a transformational rule. Thus, the then current T-rule for negation (Klima 1964), inserting a negation word ('not') transformationally in any appropriate position in the sentence, was declared illicit, since it changes meaning. If, on the other hand, the negation word is introduced as part of DS, in the form of a sentential operator, then the negative meaning of the sentence is fixed at DS level and a subsequent T-rule will then assign it its proper position in the sentence. This pays off in the syntax, according to Katz and Postal (1964), because negation controls a number of other syntactic phenomena in sentences, and it is simpler to formulate such conditions on the basis of one single well-defined structural position of the negation word, as in DS, than from the rather many different possible positions of the negation word in surface structures. Similar arguments were developed for other cases as well.

In a remarkably short time the proposal made in Katz and Postal (1964) swept through the linguistic world. By 1965 it was universally accepted by those who worked in the theoretical framework of TGG, notably also by Chomsky (1965). The principle of the semantic completeness of deep structures, and hence the meaning–invariance of T-rules, came to charac-

terize what was later called (Chomsky 1972: 66) the 'standard theory.'

Meanwhile, however, due mainly to the unhappy behaviorist past, the actual nature of meaning, and in particular the precise form of the output of the semantic projection rules, the semantic representations, remained unclear. As far as the semantic specifications were concerned, the standard theory remained, for a few years, just a program. Until the late 1960s it hardly produced any substantive descriptions. But this began to change when McCawley showed (1967; most accessible in McCawley 1973: 99–120) that, if anything, SRs must be considered to be *syntactic* structures in some semantic descriptive formal language, probably closely akin to known languages of logic. (This argument was independently presented in Seuren 1969: 219–24, where the term 'favorite synonymous language' is used.)

At the same time some linguists (e.g., Ross 1986; McCawley 1967; Seuren 1969; Lakoff 1971) realized that if the DS of any given sentence S contains all semantic information carried by S, then it is a priori plausible to assume that the DS of any S *is* the semantic representation of S. The burden of proof lies with whoever claims that the two are distinct. Since no proof or argument to that effect could be presented these linguists proposed that *all* projection rules, and hence the whole semantic component, should be eliminated from the descriptive model. The syntax itself provides the SRs required for a specification of meanings. This led to a conception of linguistic description as rendered in Fig. 2. It became known, first, as generative semantics (see *Generative Semantics*), and later, with some authors (in particular Seuren 1974), as semantic syntax.

The requirement of meaning invariance of T-rules soon resulted in the realization that DSs must be taken to be far more 'abstract' (in the sense of being remote from SS) than had hitherto been assumed. It became clear, notably, that this conception of grammar required a factorizing out of those elements that are known as 'operators' in predicate logic, i.e., elements that take sentences (propositions) or sentential (propositional) functions (i.e., structures dominated by a node labeled 'S') as input (usually called 'scope') and deliver sentences (propositions), i.e., again S-dominated structures, as output. The negation word 'not' for example, takes an S (its scope) to form an S, and likewise for the quantifiers, the modalities, and even the tenses. The factorizing out of such operator elements amounts to setting up structures that unite an operator and its scope as sisters under one dominating S-node. A subsequent transformational rule, operator lowering (see Seuren 1984), will then assign the operator its proper place in the scope-S.

The unavoidability of such factorizing out appears, for example, when one considers the passive. In early standard TGG, which worked with a T-rule 'passive'

Figure 2.

and with structures proposed in Klima (1964) and Chomsky (1965), the passive of (1a) would come out as (1b):

Not every student has read two books. (1a)

Two books have not been read by every student. (1b)

Clearly, these two sentences differ in meaning, the difference being expressible in different scopes for the operators 'not,' 'every student,' and 'two books.' Regardless of how passive is accounted for (whether by rule or as a separate DS production), a provision must be built in to ensure that the relative order of the operators in (1a) is maintained in the passive version, so that the passive will not be (1b) but rather something like the, admittedly rather awkward, sentence (1c):

Not by every student have two books been read. (1c)

And if the language in question, for independent structural reasons, does not allow for the preservation of the relative order of operators, then there must be a provision ensuring that no output is delivered.

Generative semanticists proposed to achieve the desired result by assigning to a sentence like (1a) a DS

of, in principle, the following form (disregarding tense) (2a):

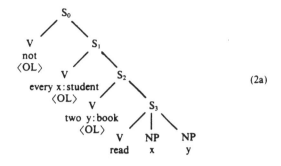

(2a)

One notes that the operators are categorized as V, i.e., verb, as proposed by McCawley (1973: 247, 277–319). This is semantically correct, since they are functions to S. Moreover, DS has the order Verb–Subject–Object, in accordance with McCawley (1970).

Each of the three operators, the negation 'not,' the universal quantifier 'every x:student,' and the existential quantifier 'two y:book,' induces the cyclic T-rule of operator lowering (OL). OL is constrained in such a way that, barring certain compensatory conditions, in principle no operator can be lowered into a position to the right of that occupied by a previously lowered operator ('scope ordering constraint' or SOC). The compensatory conditions just mentioned allow SOC to be overridden. One such condition is special lexical choice (e.g., 'some' instead of 'any' after negation indicates higher scope for 'some'). Another is tree hierarchy: *Every morning I read two poems* has no scope for ambiguity, but *I read two poems every morning* does have two readings that differ in scope. This is because in the latter sentence the constituent 'every morning,' though to the right of 'two poems,' is a very high, major constituent in the sentence and can thus take scopal precedence in spite of word order. Intonation may also override SOC. An often quoted case (Horn 1989: 226) is *All that glitters is not gold*, which means literally *not all that glitters is gold*. But note that in *All the King's horses and all the king's men could not put Humpty Dumpty back on the wall again*, SOC is again observed. The difference corresponds with different intonation contours, which probably express different topic–comment modulations. The correct syntactic analysis of such phenomena still has not been provided.

It should be stressed, in this connection, that the correspondence of scope hierarchies with left-to-right ordering in surface structures is a real fact of language, expressed in SOC, despite the conditions allowing an overriding of this principle. This fact must be stressed because it has been consistently denied in the formal semantic literature of Montagovian signature, where semantic interpretations are standardly allowed for

317

all mathematically possible permutations of scope bearing operators in sentences.

Variable binding operators, such as quantifiers, are lowered categorically onto the position of the bound variable. 'Not' is normally lowered onto the lower V but stays to the left of previously lowered operators if forced by SOC. Thus, on the S_2-cycle, 'two y:book' is lowered into the position of y in S_3, giving 'two books.' On the S_1-cycle, 'every x:student' is lowered into the position of x, giving 'every student,' and on the S_0-cycle, 'not' is lowered into the position just left of 'every student,' resulting in 'not every student' in subject position.

Passivization must now be restricted to the lowest S, i.e., S_3, which contains no operators. The same repeated cyclic application of OL on a passive S_3 will yield (stretching the resources of the grammar of English) sentence (1c), where the left-to-right order of the three operators is unchanged.

Sentence (1b), on the other hand, is generated from an underlying (2b):

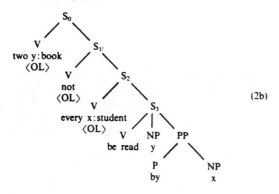

(2b)

Here the relative scope of the operators is reflected again in the left-to-right order of their SS representatives. Interestingly, with S_3 in the active form, i.e., as $_S[_V[read]_{NP}[x]_{NP}[y]]$, OL is blocked on the S_0-cycle, since the existential quantifier 'two y:book' would have to be lowered into a position to the right of the previously lowered 'not every student.' In order to express in an active sentence what is said by (2b) one has to resort to a drastic reformulation and say something like *There are two books that not every student has read.*

A significant factor in this method of analysis is the fact that the DSs of natural language sentences display structures which are directly related to well-known structures in certain forms of predicate calculus, in particular the variety known as restricted quantification theory (see, for example, McCawley 1973: 246, 264). This means that generative semantics was the first theoretical development in linguistics since the beginning of the twentieth century to bring about a serious rapprochement between logic and linguistics. The ties traditionally linking these two disciplines had

been severed with the advent of modern standard predicate calculus (classical quantification theory, CQT) as developed mainly by Russell, since it looked as if the analyses that figure in CQT lack any relevance with respect to the analyses required in grammar. Linguists thus decided that logic was no longer for them. In the context of generative semantics, however, some linguists came to the pleasantly surprising insight that, after all, even modern logic must be taken to be relevant to grammatical analysis and description. What remained unclear for the time being was the use this new logic could have for a proper semantics of natural language.

In the early 1970s generative semantics was pushed from its dominant position in theoretical linguistics by the MIT-centered development of autonomous syntax, which has so far resulted in the theory of government and binding (GB). This theory is characterized by the denial of Katz and Postal's 1964 argument that the theory of syntax gains by the assumption of the semantic invariance of T-rules, so that all semantic information of sentences is contained in their DS representations. Autonomous syntax, in fact, reverts to the position advocated in Katz and Fodor (1963), i.e., the model sketched in Fig. 1, but with much improved notions of semantic representation and projection rules. Autonomous syntax follows generative semantics in regarding SRs as syntactic structures in a formal semantic language closely akin to known logical languages. GB now speaks of the logical form (LF) of a sentence, rather than its semantic representation. It likewise follows generative semantics in concluding that, therefore, the projection rules are, in fact, transformations mapping SSs and SRs onto each other. However, while generative semantics holds that these T-rules are constitutive of the syntax, autonomous syntax distinguishes strictly between syntactic and semantic T-rules. Moreover, whereas the syntactic T-rules are usually formulated as taking a DS input and yielding an SS output ('top–down' ordering), the semantic T-rules are usually formulated as taking an SS input and giving an LF representation as output ('bottom–up'). In generative semantics, of course, no such distinction can exist. There, all T-rules are formulated as taking a DS input and yielding an SS output, i.e., in the top–down format (though the directionality of the rules is not essential).

The difference between these two schools amounts to the empirical question of whether the transformational operations required for the mapping of SRs (LF), and SSs onto each other are also instrumental in the purely syntactic definition of well-formedness conditions of sentences. Autonomous syntax gives a negative, but generative semantics a positive answer. Other than this, the differences are not essential, since generative semantics does not exclude the existence of meaning-independent structural principles or 'filters' in the grammar of a language, and Autonomous Syntax cannot exclude the possibility that the T-rules hitherto considered to be purely semantic will turn out to have a function in the syntax of the language under analysis as well, or vice versa. In fact, to the extent that the semantic component has been elaborated in GB, the mappings relating SSS and LF are remarkably similar to what was proposed earlier in generative semantics, though they are, of course, presented in the format of bottom–up directionality (cf. May 1977, where one finds quantifier raising in lieu of operator lowering).

No matter which of the two approaches, if either, will turn out to be empirically more successful, it is important to realize that the debate is more about two competing conceptions of syntax than about the relation of syntax and semantics. Yet, in the days when generative semantics was coming into its own, the question was consistently presented as being about syntax and semantics. McCawley, for example, writes (1973: 99), while commenting on his article (1967): 'It is to my knowledge the first work published... in which anyone argued for abolishing the distinction between syntax and semantics in transformational grammar.' It is now accepted that abolishing that distinction is an analytic impossibility of the same order as, for example, abolishing the distinction between the specification of a room and that of its temperature. All an 'integrated' transformational grammar, whether of the generative semantics or of the autonomous syntax persuasion, can do is relate sentence forms, SSS, to some synonymous form, the corresponding SR, formulated in a formal language that avoids ambiguities and expresses certain logical properties. The semantic function of a transformational grammar of **L** is, in other words, restricted to the translation of the sentences of **L** into a formal language which is expected to be somehow semantically relevant or 'favorite.' The question of what the meaning is of the forms or structures themselves that occur in the 'favorite' formal language of SRs is not answered. This is why some linguists prefer to speak of 'semantic syntax' rather than 'generative semantics' (see Seuren 1972 for a detailed exposé).

What is obtained is thus, in principle, nothing more than a paraphrase, not a meaning specification. In other words, a linguistic description in terms of TGG alone remains caught in a vicious 'synonymous circle.' What a semantic specification independent of paraphrases or translations could amount to was, and to a large extent still is, a question not answered in the context of linguistics proper. For an answer to that question one has to go to formal semantics, with its model theory, or, as has become clear since the early 1980s, to 'discourse semantics,' where meaning is defined as the cognitive contribution made by a linguistic element to any current domain of discourse.

2. The Logical Tradition

While linguists were caught up in their own struggles with and about meaning, a totally separate development took place in logic, a development which was soon to be applied to the semantic analysis and description of natural language. This development, known as the 'semanticization of logic,' began in the 1930s and consisted essentially of the introduction of mathematical model theory as an enrichment of logical proof theory. A 'model' is an independently defined or described state of affairs in some real or imagined 'world' whose elements are related, by means of an 'interpretation function,' to the structural elements of a language **L**. This new model theory naturally led to a definition of the notion of 'meaning of a sentence S' in terms of the conditions to be fulfilled by any world for S to be 'true.' In any world failing to fulfill these conditions S is false. In other words, the meaning of a sentence S is, in this view, exhaustively specified by a full statement of the truth conditions of S.

Moreover, the 'truth value' ('true' or 'false') of S in any one specific model M is, in the standard model-theoretic approach, considered to be 'computable' from the syntactic structure of S. This syntactic structure is taken to be a 'tree structure,' i.e., a hierarchically ordered set of n-tuples (usually pairs or triples) of linearly ordered constituents, precisely as defined and used by Bloomfield (1933) and his students in the more strictly linguistic tradition. The computation of the truth value of S, so to speak, 'works its way' through the tree **T** associated with S in the following way. Any subtree of **T** consisting of a dominating node A and dependent nodes $A_1, \ldots, A_n$ is treated as a computational unit with one of the dependent nodes, A_i $(1 \leq i \leq n)$, doing the work of a (set-theoretic) 'function' **f** and the remaining nodes providing the 'arguments' to **f**. The 'value' of **f** is passed on to the dominating node A. This value will then again become an argument to another function **f'** associated with a sister node of A, and the new value will be passed on to the node dominating A, and so on until the highest node is reached. The calculus must be organized in such a way that the eventual value assigned to the highest node in the tree **T** is the truth value of the sentence S with respect to the world specified in the model **M**. In standard formal semantics this calculus is generalized over all possible worlds (intensionalized), with the result that the final value yielded is not just one truth-value for one world but a truth-value for any one of the possible worlds or, in other words, a set of possible worlds. We thus have what is called a 'compositional calculus' yielding a truth value for any sentence S of the language **L** once a model (a world plus an interpretation function) is provided, or, in intensionalized form, a denotation for the set of possible worlds in which S is true.

Whereas this logical model theory was restricted, at

first, to the formal languages devised in logic and mathematics (a restriction strongly advocated by the logician Alfred Tarski), some of Tarski's more daring successors, in particular Donald Davidson and Richard Montague, applied it to natural language, hoping thus to lay the foundations for a mathematical theory (calculus) of natural language meaning. This development is known as formal semantics.

One feature that has consistently characterized formal semantic theories and analyses is the systematic rejection of a separate semantically and logically regular and transparent (deep structure) level of representation for sentences. The calculi are all devised for and grafted upon surface structure representations. Consequently, the grammar envisaged in formal semantic theories is entirely without transformational rules. This rejection is not essential in the sense that no formal semantics would be possible if it were given up. On the contrary, as has been said, the origins of formal semantics lie in model theory which was devised in the first place for formal logical languages such as, for example, the language of DS representations. The motivation for this rejection is, in principle, as follows. On the one hand there is the ockhamist consideration minimalizing theoretical assumptions. On the other, it is felt that the evidence for a separate level of semantic representation, with the concomitant inconvenience of T-rules, is insufficient to warrant their postulation. The more so since the formal resources afforded nowadays by logic and mathematics are sufficiently powerful to get rid of the complications that in the linguistic tradition are meant to be overcome by the assumption of DS representations and T-rules. There is no need to emphasize that the two traditions still have a great deal to sort out between themselves.

As in the structuralist linguistic tradition established mainly by Bloomfield, syntax is defined in formal semantics as the full specification of all constructions admissible in the language **L**. Unlike Bloomfieldian structuralist linguistics, however, formal semantics considers the notion of meaning to be a fully legitimate object of scientific investigation, it being captured by the notion of truth conditions. The semantics proper of a language **L**, in this view, consists of the (compositional) calculus yielding, in principle, a truth value for any given sentence of **L** in any given world with respect to which the sentence is interpreted.

It is thus clear that formal semantics has the advantage of not having been influenced by behaviorism in the way linguistics was. It, moreover, avoids the synonymous circle mentioned above, by virtue of the notions and techniques provided by model theory. The result is much greater clarity on semantic matters and also a much enriched insight, if not into the nature of human language, at least into the computational possibilities offered by tree structures.

It is also clear that, from the perspective of formal semantics, there can be no confusion about the relation between syntax and semantics: the syntax of **L** defines the combinations of form elements into all and only the well-formed sentences of **L**, whereas the semantics of **L** defines the truth conditions for all the sentences of **L** as they are defined by the syntax. It is, in effect, the distinction between specifications of objects on the one hand and of their properties on the other, or, as has been said above, very much like the distinction between the specification of a room and that of its temperature.

Despite its obvious successes it has consistently been doubted by many linguists whether formal semantics actually contributes to an improved insight into the nature of human language. These doubts are based mainly on two considerations. First, there is the fact that, due to the ungraspable character of notions like 'possible world' or, worse, 'set of possible worlds,' the values envisaged by the compositional calculus for sentences are not effectively computable in terms that specify actual worlds or situations. All that formal semantics can give is abstractions over, or schemata of, such specifications. There is, in other words, a problem of 'psychological reality.' Then, formal semantics is just too often in conflict with what linguists perceive as facts of language. The analyses are inspired by and follow modern logic, in particular CQT, i.e., its 'unrestricted' variety. And, as is well known, these analyses clash with straightforward linguistic intuitions on many different points. An example was mentioned above in connection with scopal phenomena of operators. Another example is the inability of formal semantics to come to terms with 'presuppositional phenomena'.

It is now widely accepted in formal semantic circles that objections of this nature must be taken seriously. As a result, several attempts have been made in the 1980s and early 1990s to remedy this situation. What these attempts have largely in common is a recognition of the 'context-dependency' of semantic interpretation of natural language sentences in actual use, and, in tandem with this, of the structural features that ensure a proper semantic linking up of sentences with their context (such as anaphoric devices and presuppositions). These new theories tend to incorporate a notion of 'discourse representation', mediating between sentences and what they are about. They moreover involve a much restricted notion of 'world,' more like a 'situation' or 'verification domain.' The compositional calculus, applied to syntactic trees of sentences, no longer produces truth values with respect to possible worlds, but specifications of the changes ('increments') brought about by the sentences in the representation of whatever discourse they occur in. Accordingly, the notion 'meaning of a sentence' is equated with that of its change potential with respect to any given discourse representation. Still, however, no confusion can arise, in these newer semantic theories, between the syntax and the semantics of a language, since the syntax still specifies only the possible structural combinations, and the semantics still consists of the computational procedures carried out on the syntactically defined structures.

Bibliography

Bloomfield L 1933 *Language*. Holt, New York
Chomsky N 1957 *Syntactic Structures*. Mouton, The Hague
Chomsky N 1965 *Aspects of the Theory of Syntax*. MIT Press, Cambridge, MA
Chomsky N 1972 *Studies on Semantics in Generative Grammar*. Mouton, The Hague
Harris Z S 1951 *Methods in Structural Linguistics*. University of Chicago Press, Chicago, IL
Horn L R 1989 *A Natural History of Negation*. University of Chicago Press, Chicago, IL
Katz J J, Fodor J A 1963 The structure of a semantic theory. *Lg* **39**: 170–210
Katz J J, Postal P M 1964 *An Integrated Theory of Linguistic Descriptions*. MIT Press, Cambridge, MA
Klima E S 1964 Negation in English. In: Fodor J A, Katz J (eds.) *The Structure of Language. Readings in the Philosophy of Language*. Prentice Hall, Englewood Cliffs, NJ
Lakoff G 1971 On generative semantics. In: Steinberg D D, Jakobovits L A (eds.) *Semantics. An Interdisciplinary Reader in Philosophy, Linguistics and Psychology*. Cambridge University Press, Cambridge
May R 1977 The grammar of quantification (Doctoral dissertation, Massachusetts Institute of Technology)
McCawley J D 1967 Meaning and the description of languages. *Kotoba No Uchu* **2**: 10–18; 38–48; 51–7
McCawley J D 1970 English as a VSO language. *Lg* **46**: 286–99
McCawley J D 1973 *Grammar and Meaning. Papers on Syntactic and Semantic Topics*. Taishukan, Tokyo
Ross J R 1986 *Infinite Syntax*. Ablex, Norwood, NJ
Seuren P A M 1969 *Operators and Nucleus. A Contribution to the Theory of Grammar*. Cambridge University Press, Cambridge
Seuren P A M 1972 Autonomous versus semantic syntax. *Foundations of Language* **8**: 237–65
Seuren P A M (ed.) 1974 *Semantic Syntax*. Oxford University Press, Oxford
Seuren P A M 1984 Operator lowering. *Linguistics* **22**: 573–627

Systemic Functional Grammar

M. A. K. Halliday

1. Origins of Systemic Theory

Systemic, or systemic–functional, theory has its origin in the main intellectual tradition of European linguistics that developed following the work of Saussure. Like other such theories, both those from the mid-twentieth century (e.g., Prague school, French functionalism) and more recent work in the same tradition (e.g., that of Hagège), it is functional and semantic rather than formal and syntactic in orientation, takes the text rather than the sentence as its object, and defines its scope by reference to usage rather than grammaticality. Its primary source was the work of J. R. Firth and his colleagues in London (see *Firth and the London School*). As well as other schools of thought in Europe such as glossematics it also draws on American anthropological linguistics, and on traditional and modern linguistics as developed in China.

Its immediate source is as a development of scale and category grammar. The name 'systemic' derives from the term 'system,' in its technical sense as defined by Firth (1957); system is the theoretical representation of paradigmatic relations, contrasted with 'structure' for syntagmatic relations. In Firth's system–structure theory, neither of these is given priority; and in scale and category grammar this perspective was maintained. In systemic theory the system takes priority; the most abstract representation at any level is in paradigmatic terms. Syntagmatic organization is interpreted as the 'realization' of paradigmatic features.

This step was taken by Halliday in the early 1960s so that grammatical and phonological representations could be freed from constraints of structure. Once such representations were no longer localized, they could function prosodically wherever appropriate. The shift to a paradigmatic orientation added a dimension of depth in time, so making it easier to relate language 'in use' to language being learnt; and it enabled the theory to develop both in reflection and in action—as a resource both for understanding and for intervening in linguistic processes. This potential was exploited in the work done during the 1960s on children's language development from birth through their various stages of schooling.

2. Systems and Their Realization

The organizing concept of a systemic grammar is that of choice (that is, options in 'meaning potential'; it does not imply intention). A system is a set of options together with a condition of entry, such that if the entry condition is satisfied one option, and one only, must be chosen; for example, in English grammar, [system] 'mood,' [entry condition] finite clause, [options] indicative/imperative. The option selected in one system then serves as the entry condition to another; e.g., [entry condition] indicative, [options] declarative/interrogative; hence all systems deriving from a common point of origin (e.g., [clause]) are agnate and together form a 'system network.' At the present stage of development, system networks for English grammar in computational form contain about 1,000 systems. An entry condition may involve the conjunction of different options; hence a system network is not a taxonomic structure but has the form of a lattice.

The system has one further component, namely the 'realization statement' that accompanies each option. This specifies the contribution made by that option to the structural configuration; it may be read as a proposition about the structural constraints associated with the option in question. Realization statements are of seven types:

(a) 'Insert' an element (e.g., insert subject);
(b) 'Conflate' one element with another (e.g., conflate subject with theme);
(c) 'Order' an element with respect to another, or to some defined location (e.g., order finite auxiliary before subject);
(d) 'Classify' an element (e.g., classify process as mental : cognition);
(e) 'Expand' an element into a further configuration (e.g., expand mood into subject + finite);
(f) 'Preselect' some feature at a lower rank (e.g., preselect actor : human collective); and
(g) 'Lexify' an element (e.g., lexify subject : *it*).

When paths are traced through a system network, a 'selection expression' is formed consisting of all the options taken up in the various functional components. As the network is traversed, options are inherited, together with their realizations; at the same time, new realization statements continue to figure throughout. The selection expression constitutes the grammar's description of the item (e.g., the particular clause so specified); it is also, by reference to the network, the representation of its systemic relationship to other items in the language—since the grammar is paradigmatic, describing something 'consists in' locating it with respect to the rest (showing its total lineage of agnate forms).

3. Other Basic Concepts

Systemic theory retains the concepts of 'rank,' 'realization,' and 'delicacy' from scale and category grammar. 'Rank' is constituency based on function, and hence 'flat,' with minimal layering; 'delicacy' is variable paradigmatic focus, with ordering from more general to more delicate; 'realization' (formerly 'exponence') is the relation between the 'strata,' or levels, of a multistratal semiotic system—and, by analogy, between the paradigmatic and syntagmatic phases of representation within one stratum. But in systemic theory, realization is held distinct from

'instantiation,' which is the relation between the semiotic system (the 'meaning potential') and the observable events, or 'acts of meaning,' by which the system is constituted.

The shift to a paradigmatic orientation led to the finding that the content plane of a language is organized in a small number of functionally defined components which Halliday labeled 'metafunctions.' According to this theory the grammar of natural languages evolved in simultaneously (a) 'construing' human experience (the 'experiential' metafunction) and (b) 'enacting' interpersonal relationships (the 'interpersonal' metafunction), both these being underpinned by (c) the resources of (commonsense) logic (the 'logical' metafunction; (a) and (c) are grouped together as 'ideational'). The stratal role of the lexicogrammar lies in mapping these semantic components into a unitary construct, one that is capable of being linearized; in doing this, the grammar (d) 'creates' its own parallel universe in the form of discourse (the 'textual' metafunction). These metafunctions define the dimensions of semantic space; and since they tend to be realized by different structural resources—experiential meanings segmentally, interpersonal meanings prosodically, logical meanings in iterative structures, and textual meanings in wave-like patterns—they also determine the topological formations that are characteristic of human speech.

A systemic grammar is therefore 'functional' in three distinct though related senses:

(a) Its 'explanations' are functional: both the existence of grammar (why grammar evolved as a distinct stratum), and the particular forms that grammars take, are explained in terms of the functions that language evolved to serve.
(b) Its 'representations' are functional: a structure is an organic configuration of functions, rather than a tree with nodes labeled as classes.
(c) Its 'applications' are functional: it developed as an adjunct to practices associated with language use, requiring sensitivity to functional variation in language ('register' variation). These considerations both relate it to, and at the same time distinguish it from other functional theories.

4. Other Features of the Theory

Like the Firthian linguistics from which it evolved, systemic theory is oriented towards language as social process; the individual is construed intersubjectively, through engagement in social acts of meaning. This is not incompatible with a cognitive perspective, which has been adopted in some systemic work (notably Fawcett 1980); but it does rule out any claim for 'psychological reality.' Halliday formulated this general stance as 'language as social semiotic,' thereby also locating systemic theory in the thematic context of semiotics, defined as the study of systems and processes of meaning. The relation between language and other sociocultural phenomena is then modeled on that of realization (the perspective here is Firthian rather than Hjelmslevian): language 'realizes' culture in the way that, within language, sound realizes wording, and the realization of wording in sound, in its turn, realizes meaning.

It follows from this that systemic theory gives prominence to discourse, or 'text'; not—or not only—as evidence for the system, but valued, rather, as constitutive of the culture. The mechanism proposed for this constitutive power of discourse has been referred to as the 'metafunctional hookup': the hypothesis that (a) social contexts are organic–dynamic configurations of three components, called 'field,' 'tenor,' and 'mode': respectively, the nature of the social activity, the relations among the interactants, and the status accorded to the language (what is going on, who are taking part, and what they are doing with their discourse); and (b) there is a relationship between these and the metafunctions such that these components are construed, respectively, as experiential, as interpersonal, and as textual meanings. Register, or functional variation in language, is then interpreted as systemic variation in the relative prominence (the probability of being taken up) of different options within these semantic components.

In fact such register variation (spoken/written, commonsense/technical, transactional/expository, . . . and so on) lies on the continuum between system and text; the characteristic of systemic work is that it brings all parts of this continuum under focus of attention. Analogously, it encompasses both speaker and listener perspectives (in computational terms, text generation, and parsing—there are, for example, no nonrecoverable operations such as deletion), and both synoptic and dynamic orientations; and uniquely among current theories, it assigns as much value to interpersonal and textual meaning as to ideational. On the other hand, in other respects systemic work is notably ill-balanced; there has been little study of morphology and phonology, and a disproportionate amount of research relates to English. These reflect on the one hand the contexts of its own development, especially the kinds of application for which it has been sought out; and on the other hand its requirement of comprehensiveness, demanding a coverage which is at once both broad and deep.

5. Development of Systemic Theory

The outlines of systemic theory were formulated in London in the 1960s by Halliday together with Huddleston, Hudson, and others, and in application to Bernstein's work by Hasan, Mohan, and Turner; other significant input came from the application of systemic concepts in curriculum development work, in the analysis of scientific writings and of natural conversation, and in descriptions of a number of Asian and African languages. The theory was further developed in the 1970s: by Fawcett, Berry, and Butler in the United Kingdom; by Halliday and Hasan; and by Gregory and his colleagues in Toronto. Since 1980 systemic work has expanded considerably in various directions (e.g., in artificial intelligence, child language development, discourse analysis and stylistics, and language education). It is typical of systemic practice that major extensions both to description and to theory have taken place in these 'applied' contexts: for example, the very large systemic grammars of English that now exist in computational form (PENMAN 'Nigel'; COMMUNAL), and the extensive studies of children's writing and of the language of educational texts in science, history, and other subjects that have been carried out by Martin and his colleagues in contexts such as the New South Wales Disadvantaged Schools Program.

Since 1980, further studies have been devoted to languages other than English, notably Chinese (Fang; Hu; Long; McDonald; Ouyang; Zhang; Zhao; Zhu), French (Caffarel), Indonesian (Sutjaja; Wirnani), and Tagalog (Martin); and work in text generation has begun to take in Chinese and Japanese (Matthiessen et al.) and German, French, and Dutch (Bateman; Steiner). In English, Halliday's *Introduction to Functional Grammar* brought together some of his studies begun in the late 1960s (1967/68); and advances were made in all areas of the grammar: experiential (Davidse; Martin), interpersonal (Butler; Thibault), and textual (Fries; Hasan; Matthiessen). Matthiessen (1995) presented a system-based account of English grammar, deriving from materials he had written to accompany the 'exporting' of the Nigel grammar.

Many general theoretical discussions have appeared (Fawcett; Halliday; Lemke, etc.), as well as new theoretical underpinning of key areas, especially lexicogrammar, discourse semantics, and text structure (Matthiessen; Martin; Berry; Hasan, etc.). Matthiessen's (1992) account of register theory emphasizes the integrative character of systemic work: while there are often alternative interpretations, especially where new problems are being addressed, these are not detached from their overall context in language and in linguistics. Thus there is no disjunction between grammar and discourse, or between the system and the text.

With the strengthening of what Halliday calls the 'grammatics' (that is, theory of grammar as metatheoretic resource), systemic writings have increasingly foregrounded the constructive power of grammar; this is reflected in numerous studies which began with the 'critical linguistics' of the late 1970s (Fowler et al.; Kress and Hodge; subsequently Butt; Hasan; Kress; Lemke; Martin; McGregor; O'Toole; Thibault; Threadgold; cf. Threadgold et al. 1986, and the new journal *Social Semiotics*). In a large-scale investigation of natural conversation between mothers and their preschool children, Hasan and Cloran (1990) have developed semantic networks to explore the effects of social factors on children's learning styles, and their consequences for education. Martin's work on register and genre (1992) extends the constructivist model of language to include strata of genre and ideology. It is in this overall perspective that language becomes central to the educational initiatives of Martin, Rothery, Christie, and others in Australia; compare also the work of Carter et al. in the LINC ('Language in the National Curriculum') program in the United Kingdom.

In 1974 Fawcett organized the first systemic workshop, at the West Midlands College of Education, with 16 participants from four centers in the UK. Since then the workshop has been an annual event; the first international workshop was the ninth, held in Toronto (York University) in 1982. In the 1990s, now as 'International Systemic Functional Congress,' meetings have been held in Scotland (Stirling, 1990), Japan (International Christian University, 1991), Australia (Macquarie, 1992), Canada (British Columbia, 1993), Belgium (Ghént, 1994) and China (Peking, 1995); and regular national or international seminars/workshops are held in China, in Australia and in different countries of Europe. The publication *Network* provides information on these activities, along with short articles, reviews, bibliographies and conference reports. The regularly updated bibliographical database now contains more than 1,000 books and articles. Selected conference papers from 1983, 1985, 1986 and from 1988 onwards have appeared, or are appearing, in published form (see *Bibliography*).

6. Influences and Trends

In the period from its inception in the early 1960s the main influences on systemic theory (other than those coming in via specific applications such as computational linguistics) have come from Lamb's work in stratificational grammar (see *Stratificational Grammar*) and from Sinclair's in discourse and in lexical studies. Lamb and Halliday collaborated regularly over a number of years. Sinclair had been an originator of scale and category grammar and his subsequent work exploited this, though in a complementary direction to Halliday's: Sinclair builds the grammar out of the lexis, whereas Halliday builds the lexis out of the grammar. Other input has come from Labov's quantitative methodology (though not his general perspective on language and society); from the theory and practice of corpus linguistics (Quirk; Svartvik et al.; more recently Sinclair); from other work in functional linguistics (especially Thompson); and from poststructuralist semiotics in general.

A feature of systemic work is that it has tended to expand by moving into new spheres of activity, rather than by reworking earlier positions. This reflects an ideological perspective in which language is seen not as unique or *sui generis* but as one aspect of the evolution of humans as sociocultural beings. Thus input often comes from outside the discipline of linguistics: from current theories in fields such as anthropology, literature, and neurology, and from developments in more distant sciences. Much systemic linguistics reflects transdisciplinary rather than disciplinary thinking in its approach to problems of language.

This orientation appears in some present trends and likely future directions. For example:

(a) systemic grammatics as model for other semiotic systems, especially forms of art: not only literature (Butt; O'Toole; Thibault; Threadgold) but also music (van Leeuwen; Steiner), visual imagery (Kress and van Leeuwen), and painting, architecture, and sculpture (O'Toole 1994);

(b) further developments of register theory to investigate the linguistic construction of knowledge and structures of power;

(c) using available corpus data and programs to test hypotheses about the probabilistic properties of systems (Nesbitt and Plum; Halliday and James);

(d) further development of language-based educational programs, in initial literacy, secondary 'subjects,' teacher education, language in the workplace, etc;

(e) natural language processing: modeling systems of meaning (knowledge systems); developing integrated generation and parsing programs, including multilingual ones; and processing language in 'intelligent fuzzy computing' (Sugeno);

(f) further work in deaf sign (Johnston) and development of systemic research in neurolinguistics and the discourse of aphasia, dementia, etc; and

(g) greater emphasis on studies of the expression plane in a general systemic context.

Just as systemic theory is itself a variant of a broader class of theories (functional theories, perhaps with 'system-structure theories' as an intermediate term), so it itself accommodates considerable variation. Gregory's 'communication linguistics' foregrounds structures of knowledge and presents a dynamic 'phase and transition' model of discourse; Fawcett's computational modeling contrasts in various ways with that of Matthiessen and Bateman; Martin's register theory, with genre as a distinct stratum, contrasts with Hasan's view of register as functional variation realizing different values of contextual variables. This kind of variation in 'metaregister' is one of many ways in which systemic theory appears as a metaphor for language itself.

The standard introduction to systemic linguistics has been Berry (1976/77). Other introductory or summary works are Monaghan (1979), Halliday and Martin (1981), Butler (1985), Morley (1985), and, an original work in Chinese, Hu et al. (1989). The extensive series of publications emanating from the New South Wales Disadvantaged Schools Program is an excellent source for systemic grammar of English in an educational context (see bibliography at end of Martin's paper in Halliday 1993). Further introductory books from the mid-1990s include Eggins (1994), Butt et al. (1995), Matthiessen (1995), Martin et al. (1996) and Bloor and Bloor (1995).

Bibliography

Benson J D, Cummings M J, Greaves W S (eds.) 1988 *Linguistics in a Systemic Perspective*. Benjamins, Amsterdam

Berry M 1975/77 *Introduction to Systemic Linguistics. Vol. 1: Structures and Systems. Vol. 2: Levels and Links*. Batsford, London

Berry M (ed.) 1984 *Nottingham Linguistic Circular 13*, Special Issue in Systemic Linguistics. University of Nottingham, Nottingham

Bloor T, Bloor M 1995 *The Functional Analysis of English: A Hallidayan Approach*. Arnold, London

Butler C S 1985 *Systemic Linguistics: Theory and Applications*. Batsford, London

Butt D, Fahey R, Spinks S, Yallop C 1995 *Using Functional Grammar: An Explorer's Guide*. NCELTR, Macquarie University, Sydney

Eggins S 1944 *An Introduction to Systemic Functional Linguistics*. Pinter, London

Fawcett R P 1980 *Cognitive Linguistics and Social Interaction: Towards an Integrated Model of a Systemic Functional Grammar and Other Components of a Communicating Mind*. Julius Groos, Heidelberg

Firth J R 1957 A synopsis of linguistic theory 1930–55. In: *Studies in Linguistic Analysis*, Special Volume of the Philological Society. Blackwell, Oxford

Halliday M A K 1967/68 Notes on transitivity and theme in English, Parts 1–3. *JL* **3(1)**: 37–81, **3(2)**: 199–244, **4(2)**: 179–215

Halliday M A K 1978 *Language as Social Semiotic: The Social Interpretation of Language and Meaning*. Arnold, London

Halliday M A K (ed.) 1993 *Language as Cultural Dynamic* (*Cultural Dynamics* 6.1–2). Brill, Leiden

Halliday M A K 1994 *An Introduction to Functional Grammar*, 2nd edn. Arnold, London

Halliday M A K, Fawcett R P (eds.) 1987 *New Developments in Systemic Linguistics. Vol. 1: Theory and Description*. Pinter, London

Halliday M A K, Martin J R (eds.) 1981 *Readings in Systemic Linguistics*. Batsford, London

Halliday M A K , Martin J R 1993 *Writing Science: Literacy and Discursive Power*. Falmer, London

Halliday M A K, Matthiessen C 1996 *Construing Experience through Meaning: A Language-based Approach to Cognition. Foundations of Communication and Cognition*. de Gruyter, Berlin

Hasan R, Cloran C 1990 A sociolinguistic investigation of everyday talk between mothers and children. In: Halliday M A K, Gibbons J, Nicholas H (eds.) *Learning, Keeping and Using Language: Selected Papers from the Eighth World Congress of Applied Linguistics, Sydney, August 1987*. Benjamins, Amsterdam

Hasan R, Martin J R (eds.) 1989 *Language Development: Learning Language, Learning Culture*. Ablex, Norwood, NJ

Hu Zhuanglin, Zhu Yongsheng, Zhang Delu 1989 *A Survey of Systemic Functional Grammar* (in Chinese). Hunan Educational Publishing House, Changsha

Hudson R A 1971 *English Complex Sentences*. North Holland, Amsterdam

Kress G R (ed.) 1976 *Halliday: System and Function in Language: Selected Papers*. Oxford University Press, Oxford

Martin J R 1992 *English Text: System and Structure*. Benjamins, Amsterdam

Martin J R, Matthiessen C, Painter C 1996 *Deploying Functional Grammar: A Workbook for Halliday's Introduction to Functional Grammar*. Arnold, London

Matthiessen C 1992 Register in the round: Diversity in a unified theory of register analysis. In: Ghadessy M (ed.) *Register Analysis*. Pinter, London

Matthiessen C 1995 *Lexicogrammatical Cartography: English Systems*. International Language Sciences Publishers, Tokyo

Matthiessen C, Bateman J 1991 *Text Generation and Systemic Linguistics: Experiences from English and Japanese*. Pinter, London

Monaghan J 1979 *The Neo-Firthian Tradition and its Contribution to General Linguistics*. Niemeyer, Tübingen

Morley G 1985 *An Introduction to Systemic Grammar*. Macmillan, London

O'Toole M 1994 *The Language of Displayed Art*. Leicester University Press (Pinter), London

Tench P (ed.) 1992 *Studies in Systemic Phonology*. Pinter, London

Threadgold T et al. (eds.) 1986 *Semiotics, Ideology, Language*. Sydney Association for Studies in Society and Culture, Sydney

Special Publications

Bibliography: Halliday M A K, Matthiessen C 1985 *Bibliographic Data Base for Systemic Linguistics*. Macquarie University, Sydney

Newsletter: Matthiessen C 1980 *Network: News, Views and Reviews in Systemic Linguistics and Related Areas*. Macquarie University, Sydney

Occasional papers: Hillier H 1984 *Occasional Papers in Systemic Linguistics*. University of Nottingham, Nottingham

Journal: Functions of Language 1994. Benjamins, Amsterdam

Monograph series: Monographs in Systemic Linguistics 1991. University of Nottingham, Department of English Studies, Nottingham

Papers from Workshops/Congresses

Benson J D, et al. (eds.) 1989 *Systems, Structures and Discourse. Word* **40**: 1–2

Benson J D, Greaves W S (eds.) 1985 *Systemic Perspectives on Discourse*, vols. 1 and 2. Ablex, Norwood, NJ

Benson J D, Greaves W S (eds.) 1988 *Systemic Functional Approaches to Discourse*. Ablex, Norwood, NJ

Davies M, Ravelli L (eds.) 1992 *Advances in Systemic Linguistics: Recent Theory and Practice*. Pinter, London

Halliday M A K, Peng F C C (eds.) 1992 *Current Research in Functional Grammar* (*Language Sciences* 14.4). Pergamon, Oxford

Hasan R, Cloran C, Butt D (eds.) 1995 *Functional Descriptions*. Benjamins, Amsterdam

Hasan R, Fries P H (eds.) 1995 *On Subject and Theme: A Discourse Functional Perspective*. Benjamins, Amsterdam

Hasan R, Williams G (eds.) 1996 *Literacy in Society*. Longman, London

Steiner E, Veltman R (eds.) 1988 *Pragmatics, Discourse and Text: Explorations in Systemic Semantics*. Pinter, London; Ablex, Norwood, NJ

Ventola E (ed.) 1991 *Functional and Systemic Linguistics: Approaches and Uses*. Mouton de Gruyter, Berlin

Tagmemics

Linda K. Jones

Tagmemics is a theory of language primarily, but also of all human behavior, both verbal and nonverbal. It emphasizes the hierarchical structuring of language in each of three domains—phonology, grammar, and reference. The theory was initially developed by Kenneth Pike, who named the basic units 'tagmemes,' creating a new concept for a term borrowed from Leonard Bloomfield (who had coined the term from a Greek word meaning 'rank, arrangement'). In Pike's usage, the tagmeme is a complex 'unit-in-context': it is complex because every unit embodies a number of features and it is a unit-in-context because part of its definition is its distribution in some larger context.

Theoretical development in tagmemics has always been coupled with a strong emphasis on analytical methodology. Tagmemic methodology has been frequently applied to the analysis of languages in a field situation and has proved especially useful in tackling the analysis of languages about which little or nothing has ever been written. As a result, tagmemics directly or indirectly underlies the documentation of several hundred little-known languages.

1. Historical Development

The roots of tagmemics are in American Structuralism, although it has grown beyond structuralism in some very important ways (see *American Structuralism*). The work of Edward Sapir, Leonard Bloomfield, and Morris Swadesh influenced Kenneth Pike's early work. In the 1940s he made important contributions in phonology in the areas of phonetics, phonemics, tone, and intonation. In 1948 Pike turned his attention to grammar. Having seen the fruitfulness of the concept of the phoneme in phonology, he posed a research question for himself: Might there be 'a phoneme of grammar,' that is, a minimum structural unit relevant to grammatical analysis? He named this theoretical construct a 'grameme,' meaning 'minimal emic unit of grammar.'

By 1954 Pike had worked out the broad outline of a new theory of grammar, which, in actuality, went well beyond grammar. The first major publication to present the new theory was *Language in Relation to a Unified Theory of the Structure of Human Behavior* (*LRUTSHB*), published in three parts. By the time Part III appeared in 1960, the term 'tagmeme' had come to replace the term 'grameme' for the same concept. The tagmeme was conceived of as the minimum unit of grammar and was a correlation of slot and class. The slot is the functional position that the unit occupies as its part in the larger whole. The class is the set of items which may occupy that slot. The new theory proposed that language has three simultaneously manifested structures—phonological, grammatical, and lexical—which are hierarchical in nature.

Pike was especially concerned to demonstrate the integral nature of language with human behavior in general, and so included in *LRUTSHB* detailed analyses of both verbal and nonverbal components of a church service, a football game, and a family breakfast scene. He emphasized the importance of keeping the larger context—both linguistic and behavioral—in view in proceeding with analysis. By insisting on starting with some understanding of the top levels of structure, Pike led the way in discourse analysis, in an era when anything beyond the sentence was considered outside the scope of linguistics altogether.

Through his leadership in the Summer Institute of Linguistics (SIL), Pike was able to encourage practical application of his theory. During the 1950s and 1960s many tagmemic descriptions of languages were produced, especially by SIL linguists. (Annotated listings of approximately 400 publications in tagmemics appear in Pike 1966 and Brend 1970, 1972.) This intensive study impacted the development of the theory, resulting in some changes and further elaboration.

During this period, Robert Longacre became very influential in the development of tagmemics. One of his innovations was to abandon the concept of the tagmeme as merely a minimum unit of grammar and instead to extend the notion of the tagmeme throughout the entire grammatical hierarchy. He also worked out criteria for establishing contrast between constructions and in 1964 published *Grammar Discovery Procedures*, a field manual for grammar.

Pike's magnum opus on tagmemic theory, *LRUT-SHB*, was republished in a revised second edition in 1967, and incorporated the various changes in the theory. A major new emphasis in this edition is on the complementary perspectives of 'particle, wave, and field,' imagery which was borrowed from physics to describe three different observer perspectives. The 1960s found fruitful application of the new particle, wave, field perspectives in the analysis of languages.

Stimulated by Charles Fillmore's case studies, tagmemic research began to focus on semantic roles and ways to capture these in the tagmemic formulas. Early formulas of tagmemes were simply a two-part correlation of functional slot and filler class. But now, trying to incorporate semantic roles, four-part and even nine-part tagmemes were proposed (the latter incorporated a good deal of lexical structure as well). Eventually a four-part (called 'four-cell') representation for the tagmeme was chosen by Pike, while Longacre stood by the traditional two-part tagmeme. *Grammatical Analysis* (1977), a textbook in tagmemics, utilizes the four-cell tagmeme.

In the 1970s, Pike, his wife Evelyn, and some of Pike's graduate students at the University of Michigan, focused attention on the lexical hierarchy, which had been largely neglected. Their work resulted in a substantially new understanding of this hierarchy. Since it was no longer a 'superlexicon,' the label 'lexical' for this hierarchy was discarded, replaced by the term 'referential.' A number of studies in the 1980s also contributed to the development of the referential hierarchy (see, for example, Howland 1981).

Meanwhile, Longacre had been focusing increasingly on the higher levels of the grammatical hierarchy. He has made important contributions in these areas and published a textbook *The Grammar of Discourse* (1983). Through supervising his graduate students at the University of Texas at Arlington, and in directing SIL workshops in the Philippines, New Guinea, Colombia, Mexico, and West Africa, he has stimulated numerous studies of sentences, paragraphs, and discourses in scores of languages.

2. Basic Assumptions

Tagmemic theory rests on certain basic assumptions. These have been expounded in numerous of Pike's publications, the fullest presentation being *Linguistic Concepts* (1982), while a more philosophical presentation is *Talk, Thought, and Thing* (1993). While these assumptions are formulated particularly with language in mind, they also are held to be true for all human behavior, of which language is just a part. They are statements about the nature of human behavior at a very deep level, and in fact, of the nature of human rationality. The assumptions overlap and they are not ordered.

One basic assumption is that there is always an 'observer perspective' on the data. There is no such thing as a detached, impartial perspective on any data; there is always an observer, looking at and filtering the data from his perspective. However, the observer's perspective is not fixed and by shifting perspective, he may gain new insights into the data. As already mentioned, there are three complementary observer perspectives: 'particle,' 'wave,' and 'field.' (The terms are taken from physics, where light is best explained as being simultaneously composed of particles and of waves, with its energy distributed in a field.) The three perspectives are alternant ways of viewing the same data, leading to different insights. A particle perspective focuses on the discrete, individual items in the data, the wave perspective considers the indeterminacy of borders, and the field perspective observes relationships between items and the patterns of the overall system. For example, in analyzing a stream of speech, a particle perspective views the stream as composed of a sequence of discrete sounds or phones. A wave perspective, on the other hand, recognizes the smearing of sounds into each other, which would show up on a sound spectrograph. A field perspective might make a phonetic chart inventorying the sounds found in the stream of speech in order to study patterns in the system.

There is another way in which tagmemics talks about observer perspective, and that is the difference between the alien/outsider perspective, called 'etic,' and the native/insider perspective, called 'emic.' Pike coined the terms 'etic' and 'emic,' based on 'phonetics' and 'phonemics,' to describe comparable differences in perspective on other behavioral data. An etic perspective analyzes a unit as similar in kind to units appearing elsewhere, in other languages or cultures, and in this sense, is a universal approach. An emic approach considers rather the relevance of a unit to only a single language or culture, with a concern to describe its unique system. A linguist necessarily approaches any language other than his own with an etic perspective, but through analysis, he hopes to gain an emic perspective by discovering the linguistic system as it is perceived by the native speakers.

A second set of assumptions in tagmemics concerns 'units.' In tagmemic theory, units are primitive notions, which are defined by their 'contrastive–identificational features,' their 'range of variation,' and their 'patterns of distribution in various contexts.' A unit may be shown to contrast with another unit because of certain differences in features, yet its features also help to identify a unit even in the absence of some kind of contrast. The differences between two units may be so slight as to consist of merely one feature, such as the presence or absence of aspiration on a stop, or the differences may consist of a bundle of features. Since a unit may exhibit certain variations in form and still be considered the same unit, its range of variation must be determined. Finally, a unit is defined by its privileges of occurrence, that is, its distribution patterns in context.

Spanish verbs will illustrate the assumptions regarding units. There are three major classes of verbs in Spanish, which contrast by their infinitive form endings: *ir*, *er*, and *ar*. All verbs exhibit form changes due to inflexions of person, number, and tense-mood. The greatest variation is seen in irregular verbs which show substantive stem changes, such as the verb *ir* 'to go,' with three different stem forms, as in *fuí*, *voy*, and *iré* for the past perfective, present, and future, respectively, of the first person singular. Every verb has its own distributional patterns; for example, the verb *ir* 'to go' occurs primarily in intransitive clauses.

There is yet another assumption that tagmemics makes about units: they are 'form-meaning composites.' Tagmemics differs at this point from those linguistic theories which separate form from meaning, assigning formal structures to grammar or syntax, and meaning to semantics. Tagmemic theory insists on keeping form and meaning together. Isolation of forms is untenable, since in natural language, forms always occur in some context, and it is context that shapes meaning. A form derives its meanings from its contexts, and is therefore best analyzed in relation to its meanings-in-context.

The assumption regarding units as form-meaning composites is one of a set of principles which may loosely be related under the term 'context.' One of the other principles regarding context is that 'change occurs via a shared element in a shared context.' There must always be some bridge over which the change passes. An obvious example is a portmanteau phone that results from the fusion of two sounds that are contiguous. Another example is the new meaning that a basically intransitive word acquires when it is used in a transitive clause, e.g., intransitive *hop* becomes transitive in *He hopped a train to New York*.

Another assumption regarding context is the inseparability of speech from its behavioral context. Language does not occur in a cultural or conceptual vacuum, but is contextualized in social interactions. For a text to be coherent, the words and concepts in the text must be relatable in some 'universe of discourse,' or 'frame of reference'; otherwise, communication breaks down. Shared vocabulary, shared beliefs, expectations, and cultural norms all underlie coherent communication. The universe of discourse provides the network of relationships which tie the parts of a text together into an integrated whole.

The assumptions just outlined concerning observer perspective, units, and context are sufficiently broad as to be congenial to many theories. They are not even all specifically assumptions about language; they are assumptions about human behavior, and thus could underlie a theory in some nonlinguistic field, e.g., anthropology or sociology. There are, however, some additional assumptions made in tagmemic theory that distinguish it in fundamental ways from other theories. Chief among the unique distinctives of tagmemics are the hierarchical principle and the tagmeme concept.

3. The Hierarchical Principle

The hierarchical principle is axiomatic in tagmemics. This principle makes a number of important claims. First, there is structure 'beyond the sentence,' not just loose network relations. Second, the structure that is 'beyond the sentence' is in some fundamental way the same as the structure 'below the sentence.' That is, the view is rejected that nouns, verbs, clauses, and sentences exhibit linguistic structure, but paragraphs and larger discourses either have no structure at all, or only have a radically different kind of structure that is better called something else. Tagmemics claims that all these have a similar kind of structure, which is a constituent structure characterized by part–whole relations of units in constructions.

This is where hierarchy comes in. Small units are parts of larger whole units on another level of organization, which in turn, are parts of wholes on yet another level of organization, and on up the hierarchy. This is not a taxonomic hierarchy organized by generic-specific relations; it is a 'part–whole hierarchy,' of small chunks within larger ones within yet larger ones.

A small number of specific levels are posited in the hierarchy, each level being defined by a set of form-meaning features. It is suggested that the levels are generally relevant to all languages, although not all levels are present in every language. Linguistic analysis may begin at any one of the levels. Constructions at one level in the hierarchy will be found to consist of units from other levels. Thus, analysis begins at one level but soon proceeds to other levels.

Tagmemics holds that there are three domains of language—'phonology,' 'grammar,' and 'reference'—which all are structured hierarchically. However, this is not a monistic structure building from reference to grammar to phonology (nor the opposite direction). Rather, there are three 'side-by-side' hierarchies, each independent with their own forms and meanings, yet at the same time not totally separate since they interlock as well, with some overlapping. While there are many normal correspondences of levels in one hierarchy to particular levels in the other hierarchies, there is no one-to-one isomorphism.

Of the three hierarchies, the phonological is the one that shows the most variation in which levels are present from language to language. The levels generally present are (from highest to lowest):

(a) pause group;
(b) phonological phrase (alternatively: stress group, contour);

(c) phonological word (alternatively: stress group, rhythm group, foot);

(d) syllable;

(e) phoneme.

Sometimes other higher levels are posited, such as phonological sentence, phonological period, or utterance-response. The tagmemic phonological hierarchy has been most fully developed by Eunice Pike.

In the grammatical hierarchy, the emic levels postulated are (from highest to lowest):

(a) conversation;

(b) conversational exchange;

(c) monolog discourse;

(d) paragraph;

(e) sentence;

(f) clause;

(g) phrase;

(h) word;

(i) stem;

(j) morpheme.

(A conversational exchange is defined as just one turn by each speaker, while a conversation may consist of any number of turns by the speakers.) There are both significant differences and significant similarities between contiguous levels. Longacre views the grammatical hierarchy as a simple ascent from morpheme to monolog discourse. Pike and Pike, however, have suggested that there is pairing of the levels: the levels of a pair share a similar meaning, but differ in that one comprises minimal constructions while the other comprises expanded constructions. Thus, morpheme and stem express a lexical package, but the morpheme in a minimal way, the stem in an expanded way. Word and phrase both express a term, but the word minimally, and the phrase in an expanded way. Clause and sentence both express propositions, but the clause is a minimum construction, while the sentence is an expanded one. Similarly, both paragraph, as a minimum, and monolog discourse, as an expansion, express theme-development. Finally, the conversational exchange is a minimum social interaction, while conversation is an expanded interaction.

The third hierarchy is the referential hierarchy. In tagmemic theory, reference means whatever language refers to, that is, whatever is 'talked about'—whether things, people, events, or abstractions. Note that it is not actually the 'real' world nor the 'real' thing-in-itself nor the 'real' people, since our only access to these is through observers. People observe the world about them, or ponder the world of ideas and feelings within them, or imagine something, and then talk about these things using the phonological and grammatical structures of their language. The content structure of what is said, the 'talk-concepts,' are the subject matter of reference in tagmemics. It is evident that the talk-concepts of a language are almost endless. A list of these would be rather like an encyclopedia, which may include a great deal of information about any particular entry.

The levels posited in the referential hierarchy are (from highest to lowest):

(a) performative interaction;

(b) story;

(c) event;

(d) identity (person or prop);

(e) relationships.

In addition to dealing with the content structure of stories with their events, participants, and items, certain intangibles are also dealt with in the referential domain. For instance, purpose of a person or an event, beliefs, truth and falsity, expectations and clashes with expectations, are all treated in reference, since these participate in the meaning and coherence of any text.

Referential units must not be confused with grammatical units. Any one referential unit can be expressed in multiple grammatical forms, which constitute a 'paraphrase set' for that referential unit. For example, a person might be referred to by his given name, a nickname, his family relationship (e.g., *father*), his social role (e.g., *headmaster*), or some other kind of label (e.g., *that scheming man*). There is just one man, a single referential identity, who may be referred to by numerous grammatical forms. There is another important difference between reference and grammar. In referential structure, events are in strictly chronological order, but the grammatical telling may result in reorderings of the events.

4. The Tagmeme

The tagmeme is a very basic concept in tagmemics. It was originally worked out in the domain of grammar, and later extended to phonology and reference. This section deals with the tagmeme in grammar.

Every construction, such as phrase, clause, sentence, or paragraph, is composed of units which are called 'tagmemes.' This 'Law of Composition' expresses a fundamental part–whole relationship—'tagmemes' are the parts, 'constructions' (also called 'syntagmemes') are the wholes. There are construction types which correspond to each emic hierarchical level above the 'zero,' or morpheme, level. The construction types in grammar, then, are stem, word, phrase, clause, sentence, paragraph, and on up the grammatical hierarchy. Every construction is composed of tagmemes. Tagmemes are the basic building blocks of linguistic structure.

From the beginning of tagmemic theory, however, these basic units, the tagmemes, have not been simple units. They are a complex of both form and meaning. Every tagmeme is described by its functional position 'correlated with' the class or set of words, phrases, or whatever that may occur in that position. That is, the tagmeme is a correlation of 'function slot' with 'filler class.'

The analysis of a simple example will illustrate the tagmeme concept. In a simple transitive clause in English there are generally three obligatory tagmemes: a subject slot 'filled by' or 'manifested by' the class of nouns or noun phrases, plus a predicate slot filled by the class of transitive verbs/verb phrases, plus an object slot filled by the class of nouns/noun phrases. Each of these three tagmemes is a complex of its slot or function in the clause plus the part of speech or classes of words or phrases which are found there. It is not enough to describe the parts of the transitive clause as subject, predicate, and object, nor is it adequate to list a sequence of word classes, e.g., NP VP NP. Tagmemics insists on keeping together the functional categories and the part of speech categories.

Now the relationship between a tagmeme and a construction may be elaborated. A construction is composed of tagmemes. In turn, every tagmeme is manifested either by a simple morpheme (zero-level manifestation) or by another construction. Thus, tagmemes make up constructions, on the one hand, and, on the other hand, are themselves filled by other constructions. Via the tagmeme, there is nesting of constructions within constructions, which reflects the hierarchical nature of language.

In the simplest situation, constructions on one level are composed of tagmemes which are filled by constructions from the next lower level. Longacre calls this type of simple descent 'primary exponence.' Frequently in language, however, there are other 'degrees of exponence.' Level-skipping to zero is very common, whereby a single morpheme manifests a tagmeme of some higher-level construction, e.g., *and* as the coordinating link in coordinate constructions. There is level-skipping to other than zero as well. Recursion is also common in languages, whereby a construction type nests within its same type, e.g., phrase within a phrase, as in *the life cycle of the monarch butterfly*. Backlooping occurs when a high-level construction occurs as a constituent of a low-level construction. The most prevalent form of backlooping is the embedding of a relative clause in a noun phrase.

The tagmeme was originally a two-feature unit: function slot plus filler class. Later the necessity of distinguishing tagmemes which had the same slot and class, but differed by semantic role, as for example, the subject noun phrase in *The boy hit his sister* versus *The boy was hit by his sister*, led to Pike's adding 'semantic role' to the definition of the tagmeme. With this new feature, a tagmemic analysis mentions three features: slot, class, and semantic role. In the preceding example, *the boy* is 'subject-as-actor filled by a noun phrase' in the first instance, and 'subject-as-undergoer filled by noun phrase' in the second.

About the same time, Pike added a fourth feature of the tagmeme: 'cohesion,' which expresses the 'governing–governed' relationship between one tagmeme and others in the context. For example, in many European languages, the gender of a noun requires an agreeing gender marking on its associated adjectives. In tagmemic terminology, the noun is said to 'govern gender cohesion,' while the adjectives are 'governed by gender cohesion.' Often it is useful to spell out the nature of the governing relationship in an explicit cohesion rule.

5. Notations

Notations are useful representational devices, but tagmemics attaches no theoretical significance to the formalisms it usually employs. Two notations became prevalent early in tagmemic history, which focused on representing constructions as strings of two-feature tagmemes. For example, a simple transitive clause of English might be represented as S:NP P:VP O:NP or as $S^{NP} P^{VP} O^{NP}$. Both these tagmemic formulas are read the same way: 'Subject filled by noun phrase, followed by predicate filled by verb phrase, followed by object filled by noun phrase.'

The evolution of the tagmeme in Pike's theory into a unit of four features complicated the notational system, but eventually a four-cell array was chosen to represent the tagmeme, represented in (1):

Slot	Class	
Role	Cohesion	(1)

A tagmemic formula is a linear representation of structure. For example, the sentence *The little boy was feeding some ducks* is an active transitive clause which, using four-cell tagmemes, may be formulized as in (2):

S	NP	P	VP	Ad	NP	
A	# >	Sta	> #	U	—	(2)

The abbreviations are: *S* 'subject,' *A* 'actor,' *NP* 'noun phrase,' *P* 'predicate,' *Sta* 'statement,' *Ad* 'adjunct,' and *U* 'undergoer.' The symbol # indexes a number cohesion rule (which is written in detail elsewhere). The symbol > to the right of # indicates that this tagmeme governs the cohesion rule, while > to the left of # indicates that that tagmeme is governed by the cohesion rule.

Tagmemic formulas are most useful when they represent the contrastive construction types in a language, that is, when they are formulaic generalizations which hold for all instances in the data of an emic type, e.g., all active transitive clauses. In order to handle a larger corpus of data, the class cell of each tagmeme lists all the contrastive filler classes which have been found to occur with that particular tagmeme. For example, the subject tagmeme in a generalized formula for transitive clause would need to list classes in addition to noun phrase which may occur, e.g., coordinate noun phrase, pronoun, pronoun phrase, nominalized clause, participial phrase, and so forth.

Another way to generalize a formula is to distinguish those constituents which are 'obligatory' from those that are 'optional.' A constituent is obligatory if and only if it occurs in every normal example of a construction; otherwise it is optional. Optional constituents present variants of the construction. In the English active transitive clause type, the adjunct-as-undergoer tagmeme may be deleted in certain situations, and is therefore optional. For example, the clause *A careless pilot crashes his plane* may be abbreviated to *A careless pilot crashes*. By contrast, in the passive transitive clause type, it is the adjunct-as-actor tagmeme which is optional. Passive versions would be *The plane was crashed* (*by a careless pilot*). In tagmemic notations, obligatoriness or optionality of a constituent is marked preceding it, denoted by a plus sign + for obligatory and a combined plus-minus sign ± for optional.

6. Applications

Although tagmemics is primarily a theory for linguistics, the principles of tagmemics have inspired many studies in other fields as well. The theory has been applied to other language-related fields, such as bilingual education, language learning, literature, rhetoric and composition. Anthropologists for many years have utilized the etic and emic concepts, without always realizing where they originated (cf. Headland, et al. 1990). The social structure of ethnic groups has been studied using tagmemic principles. The field of ethnomusicology (study of indigenous music systems)

has relied heavily on some of the tagmemic principles, again especially the etic–emic distinction. Even more remote fields, such as theology, have been touched by tagmemic studies.

Within linguistics, a great many languages around the world have been described in the tagmemic model. Included in the list are indigenous languages of Mexico, Guatemala, Peru, Brazil, Ecuador, Colombia, Nepal, India, the Philippines, Indonesia, Papua New Guinea, and West Africa.

Bibliography

Brend R M 1970, 1972 Tagmemic theory: An annotated bibliography, with appendix. *Journal of English Linguistics* **4**: 7–41, **6**: 1–16
Headland T N, Pike K L, Harris M (eds.) 1990 *Emics and Etics: The Insider/Outsider Debate*, Frontiers of Anthroplogy, vol. 7. Sage Publications, London
Howland L G 1981 Communicational integration of reality and fiction. *L&C* **1**: 89–148
Longacre R E 1964 *Grammar Discovery Procedures: A Field Manual*. Mouton, The Hague
Longacre R E 1983 *The Grammar of Discourse*. Plenum Press, New York
Pike K L 1954, 1955, 1960 *Language in Relation to a Unified Theory of the Structure of Human Behavior*. (2nd rev. edn., 1967) Mouton, The Hague
Pike K L 1966 A guide to publications related to tagmemic theory. In: Sebeok T A (ed.) *Current Trends in Linguistics. Vol. III: Theoretical Foundations*. Mouton, The Hague
Pike K L 1982 *Linguistic Concepts: An Introduction to Tagmemics*. University of Nebraska Press, Lincoln, Nebraska
Pike K L 1993 *Talk, Thought, and Thing*. Summer Institute of Linguistics, Dallas, TX
Pike K L, Pike E G 1977 *Grammatical Analysis. Summer Institute of Linguistics, Publications in Linguistics*, Dallas, TX

Topic, Focus, and Word Order

Rosanna Sornicola

1. Word Order: Its Controversial Nature

Throughout the history of linguistics, word order has basically been conceived as a phenomenon of a dual nature, first being related to grammar, second to style. As a phenomenon pertaining to grammar, word order is a device that codifies grammatical relations, the result being the 'basic' or fundamental word order patterns of a language. English as well as Italian, French, etc., are languages with a basic SVO order, because the functions of subject and object are, in each of these languages, carried by, respectively, preverbal and postverbal position (*John loves Mary*, where *John* is the subject, compared with *Mary loves John*, where *John* is the object). As a pragmatic phenomenon, word order encompasses those devi-

ations from basic patterns that are due to pragmatic factors, such as, primarily, marked focus placement. (Other influential factors of a pragmatic/semantic nature are the contextual dependency of sentence constituents, which is responsible for the so-called 'theme–rheme distribution,' and also the referentiality and animacy hierarchies, according to which the most referential (or the most animate) element tends to occur on the left of the sentence.)

On the whole, what is implied in this polarized view of word order as a grammatical versus a pragmatic phenomenon is that the conditions determining the word order patterns of a given natural language are formal, i.e., highly abstract and mechanical, and that functional principles, such as focus placement, contextual dependency, the referentiality and animacy hierarchies, etc., can only at a later stage affect them. This view has been supported in late twentieth-century linguistic research mainly by generative grammarians. It raises more general problems of linguistic theory, concerning the level of representation of syntactic structure on which 'order' should be placed. The idea that order is a mere realization device of structure can be traced back to Meillet and further back to Condillac and has been variously maintained by Tesnière, Halliday, and many other nongenerative linguists. The idea that structural configurations of generative grammar inherently have a linear dimension has from time to time been criticized by those who favor nonlinear models, such as Šaumjan and Soboleva, Sgall, and, in the early 1980s, in different theoretical frameworks, Bresnan and the supporters of relational grammar (see *Relational Grammar*).

The alternative view has also been defended, according to which in every language word order is determined by the interplay of both formal (i.e., strictly grammatical) and functional factors. This view can be traced back to Mathesius and to the Prague School tradition of syntactic functionalism (see *Prague School Syntax and Semantics*). In this approach every language has a certain degree of sensitivity to functional factors: word order patterns peculiar to different languages are thus the result of different dynamic interactions of such factors with grammatical ones. Grammatical factors, however, are considered as mechanical tendencies at work in every language, which are determined by the habit of always setting the same sentence constituents in the same place.

In this light, the concepts of basic versus 'nonbasic' word order, as well as the concepts of 'fixed' versus 'nonfixed' word order turn out to be idealizations of a high degree, being constructed on purely abstract sentence models rather than being arrived at by observations of real utterances. In dealing with pragmatic functions and word order, however, empirical studies of language in use should be taken into due account.

The two views are both challenged in the following discussion of topic, focus, and word order. However, any overall treatment of this subject cannot escape the fundamental difficulty that so far no unitary account has been proposed in both formal and functional terms. On the one hand, the notions of 'topic' and 'focus' have been introduced in the theoretical framework of generative grammar as terms devoid of their semantic/pragmatic import. On the other hand, the literature on word order often lacks a broader view of the set of possible syntactic structures in natural languages which are associated with functions such as topic and focus. What is more, it lacks a full understanding of formal regularities exhibited by these structures.

The following sections deal first with the crucial notions of topic and focus and second with a set of structures related to these two pragmatic functions which seem to be widely spread across natural languages: topicalization, left dislocation, right dislocation, clefting (in its various subtypes, such as *it*-clefting and *wh*-clefting), raising, passivization, extraposition. Finally, the relation between topic, focus, and syntactic structure is discussed.

2. Topic and Focus

There are no all-encompassing definitions of topic and focus in the literature. Both terms cover phenomena belonging to the whole spectrum of syntax, semantics, and pragmatics, with an extension to the phonological level.

Perhaps the most controversial concepts lie at the pragmatic level. Three (at least) definitions of topic and focus can be found with different terminology, but variants of the same thing:

(a) Topic refers to information already present in linguistic or situational context (i.e., it is the contextually bound unit or configuration of units); focus refers to information nonpresent (or partially present) in linguistic or situational context (i.e., it is the contextually unbound (or partially unbound) unit or configuration of units). With different terminology these two notions have been opposed to each other as 'given' (topic) versus 'new' (focus).

(b) Topic (or theme) is the part of the sentence conveying the lowest degree of communicative dynamism; focus (or rheme) is the part with the highest degree of communicative dynamism.

(c) Topic is presupposed information, focus is non-presupposed information.

It is a fact that has been widely recognized, but for which up till now poor theoretical explanations have been given, that across natural languages there is a high tendency in unmarked sentences to map the contextually bound stretch of the sentence on to the subject and the contextually unbound stretch on to the predicate. This tendency as well as the fact that the overwhelming majority of the world's languages are either SVO or SOV raises a problem concerning linearity. There is in fact no a priori reason why the contextually bound (given/less dynamic/presupposed) part of the sentence should come first.

The same correlation shows itself in the semantic definition associated with the two terms (note, however, that at this level the term 'comment' is often found instead of focus). Here topic is 'what is being spoken about,' focus (or comment) is 'what is being said on what is being spoken about.'

When it comes to a purely syntactic definition of topic and focus, apparently it is the linear dimension of the sentence which is essentially involved. Different models have variously assessed the property of being a topic as the occurrence of a constituent x in the first position of the sentence. This generalization, however, can be questioned. The property of being an argument of the verb is no less important as a syntactic criterion than purely linear considerations. By a large consensus in the literature only those constituents that convey grammatical functions are considered as candidates for the topic function. Thus languages may have topics that do not occur in the first position of the sentence; to take but one example, the so-called circumstantial elements that express the temporal or spatial setting (in many languages, time or place adverbs) may be placed in the first position, as in the sentence *Yesterday Mary was in a very bad mood*. Here the topic is not *yesterday*, but the constituent with the subject function. Thus the idea seems well-founded that in general a position P_1 should be differentiated from topic position $P(top)$, although there will be many cases in which $P_1 = P(top)$. Things are further complicated by the fact that the topic often coincides with a phrase with multiple constituents. An alternative and more satisfactory definition would not specify for topic just a unique position P_i, but a whole range of positions $P_j \ldots P_k$ (where $j \ldots k$ space over a set of integers ranging from 1 to k); a further condition should specify that, $P_1 \ldots P_n$ being the series of positions of syntactic structure, P_k never coincides with P_n.

Similar problems are faced in the attempt to obtain a syntactic definition of focus. Here again what is crucial is not merely the position inside the sentence, but also the categorial/functional nature of the constituent involved. Following a purely linear criterion, in fact, one could be led to assume that, at least in unmarked (i.e., nonemphatic) sentences, the focus position is the final one, since the linear dimension of the sentence can be conceived as a serial process of adding information quanta, each quantum conveying a higher information value than its antecedent. This assumption is wrong for two reasons: first, as in the case of topic, focus often does not coincide with a single constituent, but with a configuration of constituents. To resume the preceding example, in the sentence *Yesterday Mary was in a bad mood* the whole string *was in a bad mood* is the focus (or, more precisely, the 'broader focus'), although inside this domain, some constituents are more focal than others (inside the VP domain the focus proper is the NP *a bad mood*; inside the NP domain, in unmarked sentences, the general consensus would be that the focus proper is the modifier *bad* (this is what is called 'narrow focus')). Second, the final position could be occupied by a circumstantial element, which is a typical nonargument of the verb: the previous assignment of 'foci' holds true even in *Mary was in a bad mood yesterday* as well as in *Mary was in a bad mood during her stay in Rome*, when these sentences are uttered with normal intonation contours (i.e., *yesterday* and

during her stay in Rome have either no nucleus or a secondary one). Similar considerations hold true for other constituents occurring in the final position that do not have a strong dependency relation with the predicate frame and thus are extrasentential (e.g., *he said* in *John was upset by the War, he said*) or appositional (e.g., *Peter* in *I have just met my brother, Peter*; note that in *I have just met my brother Peter*, with no pause between *brother* and *Peter* and the nucleus on *Peter*, the latter constituent is the focus proper of the sentence).

One is thus entitled to think that the strength of dependency relations is a fundamental parameter in determining focus. What is suggested here is that focus is correlated to dependency structure. This formulation could be refined in terms of the relation between heads (i.e., governing constituents) and their governed constituents. In unmarked sentences, in fact, natural languages seem to show a correlation between highly focal constituents and the property of being governed. Thus, for example, in sentences with the configuration $[_S[_{NP}\ldots] + [_{VP}V + [_{NP}ART + ADJ + N_{NP}]_{VP}]_S]$ the focus would cover the NP (in many cases ADJ would be the focus proper); in sentences with the configuration $[_S[_{NP}\ldots] + [_{VP}V + [_{PP}PREP + [_{NP}\ldots]_{PP}]_{VP}]_S]$ the focus will cover the PP (with NP as the focus proper—more precisely, the governed constituent, if any, in NP).

Of course, languages vary according to the degree of conformity between the structural and the linear principle of focus assignment. This has to do with typological characteristics affecting grammar to a different extent. Consider, for example, the case of Japanese or other Altaic languages, where the predominant SOV order is systematically reflected in the general operator–operand order. In sentences such as Japanese (1–2) the focus proper (*Rōma* and *akaku*, respectively) does not occur in sentence final position. Languages of this type are thus said to have an 'unsusceptibility to functional sentence perspective' (FSP) (i.e., the linear criterion). In principle, the highest degree of conformity to FSP is exhibited by SVO (or operand–operator) languages. However, even these latter may deviate from it in some part of their grammar. Consider the case of the adjectival prenominal position in English, which results in focus not occurring in phrase-final or sentence-final position:

Kinoo	(*watashi* *wa*)		*Rōma*	*e*	*itta*	(1)
yesterday	I	TOPIC MARKER	Rome	to	have been	

'Yesterday I went to Rome'

Ano *onna* *noko*	*wa*	*kami*	*o*	*akaku*	*shite* *iru*	(2)
that girl	TOPIC MARKER	hair	OBJECT MARKER	red	has	

'That girl has red hair'

Finally, to return to the problem of assessing a relationship between linearity (order) and focus, the conclusion cannot be avoided that it is deeply affected by typological characteristics of languages. If focus tends to coincide with predication, and this, in turn, is realized at the configurational level by VP, there is no universally valid focus position. Here indeed crucial and difficult problems of syntactic theory are implied, since for languages with VSO order the major constituent VP is split. Furthermore, in SOV languages, where the governed constituents tend to occur on the left of the verb, focus seems systematically to escape the 'VP last' criterion. This in fact holds particularly for SVO languages.

However, it should be noted that a linear criterion may hold under like conditions of government. If a verb governs both an NP and a PP, the last governed major constituent in the VP is the focus (with the last governed lexical category as the focus proper).

A third criterion may impose itself. Semantic criteria may interact with both dependency and linearity. An interesting example is the so-called double-object construction of English. In *I gave a book to Mary* versus *I gave Mary a book*, a role is played by the animacy hierarchy of constituents, according to the principle of 'the most animate first.' Again, the linear criterion seems to determine the focus as the last argument of the verb.

The previous discussion has been concerned with 'unmarked' focus distribution. At this point, however, it must be noted that linear properties of 'marked' focus distribution, that is, the distribution in emphatic sentences, strongly deviate from what has been called the *ordo naturalis* principle, arranging the information increase along a left to right direction. This different distribution conforms rather to an inverse flow of information according to a decrease from left to right in the sentence. Thus, for example, in *To Rome I've never been* or in *These things we like*, focus is placed in P_1.

So far an attempt has been made at defining focus in terms of linear, structural, and semantic properties. None of these, however, is in itself sufficient. The same is true of suprasegmental correlates of focus, such as variations in pitch, length, and loudness. All these properties can be considered as realization devices of a more abstract notion of a pragmatic nature, that is, 'prominence.' A similar conclusion can be reached for the notion of topic, whose configurational and prosodic properties are envisaged in late twentieth-century literature as devices that codify the pragmatic notion of 'center of attention.'

Another possibility is to think of topic and focus as pragmatic primitives of grammar, with which particular structures can be associated in different languages (this idea has been maintained by Lakoff (1971) and by Dik (1978, 1989)). This could be especially useful in the treatment of configurational regularities concerning order, which are involved in such phenomena as topicalization, left dislocation, right dislocation, and clefting. However, the approach in terms of pragmatic primitives seems more sat-

isfactory in the framework of a formal theory than for research on empirical properties of natural languages. On the other hand, if topic and focus are defined in terms of configurations, the definition of the associated phenomena becomes rather circular.

The next section combines pragmatic and syntactic approaches in an examination of syntactic structures related to topic and focus.

3. Topic-related Structures

3.1 A General Definition

When the syntax of topic is discussed in the literature it is generally both the linear and the argumental criteria which override the pragmatic one. Thus in this section the topic will be identified as the item in one of the initial positions of the sentence which conveys a grammatical function.

Perhaps the most general syntactic property of the class of topic-related structures might be determined as the occurrence in the sentence P(top) position of a constituent with a different grammatical function from that of the subject. It can be argued, in fact, that a hierarchy of accessibility to topic position can be established in natural languages, with subject being the prime candidate for P(top):

Subject > Indirect object > Direct object
> Locative complement > Manner complement   (3)

The above definition can account for sentences such as (4–6):

To him I never said good-bye   (4)

This picture I like best   (5)

To Rome I've never been   (6)

whose structures can be thought of as derived respectively from (4′–6′):

I never said good-bye to him   (4′)

I like this picture best   (5′)

I've never been to Rome   (6′)

By adopting a phrase-structure tree of the kind used in generative grammar to represent the base structures (4′–6′), shown in Fig. 1a, it can easily be understood that sentences (4–6) are derived by a movement rule raising the nodes PP, NP, PP to the top node as shown in Fig. 1b.

3.2 Hanging Topic

The definition in example (3), however, needs to be further refined in order to be really workable for the large variety of topic-related phenomena occurring in natural languages. Consider for example the following Mandarin Chinese (7–8), Japanese (9), and Lahu (10–11) sentences (from Li and Thompson 1976: 462):

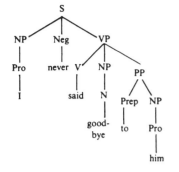 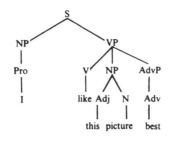 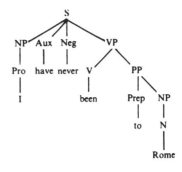

Figure 1a.

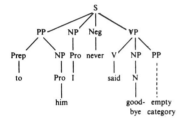 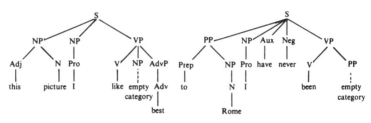

Figure 1b.

Nèi-chang   huǒ   xìngkui   xiāofáng-duì
that-classifier fire fortunate fire-brigade

           lái   de   kuài
           come ADV particle quick   (7)
'That fire, fortunately the fire-brigade came quickly'

Nèi-xie shùmu shù-shēn dà   (8)
 those tree tree-trunk big
'Those trees, the trunks are big'

Gakkoo-wa   *boku-ga*   *isogasi-kat-ta* (9)
School-topic marker I-subject marker busy-past tense
'School, I was busy'

Hɛ   chi   tê pê?   5   dàʔ   jâ   (10)
Field this one classifier rice very good
'This field, the rice is very good'

Hɔ   5   na-qhɔ̌ yɨ̄ ve   yò   (11)
elephant TOPIC nose LONG DECLARATIVE
       MARKER   PARTICLE MARKER
'Elephants, noses are long'

In these sentences the elements occupying position P(top) are ungoverned by the verb (a more technical formulation of this would be that they do not have any selectional relation to the main verb). Thus the basic representation of (7–11) would be as shown in Fig. 2. It seems reasonable then to differentiate two

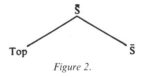

Figure 2.

fundamental classes of topic-related phenomena, the first having to do with extra sentential constituents in P(top) which constitute a kind of hanging topic, the second with sentential arguments moved or extraposed to P(top).

Languages may vary as to the permissible range of topicalization. According to a well-known hypothesis by Li and Thompson two main language types can be recognized around the world, topic-prominent and subject-prominent languages. Topicalizations of the kind shown in sentences (7–11) would be permissible in topic-prominent languages, but not in subject-prominent ones. However, the typological distinction per se is rather questionable, since the range of possible topicalization allowed by a given language seems to be related to sociolinguistic parameters such as the speaker's capability to plan the discourse (planned/unplanned discourse), different strategies in spoken versus written communication, the speaker's level of education, and so on. Spoken registers of what would be believed on the evidence of written data to be subject-prominent languages do exhibit structures like sentences (7–11). Examples (12–13) are from a corpus of spoken Italian:

La scuola, mi sono messo in congedo	(12)

The school I have taken a leave
'As to the school, I have taken a leave'

La radio, hanno trasmesso un programma interessante
The radio they have transmitted a program interesting
'On the radio they have transmitted an interesting program' (13)

3.3 Left Dislocation and Topicalization

The second class (moved sentence arguments) can be further divided into two subclasses, according to the presence (e.g., 14) or absence (e.g., 15) of anaphoric relations between the constituent moved to the top node and a coreferential pronoun filling the position which was previously occupied by it (note, however, that Italian and French sentences such as (15) and (16) would require further observations to justify the position occupied by the coreferential pronoun):

John Smith, I haven't met him for a long time (14)

Cet élève, je l'aime bien (15)
'That pupil, I like her very much'

Patrizia, l'ho vista ieri (16)
'Patrizia, I saw her yesterday'

These problems they can't deal with (17)

Il decano ho incontrato ieri (18)
The dean I met yesterday
'It is the dean I met yesterday'

Structures such as (14–16) are instances of 'left dislocation,' structures (17–18) of 'topicalization' (or 'fronting'). There seems to be, at least in many European languages, a difference in the pragmatic value of structures (14–16) and (17–18): while in the first structures the topic may not convey emphasis (unless specific suprasegmental features are associated with it), in the latter ones it seems the case that the constituent in P(top) has a contrastive value. In other words, it could be said that in sentences such as (17–18) the topic function coincides with the focus function, a peculiar property from the pragmatic point of view, related to marked word order.

From the syntactic point of view, however, rules generating both structures (14–16) and (17–18) have for a long time been recognized as being of a 'movement' nature.

An interesting problem concerns the range of constituents that may undergo movement rules of this kind. Not surprisingly, languages vary as to this range, although a strong tendency can be recognized to put in P(top) nonverbal constituents. In European languages, for example, ADJP, PP, ADVP, in addition to NP, are constituents that are allowed to move to P(top), although there is a difference from language to language as to the pragmatic value associated with the syntactic operation. For example, in both Italian and English, adjective or adverb movement to the top node results in structures conveying emphasis, as can be seen comparing the translations (19–22):

...e rosso era (19)

...and red it was (20)

volentieri venne (21)

willingly he came (22)

3.4 Raising and Passivization

Left dislocation shows the same property of constituent moving leftward to P(top), as structures which have undergone raising processes. These can be exemplified by English constructions where a NP is 'raised' out of subordinate clause subject position into main clause subject position:

Mary seems to me to be happy (23)

Another interesting similarity is shown in passivization processes, which also have the property of moving a NP constituent leftward. It has been recognized for a long time in the literature that passive sentences can be represented as structures derived from the corresponding active ones by means of movement rules (and morphological alterations of the verb, which will not be considered here). From the pragmatic point of view, passivization has convincingly been argued to be but another case of bringing into P(top) (i.e., into the 'center of attention') the NP with the grammatical function object at some underlying level of representation.

3.5 Clefting

Clefting encompasses another class of syntactic processes which are related to topic–focus distribution. The term covers various subtypes of processes, some of them more properly similar to the topic-related ones. These will be referred to as subtype A. Other clefting processes result in structures of the equative kind. These will be referred to as subtype B, to be dealt with in Sect. 4.

Languages tend to differ as to minor details in the structure generated by A-clefting, as will be clear from the following examples from typologically and/or genetically different languages (with examples (24–27) being translations each of the other):

It is me who said that		(24)
C'est moi qui l'ai dit	(French)	(25)
Soy yo quien lo he dicho	(Spanish)	(26)
Sono io che l'ho detto	(Italian)	(27)

Shì	*wǒ*	*lái*	*zhèr*	(Mandarin Chinese)	(28)
Be	I	come	here		

'It is me who comes here'

Kuṭṭiyaaṇə	*aanaye*	*nulliyatə*	(Malayalam)	(29)
Child-is	elephant	pinched-it		

'It was the child who pinched the elephant'

In all these examples the verb 'be' acts as a device assigning the focus function to the NP that immediately follows (cf. 24–28) or precedes (cf. 29). As the occurrence of a dummy subject before the verb 'be' is a feature irrelevant here—it has to do with more idiosyncratic language tendencies—it can be said that the more general A-clefting pattern is represented by (30):

$$\text{'Be'} + \text{NP} + \bar{\text{S}} \qquad (30)$$

where NP carries the focus function. Here again, as in the case of topicalization, a single constituent has both the functions of topic ('be' is no candidate for topichood) and focus.

The properties of A-clefting are similar to those of topic-related processes also from a strictly syntactic point of view. The range of constituents that may occur in postcopular position constitutes in fact a class identified by the feature [−verbal]. Note, however, that here again languages seem to vary as to the width of the [−verbal] class, i.e., as to the range of constituents that are allowed to occupy the postcopular position. For example, in languages such as English or Italian only NPs, PPs, and time and place adverbs may occur in that position (English *It is yellow that it is* and the Italian translation *È giallo che è*; English *It is well that I have found him* and the Italian translation *È bene che l'ho trovato*), whereas in Welsh adverbs and adjectives may also do so:

Bit	*chuero*	*y*	*talhaur*	(Middle Welsh)
(It) will be	bitterly	that	(it) will be paid for	(31)

More problematic is to decide whether A-clefting should be considered as a movement process (like left-dislocation and topicalization) or not. Examples such as (24–28), where a NP with the grammatical function subject occurs in postcopular position, are not generated by movement rules. Their structures could rather be base-generated with NP in P(top). This is not the case with (32):

It is you that I am looking after (32)

whose structure is obviously related to (33):

I am looking after you (33)

and could be derived from it by a movement rule.

4. Syntactic Processes that Keep the Focus in Unmarked Position

Syntactic processes whose pragmatic import is the focalization of a constituent are less homogeneous than those related to the topic. As a matter of fact, no general definition of focalization processes can be

formulated in terms of syntactic configurations, nor in terms of grammatical relations. What could be said would be rather tautological: in unmarked conditions syntactic processes related to focus either keep or move a constituent rightward in the sentence, i.e., in the domain of the unmarked focus (of course this definition would not include structures with marked focus, such as the ones in Sect. 3.5).

The normal distribution of focus as described in Sect. 2 is kept in structures such as *wh*-clefts (34–35):

The one who lies is he (34)

What is in question is his reputation as a scientist (35)

These are sentences with an equative-identifying value, which are generated by type B-clefting. The more general B-clefting pattern can be represented by:

$$X + be + Y \qquad (36)$$

where both X and Y can be any of the categories in the set (NP, $\bar{\text{S}}$). Other equative sentences conforming to pattern (36) are of a kind that is rather frequent in spoken language:

The thing is (that) they are in trouble (37)

The point is that they have never understood the situation (38)

It is worth mentioning that structure (36) has two fundamental properties: (a) reversibility, i.e., its reverse structure (36′):

$$Y + be + X \qquad (36')$$

is also well-formed (sentences like (37–38) clearly deviate from this regularity); and (b) the marking of X by the feature [−definite] (more precisely, if X = NP, the head of NP is [−definite]; if X = $\bar{\text{S}}$, the head of the NP with the subject function is [−definite]).

Sentences conforming to pattern (36) have the focus function stretching over the postcopular constituent. Note that a conflict between the linear and the semantic criteria arises in reverse sentences such as (39):

John is the one who went to Edinburgh (39)

Here in fact the feature [−definite] in the postcopular constituent is incompatible with focality (or less compatible than the feature [+definite]). It can be seen, however, how powerful the linear criterion is, as it overrides the unfavorable semantic feature, assigning the focus function to the postcopular constituent.

An interesting and peculiar effect is obtained in structures with an anaphoric pronoun anticipating either a direct object or an indirect object (or both), as in the following examples from Romance languages:

La	*he*	*visto*	*a*	*tu*	*mujer*	(Spanish)	(40)
Her	I have	seen	to	your	wife		

'I did see your wife'

Gliela	*raccontai*	*la notizia*	*ta*	*Maria*	(Italian)
To her+it	I told	the piece of news	to	Mary	

'I did tell the piece of news to Mary' (41)

| *Je* | *l'* | *ai* | *donné* | *le* | *livre* | (French) | (42) |
| I | it | have | given | the | book | | |

'I did give the book as a gift'

Here the focus is not on the last sentential argument (*a tu mujer* in (40); *a Maria* in (41); *le livre* in (42)), as in the corresponding sentences without pronominal copies before the verb (40'–42'):

He visto a tu mujer (40')

Raccontai la notizia a Maria (41')

J'ai donné le livre (42')

Rather, it is shifted leftward on the verb.

4.1 Right Dislocation and Extraposition

Structures with right dislocation of the subject, such as (43):

| *Hanno* | *considerato* | *il* | *caso* | *molti* | *esperti* | (Italian) |
| They have | considered | the | case | many | experts | |

'Many experts have considered the case' (43)

are instances of syntactic processes moving in focus what normally is a nonfocal constituent. Another case in point is extraposition, as in (44):

A critical review has just appeared of his latest book (44)

where the PP *of his latest book* is detached from NP with the subject function and moved rightward in focus.

5. Topic and Focus as Pragmatic Primitives and Syntactic Structure

In this concluding section a few general remarks will be attempted on the relationship between topic, focus, and word order as well as on the nature of topic and focus themselves.

In Sect. 2 it was pointed out that topic and focus are to be considered as pragmatic functions which should be defined neither in terms of syntactic structure nor in terms of prosodic structure. Rather, they should be conceived as independent functions with structural correlates (of a syntactic and prosodic kind). In the light of what has been observed in the last paragraphs two important correlations can be pointed out between topic, focus, and syntactic structure. The first deals precisely with word order. Topic is related to syntactic processes that keep a unit in the leftmost position, out of the sentence pattern proper, or to syntactic processes that result in moving a specific constituent leftward in the sentence. On the other hand, focus is related to syntactic processes that keep or move a constituent rightward in the sentence. This of course conforms to the linear distribution of topic and focus, as has already been pointed out in Sect. 2.

The left-to-right dimension observed, however, is to be connected to two pragmatic notions such as 'center of attention' and 'prominence,' whose import

is of a cognitive nature: constituents occurring leftward (leftmost) in the sentence belong to that part of the utterance which is the center of attention for the speaker/listener (finer considerations would be highly desirable as to possible differences between speakers and listeners in establishing centers of attention; in fact much more experimental work is needed here). On the other hand, constituents occurring rightward (rightmost) in a connected sentence will probably set up prominence peaks. As a matter of fact, it seems a fairly general property of human communication under nonemphatic conditions, to organize the information flow in the utterance according to a strategy of centering attention on specific information units first, and then giving prominence to others. This might well be a universal tendency across natural languages, which accounts for semantic or structural configurations such as topic–comment, subject–predicate, NP–VP, etc.

The second correlation between topic, focus, and syntactic structure concerns: (a) the nonverbal nature of constituents that across natural languages are more frequently allowed to occupy topic position, i.e., the center of attention in the information flow; and (b) the lack of categorial restrictions on constituents in focus. The first property could be formulated in terms of the topic position ruling out elements that bear predication and requiring referential ones. The relationship between topic and referentiality might lead to a cross-linguistic generalization of a pragmatic nature, that is, only constituents with a referential value can function as centers of attention. As to the second property, it should be noted that the lack of categorial restrictions only concerns lexical categories and not major categories: under nonemphatic conditions, VP is in fact the normal domain of the focus function in subject-initial languages. Thus the conclusion can be reached that prominence in principle is to be correlated to predication. Note that this is the case not only when focus stretches over VP, but also in marked structures such as those in Sect. 3.5, where the topic and focus functions collapse together. Predication carried out in this latter case seems to be of a special kind, which may be described as 'identifying.' Sentences with emphatic topicalization or clefting, in fact, can be analyzed as having a double predication pattern, the first associated to the leftmost NP, the second to the following stretch of utterance.

What has been said seems to have some consequences for the study of topic and focus. One of the problems in any attempt to combine pragmatic and syntactic analysis in the study of topic, focus, and syntactic structure has been the fuzziness of notions such as topic and focus themselves. It has already been pointed out in Sect. 2 that if their definition is to be kept separated from syntactic structures, no option remains but to consider them as primitives. This is far from being a satisfactory conclusion however, at least for a full understanding of how phenomena of natural languages work. On the other hand, if topic and focus are given the empirical content of center of attention and prominence, respectively, the problem of further differentiating these two notions is left open. Although an answer to this can be expected to come mainly from psycholinguistic work, the case of topic and focus collapsing together can give some provisional hints. If prominence is defined as an identifying predication, the affinity of the two pragmatic notions will show itself as a consequence. Identifying, after all, is related to referentiality. Thus, center of attention and prominence can be considered as two notions that can be differentiated in degree, being of the same nature: prominence, in fact, could be conceived as the high degree of attention centering. In this light, syntactic processes such as left-dislocation, topicalization, clefting, and the like are nothing else than effects of pragmatic and cognitive properties of the human mind and human communication.

Bibliography

Bolinger D L 1952 Linear modification. *PMLA* **67**: 1117–44
Bresnan J (ed.) 1982 *The Mental Representation of Grammatical Relations*. MIT Press, Cambridge, MA
Carlson L 1983 *Dialogue Games*. Reidel, Dordrecht
Cinque G 1977 The movement nature of left dislocation. *LIn* **8**: 397–412
Chafe W L 1970 *Meaning and the Structure of Language*. University of Chicago Press, Chicago, IL
Chafe W L 1976 Givenness, contrastiveness, definiteness, subjects, topics and point of view. In: Li Ch N (ed.) *Subject and Topic*. Academic Press, New York
Chomsky N A 1965 *Aspects of the Theory of Syntax*. MIT Press, Cambridge, MA
Chomsky N A 1981 *Lectures on Government and Binding*. Foris, Dordrecht
Daneš F 1967 Order of elements and sentence intonation. In: Bolinger D L (ed.) *Intonation*. Penguin, Harmondsworth
Dik S C 1978 *Functional Grammar*. North Holland, Amsterdam
Dik S C 1989 *The Theory of Functional Grammar*. Foris, Dordrecht
Firbas J 1964 From comparative word-order studies. *Brno Studies in English* **4**: 111–28
Firbas J 1987 On the operation of communicative dynamism in functional sentence perspective. *Leuvense Bijdragen* **76**: 289–304
Gazdar G, Klein E, Pullum G-K (eds.) 1983 *Order, Concord and Constituency*. Foris, Dordrecht
Givón T 1984 *Syntax: A Functional Typological Introduction*. Benjamins, Amsterdam
Halliday M A K 1961 Categories of the theory of grammar. *Word* **17(3)**: 1–7
Halliday M A K 1967–68 Notes on transitivity and theme in English. *JL* **3(1)**: 37–81; **3(2)**: 199–244; **4(2)**: 179–215
Jackendoff R S 1972 *Semantic Interpretation in Generative Grammar*. MIT Press, Cambridge, MA
Lakoff G 1971 On generative semantics. In: Steinberg D D, Jakobovits L A (eds.) *Semantics*. Cambridge University Press, Cambridge
Li Ch N, Thompson S A 1976 Subject and topic: A new typology of language. In: Li Ch N (ed.) *Subject and Topic*. Academic Press, New York
Marantz A 1984 *On the Nature of Grammatical Relations*. MIT Press, Cambridge, MA
Mathesius V 1939 O tak zvaném aktuálním členění větném. *Slovo a slovesnost* **5**: 171–74
Mathesius V 1941–42 Ze srovnávacích studií slovosledných. *Časopis pro moderní filologii* **28**: 181–90; 302–07
Meillet A P J 1965 *Linguistique historique et linguistique générale*. Champion, Paris
Šaumjan S K, Soboleva P A 1963 *Applikativnaja porozdajuščaja model' i iščislenie transformacij v russkom jazyke*. Akademik Nauk, Moscow
Sgall P 1972 Topic, focus and the ordering of elements in semantic representation. *Philologica Pragensia* **15**: 1–14
Sgall P et al. 1986 *The Meaning of the Sentence in its Semantic and Pragmatic Aspects*. Reidel, Dordrecht
Tesnière L V 1958 *Elements de Syntaxe Structurale*. Klincksieck, Paris

Typological and Areal Issues in Grammar

L. Campbell

'Areal Linguistics' deals with the diffusion of structural features across linguistic boundaries. A 'linguistic area' (also sometimes called *Sprachbund*, convergence area, diffusion area, adstratum, and *affinité linguistique*) is usually characterized by a number of linguistic features (thought to be due to diffusion or to convergent development) which are shared by various languages (either unrelated or from different subgroups of a language family) in a geographically contiguous area. For example, some shared grammatical traits which characterize the Balkans linguistic area (comprising Greek, Albanian, Serbo–Croatian, Bulgarian, Macedonian, and Romanian), are (a) syncretism of dative and genitive (dative and genitive cases have fused in form and function); (b) postponed articles (though not in Greek); (c) periphrastic future (futures with an auxiliary verb corresponding to 'want' or 'have'); (d) periphrastic perfect (with an auxiliary verb corresponding to 'have'); (e) no infinitive (instead with constructions such as 'I want that I go' for 'I want to go'); and (f) pleonastic use of personal pronouns (personal pronouns employed in sentences with animate objects to mark the object doubly, e.g., 'I wrote to him John' for 'I wrote (to) John'). The lack of infinitives has frequently been attributed to Greek influence, although the origin and direction of shared areal features are often not easy to determine. (Other linguistic areas are discussed below.)

'Typology,' in the broad sense, is the classification of languages in terms of their structural characteristics. The typologies which have received the most attention are those which have attempted broad classifications based on a number of interrelated features. There are, needless to say, many possible ways of categorizing languages according to their structure. Historically, languages were often classified according to their morphological tendencies as isolating, inflecting, or agglutinating. Typology as practiced in the early 1990s investigates differences, and hence also similarities, across languages, and is thus closely linked with the study of linguistic 'universals.' Typological research produces the data upon which cross-linguistic generalizations about the nature of language are made, defining the traits that languages share and the limits on language variation. A joint concern of typology and universals is with determining what the expected correlations among parts of a language's grammar are and hence with determining aspects of the nature of human language in general.

Thus, both areal linguistics and typology classify languages according to structural attributes, though for different goals. The identification of areal traits and of typological features each can have implications for the other (Comrie 1989: 204–10; Mallinson and Blake 1981: 16–18).

1. Typological Issues in the Definition of Areal Traits

Some issues concerning the definition of a linguistic area include: the number of shared traits required to establish a linguistic area, whether these must bundle (i.e., cluster at roughly the same boundaries), how areal traits are to be counted, and whether some bear more weight than others for defining a linguistic area. Typology plays a role in these issues concerning how linguistic areas are defined and how areal traits are determined. For example, Ethiopian Semitic languages exhibit a number of areal traits diffused from Cushitic languages; however, several of these individual traits are interconnected due to the borrowing of SOV (Subject–Object–Verb) basic word order from Cushitic languages into the formerly VSO Ethiopian Semitic languages. That is, typologically the orders Noun–Postposition, Verb–Auxiliary, Relative Clause–Head Noun, and Adjective–Noun tend to co-occur with SOV order in language in general. If these expected correlations in word-order typology are not taken into account, their presence in Ethiopian Semitic languages might seem to reflect several different diffused traits, which could be counted as several inde-

pendent pieces of evidence in support of a linguistic area. However, from the perspective of typologically expected word-order co-occurrences, these word-order arrangements are not independently acquired traits, but are due to the diffusion of a single complex feature, the SOV word-order type with its various expected concomitant orderings. Nevertheless, if the borrowing of SOV basic word order counts as a single areal trait, rather than many, the question remains, should the relative difficulty of acquiring a trait so central to the grammar be weighted more heavily than more easily diffused traits for definition of linguistic areas? (cf. Campbell 1985; Campbell et al. 1988; Ferguson 1976.) In another example, while most of the neighboring languages to both the North and South of Meso–America have both SOV basic word order and switch-reference markers, the languages of the Meso-american linguistic area lack both. This might be considered two independent pieces of evidence for defining the linguistic area, were it not for the fact that switch-reference systems are found for the most part only in SOV languages (with very few exceptions) (Campbell et al. 1986). That is, these are not two independent features, but are linked, and thus do not count as two distinct votes for establishing the linguistic area and to understanding the nature of the shared traits.

Clearly, typological considerations are important to the defining of linguistic areas.

2. Areal Linguistic Implications for Typology

Similarly, areal linguistics has strong implications for work in typology and universals. This is easily illustrated in word-order typology. It has been argued that certain word-order types are represented only by languages which have undergone areal diffusion and borrowing (Campbell et al. 1988). Greenberg (1966; see also Hawkins 1983) dealt with 24 possible basic word-order types, of which only 15 were thought to have actual representative languages. However, it turns out that for some of these 15 types, and for certain others for which representatives have subsequently been discovered, all the exemplifying languages owe crucial aspects of their basic word-order to areal borrowing, i.e., Greenberg's type 7, 18, 19, 20. Type 7 (Verb-first/Postposition–Noun/Genitive–Noun/Adjective–Noun) is represented only by Zoque; Zoque borrowed VOS word order from neighboring Mayan languages, as did Xinca and Pipil in the same area. Type 18 (SOV/Prepositional/Noun–Genitive/Adjective–Noun), not previously recognized to have exemplifying languages, is represented by Tigre (Ethiopian Semitic, like non-Ethiopian Semitic languages except for SOV, which it acquired from Cushitic). Type 19 (SOV/Prepositional/Genitive–Noun/Adjective–Noun) is represented by Amharic (also Ethiopian Semitic, owing its SOV and Postposition–Noun orders to borrowing from Cushitic).

(It is not clear whether Old Persian (Gathic) is type 19 or 20, while Pashto may be type 19 or 23.) Type 20 (previously with no recognized example languages, SOV/Prepositional/Genitive–Noun/Noun–Adjective) is represented by Northern Tajik, whose word order patterns were strongly influenced by borrowing from Turkic. Akkadian (Semitic) SOV is unexpected and is ascribed to Sumerian influence. Younger Avestan's Verb-final pattern is hypothesized to be the result of syntactic borrowing from the Mesopotamian linguistic area (Campbell et al. 1988).

It must be acknowledged, then, that few languages have come to have the word-order configurations of types 7, 18, 19, and 20, but most (perhaps all) languages representing these types owe aspects of their word-order patterns to borrowing from other languages. This being the case, it is clear that areal diffusion can have an impact on the study of typology and universals. Word-order universals should be framed not on these more marginal types (owing their character to borrowing), but on the typological patterns exhibited by a large number of languages and which have stronger internal explanations (i.e., explanations based on efficient functioning/processing of communication, for example the cross-category harmony principle, that modifiers tend either all to precede their heads or all to follow, aids the listener to process these structures based on their consistent position relative to one another; Hawkins 1983). Nevertheless, this is an appropriate way to view research in typology and universals, since linguists are interested in the general principles of language, in how the pieces of languages interrelate, how they function, and how they may change. Some of these principles may be reflected in absolute universals, others in statistical universals (strong tendencies); other interrelated patterns may reflect typologically significant correlations which are not normally associated with universals. The more internally motivated the universal or typological pattern, the less likely it is that areal diffusion will be permitted to introduce departures from the expected principled arrangements of elements in a language (Campbell et al. 1988).

Another issue with respect to the relevance of areal linguistics for the study of typology and universals is the problem of sampling error and the question of the limited geographical distribution of certain linguistic features. That is, areal biases in the language samples upon which cross-linguistic generalizations are framed should be avoided, since some areas exhibit a greater concentration of certain features (due to diffusion and convergence) than do others. If areal biases are not controled, the linguist runs the risk of assuming some linguistic feature to be far more typical of languages in general than it may actually be, more important for linguistic theory than it deserves to be.

This raises a related question, what is the theoretical status of linguistic phenomena which are found restricted to a particular linguistic area? For example, the clicks in the so-called Khoisan and adjacent Bantu languages of southern Africa are virtually absent as significant speech sounds elsewhere in the world. How are they to be viewed, then? Are they really part of the fundamental elements of language, a distinctive feature potentially available to all the world's languages, or are they sufficiently restricted geographically to be expected never to be found in languages elsewhere? To take a grammatical example, if virtually all languages have relative clauses except certain Australian tongues (which rather have a more general subordinating construction), what is the status of relative clauses in linguistic theory? (Comrie 1989: 144; Mallinson and Blake 1981: 266–69; Keenan 1985: 166.) Is it to be expected that other languages outside the Australian area could also lack them, although cases are unknown? How does the Australian areal lack of true relatives relate to their presence in the rest of the world's languages? How is the universal to be formulated, if at all? Can the absence of relative clauses in but a single area of the world require linguistic theory to expect their possible absence elsewhere in the world? A more telling example is that of OVS and OSV basic word order in languages of Lowland South America. Greenberg (1966) thought these to be impossible, nonoccurring orders, and indeed they are limited to languages (from a number of different families) of the Amazonian linguistic area. Theoretical errors have been committed in attempts to frame universal claims based on the assumed nonexistence of these word-order types, e.g., in an example employed to illustrate the contribution of typology to the study of universals: 'whenever the object precedes the verb the subject does likewise' (Greenberg 1978: 2; cf. Derbyshire and Pullum 1986: 16–17). That is, linguistic areas sometimes permit their languages to share unique features, not found elsewhere in the world's languages. Nevertheless, linguistic theory faces a problem in that it emphasizes universal statements that treat such language features as potentially available to all languages and not unique to specific areas.

3. Typology and Areal Linguistics as Hindrances to Linguistic History

Both typology and areal linguistics are important tools for the historical linguist. Areal linguistics helps to recover aspects of linguistic history that are due to diffusion and convergence. Typology helps to understand expected changes and constraints on possible changes. However, the two are alike in one respect, that both can hinder linguistic reconstruction. In the comparative method, similarities shared among related languages are the basis for postulating ancestral forms in the proto language. However, undetected areal borrowings can exhibit similarities that sometimes are assumed to be reflexes of common inheritance, and are erroneously reconstructed as features of the parent language (e.g., instrumental prefixes and switch-reference in a number of Indian language families of western America, where these features are ancestral to some, but borrowed into others). With respect to word-order typology, languages tend to exhibit cross-category harmony (modifiers tend either all to precede their head [e.g., Adjective–Noun] or all to follow [Noun–Adjective]). Languages which do not conform are called inconsistent and many scholars have believed that linguistic change will generally be in the direction of word-order consistency (conforming to the expected orders). This assumption, however, complicates grammatical reconstruction. Thus, if two consistent languages are compared, one may not know whether they reflect a consistent proto language or whether the two developed towards word-order consistency from some inconsistent parent as a result of the general typological tendency towards consistency which is assumed to direct linguistic change. Similarly, if a consistent language is compared with an inconsistent one, one does not know whether the proto language was inconsistent, where the consistent daughter followed the typological tendency to become consistent, or whether the parent language may have been consistent, but the inconsistent daughter developed due to other factors (e.g., borrowing). In fact, it is only when the compared daughter languages are inconsistent in the same way that a reasonably straightforward reconstruction is possible—that the proto language was inconsistent in the same way as its daughters. It is unlikely that the daughters would have developed inconsistency from a consistent proto language, since this goes against the assumption that languages tend to develop towards consistency. Paradoxically, this sort of word-order typology (frequently employed in diachronic syntax) proves helpful in reconstruction only when its underlying assumption, that languages change toward consistency, fails. When only consistent languages are compared, or where some are consistent and others not, one cannot know whether the consistency in some or all of the daughters is due to inheritance or to later conformity with the typological assumption. Thus, rather than helping with reconstruction, this sort of typological perspective on word-order change obscures the original state of affairs except in the case where inconsistent languages are compared, where the principle has not applied and therefore has not obstructed ability to recover the inherited history. Thus, areal linguistics and typology (as illustrated with the principle of word-order change towards consistency) share the similar trait that both can make grammatical reconstruction more difficult.

4. Linguistic Areas and their Grammatical Traits

Linguistic areas are often defined, surprisingly, by a rather small number of shared linguistic traits, and usually by only a few grammatical features, some of them not at all exciting. Moreover, while there is an assumption that it is diffusion among neighboring languages that shapes a linguistic area, in practice frequently traits shared by the languages of an area are merely listed with little or no attempt to distinguish between those which are actually the result of borrowing or convergence and others which may be accidental similarities, due to universal tendencies, or are even inherited in some cases. To give a general indication of how grammatical features have been treated in areal linguistics, the best-known linguistic areas are presented here together with the principal grammatical areal features that have been presented as representative of them (though each of these traits is not necessarily found in every language of the respective linguistic areas):

(a) The Balkans (see above).

(b) South Asia (Indian sub-continent, including Indo–Aryan, Dravidian, Munda, some Tibeto–Burman languages): (i) presence of a dative-subject construction; (ii) SOV basic word order; (iii) absence of a verb 'to have'; (iv) the 'conjunctive participle' (tendency for subordinate clauses to have nonfinite verbs and to be preposed); (v) morphological causatives; and (vi) compound verbs (where one portion of the compound explicates the other). Some of these proposed areal features are not limited to the Indian sub-continent (SOV), but can be found in neighboring languages, while others are not necessarily independent (e.g., SOV and conjunctive participle).

(c) The Baltic (variously defined, but including at least Balto–Finnic [especially Estonian and Livonian], Latvian, Lithuanian, Baltic German): The Baltic area is mostly defined by shared phonological features. Some borrowed grammatical features, some in only a few of the languages, include: (i) partitive case (to signal partially affected objects, e.g., 'I ate (some) apple'; Balto–Finnic, Lithuanian, Latvian, some dialects of Russian); (ii) evidential voice (modus obliquus, 'John works hard [it is said]'; Estonian, Livonian, Latvian, Lithuanian); (iii) prepositional verbs (German *aus-gehen* 'to go out'; Livonian, German, Karelian dialects); and (iv) SVO word order, plus Adjective–Noun agreement in case and number).

(d) Meso–America (Mayan, Mixe–Zoquean, Totonac, Oto–Manguean, Tarascan, some Uto–Aztecan, and others): (i) Nominal possession (of the type *his-dog the man* 'the man's dog'); (ii) relational nouns (locative expressions composed of noun roots and possessive pronominal affixes, i.e., *my-root* 'below me'); (iii) non-verb-final basic word order (no SOV) and lack of switch-reference; and (iv) borrowing of VOS among some languages (Campbell et al. 1986).

(e) Amazonia (Arawak, Tupi–Guarani, Ge, Carib, Panoan, Chibchan, and others): (i) a number of O-first (OSV, OVS) languages; (ii) nominal modifiers following their head nouns, but the constituent orders: Postposition–Noun, Genitive–Noun, Noun–Adjective, regardless of the word order of main clauses; (iii) predominantly suffixing; (iv) compounding and incorporation; (v) directional and locative markers on verbs; (vi) verb agreement with subject and object; (vii) substitution of nominalization for relative clause constructions; (viii) lack of agentive passive constructions; (ix) right-dislocated paratactic constructions; (x) use of phrasal discourse (and possibly verification) particles; and (xi) tendency towards ergatively-organized syntactic systems (Derbyshire 1986; Payne 1990).

(f) Ethiopia (Cushitic, Ethiopian Semitic, Omotic, Anyuak, Gumuz, and others): (i) SOV order, including postpositions; (ii) subordinate clause preceding main clause; (iii) gerund (nonfinite verb of a subordinate clause, often inflected for person and gender); (iv) 'quoting' construction (a direct quotation followed by some form of 'to say'); (v) compound verbs (consisting of a noun-like 'preverb' and a semantically empty auxiliary); (vi) negative copula; (vii) plurals of nouns not used after numbers; (viii) gender distinction in 2nd and 3rd person pronouns; (ix) reduplicated intensives; (x) different present tense marker for main and subordinate clauses; (xi) feminine singular for plural concord (feminine singular adjective, verb, or pronoun referring to a plural noun); and (xii) singulative (the simplest noun may be a collective or plural and require an affix to make a singular) (Ferguson 1976).

(g) The Northwest Coast of America (Salishan, Wakashan, Chemakuan, Tsimshian, Chinook, Eyak, Tlingit, Haida, Tolowa, Takelma, and others): This linguistic area is mostly defined by phonological features; additional investigation of its shared grammatical features is needed; these include: (i) pronominal plural; (ii) prefixation of nominal and verbal person markers; (iii) evidential markers on verbs; (iv) directional markers on verbs; and (v) verbal reduplication for plurality and distribution.

Bibliography

Campbell L 1985 Areal linguistics and its implications for historical linguistics. In: Fisiak J (ed.) *Papers from the Sixth International Conference on Historical Linguistics.* Benjamins, Amsterdam

Campbell L, Bubenik V, Saxon L 1988 Word order universals: Refinements and clarifications. *CJL* **33**: 209–30

Campbell L, Kaufman T, Smith-Stark T 1986 Meso-America as a linguistic area. *Lg* **62**: 530–70

Comrie B 1989 *Language Universals and Linguistic Typology, Syntax and Morphology*, 2nd edn. Blackwell, Oxford

Derbyshire D C 1986 Comparative survey of morphology and syntax in Brazilian Arawakan. In: Derbyshire D, Pullum G K (eds.) *Handbook of Amazonian Languages*, vol. 1. Mouton de Gruyter, Berlin

Derbyshire D C, Pullum G K 1986 Introduction. In: Derbyshire D C, Pullum G K (eds.) *Handbook of Amazonian Languages*, vol. 1. Mouton de Gruyter, Berlin

Ferguson C A 1976 The Ethiopian language area. In: Bender M L, Bowen J D, Cooper R L, Ferguson C A (eds.) *Language in Ethiopia.* Oxford University Press, London

Greenberg J H 1966 Some universals of grammar with particular reference to the order of meaningful elements. In: Greenberg J H (ed.) *Universals of Language*, 2nd edn. MIT Press, Cambridge, MA

Greenberg J H 1978 Introduction. In: Greenberg J H (ed.) *Universals of Human Language.* Stanford University Press, Stanford, CA

Hawkins J A 1983 *Word Order Universals.* Academic Press, New York

Keenan E L 1985 Relative clauses. In: Shopen T (ed.) *Language Typology and Syntactic Description*, vol. 2. Cambridge University Press, Cambridge

Mallinson G, Blake B J 1981 *Language Typology: Cross-linguistic Studies in Syntax.* North-Holland, Amsterdam

Masica C P 1976 *Defining a Linguistic Area: South Asia.* University of Chicago Press, Chicago, IL

Payne D L (ed.) 1990 *Amazonian Linguistics: Studies in Lowland South American Languages.* University of Texas Press, Austin, TX

Typology and Grammar

W. Croft

The term *typology* has a number of different uses in linguistics. 'Typology' is used to refer to the classification of structural types across languages; the study of linguistic patterns or generalizations that hold across languages; and a theoretical and methodological approach that contrasts with other linguistic theories. These three 'definitions' of typology correspond to the classification, generalization, and explanation of grammatical phenomena on a broad empirical base; and so constitute the typological approach to the study of grammar.

1. Basic Issues

The typological approach to grammar contrasts with the generative ('formal') approach in its inductive empirical method, and in its rejection of the *langue-parole* and synchrony-diachrony dichotomies, as will be described below. Nevertheless, these two approaches have some features in common. Both approaches take as their primary object of study the structure of individual languages; both consider the primary question of linguistics to be, 'What is a possible human language?'; and both seek answers to these questions in psychology and ultimately, biology, though in quite different ways. Both approaches make a break with American structuralism, which avoided both universalist hypotheses and language-external (e.g., psychological) explanations.

There are two important methodological issues that must be addressed before doing typological classification, the starting point of a typological analysis: the basis of cross-linguistic comparison and the nature of the language sample.

The problem of cross-linguistic comparison is to identify two grammatical phenomena in two different languages as the 'same' thing, e.g., adjective or subject. In general, this cannot be accomplished on purely formal (structural) grounds, for two reasons. First, variation across languages is too great. For example, the English subjects in (a) *She likes me*, (b) *She ran*, and (c) *She died* will be expressed by two different grammatical relations in languages such as Quiché (Mayan), Lakhota (Siouan), and even Spanish. Moreover, there is no complete agreement among these three languages: Quiché and Spanish treat (b) and (c) alike, but differ on the marking of other transitive subjects, while Lakhota treats (a) and (b) alike. Second, formal definitions are internal to the structural system of a single language, so they cannot be the basis of a language-independent definition. For this reason, typologists generally use language-external definitions of a grammatical phenomenon for cross-linguistic comparison, that is, semantic/pragmatic definitions for morphosyntactic phenomena and phonetic definitions for phonological phenomena; and then study the structural variation in their expression across languages. One can, however, use a 'derived structural' definition of e.g., 'passive' as the verb form in which the object noun phrase in the counterpart active form is expressed as the subject, once the component concepts are externally defined.

The main problem in constructing an adequate language sample is to guarantee that one has historically independent instances of the grammatical phenomenon in question. For example, a study of relative clause formation should guarantee that it is not the case that one of the languages in the sample has borrowed its relative clause structure from another language in the sample, or that the relative clause structures in two languages are descendants of the same structure in a common ancestor. For this reason, geographical and genetic diversity is the most significant factor in obtaining a useful typological sample. However, due to the stability and great age of some grammatical phenomena, it is often difficult to obtain a large sample with complete historical independence of all the instances in the languages sampled. Nevertheless, even historically related grammatical phenomena undergo separate changes once they have diverged, and with the advent of diachronic typology (see below), it is even desirable to compare the separate developments of historically related grammatical structures.

2. Typological Classification

The first step in typological analysis is typological classification. In the nineteenth century there arose a classification of languages based on the morphological structure of words; this is commonly called 'morphological typology.' In its classical formulation (by August Schleicher) languages are divided into three types: (a) isolating: no internal morphological structure to words; (b) agglutinative: words consist of several easily distinguishable morphemes, each indicating a distinct grammatical category; (c) inflexional: words involve complex internal morphological changes, so that morpheme boundaries are obscured or lost. This classification presupposes that there is only a single grammatical parameter on which languages varied, namely, the morphological structure of words; and it is a classification of languages as a whole. This represents the 'individualizing' approach to typological classification: each language is treated as a holistic type, which has its inner form or unity.

The individualizing approach eventually gave way to the 'generalizing' approach, which rejects both of these assumptions. Even the morphological typology of language contains two logically independent parameters, number of morphemes and degree of morphological complexity (allomorphy), and languages can vary independently on both parameters. Later phonological, syntactic and other typological classifications have demonstrated that there are a vast number of linguistically significant typological parameters. Thus, a language does not belong to a single holistic structural type; instead it belongs to a type that consists of values on each of many structural parameters.

Languages themselves also do not make up a single type, because they may contain constructions representing two or more types. For example, English belongs to the genitive-noun word order type by virtue of the clitic *-'s* construction in *Janet's job*, and simultaneously to the noun-genitive word order type by virtue of the prepositional *of* construction in *a window of the car*. Thus, one must say that a construction not a language belongs to a particular linguistic type. Nevertheless, one may still identify one of the constructions as representing the 'basic' construction for the function, e.g. the 'basic' declarative main clause word order. 'Basicness' appears to include high text frequency, productive use, wide grammatical distribution, and lack of specialized semantic or pragmatic connotations.

3. Unrestricted and Implicational Universals

Having made a typological classification of languages, or more precisely the constructions of languages, based on a number of grammatical parameters, one can examine the resulting distribution for cross-linguistic patterns. Typology in the usual sense of the word is the study of those patterns. The generalizations based on these patterns represent constraints on logically possible language types.

The method used to uncover cross-linguistic generalizations is empirical and inductive. The attested types in a sample are assumed to represent the actually existing language types, and the cross-linguistic generalization excludes those types not attested. A sample of extant languages should suffice, if large enough and well distributed, to make the inductive leap from 'unattested language type' to 'nonexistent language type.' Nevertheless, it is often possible to find examples of a language type that should be 'nonexistent' according to a proposed cross-linguistic generalization. Even in these cases, one still has very highly skewed distributions of language types, which itself is a significant fact to be explained; and diachronic typology requires a shift to a probabilistic approach anyway (see below).

The simplest sort of cross-linguistic generalization is the unrestricted universal, such as the universals that all languages have consonants, vowels, nouns, and verbs. Such universals make up a small proportion of the cross-linguistic universals found so far, however. The simplest type of universal that is characteristic of most typological research is the implicational universal, of the form 'If a language has P, then it also has Q,' for example, 'if a language has demonstratives that follow the head noun, then it has relative clauses that also follow the head noun,' or in logical notation, 'NDem ⊃ NRel' and its contrapositive, 'RelN ⊃ DemN.'

Implicational universals differ from unrestricted universals in a number of significant ways. An implicational universal expresses a dependency between two otherwise logically independent grammatical features (in this case, demonstrative position and relative clause position), whereas an unrestricted universal simply restricts possible values on one parameter (e.g., presence versus absence of the category 'verb'). An

implicational universal cannot be verified—or even discovered—by observing only a single language, such as English. One must do a general survey of languages to observe that the language type(s) excluded by the implicational universal, in this case a language in which the demonstrative follows the head noun and the relative clause precedes it, indeed does not exist. In contrast, one can propose ('discover') an unrestricted universal, e.g., that all languages have verbs, simply by inspecting a single language. Finally, an implicational universal does not 'predict' directly what sort of grammatical structure is found in a particular language. For example, the implicational universal given above will not tell one what the order of demonstrative and noun and relative clause and noun are in language X; it only asserts that if the demonstrative follows the noun in language X, then the relative clause is predicted to follow the noun. An unrestricted universal, on the other hand, specifies exactly what is expected to be found: language X will have verbs, nouns, consonants, vowels, etc.

An implicational universal is a low-level generalization over attested language types, and in fact, typologists beginning with Greenberg have sought deeper patterns than those described by simple implicational universals. There is a systematic correlation of word orders found in the antecedent and consequent of implicational universals; this pattern is called 'harmony.' The following correlations have been identified as harmonic patterns (S = subject, O = object, V = verb, Prep = preposition, Postp = postposition, G = genitive, A = adjective, Num = numeral):

'VO type': VO, VS [i.e., VSO], Prep, NG, NA, NNum, NDem, NRel, etc.
'OV type': OV, SV [i.e., SOV], Postp, GN, AN, NumN, DemN, RelN, etc.

However, these clusters do not describe all the possible word order types; for example, the combination DemN and NRel exists. The orders that could occur disharmonically are the 'dominant' types; they are found as the consequents of implicational universals. The major dominant patterns are SV, VO [i.e., SVO], DemN, NumN, NA, and NRel. The following high-level generalization subsumes all of the implicational universals concerning word order: 'A dominant order may always occur, but its opposite, the recessive, occurs only when a harmonic construction is likewise present' (Greenberg 1966a: 97). This is an example of a 'competing motivations' explanation: two conflicting motivations for word order patterns, dominance and harmony, are resolved according to Greenberg's rule. Hawkins (1983) also presents a competing motivation model of word order, using the concepts of modifier heaviness and mobility instead of dominance.

4. Markedness in Typology

Harmony, dominance/heaviness, and mobility are all examples of deeper and more far-reaching cross-linguistic generalizations than possible with an implicational universal of the form 'If P, then Q.' Markedness, a concept adapted from the Prague School, yields another set of cross-linguistic generalizations. Markedness in typology is a property of a grammatical category such that it displays one or more of a cluster of grammatical asymmetries cross-linguistically. The asymmetries also underlie typological hierarchies and prototypes (see below).

These asymmetries can be divided into four major types. The first is structural markedness: the marked member of a category will be expressed by at least as many morphemes as the unmarked member of a category. The simplest case, presence versus absence of a marking morpheme, can be expressed as an implicational universal, for example, 'If the singular is expressed by a nonzero morpheme on the noun, then the plural will be also.' The typical case is illustrated by English, with a nonzero plural *-s* and a zero singular; but the typological generalization also allows language types such as Latvian, with nonzero singular and plural forms, and Mandarin Chinese, with zero for both (i.e., no expression of number in the noun). Typological markedness excludes only the type with a nonzero singular morpheme and a zero plural form. Applied to syntactic constructions, one must generalize so that the marked member has at least as many morphemes as the unmarked one: thus the (agentive) passive construction in English uses three extra morphemes—the copula *be*, the passive participle *-en/-ed*, and the adposition *by*—compared to the unmarked active construction.

The second set of markedness criteria fall under the behavioral markedness type, which can be divided into three subtypes. The unmarked member of a category will have at least as many cross-cutting grammatical distinctions as a marked member. For example, the English singular pronouns *he/she/it* have a cross-cutting gender distinction that the marked plural pronoun *they* does not. This is the inflexional behavioral criterion. Its counterpart in phonology is the lack of cross-cutting phonological features in the marked member. Thus, in many languages, such as English and Haya (Grasslands Bantu), obstruents are unmarked compared to nasals because obstruents have a phonological voicing distinction while nasals do not. Closely related is the distribution of the unmarked member in syntactic (or phonological) environments: the unmarked member is found in a wider range of environments than the marked member. This is the distributional behavioral criterion. Finally, there is cross-linguistic distribution: the unmarked member will occur in language types that the marked member does not occur in. Dominant word order is an example of the cross-linguistic distributional criterion: for example, DemN word order occurs in RelN languages, but the marked (recessive) NDem order does not.

Frequency is another correlate of markedness. The unmarked member will be more frequent than the marked member, both in use (textual frequency) and across languages (cross-linguistic frequency). Greenberg's monograph on markedness (1966b) includes text counts that demonstrate that the unmarked member of a category, e.g., singular number or unglottalized consonant, is the most frequent in texts in a variety of languages. Also, a simple count of the occurrence of an unmarked type in a properly-made sample of languages should reveal that it is the most frequent overall—e.g., DemN word order is more frequent than NDem word order, regardless of associated word order types. The frequency criterion is theoretically significant because it demonstrates that typological properties cut across language structure (*langue*) and language use (*parole*).

In fact, the cross-linguistic distributional and cross-linguistic frequency criteria have a different status than the within-language criteria. The cross-linguistic criteria, used chiefly for word order patterns, do not coincide with the within-language criteria. For example, DemN order may appear to be unmarked by the cross-linguistic criteria, but in an NDem language, DemN order will be less frequent and more restricted (if it exists at all). Also, phonological markedness differs from morphosyntactic markedness in that the latter involves the encoding of concepts while the former does not. For the latter, textual frequency is the proximate causal factor (Greenberg 1966b; Bybee 1985), but for the former, phonetic properties account for both text frequency and distributional behavior. It appears that typological markedness proper is a subtype of a more general pattern of asymmetrical relationships among paradigmatic alternatives (including word order dominance and phonological markedness). However, a fourth criterion for markedness used by the Prague School linguists, the neutral value (i.e., the member of a category found in a context of neutralization), must be excluded from typological markedness. To give one of many counterexamples, the neutral-gender pronoun in colloquial English is the (marked) plural *they*, not an (unmarked) singular form. The neutral-value criterion differs conceptually as well as empirically: it is binary-valued, while the true typological markedness criteria are n-ary valued scalar properties.

5. Hierarchies and Prototypes

The concept of an unmarked member of a grammatical category is an abstraction that subsumes cross-linguistic generalizations based on grammatical structure, inflexion, distribution, and textual and cross-linguistic frequency. These diverse linguistic properties correlate quite consistently across languages. However, few if any grammatical categories fit the mold of binary-valued marked versus unmarked members. Most categories consist of multiple values, and markedness patterns for different categories frequently interact. The concepts of hierarchies and prototypes, defined in typological terms based on the markedness criteria, account for the more complex relations among members of grammatical categories.

A grammatical hierarchy is simply a ranking of members of a grammatical category, such as singular < plural < dual < trial/paucal for number or subject < object < oblique for grammatical relations. These rankings are derived from a 'chain' of implicational universals, such as 'If a language has a trial/paucal form, then it has a dual form; if a language has a dual form, then it has a plural form'; or 'If a verb in a language agrees with an oblique, then it will agree with the object; if a verb agrees with the object, then it will agree with the subject.' The grammatical properties described by these chains of implicational universals are markedness criteria; for example, the evidence given for the number hierarchy is an example of cross-linguistic distributional behavior, and that for the grammatical relations hierarchy is an example of inflexional behavior (ability to trigger verb agreement). Other markedness criteria support typological hierarchies: for example, the Chumash pronominal agreement forms have zero singular, plural *-i*, and dual *-i-s*. Thus, markedness is a relative concept: the plural is marked relative to the singular, but unmarked relative to the dual.

Typological hierarchies are manifested in many different aspects of the grammar of human languages. The number hierarchy is found in noun, adjective, and verbal inflexion. The grammatical relations hierarchy is found in case-marking, agreement, accessibility to relativization, 'promotion' of noun phrases to higher grammatical relations, and coordination-switch reference phenomena. The animacy hierarchy, loosely 1st/2nd person < 3rd person pronoun < human noun < animate noun < inanimate noun, is manifested in case marking, noun inflexions, various types of agreement patterns, promotion, and anaphora.

The grammatical relations hierarchy has attracted particular attention due to the difficulties in defining 'subject' and 'object' for many languages. In particular, many languages distinguish transitive subject ('ergative') on the one hand from intransitive subject-cum-transitive object ('absolutive') on the other in case marking, agreement, and other grammatical phenomena. (There are also a number of languages in which certain intransitive subjects—'active'—behave grammatically like transitive subjects, while the others—'stative'—behave like transitive objects.) Many other languages distinguish the direct object of ditransitive verbs ('secondary object') from the indirect object-cum-direct object of simple transitive verbs ('primary object'). In all of these languages, the absolutive and the primary object generally possess the characteristics of the unmarked category: for example, the absolutive is structurally unmarked compared to the ergative, and the primary object triggers agreement rather than the secondary object. In particular, the absolutive is textually more frequent than the ergative and the primary object is likewise more frequent than the secondary object. In other words, the construction of typological universals does not need to assume that particular grammatical categories such as 'subject' or 'direct object' are universal.

Grammatical relations involve still more complex interactions than hierarchies based on markedness patterns can describe. There are correlations between values on different grammatical categories; these correlations represent a typological prototype category. Typological prototypes can be divided into two related kinds. The first is a cluster of grammatical properties, so that a construction containing all of the properties is a prototypical member of the category. Hopper and Thompson's (1980) analysis of the prototypical transitive construction is the best-known example of the cluster prototype. The prototypical transitive clause has two or more participants, one highly volitional and agentive, the other highly affected and highly 'individuated' (animate, definite, singular, etc.), participating in an irrealis, nonnegative, punctual, bounded process. If a clause is missing one or more of these properties of subject, object, and verb, it will be more marked typologically: that is, the clause may be structurally marked, behaviorally 'defective,' and textually less frequent—or not even a transitive clause in the language. For example, reflexive constructions, in which there are not two clearly distinct participants, are frequently treated as intransitive verbs cross-linguistically. This latter property, exclusion from the category altogether, is not derived from markedness but instead from the psychological theory of prototypes.

The second kind of typological prototype is a markedness reversal, also called 'local markedness' or 'markedness assimilation.' A simple phonological example of a markedness reversal is that for obstruents, voicelessness is unmarked, but for sonorants, voicing is unmarked. Thus, the markedness of the category of voice is reversed for sonorants. A markedness reversal is simply two prototypes that are opposed to each other: the prototypical obstruent is voiceless and the prototypical sonorant is voiced. It appears that the basic grammatical notions of subject/object and noun/verb involve markedness reversals, at least in part. The prototypical subject is highly agentive, animate (in fact, first or second person), and definite, while the prototypical object is highly affected, low in animacy (at least third person, if not nonhuman or inanimate), and low in definiteness. The evidence for this is found in the phenomenon of 'split ergativity.' The prototypical noun is a physical object which is being referred to by the speaker, while the prototypical verb is a transitory process which is being predicated of some entity by the speaker.

6. Functional Motivation and Typology

Implicational universals, markedness, hierarchies, and prototypes represent the most basic types of cross-linguistic patterns discovered by typologists. All of these patterns account for various aspects of phonological and morphosyntactic behavior. In the past two decades, typologists have begun to analyze grammatical structure in terms of external motivation, that is, the typology of the relation between grammatical form and semantic/pragmatic function (Haiman 1985; Bybee 1985). This, along with the dynamicization of typology (see below) represents the search for explanatory concepts outside synchronic cross-linguistic patterns of grammatical structure.

External motivation for grammatical structure can be classified into three general types. The first type is 'economic motivation' (economy), the principle that the most frequently used expression should be expressed using the fewest morphemes. This motivation underlies most markedness patterns, including of course hierarchies and prototypes. The most frequently used forms will be the morphologically shortest (structurally unmarked). Less frequent forms will be longer, lack significant grammatical distinctions (marked inflexional behavior), and be less widely used in the grammar (marked distributional behavior).

Perhaps the most important external motivation to explain the typology of grammatical structure is 'iconic motivation' (iconicity), the principle that the structure of language should, as close as possible, reflect the structure of what is being expressed. Iconic motivation has been explored in depth in two simple cases, polysemy and conceptual distance.

Haiman uses the term 'isomorphism' to refer to the general principle of 'one form, one meaning.' While there are some violations of this principle, most notably the use of zero forms for unmarked categories in the name of economy (an example of competing motivation), the principle is generally adhered to with one significant qualification. This qualification is the existence of polysemy: closely related meanings will employ the same linguistic form, presumably for economic reasons also (otherwise the number of forms would be excessive to learn). In particular, if one finds the same apparently diverse meanings being expressed in a single form across genetically and geographically diverse languages, one must find a semantic analysis that relates those meanings. For example, polarity questions, the antecedent of a conditional, and the topic noun phrase used the same morpheme or construction in typologically diverse sample of languages; Haiman proposes an analysis to demonstrate that in fact these three functions are closely related (all involving the presentation of a topic of some sort). Syntactic polysemy is found as well. For example, in many languages focus constructions, relative clauses, *wh*-questions, and constituent negation are identical or at least very similar; all of these constructions share

the function of foregrounding a referent and backgrounding the remainder of the proposition.

Conceptual distance is reflected in morphosyntactic distance, so that if a language has two constructions that differ only in the grammatical distance between the elements of the construction, then the construction with more closely bound elements will express the conceptually more closely bound relation. For example, the inalienable possession construction, which represents the conceptually very close part-whole or inseparable relations between objects, is grammatically more close than the alienable possession construction, which describes conceptually more distant relations between objects (Haiman 1985). Other examples of iconic motivation based on conceptual distance are that the degree of integration of a complement with its main clause is correlated with degree of control or involvement that the main clause agent exerts over the action encoded by the complement (Givón 1979); and that the closeness of verbal affixes to the verb root reflects the degree of semantic interaction between the verb meaning and the affix's meaning (Bybee 1985). Conceptual distance is a rather simple measurement of grammatical structure, but it has yielded typologically significant results.

A third area in which iconic motivation has been applied with lesser success is in word order: the order of elements should reflect some conceptual ordering of ideas. Although some generalizations seem valid—subjects overwhelmingly precede objects and the antecedent of a conditional precedes the consequent—there appear to be conflicting iconic motivations, namely the principle that 'what is old information comes first, what is new information comes later' and the principle that 'what is at the moment uppermost in the speaker's mind tends to be first expressed' (Haiman 1985: 237–38), whose precise interaction is as yet unclear. Moreover, some 'free word order' languages appear to determine the order of elements through principles other than those used in European languages.

Typologists have observed patterns of competing motivation, between dominance and harmony, economy and iconicity, and even between different iconic principles. However, there are also examples of 'typological conspiracies,' in which apparently unrelated grammatical processes 'cooperate' in different ways in different languages with the same net effect. For example, it has been noted that some languages restrict the ability of noun phrases to be relativized, depending on what grammatical relation the noun phrases has in the relative clause: in some languages only subjects can be relativized, and in other languages only subjects and objects can be relativized. It turns out that those languages which restrict relativization to subjects allow virtually any nonsubject noun phrase to be 'promoted' to subject, and those that restrict it to subject and object allow virtually any oblique noun phrase to be promoted to object (Givón 1979). In addition, it has been noted that many languages with restrictions on relativization but few or no promotional processes, have a secondary relative clause formation strategy associated with the *lower* end of the grammatical relations hierarchy, used for those noun phrases not accessible to the primary strategy. The seeming purpose of these otherwise typologically unusual grammatical processes is to allow any noun phrase to be relativized. This is an example of a typo-. logical conspiracy to satisfy the principle of 'communicative motivation,' namely that a language must be able to express the full communicative range of concepts in one way or another.

7. Diachronic Typology

The typological approach to grammar has simultaneously developed in a different direction, the integration of diachrony into typology. Synchronic typology is the discovery of principles of varying degrees of abstractness to account for the pattern of existing versus nonexistent (or at least extremely rare) language types. A dynamic interpretation of synchronic typological patterns, the dynamicization of a typology, involves the reinterpretation of existing language types as possible stages through which languages can pass, and nonexistent language types as stages that languages never (or almost never) pass through. In dynamicizing a typology, the diachronic typologist attempts to find attested and unattested direct transitions from one stage to another, in order to find the allowable paths of language change.

From a dynamic point of view, language states or stages possess two properties, stability and frequency. Stability represents the likelihood that a language will exit a language state, that is, change out of a language state once it is in it; Hawkins' word order mobility is a measure of stability. An unstable language state will not persist long and therefore will be relatively rare in a sample of the world's languages; conversely, a stable state is likely to be fairly common in the world's languages. Frequency, on the other hand, represents the likelihood that the linguistic type is to occur, that is, how likely a language will enter that state. A frequently occurring language state will be quite widely distributed in a sample of the world's languages; an infrequently occurring state will have a restricted distribution. Thus, frequency and stability of language states can be inferred indirectly through the commonness and distribution of the language states across the world.

An important hypothesis regarding language change in the dynamicization of synchronic typology is the gradualness of the transition from one language state to the next. Languages pass through intermediate stages in which several correlated grammatical features change one at a time, and/or for a given grammatical feature, two constructions, the older one and a newer one, coexist, competing for the same grammatical function. It often turns out that synchronic 'exceptions' to a typological generalization are actually relatively unstable and infrequent stages in a gradual diachronic process of change from one stable state to another. For example, there are some languages in which prepositions are found with genitive-noun order, an 'exceptional' type. Closer examination of these 'exceptions' in one language family, Ethiopian Semitic, revealed that these languages have been changing from the VO to the OV order type, so that there has been a gradual shift in position in a regular sequence: first the adjective, then the genitive, then the possessive pronoun, and finally the adposition. Since the change to all the OV patterns has not yet been completed, synchronically 'exceptional' languages are attested in this family.

This example illustrates two important theoretical shifts represented by diachronic typology. First, there is a shift from the study of possible (and impossible) language states to the study of more and less probable language states, in which certain synchronically 'exceptional' language states are not truly exceptional if they are part of a possible path of language change. Second, the 'deeper' explanations sought by typologists are no longer static or synchronic, but dynamic: 'Synchronic regularities are merely the consequence of [diachronic] forces. It is not so much again that 'exceptions' are explained historically, but that the true regularity is contained in the dynamic principles themselves' (Greenberg 1969: 186). In addition, the existence of variation and change in synchronic language states has led typologists to take a dynamic perspective.

The most significant area of contemporary diachronic typological research is the study of grammaticalization (Traugott and Heine 1991; Hopper and Traugott 1993). Grammaticalization is the process by which lexical items evolve to take on grammatical functions—indication of tense, definiteness, topicality, focus, grammatical relations, etc. Grammaticalization is actually itself a correlation of several different language processes that are more or less synchronized: lexical items evolve phonologically and morphosyntactically as well as functionally when they become grammatical elements. Phonological grammaticalization processes involve the gradual reduction of the phonological size of the former lexical item, and its attachment and phonological adaptation to an associated root. Morphosyntactic processes involve the former lexical item's becoming obligatory, fixed in word order, syntactically bound to an associated root, and fitting into a small paradigm of other grammatical elements. Functional processes involve an as yet ill-understood shift in semantic/pragmatic content of the former lexical item to a more 'grammatical meaning,' and also an expansion of the semantic or functional range of the item.

Practitioners of the typological approach to grammar have attempted to draw together the various strands of typological research—cross-linguistic synchronic patterns, functional motivation, and diachronic typology (see for example Givón 1979, 1984/1991; Haiman 1985). The typological approach views language as an adaptive evolutionary phenomenon. Economic, iconic, and communicative motivation represent adaptive pressures that constrain language structure. Language evolution operates within the space of allowable language states determined by these adaptive pressures. Evolution is a probabilistic process; less-adaptive variants can arise in the population of language states, but shift or disappear over time. A speaker's knowledge of language represents the interaction between grammatical structures 'inherited' (acquired) from the language community—already variable—and the aforementioned adaptive constraints which are also part of linguistic competence.

Bibliography

Bybee J L 1985 *Morphology*. Benjamins, Amsterdam

Comrie B 1989 *Language Universals and Linguistic Typology*, 2nd edn. University of Chicago Press, Chicago, IL

Croft W 1990 *Typology and Universals*. Cambridge University Press, Cambridge

Givón T 1979 *On Understanding Grammar*. Academic Press, New York

Givón T 1984/1991 *Syntax: A Functional-Typological Introduction*, 2 vols. Benjamins, Amsterdam

Greenberg J H 1966a Some universals of grammar with particular reference to the order of meaningful elements. In: Greenberg J H (ed.) *Universals of Grammar*, 2nd edn. MIT Press, Cambridge, MA

Greenberg J H 1966b *Language Universals, With Special Reference to Feature Hierarchies*. Mouton, The Hague (Janua Linguarum, Series Minor 59)

Greenberg J H 1969 Some methods of dynamic comparison in linguistics. In: Puhvel J (ed.) *Substance and Structure of Language*. University of California Press, Berkeley, CA

Greenberg J H 1974 *Language Typology: A Historical and Analytic Overview*. Mouton, The Hague (Janua Linguarum, Series Minor 184)

Greenberg J H, Ferguson C A, Moravcsik E A (ed.) 1978 *Universals of Human Language*, 4 vols. Stanford University Press, Stanford, CT

Haiman J 1985 *Natural Syntax: Iconicity and Erosion*. Cambridge University Press, Cambridge

Hawkins J A 1983 *Word Order Universals*. Academic Press, New York

Hopper P, Thompson S A 1980 Transitivity in grammar and discourse. *Lg* **56**: 251–99

Hopper P, Traugott E C 1993 *Grammaticalization*. Cambridge University Press, Cambridge

Shopen T (ed.) 1985 *Language Typology and Syntactic Description*, 3 vols. Cambridge University Press, Cambridge

Traugott E C, Heine B 1991 *Grammaticalization*, 2 vols. Benjamins, Amsterdam

Typology and Word Order Change

K. Burridge

Because all languages of the world show a range of similarities and differences in their structure, it is possible to set up language types; that is, groups of languages classified according to the features which they have in common and which in turn differentiate them from other languages. This is a 'typological classification.' Typological classifications of this sort have been especially important for historical linguists studying language change by defining parameters for potential change.

At first, the typological approach might seem fundamentally different from research into universals, which concentrates on what characterizes all human language. In effect, however, the typological and universalist approaches are complementary—they share a general interest in identifying the possible and impossible properties of natural language and relationships between these properties. The overlap between them is particularly evident in the area of word order typology and the so-called implicational universals.

1. Word Order Typologies

The typological approach is by no means new. As early as the seventeenth century, European scholars (principally philosophers and linguists) were collecting material which provided the basis for typologies of the eighteenth and nineteenth centuries. These early typological classifications (like those of August and Friedrich von Schlegel) differentiated languages on the basis of their morphological structure. The approach at this time was strongly influenced by Darwin's ideas. Language types were viewed as representing different stages in linguistic evolution, and change was in terms of growth and decay. While these classifications are still useful in the late twentieth century, language typologies have since taken a much less prescriptive approach. Language types are no longer viewed as being better or worse than others. They also concentrate less on morphology and more on syntactic characteristics like basic word order patterns—in particular, the positioning of major sentence constituents like subject, object, and verb, and of phrasal constituents like noun and adjective. This research has revealed that, of all the mathematically possible word order combinations across different phrasal categories, languages utilize surprisingly few and with very different frequencies (see Hawkins 1983). For example, with respect to ordering within major sentence constituents, the majority of the world's languages fall into only three types: subject verb object (SVO), subject object verb (SOV), and verb subject object (VSO). Of these, SVO and SOV are the most and VSO the least frequent. The three other logically possible orders, VOS, OSV, and OVS (i.e., those where the object precedes the subject), are rare. A factor here may be the greater saliency of the subject as the topic of a sentence, which places it more naturally in initial position. This would also explain the strong tendency toward SVO as a favorite alternative order in VSO languages.

Although there are occasions when these shared features are the result of 'genetic relationship,' this does not have to be the case. For example, English shares basic SVO ordering with a number of genetically related languages like Norwegian, French, and Greek, but also with many unrelated languages like Malay, Thai, and Swahili. In the same way, languages belonging to one genetic family can show vastly different word order typologies. Welsh, for example, is related to English, but true to its Celtic origins has a basic word order pattern of VSO.

Typological homogeneity can exist between genetically diverse languages, because over time they have undergone the same sorts of changes. It can also result from 'forced change' or language change through contact (a striking example of this is the shift in Amharic from basic VO to OV type as a result of contact with Cushitic). Unfortunately, it is often difficult to distinguish between this sort of change and a case of parallel but independent change. For example, the increasing VO character of Old English may have been due to the internal dynamics of the language, or contact with French—or it may also be that the contact simply accelerated changes already underway in the language.

Word order typologies such as these assume the viability of categories like subject, verb, object, noun, and adjective as basic linguistic entities of all languages. They also assume the viability of basic word ordering in natural language (Hawkins 1983: ch. 1.5; Comrie 1989: ch. 4). Basic orders do not, however, exclude the possibility of other word orders. For example, though the basic positioning for major sentence constituents in English is SVO, speakers can deviate from this order if they want to highlight a particular part of the message. For example, fronting elements is a common strategy for emphasis, as in *Mango ice-cream I adore!* (OSV). Variation on basic ordering relates to the communicative function of sentences (or the discourse structure), and affects more particularly the positioning of the verb and its arguments and not the ordering within other phrasal categories, like noun phrases and prepositional phrases.

Sometimes it is not easy to decide on a basic word order. For example, the English possessive construction allows two possible orders: noun genitive and genitive noun (*the cover of the book* versus *the book's cover*). Frequency, both in terms of language use and grammar, markedness (for instance, a marked construction may have a specific meaning associated with it), and also historical considerations can help in deciding the question of basicness. Even so, there are still times when these criteria conflict (as in the English possessive construction), and consequently no order emerges as being truly basic (see also Sect. 3.3 on the problem of 'free word order' languages for this approach).

2. Language Change—the Problem of Syntax

Like all aspects of human life, language is constantly changing. Sounds, meanings, vocabulary, and grammatical structure are all in a constant state of flux. This is both natural and inevitable and is not to be regarded as a form of linguistic decay, as is sometimes believed.

As intimated earlier, a language's basic type is just as prone to the process of change. For example, a decline of SOV order in the world's languages is due to the fact that many languages of continental Europe and Africa have undergone a shift from SOV to SVO type. English has completed this shift, and one must look at very old documents to find evidence of this earlier pattern; for example (Old English), *Se here it besæt* 'The (enemy) army it besieged.' Other Germanic languages like Dutch and German, however, retain more of the early SOV character. For example, conservative SOV order remains in these languages as a marker of subordinate clauses: Dutch *Hij zegt dat hij een auto koopt*, literally 'He says that he a car buys.' Main clauses also show evidence of this earlier pattern in what has been termed the 'sentence brace' or 'two-pronged predicate'—only finite verbs have moved to second position in the clause, while all nonfinite verbs remain in final (or near-to-final) position; for example, Dutch *Ik heb een auto gekocht*, literally 'I have a car bought.' Consequently, there is debate as to whether SOV or SVO is the basic word order in these languages.

Until the 1960s, emphasis within historical linguistics was very much on sounds and the way in which they change over time. As a consequence, historical grammar, more particularly syntax, has been a relatively neglected area of study. The problem is that there is simply not the same knowledge about syntax and its workings as there is about sounds. There are also practical problems which make studying sound change easier than syntactic change. For one, the nature of sounds means that they can be listed and, because of the finiteness of their inventories, full descriptions can be gained of lost sound systems, sometimes on the basis of a very limited corpus. This is not the case for syntax, however—no finite corpus of utterances, no matter how large, will provide full descriptions of early syntactic systems. There will always exist gaps in linguists' knowledge, and uncertainty about conclusions made will always be greater for syntax than for phonology.

3. Typology and Word Order Change

Typology, with its natural application to the study of language change, has provided a useful theoretical foundation for research within diachronic syntax. The work of several highly influential researchers is considered below.

3.1 The Contribution of Joseph Greenberg

It was during the early days of generative grammar, but not within its framework, that the American linguist Joseph Greenberg wrote his famous essay 'Some universals of grammar with particular reference to the order of meaningful elements' (1963). This proved to be a turning point in the study of diachronic syntax, in that it provided a useful synchronic framework for a theory of syntactic change to emerge. This approach, and those which it has inspired, use typology and typological universals to account for existing syntactic patterns and their historical development.

Greenberg examined selected grammatical features (for the most part word order patterns) from 30 languages of the world. He divided these languages into the three basic types; SVO, SOV, and VSO. Data in his research showed correlations between certain word order patterns and other grammatical properties. From his findings, he listed 45 implicational universals of the type—'If a language A has feature F1, then (with more than chance frequency) it also has feature F2.' For example, his Universals 3 and 4 read:

Universal 3: Languages with dominant VSO order are always prepositional.
Universal 4: With overwhelmingly greater than chance frequency, languages with normal SOV order are prepositional.

Implicational statements of this sort seek to establish constant relationships between different grammatical features of language. They represent near-universals, tendencies based on those properties which emerge from the data as being the statistically predominant ones, and against which patterns of change may be studied.

3.2 The Contributions of Winfred P. Lehmann and Theo Vennemann

Since the appearance of Greenberg's work, there have been a number of proposals which seek to account for these word order correlations by appealing to the existence of a basic ordering of elements to which all languages naturally conform. The work of two linguists in particular exemplifies this position; namely Winfred P. Lehmann and Theo Vennemann.

Both Lehmann and Vennemann reformulated Greenberg's original classification into only two types: OV and VO. On the basis of his findings, they made one overall generalization which correlated the position of all sentential elements to the relative ordering of the verb and its direct object. Those languages conforming to either OV or VO type in their word order patterns were therefore described as typologically 'consistent' or 'harmonious' and those not typologically 'inconsistent.' A consistent VO language, for example, would show patterns in which the items in the A column below precede those in the B column (consistent OV languages would naturally show the reverse of these patterns):

A	B
verb	object
auxiliary	main verb
modal	main verb
verb	adverb
preposition	noun
noun	demonstrative
noun	genitive
noun	numeral
noun	relative clause
noun	descriptive adjective
comparative adjective	standard of comparison

According to this schema, then, English is an inconsistent VO language by showing some noun phrase patterns harmonious with OV type (the exceptions are relative clauses and prepositional genitives, which *follow* their head nouns). The modern Romance languages are more consistently VO by placing most modifiers after the noun.

Both Vennemann and Lehmann offer structural principles ('the principle of natural serialization' and 'the structural principle of language,' respectively) to account for the correlations which they draw from Greenberg's data. Accordingly, constituents in the A list above are assigned the status of 'operand' and those in the B list the status of 'operator.' Operands and operators correspond to the heads and modifiers (or dependents) of traditional and innovative linguistic theory (for example, in the cross-categories central to X-bar theory).

This, then, is a level of 'pure type.' Pure OV and VO languages represent a consistent implementation of the modifier:head relationship. This then has historical application: the pressure to conform to this basic ordering is viewed as strong enough to initiate change. Accordingly, structural changes are explained teleologically, in terms of movement toward the consistent implementation of these structural principles. The ordering relationship between the syntactic patterns in both the verb phrase and the noun phrase and the fact that they exhibit parallel development is therefore explained by both linguists in terms of direct 'analogy'; that is, the modifier stands in precisely the same relationship to its noun as the complement or object stands to the main verb; that is, modifier:noun: object:verb. According to both linguists, only a change in verb position (brought about through language contact, for example, or the breakdown of a language's case system; see Lehmann (1973) and Vennemann (1974)), can trigger a typological shift. This change will facilitate analogical changes in the ordering of other constituents in the direction of greater consistency of type. There may be considerable lag between this initial change and later 'harmonic' changes in other phrase types. English, for example, has completed a shift from OV to VO, although the noun phrase ordering still remains principally that of modifier:noun. This schema predicts that changes will eventually take place in the noun phrase patterns which will make English typologically more harmonious. Evidence that this is already beginning to happen is the appearance of a new prepositional possessive showing noun genitive order (e.g., *cover of the book*). Noun adjective ordering in French has been interpreted as a similar move towards greater typological harmony. The handful of common-usage adjectives (like *grand* 'large' and *petit* 'small') which appear before the noun and not after are explained as remnants of the OV type which characterized early Romance (see criticism of this position in Sect. 3.3).

This schema offers a means of linking together a number of changes, at the same time giving them meaning by showing them to be part of some overall long-term trend; that is, toward consistency of type. But there are problems, not so much with the typological approach itself, but rather the misuse of it.

3.3 The Misuse of Typology

Greenberg's initial statements were extremely cautious, based only on the data from his sample of 30 languages. For example, on the basis of these data, he found only one verb phrase pattern implicationally related to a noun phrase pattern; namely, the correlation between VSO order and noun adjective order. There is therefore nothing justifying Vennemann's and Lehmann's move to correlate the ordering of *all* sentence constituents to the head/modifier ordering as described above. This correlation has also been interpreted as bidirectional, although Greenberg's initial statements were largely unidirectional. For example, OV order is a good predictor of a case system (Greenberg's Universal 41). However, a case system

does not necessarily predict OV order, nor does the lack of a case system necessarily imply VO order. This reinterpretation of Greenberg's implicational universals is methodologically unsound.

Another major weakness comes from the collapsing of Greenberg's initial three word order types SVO, SOV, and VSO into only OV and VO. The fact is that SVO order is not a reliable predictor for word order arrangements elsewhere, and the conflation of SVO and VSO has severely weakened Greenberg's initially strong correlations. For instance, while there were no exceptions to Greenberg's Universal 17, which correlated VSO order and noun adjective order, there is no clear correlation between VO order and noun adjective order (5 out of 19 cases) or between OV order and adjective noun order (6 out of 11). The main problem is simply that the implicational universals vary considerably in strength. Some correlations, like that between adpositions and verb phrase order, are very strong. Others are comparatively weak.

There is also a problem with the initial trigger for a typological shift. There are a number of languages where changes in the noun phrase have occurred *prior* to any changes in the verb phrase. For example, Germanic changed to preposition noun while it still had OV syntax (as did Latin and Lithuanian). This evidence suggests that it is not only the verb which can motivate change.

Other problems arise when one tries to include flexible or free word order languages in this schema. For example, most Australian languages (like Yulparija and Dyirbal) show extraordinary freedom of word order. Theoretically, it is possible for words (even words belonging to the same notional phrase) to appear in any order with no grammatical significance. While an analysis of discourse may reveal word order preferences based on thematic organization (considerations of topic and focus, for example), it is still not possible in these languages to distinguish a basic word order. Also problematic are languages where functional categories like S and O may not be equivalent to those in other languages (for example, ergative languages), or those which show ellipsis of these categories (for example, languages like Eskimo allow 'missing' subjects). More work needs to be done to accommodate these sorts of languages.

In addition to these specific problems, there are more general questions relating to the approach as a whole, concerning what these sets of near-universals can contribute to an explanatory theory of change; whether it is valid to view 'pure type' as some sort of ideal or goal towards which all languages are seen to strive; and whether showing a change to be part of a drift towards typological consistency constitutes an explanation for the change.

Certain word order patterns do seem compatible, and languages do seem to motivate changes favoring such patterns. This cannot be denied, and even the greatest critics of the approach do not attempt to do so. However, as many critics have pointed out, because the so-called universals are really only statements of likelihood or tendency and therefore only hold for part of the time (that is, they do not meet the requirements of absolute universals or 'laws'), they cannot be used as an explanation. Typological drift has no explanatory force in it per se. Typological universals can themselves never answer the question 'why.' What they can do, however, is give an idea of what constitutes likely and unlikely changes and therefore point to the preferred directions of change. In this way, typological universals can at least provide a weak theory of change (see Harris 1984, who also argues this position).

In fact, because of the unpredictable and inexplicable elements in language, typology may never be able to offer more than this. Because of social, cultural, and psychological factors, languages will never behave 'lawlike,' and this human element will always militate against absolute universals that hold 100 percent of the time. Clearly, a word order shift, like any sort of language change, is going to involve a complex interaction of social, psychological, contextual, internal structural, and geographical factors which can bring about, accelerate, retard, and even reverse changes of a typological drift. As usual, the factors involved are going to be far more numerous than is typically recognized.

Whatever criticism might be leveled at the typological approach, however, it cannot be denied that the pioneering work of Greenberg and the subsequent theories of change provided by linguists like Vennemann and Lehmann have given the necessary basis which had hitherto not existed for the description and evaluation of syntactic change in language, and consequently has encouraged many more studies in this field. This has obviously contributed considerably to an improvement of the original position—one striking example is the work of John A. Hawkins.

3.4 The Contribution of John A. Hawkins

Using a sample of 350 languages, Hawkins (1983) attempts to establish a set of typological universals which are absolute. As with Greenberg's original universals, his are also unidirectional. They also differ from both Vennemann's and Lehmann's universals (and also some of Greenberg's) by relying on implicational relationships between three or more parameters. The following are two examples of his complex implicational statements (Hawkins only uses SOV and VSO as predictors of other word order patterns):

> If a language has SOV word order, and if the adjective precedes the noun, then the genitive precedes the noun; that is, SOV ⊃ (Adj + N ⊃ Gen + N)

> If a language has VSO word order, and if the adjective

follows the noun, then the genitive follows the noun; that is, VSO ⊃ (N + Adj ⊃ N + Gen)

He also proposes four hypotheses which prescribe the way in which word order changes may take place without any violation of his universals. The last of these hypotheses, 'the principle of cross-category harmony' (a weaker version of Vennemann's 'principle of natural serialization') predicts that the more a language departs from harmonic ordering, the rarer the language. Accordingly, shifts in head/modifier patterns (for example, a change in verb position) will be matched by adjustments elsewhere to reintroduce cross-category harmony.

In later work, Hawkins (1990) examines the whole question of these word order universals from a performance perspective. By showing that a number of his cross-categorial ordering regularities arise from innate processing mechanisms, he is able to offer a more explanatory account of these universals. Hawkins's work represents a successful attempt to refine and further clarify the original implicational universals and also find a rationale for them, and has contributed greatly to linguists' understanding of historical change in language.

3.5 The Consequences of Typology for Historical Reconstruction

Typology has important consequences for the reconstruction of past syntactic systems. Unfortunately, because syntactic patterns are not symbols and do not evolve in the same way as sounds, one cannot apply the usual comparative method for reconstruction; diverging syntactic constructs simply do not compare in the same way. Here, typology can help by showing the preferred avenues of change. In this way, linguists can use their knowledge of syntactic types in reconstruction, much like the use made of the understanding of phonological systems. There is a danger, however. In the past, the assumed typological 'purity' of the protolanguage forced reconstructions based not on the comparative evidence available but on what was demanded by the method itself, to the extent that features present in daughter languages were even overlooked if they represented typological inconveniences. Given that a great many of the world's languages are typologically impure, this is a very dangerous practice. However, this is once more a fault in the application of typology, rather than in the approach itself—it is important that typology is used only as a guideline and not as 'an intellectual straitjacket into which the facts...must be fitted, willy-nilly, rightly or wrongly' (Watkins 1976: 306). It follows, however, that as linguists' understanding of typology and typological universals grows, so too will the understanding of typology's role in the reconstruction process for syntax.

Bibliography

Comrie B 1989 *Language Universals and Linguistic Typology.* Blackwell, Oxford

Croft W 1990 *Typology and Universals.* Cambridge University Press, Cambridge

Greenberg J H 1963 Some universals of grammar with particular reference to the order of meaningful elements. In: Greenberg J H (ed.) *Universals of Language.* MIT Press, Cambridge, MA

Harris M 1984 On the strengths and weaknesses of a typological approach to historical syntax. *Current Trends in Historical Linguistics.* Mouton, The Hague

Hawkins J A 1983 *Word Order Universals.* Academic Press, New York

Hawkins J A 1990 A parsing theory of word order universals. *LIn* **21**: 223–61

Lehmann W P 1973 A structural principle of language and its implications. *Lg* **49**: 47–66

Mallinson G, Blake B J 1981 *Language Typology Crosslinguistic Studies in Syntax.* North-Holland, Amsterdam

Vennemann T 1974 Topics, subjects and word order: From SXV to SVX via TVX. In: Anderson J, Jones C (eds.) *Historical Linguistics,* vol. 1. North-Holland, Amsterdam

Watkins C 1976 Towards P–I–E syntax: Problems and pseudo-problems. In: Steever S B, Walker C A, Mufwene S S (eds.) *Papers from the Parasession on Diachronic Syntax.* Chicago Linguistic Society, Chicago, IL

Universals of Language

J. R. Payne

The term 'language universal' is used to describe statements which are true of all languages. Research into language universals has essentially taken place within two frameworks: the Greenbergian framework, in which large samples of languages have been tested at a relatively superficial level of analysis, and the Chomskyan framework, in which a very small sample of languages have been analyzed in greater depth. Both approaches have their advantages and disadvantages: while Greenbergian language universals have statistical validity, an explanation of them is often difficult to find. On the other hand, Chomskyan universals are motivated by the need for explanation, but the sample is invariably not large enough to test whether the claims which are made have any genuine significance. In the future, one may expect to see a fruitful combination of the two frameworks as deeper analysis is combined with the statistical advantages of greater sample sizes.

1. Greenbergian Universals

The term 'Greenbergian Universal' (see *Greenberg Universals*) owes its origin to the 'Memorandum Concerning Language Universals' written by Joseph Greenberg, Charles Osgood, and James Jenkins as an introduction to the report (see Greenberg 1963) on the Dobbs Ferry conference on language universals held in 1961. This memorandum treats language universals as statements of the form:

For all x, if x is a language, then . . .

The simplest form that such a statement can take is that of an 'unrestricted' universal:

For all x, if x is a language, then x has property P.

Typical unrestricted universals concern the status of basic categories as universal properties of language, for example, the existence in all languages of a phonological distinction between vowels and consonants, or a grammatical distinction between nouns and verbs. Some putative basic categories are now known not to be universal: for example, in many languages the words corresponding to English adjectives can be argued to be either nouns or verbs (Dixon 1982).

A 'statistical' universal takes the form:

For all x, if x is a language, then the probability that x has property P is greater than the probability that x has property Q.

A typical example is the statement that a language is more likely to have at least one nasal stop (e.g., a segment like /m/ or /n/) than to have no nasal stops at all. The presence of nasal stops can very nearly be stated as an unrestricted universal, but the existence of a few languages without nasal stops forces a probabilistic statement.

The greatest attention within the Greenbergian framework has been devoted to 'implicational' universals. A 'universal' (or 'exceptionless') 'implication' takes the form:

For all x, if x is a language, then if x has property P, x has property Q.

A 'statistical implication' (referred to by Greenberg, Osgood, and Jenkins as a 'statistical correlation'), then has the form:

For all x, if x is a language, then if x has the property P, the probability that x has property Q is greater than the probability that x has property R.

Typical examples of implicational universals are word-order universals relating the dominant order of basic sentence elements (subject, verb, object) to the order of other constituents. For these purposes, languages are usually divided into V-final languages (which have dominant word order SOV), SVO languages, and V-initial languages (which have the dominant word order VSO or VOS). On the basis of a pioneering sample of 30 languages, Greenberg (1963) proposed a set of word-order universals which have greatly influenced subsequent research. However, while many of these universals were initially formulated as universal implications, exceptions have almost invariably been found as larger and larger samples of languages have been analyzed. It is not implausible, indeed, that all implicational universals will turn out to be statistical.

A statement of word-order universals based on a sample of 603 languages (Dryer 1991) includes the following correlations:

	V-final	SVO	V-initial
Noun-Postposition	0.96	0.14	0.09
Verb-Tense/aspect auxiliary	0.94	0.21	0.13
Genitive-Noun	0.89	0.59	0.28

These figures, computed using an algorithm which controls for the most severe kind of genetic bias in the selection of the sample, are to be interpreted as the probabilities of a language with the given dominant word order (V-final, SVO, V-initial) having the order of elements indicated in the left-hand column: for example, a randomly chosen V-final language has a 96 percent chance of having the order noun-postposition rather than preposition-noun, a 94 percent chance of having the tense/aspect auxiliary follow the main verb rather than precede it, and an 89 percent chance of having a genitive phrase precede rather than follow the noun which it modifies. On the other hand, V-initial languages are more likely to have the opposite orders: preposition-noun, tense/aspect auxiliary-main verb, and noun-genitive phrase. SVO languages turn out for the most part to pattern with V-initial languages (the unpredictability of the noun-genitive order being one of a few notable exceptions).

It is interesting to note that a few of the universals originally proposed by Greenberg (1963) cannot even be considered to be statistical implications when larger samples are taken into consideration. There turns out, for example, to be no significant correlation between dominant word order and the order of adjective and noun, or the order of demonstrative and noun. The figures from Dryer (1991) are as follows:

	V-final	SVO	V-initial
Adjective-Noun	0.40	0.41	0.34
Demonstrative-Noun	0.68	0.74	0.58

While the large samples which are being analyzed at the time of writing are able to show which universals have statistical validity, explaining the valid universals is a difficult task. A number of factors have been suggested involving a variety of domains (gram-matical, semantic, pragmatic, psycholinguistic, etc.). Perhaps the most significant type of explanation can be found at a diachronic level: Greenbergian universals tend to hold because language categories develop historically in fixed patterns: for example, the category of adposition (preposition or postposition) can develop from the category of verb by a process of grammaticalization (the English preposition *regarding* is an example of this). It is natural, therefore, that the order of verb and object noun should coincide with the order of adposition and noun. However, checking the validity of diachronic (and other) explanations of Greenbergian universals is a formidable task which in the early 1990s had hardly begun.

2. Chomskyan Universals

Within the Chomskyan framework, the goal of linguistic theory is to characterize I-language, the internalized knowledge incorporated in the brain of individual native speakers. Part of this knowledge, a set of linguistic principles known as 'universal grammar,' is claimed to be an innate property of the human mind. The properties of particular languages then derive from the setting of various 'parameters' permitted by the principles of universal grammar. This overall approach to language is known as the 'principles and parameters' approach (see *Generative Grammar: Principles and Parameters*).

As a simple illustration of the principles and parameters approach, one can take the ways in which word-order variation between languages is determined. According to Ouhalla (1991), the distinction between VSO and SVO word order is closely related to a parameter called the AGR/TNS (agreement/tense) parameter. In TNS-initial languages, the basic sentence structure has the tense element higher than the agreement element (Fig. 1a), while in AGR-initial languages the agreement element is higher than the tense element (Fig. 1b). The two structures share the proposed universal principle that all categories, whether they be lexical categories like V (verb) or functional categories like TNS (tense) and AGR (agreement), have a phrasal projection (VP, TNSP, and AGRP) with a SPEC (specifier) position. The specifier position of VP is the initial position of the subject in all languages. Universal principles of movement then permit the verb to move up the tree into the TNS and AGR positions, acquiring tense and agreement affixes as it does so, while the subject moves from specifier position to specifier position until it ends up in the 'canonical' subject position, the specifier of AGRP where it can trigger verb-agreement. The result of these movements in a TNS-initial language like Berber is that the subject ends up in a position where it follows the verb (Fig. 2a), while in an AGR-initial language like French, the canonical subject position will follow the verb (Fig. 2b).

One consequence of a deeper analysis of word-order

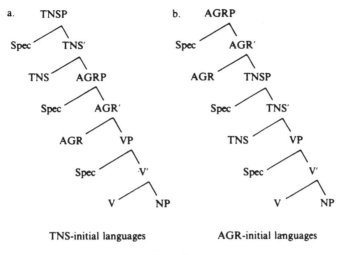

TNS-initial languages   AGR-initial languages

Figure 1.

of this kind is that it permits further predictions, akin to Greenbergian implicational universals, about correlations between SVO- and VSO-dominant word orders and other properties of the languages under consideration. For example, the presence of a higher specifier position (specifier of TNSP) into which the subject might subsequently move suggests that SVO should always be an alternative order in languages which have dominant VSO order (a correlation originally suggested by Greenberg on purely empirical grounds). In the case of SVO languages, however, no higher position is available and hence no alternative word order is possible. Another prediction is that VSO- and SVO-dominant word orders will correlate with the order in which tense and agreement morphemes attach to the verb. In VSO (TNS-initial) languages, the order of morphemes within the verb should be TNS–AGR–V or V–AGR–TNS, while in SVO (AGR-initial) languages the order should be AGR–TNS–V or V–TNS–AGR. This is correct in Berber and French; however, in this case, it is simply not known to what extent the correlation genuinely holds. Exceptions such as the Celtic languages, which have VSO word order without SVO as an alternative, and which have V–TNS–AGR as the order of verbal morphemes, require the postulation of alternative analyses of word order which weaken the predictive power of the original analysis.

A radical rethink of the 'principles and parameters' model has resulted in the 'minimalist program' (Chomsky 1995; see *Generative Grammar: The Minimalist Program*), in which the representation of each sentence consists solely of a phonetic form (PF) and a logical form (LF). The central component of the human language computation system is the com-

putation which assembles lexical items and particularly their associated grammatical and semantic features into LF representations, which are interpreted at the 'conceptual–intentional' interface of the human mind. Given the assumption that interpretation should be maximally simple, the conjecture is made that, across languages, LF representations should be as similar as typological variation permits, and indeed unique if possible. In this model, the whole computational procedure which assembles logical forms essentially represents what is universal about human language. Language variation arises from the procedure which derives PF representations. At some point in the LF computation there is an operation called 'Spell-Out' which applies to the structure already formed and strips away those elements relevant only to PF. For example, in an SVO language like French, Spell-Out applies at the point at which subject and verb have both been moved to higher positions in the tree, whereas in a VSO language like Berber, Spell-Out applies at a point where the verb alone would have moved to a higher position.

It is worth noting that the requirement that logical forms be the same across languages means that word-order variation cannot be derived, as in Ouhalla's system, by arranging functional categories in different hierarchical positions: instead, the functional categories must be hierarchically arranged in the same way across languages, and what differs is whether the movement of items like subject and verb takes place overtly, before Spell-Out, or covertly as part of the LF computation. There is also no correlation predicted between word-order and the morphological properties of verbs.

The full consequences of the minimalist program

357

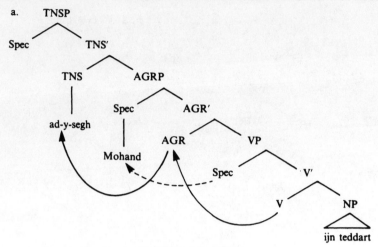

ad -   y - segh Mohand ijn teddart
FUT - 3ms buy Mohand a   house
'Mohand will buy a house'

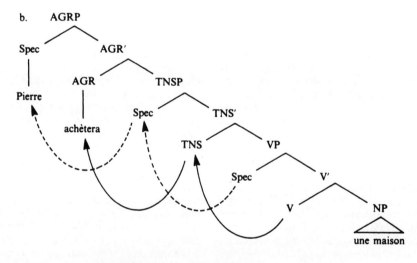

Pierre achèt - er - a   une maison
Pierre buy - FUT - 3s a   house
'Pierre will buy a house'

Figure 2.

for research into language universals are at the time of writing still being worked out. Subtle and new predictions are made by the model, and it remains to be seen whether they have typological validity.

Bibliography

Chomsky N 1988 *Language and Problems of Knowledge*: *The Managua Lectures*. MIT Press, Cambridge, MA

Chomsky N 1995 *The Minimalist Program*. MIT Press, Cambridge, MA

Comrie B 1989 *Language Universals and Linguistic Typology: Syntax and Morphology*, 2nd edn. Blackwell, Oxford

Croft W 1990 *Typology and Universals*. Cambridge University Press, Cambridge

Dixon R M W 1982 *Where Have All the Adjectives Gone? and Other Essays in Syntax and Semantics*. Mouton, The Hague

Dryer M S 1991 SVO languages and the OV:VO typology. *JL* **27(2)**: 443–82

Greenberg J H (ed.) 1963 *Universals of Language: Report of a Conference Held at Dobbs Ferry, New York, April 13–15, 1961.* MIT Press, Cambridge, MA

Ouhalla J 1991 *Functional Categories and Parametric Variation.* Routledge, London

Payne J R 1990 Language universals and language types. In: Collinge N E (ed.) *An Encyclopaedia of Language.* Routledge, London

Valency and Valency Grammar

David J. Allerton

'Valency' (also known as 'valence,' especially in the USA) is the name given in various syntactic theories (such as valency grammar, dependency grammar, and some kinds of functional grammar), to a particular kind of dependency property of lexical items. This kind of lexico–syntactic property involves the relationship between, on the one hand, the different subclasses of a word-class (such as verb) and, on the other, the different structural environments required by those subclasses, these environments varying both in the number and in the type of elements. Valency is thus seen as the capacity a verb (or noun, etc.) has for combining with particular patterns of other sentence constituents, in a similar way to that in which the valency of a chemical element is its capacity for combining with a fixed number of atoms of another element (for example, one in the case of monovalent hydrogen or sodium, two in the case of bivalent oxygen or calcium, etc.). Such information is vital for language learners but was never adequately presented in traditional grammars and dictionaries.

1. The Basic Idea of Valency

Although verbs, for instance, in most languages share syntactic features of a very basic kind, and often inflectional ones too, they differ radically in the number of accompanying noun phrases, prepositional phrases, etc. they require and/or permit (such as subjects, (prepositional) objects, etc.). (Points in the following discussion will be exemplified mainly from English and French, but they should be taken as having more general validity.)

In English the verbs *stumble, jolt,* and *thrust* occur in distinctive environments in sentences like *Alfred stumbled, Alfred jolted the door,* and *Alfred thrust the key into the lock,* with the result that putting one of these verbs into the distinctive syntactic context of one of the others gives an ungrammatical sequence like **Alfred stumbled the door,* or **Alfred jolted the key into the lock.* Such restrictions mean that verbs need to be subclassified according to their syntactic potential, a fact recognized by traditional grammar in the (inadequate) division into transitive and intransitive verbs, and in transformational grammar in the

notion of 'strict subcategorization,' or selectional properties in the lexicon. The special contribution of valency grammarians to the study of this type of subselection has been a thorough investigation of just how much is determined by the verb (or noun, etc.), and of how different potentials of the same verb (e.g., *Alfred pushed/—pushed the key/—pushed the key into the lock*) are related.

2. Varying Views of Valency

The invention of the notion of *valency* (French *valence,* German *Valenz,* Dutch *valentie*), is often credited to Lucien Tesnière, whose *Esquisse d'une syntaxe structurale* appeared in 1953, but whose main work, *Eléments de syntaxe structurale* was only published posthumously in 1959. The notion had, however, been clearly expounded by A. W. de Groot in his Dutch work, *Structurele syntaxis* (1949), and is even hinted at by Karl Bühler in an oft-quoted remark from his *Sprachtheorie* (1934), to the effect that '...words of a particular word-class open up around them one or several "empty places," which have to be filled by words of certain other word-classes' (1934: 173).

It is nevertheless preeminently Tesnière's notion of valency that has been studied and developed in continental Europe, especially Germany, since the 1960s. On the one hand valency has been integrated with 'dependency theory' by such scholars as J. Ballweg, U. Engel, B. Engelen, H.-J. Heringer, J. Kunze, H. Schumacher, and H. Vater; on the other it has been applied to the detailed description of, most notably, German by G. Helbig and the Leipzig school, but also of English (D. J. Allerton, R. Emons, and T. Herbst), and French (W. Busse and J.-P. Dubost). (For a historical survey up to the mid-1970s, see Korhonen 1977.) The following review of the problems of valency theory will take Tesnière's proposals as a starting point.

3. Tesnière's Approach

Valency can be incorporated into a functional type of constituency grammar (involving relationships between the subcategorization of neighboring constituents), but for Tesnière it was one aspect of dependency grammar. His semantically based syntax is concerned with establishing the hierarchy of word 'connexions' within a sentence, which make up the structural order of words (as opposed to their linear order). The structural order of each sentence is given in terms of a 'stemma,' a two-dimensional display, in which the top-to-bottom dimension represents a series of relationships between 'governors' (or 'heads,' French *régissants*) above and 'dependents' (French *subordonnés*) below. Typically in a 'governor-dependent relationship' the governor may occur without the dependent but not vice versa, and the governor provides the central semantic element whereas the dependent only represents a modification of this.

Considering the partial structural stemma of (1a) in Fig. 1, a number of points in Tesnière's account can be appreciated: first, the governor-dependent relationship can operate at different levels (with *old* acting as dependent of *the grammarian* but as governor of *very*); second, one governor (like *the grammarian*), can have more than one dependent (*old* and *French*, in this case) but not vice versa; third, an 'empty word' like *the* can combine with a 'full word' like *grammarian* to form a single 'nucleus' (marked with a so-called 'circle'), that is, a single point on the stemma. Each governor is said to act as a 'node' (French *noeud*) for all of its direct and indirect dependents, so that *the grammarian* acts as a node for the whole of the stemma of (1a) in Fig. 1.

In a typical sentence, like that of (1b) in Fig. 1, Tesnière sees the main verb as the 'central node' (*noeud des noeuds*). The verb achieves this central role through its high position in the hierarchy of connexions but also through its ability to determine the number and variety of its dependents. But the question of how many dependents a verb has is no simple matter. In fact Tesnière distinguishes two types of dependent for verbs, to which he gives the labels *actants* and *circonstants*. From a semantic point of view the *actants* represent the participants, while the *circonstants* represent the setting and incidental details of the process or state expressed by the verb, the whole sentence portraying a mini-drama. In the example of (1b), where *offered* represents the process, *Alfred*, (*that*) *Bible*, and *to Charles* would be *actants*, while *repeatedly*, *in Strasbourg*, and *on Tuesday* would be *circonstants*.

4. An Essential Distinction: *Actants* versus *Circonstants*

Everything so far noted about Tesnière's views has been a matter of general dependency theory, but the distinction between *actants* and *circonstants* is distinctively the preserve of valency theory. *Actants* belong to the valency of individual verb types, whereas *circonstants* are in principle potential dependents in any sentence, regardless of the verb. Thus the con-

stellation of *actants* represented in (1b) is characteristic of one subclass of English verbs that includes not only *offer* but also *give*, *lend*, *refuse*, *sell*, *send*, and a couple of dozen others.

In (1b) *Alfred*, *that Bible*, and *to Charles* would be termed by Tesnière first, second and third *actant* respectively, and these terms correspond to what in English grammar are normally called subject, (direct) object, and indirect object respectively. These are the only elements that Tesnière recognizes as *actants* in active sentences, which is unfortunate, because many prepositional phrases are equally essential to the verb, such as the prepositional object *on Barbara* in *Alice relied on Barbara*, and even purely adverbial phrases are required by certain verbs, such as *live* (*at home*, etc.), *last* (*two hours*, etc.) or *thrust*, which, as noted earlier, needs both an object and a specification of place.

The subclass of verbs that includes *offer*, *give*, etc. is described as 'trivalent,' because its members require three *actants*; the same could be said of the subclass of *thrust*, *put*, etc., although Tesnière did not recognize this. Ordinary transitive verbs like *jolt* or *like*, *kill*, etc., which merely require a subject and a direct object, are termed 'bivalent' (or 'divalent'); and the same could be said of copular verbs like *be*, *seem*, or *become* that take an adjectival or nominal predicative (complement) such as *beautiful* or *a beauty*. Finally, ordinary intransitive verbs like *stumble* or *deteriorate*, *sneeze*, etc. are described as 'monovalent' (for 'zero-valent' (= 'avalent') verbs, see Sect. 7).

By contrast with *actants*, the adverbials of (1b) are not relevant to valency classification. Thus *repeatedly*, an adverbial of frequency, *in Strasbourg*, a positional adverbial of place, and *on Tuesday*, a punctual adverbial of time, could all just as well have occurred with the different verb subclasses represented by *stumble*, *jolt*, and *thrust*, in fact with any verb at all. Tesnière (1966: 125) mistakenly insists that such adverbials are unlimited in number (by contrast with the fixed number of *actants*), but the essential point is their universality, their freedom to occur in any sentence.

Through the history of valency theory and grammatical theories such as transformational grammar (cf. Baker 1989: 266–67), and systemic grammar (cf. Halliday on 'participant roles and circumstantial roles'), various technical terms have been used to refer to the distinction between these two kinds of dependent of a governor (or head). These are listed in (1c) in Fig. 1. For clarity's sake the terms 'verb elaborator' and 'free modifier' will henceforth be used for the post-Tesnièrian equivalents of *actant* and *circonstant*. (Although the term complement is commonly used in the sense of elaborator, it has the disadvantage that for traditional grammarians and many modern ones it has a quite different meaning and may exclude the subject, which the terms elaborator and *actant* never do.)

(1a)

Stemma for *the very old French grammarian* (after Tesnière)

(1b)

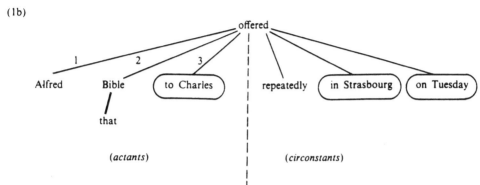

Stemma for *Alfred repeatedly offered that Bible to Charles in Strasbourg on Tuesday* (after Tesnière)

(1c)

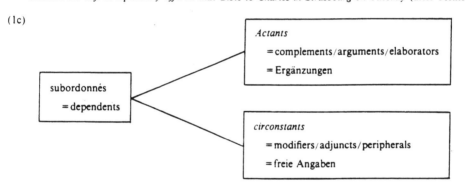

Figure 1. Stemmas and types of dependent.

Whatever the terminology, there is a consensus about the need for a distinction between elaborators and free modifiers; but there are certain problems associated with it. Clearly Tesnière oversimplified matters by insisting that, in principle, elaborators (*actants*), were essentially nominal in form and semantically necessary to the verb, while free modifiers (*circonstants*) were adverbial in form (including prepositional phrases), and semantically not required by the verb. German valency theorists, such as Helbig, Heringer, and Herbst, have proposed tests for distinguishing the two kinds of dependent. Helbig, for instance, suggested that in sentences like the following:

Alice ate the sandwich in the train. (1)

Alice put the sandwich in the fridge. (2)

the status of the adverbial phrases differs partly because *in the train* is omissible while *in the fridge* is not, but also because the first phrase, but not the second, has regularly corresponding sentences of the form:

Alice was in the train when she ate the sandwich. (3)

What Alice did in the train was $\begin{smallmatrix}(to)\,eat\\she\,ate\end{smallmatrix}$ a sandwich. (4)

These correspondences to related sentences seem to indicate that *in the train* in (1) is a free modifier or 'adjunct,' whereas *in the fridge* in (2), though an adverbial, is verb elaborator, just like the earlier examples of obligatory adverbials with the verbs *live*, *last*, and *thrust*.

361

All obligatory elements are therefore verb elaborators, but this does not mean that all optional elements are free modifiers. Even Tesnière only suggested that elaborators (*actants*), are 'often indispensable to complete the sense of the verb' (1966: 128). Helbig, in fact, proposes a three-way division into 'obligatory elaborators,' 'optional elaborators,' and free modifiers ('*obligatorische/fakultative Ergänzungen, freie Angaben*'). The following examples suggest the need for an even more subtle analysis:

Alfred was editing the play. (5)

Alfred was watching [the play]. (6)

Alfred was reading (the play). (7)

Alfred was idling. (8)

The first three have *the play* as the object of the verb and therefore as a potential part of its valency; but it is only in the first sentence that the object is obligatory. In both the second and the third sentences *the play* may be omitted, but under different conditions: whereas in (6) the objectless version of the sentence always requires the listener to identify the thing watched from what is evident in the context, in (7) the objectless sentence leaves the thing read totally open as a matter of no immediate interest (cf. Allerton 1982: 68–70). Thus while the optional object is clearly part of the valency of *watch* in all its uses, the verb *read* appears to have two different valencies, only one of them involving an object. In (8), finally, no object is possible with the unequivocally intransitive verb *idle*; an object can therefore be no part of its valency. This truism suggests a useful general test: if an element, such as an object noun phrase, can only be added to certain verbs and not to others, then it participates in verb valency, in contrast to, say, a time adverbial like *yesterday* or *today*, which can be freely added to any sentence (given an appropriate tense form). The test of insertion, rather than that of omission, is therefore most useful for distinguishing elaborators from free modifiers.

5. The Diversity of Elaborators

Further tests are needed for deciding what kinds of elaborator need to be distinguished. A substitution test, for instance, is useful in assessing combinations of verb and prepositional phrase. All the prepositional phrases in the following sentences are omissible elaborators, and yet they do not all have the same status:

Alice listened to the big waves. (9)

Alice concentrated on the big waves. (10)

Alice swam to the big waves. (11)

Alice floated on the big waves. (12)

A comparison of the first two sentences (9–10) shows not only that the preposition is selected by the verb but even that no other preposition is possible without a change in the nature of the combination; the prepositional phrase is therefore some kind of prepositional object (a category not allowed for by Tesnière but standard in German valency grammar). The prepositional phrases in (11) and (12) are, however, different for a number of reasons: first, the preposition can be replaced with a range of other prepositions to give a series of regular semantic contrasts (*to → into, towards, under*, etc.; *on → over, near, behind*, etc.); second, while the prepositional phrases of (11) and (12) demonstrate their place-adverbial nature through their capacity for being preceded by particles like *right*, those of (9) and (10) reject this possibility; finally, the latter phrases show their partly nominal nature through their elicitation with a *What*-+preposition question, as compared with the *Where* (*...to*) question typical of the adverbials of (11) and (12).

These and similar criteria have been referred to by valency grammarians establishing the various possible elaborators of verbs. It has become clear that these include not only noun phrases but also prepositional phrases and adverbs. They also include adjective phrases, as in the first two (13–14) of the following sentences:

Alfred kept fit. (13)

Alfred remained fit. (14)

Alfred remained an athlete. (15)

Alfred insulted an athlete. (16)

The first three of these sentences illustrate the pattern of a verb with what is in traditional grammar called a complement but in most modern works is referred to as a 'predicative' (following Jespersen). Most typically this is an adjective phrase, as in (13) and (14), but where it is a noun phrase, as in (15), this may generally be replaced with an adjective phrase. One way in which predicatives differ from objects is in their non-acceptance of 'clefting,' with the result that **It was an athlete that he remained* is not a possible sentence, while *It was an athlete that he insulted* is perfectly natural.

Clearly predicatives and objects are noun phrases with rather different functions, and it can be argued that function is a vital ingredient in the specification of elaborators, particularly in a noncase language like English. 'Passivization' of a sentence, in particular the moving of an active object to subject position in the corresponding passive (e.g., changing (16) above to *An athlete was insulted by Alfred*), can play a part in evaluating such functions. In a language like German, on the other hand, it might be sufficient to define elaborators with such labels as accusative object, dative object, prepositional object, etc. and regard the predicative as nominative kind of object, since

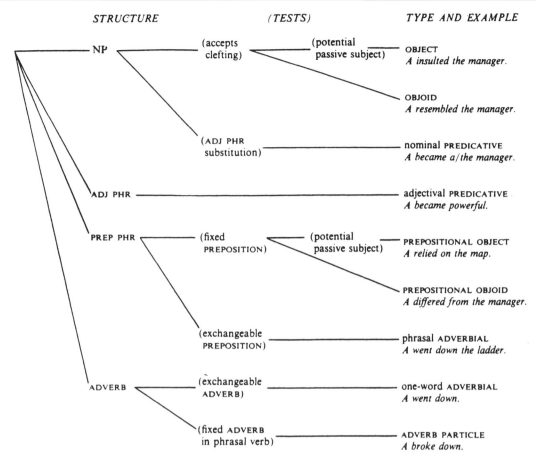

STRUCTURE (TESTS) TYPE AND EXAMPLE

NP — (accepts clefting) — (potential passive subject) — OBJECT
A insulted the manager.

OBJOID
A resembled the manager.

(ADJ PHR substitution) — nominal PREDICATIVE
A became a/the manager.

ADJ PHR — adjectival PREDICATIVE
A became powerful.

PREP PHR — (fixed PREPOSITION) — (potential passive subject) — PREPOSITIONAL OBJECT
A relied on the map.

PREPOSITIONAL OBJOID
A differed from the manager.

(exchangeable PREPOSITION) — phrasal ADVERBIAL
A went down the ladder.

ADVERB — (exchangeable ADVERB) — one-word ADVERBIAL
A went down.

(fixed ADVERB in phrasal verb) — ADVERB PARTICLE
A broke down.

Figure 2. Types of English phrasal elaborators (excluding the subject) for bivalent verbs (after Allerton 1982).

passivization is not limited to sentences with any one kind of object (though, admittedly, only the accusative object can become the passive subject). One view of the total range of English verb elaborators other than the subject is given for bivalent verbs in Fig. 2.

6. The Special Status of Subjects

The range of English verb elaborators displayed in Fig. 2 expressly excludes the subject. But, as noted above, valency grammarians differ from other grammarians in seeing the subject not as standing apart from the predicate or verb phrase but rather as standing alongside the object as an elaborator. As Tesnière puts it (1966: 109): '... *du point de vue structural... le sujet est un complément comme les autres*'; but this is something of an oversimplification.

The subject has a special place as regards inflexional morphology. In languages that have grammatical case frequently there is a case such as nominative that is selected regardless of the lexical verb used, whereas verbs may govern objects in at least two different cases

(as in German or Russian). As for the verb's own inflexions, these commonly agree with the number, person, etc. of the subject but not the object, whereas the reverse never obtains. Languages with an ergative case, like Basque, are slightly different in these two respects.

In terms of syntactic form subjects, first, have greater positional prominence in the sense that, in the absence of a specially marked theme, the subject occurs typically as the first noun phrase in the sentence—a feature shared by SOV, SVO, and VSO languages, that is, well over 90 percent of the world's languages. Second, as regards syntactic dependence for occurrence, the subject normally has a higher priority than the object, in the sense that with all verbs or (depending on the language) the vast majority of them a subject is obligatory, while an object is only required by a proportion of verbs (transitive ones). It is of course true that many languages—so-called 'prodrop languages' like Spanish, Italian, or Japanese—allow the subject to be omitted when it is

363

identifiable from the linguistic or situational context (e.g., Spanish *vino* 'he/she/it came'); but these languages further allow the objects of many verbs to be omitted with no requirement of contextual recoverability (just like English *read*, discussed above, cf. Spanish *leyó* 'he/she/it read (something)'), and of course purely intransitive verbs (like Spanish *venir* 'come') reject objects altogether.

Finally, the subject (but not the object) has a textual role in being the typical sentential theme, one often carried forward from previous sentences, and is often phonologically marked as such (in English, for instance, often through a separate intonation unit). On the whole, then, subjects stand apart from other verb elaborators and need to be accorded a special status vis-à-vis the verb; but they are elaborators nonetheless.

7. Levels of Analysis

The above discussion of subjects and objects partly presupposes a clear definition of these categories. But this is a complex issue, in which much hinges on the relationship between transitive active sentences and passive sentences as well as sentences with other formats. Consider a pair of sentences like:

Alice attacked Barbara. (17)

Barbara was attacked by Alice. (18)

According to most criteria (position, agreement, obligatoriness, for instance) *Alice* is the subject of (17), whereas *Barbara* is the subject of (18) despite the virtual synonymy of the two sentences. Tesnière accepts such an analysis but notes that the subject of the passive, *Barbara*, has the same semantic role ('patient' or 'sufferer' of the verbal action) as the object of the active sentence; whereas the subject of the active sentence, *Alice*, has the same semantic role ('agent') as the passive agentive phrase, *by Alice*, which he terms 'counter-subject.' What Tesnière fails to note is that these semantic roles are not valid for all active and passive subjects, objects, and counter-subjects; rather it is a matter of the semantic valency requirements of individual verbs, as exemplified by the similar correspondences observable in the following sentences:

Alice liked Barbara. (19)

Barbara was liked by Alice. (20)

Alice pleased Barbara. (21)

Barbara was pleased by Alice. (22)

Thus, while in the first two sentences (19–20) with *liked*, the active object and the passive subject, *Barbara*, agree in being the causer or stimulus of the emotion described by the verb, in the last two sentences (21–22) with *pleased*, it is the active subject and passive counter subject, (*by*) *Alice*, that have this kind

of role. There is a similar exchange of syntactic functions between the *liked* sentences and the *pleased* sentences for the other semantic role of 'mental experiencer.' So while precise semantic roles are determined by the meaning of individual verbs (cf. also *defeat* and *lose* (*to*)), there is, given sentences containing any particular verb, a crucial correspondence between the syntactic functions of the active and the passive format of related sentences, and therefore a need to recognize a level of analysis independent of and intermediate between superficial subjects and objects on the one hand and purely semantic roles on the other. This is the level of deep or underlying subjects and objects.

A further reason for recognizing this underlying level of description is the behavior of certain meteorological verbs, as exemplified by English *It was raining*, French *Il pleuvait*, and Spanish *Llovía*. In Spanish (and other prodrop languages), it is impossible to have a subject with such verbs in their normal use, and the verb *llover* can be said to be zero-valent (or 'avalent,' to use Tesnière's term). In English and French the words *it* and *il* respectively fulfil the requirements discussed above to qualify as superficial subjects; but such a subject has no clear semantic role and is not replaceable (by *the weather*, etc.), and it seems that it may simply be part of the required surface structure for English and French sentences without corresponding to a true valency subject. For the corresponding German form *Es regnet* the situation appears to be slightly different, because sentences without a (nominative) subject do occur (e.g., *Mich friert* 'Me is freezing = I am freezing,' *Mir ist kalt* 'To-me is cold = I am cold,' *Mir wurde geholfen* 'To-me was helped = I was helped'). (NB The initial pronoun in these sentences is the theme but not the subject.) It could therefore be argued that, since this empty German *es* is not required by any general rule of sentence structure but is demanded by such meteorological verbs, it is a required (though empty) elaborator.

A summary of the relationships between valency functions and surface form in English meteorological sentences, ordinary intransitive and transitive sentences, both active and passive, is given in Fig. 3. Trivalent verbs of the indirect object type discussed (like *offer* and *give*), also appear in two formats in English, as exemplified by:

Alfred handed that Bible to Charles. (23)

Alfred handed Charles that Bible. (24)

These two formats can be regarded as variant realizations of the same valency pattern, with the indirect object appearing either after the object and with a preposition (as in (23)) or before it and without a preposition (as in (24)).

8. Reflexive and Causative Verb Patterns

Rather different in its valency implications is the kind of obligatorily reflexive verb exemplified by *absent*

Sentence with:	Valency gap	Valency subject	Valency object
Zero-valent verb e.g., *rain*	SURFACE SUBJECT	—	—
Monovalent verb e.g., *stumble*	—	SURFACE SUBJECT	—
Divalent verb e.g., *jolt*:			
—active	—	SURFACE SUBJECT	SURFACE OBJECT
—passive	—	SURFACE COUNTER SUBJECT	SURFACE SUBJECT

Figure 3. Correlation of English valency and surface functions.

oneself in (25), compared with the incidentally reflexive verb of (26):

Alice absented herself from the meeting. (25)

Alice criticized herself at the meeting. (26)

Since a nonreflexive object is impossible with the verb *absent*, the *herself* of (25) cannot be said to express an independent semantic role beyond that of the subject, which in this case can be described as agent. In (26), on the other hand, *herself* has the role of patient (or affected entity), with the subject again having the role of agent. But in both cases the reflexive pronoun fulfils the valency function of object, a (prepositionless) noun phrase immediately following the lexical verb, so that both verbs can be regarded as bivalent.

This view of the valency of reflexive verbs differs from that of Tesnière, who saw reflexive verbs as manifestations of a different kind of verbal voice, the so-called 'recessive' (French *récessif*), which reduced the valency of a verb by one, so that bivalent verbs like *lever* 'raise,' or *ouvrir* 'open (transitive)' become monovalent when reflexive (*se lever* 'rise, stand up,' *s'ouvrir* 'open (intransitive)'). Although this is an interesting view, it is something of an oversimplification.

In fact reflexive verbs in French (and many other languages, including German), seem to have at least four different kinds of status. First, verbs like *se laver* 'wash oneself,' or *se critiquer* 'criticize oneself' are ordinary transitive verbs that can have a reflexive object as an alternative to a normal one, but the reflexive one has no special significance for verb valency. Second, verbs like *s'absenter* 'absent oneself,' or *se souvenir* (*de*) 'remember' do not have a non-reflexive use, and thus the reflexive pronoun is an empty elaborator, even though an essential one, rather similar to the *es* of German *Es regnet* (discussed in Sect. 7). Third, there are verbs like *douter/se douter* 'doubt/imagine, suspect,' or *résoudre/se résoudre* (*à*) 'solve/decide,' which have both a nonreflexive and a reflexive use, but where the semantic difference is too great for them to be simply counted as the same verb; in fact, reflexivization is used almost like a device of

word-formation for producing a new lexical item, one which has to count as a compulsorily reflexive verb. Fourth, there are verbs like *ouvrir* and *vendre*, for which the reflexive pattern is used to convey the idea that the subject is semantically the patient (and hence also object), and that there is no explicit agent, which is why the patient has to fill the subject position too, as in *La porte s'ouvre* 'The door opens (itself).' This reflexive use truly is a way of coping with a reduced number of semantic roles and gives rise to 'poly-valency,' that is, a verb displaying the same meaning in two quite different grammatical uses.

Tesnière also recognized syntactic devices for increasing the valency of verbs, such as French causative constructions with *faire*. English causative constructions with *have*, *make*, and *cause*, etc. preserve subject and object functions in the embedded infinitive clause of sentences like those of (27) and (28) below, so that *Alfred* remains the subject and *Balzac* the object of the verb (*to*) *read*, just as they would have been in a full sentence with the same content (*Alfred reads Balzac*, for instance):

John had Alfred read Balzac. (27)

John caused Alfred to read Balzac. (28)

In French, on the other hand, *faire* seems to combine with infinitives to form complex verbs like *faire mourir* 'have ... die,' *faire apprendre* 'have ... learn,' *faire ... donner* 'have ... give,' to give sentences like the following (adapted from Tesnière), in which *Jean* is introduced as the causer or instigator and as subject of the whole *faire* + VERB complex, displacing *Alfred* from subject position:

Jean fait mourir Alfred. (29)
(cf. Alfred meurt.)

Jean fait apprendre le bulgare à Alfred. (30)
(cf. Alfred apprend le bulgare.)

Jean fait donner la Bible à Charles par Alfred. (31)
(cf. Alfred donne la Bible à Charles.)

As Tesnière points out (1966: 260–62), French requires that the displaced subject should occupy the next available place down the hierarchy, starting with the object (= second *actant*) as in (29), going on to the indirect/prepositional object (= tierce *actant*) as in (30), and going on as far as the agent phrase (= quatrième *actant*) as in (31).

Other languages have different ways of dealing with the valency of causative relationships. One possibility is to have a morphologically related verb derived with an affix to create a verb of different valency: the German prefix *be-*, for instance, often has the effect of converting an intransitive verb into a transitive one, as in the pairs *arbeiten/bearbeiten* 'work/work on, process,' *enden/beenden* '(come to an) end/end, complete.' A further possibility is to allow polyvalency in such a way that the same verb may be used intransitively and transitively in a causative sense without change of form, as with the many so-called ergative verbs of English, which typically refer to a change of state or position. Verbs such as *break*, *cook*, *open*, *roll*, and *sink* have a monovalent use as in (32) below beside a bivalent one with a causative meaning as in (33):

> The glass broke. (32)

> John broke the glass. (33)

With such verbs the subject of the intransitive pattern and the object of the transitive pattern have a similar semantic role of patient affected, while the transitive subject has the role of agent.

9. Adjective and Noun Valency

Although Tesnière confined valency to verbs, it has been naturally extended to adjectives and nouns by later valency grammarians. Predicative adjectives combine with copular verbs to form a unit that has many features in common with verbs, including similar valency requirements: for instance, *be afraid (of)* can be compared with *fear*. Admittedly the adjective (phrase) *afraid (of)* can be regarded as an elaborator of the verb *be*; and it is true that predicative adjective phrases occur with various verbs other than *be*, such as *become*, *remain*, *seem* (not to mention the trivalent *make (someone/something...)*, *keep (someone/something...)*, etc.), and thus involve a second order valency. On the other hand, the adjective's valency extends beyond what is normally termed adjective complementation, as in *afraid of the dark*, to cover the subject of its companion verb. An adjective like *afraid*, for instance, requires an animate subject with the role of experiencer. Other predicative adjectives have requirements that link subjects with other elaborators, as the following examples demonstrate:

> Alfred is similar to Alice. (34)

> Alice and Alfred are similar (to each other). (35)

> [Alice is mad about cars.] Alfred is similar. (36)

Clearly *similar (to)* implies two entities, but these can be referred to in three different patterns: in (34) one entity is the subject and the other occurs as an adjectival 'postelaborator'; in the (35) pattern, which involves a reciprocal meaning, the subject must be plural, and the postelaborator is freely omissible; in the (36) pattern, finally, the postelaborator element must be supplied from the context (just like the object of the verb *watch*, discussed in Sect. 4). The elaboration patterns of such adjectives thus cannot be adequately described without reference to the subject.

Most English adjectival elaborators are like verb elaborators in that they follow the word they elaborate. There is, however, one important difference: while the majority of verb objects have no preposition in English, virtually all adjectives do require a preposition before their complement (the one clear exception being *worth*). As in the case of prepositional verbs, the adjectives each select a particular preposition, in an often arbitrary way, for example, *keen on, eager for, dependent on, independent of, free of/from*. Sometimes the adjective's choice of preposition agrees with that of a corresponding verb, sometimes the verb has a different preposition, or no preposition at all:

> Alice was hopeful of success. (37)
> (cf. Alice hoped for success.)

> Alice was hungry for power. (38)
> (cf. Alice hungered for power.)

> Alice was desirous of wealth. (39)
> (Alice desired wealth.)

Adjectives with more than one postelaborator are relatively rare but can be found, for example, *responsible to (someone) for (something)*.

In case languages some elaborators of adjectives occur without a preposition, but instead they occur in a particular case form required by the adjective. In German this is most commonly the dative, and such elaborators most commonly precede the adjective, as in (40) below; on the other hand, *anders* 'different,' is complemented with the case-neutral subordinator *als*, which follows, as in (41):

> Alfred ist seinem Bruder sehr ähnlich. (40)
> (cf. Alfred is very similar to his brother.)

> Alfred ist ganz anders als sein Bruder. (41)
> (cf. Alfred is quite different to/from his brother.)

(Note that *sehr/very* and *ganz/quite* are free modifiers and thus strictly outside adjective valency; the preference for the one or the other in these cases is determined semantically rather than lexico-grammatically.)

Noun valency can be compared with adjective valency, particularly for nouns derived from adjectives, though the selection of prepositions in noun complements, too, only partly corresponds to that in related words (i.e., adjectives and verbs), as illustrated by these examples:

> Alice's dependence on her parents (was obvious). (42)
> (cf. Alice was dependent on her parents.
>   Alice depended on her parents.)

Alfred's pride in the project (was obvious).   (43)
(cf. Alfred was proud of the project.
        Alfred prided himself on the project.)

Noun valency therefore also needs to be specified independently. It even has special features of its own. First, there are many nouns without a corresponding verb or adjective that take a complement, for example, *daughter (of . . .), president (of . . .), headquarters (of . . .), advantage (of . . .), appetite (for . . .).* Second, as the above examples make clear, English *of,* often corresponding to a genitive case in case languages, is the favored preposition; thus an *of* noun complement often corresponds to the simple object of a transitive verb (without a preposition), for example, *bombardment/defence/besiege of the castle* (cf. *bombard/defend/besiege the castle*), but even here there are exceptions, such as *attack on the castle.* The most striking feature of noun valency, however, is the fact that the item corresponding to the subject of a verb, particularly of a transitive one, can appear in a language like English as a possessive determiner (i.e., in place of an article), as an alternative to its occurrence as a prepositional complement, as the following examples show:

a/the defeat, a/the collapse [simple *determiner*   (44)
    + NOUN].

Alfred's collapse, the collapse of Alfred, *the   (45)
    collapse by Alfred.

Bernard's defeat (?by Alfred), the defeat of Bernard   (46)
    by Alfred, Alfred's defeat of Bernard, *the defeat
    of Alfred of Bernard.

Although complex interrelationships are involved in the above, and border lines are not always clear, it can be said that *by* complements normally correspond to transitive subjects, possessives to transitive or intransitive subjects (and occasionally objects), and *of* phrases to intransitive subjects or to objects. Furthermore, two complements of the same kind are not allowed.

10. Embedded Clauses as Part of Valency

Many verbs, adjectives, and nouns, besides their normal complementation with phrases (whether nominal, prepositional, or adjectival) also allow complementation with finite or nonfinite clauses. Alongside phrasal complementation like *Alice wanted a holiday* or *Alice realized her mistake,* verbs like *want* or *realize* also permit clausal complementation as in (47) and (48) respectively:

Alice wanted to go to Switzerland.   (47)
Alice wanted Angela to go with her.

Alice realized that she had made an error.   (48)
Alice realized how she had gone wrong.

It is part of the valency of the verb *want* that it can occur with a following infinitive, with the further possibility of specifying a different subject (here *Angela*) for this infinitive, whereas *enjoy,* for instance, is impossible with the infinitive but natural with a gerund construction (e.g., *going to Switzerland*). The verb *realize* is impossible with both infinitive and gerund but does occur with a finite clause as in (48) above. Both nonfinite and finite clausal complementation can be regarded as cases of 'embedding,' that is, downgrading of a sentential structure to play a lower level role as a verb elaborator. But in any case verbs need to be lexically specified for the types of embedded pattern they accept. Some verbs, moreover, are restricted to clausal complementation: the verb *condescend,* for instance, always requires a following infinitive. Finally, the above points concerning verbs apply equally to adjective and noun complementation, as these phrases show: *able to speak French, capable of speaking French, confident that she could speak French; a tendency to speak French, a habit of speaking French, the fact that she spoke French.*

11. The Limits of Valency

Verbs, adjectives, and nouns are the three major lexical word classes for which the concept of valency is clearly appropriate and for which detailed language studies have been made and preliminary dictionaries compiled. An important issue is whether the concept be extended further, beyond the occasional adverb directly derived from an adjective and copying its valency (e.g., *independently of Alfred*). Transformational grammarians have suggested grouping together spatio–temporal adverbs and prepositions respectively as intransitive and transitive particles (or 'prepositions' in a new sense), transitive ones involving complementation with noun phrases and prepositional phrases. This insight could be applied to valency to give a classification something like the following:

Particles (or new prepositions)
(a) *zero-valent*:   nearby, home; soon,
                                              previously
(b) *monovalent*
    (obligatory simple object):   at, to(wards), from;
                                              during
    (omissible simple object):   in, above, off; after,
                                              before
    (omissible prepositional object): out (of), in front (of)
(c) *bivalent*:   between (. . . and . . .)

But there are problems with such an analysis: for instance, whether the situated entity (the subject or object of the sentence), should be included as a further elaborator, thus increasing all the above valencies by one; whether *out of* (or *away from*) really contains two words of the same word class particle/'preposition' (albeit of different subclasses); whether *above* and *out* (etc.), in their unaccompanied uses always imply an omitted object.

Although the application of valency grammar can thus be extended, it is not really intended to account for the whole of a syntactic system, any more than Fillmore's 'case grammar' (see *Case Grammar*). Valency is a matter of the subcategorization of lexical categories, and therefore in a strict sense would exclude:

(a) coordinate structures, which are treated separately both by Tesnière (under the heading of French *jonction*) and in Hudson's *Word Grammar* (where they are basic and not derived from word–word relations);

(b) grammatical 'specifiers,' such as auxiliaries and (nonpossessive) determiners, which although treated as dependents (or even governors) by many dependency grammarians, were regarded by Tesnière as involving a different relationship to main verbs and nouns respectively—a view still valid today;

(c) 'subordinators' in Tesnière's interpretation, which embraced prepositions and subordinating conjunctions, these being for him convertors (French *translatifs*), of noun phrases or clauses to adverbial or adnominal function (e.g., adverbial (*Alfred arrived*) *before the concert/before I arrived*; adnominal (*Alfred liked the book*) *in the window/which he'd seen in the window*)—again a theoretically tenable position.

Valency can thus evidently be included in a dependency grammar; for Engel (1977: 116), in fact, valency is simply a matter of dependency on subclasses. Equally valency can be incorporated into a functional grammar or a functionally enriched constituency grammar, albeit under a different rubric. Furthermore, valency characteristics have, in recent years, increasingly been incorporated into dictionary entries, and improved specialist valency dictionaries are being prepared (for instance the Augsburg one for English, initiated by T. Herbst and D. Heath). One thing is clear: valency relationships must find a place in every complete linguistic description.

Bibliography

Abraham W (ed.) 1978 *Valence, Semantic Case and Grammatical Relations.* Benjamins, Amsterdam

Allerton D J 1982 *Valency and the English Verb.* Academic Press, London

Baker C L 1989 *English Syntax.* MIT Press, Cambridge, MA

Bühler K 1934 *Sprachtheorie.* Fischer, Jena

Busse W, Dubost J-P 1977 *Französisches Verblexikon.* Klett, Stuttgart

Emons R 1976 *Valenzgrammatik für das Englische: Eine Einführung.* Niemeyer, Tübingen

Engel U 1977 *Syntax der deutschen Gegenwartssprache.* Schmidt, Berlin

Fillmore C J (1977) The case for case re-opened. In: Cole P, Sadock J M (eds.) *Syntax and Semantics 8: Grammatical Relations*, pp. 59–81. Academic Press, New York

Groot A W de 1949 *Structerele syntaxis.* Servire, The Hague

Helbig G (ed.) 1971 *Beiträge zur Valenztheorie.* Mouton, The Hague

Helbig G, Schenkel W 1973 *Wörterbuch zur Valenz und Distribution deutscher Verben.* VEB Bibliographisches Institut, Leipzig

Herbst T 1983 *Untersuchungen zur Valenz englischer Adjektive und ihrer Nominalisierungen.* Narr, Tübingen

Herbst T 1988 A valency model for English nouns. *JL* **24**: 265–301

Heringer H-J 1973 *Theorie der deutschen Syntax*, 2nd edn. Hueber, Munich

Hudson R A 1984 *Word Grammar.* Blackwell, Oxford

Korhonen J 1977 *Studien zu Dependenz, Valenz und Satzmodell*, vol. I. Lang, Berne

Schumacher H (ed.) 1976 *Untersuchungen zur Verbvalenz.* Narr, Tübingen

Tesnière L 1953 *Esquisse d'une syntaxe structurale.* Klincksieck, Paris

Tesnière L 1966 *Eléments de syntaxe structurale*, 2nd edn. Klincksieck, Paris

Word Grammar

R. A. Hudson

Word Grammar (WG) is a theory of language structure. Its most important distinguishing characteristics are the following:

(a) that knowledge of language is assumed to be a particular case of more general types of knowledge, distinct only in being about language; and

(b) that most parts of syntactic structure are analyzed in terms of dependency relations between single words, and constituency analysis is applied only to coordinate structures.

To take a simple example, the grammatical analysis of *Fred lives in London* can be partially shown by the diagram in (1):

$$\leftarrow \text{ subject}\ulcorner\quad\ulcorner\text{complement} \rightarrow \ulcorner \text{ complement} \rightarrow$$

Fred　　　　lives　　　　　　　in　　　　　London.

(1)

Each arrow in this diagram points from a word to one of its dependents, but there are no extra nodes for phrases or clauses. The similarities between linguistic and nonlinguistic knowledge are of various kinds which are outlined in the first section.

1. Linguistic and Nonlinguistic Knowledge

WG is an example of what has come to be called cognitive linguistics (Taylor 1989), in which the similarities between language and other types of cognition are stressed. These similarities are of three main types:

(a) in the data structures;
(b) in the categories of grammar; and
(c) in the processing mechanisms.

In each case it is possible to find at least *prima facie* evidence of nonlinguistic knowledge which parallels the knowledge of language. Although the analysis of both the linguistic and the nonlinguistic examples is a matter for further research and discussion, the extreme 'modularity' assumed by Chomskyan linguists appears at present to be untenable. On the other hand, if it should turn out that even the cognitive linguistics research program cannot find a convincing nonlinguistic parallel for some part of language structure, then this evidence will be all the more convincing for not having arisen out of the initial assumptions.

A WG grammar consists of an unordered list of propositions called 'facts.' All WG propositions have just two arguments and a relation, ' = ,' 'isa' and 'has.' Examples follow (2a–c):

type of object of verb = noun (2a)

DEVOUR isa verb (2b)

DEVOUR has an object (2c)

These facts are self explanatory except for a few technical expressions ('isa' means 'is an instance of'). This very simple database defines a network of concepts whose links are of many different types (e.g., 'type of object of'). It is a commonplace of current cognitive psychology that knowledge in general is organized in this way, so the data-structures of language are similar in fundamental respects to those of general knowledge.

Furthermore the 'isa' relations (e.g., between DEVOUR and 'verb,' and between 'verb' and 'word') are exploited by inheritance, whereby DEVOUR inherits all the properties of 'verb,' and via 'verb' all those of 'word.' It is quite uncontroversial to assume that this is also how general knowledge is organized, so here too is a similarity between the data-structures of language and of nonlanguage. Section 3 discusses inheritance in more detail.

The second similarity between language and nonlanguage involves the categories to which the grammar refers. Specifically it can be shown that every category referred to in the grammar is a special case of some general category which is part of general knowledge. For example in (3a–c):

'word' is a special kind of 'action' (3a)

'dependent' is a special kind of 'companion,' a relation between two events linked in time (e.g., between the two events referred to by *John followed Mary into the room*) (3b)

'conjunct' (a relation used in the syntax of coordination) and 'stem' (referred to in morphology) are each a special kind of 'part.' (3c)

Thus every linguistic concept inherits some properties which are also available for nonlinguistic concepts, so an analysis of a grammar is incomplete unless it is part of a more general analysis of these parts of general knowledge.

These parallels are supported by other connections between the categories of language and those of general knowledge. Although syntactic dependencies typically link one word to another, there are a few points in a grammar which allow a dependency to link a word to something which is not a word. The clearest example of this in English is the word *go*, whose complement may be some nonlinguistic action (e.g., *He went* [wolf whistle]). In this example nonlinguistic categories function like linguistic ones; but the converse can also be found, with linguistic categories replacing the more normal nonlinguistic ones. This is the case when language is used to talk about language; for example, the meaning of *Fred said a word* contains the concept 'word,' which is part of the grammar, alongside clearly nonlinguistic concepts like 'Fred.'

The third similarity between linguistic and nonlinguistic knowledge involves the processes by which they are exploited. According to WG, sentences are parsed by applying the same general procedures used when understanding other kinds of experience: a complex mixture of segmentation, identification, and inheritance. This is probably the weakest part of WG theory because so little is known about processing that it is hard to show close similarities between language and nonlanguage.

One particular kind of processing of knowledge is learning. According to WG the cognitive structures that a child has developed before it learns to talk are similar to the grammatical structures which it has to learn. This makes the feat of learning language much less impressive and mysterious than in the modular view where the grammar is a unique structure which would have to be built from scratch if it were not innate. At the same time, however, it has to be recognized that some research challenges arise under either assumption; in particular, it is hard to explain how children learn that some structure is not possible (e.g., * *I aren't your friend*; cf. *Aren't I your friend?*) in the absence of negative evidence.

2. Enriched Dependency Structures

The other highly controversial characteristic of WG is its use of dependency analysis as the basis for syntax. It makes no use of phrases or clauses. 'Dependency analysis' is an ancient grammatical tradition which can be traced back in Europe at least as far as the Modistic grammarians of the Middle Ages, and which makes use of notions such as 'goverment' and 'modification.' In America the Bloomfieldian tradition (which in this respect includes the Chomskyan tradition), assumed constituency analysis to the virtual exclusion of dependency analysis, but this tradition was preserved in Europe, particularly in Eastern Europe, to the extent of providing the basis for grammar teaching in schools. However, there has been very little theoretical development of dependency analysis, in contrast with the enormous amount of formal, theoretical, and descriptive work on constituent structure.

In one respect WG is stricter than typical European dependency grammar, namely in its treatment of word order. According to WG all dependency structures (in all languages) are controlled by an 'adjacency principle' (also known in Europe as the principle of 'projectivity'; it should be distinguished carefully from the adjacency principle of government–binding theory). The adjacency principle can most easily be explained by referring to the derived notion 'phrase.' A dependency analysis defines 'phrases' as by-products (rather than as the basic categories of the analysis): for each word (W) there is a phrase consisting of W plus the phrases of all the words that depend on W. (W is called the 'root' of this phrase.) For example, in *He lives in London* dependency analysis defines *in London* as a phrase because only *London* depends on *in*; but it also defines the whole clause as a 'phrase' with *lives* as its root.

Given this definition of 'phrase,' the adjacency principle requires all phrases to be continuous (with one important exception discussed below). For example, the phrase *in large cities* is fine, but *large* cannot be placed before *in* (*large in cities*) because this would produce a phrase (*large cities*) separated by a word which is not part of that phrase. The adjacency principle is assumed to apply to all languages, but it remains to be seen whether the apparent counterexamples can all be explained.

This version of the adjacency principle is roughly equivalent to a context-free phrase-structure grammar, so even English contains a great many structures which cannot be analyzed, and which show that this version of the adjacency principle is too strict. Take a so-called 'raising' example like (4):

It kept raining   (4)

It is generally agreed that *it* is the subject of *raining* as well as of *kept*. But this means that the phrase whose root is *raining* contains *it* but not *kept*, so this phrase is discontinuous but grammatical. To allow for such counterexamples, without abandoning the adjacency principle, the rules of traditional dependency grammar are relaxed in various ways.

First, one word is allowed to be a dependent of more than one other word, a move which is needed in any case for (4) in order to show that *it* is the subject

of the participle as well as of *kept*. This gives the structure in (5):

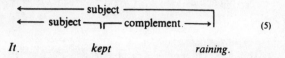

(5)

Second, discontinuity is permitted just in case the interrupter is the head both of the phrase-root and also of its separated dependent, as in (5). This is the exception to the simple adjacency principle mentioned above, and it is built into the universal adjacency principle.

The dependency configuration in (5) can be described as the 'raising pattern' (Hudson 1990b). The raising pattern is responsible for many of the complexities of syntax, in addition to raising structures themselves (and the closely related 'control structures'). It is responsible for the extraction found in examples like *Beans you know I like*, where *beans* is the object of *like*. The WG structure for this example is shown in (6):

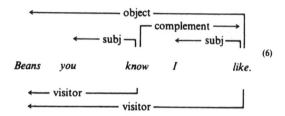

(6)

The crucial innovation in (6), compared with traditional dependency analyses, is the dependency relation 'visitor,' which is functionally equivalent to the '(spec of) comp' relation which is provided for extractees in PSG-based analyses. The visitor dependency defines the extractee as a part of a series of phrases: first, the phrase whose root is *know*, and, second, the one whose root is *like*. Although the latter is discontinuous, it is permitted by the adjacency principle because the interrupter, *know*, is the head of both *beans* and *like*.

The example (6) illustrates the way in which the relatively rich dependency structures of WG combine both 'deep' and 'surface' information into a single structure, thereby making transformations unnecessary. Similar analyses are provided for other structures which are often taken as evidence for multiple levels of structure related by transformations. Passives, for example, are given a structure in which the subject also has the dependency relation 'object' as in (7).

Section 3 will show how structures like this are generated, but the main point to be noted here is that the power of WG comes from the possibility of multiple dependency analyses applied to a single, completely surface, structure. As will be seen in Sect. 4, this kind

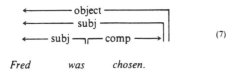

Fred   was   chosen.

(7)

of analysis promises to be very suitable for mechanical parsing.

3. Inheritance and *Isa* Relations

It has already been seen that a WG grammar consists of a list of propositions, and that some of the propositions have the predicate 'isa,' which links concepts hierarchically in so-called 'isa-hierarchies.' One isa-hierarchy contains all the various word-types, from the most general type, 'word,' through subtypes like 'noun,' 'pronoun,' and 'reflexive-pronoun,' down to individual lexical items (and even further). Another hierarchy contains all the different dependency relations, from 'dependent' at the top down through relations like 'postdependent' and 'complement' to the most specific concepts like 'indirect object.' These are the richest hierarchies involved in grammar, but there are many more smaller ones. So the isa-hierarchy plays a fundamental part in a WG grammar.

Isa-hierarchies are exploited by means of 'inheritance,' whereby facts about higher categories automatically apply to categories below them in the hierarchy. For example, suppose a grammar contained the following facts as in (8a–c) (where 'it' is a variable standing for the italicized word):

position of predependent of *word* = before it   (8a)

subject isa predependent   (8b)

RUN isa word   (8c)

By inheritance it can be inferred from (8) that (9) is also true:

position of subject of *RUN* = before it   (9)

Not only grammars but also sentence structures consist of lists of facts; dependency diagrams are just convenient summaries of a small subset of these facts. Since the words in a sentence are different from the lexical items of which they are instances, they are given different names as well—names like W1, W2, and so on. The structure of the sentence *Fred ran* is thus given in part by the following propositions (10a–e):

structure of W1 = ⟨Fred⟩   (10a)

structure of W2 = ⟨ran⟩   (10b)

W1 isa FRED   (10c)

W2 isa RUN   (10d)

subject of W2 = W1   (10e)

It is probably easy to see how a grammar acts as a set of well-formedness conditions on sentence structures. A structure is generated provided that each word in the sentence can be assigned, as an instance, to some word in the grammar, and that all the facts which are true of that grammar–word can be inherited onto the sentence–word without contradiction. For example, the subject of RUN should precede it (9), so since W2 isa RUN (10d) the subject of W2 should also precede it; and since W1 is the subject of W2 (10e) it should therefore be the case that W1 precedes W2. Grammars are applied to sentences, by ordinary logic, which again supports the claim that language is similar to nonlinguistic knowledge.

One consequence of locating all grammatical facts in isa-hierarchies is that there is no distinction, either in principle or in practice, between 'the grammar proper' and 'the lexicon.' To the extent that the lexicon can be identified at all, it is just the set of facts that refer to categories in the lower regions of the total isa-hierarchy. It is tempting to classify WG as an extremely 'lexicalist' theory of grammar, because of the central role assigned to individual words, but this is a meaningless claim in the absence of a boundary between the lexicon and the rest of the grammar.

4. Applications

This article has concentrated on the syntax of WG, but it should be emphasized that the theory has already been extended to some parts of morphology, and to large areas of semantics. On the other hand, it has not yet been applied to phonology, nor has it been applied extensively to languages other than English; so the theory is still in some respects in an early stage of development. It is not too soon, however, to anticipate some possible applications: (a) computer systems, (b) lexicography, and (c) language teaching.

Regarding computer applications, any dependency-based system has the attraction of requiring less analysis than a constituency-based one, because the only units that need to be processed are individual words. Furthermore the relatively rich dependency structures allowed by WG mean that the completely surface analysis gives a lot of structural information, of the kind shown in other theories by empty categories or underlying structures. This rich dependency structure is relatively easy to identify, because the additional structure is generally predictable from a simple basic structure; and once it is built, it is very easy to map onto semantic structure. It also provides a much more suitable basis for corpus analysis aimed at establishing cooccurrence statistics than constituency structure does. The logical basis of the inheritance system makes WG grammars particularly easy to use in a logic-based computer system, and encourages a very clear conceptual distinction between the grammar and the parser. Various small WG parsers have already been written in Prolog (Fraser 1992).

As far as lexicography is concerned, WG theory is nearer than most linguistic theories to the practice of modern lexicographers. Some general trends in lexicography can be identified:

    (a) the blurring of the distinction between grammars and dictionaries;

    (b) the blurring of the distinction between dictionaries and encyclopedias;

    (c) the treatment of dictionaries as databases with a network structure rather than as lists of separate lemmas;

    (d) the inclusion of rich valency information in terms of dependency types like 'object'; and

    (e) the incorporation of increasingly sophisticated sociolinguistic information about words.

In all these respects lexicography has followed the same path as WG, so the latter may provide some helpful theoretical underpinnings for lexicography (Hudson 1988b).

Language teaching is another area in which WG may prove useful, though this remains to be demonstrated. It is still a matter of debate what role, if any, explicit facts should play in language teaching, but it seems beyond doubt that at least the teacher should 'know' the facts of the object-language quite consciously, and should also know something about how language, in general, is structured. Even in the present rather early stage in the development of linguistic theory agreement has been reached on a great many issues which teachers ought to know about (Hudson 1992). Some of WG's attractions are similar to those listed above for lexicography, but dependency analysis also provides a convenient notation for sentence structure which allows the indication, for example, of selected grammatical relations without the building of a complete sentence structure. This is not surprising considering that WG, and dependency theory in general, is a formalization of traditional school grammar. It is worth remembering that the classic of dependency theory (Tesnière 1959) was written explicitly in order to improve the teaching of grammar in schools.

Bibliography

Fraser N 1992 The theory and practice of dependency parsing (Doctoral dissertation, London University)
Hudson R A 1984 *Word Grammar*. Blackwell, Oxford
Hudson R A 1985 The limits of subcategorization. *LAn* **15**: 233–55
Hudson R A 1986 Sociolinguistics and the theory of grammar. *Linguistics* **24**: 1053–78
Hudson R A 1987 Zwicky on heads. *JL* **23**: 109–32
Hudson R A 1988a Coordination and grammatical relations. *JL* **24**: 303–42
Hudson R A 1988b The linguistic foundations for lexical research and dictionary design. *IJLex* **1**(4): 287–312
Hudson R A 1988c Extraction and grammatical relations. *Lingua* **76**: 177–208
Hudson R A 1989a English passives, grammatical relations and default inheritance. *Lingua* **79**: 17–48
Hudson R A 1989b Gapping and grammatical relations. *JL* **25**: 57–94
Hudson R A 1990a *English Word Grammar*. Blackwell, Oxford
Hudson R A 1990b Raising in syntax, semantics and cognition. *UCL Working Papers in Linguistics* **2**
Hudson R A 1992 *Teaching Grammar*. Blackwell, Oxford
Taylor J R 1989 *Linguistic Categorization: An Essay in Cognitive Linguistics*. Oxford University Press, Oxford
Tesnière L 1959 *Eléments de Syntaxe Structurale*. Klincksieck, Paris

Word Order and Linearization

A. Siewierska

Word order and linearization are major areas of linguistic inquiry within all linguistic traditions: descriptive, theoretical, and typological. This article concentrates on the typological perspective centering on the notion of 'basic order.' It begins with a consideration of the notion of basic order, then proceeds to review the distribution of word order patterns on a cross-linguistic basis, and next presents a brief account of the host of interrelated factors deemed to underlie the recurring linearizations. The article closes with a specification of the major problems posed for theory specific accounts of universal word order phenomena.

1. The Notion of Basic Order

In the wake of Greenberg's (1963) seminal investigation, the order of major clausal constituents has been characterized in terms of the relative positioning of the subject (S), object (O), and verb (V), giving rise to a typological classification of languages into SVO, SOV, VSO, OVS, VOS, and OSV. Since most, if not all, languages exhibit some variation in the ordering of major clausal constituents, the characterization of a language with respect to the above six-way typology is achieved in relation to the meta-theoretical concept of basic order. Within the context of typological studies the term basic order, at the sentence level, is typically identified with the order that occurs in stylistically neutral, independent, indicative clauses with full noun phrase (NP) participants, where the subject is definite, agentive, and human, the object is a definite semantic patient, and the verb represents an action, not a state or an event. It is important to note that for reasons to be specified presently, the basic order, defined as above, may, but need not, correspond to the statistically dominant word order in a language. The identification of the basic order of a language has a limited heuristic value in that it does not correlate with a unified set of word order properties on a cross-linguistic basis. Nonetheless, enough significant sub-regularities of order have been observed to follow from the basic order to warrant taking the Greenbergian typology as a point of departure for further examinations of universal word order phenomena (see *Greenberg Universals*).

In view of the above-mentioned requirements imposed on the constituents of clauses in terms of which the basic order is defined, the determination of the basic order of a language is not always a straightforward matter. For instance, in some ergative languages it is not always clear which constituent of a transitive clause should be considered as subject and which as object, owing to the conflicting results obtained from the typical subject identifying criteria. Another problem arises in connection with the necessary presence of two full NP participants. There are languages in which such transitive clauses are nonexistent (e.g., Puget Salish) or uncommon (e.g., Apalaí, Gunwinggu, Yatzachi, Zapotec) since the subject and/or object must or tends to be expressed solely by pronominal affixes on the verb or by clitics elsewhere in the clause. Two or more word order patterns may be in competition for basicness as in languages such as Guugu–Yimidhirr, Sahaptin, or Samoan, which exhibit considerable word order variation at the sentence level. This variation is conditioned by the distribution of given and new information or the relative newsworthiness of the informational content of the constituents of the utterance. Furthermore, some languages display different word order preferences dependent on text types. Russian is a case in point, as it is seen to favor SVO order in the formal written language but SOV in the colloquial spoken language.

Due to the above problems, some languages are nowadays assigned a basic order only for the verb and subject (SV or VS) and/or verb and object (OV or VO) or even classified as not displaying a basic order at all.

2. Distribution of Basic Orders of Major Clausal Constituents

For the languages which do manifest a basic order in the Greenbergian sense, the relative frequency of occurrence of the six basic orders has been established

and confirmed by several independent investigations. Table 1 lists the percentage of languages exhibiting

Table 1. Frequency of six basic orders in the world's languages.

	SOV	SVO	VSO	VOS	OVS	OSV
Greenberg (142)	45.0	36.6	18.3	—	—	—
Ruhlen (427)	51.5	35.6	10.5	2.1	—	0.2
M & B (100)[1]	41.0	35.0	9.0	2.0	1.0	1.0
Hawkins (336)	51.8	32.4	13.3	2.3	—	—
Tomlin (402)	44.8	41.8	9.2	3.0	1.2	—

[1] In Mallinson and Blake's sample 11 languages are not classified in terms of this typology. Therefore the percentages in this row do not add up to 100.

each of the six basic orders in the language samples of Greenberg (1963), Ruhlen (1975), Mallinson and Blake (1981), Hawkins (1983), and Tomlin (1986).

As suggested by the figures in Table 1, in terms of frequency of occurrence, the six basic orders fall into two subgroups: subject-before-object languages and object-before-subject ones. The former are widely attested, while the latter did not feature in Greenberg's original sample at all, and subsequently have been found to occur in less than 5 percent of the world's languages. Of the subject-before-object languages SOV and SVO by far outnumber the VSO ones, and among the three linearization patterns in which the object precedes the subject, OSV is the rarest.

2.1 Sampling Techniques

The language frequencies reflected in the data in Table 1, with the exception of Tomlin's (1986) figures, are based on random language samples. Consequently, though the above figures provide a good indication of the frequencies of the six basic orders among the world's languages, the cross-linguistic preferences and to a lesser extent dispreferences that they define cannot be automatically assumed to be due to inherently linguistic factors underlying the nature of human language, as opposed to nonlinguistic forces such as genetic affiliation, areal distribution, typological structure, and cultural identification. Particularly in need of investigation is the impact of nonlinguistic influences on the frequency of basic orders displaying relatively similar levels of occurrence such as SOV versus SVO or the three object-before-subject orders. For example, it is generally claimed that there is no linguistic preference for SOV as compared to SVO order, since the slightly higher frequency of SOV languages is not statistically significant. Yet several linguists have pointed out that in Tomlin's (1986) language sample, which is the most representative of the language samples cited in Table 1, 40 percent of the SVO languages are Niger–Congo. Therefore, had it not been for various historical factors which led to the expansion of the Niger–Congo language family, the frequency of SVO would have been markedly lower, and by the same token the linguistic preference for SOV languages much clearer. Historical factors may also be responsible for the relatively high frequency of occurrence of VSO as compared to the object-before-subject languages, since the majority of VSO languages belong to the Austronesian language family.

In order to minimize the genetic, areal, and cultural biases inherent in random sampling, new sampling methodologies are being applied involving stratified language samples as discussed by Perkins (1989). The proposed language samples, such as those developed by Rijkhoff et al. (1993), seek to select a proportional number of maximally differentiated languages, both areally and genetically, the latter criterion being sensitive not only to variation across language families, but also to variation within individual phyla. These more representative language samples will provide a better understanding of the interplay between linguistic and nonlinguistic determinants of order and thus contribute substantially to a fuller appreciation of the universal and particular features of human language.

2.2 Typological Markedness

Since the vast majority of the world's languages display basic orders in which the subject precedes the object, such ordering is seen to be typologically unmarked, while the converse object-before-subject order is labeled as marked. The source of the difference in markedness of the two word-order patterns is a topic of continuing debate. The dominant view associates the different markedness values with differences in ease of processing, and the adoption of the respective linearizations with the instantiation of an addressee-oriented principle of communication in the case of subject-before-object languages as opposed to a speaker-oriented communicative strategy in the case of object-before-subject ones.

The basic properties of subjects and objects in the two groups of languages are by and large the same: subjects tend to be human, semantically agentive, and moreover topical and therefore they typically convey given information, whereas objects are generally inanimate, semantically nonagentive, frequently focal and thus informationally new. Psycholinguistic research summarized in Bock (1982) suggests that the processing of easily accessible language data, where high accessibility correlates with the above-mentioned features of subjects, involves an 'automatic' processing mode and contrasts with the 'controlled' processing of less accessible language material. It is therefore argued that the presentation of easily accessible language data before less accessible information, as is the case in subject-before-object orders, facilitates syntactic processing since it frees both the speaker's and the addressee's processing resources for the controlled processing of the less accessible material. Moreover, the automatically processed data provides

the basic frame or perspective for the interpretation of the utterance; hence the processing task of the addressee is made easier if this perspective is presented first. Conversely, presenting new or more newsworthy and thereby less accessible information first, as in object-before-subject orders, is seen to impede the addressee's cognitive processing, in view of the fact that the relevance of the material delivered earlier in the utterance does not become apparent until the whole utterance is complete.

The communicative strategy adopted by the dominant subject-before-object languages is viewed as addressee-oriented because the speaker, having some new or newsworthy information to deliver, places the addressee's need for clarity and distinctiveness above his own need to divulge the message. In object-before-subject languages, on the other hand, the addressee's need of a prior perspective for the interpretation of the utterance is sacrificed to the immediate interests of the speaker, and hence the speaker-oriented view of such word-order patterns. The addressee versus speaker orientation underlying the markedness value of subject-before-object as compared to object-before-subject ordering is currently regarded as a major source of typological markedness in general. It is argued that though human language is geared to serve both speakers and listeners, it is intrinsically more difficult for the listener to decode the message than for the speaker to encode it, since the speaker has knowledge of what is going to be said, but the listener does not. Consequently, an optimal communicative system should be biased toward the addressee rather than the speaker. Though requiring further verification, the fact that the source of the markedness contrast between subject-before-object as compared to object-before-subject languages may follow from a more general principle of markedness must be regarded as a significant finding of typological research.

3. The Natural Serialization Principle

Greenberg's (1963) six-way division of languages into SOV, SVO, VSO, OVS, VOS, and OSV has been supplemented by a two-way typology of VO and OV languages originating in the dependency tradition and the work of the nineteenth-century German typologists. This two-way typology is based on the division of constituents into head/modifier pairs such as: verb/object, verb/adverbial, auxiliary/main verb, noun/adjective, noun/relative clause, noun/genitive, noun/determiner, adposition/noun phrase, adjective/adverbial (where the first member of the pair is the head and the second the modifier).

The basic insight of the VO/OV typology is expressed by Vennemann's (1972) natural serialization principle (NSP) and its analogues, which stipulate that languages show a preference for serializing constituents in terms of either the head > modifier schema

(VO, centrifugal) or, modifier > head pattern (OV, centripetal). Languages exhibiting linearization patterns in complete conformity with the NSP are termed 'consistent.' Consistency, however, is currently viewed not as a norm, but as an ideal which languages approximate to various degrees. Thus, for example, given that the subject qualifies as a modifier of the verb, all SVO languages are by definition inconsistent. And of the languages in Greenberg's Appendix II, 95 (67 percent) are inconsistent in terms of just five head/modifier pairs, i.e., verb/object, verb/subject, adposition/noun, noun/adjective, and noun/genitive. Of these 95 languages, 57 are inconsistent with respect to 1 of the 5 head/modifier pairs, and 38 with respect to 2. Both the number of inconsistent languages and the degree of inconsistency increase once other head/modifier pairs are considered.

In view of the fact that the vast majority of languages, if not all, exhibit a measure of inconsistency, the word order predictions incorporated in the NSP have been refined by supplementary principles which seek to specify among the inconsistent orderings the regularities that do obtain.

3.1 Supplementing the NSP

A number of subregularities of order of a high level of generality have been captured by Hawkins (1983) in the principle of cross-category harmony (PCCH). The PCCH states that languages display a preference to generalize the order obtaining in one head/dependent category to that of other categories. Departures from this preference in one head/dependent category are in turn likely to induce comparable departures in other head/dependent pairs. Thus, for example, Hawkins notes that the continuum in verb position, verb-initial, verb-medial, verb-final, is reflected in the position of the noun in relation to its modifiers. This is shown by the fact that VSO languages are more consistently noun-initial than SVO languages, in which the preposing of the subject in relation to the verb is often mirrored by the preposing of the adjective and/or genitive and/or determiner before the noun. Moreover, nonrigidly verb-final SOV languages (SOV languages which allow for the placing of some modifiers to the right of the verb) tend to have some nominal modifiers following the noun, while rigidly verb-final SOV languages generally serialize all their modifiers prenominally.

Recurrent patterns have also been found to underlie the inconsistent placement of modifiers relative to the noun, negative elements relative to the verb or verb stem, and the location of conjunctions and subordinators. Of particular interest is the cross-linguistic distribution of noun/modifier pairs. Hawkins (1983: 75, 86), using a typological division of languages based on the presence of prepositions (prepositional languages) vs. postpositions (postpositional languages)—which he takes to be superior to the two-way verb-

based typology—considers the statistical frequency of the ordering of noun/modifier pairs and in particular the patterns of preposing a modifier before the noun in prepositional languages, and of postposing a modifier after the noun in postpositional languages. He observes that in the case of prepositional languages, the first to be preposed are the demonstrative or numeral; then both; next comes the adjective; followed by the genitive; and finally the relative clause. This is captured in the prepositional noun modifier hierarchy (PRNMH) (1):

$$\text{Prep} \supset ((\text{NDem} \lor \text{NNum} \supset \text{NA}) \,\&\, (\text{NA} \supset \text{NG}) \,\&\, (\text{NG} \supset \text{NRel}))$$

$$(1)$$

The postposing of modifiers in postpositional languages begins with the adjective; then comes the relative clause; then the demonstrative or numeral; and finally the genitive. The order of modifier postposing is represented in the postpositional noun modifier hierarchy (PONMH) (2):

$$\text{Post} \supset ((\text{AN} \lor \text{RelN} \supset \text{DemN} \,\&\, \text{NumN})$$

$$\&\, (\text{DemN} \lor \text{NumN} \supset (\text{GN}))$$

$$(2)$$

The principle underlying the two-noun modifier hierarchies is the preference for placing 'lighter' constituents to the left of 'heavier' ones (see Sect. 4.3). Given the progressive increase in length and complexity and thereby heaviness from the demonstrative to the relative clause, the PRNMH is fully consistent with the light > heavy principle, the PONMH only partially so, namely in that relative clauses tend to be postposed earlier than demonstratives or numerals. Significantly the predictions captured in the two-noun modifier hierarchies are corroborated by the actual quantities of languages displaying the stipulated co-occurrences. Thus, for example, there are more prepositional languages in Hawkin's sample in which a numeral is placed before the noun (44), than those with a prenominal demonstrative (38) or genitive (19), and there is only one language with a preposed relative clause.

An alternative explanation for the inconsistent placement of modifiers relative to the head has been advanced by Dryer (1992) whose Branching Direction Theory predicts a preference for consistent ordering only in cases where the head is a lexical and the modifier a phrasal category.

4. Ordering Relations Among Modifiers

The NSP stipulates a preference for serializing modifiers either to the right or to the left of the head, but it says nothing about the relative ordering of modifiers among each other. The most general principle pertaining to the sequencing of modifiers (as compared to the ordering of modifier pairs) takes the form of a constraint against discontinuous constituents which ensures that a modifier will be separated from its head only by other modifiers of the same head. The most notable departures from this norm leading to discontinuities within noun phrases and adjectival phrases are to be found among the languages of the Australian continent, and also in several European languages such as Russian, Polish, or Latin. More widespread are instances of discontinuity involving relative clause and PP extraposition, subject-raising, and parenthetical placement, all of which require special pragmatic motivation. The ordering characteristics of modifiers among each other have been captured in the form of several related principles, the most important of which are discussed briefly below.

4.1 Iconicity

Any facet of structure—thus also any word order pattern—which corresponds to the order of things in the real world and which reflects generally accepted perceptions of dominance and salience and/or established semantic dependencies may be viewed as iconic (Haiman 1985). One of the manifestations of iconicity (see *Iconicity*), thus broadly conceived, is subject and/or object selection, and linearization in line with what is known as the personal hierarchy (3):

1person > 2person > 3person human > higher animals

> other organisms > inorganic matter > abstracts

(3)

The personal hierarchy reflects the unqualified interest of humans in the ego, their conversational partners, and other humans over and above nonhuman entities or abstract situations and events. It predicts a preference for clauses with human or animate subjects such as *People are dying of starvation* rather than inanimate or abstract ones such as *Starvation is killing people* which is consistently adhered to on a cross-linguistic basis. Apart from the effect that the personal hierarchy exerts on linearization via subject and also object selection, its influence is often observed in the linear arrangement of clitics and bound pronouns, and in the order of conjuncts. In the latter case, however, it may interact with considerations of social status, relative authority, and politeness as evinced by the formal *you and me* as compared to the colloquial *me and you*. Essentially iconic is also the strong correlation between subjecthood and agentivity mentioned in Sect. 2.2, which is seen to reflect a preference for presenting events and situations in line with the actual development of things in the real world. Our perception of natural progression in the case of an action event is from the agent to the patient and for an act of giving from giver to receiver. The choice of agent for subject over that of patient or recipient is

thus consistent with both the perceived directionality of events and the dictates of the personal hierarchy.

Under the broad view of iconicity may be subsumed virtually all of the other principles of order that have been proposed to date including the ones to be mentioned in the following sections. More commonly, however, by iconic ordering is meant ordering in line with actual temporal succession. The effect of temporal ordering is discernible particularly in the placement of adverbials and conjuncts. For example, in Mandarin a projected destination is positioned preverbally, a destination already reached postverbally. In English source tends to be placed before destination or goal as in *on the road from Amsterdam to Rotterdam* rather than *on the road to Rotterdam from Amsterdam*. As for conjuncts, in numerous languages, conjuncts generally serialize in ordered sequences such as: first, second... last; beginning, middle, end; anterior, posterior; or a, b, ... z, etc., as reflected in expressions like: *in and out*; *there and back*; or *at sixes and sevens*.

4.2 Semantic Bonding

The claim inherent in the principle of semantic bonding is that the tighter the semantic link between a modifier and the head, the closer the modifier is likely to be located to the head. The influence of this principle may be observed in the sequencing of the verbal arguments and adjuncts, the ordering of different types of adjectives and adverbials and also in the placement of bound morphemes relative to the stem.

As regards the verbal arguments, the direct object and verb are seen to form a more cohesive semantic and syntactic whole than the subject and verb. This fact in turn is taken to underlie the cross-linguistic infrequency of basic VSO as compared to SOV and SVO orders and the extreme rarity of OSV vis-à-vis the slightly less rare OVS and VOS. To the tight semantic bond between the object and verb is also attributed the tendency to place indirect objects and verbal adjuncts either to the left or to the right of the verb–object sequence. This tendency is especially strong in SVO languages in which SVXO orders are found only in heavily restricted sets of circumstances. SOV languages are more permissive in this respect; there are some SOXV languages, and the ones which display SXOV basic order may have SOXV as an option. Nonetheless, the preservation of the integrity of the verb and object combination may be assumed to provide the motivation for the relatively frequent SOVX ordering.

Differences in semantic bonding have also been observed between the verb and its adjuncts. For example, adjuncts designating instruments, speed, or manner specify additional properties of the situation or event denoted by the predicate and its arguments and thus may be viewed as entering into a close semantic relation with the nucleus of the predication. A looser semantic bond exists between the nucleus predication and adjuncts of location, time, or frequency since they do not affect the nature of the designated situation or event, but merely define its spatial or temporal location. Even more loosely related to the predication are epistemic, evaluative, and evidential adjuncts which reflect the speaker's evaluation of or attitude towards the content of the predication while not actually contributing to the semantic content of the predication itself. And the most distinctly linked to the predicate nucleus are illocutionary adjuncts which modify the force of the basic illocution of the utterance. Though the order of verbal adjuncts even more so than that of the arguments is subject to the effect of pragmatic factors, a preference has been discerned for linearizations reflecting the just-noted degrees of semantic bonding. For instance, in the English clause *Honestly, you certainly performed brilliantly yesterday* the illocutionary adverb *honestly* precedes the subjective epistemic adverb *certainly*, and the manner adverbial *brilliantly* is placed closer to the predicate than the temporal adverbial *yesterday*. The semantic modifications introduced by adjuncts can also be expressed morphologically by bound forms, the ordering of which relative to the stem tends to reflect the same semantic scope relations as in the case of adjuncts. For example, the preferred order of application of 'aspect,' 'tense,' and 'modality' markers relative to the stem of the verb is either verb–ATM or MTA–verb.

Turning to the modifiers of the noun, the adjective and noun form a semantic whole, while the numeral adds only cardinality, and the demonstrative designates proximity and/or identifiability. In keeping with the principle of semantic bonding, the preferred order of prenominal modifiers is ADJNUMDEM–N and the most frequent order of postnominal ones is N–ADJNUMDEM (Hawkins 1983: 119–20).

4.3 Length and Complexity

The length and complexity of an element is seen to covary inversely with the ease with which its referent can be identified. Identifiability in turn correlates closely with frequency of occurrence and high topicality. Since easily accessible and topical information tends to be placed prior to less accessible material (see Sect. 2.2), by the same token shorter and less complex constituents tend to precede longer and more complex ones.

There is compelling cross-linguistic evidence for the preference to place informationally and structurally light constituents before heavy ones. The following are just a few cases in point:

(a) the tendency for clitics to occur in second position in the utterance, known as Wackernagel's Law;

(b) the earlier placement of pronominal as compared to nominal subjects or objects in languages such as Bimoba, Cairene Arabic, German, Grebo, Ila, Karen, Twi, and Uzbek;

(c) the preference for final placement of sentential NPs observed in, for example, Blackfoot, Tuscarora, Kinyarwanda, Malagasy, Sherpa, Persian, Latin, and English;

(d) the phenomena of heavy NP shift as in *Fred sent to his client several brochures with all the accommodation details* and extraposition from NP as in *I met a man last night who reminded me of you*;

(e) the prehead vs. posthead placement of shorter as compared to longer forms of a modifier as is the case with: relative clauses in, for example, Finnish, German, and Tagalog; inflexional and prepositional genitives in several Germanic languages (e.g., *the boy's uncle* vs. *the uncle of my next-door neighbor*); and simple as opposed to complement-taking adjectives in English (e.g., *a proud man* vs. *a man proud of his son*). It may even be the case that length is the most significant determinant of linear order, as recently argued by Hawkins (1994).

5. Word-order Variation

The significance attributed to the concept of basic order follows from the assumption that the basic location of functional categories will be maintained unless there are reasons to do otherwise. These reasons may involve pragmatic highlighting, the varying identifiability or salience of the constituents of the clause, or language-specific considerations such as those following from the verb-second constraint in some of the Germanic languages. Variations in order resulting from the above, typically involve major clausal constituents rather than the elements of noun, adjective, or adpositional phrases, which on the whole display rather stable word-order characteristics.

The number and type of permissible word-order permutations at the sentence level differs from language to language. All languages appear to allow for the initial placement of at least some temporal and spatial adverbials and for the fronting of emphatic and contrastive constituents. Also common are variations in order resulting from the placement of heavy material to the right, mentioned earlier. Interestingly enough, variations in order induced by this tendency even occur in object-before-subject languages which on the whole exhibit word order preferences counter to those displayed by subject-before-object languages.

The potential variations in the positioning of the verb, its arguments, and adjuncts are not predictable from the basic order that a language displays. Linguists have, however, noted a close relationship between a language's basic syntactic order and its positional strategies for the topic and the focal part of the comment; the subject position is the most common location of the topic, and the object position the characteristic location of items in focus. Therefore certain predictions can be made in regard to the most likely placement of constituents bearing particular pragmatic functions, though not concerning the extent to which such placement is actually utilized or the range of constituents that it typically affects. For example, both English and Polish are typically classified as SVO languages, and as one would expect, in both languages the initial position is viewed as the favored location of the topic. Yet in English the placement of nonsubject topics in initial position (particularly of verbal arguments and instruments and benefactives) is highly constrained; OSV and XSV orders as in *Max I like* or *In Kuwait he was born* are unquestionably marked. Whereas in Polish the initial placement of topical objects or adjuncts occurs regularly and is conditioned by the same factors as those affecting the initialization of subjects. Needless to say, Polish sanctions much greater variation in order than English does; in fact in Polish virtually any sequence of the verb and its arguments and adjuncts is possible.

6. Accounting for Word Order in Grammatical Theory

The typological classification of languages in terms of the basic location of the subject, object and verb, and the preference for modifier/head or head/modifier ordering offers only a restricted amount of information about the word-order patterns to be found in any given language. Nevertheless, it constitutes a good point of departure for theory-specific accounts of linearization. However, since most languages are not consistent in the NSP sense of the term and moreover allow for some variations on the basic order, the formulation of linearization rules capable of capturing the full range of word-order patterns encountered in languages has so far met with comparatively little success. Most grammatical frameworks, for instance, government and binding, lexical functional grammar (see *Lexical Functional Grammar*), generalized phrase structure grammar (see *Generalized Phrase Structure Grammar*), categorial grammar (see *Categorial Grammar*), word grammar (see *Word Grammar*), and relational grammar (see *Relational Grammar*) seek to provide an account only of a limited subset of word-order facts, typically those which the theories in question define as syntactic as opposed to pragmatic. And even within such reduced domains they have encountered problems, arising in the main from the failure to include an appropriately wide range of information in the specification of rules of order. For instance, the constituency-based rules of order proposed in the context of lexical functional grammar, do not allow for the inclusion of functional information, nor information pertaining to semantic roles or semantic features such as animacy or definiteness. Since the order of objects in ditransitive clauses and often also the sequencing of clitics is in many languages affected by the above factors, no adequate

account of the relevant ordering can be given within the proposed system of rules. To give another example, the linear precedence rules of generalized phrase structure grammar do not make reference to the internal composition of phrases. Therefore the possibility of PP > NP order with heavy NPs in English cannot be accounted for, nor the postnominal location of adjectives taking PP complements.

The complex array of factors that affect word order cross-linguistically and the interrelationships among these factors suggest that the word-order patterns occurring in languages are best viewed not in terms of dichotomous grammaticality judgments, but in terms of a series of choices defining a preferential ranking among the set of word-order possibilities available in a given language. This needs to be captured in any word-order rules that aspire to provide a comprehensive statement of order. Currently, ways of doing this are being elaborated, which assign a relative weighting to each of the possible orderings and specify how conflicting tendencies defining mutually exclusive linearizations are likely to be resolved within individual languages and across languages. This line of research represents the first serious attempt to integrate syntactic, semantic, and pragmatic aspects of order within specific models of grammar and therefore, in view of the far from satisfactory treatment of word order in modern grammatical theory, undoubtedly, is a step in the right direction.

Bibliography

Bock K 1982 Toward a cognitive psychology of syntax: Information processing contributions to sentence formulation. *Psychological Review* **89**: 1–47
Dryer M S 1992 The Greenbergian word order correlations. *Lg* **68**: 81–138
Greenberg J H 1963 Some universals of grammar with particular reference to the order of meaningful elements. In: Greenberg J H (ed.) *Universals of Language*. MIT Press, Cambridge, MA
Haiman J 1985 *Natural Syntax: Iconicity and Erosion*. Cambridge University Press, Cambridge
Hawkins J A 1983 *Word Order Universals*. Academic Press, New York
Hawkins J A 1994 *A Performance Theory of Order and Constituency*. Cambridge University Press, Cambridge
Mallinson G, Blake B J 1981 *Language Typology: Cross-Linguistic Studies in Syntax*. North-Holland, Amsterdam
Perkins R D 1989 Statistical techniques for determining language sample size. *SLang* **13(2)**: 293–315
Rijkhoff J et al. 1993 A method of language sampling. *SLang* **17(1)**
Ruhlen M 1975 *A Guide to the Language of the World*. Stanford Language Universals Project, Stanford University, CA
Tomlin R S 1986 *Basic Word Order*. Croom Helm, London
Vennemann T 1972 Analogy in generative grammar, the origin of word order. In: Heilmann L (ed.) *Proceedings of the Eleventh International Congress of Linguistics*, vol 2. Il Mulino, Bologna

X-bar Syntax

R. Cann

X-bar syntax is a theory of syntactic categories and their associated syntactic structures which provides a way of formally associating lexical and phrasal expressions of the same general type (like nouns and noun phrases) and capturing the notion 'head of a phrase' within a phrase structure grammar. Although often giving rise to controversy, the theory has had a significant influence on the development of theories of constituent structure and, in the early 1990s, finds a place within most syntactic frameworks.

1. Inception

The X-bar notation was introduced into syntactic theory in Chomsky (1970), developing an idea put forward in Harris (1951), and was designed to account for the structural similarities between certain derived nominal phrases in English (e.g., *John's proof of the theorem*) and their associated full sentences (e.g., *John proved the theorem*) without recourse to a transformational derivation of the former from the latter. If nominals are not syntactically derived from their associated verbs, they must be listed in the lexicon and inserted into the appropriate syntactic environments at deep structure. Such an approach entails the existence of a full set of almost identical phrase structure rules introducing the major lexical categories, N (noun), A (adjective), and V (verb) and their complements. In order to capture the generalization that similar complement structures are found across the major categories (including prepositions), Chomsky proposes the single phrase structure schema in Fig. 1 where the X is to be interpreted as a variable over the major categories, N, V, A, and P, X′ (read as 'X-bar' after the notation, X̄, used in the original article) stands for 'a phrase containing X as its head' (Chomsky 1970: 210), and the functional label 'Complements' covers the set of all possible complement expansions (NP, NP PP, NP S, etc.).

$$X′ \rightarrow X \text{ Complements} \tag{1}$$

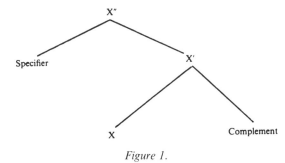

Figure 1.

In order to capture further similarities across category structures, this notation is extended up another level, expanding X″ ('X double-bar') as X′ (its head) together with its 'Specifiers.' The latter is another functional label, covering minor categories like determiners and major categories like noun phrase in subject position:

$$X″ \rightarrow \text{Specifiers } X′ \tag{2}$$

The two schemata in (1) and (2) together derive the general syntactic structure shown in Fig. 1 which is taken to hold for all the major categories N, A, V, and P. The tree shows how X′ and X″ are interpreted as phrasal 'projections' of the lexical category X. The parallelism of syntactic structures for all major categories determined by the X-bar schemata enables interesting generalizations to be made. For example, subcategorization and selectional restrictions can be generalized across related lexical items that have different categorial specifications (e.g., the verb *destroy* and the noun *destruction* both take NP objects). Generalized grammatical functions may also be defined over the structure in Fig. 1, allowing grammatical function changing rules to operate over any relevant domain whatever the categorial properties of the head. For example, the grammatical function 'object' can be defined as any N″ dominated by X′ and that of 'subject' as N″ dominated by X″. An implication of this is that a grammatical function changing rule like passivization does not need to make reference to the category of the structure it applies to but only to the relevant structural configuration.

The X-bar schemata in (1) and (2) constitute the 'standard theory' of X-bar syntax (cf. Radford 1988: 253–78) which has five main characteristics that differentiate it from standard phrase structure grammar:

(a) Phrasal categories are defined as projections of lexical ones using the bar level notation.

(b) Every major category (N, A, V, and P), but possibly excluding S, participates in the X-bar schemata.

(c) There are two phrasal categories, X′ and X″.

(d) Every phrase structure rule (with possible specified exceptions) contains a unique head and each head has one fewer bar level than its mother.

(e) Specifiers are introduced as sisters to X′ and complements as sisters to X.

During the development of the theory further characteristics have been added in the form of other constraints on heads and their satellites. The most important of these are:

(f) Every category introduced by a phrase structure rule that is not a head must be a maximal projection (Jackendoff 1977).

(g) Every nonhead category is optional (Emonds 1976).

(h) Every head must appear adjacent to one of the boundaries of X′ (Stowell 1981).

Each of these properties has engendered considerable debate which still continues. However, despite changes in the interpretation of the theory from constraints on phrase structure rules to a set of principles governing the construction of well-formed syntactic structures, the fundamentals of the theory have been remarkably persistent and continue to be assumed in syntactic frameworks like Transformational Grammar, Generalized Phrase Structure Grammar, and Lexical Functional Grammar (see *Transformational Grammar*; *Generalized Phrase Structure Grammar*; *Lexical Functional Grammar*).

2. X-Bar Categories

In standard Phrase Structure Grammar, category symbols are atomic (and arbitrary) so that no formal relation between different categories can be defined. There is, however, an intuitive relation between phrasal categories like NP, AP, PP, and VP and their lexical (preterminal) counterparts N, A, P, and V, which is that noun phrases (NP) contain nouns (N), adjective phrases contain adjectives, verb phrases contain verbs, and prepositional phrases contain prepositions. The X-bar notation for categories formally captures this intuition by factoring syntactic categories into a categorial label (like N, V, A, and P) and an index that indicates the phrasal type of the category. Phrasal types are interpreted as projections from the lexical category which has an index of 0, so that a lexical noun has the category $\langle N,0 \rangle$, its first projection is $\langle N,1 \rangle$, its second $\langle N,2 \rangle$, and so on. For this reason, X-bar categories are often written with the category label followed by a numerical superscript, e.g., N^1, N^2 etc., especially if more than two levels of projection are hypothesized. In Gazdar et al. (1985), the ordered pair structure of X-bar categories is dispensed with in favor of treating the bar level as a syntactic feature, 'BAR' with three values 0, 1, and 2.

A further debate has emerged over the range of categories that may project in the sense of X-bar theory. Chomsky (1970) and many others assume that only the major categories, noun, verb, adjective, and (following the arguments of Ray Jackendoff) preposition have phrasal counterparts. The sentence category has also been analyzed as a phrasal category, but one possibly lacking in a lexical counterpart. Minor categories like determiner, quantifier, complementizer, degree words, etc., have been defined as in Gazdar et al. (1985) as those that contain no bar level specification at all. In current Transformational Grammar, however, it has been suggested that certain

minor categories do project in the same way as major ones. For example, traditional noun phrases have been analyzed as projections of the determiner rather than the noun, the latter heading N″, interpreted as a common noun phrase complement of Det. Taking the X-bar analysis of minor categories further, Pollock (1989) suggests that categories that have no full lexical exemplars like agreement and tense also project in the syntax, yielding very abstract and complex phrase structure trees. As yet it is not clear what constraints there are on what categories may have bar levels (apart from the major ones), but the theory does allow for cross-linguistic variation in categories which project while maintaining the generalization that syntactic structures are constant.

3. Phrasal Projections

Although the standard theory assumes only two levels of projection, the theory imposes no upper limit on the possible number of bar levels. There have been various suggestions for the maximal value of the index, from the logical minimum of 1 (Stuurman 1985), through 3 (Jackendoff 1977), and up to 6 or more. It has also been suggested that there is no necessary maximum value at all and that categories project as far as is required to account for the structure of a phrase (Verkuyl 1981). Since adjectives can be theoretically iterated an infinite number of times, a nonrecursive analysis of the structure of such phrases entails that the index may itself be infinite. Most researchers, however, reject this interpretation and argue that there is a specific and identifiable maximal number of phrasal projections. The argumentation for this follows structuralist methodology in assigning expressions with the same syntactic distribution to the same category, including bar level. For example, the fact that a phrase like *cloudy blue sky* can be substituted felicitously for *blue sky* in all syntactic contexts may be captured by assigning both phrases to the same category, N′ and generating them by recursive application of the rule in (3):

$$N' \rightarrow AN' \tag{3}$$

Such a rule is not well-formed according to the X-bar schemata already given and entails the introduction of the recursive schema (4) into X-bar theory. This schema in effect adopts into X-bar syntax Harris's repeatable substitution equations, making the theory even more 'reminiscent of the system of phrase structure analysis developed by Harris in the 1940s' (Chomsky 1970: 211; see Stuurman 1985: 16–26 for a fuller discussion of the resemblances between the two proposals).

$$X' \rightarrow \text{Modifier} \, X' \tag{4}$$

The structuralist methodology adopted to justify the schema in (4) also provides an empirical way of identifying the number of bar levels exhibited by different categories along the lines discussed by Harris. Thus, different phrasal levels are postulated only where expressions of some category may be combined with other elements to form well-formed expressions of the same general category but with a different distribution. Where no further combinations lead to a phrase of the same general type then a maximal bar level has been reached. Such an approach adopts a strongly empirical stance towards the definition of phrasal categories which not only allows projection levels to vary from category to category, but also for the same lexical category across languages. On such an interpretation, while there may be similarities within a language across certain projection levels, these are not required and do not necessarily carry over into the descriptions of other languages, so that the universality of the X-bar system reduces to the idea that lexical categories project (i.e., that phrasal categories have heads with the same categorial label). The specification of the number of bar levels becomes a purely descriptive matter.

This latter interpretation of projection types is associated primarily with monostratal theories of syntax like Generalized Phrase Structure Grammar and Lexical Functional Grammar (see *Generalized Phrase Structure Grammar*; *Lexical Functional Grammar*). A good deal of work in X-bar syntax, however, adopts Chomsky's original assumption that there is a single number of bar levels that is relevant for all projecting categories, a proposal that has been dubbed the 'Uniform Level Hypothesis.' Jackendoff (1977) adopts a strong version of this hypothesis, maintaining a uniform three-level projection even for minor categories, where all projections are nonbranching. Generally, however, exceptions to the Uniform Level Hypothesis are permitted where the category in question is a specified grammatical formative, a minor category, or the sentential category. Some attempts at providing a more explanatory characterization of the numbers of bar levels have been made and thus provide a more reasoned basis for the adoption of the Uniform Level Hypothesis into Universal Grammar. One such attempt is given in Muysken (1982) which provides a feature analysis of bar levels based on the perceived primitive properties of the X-bar system. Muysken suggests that there are two primitive properties underlying the X-bar convention: the notion of 'projection,' that categories project up trees from lexical categories, and the notion of 'maximality,' that there is a maximal number of projections that can be made from any one category. Treating these properties as binary-valued features yields four possible types of category, three equivalent to the three bar levels of the standard theory plus a nonprojecting maximal category that may be used to analyze minor categories like Determiner, Modal, Quantifier, etc.

$$[+\text{maximal}, +\text{projection}] = X'' \quad\quad (5)$$
$$[-\text{maximal}, +\text{projection}] = X'$$

$$[-\text{maximal}, -\text{projection}] = X$$
$$[+\text{maximal}, -\text{projection}] = \text{minor grammatical category}$$

More recent suggestions in Kayne (1994) and Chomsky (1995a, 1995b) provide a more restricted basis for the theory without using feature decomposition. Kayne proposes that there is only a single phrasal projection, XP, which dominates a lexical head plus a complement. To incorporate a second level of structure, adjunction is allowed to XP, as in (6):

$$XP \rightarrow TPXP \quad\quad (6)$$

Using an algorithm for deriving linear order from hierarchical relations, Kayne argues that there can be one and only one adjunct per projection and thus reconstructs, from more general principles, the strict version of the X-bar structure without recursion that was shown in Fig. 1. Chomsky (1995a) takes a somewhat different approach. Bar levels of any sort are rejected and structures are defined through a projection of the label one of two sister expressions, essentially giving rise to one type of rule only, that in (7) where x and y are the labels (lexical features) of lexical items. (One of the effects of this move is to make transformational syntax more similar to Dependency and Categorial Grammar.) The schema is fully recursive, allowing multiple specifiers, and is thus very similar to Verkuyl (1981)'s proposals, but without the enumeration of phrasal levels.

$$x \rightarrow xy \qu\quad (7)$$

4. Endocentricity

The schematic X-bar structure in Fig. 1 shows how the theory captures the traditional notion that phrases are typically 'endocentric,' i.e., that phrases contain expressions of the same categorial type. This solves the problem noted in Lyons (1968) concerning the formal possibility of phrase structure rules which violate the endocentricity of the phrase, as there can be no rules in a grammar, for example, that rewrite N′ (= Nom) as V S or V″ (= VP) as N. X-bar theory, therefore, seems to impose a strong and desirable constraint on the type of base rules found in any natural language. However, a debate arises over the precise relationship between mothers and their heads, a question which is intimately connected with the questions about the number and domain of projection types. The three schemata in (1), (2), and (4) all conform to the general pattern in (8) where m and n stand for indices representing bar levels:

$$X^n \rightarrow \ldots X^m \ldots \qu\quad (8)$$

The previous section discussed the values that n and m may take, but the relation between n and m in (8) is also an important and controversial matter. In Chomsky (1970) and many works thereafter, m is equal to $n-1$ in all cases. Kornai and Pullum (1990) refers to this property as 'succession' and point out that the assumption is incompatible with any adoption of directly recursive rules like (3). If the latter type of rule is adopted then m must be equal to $n-1$ or to n itself. This is the commonest assumption, but it has been argued that an even weaker constraint on the relation between m and n should be adopted. This requires m only to be less than or equal to n, thus allowing, for example, double-bar categories to be headed directly by a lexical head. Such rules are proposed in Emonds (1976) and Gazdar et al. (1985) amongst others and are particularly useful where a lexical head admits of no specifiers, e.g., the auxiliaries in English which may be analyzed as taking a verb phrase complement but no specifier, as in the rule in (9):

$$V[+Aux]'' \rightarrow V[+Aux]V'' \qquad (9)$$

More dramatic violations of succession have been proposed, but generally such rules are eschewed and the most common assumption is that a head must have an identical or lower bar level than its mother, with the possible additional stipulation that a lower bar level must be only one less than the mother's.

Another constraint implied by the X-bar schemata is that all phrase structure rules are endocentric. Chomsky (1970) violates this constraint by adopting the position that sentences are nonendocentric and that S does not participate in the X-bar system. Jackendoff also allows 'exocentric' rules as 'systematic exceptions to the Uniform Three Level Hypothesis' (Jackendoff 1977: 221), but the current orthodoxy takes the view that all rules or structures are indeed endocentric. The problem of the apparent nonendocentricity of the sentence has been solved in various ways. One solution is to take S as a projection of the verb and analyze it as V^{max} for some maximal bar level. Problems arise with this analysis, however, with regard to structural parallelism, the position of the auxiliary node and the analysis of the clausal category, often written S'. Chomsky (1986), following Stowell (1981), adopts the hypothesis that S is (universally) headed by a remnant of the Aux node, renamed inflexion (I), which possibly contains tense and agreement information, has the subject as its specifier, and V'' as its complement. The clausal category, S', is then defined as a projection of Complementizer (C), which yields the abstract structure in Fig. 2 as the analysis of full clauses. The insistence that all rules and structures are properly endocentric has led within transformational grammar to the postulation of heads like Agr and Tense which are often empty at d-structure. The argumentation for such abstract structures must of necessity depart from the general methodology for determining the heads of constituents and may lead to a situation where the content of the endocentricity constraint becomes obscure (see *Head-driven Phrase Structure Grammar*).

A final constraint exemplified by the X-bar schemata is that heads are apparently unique in their constructions. While it is recognized that most constructions do indeed conform to this principle of uniqueness, it has been argued that not all constructions observe it. Gazdar et al. (1985), for example, adopt an analysis of coordinate constructions as multiheaded, presupposing the new X-bar schema (10), where X^{i+} indicates one or more instances of the category X^i.

$$X^i \rightarrow X^{i+} X^i \qquad (10)$$

The introduction of such a schema into X-bar syntax does not pose a theoretical problem beyond expanding the number of rule schemata required. However, it has been argued that there are constructions, e.g., Det+N and Comp+S in English, that must be analyzed as doubly headed according to common criteria for identifying heads, but that the two heads are not identical categorially (Cann 1993). If this is true, then the foundations of X-bar theory would be seriously compromised as there is no provision for relating mothers to their heads where different category labels are involved.

5. Specifiers, Adjuncts, and Complements

In addition to imposing constraints on the relation between mothers and their heads, conditions may also be imposed on their sisters. The most frequently cited constraints are that nonhead daughters must be maximal projections and that they are optional. The formal content of these constraints may be questioned but the intuition behind the claims is clear. With respect to the maximality constraint, the idea is that where an expression of category X may appear as a nonhead daughter in a rule then all possible structures in which X is the head may also appear in that position. For example, where a rule allows a verb to head a constituent containing a nominal phrase, the maximality constraint entails that that nominal phrase can be realized minimally as a noun as in *drink water* or as any maximal expansion of N, including specifiers, modifiers, and complements, e.g., *drink some clear water from the well*. Maximality rules out analyses that, for example, require a specifier in a nonhead daughter to be omitted as in the appearance of verb phrase (V') complements in a two-bar level grammar where S is the maximal projection of V or a sentential analysis of nonfinite complements to verbs that do not allow subjects of those complements (as in *try to sing* versus **tried Kim to sing*). Analyses like the latter, which are often assumed in the literature, must seek to rule out the appearance of subjects through the action of other grammatical rules or principles.

The optionality constraint also has strong intuitive appeal. In all constructions, adjuncts are always optional and, in noun and adjective phrases, so are complements and most specifiers. Although complements are not generally optional in prepositional

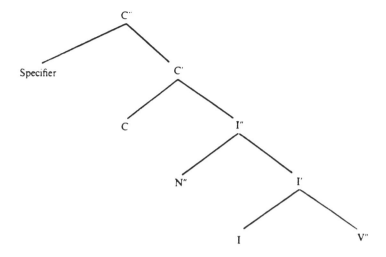

Figure 2.

and verb phrases, one may attribute this to other factors (e.g., case requirements) and not to the property of the rule or rules expanding V′ or P′, i.e., to X-bar theory. If other factors are allowed to override the optionality of nonhead daughters, either parochially via the lexicon or universally through the operation of a general principle, then the condition really reduces to a statement that there is some head (of any projecting category) in a language that may appear without any sisters at all (e.g., intransitive verbs, prepositions, and mass nouns). Since this is one of the ways of determining the head of a construction, it is not clear that the optionality constraint has any important consequences in the grammar beyond what is already embodied in the claim that all constructions are endocentric.

In some of the earliest work within X-bar syntax, the terms 'specifier' and 'complement' referred to ordered positions with respect to the head: specifiers preceded, and complements followed, the head (cf. Jackendoff 1977: ch. 3). Ordering relations amongst constituents, however, are currently factored out of phrase structure rules (see below) and so these two functional labels have come to refer to the unordered positions within the X-bar tree shown in Fig. 1. Elements occupying these positions have different functions within the grammar and exhibit different properties. The complement position is associated with the argument positions of the head. Complements are subcategorized for and are given semantic argument status, for example by being θ-marked. Complements also have the property that they can generally be displaced from their expected position, a fact that is accounted for in current Transformational Grammar by the Empty Category Principle and in Generalized Phrase Structure Grammar by the Lexical Head Constraint on metarule application. Both theories crucially rely on a fundamental sisterhood relationship between displaced constituents and their lexical heads being stated somewhere in the grammar (see *Generalized Phrase Structure Grammar*).

The specifier position, on the other hand, not being sister to X, is not subcategorized for, and displacement from this position is less frequent, and subject to more restrictions, than that from complement position. In addition, elements in specifier position may be required to agree with the lexical head of the containing constituent. The definition of a specifier is not, however, easy to pin down. In the earliest research into X-bar syntax, specifiers were usually minor categories like determiners, auxiliaries, degree words, etc. Often the addition of expressions of such categories changes the nature of the phrase quite considerably (e.g., the addition of the determiner *the* to the nominal phrase *happy gardener* yields an expression *the happy gardener* with a different distribution) and this has led to the suggestion that specifiers take a nonmaximal category into a maximal one (i.e., one that can head no more inclusive phrases). Under such an interpretation noun phrases that saturate a predicate, like sentential subjects, may also be construed as specifiers. This captures the parallelism between deverbal nominal expressions with possessive subjects (e.g., *The barbarians' destruction of the city*) and full sentences (e.g., *The barbarians destroyed the city*) where the N″ *the barbarians* is in specifier position in both cases, of N′ in the former case and V′ or I′ in the latter. From the analysis of specifiers as subjects follows the hypothesis that this position should be available as a landing site for movement in transformational analyses. Thus, it is generally assumed that question phrases are moved to the specifier position of C″ (cf. Fig. 2) rather than to the complement position itself (cf. Chomsky 1986). The specifier position may, therefore, contain elements that perform one of three functions: minor categories that alter the distributional properties of a phrase; phrasal expressions that saturate predicates; and displaced constituents. Attempts are currently being made in transformational theory to unify the nature of specifiers by taking the specifier position to be a landing site for movement and the position of external θ-marking whilst analyzing grammatical formatives as heads of their own phrases (as in the Determiner Phrase analysis of traditional noun phrases mentioned above). A fully coherent theory of specifiers has still, however, to be developed.

The third type of functional category in X-bar syntax includes adjuncts of all sorts (attributive adjectives, adverbial expressions, nonargument prepositional phrases, relative clauses, purpose clauses, etc.). These are generated recursively as daughter and sister to X′, thus inhabiting an intermediate position between specifiers and complements. This intermediate status also seems to be reflected in their syntactic properties: they do not receive a θ-role from the head (and are not therefore arguments), are displaced less freely than complements but more freely than specifiers, and are always optional.

In both Kayne (1994) and Chomsky (1995a, 1995b), the structural distinctions between the three functional types are obscured. Both essentially reduce specifier and (phrasal) adjunct to the same relation, (6) and (7), respectively. For Chomsky, there is a further reduction in that the complement relation is also structurally identical to that of the specifier with differences between the two functions being reconstructed through locality with a head (complements being closest, i.e. most local, to the head). It remains to be seen whether the more restricted theories of the three functional relations of X-bar theory will turn out to be adequate.

6. Word Order Typology and Configurationality

In earlier research, the X-bar convention was presumed also to account for word order within phrase structure trees as well as hierarchical relationships between constituents. Following the suggestion of Gazdar and Pullum that phrase structure rules should be factored into hierarchical combination rules and word-order statements, most research within the X-bar framework assumes that word order is not determined by the X-bar schemata but by other rules or principles. In Generalized Phrase Structure Grammar (cf. Gazdar et al. 1985), hierarchical relationships are determined by 'Immediate Dominance Rules' and word order is determined by 'Linear Precedence Rules.' In transformational theory, constraints on word order are postulated to follow from principles like Case Theory and Theta Theory (cf. Stowell 1981) except that X-bar theory still allows a parameter of

word-order variation: the linear relationship between heads and their sisters. Thus, a typology of 'head-first' and 'head-final' languages is implied by the fixing of this parameter which acts as a default rule for ordering constituents where no other principles determine linear relations. It is interesting to note that while earlier studies within Generalized Phrase Structure Grammar postulated linear precedence rules that refer to heads, in the early 1990s such rules are rejected in favor of rules that refer to category specifications only.

Although variation in constituent order cross-linguistically is not in principle problematic for X-bar syntax, free word order does pose a considerable problem for the theory. Hale (1983) puts forward the case that there is too little evidence to give hierarchical analyses to very free word order languages like the Australian Aboriginal language, Warlpiri. Such languages, it is argued, are best given 'flat' syntactic structures, allowing words to appear in many different orders even to splitting semantic constituents. These have been called 'W*' (W-star) languages after the suggestion that their grammars contain only the rule in (11):

$$X' \to XW^* \tag{11}$$

This expands X′ as a head and a string of zero or more words. Where X is equivalent only to the sentential category, the only hierarchical structure in the language is between the sentence, its head (Inflexion or Auxiliary) and any number of other words. Work within current transformational theory tries to solve the problem by using projections of functional (minor) categories (see Kayne 1994). Apparent nonconfigurational languages are hypothesized to be defined by the same structural rules as configurational ones, but have sytactic projections that provide more positions for expressions to appear in. This approach remains controversial, but some version of the idea will be necessary to support the candidacy of X-bar syntax as a fundamental principle of Universal Grammar. Without a robust solution to the problem, the status of the theory will be open to serious doubt (see *Word Order and Linearization*; *Typology and Word Order Change*).

Bibliography

Cann R 1993 Patterns of headedness. In: Corbett G, Fraser N M, McGlashan S (eds.) *Heads in Grammatical Theory*. Cambridge University Press, Cambridge

Chomsky N 1970 Remarks on nominalization. In: Jacobs R A, Rosenbaum P S (eds.) *Readings in English Transformational Syntax*. Ginn, Waltham, MA

Chomsky N 1986 *Barriers*. MIT Press, Cambridge, MA

Chomsky N 1995a Bare phrase structure. In: Webelhuth G (ed.) *Government and Binding Theory and the Minimalist Program*. Blackwell, Oxford

Chomsky N 1995b *The Minimalist Program*. MIT Press, Cambridge, MA

Emonds J E 1976 *A Transformational Approach to English Syntax*. Academic Press, New York

Gazdar G, Klein E, Pullum G K, Sag I A 1985 *Generalized Phrase Structure Grammar*. Blackwell, Oxford

Hale K 1983 Warlpiri and the grammar of non-configurational languages. *NLLT* 1: 5–47

Harris Z S 1951 *Structural Linguistics*. University of Chicago Press, Chicago, IL

Jackendoff R 1977 *X′ Syntax: A Study of Phrase Structure*. MIT Press, Cambridge, MA

Kayne R 1994 *The Antisymmetry of Syntax*. MIT Press, Cambridge, MA

Kornai A, Pullum G K 1990 The X-bar theory of phrase structure. *Lg* **66**: 24–50

Lyons J 1968 *An Introduction to Theoretical Linguistics*. Cambridge University Press, Cambridge

Muysken P 1982 Parameterizing the notion 'head.' *JLR* **2**: 57–76

Pollock J-Y 1989 Verb movement, universal grammar and the structure of IP. *LIn* **20**: 365–424

Radford A 1988 *Transformational Grammar: A First Course*. Cambridge University Press, Cambridge

Stowell T 1981 Origins of phrase structure (Doctoral dissertation, Massachusetts Institute of Technology)

Stuurman F 1985 *Phrase Structure Theory in Generative Grammar*. Foris, Dordrecht

Verkuyl H 1981 Numerals and quantifiers in X-bar syntax and their semantic interpretation. In: Groenenbijk J A G, Janssen T M V, Stokhof M B J (eds.) *Formal Methods in the Study of Language*. Mathematisch Zentrum, Amsterdam

Glossary

(A selection of terms taken from the original Glossary edited by M. G. Dareau, *University of Edinburgh,* which appeared in The *Encyclopedia of Language and Linguistics*).

The alphabetical arrangement is word by word, and hyphens are ignored.

Brackets in the entry enclose alternative terms, parts of terms or the symbol/abbreviation used for that term.

Small capitals refer to fields or subfields in the main encyclopedia.

Terms in bold type refer to other entries within the glossary or provide other related usages.

Abbreviations

esp.	especially
freq.	frequently
Gmc	Germanic
Goth	Gothic
ME	Middle English
med.	medieval
mod.	modern
OE	Old English
OF	Old French
orig.	originally
OSc	Old Scottish
specif.	specifically
trad.	traditionally
transf.	transferred

A = **adjective, adverbial, argument**

A-bar-binding In **binding theory**, the **coindexing** of a category with a c-commanding (see **c-command**) category in A-bar position. See **bar 1**.

A-binding In **binding theory**, the **coindexing** of a category with a c-commanding (see **c-command**) noun phrase in A-position.

A-over-A A constraint on transformational rules in GENERATIVE GRAMMAR, which says that in a construction when a category A is embedded within a larger instance of the same category A, then a rule that refers to the category A may only apply to the larger (higher) instance of A. The rule would, for example, prevent the movement of an NP out of a relative clause: *I know [$_{NP}$ a man who grows [$_{NP}$ roses]]: *roses, I know a man who grows—*

A-position In GENERATIVE GRAMMAR, a position in which an **argument** (sense **2**) can occur.

abessive In **inflecting** and **agglutinating languages**, e.g.,

Finnish, the **case** denoting lack of accompaniment, 'without.'

ablative In **inflecting** and **agglutinating languages**, the **case** expressing **locative** and **instrumental** meanings, separation, origin, etc.; equivalent to prepositions, 'by,' 'with,' 'from.'

absolute universal A **universal** which characterizes all languages without exception, e.g., every language has nouns.

absolutive Said of the object of a transitive verb and the subject of an intransitive verb in an **ergative** language, e.g., Eskimo, which display the same case.

abstract 1 Describes a **noun** which denotes a quality or state, e.g., *domesticity, poetry.* (Contrasts with **concrete**.) **2** A summary. **3** In the study of **narrative**, a summary of the story, optionally present.

acceptability The possibility or normality of an utterance, usage, etc., in a language as judged by a native speaker; in GENERATIVE GRAMMAR, the acceptability of an utterance is seen as a matter of **performance** (contrasting with **grammaticality** which is a matter of **competence**). (**Unacceptable** examples are indicated by a preceding asterisk.)

acccessibility A measure of the ease with which a speaker can retrieve a linguistic unit from his/her memory, some sorts of unit being retrieved more easily than others.

accessibility hierarchy In RELATIONAL GRAMMAR, the hierarchical ordering of the grammatical relations **subject, direct object, indirect object,** etc., with regard to the syntactic processes, e.g., relativization, they take part in; postulated as a linguistic **universal**.

accidence The part of a grammar dealing with **inflections**.

accusative, objective 1 In **inflecting** and **agglucinating languages,** the **case** of the noun when it is the object of a verb; trad. applied to the object in English (the inflected pronominal forms *him, her,* etc., are now usually said to be in the **objective** case). **2** Said of a language in which the objects of transitive and intransitive verbs are treated alike. (Contrasts with **ergative 1**.)

acquisition see **language acquisition**

across-the-board phenomena Effects which apply 'across the board' to the whole of a linguistic system, specif. In GENERATIVE GRAMMAR, phenomena which affect all the constituents in a coordinate structure.

actant also **(verb) elasborator** In VALENCY GRAMMAR,

387

a functional unit determined by the **valency** of the verb, e.g., subject, direct or indirect object, essential adverbial, etc. (Contrasts with **circonstant**.)

action 1 also **activity** Something which happens under the control of an **agent** or **actor**, trad. also used of events or processes not attributable to an agent. **2** Descriptive of what a **verb** 'does', freq. in the phrase 'the action of the verb'.

active 1 In the analysis of **voice**, a sentence or clause in which the **subject** is also the **actor**, e.g., *Mary drove the car*; the verb form in such a sentence or clause. (Contrasts with **passive**.) See also **middle voice**. **2** Describes a possible state of a piece of information in the mind of a speaker or listener, e.g., something already known, **given** material, is considered to be active, other levels of awareness on the part of the speaker or listener may be termed **semi-active** and **inactive**.

activity A type of **action**, a **process** that occurs under the control of an **agent** or **actor**, e.g., *John runs every day*.

actor 1 The entity which puts into effect the action of the verb, sometimes equated with the **subject** of a sentence, e.g., *Susan ate the cake*. Cf. **agent 2** In ROLE AND REFERENCE GRAMMAR, the primitive **macro-role** which expresses the participant which instigates, performs, controls the action or situation. (Contrasts with **undergoer**.)

actor-action-goal The sentence pattern typical of **statements** in many languages, e.g., in *Ivor took a book*, *Ivor* is the **actor**, *took* the **action** (sense **1**) and *book* the **goal** (see **patient**).

adequacy Evaluation of success in the writing of a **grammar** according to various criteria. See also **descriptive adequacy**, **explanatory adequacy**, **external adequacy**, **internal adequacy**, **observational adequacy**. Cf. also **strongly adequate** (see **strong generative capacity**).

adessive In **inflecting** and **agglutinating languages**, the **case** expressing the meaning 'on' a place.

ADJ = adjective

adjacency principle (condition) In GOVERNMENT AND BINDING THEORY, the general principle that a case assigner, e.g., a verb phrase, and its assignee, e.g., a noun phrase, may not be separated by another linguistic element, i.e., *I killed a duck today* where *killed* and *a duck* are adjacent, is well-formed but **I killed today a duck* is not.

adjectival (adjective) phrase A **phrase** which functions like an adjective.

adjectivalization In TRANSFORMATIONAL GRAMMAR, the process of transforming a predicative structure into an attributive adjective or adjectival phrase or clause, e.g., *laughing jackass < The jackass is laughing*.

adjective (adj, ADJ, A) A member of the word class

whose main function is to specify an attribute of a noun, e.g., *a fat cat*, *The cat is fat*, in many languages displaying contrasts of degree: *fat, fatter, fattest*.

adjoin see **adjunction**

adjunct 1 *gram* An optional element in a grammatical construction which may be added or omitted without any consequent syntactic change, e.g., *She came home afterwards*; *They went for a walk in the park*. **2 In** X-BAR SYNTAX, one of the functional categories, beside **specifiers** and **complements**, including attributive adjectives, adverbials, etc.; they are always optional.

adjunction In TRANSFORMATIONAL GRAMMAR and GOVERNMENT AND BINDING THEORY, a **movement rule** or **transformation** which **adjoins** or attaches a constituent which has been moved to a category at the point (**landing site**) to which it has been moved thereby creating a new node of that category whose immediate constituents are the moved constituent and the original category; **extraposition** is one example of **adjunction**. See also **Chomsky adjunction**, **daughter adjunction**, **sister adjunction**.

adnominal Any element in a noun phrase which modifies a noun as an adverbial modifies a verb, e.g., *a big cat*, *a cat in a hat*, *Jane's cat*.

adposition A **preposition** which typically takes a noun phrase complement.

ADV = adverb, adverbial

advancement In RELATIONAL GRAMMAR, a class of processes used to change grammatical relations, e.g., passivization, which converts object to subject, moving the noun phrase in object position up the relational hierarchy.

adverb, (adv, ADV) A member of the word class whose main function is to specify the mode of action of a verb, e.g., *She ate quickly*; other functions include sentence connector, e.g., *Besides, it's blue*, and intensifier, e.g., *very good*.

adverbial, (ADV, A) An element of clause structure functioning like an adverb, said esp. of phrases or clauses, e.g. *He telephoned at once/last year/when he got home*.

adverbial clause A clause which functions like an adverb to express various relationships. See also **causal clause**, **concessive clause**, **conditional 1**, **degree 2**, **manner 1**.

adverb(ial) phrase A **phrase** which functions like an adverb; a phrase with an adverb as its head, e.g., *very quickly*.

adversative Describes a construction which expresses an unfavourable or antithetical effect or circumstance, e.g., *but* is an adversative conjunction.

affected Describes the **participant role** of the direct object, being the entity usually affected by the action of the verb. (Contrasts with **agentive 3**, **recipient**.)

affirmative, positive Said of a sentence or verb which

is not negative (see **negation**), i.e., which expresses an assertion, e.g., *It is raining.*

affix 1 A **formative** capable of being added to a **root** or **stem** to make a more complex word, e.g., *unfriendly.* See also **infix**, **prefix**. **2** In GENERATIVE GRAMMAR, the term has been extended to include present and past tense markers, *-ing*, *be*, *have*, etc.

affix hopping In GENERATIVE GRAMMAR, an obligatory transformation which ensures that an **affix** (sense **2**) is attached correctly, e.g., *ing + fly* becomes *fly + ing*, in a string.

affixing language A language which expresses grammatical relations mainly through the use of affixes, e.g., Latin. Cf. **inflecting** and **agglutinating languages**.

agent(ive) 1 A clause element whose function is to specify the means whereby an action, etc., comes about, e.g., in the passive the **agent** is the nominal, etc., occurring in the 'by' phrase: *The cake was eaten by the dog.* **2** In CASE GRAMMAR and GOVERNMENT AND BINDING THEORY, one of a fixed set of 'semantic cases' or **theta roles** (along with **dative**, **objective**, etc.). **3** The **participant role** typically of the subject, the instigator of what is denoted by the verb. (Contrasts with **affected**, **recipient**.)

agglutinating language A language in which words are made up of a sequence of morphs, each expressing a separate item of meaning as, number, person, tense, etc. Cf. **inflecting language**.

agreement 1 also **concord** A formal relationship in which the form of one element requires a corresponding form in another, e.g., between subject and verb: *the cat sits*, *the cats sit*. **2** also **AGR** In GOVERNMENT AND BINDING THEORY, the component of **INFL** (**inflection 2**) concerned with **agreement** (sense **1**), specif. the coindexing mechanism responsible for agreement between subject and verb. **3** also **AGR** In GENERALIZED PHRASE STRUCTURE GRAMMAR, the head feature (see **head feature convention**) which ensures agreement wherever this is appropriate.

Aktionsart A term applied to various distinctions lexical and grammatical, in the types of actions, etc. denoted by verbs, sometimes equated, more or less, with **aspect**.

algorithm A procedure in which a complicated operation is resolved into a number of clearly defined simpler steps.

alienable Describes a type of possessive where the item possessed is so in a nonessential or temporary fashion, e.g., *the girl's hat* vs *the girl's hair*, which is **inalienable**.

allative In **inflecting** and **agglutinating languages**, the **case** expressing the meaning of motion 'to' or 'towards' a place.

allo- Refers to the non-distinctive realizations of a linguistic unit, e.g., **allophone**, **allomorph**, etc.

allomorph One of a number of alternative realizations

of a morpheme which are, e.g., conditioned by their phonetic environment, as in the case of the plural morpheme in English, realized by the allomorphs /s/, /z/ and /iz/.

alpha notation In GENERATIVE GRAMMAR, a simplification made in the statement of a rule by the introduction of a variable (α).

alternant see **alternation**

alternation The relationship between variant forms of any sort. The forms or **alternants** freq. vary predictably, e.g., *girl ~ girls*, *profound ~ profundity*, or not, e.g., *go ~ went*.

ambient clause A **clause** which refers to the weather or environment, e.g., *It is cold.*

ambiguity Said of a word, phrase, etc., which has two or more meanings leading to the necessity for more than one lexical or grammatical analysis.

ambivalent Describes a verb whose valency can be expressed according to two or more different valency schemata, e.g., *Mary killed Bob* can be described either as **operative** or **factitive**.

analyzable In GENERATIVE GRAMMAR, of a string which satisfies the structural description of a transformational rule, the rule being, therefore, applicable.

anaphor In GOVERNMENT AND BINDING THEORY, a noun phrase which has no external reference but refers to some linguistic antecedent, specif. **reciprocal pronouns** (see **reciprocal**), e.g., *each other*; **reflexive pronouns**, e.g., *himself*; **NP-traces**.

anaphora Reference back to something previously expressed, as by use of a pronoun or pro-verb, e.g., *John went home, **he** really **did that**.* (Contrasts with **cataphora**.)

animate A feature of nouns whose reference is to living things. (Contrasts with **inanimate** which refers to objects or concepts.)

antecedent A word, phrase, etc. referred to by a pronoun, etc. occurring later in the text, e.g., ***The hat** he wore is this one.*

anthropological linguistics 1 = **linguistic anthropology** **2** The study of non-Western languages (esp. of the Americas) focusing on their interaction with regard esp. to areal groupings, language contact, and linguistic typology.

antipassive In **ergative** languages, the functional equivalent of the **passive** in non-ergative languages.

apodosis The consequence or result expressed in the main clause in a conditional sentence, e.g., *If I come **he must go**.*

application The range of use of a word, etc., in relation to extralinguistic entities, situations, etc.

application grammar A type of **generative categorial grammar** whose basic units are **term** (α) and **sentence** (β).

applicative Describes the double-object construction in some languages, e.g., Bantu, where various participant roles can be indicated as an object by the addition of an affix.

apposition Two or more noun phrases having the same referent and standing in the same syntactical relation to the rest of the sentence, e.g., *Dylan Thomas, poet, playwright, drunk*.

appropriate Of language in general: suitable in a given situation, e.g., *Dear Sir* is appropriate in a formal letter to a newspaper, *Dear Jimmy* is not.

arbitrariness 1 The lack of physical correspondence between linguistic forms and their referents in the real world. **2** In SAUSSUREAN linguistics, the conventional nature of the relationship between **sign** and **signified** is termed **arbitrary**. (Contrasts with **iconicity** (see **icon**).)

arbitrary reference In GOVERNMENT AND BINDING THEORY, an empty subject, indicated by **PRO**, whose reference is unattributable, e.g., the subject of the infinitive in *It is easy to frighten Alison*.

arboreal 1 In GENERATIVE GRAMMAR = **tree** structure.

arc In RELATIONAL GRAMMAR and ARC PAIR GRAMMAR, a curved arrow indicating a relationship of dependency on a linguistic level, e.g., of **subject** with the clause of which it is subject.

arc pair grammar A linguistic theory deriving from RELATIONAL GRAMMAR and concerned with constructing a highly explicit, formalized account of the linguistic relationships (i.e. subject, object, etc.) that make up linguistic constructions.

area = **(linguistic) area**

areal linguistics An aspect of **dialectology**, the study of the linguistic characteristics of a (**linguistic**) **area**.

argument (A) 1 An independent variable upon whose value that of a **function** depends, e.g., *x*, *y* or *z* in *x-y+z*. **2** In GENERATIVE GRAMMAR and CASE GRAMMAR, a position filled by a noun or noun phrase within a sentence or noun phrase, i.e., a subject, direct object, etc. See also **nuclear argument**. **3** In GOVERNMENT AND BINDING THEORY, the expressions within a linguistic structure that receive **theta roles**. **4** A prose statement of the sense of a poem.

argument slot In CASE GRAMMAR, the possible positions of noun phrases (or **arguments**) in a sentence (or **proposition**), labeled or identified according to their semantic relationships with the verb phrase (or predicate word).

arity = **valency**

arrangement A sequence of linguistic elements according to their relative position or distribution, the possible combinations of phonemes within words, words within sentences, etc. Cf. **item and arrangement**.

article A **determiner** which differentiates nouns according to their definiteness: *the* is the **definite article** in English, *a(n)* the **indefinite**.

ascension In RELATIONAL GRAMMAR, the process of **raising**, e.g., in the analysis of *Mary seems to smile*, Mary ascends from being subject of *Mary smiles* to being subject of *Mary seems to smile*.

ascriptive Of a type of sentence where the subject noun phrase and the post-verbal complement are attributively identical but not exchangeable, e.g., *Jane is happy*, *Happy is Jane.

aspect A category of description referring to the way in which the performance of an action, esp. its duration or completion, is denoted by the verb, e.g., *I am going/I go*. Other possible aspectual distinctions include **attenuative**, **habitual**, **inceptive**, **iterative**, **mutative**, **resultative**, **progressive**, etc. Cf. **Aktionsart**.

aspectualizer In GENERATIVE GRAMMAR, a **formative** indicating **aspect**.

assertive Used to describe collectively the grouping of adjective, pronoun and adverb, *some*, *somebody*, *something*, *sometimes*. (Contrasts with the **non-assertive** *any*, *anybody*, *anything*, *ever* and the **negative** *no*, *nobody*, *nothing*, *never*.)

assign In GENERATIVE GRAMMAR, describes the action of rules, in attributing structure to sentences.

asterisk (*) A mark used to indicate **1** A grammatically **unacceptable** usage, e.g., *Is good he. **2** A reconstructed form hypothesized as underlying known forms but for which there is no written evidence, e.g., OTeut *dômjan (Goth *dôm-s* judgement, doom). **3** In X-BAR SYNTAX, an operator used to indicate any number (including zero) of examples of a category, e.g., YP* = any number of phrases of any sort. **4** **non-configurational languages** are also called **W*** (**w-star**) **languages**.

asterisked form = **starred form**

attested Of linguistic forms, evidenced in actual (past or present) usage.

attribute = **feature 4**

attributive Describes an adjective or other modifier when it occurs whin the noun phrase, e.g., *the red nose*, **city** *streets*, **never to be forgotten** *occasion*. (Contrasts with or, in some approaches, is viewed as including **predicative**.)

autolexical syntax An analysis which treats syntax and morphology as separate parallel organizations of the same surface structure data.

autonomous syntax In STANDARD THEORY, the independence of the syntactic component from the semantic component.

auxiliary (verb), (Aux) A non-lexical verb used in conjunction with a **lexical verb** to make distinctions of aspect, mood, voice, etc., e.g., *We are going*, *I can/ may/shall come*.

avalent see **valency**

axiom, **postulate** One of the set of basic propositions which a linguistic theory assumes to be true and from which the rest of the grammar may be deduced.

axis 1 In SAUSSUREAN linguistics, intersecting dimensions of linguistic analysis, e.g., synchronic vs diachronic is termed 'axis of simultaneities' vs 'axis of successions'. **2** In some models of grammatical classification, the second or directed element in an **exocentric construction**, e.g., *hit* **the ball**, *in* **the house**.

bar 1 In X-BAR SYNTAX, a syntactic category; specif. **zero-bar** categories are word-level categories, **single-bar** and **double-bar**, phrase-level. Further specifications can be indicated as A-bar. **2** In GENERALIZED PHRASE STRUCTURE GRAMMAR, an integer-valued feature taking the values {0,1,2} where these stand for the same syntactic categories as in **1** above.

bar (number, prime) notation In GENERATIVE GRAMMAR, in the analysis of the phrase, equivalent notations which distinguish the full phrase, e.g., *the Queen of Scots* as $\bar{\bar{N}}$ (N-double bar) (N^2 or N'') from the **small phrase** *Queen of Scots*, $\bar{N}$ (N-single bar) (N^2 or N') and the noun which is the head of the phrase, *queen* (N, N^0), the **zero-level category**.

bar projection = **projection 2**

barrier In GOVERNMENT AND BINDING THEORY, a category whose boundaries block certain processes, specif. a single barrier blocks government, two barriers block movement.

base (component) In STANDARD THEORY, the part of the syntactic component which generates the basic sentence patterns; the **phrase structure component** (see **phrase structure grammar**). Cf. **deep structure**, **transformational grammar**.

behaviorism A doctrine holding that objective evidence observable in behavior is the proper study of psychology, applied to linguistics by BLOOMFIELD.

benefactive In analysis in terms of **participant roles**, the entity benefiting from an action, e.g., *you* in *I have a present for you*.

binary also **boolean** Describes classifications in terms of mutually exclusive alternatives ($\pm$), i.e., the presence or absence of any particular **feature**, e.g., [$\pm$ singular].

binary branching The technique, illustrated in tree diagrams, of dividing sentences into their **immediate constituents** (see **constituent analysis**) successively in pairs, e.g. $\Sigma \to NP + VP/VP \to V + NP$ etc.

binary feature A **feature** classifying linguistic units in terms of mutually exclusive pairs [$\pm$ animate]. (Contrasts with **unary feature**, **multivated feature**.)

binding inheritance principle In HEAD-DRIVEN PHRASE STRUCTURE GRAMMAR, the correlate of GENERALIZED PHRASE STRUCTURE GRAMMAR'S **foot feature principle**.

binding theory In GOVERNMENT AND BINDING THEORY,

the sub-theory which sets out the conditions which direct the formal relations among the elements of a sentence, esp. in determining the positions of noun phrases and their **coindexation** (see **coindexing**). See also **A-binding**, **A-bar-binding**, **government and binding theory**.

blocking In TRANSFORMATIONAL GRAMMAR, the failure of a rule to apply to a derivation.

boolean = **binary**

bottom-up Describes a **grammar** (sense **3**) or grammatical **formalism** which takes as basic lists of words and expressions belonging to different categories, noun, adjective, etc. and develops a body of rules which specify how these expressions may combine, e.g., **Montague grammar**. (Contrasts with **top-down**.)

bound 1 Describes a **morpheme** which is not able to function independently as a separate word, e.g., an affix: *re-*, *-ed*, etc. (Contrasts with **free**.) **2** In GOVERNMENT AND BINDING THEORY, **constituents** which have been formally related by **coindexing**. (Contrasts with **free**.) **3** Describes a variable which has been assigned a value.

boundary-symbol (-marker), (#) In TRANSFORMATIONAL GRAMMAR, the symbol or marker indicating the boundaries between structural units, e.g. #S#. Cf. **concatenation symbol**.

bounding theory In GOVERNMENT AND BINDING THEORY, a sub-theory which determines the limits of movement, esp. the **subjacency condition** that no movement operation can cross more than one **barrier**.

bracketing 1 A means of displaying linearly (as in mathematics, etc.) the structure of a string of elements, e.g., [[*the lady*] [*wore*] [*a red hat*]]. **2** In GENERATIVE SYNTAX, (a) parentheses ( ) enclose optional elements, e.g., D(Adj)N = DN or DAdjN; (b) braces { } enclose alternatives, e.g., $D\{^{Adj}_N\}N = DAdjN$ or DNN; (c) square brackets [ ] require horizontal matching, e.g. $[^A_B] \to [^C_d] = A \to C$ and $B \to D$. See also **conjunctive ordering**.

branching The linear connections in a **tree** (**diagram**). Cf. **binary branching**.

C = **complementizer**

c-command, constituent command In GOVERNMENT AND BINDING THEORY, the relationship between an element in a phrase-marker and those elements with which it shares a dominating node, i.e., A c-commands B if an only if the node dominating A also dominates B, and A does not dominate B or B A.

c-structure In LEXICAL-FUNCTIONAL GRAMMAR, **constituent structure** characterizing phrasal and sentential syntax by means of a simple set of phrase structure rules. Cf. **f-structure** and **lexical-functional grammar**.

capacity see **strong generative capacity**, **weak generative capacity**

case 1 In **inflecting** and **agglutinating languages**, the inflectional forms of the noun, pronoun or adjective used to identify syntactic relationships within the sentence, e.g., the **nominative** case identifies the **subject**, the **accusative** the **object**, the **genitive** the relation of possession, etc. **2** In **case theory**, a sub-theory of **government and binding theory**, the inflectional categories (Nominative, Accusative, Genitive and Oblique) assigned to all NPs (noun phrases). **3** The corresponding grammatical relationships of case in **inflecting languages**.

case filter In GOVERNMENT AND BINDING THEORY, the mechanism which designates a noun phrase (NP) as not well-formed (*NP) if it has no **case** assigned to it.

case frame In CASE GRAMMAR, the array of **cases** specifying the structural context for verbs.

case grammar A **grammar** (sense 3) based on the assumption that semantic functions are at least relevant and probably basic to the expression of syntactic generalizations.

case phrase In CASE GRAMMAR, a noun phrase plus an indicator of the **case** to which the noun phrase belongs and which becomes in the surface structure subject, object or adjunct.

case relation In CASE GRAMMAR, the semantic functions basic to the lexicon or syntax, e.g., **agentive**, **neutral**, **instrumental**, etc.

case theory In GOVERNMENT AND BINDING THEORY, a subtheory which assigns **case** to every well-formed NP under a variety of rules, e.g., the category INFL (**inflection**) assigns nominative case to the subject.

cataphora Reference forward, e.g., *This is what I want you to do . . .* (Contrasts with **anaphora**.)

categorial component In GENERATIVE SYNTAX, the part of the **base component** which specifies syntactic categories such as S (sentence), NP (noun phrase), VP (verb phrase).

categorial grammar A **grammar** (sense 3) based on the recognition of just two fundamental categories, sentence and noun, all other categories (verb, adjective, etc.) are derived in a quasi-arithmetical fashion from sentence (Σ) and noun (n), e.g., verb is identified as Σ/n indicating an element that combines with a noun to form a sentence.

categorial rule In GENERATIVE GRAMMAR, a rule which develops a category into further categories, e.g., NP → Det + N.

category 1 Any 'class' or group of linguistic elements recognized in the description of a language, e.g., phoneme, noun etc. **2** = **part of speech 3** Restricted to features associated with parts of speech, e.g., mood, tense, person, etc. **4** In SCALE AND CATEGORY GRAMMAR and SYSTEMIC GRAMMAR, one of the fundamental parameters of the linguistic description (consisting of the categories of **unit**, **structure**, **class** and **system**); the other being **scale**.

category feature In GENERATIVE SEMANTICS, a **contextual feature** which specifies the node which will dominate a lexical item in the phrase-marker.

catenative Describes a lexical verb which governs another non-finite lexical verb, e.g., *He loves to swim*, *She needs to eat*. Cf. **control 2** and **raising**.

causal clause A variety of **adverbial clause** expressing the reason for something, e.g., *Because the bus was late they missed the first act.*

causative A class of verbs incorporating the notion of causality in their (lexical) meaning, e.g., *lay* is the causative of *lie*, *kill* of *die*, etc/

center-embedding = **self-embedding**

chain In GOVERNMENT AND BINDING THEORY, the pairing of a noun phrase (NP) and its coindexed **trace**, i.e., (NP,e).

chain vs choice Describes essential characteristics of the main axes of linguistic organization, i.e., the sequential character of the **syntagmatic** axis as against the substitutional nature of the **paradigmatic** (see **paradigm 2**) axis.

CHO = **chomeur**

choice see **chain vs choice**

chomeur (CHO) In RELATIONAL GRAMMAR, a nominal displaced from its role in the sentence, e.g., the subject of an active sentence when this is passivized.

Chomsky adjunction In some versions of TRANSFORMATIONAL GRAMMAR, a type of **adjunction** whereby, e.g., in the derivation of the passive, *by* is linked to the agent complement NP (the former subject) by a copy of the NP being made on the level above the original NP, which copy NP dominates both *by* and the agent NP and is **sister** adjoined to the VP.

Chomsky hierarchy A list of increasingly comprehensive **formalisms** i.e., **finite-state grammar**, **context-free context sensitive**, **recursive** rules.

circonstant, free modifier In VALENCY GRAMMAR, a non-essential dependent, e.g., adjunct, modifier. (Contrasts with **actant**.)

class 1 A set of words, morphemes, etc. which have properties in common, see specif. **form class**. **2** In SCALE AND CATEGORY GRAMMAR and SYSTEMIC GRAMMAR, a set of words, etc. which function in the same way, e.g., the class of nominal groups function as subject, object, etc., making up, together with **structure**, **system** and **unit** the basic categories of the theory.

classifier 1 A morpheme functioning to indicate the **class** (sense **1**) to which a word belongs, e.g., in French, *-eau* and *-elle* are gender classifiers, as in *beau* and *belle*, in English *-ly* distinguishes adverbs, as in *really*. **2** A word in various languages, e.g., Mandarin Chineses, Tzeltal, used to characterize entities as being of a particular sort, e.g., as 'human', 'plant', 'flat', etc., in transf. use, a means of analyzing various aspects of the semantic structure of nouns in non-classifier languages. **3** In **sign language**, a handshape which designates a class of objects.

clause 1 A syntactic unit consisting of subject and predicate which alone forms a **simple sentence** and in combination with others forms a **compound sentence** or **complex sentence**. See also **adverbial clause, main clause, noun clause, relative clause. 2** In modern grammars, sometimes expressed as a unit larger than a phrase but smaller than a sentence, to account for clauses which fall outside the traditional 'subject, predicate' pattern. See also **wh-clause, small clause, exceptional clause.**

clause chaining language A language in which clauses are combined in such a way as to blur the distinction between **coordination** and **subordination.**

clause-mates In GENERATIVE GRAMMER, elements dominated by the same S **node.**

clause object A clause functioning as **object.**

clause relations Connections, sometimes evidenced formally, e.g., *if . . . then, either . . . or*, sometimes merely by implication, between clauses or sentences seen as an aspect of textual **coherence.**

cleft sentence A sentence in which a particular emphasis or focus is achieved by splitting a simple sentence into two clauses, e.g., *Mary wore a red hat → It was Mary who wore a red hat* or *It was a red hat which Mary wore.*

clefting, theme predication The process described at **cleft sentence.**

cline In SCALE AND CATEGORY GRAMMAR and SYSTEMIC GRAMMAR, a graded scale or continuum of contrasts, e.g., between rising and falling pitch. Cf. **gradience.**

clitic A word or form dependent on the preceding or following word, respectively, **enclitic**, e.g., English *the, a*, French *je, j'*, and **proclitic**, e.g., English *n't* in *can't*, etc.

closed (finite) class A class whose members can (at least in theory) be listed, e.g., the class of articles in English or cases of the noun in Finnish. (Contrasts with **open (infinite) class.**)

cognate object An object closely related derivationally or semantically to the verb which governs it, e.g., *to dream **dreams**, to die the **death**, to run a **race**.*

cognitive grammar A theory based on a view of language as facet of cognition, grammar being the means whereby conceptual content is structured and functioning solely as a link between phonological and semantic structures. Cf. **cognitive semantics.**

cognitive (descriptive, conceptual, referential) meaning Meaning of a denotative or propositional sort, objectively or intellectually verifiable. (Contrasts with **affective meaning.**)

cognitive semantics In COGNITIVE GRAMMAR, a view of meaning that identifies it with mental structures and processes rather than **truth conditions.**

cohesion The ability of some linguistic constructions to bind together in units larger than the word, e.g., article + noun **anaphora**: *The girl went out. She shut the door.*

coindexing, coindexation In GENERATIVE GRAMMAR, the process of marking the identity of constituents by using subscript letters or numbers, as, e.g., I_1 *said* I_1 *could come* or He_1 *could come* but *John said Alan could come*: He_1 *said* he_2 *could come.*

collapse In GENERATIVE GRAMMAR, the conflating of rules to provide a more general statement, e.g., NP → DN and NP → DAdjN may be collapsed into NP → D(Adj)N.

collective noun A noun denoting some entity made up of a collection of parts seen at any particular time as individual parts acting separately or as a combination acting as one, and taking respectively, a plural or singular verb, e.g., *The crowd were dispersing*; *Parliament is in session.*

colligation In FIRTHIAN linguistics, the occurrence of groupings among words according to the sorts of grammatical relations they enter into; the ordering of words on this basis, e.g., *enjoy* belongs to the group of verbs taking the *-ing* form of the verb: *I enjoy fishing*; whereas *agree* takes the infinitive: *I agree to fish.*

collocation Orig. in FIRTHIAN linguistics, the habitual cooccurrence of particular lexical items, sometimes purely formally, e.g., *eke out*; sometimes with some semantic implication, e.g., *slim chance.*

combinatorial Relating to the property of linguistic units combining into more complex units.

comitative In **inflecting** and **agglutinating languages**, the **case** expressing the meaning 'along with'.

command 1 In the classification of sentences in terms of **function**, a sentence which conveys an order, in **form**, typically, an **imperative sentence**. (Contrasts with **exclamation, question, statement.**) **2** see **c-command.**

comment The part of a sentence which says something about the **topic** of the sentence, e.g., *His spectacles were on his head.*

comment clause A comment added, often parenthetically, to another clause, e.g., *The answer, **you know**, is in the soil*; *To be honest, I don't believe it.*

common Applying to the unmarked form of a grammatical category (as in **common case**, in English contrasting with the **genitive**, the only marked case).

common noun A noun denoting a class of objects, places, etc., e.g., *the boy, the cottage*. (Contrasts with **proper noun.**)

communicative competence, pragmatic competence The ability of a speaker to use language appropriately.

communicative dynamism (CD) In the **functional sentence perspective** of the PRAGUE SCHOOL, the degree to which different parts of an utterance add new meaning. Cf. **theme**, **rheme**.

commutation In GLOSSEMATICS, restricted to one sort of relationship between members of a **paradigm**. (Contrasts with **substitution**.)

comp = comparative, complement

Comp or **COMP** = complementizer

comparative (comp) The **degree** of comparison of two entities expressed formally as, e.g., *louder*, *more astonishing* vs *loud*, *astonishing*.

competence Esp. in GENERATIVE GRAMMAR, the native speaker's innate knowledge of his or her language. (Contrasts with **performance**.) Cf. **communicative competence**, **langue**.

competence grammar A **grammar** (sense **3**) which defines the entire set of rules available to a speaker for the generation of sentences.

complement (comp) 1 An element in a clause which completes the action indicated by the verbs *be/seem/become* and **intransitive** verbs, e.g., *John was/seemed/became/fell **ill**, John was/became **a violinist**.* These are **subject complements** referring to the same entity as the subject. **2** In some theories, any obligatory element in the predicate excluding the verb, e.g., *She ate **a banana**, She went **home to Stockholm**.* **3** An **object complement** makes reference to a direct object, completing the action of a **transitive** verb, e.g., *She called the man **a liar**.* **4** In GENERATIVE GRAMMAR, a **sister** constituent of a zero-level category. **5** In X-BAR SYNTAX, one of the major components of a phrasal category. **6** Sometimes applied to categories other than the verb, e.g., the *of* phrase in *Spirit of St Louis* may be termed the complement of *spirit*.

complement clause 1 A clause following the verb *be*, e.g., *This is **what I want**.* **2** In some views, any **subordinate clause**.

complementizer (Comp, COMP, C) 1 In GENERATIVE SYNTAX, a subordinating conjunction marking an embedded sentence of complement type, e.g., *I said **that** he was nice.* **2** In GOVERNMENT AND BINDING THEORY, **COMP (C)** is a zero-level category whose maximal projection **(CP)** is the highest level grammatical construction, see next.

complementizer phrase (CP) In GOVERNMENT AND BINDING THEORY, the **maximal projection** of C, i.e., C″ (see **double-bar**), which is the largest unit of grammatical analysis recognized by the theory.

complex noun phrase (NP) In GENERATIVE SYNTAX, a noun phrase including a clause functioning as complement or adjunct, e.g., ***The hat that she wore** was red.*

complex sentence A sentence consisting of **1** a main clause and one or more subordinate clauses. **2** more than one clause. (Contrasts with **compound sentence**, **simple sentence**.)

complex symbol In GENERATIVE GRAMMAR, a symbol in a phrase-marker with the specification of its internal structure, usually a set of syntactic features, e.g., [+V], [+transitive], [+past], etc., identifying *took*.

component In GENERATIVE GRAMMAR, a major section of the theory: the **base component**, **semantic component**, **transformational component** (see **transformational grammar**), etc.

Compositional 1 Esp. in SCALE AND CATEGORY, TAGMEMIC, STRATIFICATIONAL and PHRASE STRUCTURE GRAMMARS, hierarchical; larger units being composed of smaller units, as a sentence of clauses, a word of morphemes, etc. **2** In MONTAGUE GRAMMAR, of the meaning of a phrase, etc., composed of the meanings of its constituent parts.

compound noun A noun made up of at least two free morphemes, e.g., *bedroom*, *hatstand*.

compound sentence A sentence composed of two or more main clauses. Cf. **complex sentence 2**. (Contrasts with **complex sentence**, **simple sentence**.)

concatenation Esp. in GENERATIVE GRAMMAR, (the formal representation of) the linking together of linguistic elements to form strings in linear succession, e.g., $N + V + N$ or $N \char`^ V \char`^ N$.

concatenation symbol In TRANSFORMATIONAL GRAMMAR, the symbol which links structural units, usu., + e.g., $N + V$. Cf. **boundary-symbol**.

concessive (clause) A variety of **adverbial clause** expressing concession, e.g., *She went **although she was ill**.*

concord = agreement

concrete Describes a **noun** which denotes a real or physical entity, e.g., cat, house, poem. (Contrasts with **abstract**.)

condition 1 A factor to be taken into account in the evaluation of a grammar, e.g., **adequacy**, **simplicity metric**. **2** Esp. in GENERATIVE GRAMMAR, a criterion to be met before a rule becomes operative. Cf. **constraint**.

conditional Of a **sentence** or **clause**, expressing a hypothesis, typically contained in an *if*-clause (the **protasis**), or the conditions whereby what is expressed in the main clause (the **apodosis**) may be valid, e.g., ***If it rains** I shall go home, **If it had rained** I would have gone home.* See also **adverbial clause**.

configuration 1 An identifiable **arrangement** of elements. **2** In STANDARD THEORY, the phrase-marker is regarded as a configuration of syntactic categories linearly arranged.

configurational languages Languages in which the word order is (relatively) fixed and the constituent structure hierarchical, e.g., English.

congruence Agreement between **levels** of analysis. Maximum congruence of levels occurs in the sentence, i.e., grammar, phonology and semantics all tend to agree as to the boundaries of the sentence, this is not necessarily so for other linguistic units.

CONJ = conjunction

conjoining In GENERATIVE GRAMMAR = **coordination**

conjugation In **inflecting** and **agglutinating languages**, the set of verbs that vary according to the same model of formation or **paradigm**.

conjunct In TRANSFORMATIONAL GRAMMAR, a conjoined (see **conjoining**) element.

conjunction (CONJ) One of the class of words whose main function is to connect clauses, phrases or words; trad. **coordinating conjunctions**, e.g., *and*, *but*; and **subordinating conjunctions**, e.g., *that*, *when*.

conjunction reduction = **non-constituent coordination**

conjunctive ordering In GENERATIVE GRAMMAR, the obligatory selection of one of a set of choices enclosed in braces, e.g., A {B,C} = AB or AC. Cf. **disjunctive ordering**.

connective A word whose main function is to link linguistic units, chiefly a conjunction or adverb, e.g., *and*, *but*, *however*, *nonetheless*, also, copula verbs, such as *be*, *seem*.

constituency grammar = **constituent structure grammar**

constituent A linguistic **unit** (sense **1**) which is a component of a larger linguistic construction (as, a word of a phrase, a phrase of a clause, etc).

constituent analysis The analysis of a sentence, etc. into its constituents, hierarchically arranged as **immediate constituents** (ICs), the major divisions, e.g., [[the visitor][has arrived]] and **ultimate constituents** (UCs), the smallest divisions possible on the syntactic level, e.g., [[the][visit[-or]]][[has] [arrive[-ed]]]. This can also be displayed in a **tree diagram**.

constituent command = **c-command**

constituent sentence = **embedded sentence** (see **embedding**).

constituent structure The structure of a sentence, etc., as represented in a tree diagram or by bracketing, displaying the grammatical relationships of the constituents.

constituent structure grammar, constituency grammar A grammar taking the **constituent** as basic to its analysis (see **constituent analysis**).

constraint A restriction on the application of specific rules to avoid the generation of ill-formed sentences. (Cf. **condition 2**, **filter 1**.

construction 1 The syntactic arrangement or patterning within a grammatical unit. **2** In the theory of **comprehension**, the process of constructing an interpretation of a sentence, etc.

construe 1 To analyze a **construction** (sense **1**) in terms of its syntactic relationships. **2** In recent GENERATIVE SYNTAX, a **rule of construal** defines the relationship between **anaphors** and their **antecedents**.

context-free In GENERATIVE GRAMMAR, describes rules which apply without restriction. (Contrasts with **context-sensitive**.)

context-sensitive In GENERATIVE GRAMMAR, describes rules which only apply if they satisfy some contextual restriction. (Contrasts with **context-free**.)

contextual feature In THE STANDARD THEORY of GENERATIVE SEMANTICS, a syntactic feature which specifies the conditions as to where in the deep structure a lexical item can occur. Cf. **rule feature**.

contrast 1 also **distinctiveness** Difference, esp. of a **contrastive** sort serving to distinguish difference in meaning, observable between linguistic units of any sort. **2** In some approaches, restricted to syntagmatic differences.

control The mechanism whereby correct agreement is ensured. **1** In GENERALIZED PHRASE STRUCTURE GRAMMAR, see **control agreement principle**. **2** In GOVERNMENT AND BINDING THEORY, see **control theory**.

control agreement principle (CAP) In GENERALIZED PHRASE STRUCTURE GRAMMAR, the means of ensuring the agreement of appropriate linguistic elements, e.g., subject and verb, noun and adjective, etc.

control theory In GOVERNMENT AND BINDING THEORY, the means whereby the referential identity of the main clause subject or object and the subject of an embedded infinitive clause (**PRO**) is ensured after different lexical verbs, e.g., after *promise* the main clause subject determines the reference of PRO, after *persuade*, the main clause object, e.g., I_1 *promised Gloria PRO_1, to buy it, I persuaded Gloria_2 PRO_2 to buy it*.

controller 1 In **control theory**, the antecedent noun phrase which has the same reference as the subject of a following embedded infinitive clause (**PRO**). **2** = **governor 2**

cooccurrence Refers to any permitted syntagmatic combination of units, e.g., *a baby* but **a butter*; *eke out* but **eke in*; *feed the cat*, but **fall the cat*.

coordinate clause One of a number of clauses linked by **coordinating conjunctions**, e.g., *Boys danced and girls sang*.

coordinating conjunction, coordinator, (CONJ) A conjunction used in **coordination**, e.g., *and*, *or*, *but*, etc.

coordination The linking of linguistic units of the same syntactic status, e.g., *John and Mary; tired but happy; to go home or stay away*, etc. See also **coordinate clause**.

copula, linking verb A verb with very little independent meaning, used to link subject and complement and serve as the vehicle for tense, etc., e.g., in English, *be*, *seem*, *become*. Cf. **intensive**.

copy tag A **tag question** which copies the positive or negative status of the main clause, acting to question what is being said, e.g., *You like this, **do you?*** (Contrasts with **checking tag**.)

copying In TRANSFORMATIONAL GRAMMAR, a syntactic operation which duplicates a phrase-marker constituent in some other part of the phrase-marker, e.g., in **tag questions**.

core grammar In GENERATIVE GRAMMAR, the unmarked grammatical principles of (a) language.

coreference In GENERATIVE GRAMMAR, identity of reference between two (or more) constituents of a sentence, e.g., *I said I knew*. Cf. **coindexing**.

corepresentational grammar An approach which analyzes linguistic structure by means of two representations, one displaying the basic constituent structure, the other structural information, e.g., grammatical relations, of other sorts. Cf. **lexical-functional grammar**.

corpus Written texts, transcriptions, recorded data, etc. used as a basis for any sort of linguistic or language related investigation; a **computer** or **computerized corpus** is a body of such data in a machine-readable form.

count(able) noun A noun denoting a separate entity, one of a number of such entities which can be counted, e.g., *an apple*, *many ducks*, *three pineapples*. (Contrasts with **mass noun**.)

counter-agent In CASE GRAMMAR, the resistance or force against which an action is carried out.

crossover constraint In GENERATIVE GRAMMAR, a restriction on the movement of a noun phrase in the phrase-marker, specif. to prevent one noun phrase crossing another with which it is coreferential, e.g., to prevent the passivization of reflexives.

cycle, transformational cycle In TRANSFORMATIONAL GRAMMAR, the application of a complete set of rules in a particular **domain**. Cf. **cyclic rules**.

cyclic node In TRANSFORMATIONAL GRAMMAR, a node which can function as the **domain** of a **cycle** of rules, esp. S and NP.

cyclic rules In TRANSFORMATIONAL GRAMMAR, rules in the transformational component which are always applied in the same order and not re-applied until each member of the sequence has operated, the cyclic principle is a means of causing rules to interact correctly, e.g., in deriving **embedded sentences** (see **embedding**).

D = determiner

D-structure In GOVERNMENT AND BINDING THEORY, a conception of deep structure where the structural aspects of a sentence in which thematic roles (see **theta role**) are directly assigned is represented. D-structures derive from the categorial component and the lexicon and are mapped onto **S-structures** by a single-mapping, **move alpha**.

dative 1 In **inflecting** and **agglutinating languages**, the **case** expressing the relationship of **indirect object** or the meanings *to* or *for*. **2** also **experiencer** In CASE GRAMMAR, the case of an entity or person affected by the action or state of the verb, e.g., *The dog caught the rat*.

daughter In GENERATIVE GRAMMAR, a node immediately dominated by another node (its **mother**). See also **sister**.

daughter adjunction In some versions of TRANSFORMATIONAL GRAMMAR, a derivation whereby some constituent is adjoined in such a way as to be a **daughter** of some other constituent, e.g., in one derivation of the VP, *be* and its past participle marker are adjoined as daughters of Aux (**auxiliary**).

declarative The sentence type or verb form typically used in making a statement, e.g., *John is arriving at three*. Cf. **imperative**, **interrogative**, **indicativee**.

declension A set of nouns, pronouns or adjectives which have the same inflections. Cf. **decline**.

decline To state in a prescribed order the inflected forms of a noun, pronoun or adjective. Cf. **declension**.

deep structure (grammar), remote structure In TRANSFORMATIONAL GRAMMAR, the abstract representation of a sentence specifying the syntactic facts which govern how the sentence is to be interpreted, disambiguating, e.g., *Flying planes can be dangerous* as between *planes which fly* and *the flying of planes*; or assigning the same underlying form to, e.g., active and passive sentences such as *John loves Mary* and *Mary is loved by John*. Cf. **surface structure**.

defective 1 Describes a word which lacks its full set of inflectional forms, e.g., Latin verbs *coepi*, *memini*. **2** Describes a writing system which uses only consonant symbols.

definiteness A feature characterizing nouns or noun phrases which refer to (specific, identifiable) entities, usu. accompanied by the **indefinite article** (see **article**), e.g. *the boy*, *the black cat*. (Contrasts with **indefinite** entities, freq. accompanied by the **indefinite article** (see **article**), e.g., *a boy*, *any boy*.)

degree 1 A grammatical category specifying the level of comparison of an adjective or adverb, specif. **positive**, **comparative**, and **superlative**, e.g., *hot*, *hotter*, *hottest*, also **equative**, e.g., *as hot as*. **2** also **comparison** A variety of **adverbial clause**, e.g., *She eats almost as quickly as you do*.

deletion In TRANSFORMATIONAL GRAMMAR, an operation allowing the elimination of a constituent of a phrase-marker, e.g., deletion of the subject in one derivation of imperatives in English, *do*-deletion, etc. Cf. **dummy** and **equi NP deletion**, **insertion**.

delicacy In SCALE AND CATEGORY GRAMMAR and SYSTEMIC GRAMMAR, the **scale** of analysis concerned with depth of detail: more delicate = increasingly detailed. Cf. **exponence** (or **realization**) and **rank**.

delta symbol (Δ) In some models of TRANSFORMATIONAL GRAMMAR, a **dummy symbol** marking the places in the phrase-marker later to be filled by the complex symbols of lexical items.

demonstrative (adjective, pronoun) *gram, trad* An adjective or pronoun which serves to distinguish between members of a class, specif. *this (these), that (those)*, e.g., **This** *rose not* **that** *one, or* **these** *if you prefer. No I'll have* **those**.

demotion In RELATIONAL GRAMMAR, a class of relation-changing processes which alter positions within the relational hierarchy, e.g., altering the relation of subject and verb **demotes** the subject of an active verb to become object of a passive.

dependency grammar A **formal grammar** in which grammatical relations are explained in terms of dependencies, e.g., syntactic structures are represented by dependency trees or sets of nodes whose interconnections specify structural relations, i.e., a **governor** controls its **dependents** by **dependency rules** which specify the correct structural relations for each class of unit.

dependent see **dependency grammar**

dependent clause = **subordinate clause**

derivation 1 In GENERATIVE GRAMMAR, the stages through which the initial symbol, standing for 'sentence' passes to produce a **terminal string**. **2** = **etymology**

derivational morphology (The study of) the process of word-formation whereby new words are created by the addition of an affix to an already existing word, e.g., *rare/rarity; arrange/arrangement*. (Contrasts with **inflectional morphology**.)

derived structure In GENERATIVE GRAMMAR, an output phrase-marker after the application of a transformational rule or rules.

descriptive adequacy The description by a **grammar** (sense **3**) of which sentences in a language are (or are not) well-formed and the supplying of a set of linguistic structures for the well-formed sentences which accord with the intuitions or **competence** of the native speaker. Cf. **adequacy**.

descriptive grammar (linguistics), synchronic linguistics The study of a language or variety of language at a given point in time with the intention of producing a **description** of the language, i.e., a systematic, comprehensive and precise account, based on objective observation, of its structures and usages. Cf. **perspective grammar**.

det, DET = **determiner**

determinant In FUNCTIONAL GRAMMAR, a **satellite** which functions to **determine** the **nucleus** (or another satellite), e.g., *hot* and *very* in *a very hot day, up* in *go up*.

determiner (det, DET, D) *gram* A sub-class of modifiers cooccurring with nouns and pronouns to express semantic contrasts such as number or quantity, e.g.,

specifying count or mass nouns; specif. the articles *a/the*, also, items which occur in 'article position' in the noun phrase, e.g., *some, every, much, this*, etc. In some approaches the term is extended to cover other sorts of modifier.

determiner phrase (DP) In some models of GENERATIVE GRAMMAR, a noun phrase including a determiner where the determiner is regarded as the head.

device In GENERATIVE GRAMMAR, a quasi-mathematical model or construct designed as a means of analysis, e.g., grammar is a device for generating sentences. See also **language acquisition device**.

diachronic (historical) linguistics The study of languages as they change through time.

direct object (DO) A noun or its equivalent on or towards which the action of a transitive verb is directed, e.g., *My daughter eats* **eggs**; freq., with active verbs, **patient** of the verb; in **inflecting** and **agglutinating languages** taking the **accusative** case. Cf. **indirect object**.

disambiguation In TRANSFORMATIONAL GRAMMAR, the provision of alternative formal structural analyses for superficially similar sentences, e.g., *The food is ready to eat/The guest is ready to eat*, or surface structures with more than one possible interpretation, e.g., *They can fish in Alberta*.

discontinuity The splitting of some grammatical constituents, as phrasal verbs, e.g., *eat up*, in *Eat your dinner up*; negative particles, e.g., French *ne . . . pas*; the question form of the verb, e.g., *Are you laughing at me?*, etc.

discovery procedure Esp. in BLOOMFIELDIAN linguistics, a set of techniques to be applied to a sample of language which would automatically produce a correct grammatical analysis.

disjunctive ordering In GENERATIVE GRAMMAR, the ordering of optional elements (as $X \rightarrow (M)Z$) whereby a bracketed choice may be taken up. ($X \rightarrow MZ$), or not ($X \rightarrow Z$); if the latter is chosen the former may no longer apply. Cf. **conjunctive ordering**.

distribution The set of linguistic environments in which a linguistic unit can occur.

ditransitive (three-place) verb *gram* A **transitive** verb which takes two objects, e.g., *She* **gave** *the cat some milk*. Cf. **indirect object**.

DO = **direct object**

domain In GENERATIVE GRAMMAR, the parts of a tree diagram **dominated** (see **dominance**) by any particular node, e.g., the domain of any particular rule consists of just those constituents affected by the rule.

dominance, domination In GENERATIVE GRAMMAR, the relationship between a node and everything which derives from it, a node **dominates** everything in a tree diagram traceable back to it, usu. termed **precedence**. See also **immediate dominance**.

397

double-bar In the **X-bar theory** of GOVERNMENT AND BINDING THEORY, the **maximal projection** of a **zero-level category**, a full phrasal category, i.e., the whole noun phrase (NP) *the Queen of Scots* is N̄ (N-double bar) or, more frequently, N″ (see **bar notation**).

double-base transformation generalized transformation In GENERATIVE GRAMMAR, a rule which has an input of two or more terminal strings.

doubly-filled COMP filter In EXTENDED STANDARD THEORY, a filter allowing exclusion of sentences like *I asked who that Amy met* where *who* and *that* both occupy the COMP position.

DP = determiner phrase

dummy symbol 1 In TRANSFORMATIONAL GRAMMAR, one of a variety of symbols used in the deep structure to stand for or mark the place of a category or element which replaces it at a later stage of the derivation, e.g., **delta symbol**. **2** also **expletive** In GOVERNMENT AND BINDING THEORY, an element in A-position (i.e., argument position) with no **theta role**.

dummy, empty (null) element, prop A grammatical element retaining no or only vestigial traces of lexical meaning, e.g., *is* in *Mary is beautiful*; *do* in *Do you want some?*; *there* in *There is a cat in the house*; *it* in *It is snowing*.

e = empty category

E-language, externalized language A CHOMSKYAN term for a collection of sentences understood without reference to the speaker's internalized language or **I-language**; language viewed as a set of utterances, forms, etc. paired with meanings, which it is the purpose of a grammar to describe.

ECM = exceptional case marking

economy The principle that any analysis should contain as few rules, symbols, etc. as possible, e.g., the ordering 1. S → NP + VP 2. V → V + NP 3. NP → Def + N is prefered to 1. S → NP + VP 2. NP → Def + N 3. VP → V + NP$_2$ 4. NP$_2$ → Det + N. Cf. **simplicity metric**.

ECP = empty category principle

elative In **inflecting** and **agglutinating languages**, the **case** denoting motion 'away from (inside)' a place, sometimes contrasting with **ablative** 'from outside'.

element 1 A general term for any part of linguistic structure. **2** An immediate constituent of a hierarchical unit, e.g., the elements of sentence structure are subject, verb, complement, object and adverbial; an affix is an element of word structure, etc.

embedding In GENERATIVE SYNTAX, describes a process or construction where part of the structure which might have functioned as an independent sentence functions as a constituent in another sentence, e.g.,

The girl who went away way my best friend where *who went away* is an **embedded sentence**.

emic Esp. in TAGMEMICS, describes an approach which sets up a system of meaningfully distinct units (phonemes, morphemes) and describes the linguistic data in terms of these units. Cf. **etic**.

empty category (e) 1 In GENERATIVE GRAMMAR, a **category** which, for any reason, is missing, e.g., in the case of ellipsis: *Who will do the flowers? I will*, i.e., *Who* [VP [M + V *do*] *the flowers*] *I* [VP [M + E]]. **2** In GOVERNMENT AND BINDING THEORY, mechanisms to ensure the maintenance of correct relationships throughout the derivation of a structure, e.g., **PRO**, **pro** and **trace**. **3 = slash**

empty category principle (ECP) In GOVERNMENT AND BINDING THEORY, a principle of the theory of government which requires a trace to be identifiably governed, either by a lexical category or by a category with the same index, i.e., its antecedent.

enclitic An unstressed word which has become attached to a preceding word, e.g., *cannot*, *aren't*, *prithee*.

endocentric (headed) construction A construction whose distribution is identical with that of one or more of its constituents, e.g., the noun phrase *pretty Polly* is identical in distribution to the noun *Polly*.

entry condition In SYSTEMIC GRAMMAR, the criterion which must be satisfied for any grammatical system to become operative, e.g., the system offering the choices declarative/interrogative/imperative requires as its entry condition that the input be a main clause.

equi NP deletion (EQUI) In early models of TRANSFORMATIONAL GRAMMAR, an obligatory rule deleting a noun phrase from a complement clause when it is coreferential with a noun phrase in the main clause, e.g., *Jim wants to take a bath* where *Jim* is the underlying subject of both *wants* and *to take*. Cf. **control theory**, **raising**.

ergative 1 Said of a language (e.g., Basque), construction, etc. where the object of a transitive verb and the subject of an intransitive verb display the same case. **2** In such a language, said of the subject of a transitive verb. Cf. **absolutive**. **3** In transferred use, applied to languages not traditionally regarded as 'ergative', relating sentences such as *The glass broke* and *The boy broke the glass* in a similar fashion, the **agent** of the action being referred to as the 'ergative subject'. Cf. **unaccusative**.

essive In **inflecting** and **agglutinating languages**, the **case** expressing the meaning 'at' a place.

EST = extended standard theory

etic Esp. in TAGMEMICS, describes an approach to the study of linguistic data where all aspects of the data are described whether or not they are meaningful in terms of the phonological system of the language under consideration. Cf. **emic**.

evaluation procedure, decision procedure A means, ideally automatic, of choosing between alternative analyses or grammars.

exceptional case marking (ECM) In GOVERNMENT AND BINDING THEORY, the mechanism used to deal with **subject-to-object raising** (see **raising**) in classical TRANSFORMATIONAL GRAMMAR. The verbs involved, e.g., *believe, consider* are interpreted as having the lexical property of assigning accusative **case** to a complement in just those cases where S is 'pruned' (**S-pruning**), e.g., in *Sheila believes him to be a genius* but not in *Sheila believes he is a genius*. A similar technique is used in the derivation of, e.g., *She liked him kissing her* (as opposed to *She linked his kissing her*).

exceptional clause In GOVERNMENT AND BINDING THEORY, a clause occurring as the complement of a particular subset of verbs, esp. verbs of saying or thinking (*believe, persuade*, etc.) which is typically of the form [NP *to* VP], e.g. *I believe the cat to be hurt*. (Contrasts will **ordinary clause**, **small clause**.)

existential Describes a sentence beginning *There is/are*, expressing the fact, belief, etc. that something exists, e.g., *There is a car in the drive*.

exocentric construction *gram* Any construction which is not **endocentric**, i.e., no part of it can substitute for any other part in distribution, e.g., *Polly flies*.

experiencer 1 *sem* The entity which, or more commonly, who experiences something, the subject of a state. **2** = **dative 2**

explanatory adequacy The level of **adequacy** attained by a linguistic theory which is capable of providing a grammar which is descriptively adequate (see **descriptive adequacy**) for every natural language, is capable of differentiating between natural languages and other semiotic systems, and is psychologically plausible.

expletive In GOVERNMENT AND BINDING THEORY, a label for a **dummy** (see **dummy symbol**) element.

exponence 1 In a hierarchical linguistic analysis, the correspondence between linguistic units at different levels of the hierarchy, e.g., words have phonological units (phonemes) as their **exponents**. **2** In SCALE AND CATEGORY GRAMMAR and SYSTEMIC GRAMMAR, the **scale** of analysis which relates the categories of the theory to the data, e.g., *child* is an exponent of the class of nouns. Cf. **delicacy** and **rank**.

expression rules In FUNCTIONAL GRAMMAR, a final stage in the generation of sentences.

extended standard theory (EST) The model of GENERATIVE GRAMMAR developed from **standard theory** by the addition of semantic rules functioning with the surface structure as input, e.g., in relation to stress, intonation, focus, etc. Cf. **revised extended standard theory**.

external adequacy The evaluation of a **grammar** according to how well it corresponds to the **data**. Cf. **adequacy**.

extraposition 1 The process or result of relocating an element close to the end of a sentence, e.g., by **fronting** the construction with an **extrapositive** or **anticipatory** *it*, e.g., *It became apparent that the cat was in the house* rather than *That the cat was in the house became apparent*. **2** In later versions of TRANSFORMATIONAL GRAMMAR, a **movement rule** or **transformation** involving **adjunction** whereby, e.g., a PP (prepositional phrase) complement can be moved out of the NP (noun phrase) and attached to the end of the clause, e.g., *An example of a very rate plant has just been discovered in Tibet → An example has just been discovered in Tibet of a very rare plant*.

extrinsic ordering In GENERATIVE GRAMMAR, the explicit ordering of rules to produce well-formed sentences, the ordering being determined by constraints imposed by the language, e.g., if the rules $N → Adj + N$ and $N → N + and + N$ are ordered 1 and 2 strings like *happy* (*boys and girls*) is produced (where the ambiguity is unresolved) whereas if they are ordered 2 and 1 *happy boys and happy girls* is produced. Cf. **intrinsic ordering**.

---

f-structure, functional structure In LEXICAL-FUNCTIONAL GRAMMAR, the functional analysis of a sentence in terms of subject, object, etc.

feature 1 Any, esp. meaning-bearing, property of spoken or written language. **2** = **distinctive feature 3** In GENERATIVE GRAMMAR, the (grammatical or semantic) properties used to classify words in the **lexicon**, e.g., [countable], [animate], [human], etc. **4** In TRANSFORMATIONAL GRAMMAR, GOVERNMENT AND BINDING THEORY, LEXICAL FUNCTIONAL GRAMMAR, etc., properties used to classify syntactic categories, e.g., [±N] (noun), [±Det] (determiner), [±Pas] (passive), etc. **5** see **head feature**, **foot feature**

feature cooccurrence restriction (FCR) In GENERLIZED PHRASE STRUCTURE GRAMMAR, a restriction constraining possible combinations of **feature specifications**.

feature instantiation In GENERALIZED PHRASE STRUCTURE GRAMMAR, a mechanism which allows features to be freely assigned to categories in a local tree according to a general rule provided they do not violate any condition laid down by the grammar. Cf. **inherited feature specification**.

feature specification In PHRASE STRUCTURE GRAMMARS, a means of specifying grammatical categories by an ordered pair of **feature** and **feature value**, e.g., [case/nominative].

FFP = **foot feature principle**

field 1 In TAGMEMICS, part of an analogy with physics whereby language is viewed as a combination of **particle**, **wave** and **field**, the field being the functional perspective of the text as part of the wider linguistic memory. **2** In **field theory**, a network of interrelated **lexemes**. **3** An area in a record containing a specific category of data. **4** The smallest unit of data in a **data base**.

filler In **slot-and-filler models** of grammar, esp. TAG-MEMICS, a form suitable for use at a particular place or **slot** in a construction, e.g., a noun phrase or construction substitutable for a noun phrase will fill the subject **slot**.

filter 1 also **output constraint** In GOVERNMENT AND BINDING THEORY, a **constraint** which prevents the generation of ill-formed sentences by stating that any particular construction of the surface structure is ill-formed, e.g., the FOR FOR filter which allows *What we are aiming for is for this to succeed* but not **We are aiming for for this to succeed*. **2** A device for separating the frequency components of a sound wave.

finite-state grammar In GENERATIVE GRAMMAR, a simple type of generative device which works by selecting an initial element (from the set of possible initial elements) and generates a string by continuing the process of selection in a rightwards direction choosing each subsequent element from the possibilities available, e.g., *the* is a possible initial element in English, thereafter a noun must be chosen, and so on.

fixed word order Not open to variation, e.g., where a change of word order involves a change of meaning, cf. *The girl loves the dog/The dog loves the girl* and Latin *Puella amat canem* (the girl loves the dog/*Canem amat puella* (the girl loves the dog). (Contrasts with **free word order**.

focus The **new** material in a sentence, e.g., if *John fell* is the answer to *Who fell? John* is the focus, not so if the question is *What happened?* (Contrasts with **presupposition**.)

foot feature In GENERALIZED PHRASE STRUCTURE GRAMMAR, one of a set of features used in the derivative of **unbounded dependencies** to ensure the identity of the constituent that is lost, specif. {SLASH, WH, RE}, i.e., {a missing constituent, *who/which/what* constituents, reflexives}.

foot feature principle (FFP) In GENERALIZED PHRASE STRUCTURE GRAMMAR, the principle of feature instantiation which ensures the maintenance of correct relationships in **unbounded dependencies**, e.g., wh-questions and topicalizations; this requires that any **foot feature** instantiated on the mother of a local tree be marched by the instantiation of the same foot feature on at least one daughter. Cf. **control agreement principle**, **head feature convention**.

foregrounding, actualization 1 The relative prominence of particular elements, e.g., the main events of a story in a narrative or the rhymes or alliterating words in verse are foregrounded. (Contrasts with **back-grounding** which refers to the rest of the text.)

form 1 The phonological or grammatical structure or appearance of (the units of) a language (see **linguistic form**) in contradistinction to their semantic meaning. **2** One of the accidental or inflectional variants a **word** (or lexeme) displays in different linguistic situations, e.g. *sing* and *sang* are different forms of the same lexeme, *sang* being the past tense form of the verb; *sang* is also a dialect form of the noun *song*. Cf. **function**. **3** also **expression** In SAUSSUREAN linguistics, the linguistic structure, i.e., the phonological, grammatical and semantic structure of a language imposed on the phonic or cognitive continuum or **substance**. **4** In SCALE AND CATEGORY GRAMMAR and SYSTEMIC GRAMMAR, the **level** of grammatical and lexical organization (in contradistinction to **substance** and **context**). **5** The essential characteristics of a linguistic theory stated explicitly, esp. in logical or mathematical terms. **6** The structure of a (literary) text, as opposed to its content.

form class 1 A class whose members are syntactic equivalents, i.e., they have the same distribution throughout the sentences of the language. **2** Used in place of the trad. term **part of speech**.

formal grammar 1 Contrasting with **notional grammar**, a description of language in sense **2** of **grammar** where no assumptions about the universality of such categories as parts of speech, mood, etc. is made, the structure of each language being in sense **2** of **formal**.

formal universal In GENERATIVE GRAMMAR, any condition put on the way in which the rules of a grammar operate or how different units combine with each other, e.g., the type of **components**, **rules**, **rule ordering**, etc. allowed, the **constraints** imposed, etc. (Contrasts with **substantive universal**.)

formalism 1 An artificial language whose purpose is the precise characterization of other languages, artificial or natural, specif. in linguistic theory has a method of defining explicitly the grammatical properties of individual languages.

frame feature In CASE GRAMMAR, in lexical entries for verbs, the feature specification indicating the appropriate **case frames** for different verbs.

free variation Substitutability of one element for another in a given context without a change in meaning, esp. in phonology, e.g., /iː/ and /aɪ/ can be free variants in *either* or *neither*.

free word order A characteristic of **inflecting** or **agglutinating languages** where the order in which the words in a sentence occur does not affect the meaning. (Contrasts with **fixed word order**.)

FSP = functional sentence perspective

function 1 How a constituent works, its relationship with the other constituents in a larger unit, as, a noun or noun phrase in relation to a sentence can work or noun phrase in relation to a sentence can work or function as subject, object, complement, modifier, etc., freq. seen in contradistinction to **form 1**. **2** A mathematical expression connecting a number of **arguments** in a particular relationship and dependent on the individual values of the arguments for its own value, e.g., $a + b$ is a function whose value is dependent on the values of a and b.

functional grammar A type of **grammar** based on a view of language as social interaction and particularly concerned with the rules which govern linguistic expressions as used in such activity.

functional sentence perspective (FSP) A theory deriving from the PRAGUE SCHOOL, which is concerned with utterance or text analysis in terms of the information an utterance conveys and evaluating it in terms of its semantic contribution to the discourse as a whole. Cf. **given**.

functional structure = f-structure

gap 1 The absence of a linguistic unit at a particular place in a pattern of semantic, syntactic or phonological relationships **2** In GENERATIVE GRAMMAR, a phonologically **empty category** (sense **1**) standing for a missing or deleted category.

gapping = non-constituent coordination

GB = government and binding theory

gender 1 A grammatical category in which nouns are classified as belonging to a number of sub-classes based on properties related to some extent to natural properties: the trad. genders are **masculine**, **feminine**, and **neuter**, others are also required (based, e.g., on shape, edibility, animacy, in, e.g., the Bantu languages). Gender concord is required between noun and adjective, etc. and in the selection of pronouns. Note the distinction between **natural gender** where the sex of the referent is taken into account and **grammatical gender** where the classification is arbitrary. *Elle est belle, le nouveau professeur* illustrates both sorts. **2** Sex, e.g., *the feminine gender* = women, females.

general (theoretical) linguistics Linguistic theory or method in any sphere (descriptive, comparative, etc.) as it may be applied universally, in contradistinction to specific applications of theory and method as in **applied linguistics, sociolinguistics**, etc.

generalized phrase structure grammar (GPSG) A linguistic theory without transformations, in which the syntactic structure of a sentence is a single phrase-marker and categories are specified as sets of features and feature values. See also **head-driven phrase structure grammar**.

generalized transformation = double-base transformation

generative grammar (linguistics) A system of rules which operates upon a set of elements to define a subset of the total number of possible combinations of the elements as grammatically well-formed and its

complement as grammatically ill-formed; applied to natural languages, a generative grammar defines the set of grammatically well-formed sentences, assigning to each a set of explicit structural descriptions.

generative semantics A particular view of the semantic component of a generative grammar in which no distinction is drawn between the deep structure of a sentence and its semantic interpretation, thus proposing a model which is semantically based. Cf. **interpretive semantics** (see **interpretive**).

generative syntax The component of a generative grammar which assigns syntactic descriptions.

generic Describes a word or usage referring to a class of entities, e.g., *The whale is a mammal/Whales are mammals* or states of affairs, e.g., *Birds build nests*.

genericity A type of **aspect** or **Aktionsart** expressing a **generic** property.

genitive In **inflecting** and **agglutinating languages**, the **case** expressing possession or origin and related concepts, e.g., *the dog's bone*, *a night's fishing*. Cf. **postmodifying genitive**.

gerund = verbal noun

gerundive The future passive participle in Latin, functioning as a verbal adjective and expressing the fitness or necessity of the action to be performed, e.g., *amandus* deserving or requiring to be loved; sometimes used of similar usages in other languages.

given In the analysis of utterances in terms of information structure, the information already supplied, contrasting with what is **new**. Cf. **focus, theme**.

glossematics Developed by HJELMSLEV and the COPENHAGEN SCHOOL, a view of language as a purely deductive system, one of a number of symbolic systems in human interaction and only fully comprehensible in relation to others, e.g., logic, dancing.

glosseme The abstract minimal term proposed in **glossematics**.

goal 1 In a **localistic** (see **localism**) view of meaning, the end point of movement, grammaticalized in the **dative** case. (Contrasts with **source 1**.) **2** In CASE GRAMMAR, the place to which something moves. (Contrasts with **source 2**.) **3 = patient**.

governing category In GOVERNMENT AND BINDING THEORY, the smallest structure, i.e. noun phrase or sentence, in which the relationship of **binding** (see **binding theory**) occurs. A functions as governing category for B if and only if A and B are dominated by the same **maximal projections**.

government, rection 1 In **inflecting** and **agglutinating languages**, the morphological control imposed by a word (class) on another, e.g., in Latin, prepositions **govern** or determine the case of the following noun: *ad Romam* but *ab Roma*. **2** In STANDARD THEORY, a rule is **governed** if it has lexical exceptions (**ungoverned** if not), e.g., *Green suits you* is an exception to the passivization rule, passivization is, therefore, **governed. 3** In GOVERNMENT AND BINDING THEORY, a particular instance of **c-command**, the circumstance where a lexical head (Noun, Verb, Preposition) is able to assign **Case** to its NP Complement; government is a prerequisite of Case-assignment, thus, e.g., a verb cannot govern a NP complement in another clause.

government and binding theory (GB) A theory of **universal grammar** in which the content of the basic components is kept to a minimum and the language-specific information is contained in a series of sub-theories (**binding theory, bounding theory, case theory, control theory, government theory, X-bar theory** (see **X-bar syntax**) and **theta theory**). A derivation of the theory consists of **D-structure** which becomes **S-structure** via **move alpha**; S-structure in turn is acted upon by **phonetic form** and **logical form** to produce a grammatical representation.

government theory In GOVERNMENT AND BINDING THEORY, the sub-theory principally concerned with the **empty category principle**.

governor 1 In GOVERNMENT AND BINDING THEORY, the lowest **c-command** node in a tree, providing that there is no intervening noun phrase. **2** also **controller** In DEPENDENCY GRAMMAR, the superordinate node in a dependency tree which controls a set of dependent nodes, thereby defining a specified structural relationship, e.g., in clause structure the verb is the governor of the noun phrases.

GPSG = generalized phrase structure grammar

gradience, serial relationship The lack of sharp boundaries between linguistic categories; a **gradient** or **cline** being the series of gradations between an instance clearly belonging in one category and an instance clearly belonging in another, e.g., *for* lies somewhere between the coordinating and subordinating conjunctions *and* and *if*.

grammar 1 The study of language and the rules that govern its usage. **2** A description of the forms of words and the manner in which they combine to form phrases, clauses or sentences, = **morphology + syntax**. **3** A systematic and explicit account of the structure of (a) language according to the tenets of one or other of the theories of modern linguistics, freq. taken to include **phonology** as well as **morphology** and **syntax**, e.g., **transformational grammar, case grammar**, etc. **4** In STRATIFICATIONAL GRAMMAR, the **two stratal system** consisting of the **morphemic system** and the **lexemic system** intermediate between **phonology** and **semology**. See also **competence grammar, descriptive grammar, formal grammar, functional grammar, generative grammar, notional grammar, performance grammar, reference grammar, universal grammar**.

grammatical form In American STRUCTURALIST LINGUISTICS, a **tactic form** (see **tazeme**) plus its meaning, i.e., those aspects of a **linguistic form** which relate strictly to grammatical arrangement, i.e., whether it is a subject/question, etc. (Contrasts with **lexical form**.)

grammatical gender see **gender**

grammatical (structural) meaning The aspect of meaning conveyed in the grammatical parts of linguistic structures, e.g., in the form *-ing* (verbal + nominal or + participial), *-ed* (past tense), *-s* (plural), etc.

grammatical (empty, form, function) word, functor A word without significant lexical meaning which functions to express grammatical relationships, e.g., *a, the, to, at*, etc. (Contrasts with **lexical word**.)

grammaticality, well-formedness The conformity of a linguistic structure (phrase, clause sentence, etc.) to the rules of (a particular) grammar. (Contrasts with **ungrammaticality**.) Cf. **acceptability**.

grammaticalization, grammaticization The attribution of **grammatical meaning** to a lexical item, e.g., Scots *ane*, the lexical item 'one' is also the indefinite article 'a, an'.

group In SCALE AND CATEGORY GRAMMAR and SYSTEMIC GRAMMAR, the **unit** on the rank scale between word and clause, e.g., *the fat cat* is a **nominal group**, *has lapped*, a **verbal group**.

habitual Describes a form or **aspect** expressing repetition, e.g., *He comes frequently, He leaves at six*.

head 1 In an **endocentric construction**, the element distributionally equivalent to the whole phrase, e.g., *cat* in *John's car, the tabby cat, the cat which I bought my daughter* and *lapped* in *has lapped the milk*. **2** In GENERALIZED PHRASE STRUCTURE GRAMMAR, the **daughter** which characterizes the identity of its constituent.

HEAD In GENERALIZED PHRASE STRUCTURE GRAMMAR, a term dominating the collection of features specifying the **head** in a **headed construction** (see **head 1**), specif. **HEAD** = {N, V, PLU, PER, VFORM, SUBJ, PFORM, AUX, INV, PAST, PRD, ADV, SLASH, AGR, SUBCAT, BAR, LOC}.

head-driven phrase structure grammar (HPSG) A model deriving esp. from GENERALIZED PHRASE STRUCTURE GRAMMAR and CATEGORIAL GRAMMAR and consisting of grammar principles, grammar tules and lexical entries all of which are represented in terms of feature structures, or sets of features (consisting of an attribute and a value) which are its sole descriptive device and which are used to describe phrasal constituents and lexical constituents alike.

head feature In GENERALIZED PHRASE STRUCTURE GRAMMAR, the **feature** (sense **3**) which are the necessary properties of the **head** of a phrase, e.g., second person singular NP which is the subject of a sentence is characterized as [BAR, 2]; [N, +]; [V, −]; [PER, 2]; [PLU, −]; [CASE, NOM].

head feature convention (HFC) In GENERALIZED PHRASE

STRUCTURE GRAMMAR, a **feature instantiation** principle which imposes conditions on the assignment of categories to nodes in a **local tree**, requiring a correspondence between the feature specification of the **mother** and a **daughter** which is a head in those features which can be freely equated, e.g., tense, number, etc.

head feature principle In HEAD-DRIVEN PHRASE STRUCTURE GRAMMAR the rule equivalent to the **head feature convention** in generalized phrase structure grammar.

head-first language see **head parameter**

head-last language see **head parameter**

head parameter In GENERATIVE SYNTAX, esp. with reference to **universal grammar**, the proposition that in a language the head always occurs on the same side in all phrases: **head-first languages** have the head leftmost in the construction, e.g., *in Dublin, eat the cake*; **head-last languages** have the head to the right.

headed construction = **endocentric construction**

heavy noun phrase In GENERATIVE SYNTAX, a noun phrase with a relatively long and complex construction, one allowing **postposing**, i.e., *Gillian finds friendly all the children in her class* as against **Gillian finds friendly all the children.*

hierarchy 1 In the classification of linguistic units, a series of subordinate levels each successively consisting of the next one down, i.e., a sentence consists of clauses and a word consists of morphemes. **2** see **accessibility hierarchy 3** The relationship of the elements of a structure organized as a series of levels, higher level elements having precedence over lower level elements.

horizontal grouping In STRATIFICATIONAL GRAMMAR, an operation of **realizational analysis** which analyzes, e.g., *dog* as a structural unit of *doglike* and *dogged* but not of *dogmatic*.

horizontal splitting In STRATIFICATIONAL GRAMMAR, an operation of **realizational analysis** which analyzes, e.g., French *du* as the realization of underlying *de* + *le*.

HPSG = **head-driven phrase structure grammar**

hypotaxis A variety of **subordination**, specif. of clauses, where a dependent construction is connected to the main clause by a subordinating conjunction, e.g., *I will go home when the bus comes*. (Contrasts with **parataxis**.)

I, INFL = **inflection 2**

I-language, internalized-language A CHOMSKYAN term for language seen as an element of the speaker's or hearer's mind. (Contrasts with **E-language**.)

I-movement In some later versions of TRANSFORMATIONAL GRAMMAR, **a movement rule** involving **substitution** whereby I (modal verb + inflection) is moved, in, e.g., the derivation of questions, *Gloria*

likes oysters/Does Gloria like oysters? Cf. **NP-movement**, **V-movement**, **extraposition**.

IA = **item and arrangement**

IC = **immediate constituent**

icon A **sign** displaying non-arbitrary characteristics, e.g., a map; rising pitch and loudness are **iconic** of anger; instances of **onomatopoeia** display **iconicity**. Cf. **arbitrariness**.

idealization The discounting of certain aspects of the raw data of speech, e.g., error, memory-lapse, hesitation, in the production of as generally applicable an analysis as possible; underlying, in GENERATIVE GRAMMAR, the concept of **competence**.

ill-formedness = **ungrammaticality**

illative In some **inflecting** and **agglutinating** languages, e.g., Finnish, the **case** expressing 'motion into', 'direction towards'.

illocutionary act, speech act In the theory of SPEECH ACTS, an act performed in saying something, i.e., making a promise, asking a question, giving a name; the **illocutionary force** of an utterance is its status as a promise, inquiry, etc.

immediate constituent see **constituent analysis**

immediate dominants (domination) (ID) In GENERATIVE GRAMMAR, the situation where **dominance** occurs between nodes in a phrase-marker without the intervention of any other node.

immediate dominance (ID) rules The component of GENERALIZED PHRASE STRUCTURE GRAMMAR which specifies the relationships between **nodes** (**mothers** and **daughters**) in a phrase-marker, e.g., specifying that A can dominate B, C and D ($A \rightarrow B,C,D$) not, however ordering B, C and D which is done by the **linear precedence rules**.

imperative 1 The inflectional **mood** which expresses the will to control or influence, e.g., in Latin *ama*, the command 'love!' Cf. **indicative**, **jussive**, etc. **2** The sentence type or verb form typically used in commands, exhortations, entreaties, etc. Cf. **declarative**, **interrogative**.

imperfect A form of the verb in some languages expressing past time usually with some aspectual element of duration or continuity. Cf. **perfect**.

imperfective An **aspect** of the verb indicating non-completion or continuation of an action. (Contrasts with **perfective**.)

impersonal A verbal construction without specification for **person**, a construction lacking an **agent**, e.g., *It is sunny, So be it.*

implication, conditional The **logical connective** p implies q ($p \rightarrow q$ or $p \supset q$), if then q.

implicational universal Truths about linguistic structure that can be deduced or that are implied in what is already known, e.g., if a language has free word order it will use inflections or affixes to express subject, object, etc. relations.

inchoative 1 = **ingressive** 2 In some approaches, used of the process of change from one state to another, e.g., in *The track narrows at this point*.

incorporating language A language which uses long, morphologically complex words, typically nouns (cf. **noun incorporation**), as a preferred construction, the ratio of word to morpheme being one-to-many and lexical morphemes being able to combine in a single word, as e.g., in many American Indian languages. Cf. **polysynthetic language**.

indicative The inflectional **mood** expressing **factivity** and simple assertion used in the verb forms of statements and questions (**declarative** and **interrogative** sentence types), e.g., in Latin *amat* (he is loving). Cf. **imperative**, etc.

indirect object (IO) The recipient or beneficiary of the action of the verb, usu. so termed when no preposition is present, as *I gave/got my daughter a cat*, the equivalent of or equated with *to/for my daughter* in *I gave/got a cat to/ for my daughter* (= **dative** function in **inflecting** and **agglutinating languages** and sometimes trad. so termed in English).

indirect question A **question** related in a subordinate clause, e.g., *He asked me if I was going home*. (Contrasts with **direct question** (see **direct speech (question)**).)

indirect (reported) speech, oratio obliqua An utterance related in a subordinate clause, e.g., *I told him that I was going home*. (Contrasts with **direct speech**.)

indirect speech act In the theory of SPEECH ACTS, an utterance in which the communicative intention is not reflected in the linguistic form used, e.g., *It is very cold in here* may express a request to have the windows closed.

inessive In some **inflecting** and **agglutinating languages**, e.g., Finnish, the **case** expressing location or position within a place.

infinitive The **non-finite** form of the verb regarded as the unmarked or base form and used to cite a particular verb, e.g., the verb *go* (= the bare or **zero infinitive**) or, in English, with the particle *to*, the verb *to go* (= the *to*-**infinitive**).

infinitive clause In GOVERNMENT AND BINDING THEORY, the *to*-**infinitive** form of the **infinitive**.

infix An **affix** inserted within a root or stem, e.g., in Tagalog *sumulat* (wrote < *sulat* (write).

inflecting (fusional) language A language in which words cannot be readily separated into morphs, the inflections indicating grammatical changes being to some extent fused with the stem.

inflection, inflexion 1 A change made in the form of a word (chiefly by the addition of a suffix or prefix) to indicate variations in the grammatical relations between words in a sentence without changing the class to which they belong, e.g., in the declension of nouns and conjugation of verbs. Cf. **derivation** 1. 2 also **I**, **INFL** In GOVERNMENT AND BINDING THEORY, a category, containing information about **tense** (TNS) and **agreement** (sense 2) (**AGR**).

inflectional morphology (The study of) the process undergone by words by the addition of **inflections** whereby distinctions of category, case, etc. are achieved, e.g., *like*, *likes*, *liking*; *cat*, *cats*.

ingressive also **inceptive, inchoative** A type of **aspect** or **Aktionsart** where the beginning of an action is marked grammatically, indicated in English by, e.g., *be on the point of*, *be just about to*: *I'm just about to go out*; or in Russian *pet'* (sing) > *zapet'* (being to sing).

inherited feature specification In GENERALIZED PHRASE STRUCTURE GRAMMAR, a feature specification whose presence on the category in a tree is directly determined by the **immediate dominance** (ID) **rule**. Cf. **feature instantiation**.

initial symbol In GENERATIVE GRAMMAR, the symbol for 'sentence', the highest-level structure in generative grammar, occurring in the left in the first **rewrite rule**, symbolized as Σ, S′ or CP.

insertion In TRANSFORMATIONAL GRAMMAR, the operation which introduces a new grammatical element into a string, e.g., *do*-insertion in *She wants to go → Does she want to go?* Cf. **deletion**.

instrumental 1 The **case** taken by a noun phrase expressing 'by means of'. 2 In analysis in terms of **participant roles**, the entity used to carry out an action, e.g., *penknife* in *Fred cut the string with a penknife*. 3 In CASE GRAMMAR, a **case relation** or **theta role** of the inanimate entity occurring in a causal relationship with a verb, e.g., *the stone* in *The stone shattered the vase*. Cf. **agentive**, **dative**, etc.

intensifier 1 A class of adverbs used to emphasize, amplify or tone-down the meaning of another element, e.g., *a very good boy*, *deeply anxious*, *well enough*; **intensifying adjectives** have a similar function, e.g., *certain* victory, a *complete* fool. 2 Linguistic and non-linguistic expressions more generally used for a similar purpose, e.g., gesture.

intensive Describes a construction where there is semantic identity or attribution between its parts, e.g., between subject or object and complement as in *She is an old bat*, *He called her an old bat*; nouns in apposition as in *Fred, the fireman*; verb and object as in *sail the sea*.

intermediate projection In X-BAR SYNTAX, a **phrase**, i.e., a **projection** larger than zero-level (a word) and smaller than the maximal projection (a sentence).

interpretive In STANDARD THEORY, the status given to the phonological and semantic (**interpretive semantics**) components, generative power being seen purely as a property of the syntax.

interrogative 1 The sentence type or verb form typically used in asking a question, e.g., *Is John coming?* Cf. **declarative**, **imperative**. **2** also **dependent** The inflectional **mood** used in some question forms in some Celtic languages.

interrogative pronoun (adjective, adverb) A **pronoun**, e.g., *who*, etc. (**adjective**, e.g., *which*, etc., **adverb**, e.g., *why*, etc.) marking interrogative constructions.

intransitive (one-place) verb A verb which combines with only one nominal, e.g., *Adam died.* (Contrasts with **transitive verb**.)

intrinsic ordering In GENERATIVE GRAMMAR, the ordering of rules determined as a consequence of how rules are formulated, e.g., if the rule P_1 introduces the symbol M and P_2 analyzes M, P_1 must logically come before P_2. Cf. **extrinsic ordering**.

inversion A reversal in sequence of linguistic elements, e.g., *He is laughing* → *Is he laughing?*

IP = item and process

island In TRANSFORMATIONAL GRAMMAR, a construction whose constituents cannot be separated, specif. a construction to which wh-movement rules cannot apply, i.e., subject phrases and adjunct phrases, e.g., **Who did the fall of cause public rejoicing ← The fall of the dictator caused public rejoicing* or **Who did the regime fall after the death of ← The regime fell after the death of the president*.

island condition In TRANSFORMATIONAL GRAMMAR, the condition that constituents of complement phrases can be separated, e.g., *What did he arrange the collapse of ← He arranged the collapse of the coalition*, but not those of subject/adjunct phrases, see also **island**.

item 1 An individual linguistic form, esp. a **lexical item**, a word as listed in an inventory or dictionary. **2** A member of a group; a unit composed of a number of related characteris.

item and arrangement (IA) The model of morphological description in which words are seen as linear sequences of morphs, e.g., *laughed* is *laugh + ed*. Cf. **item-and-process**.

item and process (IP) The model of morphological description in which words are seen as part of a derivational process, e.g., *laughed ← laugh*, *sang ← sing*.

iterative, frequentative A type of **aspect** or **Aktionsart** which expresses the repeated occurrence of an action on a single occasion, e.g., *He kept on bouncing the ball*, *The ball kept bouncing.* (Contrasts with **semelfactive**.)

jussive The verb form or sentence type expressing a command (or prohibition) in some languages, adopted more generally in some approaches as the term paralleling **imperative** as **declarative** parallels **indicative** and standing in the same relationship to **command** or **mand** as **declarative** and **interrogative** stand to **statement** and **question**.

Katz-Postal hypothesis In GENETATIVE GRAMMAR the hypothesis that transformations should not change meaning.

kernel sentence 1 In GENERATIVE GRAMMAR, a simple sentence, unmarked in respect of **mood**, **voice** or **polarity** and which contains no omissible or optional elements, i.e., in English, a kernel sentence is declarative, active and affirmative. **2** In early TRANSFORMATIONAL GRAMMAR, a sentence generated from a single **kernel string** without the application of any optional transformations, i.e., in English a simple, active, declarative sentence as in **1** above.

kernel string In (early) GENERATIVE GRAMMAR, the output of the phrase-structure rules.

labeled bracketing Bracketing in which the constituents are indicated by superscript or subscript labels, e.g., $[_S[_{NP}[_{Det}$ the] $[_N$ lady] $[_{VP}[_V$ wore] $[_{NP}[_{Det}$ a] $[_{Adj}$ red] $[_N$ hat]]].

landing site In TRANSFORMATIONAL GRAMMAR, the position in a phrase-marker to which a constituent is moved.

language 1 also **natural language** The principal signaling-system or instrument of communication used by humans for the transmission of information, ideas, etc., the central element of which is verbal but which contains as an essential component a substantial non-verbal element, e.g., intonation, stress, punctuation, etc. Communication by means of language is carried out in a number of **media**, viz., speech (regarded by modern linguists as primary), writing and traditionally less centrally, signing (**sign language**). Human language may be distinguished from the signaling systems of other species chiefly by its grammatical and semantic complexity and flexibility and by its descriptive and creative function but whether this is a difference of degree or kind is open to argument. **2** A variety of speech, writing, etc. used in particular circumstances, e.g., the language of literature, the courts, the streets, science, etc. **3** Non-verbal or artificially constructed communicative symbol systems, e.g., the language of bees, mathematics, computers. **4** An instance of **1** above, the verbal means of communication of a particular community; definable in linguistic or (in part) political terms, i.e., a language is the dialect of a nation, usu. (but not always) different enough from other languages to preclude mutual comprehensibility, e.g., English, Latin, Chinese. **5** A distinction is sometimes made with regard to handicap between 'language' and 'speech', the former referring to those aspects of language concerned with the formulation and structuring of meaning, the latter, restrictively, to the use of sounds. **6** The characters, conventions and rules used to convey information, e.g., in a **programming language** like BASIC or a **machine language**.

language acquisition 1 The process or result of learning (a particular aspect of) a language, esp. in childhood. **2** The process of acquiring a second language.

language acquisition device (LAD) In GENERATIVE GRAMMAR, a model of language learning which credits the young child with an **innate** predisposition to acquire language.

language-independent preferred order of constituents (LIPOC) In FUNCTIONAL GRAMMAR, the ordering of constituents according to their categorical complexity, i.e., word/phrase/clause.

langue Orig. in SAUSSUREAN linguistics, the language system, lexical, grammatical and phonological, underlying language behavior or **parole**. Cf. **competence**.

layering 1 The successive hierarchical levels in immediate constituent analysis. **2** In TAGMEMICS, the inclusion of one construction within another of the same type, e.g., a phrase within a phrase, as in *the girl on the roof*. (Contrasts with **level-skipping** and **backlooping**.)

learnability (learning) theory, grammar induction, grammatical inference A mathematical approach to the process of language acquisition which constructs idealized learning procedures.

left branching In GENERATIVE GRAMMAR, describes a construction whose representation in a tree-diagram shows complexity in the left side of the diagram, e.g., *the mouse's hole's entrance's location*. (Contrasts with **right branching** as in *the location of the entrance of the hole of the mouse*.)

left dislocation A variety of **topicalization**, specif. the transposition of a constituent from its canonical position where it is replaced by a pronoun (or a noun phrase with the same referent) to initial position in a sentence, e.g., *The mouse, I saw it (the horrible little rodent)*. (Contrasts with **right dislocation**: *I saw it, the mouse*.)

level 1 The major branches of linguistic analysis, esp. phonology, grammar and semantics. **2** A layer or stratum of a hierarchical structure, as word, phrase, clause, level of prosody, etc. **3** In SCALE AND CATEGORY GRAMMAR and SYSTEMIC GRAMMAR, one of the three basic divisions of the subject matter of linguistics: **substance**, **form** and **context**.

level of representation In GENERATIVE GRAMMAR, a particular point in a derivation, e.g., deep structure, surface structure, phonological representation, etc.

level-skipping In TAGMEMICS, describes a situation where a level of construction is missing and a **filler** from a lower level is used to fill a higher level **slot**, e.g., where *'s* (a morepheme- level ending) is attached to a phrase (skipping word-level), e.g., *Joan of Arc's visions*. (Contrasts with **layering** and **backlooping**.)

lexeme 1 The minimal distinctive unit in the semantics of a language, a word in the sense of a unit of meaning incorporating all the grammatical variations or forms in which it is liable to occur, e.g., the verb *sing* (incor-porating *sings*, *singing* the present participle, *sang*, *sung* but not *song*, *singer* or *singing* the verbal noun); *good* (including *better*, *best*). Cf. **lexical item**. **2** In STRATIFICATIONAL GRAMMAR, a grammatical unit which functions on the **lexemic stratum** = **1** above.

lexemic stratum In STRATIFICATIONAL GRAMMAR, the stratum concerned with the structure of words and phrases, e.g., the morphological and semantic relationships between *draw*, *withdraw*, *draw up*, etc.

lexical entry A listing in a dictionary or **lexicon** (sense **1**).

lexical form In American STRUCTURALIST LINGUISTICS, a **morpheme** plus its meaning (a **sememe**), i.e., those aspects of a **linguistic form** which are strictly lexical in character. (Contrasts with **grammatical form**.)

lexical-functional grammar (LFG) The theory proposes a model of syntax not purely structurally based. It takes the grammatical functions 'subject' (SUBJ), 'object' (OBJ), etc. as primitives, the representations displaying them being known as **f-structures**. A level of constituent structure, **c-structure**, expresses these aspects, e.g., word order, phrasal structure, which seem to display the greatest variation from language to language. Most grammatical constraints, e.g., agreement, anaphora, being regarded as expressing least variation across languages are stated on f-structure representations. The lexical part of the theory, the **lexicon**, is central and much of the work done by transformations in other approaches, here, is carried out by lexical rules, e.g., active → passive is seen as a lexical process.

lexical insertion rules In GENERATIVE GRAMMAR, the rules which insert appropriate lexical items at the correct place in grammatical structure.

lexical item An **item** (sense **1**) of vocabulary, commonly used as an equivalent of **lexeme**.

lexical syntax In GENERATIVE GRAMMAR an approach which includes syntactic information in the **lexicon**.

lexical (full) verb A verb with lexical meaning, e.g., *arrive*, *go*. (Contrasts with **auxilliary verb**.)

lexical (full, content) word, contentive A word having lexical meaning, e.g., *fox*, *arrive*. (Contrasts with **grammatical word**.)

lexicalist hypothesis In REVISED EXTENDED STANDARD THEORY, a **lexicalist morphology** whereby the rules for word formation are no longer transformational but are treated lexically, e.g., by listing morphemes, word formation rules, etc. and using these in conjunction with a dictionary of the words existing in the language.

lexicalist morphology In GENERATIVE GRAMMAR, one of a number of developments in **morphology**, specif. in connection with the handling of word formation and the nature of the **lexicon**.

lexicalization The provision of a word for a meaning distinction.

lexicase A type of **valency grammar**.

lexicon 1 The vocabulary or word-stock of a language, a listing of this, as in a dictionary. **2** In GENERATIVE, etc. LINGUISTICS, the lexical component of a generative grammar or other modern grammatical theory, containing morphological, syntactic and semantic information relevant to individual **lexical entries** and to the organization of the particular grammar.

lexis The vocabulary of a language. Cf. **lexeme**.

lexotactics In STRATIFICATIONAL GRAMMAR, the rules governing the **lexemic stratum**.

LF = logical form

LFG = lexical-functional grammar

licensing In GOVERNMENT AND BINDING THEORY, the effect of the **projection principle** is that a position will exist in the syntactic structure because a lexical item requires it (or may require it), the lexical item is, thus, said to **license** the category.

linear precedence (LP) rule In GENERALIZED PHRASE STRUCTURE GRAMMAR, a statement of the ordering of sister elements in a local tree, i.e., A < B states that a node labeled A always appears to the left of a node labeled B in a local tree.

linearity 1 Describes the structure of the sentence, i.e., a sentence is a unidimensional string or sequence of concatenated constituents, which is a description of a **linear** structure. **2** Also applies to the rules of the grammar, i.e., they apply singly and in an ordered fashion.

linguistic form 1 A linguistic unit or element of any sort (sentence, lexeme, phrase-structure tree, etc.) treated with regard to its grammatical, phonological, etc. structure in contradistinction to its **function** (sense **1**). See also **form**. **2** In American STRUCTURALIST LINGUISTICS, a phonetic form with its meaning, e.g., the linguistic form of *Go!* includes its pronunciation [go] plus exclamatory final-pitch indicating its status as a command, and its lexical meaning.

linguistically significant generalization Esp. in GENERATIVE GRAMMAR, one of the criteria for the **adequacy** of a grammar, its ability to characterize those linguistic relationships found to be significant by native speakers, e.g., that the interrogative is significantly related to the declarative.

linking verb = copula

LIPOC = language-independent preferred order of constituents

loc, LOC = locative

local transformation In TRANSFORMATIONAL GRAMMAR, a transformation which applies only to a sub-string dominated by a single category symbol.

local tree In GENERALIZED PHRASE STRUCTURE GRAMMAR, a **tree** with only two sets of **nodes**, the **root** or topmost node and the **daughter** nodes.

localism The proposition that expressions of location in time or space are more basic grammatically and semantically than non-spatial expressions; tense, aspect, possession and existence are viewed as reflecting underlying **locative** features.

locative (loc, LOC) 1 In **inflecting** and **agglutinating languages**, the **case** expressing place. **2** Describes an adjunct, complement, etc., expressing place or **location**, e.g., *in the street*. **3** In CASE GRAMMAR, a **case relation** identifying the location or spatial orientation of the state or action identified by the verb.

logical form (LF) In GOVERNMENT AND BINDING THEORY, the level of the theory representing the 'meaning' aspect of the strings that are the output of the grammar. The equivalent of the semantic component in other models.

LP = linear precedence

M = modal

mad magazine sentence In TRANSFORMATIONAL GRAMMAR, an echoic sentence of the form [NP XP], e.g., in the reply to the statements *I think you should know I am leaving you/The dog is dead/Susan is quite brilliant*, *What! You leaving me/The dog dead!/Susan brilliant?*

main clause A clause which has a finite verb and can function independently as a sentence.

main verb The most important verb in a clause, usu. a **lexical verb**, e.g., *came* in *He came home at three*; *come* in *He hasn't come home yet*; *is* in *He is late*. (Contrasts with **auxiliary** (verb).)

manner 1 A variety of **adverbial clause**, e.g., *He took to wealth **as if he were born to it***. **2** A category of **adverbs** and **adverbials** which express something qualitative about the verb or adjective modified or how something occurred, e.g., *He ran **quickly** and **with ease***, *She came **precariously** close to falling*.

mapping 1 The establishment of defined correspondences between two sets of quantities or values, specif. in **linguistics**, the correspondences between the elements in a linguistic model and the elements of the actual language. **2** In TRANSFORMATIONAL GRAMMAR, the process relating one stage of a derivation to another.

markedness 1 The presence of some linguistic feature in an element as opposed to its absence, e.g., /b/ is **marked** for voice, /p/ **unmarked**; *god* is unmarked vis à vis *gods* which is marked for plurality and *goddess* which is marked for gender; *bitch* is marked for gender vis à vis *dog* which is unmarked. Markedness is freq. indicated by the presence of an affix or by restriction in distribution, e.g., *dog* = male/female canine, *bitch* = female canine. **2** Any prominent or unusual feature or pattern, e.g., **alliteration**.

mass (non-count(able), uncountable) noun A noun which denotes a quantity or mass of unindividuated material, e.g., (*some*) *butter*, *duck*, *pineapple*. (Contrasts with **count(able) noun**.)

matching condition In GOVERNMENT AND BINDING THEORY, a **condition** (sense **2**) of **binding theory** that noun phrases which are **coindexed** (see **coindexing**) must be compatible as regards the features assigned to them (gender, plurality, etc).

matrix 1 A rectangular array of elements arranged in columns and rows, e.g., an array of segments and features indicating the presence or absence of a feature in a particular segment. **2** In GENERATIVE SYNTAX, the sentence in which another sentence is embedded, e.g., *The man* who fell down *was drunk*.

maximal projection (phrase expansion), (X) In the **X-bar theory** of GOVERNMENT AND BINDING THEORY, the highest level of **phrasal projection** (see **projection 2**) for any particular category, i.e., the largest constituent required to account for all the possible dependents of a lexical category, e.g., *Jean is* **a teacher of physics** is the maximal projection of a noun phrase, including both **complement** (sense **5**) *of physics* and **specifier** *a*, similarly for *Jean is* **very keen on her job** (adjective phrase), *will go* **quite independently of me** (adverbial phrase), *She might* **be thinking of you** (verb phrase). Cf. **double-bar**.

MDP = **minimal distance principle**

metarule 1 A rule defined in terms of other pre-existent rules. **2** In GENERALIZED PHRASE STRUCTURE GRAMMAR, a set of **immediate dominance** (**ID**) rules defined on the basis of the properties of others already in the grammar, whose function is to capture the sorts of generalizations dealt with by transformations in other approaches, e.g., the passive metarule states that in a grammar where every ID rule which permits VP to dominate NP and other material there is also a rule which allows the passive category to dominate the other material from the original rule.

middle voice A **voice** of the verb in Greek, used specif. where the action or state expressed in the verb affects the subject of the verb or the subject's interests, i.e., that the action is being carried out by the subject for his or her benefit, e.g., *loúomai khitona* 'I am washing (my) shirt'. (Contrasts with **active 1** and **passive**.)

minimal distance principle (MDP) In the analysis of complement clauses, the assumption that the closest noun phrase to its left is its subject, e.g., in *James asked John to come*, *John* is the subject of *to come*.

minimal free form The BLOOMFIELDIAN definition of a word, the smallest linguistic form capable of occurring on its own as an utterance.

modality 1 A medium of communication, e.g., speech, writing. **2** The system expressing **mood** (sense **1**). **3** In CASE GRAMMAR, the sentence constituent which consists of the elements of tense, mood and aspect. **4** The classification of **propositions** according to whether they are necessary, possible, contingent, obligatory, etc.

mode In TAGMEMICS, describes the three different ways in which the units of the theory are regarded, specif. the **feature mode** in which the units are viewed as contrasting, e.g., phonemes; the **manifestation mode** in which the physical variation of units is dealt with, e.g., phonetic variants; the **distribution mode** which is concerned with the relations between units, e.g., their distribution in classes, etc.

modification 1 The limiting of a linguistic element by another dependent linguistic element (the **modifier**), restricted to the use of adjectives and adverbs, or extended to any dependent structure, e.g., in *the small house on the prairie*, *house* is **modified** by *small*, also, in some approaches, by *on the prairie*. **2** In SYSTEMIC GRAMMAR, restricted to premodifying dependents, e.g., *the small house*, *the America's Cup*. Cf. **qualification**. **3** Any alteration of (a) the airstream in the vocal tract (b) the typical action of the vocal organs, as in **secondary articulations**, etc. **4** Formal change within a word, e.g., *man > men*.

modifier 1 A limiting dependent structure, see **modification 1** and **2**. **2** In FUNCTIONAL GRAMMAR, a particular class of **satellites**, e.g., *a/the*, *-ed*, *-s*, etc. Cf. **determinant**.

moneme In FUNCTIONAL GRAMMAR, the minimal significant unit of meaning, e.g., *-s*, *-en*, etc. make up a single moneme meaning 'plural', which, being unable to function freely, is termed a **joint moneme**; *hand*, *boy* are **free monemes**.

monostratal Of a **grammar** (sense **3**), having a single level of representation.

monovalent see **valency**

Montague grammar An approach to linguistic analysis based on **formal semantics** in which the syntactic element is subordinated to and required to serve the analysis of meaning in terms of truth-values, e.g., the constituents identified by the syntax should be just those constituents from which the meaning of the whole can be determined, e.g., *the man who fell down* is analyzed in such a way that the class of men and the class of those who fell down are combined: NP → DET + NOM → ART + [NOM + S] → the + [man + who fell down], explicating the truth-value meaning of the phrase by the actual process of the syntax.

mood 1 The category whereby the attitude of the speaker towards what is said (uncertainty, etc.) is expressed by verbal inflections or the use of **modal (auxiliary) verb (M)** forms, e.g., *would*, *should*, *ought*, etc. See **indicative**, **imperative**, etc. **2** In the study of **narrative**, the type or **register** of discourse used by a narrator.

morph The substantial exponent of a morpheme, e.g., in *kicked* two morphs represent the morphemes 'kick' and past tense 'ed', in *went* one morph represents 'go' and past tense.

morpheme The minimal unit of grammatical analysis one or more of which make up a **word**, e.g., *cat* is one morpheme, *cats* (*cat*+*s*), *catkin* (*cat*+*kin*) two. See also **morph**, **allomorph**, **bound 1**.

morphology 1 The study of the structure of words. See also **derivational morphology**, **inflectional morphology**. **2** A level of linguistic organization, comparable with **phonology**, **syntax**, etc.

morphophonemics, morphophonology The study of how phonological factors affect the phonetic realization of morphemes, e.g., the past tense morpheme <ed> is realized as /t/, /d/, /əd/ in different phonetic environments, as, in *tipped, ribbed, knitted.*

morphosyntax That area of grammar whose categories may be defined in terms both of morphology and syntax, e.g., number, tense, etc. have morphological aspects, e.g., plural requires the addition of -*s*, past tense of -*ed*, etc., and syntactic aspects, e.g., plural nouns require plural verbs, etc.

mother In GENERATIVE GRAMMAR, a **node** that immediately dominates another node (its **daughter**).

move α (move alpha) In GOVERNMENT AND BINDING THEORY, a transformational operation which allows the movement of anything anywhere, actual moves being allowed or disallowed by other constraints, it is the derivational process that connects **D-structure** and **S-structure**.

movement, permutation, reordering In TRANSFORMATIONAL GRAMMAR, a type of transformation which moves a constituent from one part of a phrase-marker to another. See also **adjunction** and **substitution**.

movement rule In TRANSFORMATIONAL GRAMMAR, a type of **transformation** involving the movement of elements of structure which links deep structure (or D-structure) and surface structure (or S-structure). In later versions of the theory, specif. **V movement, I movement, NP movement** and **extraposition**.

N = noun

negation 1 The process of denial or contradiction of or dissent from something asserted, in English freq. by means of the **negative particle** *not*. **2** The **logical connective** *not p*, where *p* is a proposition, having the truth value 'false'.

negative 1 Describes a word (adjective, pronoun, adverb), particle, sentence, etc. which exhibits **negation**, e.g., *no, nobody, nothing, nowhere, not at all, I never went there*, etc. See also **assertive**. **2** see **polarity**

nesting, incapsulation, inclusion A type of construction in which modifiers may be inserted recursively into an endocentric construction, e.g., *the dog*+*on the pave-ment*+*near the station . . .* etc.; *the dog*+*which chased the cat*+*which ate the mouse . . .* etc/. Cf. **embedding**.

node In a **tree diagram** the point where two (or more) branches meet, i.e., the point of origin of subordinate items of data.

NOM = nominative

nominal 1 Of or relating to a **noun** or **noun phrase**. **2** A lexical item which lacks some of the characteristics of a noun, e.g., *the wealthy*, which has no plural *the *wealthys*.

nominal group 1 = **noun phrase 2** see **group**

nominalization 1 The process of noun formation, the noun so formed, e.g., *sad > sadness, kill > killing*. **2** In TRANSFORMATIONAL GRAMMAR, the transformation of a sentence (S) into a noun phrase (NP), the NP so formed, e.g., *the establishment of a frame of reference < that a frame of reference is established.*

nominative (NOM) 1 also **subjective** In **inflecting** and **agglutinating languages**, the **case** of the subject of a verb; usu. the unmarked form. **2** In GENERATIVE SYNTAX, the **case** of the subject NP in a finite clause.

non-configurational languages also, in GOVERNMENT AND BINDING THEORY, **W* (W-star) languages** Languages with (relatively) free word order and lacking hierarchical constituent structure.

non-constituent (reduced, incomplete conjunct) coordination, conjunction reduction, gapping In GENERATIVE SYNTAX, the omission of some part of a construction as, e.g., in *Gloria stole a handbag, Mavis a hat.*

non-finite A form of the verb capable of functioning only in dependent clauses. In English, the infinitive, past and present participles, e.g., *To go to school John passed the park*, *Going to school John . . .*, *Gone to school by eight John went through the park.*

non-terminal symbol In GENERATIVE GRAMMAR, a node in a phrase-marker which dominates other nodes. (Contrasts with **terminal symbol**.)

notional grammar A description of language in senses **1** or **2** of **grammar** based on the view that there exist extralinguistic categories (parts of speech, mood, tense, etc.) which hold true for all languages. (Contrasts with **formal grammar**.)

noun (N) A member of the word class trad. defined as naming a 'person, place or thing', or, in modern linguistics, with reference to its distribution (preceding the predicate, etc.), function (as subject, object, etc. of a verb) and the morphological properties it displays (inflecting for case, number, etc.). See also **common noun, proper noun**.

noun clause A clause which functions as a **noun**, e.g., *He told her **that he was ill**; **What her job was** determined her place of residence.*

noun incorporation The incorporation in a verb form of an object noun, e.g., *to tale-tell*. In some languages, specif. a generic noun functioning as a cross-reference to the particular noun governed by the verb.

noun phrase (NP), nominal (group) *gram* A word or group of words which functions as a **noun**, having the same distribution as a noun and whose **head** is a noun. Cf. **group**.

NP-movement In some later versions of TRANS-FORMATIONAL GRAMMAR, a **movement rule** involving **substitution** whereby an NP (noun phrase) is moved into an empty NP position, e.g., in the derivation of the passive. Cf. **I-movement, V-movement, extraposition**.

NP-trace In GOVERNMENT AND BINDING THEORY, the **trace** of an NP moved by **NP-movement**.

nuclear argument In GENERATIVE SEMANTICS, the intransitive subject, transitive subject (or **agent**) and transitive (direct or indirect) object (or **patient**) functioning in a sentence. Cf. **argument 2**.

number A grammatical category dealing with the analysis of word forms in so far as they express **singularity, plurality** or **duality**.

object 1 also **direct object (DO)** The noun (phrase) following and dependent on a finite transitive verb, in simple declarative sentences freq. identified with the patient or goal, e.g., *The cat chased the mouse.* In **inflecting** and **agglutinating languages** freq. identified by the **accusative** case. Cf. **indirect object. 2** The noun (phrase) governed by or following a preposition, e.g., *between us, down the street.* **3** In the theory of C S PEIRCE, a member of a triadic relationship with **sign** and **interpretant**, whatever determines a sign, e.g., the presence of a person causes the existence of a footprint which functions as a sign of that presence, its object. **4 = frame. 5 = neutral**

object complement see **complement 3**

object raising see **raising**

objective = accusative

obligatory transformation (rule) In TRANS-FORMATIONAL GRAMMAR, a transformation or rule which must apply if the circumstances for its application are met. (Contrasts with **optional transformation (rule)** where a choice exists as to whether to apply the rule or not.)

oblique In **inflecting** and **agglutinating languages**, applied to any **case** except the **nominative. 2** In RELATIONAL GRAMMAR, used to describe functional relationships other than subject, direct object and indirect object, e.g., **locative, instrumental, benefactive**, etc.

observational adequacy The generation by a **grammar** (sense 3) of the whole of a corpus, specifying which sentences are well-formed.

obviative A **fourth person** form, used to distinguish a

further entity from a **third person** (see **person**) entity already mentioned.

one-place verb = intransitive

operator binding In GOVERNMENT AND BINDING THEORY, the binding (see **binding theory**) by an **operator** of a **variable** (sense **2**), as part of the mechanism of *wh*-**movement**.

optative The inflectional **mood** expressing **counterfactivity** and remote possibility (in Greek and Sanskrit formally distinct from the **desiderative**). Cf. **indicative**, etc.

optional transformation (rule) see **obligatory transformation (rule)**

output In GENERATIVE GRAMMAR, the string resulting from the action of a rule or set of rules.

output constraint = filter 1

overgeneration In GENERATIVE GRAMMAR, the situation where a rule generates ungrammatical as well as grammatical structures.

overt Linguistic relationships observable in the surface structure, e.g., concord. (Contrasts with **covert**.)

P = particle, phrase, predicator, preposition

paradigm 1 An example of pattern illustrating the inflectional forms of a part of speech, usu. set out in a table. **2** More generally, a set of relationships between linguistic units where one unit substitutes for another according to different linguistic environments, e.g., in *I ate an orange/The orange was eaten by me*, *I* and *me* are in a **paradigmatic** relation, substituting for each other in nominative/oblique or actor/patient contexts, also *an* and *the* can be seen as part of a paradigm functioning in the context *-orange* and substitutable for each other. (Contrasts with **syntagmatic**.)

parameter In GOVERNMENT AND BINDING THEORY, a means of universalizing parallel but not identical constraints or variations of construction observed in different languages, an aspect of **universal grammar**. The range of modifications in form allowable within a **principle**. Cf. **head parameter, principles and parameters**.

paraphrase 1 The restatement of the meaning of a piece of text in other words. **2** In TRANSFORMATIONAL GRAMMAR, the view that different syntactic structures, e.g., active and passive, essentially paraphrase each other, justifying the notion of transformations which do not alter meaning.

parasitic gap In GENERATIVE SYNTAX, a **gap** caused by or depending on another gap in the structure of the sentence.

parataxis The linking of clauses by juxtaposition, e.g., *Go home. It's already dark.* (Contrasts with **hypotaxis** and **coordination**.)

parole Orig. in SAUSSUREAN linguistics, language seen

as behavior, in usage, in speech or writing; specific instantiations of **langue** (freq. identified with the Chomskyan **performance** vs **competence**).

parsing The process of labeling the elements of a sentence according to their part of speech and syntactic relationships.

part of speech A grammatical class of words, noun, verb, etc = **word class**

participant role The functions attached to noun phrases within a sentence, as, agent, patient, etc.

participial adjective A present or past participle used as an adjective, e.g., *flying doctors*; *cooked chicken*.

participle A form of the verb which participates in some characteristics of verb and adjective, e.g., in *He was running* and *He was cheated*, *running* and *cheated* are respectively present and past participles, or *ing*- and *ed*- forms. Cf. **participial adjective**.

particle (P, prt) 1 An **invariable** word with a grammatical function and difficult to classify in terms of parts of speech, includes, e.g., the **negative particle** (see **negation 1**), *not*, *to* in the infinitive form *to go*, the adverbial component in phrasal verbs, e.g., *away* in *Go away*, etc. **2** In TAGMEMICS, part of an analogy with physics whereby language is viewed as a combination of **particle**, **wave** and **field**, the particle being the linguistic unit, e.g., phoneme, morpheme.

partitive 1 (A form) serving to denote a part or quantity, e.g., *some*, *section*, *pint*. **2** In some **inflecting** and **agglutinating languages**, e.g., Finnish, the **case** expressing a part of something.

passive (PAS) In the analysis of **voice**, a sentence or clause in which the subject is the **patient** or **recipient** in relation to the action, e.g., *The car was driven by Mary*; the verb form in such a sentence or clause. (Contrasts with **active 1** and **middle voice**.)

path 1 In GENERATIVE GRAMMAR, a route in a tree diagram consisting of an unbroken series of branches and nodes which when traced upwards identifies the pattern of **dominance** obtaining in the tree. **2** The route taken by an entity from **source** to **goal**, e.g., in *James came towards him*, *towards* expresses the 'path'.

patient in some approaches also **goal** The entity **affected** by the action of the verb, sometimes to be equated with the **object**, e.g., *the cake* in *Susan ate the cake* or *The cake was eaten by Susan*, but *the prize* in *The cake was the prize*.

patois A provincial or illiterate dialect.

perfect, present perfect A form of the verb, sometimes regarded as a **tense**, sometimes as **tense + aspect**, which expresses some variety of past time, in English, the verb form conjugated with *have*, e.g., *He has written*, and regarded as pastness having some relevance to the present, contrasting, e.g., with *He wrote*. Cf. **pluperfect**, **imperfect**, **aorist**.

perfective (PERF) An **aspect** of the verb indicating completion of an action. (Contrasts with **imperfective**.)

performance Esp. in GENERATIVE GRAMMAR, language as exemplified in the corpus of utterances produced by a native speaker. (Contrasts with **competence**.) Cf. **parole**.

performance grammar A **grammar** (sense **3**) whose aim is the description of a corpus or sample of output, also taking account of various aspects of speech production and perception. Cf. **competence grammar**.

periphrasis 1 The expression of a grammatical relationship by the use of a phrase or **periphrastic** form rather than an inflection, e.g., *of John* or *more lovely* rather than *John's* or *lovelier*. **2** also **circumlocution** An elaborate or roundabout way of putting something, freq. characteristic of **euphemism** or **jargon**.

person A grammatical category used to identify the participants in a situation: **first person**, **second person**, **third person** referring respectively to the speaker (and associates) (*I*, *we*); hearer(s) (*you*); persons and things other than the speaker and hearer (*it*, *they*, *someone*, etc.).

personal pronoun The **pronoun** referring to **person**, *I*, *me*, *you*, *she*, etc.

PF = **phonetic form**

phonological component In GENERATIVE GRAMMAR, the part of the theory concerned with **phonology** and **phonetics**. (Contrasts with **syntactic component**, **semantic component**.)

phrasal verb A verb which consists of a lexical verb and an adverbial or prepositional particle functioning as a syntactic unit, e.g., *go away*, *come up*.

phrase (P) Two or more words in a syntactic relationship that function like a word (as opposed to a clause or sentence), specif. **noun phrase**, e.g., *She wore **the red hat***, **verb phrase**, e.g., *They **have gone swimming***, **adjectival phrase**, e.g., *The tramp, **wet and rejected** turned away*, **adverb(ial) phrase**, e.g., *They cooperated **very happily***, **prepositional phrase**, e.g., *I saw you **on television***.

phrase marker (PM) In GENERATIVE GRAMMAR, **labeled bracketing** or a **tree diagram** representing (some part of) the derivation of a **string**.

phrase structure analysis In GENERATIVE GRAMMAR, the analysis of the structure of a sentence, etc. into its phrasal components (NP, VP, etc.) or **constituent structure** by means of **phrase structure rules**.

phrase structure (PS) grammar (component) In GENERATIVE GRAMMAR, a grammar or component of a grammar consisting of a set of **phrase structure rules** or concatenating **rewrite rules** of the sort $\Sigma \rightarrow NP + VP$ by which the correct constituent structure may be assigned to sentences.

phrase structure rules see **phrase structure grammar**

pied piping In GENERATIVE GRAMMAR, the movement

of a preposition to the front of the clause in such derivations as *To which category do you refer?* (Contrasts with **stranding**.)

pluperfect, past perfect The **perfect** located in past time, i.e., a form of the verb expressing completion of an action in the past, e.g., *He had written*.

plural(ity) A contrast of **number** referring to two or more than two, e.g., *six cats*. (Contrasts with **dual(ity)**, **trial(ity)**, **singular(ity)**.)

polarity The contrast **negative/positive** realized syntactically by the negative particle *not*; morphologically by *un-*, *dis-*, etc, e.g., *happy/unhappy*, *loyal/disloyal*; and lexically, in spatial expressions, where a particular point is seen as zero (negative), e.g., the ground or a source, etc., and its opposite, e.g., above the ground or a goal is seen as positive, giving negative/positive oppositions in *down/up*, *low/high*, *back/front*. The concept may be extended beyond any link with its spatial origins to encompass negative vs positive in other lexical fields as, e.g., *black/white* or perhaps even *fat/thin*.

polysynthetic language An extreme variety of **incorporating language** in which lexical and grammatical morphemes can combine to form a single word, or even a sentence, e.g., in Eskimo.

possessive A linguistic form indicating ownership or possession, e.g., *my*, *mine*, including **genitive** and **postmodifying genitive**, and, in some languages, closely related to **locative** (senses **1** or **2**).

possessive pronoun (adjective) The **pronoun (adjective)** indicating possession, *mine*, *yours*, *his*, *hers*, etc. (*my*, *your*, *his*, *her*, etc.).

postcyclic rules 1 In EXTENDED STANDARD THEORY, transformations which apply after the application of **cyclic rules** has been completed. **2** In LEXICAL PHONOLOGY, the rules which apply after the application of the **cyclic rules** is complete, they apply only to underived forms and take no account of morpheme boundaries.

postmodification Any part of a construction which comes after the head in an **endocentric** phrase, e.g., *smelling of soap* in *skin smelling of soap* or *in the bath* in *children in the bath*.

postmodifying genitive A construction expressing ownership, an alternative to the **genitive**, e.g., *the bone of the dog*. Cf. **possessive**.

postposing The removal to the end of part of the construction in certain circumstances, e.g., *Gillian finds all the children friendly/Gillian finds friendly all the children in her class*.

postposition A particle in, e.g., Japanese, Turkish, etc.which fulfils the functions of a **preposition** in English but comes after the noun it modifies, e.g., Japanese *Tokyo e* (to Tokyo).

pragmatics also **general pragmatics** The study of language use in relation to its social context, specif. the meanings of utterances occurring in situations.

precedence In GENERATIVE GRAMMAR, the relationship between nodes in a phrase-marker where a node to the left of another is said to **precede** it. Cf. **dominance**, **linear precedence rule**.

predeterminer A **modifier** (sense **1**) which comes before the determiner in a noun phrase, e.g., *all* in *all the roses*, *half* in *half a pound*.

predicate 1 In the analysis of the sentence, the second part of a two-part analysis: **subject + predicate**, specif. the verb + object + adjuncts (some approaches, however, would exclude the adjuncts from the predicate), e.g., in *Susanna fell, fell* is the predicate, similarly *ran away*, *ate an apple*, *lay on the grass in the park* might fill that slot. Semantically, the predicate can frequently be equated with the **comment**. **2** In FUNCTIONAL GRAMMAR, the **nucleus** of a complete utterance, in English usu. the verb, e.g., in *We ate a goose at Christmas*, *eat* is the predicate.

predicate calculus A means of representing in symbolic form the internal structure of **propositions**, used to display the underlying logical structure of sentences.

predicate frame In FUNCTIONAL GRAMMAR, the listing in the **lexicon** (sense **2**) of the **predicate** (sense **2**).

predication theory In some versions of GOVERNMENT AND BINDING THEORY, an alternative way of analyzing **small clauses**, i.e., in *I think Jane terribly funny*, *Jane* is interpreted as the main clause object of which *terribly funny* is predicated.

predicative Describes an **adjective** or other **modifier** in post-verbal position, e.g., *Susanna is happy*. (Contrasts with or, in some approaches, is viewed as included in **attributive**.)

predicator (P) In LOGICAL SEMANTICS, the verb, viewed as functioning pivotally in the clause; the verb may be a one-place or two-place predicator, i.e., **intransitive** or **transitive**, having one or two **arguments** (sense **2**), the equivalent of a one- or two-place **predicate** in **predicate calculus**.

prefix An **affix** attached to a root or stem in initial position, e.g., *re-* in *return*; in some languages **inflections** may be **prefixed**, e.g., in ʒe- in Old English or *ge-* in German.

premodification **Modification** occurring before the head of an endocentric phrase, e.g., *Many of the city of London* in *Many of the city of London buses arrive late*.

PREP = preposition

preposing In GENERATIVE SYNTAX, the movement of a constituent of a sentence to a position earlier in the sentence than it would normally occur, e.g., *Tomorrow I leave for Spain*; *I told her to finish at once but **finish** she did not*.

preposition (P, PR, PREP) A **particle** which has a

grammatical or local function, acting usu. in combination with a following noun phrase (see **prepositional phrase**), e.g., *in the house*, *beyond reason*, *from Venice*, etc. See also **postposition**.

prepositional group In SCALE AND CATEGORY GRAMMAR and SYSTEMIC GRAMMAR, a **prepositional phrase**.

prepositional phrase (PP, prep phr) A **phrase** consisting typically of preposition + noun phrase, of which the preposition is head, and which functions like an adverb, e.g., *He appeared **at the window***.

prescriptive grammar, prescriptivism A grammar which lays down rules for correct usage; a view of grammar which sees it as having this function. Cf. **descriptive grammar**.

present perfect = perfect

present tense The unmarked **tense** of the verb, referring to things as they are at the present moment (now), e.g., *He takes his first extraterrestrial step*, sometimes inclusive of past time (up to and including now), e.g., *He takes a packed lunch*, and sometimes, also, future time, e.g., *The dodo is extinct*.

presentational Describes a type of construction which introduces new material into the discourse, e.g., sentences beginning with *here* or *there*: *Here is the shipping forecast*; *There is a cat on the roof*.

preterite The simple past **tense** form of the verb, e.g., *He fell*.

primary predication The relationship of the **predicate** with the **subject** of a sentence, e.g., *fell* in *Susanna fell*. (Contrasts with **secondary predication**.)

primitive 1 Describes the **axiomatic** (see **axiom**) terms in linguistic theory, e.g., 'meaningful', 'sound'. **2** Applied to specific theories, each theory defines certain terms as primitive the rest being derived from them, e.g., in X-BAR SYNTAX the features N and V are primitive, 'noun' being derived: defined as [+ N, − V].

principle In GOVERNMENT AND BINDING THEORY and GENERALIZED PHRASE STRUCTURE GRAMMAR, a grammatical statement less specific in scope than a **rule** and applying with modifications to many different languages. See also **principles and parameters**.

principle parts (of a verb) The main forms of the verb which assign it to a **conjugation**, i.e., first person present tense, infinitive, first person preterite, past participle, e.g., Latin *amo/amare/amavi/amatum*.

principles and parameters The theory of **universal grammar** put forward in GOVERNMENT AND BINDING THEORY and GENERALIZED PHRASE STRUCTURE GRAMMAR. See **parameter, principle**.

PRO (big PRO) In GOVERNMENT AND BINDING THEORY, an **empty category** standing for the 'missing subject' of an infinitive, e.g., *Lucy loves to jump*, may be analyzed *Lucy + loves + PRO + to jump* where PRO functions to identify the 'missing subject' and coindex it as identical with *Lucy*.

pro (little pro) In GOVERNMENT AND BINDING THEORY, an **empty category** standing for a 'missing pronoun' in some languages, e.g., Spanish *llegué* (I arrived)/*llegó* (he/she arrived), Latin *amo* (I love)/*amat* (he/she loves).

pro-drop language In GOVERNMENT AND BINDING THEORY, a language, e.g., Latin, Italian, Malayalam which can have subjectless sentences. See **pro**. (Contrasts with **non-pro-drop languages**, e.g., English.)

pro-form, pro-constituent, pro-NP, pro-verb On the analogy of **pronoun**, an element in a sentence that substitutes for another form, constituent, noun phrase or verb, e.g., *some* and *did* in *Colin ate the sweets*; *Ron had some, too and so did Seumas*.

process 1 The concept of the production of one linguistic element or construction by means of an operation applied to another, e.g., *boys ← boy*, *Golf is enjoyed by Harry ← Harry enjoys golf*. Cf. **item-and-process**. **2** A dynamic situation, as expressed by a verb, which exists over time, e.g., *fly*, *run*. (Contrasts with **event**.)

proclitic An unstressed word in a syntactic relationship and pronounced with a following word, e.g., *an*.

progressive (PROG), continuous An **aspect** of the verb (trad. treated as a **tense**), expressing duration or frequency of repetition over time, e.g., *I was traveling to Glasgow for three hours* or *every day*. (Contrasts with **punctual, simple**.)

projection 1 In GENERALIZED PHRASE STRUCTURE GRAMMAR, the process of mapping the lexical categories specified in a **rule** into **legal extensions** of these categories in a **tree (diagram)**, i.e., a diagram of a linguistic structure is **projected** by a rule. **2** also **bar projection, phrasal projection**, in X-BAR SYNTAX, the connection between a lexical entry in the lexicon and its syntactic representation, specif. the constituent (consisting of **(specifier) head** (sense 1) and **complement**) set up to account for the distribution of the dependents of a lexical category. See **projection principle**. See also **maximal projection**.

projection principle In X-BAR SYNTAX, a fundamental tenet of the theory, which states that representations at the level of syntax observe the subcategorization properties of lexical items, in this sense they are **projected** from the lexicon.

projection rules In STANDARD THEORY, the rules in the semantic component which link all the semantic features of lexical items and associate them with the grammatical relationships formulated in the deep structure to produce a semantically correct derivation.

promotion In RELATIONAL GRAMMAR, a process, specif. **advancement** or **ascension** which increases the prominence of a noun phrase (NP).

pronominal In GOVERNMENT AND BINDING THEORY, one of the types of noun phrase classified with regard to their function in **binding theory** (the others being **anaphor** and **r-expression**), specif. includes **personal**

pronouns, reflexives, pro. A pronominal [+p] in contrast with an **anaphor** is **free** in its governing category.

pronominalization In TRANSFORMATIONAL GRAMMAR, the rule allowing a **pronoun** to replace a lexical noun phrase.

pronoun A word that can substitute for a noun or noun phrase (or clause) or words of similar type, e.g., *it* and *what* in *What fell? It did, that clock on the shelf* or *he* in *John left work, he went home*. See also **demonstrative, interrogative, personal, possessive, prepositional, reciprocal, reflexive, relative pronoun, T/V forms**.

proper government In GOVERNMENT AND BINDING THEORY, part of the **empty category principle**, that the **empty category** must be governed by a lexical category.

proper noun (name) A **noun** which refers to an individual person, place, etc., e.g., *Thomas, Boston*. (Contrasts with **common noun**.)

proportional In PRAGUE SCHOOL phonology, an **opposition** which is one of a number of similar oppositions, e.g., /f/ vs /v/, /s/ vs /z/, /ʃ/ vs /ʒ/. (Contrasts with **isolated**.)

proposition In CASE GRAMMAR, a sentence constituent, a proposition being analyzable into a verb and a set of **case phrases**.

PRT = particle

PS = phrase structure

pseudo-cleft sentence A construction resembling a **cleft sentence** but where the relationship of **main clause** and **subordinate clause** is evident, e.g., *What she wore was a red hat* or *A red hat was what she wore* are **pseudo-cleft** and **inverted pseudo-cleft** versions of *She wore a red hat*.

PSG = phrase structure grammar

punctual A type of **aspect**, describing an event regarded as happening momentarily (**momentary**) or having no duration in time (**transgressive**). (Contrasts with **durative** and **progressive**.)

Q = quantifier, question

QR = quantifier raising

qualification 1 A type of **modification**, specif. of a noun or noun phrase: a noun is **qualified** by an adjective, noun, noun clause (the **qualifier**), etc. (whereas a verb is **modified** (see **modification 1**) by an adverb, etc.). **2** In SYSTEMIC GRAMMAR, **modification** occurring after the **head** of a noun phrase, e.g., *in the red hat* in *the woman in the red hat*. Cf. **postmodification**.

qualifier see **qualification**

quantifier (Q) One of a set of lexical items which expresses quantity, e.g., *all, every, some, a number*, etc.

quantifier floating In TRANSFORMATIONAL GRAMMAR, the rule permitting the movement of a quantifier as

between, e.g., *All the cats are black* and *The cats are all black*.

quantifier raising (QR) In GOVERNMENT AND BINDING THEORY, a type of **adjunction**, the movement of a quantified noun phrase to initial position in the clause during mapping from **S-structure** to **logical form**, during which process the scope of the quantifier (**quantifier scope**) is established, e.g., in the derivation of *Everyone kisses his girl* the distinction is made between *Everyone kisses his* (*own*) *girl* and *Everyone kisses* (*some specified person's*) *girl*.

question (Q) In the classification of sentences according to function, a sentence used to elicit a response, information, etc., usu. expressed in the form of an **interrogative**. See also *wh-***question** (see *wh-***form**). (Contrasts with **command, exclamation, statement**.)

R = root

R-expression, referring expression In GOVERNMENT AND BINDING THEORY, a class of noun phrases (NPs), classified as to their characteristics vis-à-vis **binding** (see **binding theory**); **R-expressions** or 'referential' expressions are classified as all NPs which are neither **anaphoric** (see **anaphor**) nor **pronominal** [−a, −p], e.g., the empty category *wh-***trace** is an R-expression.

R-graph, relational graph In ARC PAIR GRAMMAR, using terminology taken from mathematical graph theory, a description of grammatical relations in terms of **arcs**.

raising In some versions of TRANSFORMATIONAL GRAMMAR and GOVERNMENT AND BINDING THEORY, the movement of a constituent to a higher position in a phrase marker, specif. **subject-to-subject raising** as in the movement of an embedded subject to subject position in the main clause, e.g., *It seems that Mary is missing → Mary seems to be missing*; and **subject-to-object raising** where the subject of a complement clause is raised to object of the main clause, e.g., *I believe that Alan is French → I believe Alan to be French* where *Alan* is construed as the object of *believe*. See also **quantifier raising, right mode raising**.

rank 1 In SCALE AND CATEGORY GRAMMAR and SYSTEMIC GRAMMAR, a **scale** of the analysis (see also **exponence** (or **realization**) and **delicacy**), specif. the hierarchical ordering of units within any particular **level** (sense 1), **grammar** (sense 3), etc.) of the theory, e.g., the **rank scale** of the grammar consists of **sentence, clause, group, word, morpheme**, each consisting of one or more than one of the unit next below. See also **rank shift**. **2** In the analysis of **lexical fields**, a strict **serially ordered set** of ungradable and incompatible lexemes, usu. in technical language, e.g., in the allocation of examination grades: *excellent, good, average, fair, poor* where these are the only allowed terms.

rank shift In SCALE AND CATEGORY GRAMMAR and SYSTEMIC GRAMMAR, the process whereby a linguistic unit operates within the structure of a unit of lower, or the same **rank** (sense **1**), e.g., *city lights*, *the woman who wore a red hat*.

realization, actualization, manifestation 1 The physical or substantial expression in sound or writing (phonic or graphic substance) of abstract linguistic units, e.g., a phoneme /b/ is realized as ⟨b⟩ on the page or [b] as spoken. Cf. **representation 1**. **2** In SYSTEMIC GRAMMAR, the equivalent of **exponence** in **scale and category grammar**.

realizational analysis In STRATIFICATIONAL GRAMMAR, the aspect of the grammar which deals with the way the conceptual correlations of linguistic elements are connected to their phonic correlations, specif. in the operations of **horizontal grouping**, **horizontal splitting**, **vertical splitting** and **vertical grouping**. (Contrasts with **tactic analysis**.)

reanalysis, restructuring In GENERATIVE GRAMMAR, a process whereby sequences of linguistic categories are grouped into units, e.g., the proposition is attached to V to compose a phrasal verb rather than continuing to be attached to the prepositional node P, *look + down + on* → look down on.

recipient In analysis in terms of **participant roles**, the entity passively implicated in the event denoted by the verb, characteristically the indirect object, e.g., *James* in *Mary fed James a story*. (Contrasts with **affected**, **agentive**.)

reciprocal Describes a relationship of mutuality as expressed by various word classes, e.g., the **reciprocal pronouns**, *each other*, *one another* or **reciprocal verbs**, e.g., *interact*, *meet*.

rection = **government 3**

recursion The repetition of syntactic structure, e.g., *a big, fat, happy man*; *a doll and a book and a skateboard . . .* ; *the man that kept the dog that killed the cat that . . .*

recursive (iterative) rules In GENERATIVE GRAMMAR, rules which may be applied repeatedly, in generating, e.g., more than one adjective, *a large red hat*.

recursive transition network (RTN) grammar A development of **transition network grammar** consisting of a hierarchy of networks each of which describes the structure of a category. Each network corresponding to one of these categories is invoked in turn so allowing the recovery of a hierarchical structure for the sentence.

reduced coordination = **non-constituent coordination**

redundancy rules In GENERATIVE GRAMMAR, the rules specifying features which can be predicted from their context (**redundant features**) and thus need not be specified.

reference 1 The relationship that obtains between a linguistic expression and what it stands for or **denotes** on any particular occasion of utterance, e.g., *the cat* may mean the cat I own/have just been talking about, etc. **2** A relationship of identity obtaining between grammatical units, e.g., in *The cat went out, it likes to hunt*, 'it' **refers** to 'cat'. Cf. **anaphora**, **cataphora**.

reference grammar = **grammar 2**; a textbook providing this.

referent, denotation The entity in the real world referred to by a linguistic expression, e.g., a particular pencil is the **referent** of the referring expression '*this pencil*'; or Socrates is the referent of the name '*Socrates*'.

referential index In GENERATIVE GRAMMAR, a marker indicating sameness or difference of reference, e.g., *The woman₁ took her₁ hat* (i.e., her own) or *The woman₁ took her₂ hat* (someone else's).

referential meaning 1 = **cognitive meaning 2** The sort of meaning that identifies or **refers** to an entity in the real world (its **referent**), e.g., in *I spoke to the sergeant whoever is sergeant is intended*. (Contrasts with **attributive meaning**.)

referential opacity Describes the circumstance in which a construction or context fails to preserve its truth-functionality when certain sorts of coreferential substitution are made, e.g., *Lois Lane believes that Superman can fly* is true but *Lois Lane believes that Clark Kent can fly* is not true even though Superman is Clark Kent.

referring expression 1 An **expression** used to identify what is being talked about (the **referent**), e.g., *Jimmy's* in *Jimmy's cat is tabby*. **2** = **R-expression**

reflexive Describes a construction where subject and object refer to the same entity, explicitly with the **reflexive pronoun**, e.g., *John killed himself* or implicitly, e.g., *John never shaves*.

reflexive pronoun A pronoun which refers to the same person or thing as the subject of the verb, e.g., *myself*, *yourself*, etc.

regular Describes a linguistic form which conforms to the usual patterns or rules of a language, e.g., *-ed* is the regular past tense form in English: *loved*, *parted*. (Contrasts with **irregular**.)

regular grammar = **linear grammar**

relational grammar A **grammar** (sense **3**) which takes grammatical relations rather than categories as its central concept, i.e., **subject**, **object** (sense **1**) rather than **noun**, **verb**.

relational network In RELATIONAL GRAMMAR, the representation of a sentence expressing the grammatical relations obtaining between the elements of a sentence and the syntactic levels at which these occur.

relative clause A **clause** (sense **1**) functioning as a modifier within a noun phrase, introduced in some languages by a **relative pronoun**, e.g., *the woman that wore the red hat*. See also **adnominal**, **restrictive relative**.

relative pronoun A **pronoun** used to introduce a **relative clause**, e.g., *who, which, that.*

relator, functional In FUNCTIONAL GRAMMAR, a **moneme** which connects other monemes, e.g., conjunctions, prepositions, postpositions, case endings.

renewal of connection In FIRTHIAN linguistics, the validation of an analysis by checking it against a second set of data thus renewing the connection between the units of the analysis and their exponents in the data.

reordering 1 = movement **2** In the **transformational analysis** of historical phonological change, the postulation that the differences between dialects can be explained by re-ordering the sequence of rules leading to a change.

representation Chiefly in GENERATIVE GRAMMAR, the way in which each successive level (see **level of representation**), of the analysis is manifested or symbolized in the process of generating a sentence, e.g., a phonetic representation will be in terms of a matrix of phonetic features.

restrictive Describes a type of **modification** where the **modifier** is part of the essential identification of the noun, etc. that it modifies, e.g., in *A black cat crossed his path*, seen as a symbol of good luck, *black* is essential to the identification 'black cat'; *a white, tabby*, etc. *cat* has not the same significance. A restrictive modifier is stressed, *a black cat*. (Contrasts with **non-restrictive**, as in, e.g., *Look at the little black cat* where *black* is unstressed.)

restrictive (defining) relative A **relative clause** which defines the noun with which it occurs, e.g., *The mountain which he climbed was Mont Blanc*. (Contrasts with the **indefinite** or **non-defining relative**, e.g., *He got injured on Mont Blanc, which he was climbing*.)

restructuring = reanalysis

result also **resultative, resulting, resultant** A clause or sentence element expressing outcome or consequence, e.g., *so that it would work*; *with the result that*, etc.

resumptive (shadow) pronoun (relative) A **pronoun** or **relative clause** which reiterates or recapitulates something expressed previously, e.g., *John Smith, surely you've heard of him*; *She went into a street, a street which she knew of old.*

revised extended standard theory (REST) In GENERATIVE GRAMMAR, the revised version of the **extended standard theory** incorporating the notion of **trace** into the process of **movement**; other changes include the incorporation into the **base component** of the **lexicalist hypothesis** and **X-bar theory, shallow structure**, etc.

rewrite (rewriting, expansion) rule In GENERATIVE GRAMMAR, a rule of the type X → Y, e.g., NP → Det + N whereby the structure to the left of the arrows is expanded into that to the right, the arrow being the instruction for the expansion.

rheme 1 In FUNCTIONAL SENTENCE PERSPECTIVE, the part of a sentence having the greatest semantic input, usu. of new information. (Contrasts with **theme** (sense **1**) which is the part containing least communicative material.) **2** In more general use, equated with **predicate** (sense **1**) or **comment** or schematized as non-initial in the sentence.

right branching see **left branching**

right dislocation see **left dislocation**

right node raising, shared constituent coordination In GENERATIVE SYNTAX, describes a type of coordinate construction, e.g., *One loves, the other hates, the movies.*

role and reference grammar A lexically based grammar which regards the functional role of grammatical units as primary, taking the **macro-roles actor** and **undergoer** as primitives.

role structure analysis In various theories, e.g., CASE GRAMMAR, SYSTEMIC GRAMMAR, the analysis of linguistic elements, etc., according to their semantic relationships, e.g., a **subject** with human reference usu. has an **agentive** role.

root transformation In TRANSFORMATIONAL GRAMMAR, a **transformation** applying exclusively to full sentence structures, not to embedded sentences or subordinate clauses, e.g., in *yes/no* **questions** where only the main clause is affected.

rule 1 A usually valid generalization as to relationships holding between linguistic elements or structures. **2** The **formal** statement of **1** above, esp. in GENERATIVE GRAMMAR, a **generative rule** which not only states a relationship formally but predicts that the relationship is true for all similar instances in the language. See also **phrase-structure rule** (see **phrase structure grammar**), **rewrite rule, transformation**.

rule feature In the STANDARD THEORY of GENERATIVE SEMANTICS, a feature listed in the lexicon specifying whether the lexical item is exceptional as regards the application of non-lexical transformations.

(rule) ordering In GENERATIVE GRAMMAR, the application of rules in a particular sequence. Cf. **cyclic rules, extrinsic ordering**.

rule-to-rule hypothesis (program) A program based on the view that for each syntactic rule of a language there is an associated semantic rule which specifies the meaning of the constituent whose form is determined by the syntactic rule.

S = sentence, subject

S-structure In GOVERNMENT AND BINDING THEORY, the output of the syntactic component developed to include **empty categories** such as **pro** and **trace** which are required by the principle that a syntactic position which exists at all is considered always to have existed in the derivation and is required to continue to exist at all stages of the derivation, thus all positions that occur at S-structure are required to occur at **D-structure** (in the form of empty categories). S-structure is derived by **move α** from D-structure and is in turn the stage of the derivation preceding **phonetic form** and **logical form**. Cf. **surface structure**.

satellite In FUNCTIONAL GRAMMAR, every unit in an utterance which may be regarded as dispensable, i.e., everything except the **nucleus** and the **subject** of the sentence, e.g., in *We ate a goose at Christmas* the satellites are *past tense, a, goose, at Christmas*.

SC = small clause, structural change

scale In SCALE AND CATEGORY GRAMMAR and SYSTEMIC GRAMMAR, one of the fundamental parameters of the theory, consisting of the scales of **rank**, **delicacy** and **exponence**, the other being **category**.

scale and category grammar, Hallidayan (neo-Firthian) grammar A theory of linguistic description that relates linguistic form (**grammar** (sense **2**) and **lexis**) to **phonic** or **graphic substance** on the one hand and to the **extra-linguistic** situation on the other by means of the **inter-levels** of **phonology** or **orthography** and **context of situation**; linguistic form itself is analyzed as four **categories** (**unit**, **structure**, **class** and **system**) related to each other along three **scales** (**rank**, **delicacy** and **exponence**).

scope The extent of the influence of a particular form over the stretch of language in which it occurs, esp. of negatives, quantifiers, adverbials and interrogatives, e.g., a negative influences everything that comes after it in the clause, cf. *not distinguishable from the rest*.

SD = structural description

selectional feature (restriction, rule) In GENERATIVE SEMANTICS, a **feature** specifying a restriction on the collocations of lexical items, e.g., *sleep* generally has an animate subject, !The stone slept.

self-embedding, center-embedding In GENERATIVE SYNTAX, a construction involving a rule of the sort A → B(+A)+C, e.g., in *The girl that the boy kissed blushed*.

sentence (S) The largest unit of structure in the organization of the grammar of a language, regarded, along with the **word** as one of the two fundamental units of grammatical description. The sentence is classified formally as **declarative, exclamative, interrogative, imperative** types (corresponding to the functional classifications **statement, exclamation, question** and **command**); **simple, complex** and **compound sentences**. See also **main clause, clause**.

sentence function How a sentence works or functions, i.e., as **statement, command, question**, etc. (in contra-distinction to its form: **declarative, imperative, interrogative**, etc.).

simplicity metric In GENERATIVE GRAMMAR an elevation of an analysis in terms of the number of rules, features, etc. it requires; the fewer the number, the simpler the analysis. Cf. **economy**.

sister In GENERATIVE GRAMMAR, one of a set of **nodes** immediately dominated by the same (**mother**) node.

sister adjunction In GENERATIVE GRAMMAR, a type of **adjunction** in which two elements are adjoined under a node as **sister** constituents of the node.

slot 1 In a **slot-and-filler model** of grammar, esp. TAG-MEMICS, the position in a construction 'filled' by a particular category of word, e.g., object slot. **2** Part of a **frame**, one component of an object functioning to contain one defining **feature** of the object.

slot-and-filler model A model of grammar which makes use of the notions of **slots** and **fillers**, e.g., **tagmemics**.

small clause (SC) In GOVERNMENT AND BINDING THEORY, an interpretation as a type of clause of constructions lacking a finite or non-finite verb and consisting only of a noun phrase + adjective phrase/noun phrase/prep phrase, etc., e.g., *I think **Jane terribly funny**, I used to think **you a bore**, They want **their parents out of the house***, etc. (Contrasts with **ordinary clause, exceptional clause**.)

small phrase In GENERATIVE GRAMMAR, in the analysis of the **phrase**, the full phrase minus its **specifier**, e.g., *Queen of Scots* in the NP *the Queen of Scots*; *independently of you* in the adverbial phrase *quite independently of you*. See also **bar notation, maximal projection**.

source 1 In the analysis of spatial aspects of meaning, one of the two dynamic relations, the origin of movement, grammaticalized in the **ablative** case. (Contrasts with **goal 2**.) **2** In CASE GRAMMAR, the place from which something moves. (Contrasts with **goal 3**.)

specified subject condition In EXTENDED STANDARD THEORY, a type of **constraint** that prevents movement of a constituent which is not a subject or part of a subject out of a clause or noun phrase which contains a specified subject, e.g., in deriving *Mary wants to see John* from the underlying *comp NP wants [`comp Mary to see John]* the constraint prevents *John*, which is not a subject from being moved to the empty NP position, thus **John wants Mary to see*.

specifier In X-BAR SYNTAX, the item which precedes the **head** (sense **1**) of a phrase, i.e., a **double-bar** category functioning with a small phrase or **single-bar** category to make up the (maximal) phrase, e.g., in the noun phrase *the queen of Holland*, *the* is the specifier of the noun *queen*, in the adjective phrase, *vastly sure of himself*, *vastly* is the specifier of the adjective *sure*, etc.

sponsor In ARC PAIR GRAMMAR, a primitive relation holding between linguistic states, i.e., state S_A sponsors state S_B if the occurrence of S_B is justified by or dependent on the occurrence of S_A. (Contrasts with **erase**.)

standard theory The model of generative grammar developed by Chomsky in *Aspects of the Theory of Syntax*. See also **extended standard theory**.

stratal system In STRATIFICATIONAL GRAMMAR, a subsystem of relationships with its own internal syntax or **tactics**, specif. the **hypophonemic**, **phonemic**, **morphemic**, **lexemic**, **sememic** and the **hypersememic** (or **gnostemic**) **systems**, paired in **two-stratal systems** in the major components of **phonology**, **grammar** and **semology**.

stratificational grammar A theory which treats linguistic structures as a series of **strata**. For English six strata are proposed, grouped as three major components, viz. **semology** which is concerned with meaning, **phonology** with speech and **grammar** which is intermediate between the two. See also **stratal system**.

strict subcategorization In GENERATIVE SEMANTICS, specifies restrictions placed on the choice of lexical items within the categories of nouns, verbs, etc.

string Esp. in GENERATIVE GRAMMAR, a linear sequence of constituents combined in a particular order, in the case of language, usu. taken to be words, e.g., *the + man + was + bald* (but not **man + the + bald + was*).

strong generative capacity (power) In GENERATIVE GRAMMAR, the capacity or power of a grammar not only to generate a desired set of sentences, but to assign satisfactory **structural descriptions** to the sentences generated; such a grammar is said to be **strongly adequate** (see **adequacy**).

strongly adequate see **strong generative capacity**

structure 1 The rule-governed arrangement that linguistic units enter into to form a meaningful whole, the patterns of interrelationships available to any particular unit, e.g., clause structure, word structure. **2** also **element of structure** In SCALE AND CATEGORY GRAMMAR and SYSTEMIC GRAMMAR, a **category** of the theory: the entities which function together to form the **structure** (sense **1**) of a language, e.g., subject, complement. (Contrasts with **unit**, **class**, **system**.)

structure dependency In GENERATIVE GRAMMAR, the principle that a rule can only be applied to a sentence of its syntactic structure is known, i.e., the rule of inversion in questions which applies to NP + Aux is known to be such, e.g., only if *Jane is* is recognized as an example of NP + Aux can the rule produce *is Jane*; from this it is inferred that the native speaker understands his or her language in terms of its syntactic structure.

subcategorization In GENERATIVE GRAMMAR, RELATIONAL GRAMMAR, etc., the classification of lexical items according to how they may co-occur with other lexical items, e.g., a verb that may take an object is **subcategorized** as transitive; transitive is a **subcategorization feature**.

subcategorization frame In GENERATIVE GRAMMAR, the specification of the range of **sister** constituents which can co-occur with a lexical item, e.g., the subcategorization of *put* specifies NP and PP(LOC) complements, as, *put + the money + in your pocket*.

subjacency condition In GOVERNMENT AND BINDING THEORY, a restriction or bounding (see **binding theory**) condition specifying how far a constituent may move in a single rule-application, specif. that no constituent may move across more than one bounding node in a single movement, e.g., in the process of **wh-movement** generating *What did you think that you would do* the wh-movement rule must act successively, or cyclically from *You did think that you would do what* → *You did think what that you would do* → *What did you think that you would do*.

subject-to-object raising see **raising**

subject-to-subject raising see **raising**

subjective = nominative 1

subjunct In QUIRKEAN linguistics, a group of **adverbials** which function in a subordinate role in relation to other clause elements, relating to the whole clause or some part of it, and expressing variously viewpoint, courtesy, volition, etc., e.g., *Frankly, I couldn't care less*, *Can we go*, *please*, *She pushed him over deliberately* (= 'intentionally' rather than 'with deliberation').

substantive universal In GENERATIVE GRAMMAR, the primitives of a grammar used in the analysis of the data, e.g., NP, VP, the sets of distinctive features used, e.g., count, human, transitive, etc. (Contrasts with **formal universal**.)

substitution 1 The replacement of one element by another at any place in a linguistic structure. **2** In TRANSFORMATIONAL GRAMMAR, a **movement rule** whereby an element of structure is moved from the position it occupies to some other empty position, specif. in **I-movement**, **NP-movement** and **V-movement**. (Contrasts with **adjunction**.) **3 = commutation 4** In GLOSSEMATICS, contrasts with **commutation**.

substring A constituent of a **string** which is itself a **string**, e.g., *The man who came to dinner was bald*.

surface structure 1 In TRANSFORMATIONAL GRAMMAR, the stage in the derivation of a sentence that comes after the application of transformational rules and provides the input for the phonological component. **2** also **surface grammar** More generally, the form an utterance or sentence takes as spoken or as it appears on the page, freq. in relation to the ambiguities evident in such material, e.g., the surface structures of *Germs are too small to see without a microscope* and *They are too much involved in the affair to see without help* are similar (though their **deep-structures** are not).

syntagmeme In TAGMEMICS, a unit in a grammatical hierarchy viewed as a sequence of the **tagmemes** it consists of, e.g., a sentence is a syntagmeme for the clauses it is made up of.

system 1 A linguistic network of any sort the meaning of whose terms is determined by their relationships of equivalence or contrast with each other, e.g., the vowel system, verbal system, system of kinship terms, etc.;

the interrelated sets of such networks make up the system of the language as a whole. **2** One of the four central categories of **scale and category grammar** (contrasting with **unit**, **structure** and **class**), becoming in **systemic grammar** the central category of the theory, a refining or redefining of sense **1** above, a finite set of items paradigmatically related to each other, and functioning in classes.

tactic (tactical) analysis In STRATIFICATIONAL GRAMMAR, one of the two basic types of analysis recognized by the grammar, concerned with the combinatory possibilities of linguistic elements. (Contrasts with **realizational analysis**.)

tagmeme 1 In American STRUCTURALIST LINGUISTICS, the minimal distinctive unit of **grammatical form**, e.g., the information contained in the 'exclamatory final-pitch' or the exclamation point in *Go!* **2** In TAGMEMICS, the basic unit of the grammar, being a place in a structure together with the class of linguistic elements that occurs there, i.e., a **slot and filler**.

tagmemics An American STRUCTURALIST model of linguistic description which proposes the **phoneme**, **morpheme** and **tagmeme** as the basic units, respectively, of phonology, lexicon and grammar, the **tagmeme** being used as a cover term for all grammatical units, which are distinguished in the analysis by differences in **slots** and the **fillers** which can fit into them, e.g., a noun/pronoun or subject in _____ *wore a hat* (e.g., *She, Joan, The old man*) or a clause/phrase in *the boy* _____ *was caught* (e.g., *who skipped school, running away*).

taxeme In American STRUCTURALIST LINGUISTICS, the minimal distinctive unit of grammatical form, a grammatical feature, of the same status in the grammar as the **phoneme** in the lexicon. Combinations of taxemes or single taxemes used in grammatical arrangements are called **tactic forms**, e.g., *Go!* contains two taxemes: 'exclamation' realized in its pitch if spoken or an exclamation point if written and 'verb' (as opposed to 'noun', etc. in, e.g., *bad boy!*). Such an arrangement, combined with meaning, is a unit of **grammatical form** or **tagmeme**.

theme 1 In FUNCTIONAL SENTENCE PERSPECTIVE, the **given** information in a sentence. (Contrasts with **rheme**.) **2** In analysis in terms of **participant roles**, a necessary participant in the action of the sentence which is neither **agent** nor **patient**, e.g., *the window* in *Tony opened the window* or *The window was open*, or *Susan* in *A friend takes care of Susan after school*.

theta (θ) criterion In GOVERNMENT AND BINDING THEORY, the main principle of **theta theory**, the stipulation that each argument be assigned only one **theta role** and vice versa.

theta (θ) marking In GOVERNMENT AND BINDING THEORY, the principle relating subcategorization and the assignment of **theta roles**, subcategorization applies to a position, e.g., NP, the theta marking of the position refers to its lexical content, e.g., whether it is **agent**, **patient**, etc.

theta (θ) role, thematic role In GOVERNMENT AND BINDING THEORY, the semantic role borne by an **argument**, e.g., **agentive**, **source**, **goal**, etc.

theta (θ) theory In GOVERNMENT AND BINDING THEORY, the theory concerned with the functioning of **theta roles**.

trace (t) In TRANSFORMATIONAL GRAMMAR, the co-indexed empty node left behind by a constituent moved to some other place in the structure, e.g., in *wanna*-**contraction**, this concept is used to explain why in examples like *You might want who to win?* → *Who might you want to win?* *want to* cannot be contracted to *wanna*.

transformation, transformational rule, transform In TRANSFORMATIONAL GRAMMAR, One of a number of processes that act on the phrase-structure input (**deep structure** or **D-structure**) of the grammar to reorder it in such a way as to produce the **surface structure** or **S-structure** output, thereby expressing the perceived linkage between, e.g., active and passive, declarative and interrogative, etc. See also **movement rule**, **adjunction**, **deletion**.

transformational grammar (TG) In GENERATIVE GRAMMAR, a grammar which includes a **transformational component** in which, by means of **transformations**, elements of structure are reorganized, the **deep structure** of sentences thereby being linked to the **surface structure**; by this process structural relationships are confirmed, e.g., *I love Lucy* is shown to be closely related to *Lucy is loved by me*, and structural ambiguities are resolved, e.g., *Flying planes can be dangerous* is shown to be derivable from either *planes which fly* or *people who fly planes*. See also **transformation**.

unaccusative Describes an **intransitive** verb whose **subject** can be understood as originally an **object** (sense 1), i.e., as a **recipient** or **patient** in relation to the action, e.g., *broke* in the *The jug broke*. Cf. **ergative 3**.

unbounded dependency construction (UDC) In GENERALIZED PHRASE STRUCTURE GRAMMAR, etc., a construction in which a syntactic relationship exists between linguistic elements which may occur at an indefinably great distance from each other, e.g., in *wh*-**questions** (see *wh*-**form**): *what* in *What did he take out of the cupboard?* is the object of *take* but is distanced from it by its interrogative position, similarly in **topicalization**, **cleft sentences**, etc.

undergoer In ROLE AND REFERENCE GRAMMAR, the

primitive **macro-role** which expresses the participant which is acted upon.

unification In GENERALIZED PHRASE STRUCTURE GRAMMAR, a process of combining **categories** whereby the resulting category is the smallest category which is an **extension** of every category included in the process, providing they do not contain contradictory features, e.g., the unification of { <N, + >, <PRD, + >} and { <N, + >, <V, − >} is { <N, + >, <V, − >, <PRD, + >}.

uniformity of theta assignment hypotheses = universal alignment hypothesis

unit 1 A general term for an entity which is the focus of interest, e.g., phonological unit, grammatical unit, etc. **2** in SCALE AND CATEGORY GRAMMAR and SYSTEMIC GRAMMAR, one of the four main categories of the theory: the linguistic entities at any level of analysis, i.e., the units on the level of grammar are, morpheme, word, group, clause, sentence; on that of phonology, phoneme, syllable, foot, tone group. The units relate to each other hierarchically the one below being included in the next above. (Contrasts with **structure**, **class**, **system**.) **3** A **count(able) noun**.

universal alignment hypothesis, uniformity of theta assignment hypothesis The hypothesis that grammatical relations of a functional sort, i.e., **subject**, **object** (sense 1) are in one to one correspondence with thematic relations such as **agentive**, **patient**.

V-movement In the later versions of TRANSFORMATIONAL GRAMMAR, a **movement rule** (see **transformation**) involving **substitution** whereby V (verb) is moved out of the VP (verb phrase) into an empty finite I (inflection), a technique for attaching the inflections to finite verbs, e.g., *Gloria* [I e] [VP *eat*] *oysters*] → *Gloria* [I *eats*] VP *oysters*]. Cf. **I-movement**, **NP movement**, **extraposition**.

valency, valence, ARITY Esp. in CASE GRAMMAR and DEPENDENCY GRAMMAR, a weighting or quantification of verbs in terms of the number of dependents (or **arguments** or **valents**) they take, i.e., an intransitive verb is **monovalent**, it has a valency of 1, e.g., *John fell*; a transitive verb is **bivalent** with a valency of two, e.g., *John chased the cat*; a verb which also takes an indirect object or some other nondeletable dependent is trivalent with a valency of 3, e.g., *John gave the cat some milk*, *John put the cat in its basket*; a verb with no arguments, in e.g., *It rains* is **zero-valent** or **avalent**.

valency grammar An approach to syntactic theory which takes **valency** as its central thesis.

valency set In DEPENDENCY GRAMMAR and CASE GRAMMAR, verbs classified by their **valency**, i.e., **monovalent**, **bivalent**, etc.

valent see **valency**

variable 1 A term which may assume different values, any member of a set of individuals chosen randomly from within the set, e.g., $x = 1, 2 \ldots$, or the element which takes a particular position in a linguistic structure, e.g., X VP might stand for any sort of construction that can assume subject position. **2** also *wh*-**trace** Specif. in GOVERNMENT AND BINDING THEORY, as part of the **binding theory**, the **empty category** left behind after **wh-movement**.

vertical grouping In STRATIFICATIONAL GRAMMAR, an operation of **realizational analysis** which relates, e.g., the abstract concept past participle to a variety of realizations, *-ed, -en*, etc.

vertical splitting In STRATIFICATIONAL GRAMMAR, an operation of **realizational analysis** which recognizes that a single realization, e.g., English *-ed* may be identical with more than one linguistic unit, i.e., past tense and past participle.

wave In TAGMEMICS, part of an analogy with physics whereby language is viewed as a combination of **particle**, **wave** and **field**, the **wave** being language as a dynamic system, constantly moving, merging and overlapping.

weak generative capacity (power) In GENERATIVE GRAMMAR, the capacity or power of a grammar to generate grammatical sentences, languages, etc. (Contrasts with **strong generative capacity**.)

wh-**form** (-clause, -complement, -noun phrase, -question, -word, etc.), *wh*-**movement** (-fronting, etc.) A **clause**, etc. introduced by involving, consisting of, etc. the class of items chiefly beginning with *wh*-, i.e., *why*, *what*, *where*, *how*; *who*, *what*, etc.

wh-**trace = variable 2**

X-bar ($\bar{X}$, X′) syntax (theory) In recent versions of GENERATIVE GRAMMAR, esp. GOVERNMENT AND BINDING THEORY, and in a modified form in GENERALIZED PHRASE STRUCTURE GRAMMAR, a theory which draws the generalization from the structure of phrases (noun phrase (NP), verb phrase (VP), adjective phrase (AP), prepositional phrase (PP), etc.) that all of them have the structure **head** (sense 1), from which the essential character of the phrase derives, and **complement** (sense 5) described as the **projection** of the head. Thus the head of any phrase, i.e., the category itself, may be termed X (=N, V, A, P, etc.) and the projection of the phrase, X-bar ($\bar{X}$, X′) or X-double-bar ($\bar{X}$, X″), being respectively an intermediate 'semi-phrasal' level and the full phrase (the **maximal projection** of the phrase). Thus in the phrase *the pleasure of going home*, *pleasure* = X (in this case = N), *pleasure of going home* = X′ or N′, and *the pleasure of going home* = X″

or N″ or NP; similarly, in *very happy to see you,* *happy* = X or A, *happy to see you* = X′ or A′ and *very happy to see you* = X″ or A″ or AP, and so on for verb and prepositional phrases. Sentences are analyzed in the same way taking a category **INFL** (inflection) as the **head**.

X-double bar (X̄, X″) = maximal projection

zero level (zero-bar) category In X-BAR SYNTAX, in the analysis of the phrase, the lexical **head** of the phrase, identified as N(noun), V(verb), etc. without any further marker (see **bar notation**).

List of Major Language and Linguistics Journals

The list of journals given below is a representative selection of periodical publications, particularly those published in English, devoted primarily to the dissemination of research on languages and linguistic theory and includes all those frequently referred to in this Encyclopedia. A more comprehensive listing can be found in the *Bibliographie linguistique de l'année/Linguistic Bibliography for the Year* (Kluwer, Dordrecht). With a few exceptions the abbreviations given below are those used in this annual publication. A somewhat different and slightly less extensive listing can be found in *Linguistics and Language Behavior Abstracts* (LLBA, San Diego, CA).

AJL	Australian Journal of Linguistics: journal of the Australian Linguistic Society. St Lucia, Queensland
AJPh	American Journal of Philology. Baltimore, MD
AmA	American Anthropologist. Menasha, WI
AnL	Anthropological Linguistics. Bloomington, IN
AP	Applied Psycholinguistics. Cambridge
BLS	Berkeley Linguistics Society: proceedings of the annual meeting. Berkeley, CA
CJL	Canadian Journal of Linguistics/Revue canadienne de Linguistique. Toronto
CL	Computational Linguistics. Cambridge, MA
CLS	CLS . . . : papers from the . . . annual regional meeting of the Chicago Linguistic Society. Chicago, IL
Cognition	Cognition: international journal of cognitive science. Amsterdam
CognL	Cognitive Linguistics. Berlin
FoL	Folio Linguistica: acta Societatis Linguisticae Europaeae. The Hague
IJAL	International Journal of American Linguistics. Chicago, IL
IJLex	International Journal of Lexicography. Oxford
JChL	Journal of Child Language. Cambridge
JEGP	Journal of English and Germanic Philology. Urbana, IL
JL	Journal of Linguistics. Cambridge
JLR	Journal of Linguistic Research. Bloomington, IN
JPrag	Journal of Pragmatics: an interdisciplinary quarterly journal of language studies. Amsterdam
LA	Linguistische Arbeiten. Tübingen
LAcq	Language Acquisition. Hillsdale, NJ
LAn	Linguistic Analysis: a research journal devoted to the publication of high quality articles in formal phonology, morphology, syntax and semantics. Seattle, WA
Langages	Langages. Paris
LBer	Linguistische Berichte. Braunschweig
L&C	Language and Communication: an interdisciplinary journal. Oxford
LCProc	Language and Cognitive Processes. London/Utrecht
LeSt	Lingua e stile: quaderni dell'Instituto di Glottologia dell'Università degli Studi de Bologna. Bologna
LFr	Langue française. Paris
Lg	Language: journal of the Linguistic Society of America. Baltimore, MD
LIn	Linguistic Inquiry. Cambridge, MA
Lingua	Lingua: international review of general linguistics. Amsterdam
Linguistics	Linguistics. Berlin

Linguistique	La Linguistique: revue de la Société Internationale de linguistique fonctionnelle. Paris
L&P	Linguistics and Philosophy: an international journal. Dordrecht
LRev	The Linguistic Review. Dordrecht
LS	Language Sciences: a world journal of the sciences of language. Tokyo
NLLT	Natural Language & Linguistic Theory. Dordrecht
PBML	The Prague Bulletin of Mathematical Linguistics. Praha
PMLA	Publications of the Modern Language Association of America. New York
PSML	Prague Studies in Mathematical Linguistics. Praha
QSem	Quaderni di semantica: rivista internazionale de semantica teorica et applicata. Bologna
RRL	Revue roumaine de linguistique. Bucharest
RQLTA	Revue québécoise de linguistique théorique et appliquée. Trois-Rivières, Québec
SLang	Studies in language: international journal sponsored by the foundation 'Foundations of Language.' Amsterdam
SLS	Studies in the Linguistics Sciences: publication of the Department of Linguistics, University of Illinois. Urbana, IL
Word	Word: Journal of the International Linguistic Association. New York

List of Contributors

ALLERTON, David J. (University of Basle, Basle, Switzerland)
Valency and Valency Grammar: 359

ANDERSON, John M. (University of Edinburgh, Edinburgh, UK)
Case Grammar: 19

ATKINSON, Martin (University of Essex, Colchester, UK)
Generative Grammar: The Minimalist Program: 137; *Language Acquisition: Formal Models and Learnability Theory*: 209

BENNETT, David C. (University of London, London, UK)
Stratificational Grammar: 294

BLAKE, B. (La Trobe University, Bundoora, Victoria, Australia)
Relational Grammar: 273

BURRIDGE, K. (University of British Columbia, Vancouver, British Columbia, Canada)
Typology and Word Order Change: 350

CAMPBELL, L. (University of Christchurch, Christchurch, New Zealand)
Typological and Areal Issues in Grammar: 339

CANN, R. (University of Edinburgh, Edinburgh, UK)
X-bar Syntax: 379

CARSTON, R. (University College London, London, UK)
Syntax and Pragmatics: 306

COOPER, Richard P. (University College London, London, UK)
Head-driven Phrase Structure Grammar: 191

CROFT, W. (University of Michigan, Ann Arbor, MI, USA)
Typology and Grammar: 343

†DIK, Simon C. (University of Amsterdam, Amsterdam, The Netherlands)
Functional Grammar: 84

FOLEY, W. A. (University of Sydney, Sydney, New South Wales, Australia)
Information Structure: 200

FOUGHT, John G. (University of Pennsylvania, Philadelphia, Pennsylvania, USA)
American Structuralism: 1

FRASER, N. M. (University of Surrey, Guildford, UK)
Dependency Grammar: 71

FREIDIN, R. (Princeton University, Princeton, NJ, USA)
Generative Grammar: Principles and Parameters : 119

FUDGE, Erik C. (University of Reading, Reading, UK)
Glossematics (Hjelmslev): 169

GOLDBERG, Adele E. (University of California, San Diego, La Jolla, CA, USA)
Construction Grammar: 68

GROSS, Maurice (Blaise Pascal Institute, Paris, France)
Lexicon Grammar: 244

HAIMAN, J. (Macalester College, St Paul, MN, USA)
Iconicity: 196

HAJIČOVÁ, Eva (Charles University, Prague, Czech Republic)
Prague School Syntax and Semantics: 265

HALLIDAY, M. A. K. (University of Sydney, Sydney, New South Wales, Australia)
Systemic Functional Grammar: 321

HARLOW, Stephen J. (University of York, York, UK)
Generative Grammar: Transformational Grammar: 147

HERVEY, S. G. J. (University of St Andrews, St Andrews, UK)
Functionalism, Axiomatic: 110

HEWITT, B. G. (University of London, London, UK)
Greenberg Universals: 187

HUDSON, R. A. (University College London, London, UK)
Word Grammar: 368

HUMPHREYS, R. L. (University of Essex, Colchester, UK)
Lexicon in Formal Grammar: 241

JACOBSON, P. (Brown University, Providence, RI, USA)
Constituent Structure: 54

JONES, Linda K. (Summer Institute of Linguistics, Jakarta, Indonesia)
Tagmemics: 326

KASHER, A. (Tel-Aviv University, Tel-Aviv, Israel)
Chomsky and Pragmatics: 44

LANGACKER, Ronald W. (University of California, San Diego, CA, USA)
Cognitive Grammar: 51

LONGACRE, R. E. (University of Texas, Arlington, TX, USA)
Grammatical Units: 175

MACKENZIE, J. Lachlan (Vrije Universiteit, Amsterdam, The Netherlands)
Functional Grammar: 84

MARTINET, André (Université René Descartes, Paris, France)
Functional Grammar: Martinet's Model: 92

McCAWLEY, James D. (University of Chicago, Chicago, IL, USA)
Generative Semantics: 164

MILLER, Jim (University of Edinburgh, Edinburgh, UK)
Applicational Grammar: 11

NEIDLE, C. (Boston University, Boston, MA, USA)
Lexical Functional Grammar: 223

NEWMEYER, F. J. (University of Washington, Seattle, WA, USA)
Chomsky's Philosophy of Language: 45

PALMER, F. R. (University of Reading, Reading, UK)
Firth and the London School: 81

PAYNE, J. R. (University of Manchester, Manchester, UK)
Universals of Language: 355

SADLER, Louisa (University of Essex, Colchester, UK)
New Developments in Lexical Functional Grammar: 259

SADOCK, Jerrold M. (University of Chicago, Chicago, IL, USA)
Autolexical Syntax: 15

SEUREN, P. A. M. (Catholic University, Nijmegen, The Netherlands)
Syntax and Semantics: 314

SIEWIERSKA, A. (University of Amsterdam, Amsterdam, The Netherlands)
Word Order and Linearization: 372

SORNICOLA, Rosanna (University of Naples Federico II, Naples, Italy)
Topic, Focus, and Word Order: 331

STAROSTA, Stanley (University of Hawaii, Honolulu, HI, USA)
Lexicase: 231

STEEDMAN, Mark (University of Pennsylvania, Philadelphia, PA, USA)
Categorial Grammar: 31

STUURMAN, F. (University of Utrecht, Utrecht, The Netherlands)
Descriptive Grammar and Formal Grammar: 75

TAGER-FLUSBERG, H. (University of Massachusetts, Boston, MA, USA)
Language Acquisition: Grammar: 216

TRAUGOTT, Elizabeth C. (Stanford University, Stanford, CA, USA)
Grammaticalization and Lexicalization: 181

VAN VALIN, Jr, R. D. (State University of New York, Buffalo, NY, USA)
Functional Relations: 98; *Role and Reference Grammar*: 281

WARNER, A. R. (University of York, York, UK)
Generalized Phrase Structure Grammar: 113

ZWICKY, Arnold M. (Ohio State University, Columbus, OH, USA)
Syntax and Phonology: 300

Name Index

Subject Index